STRATEGIES for *e*-BUSINESS

A comprehensive companion website is available at

www.booksites.net/jelassi

For students

- Extra FT articles are added each semester providing current commentary on a fast-changing subject
- Weblinks relating to organizations mentioned in the text facilitate straightforward searching

Further resources for instructors are also available on this site.

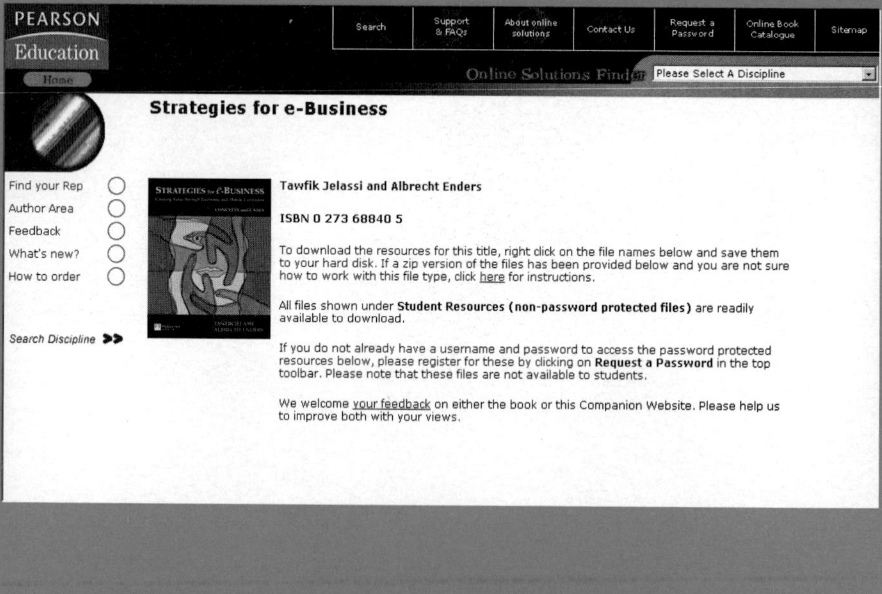

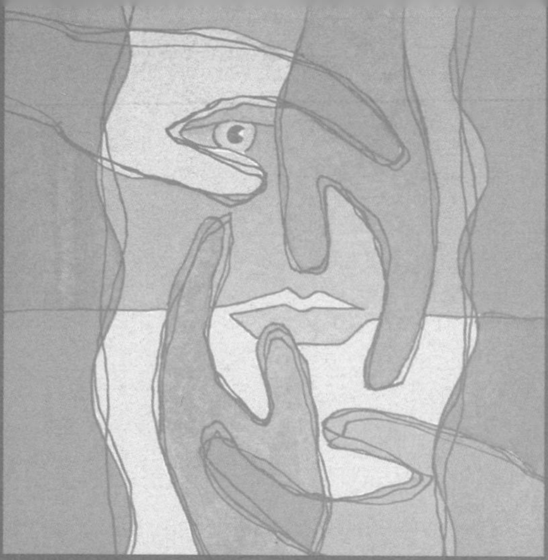

STRATEGIES for *e*-BUSINESS

Creating Value through Electronic and Mobile Commerce

CONCEPTS and CASES

Tawfik Jelassi

Albrecht Enders

FT Prentice Hall
FINANCIAL TIMES

An imprint of Pearson Education
Harlow, England • London • New York • Boston • San Francisco • Toronto • Sydney • Singapore • Hong Kong
Tokyo • Seoul • Taipei • New Delhi • Cape Town • Madrid • Mexico City • Amsterdam • Munich • Paris • Milan

Pearson Education Limited

Edinburgh Gate
Harlow
Essex CM20 2JE
England
and Associated Companies throughout the world

Visit us on the World Wide Web at:
www.pearsoned.co.uk

First published 2005

ISBN 0 273 68840 5

British Library Cataloguing-in-Publication Data
A catalogue record for this book is available from the British Library

Library of Congress Cataloging-in-Publication Data
A catalog record for this book is available from the Library of Congress

10 9 8 7 6 5 4 3 2 1
09 08 07 06 05

Typeset in $10\frac{1}{2}/12\frac{1}{2}$ pt Minion by 30
Printed and bound by MateuCromo Artes Graficas, Spain

The publisher's policy is to use paper manufactured from sustainable forests.

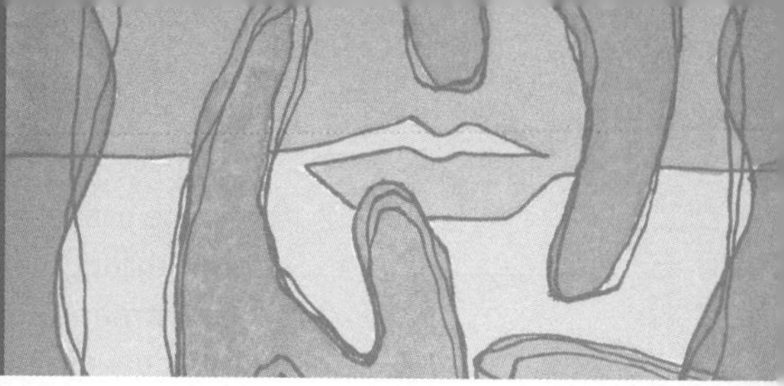

BRIEF CONTENTS

DETAILED CONTENTS

PART 4 Case studies

Case studies

Companion Website resources

A comprehensive companion website is available at **www.booksites.net/jelassi**

For students

- Extra FT articles are added each semester providing current commentary on a fast-changing subject
- Weblinks relating to organizations mentioned in the text facilitate straightforward searching

For instructors

- PowerPoint slides of figures and tables from the book, as well as some textual slides with key points from the chapters, to help lecture preparation
- Teaching notes for the case studies to save valuable preparation time
- Suggested syllabi for alternative courses draw on the authors' experience of teaching the subject to a range of students in different countries

LIST OF EXHIBITS

FOREWORDS

e-Business – the genesis of an advantage

By Professor Dr Bolko von Oetinger
Senior Vice-President and Director of the Strategy Institute of The Boston Consulting Group

e-Business? Doesn't that sound like a fairytale from a golden age? From an age when the revolutionaries of the 'new economy' stormed the Bastille of the 'old economy' and rashly, and all too self-confidently, announced the demise of supposedly obsolete areas of business. From an age when the cash-burning rate was all too often taken as a sign of entrepreneurial courage. These days, it should be neither a sense of *schadenfreude* nor nostalgia, which comes with hindsight, that ought to shape our analysis of e-business. Instead, we should ask a serious strategic question. Beyond all the narcissism and glamour, has there not been a considerable change underway in our economic world which has irrevocably and fundamentally changed many businesses? And if so, what lesson should it teach us for the future? Is the real world of e-business possibly still just around the corner?

In the shortest possible time span, e-business offered a new opportunity for the creation of competitive advantage. The surprising novelty of the approach first shook up the markets, until the bubble (caused by rash extrapolations) finally burst. Now that the clouds of dust have settled again, and more rapidly than many investors may have wished, it has become clear that nothing is the same any more; in fact, that the most fundamental ways of conducting business have been profoundly and irrevocably altered.

If we look back at the structural changes brought about by e-business, the example of the French Revolution springs to mind. One is tempted to say that we find ourselves in a post-revolutionary age which perhaps may not fulfill the visions of a Robespierre or a Saint-Just, but which has nonetheless made it impossible to return to pre-revolutionary conditions. The reign of terror of the Jacobins, that is, the irrational hype and hysteria surrounding the dot.com industries, now belongs to history. Robespierre, and along with him hundreds of other dot.coms, have been led to the scaffold. And yet still the legitimate cry goes up anew: the revolution is dead - long live their revolutionary ideas! Or, to put it in more modern terms: the excesses may be over, but the guiding principles remain. Principles, which possibly still await the coming of their Napoleon.

The development of e-business is a veritable case study of the management of advantage and thus of the development of strategy. To my mind, this presents also the value and the significance of the work of Tawfik Jelassi and Albrecht Enders, which is based on the principal insight that it is time to differentiate between the short-lived hype surrounding e-commerce, and its real and lasting durability.

The critical and risky initial stage of any technology-driven strategy consists of transforming technologies into commercial advantages. Technological innovations can provide an attractive basis for growth strategies, new customer value, new business

models and innovative products. Of crucial importance during this early stage is the ability to determine where technological innovations can be applied. That is the way it was in the past, and that is how it remains today in the case of e-business. If we differentiate between Internet technology and its commercial application in e-business, we soon notice that there are two main strategic options: on the one hand, it is obvious that within e-business itself there are still massive untapped possibilities. The impact that e-business applications will have in the areas of health care, education or in the public sector, to name but three areas, is still not completely clear. In these areas, we find ourselves still at the beginning of potentially revolutionary changes to existing business models. On the other hand, the technological innovation potential of the Internet itself is in no way fully exploited yet. A glance at the future of broadband technology, which is already being put to good use in Korea and Japan points the way to many new applications of the high-speed Internet. Consider also the more distant possibilities that will arise from the synergies between the Internet and mobile phone technologies. These applications will not only create new business opportunities, but they will also fundamentally change the strategies of many companies, particularly in the communication and media industries.

Thus, technological platforms and innovations provide an important foundation for competitive advantages, which in turn manifest themselves in commercial applications. But e-business technologies have opened up even more business opportunities: they have also changed the way we think about business strategies and sources of competitive advantage. The once self-contained value chain has been transformed into a network of value elements, and has thus made possible an organizational deconstruction of previously unimaginable extent. Those who do still think in terms of value chains are not only using the wrong term, they are also missing out on a great opportunity, since an open network offers far greater opportunities than a single chain. The Internet creates the communication links that open up the creative space for new businesses to grow into.

In 1911, Schumpeter already referred to these kinds of new combinations of different value chains in his *Theory of Economic Development*. Today, almost 100 years later, technological development is accelerating this unending succession of creative destruction and reconstruction in a previously unheard of way. Today, it is becoming increasingly easy to interlink the different parts of a value chain across companies and across geographical boundaries. Supported by increasingly sophisticated IT solutions in the supply chain management process, the concept of deconstruction has shaped many organizations. Thus, the world appears today as if encompassed by a single production line, allowing us to connect individual stages of production around the globe. We can also replace vertical organizational structures with horizontal layers, thereby transforming a company into one that can compete at different stages of the value structure. Those who do not include such considerations in their thinking are committing a strategic error that will negatively influence the efficiency and effectiveness of their business. It is clear that the Internet and the accompanying structural and organizational changes have become the backbone of the economy. And yet, most likely, this is only the beginning. We are entering an era of growing economic freedom, where the multitude of possible value chain combinations reminds us of the Lego® system. And, as the freedom for recombining different parts of the value structure increases, the space for innovations and real surprises also grows.

For the majority of businesses that adopted e-business, it has proven advantageous not to get rid of existing structures and to replace everything with the new (that is,

with e-business) but, rather, to skillfully merge the old and the new. This combination of tried and tested tradition and sensible innovation leads to an increase in efficiency, improvement in quality and higher customer retention. Just think of online portals, CRM or the design of internal business processes. Since almost all companies pursue the above goals, in theory the advantage relative to each other is only limited. In practice, however, it has become obvious that companies implementing e-business strategies have achieved very different results, always depending on how they executed their strategies.

The best results have always been achieved when operational excellence, attention to the smallest details, step-by-step change and careful experimentation over a long period of time have driven the implementation of e-business. The successful e-business companies did not fall into the trap of believing that being first in the market would be sufficient for guaranteeing lasting competitive advantage. They had internalized one of the most important strategic insights: it is not enough just to be the first; one must also be the best. Many dot.coms grew faster than demand, thereby creating over-capacity, which ultimately led to their demise. A more realistic appraisal of the evolution of the online market, which was slower than many of the start-ups had anticipated, could have helped to avoid many disappointments. If there is an important lesson to be learned from this period of hype, then it is this: only the integration of old and new, combined with superior execution - which was more important than just speed - turned technological innovations into sustainable competitive advantage.

e-Business has also created entirely new types of innovative business models, thereby providing the strategic theme of 'disruptive innovation' with some instructive examples of strategic excellence. Business models have sprung up which would formerly have been unthinkable. Think of eBay, Google and Amazon, enterprises that have disruptively stirred up the market like no others. The distinctive trait that sets these three companies apart is the fact that they were not only innovative in the past, but that they continue to be so today. They did not just create new companies, but they also built strong global brands. They were able to do this because they deliver superior customer value. There were numerous competitors who had also recognized the potential of these new business opportunities, but they were unable to act accordingly. The courage of the entrepreneur, the courage to experiment, as well as the courage to hold on to a vision when the figures don't yet add up, the courage to swim against the tide but at the same time always to retain a grasp of the economic reality is reminiscent of a classical recipe for success for laying the foundations of successful businesses.

The history of the three above-mentioned companies indicates a high level of flexibility, an unmistakable sign of good strategy management. eBay began as an electronic flea market and has become one of the largest retailing companies, constantly winning new customers and expanding into new product categories. Today, Amazon is not only a mail order company, but also a software provider that markets its own software and business processes. Both companies have realized that, at the edges of their existing business models, there often lurks a new strategic option just waiting to be discovered. In the online music industry, the story which began with Napster and is now continued by Apple against Microsoft and Sony shows just how strong the innovative will of the visionary entrepreneur has to be, what an eye he or she has to have for the quality of the future business model, how much energy is required for it to be put into practice, and finally how risky the attempt to transform a business idea into an actual business really is. Through an extensive strategy framework and 28 detailed case studies from many different industries and countries, Jelassi and Enders illustrate powerfully that a

successful strategy consists of the combination of many factors rather than one single element. This is also, and in particular, true for e-business.

The emergence and development of e-business is a chapter from that great story which deals with the question of how something new comes into being. It is a chapter from the history of innovation, and for that reason alone it deserves to be examined in detail. It was not the established firms who seized the new opportunities, but rather the outsiders. The outsider as innovative strategic genius is not an unusual phenomenon. Because venture capital for e-business start-ups was seemingly unlimited, droves of inexperienced entrepreneurs, many of them with unsustainable business plans, managed to reach the starting block and simply took off. The laws of the market have caught up with all of them. Only the best managed to survive.

It is important to have a precise understanding of the history of e-business, as the world of e-business has given the whole economy an extraordinary boost of motivation. The fact that so many people, young and old, felt the call to become entrepreneurs is in, and by, itself worth more than the resulting ventures. There is no growth, no value creation and no employment without innovation and without entrepreneurs. And there is no innovation without advantage. E-business is the story of the creation of an advantage. It is important that this story is remembered and told.

Professor Dr Bolko von Oetinger
Senior Vice-President and Director of the Strategy Institute of The Boston Consulting Group 2nd April 2004

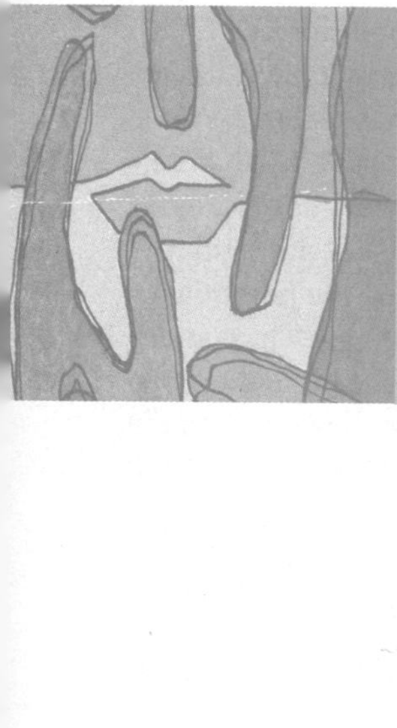

How companies can gain business value from e-technologies – information and communication technologies and productivity

By Erkki Liikanen
European Union Commissioner for Enterprise and Information Society

Information and communication technologies (ICT) are opening up new opportunities for businesses and government. They are allowing them to streamline the way they work and add value to the goods and services they offer. They are boosting productivity, creating new business value and enhancing competitiveness. Investing in ICT, in line with business objectives, is therefore vital for driving the productivity growth that Europe needs if it is to achieve its strategic goal of becoming a dynamic, competitive, knowledge-based economy.

Europe's productivity growth is increasingly being driven by e-business. The West European market for ICT is set to grow by over 3% in 2004, according to the latest report by the European Information Technology Observatory (EITO)[1]. But, to deliver this productivity dividend, ICT goods and services must be put to work throughout the economy. The EITO report also sounds the warning that these benefits risk being held back if Europe faces a weak economic recovery, budget restrictions, and a lack of skills and technology culture. This will inhibit ICT investment, especially by small and medium-sized enterprises (SMEs).

---

1 http://www.eito.com/index-eito.html

So what is 'e-business'? It covers e-commerce (buying and selling online) and also the restructuring of business processes to make the best use of digital technologies. It is starting to have a profound effect on every aspect of the European economy and the way people work. It offers opportunities, but also poses challenges for both companies and consumers. However, e-business is not just about making Internet connections or selling online. Businesses have to move beyond that if they want to boost their competitiveness. They have to pump ICT for its full potential if they are to see their overall performance strengthened.

Reaping the benefits of e-Business

The November 2003 e-Business W@tch[2] survey identified two factors for e-business maturity: a company's size and the sector in which it operates. Large companies are generally still ahead of smaller ones, especially in their use of more advanced e-business applications. Manufacturing industries, such as automotive or electronics and electrical machinery, are using ICT to improve their supply chain efficiency, while consumer-oriented services, like tourism or retail, are still using e-business mainly to improve their customer relations.

This impact is also reflected if we compare overall EU and US productivity growth. Slower labour productivity growth in the EU since the mid 1990s is making us less competitive. Comparisons show how US productivity has grown fastest in ICT-producing and ICT-using sectors like wholesale and retail trade. They are the ones who have invested most in new technologies, re-organized how they do things and provided their employees with the skills needed to make the most of these investments. They are reaping the benefits of both technology and, in many cases, e-Business.

But we should not forget that there are areas where EU productivity growth is better, for example, in electronic communications. This is the result of deregulation-driven competition, strong investment, reorganization of enterprises and the wide take-up of new services. This is where policy-makers have a role to play – creating the regulatory and other conditions in which businesses of all sizes and across a wide range of sectors can make the most of e-business.

So, this is the e-business challenge for small and medium-sized firms today. They need not only to trade online, but to build ICT effectively and productively into the way their businesses operate. This entails at least three things. Firstly, *re-thinking* and adapting the way that they use ICTs. Secondly, *joining* in the economy-wide trend for business clusters to change from mere informal alliances of business partners into 'virtual organizations' with highly interlinked infrastructure and business processes. And thirdly, *equipping* management and employees with the skills they need to work in this dynamic environment.

Re-thinking ICTs

e-Business is about creativity and innovation. It is enabling people and knowledge to generate new business opportunities. To spot a market, it takes an entrepreneur. But technological progress is certainly revealing some of the best places to look.

---

2 http://www.ebusiness-watch.org/

Developments in broadband access and third-generation mobile communications are opening up new ways to create and exploit ideas. Inter-operable technologies and new business applications are lowering transaction costs and enabling businesses to switch easily among networks of business partners, so as to keep pace with changes in demand. Tools such as intranets and portals, and technologies for managing content and communications are enhancing profitability, while the progress of high-speed mobile and wireless communications allows these tools to be used in a seamless information society almost anywhere in the world.

Innovative firms are showing how these tools can be used to:

- transform businesses, letting them compete in new, faster and better ways;
- facilitate the development of goods and services and bring them to the market faster;
- create, develop and use knowledge to win more business, change the nature of business won, increase efficiency and reduce risk;
- serve customers through many different and better co-ordinated channels;
- create new brand experiences for customers, suppliers and business partners; and
- optimize exchanges with all stakeholders – customers, suppliers, business partners and staff.

Hundreds of small businesses across Europe have taken part in EU-funded 'take-up' projects, which demonstrate what e-business tools can do. With the help of local or regional 'catalyst' organizations and by sharing development work and results, these businesses have been able to re-think and adapt emerging technologies to their business needs.

Of course, any SME investing in ICT needs to think hard about how long it will take to recoup its investment. The average return-on-investment time for companies in a recent EU ICT take-up showcases study[3] was 19 months, but many managed it in under a year. (ROI times ranged from 6 to 36 months). Although this study does not generalize about the impact of ICT take-up on sales, 18 out of the 22 showcase firms reported that their competitiveness had either increased significantly or 'sky-rocketed'.

Joining networks

To make the most of ICT, small firms often need to be part of collaborative networks made-up of different enterprises. These networks are effectively becoming 'virtual organizations'. Their close inter-linkage and business processes needed to supply value-adding goods and services on demand. Small firms can contribute their specific strengths and skills, and at the same time access the competitive advantages of a large business network.

Today, firms are working in networks in almost all industrial sectors, mainly to improve their supply chains from both the customer and supplier sides. This brings benefits from improving supply chains, faster response times and lower costs from better logistics and customer management. The next 'big thing' in collaborative networks is to stimulate the creation and innovation process within these networks. Each partner contributes his expertise and know-how, and the network creates value together. This degree of collaboration requires all participating firms to share some of their knowledge with other firms that they trust. They must not only share technology, but also be prepared to transform their traditional forms, structures and practices.

---

3 European e-Business Showcases, ISBN 92-894-5057-6 © European Communities, 2003. Luxembourg: Office for Official Publications of the European Communities, 2003.

Business-to-business (B2B) e-marketplaces, for example, bring together many buyers and sellers, facilitating new partnerships and streamlining business processes. Larger enterprises use them mainly to save transaction costs and reduce prices. But they also enable small firms to find new business partners and to establish new niches in bigger companies' value chains.

Large firms often find that small ones are working on the same issues. It may be in their own interest to help the small firms to come up with new solutions. Networking through e-marketplaces can thus pave the way for a more intelligent and productive use of technology with all the businesses concerned coming out on top, leading to increased productivity, efficiency and competitiveness.

Small firms that are reluctant to join B2B e-marketplaces may eventually be forced to do so. The large companies and public authorities to whom they supply goods and services are doing a growing share of their transactions electronically, either via their own Internet trading platforms or in third party e-marketplaces. Small suppliers could eventually be obliged to take part in electronic auctions and tenders just to stay in business.

Reluctance to join these e-marketplaces may reflect a lack of awareness among small firms of the potential benefits. But there are real barriers too. These include the difficulty of judging which of the many e-marketplaces can be trusted or suits a small firm's business needs, and the lack of commonly-agreed standards for goods and services supplied. Finally, many small firms worry about the possibility of unfair practices, such as price-fixing, in online auctions.

Policy makers can help, by removing barriers to the use of e-marketplaces, raising awareness of their benefits, improving market transparency and promoting fair business practices. To build trust, they should strive to improve access to neutral information on these marketplaces. European standardization initiatives to develop electronic catalogues of goods and services can enhance market transparency. To counter concerns about electronic auctions, codes of conduct should be drawn up to ensure fair and transparent business practices. In addition, practical solutions like 'hotlines' could enable small firms to lodge any complaints about unfair behaviour.

e-Skilling

The European Commission is allocating €250 million, a substantial amount from within its sixth research framework programme, to research innovative forms of e-business and e-work. The results of this research will feed into new policies, which will be taken forward in co-operation with the EU Member States.

The European e-Skills Forum[4] is one example. It aims to foster an open dialogue among stakeholders and to push action that can help to narrow the e-skills gap and to address skills mismatches. One way of helping to do this is its preparation of common e-skills certification arrangements across Europe.

e-Government applications

The right combination of ICT, re-organization and training is also bringing improvements to productivity within governments and public administrations, allowing them to do more for less money. However, the full effects of investments in new technology depend on accompanying it with a reorganization of the way in which services are delivered, and different departments and agencies inter-operate at

4 http://europa.eu.int/comm/enterprise/ict/policy/ict-skills.htm

regional, national and European level. A recent survey[5] provides a helpful guide for public administrations wanting to improve the quality and take-up of their own online public services through back-office reorganization.

Administrative reorganization that harnesses the full potential of ICT can cut costs, boost productivity, and provide simpler and more flexible organizational structures. It can also help to ensure that systems work together across the administration and can improve the working environment for staff.

The practical results for the public and for businesses are fewer visits to administrations, together with faster, cheaper, more accessible and efficient services. Benefits are also reflected in fewer errors, more openness, easier to use systems and greater user control.

Examples of good practice included substantial savings in enrolment in higher education in Finland and the UK. In the Finnish case, self-service by students accessing the online service has reduced the burden imposed by enrolment on administrative staff. In the University of Helsinki alone, this has reduced the number of desk visitors by about 16,000 per annum.

The design of a Danish citizens' portal makes it easier to measure benefits. The most common result is that the technology itself may give 20% of a given saving while the redesign of organizational processes provides the remaining 80% of the saving.

The survey, financed by the European Commission as part of the 'benchmarking' of eEurope, includes 29 in-depth "best practice" case studies. Covering EU Member States (plus Iceland, Norway and the European Commission itself), it looks at a common list of 20 basic public services and offers a set of recommendations to public online service providers.

Improving our productivity performance is essential if Europe's companies are to remain globally competitive and power economic growth and new jobs. The adoption by businesses of all sizes of new technologies will help them to add value to their activities and transform what they do. This is an essential part of our response to global competition. It will also create a long-lasting process of innovation which will help to fuel sustainable improvements in our economy over the years head.

For the economy as a whole, high levels of investment in ICT, a strong ICT-producing industry, and ICT-driven innovation will be crucial to raising the Union's overall potential for growth. At company level, those who embrace ICT, and with it innovation and improved performance, should see this reflected in higher profits and increased market share, provided it is combined with organizational change and upgrading of skills. This does not happen overnight. It can take five years or more for this combination of ICT and organizational capital deepening to pay off, but once it does the returns achieved are above average.

With the right regulatory, financial and business conditions, constant technological advances combined with organizational and business innovation, will deliver a lasting transformation of the economy and the business environment over the decade ahead. This is an exciting challenge, but one which business and Europe must undoubtedly pursue.

Erkki Liikanen
European Union Commissioner for Enterprise and Information Society
Brussels, April 2004

---

5 'Reorganisation of Government Back Offices for Better Electronic Public Services – European Good Practices' http://europa.eu.int/egovernment_research

PREFACE

'People tend to overestimate new technology in the short run and underestimate it in the long run.'

Bo Harald, Head of e-banking at Nordea Bank, Finland[1]

Context and positioning of the book

When we talked to colleagues and friends during the last few months about our e-business book project, many of them asked whether we were arriving too late with this book. They reminded us that the Internet bubble had burst three years ago and that most online companies had since gone bankrupt. This is certainly true, yet we nonetheless believe that it is indeed a very timely moment to publish a book on e-business and strategy.

Since the spectacular burst of the bubble in 2000, companies all over the world have continued to develop and implement e-business strategies, albeit with much less public attention and media coverage than before. Similar to other important technological revolutions such as railways or steam engines, the Internet has also undergone a typical cycle of boom and bust. Following a bust, technological revolutions rebound, and it is only then – during the 'golden age' – that they show their true impact. At the time of the writing of this book, it looks as if e-business has entered this golden age.

However, this development is not adequately mirrored in the e-business literature. During the boom and bust years, there was plenty of interest in the academic and business communities about Internet start-ups, their value-creation potential, the rising stock valuations and, subsequently, the bankruptcies of many fallen stars. Ever since the bubble burst, though, this interest has waned considerably. During our research, we found very few books published after the collapse of the dot.com bubble that specifically address e-business strategy issues. We also noticed that there were many excellent books on strategy and many books on e-business, yet there were relatively few books that attempted to bring the two fields together in a comprehensive and rigorous manner.

This book, as its title suggests, attempts to close these gaps. It aims at providing readers with a holistic and integrated view of the realms of strategy and e-business by focusing on strategic concepts and linking them to actual cases of companies engaged in e-business activities. It also aims at going beyond the hype by closely analyzing examples of failure as well as success in order to help readers assess the underlying drivers for a successful e-business strategy.

1 Personal interview with Bo Harald, 20 September 2003.

Target readers

Strategies for e-Business is a textbook targeted at senior managers, business strategists, entrepreneurs, consultants, participants enrolled in MBA, Masters and executive education programmes and students in the final year of their undergraduate education. It should be of interest to general management programmes and seminars as well as to those specializing in e-business, e-commerce, technology management, marketing, entrepreneurship and business strategy.

Key features

The key differentiating features of this book include the following:

- *A detailed study approach for e-business strategy.* Creativity and analytical ability are of fundamental importance in the strategy formulation process. Chapter 2 of this book discusses how to improve these qualities through the use of concepts and cases.
- *A comprehensive e-business strategy framework.* This framework serves as a comprehensive basis for e-business strategy formulation. It is based on rigorous and time-proven concepts from the field of strategic management, which were adapted to the specific context of e-business.
- *An e-business roadmap.* Part 3 of the book contains an e-business roadmap that is meant as a guide to help in the formulation process of an e-business strategy. It provides an overview of the key issues in strategic management. At the same time, extensive cross-references to the more detailed e-business strategy framework allow the reader to obtain more in-depth information when needed.
- *In-depth case studies.* The book contains 28 real-world case studies, which provide in-depth accounts of how companies in several industries and different countries have developed and implemented electronic and mobile commerce strategies. All the cases result from first-hand field-based research, which the case authors have personally conducted, in most cases in co-operation with executives and top-level managers of the companies involved.
- *Broad coverage of the time horizon covered by the cases.* The time period that the cases cover spans from the grassroots of e-commerce (1993–95), to the rise of the Internet (1996–2000), to the subsequent burst of the bubble (in 2000), to the current consolidation period (from 2001 to the present). With this time span, we hope to provide a much broader perspective and thereby offer a more longitudinal and enriching view of the subject and the way it has evolved over time in terms of concepts and frameworks as well as strategies and practices.
- *Geographic focus on Europe.* While most of the existing e-business casebooks focus on companies that are based in the USA, this book focuses primarily on companies operating in Europe. In addition to the USA and Japan, European countries covered by the case studies of the book include Denmark, France, Germany,

Finland, Italy, Norway, Portugal, Spain, Sweden, the Netherlands and the UK. In addition to the technological aspects discussed in the cases, the wide variety of countries helps to provide insights into the specific business environment and national culture that characterize the different countries covered.

Structure and content

Content-wise, Part 1 presents the context of the book. Chapter 1 introduces the key terminology and evolution of e-business. It emphasizes the distinct phases that technological revolutions go through before reaching their full potential. Chapter 2 looks at how the concepts and cases presented in the book can help managers and students interested in e-business strategies to expand their skills along the dimensions of creativity and analytical ability.

Part 2 suggests a strategy framework for the formulation of e-business strategies. Chapter 3 presents the external environment of e-business ventures. This includes an analysis of the macro-environment and the industry structure. Chapter 4 focuses on market segmentation and market targeting for e-business. Chapter 5 is concerned with understanding the generic concept of value and the Internet-impacted value chain. It also discusses the conflict between the market-based and the resource-based view of strategy formulation. Chapter 6 analyzes different strategy options for creating value in the market space. Chapter 7 is concerned with the impact of the Internet on the horizontal boundaries of a firm. In particular, it deals with the concepts of economies of scale and scope and the optimal timing of market entry. Chapter 8 considers the impact of the Internet on the vertical boundaries of a firm. Chapter 9 outlines the internal organization of a firm's e-business activities.

Part 3 provides a road map for the formulation of an e-business strategy. Through the use of cross-references, this roadmap is closely linked to the e-business strategy framework presented in Part 2.

Part 4 contains the case studies on e-business. To provide an overview of all case studies, it starts with a brief synopsis of each case, and is then followed by the full-length case studies. At the end of each case study, we suggest a number of questions for personal reflection and group discussion. These questions are meant to guide the analysis among colleagues (and classmates) of the case study at hand.

Getting the most from *Strategies in e-Business*

In order to gain the most benefit from this book, we recommend that you try to achieve the following when working through the book chapters:

- Thoroughly understand the theoretical concepts presented in the e-business strategy framework.
- Critically assess the strengths and weaknesses of each concept and determine the context for its appropriate use.

- Apply the concepts when analyzing the cases and make action-oriented recommendations backed up by logical reasoning and supporting arguments.
- Expand the usage of the concepts and the frameworks into other business situations that you encounter in your daily work or study.

To make your learning experience more effective and enriching, the book contains the following features:

- *Chapter at a glance* at the beginning of each chapter provides a quick overview of the most important topics discussed in the chapter.
- *Related case studies* are included at the beginning of each chapter to illustrate which cases are most relevant for the topics discussed. For more information on this, Exhibit P.1 illustrates the relationships between the case studies and specific chapters and sections of the book.
- *Learning outcomes* offer a brief description of what you should have achieved after reading the chapter.
- Different types of boxes are contained in the text body of each chapter to provide added information about the concepts that are discussed.
  - *FT articles* are taken from the *Financial Times* to provide a journalistic perspective (within the timeframe context) of the issue discussed in the section.
  - *Critical Perspectives* present a different, if not opposing, view to the position taken in the main text of the chapter. For instance, the resource-based view is presented as a critical perspective on Porter's market-based view to strategy formulation. Weighing the merits of each view is a valuable exercise for gaining a more in-depth understanding of the concept that is presented.
  - Additional *e-Business Concepts*, such as e-CRM or the 'blow up' between richness and reach, are intended to expand the conceptual thinking presented in the chapter.
  - *Strategy in Action* boxes are mini-case examples that provide an additional illustration of the concepts discussed in the chapter. These examples feature specific e-business strategy issues at companies such as easyJet, FedEx or Amazon.com.
- *Summaries* at the end of each chapter allow you to review the most important points that were discussed in the chapter.
- *Review questions* help you assess your understanding of the material presented in the chapter. In general, the answers to these questions are straightforward since they are based on the material presented in the chapter.
- *Discussion questions* help you to transfer the concepts from the chapter into different business contexts. They are also meant as a starting point for discussion with your colleagues and peers.
- *Recommended key reading* provides a select list of additional books and articles that you can read if you wish to find out more about a specific topic.
- *Useful weblinks* provide either the source or additional information on some material contained in the chapter.

Exhibit P.1 The cases cover different industries and focus on a variety of different themes

	Case name		Chapter 3		Chapter 4			Chapter 5		Chapter 6	Chapter 7		Chapter 8	Chapter 9	
			Macro-environment	Industry structure	B2C market segmentation	B2B market segmentation	Mass customization	Value creation	e-CRM/virtual value chain	Competitive advantage	Economies of scale and scope	Early-mover (dis-) advantages	'Make-or-buy' decisions	online/offline channel management	e-Business organizational structure
IT infrastructure and services	1 Minitel	209	●●					●		●		●●			
	2 CompuNet	224	●				●●	●●	●	●					
e-Government and e-education	3 e-Government	237	●●					●							
	4 Euro-Arab Management School	247									●●		●●		
B2C in retailing	5 Alcampo *vs.* Peapod	253						●				●●		●	●●
	6 Amazon *vs.* BOL	269		●●			●●	●●		●●	●●		●●	●	●●
	7 Nettimarket	288			●●										
	8 Tesco	298						●		●●	●●			●●	
	9 ChateauOnline	310			●●			●		●●					
B2C in financial services	10 Advance Bank	325					●●		●●				●●	●	
	11 Electronic purse	341	●●					●							
	12 Nordea	355	●					●	●●	●●				●●	
B2C in manufacturing	13 Ducati	371						●●						●●	
	14 Ducati *vs.* Harley	386					●●	●					●●		●●
B2C in media	15 Terra Lycos	400		●●					●●						
	16 Google	420		●				●●				●			
	17 DoubleClick	433						●		●●		●			
B2B e-commerce and B2B e-marketplaces	18 Brun Passot	449		●		●●				●					
	19 CitiusNet	462				●●		●	●						
	20 mondus	480				●●									
	21 Covisint	499				●●		●			●				●●
C2C e-commerce	22, 23, 24 eBay (A, B, international)	514–538						●●				●●			
P2P e-commerce	25 Online file-sharing	539		●●				●		●●				●	
Mobile e-commerce	26 12Snap	554			●●			●	●			●●			
	27 paybox	570	●					●		●		●			
	28 NTT DoCoMo	584	●●					●				●			

●● Primary focus of the case study ● Secondary focus of the case study

GUIDED TOUR OF THE BOOK

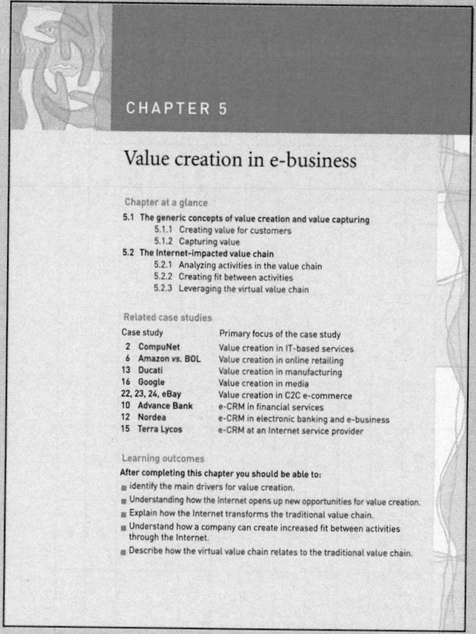
CHAPTER 5

Value creation in e-business

Chapter at a glance

5.1 The generic concepts of value creation and value capturing
5.1.1 Creating value for customers
5.1.2 Capturing value
5.2 The Internet-impacted value chain
5.2.1 Analyzing activities in the value chain
5.2.2 Creating fit between activities
5.2.3 Leveraging the virtual value chain

Related case studies

Case study	Primary focus of the case study
2 CompuNet	Value creation in IT-based services
6 Amazon vs. BOL	Value creation in online retailing
13 Ducati	Value creation in manufacturing
16 Google	Value creation in media
22, 23, 24, eBay	Value creation in C2C e-commerce
10 Advance Bank	e-CRM in financial services
12 Nordea	e-CRM in electronic banking and e-business
15 Terra Lycos	e-CRM at an Internet service provider

Learning outcomes

After completing this chapter you should be able to:

- identify the main drivers for value creation.
- Understanding how the Internet opens up new opportunities for value creation.
- Explain how the Internet transforms the traditional value chain.
- Understand how a company can create increased fit between activities through the Internet.
- Describe how the virtual value chain relates to the traditional value chain.

Each chapter opens with a **brief summary** of the key points to aid readers' assessment of the benefit of the chapter.
Learning outcomes highlight core coverage, helping the reader to structure their learning and evaluate their progress.

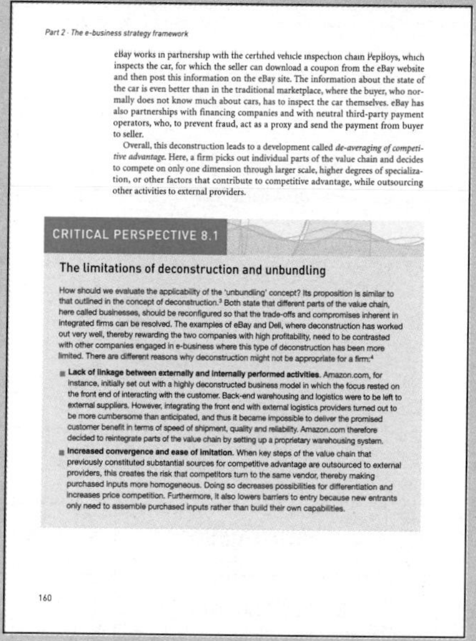
Part 2 · The e-business strategy framework

eBay works in partnership with the certified vehicle inspection chain PepBoys, which inspects the car, for which the seller can download a coupon from the eBay website and then post this information on the eBay site. The information about the state of the car is even better than in the traditional marketplace, where the buyer, who normally does not know much about cars, has to inspect the car themselves. eBay has also partnerships with financing companies and with neutral third-party payment operators, who, to prevent fraud, act as a proxy and send the payment from buyer to seller.

Overall, this deconstruction leads to a development called *de-averaging of competitive advantage*. Here, a firm picks out individual parts of the value chain and decides to compete on only one dimension through larger scale, higher degrees of specialization, or other factors that contribute to competitive advantage, while outsourcing other activities to external providers.

CRITICAL PERSPECTIVE 8.1

The limitations of deconstruction and unbundling

How should we evaluate the applicability of the 'unbundling' concept? Its proposition is similar to that outlined in the concept of deconstruction.[3] Both state that different parts of the value chain, here called businesses, should be reconfigured so that the trade-offs and compromises inherent in integrated firms can be resolved. The examples of eBay and Dell, where deconstruction has worked out very well, thereby rewarding the two companies with high profitability, need to be contrasted with other companies engaged in e-business where this type of deconstruction has been more limited. There are different reasons why deconstruction might not be appropriate for a firm:[4]

- **Lack of linkage between externally and internally performed activities.** Amazon.com, for instance, initially set out with a highly deconstructed business model in which the focus rested on the front end of interacting with the customer. Back-end warehousing and logistics were to be left to external suppliers. However, integrating the front end with external logistics providers turned out to be more cumbersome than anticipated, and thus it became impossible to deliver the promised customer benefit in terms of speed of shipment, quality and reliability. Amazon.com therefore decided to reintegrate parts of the value chain by setting up a proprietary warehousing system.
- **Increased convergence and ease of imitation.** When key steps of the value chain that previously constituted substantial sources for competitive advantage are outsourced to external providers, this creates the risk that competitors turn to the same vendor, thereby making purchased inputs more homogeneous. Doing so decreases possibilities for differentiation and increases price competition. Furthermore, it also lowers barriers to entry because new entrants only need to assemble purchased inputs rather than build their own capabilities.

160

Critical Perspective boxes present alternative viewpoints and encourage the reader to critically evaluate key ideas and practices.

Where possible **figures and artwork** are used to illustrate concepts and provide useful learning aids.

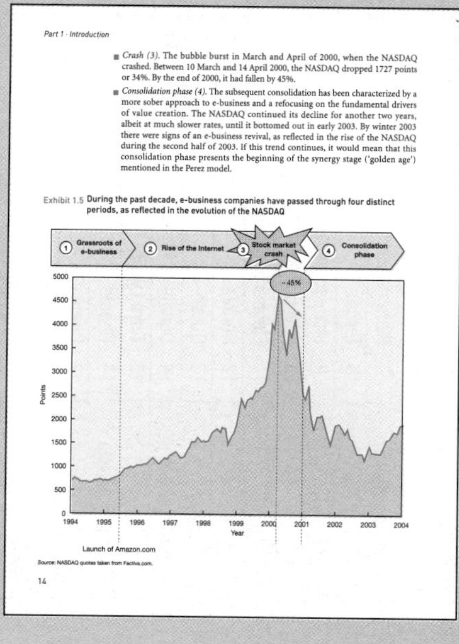
Part 1 · Introduction

- *Crash (3).* The bubble burst in March and April of 2000, when the NASDAQ crashed. Between 10 March and 14 April 2000, the NASDAQ dropped 1727 points or 34%. By the end of 2000, it had fallen by 45%.
- *Consolidation phase (4).* The subsequent consolidation has been characterized by a more sober approach to e-business and a refocusing on the fundamental drivers of value creation. The NASDAQ continued its decline for another two years, albeit at much slower rates, until it bottomed out in early 2003. By winter 2003 there were signs of an e-business revival, as reflected in the rise of the NASDAQ during the second half of 2003. If this trend continues, it would mean that this consolidation phase presents the beginning of the synergy stage ('golden age') mentioned in the Perez model.

Exhibit 1.5 During the past decade, e-business companies have passed through four distinct periods, as reflected in the evolution of the NASDAQ

Source: NASDAQ quotes taken from Factiva.com.

14

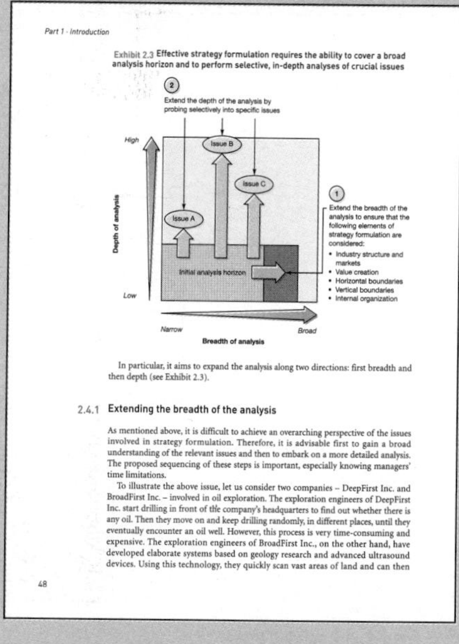
Part 1 · Introduction

Exhibit 2.3 Effective strategy formulation requires the ability to cover a broad analysis horizon and to perform selective, in-depth analyses of crucial issues

In particular, it aims to expand the analysis along two directions: first breadth and then depth (see Exhibit 2.3).

2.4.1 Extending the breadth of the analysis

As mentioned above, it is difficult to achieve an overarching perspective of the issues involved in strategy formulation. Therefore, it is advisable first to gain a broad understanding of the relevant issues and then to embark on a more detailed analysis. The proposed sequencing of these steps is important, especially knowing managers' time limitations.

To illustrate the above issue, let us consider two companies – DeepFirst Inc. and BroadFirst Inc. – involved in oil exploration. The exploration engineers of DeepFirst Inc. start drilling in front of the company's headquarters to find out whether there is any oil. Then they move on and keep drilling randomly, in different places, until they eventually encounter an oil well. However, this process is very time-consuming and expensive. The exploration engineers of BroadFirst Inc., on the other hand, have developed elaborate systems based on geology research and advanced ultrasound devices. Using this technology, they quickly scan vast areas of land and can then

48

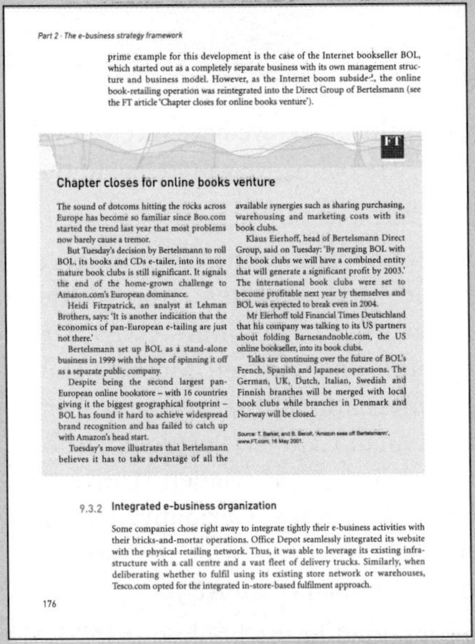

Part 2 · The e-business strategy framework

prime example for this development is the case of the Internet bookseller BOL, which started out as a completely separate business with its own management structure and business model. However, as the Internet boom subsided, the online book-retailing operation was reintegrated into the Direct Group of Bertelsmann (see the FT article 'Chapter closes for online books venture').

FT

Chapter closes for online books venture

The sound of dotcoms hitting the rocks across Europe has become so familiar since Boo.com started the trend last year that most problems now barely cause a tremor.

But Tuesday's decision by Bertelsmann to roll BOL, its books and CDs e-tailer, into its more mature book clubs is still significant. It signals the end of the home-grown challenge to Amazon.com's European dominance.

Heidi Fitzpatrick, an analyst at Lehman Brothers, says: 'It is another indication that the economics of pan-European e-tailing are just not there.'

Bertelsmann set up BOL as a stand-alone business in 1999 with the hope of spinning it off as a separate public company.

Despite being the second largest pan-European online bookstore – with 16 countries giving it the biggest geographical footprint – BOL has found it hard to achieve widespread brand recognition and has failed to catch up with Amazon's head start.

Tuesday's move illustrates that Bertelsmann believes it has to take advantage of all the available synergies such as sharing purchasing, warehousing and marketing costs with its book clubs.

Klaus Eierhoff, head of Bertelsmann Direct Group, said on Tuesday: 'By merging BOL with the book clubs we will have a combined entity that will generate a significant profit by 2003.' The international book clubs were set to become profitable next year by themselves and BOL was expected to break even in 2004.

Mr Eierhoff told Financial Times Deutschland that his company was talking to its US partners about folding Barnesandnoble.com, the US online bookseller, into its book clubs.

Talks are continuing over the future of BOL's French, Spanish and Japanese operations. The German, UK, Dutch, Italian, Swedish and Finnish branches will be merged with local book clubs while branches in Denmark and Norway will be closed.

Source: T. Barker, and B. Benoit, 'Amazon sees off Bertelsmann', www.FT.com, 16 May 2001.

9.3.2 **Integrated e-business organization**

Some companies chose right away to integrate tightly their e-business activities with their bricks-and-mortar operations. Office Depot seamlessly integrated its website with the physical retailing network. Thus, it was able to leverage its existing infrastructure with a call centre and a vast fleet of delivery trucks. Similarly, when deliberating whether to fulfil using its existing store network or warehouses, Tesco.com opted for the integrated in-store-based fulfilment approach.

176

***Financial Times* articles** illustrate theory, offering the reader comment from the business press to complement the academic debate.

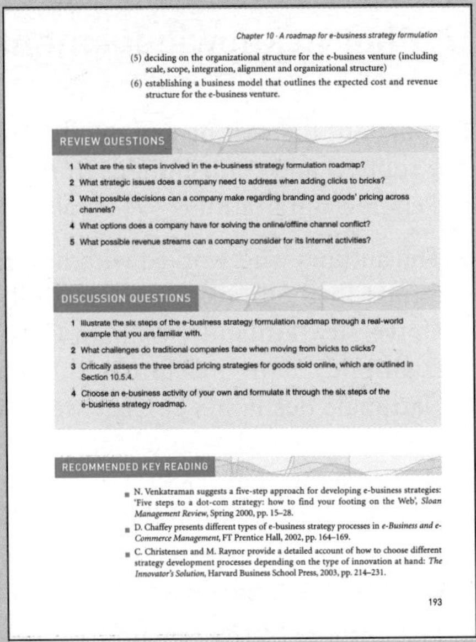

Chapter 10 · A roadmap for e-business strategy formulation

(5) deciding on the organizational structure for the e-business venture (including scale, scope, integration, alignment and organizational structure)

(6) establishing a business model that outlines the expected cost and revenue structure for the e-business venture.

REVIEW QUESTIONS

1 What are the six steps involved in the e-business strategy formulation roadmap?
2 What strategic issues does a company need to address when adding clicks to bricks?
3 What possible decisions can a company make regarding branding and goods' pricing across channels?
4 What options does a company have for solving the online/offline channel conflict?
5 What possible revenue streams can a company consider for its Internet activities?

DISCUSSION QUESTIONS

1 Illustrate the six steps of the e-business strategy formulation roadmap through a real-world example that you are familiar with.
2 What challenges do traditional companies face when moving from bricks to clicks?
3 Critically assess the three broad pricing strategies for goods sold online, which are outlined in Section 10.5.4.
4 Choose an e-business activity of your own and formulate it through the six steps of the e-business strategy roadmap.

RECOMMENDED KEY READING

- N. Venkatraman suggests a five-step approach for developing e-business strategies: 'Five steps to a dot-com strategy: how to find your footing on the Web', *Sloan Management Review*, Spring 2000, pp. 15–28.
- D. Chaffey presents different types of e-business strategy processes in *e-Business and e-Commerce Management*, FT Prentice Hall, 2002, pp. 164–169.
- C. Christensen and M. Raynor provide a detailed account of how to choose different strategy development processes depending on the type of innovation at hand: *The Innovator's Solution*, Harvard Business School Press, 2003, pp. 214–231.

193

Review and discussion questions at the end of each chapter help the reader to test the theory they have learned and develop their ideas in debate with others.

Recommended key reading provides a select list of specialist books and articles for the reader, enabling them to find out more about specific topics introduced in the chapter.

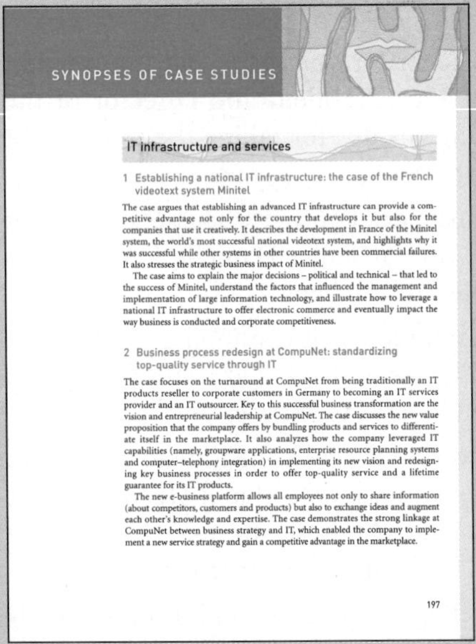

SYNOPSES OF CASE STUDIES

IT infrastructure and services

1 Establishing a national IT infrastructure: the case of the French videotext system Minitel

The case argues that establishing an advanced IT infrastructure can provide a competitive advantage not only for the country that develops it but also for the companies that use it creatively. It describes the development in France of the Minitel system, the world's most successful national videotext system, and highlights why it was successful while other systems in other countries have been commercial failures. It also stresses the strategic business impact of Minitel.

The case aims to explain the major decisions – political and technical – that led to the success of Minitel, understand the factors that influenced the management and implementation of large information technology, and illustrate how to leverage a national IT infrastructure to offer electronic commerce and eventually impact the way business is conducted and corporate competitiveness.

2 Business process redesign at CompuNet: standardizing top-quality service through IT

The case focuses on the turnaround at CompuNet from being traditionally an IT products reseller to corporate customers in Germany to becoming an IT services provider and an IT outsourcer. Key to this successful business transformation are the vision and entrepreneurial leadership at CompuNet. The case discusses the new value proposition that the company offers by bundling products and services to differentiate itself in the marketplace. It also analyzes how the company leveraged IT capabilities (namely, groupware applications, enterprise resource planning systems and computer–telephony integration) in implementing its new vision and redesigning key business processes in order to offer top-quality service and a lifetime guarantee for its IT products.

The new e-business platform allows all employees not only to share information (about competitors, customers and products) but also to exchange ideas and augment each other's knowledge and expertise. The case demonstrates the strong linkage at CompuNet between business strategy and IT, which enabled the company to implement a new service strategy and gain a competitive advantage in the marketplace.

197

Synopses of the case studies provide an overview of the content of each case and draw out the most important themes.

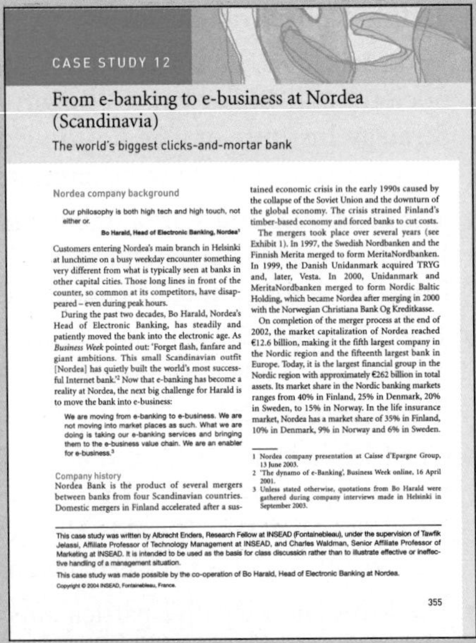

CASE STUDY 12

From e-banking to e-business at Nordea (Scandinavia)

The world's biggest clicks-and-mortar bank

Nordea company background

Our philosophy is both high tech and high touch, not either or.

Bo Harald, Head of Electronic Banking, Nordea[1]

Customers entering Nordea's main branch in Helsinki at lunchtime on a busy weekday encounter something very different from what is typically seen at banks in other capital cities. Those long lines in front of the counter, so common at its competitors, have disappeared – even during peak hours.

During the past two decades, Bo Harald, Nordea's Head of Electronic Banking, has steadily and patiently moved the bank into the electronic age. As *Business Week* pointed out: 'Forget flash, fanfare and giant ambitions. This small Scandinavian outfit [Nordea] has quietly built the world's most successful Internet bank.'[2] Now that e-banking has become a reality at Nordea, the next big challenge for Harald is to move the bank into e-business:

We are moving from e-banking to e-business. We are not moving into market places as such. What we are doing is taking our e-banking services and bringing them to the e-business value chain. We are an enabler for e-business.[3]

Company history

Nordea Bank is the product of several mergers between banks from four Scandinavian countries. Domestic mergers in Finland accelerated after a sustained economic crisis in the early 1990s caused by the collapse of the Soviet Union and the downturn of the global economy. The crisis strained Finland's timber-based economy and forced banks to cut costs.

The mergers took place over several years (see Exhibit 1). In 1997, the Swedish Nordbanken and the Finnish Merita merged to form MeritaNordbanken. In 1999, the Danish Unidanmark acquired TRYG and, later, Vesta. In 2000, Unidanmark and MeritaNordbanken merged to form Nordic Baltic Holding, which became Nordea after merging in 2000 with the Norwegian Christiania Bank Og Kreditkasse.

On completion of the merger process at the end of 2002, the market capitalization of Nordea reached €12.6 billion, making it the fifth largest company in the Nordic region and the fifteenth largest bank in Europe. Today, it is the largest financial group in the Nordic region with approximately €262 billion in total assets. Its market share in the Nordic banking markets ranges from 40% in Finland, 25% in Denmark, 20% in Sweden, to 15% in Norway. In the life insurance market, Nordea has a market share of 35% in Finland, 10% in Denmark, 9% in Norway and 6% in Sweden.

1 Nordea company presentation at Caisse d'Epargne Group, 13 June 2003.
2 'The dynamo of e-Banking', Business Week online, 16 April 2001.
3 Unless stated otherwise, quotations from Bo Harald were gathered during company interviews made in Helsinki in September 2003.

This case study was written by Albrecht Enders, Research Fellow at INSEAD (Fontainebleau), under the supervision of Tawfik Jelassi, Affiliate Professor of Technology Management at INSEAD, and Charles Waldman, Senior Affiliate Professor of Marketing at INSEAD. It is intended to be used as the basis for class discussion rather than to illustrate effective or ineffective handling of a management situation.

This case study was made possible by the co-operation of Bo Harald, Head of Electronic Banking at Nordea.

Copyright © 2004 INSEAD, Fontainebleau, France.

355

28 in-depth case studies from a variety of industries and organisations in Europe and beyond offer the reader a wealth of research and experience on a relatively new area of business. These cases (many from INSEAD) are written by acknowledged experts and many have won awards. Each are followed by suggested discussion questions.

Author acknowledgements

Throughout the writing and publication process of this book, we have received valuable support and contributions from many people. Therefore, we would like to thank and express our gratitude to the following individuals:

- The authors who worked with us during the development of the case studies contained in the book. These are Bill Anckar and Pirkko Walden (Abo Akademi University, Finland), William Cats-Baril (University of Vermont, USA), Leslie Diamond, Hans-Joachim Jost, Timothy Lennon and Morven McLean (Ecole Nationale des Ponts et Chaussées School of International Management, Paris), Carlos Faria and Manuel Joåo Pereira (Universidad Catolica Portugal, Lisbon), Han-Sheong Lai (KPMG, USA), Stefanie Leenen (St Gallen University, Switzerland), Philipp Leutiger (Nuremberg University, Germany), Claudia Loebbecke (University of Cologne, Germany), Michael Müller (McKinsey, Germany), as well as James Téboul and Charles Waldman (INSEAD).
- The authors of the remaining case studies contained in the book: our INSEAD colleagues Ben Bensaou, Soumitra Dutta, Chan Kim, Renée Mauborgne, David Midgley, Subramanian Rangan and Theodoros Evgeniou; also Timothy Devinney from the Australian Graduate School of Management, Sid Huff from the University of Wellington (New Zealand), Michael Wade from the Schulich School of Business at York University (Canada), S. S. George and A. Mukund from the Center for Management Research in Hyderabad (India), and Patricia Reese and Yasushi Shiina from INSEAD.
- Erkki Liikanen (European Union Commissioner for Enterprise and Information Society) and Bolko von Oetinger (Senior Vice-President and Director of the Strategy Institute of The Boston Consulting Group) for taking the time out of their busy schedules to write forewords for the book.
- The colleagues and staff at the Ecole Nationale des Ponts et Chaussées School of International Management (ENPC MBA), in particular Danielle Colletti who helped with the editing of some of the chapters of this book.
- The colleagues at The Boston Consulting Group for their continuing support and their helpful feedback. In particular, we would like to thank Ralf Ermisch, Thomas Röhm, Gunther Schwarz, Just Schürmann and Pierre Yogeshwar.
- Our friends in academia and the business world who took the time to review the manuscript of the book. In particular, we would like to thank Hervé Bousset (Madras Digital), Harald Hungenberg and Andreas König (Nuremberg University), Andreas Keck (Premedion) and Paul Smith (PSA International).
- The MBA and executive participants of several programmes and business schools who, through their analysis and discussion of the case studies, contributed to the shaping of the book.
- The executives and managers of the companies featured in the case studies contained in the book.
- The R&D department of INSEAD, in particular Isabel Assureira.

- The staff at Pearson Education. In particular, we would like to thank our editors Jacqueline Senior and Sarah Wild for their outstanding support throughout the whole publication process.
- The numerous reviewers who provided valuable insights through their detailed feedback on the book proposal. These were: Simon Snowden, University of Liverpool Management School; Dr Mark Xu, Department of Accounting, Law and Management Science, Portsmouth Business School; Prof. Yves Pigneur, Ecole des HEC, Université de Lausanne; Dr Neil Pollock, School of Management, University of Edinburgh; Dr Dave Chaffey, Director, Marketing Insights Limited; Martyn Kendrick, Principal Lecturer and Deputy Head of Department, Department of Strategy and Management, Leicester Business School; Dr Rana Tassabehji, Lecturer in Information Systems and e-Business, Bradford University School of Management.
- Last but not least, special thanks go to our families for their unlimited support and much appreciated encouragement of this book project. It is to our dear ones (Rafia, Samy, Sélim, Mehdi, Kim and Megan as well as to the larger Chadli Jelassi and Dietrich Enders families) that we dedicate this book.

Feedback

We are interested in hearing your comments about this book. We appreciate both critical and supportive feedback, which can help us to improve our future research work. You can reach us via e-mail at **jelassi@enpcmbaparis.com** and **albrecht_enders@web.de**.

Tawfik Jelassi
Albrecht Enders
April 2004

THE AUTHORS

Tawfik Jelassi

Tawfik Jelassi (right) is Professor of e-Business and Information Technology and Co-Dean of the School of International Management at the Ecole Nationale des Ponts et Chaussées (Paris). He is also Affiliate Professor of Technology Management at INSEAD (Fontainebleau). Dr Jelassi holds a PhD from New York University (Stern School of Business), graduate degrees from the Université de Paris-Dauphine and an undergraduate degree from the Institut Supérieur de Gestion (Tunis). His research focuses on e-business and the strategic use of IT. This research has appeared in his books: *Competing through Information Technology: Strategy and Implementation* (Prentice Hall, 1994), and *Strategic Information Systems: A European Perspective* (Wiley, 1994). Professor Jelassi has also published over 80 research articles in leading academic journals and conference proceedings, and was awarded several teaching and research excellence awards. He has taught extensively on MBA and executive programmes in over a dozen countries around the world and has served as an adviser to several international corporate and government organizations.

Albrecht Enders

Albrecht Enders (left) is an Associate with The Boston Consulting Group in the company's Cologne office. Previously, he worked as a Research Fellow at INSEAD where he conducted research on mobile and electronic commerce. He has written numerous articles and case studies on e-business and strategy. Albrecht Enders holds a graduate degree and a PhD in strategic management from the Leipzig Graduate School of Management in Germany and a BA in economics from Dartmouth College in the USA.

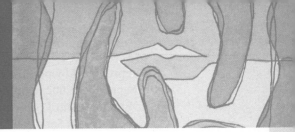

PUBLISHER'S ACKNOWLEDGEMENTS

We are grateful to the following for permission to reproduce copyright material:

Front cover painting from The Boston Consulting Group. The painting is part of a series used in a BCG recruiting campaign throughout Germany and Austria and was painted by Andreas Bogdain who lives and works in Eberswalde, near Berlin; Exhibit 1.1 adapted from *E-business and E-commerce Management*, Financial Times Prentice Hall (Chaffey, D. 2002); Exhibit 1.3 and 1.4 adapted from *Technological Revolutions and Financial Capital: The Dynamics of Bubbles and Golden Ages*, Edward Elgar Publishing (Perez, C. 2002); Exhibit 1.7 adapted from *Net Gain*, Harvard Business School Press (Hagel, J. and Singer, M. 1997); Exhibit 3.1 adapted with the permission of The Free Press, a Division of Simon & Schuster Adult Publishing Group, from *Competitive Strategy: Techniques for Analyzing Industries and Competitors* by Michael E. Porter, Copyright © 1980, 1998 by The Free Press. All rights reserved. Exhibits 3.2 and 5.5 from Strategy and the Internet, *Harvard Business Review*, March 2001, Harvard Business School Publishing Corporation (Porter, M. 2001); Exhibit 3.3 from *Co-opetition* by Adam M. Brandenburger and Barry J. Nalebuff, copyright © 1996 by Adam M. Brandenburger and Barry J. Nalebuff. Used by permission of Doubleday, a division of Random House, Inc. and with kind permission from the authors; Exhibit 4.2 adapted from E Hubs: The new B2B marketplaces, *Harvard Business Review*, May–June 2000, Harvard Business School Publishing Corporation (Kaplan, S. and Sawhney, M. 2000); Exhibit 4.4 from *Marketing Management*, Prentice Hall (Kotler, p. 2000); Exhibits 5.3 and 6.1 adapted with the permission of The Free Press, a Division of Simon & Schuster Adult Publishing Group, from *Competitive Advantage: Creating and Sustaining Superior Performance* by Michael E. Porter, Copyright ©1985, 1998 by Michael E. Porter. All rights reserved. Exhibit 5.6 from Exploiting the Virtual Value Chain, *Harvard Business Review*, Nov.–Dec. 1995, Harvard Business School Publishing Corporation (Rayport, J. and Sviokla, J. 1995); Exhibit 6.2 adapted from Creating new market space, *Harvard Business Review*, Jan.–Feb. 1999, Harvard Business School Publishing Corporation (Kim, C. and Mauborgne, R. 1999); Exhibit 7.2 adapted from *Blown to Bits*, Harvard Business School Publishing Corporation (Evans, P. and Wurster, T. 1999); Exhibits 8.2 and 8.3 adapted from Unbundling the Corporation, *Harvard Business Review*, Mar.–Apr. 1999, Harvard Business School Publishing Corporation (Hagel, J. and Singer, M. 1999); Exhibit 9.1 adapted from *European Management Journal*, Vol. 21, Issue 1, Angehrn, A., Designing mature Internet strategies: The ICDT model, p. 367, 1997, with permission from Elsevier; Exhibit 9.3 adapted from Get the right mix of bricks and clicks, *Harvard Business Review*, May–June 2000, Harvard Business School Publishing Corporation (Gulati, R. and Garino, J. 2000).

Text extracts: 'It's too early for e-business to drop its 'e', May 21, 2002, reproduced by permission from David Bowen; 'Burning money at Boo: the founders of the infamous internet company were fools rather than knaves', November 1, 2001,

reproduced by permission from Tim Jackson; 'Breaking the barriers to creativity', 5 September, 2002, reproduced by permission from W. Altier; 'Business Thinking', and 'Probing' from *Perspectives on Strategy*, Stern, C. and Stalk, G. (editors), Copyright © John Wiley & Sons 1998. This material is used by permission of John Wiley & Sons, Inc.

We are grateful to the Financial Times Limited for permission to reproduce the following material: 'Minitel proves a mixed blessing', © *Financial Times*, 8 February, 2000; 'A billion-dollar mistake: Webvan's failure has been an expensive lesson for the Internet, © *Financial Times*, 10 July, 2001; 'eBay leads online revival as net hits the refresh button', © *Financial Times*, 9 May, 2003; 'Amazon aims to be king of the online retail jungle', © *Financial Times*, 21 October, 2003; 'Covisint fails to move up into the fast lane', © *Financial Times* 4 July, 2002; 'Dell aims to stretch its way of business', © *Financial Times* 13 November, 2003; 'E-marketing in a straitjacket', © *Financial Times*, 1 December, 2003; 'Amazon sees off Bertelsmann', © Financial Times, 16 May, 2001.

Case studies: We are grateful to INSEAD for permission to use the following case studies: Case study 1, Establishing a national IT infrastructure: The case of the French videotex system, Minitel (case and discussion questions); Case study 2, Business process redesign at Compunet: standardizing top-quality service through IT; Case study 8, The Tesco.com experience: is success at hand?; Case study 9, ChateauOnline; Case study 12, From e-banking to e-business at Nordea (Scandinavia): the world's biggest clicks-and-mortar bank; Case study 13, Ducati motorcycle (Italy): riding traditional business channels or racing through the Internet; Case study 14, Ducati (Italy) *vs.* Harley-Davidson (USA): innovating business processes and managing value networks; Case study 15, Terra Lycos: creating a global and profitable integrated media company; Case study 17, DoubleClick Inc.: a strategic transformation; Case study 18, Competing through EDI at Papeteries Brun Passot: making paper passé; Case study 19, CitiusNet: the emergence of a global electronic market; Case study 20, Business-to-business electronic commerce: mondus.com – an e-marketplace for small and medium-sized enterprises; Case study 21, B2B e-marketplace in the automotive industry: Covisint – a co-opetition gamble?; Case study 22, eBay strategy (A); Case study 23, eBay strategy (B); Case study 24 eBay international; Case study 26, 12Snap (Germany, UK, Italy): from B2C mobile retailing to B2B mobile marketing; Case study 27, Paybox.net (Germany): a mobile payment service; Case study 28, NTT DoCoMo i-mode: value innovation at DoCoMo. We are grateful to the following for permission to use their case studies: Case study 4, The Euro-Arab Management School, reproduced by permission from Michael Wade; Case study 16, Google.com: the world's number-one Internet search engine, reproduced by permission from ICFAI Center for Management Research (case and discussion questions).

In some instances we have been unable to trace the owners of copyright material and we would appreciate any information that would enable us to do so.

Part 1

INTRODUCTION

PART OVERVIEW

This introductory part sets up the overall context for the book. It contains the following elements:

- A definition of the key terminology used throughout the book
- An overview of the evolution of e-business over time
- A discussion of how concepts and cases contribute to building e-business competence.

The goal of this introductory part is to provide a guide and a context for the content of the book. Chapter 1 starts out with definitions of the most important terms used in the book, such as e-business, electronic commerce and mobile e-commerce, and the concepts of strategy and value creation. It then provides an overview of the evolution of e-business over the past decade and recognizes four distinct periods: (1) the grassroots of e-business, (2) the rise of the Internet, (3) the crash and (4) the consolidation phase. Chapter 2 shows how cases and concepts help to enhance creativity and analytical abilities, leading to increased overall e-business competence.

CHAPTER 1

Key terminology and evolution of e-business

Chapter at a glance

Learning outcomes

After completing this chapter you should be able to:

- Understand what the terms of 'e-business', 'electronic commerce' and 'mobile e-commerce' mean.
- Define the concept of strategy and differentiate between different levels of strategy development.
- Describe the life cycle of technological revolutions and illustrate it through different historic examples.
- Recognize the four main periods of the e-business evolution over the past decade and explain the peculiar characteristics of each period.

INTRODUCTION

The purpose of this chapter is to set up the stage for the remainder of the book. Since, due to the relative novelty of e-business, there is not yet a clear and shared view of what this domain entails, we first want to ensure a common understanding of the key terminology used throughout the book. Section 1.1 includes the definition of e-business-related terms and concepts as well as some strategy-specific perspectives. Following that, Section 1.2 provides a framework that describes the typical stages of technological revolutions and positions the evolution of electronic business during the past decade within this framework.

1.1 Key terminology

1.1.1 e-Business

The term *e-business* is defined here as the use of electronic means to conduct an organization's business internally and/or externally.[1] Internal e-business activities include the linking of an organization's employees with each other through an intranet to improve information sharing, facilitate knowledge dissemination, and support management reporting. e-Business activities also include supporting after-sales service activities and collaborating with business partners, e.g. conducting joint research, developing a new product and formulating a sales promotion.

In spite of the distinct terminology that is used, e-business should not be viewed in isolation from the remaining activities of a firm. Instead, an organization should integrate online e-business activities with its offline business into a coherent whole. The *Financial Times* (FT) article 'It's too early for e-business to drop its "e"', provides a further discussion of the importance of the 'e' in e-business.

1.1.2 Electronic commerce

Electronic commerce, or *e-commerce*, is more specific than e-business and can be thought of as a subset of the latter (see Exhibit 1.1). Electronic commerce deals with the facilitation of transactions and selling of products and services online, i.e. via the Internet or any other telecommunications network. This involves the electronic trading of physical and digital goods, quite often encompassing all the trading steps such as online marketing, online ordering, e-payment and, for digital goods, online distribution (i.e. for after-sales support activities). e-Commerce applications with external orientation are buy-side e-commerce activities with suppliers and sell-side activities with customers.

1.1.3 Mobile e-commerce

Mobile e-commerce, or *m-commerce*, is a subset of electronic commerce. While it refers to online activities similar to those mentioned in the electronic commerce category, the underlying technology is different since mobile commerce is limited to mobile telecommunication networks, which are accessed through wireless hand-held devices such as mobile phones, hand-held computers and personal digital assistants (PDAs).

Exhibit 1.1 **Electronic business includes electronic commerce and mobile electronic commerce**

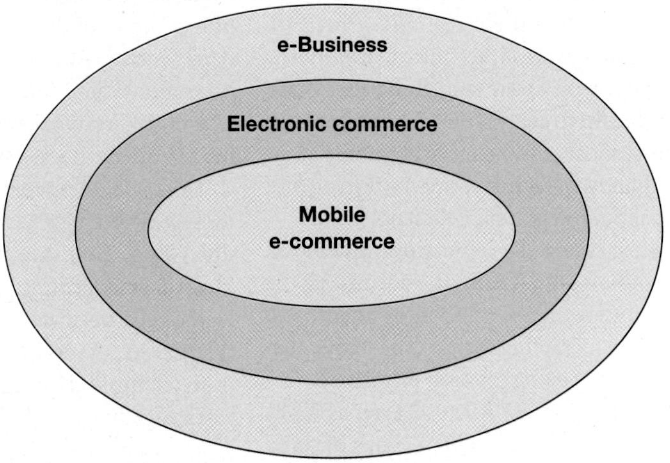

Source: Adapted from D. Chaffey, *E-Business and E-Commerce Management*, FT Prentice Hall, 2002, p. 9.

FT

It's too early for e-business to drop its 'e'

Jargon is used to make the banal sound enthralling, the simple sophisticated. It is often used to disguise the fact that the speaker, or writer, does not know what he is talking about, or cannot be bothered to find a more precise word. In the past five years, one letter has come to symbolize the worst of jargon. The fifth letter in the Roman alphabet, it has been used in front of business, commerce, finance, procurement, learning, enablement, government. Almost any noun you can think of has probably been an e-noun. Companies have used 'e' liberally to give themselves a buzz on the stock market.

Now, 'e' is on its way out. Yet, despite everything I have said, this is bad news. The 'e' has been chased away by the dotcom crash, which transformed it from magic drug to kiss of stock market death. But, even before that, it was going out of fashion. One senior consultant told me in 2000 that the 'e' would be dropped by his organization within a year or two (it was). His argument – widely accepted – was that internet-based business would become so pervasive that it would be pointless, indeed damaging, to talk about it as a separate discipline.

E-business would and should disappear into business. And so it should; but not yet. At the Richmond Events e-forum last October, several hundred senior managers from blue-chip companies gathered on a cruise ship to be assaulted by a mixture of cabernet sauvignon and hard sell from vendors of e-services of various sorts. There was a 'last days of Rome' feeling about it, as delegate after delegate let slip that he or she had either just left their e-job, or was about to.

What was particularly interesting was that people were revealing their 'real selves' beneath their e-titles: they were either information technology people, or they were something else. While a few could talk strategy and technology with equal fluency, most gave their backgrounds away. They were happy speaking about marketing and strategy, or about integration issues; not both.

I have since received a letter from Richmond Events announcing the death of e-forum, saying that its functions would be rolled into either the IT directors or the marketing forum. The divide that was apparent at the event has been formalized.

Why does this matter? Because, even as it has crumbled, the value of the letter 'e' has become ever more clear. It is, or has been, a bridge between technical and non-technical managers.

From the earliest days of the commercial internet, proponent after proponent of the strange new medium said the same thing: 'Don't let the IT people run it.' They believed the effective use of the internet depended not on the technology but on a strategic understanding of what it could do.

Technologists were, of course, vital for implementing the strategy, but they often knew too much about the trees to be able to see the wood. Also, most IT directors had a 'supplier' role to an organization; they were rarely involved in strategic decision-making.

As the commercial internet became e-commerce and then e-business this view held, though there were tensions. Many companies put their trust in new media consultancies led by marketing people who loved to talk strategy. 'Leave your strategy to us; we understand it better than you can,' they would tell their open-walleted clients. They hired technical people – indeed, the real skills shortage was at the technical end – but they kept control.

Sadly, these agencies also sowed the seeds of their own destruction, because they could not match either the technical skills of systems integration specialists, or the strategic skills of the big consultancies. Meanwhile, a sizeable minority of organizations kept their e-business strategy in-house and under the control of their IT departments. Add to this the rush by boards to pour money into Internet ventures simply for the sake of tickling the share price and it is not surprising that so much was wasted so fast by so many.

How is it, then, that any companies managed to exploit the new technology effectively? How did Cisco, Dell, Electrocomponents, General Electric manage it?

Largely, because people at the summit saw that the secret was in bringing technologists and non-technologists together and making them work together – and often they used the banner 'e' as a marshalling-point. The good e-business managers I have met are (or were) either technologists on the way to becoming strategists, or non-technologists with an increasing understanding of IT. On the way, I stress; rarely close to achieving fluency in both.

The new media agencies, for all their arrogance, were also attempting to master both skills. Again, they had a long way to go; so it is a shame that they have been humbled so brutally. The danger, as the e-bridge crashes into the river, is that the great unrealized possibilities of the internet will be swept away with it. When an organization has a cadre of managers with a real understanding of both strategy and technology, fine – let the bridge collapse. But until then, some form of e-business department and function – labeled with whatever jargon – should remain essential to any intelligent group's structure.

Source: D. Bowen, 'It's too early for e-business to drop its "e"', *Financial Times*, 21 May, 2002.

1.1.4 The concept of strategy

In addition to e-business, *strategy* is the second key thrust of this book. More specifically, we analyze and illustrate how firms develop and implement strategies for their e-business activities and draw lessons and guidelines from the studied practices. However, we should recognize that the term 'strategy' means different things to different people. To get a clear understanding of the meaning of strategy the way it is used in this book, let us first consider the following definitions of strategy and then suggest a common foundation.

Strategy is:

> ... the direction and scope of an organization over the long-term, which achieves advantage for the organization through its configuration of resources within a changing environment to the needs of markets and fulfill stakeholder expectations.
>
> **Gerry Johnson and Kevan Scholes**[2]

> ... the determination of the basic long-term goals and objectives of an enterprise, and the adoption of courses of action and the allocation of resources necessary for carrying out theses goals.
>
> **Alfred Chandler**[3]

> ... the deliberate search for a plan of action that will develop a business's competitive advantage and compound it.
>
> **Bruce Henderson.**[4]

> ... the strong focus on profitability not just growth, an ability to define a unique value proposition, and a willingness to make tough trade-offs in what not to do.
>
> **Michael Porter**[5]

Based on the above definitions, we would like to stress the following aspects that are crucial for strategy formulation:[6]

- Strategy is concerned with the *long-term direction* of the firm.
- Strategy deals with the *overall plan for deploying the resources* that a firm possesses.
- Strategy entails the willingness to make *trade-offs*, to choose between different directions and between different ways of deploying resources.
- Strategy is about achieving *unique positioning* vis-à-vis competitors.
- The central goal of strategy is to achieve sustainable *competitive advantage* over rivals and thereby to ensure lasting profitability.

Having defined the concept of strategy, we can now differentiate it from the concept of *tactics*, a term that is often used interchangeably with strategy. Tactics are schemes for individual and specific actions that are not necessarily related to one another. In general, specific actions can be planned intuitively because of their limited complexity. A firm can, for instance, have a certain tactic when it launches a marketing campaign.

Strategy, on the other hand, deals with a more overarching formulation that affects not just one activity at one point in time but all activities of a firm over an extended time horizon. To achieve consistency between different activities over time, intuition is generally not sufficient; it also requires logical thinking. Drawing an analogy with

warfare, we could say that while tactics are about winning a battle, strategy is concerned primarily with winning the war.

It has often been argued that the increasing importance of technology reduces the need for clear strategies. Firms should instead focus on getting their technology to work. This is especially true for the technology underlying e-business and electronic commerce. Yet, technology is not, and cannot be, a substitute for strategy. Overlooking strategy and how a firm can create sustainable competitive advantage is a likely recipe for failure. Just because certain activities are feasible from a technological perspective does not mean that they are sensible from a strategic perspective. Ultimately, information technology (IT) and the Internet should be used not for the sake of using them but instead to create benefit for customers in a cost-efficient way.

Formulating long-term strategies has become more difficult due to the continuously changing business environment. How long-term can a strategy be when the technological environment is permanently changing? This is obviously a difficult question that has no clear-cut answers. When a disruptive innovation emerges and redefines the basis of competition, previous strategies become all but worthless. This was the case, for instance, when Amazon.com entered the book-retailing market with its online bookstore and when Napster launched its file-sharing platform for online music distribution. Nonetheless, it is important to be aware of the trade-offs that arise when a firm gives up long-term strategy in return for short-term flexibility.

Within organizations, we typically recognize the following three different levels of strategy (see Exhibit 1.2). They are (1) *corporate-level strategy*, (2) *business unit strategy* and (3) *operational strategy*.[7] It is important to note here that most of the cases featured in this book deal primarily with issues related to the first two levels of strategy.

Corporate-level strategy

The highest strategy level, i.e. the corporate-level strategy, is concerned with the overall purpose and scope of the firm. It typically involves the chief executive officer (CEO) and top-level managers. Corporate strategy addresses issues such as how to allocate resources between different business units, mergers, acquisitions, partnerships and alliances.

Consider, for instance, the merger in 2000 between AOL and Time Warner, where the CEOs of both firms looked across all the businesses of their respective companies before deciding to merge the two corporations. Another example of corporate strategy that is important in the e-business context is the choice of distribution and sales channels. For example, the top management of Tesco plc first made the decision in 1995 about whether to use the Internet to sell groceries online and then on how to set it up organizationally (see Section 9.3 for a discussion of the different ways of organizing e-commerce ventures). Only then was the responsibility delegated from the corporate level to the Tesco.com business unit.

Business unit strategy

Business unit strategy is concerned primarily with how to compete within individual markets. Dell, for instance, operates distinct business units that target large corporate

customers, private households and public-sector customers. Since these are very separate markets, with differing needs and preferences, it is also necessary to formulate a distinct business unit strategy for each one of these markets (see Section 4.1.2 on market segmentation for e-commerce).

At a more detailed level, a business unit strategy deals with issues such as industry analysis, market positioning and value creation for customers. Furthermore, when formulating a business unit strategy, it is also necessary to think about the desired scale and scope of operations.

Operational strategy

Operational strategy deals with how to implement the business unit strategy with regards to resources, processes and people. In the context of e-business, this includes issues such as optimal website design, hardware and software requirements, and the management of the logistics process. Furthermore, this also includes operational effectiveness issues, which are addressed by techniques such as business process re-engineering (BPR) and total quality management (TQM).

Although these approaches are important, they do not belong intrinsically to strategy formulation, since, as stated above, strategy is about making trade-offs; that is, about deciding which activities a firm should perform and which ones it should *not* perform. Operational issues are of high importance for any organization; however, they are not the primary focus of this book, and covering them in-depth would overextend the scope of the book.[8]

Exhibit 1.2 **The focus area of the cases is on corporate level and business unit strategy**

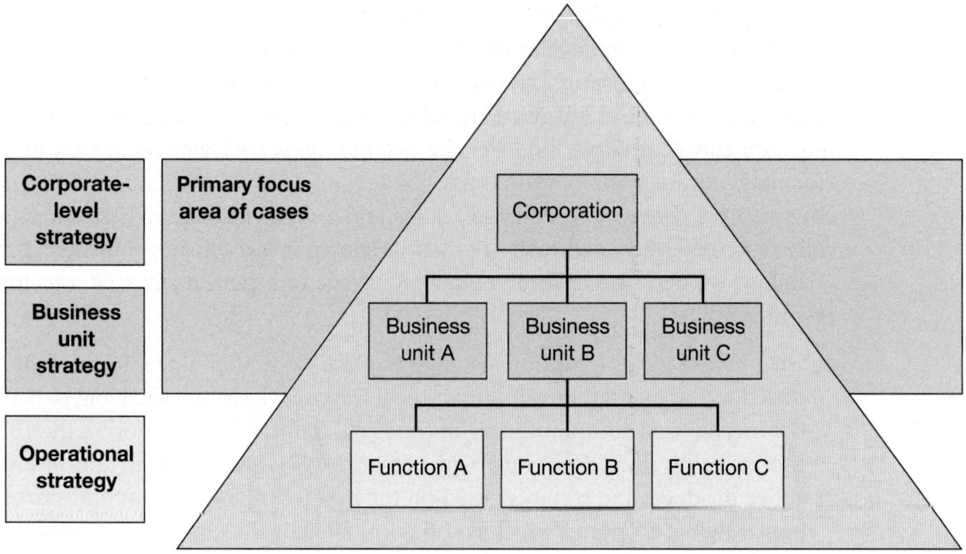

1.1.5 The concept of value creation

The ability of a firm to create value for its customers is a prerequisite condition for achieving sustainable profitability. In the context of e-business strategies, the concept of *value creation* deserves special attention because many Internet start-ups that ended up in bankruptcy at the end of the Internet boom years did not pay enough attention to this issue. Instead, they were frequently concerned mainly with customer acquisition and revenue growth, which was sustainable only as long as venture capitalists and stock markets were willing to finance these firms.

Nowadays, however, in a harder and more turbulent business environment, it is imperative that strategies focus on what value to create and for whom, as well as how to create it and how to capture the value in form of profits. In economic terms, value created is the difference between the benefit a firm provides to its consumers and the costs it incurs for doing so. Because of the importance of value creation, we devote all of Chapter 5 to this topic and address the various issues related to this concept.

1.2 The evolution of e-business

Before discussing e-business from a structural perspective through the e-business strategy framework presented in Part 2, we first want to analyze the evolution of e-business over the past decade and compare it with the life cycle of other *technological revolutions*. Carlota Perez defines a technological revolution as a 'powerful and highly visible cluster of new and dynamic technologies, products and industries, capable of bringing about an upheaval in the whole fabric of the economy and of propelling a long-term upsurge of development'.[9]

Whether the printing press, steam engine, railway or car, all technologies have gone through similar surges. Perez divides the surge of a technological revolution into two consecutive periods: (1) the *installation period*, which consists of an *irruption* stage and a *frenzy* ('gilded age') stage, and (2) the *deployment period*, which consists of a *synergy* ('golden age') stage and a *maturity* stage. These stages are typically separated by a downturn or crash, as shown in Exhibit 1.3.

Below, we describe in more detail each stage of a typical surge of a technological revolution:[10]

- *Irruption (1)*. The irruption stage takes place right after a new technology is introduced to the market. Revolutionary new technologies, also called 'big bangs', include the mechanized cotton industry in the 1770s, railway construction in the 1830s, and, more recently, Intel's first micro-processor in 1971. During the irruption stage, innovative products and services based on the new technology appear and start slowly to penetrate the economy, which is still dominated by the previous technology.
- *Frenzy (2)*. The frenzy stage, also called the 'gilded age', is characterized by a sense of exploration and exuberance as entrepreneurs, engineers and investors alike try to find the best opportunities created by the technological big bang irruption. Using a trial-and-error approach, investors fund numerous projects, which help

Exhibit 1.3 **Technological revolutions move through different stages as their diffusion increases**

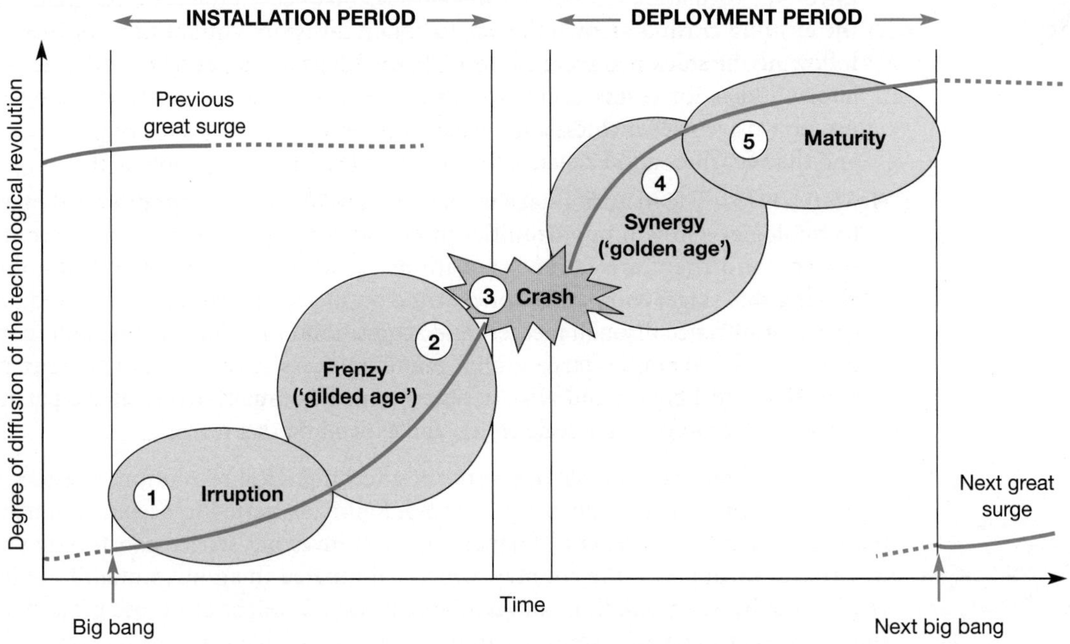

Source: Adapted from C. Perez, *Technological Revolutions and Financial Capital: The Dynamics of Bubbles and Golden Ages*, Edward Elgar, 2002, p. 48.

quickly to install the new technology in the economy. However, as investors become increasingly confident and excited, they start considering themselves to be infallible. Depending on the technological revolution, they have financed digging canals from any river to any other river, building railway tracks between every city and village imaginable, and, more recently, creating online retailing websites for every conceivable product, be it pet food, medicine or furniture. This process typically continues until it reaches an unsustainable exuberance, also called 'bubble' or 'mania'. At that point, the 'paper wealth' of the stock market loses any meaningful relation with the realistic possibilities of the new technology to create wealth.

- *Crash (3)*. The gilded age is followed by a crash, when the leading players in the economy realize that the excessive investments will never be able to fulfil the high expectations. As a result, investors lose confidence and pull their funds out of the new technology. Doing so sets off a vicious cycle, and, as everyone starts to pull out of the stock market, the bubble deflates and the stock market collapses.
- *Synergy (4)*. Following the crash, the time of quick and easy profits has passed. Now, investors prefer to put their money into the 'real' economy, and the successful firms are not the nimble start-ups but instead established incumbents. While, during the frenzy stage, there were many start-ups competing within an industry, the crash led to a shake-out where most of these ventures went out of business. During the synergy stage, a few large companies start to dominate the markets and leverage their financial strength to generate economies of scale and scope. Now, the emphasis is no longer on technological innovation but instead on how to make technology easy to use, reliable, secure and cost-efficient.

In order for the synergy stage to take hold, governmental agencies need to introduce regulations to remedy the fallacies that caused the previous frenzy and the ensuing crash and, by doing so, to regain investors' confidence. For instance, following the stock market crash in 1929, the US government set up separate regulatory bodies for banks, securities, savings and insurances, and also established protective agencies including the Federal Deposit Insurance Corporation (FDIC) and the Securities and Exchange Commission (SEC).

- *Maturity (5):* The maturity stage is characterized by market saturation and mature technologies. Growth opportunities in new and untapped markets are becoming scarcer, and there are fewer innovations resulting from the new technology. During this stage, companies concentrate on increasing efficiency and reducing costs, for instance through mergers and acquisitions. In today's mature automobile industry, for example, large global manufacturers such as Daimler Benz and Chrysler, and Renault and Nissan, have merged or established strategic partnerships in order to generate scale effects and expand market reach.[11]

For a more extensive example of a surge of a technological revolution, consider the evolution of the railway industry in England. Railroads started to become popular in the 1830s. Many entrepreneurs, financed by eager investors, started constructing railway routes throughout the country, which culminated in an investment bubble in 1847. Initially, when building railway tracks, investors sought out those projects that showed a clear need and were easy to build. As the bubble kept growing, investors, searching desperately for investment opportunities, started to fund projects for which there was hardly any demand and that were complicated and costly. Ultimately, railway companies were even building tracks that were running in parallel to one another, even though it was obvious that only one track could be operated profitably in the long term.

Inevitably, the railway bubble burst; after the dust had settled, the stocks of railway companies had lost 85% of their peak value. After the crash in 1847, when a large number of railroad companies went bankrupt, the industry bounced back, rapidly increasing mileage and passengers, and tripling revenues in just five years after the bust. After 1850, railways drove much of England's economic growth, and they continued to dominate the transportation market until the automobile became a medium of mass-transportation in the middle of the twentieth century.[12]

We can observe similar evolutions with other technological revolutions, such as steel production, steam energy and, more recently, the automobile (see Exhibit 1.4).

The above perspective illustrates that the time from the first commercial usage of a new technology to its widespread application can stretch over a period lasting up to 50 years. Within these long periods, the technology's diffusion and growth are not continuous. Instead, they are often marked by a crash, when the initial exuberance and optimism about a new technology fades.

One of the main reasons for these long gestation periods between the irruption and the synergy stages is that it is not sufficient just to have the appropriate technology in place. In addition, managers need to be willing and able to abandon previous ways of doing things and start using the new technology in such a way that it actually creates value. This takes time and requires a lot of experimenting and fine-tuning.

The development of e-business has been quite similar to that described above. During the past decade, e-business has changed dramatically, evolving through the

Exhibit 1.4 Major technological revolutions during the past two centuries show similar patterns of evolution

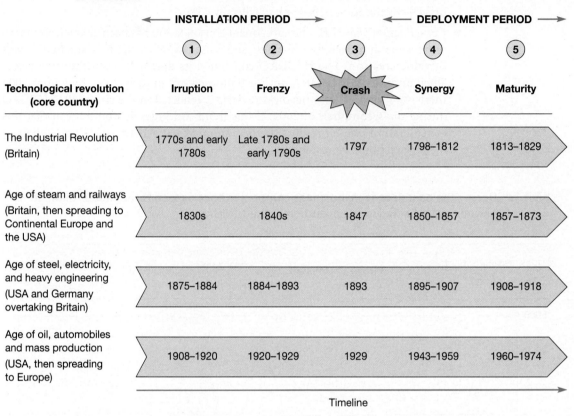

	← INSTALLATION PERIOD →			← DEPLOYMENT PERIOD →	
Technological revolution (core country)	(1) **Irruption**	(2) **Frenzy**	(3) **Crash**	(4) **Synergy**	(5) **Maturity**
The Industrial Revolution (Britain)	1770s and early 1780s	Late 1780s and early 1790s	1797	1798–1812	1813–1829
Age of steam and railways (Britain, then spreading to Continental Europe and the USA)	1830s	1840s	1847	1850–1857	1857–1873
Age of steel, electricity, and heavy engineering (USA and Germany overtaking Britain)	1875–1884	1884–1893	1893	1895–1907	1908–1918
Age of oil, automobiles and mass production (USA, then spreading to Europe)	1908–1920	1920–1929	1929	1943–1959	1960–1974

Timeline →

Source: Adapted from C. Perez, *Technological Revolutions and Financial Capital: The Dynamics of Bubbles and Golden Ages*, Edward Elgar, 2002, p. 57.

following four periods (see Exhibit 1.5), which mirror the evolution of the National Association of Securities Dealers Automated Quotations (NASDAQ)[13] during the same time period.

- *Grassroots of e-business (1).* Before the widespread commercial use of the Internet, the NASDAQ showed only modest increases. Between 1983 and 1993, it hardly doubled from 350 to 700 points. We refer to this period as the grassroots of e-business which corresponds to the irruption stage in the Perez model.
- *Rise of the Internet (2).* Even though the beginning of the dot.com boom cannot be determined precisely, we chose 1995, the year when Amazon.com was launched, as the starting point of the rise of the Internet period.[14] The year 1995 also saw the going public of Netscape, the maker of the Netscape Navigator web browser, which presented the first initial public offering (IPO) of a major Internet company. This period, which corresponds to the 'gilded age', finds its reflection in the strong rise of the NASDAQ, especially during the late 1990s. At the peak of this frenzy stage, the NASDAQ traded at price/earning (p/e) ratios of 62, after it had not exceeded p/e ratios of 21 in the years between 1973 and 1995.[15]

- *Crash (3).* The bubble burst in March and April of 2000, when the NASDAQ crashed. Between 10 March and 14 April 2000, the NASDAQ dropped 1727 points or 34%. By the end of 2000, it had fallen by 45%.
- *Consolidation phase (4).* The subsequent consolidation has been characterized by a more sober approach to e-business and a refocusing on the fundamental drivers of value creation. The NASDAQ continued its decline for another two years, albeit at much slower rates, until it bottomed out in early 2003. By winter 2003 there were signs of an e-business revival, as reflected in the rise of the NASDAQ during the second half of 2003. If this trend continues, it would mean that this consolidation phase presents the beginning of the synergy stage ('golden age') mentioned in the Perez model.

Exhibit 1.5 During the past decade, e-business companies have passed through four distinct periods, as reflected in the evolution of the NASDAQ

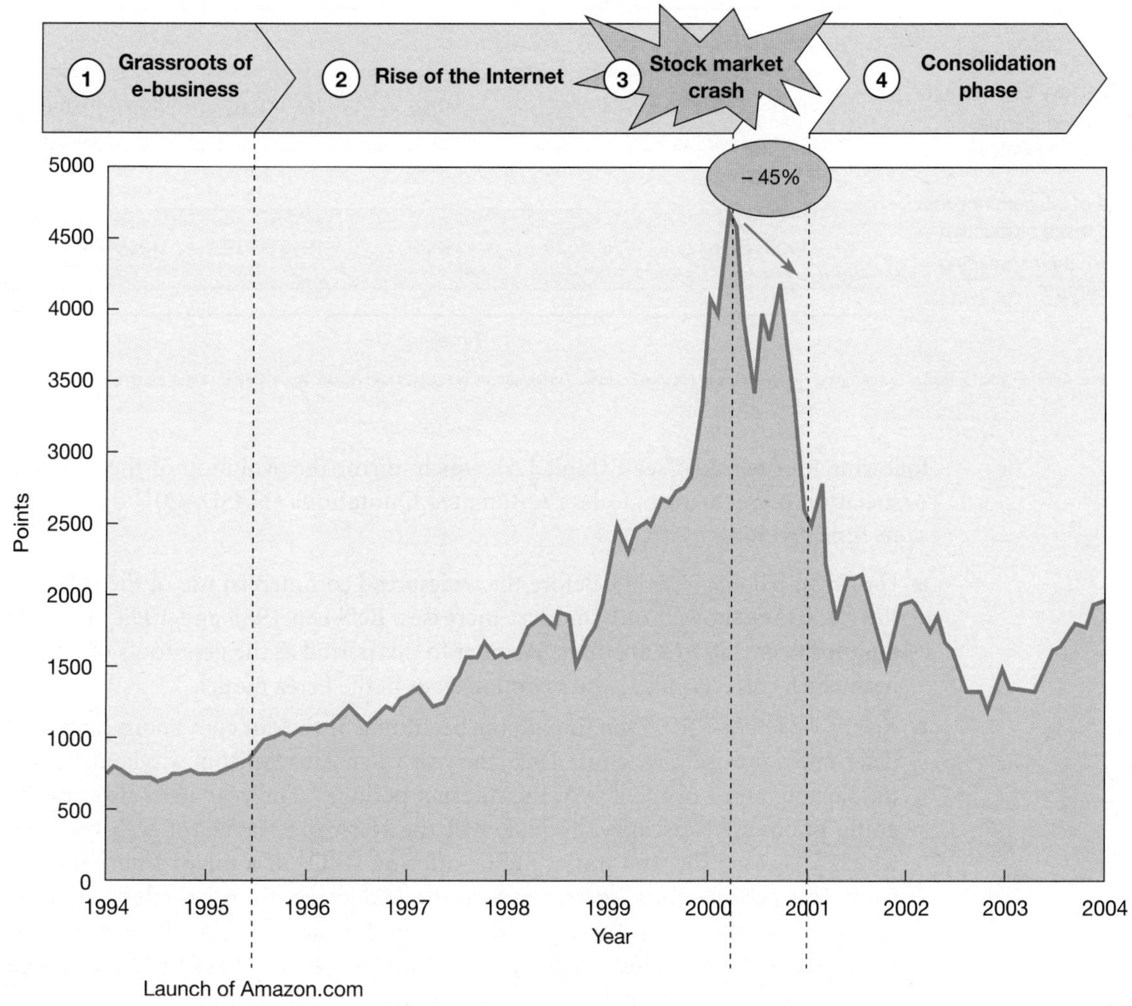

Source: NASDAQ quotes taken from Factiva.com.

In the following sections, the above four time periods are discussed in more detail. The purpose of doing so is twofold:

- First, to provide a longitudinal context for the case studies that are presented in Part 4 of this book (see also Exhibit 1.6). Each case study presents unique insights into the main characteristics of each specific period. These are demonstrated by the content of each case and also the quotes provided by the top management of the companies featured in the case. For instance, the following statement, made by Jeff Bezos, CEO of Amazon.com, in 1998, was perfectly acceptable at that time, but it would hardly be welcomed by investors in today's business climate: 'We are going through a critical stage right now. We want to extend our offer on a global scale and we want to invest even more in customer service; that's all very expensive. This would be a miserable moment to make profits.'

  Also, the chief technology officer of 12Snap, a German start-up company offering mobile marketing services, would have probably made a more exuberant statement during the boom years than the one he made in 2001, when he commented on the strategy of his firm: 'In the next couple of quarters, there is no such a thing as a high growth, high-risk business model. It's our job to create money and a viable business, and that's the focus for now.' Thus, while focusing on the content issues of the cases presented in the book, we also find it particularly revealing to notice how different economic situations influence the actions and statements of the executives and managers who are portrayed throughout the cases.
- Second, to explain with hindsight some of the underlying characteristics of each time period using concepts such as the five forces industry framework, value creation and capturing, and economies of scale and scope. These concepts are explained in more detail in Part 2.

1.2.1 The grassroots of e-business

Before the Internet became a widely used platform for conducting e-business transactions, companies were already using other information and communication technologies (ICT) infrastructures. These included electronic data interchange (EDI), inter-organizational information systems (IOS), and public IT platforms such as the Minitel videotext system in France. They enabled companies to connect their business functions internally and also to reach out to their suppliers, customers and third-party partners.

However, the value-creation potential of these technologies was limited due to the high costs involved and the limited benefits that were achieved. System implementation costs were high since most of these ICT infrastructures were more or less proprietary and had to be adapted extensively to the individual needs of each company.

The benefits of these systems were limited due to two factors. First, the number of companies using these IT systems was relatively low compared with today's ubiquitous Internet, thus limiting the number of potential partners. Second, even if a company used an ICT infrastructure, its IT systems and applications were not compatible with those of its business partners. This made it difficult at best, if not impossible, to inter-connect different 'islands of technology'. As a result of the above

Exhibit 1.6 **The case studies in the book cover the four periods of the e-business evolution**

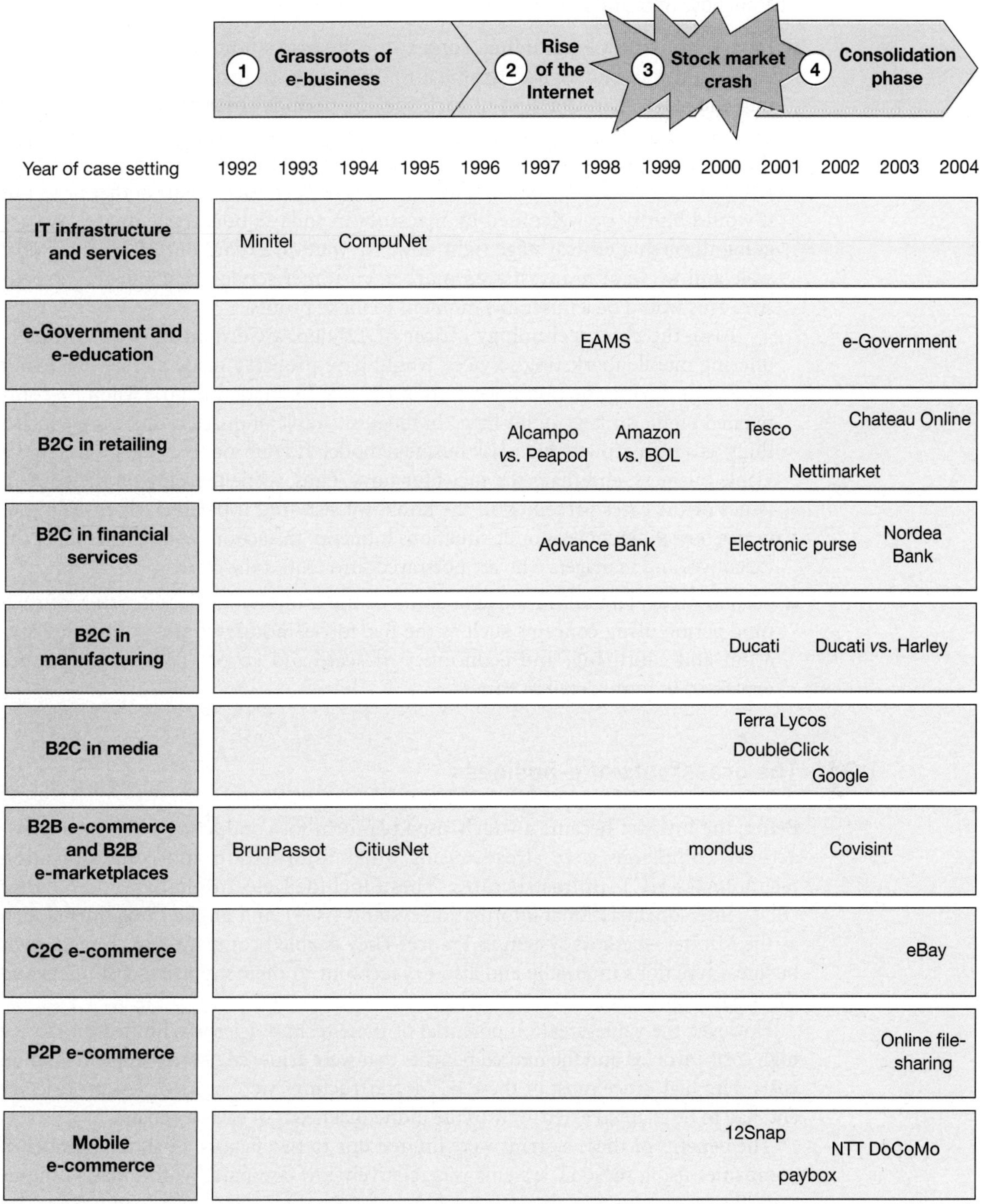

factors, e-business existed only to a limited extent within and across companies or even beyond national boundaries (see the FT article 'Minitel proves a mixed blessing').

The case studies of Brun Passot, a French paper manufacturer and office supplies distributor, and of CitiusNet, a horizontal e-marketplace, illustrate how in the late 1980s and early 1990s e-business enabled electronic trading between companies. At that time, the Internet was not yet available for commercial use. These companies leveraged an alternative platform, the Minitel system, which was developed by the French government and rolled out nationwide in 1982.

The case study of CompuNet, a German IT product reseller and service provider, shows how a firm used IT before the advent of the Internet to provide top-quality service to its corporate customers. CompuNet relied on technologies such as computer–telephony integration (CTI), enterprise resource planning (ERP) systems and groupware to service its customers' IT network remotely and offer a unique life cycle guarantee of the personal computer (PC) product.

FT

Minitel proves a mixed blessing

When Internet service providers began to promote their services in France in 1996, France Telecom, then a state-run monopoly, immediately stepped up advertising for Minitel, the French online service, in an effort to shield it from the competition.

Four years later, Wanadoo, France Telecom's internet arm, is the country's biggest ISP and the former monopoly – now the largest market capitalisation on the Paris Bourse – is selling ADSL high-speed internet connections to the country's households and small businesses.

'In France, you cannot dissociate the internet from Minitel,' says Philippe Guglielmetti, chief executive of Integra, the country's pioneer in e-commerce services and infrastructure.

Minitel, launched in 1983, was a rudimentary equivalent of today's net-PC. Roughly double the size of a table-top telephone set, it had no storage capabilities, a black and white screen displaying text only, and an in-built modem that was slow by today's standards. Millions of terminals were handed out free to telephone subscribers, resulting in a high penetration rate among businesses and the public. Paradoxically, Minitel is now blamed for the country's slow take-up of the internet, and hailed as the platform from which France can leap on to the worldwide web.

'French consumers have been making online purchases for more than 15 years,' says Ramzi Nahas, managing director of Fimadex, a venture adviser. 'Minitel has played an important role in dispelling consumers' fears about making payments on a screen.'

The French still feel that credit card details are more secure on a less open system. In 1995, before net access was widely available, 16 per cent of train reservations on the SNCF national railway were made through Minitel. France Telecom estimates that almost 9m terminals – including web-enabled PCs – had access to the network at the end of last year. In the past few years, Minitel connections were stable at 100m a month plus 150m online directory inquiries, in spite of growing internet use.

A recent survey of Wanadoo customers showed that 82 per cent also used Minitel regularly. More significantly, 14 per cent started logging on to Minitel after they became web users.

▶

Other surveys show that Minitel is more efficient than the net for some uses. According to France Telecom, a train reservation takes on average 3.5 minutes on Minitel, compared with 4.5 minutes on SNCF's website. Directory inquiries take 30 seconds and 1.5 minutes respectively. But there are signs that sophisticated users of Minitel are switching to the Internet.

Customers of Cortal, the online brokerage of Paribas bank, have been trading securities on Minitel since 1993. Barely a year after Cortal launched internet trading in October 1998, two-thirds of online trades had shifted to the new service, with Minitel handling the remaining third.

France Telecom, which has invested large sums to develop Minitel, believes it will co-exist – and gradually converge – with the net in the coming years. Software to access Minitel has been embedded in the French version of the Windows 98 operating system, alongside Microsoft's Internet Explorer web browser.

France Telecom is not alone in hanging on to Minitel. Most French companies are also attached to the network, partly because of the investment they have made but mainly because they have perfected the methods to generate revenues from online activities.

France Telecom charges Minitel users, at rates of up to $1 a minute, on their monthly telephone bill. It then pays back part of the sum to the companies that operate Minitel servers.

In 1998, Minitel generated €832m ($824m) of revenues, of which €521m was channelled by France Telecom to service providers. Wanadoo's sales (which are not published) are 'insignificant in comparison', according to a company official.

Analysts say Minitel's structure, a monopoly operated by a governmental organisation, was a blessing and a curse. 'That it operated on a single network made it safe and allowed e-commerce to take off in France,' says Mohamed Lakhlifi, sales manager at Unilog, a Paris-listed computer services company. 'But regulatory hurdles and the absence of competition stifled innovation.'

Another consultant says habits acquired in the Minitel age are tempering managers' enthusiasm for the internet. 'Almost two-thirds of projects that start as ambitious internet operations end up being scaled down to a website that connects users to the company's existing Minitel server,' says an IT specialist.

Mr Nahas at Fimadex says the average age of French senior managers is higher than in the US, 'which means they are less computer literate. Most of these managers see the internet as just another way of channelling orders for their products. Very few are aware that their whole marketing strategy must be reviewed.'

But Minitel's most important contribution to French e-business will undoubtedly be in the form of lessons learnt. Minitel provides more than 15 years of statistics about retailing and online usage habits.

'A lot of what is happening on the internet today took place locally [in France] in the 1980s,' says an information technology consultant. 'We have known for years that sex chat rooms, dating services and financial applications are the engines of innovation and revenue generation in an online environment.'

Integra says the Minitel experience can be transposed into internet business practices. 'Early studies in the US predicted that internet transactions would stabilise at 1 per cent or 1.5 per cent of consumer goods retailing,' says Mr Guglielmetti. 'Our experience with Minitel leads us to think that e-commerce could make up some 10 per cent of sales of products adapted to distance selling.'

Minitel sales in recent years accounted for almost 15 per cent of turnover at La Redoute and Les Trois Suisses, France's biggest mail order companies. Integra estimates that Minitel represents 7–8 per cent of all French distance selling.

One of the biggest barriers to greater internet use is the French language. Integra, which operates web hosting services in several countries, says 90 per cent of its servers are in the language of the country they are based in. 'This is not a problem when your language is English,' says an executive. 'It becomes a problem when your language is less widely used.'

Conversely, French e-business is expected to benefit from a number of national factors. The country is more advanced than most of its neighbours – and the US – in its use of smart-cards. All credit and debit cards issued in France have an embedded chip with a dedicated identification code, which makes online payments more secure.

Source: 'Minitel proves a mixed blessing', www.FT.com, 8 February 2000.

1.2.2 The rise of the Internet

In July 1995, the Internet boom years began with the launch of Amazon.com, today's best-known online retailer. The subsequent five years were characterized by great exuberance and the belief in the seemingly unlimited potential of the Internet. During that time period, the profitability and economic viability of companies and business models did not seem to matter much. Instead, metrics such as 'click-through rates', or 'number of eyeballs', i.e. the number of visitors to a site, were the main determinants for stock market success and media coverage. In the case of the fashion retailer Boo.com, the founder Ernst Malmsten did not even have to provide investors with these kinds of metrics. The mere hope of high future profits allowed Boo.com to spend $30 million of venture capital money, even before launching its website (see the FT article 'Burning money at Boo').

For a more detailed insight into this period, consider the example of Priceline.com, which allowed people to purchase airline tickets through the Internet. Priceline.com went public on 30 March 1999, and the shares that were issued at $16 each soared immediately to $85 each. At the end of the day, Priceline.com had reached a valuation of almost $10 billion, which was more than those of United Airlines, Continental Airlines and Northwest Airlines combined.[16] While these airlines had a proven business model, valuable brands and substantial physical assets, Priceline.com owned only a few computer servers and an untested business model.

In fact, the company even stated in its IPO prospectus that it did not expect to be profitable at any time in the near future, that the business model was new and unproven, and that the brand might not be able to achieve the required brand recognition. Investors ignored these warnings because they believed that they would always be able to sell the stock to someone else at an even higher price. This investment approach during the Internet boom years became known as the 'Greater Fool Theory'.[17] In the USA, some 100 million people, about half of the adult population, had invested in stocks at the peak of the bubble. As the stock market kept soaring, more and more people – who had seen their colleagues and friends get rich – also started investing in Internet stocks. This meant that the chances of finding a 'greater fool' were high – at least during the Internet boom years.

The case studies in this book dating from the above time period and featuring companies such as Advance Bank, Amazon.com BertelsmannOnline (BOL), Alcampo.es, Peapod.com and mondus.com, illustrate this very same spirit of almost boundless excitement and optimism.

The fundamental driver of the e-business boom was the belief that it would be possible to increase value creation multifold because, as explained below, the Internet would lower costs while, at the same, time increasing consumer benefits:

- *Lower costs.* Costs were expected to decrease significantly because managers and analysts alike believed that Internet ventures would not require heavy investments in expensive bricks-and-mortar infrastructure, such as warehouses, retail outlets and delivery trucks. Instead, they believed that all physical activities could be outsourced to external providers while they focused on the technology aspect of the business and on customer interactions.
- *Higher benefits.* At the same time, the belief was that compared with their more traditional bricks-and-mortar competitors, Internet 'pure-play' companies would provide far superior consumer benefits. It was thought that coupling the two-way connectivity of the Internet with database capabilities and customer relationship management (CRM) systems would create much higher benefits than traditional outlets ever could.

The result of this increase in the value created, so the logic went, was an outward shift in the traditional supply and demand curves, as shown in Exhibit 1.7.[18] First, as a result of lower marketing and distribution costs achieved through the Internet, supply has expanded because suppliers are willing to pass some of their cost savings on to their customers and offer their goods at a lower price. Second, due to customers' lower transaction costs, demand has also expanded. That is, at any given price, customers request more goods. The overall effect of these two movements is an expansion of the market volume, which is shown in Exhibit 1.7 by the new intersection of the e-supply and the e-demand curves.

Exhibit 1.7 The Internet shifts the traditional supply and demand curves outward, thereby expanding the market volume

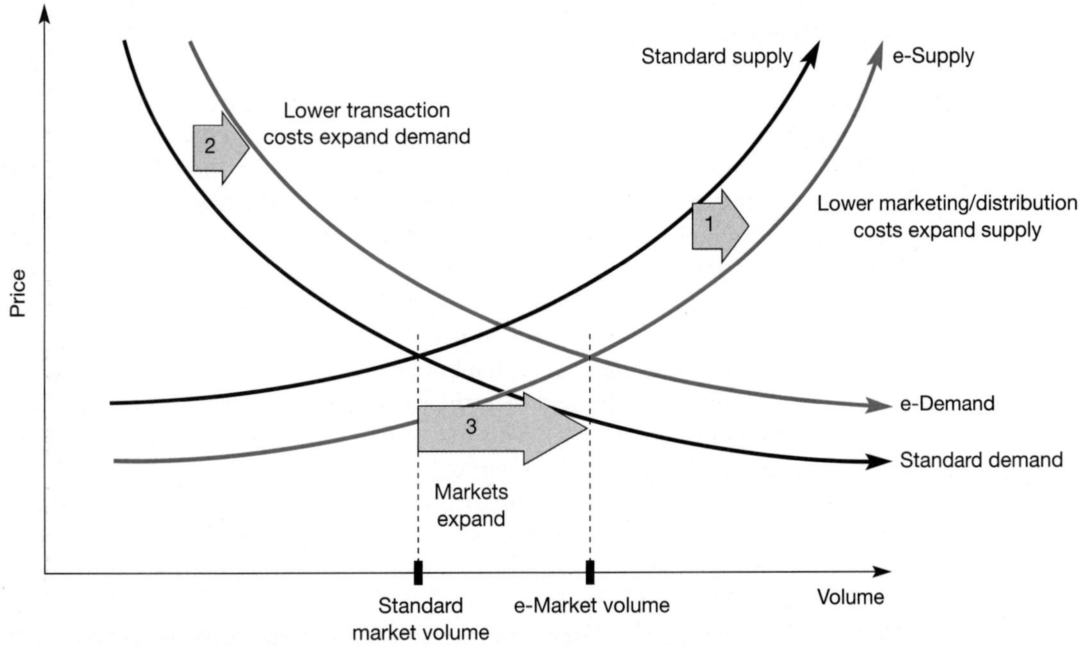

Source: Adapted with permission of Harvard Business School Press. [Exhibit 7595] from *Net Gain* by J. Hagel and M. Singer. Boston, MA, 1997, p. 35.

This still leaves us with the question of why so many companies rushed into this e-market so rapidly during the Internet boom years. Several factors can explain this new 'gold rush' (see also Section 7.2 for a more detailed discussion of early-mover advantages and disadvantages in e-business).

By entering the e-market early, companies were trying to generate scale effects through large sales volumes. They wanted to attract new customers quickly and build up a large customer base. The underlying hope was that once customers had used a website a number of times, then they would be unlikely to switch to a competitor, since they would have to get used to a new website layout and functioning. Furthermore, data-mining techniques would allow online companies to customize their offerings to the specific preferences of the individual customer. By switching to another provider, customers lose this level of customization, at least over the short term.

Internet ventures also expected to create a customer lock-in through network effects. As more and more customers sign up and provide information about themselves, as is the case at eBay and through Amazon.com's book reviews, customers are less likely to switch to competitors unless the latter offer better (or at least similar) network effects. Because of these effects, there was a 'winner-takes-all' expectation, whereby a dominant player would outperform competitors through high-scale economies and network effects.

Finally, and probably most importantly, the peculiar investment climate pushed companies to spend and expand rapidly instead of taking a more cautious approach. In 1999, Silicon Valley venture capitalist firms such as Sequoia Capital and Benchmark Capital invested an all-time high of $48.3 billion. This presented a 150% increase over 1998, and 90% of this money went towards high-tech and Internet companies.[19] In order to qualify for venture capital funding, companies had to convince investors that they would be able to grow big and fast and so fuel the hope of a rapid payback on investment.

These investors did not necessarily believe in the future of the start-ups they funded. Yet they knew that as long as stock markets kept going up and people kept buying Internet stocks, regardless of the underlying business model, they could not go wrong. At the same time, investment bankers and venture capitalists who refused to play this 'game' also knew that they would fall behind their less scrupulous competitors. These perverted incentives contributed significantly to the build-up of the stock market bubble.

FT

Burning money at Boo: the founders of the infamous Internet company were fools rather than knaves

When Boo.com went into liquidation on May 17 last year, barely six months after its launch, the question was not why the global online fashion retailer had closed. Rather, it was why investors had allowed the company to burn through $100m before it did so.

It takes only a few chapters of this enthralling book to realise that the answer began with the ▶

personality of Ernst Malmsten, a 6ft 5in Swede of 27, with nerdy glasses. Malmsten, the founder and chief executive of Boo, had already proved himself spectacularly skilled at getting big companies to put money behind strange ideas when he set up a festival of Nordic poetry in New York, signing up as sponsors Ericsson, Saab, Ikea, Carlsberg and Absolut. He later created and then sold a pioneering online book store in Sweden.

When Malmsten turned his attention to selling clothes online in spring 1998, his natural fluency, passion and authority became the fuse that ignited an explosive mixture of investor greed and uncertainty as to whether the web would be earth-changing or merely very big.

Malmsten's partners were Kajsa Leander, a kindergarten playmate turned model turned girlfriend turned business partner, and Patrik Hedelin, an investment banker who had helped them to sell their stakes in the online book store.

The three talked the investment bank JP Morgan into helping them find investors to put up $15m for the plan – and brought in blue-chip lawyers, headhunters, technology providers and public relations and advertising agencies to add further credibility.

Despite JP Morgan's roster of contacts, they were turned away by venture capitalists with a record in backing technology start-ups. Instead, it was less expert investors who took the bait – notably a small British investment firm called Eden Capital, the luxury-goods magnate Bernard Arnault, the Benetton family and a rag-bag of Middle Eastern investors.

As the company approached its target launch date of June 1999, the glamorous young founders generated more and more positive media coverage. Given the received wisdom at that time that only funky young people understood the Internet, the investors left their dream team to get on with opening offices in cool warehouse spaces around the world and hiring hundreds of staff.

But there was a problem: beneath the buzz and excitement, not one of the founders was a capable manager, let alone up to the Welchian task of getting a highly complex international launch project finished on time and on budget.

Instead, they devoted their energies to talking at conferences in Venice, shooting television commercials in Los Angeles, entertaining journalists at Nobu in London and the SoHo Grand in New York, spending $10,000 on clothes at Barneys so they would look the part on the cover of *Fortune*, holding staff parties in smart nightclubs before the company even had a product, and flying around the world to investor meetings on Concorde and private jets.

As the schedule began to slip, Malmsten lost faith, one by one, in his partners and underlings. Ericsson was no good at systems integration, he concluded. Hill and Knowlton did not know how to sell the story to the media. JP Morgan was not bringing in investors fast enough. The chief technology officer was not up to his job. Even Patrik, his fellow founder, was too much of an individual to be a good chief financial officer.

With five launch deadlines passed and $30m spent, Malmsten took all his staff out to lunch at the Cafe Royal in August 1999 to announce that another of his managers would create Project Launch, with a new deadline set for three months later.

It was a measure of the height to which the internet craze had grown that the company's investors, told of the delays at a board meeting three weeks later, did not fire Malmsten and his two co-founders on the spot. Instead, they accepted the assurance that the new November deadline would be met, allowing the company to go public a few months later, and agreed to put up more cash. Astonishingly, a Lebanese investment fund then put in another $15m at a price that valued the business at $390m.

Boo.com did open, as promised, in November. But only 25,000 people visited its website on day one, compared with an expected 1m, and it soon became clear that sales would be less than a 10th of the promised target of $37m in the first seven months. The conclusion seemed clear: Boo's founders had wildly overestimated the market size, their ability to penetrate it, or both.

The company needed another $20m to last until February and the strategic investor that JP

Morgan wanted to bring in – Federated Department Stores of the US – postponed a deal to put up $10m until it saw how Christmas sales went. Despite this, the company's investors, still driven more by greed than by fear, provided more cash in the hope of doubling their money in a forthcoming initial public offering. Their new investment valued at $285m a business that had annualised sales to date of $3m.

Not even the market crash of March 2000, which killed forever any hope of a quick exit at a profit, managed to restore sanity to investors or management. The Boo founders continued to bicker internally about the depth of the cuts they should be making, while the core investors talked seriously about putting in another $30m at a price that valued the existing shareholdings at $20m.

In Malmsten's account, the Boo story is more comic opera than tragedy and its leading characters are fools rather than knaves. The lesson, if there is one, is that the Boo people copied every detail of the fast-growing Silicon Valley start-up except for one key point. The private-jet lifestyle and global partying are what you do after becoming a billionaire. Before getting to profit, you fly economy and spend money for the benefit of customers, not staff.

Source: T. Jackson, 'Burning money at Boo: the founders of the infamous internet company were fools rather than knaves', *Financial Times*, November 1 2001.

1.2.3 The crash

During 1995–99, investors and managers had artificially inflated market sizes for dot.com companies and overlooked a number of important issues that led to the subsequent end of the Internet boom years.[20]

On the one hand, revenues were artificially inflated through a number of ways. First, in order to gain market share, Internet ventures subsidized customers' purchases of their products. For instance, Internet retailers such as Amazon.com and the pet-food supplier pets.com provided free shipping and delivery to their customers – even for 20-pound dog-food bags. Second, many customers bought products and services online more out of curiosity than to fulfil an actual need. After the novelty wore off, many customers reverted to their traditional buying behaviour. Third, in many instances, revenues for the Internet ventures were generated through stocks from partner companies that enjoyed equally high market valuations.

On the other hand, costs were not represented realistically, which further distorted the true state of the underlying business. In many cases, dot.com companies received subsidized inputs because suppliers were eager to do business with them, which helped them to reduce costs. More importantly, many suppliers and employees accepted equity as payment, expecting that the stock market boom would continue to rise.

The above-mentioned factors resulted in bad operating financials, which did not reflect the actual Internet ventures' business model in terms of costs and revenues. Furthermore, bank analysts, such as Mary Meeker from Morgan Stanley, who, in 1996, wrote the highly publicized *Internet Report*, had pointed out that the focus of investors should be not on current earnings but on earnings potential.[21] Instead, investors were supposed to emphasize the numbers of online customers, unique website visitors and repeat online buyers. Consequently, e-managers, trying to meet investors' expectations, spent heavily on marketing and advertising to attract site visitors and customers, regardless of costs. As it turned out, however, these metrics

might have been a good indicator for spectator traffic on a website, yet they did not represent a reliable indicator of profitability.

On Monday, 13 March 2000, the dot.com bubble started to burst. Within three days, the NASDAQ slid by almost 500 points. At that time, Jack Willoughby, a journalist for *Barron's*, published an article in which he calculated the 'burn-rate' of Internet companies, which measured the rate at which these companies were spending money. He concluded that most of the Internet companies would run out of money within a year:

> When will the Internet bubble burst? For scores of Net upstarts, that unpleasant popping sound is likely to be heard before the end of this year. Starved for cash, many of these companies will try to raise fresh funds by issuing more stock or bonds. But a lot of them won't succeed. As a result, they will be forced to sell out to stronger rivals or go out of business altogether. Already, many cash-strapped Internet firms are scrambling for funding.[22]

This article shattered the hope of investors that, regardless of their economic viability, Internet firms would always be able to raise more money.

Along with most other Internet firms, the stock of the above-mentioned Priceline.com started to slide from $150 at its peak down to less than $2. At this valuation level, the capitalization of Priceline.com would not even have sufficed to purchase two Boeing 747 jets. Other Internet companies faced similar fates and either went bankrupt (see the FT article 'Webvan's billion-dollar mistake'), or were acquired by a larger competitor, often a traditional bricks-and-mortar company from the so-called 'old economy'. For instance, K·B Toys, an 80-year-old, bricks-and-mortar toy retailer, purchased the intellectual property, software and warehouses of bankrupt eToys.com – once one of the most highly praised online start-ups and valued at $10 billion – and relaunched eToys.com in October of 2001.

FT

Webvan's billion-dollar mistake

The demise of Webvan ends the hope that a business as mundane as grocery shopping could be transformed by a standalone Internet company.

Webvan was the best funded and the most hyped of the online grocers, soaring to an $8.7bn market valuation on its first day of trading in November 1999. Now it has burned through more than $1bn of cash in less than two years.

The rise and fall of Webvan is a study in the illusions of the dotcom boom and the wishful thinking of Wall Street. It is leaving little in its wake but a stain on the reputations of the blue-chip backers it attracted in its early days.

Founded in 1996 by Louis Borders of Borders Books, Webvan managed to lure George Shaheen, managing partner of Andersen Consulting, to be its chief executive. Its board was filled with some of the most revered names of the era: Christos Cotsakos of E*Trade, Tim Koogle of Yahoo and Michael Moritz of Sequoia Capital. Its money came from such Silicon Valley powerhouses as Softbank Capital Partners and Benchmark Capital and its shares ▶

were touted by Wall Street's best- known investment banks.

Goldman Sachs said in February 2000 that Webvan could become an Internet franchise to rank alongside AOL and Yahoo. 'Webvan has re-engineered the backend fulfilment system to create a scalable solution to the last-mile problem of e-commerce,' its analysts wrote. Having such names behind it ensured that Webvan was able to come to market – with Goldman as lead underwriter – after only a few months of trading in which it had managed to sell just $3.2m worth of goods.

Nonetheless, its executives assured investors it had a vast opportunity. Groceries represented a far larger market than books, videos or music – areas in which e-commerce made its first forays. The typical US household spends $5,000 a year on groceries and goes food shopping more than twice a week.

From the start, the company had big ambitions. Rather than starting off in a large city or two, learning from its mistakes and perhaps making a small profit before expanding, it decided to open in 26 markets within three years.

Each distribution centre would be 18 times the size of a typical supermarket and would cost $35m. Almost 5 miles of conveyor belts would bring products to the packers at each site and refrigerated vans fitted with sophisticated global satellite positioning systems would allow each warehouse to serve a 50-mile radius.

It soon became obvious that Webvan was overbuilding – but by then it had nine centres open, each bleeding cash and operating at a fraction of capacity. 'I believe they were doomed from the start because their business model was one that was predicated on reinventing the entire system rather than using any of the existing structure,' says Robert Mittelstaedt, vice-dean of executive education at the Wharton School. Webvan's profligate plan 'defied economic sense in a low-margin business,' he adds.

Groceries did not offer the prospect of fat margins that a smart new entrant could try to undercut. Kroger's return on sales in 1999 was just 2.2 per cent and Ahold achieved a 4.5 per cent operating margin in the same year. Many online retailers have got round such issues by charging above-market prices for convenience but this was always likely to be a challenge. Most families watch their weekly food bills carefully, as food manufacturers that have raised prices know to their cost.

The hope that e-tailers' gross margins could exceed those of traditional retailers was punctured not only by high fulfilment costs but also by online grocers' lack of purchasing power and the heavy discounting many had to offer to attract customers.

The cost of Webvan's infrastructure, however impressive, eventually prevented it from competing with traditional supermarkets. Mr Mittelstaedt says this problem was not unique to online grocers. 'The places you see where (e-tailers) successfully changed the business model have nothing to do with physical distribution – such as recruitment sites,' he says.

Shoppers were not crying out for an alternative way to buy groceries and it is notable that the supermarket model had not been challenged by previous innovations such as catalogues.

Whether Webvan truly offered convenience is also questionable. Although it guaranteed delivery within a 30-minute window chosen by the customer – although not the same day – this still required somebody to be at home to accept the goods.

The one factor that cannot be blamed for Webvan's failure is online competition from traditional grocers such as Safeway, Kroger and Albertson's. All were slow to the Internet and all invested only small sums in online operations.

The big retailers are slowly showing signs of learning from Webvan's mistakes. Ahold invested last year in Peapod, an online-only grocer that now picks merchandise from Ahold's US chains. Safeway last month gave up its warehouse model in favor of a partnership with Tesco, the UK retailer that has built the world's largest online grocery business by using a model whereby orders are assembled in its stores.

Meanwhile, more than 200 of Webvan's delivery vans currently sit outside its closed plant in Lawrence-ville, Georgia, awaiting

auction next month. They are expected to fetch a fraction of what Webvan paid for them.

Webvan's investors now face an anxious wait to see whether they can salvage anything from the physical assets left behind by this supposedly virtual business. For now, it seems, few people apart from the time-stressed technophiles who founded the company really need Webvan.

There were a few mourners yesterday. Sarah Lonsdale, a San Francisco freelance writer, was until yesterday a devoted user of the service. Now she will have to lug her two children to the grocery store. 'I'm disappointed,' she says. 'Webvan had really got its act together. The convenience of ordering was fantastic.' But in the end, that was not enough.

Source: P. Abrahams and A. Edgecliffe-Johnson, 'A billion-dollar mistake: Webvan's failure has been an expensive lesson for the Internet', *Financial Times*, 10 July 2001.

1.2.4 The consolidation phase

The consolidation phase began in late 2000, subsequent to the burst of the Internet bubble, which took place in March and April of 2000. e-Business entrepreneurs, managers, investors and the media awoke to the new reality and started reflecting on what had really happened. More importantly, they tried to understand the reasons that led to the failure of so many Internet ventures, as well as the flaws in their business models.

In addition to the hysteria that had distorted valuations, many of these ventures did not create as much value as was anticipated, and they were also unable to capture the value they created in the form of profits. Let us look at each of these points in turn.

Overall, the value created by Internet ventures turned out to be lower since costs were higher and benefits were lower than it was thought throughout the boom years. The belief that e-business would be comparatively low-cost stemmed mainly from the idea that it required only a couple of computer servers and a website to set up an online company. Furthermore, it was thought that doing business through the Internet would be highly scalable since it required only setting up additional computer processing capability to cater for new customers around the globe.

Yet for many online businesses the costs of developing a website turned out to be only a small fraction of the total costs. For instance, during the boom years, Amazon.com, on average, paid around \$16 for buying and shipping a book. On top of that came \$8 for marketing and advertising and \$1 for overheads (which included the website development), raising overall costs per book to \$25. Average price per book sold, however, was only \$20.[23] The main reason for the high costs was that most costs, including marketing and sales, were not nearly as scale-sensitive as the set-up of a website. In fact, the acquisition costs of online customers were, in general, much higher than those of traditional bricks-and-mortar companies. Internet 'pure-player' companies had first to build up their brand name and then win over the trust of online customers.

Furthermore, the notion of the unbundled corporation in which external providers manage the high fixed-cost logistical processes did not work out as expected. In order to maintain high levels of quality and reliability, online companies such as Amazon.com reverted to setting up their own warehouses and distribution centres, thereby adding significantly to overall costs.

It also turned out to be difficult for most Internet companies to establish a sustainable revenue model. As a result, they were unable to ensure a high enough return on investment to justify their stock market valuation. For instance, after starting operations in April 1998, Priceline.com managed, by the end of that year, to sell $35 million worth of airline tickets – at an overall cost of $36.5 million!

The inability of many firms to charge appropriate prices for products and services was due to the following factors. First, the Internet lowered barriers to entry (see Section 3.2.2). While, in the past, it was necessary to operate an extensive physical network to compete in the retailing sector, many companies from all realms, such as Boo.com and eToys.com, attempted to grab market share by leveraging the Internet. In the online market for pet food, more than half a dozen web retailers were competing for customers. This led to a price war to attract customers, with some companies giving away products or services for free.

Second, the strategic stakes that were involved further aggravated the competitive situation. Knowing that only a few online companies per sector would be able to stay in business, these companies invested heavily and sacrificed profits for market share. They also hoped that market share would translate into durable customer relationships. After all, e-business was supposed to be a winner-takes-all market. Yet, ultimately the lock-in effect created through high switching costs and network effects occurred only in a few cases (see also Section 7.2.1). As websites became user-friendlier, it also became easier for customers to switch from one provider to another.

Regarding network effects, only companies that rely heavily on consumer interactions, such as eBay, were able to leverage the power of their installed customer base. However, at most other online companies, individual customers usually do not care much about the size of the installed user base. For instance, now that other large players, such as Microsoft, have moved into the search engine market, Google.com, today's undisputed leader in this market, faces the risk of losing its dominance. This is due to the fact that search engines are not well suited for creating a lock-in effect.[24] In most cases, users prefer the search engine that delivers the best results. If that happens to be Microsoft because it integrates its search engine with information from the browser or the operating system, then users are likely to switch.

The final dark side of the boom years was that many companies, most notably the energy trader Enron, once hailed as the model Internet-based company, and the telecom operator Worldcom, applied illegal accounting practices to boost profits. This worked out as long as the boom persisted and the stock market kept going up. However, once the market had collapsed and investors started to scrutinize accounts more closely, the extent of the criminal activities became obvious, forcing these companies and numerous others to file for bankruptcy.

What messages can we take away from looking at these boom and bust cycles across history? First, during the consolidation phase it is essential to return to business fundamentals. This entails paying close consideration to issues such as industry structure, value creation, and ways to create profits and a sustainable competitive advantage through the Internet.

Second, just like the railway, steel and automobile industries underwent boom and bust phases before releasing their true economic potential, it is likely that we are observing a similar evolution in the e-business sector. The booming installation years

of the Internet were followed by a bust. Now the time has come for the less exciting, yet in all likelihood much more profound, deployment period of e-business.[25]

Just like after previous crashes, regulatory agencies also reacted this time to improve investor protection. In July 2002, President George W. Bush signed the Sarbanes-Oxley Act of 2002, which mandates a number of reforms to enhance corporate responsibility and financial disclosures and to combat corporate and accounting fraud. In addition, this act also created the Public Company Accounting Oversight Board (PCAOB), which has the role of overseeing the activities of the auditing profession.

Recent developments, documented by some of the cases in the book (such as Tesco.com, eBay, Ducati, Nordea and NTT DoCoMo), confirm that if firms have consistent e-business strategies and implement them superiorly, they can create significant value for their customers while at the same time being highly profitable. As a result, the stock valuation of some highly successful Internet ventures, such as eBay and Amazon.com, have already soared back to levels that we witnessed last during the Internet boom years (see the FT article 'eBay leads the online revival').

FT

eBay leads online revival as net hits the refresh button

It all looks so Last Century.

EBay, the Internet flea-market, is once again worth as much as Sears, The Gap and Federated Department Stores combined. Online travel service Expedia is worth more than the six biggest US airlines put together. And Amazon.com stock is trading at four times Barnes & Noble and Borders.

The Internet's boom-time stock prices are back, as a handful of survivors has emerged from the wreckage. Only this time around, the web has become a very different place to do business.

Real sales and earnings, not eyeballs or click-through rates, are now the main yardsticks for stock prices – even if those measures have been stretched almost to the point of incredulity.

In some ways, things seem to have changed little since the bubble. Share prices are still based on a belief that the infant web will consume vast swathes of the retail, travel and media industries.

Take USA Interactive, the corporate vehicle of Barry Diller, the media entrepreneur, who this week pulled off the latest in a string of web deals with an agreement to acquire financial services site LendingTree. Through Expedia and Hotels.com, Mr Diller is already the world's biggest online travel agent. Yet he claims this is just the beginning; with less than 15 per cent of US travel sales conducted online – and in Europe only 1 per cent – there is plenty of room to grow. Some time over the next decade, Americans will be booking more than half of their personal travel online, industry forecasters say.

The current level of share prices already treats much of this growth as a certainty. EBay's shares have now touched a level they topped only during a dizzy two-week spell at the peak of the dotcom bubble.

Internet stocks are the only corner of the tech sector to have gone up over the past 12 months, according to Merrill Lynch.

Three years on, the few remaining dotcoms have at least notched up a record that makes the grand promises of the bubble seem a little less pie-in-the-sky.

EBay has lifted its revenues from around \$200m (£128m) to \$1.2bn, while its profits have jumped from \$10m to \$250m. Amazon, though ▶

yet to turn a full-year profit, has more than doubled revenues and is now edging into the black.

'The internet's for real,' says Steve Milunovich, technology strategist at Merrill Lynch. Other technologies have shaken off early disappointments to create huge new markets, he adds.

'People were writing off the PC before Microsoft even went public.'

At 70–80 times expected earnings this year, the internet companies are still off the charts compared with traditional stocks – although at least they are being compared on the same scale. But to keep growing at exponential rates the internet survivors will have to master new skills. Three that have bedevilled many traditional companies stand out.

- One is acquisitions. The dotcoms have started to mop up smaller rivals in a bid to consolidate their foothold and extend their reach into new markets. Besides Mr Diller's acquisition spree, Yahoo has bought internet search and online recruitment companies, while eBay bought the biggest online payments company.
- A second new skill, as they move into new markets, involves cross-selling to existing customers. Part of Mr Diller's promise is that he can sell hotel rooms and sports tickets to people who come to Expedia for airline seats – something that sounds easy but which few broad-based consumer companies have managed.
- Third, and perhaps most difficult, they must now conquer the world. Though far from mature, the US internet market is slowing; the best chance to keep the exponential expansion going is by exporting America's dotcom successes. 'For Hotels.com and Expedia, the biggest growth drivers are overseas,' says Peter Mirsky, an analyst at Fahnestock.

EBay's international revenues are soaring, while Yahoo plans to reproduce its US businesses in the biggest overseas markets.

It may be that not all consumers are as ready as Americans to love the net. Europeans have fewer credit cards and PCs and more suspicion of technology, says Mr Mirsky. A setback such as a big security breach could stop international expansion in its tracks.

But Wall Street's 'buy' signs are already signalling that the next generation of multinationals is ready to reach out to the world.

Source: R. Waters, 'eBay leads online revival as net hits the refresh button', *Financial Times*, 9 May 2003.

SUMMARY

- This chapter first introduced the definitions of e-business-related terms, including 'e-business', 'electronic commerce' and 'mobile e-commerce', definitions of strategy and value creation.
- Second, this chapter provided a framework that describes the typical periods of technological revolutions. It also positions within this framework the evolution of e-business during the last decade. The four main periods that characterize this evolution are:
  - the *grassroots of e-business* period, which took place before the widespread commercial use of the Internet;
  - the *rise of the Internet* period, which started with the launch of Amazon.com in 1995 and continued until 2000;

- the *crash*, which started in March and April 2000 and caused a 45% decline of the NASDAQ by the end of that year;
- the *consolidation phase*, which followed the stock market crash and continues until today.

REVIEW QUESTIONS

1 Define the terms 'e-business', 'electronic commerce' and 'mobile electronic commerce', and describe how they differ from one another.

2 Provide a definition of strategy the way it is used in this book.

3 What are the three levels of strategy that can be distinguished?

4 Describe the different periods of the life cycle model, as proposed by Carlota Perez.

5 What are the four time periods of the e-business evolution? What are the peculiar characteristics of each period?

DISCUSSION QUESTIONS

1 Referring to the FT article 'It's too early for e-business to drop its "e"', discuss whether it is sensible to still speak of e-business strategies. Defend your arguments.

2 What do you think are the main elements of strategy formulation? Does the perspective chosen in this chapter correspond to your own experiences and observations?

3 Discuss the evolution of two technological revolutions using the framework proposed by Carlota Perez. To what extent is it possible to apply this framework to the evolution of e-business?

4 Are we about to enter the golden age of e-business? Defend your argument.

RECOMMENDED KEY READING

- B. Henderson uses the metaphor of biological evolution to describe the essence of strategy in 'The origin of strategy', *Harvard Business Review*, 1989, November–December, pp. 139–143.
- A detailed account of different levels of strategy can be found in G. Johnson and K. Scholes, *Exploring Corporate Strategy*, Prentice Hall, 2002, pp. 10–11.
- H. Mintzberg is one of the most prominent critiques of the design or positioning school. For further reading, see *Strategy Safari – A Guided Tour Through the Wilds of Strategic Management*, Prentice Hall, 1998, pp. 114–118, which offers no less than ten different approaches to explaining strategy. His article 'The design school: reconsidering

the basic premises of strategic management', *Strategic Management Journal*, 1990, Vol. 11, No. 3, pp. 171–195 provides a more condensed criticism of the design school.
- M. Porter's article 'Strategy and the Internet' *Harvard Business Review*, 2001, March, pp. 63–78 provides an excellent overview of the impact of the Internet on strategy formulation.
- C. Perez developed the five-stage model of technological revolutions presented in this chapter: see *Technological Revolutions and Financial Capital: The Dynamics of Bubbles and Golden Ages*, Edward Elgar, 2002. She draws heavily on the writings of twentieth-century economist J. Schumpeter. Among his important works rank the books *Business Cycles*, Porcupine Press, 1982 and *Capitalism, Socialism and Democracy*, Harper&Rank, 1975.
- B. Arthur builds on the insights of C. Perez in the article 'Is the information revolution dead?' *Business 2.0*, 2002, pp. 65–73 March, where he suggests that the Internet economy is undergoing the same evolutionary phases as previous technological revolutions.
- In 'Profits and the Internet: seven misconceptions', *Sloan Management Review*, 2001, Summer, pp. 44–53, S. Rangan and R. Adner analyze why the promises of the Internet economy were not fulfilled.
- J. Cassidy takes a critical perspective of the development of the Internet economy in *Dot.con*, Perennial, 2003.
- E. Malmsten (the co-founder of Boo.com), E. Portanger and C. Drazin provide an account of the rise and fall of the Internet fashion retailer Boo.com. in their book *Boo Hoo*, Arrow Books, 2002.

USEFUL WEBLINKS

- **www.aol.com**
- **www.boo.com**
- **www.expedia.com**
- **www.hotels.com**
- **www.priceline.com**
- **www.timewarner.com**
- **www.law.uc.edu/ccl/soact/soact.pdf** Contains the full text of the Sarbanes-Oxley Act of 2002.

NOTES AND REFERENCES

1 For definitions of e-business and e-commerce, see A. Bartels, 'The difference between e-business and e-commerce', www.Computerworld.com. Accessed 30 October 2000.
2 G. Johnson and K. Scholes, *Exploring Corporate Strategy*, Prentice Hall, 2002, p. 10.
3 A. Chandler, *Strategy and Structure in the History of the American Industrial Enterprise*, MIT Press, 1962, p. 13.

4 B. Henderson, 'The origin of strategy', *Harvard Business Review*, 1989, November–December, p. 141.
5 M. Porter, 'Strategy and the Internet', *Harvard Business Review*, 2001, March, p. 72.
6 Researchers of strategy have been engaging in a heated debate about what strategy entails. Most notably, there are two different schools of strategy. The 'design view' of strategy considers strategy as characterized by deliberate planning and objective setting. The 'experience view' suggests that strategies develop in an adaptive fashion and depend to a large extent on existing strategies. See also G. Johnson and K. Scholes, *Exploring Corporate Strategy*, Prentice Hall, 2002, pp. 39–46. The frameworks and concepts proposed in this book focus on the design view of strategy.
7 For a detailed discussion of different levels of strategy, see G. Johnson and K. Scholes, *Exploring Corporate Strategy*, Prentice Hall, 2002, pp. 10–11.
8 For a discussion of operational issues in e-commerce, including topics such as website design and HTML programming, see D. Chaffey, *e-Business and e-Commerce Management*, FT Prentice-Hall, 2002, pp. 143–156.
9 C. Perez, *Technological Revolutions and Financial Capital: The Dynamics of Bubbles and Golden Ages*, Edward Elgar, 2002, p. 8.
10 Ibid, pp. 90–137.
11 Note that as one technology reaches its maturity, the next technological revolution is about to emerge. As a result, there can be considerable overlap between two technology surges.
12 C. Perez, *Technological Revolutions and Financial Capital: The Dynamics of Bubbles and Golden Ages*, Edward Elgar, 2002, pp. 90–137.
13 The NASDAQ is the main USA-based stock exchange for high-tech companies.
14 Amazon.com was the first firm to add the suffix '.com' to the end of its name, thereby establishing the expression 'dot.com', which refers to all types of Internet ventures.
15 The p/e ratio of a company's stock is calculated by dividing its stock price by its earnings per share. For instance, if a company made €5 per share in the past year and the share sells for €50, then the p/e ratio for this share is 10.
16 J. Cassidy provides a detailed account of the exuberance and hysteria during the Internet boom years in *Dot.con*, Perennial, 2003, pp. 2–5.
17 Ibid, p. 5.
18 J. Hagel and M. Singer, *Net Gain*, Harvard Business School Press, 1997.
19 M. Pandya, H. Singh, R. Mittelstaedt, *et al.*, *On Building Corporate Value*, John Wiley, 2002, p. 8.
20 For an excellent discussion of the flawed thinking during the boom years of the Internet, refer to M. Porter, 'Strategy and the Internet', *Harvard Business Review*, 2001, March, pp. 63–78.
21 M. Meeker and C. DePuy, *The Internet Report*, Harper Business, 1996.
22 J. Willoughby, 'Burning up: Warning: Internet companies are running out of cash', *Barron's*, 20 March 2000, p. 29.
23 J. Cassidy, *Dot.con*, Perennial, 2003, p. 148.
24 F. Vogelstein, 'Can Google grow up', *Fortune*, 8 December, 2003, pp. 38–43.
25 See also T. Mullaney and H. Green, 'The e-Biz surprise', *BusinessWeekOnline*, 12 May 2003.

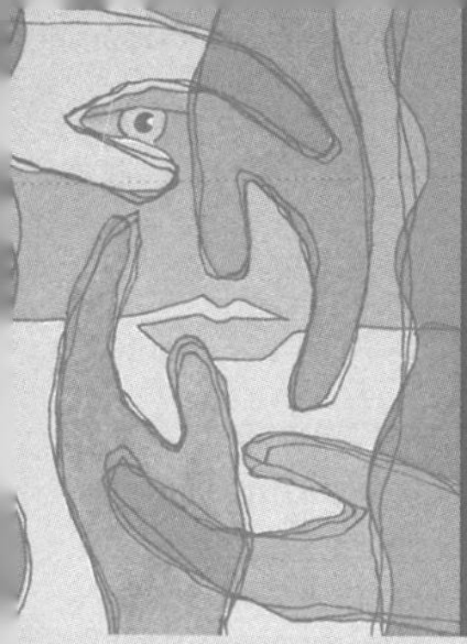

CHAPTER 2

Building e-business competence through concepts and cases

Chapter at a glance

Learning outcomes

After completing this chapter you should be able to:

- Understand how creativity and analytical abilities contribute to the strategy development process.
- Recognize the value of case studies for learning about e-business.
- Explain the value of concepts and frameworks for learning about e-business.

INTRODUCTION

Let us venture out from the e-business world for a moment and compare managers in charge of strategy development with architects who are designing new buildings.[1] We will consider first what kind of qualities good architects need to have and determine in a following step to what extent this analogy is relevant for managers.

Good architects are those who bring new, creative and surprising elements into their work. While planning buildings, they do not just copy what has always been around within their cultural area. Instead, they develop a unique style that combines well-proven, generally accepted solutions with new, individual and creative ideas. It is this way of solving technical and artistic problems that sets their work positively apart from others. They design buildings where bypassers recognize and appreciate immediately who the architect was.

How do good architects develop their ideas? Architects need to get inspired and find 'food' for their mind to work and play around with. They derive their inspiration from many different sources. They can turn to the leading architects within their own country and culture and learn from their styles. To expand their horizon further, they might travel around the world to see other settings and cultures to find out more about other architectural styles. On a more abstract level, they might also turn to nature to see how plants and trees have solved their own 'architectural' challenges.

Yet good architects are not only creative; they also have the analytical ability to assess critically the feasibility of the ideas they develop. This includes finding answers to questions such as 'Will the building be structurally sound?', 'What will the construction costs be?', 'Will people enjoy living in this building?' and 'Will my client be able and willing to pay for it?' To answer these questions, good architects need to be able to conduct their analysis both on a broad level to cover all relevant issues (such as structural soundness of the building design, legal restrictions and financial considerations) and also on a detailed level to address the specific problems of the project at hand. The critical ability is that they are able to switch back and forth between broad overall considerations and important detailed issues that require in-depth analysis.[2]

The essence of this analogy is to point out that, just like good architects, successful managers are likely to be those who come up with innovative strategic ideas. Additionally, they are able to determine whether their ideas hold when scrutinized from an analytic business perspective.

We start this chapter by briefly outlining the dimensions of creativity and analytical ability.[3] Following that, we discuss how the conceptual e-business strategy framework and the case studies contained in this book can help students and managers involved with e-business strategy development to expand their skills and knowledge along the dimensions of creativity and analytical ability.

2.1 Defining creativity and analytical ability

2.1.1 Creativity

In its broadest sense, creativity can be defined as the ability to develop new ideas. Just like it is inherently difficult to determine what makes some people more intelligent than others, it is also difficult to determine why some people are more creative than others. However, in spite of this uncertainty, one predominant characteristic among creative people is that they have been exposed to different experiences, thinking styles and disciplines from which they draw in their search for new ideas.

Consider, for example, the great German baroque composer, Johann Sebastian Bach, who lived in the eighteenth century. Even though he led a rather provincial life, never travelling outside Germany, his music was inspired by other great European composers of the baroque period. Most importantly, Bach transcribed the orchestral work of Italian composers such as Antonio Vivaldi, which later had a profound influence on Bach's style of composition, as can be witnessed, for example, in his *Italian Concerto* for harpsichord.

The American inventor Thomas Edison, who invented the electric light bulb and the telegraph, also immersed himself in a broad variety of knowledge from an early age. At age 11, Edison's parents taught him how to use the resources of the local library. He started with the last book on the bottom shelf and planned to read every book in the building. At age 12, he had read Gibbon's *Rise and Fall of the Roman Empire*, Sears' *History of the World* and Burton's *Anatomy of Melancholy*, in addition to *The World Dictionary of Science* and books on practical chemistry.[4]

These two examples are meant to illustrate that a broad knowledge or experience pool – a characteristic that Csikszentmihaly, a researcher of creativity, calls 'differentiated mind' – seems to be a prerequisite for creativity.[5] Based on this knowledge, creative individuals are able to produce many new ideas, mostly by taking existing ideas that are seemingly unrelated and then connecting them in new ways.

The inevitable question is then: how can we improve our creativity in order to be able to develop innovative ideas? There exists a vast literature on creativity that suggests detailed methods on how to think creatively individually or in team settings.[6] In the context of this book, we consider the following steps to be of special importance:

- *Create a vast and diverse pool of knowledge and experiences.* Search outside your domain of expertise to provide your mind with enough 'food' for developing creative ideas. A good starting point is to capture interesting ideas from different settings (industrial, organizational, geographical, cultural, etc.). In most cases, it will probably not be clear what this information will be good for, or even whether it will ever be good for anything. The problem with creativity is that you just do not know beforehand which ideas will turn out to be valuable and which ones will not. The collection of case studies in this book provides some examples of good (and bad) ideas and successful (and failed) implementations. You might also want to look across disciplines by studying, for instance, history or biology.

- *Produce as many different ideas as possible.* Play around with the existing ideas from others, get a feeling for why they work, or do not work, and try to connect ideas that are seemingly unconnected (see the FT article 'Breaking the barriers to creativity'). Creativity is not a plug-and-play affair; rather, it requires time and patience. However, to look for new applications of old ideas is a good way to jump-start a creative thinking process. Consider, for instance, the deployment of the steam engine in the nineteenth century. At first it was used only in mines, and it took 75 years for someone to work out that it could also be used to power steamboats. For a more recent example, consider Jeff Bezos, the founder of Amazon.com. He saw the potential of the Internet and connected that with book retailing to create the idea of Amazon.com, which, in a matter of a few years, has turned into the largest book store in the world. To connect existing ideas in new ways requires one to break out of the known reality by making a mental leap into new and uncharted territory.
- *Produce unlikely ideas.* At this early stage, there is no need to think about implementation; instead, all that matters is creation. Just ensure that the ideas you produce are unlikely ideas, i.e. ideas that are very different from what other people come up with and that diverge from traditional thinking. That is what constitutes their novelty and uniqueness. At the same time, these ideas are not bizarre. Once others see them, they say: 'Oh, that's so obvious. I could have thought of that myself.' Maybe they could have, but they did not; they were unable to make this seemingly obvious connection between A and B. That is the big difference between creative and not-so-creative people – it is the almost-but-not-quite dimension that sets them apart. For instance, with hindsight it is easy to see that an online auction house such as eBay would be highly successful. Yet someone had to have the creative insight to come up with this idea and, later, the courage to implement it.

FT

Breaking the barriers to creativity

Creativity, a philosopher once remarked, is whatever you choose to make of it. Creativity begins with recognizing opportunities as they present themselves in everyday life. Once these 'triggers' for creativity have been spotted, the manager then needs to assess the problem, often overcoming barriers to new solutions.

Creativity is achieved through breaking down existing relationships and analyzing the elements of the problem, then moving these into new patterns until a solution is found. Creativity requires a desire to experiment, an ability to understand problems and ask questions, and a refusal to be afraid of failure. Developing these traits is not easy, but it can be done. Every person in an organization has the potential to make new and better things happen, to bring into being new ideas regardless of their job or background. Whether they do so is a matter of their ability to see the world around them and whether they can recognise the opportunities or 'triggers' for creativity that can be found in everyday life.

Triggers for creativity

Intermittent windshield wipers for automobiles were not invented by an auto engineer, but by someone who tinkered with cars in his spare time. Collectively, the major automakers had thousands of engineers on their payrolls, most of whom would at some time have had the experience of driving in the rain. Yet none of these 'experts' saw this situation as an opportunity to do something new.

We are exposed to these moments every day; if we fail to notice them, they pass us by. If we pause to reflect and question, the situation might become a trigger, an impulse to creative action.

History has recorded other triggers. While on vacation, Edwin Land took pictures of his daughter. When she showed her disappointment that she couldn't see the results right then and there, he set his mind to the task of developing instant photography. Art Fry sang in a church choir for years. As many choir members did, he put slips of paper in his hymn book to mark each selection. His technique was not foolproof, however; the slips of paper often fell out. Taking his dissatisfaction back to his job, he developed what became 3M's Post-it note pads.

The non-stick coating Teflon was an accident. However, its subsequent application to a myriad of products happened because a curious chemist didn't throw away the accident; he played with it to learn more about its properties. He found that the new product could have many uses, such as non-stick frying pans.

These events probably happened to hundreds of other fathers, choir members, and chemists. The only difference is they were triggers to these people, and events to be forgotten by the others.

Defining the problem

It has been said that 'a problem correctly stated is half solved'. Edward de Bono talks about an office building where people complained about the time they had to wait for the elevators. Seeing the problem as one of 'How can we speed up the elevators?' the building's owners felt they were up against a brick wall of prohibitive costs. In a triumph of lateral thinking, it was suggested that mirrors be placed on the walls around the elevators. Thus people would spend the time looking at themselves, combing their hair, and would be oblivious to the wait.

However, suppose the problem had originally been stated in terms of the true choice: 'How can we eliminate the complaints about the elevators?' Speeding them up would have been an idea; mirrors might have been recognized as an idea, as well as mounting television sets on the wall or piping in news broadcasts. The problem was first looked at in terms of changing the performance of the product (the elevators). It was solved by creating change in how the product was perceived, by changing the product's environment.

Barriers to creativity

An important first step in developing creative abilities is to recognize what stands in the way of creating ideas.

- The foremost of these barriers is your own *experience*. The advertising guru David Ogilvy once commented that 'The majority of businessmen are incapable of original thought because they are unable to escape from the tyranny of reason.' As an example, Kenneth Olsen, the president of Digital Equipment Corporation, relied on his extensive experience in computers when he told attendees at the World Future Society's 1977 Convention: 'There is no reason for any individual to have a computer in their home.' Relying on what he himself knew about the industry meant that Olsen lost out in the race to enter the home computer market, as his company was overtaken by rivals such as Apple.
- The *assumptions* you make are another barrier to creativity. For years, the greeting card companies assumed that their competition was other greeting card companies. However, research showed that companies in other sectors, such as telecommunications company Florists Telegraph Delivery (FTD), were also significant competitors.

- The *judgements* we make are a third barrier to creativity. When was the last time you reacted to an idea with: 'It will never work', or 'We tried that before', or 'They'll never buy it?' Think about judgments you've laughed at like, 'He'll fall off the end of the earth' (said about Christopher Columbus) or 'They'll never replace horses' (said about automobiles). Often judgements are passed on a situation before all the information is known, and thus opportunities are lost.
- Your *thinking patterns* can be another barrier to creativity. However, while these can inhibit creativity, you could not survive without them. Like experience, thinking patterns can be both an asset and a liability. The key lies in knowing when to depend on them and when to lock them away. If you are driving down a highway and you hear a siren, a stored thinking pattern immediately takes over. You locate the source and, if it is in your line of travel, you pull over to get out of the way of an emergency vehicle – or to receive your speeding ticket. At other times, though, thinking patterns tend to lead us to routine behaviour and thought, so that we fail to recognize the new as a source of opportunity.
- A fifth barrier is the *right answer syndrome.* So much of current education emphasizes the need to 'get the right answer'. Answers are just arrangements of information. For example, the game of tic-tac-toe has nine boxes. If each box contains a piece of information, how many combinations are there of these nine pieces of information? There are 362,880 possible combinations of these nine pieces of information. (The answer is 9 factorial, which means it is determined by multiplying $9 \times 8 \times 7 \times 6 \times 5 \times 4 \times 3 \times 2 \times 1 = 362{,}880$.) However, knowing this answer does not help us to win at tic-tac-toe. In the same way, knowing how many units of product we are selling does not help us to sell more. Creativity involves looking beyond the simple facts.
- The last barrier is *fear of failure.* Failure is actually a great learning tool. Unfortunately, too many managers are graduates of the right-answer school and are oblivious to the value of failure. The best answer to the fear of failure syndrome was expressed by Thomas Edison. When a friend suggested that Edison's attempts to develop an electric storage battery were a failure since he had tried thousands of materials without success, Edison replied: 'Why, I've got a lot of results. I know several thousand things that won't work.'

An approach to creativity

The path to creative ideas has three stages, which involve breaking down the previously perceived relationships between parts of the problem; then re-examining the pieces individually; then rearranging the pieces to form new relationships until we find a pattern that works and solves the problem. The first step in creating ideas is to destroy the familiarity, the relationships of everything you know about the problem. Before Edwin Land invented instant photography, every consumer knew that seeing the results of a picture-taking session was related to developing the film, which was related to a place called a darkroom, which was related to the local drugstore as its contact point.

Everybody was a prisoner of that familiarity, including Edwin Land himself, until he let his mind destroy those relationships. Once this act of destruction has happened, you have a rich reservoir of bits and pieces of information, of unconnected facts and fantasies. However, just like the words in a dictionary, they do nothing until they are selected and assembled to become a coherent sum. The value of these pieces was neatly summed up by Albert Szent-Gyorgyi: 'Discovery consists of seeing what everybody has seen – and thinking what nobody thought.'

The final step is to look for new ways of assembling the pieces. The value and simplicity of this step was succinctly described by the painter Sir Joshua Reynolds in the eighteenth century: 'Invention is little more than new combinations of those images which have been previously gathered and deposited in the

memory.' It is this development of new patterns and pictures which is the final act of creativity.

In summary

The fundamental steps to developing your own creative-thinking capabilities can be summarized as follows:

1. Recognize the triggers you are exposed to every day and see the opportunities presented.
2. Define the problem in terms of the 'true choice', and make sure the right questions are being asked.
3. Recognize your barriers to creativity and overcome them.
4. Forget everything you know in terms of relationships between the elements of the problem.
5. Remember everything you know and assess all the pieces of the problem.
6. Rearrange everything you know by moving the same pieces into new relationships with each other.

Source: W. Altier, 'Breaking the barriers to creativity', www.FT.com, 5 September 2002

2.1.2 Analytical ability

Analytical ability refers to the skills that are necessary to integrate the knowledge that one possesses into a coherent whole. Thus, while creativity is concerned with *divergent thinking*, i.e. coming up with ideas that are out of the ordinary, analytical ability is concerned with *convergent thinking*, i.e. relating multiple parts of one's thinking and integrating them into a coherent whole.[7] Managers with an integrated mindset are able to break down a complex business problem into its manageable parts and identify crucial variables and questions. They do so by first looking at the 'big picture' that encompasses a broad overview over all involved issues and then focusing on those issues that are of special relevance to the problem at hand.

2.2 Becoming a 'catalyst for change'

By nature, not all managers are endowed with the genius of creativity and profound analytical ability. Instead, they differ along these two dimensions, leading to the classification of manager types explained below, which include (1) the *novice*, (2) the *visionary*, (3) the *efficient performer* and (4) the *catalyst for change* (see Exhibit 2.1).

- *Novices* have a low level of both creativity and analytical ability. In order to develop innovative yet sound strategies, they need to expand their abilities along the creativity and analytical ability dimensions. Note that novices as referred to in this context must not be confused with novices who are new to a company. The latter type of novice might well have had varied experiences and honed their analytical skills before joining the company. Thus, they already possess the skills and knowledge to become a catalyst for change. In the proposed classification, however, the novice does not possess these skills and knowledge.

- *Visionaries* are characterized by an immense level of creative energy yet little analytical ability. Throughout their lives and careers, they have collected many different ideas and they continually develop new ideas. They have a very differentiated mindset. Yet, because they are unable to integrate the many different ideas and evaluate them by means of structured, logical reasoning, their endeavours often tend to end up in chaos and are frequently abandoned prematurely.
- *Efficient performers* possess the opposite characteristics of the visionary. While they do not have the ability to develop creative new ideas, they dispose of strong analytical abilities. This is reflected in the way they perform qualitative and quantitative analyses with rigour and depth.
- *The catalysts for change* combine the positive traits of both the visionary and the efficient performer. Thus, they have high levels of creativity and of analytical ability. They know that strategy formulation is more than just crunching numbers and hoping that something will come out that ensures value creation and competitive advantage. They also know that ideas by themselves are not enough to build a sustainable, profitable business. Instead, to them, strategy formulation is a mix between creativity and analysis.

These manager types are characterized by a number of opposing attributes, which are effectively united in one person. Catalysts for change have the ability to (1) alternate between *imagination and fantasy* and a *rooted sense of reality*, (2) be very *playful* at certain times yet return to a very *disciplined* working style within a matter of minutes, and (3) shift quickly from *openness*, where they work closely together with others, to *closure*, where they seclude themselves to work out the details of their thinking.[8]

Exhibit 2.1 Fostering creativity and analytical ability helps a manager to become a catalyst for change

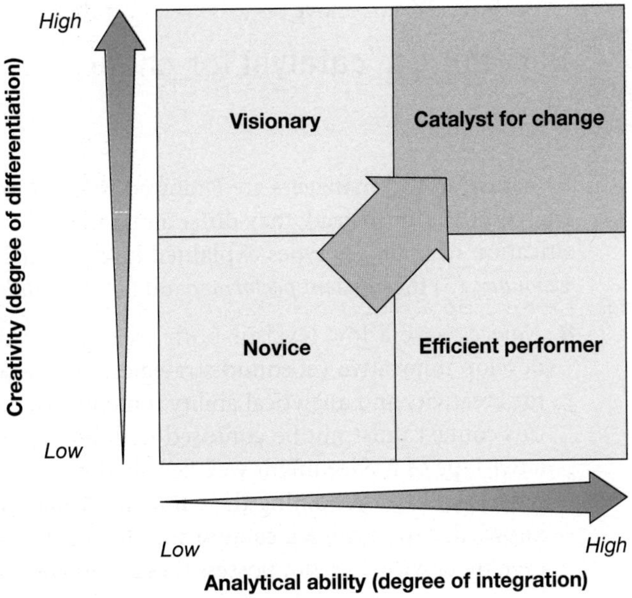

The proposed classification of different types of manager is helpful in two ways. First, at an individual level you can think where you would place yourself within this matrix. You can also discuss with your colleagues or classmates where they would place you within the matrix. Doing so also allows you to determine which abilities you need to develop further in order to become a catalyst for change.

Furthermore, when working in a team, you can also think about the different people needed to ensure a high level of both creativity and analytical ability. Selecting individuals with complementary abilities can then help your team, as a whole, to become a catalyst for change.

2.3 Learning about e-business through case studies

This book is an integrated, case-study-based learning package, as is demonstrated by the large number of cases included in it. When writing this book, we had three primary aims in mind: the case studies should provide (1) a *context for the analysis of e-business issues*, (2) a *context for the application of e-business concepts*, and (3) a *stimulus for creative e-business strategies.*

2.3.1 Case studies as a context for the analysis of e-business issues

The first aim of the case studies in the book is to provide a broad overview of the critical issues and challenges that organizations face when developing their e-business strategies and, subsequently, conducting their online activities. The diversity of settings and contexts of the cases provides insights on different issues, including e-procurement, online/offline channel conflicts, e-logistics, e-payment, one-to-one marketing, and the move from mass production in the physical world to mass customization through the Internet.

We hope that, after working through these case studies, you will have a richer pool of experiences. However, instead of providing ready-made answers to the questions they raise, these cases studies aim at giving you a deeper understanding of the issues involved and the choices and trade-offs that need to be made when you are faced with making similar decisions of your own.

2.3.2 Case studies as a context for the application of e-business concepts

The second aim of the cases is to provide real-world situations for applying the conceptual frameworks described in the e-business strategy framework part of the book. Compared with typical strategy textbooks, this 'laboratory' setting offers a number of advantages. Just like in the real world, information is not neatly packaged and presented. Instead, you have to sift through the rather large amounts of information provided in the cases and distil from it the most important facts. You need then to determine which framework is most applicable to a given situation. In order to arrive

at a conclusion and make recommendations, you will have to collect more data and build supporting arguments to defend your stance in front of colleagues.

However, be cautious: there is no single right answer to the questions raised in the cases. As alluded to above, strategy formulation is not maths, where you plug in the numbers and get just one clear answer. There are, however, answers that are better supported by factual evidence than others, and there are answers that use logical reasoning more stringently than others. Thus, the case setting with its inherent ambiguity provides an excellent environment for practising the development and exchange of arguments and the sharpening of analytical skills.[9]

2.3.3 Case studies as a stimulus for creative e-business strategies

In addition to providing factual information and a basis for applying the proposed frameworks, the cases in this book are also meant to serve as a source for creative idea development. As discussed above, it is important to collect ideas from many different sources as to provide 'food' for the creative thought development process.

Just like the architect who studies different building styles from different countries, the cases from different industries and organizations aim at providing you with the opportunity to gain insights into different ways of conducting e-business. For example, consider a group of managers in the strategy division of a large German bank. How do they get inspired to develop innovative strategies? Essentially, the case studies enable the following three possibilities (see also Exhibit 2.2):

- *Intra-industry benchmarking (within own culture).* The above-mentioned bank managers can first benchmark other banks in Germany. This might provide them with either the comforting feeling that the competition is lagging behind or the feeling that there are some relatively minor adjustments that need to be made. In any case, the closed-in perspective of looking within an industry in one's own culture is often unlikely to provide the creative ideas that would give the bank a lasting source of competitive advantage.
- *Intra-industry benchmarking (across cultures).* The potential for relevant new insights increases as the bank's managers start looking outside their own business culture. For example, they may focus on countries with an established 'e-habit', i.e. having a large portion of the population frequently using the Internet for a wider variety of activities than in Germany. Finland, where e-banking has been customary over the past two decades and where customers are now heavily into using mobile banking, represents an interesting case. The German managers could focus on this country to scout out the recent developments, which will most likely also take place in Germany in the not-so-distant future. Studying Finnish banks, such as Nordea, which is at the cutting edge of electronic and mobile banking, would thus offer an interesting benchmark to analyze in more detail.
- *Cross-industry inspiration.* A far more innovative and ground-breaking, albeit more challenging, source of new ideas is to look across different industries and think about how their way of conducting e-business could be transferred to one's own industry. A bank might ask: 'What can we learn from the way Ducati sells some of its motorcycle products exclusively online, or from how 12Snap manages

Exhibit 2.2 **New ideas can be found by analyzing state-of-the art companies within one's own industry and also across industries**

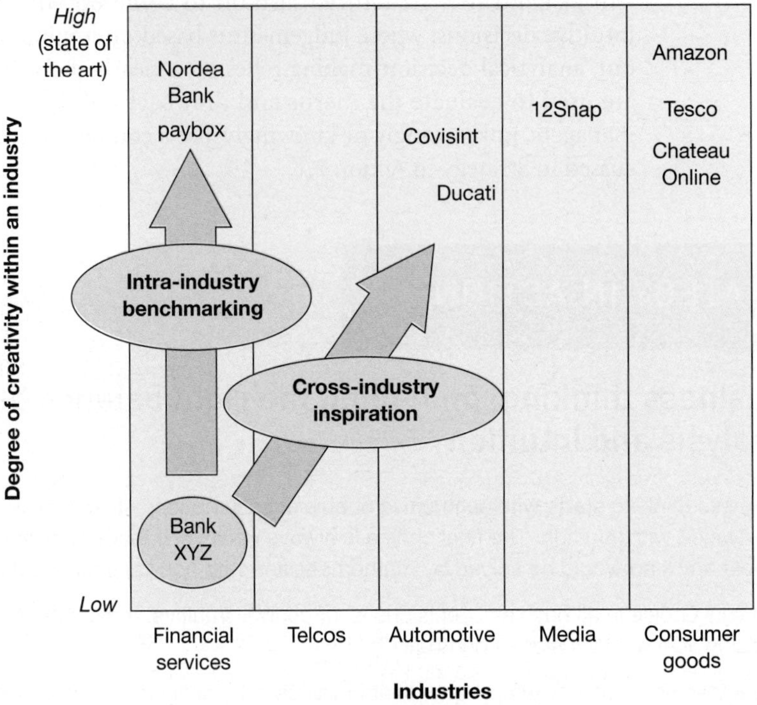

its one-to-one mobile marketing operations?' Building bridges requires creative leaps; that is ultimately the source of competitive advantage, since there are only a few companies willing and able to make such leaps.

The case studies in the book are meant to be a source of inspiration for cross-industry fertilization. For example, during our teaching we found out that managers from a global insurance company were able to derive interesting and valuable insights from analyzing the Ducati case study. Obviously, these cross-industry comparisons should not be adopted 'as is' in one's own industry but rather used to stimulate new and unconventional thinking and to raise the simple, yet powerful question: 'Would it not be possible for our company to do something similar if …?'

2.4 Learning about e-business through concepts and frameworks

After discussing the creative element of strategy formulation, we also need to find ways to evaluate creative ideas and strategies and determine whether it is sensible to implement them. What are the possibilities to test the usefulness of strategy ideas? What makes one strategy more likely to succeed than another? Essentially, there are two different routes that managers can choose from.

At one end of the spectrum, managers rely solely on their intuition, which is based mainly on their past experiences. At the other end, they rely on analyzing the problem at hand in a structured fashion to come up with a solution. In contrast to intuitive decisions, where judgement is based on implicit criteria that are not spelled out, analytical decision-making relies on a clearly defined set of explicit criteria that are used to evaluate the merits and drawbacks of different options. In most cases, managers, unknowingly or knowingly, use a combination of these approaches, as discussed in Strategy in Action 2.1.

STRATEGY IN ACTION 2.1

Business thinking: on finding the right balance between analysis and intuition

Business thinking starts with an intuitive choice of assumptions. Its progress as analysis is intertwined with intuition. The final choice is always intuitive. If that were not true, all problems of almost any kind would be solved by mathematicians with non-quantitative data.

The final choice in all business decisions is, of course, intuitive. It must be. Otherwise it is not a decision, just a conclusion, a printout.

The trade-off of subjective non-quantifiable values is by definition a subjective and intuitive choice. Intuition can be awesome in its value at times. It is known as good judgment in everyday affairs. Intuition is in fact the subconscious integration of all the experiences, conditioning and knowledge of a lifetime, including the emotional and cultural biases of that lifetime.

But intuition alone is never enough. Alone it can be disastrously wrong. Analysis too can be disastrously wrong. Analysis depends upon keeping the required data to manageable proportions. It also means keeping the non-quantifiable data to a minimum. Thus, analysis by its very nature requires initial oversimplification and intuitive choice of starting assumptions with exclusion of certain data. All of these choices are intuitive. A mistake in any one can be fatal to the analysis. Any complex problem has a near infinite combination of facts and relationships. Business in particular is affected by everything, including the past, the non-logical and the unknowable. This complexity is compounded by multiple objectives to serve multiple constituencies, many of whose objectives must be traded off. Problem solving with such complexity requires an orderly, systematic approach in order to even hope to optimize the final decision.

When the results of analysis and intuition coincide, there is little gained except confidence. When the analysis reaches conclusions that are counter-intuitive, then more rigorous analysis and reexamination of underlying assumptions are always called for. The expansion of the frame of reference and the increased rigor of analysis may be fruitful.

But in nearly all problem solving there is a universe of alternative choices, most of which must be discarded without more than cursory attention. To do otherwise is to incur costs beyond the value of any solution and defer decision to beyond the time horizon. A frame of reference is needed to screen the intuitive selection of assumptions, relevance of data, methodology and implicit value judgments. That frame of reference is the concept.

▶

Conceptual thinking is the skeleton or the framework on which all the other choices are sorted out. A concept is by its nature an oversimplification. Yet its fundamental relationships are so powerful and important that they will tend to override all except the most extreme exceptions. Such exceptions are usually obvious in their importance. A concept defines a system of interactions in terms of the relative values that produce stable equilibrium of the system. Consequently, a concept defines the initial assumptions, the data required and the relationships between the data inputs. In this way it permits analysis of the consequences of change in input data.

Concepts are simple in statement but complex in practice. Outputs are almost always part of the input by means of feedback. The feedback itself is consequently a subsystem interconnected with other subsystems.

Theoretically, such conceptual business systems can be solved by a series of simultaneous equations. In practice, computer simulation is the only practical way to deal with the characteristic multiple inputs, feedback loops and higher order effects in a reasonable time at reasonable cost with all the underlying assumptions made explicit. Pure mathematics becomes far too ponderous.

Concepts are developed in hard science and business alike from an approximation of the scientific method. They start with a generalization of an observed pattern of experience. They are stated first as a hypothesis, then postulated as a theory, then defined as a decision rule. They are validated by their ability to predict. Such decision rules are often crystallized as policies. Rarely does a business concept permit definitive proof enough to be called a 'law' except facetiously.

Intuition disguised as status, seniority and rank is the underlying normative mode of all business decisions. It could not be otherwise. Too many choices must be made too often. Data is expensive to collect, often of uncertain quality or relevance. Analysis is laborious and often far too expensive even though imprecise or superficial.

Yet two kinds of decisions justify rigorous and painstaking analysis guided by intuition derived from accumulated experience. The irrevocable commitment of major reserves of resources deserves such treatment. So do the major policies which guide and control the implementation of such commitments.

All rigorous analysis is inherently an iterative process. It starts with an intuitive choice and ends with an intuitive decision. The first definition of a problem is inescapably intuitive. It must be in order to be recognized as a problem at all. The final decision is intuitive. It must be or there is no choice and therefore no need for decision.

Between those two points of beginning and ending, the rigorous process must take place. The sequence is analysis, problem redefinition, reanalysis and then even more rigorous problem redefinition, etc. until the law of diminishing returns dictates a halt – intuitively.

The methodology and sequence of business thinking can be stated or at least approximated.

- State the problem as clearly and fully as possible.
- Search for and identify the basic concepts that relate to the perceived critical elements.
- Define the data inputs this conceptual reference will require. Check off and identify any major factors, which are not implicitly included in the conceptual base.
- Redefine the problem and broaden the concept as necessary to include any such required inputs.
- Gather the data and analyze the problem.
- Find out to which data inputs the analysis is sensitive. Reexamine the range of options with respect to those factors and the resulting range of outputs.

- Based on the insights developed by the analysis, redefine the problem and repeat the process.
- Reiterate until there is a consensus that the possible incremental improvement in insight is no longer worth the incremental cost. That consensus will be intuitive. It must be. There is no way to know the value of the unknown.

It is a matter of observation that much of the value of a rigorous and objective examination of a problem will be found in one of three areas:

- First, the previously accepted underlying assumptions may prove to be invalid, in fact, or inadequate as the problem definition is changed.
- Second, the interaction between component functions may have been neglected, resulting in suboptimization by function.
- Third, a previously unknown or unaccepted or misunderstood conceptual framework may be postulated which both permits prediction of the consequence of change and partially explains these consequences.

It is also a matter of common observation that the wisest of intuitive judgments come after full exploration and consensus on the nature of the problem by peers of near equal but diverse experience.

Finally, it is also a matter of general experience that implementation of the optimum decision will prove difficult if that discussion and consensus have not been continued long enough to make the relationship between the overall objective and the specific action seem clear to all who must interpret and implement the required policies. Otherwise, the intuition of those who do the implementation will be used to redefine the policies that emerged from analysis. This is one reason planned organization change is so difficult, and random drift is so common.

Here are some fundamental procedural suggestions. Define the problem and hypothesize the approach to a solution intuitively before wasting time on data collection and analysis. Do the first analysis lightly. Then and only then redefine the problem more rigorously and reanalyze in depth. (Don't go to the library and read all the books before you know what you want to learn.) Use mixed project research teams composed of some people with finely honed intuitions from experience and others with highly developed analytical skills and too little experience to know what cannot be done. Perhaps in this way you can achieve the best of both analysis and intuition in combination and offset the weaknesses of either.

Source: B. Henderson, 'Business thinking', in C. Stern and G. Stalk (eds), *Perspectives on Strategy*, John Wiley, 1998, pp. 260–263.

Intuition is valuable because it provides a quick solution to a problem. However, its value is somewhat limited when the environment changes as quickly and drastically as is the case with e-business. Then, managers risk overlooking or misjudging important factors, which results in misguided strategies.

An analytical approach to strategy formulation, on the other hand, allows for a broader and more profound analysis of the issues at hand. However, it is time-consuming and difficult, since it is not immediately obvious which factors need to be analyzed when evaluating strategies in a systematic way. Questions such as 'Should we start selling our products online?' and 'How should we position ourselves vis-à-vis our competitors and how should we organize our firm?' cannot be answered by just looking at individual and isolated factors. Instead, it is necessary to acquire a thorough and comprehensive perspective.

How can this be done? One possible approach is to use conceptual frameworks that break down the problem at hand into manageable subunits, which can be analyzed individually. The goal of a framework is to facilitate thinking through a problem by providing a structured approach that is independent of industry or starting position. A good framework has the following qualities:[10]

- *It captures the most important dimensions of the problem.* This means that all the important elements that constitute an integral part of the real world are included in the framework. One of the reasons why, for instance, Porter's industry analysis framework, which is defined in Section 3.2, has been used widely in the business and academic communities is that it has captured the essential factors that determine the attractiveness of an industry. At the same time, a good framework captures the essential variables with the least number of dimensions, which in turn helps manage complexity. A framework with hundreds of variables might cover all dimensions, yet it is not practical in everyday problem-solving. Thus, finding the right balance between being exhaustive on the one hand and keeping the framework as simple as possible on the other hand is a crucial challenge in framework building.
- *All the elements that the framework contains are mutually exclusive.* This means that the elements or dimensions in the framework differ systematically from each other and do not overlap. To a large extent, this criterion determines the clarity of frameworks. Consider, for example, the value chain concept, which is discussed in more detail in Section 5.2. This concept helps a manager to separate distinctive, albeit interrelated, activities within a firm such as inbound logistics, production, outbound logistics, marketing and sales, and after-sales service. The separation into discrete activities opens up the way to a more rigorous analysis and to raising questions such as 'Which of our activities should we perform internally and which should we outsource?' and 'Through which activities can we differentiate ourselves from our competitors?'

Frameworks such as Porter's five forces and the value chain are frequently criticized for being too rigid and leaving too little room for creativity.[11] There are essentially two alternatives to a framework-based approach. First, to rely solely on intuition, which presents its own set of problems as was discussed above. Second, to use an analytical approach without a structured framework and to start from scratch every time. Doing so entails two main risks.

First, you might forget an important dimension that, in the end, may turn out to be crucial for the problem-solving process. Second, it requires substantially more effort because you need to determine the most important variables that drive the analytical process. Doing so might force you to consider every variable involved but never to achieve any real depth in your analysis.

Instead of the above-mentioned approaches, it is more sensible to familiarize yourself with key frameworks and concepts and then adapt them to the needs of the specific situation at hand. The goal of the e-business strategy framework (presented in Part 2) is to make you more familiar with the most important strategy frameworks and to show, through examples, how they can be used in an e-business context. However, the proposed framework is not meant to provide any ready-made answers. Instead, it aims to raise questions and providing a structured approach to asking 'Why?' and 'Why not?'

Exhibit 2.3 Effective strategy formulation requires the ability to cover a broad analysis horizon and to perform selective, in-depth analyses of crucial issues

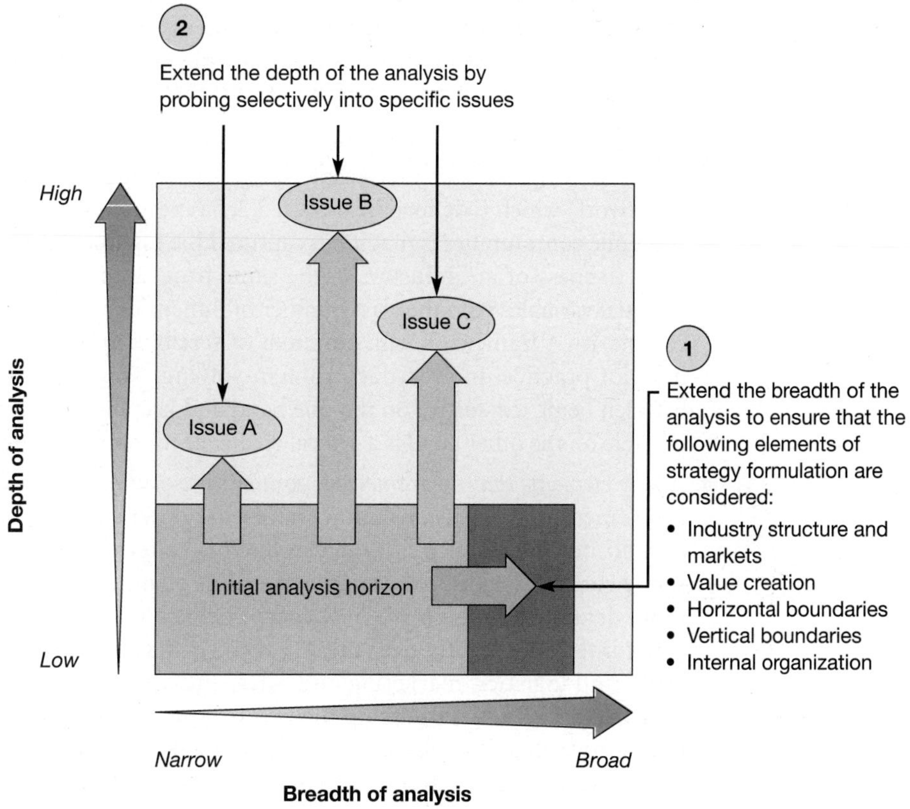

In particular, it aims to expand the analysis along two directions: first breadth and then depth (see Exhibit 2.3).

2.4.1 Extending the breadth of the analysis

As mentioned above, it is difficult to achieve an overarching perspective of the issues involved in strategy formulation. Therefore, it is advisable first to gain a broad understanding of the relevant issues and then to embark on a more detailed analysis. The proposed sequencing of these steps is important, especially knowing managers' time limitations.

To illustrate the above issue, let us consider two companies – DeepFirst Inc. and BroadFirst Inc. – involved in oil exploration. The exploration engineers of DeepFirst Inc. start drilling in front of the company's headquarters to find out whether there is any oil. Then they move on and keep drilling randomly, in different places, until they eventually encounter an oil well. However, this process is very time-consuming and expensive. The exploration engineers of BroadFirst Inc., on the other hand, have developed elaborate systems based on geology research and advanced ultrasound devices. Using this technology, they quickly scan vast areas of land and can then

predict precisely where it is worthwhile drilling. In effect, they look at the bigger picture first before investing substantial efforts in drilling, thereby reducing cost and increasing the likelihood of success.

Often, however, managers behave more like the engineers from DeepFirst Inc., overlooking the 'bigger picture' and instead focusing first on isolated issues, which often turn out to be of only marginal importance. In doing so, they collect vast amounts of data and build elaborate quantitative models only to find out later that the issue they were working on so diligently did not really matter in the broader context. However, while getting immersed in a side issue, they forgot to move on to other areas of analysis that were significantly more important.

In order to reduce the danger of missing key variables in the strategy-formulation process, it is important to have a clear understanding of the overall dimensions that are likely to be relevant. In the e-business strategy framework, there are three main dimensions, which are all closely interrelated. These are: (1) external environment and markets, (2) value-creation and strategy options, and (3) firm structure and organization. Depending on the strategic context at hand, certain dimensions are more relevant than others. In any case, however, it is important to have the broad picture at the outset and only then to drill deeper into more specific issues.

2.4.2 Extending the depth of the analysis

In addition to expanding the breadth of the analysis, a second goal of the concepts discussed in the e-business strategy framework is to expand the depth of the analysis. To illustrate this point, let us consider the case of a firm that wants to enter the online auction market. At first glance, this market might seem attractive because existing players, such as eBay, are highly profitable. Digging deeper, we would then ask 'Why is this so?', a question to which there are several answers. First, there are high economies of scale, which limits costs. Second, there are also high barriers to entry, which allows incumbent firms to charge healthy margins.

Moving down to the next level of analysis, we can determine the reasons for the high barriers to entry. They result largely from network effects. Once an e-auction place has managed to attract a critical number of users, it is unlikely that customers will switch to a new competitor. This is due to the fact that much of the value of an e-auction place depends on how many other customers use it, which creates a liquid market where it is easy to sell and buy things.

Moving down one more level, we could ask how the firm was able to create strong network effects and whether these effects could be replicated. This probing can continue by always asking 'Why?' Eventually, however, there will be a point where it is not sensible to keep raising questions any more because the effort of doing so will outweigh the expected benefit. Yet, more often than not, we tend to stop asking 'Why?' too soon rather than too late (see Strategy in Action 2.2).

Furthermore, with today's advanced IT capabilities, companies can more easily collect relevant data to answer deeper-seated questions. For instance, when analyzing customer service at Amazon.com, Jeff Bezos requires detailed quantitative run-downs of numbers regarding the average customer contacts per order, average contact length, breakdown of e-mail and telephone contacts, and total cost of each contact.

The move along the chain of causality by asking 'Why?' helps you to understand the root causes of successes and failures. You can then use these insights for evaluating your own ideas and making more informed strategy decisions. To foster the analysis, the concepts discussed in this book represent the following three levels of thinking:

- *e-Business specific concepts.* On the first level, concepts such as a company's virtual value chain (see Section 5.2.3), the unbundling of the traditional organization (see Section 8.3), and the ICDT (information, communication, distribution and transaction) model (see Section 9.1) are specific to e-business. Frequently, these concepts implicitly or explicitly build on concepts from strategic management literature (such as the value chain concept) and also on fundamental economic thinking (such as the concept of transaction costs).

  The strength of these concepts is that they are tailored to the e-business context; therefore, their applicability is rather straightforward. However, this specific tailoring presents, at the same time, their main weakness, since, as the experiences of the last few years have shown, these concepts often fall short of explaining more complex cause–effect relationships, thereby possibly misguiding managers into seemingly obvious yet faulty strategies.

  Consider, for instance, the concepts of deconstruction and unbundling that became popular during the Internet boom years (see Sections 8.2 and 8.3). Managers were supposed to take apart their company's value chains and focus on individual activities or businesses where they possessed a competitive advantage. The initial logic was, in many cases, compelling. In other cases, however, it did not turn out to be fitting because crucial linkages between different activities within the firm were overlooked. Probing beyond the initial level of analysis might have provided a more profound explanation and, in turn, would have led to more sensible conclusions and better strategies.

- *Generic strategic concepts.* In order to move beyond the initial level of analysis and find deeper cause–effect relationships, it is useful to have a good understanding of the key strategic concepts, such as the five forces industry model, the concept of co-opetition, the generic strategy options and the value chain. These concepts can be applied irrespective of the industry or firm at hand. The common characteristic of these concepts is that they do not provide any ready-made answers. Instead, they define the relevant variables and thus help managers to raise the right questions. We discuss these concepts at length in the e-business strategy framework and link them to some real-world examples to illustrate how they can be applied in the specific e-business context.

- *Fundamental economic concepts.* Underlying the strategy concepts there is another level of thinking based on fundamental economic concepts. These include economies of scale and scope, transaction costs and value creation. They are also relevant in the e-business context and provide a strong basis for more in-depth analysis.

Summing up this section on conceptual thinking, we would like to stress again that concepts and frameworks are not meant as a substitute for the development of creative ideas. Creative ideas are a prerequisite for any innovative strategy. Conceptual thinking is the next step to help select those creative ideas that are likely to succeed.[12]

STRATEGY IN ACTION 2.2

'Why?' – the importance of questions in strategy formulation

The single most important word in strategy formulation is *why*.

Asking why is the basic act of probing. Searching for root causes takes strategy formulation away from the unconscious repetition of past patterns and mimicry of competitors. Asking why leads to new insights and innovations that sometimes yield important competitive advantages.

Asking why repeatedly is a source of continuous self-renewal, but the act of inquiry itself is an art. It can evoke strong reactions from the questioned. It is only rarely welcomed. It is sometimes met with defensiveness and hostility, on the one hand, or, on the other, the patronizing patience reserved by the knowledgeable for the uninformed.

To ask why – and why not – about basics is to violate the social convention that expertise is to be respected, not challenged. Functional organizations in mature industries have a particular problem in this regard. One risks a lot to challenge the lord in his fiefdom.

Questioning the basics – the assumptions that 'knowledgeable' people don't question – is disruptive. Probing slows things down, but often to good effect. It can yield revolutionary new thoughts in quite unexpected places.

To probe to the limits is to simplify the problem to its essentials and solve one problem rather than many. To pursue such probing takes a special, strongly motivated person, unless one makes it the norm for the organization. Asking why five times is easy to say, but hard to do. It challenges people's knowledge and even self-respect. It can call into question their diligence and the basis of their expertise. It requires fresh thinking on all sides. Yet it's so basic to learning, to seeing new things from the familiar. In the early 19th century, doctors routinely went, without washing, from autopsies to the treatment of patients – with disastrous results. Ignaz Semmelweis is the man who first hypothesized the basic relationship and proposed and tested a change to clean hands – yet in his own time he had to struggle with his peers because he questioned the accepted practice.

Probing takes us beyond data analysis

Good strategy depends critically on knowing the root causes. Finding them is often a task beyond quantitative analysis. One must look to broader frames of reference and bring basic judgment and common sense to bear. Probing – asking why – is the often intuitive search for the logic that heavy data analysis can miss or bury.

Asking why is a qualitative act. It is different from quantitative analysis, but the one gains power from the other. It propels analysis forward by raising new questions to be subjected to rigorous analysis. It takes us beyond the numbers to new answers, new solutions, and new opportunities. Quantitative analysis should not become both the means and the end.

Asking why can raise the questions that are fundamental, but not necessarily answerable through rigorous analysis itself. These are the basic questions of leadership and common sense. They are the search for 'the point.' For example:

- Why do we continue in this business?
- Why should anyone buy this product?

- What will prevent competitors from matching us? What will we do then?
- Why are we making so much money?
- Why won't it eventually come to an end?
- What must we do now to prepare for or moderate that change?

These sorts of probes search for the bedrock reasons for value and advantages to test how enduring they may be. They ask whether the shape and character of the business and its strategy make sense.

Asking why is easy in concept, but harder in practice. It can be very rewarding. Why not do it?

Source: J. Isaacs, 'Probing', in C. Stern and G. Stalk (eds), *Perspectives on Strategy*, John Wiley, 1998, pp. 276–278.

SUMMARY

- First, this chapter outlined the dimensions of creativity and analytical ability and pointed out the importance of these two qualities in the strategy-development process.
- Second, this chapter suggested a categorization of different manager types along the dimensions of creativity and analytical ability. The resulting four manager types are (1) the novice, (2) the efficient performer, (3) the visionary and (4) the catalyst for change. The goal of the concepts and case studies presented in this book is to help you move closer towards becoming a catalyst for change.
- Third, this chapter showed how case studies can serve as an inspiration for creative strategy development. Readers can use them to conduct intra-industry benchmarking (within one's own culture and across cultures) and as a source for cross-industry inspiration.
- The chapter then discussed the value of frameworks in the strategy-formulation process and outlined the key requirements that a good framework needs to fulfil. First, it must capture the most important dimensions of the problem at hand. Second, all the elements contained in a framework must be mutually exclusive.
- The last section of this chapter outlined two analytical techniques to evaluate strategies. First, this includes expanding the breadth of the analysis to ensure that each important element is considered thoroughly. Second, it includes expanding the depth of the analysis to ensure that the most important issues for the problem at hand are assessed rigorously.

REVIEW QUESTIONS

1 What are the three possibilities mentioned in this chapter that can help you to improve your creativity?

2 How do the four types of managers mentioned in this chapter differ? What are the specific qualities of the 'catalyst for change'?

3 What are the three ways in which case studies can help you to learn about e-business?

4 What are the key characteristics of a good framework?

5 What are the three levels of conceptual thinking presented in this book?

DISCUSSION QUESTIONS

1 Where do you position yourself within the 'catalyst-for-change' matrix?

2 Discuss your above assessment with colleagues. In light of their feedback, in which area would you especially like to improve your abilities?

3 Discuss how case studies can help you to develop creative strategies. Provide some examples.

4 Is it always sensible to try to get a broad understanding of a problem before addressing more detailed issues? What problems do you foresee with this approach?

5 How can you increase the depth of analysis through the concepts and frameworks presented in this book?

RECOMMENDED KEY READING

- B. Nalebuff and I. Ayres outline an approach to creative problem solving in *Why Not? How to Use Everyday Ingenuity to Solve Problems Big and Small*, Harvard Business School Press, 2003.
- M. Csikszentmihalyi analyzes different dimensions of creativity in *Creativity*, HarperPerennial, 1997.
- E. de Bono, one of the leading thinkers in the field of creative thinking, proposes 'lateral thinking' as a way for creative idea development in his book *Lateral Thinking – A Textbook of Creativity*, Penguin Books, 1990.
- For a practical and very insightful discussion of structuring and problem solving, see B. Minto, *The Pyramid Principle*, FT Prentice Hall, 2002.
- M. Porter discusses the importance and value of frameworks in the article 'Towards a dynamic theory of strategy', *Strategic Management Journal*, 1991, Vol. 12, No. 8, pp. 95–117. For further reading on M. Porter's thinking about frameworks, see also

N. Argyres and A. McGahan, 'An interview with Michael Porter', *Academy of Management Executive*, 2002, Vol. 16, No. 2, pp. 43–52.

- R. Rumelt, D. Schendel and D. Teece discuss the tension between case-based approaches and theoretical constructions for the strategy formulation process in 'Strategic management and economics', *Strategic Management Journal*, 1991, Vol. 12, No. 8, pp. 5–30.

USEFUL WEBLINKS

- **www.creativitypool.com** Database with creative and original ideas.
- **www.pyramidprinciple.com** Website of Barbara Minto. She invented the Pyramid Principle, which provides a structured approach to problem solving.
- **www.thomasedison.com** Website containing biographical information about the inventor Thomas Edison.
- **www.trendwatching.com** Website that spots emerging consumer trends and related new business ideas on a global basis.
- **www.whynot.net** Online forum for people to share and talk about their ideas.

NOTES AND REFERENCES

1 T. V. Ghyczy describes the usefulness of metaphors for strategy development in the article 'The fruitful flaws of strategy metaphors', *Harvard Business Review*, 2003, September, pp. 86–94. One of his key messages is that, contrary to popular thinking, the true value of a metaphor for generating new strategic perspectives becomes apparent when the metaphors themselves stop working, which is the case when a metaphor is not entirely transferable to the problem depicted. Attracted by the familiar and repelled by the unfamiliar connections, one is, at the same time, left in a state of understanding and incomprehension. In this state of mind, the likeliness of looking at things in new and creative ways increases.

2 Obviously, strategy development is not the same as designing a building. Most importantly, architects face nowhere near as much uncertainty regarding environmental changes as managers do in the still rapidly evolving e-business environment. If we were to include this business-like level of uncertainty, this would mean that the architects would not know whether the buildings they are designing will be built on quicksand or on rock, in the tropical rainforest or in the Arctic Circle.

3 Due to the length limitation of this book, this chapter might not cover many of the aspects that pedagogues or psychologists would want to see discussed in this context. Nonetheless, for students who have previously had only little exposure to the case method and conceptual approaches to problem-solving, we believe that this chapter can provide a valuable context for their learning experience.

4 For more information on Thomas Edison's life, visit www.thomasedison.com

5 See M. Csikszentmihaly, *Creativity*, HarperPerennial, 1997, pp. 368–370.

6 For a good discussion on idea development and creativity, see A. Hargadon and R. I. Sutton, 'Building an innovation factory', *Harvard Business Review*, 2000, May–June, pp. 157–166 and B. Nalebuff and I. Ayres, *Why Not?* Harvard Business School Press, 2003. For more recommended reading on this topic, refer to the list at the end of this chapter.
7 M. Csikszentmihalyi, *Creativity*, HarperPerennial, 1997, pp. 362–363.
8 Ibid, pp. 360–363.
9 See R. Bruner, B. Gup, B. Nunnally, *et al.*, 'Teaching with cases to graduate and undergraduate students', *Financial Practice and Education*, 1999, Vol. 9, No. 2, pp. 138–147.
10 For an excellent discussion of the value of frameworks in strategy research, see M. E. Porter, 'Towards a dynamic theory of strategy', *Strategic Management Journal*, 1991, Vol. 12, No. 8, pp. 95–117. For a practical discussion of structuring and problem solving, see B. Minto, *The Pyramid Principle*, FT Prentice Hall, 2002.
11 R. Grant criticizes Porter's frameworks in *Contemporary Strategy Analysis*, Blackwell, 2002, p. 89.
12 R. Grant offers an excellent explanation of the value of analysis in the strategy development process in his book *Contemporary Strategy Analysis*, Blackwell, 2002, pp. 31–32.

Part 2

THE E-BUSINESS STRATEGY FRAMEWORK

PART OVERVIEW

This part proposes an e-business strategy framework that consists of the following elements:

- The macro-environment, industry structure and markets
- The concepts of value creation, the value chain and the virtual value chain
- Generic strategy options and strategies for opening up new market spaces
- Horizontal boundaries of the firm
- Vertical boundaries of the firm
- Internal organization of the firm.

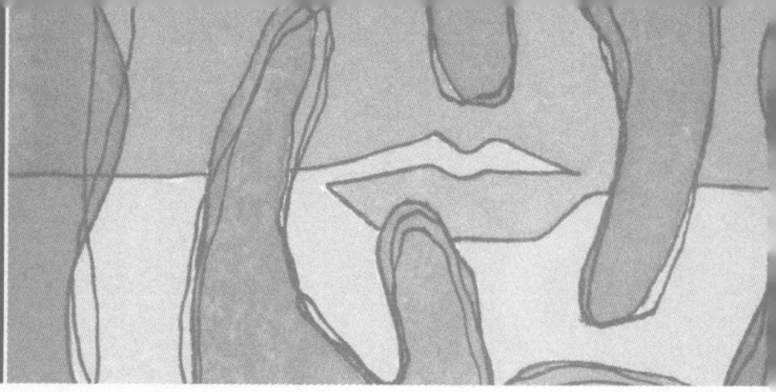

INTRODUCTION TO PART 2

The goal of this part is to provide an overarching framework that can serve as a comprehensive basis for e-business strategy formulation. To do so, we believe that it is valuable to begin with rigorous and time-proven concepts from the field of strategic management and then to adapt them to the specific context of e-business. This adaptation takes places in three ways.

First, although the conceptual chapters provide a broad strategy, they highlight specific concepts that are important for e-business and help us to understand recent successes and failures in the field. These include economies of scale and scope, switching costs, network effects and transaction cost theory. Second, the framework presents some e-business specific concepts such as the virtual value chain (see Section 5.2.3) and the ICDT (information, communication, distribution and transaction) model (see Section 9.1). Third, all the concepts and frameworks that are presented in the conceptual chapters are illustrated through the e-business-specific examples. By doing so, we want to link real-world examples with theoretical considerations, hoping to make the material more accessible and applicable.

The e-business strategy framework addresses three broad sets of questions. These are:

- Where do we (as a company) want to compete?
- What type of value do we want to create?
- How should we set up and organize our company to deliver the desired value?

Obviously, these three areas are very much interlinked (see Exhibit II.1). We cannot answer one question without considering the other two. Strategies are thus more likely to be successful if managers take into consideration all relevant dimensions. Yet, in order to do so, it is helpful to break down the above questions into separate issues.

The first broad section in the e-business strategy framework deals with a firm's external environment. The key question here is: 'Where do we want to compete?' Answering this question depends in part on the following factors:

- *The macro-environment* (*Section 3.1*). Analyzing the macro-environment helps us to gain an understanding of trends within the political, economic, social or technological spheres.
- *Industry structure* (*Section 3.2*). Porter's five forces provide a guiding framework for determining the attractiveness of an industry. This includes an analysis of industry rivalry, barriers to entry, substitute products and bargaining powers of buyers, and bargaining power of suppliers. In addition, the co-opetition value net is presented to complement the five forces framework.
- *Markets* (*Chapter 4*). Customers have different preferences and expectations. It is therefore helpful to break down markets into individual segments, which reflect customers' purchasing characteristics, such as age, gender, income level, etc.

Exhibit II.1 The e-business strategy framework addresses three main questions

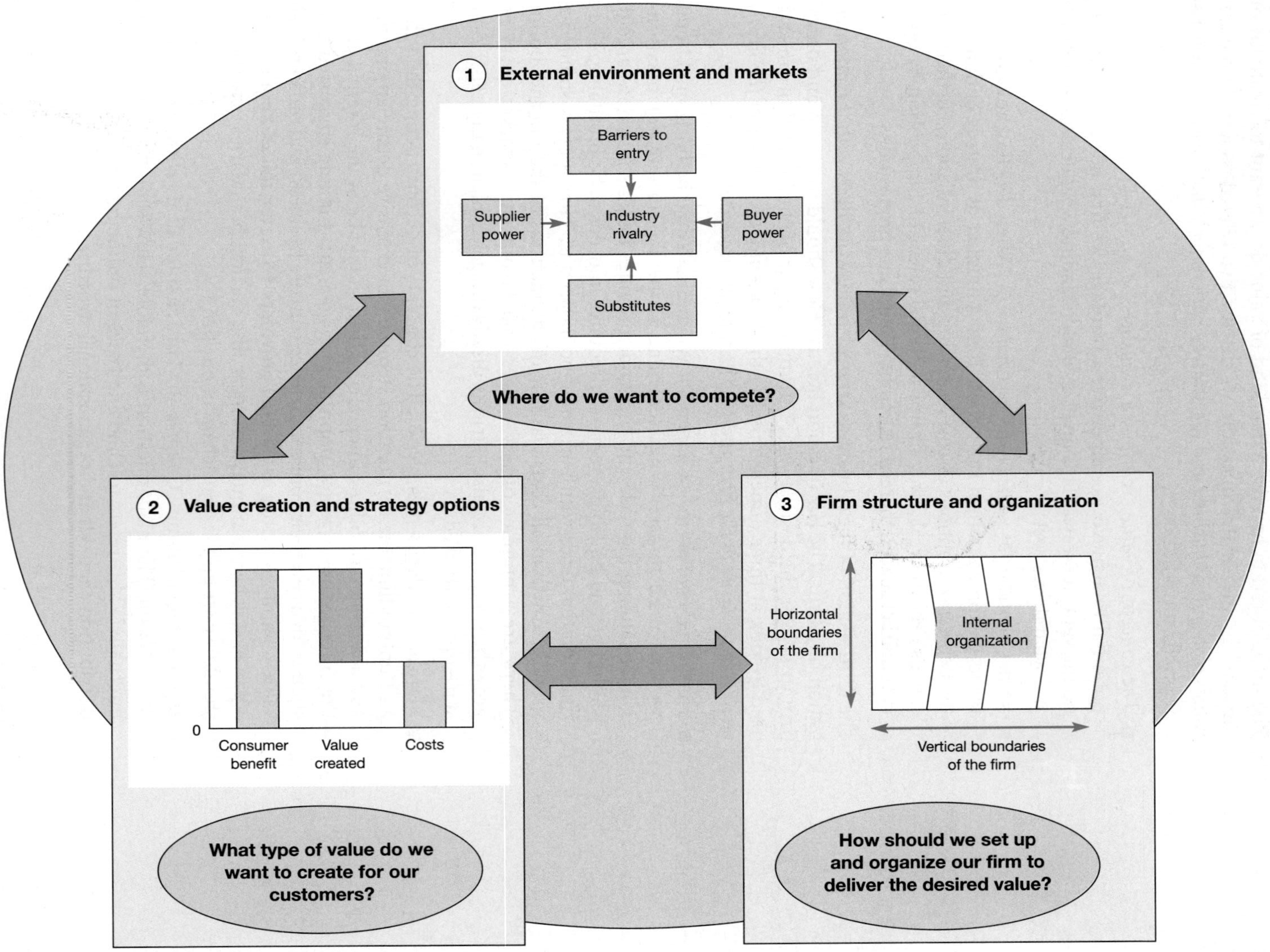

The second section of the e-business strategy framework deals with value creation. The main question here is: 'What kind of value do we want to create for our customers?' To answer this question, we discuss two related issues: (1) the *concept of value creation in e-business* and (2) *strategy options for value creation*. These issues are now briefly introduced.

- *The concept of value creation in e-business* (*Chapter 5*). To understand a firm's potential to achieve a competitive advantage, we first need to analyze the economic value it creates. This involves understanding what drives consumer benefits and what drives costs.
- *Strategy options for value creation* (*Chapter 6*). When deciding how to create value for its customers, a firm can choose from a number of strategy options. These are the two generic options of cost leadership and differentiation. Furthermore, firms can also try to break away from traditional forms of competition by opening up new market spaces, thereby redefining their value propositions.

The third section of the e-business strategy framework deals with the internal organization of a firm. The key question here is: 'How should we set up and organize our firm to deliver the desired value?' In the context of the internal organization, we need to look at three dimensions: (1) the *horizontal boundaries of the firm*, (2) the *vertical boundaries of the firm* and (3) the *internal organization*.

- *Horizontal boundaries*[1] (*Chapter 7*). When discussing the horizontal boundaries, we first need to ask: 'What scale and scope should our organization have?' Understanding the scale and the scope provides insights into how large the firm should be and how big a market it requires in order to be profitable. The second question that deals with horizontal boundaries is: 'How quickly should we try to grow?' Growth at all costs was one of the mantras of the Internet boom years. There are a number of advantages that favour early market entry and fast growth. Yet there are also various disadvantages, which many eager e-business start-ups overlooked.
- *Vertical boundaries* (*Chapter 8*). The concepts of deconstructing the value chain and unbundling the corporation stemmed an extensive debate among managers and academics as to how integrated a firm should be in the Internet era. During the Internet boom years, popular management thinking suggested that firms should focus on their core competence (or core business) and outsource all other value-creating activities to external providers. However, this did not turn out to be a panacea. The main question regarding vertical boundaries is therefore: 'How should we set up the value chain of our firm?'
- *Internal organization* (*Chapter 9*). This chapter deals with the firm's internal organization. The main question is therefore: 'How should we organize our firm internally?' This refers to choosing types of online interactions with customers, distribution channels and organizational structures.

---

1 We should mention at this point that the standard vocabulary used in the management literature to refer to a firm's horizontal and vertical boundaries could be confusing, since the typical visual representation of these concepts (as shown in Exhibit II.1) is actually opposite to the meaning of the vocabulary used.

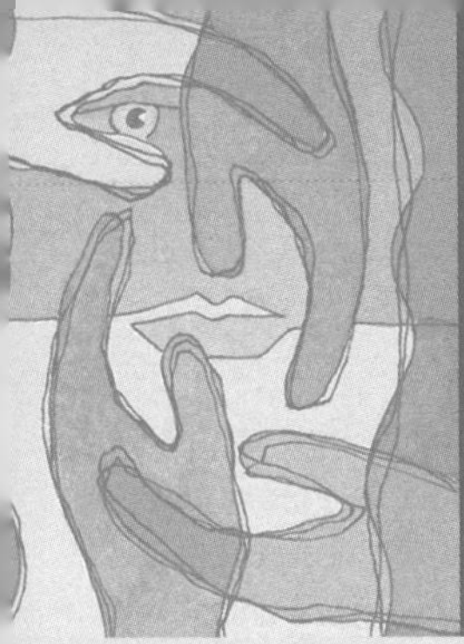

CHAPTER 3

The impact of the Internet on the macro-environment and on the industry structure

Chapter at a glance

3.1 Examining trends in the macro-environment

- 3.1.1 The political and legal environment
- 3.1.2 The economic environment
- 3.1.3 The social environment
- 3.1.4 The technological environment

3.2 Examining industry structure with the five forces framework

- 3.2.1 Industry rivalry
- 3.2.2 Barriers to entry
- 3.2.3 Substitute products
- 3.2.4 Bargaining powers of buyers and suppliers

Related case studies

Case study		*Primary focus of the case study*
1	**Minitel**	Political macro-environment
3	**e-Government**	Political macro-environment
11	**Electronic purse**	Technological macro-environment
28	**NTT DoCoMo**	Technological macro-environment
6	**Amazon *vs.* BOL**	Industry structure
15	**Terra Lycos**	Industry structure
25	**Online file-sharing**	Industry structure

Learning outcomes

After completing this chapter you should be able to:

- Analyze trends in the macro-environment and explain their implications for e-business ventures.
- Understand the value of the five forces framework for the analysis of industry attractiveness.
- Explain the key characteristics of the co-opetition framework and show how it expands on the five forces framework.

INTRODUCTION

e-Business ventures, or any ventures for that matter, do not operate in isolation from their environment. Their ability to create value for their customers and to generate profits for themselves depends to a large extent on circumstances outside their direct influence. In order to assess how the Internet influences the environment, this chapter first provides a systematic approach for analyzing the macro-environment. Second, it presents Porter's five forces framework for analyzing the attractiveness of an industry and also the co-opetition framework, which offers an alternative perspective for industry analysis.

3.1 Examining trends in the macro-environment

The macro-environment takes a broad perspective of the factors that influence a firm's strategy and performance.[1] Evolving trends in the macro-environment can present significant opportunities and threats to a firm's strategy. Therefore, at the outset of any strategy formulation, it is useful to analyze the trends that characterize the macro-environment in its different dimensions: *political, legal, economic, social* and *technological.*

3.1.1 The political and legal environment

The political and legal environment relates to issues on different organizational levels. At country and industry levels, it includes issues such as governmental subsidies, taxation, monopoly legislation and environmental laws.

Consider the Minitel system featured in the case studies section of this book. This system was financed to a large degree by the French government in the late 1970s in order to computerize French society. For instance, users received the Minitel terminal free of charge.

Because of the difficulty of agreeing on cross-border agreements, taxation has been a difficult issue in electronic commerce. Regarding monopoly legislation, Microsoft has been accused of violating its dominant position in the operating system market by leveraging it to move into other software markets at the expense of competitors.[2]

When Amazon.com entered the German market, it was confronted with the price-fixing regulation, which sets a common price for all new books sold in the country. This made it impossible for Amazon.de to compete with rival bookstores on the price dimension.

In the environmental sphere, governments in many countries, such as Spain and the UK, have zoning laws, which make it difficult, if not impossible, for grocery

retailers to set up new hypermarket stores. Thus, some retailers in these countries thought of the Internet and online sales as a possible alternative for business growth.

At the individual level, political and legal debates revolve around the extent to which companies should be allowed to intrude into the private lives of Internet users. This includes topics such as the placement of cookies (text files stored on the PC that allow the website operator to identify them) and aggressive marketing via so-called spam mails (unsolicited e-mail messages). For more details on this matter, see Section 9.1.1.

3.1.2 The economic environment

The economic environment refers to broader economic developments within the context of a country, a regional dimension or a global dimension. Important factors in the economic environment are interest and exchange rates, evolution of stock markets and, more generally, economic growth rates. The favourable economic environment of the 1990s and the resulting cheap availability of capital contributed strongly to the quick rise of Internet companies.

This rise found its abrupt halt in the burst of the bubble in March 2000 and the subsequent demise of most of these Internet start-ups. The launches of some start-ups discussed in Part 4 of this book, such as mondus.com and 12Snap, were feasible only because capital was accessible so easily at the time. During the ensuing consolidation phase, on the other hand, which was characterized by depressed stock markets and cautious venture capitalists, it became much more difficult to gain access to capital, even if the underlying business idea was sound.

3.1.3 The social environment

The social environment considers factors such as population demographics, income distribution between different sectors of society, social mobility of people, and differing attitudes to work and leisure. Social developments were the main driver behind the development of numerous e-business applications. For instance, if, due to their careers, members of a developed society increasingly become cash-rich but time-poor, then businesses that address this problem for the individual consumer can create substantial benefit. The online retailer Tesco.com, for example, primarily targets customers who do not have the time or the desire to shop systematically in a physical grocery store.

Other important dimensions of the social environment that impact the development and use of electronic business are Internet usage patterns. These are measured by the percentage of the population using e-mail or the Web for information purposes and doing transactions online. These types of measurements provide good indications of the evolution of a society towards establishing an e-habit. An additional indicator of changes in the social environment is the degree of usage of online communities, such as iVillage.com, where Internet users come together to discuss issues that interest them (see Section 7.2.1 for a detailed discussion of network effects and virtual online communities).

3.1.4 The technological environment

The technological environment is of significant importance in the context of e-business. Technological innovations (such as the Internet or wireless devices) led to the emergence of new market opportunities and business models. Other important drivers of technological developments are standards and languages such as the TCP/IP (Transmission Control Protocol/Internet Protocol), HTTP (Hypertext Transfer Protocol), HTML (Hypertext Mark-up Language) and, more recently, XML (Extended Mark-up Language).[3]

After most of the technological standards have become more common-place in wireline e-business applications, much attention has been paid to the evolution of new technology standards for wireless devices. This includes, for instance, the security features for mobile phones, an issue that is discussed in the paybox case study (see p. 570). The case on NTT DoCoMo (p. 584) also illustrates how an individual company can establish new technological standards in the mobile commerce industry, as happened with i-Mode in the case of NTT DoCoMo.

The exemplary factors mentioned within the above four dimensions should serve only as a starting point for a careful analysis of the macro-environment. Depending on the industry and country at hand, the importance of these dimensions will obviously differ. Needless to say, though, a good understanding of the macro-environment is essential for the formulation of sound business strategies.

3.2 Examining industry structure with the five forces framework

What does the profitability of any given firm depend on? First, a firm needs to be able to create higher value than its rivals. (For a detailed discussion of value creation, see Chapter 5.) Second, it also needs to be able to capture the value that it creates in the form of prices that exceed its costs. If a firm can charge high prices for its products or services, then it captures large parts of the value it creates. If, on the other hand, prices are driven down by competition, then consumers will capture most of the value.

This highlights the fact that profitability depends not only on the internal activities of a firm but also on its surroundings, i.e. the industry it competes in. In this context, an industry is defined as a group of firms that produce products that are close substitutes for each other.[4] This environment differs from industry to industry.

As an example, let us consider the personal computer (PC) industry. During the past decades, this has created immense value for consumers as PC capabilities, in the form of both desktops and laptops, have increased multifold every year. While benefits to consumers have increased, prices have not risen; instead, they have actually decreased significantly over time. On the other hand, there are industries such as software development where a firm like Microsoft captures large parts of the value it creates (e.g. for computer operating systems), thus turning it into one of the most profitable companies in the world. This raises the question as to what determines the ability of a company to capture value.

Porter proposes a five-forces framework, which outlines the main factors determining a firm's ability to capture the value it creates.[5] In essence, this ability is determined largely by the attractiveness of the industry in which a firm competes. Obviously, the advent of the Internet has profoundly impacted the structure of many industries. Yet there are no general conclusions regarding how the Internet affects the structure of different industries. Instead, it is necessary to analyze each industry individually.[6]

The five forces shown in Exhibits 3.1 and 3.2 are meant as a guiding framework to explain the sustainability of profits against bargaining and competition. The five structural features that determine industry attractiveness are: (1) *industry rivalry*, (2) *barriers to entry*, (3) *substitute products*, (4) *bargaining power of suppliers* and (5) *bargaining power of buyers.*

Exhibit 3.1 **Five forces influence the attractiveness of an industry**

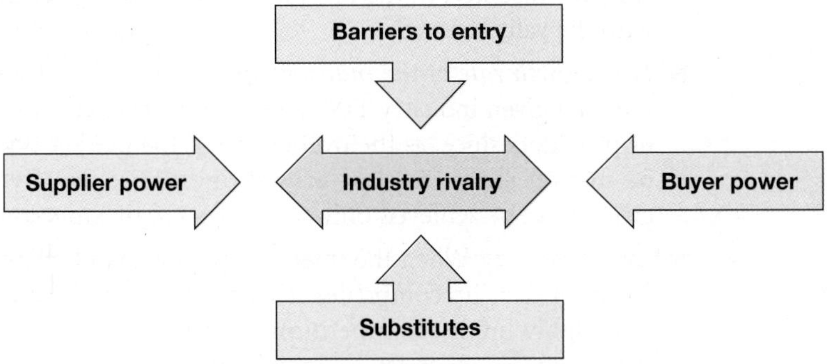

Source: Adapted from M. Porter, *Competitive Strategy*, Free Press, 1998, p. 4.

3.2.1 Industry rivalry

Industry rivalry occurs when firms within an industry feel the pressure or the opportunity to enhance their existing market position. High intensity of rivalry within an industry results from the following structural factors:

- *Large number of competitors.* If there are numerous competitors, then individual firms may want to make a competitive move, e.g. by lowering prices. Furthermore, the Internet has reduced the importance of geographic boundaries, which traditionally limited the number of competitors within a region. For instance, business-to-business (B2B) e-marketplaces, such as mondus.com (featured in the case studies section), quickly expanded into new locations. Since competitors followed the same strategy, competition became more intense.
- *High fixed costs.* High fixed costs (such as extensive physical infrastructure) create strong pressure to fill capacity, even at the expense of having to cut prices. Consider bricks-and-mortar retail stores, which have specific capacities that must be utilized. To create the necessary turnover, retailers often find themselves in highly competitive price wars. Through the Internet, the ratio between fixed and variable costs shifts more towards fixed costs. Developing software has initially high costs, but rolling it out across different markets is comparatively cheap. Thus,

industry rivalry tends to increase because e-business ventures want to optimize the use of their capacity.

- *High strategic relevance.* Rivalry increases when firms have a strategic stake to succeed in a given industry. One of the most prominent examples is Microsoft's decision in 1996 to design all its new products for Internet-based computing. This decision led to the browser competition between Netscape's Navigator, the incumbent browser software, and Microsoft's Explorer, a competition that Microsoft was determined to win. In order to beat Netscape, Microsoft offered the Web server software, which cost $1000 at Netscape, for free and put 800 people to work on an upgraded version of the Explorer.[7] Ultimately, Explorer pushed most competing products out of the market and became the dominant browser software in the market.
- *Little differentiation between products.* Rivalry also increases when there is little differentiation among products, which become more like commodities. This is the case, for instance, in the computer-chip industry, where profits are low compared with the value created.
- *Low growth rate of the industry.* Intensity of rivalry also depends on the growth rate of a given industry. Fast-growth industries can accommodate a larger number of providers since, as the overall size of the market expands, each competitor gets its market share. In slow-growth industries, rivalry tends to be intense since growth can be achieved only at the expense of some competitors.
- *Excess capacity.* When the Internet became an online platform for commercial use, scores of start-up companies started using it in different industries, which resulted in a highly intense competition. Venture capitalists and stock markets provided cheap capital, which led to an overinvestment in Internet start-ups, thereby creating overcapacities. This has changed since the crash of the stock market in 2000, which has led to the demise of most of these start-ups.

However, companies need not always be rivals and just that. As explained in Critical Perspective 3.1 at the end of this chapter, some competitors co-operate with each other, hence the term 'co-opetition'. As an example of this business concept, see the FT article 'Will Amazon.com's co-opetition gamble pay off?'

3.2.2 Barriers to entry

Barriers to entry determine the threat of new competitors to enter the market of a specific industry. New entrants, bringing new capacity and the desire to gain market share, have two negative effects on the attractiveness of an industry. First, new entrants take away market share from existing incumbents. Second, they bid down prices, which in turn reduces the profitability of the incumbent companies. Consequently, profitability of any given industry tends to decrease as barriers to entry are lowered, and vice versa. The impact of the Internet on barriers to entry, however, has been more ambivalent than initially assumed, when it was commonly thought that the Internet would wipe out most barriers to entry. In general, high barriers to entry result mainly from the following factors:

- *High fixed costs* deter many potential entrants because they do not have the required capital and/or the willingness to invest large amounts of money into a

risky market entry. While it was necessary in the past to set up an extensive bricks-and-mortar infrastructure to reach out to a large number of customers, the Internet has reduced this requirement. This is especially true for digital goods, which can even be distributed online. For example, the distribution of music CDs used to take place fully through a large network of physical stores.

The rise of the online file-sharing systems, such as Napster, illustrates how a single person (Shawn Fanning in this case) with an ingenious idea can threaten a whole industry, with its elaborate and high fixed-cost distribution system. Through the Napster platform, individual Internet users were able to exchange music files of their favourite songs, which undermined the traditional business model of the record industry. Subsequently, music companies attempted to raise barriers to entry again by declaring file-sharing services illegal, yet it is clear that the Internet has profoundly changed the way music will be distributed in the future (for a more detailed account of how the Internet has caused a paradigm shift in the music industry, see the case study on online file-sharing, p.539). Pressure on music companies that rely on physical distribution infrastructure has become so strong that some of them – Bertelsmann's BMG and Sony – announced in December of 2003 that they would merge their music divisions.[8]

In industries that involve the distribution of physical goods or require a high level of personal interaction, the impact of the Internet on barriers to entry is more ambiguous. Amazon.com, for instance, initially also thought that it could focus solely on the customer interaction aspect of its business and outsource to external providers all distribution logistics, which would have required substantial investments. However, Amazon.com soon found out that in order to guarantee a high level of reliability, it had to operate its own warehouses, which in turn increased the required investments. Set-up costs for a warehouse averaged at \$50 million, and operating costs were also significant. In order to finance these infrastructure investments, Amazon.com was forced to issue more than \$2 billion in bonds.[9]

Similarly, in banking, direct banks initially thought that they could acquire and service customers solely through online channels. The case study of Nordea Bank, however, illustrates that an extensive branch network can be crucial for the acquisition of online customers and the selling of more complex financial products. As a result, such physical assets created effective barriers to entry for new online competitors.

- *Trust and brand loyalty* are essential for customer acquisition and retention. Bricks-and-mortar companies were able to launch their online activities more easily than Internet 'pure-play' ventures, since they already possessed a respected brand and consumers trusted them. Pure online businesses, on the other hand, have to invest heavily in marketing activities to build up their brand. Building trust is even more difficult for a pure online business since, in case of problems, customers do not have a nearby physical branch that they can go to or a customer adviser with whom they can interact face-to-face. For example, Advance Bank, the German branchless bank featured in the case studies section of this book, invested heavily in creating brand loyalty.
- *A steep learning curve* allows a firm to reduce its cost structure quickly or to find ways to create more customer benefits. Any competitor that wants to move into an industry needs to accept low returns while it goes through the same learning experience as incumbents. Otherwise, it has to find ways to make the incumbents'

learning experience obsolete by offering a new way of running the business (see Section 6.2 on opening up new market spaces). Amazon's early start in online retailing helped the company to stay ahead of other competitors, such as BOL. The latter was never able to catch up with Amazon.com and ultimately withdrew from the online book retailing business.

- *High switching costs and strong network effects* help an incumbent to keep its customers, even if a new entrant offers higher value (for a more detailed discussion of this issue, see Section 7.2.1). Think about the retail banking industry. If customers want to switch from one bank to another, they have to change all their automated bill payment procedures to the new account, and also inform relevant companies and individuals about the change. The effort associated with doing so could be an effective deterrent for many customers to move to another bank even though the latter offers higher value. In the Internet context, the so-called 'stickiness' of a website refers to the switching costs involved with moving from one site to the next. High stickiness makes it unlikely that a user will move from one site to the next. Similarly, strong network effects also tend to increase barriers to entry.

  eBay, for instance, has created strong barriers to entry for potential competitors through the large customer base it has created over the past few years. For individual customers, it makes sense to switch to a new provider only if they know that all or at least most other current users would switch as well. Only then would they be able to enjoy the same type of market liquidity as they did before (see the eBay case study, p. 514).

- *Strong intellectual property protection* is essential for firms that sell products with high development costs but low reproduction costs. This is the case with digital goods such as music, video and software. When intellectual property rights are not enforced rigidly, barriers for new (albeit illegal) entrants are lowered, thus allowing them to push cheap, pirated copies into the market. Furthermore, without strong intellectual property protection, it will be increasingly difficult in the future to entice authors or artists to write and compose, since they will not get compensated adequately.

3.2.3 Substitute products

The intensity of pressure from substitute products depends on the availability of similar products that serve essentially the same or a similar purpose as the products from within the industry. As the availability and quality of substitute products increase, so profits generated within the industry tend to decrease. This is due to the fact that substitutes place a ceiling on prices that firms within the industry can charge for their products. The Internet has helped to increase the pressure from substitute products, as it tends to increase the variety of products available to customers.

For instance, online music-sharing is evolving so quickly that it has become a formidable substitute for CDs, thereby threatening the traditional music industry in its foundations. In the software arena, Microsoft, the dominant producer of software for desktop PCs, is facing new substitutes in the form of mobile devices that increasingly provide many of the same functionalities as traditional PCs. However, the software for these products is not primarily Microsoft-based.[10]

3.2.4 Bargaining powers of buyers and suppliers

The bargaining powers of buyers and suppliers are the two sides of the same coin; that is why we discuss them jointly. The bargaining power of buyers tends to be high (and that of suppliers low) if the industry displays the following characteristics:

- *High concentration of buyers*, which allows them to leverage their purchasing power through pooling. One important function of many B2B e-marketplaces – such as Covisint, discussed on page 499 – is the aggregation of buyers. This helps them to achieve better terms from suppliers than they could obtain individually.
- *Strong fragmentation of suppliers*, which makes it difficult to establish a joint approach to pricing. In the PC industry, many producers are constantly trying to gain market share at the expense of other competitors by undercutting each other's prices. This, in turn, undermines the pricing power of the whole industry.
- *A high degree of market transparency*, which allows buyers to easily compare offers between different suppliers. Today, advanced search tools available on the Internet allow customers to choose from a larger pool of suppliers and to compare prices instantaneously, thus making it easier for them to find the best deal.
- *Products are increasingly becoming commodities*, resulting in little or no differentiation between different providers. The pricing of commodity products that do not require extensive purchasing advice or after-sales service are especially affected by higher degrees of market transparency, since customers can then safely choose the lowest price provider.
- *Low switching costs and weak network effect*, which make it easy for buyers to change suppliers. Switching costs and network effects are discussed in detail in Section 7.2.1.

Conversely, the bargaining power of suppliers is high if the opposite of all or some of the above characteristics holds true.

The impact of the Internet on the five forces is depicted in more detail in Exhibit 3.2.

The perspective offered by the five forces framework might seem to be too static in a rapidly changing business world, where industries are in constant flux. It is, indeed, increasingly difficult to define industry boundaries, which are becoming more and more blurred due to, among others, mergers and acquisitions. However, this does not mean that the five forces framework has become irrelevant, since it still helps to pinpoint competitive and industry conditions that are subject to change.

With the rising importance of the Internet, it has become more important to think about its business impact. This entails thinking about industry positioning and how it may be altered as a result of changing barriers to entry, power distribution between suppliers and buyers, forms of substitution and industry rivalry. In spite of these changes, the underlying strategic questions remain the same: 'How and where should (and can) a firm gain competitive advantage, thereby creating superior profit generation potential?'

Exhibit 3.2 The Internet has a profound impact on the five forces that influence industry attractiveness

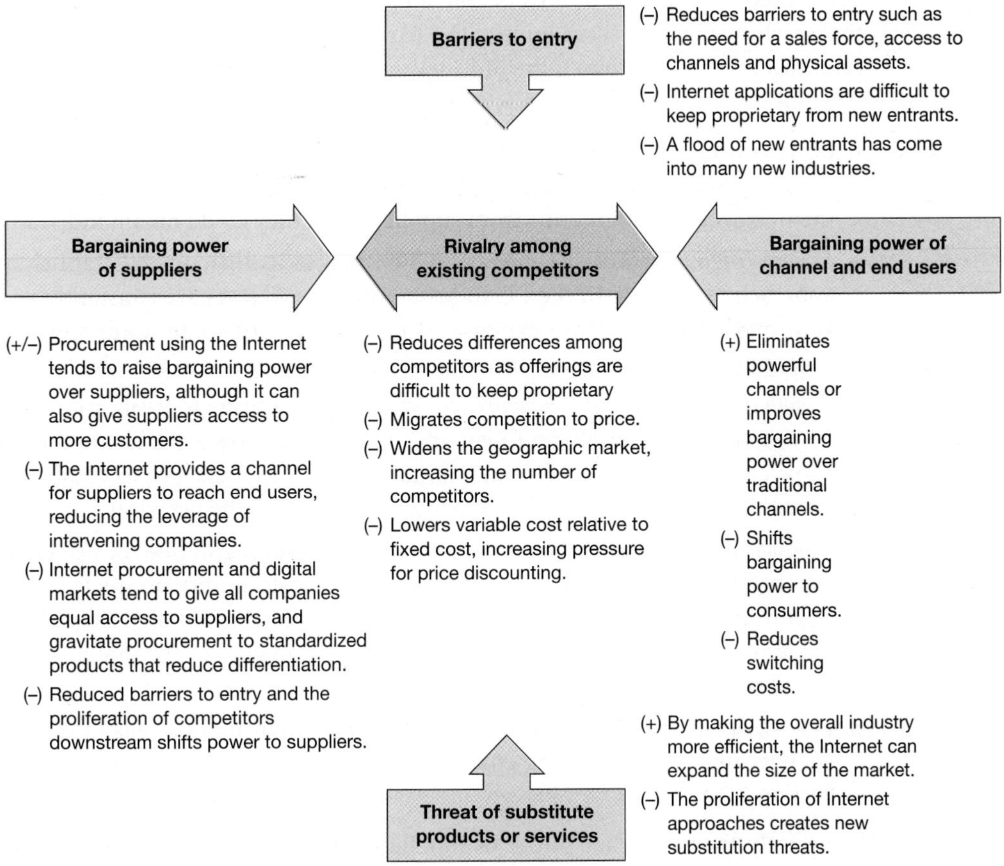

Source: Reprinted by permission of *Harvard Business Review* [Exhibit RO 103D]. From 'Strategy and the Internet' by M. Porter, March 2001. Copyright © 2001 by the Harvard Business School Publishing Corporation, all rights reserved.

CRITICAL PERSPECTIVE 3.1

Co-opetition in e-commerce

While the five forces industry framework focuses on the negative effects that market participants might have on industry attractiveness, the co-opetition framework enriches this perspective by highlighting that interactions with other players can also have a positive impact on profitability.[11] These interactions can include (1) joint setting of technology and other industry standards, (2) joint developments and (3) joint lobbying.

- **Joint setting of technology and other industry standards** is often a prerequisite for ensuring the growth of an industry. For instance, the wireless marketing company 12Snap (featured in the case studies section of this book) joined other wireless marketing providers to set up industry standards on how to conduct marketing campaigns over the mobile phone.

- **Joint developments** between different firms can offer the opportunity for improving quality, increasing demand or streamlining procurement. Through its Zshops, Amazon.com has made it possible for other sellers, who are, in principal, competitors, to sell through the Amazon.com website. Similarly, competing car manufacturers teamed up to set up the common purchasing platform Covisint to streamline their purchasing processes.
- **Joint lobbying** for favourable legislation is also frequently a prerequisite for growth and for the erection of barriers to entry.

The value net framework (Exhibit 3.3), which is similar to the five forces industry framework, focuses on the positive aspects of interactions and seeks to identify opportunities for value creation through collaboration.[12] Therefore, it provides a complementary perspective to the one offered by the five forces model. The value net framework looks at four 'players', which, through their interactions, characterize the market environment. These players consist of customers, suppliers, competitors and complementors.

- **Customers** (sometimes the end consumers) are the recipients of products or services produced by the firm.
- **Suppliers** are companies that supply the firm with resources, including labour and (raw) materials.
- **Competitors** are companies whose products are considered to be substitutes to the firm's own products.
- **Complementors** are companies whose products are complementary to a firm's own offerings. The underlying idea is that customers value a given product more if they can also buy a complementing product from somebody else. This is the case, for example, with CD and DVD players, or game cartridges and consoles.

The role of competitors and complementors can change depending on the context. For instance, with the above-mentioned Zshops, Amazon.com has changed competitors into complementors. Instead of looking at them only from a 'negative' perspective, Amazon.com decided that allowing these companies to offer their products on the Amazon.com website would improve its overall value proposition.

Similarly, different car manufacturers, such as General Motors and DaimlerChrysler, joined forces to create the online purchasing platform Covisint (featured in the case studies section of the book) to pool purchasing and thereby to reduce input costs.

Exhibit 3.3 The value net outlines the main players in the co-opetition framework

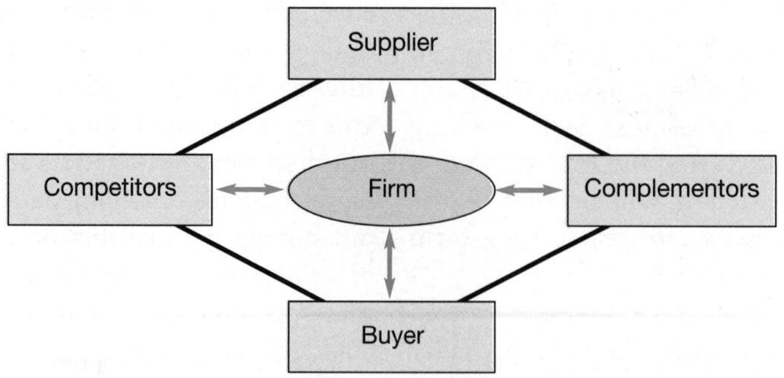

Source: Adapted from A. Brandenburger and B. Nalebuff, *Co-opetition*, 1998, Currency Doubleday, p. 17.

FT

Will Amazon.com's co-opetition gamble pay off?

When Jeff Bezos launched Amazon.com in 1995, he wanted it to be 'Earth's largest bookstore'. Now it has an even grander-sounding ambition: to be 'Earth's most customer-centric organization'. Amazon is no longer just an online book and music retailer, but has transformed into a virtual 'mall' selling golf balls to plasma screen TVs. Many are sold through its site by other retailers such as Gap, the fashion chain, Nordstrom, the department store retailer, or Target, the discounter.

That strategy, launched with a partnership with Toys Я Us in August 2000, has accelerated in the past year. Click on Amazon's US website today and find a clothing store with partners ranging from Eddie Bauer to Urban Outfitters, and its sporting goods store, launched last month, with more than 3,000 brands covering 50 sports.

Unlike its books business, Amazon does not hold these products in its warehouses and fulfil customers' orders: its partners do that. Amazon takes the orders and rakes off a commission. Roger Blackwell, professor of marketing at the Fisher College of Business at Ohio State University, says Amazon has shifted from a business-to-consumer operator to more of a business-to-business operator.

Amazon calls it going from retailer to 'retail platform'. The market approves. From a low of $5.97 two years ago, when investors fretted it might run out of money, Amazon's shares have mushroomed to almost $60, reaching valuations last seen during the Internet boom. Investors have betted it will be one of the few Internet pioneers to reach long-term profitability.

'Amazon could not survive unless it evolved to a business-to-business service provider model,' says Mr Blackwell. 'There's certainly more money to be made from selling [services] to Target and Nordstrom than selling books to consumers.' Its retail partnerships take several forms:

- First is the so-called *'merchants@' program*, including its clothing, sporting goods and toy stores, where Amazon earns fees or commissions for taking orders. This also includes its Marketplace area, where small businesses and individuals can sell new and used goods. Transactions here account for about 20 per cent of Amazon's unit sales.
- Second is *'merchants.com'*. Here Amazon operates websites for other retailers under their names, using its e-commerce expertise, again earning fees or commissions.
- Third are co-branded *'syndicated' stores*, where Amazon sells its products through someone else's site. Consumers clicking on Borders.com, website for one of the biggest US bricks-and-mortar bookstores, for example, find themselves at a site styled 'Borders teamed with Amazon.com'. A similar arrangement applies at Waterstones, the UK bookseller.

Amazon claims to be indifferent to whether customers buy goods new or used from its own business, from partners or individuals. It makes money from each transaction, it says, aiming simply to be a 'place where people can find, discover, and buy anything they want to buy online'. That makes it potentially the dominant Internet shopping destination. Respective margins on its own and third-party transactions are not disclosed. But analysts suggest it can earn bigger margins on selling partners' goods, without storage and distribution costs. Heath Terry of CSFB estimated in a recent research report that operating margins on third-party business could top 30 per cent.

The strategy has risks. Amazon has worked hard to build up its customer base by shifting to a lower-priced strategy, offering free shipping ▶

and price discounts. It has no control, however, over partners' pricing, while some manufacturers such as Nike have attempted to keep their products off a site they see as an inappropriate sales channel for their brand. The strategy also brings Amazon into closer competition with another Internet pioneer: eBay. eBay's 'Buy it now' function increasingly allows consumers to purchase at fixed prices rather than at auction, and it also has partnerships with other retailers.

Source: N. Buckley, 'Amazon aims to be king of the online retail jungle', *Financial Times* 21 October 2003.

SUMMARY

- First, this chapter addressed the question of where a firm should compete, by offering frameworks for analyzing the macro-environment, which includes factors such as the political and legal, the economic, the social and the technological environment.
- Second, the chapter discussed Porter's five forces as a guiding framework for determining the attractiveness of an industry. This also included an analysis of the influence of the Internet on industry rivalry, barriers to entry, substitute products, and the bargaining powers of buyers and suppliers.
- Third, the chapter introduced the concept of 'co-opetition', which refers to companies that co-operate and compete with each other at the same time. It illustrated how the Internet enables the implementation of such a concept and how it supports the underlying interactions between the companies involved.

REVIEW QUESTIONS

1. Explain the impact of the Internet on the macro-environment.
2. Review the impact of the Internet on the five forces industry framework.
3. How can the Internet enable companies to implement co-opetition in electronic commerce?

DISCUSSION QUESTIONS

1. Illustrate the five forces industry framework through two e-commerce examples from the same industry: one of a dot.com start-up and the other of an established company.
2. Choose an e-commerce example and discuss how a company can use the Internet to implement the 'co-opetition' concept.
3. Will eBay become Amazon.com's most powerful competitor in the future? Defend your argument.
4. Suppose that you want to launch an e-commerce venture. Which framework/concept from those introduced in this chapter would you use most to analyze and refine your ideas, and why?

RECOMMENDED KEY READING

- G. Johnson and K. Scholes discuss the macro-environment of firms in Chapter 3 of *Exploring Corporate Strategy*, Prentice Hall, 2002, pp. 97–138.
- For a more in-depth analysis of the five forces, see M. Porter, *Competitive Strategy*, Free Press, 1998.
- A. Brandenburger and B. Nalebuff introduce the concept of co-opetition in their book *Co-opetition*, Currency Doubleday, 1998.

USEFUL WEBLINKS

- www.bmg.com
- www.borders.com
- www.ivillage.com
- www.microsoft.com
- www.netscape.com

NOTES AND REFERENCES

1 A good discussion of macro-environmental influences can be found in G. Johnson and K. Scholes, *Exploring Corporate Strategy*, Prentice Hall, 2002, pp. 99–110. A more e-commerce-specific discussion of environmental factors is contained in D. Chaffey, *e-Business and e-Commerce Management*, FT Prentice Hall, 2002, pp. 143–156.

2 'Windows of opportunity', *The Economist*, 15 November 2003, p. 61.

3 TCP specifies how information should be separated into individual packets and reassembled at the destination. The IP specifies how individual packets should be sent over the network. The HTTP is a method of jumping back between different files. The HTML is a computer language for formatting hypertext files. J. Cassidy provides a very readable and informative account of the most important Internet standards and technologies in his book *Dot.con*, Perennial, 2003, pp. 16–24.

4 For a detailed discussion of industry analysis, see M. Porter, *Competitive Strategy*, Free Press, 1998, pp.3–34.

5 The five forces framework is contained in M. Porter, *Competitive Strategy*, Free Press, 1998, p. 5.

6 R. D'Aveni suggests that levels of competition have risen in the past decade, leading to a phenomenon that he calls 'hypercompetition'; see R. D'Aveni 'Coping with hypercompetition: utilizing the new 7S's framework', *Academy of Management Review*, 1995, Vol. 9, No. 3, pp. 45–57. However, G. McNamara, P. Vaaler and C. Devers have tested this thesis empirically and have not found conclusive evidence for an intensification of competition: 'Same as it ever was: the search for evidence of increasing hypercompetition', *Strategic Management Journal*, 2003, Vol. 24, No. 3, pp. 261–278.

7 J. Cassidy, *Dot.con*, Perennial, 2003, pp. 105–106.
8 T. Burt and P. Larsen, 'Sony and BMG sign music merger deal', www.FT.com, 12 December 2003.
9 F. Vogelstein, 'Mighty Amazon', *Fortune*, 26 May 2003, p. 64.
10 'Software's great survivor', *The Economist*, 22 November 2003, p. 70.
11 The concept of 'co-opetition' was developed by A. Brandenburger and B. Nalebuff, *Co-opetition*, Currency Doubleday, 1998. It entails simultaneously co-operating and competing with other companies.
12 Ibid.

CHAPTER 4

Markets for e-business

Chapter at a glance

4.1 Market segmentation for e-business

4.1.1 Segmenting consumer markets for e-business

4.1.2 Segmenting business markets for e-business

4.2 Market targeting for e-business

Related case studies

Case study	*Primary focus of the case study*
7 **Nettimarket**	B2C market segmenting: case of senior citizens
9 **ChateauOnline**	B2C market segmenting: case of wine buyers
26 **12Snap**	B2C market segmenting: case of youngsters
18 **Brun Passot**	B2B market segmenting: case of SMEs
19 **CitiusNet**	B2B market segmenting: case of large companies
20 **mondus**	B2B market segmenting: case of SMEs
21 **Covisint**	B2B market segmenting: case of large companies
2 **CompuNet**	Mass customization of IT services
6 **Amazon *vs.* BOL**	Mass customization of customer interaction
10 **Advance Bank**	Mass customization of financial services
14 **Ducati *vs.* Harley**	Mass customization of manufactured products

Learning outcomes

After completing this chapter you should be able to:

- Understand the reasons for segmenting markets and the specific requirements that a market segmentation should fulfil.
- Explain different possibilities for segmenting consumer markets.
- Differentiate B2B e-marketplaces based on the 'what' and the 'how' of purchasing and also based on their degree of openness.
- Explain the different possibilities for market targeting.

INTRODUCTION

Porter's five forces framework, which we discussed in Chapter 3, is a generic framework for analyzing any industry and drawing conclusions regarding its attractiveness. Industries as a whole, however, are frequently too broad of category to allow for any meaningful analysis.

Consider the car industry, which consists of a broad array of different car manufacturers, which cater to different types of customers. To conduct an industry analysis that contains both high-end manufacturers, such as Porsche and Jaguar, and mass producers, such as Toyota and Skoda, would provide only very limited insight into the attractiveness of the industry. Similarly, lumping together different types of customers, such as private consumers and corporate customers, also does not provide much insight, since their needs are completely different. To remedy this, we need to segment industries and markets within a specific industry into finer units and then decide which ones to target.

4.1 Market segmentation for e-business

4.1.1 Segmenting consumer markets e-business

Why is it sensible to divide markets into finer segments?[1] We need to do so because different people have different preferences regarding product features and, therefore, appreciate different value propositions. Let us look at the example of mobile telephones. A busy, young management consultant might value the possibility of checking their bank balance via their mobile phone, while a senior citizen with eyesight problems may not be attracted by mobile banking. However, the latter might find mobile phones with enlarged dialling pads valuable, allowing them to key in phone numbers more easily. This example illustrates how differences in customer preferences are the foundation for market segmentation. According to this, a market segment is defined as a group of customers who have similar needs.

Historically, segmenting markets and catering to different needs has not always been as important as it is nowadays. For instance, in 1909 Henry Ford started to offer car buyers in the USA the Model-T Ford car 'in any colour, as long as it is black'. By 1926, Ford had sold over 14 million Model-T cars. Obviously, with the advent of more sophisticated production technologies and, more recently, the Internet, it has become possible and necessary to segment markets in a much finer way and to offer different products and services to different customer segments (see e-Business Concept 4.1).

There are two main reasons why it is useful to segment markets. Segmentation of markets provides (1) insights into customer preferences and (2) information about the potential segment size. These two factors are now explained briefly.

E-BUSINESS CONCEPT 4.1

The e-business market segmentation matrix

The e-business market segmentation matrix[2] provides an overview of the different participants in electronic business. It differentiates three types of participants – consumers, businesses and government – who can act as both suppliers/providers and buyers/recipients. This results in the nine quadrants shown in Exhibit 4.1. Below, we shall explain each one of these configurations, taking the perspective of a supplier/provider who is dealing respectively with a buyer/recipient, who can be a consumer, a peer or a citizen, as well as a business, or a governmental agency. In other words, we shall proceed with the description of the proposed matrix row by row, rather than column by column.

The consumer/peer/citizen as a supplier/provider

Through the Internet, consumers can act as suppliers themselves. Consumer-to-consumer (C2C) relationships are those where one consumer acts as a supplier and sells goods to other consumers. The most prominent examples for C2C interactions are Internet auction places, such as eBay, where consumers can sell used and new products to other consumers. When interactions between consumers are not of a commercial nature, we call them peer-to-peer (P2P) interactions. These are voluntary in nature and are free of charge. Examples of P2P sites include online music-sharing platforms, such as Kazaa and Gnutella.

The second relationship type in this segment is the consumer-to-business (C2B) relationship, where, in general, consumers supply businesses with information about their experiences with products or services. Examples of C2B interactions are the book reviews at Amazon.com and consumer opinions at Ciao.com, a product-comparison platform. The information that consumers provide is then shared with other consumers to help them make more informed purchasing decisions.

The third category in this segment contains consumer-to-government (C2G) interactions, such as the online submission of tax return forms, and citizen-to-citizen interactions. An example of the latter is the partly Internet-based campaign that Howard Dean ran in the USA for the 2004 presidential election. During the primaries of the Democratic Party, Dean leveraged the Internet as a platform for interacting with supporters and citizens, outlining his viewpoints on different policy issues and raising funds.

The business as a supplier/provider

The most typical form of interaction is one where businesses act as suppliers to other parties. In business-to-consumer (B2C) interactions, firms sell products and services through online means directly to their customers. A number of case studies featured in the book, such as Tesco.com, Amazon.com, Advance Bank, Nettimarket, Ducati and ChateauOnline, focus on B2C interactions.

Business-to-business (B2B) interactions are platforms for the online purchase of operating or manufacturing inputs that other businesses need for making their products and services. The e-marketplace platform Covisint, which serves car manufacturers (as buyers) and component suppliers (as sellers), is a prominent example of a B2B platform.

Business-to-government (B2G) interactions include, for instance, the online submission of corporate tax return forms.

The government as a supplier/provider

Compared with the above two categories (i.e. consumers and businesses), government activities in e-commerce have so far been relatively low. However, this is changing, and it can be expected that in the future a significant part of governmental agencies' interactions with citizens and businesses will be conducted online (for a detailed discussion of e-government applications, see the e-government case study, p. 237).

The e-business market segmentation matrix shown in Exhibit 4.1 provides a classification of the different interaction types made possible through the Internet. This allows e-business players to position their own Internet operations within one or more quadrants of this matrix, and also to consider the option spaces into which they may want to expand.

For instance, Amazon.com started out in July 1995 as a pure B2C firm, selling books online to customers. It soon added a C2B component through the online reviews, which customers posted on the company's website. Later, Amazon.com expanded into C2C, when it allowed customers to sell used books through its website, using the Amazon.com online payment mechanism.

Exhibit 4.1 The e-business market segmentation matrix classifies different types of interaction between consumers, businesses and governmental agencies

Supplier/provider \ Buyer/recipient	Consumer/peer/citizen	Business	Government
Consumer/peer/citizen	**Consumer-to-consumer** e.g. eBay Peer-to-peer e.g. Napster Citizen-to-citizen (e.g. US 2004 election campaign)	**Consumer-to-business** e.g. Amazon.com	**Citizen-to-government** e.g. online tax return forms
Business	**Business-to-consumer** e.g. Ducati.com	**Business-to-business** e.g. Covisint.com	**Business-to-government** e.g. online filing of corporate tax returns
Goverment	**Government-to-citizen** e.g. information about pension statements of citizens	**Government-to-business** e.g. information about most recent legal regulations	**Government-to-government** e.g. exchange of diplomatic information

Another example is Nordea, which, like most other banks, was primarily offering retail (B2C) and corporate (B2B) banking services. Through the Internet, Nordea now enables government-to-citizen (G2C) interactions through an online connection with the Finnish government database that maintains the pension records of Finnish citizens. Through this online link, Nordea customers have instant access to their pension statements, an important feature when deciding, for instance, on a savings plan for retirement. Coincidentally, Nordea bank also offers savings plans for retirement.

- *Insights into customer preference.* Segmentation enhances the understanding of the target customer group and its preferences. First, this knowledge is helpful in determining how to shape a product and what kind of features to include. These features differ, depending on the target customer. Second, customer preferences help in deciding which distribution channels to select. For instance, Nordea Bank found out that older customers were more likely to start using the Internet for online banking services if they were enticed to do so during a personal face-to-face conversation at a bank branch.
- *Information about the potential segment size.* Segmentation also helps to assess the potential market. To have an approximate idea of how many customers might be using a product or a service is crucial for estimating possible scale effects and overall return on investment. Webvan in the USA is an interesting case, since it illustrates the disastrous effects of faulty market segmentation and sizing. Assuming an immense market potential, Webvan built large, centralized warehouses that could serve a huge customer base. As it turned out, however, the market segment attracted to this service was much smaller than expected. As a result, the picking and packing facilities were underutilized and most of the delivery trucks drove around half-empty.

Effective market segmentation that actually helps to meet customer preferences is by no means easy. There are many different ways in which a market can be segmented. Kotler proposes a number of different requirements that any type of segmentation should fulfil.[3] A market segment should be:

- *Measurable.* It should be possible to measure the size of a defined segment in order to determine its purchasing power and its peculiar characteristics.
- *Substantial.* A segment should be large enough to justify that it is addressed separately. During the Internet boom years, many category specialists entered specific market segments with a very targeted offering. Yet, as it turned out, the targeted segments were not large enough – at least then – to be served profitably.
- *Differentiable.* The segments must be exclusive and react differently to a variety of marketing approaches.
- *Actionable.* It should be possible to develop sales and marketing approaches to serve specific segments. For instance, the case study of 12Snap illustrates how mobile marketing campaigns can be designed specifically to target the segment of 15–25-year-old mobile phone users.

As mentioned above, there are myriad ways of segmenting any market. However, depending on the specific product and context, some ways are obviously better than

others. For instance, it might be possible to segment the market of ChateauOnline's wine customers based on hair colour and come up with blond, brown, black-haired and bald customers. In all likelihood, doing so will not provide much insight regarding different preferences and will thus also not be actionable. In this case, a segmentation between male and female groups or between income groups would probably be much more valuable. The point is that segmentation is not one-size-fits-all. Instead, it requires creative and innovative thinking to differentiate meaningful market segments.

Below, we outline the main possibilities for segmenting a given market (see also e-Business Concept 4.2 on segments of one and mass customization). These possibilities include *geographic, demographic, psychographic* and *behavioural* segmentations.

- *Geographic segmentation* entails the selection of specific geographic regions – for example, continents, countries or states – and tailoring offerings according to the preferences of customers within that region. For instance, in Europe, certain countries, such as Finland and Sweden, have a very high Internet penetration rate while others, such as Italy and Greece, do not. Segmenting according to countries or regions can bring out these differences and help to design custom-fit strategies for each region.
- *Demographic segmentation* focuses on different personal attributes of population segments. Demographic segmentation can be done, for instance, by looking at (1) age, (2) gender, (3) income and (4) life-style. For instance, regarding the age dimension, 12Snap has positioned itself clearly to attract to its mobile marketing services the segment of young mobile phone users, while Nettimarket in Finland segmented targeted senior citizens for its online grocery delivery service.

  Regarding the gender dimension, the virtual community ivillage.com initially aimed at serving both men and women. However, as it turned out that women were much more interested in ivillage's offering, the company decided to focus on the female segment.

  On the income dimension, Advance Bank wanted to focus exclusively on the upper-income segment of the German market. However, it failed to realize that this segment was too small (or unwilling to use a branch-less bank), which led Advance Bank to branch out into other segments. This action eventually undermined the overall strategy of the bank.
- *Psychographic segmentation* entails lifestyle issues such as personality type and personal interests. For instance, the 'cash-rich, time-poor' segment of customers has been a primary target for online grocery shopping services such as Tesco.com. In order to save time for their social activities and hobbies, members of this segment are more inclined to shop online (and pay the delivery fees) than spend hours in a supermarket store.
- *Behavioural segmentation* divides customers into segments based on their use of a product or service. This can be done, for instance, according to usage occasions or usage rates. Dell uses an occasion-based segmentation to group its customers into the following segments: home office, small business, medium to large business, government, education and healthcare.[4] Segmenting according to usage rates is often useful when different customers show vastly different shopping behaviours. For many firms, 20% of customers make up 80% of revenues. Placing frequent and less frequent customers into different segments and providing them with different levels of service or marketing efforts can then be appropriate.

E-BUSINESS CONCEPT 4.2

Segments of one and mass customization in the Internet world

During the past few years, the ability of firms to segment their markets to an increasingly fine degree has culminated in some cases in mass customization, or the so-called 'segment of one'.[5] The goal of mass customization is to offer a customized product that meets individual needs, while still maintaining a low-cost position through a mass-market operation.

Before mass production started in the twentieth century, segments of one were common-place. Many products, such as clothes and shoes, were fitted and customized to meet the specific needs of each individual customer. At the local food store around the corner, the store owner knew about the likes and dislikes of each customer. Customization was the norm because there was no other way to produce goods or provide services.

When production moved away from human labour to be handled by automated machinery, this type of customization was sacrificed in order to reduce costs. As a result, individual customers had to search among the existing mass-produced offerings to find styles and sizes that fitted their needs and preferences. In fact, mass production became the norm in most realms of business. Nowadays, department stores carry only a certain number of different styles and sizes. At large grocery chains, check-out agents know how to scan in the product codes but do not necessarily know about, for example, the wine or organic food preferences of their customers.

Today, we observe an increasing trend towards mass customization, which is characterized by low-cost mass production yet individually designed products and services.

The introduction of mass customization into business processes is driven by a number of developments. First, customers lead increasingly individualized lives, where everyone has a unique set of needs and wants. Second, the rapid developments in information and production technologies make it possible to meet these individualized needs to an ever-higher degree. The advent of the Internet and its integration into customer relationship management (CRM) applications has accelerated this development further.

The Internet makes it possible to determine specific customer needs by capturing and analyzing customers' clickstreams, i.e. by monitoring customers' behaviour when they surf around a website and make purchases. For instance, through its personal recommendation lists, Amazon.com provides customers with information about books they might be interested in based on their previous purchases. You may receive similar personalized information and proactive advice from a bookstore if you are a frequent, repeat-purchase customer and have always interacted with the same, knowledgeable salesperson.

The Internet also enables the customization of production processes. One of the classic examples here is the way in which Dell has customized its production to meet specific customer needs and preferences. A somewhat less known example is the online vitamin supplier Acumins.com. Many people need to take a wide variety of different vitamin supplements every day. Buying individual vitamin packages at the local store is a costly and cumbersome affair. Acumins.com has set out to solve this problem by offering online nutrition analysis to consumers, manufacturing custom-mixed varieties of vitamins and shipping them out to customers.

There are two main benefits of mass customization. First, if it is done properly, it leads to higher levels of customer satisfaction, because only product and services that actually create customer benefit are provided, while those that only generate costs and no benefit are left out. Second, mass customization provides the potential to lock customers into one's own products or services. Take the example of Amazon.com again. If you find the personalized recommendations useful, then you are less likely to switch to a competing online bookstore, since the database of the new bookstore would have to be 'trained', which means that you have to make a number of purchases before it can provide you with the same type of personalized book recommendations.

4.1.2 Segmenting business markets for e-business

Classification of B2B e-marketplaces based on the 'what' and 'how' of purchasing

To systematize the landscape of rapidly changing B2B markets, Kaplan and Sawhney propose a classification of B2B electronic marketplaces based on *what* businesses purchase and *how* they purchase it.[6] 'Regarding the *what*, there are essentially two different types of goods:

- *Operating inputs.* These goods are also often called MRO (maintenance, repair and operations) goods, which include items such as office supplies, airline tickets and services. MRO goods are not industry-specific. For instance, companies such as 12Snap and Ducati, which are in very different industries, both need computers and office supplies for their employees. MRO goods are usually purchased from horizontal vendors and shipped through third-party logistics providers.
- *Manufacturing inputs (raw materials and components).* These goods are industry-specific and are usually purchased from vertical suppliers/distributors. To handle and deliver these manufacturing inputs, it is usually necessary to set up specific fulfilment mechanisms. For instance, a motorcycle manufacturer, such as Ducati, that sources engine parts on a continuous basis from an external supplier is unlikely to use courier services, such as Federal Express, DHL or UPS, for delivery.

The second determining dimension is *how* these goods are purchased from suppliers. There are two main types of sourcing:

- *Systematic sourcing.* This type of sourcing involves negotiated contracts with qualified suppliers. Contracts are usually long-term and built on mutual trust, hence leading to lasting relationships between buyer and seller. The goal of systematic sourcing is to create value for both buyer and seller, by sharing, for instance, sales forecasts, customer data and production statistics. Thus, systematic sourcing relationships are usually about more than optimizing just price. To corporate customers, it is more important to get the right product at the right time with the right service than to save an additional 1–2%. Usually, it is advisable to set up systematic sourcing contracts when (1) complicated products are involved that need specific adjustment and service and (2) it is necessary to make investments that are

specific to the relationship. The relationship that Dell maintains with external suppliers of PC components is an example of systematic sourcing.

- *Spot sourcing*. Firms typically use this type of sourcing to fulfil an immediate need at the lowest possible price. Commodities such as oil, gas and iron are typically purchased via spot sourcing. Thus, it rarely involves a long-term relationship between buyer and seller. In contrast to systematic sourcing, spot sourcing focuses primarily on price, so that both buyer and seller try to maximize their own benefit at the other party's expense.

Based on the above dimensions, it is possible to construct a B2B Internet matrix depicting the following four different types of B2B e-marketplaces (see also Exhibit 4.2):

- *MRO hubs* are horizontal e-marketplaces with long-term supply relationships for operating inputs. For instance, Grainger in the USA sells goods that companies need to keep their plants and facilities running. CitiusNet, a case study featured in this book, is another example of an MRO hub that sells non-strategic, low-value items.
- *Catalogue hubs* sell manufacturing inputs through a systematic sourcing system. Goods sold through catalogue hubs are tailored specifically to meet the individual needs of the purchasing company. An example here is Covisint, which is a vertical e-hub for the automotive industry, linking car manufacturers with their suppliers of component suppliers (see the Covisint case study, p. 499).
- *Yield managers* are horizontal e-marketplaces for spot sourcing of operating inputs. They are most valuable for operating inputs that display high fluctuations in price and/or demand. An example here is mondus.com, which is a horizontal e-marketplace for small and medium-sized enterprises (see the mondus.com case study, p. 480).
- *Exchanges* are closely related to more traditional commodity exchanges. They are used primarily for the selling of commodities, such as steel and copper, that are used in the production process. An example of such an Internet-based exchange is e-steel.com.

Exhibit 4.2 **The business-to-business (B2B) e-commerce matrix classifies different types of B2B e-marketplaces**

How do firms buy? / What do firms buy?	Operating inputs	Manufacturing inputs
Systematic sourcing	**MRO hubs** Horizontal markets that enable systematic sourcing of operating inputs	**Catalogue hubs** Vertical markets that enable systematic sourcing for manufacturing inputs
Spot sourcing	**Yield managers** Horizontal markets that enable spot sourcing of operating inputs	**Exchanges** Vertical markets that enable spot sourcing for manufacturing inputs

Source: Adapted with permission of *Harvard Business Review* [Exhibit ROO 306]. From 'E Hubs: The New B2B Marketplaces' by S. Kaplan and M. Sawhney, May–June 2000.

Classification of B2B e-marketplaces based on their degree of openness

This classification focuses on the degree of openness of B2B e-marketplaces.[7] At one end of the spectrum, e-marketplaces with a high degree of openness are those that are publicly accessible to any company. At the other end of the spectrum, e-marketplaces with a low degree of openness are accessible only upon invitation. Based on this distinction, we recognize three main types of e-marketplaces: public e-markets, consortia and private exchanges (see Exhibit 4.3).

- *Public e-markets* are generally owned and operated by a third-party provider. They are open to any company that wants to purchase or sell through the e-marketplace. Because it is easy to enter and leave public e-markets, businesses processes are primarily standardized and non-proprietary. Products that are most likely to be sold through public e-marketplaces are commodities that need little or no customization. An example of a public e-market is mondus.com.

Exhibit 4.3 Different B2B e-marketplaces display varying degrees of openness

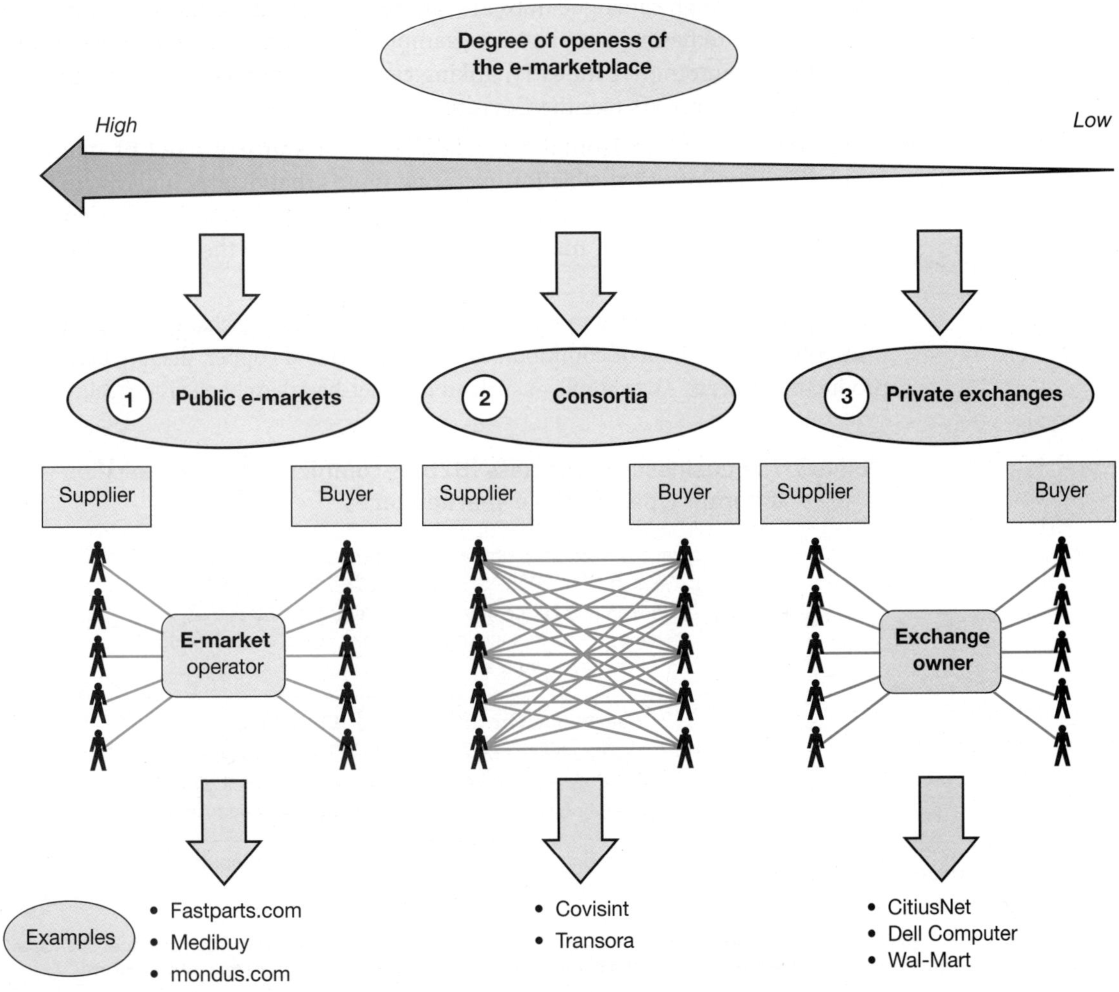

Source: Adapted from W. Hoffman, J. Keedy and K. Roberts, 'The unexpected return of B2B', *McKinsey Quarterly*, 2002, No. 3, p. 99.

- *Consortia* are typically jointly owned and operated by companies that participate in the online B2B exchanges. Access is much more limited than in public e-markets, since only equity holders and selected trading partners are admitted. Covisint, founded by General Motors, Ford and DaimlerChrysler, is an example of a B2B consortium (see the FT article 'Covisint fails to move up into the fast lane').

FT

Covisint fails to move up into the fast lane

When Covisint was launched at the height of the dotcom boom, it boasted of 'a place where people, products, information, and services come together to transform the automotive industry'. Two years later, the industry is still waiting for that transformation. Formed by General Motors, Ford and DaimlerChrysler, Covisint was designed to be a giant electronic marketplace where they would carry out procurement through online auctions at a fraction of the cost of traditional methods. Suppliers and carmakers would work seamlessly squeezing inefficiencies out of the system.

Offices sprouted in Europe, Japan and South America. Buoyed by their vision, the founders – principally the big three US carmakers, later joined by Renault-Nissan, Peugeot-Citroën, Commerce One and Oracle – laid plans for a stock market flotation bankers believed could raise $5bn. Today, however, its listing plans are a distant dream and Covisint is struggling to redefine itself.

Last week, the company lost Kevin English, its chief executive, although both sides said his departure was unrelated to company strategy. One quarter of Covisint's workforce was also cut, leaving a total of just under 300. 'When it was formed it was in the heyday of internet valuations and this was a whole new way of [doing] business that turned out to be wrong,' says John Henke, professor of marketing at Oakland University in Michigan. One of the main aims of Covisint was to offer a one-stop online shop that allowed manufacturers and suppliers to communicate with each other, sharing information such as inventory levels and parts usage patterns.

However, it soon became apparent that suppliers had little trust in a system where price-sensitive information about their business model was readily available to competitors. Indeed, lack of trust between motor manufacturers and parts suppliers was – and remains – Covisint's biggest problem. Parts suppliers object to the fact that manufacturers will select 'preferred bidders' who then bid against each other for the supply contract on offer. 'There are a lot of emotional feelings about it,' says Neil de Koker, managing director of the Michigan-based Original Equipment Manufacturers Association, a body that represents parts suppliers. 'It's perceived by many as a tool to beat the incumbent suppliers' prices down without really doing anything. If that [motor manufacturing] customer represents 30 per cent of your business and you walk away they could tell you you'll never be a preferred bidder again.'

Daniel Garretson of Forrester Research in Boston says: 'There's a lot less ability for the auto industry to co-operate than everyone thought. There's a lot of entrenched distrust so it's difficult to bring the layers together in a collaborative process.' He believes Covisint should 'cede' the auctions back to the manufacturers, and downgrade the internet hub to a medium for exchanging information and selling systems integration services.

Observers say incoming chief executive Harold Kutner's biggest challenge will be to mollify the estimated 7,000 parts suppliers that ▶

use Covisint. Parts suppliers can still take their business to competing sites with no links to the manufacturers. 'The manufacturers have not put a strategy out there that lays out for suppliers how they will do business with the customer through Covisint,' says Kevin Prouty, automotive research director at AMR Research in Boston. 'How will Covisint act between the supplier and the manufacturer? There's no roadmap for that yet.'

Mr Kutner, a former executive in charge of worldwide purchasing at GM, insists that Covisint is on track for profitability by the fourth quarter. But the broader issue is whether Covisint has a future at all. The carmakers, who are estimated to have invested $270m in launching Covisint, are standing by the concept. DaimlerChrysler says Covisint is 'one of many key tools that we use in B2B in order to manage relations with our suppliers' because it reduces the amount of time needed to decide where to source parts. Most observers seem to agree that it does have a future, but that the much vaunted industry transformation was, in the end, hopelessly misplaced. 'The purpose is to take costs out of the system, and it's doing that – just not nearly as quickly as we'd like,' says Mr de Koker. 'It's a lot more difficult than people thought.'

Source: J. Grant, 'Covisint fails to move up into the fast lane', *Financial Times*, 4 July 2002.

- *Private exchanges* are the most restrictive e-marketplaces in providing access to other parties. They are typically operated by a single company that wants to optimize its sourcing activities by tying its suppliers closely into its business processes. The operator of the private exchange invites selected suppliers to participate in the private exchange and provides them with detailed information about, for instance, sales forecasts or production statistics. In turn, this helps the supplier to optimize its supply chain. In order to achieve this type of close integration, it is generally necessary to build a customized system that tightly integrates the information systems of both buyer and seller. As a result, business relationships in private exchanges tend to last longer than in public e-marketplaces. The most prominent example of a highly successful private exchange is that of Dell with its suppliers.

4.2 Market targeting for e-business

After dividing markets into individual segments, it is still necessary to determine how to target a specific market segment. There are two main choices associated with market targeting. First, we need to determine which segment(s) to target. Second, we need to determine how many different products and services to offer to the selected segment(s). As a manager at a car manufacturer, for example you could decide to produce just limousines for the upper-income class. Another manager might decide that it is more appropriate to produce also sports utility vehicles (SUVs) and family vans for other market segments. When deliberating the choices, managers always need to keep two main questions in mind:

- *Is the market segment or the group of market segments attractive?* The attractiveness of market segments can be analyzed through the five forces framework (discussed in Chapter 3). To find out about the attractiveness of a segment, one could, for

instance, analyze the overall growth of the segment, its current profitability and current competition within the segment.

- *Can we compete successfully in this market segment?* This depends on the ability to create value through the resources and skills that a firm possesses. (For a more detailed discussion of value creation, see Chapter 5.)

  Companies can choose from five main possibilities to target market segments (see Exhibit 4.4). These possibilities are: (1) *single-segment concentration,* (2) *selective specialization,* (3) *product specialization,* (4) *market specialization* and (5) *full market coverage.*

- *Single-segment concentration.* Premium providers, such as Ducati, which specializes in the production of motorcycles for the higher-income motorcycle market, frequently concentrate on single segments of a market. This allows them to gain profound knowledge of customers, to develop specialized production know-how and to serve exactly the needs of their specific customer segment. Their brand is positioned clearly as a premium brand, undiluted by lower-class products, which allows them to charge a price premium for their products. Competitors with a broader positioning are likely to over- or underserve this specific customer segment. The downside of single-segment concentration is that if the targeted segment fails to generate the required revenues, then the whole firm is endangered.

Exhibit 4.4 Target-market selection depends on the number of markets served and the number of different products and services offered

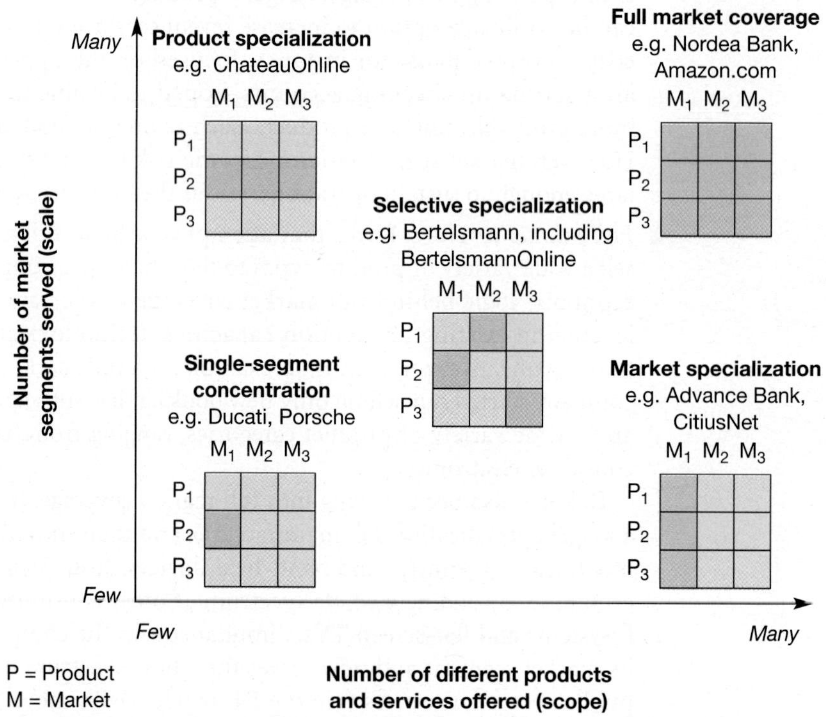

Source: Adapted from P. Kotler, *Marketing Management*, Prentice Hall, 2002, p. 299.

- *Selective specialization.* A company that pursues selective specialization targets different market segments with different product types. Doing so has the advantage of spreading out the business risk. However, it also poses the danger that the firm loses focus, thereby becoming vulnerable to attacks by more focused competitors. The German media group Bertelsmann, for instance, offers a wide variety of media products in the online, print, TV and radio areas, which target different customer groups.
- *Product specialization.* A category specialist such as ChateauOnline, which focuses primarily on wine retailing, concentrates on one product but wants to reach out to as wide a market as possible. The goal of product specialists is to generate either economies of scale or special learning effects that set them apart from their competitors. The risk of product specialists is that if their specific product loses favour with customers, then they would not be able to make up for a fall in revenues through other products. For instance, ChateauOnline (see p. 310) would face major challenges if new medical research were to show that wine consumption has severe detrimental health effects.

  The mobile payment provider paybox.net (also featured in the case studies part of the book) failed with its mobile payment service for online and offline transactions because the uptake by customers and merchants was not large enough to cover costs. Since paybox.net had focused only on the mobile payment service, it was unable to generate enough revenues as to sustain its business.
- *Market specialization.* Firms that concentrate on a specific market segment aim at gaining a strong reputation and trust with members of the targeted segment, and then expanding by offering a range of products to the same segment. Cross-selling can be a valuable option to increase revenues, since it limits customer acquisition costs. Advance Bank, for instance, focused on the upper-income segment and, after setting up checking accounts, hoped to be able to branch out into other, more profitable, financial products, such as mutual funds and insurance products. However, market specialization poses the risk that the segment in question is not large enough to sustain operations, as was the case with Advance Bank.
- *Full market coverage.* Firms that attempt to achieve full market coverage want to sell a wide variety of product types to the whole spectrum of target segments. The economic logic behind full market coverage is to create economies of scope by leveraging existing production capacities, technological platforms or a strong brand name. Amazon.com is an example of a full market provider. Although the company started out selling only new books, it has subsequently added used books and a wide variety of product categories, ranging from baby toys, to pet food, to consumer electronics.

  Dell has also been moving into full market coverage. It started its operations as a single specialization PC manufacturer and then moved into peripheral equipment, such as printers and hand-held devices. Now, Dell is broadening its scope even more by adding a whole spectrum of other consumer electronics, such as hi-fi systems and flat-screen TVs. Simultaneously, the company has been expanding its market segment and now serves the whole spectrum of corporate, private and public-sector customers (see the FT article 'Dell's move from PCs into complementary products' on page 129).

SUMMARY

- This chapter addressed market issues in e-business. First, it analyzed two market segments that Internet ventures can target: (1) consumer markets and (2) business markets
- Second, it proposed an e-business market segmentation matrix, in which a taxonomy of Internet-enabled interactions is suggested. These interactions take place between suppliers/providers and buyers/recipients of products and services. Depending on the context at hand, the players involved include businesses, governmental agencies and consumers/citizen/peers.
- Third, the chapter suggested different criteria for market segmentation and highlighted the increasing move, through the Internet, from mass production to mass customization. It then proceeded with a classification of business-to-business (B2B) e-markets based on *what* and *how* companies purchase goods from suppliers. It also discussed varying degrees of openness in B2B e-marketplaces.
- Finally, the chapter outlined different possibilities for targeting market segments in e-business. There are essentially five different options, which differ depending on the number of different products offered and the number of target segments served. The options include: (1) single-segment concentration, (2) selective specialization, (3) product specialization, (4) market specialization and (5) full market coverage.

REVIEW QUESTIONS

1. Outline the e-business market segmentation matrix based on its two underlying dimensions.
2. Describe the underlying reasons for the move from mass production to mass customization in the Internet world.
3. Outline the business-to-business (B2B) e-commerce matrix based on its two underlying dimensions.
4. What B2B purchasing models do companies use? What criteria determine what specific model to use?
5. Explain the concept of openness in B2B marketplaces. What different types of marketplace can you differentiate based on their degree of openness?
6. Which possibilities can a company choose from to target market segments for e-commerce?

DISCUSSION QUESTIONS

1 Provide a real-world example of your choice for each one of the nine quadrants that make up the e-business market segmentation matrix.

2 Discuss the increasing move from mass production to mass customization in the Internet world through two actual examples that you are familiar with.

3 What issues and challenges do companies generally face when moving from mass production to mass customization through the Internet? Are there specific industries where such a move is easier to make than in others?

4 Illustrate each quadrant of the business-to-business (B2B) e-commerce matrix through a real-world example.

5 Provide an example of a B2B e-marketplace for each one of the B2B purchasing models outlined in this chapter.

6 Discuss the advantages and disadvantages of the varying degrees of openness in B2B marketplaces, i.e. public e-markets, consortia and private exchanges.

RECOMMENDED KEY READING

- S. Kaplan and M. Sawhney developed the concept of e-hubs in 'e-Hubs: the new B2B marketplaces', *Harvard Business Review*, 2000, May–June, pp. 97–103.
- W. Hoffman, J. Keedy and K. Roberts differentiate e-marketplaces according to their degree of openness in 'The unexpected return of B2B', *McKinsey Quarterly*, 2002, No.3, pp. 97–106
- P. Kotler provides a more detailed account of market targeting in *Marketing Management*, Prentice Hall, 2002, p. 299–303.

USEFUL WEBLINKS

- www.acumins.com
- www.ciao.com
- www.dell.com
- www.deanforamerica.com
- www.ghx.com
- www.gnutella.com
- www.grainger.com
- www.napster.com

NOTES AND REFERENCES

1 For an extensive discussion of market segmentation, see P. Kotler, *Marketing Management*, Prentice Hall, 2002, pp. 279–306.

2 See also T. Hutzschenreuter, *Electronic Competition*, Gabler, 2000, pp. 28–29.

3 P. Kotler, *Marketing Management*, Prentice Hall, 2002, pp. 286–287.

4 This segmentation becomes apparent on the opening page of www.dell.com, where visitors can choose between different segments.

5 For more detailed discussions of one-to-one marketing see P. Kotler, *Marketing Management*, Prentice Hall, 2002, pp. 282–285, and also D. Peppers, M. Rogers, and B. Dorf, 'Is your company ready for one-to-one marketing', *Harvard Business Review*, 1999, January–February, p. 152.

6 S. Kaplan and M. Sawhney, 'e-Hubs: the new B2B marketplaces', *Harvard Business Review*, 2000, May–June, pp. 97–103.

7 W. Hoffman, J. Keedy and K. Roberts, 'The unexpected return of B2B', *McKinsey Quarterly*, 2002, No. 3, pp. 97–106.

CHAPTER 5

Value creation in e-business

Chapter at a glance

Related case studies

Case study		*Primary focus of the case study*
2	**CompuNet**	Value creation in IT-based services
6	**Amazon *vs.* BOL**	Value creation in online retailing
13	**Ducati**	Value creation in manufacturing
16	**Google**	Value creation in media
22, 23, 24,	**eBay**	Value creation in C2C e-commerce
10	**Advance Bank**	e-CRM in financial services
12	**Nordea**	e-CRM in electronic banking and e-business
15	**Terra Lycos**	e-CRM at an Internet service provider

Learning outcomes

After completing this chapter you should be able to:

- Identify the main drivers for value creation.
- Understand how the Internet opens up new opportunities for value creation.
- Explain how the Internet transforms the traditional value chain.
- Understand how a company can create increased fit between activities through the Internet.
- Describe how the virtual value chain relates to the traditional value chain.

INTRODUCTION

In essence, strategy formulation revolves around the concepts of value creation and value capturing. During the Internet boom years, Internet ventures often did not pay enough attention to these fundamental economic concepts. Nowadays, though, economic viability of any e-business venture is of paramount importance to managers and investors alike. This is why we devote a full chapter to these concepts.[1]

This chapter starts out with a generic discussion of value creation and value capturing. The value chain concept is then presented as a way to analyze the individual steps in the value-creation process. Finally, this chapter discusses the concept of the virtual value chain.

5.1 The generic concepts of value creation and value capturing

5.1.1 Creating value for customers

The concept of value creation is at the core of what a firm does, since only superior value creation vis-à-vis rivals opens up the opportunity for superior profitability. What does value creation depend on? In order to understand and apply the value-creation concept, let us first consider the underlying economics.

Value created is the difference between the consumer's perceived benefit from a given product and the firm's cost for providing that product. In the strategy and economics literature, there are numerous, often times divergent, definitions of some closely related concepts such as value, consumer benefit, utility and value created. To establish a common understanding of some key terms for the remainder of the book, we now provide definitions of *consumer benefit*, *costs* and *value created*. The relationship between these terms is shown in Exhibit 5.1.

Consumer benefit

Consumer benefit consists of all the characteristics that an individual consumer values in a product or service. In economic terms, consumer benefit is approximated by the buyer's maximum willingness to pay for a given product. The crucial question that needs to be asked is: 'When is the buyer indifferent between buying and not buying a specific product or service?'

To illustrate this concept, consider the automatic bidding agent at eBay, the online auction company. Imagine you want to purchase a laser printer at eBay. After picking out a printer, you have the possibility of entering into the bidding agent a maximum price at which you would still be willing to buy the printer. This particular printer might have a perceived worth to you of €200. The bidding agent then starts at the lowest offering price of, say, €20. Any time another bidder enters the race and trumps your bid, the bidding agent is automatically activated and places a bid just above the previous one, until it

Exhibit 5.1 Value creation depends on benefit and cost positions

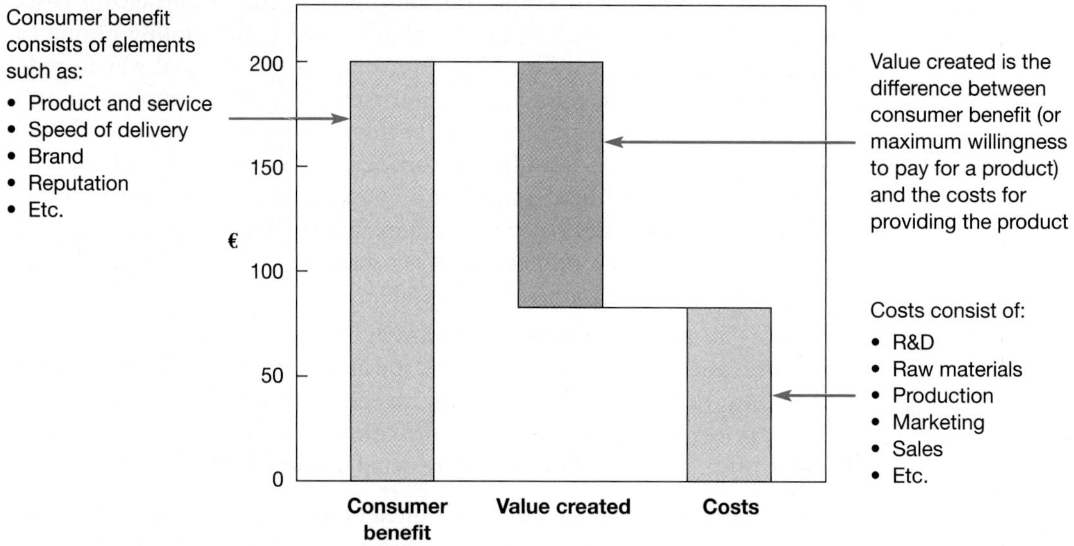

Source: Adapted from D. Besanko, D. Dranove, M. Shanley and S. Schafer, *Economics of Strategy*, John Wiley, 2003, p. 368.

reaches your maximum price of €200. When someone else goes over this amount, you drop out. The implicit meaning behind this is that the benefit that you expect from the printer does not justify the higher price that is now being charged. Your consumer benefit and, therefore, also your maximum willingness to pay are €200.

Costs

Costs, in this context, include all the expenses that are incurred in providing a product to the consumer. This includes different cost items, such as technology development, raw materials, production, marketing, sales and delivery.

Variable costs, such as raw materials for a product or postage, can be attributed directly to an individual product, whereas fixed costs, such as the costs for the development of a website or the construction of a warehouse, need to be spread out across all the products that are sold through this website. The costs of firms depend on different cost drivers, such as economies of scale and scope, capacity utilization, previous experience or input prices (see Section 7.1, which deals with economies of scale and scope).

Value created

Value created is the difference between the benefit that consumers get from using a product and the costs that are incurred to produce the product. (Note that value created by itself does not state anything yet about price or profits. Determining price will be the next step.) There are two necessary requirements that a firm needs to fulfil in order to compete successfully in the marketplace. The value that it creates:

- *Must be positive.* The costs must be lower than the benefit it provides to consumers. This requirement is straightforward, even though during the Internet

boom days many companies did not pay sufficient attention to it when they offered through the Internet doubtful consumer benefits at outrageous costs. An example of a product with negative value created is the mobile phone called 'Iridium', which was introduced by Motorola in 1998. Its goal was to redefine mobile telephony by introducing uninterrupted wireless communication anywhere in the world. Development costs for this service were a staggering $5 billion. However, this phone model suffered from several drawbacks: it did not work in cars or buildings, it required a number of attachments, and it was heavier than a traditional mobile phone. Faced with comparatively low consumer benefits, high costs, and low subscriber numbers of fewer than 50 000 people, Motorola decided to terminate the project prematurely in 2000.[2]

- *Must be higher than the value that is created by competitors.* Unless a firm can create similar or higher value than competitors, it will not be able to stay in business over the medium to long term. This is due to the fact that competitors can either undercut prices due to lower costs or offer consumers more benefit while charging the same price. This is discussed in more detail in Section 5.1.2.

Let us return to the printer example auctioned on the eBay website to illustrate the concept of value created. Your reservation price of, say, €200, which you stated for the laser printer, is a monetary reflection of your expected benefit from buying this printer. At €201, you would not be willing to purchase the printer any more. At €200, you are indifferent between buying it and keeping the €200 for other purposes. At any price below €200, you would be capturing part of the value created. Assume that the seller has incurred costs of €80 for the printer (for the initial purchase of the printer and the costs of displaying it on eBay). Then, the overall value created is €120, i.e. consumer benefit of €200 minus the €80 of costs.

What exactly constitutes consumer benefit? It is inherently difficult to measure, because consumer benefit cannot be quantified objectively, regardless of place, time and person. Instead, it varies from individual to individual, depending on:

- *Personal preferences*: you might derive a high benefit from driving a shiny sports car, whereas your next-door neighbour, who has three children, will get much more benefit from a mini-van.
- *Place*: think of a freezer in the Arctic versus a freezer in the Sahara.
- *Time*: think of the benefit of electric light during the day versus at night.

What elements need to be considered when determining levels of consumer benefit?[3] There is a wide range of sources for consumer benefit, which can be divided into *tangible* and *intangible* sources, depending on whether they can be observed directly.

Tangible sources of consumer benefit include the following:

- *Product quality.* This characteristic refers to the objective traits of a product, such as its functionality, durability (or reliability) and ease of installation. For instance, the quality of Ducati motorcycles can be determined accurately by metrics such as maximum speed, acceleration, kilometres per litre, or breakdown rate. Likewise, the quality of Tesco.com's online grocery business can be measured by the freshness and overall quality of the goods delivered.
- *Degree of product or service customization.* The more a product or service can be adapted to specific customer needs, the more benefit it creates for the individual

user. Dell manufactures its PCs to customer specifications, resulting in two types of benefit. First, all the components that an individual customer values in a PC are included; second, all components that are not valued are left out, thus helping to keep down PC prices (see also e-Business Concept 4.2, p. 83).

- *Convenience.* The mental energy, effort and time that buyers have to expend during the purchasing process need to be taken into account when comparing different providers.[4] This is why people do not drive 10 km to the discount supermarket just to buy a bag of coffee, but instead go to the local corner store, even though the coffee there might be more expensive. Through its online grocery service, Tesco.com aims to increase convenience for shoppers, and especially for very busy people.
- *Service quality.* This characteristic refers to the friendliness and know-how of salespeople or, in the case of a website, the degree of personalization, ease of use, and response time and information quality of online enquiries. ChateauOnline, the French wine retailer featured in the case study on p. 310, provides a superior service to its customers by offering extensive wine reviews, wedding and party services with recommended wines to go with the menu, venue and chosen budget, and webmiles for frequent buyers.
- *Speed of delivery.* The ability to deliver products and services quickly is an important source of consumer benefit. Speed depends on the availability of products, location of the seller, and quality of the logistical process. A firm that has the ability to deliver faster than its competitors because of its management approach, superior process flow, and IT systems and applications can create a significant competitive advantage. Amazon.com, for instance, installed proprietary warehouses to be able to ensure that products are available and get shipped out in a timely fashion.
- *Product range.* A broad and deep selection provides an important source of differentiation since it allows convenient and quick one-stop shopping. Amazon.com is a prime example of a retailer with a deep and broad product range, since customers can find, for example, most book titles that are currently in print (and out of print).

Intangible sources of consumer benefit include the following:

- *Brand.* This characteristic refers to the perceived traits that consumers associate with the company that is selling a product or a service. A strong brand tends to result from products that meet high-quality standards, yet this may not necessarily be so. It might also come as a result of intensive and innovative marketing activities. Brands need to be built and nurtured in order to use them as a differentiating characteristic in the marketplace.

  Most online firms had to invest heavily into the creation of their brand, as is shown in the case studies section of this book through the examples of 12Snap, Advance Bank and ChateauOnline. On the other hand, for established physical firms such as Tesco, Nordea and Ducati, it was much easier to acquire online customers, since they already benefited from a strong brand through their store outlets, office networks or physical dealerships.
- *Reputation.* The perceived historic performance of a company is a major factor influencing reputation. Customers value reputation because it decreases their

purchasing risk. Especially when it comes to making online payments with a credit card, a company's reputation is critical, since many online customers still feel uneasy providing this information to an unknown vendor.

It is important to note that consumer benefit does not happen in a vacuum. It depends on what other firms in the industry offer, since consumers constantly compare different product providers. To bring in this dimension, we need to differentiate between *threshold features* and *success factors*.[5]

- *Threshold features* are the minimum requirements that a firm must fulfil in any product or service. If a firm cannot meet these minimum requirements, then it will get excluded from the market because buyers will not even take it into consideration. A threshold feature might be, for example, a website with functioning links or a secure payment mechanism for online transactions. These are required features that do not differentiate a product.
- *Critical success factors*, on the other hand, are those benefits that are crucial for the buyer's decision to purchase a given product. At Amazon.com, these features include the wide variety of goods, the reviews, and the convenient and fast shopping experience made possible through the company's one-click shopping application. At Nordea Bank, critical success features are the ease of use of the online banking site and the e-business services.

To summarize, both threshold features and critical success factors create consumer benefit, but only the latter help a firm to differentiate itself from its competitors by creating superior consumer benefit.

5.1.2 Capturing value

While it is important for a firm to create value that is superior to the value created by its competitors, it is equally important to capture parts of the value it creates in the form of profits (or producer surplus, as it is called here). As stated above, value creation by itself does not provide any information about how the value is distributed between consumers and producers, as is shown in Exhibit 5.2. This distribution takes place through the price that a firm can charge for the product or a service. Price splits the value created into two separate entities: the *producer surplus* and the *consumer surplus*.

- The *producer surplus* represents the profits that a firm generates when selling a product. Profits are the difference between the price at which the product is sold and the costs of producing it.
- The *consumer surplus* represents the difference between the consumer benefit, which is the maximum willingness to pay, and the price the customer has actually paid for a product. In general, customers will seek out those products that offer them the greatest surplus, which can be achieved either through a higher customer benefit level at the same price as other products or through lower price with comparable quality.

To illustrate the concept of producer and consumer surplus, let us look again at the example of the printer auction at eBay. If the auction ends at €160, which is below

Exhibit 5.2 Value created is distributed between producers and consumers

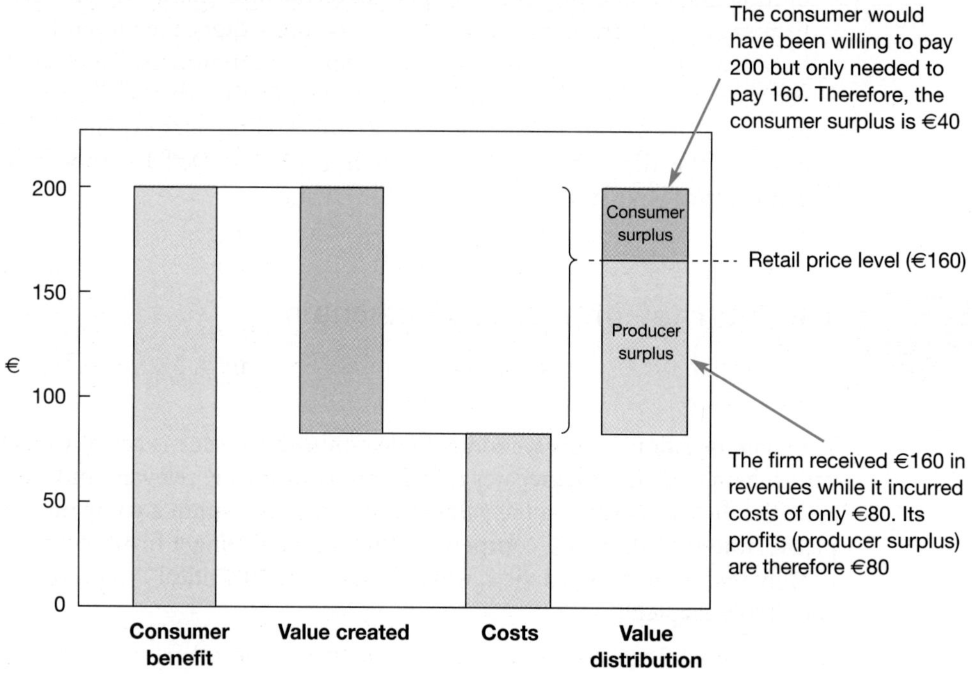
The consumer would have been willing to pay 200 but only needed to pay 160. Therefore, the consumer surplus is €40
200
150
100
50
0
€
Consumer surplus
Retail price level (€160)
Producer surplus
The firm received €160 in revenues while it incurred costs of only €80. Its profits (producer surplus) are therefore €80
Consumer benefit
Value created
Costs
Value distribution

Source: Adapted from D. Besanko, D. Dranove, M. Shanley and S. Schaefer, *Economics of Strategy*, John Wiley, 2003, p. 368.

your maximum willingness to pay, then the purchase goes to you. How does the value created get distributed? For the seller, the surplus is the difference between the price of €160 and the cost of €80, which comes out to be €80. Your consumer surplus is the difference between your maximum willingness to pay €200 and the price you have actually paid (€160). This comes out to be €40. In this example, the seller captured the larger part of the value created (€80) while the customer captured the smaller part (€40).

Now, we can answer the overarching question regarding which factors influence the distribution of value between buyers and sellers. There are two factors that influence a firm's profitability: (1) *the industry structure* and (2) the *relative level of a company's value creation.*

- *Industry structure.* The distribution of value depends on the industry in which a firm is competing. Porter's five forces industry framework (discussed in Section 3.2) helps to determine how value created is distributed. Industries with highly intense competition, low entrance barriers and readily available substitutes tend to be less attractive and, therefore, less profitable. This is due to the fact that existing and new competitors bid down prices in order to gain market share from their competitors. This means that the value created typically goes to consumers in the form of low prices. Thus, in general, it is difficult for a firm to earn attractive profits in an industry that is characterized by the above-mentioned factors. The PC industry is a prime example of an intensely competitive industry, where value created is high yet profits remain low for most firms.

- *Relative level of a firm's value creation.* A firm's own value creation relative to that of its competitors is the second important factor that determines profitability. If a firm manages to create higher value than its competitors, then it has the potential to earn attractive profits, even in highly competitive industries. For example, in the very competitive PC industry, Dell has been able to earn above-average profits because of its unique direct-sales model, which eliminates expensive intermediaries in the distribution chain. This has allowed Dell to underprice most competitors while still maintaining healthy margins.

5.2 The Internet-impacted value chain

The main question in this section is to determine how value is actually created. The value chain, which disaggregates a firm into strategically relevant and interrelated activities, helps to examine the value-creation process within a company.[6] However, please note that there are competing views on analyzing a firm's activities, most notably the resource-based view, which is discussed in Critical Perspective 5.1 at the end of this chapter.

5.2.1 Analyzing activities in the value chain

Ultimately, competitive advantage rests on activities that a firm can perform better or more efficiently than its competitors. There is no general blueprint prescribing which activities should be included in analyzing a company's value chain. However, the following criteria should be used when including specific activities. An activity should:

- *Display different economics.* For instance, the development activity of a new software program displays very large economies of scale since the software can be replicated at negligible cost.
- *Provide high differentiation potential.* These are activities that can greatly increase tangible and intangible consumer benefits, such as product and service quality, convenience and reputation.
- *Present sizeable costs.* These are activities that add significantly to the overall cost structure of the firm. For instance, in the case of Ducati, these might be activities related to product development and manufacturing. In the case of 12Snap, major costs are incurred for marketing.

On an aggregate level, a company's value chain contains primary and support activities (see Exhibit 5.3).

To get a better understanding of the ways in which the Internet can change the value chain, we will take a closer look at how Dell has transformed its value chain.

- *Inbound logistics* consist of receiving, storing and distributing incoming goods within the company. On a more detailed level, this might include activities such as checking inventory levels and order placement. Through close linkage with its

Exhibit 5.3 A company's value chain consists of distinct value-adding activities

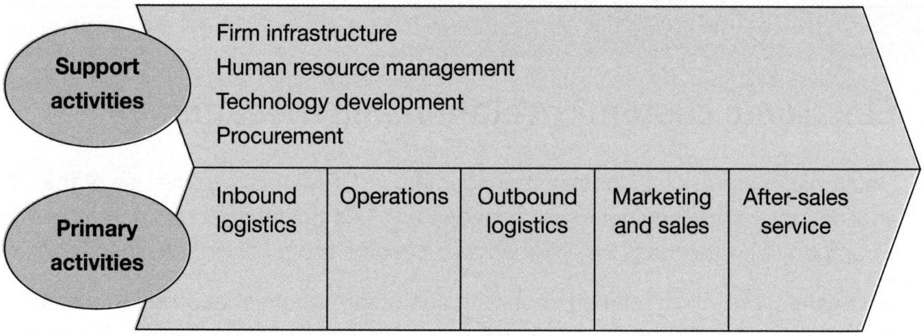

Source: Adapted from M. Porter, *Competitive Advantage*, Free Press, 1998, p. 37.

suppliers, Dell has managed radically to change its inbound logistics. For instance, when Dell sources monitors from Sony, the boxes are not shipped to a Dell plant from where they are distributed. Instead, Dell has made arrangements with logistics companies, such as UPS, to pick up the monitors as needed from the Sony manufacturing plant, match them with the corresponding computers, and then deliver them to customers. Doing so reduces the need for warehousing capacity and inventory, and cuts out transportation steps.[7]

- *Operations* consist of those activities necessary for the making of a product or a service. The Internet has, in many cases, drastically changed a company's production activities. By taking orders online, companies can significantly shrink the time between order placement and productions, enabling them to start production in 'real time'. For instance, through the close linkage between the ordering website and the production facilities, Dell can build products that match orders, thus increasing turnover and reducing inventory costs.[8]
- *Outbound logistics* consist of activities required for getting the product to the buyer, which can be done either physically or electronically (for digital goods). For example, the reduction of inbound logistics by leaving products with suppliers also reduces Dell's efforts and expenses for outbound logistics. Complementary components, such as PC monitors, are shipped directly from the supplier to the final customer.
- *Marketing and sales* activities aim at enticing customers to buy a product and to provide the means for doing so. This includes activities such as providing online catalogues and running online marketing campaigns (see also e-Business Concept 5.1 for a discussion of customer relationship management as part of online marketing activities). For example, the Internet has enabled Dell to move online most of its marketing and sales activities. Dell has thus offered customers a fast and comprehensive way to place orders, while at the same time keeping down costs (since it does not have to pay for an expensive sales force and retail outlets).

One of Dell's main competitors Compaq, which relied on in-store sales as its main distribution channel, was affected severely by Dell's direct model, yet it was largely unable to replicate it because of conflicts with its existing physical channels. In other industries, physical sales channels are much more valuable than it was initially anticipated at the beginning of the Internet boom years. Consider the banking industry,

E-BUSINESS CONCEPT 5.1

Electronic customer relationship management

Electronic customer relationship management (e-CRM) refers to the use of the Internet and IT applications to manage customer relationships.[9] As the Internet has permeated different activities of a company's value chain, e-CRM has also become more important. Specifically, it aims at:

- Creating long-term relationships with customers to offset acquisition costs.
- Reducing the rate of customer defections.
- Increasing the 'share of wallet' through cross-selling and up-selling.
- Increasing the profitability of low-profit customers.
- Focusing on high-value customers.

e-CRM comprises the following four main elements (see Exhibit 5.4): (1) **customer selection,** (2) **customer acquisition**, (3) **customer retention**, and (4) **customer extension.**

- **Customer selection** refers to customer segment targeting, which was discussed in Section 4.2.
- **Customer acquisition** includes promotions and other incentives to (1) acquire completely new customers and (2) entice existing customers to move to the Internet. In order to engage a customer in a relationship through the online channel, a firm needs to have at least the customer's e-mail address. More detailed customer profiles include information such as a customer's personal interests, age, financial status and role in the purchasing process. To acquire this more detailed information, it is usually necessary to offer customers an incentive, e.g. a gift certificate or a free product sample. e-Commerce companies use a number of

Exhibit 5.4 **Customer relationship management consists of four elements**

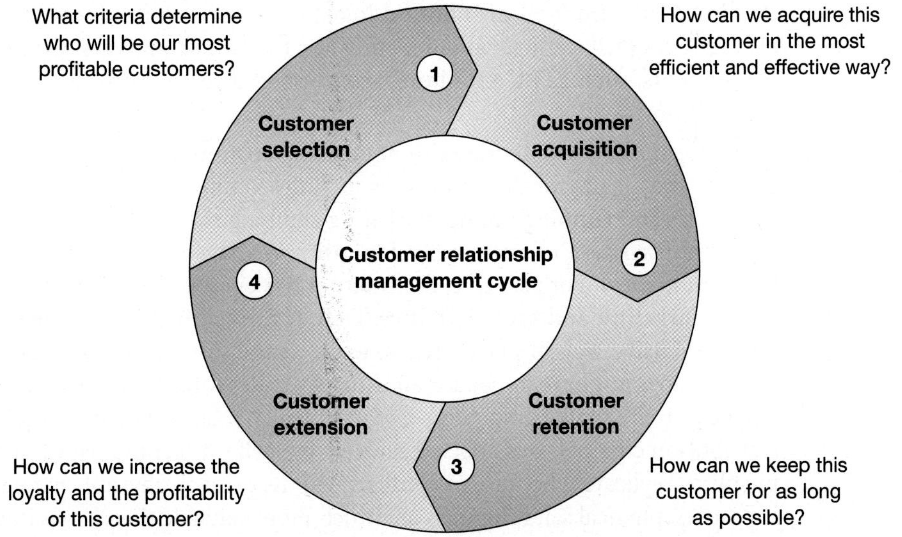

different tools to get the attention of potential customers. Initially, this was done primarily through banner advertising.

More recently, marketers have added more sophisticated tools such as 'viral marketing', where customers forward a website address or other types of company information to each other via e-mail or SMS. 12Snap, which is featured in the case studies part of the book, uses this approach intensely in its mobile marketing campaigns. Another effective way of customer acquisition is link building, which Amazon.com does in partnership with affiliate sites that refer to the Amazon.com site. For instance, the alumni club of the Leipzig Graduate School of Management in Germany maintains an affiliate relationship with Amazon.de. As part of this agreement, the alumni club's homepage hosts a link to the Amazon.de website and receives a 5% commission on all sales that take place through this link.

- **Customer retention** has the goal of (1) turning one-time customers into repeat-purchase customers and (2) keeping customers for as long as possible in the online channel. Customer retention is achieved primarily through two features: personalization and communities (these are discussed in detail in Section 7.2.1). The personalization of a website designed to meet specific customer needs helps to create 'stickiness'. If customers want to change their online provider, then they will incur switching costs. Strong online communities with many different users help to create network effects. Both personalization and online communities entice users to stay with a particular website.
- **Customer extension** focuses on maximizing the lifetime value of a customer. Companies achieve this primarily by expanding the scope of an existing customer relationship through cross-selling. Nordea, for instance, is turning towards triggered data-mining to cross-sell additional financial products to existing customers. Triggered data-mining works as follows: when there is a change in a customer account – for instance, a large incoming money transfer, an address change or a marital status change – a trigger in the database is set off and informs the bank about this change. This, in turn, raises the following question: 'What does this change mean for financing, for long-term payments, for insurance and e-services?'

where most industry experts assumed then that virtual banks with no physical presence would be able to outperform their cost-intensive bricks-and-mortar competitors both on the cost and the benefit dimensions. As it turned out, however, bank customers actually valued the presence of bricks-and-mortar branches, to which they could turn and where they could meet with an adviser in a face-to-face setting. The case of Nordea shows how success in the online world depended to a large degree on integrating online activities with sales activities in the branches.

- *Service* activities deal with the after-sales phase, which includes the installation of a product, supplying spare parts and exchanging faulty products. Dell's corporate customers can go to Dell's intranet and access the same internal support tools that Dell's own technical support teams use.

The importance of the different activities in the value chain varies from one industry to another. For service firms, operations and marketing/sales activities are crucial. A retailer of physical goods such as Amazon.com places a major emphasis on inbound and outbound logistics as well as marketing and sales. To create high levels of consumer benefit, Amazon.com offers sophisticated sales and marketing tools, such as the personalized recommendation list, which is based on a customer's previous

purchases. As part of sales, Amazon.com has patented the one-click payment mechanism, which allows customers, after having gone through a one-time registration process, to make a purchase simply by clicking on an icon and without having to provide any further information about themselves. Thus, the above-outlined value chain is not a blueprint for analyzing any individual business. Instead, it should be set up based on the individual context of the firm and with the goal of providing a good understanding of how the business operates.

In addition to the primary activities that are related directly to the production and sales process, the value chain also comprises the following support activities:

- *Procurement deals* with the primary inputs for different processes within the organization. This includes the purchasing of, for example, machinery, PCs, servers and office equipment. Procurement is often a crucial element of the overall cost structure of a company. The case studies of Brun Passot and Covisint deal specifically with how procurement processes can be made more efficient through the use of electronic platforms (see also Section 4.1.2 for a discussion of B2B e-marketplaces).
- *Technology development* includes specific R&D (research and development) for product design. It also refers to development activities that optimize the functioning of other activities of the firm. For instance, to develop its auctioning technology platform for mobile phones, 12Snap set up its own programming lab.
- *Human resource management* consists of recruiting, managing, training and developing people. The Internet transformed this activity through online recruiting, web-based training and intranet-based knowledge management. Human resources issues also influence Internet-based companies to make conscious choices regarding their geographical location, because employees represent the least mobile asset. Amazon.com, for example, set up its headquarters in Seattle, USA, to be able to attract qualified IT specialists. The Advance Bank in Germany decided to build up its call centres in Wilhelmshaven, a city with high unemployment, where it could find cheap yet qualified call-centre agents. Similarly, 12Snap set up its technology development centre in Prague, Czech Republic, one of the few places at the time where the firm could find qualified yet comparatively cheap labour.
- *Infrastructure* refers to a firm's physical premises, including offices, plants, warehouses and distribution centres. In spite of being an online retailer, Amazon.com operates a network of its own warehouses in its key markets to co-ordinate the logistics of delivery.

Exhibit 5.5 shows examples of how the Internet influences the different activities of a value chain.

In order for a firm to be able to perform certain activities within the value chain, it needs to dispose of certain assets and skills such as physical and financial assets, human resources, technology and know-how. This asset and skill portfolio is not static, however. As a firm performs certain activities during an extended period of time, it also builds up skills internally, as the different departments improve their processes and create assets. These include internal assets such as improved technology or employees' know-how, and external assets such as a superior brand reputation or strong relationships with suppliers and buyers.[10]

Exhibit 5.5 The Internet impacts all activities in the value chain

Firm infrastructure
- Web-based, distributed financial and enterprise resource planning (ERP) systems
- Online investor relations, e.g. information dissemination, broadcast conference calls

Human resource management
- Self-service personnel and benefits administration
- Web-based training
- Internet-based sharing and dissemination of company information

Technology development
- Collaborative product design across locations and among multiple value-system participants
- Knowledge directories accessible from all parts of the organization
- Real-time access by R&D to online sales and service information

Procurement
- Internet-enabled demand planning
- Other linkage of purchase, inventory and forecasting systems with suppliers
- Direct and indirect procurement via marketplaces, auctions and buyer–seller matching

Inbound logistics	Operations	Outbound logistics	Marketing and sales	After-sales service
• Real-time integrated scheduling, shipping, warehouse management, demand management and planning, and advance planning and scheduling across the company and its suppliers • Dissemination throughout the company of real-time inbound and in-progress inventory data	• Integrated information exchange, scheduling and decision-making in in-house plants and components suppliers	• Real-time transaction of orders • Automated customer-specific agreements and contract terms • Customer and channel access to product development and delivery status • Collaborative integration with customer forecasting systems • Integrated channel management	• Online sales channels, including websites and marketplaces • Real-time inside and outside access to customer information, product catalogues, dynamic pricing, inventory availability, online submission of quotes and order entry • Online product configurators • Customer-tailored marketing via customer profiling	• Online support of customer service representatives • Customer self-service via websites and intelligent service request processing • Real-time field service, access to customer account review, work-order update, etc.

Source: Reprinted by permission of *Harvard Business Review* [Exhibit RO 103D]. From 'Strategy and the Internet' by M. Porter, March 2001.

5.2.2 Creating fit between activities

Activities in the value chain are not performed in isolation; instead, they are linked to each other throughout the value chain.[11] A firm's ability to create a better and unique fit between activities is ultimately responsible for its competitive advantage. Thus, the whole of the value chain is more important than the sum of its individual activities. Sustainability also results from a unique fit, since it is much more difficult for competitors to imitate a set of interrelated activities than just to put together different elements and effectively replicate that same model.

There are three main levers that determine the fit of activities within a firm: (1) *consistency between activities*, (2) *reinforcement of activities* and (3) *optimization of efforts.*

Consistency between activities

Consistency ensures that individual activities with their respective advantages build on each other instead of cancelling themselves out. If a firm aims for a differentiation advantage, then the goal should be to design activities such that each activity adds to the differentiation advantage. On the other hand, if the goal is to be a low-cost provider, then costs of each activity should be kept to a minimum while still maintaining the threshold features that are required to stay in the market. Lack of consistency dilutes the positioning of a firm. The need for consistency emphasizes the requirement that strategy is not just about deciding which activities a firm should perform but also, and equally important, which activities not to perform. If a firm wants to be everything to everyone, then it runs the risk of not being able to do anything better than the competition and will end up being 'stuck in the middle'.

Why is that so? Porter argues that strategic positions are not sustainable if there are no trade-offs with other positions.[12] If a firm wants to provide highest-quality standards, then this usually entails higher costs, while the desire for lower costs usually results in a decrease of quality. This trade-off arises from the following sources:

- *Activities.* The trade-off results in part directly from the activities involved. Different positions require different processes, resources, skills and value-chain set-ups. A firm that wants to achieve a differentiated positioning needs to invest heavily to ensure highest-quality standards (and, hopefully, to be able to command a price premium). Cost leaders, on the other hand, need activities that provide the lowest possible cost structure because they want to compete through low prices. Customers of these firms want to receive the basic service at the lowest possible price. Thus, a firm that wants to be a cost leader and unnecessarily bloats its costs by overengineering its activities is actually destroying value.
- *Image and reputation.* Trying to be both a low-cost and a differentiated provider can easily cause inconsistencies in a firm's image and reputation. It is much easier for a firm to communicate its strategy credibly to its different stakeholders (such as customers and shareholders) when it has a clear positioning. Think of the car manufacturer Porsche. To build up and maintain the reputation of premier sports car manufacturer, Porsche needs to position itself clearly with its products and services. Similarly, a low-cost provider such as the US retailer WalMart focuses its efforts on providing its products at the lowest possible costs.

- *Strategy implementation.* It is much easier to implement a strategy within a firm if employees have a clear guiding vision of the strategy and if they do not have to ask themselves with every decision: 'Are we competing on low cost, or are we trying to be a differentiated provider?'

The European low-cost airline easyJet.com is a good example of a firm that is continuously striving for consistency across different activities of its value chain. To minimize costs, easyJet.com forgoes many of the features, frills and perks that are offered by traditional airlines. While the latter rely heavily on expensive ticketing offices and sales agencies, easyJet.com sells almost solely through the Internet (see also Strategy in Action 5.1). Furthermore, customers do not receive printed tickets. Instead, they show up at the airport's check-in counter where they receive their boarding pass upon passport identification. On board, passengers are not offered free meals and drinks, but instead they have to pay for each drink or snack. Finally, after landing, planes are turned around much faster than the industry average, which helps to reduce standing fees and increase capacity utilization.[13]

STRATEGY IN ACTION 5.1

easyJet.com's low-cost strategy and the Internet

The Internet plays a vital part in the easyJet business plan and is critical to its ongoing success. As a low-cost operation, controlling the cost of doing business is crucial to the airline's ability to offer low fares. Because the Internet provides the most cost-effective distribution channel, easyJet has aggressively pursued its strategy of encouraging passengers to book their seats online. Here are some examples of the ways in which easyJet incentivizes people to book via the Internet:

- Passengers booking online receive a discount of £5.00 for each leg of a journey. easyJet first pioneered the concept of offering a discount to Internet customers, an initiative that has been widely copied by competitors.
- Any easyJet promotions are exclusive to the Internet, so that customers must get online if they wish to take advantage of discounted fares.
- If customers wish to book seats more than two weeks in advance of the departure date of the flight, they can only do so by booking online. As fares generally increase as the departure dates gets closer, this means that the best fares are first available to those who book via the Internet.

Since easyJet started selling seats via the Internet in April 1998, the airline has enjoyed dramatic growth in its online sales. The airline reached the one-million seat mark in October 1999, and celebrated this important landmark by giving that lucky passenger unlimited free flights for a whole year. Five months later in March 2000, easyJet reached two million seats, and it only took another three months after that to reach the three-million seat mark, indicating a huge acceleration in the growth of online sales. easyJet has now sold many millions of seats online. The proportion of all sales made online has also shown impressive growth. easyJet now sells around 90% of its seats online every week, which is a higher percentage than any other airline, reinforcing its position as the 'web's favourite airline'.

Source: www.easyjet.com

The case of the Advance Bank in Germany, which wanted to be a premium provider of direct banking services in Germany, is a good example of inconsistent positioning that led to persistently low levels of profitability. Based on its initial differentiation strategy, the bank set up large call centres, hired skilled call centre agents (most of them with a university degree), and developed a highly sophisticated IT infrastructure and website. When customer acquisition did not meet expectations, the bank attempted to broaden its customer base and expanded into less affluent segments by offering cheque accounts for free. This move, however, was not consistent with the initial set-up of the company's differentiated set of activities, since the low-cost customers were not bringing in sufficient margins to finance the cost-intensive activities of the bank.

Reinforcement of activities

Reinforcement is the second important characteristic of a good fit between the different activities of a firm. Its underlying thinking is that competitive advantage comes as a result of how some activities influence the quality of other activities to create higher quality in products or service.

Take, for instance, the sales activities. If a firm has a highly motivated and skilled sales force, it is much more effective if the firm also has excellent R&D and production facilities to produce a top-quality product. Similarly, a sophisticated website, such as the one of Amazon.com, becomes more valuable when it is combined with a warehouse system that allows for fast, reliable and efficient deliveries. During the Internet boom years, firms that only built up a flashy website without working out the detailed logistics in the back end were unable to create this type of reinforcement (although they were able to raise substantial capital from venture capitalists and stock markets). Reinforcement between separate activities is difficult to pinpoint from the outside. Therefore, it is difficult to imitate a position that is built on strong reinforcement across activities.

The case of Nordea illustrates the importance of reinforcement. Among other reasons, Nordea is successful because it managed to create a tight fit between all its online and offline banking activities, which allowed the bank to move quickly online a large number of their branch customers. Pure online banks cannot imitate this effective customer-acquisition approach, since they do not have a physical branch network. Other bricks-and-mortar banks that tried to follow suit did not realize the importance of closely connecting the online and offline businesses. They opted instead for distinct profit-centre structures, thereby creating competition between their online and offline activities. A firm's ability to cross-sell and/or sell through complementary distribution channels is critical, since, especially in the service industry, the cost of acquiring a new customer can be two- to threefold the cost of selling to an existing customer.

For example, Dresdner Bank, the owner of Advance Bank, chose to maintain its direct banking operation in a separate business unit. As a result, it could not leverage the physical branch network for customer acquisition and services. This lack of reinforcement between different channels also contributed to the decision to close down Advance Bank at the end of 2003 and to move all its customers to the multi-channel banking offerings of Dresdner Bank.

Optimization of efforts

The third characteristic of good fit is optimization of efforts. While reinforcement focuses primarily on improving the customer experience by linking up separate activities, optimization emphasizes the importance of cost reduction through the elimination of redundancy and wasted activity. For instance, Internet companies that have optimized their order-taking process can reduce the cost for truck fleet and personnel. Dell currently presents the best practice in optimization of efforts. Activities such as sourcing, production, sales and service are connected in such a way as to minimize costs while still providing superior customer benefits.

Creating fit between activities through consistency, reinforcement and optimization creates the link between strategy formulation, which takes place on a rather abstract level, and implementation, which deals with determining how to choose and structure a firm's activities. Creating fit is a time-consuming effort, especially as a firm moves from consistency to reinforcement and optimization. It is necessary to analyze closely the vertical and horizontal boundaries of a firm and to set up the internal organization accordingly, in order to create fit among activities. This requires substantial resources and managerial skills, which also explains why strategy has long-term implications. Changing strategies randomly makes it hard to obtain a competitive advantage, because creating fit takes time and effort. This does not mean that new tools and concepts such as total quality management (TQM), which might help to increase operational effectiveness, should generally be discarded, yet it is important to realize that it is sensible to implement these tools only as long as they do not alter the fundamental basis of the strategic position and its trade-offs.

5.2.3 Leveraging the virtual value chain

In the context of the value chain discussion, it is also of interest to introduce the concept of the virtual value chain,[14] which emphasizes the importance of information in the value-creation process (see Exhibit 5.6). The key drivers behind this concept are advances in information technology and the evolution of CRM systems, which have increasingly provided firms with vast amounts of information.

The concept of the virtual value chain suggests that information captured in the physical value chain for activities such as order processing and logistics should be used to offer enhanced quality of customer service. Based on this concept of recycling information, the virtual value chain illustrates new opportunities to create value by using information captured in the physical value chain. In the past, a lot of information was captured only to support the value-adding processes in the physical value chain, although this information in itself presented potential value to customers.

Opening up new opportunities to make this information available to customers, thereby increasing the value created, is the main goal of the virtual value chain. The latter comprises the following steps: gathering and organizing information, selecting and synthesizing relevant pieces of information that are of value for the customer, and finally choosing appropriate formats for distributing the information.

Exhibit 5.6 The virtual value chain illustrates how information captured in the physical value chain can be used to enhance customer service

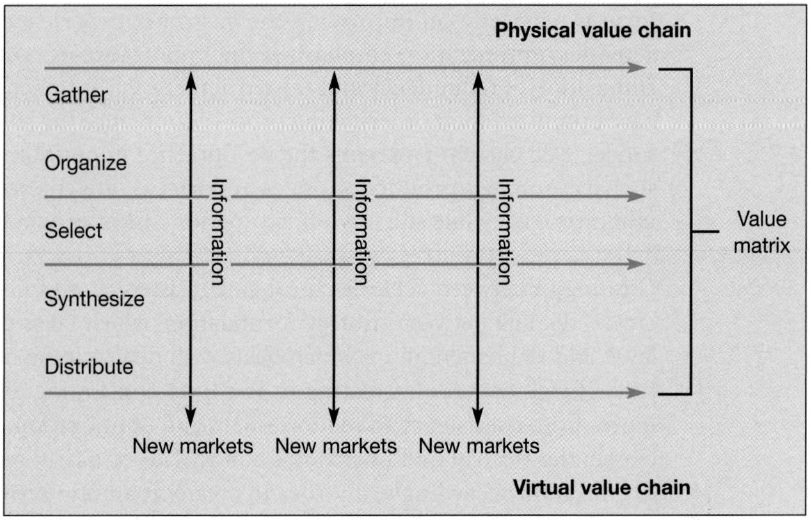

Source: Reprinted by permission of *Harvard Business Review* [Exhibit 95610]. From 'Exploiting the Virtual Value Chain' by J. Rayport and Sviokla, Nov.–Dec. 1995.

At Dell, corporate customers can access customized intranet sites, called Premier Pages, where they can find information on purchasing and technological configurations that they buy from Dell. FedEx has implemented technology through which it can track exactly where a package is located at any given moment during the delivery process. It created additional value for customers when it made this information available on the Internet, so that customers always know where their package is and when they can expect to receive it (see Strategy in Action 5.2).

The virtual value chain framework can be used to analyze several of the cases studies in this book. Nordea Bank, for instance, has used information that it had access to or already owned to create value for its customers. For example, the bank allowed its customers to access their pension statements electronically, which are maintained by a governmental agency. The bank also made its customer-identification process available to other companies that need to use Nordea's e-identification and e-signature services.

Amazon.com has also extensively used information captured throughout its physical value chain to create value. Customers have the possibility of tracking online past purchases and checking the status of delivery. The personalized book-recommendation list, where customers get recommendations based on what other people have bought, is another example of how Amazon.com has also tapped into the previously unused information stored in its databases. Furthermore, including reviews from other customers and providing sample pages of selected books create value for customers while requiring only marginal investment, since the required information-capturing systems are already in place.

STRATEGY IN ACTION 5.2

The virtual value chain at FedEx

FedEx InSight is a technological milestone for businesses needing solutions that speed fast-cycle orders and production, reduce inventory costs and add customer-satisfaction value.

'FedEx InSight gives us the ability to solve important issues before they become problems for our customers', said Stephen Egerton, International Logistics Analyst for Millipore Corporation, a high-tech bioscience company based in Bedford, Mass. 'If there is missing clearance information or shipping documentation that is causing a clearance delay, FedEx InSight sends an e-mail alert. This alert shows us the critical shipment details and the proposed resolution of the issue, keeping our logistics channels running at peak efficiency.'

Using FedEx InSight, customers can create a customized view of shipment information, and request to be notified via e-mail, fax or wireless device of critical shipping events as they occur during transit. Information provided in the enhanced visibility solution can give customers the ability to plan their operations more efficiently to save time and money for their inbound, outbound and third-party shipments.

'Managing inventory in motion across global supply chains requires a high level of detailed information that companies need to strengthen their competitive advantage', said Karen Rogers, Vice-President, e-Commerce Marketing, FedEx Services Corp. 'The unsurpassed technology in FedEx InSight can give companies of any size critical data visibility to manage the movement of parts and products over any period of time.'

The application meets a growing need of companies for quick, visible access to more comprehensive shipping and tracking data. For example, 76% of those in a Forrester Research Inc. survey that said they could not track their shipments en route or get shipment updates via wireless device, fax or e-mail. FedEx InSight arms these customers with complete data to manage their shipment process more efficiently.

How FedEx InSight works

FedEx InSight identifies FedEx Express and FedEx Ground shipments by associating them to a customer and matching an account number or company name and address. This places greater flexibility and control of information in the hands of each customer.

For example, a company may need to view international inbound shipments for a six-day period, in addition to shipments that are outbound during the same period or beyond. The company may also require a complete view of in-transit shipments billed to a third party. FedEx InSight allows this customized view of information, plus the ability to add more levels of tracking details a customer may need.

Because the information is displayed and updated as events occur, customers can better plan business efficiencies, such as adding more employees to a particular production line or resolving problems by providing missing customs documents. In addition, FedEx InSight provides quick visibility status of multiple shipments to different destinations.

Source: FedEx press release from 1 April 2001, taken from www.fedex.com

CRITICAL PERSPECTIVE 5.1

The resource-based view and core competencies

Since the beginning of the 1990s, Porter's approach to creating competitive advantage, which is also called the *market-based view*, has been criticized primarily because of its seemingly one-sided market orientation.[15] The focus of the criticism is that Porter's approach might help to diagnose a specific competitive problem but it does not provide any means to solve it. Other factors that have an important impact on a firm's competitive positioning, such as internal structure, processes, resources and capabilities, do not receive adequate attention. To alleviate these shortcomings, a *resource-based view* was developed, which focuses on the internal perspective of a firm, namely its *core competencies*.

The terms 'competence' and 'core competency' have been used widely, meaning different things to different people. Let us therefore establish some basic definitions before proceeding. First, a *competence* is a combination of different resources and skills:

- **Resources** are all the tangible and intangible assets of a firm that can be used in the value-creation process. Tangible resources include assets such as IT infrastructure, bricks-and-mortar infrastructure and financial capital. Intangible resources include employee knowledge, licences, patents, brand name and reputation of a firm.
- **Skills** represent the ability of a firm to use resources efficiently and effectively. Skills are manifest in the design of processes, systems and organizational structures. Even before the Internet became a mainstream technology, Dell had already built up significant skills in managing the process flow of its direct business model. Adding the Internet was relatively easy, since the necessary skills were already in place.

However, not all competencies that a firm has are necessarily *core competencies*. Instead, in order for a competence to be considered as core, it needs to be:

- **Valuable**. Customers have to appreciate the value of what the competence produces. This can be achieved through either the lowering of costs or the increasing of customer benefit, as perceived by customers.
- **Unique**. The competence needs to be unique so that it not only offers a source of value creation but also allows the firm to capture the value it creates in the form of profit. If a competence is not unique, then competition with other firms will drive down profits.
- **Hard to imitate**. Uniqueness of a core competence is sustainable only if other firms find it difficult to imitate the competence. First, competencies are hard to imitate if they require the tightly inter-linked participation of many functions or divisions of the firm. Nordea's core competence in the integration of offline and online banking, for instance, is hard to imitate because it requires the alignment of activities across multiple functions and channels. Second, causal ambiguity also increases the barriers to imitation. Causal ambiguity exists when there is no clear understanding of the sources of a core competence, which makes it hard for an outsider to imitate the competence.

- **Valuable across different products or markets.** A competence is of major value to the firm only if it is not limited to one product or to one market. One of Amazon.com's core competencies is its ability to manage the flow of merchandise from receipt of a customer's online order to shipping the product to the customer. To create this core competence, it built up resources in the form of warehouses and IT infrastructure and created internal skills. As the company moves into different product categories such as toys, home electronics and clothes, it can reuse its skills and resources.

Both skills and resources are required in processes that run across different functional units of a firm. In fact, an important building block of the competence-based approach is that strategy rests less on functional divisions and products but rather more on processes that cut across different divisions (see Exhibit 5.7).

Compatibility between the resource-based view and the market-based view of strategy

For a moment, let us venture out into the theory of strategic management and discuss the relationship between the *resource-based view* and the *market-based view*. While many authors assume that the approaches are fundamentally different, there is a growing strand of research that suggests that the two approaches are not in competition with one another but rather complement each other.[16]

Although the resource-based view and the market-based view approach strategy formulation from two different angles, they share a common underlying thinking. This reduces the gap between the market-based view (which focuses on the external environment and is activity-focused and functionally oriented) and the resource-based view (which is internally oriented and competence-focused and takes on a cross-functional perspective). Upon closer scrutiny, the perceived dichotomy between the two views does not hold any more, as is shown below.

Exhibit 5.7 **The core competence approach cuts across different functional areas within a firm**

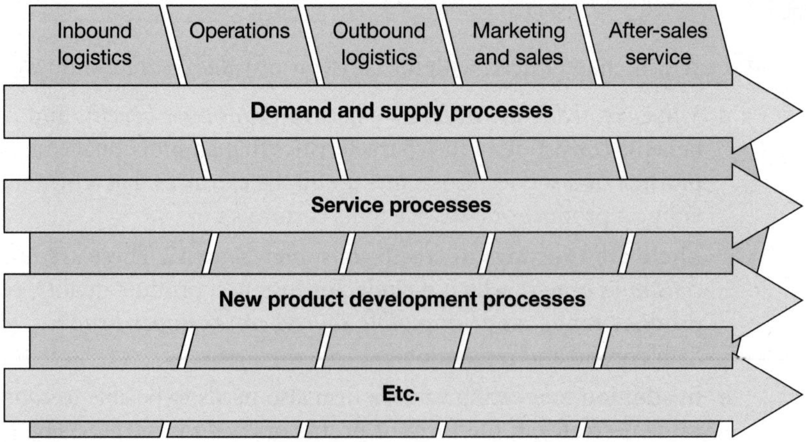

- **Dichotomy between external and internal focus.** On the one hand, the market-based view emphasizes the competitive landscape in terms of industry structure (see Section 3.2), which is external to the firm. However, it also emphasizes the creation of competitive advantage through internally executed activities, and the ability to create value through activities is ultimately determined by the quality of internal resources and skills. The resource-based view, on the other hand, starts out with internal considerations of resources and skills. However, any given core competence needs to fulfil the requirements of creating value and being unique and sustainable. This, in turn, requires considerations that are external to the firm and that provide insights into consumer preferences and the competitive landscape.
- **Dichotomy between activities and competencies.** The market-based view starts out with the definition of activities such as operations or marketing and sales. Yet, to perform these activities in such a way that they create competitive advantage, a firm ultimately needs to possess superior resources and skills because they are the building blocks of superior activities. The resource-based view, on the other hand, starts out with the core competence as the main building blocks of competitive advantage. However, competences that consist of resources and skills create value only as part of activities. A strong brand, for instance, is not valuable in and of itself. Instead, it creates value when a firm is able to spend less money on marketing activities while still achieving the same results in consumer awareness as other firms that need to spend more heavily because they do not possess the same brand reputation. Thus, competencies ultimately also rely on activities as sources of competitive advantage.
- **Dichotomy between functional and cross-functional perspective.** Through the analytical framework of the value chain, the market-based view starts out with functional divisions that perform discrete activities. Yet, building on the divisional structure, it also includes a cross-functional perspective when it emphasizes the requirement of fit between different activities that can be achieved via consistency, reinforcement and optimization. The resource-based view, on the other hand, begins with competences that are generally cross-functional processes. Yet processes, in the end, also consist of individual activities, which are located in functional units.

SUMMARY

- First, this chapter dealt with the concepts of *value creation* and *value capturing:*
  - *Value created* is the difference between *consumer benefits* and *costs.* Consumer benefits consist of all the characteristics that an individual consumer values in a product or a service. Costs include all the expenses that a firm incurs when providing a product or a service to its customers.
  - There are two ways to create consumer benefits. These are *tangible sources of consumer benefit,* which include, for instance, product quality, convenience and product range, and *intangible sources of consumer benefits,* which include a firm's brand and reputation.
  - In addition to creating value, a firm also needs to be able to *capture* parts of the value it creates in the form of profits or *producer surplus.* The price at which a product is sold determines what portion of the value created goes to the producer as *producer surplus* and what goes to the consumer as *consumer surplus.*

  - The ability of a firm to generate profits depends on the *structure of the industry* where it competes and its level of value creation relative to that of its competitors.
- Second, this chapter discussed the *value chain*, which disaggregates a firm into strategically relevant activities:
  - Two types of activities can be distinguished within a firm. First, *primary activities*, which include *inbound logistics, operations, outbound logistics, marketing and sales* and *service.* Second, support activities, which include firm infrastructure, human resources, *technology development and procurement.*
  - There are three main levers that determine the fit of activities within a firm: (1) *consistency between activities*, (2) *reinforcement of activities* and (3) *optimization of effort.*
- Third, this chapter presented the concept of the virtual *value chain*, which suggests that information captured in the physical value chain (e.g. for activities such as order processing or logistics) should be used as a new source of value creation to enhance the quality of customer service.
- Finally, this chapter also provided a critical perspective of the *market-based view* of strategy formulation. This critique is based on the *resource-based view*, which builds on the *core competences* that cut across different activities.
  - Competences consist of a combination of different *resources* and *skills.*
  - In order for a competence to qualify as a core competence, it needs to be (1) *valuable*, (2) *unique*, (3) *hard to imitate* and (4) *valuable across different products or markets.*

REVIEW QUESTIONS

1. Outline the concept of value creation. Describe how a firm can use the Internet to increase its value creation.
2. Explain the concept of value capturing, and describe how it influences the profitability of a firm.
3. What are the primary and supporting activities in the value chain, and how does the Internet influence them?
4. Through which measures can a firm improve the fit between activities in the value chain? Explain how the Internet can influence these measures.
5. Outline the main concept of the virtual value chain, and explain how it relates to the traditional value chain.
6. What is a competence? What criteria does a competence need to fulfil in order to qualify as a core competence?

DISCUSSION QUESTIONS

1 Consider the examples of Webvan and Tesco.com. Explain the different fates of these two companies using the concepts of value creation and value capturing.

2 Analyze the value chain of an e-commerce venture that you are familiar with. Explain how the Internet has impacted the primary and support activities of its value chain.

3 Based on the above example, think of ways in which this firm could further improve the fit among activities through consistency, reinforcement and optimization.

4 Think critically about application possibilities of the virtual value chain. Are there industries where the virtual value chain concept is more applicable than in others? If so, explain why.

5 Discuss whether competence-based thinking is more suitable for strategy formulation than the activity-based approach outlined in the value-chain concept.

6 How do the market-based view and the resource-based view differ, and to what extent can they be reconciled?

RECOMMENDED KEY READING

- D. Besanko, D. Dranove, M. Shanley and S. Schaefer provide a detailed discussion of value creation and value capturing in *Economics of Strategy*, John Wiley, 2003, pp. 358–402.
- M. Porter's book, *Competitive Advantage*, Free Press, 1998, is a seminal work on value creation and the value chain. M. Porter expands on his thinking about competitive advantage in 'What is strategy', *Harvard Business Review*, 1996, November–December, pp. 70–73.
- R. Amit and C. Zott specifically discuss this chapter's topic in 'Value creation in e-business', *Strategic Management Journal*, 2001, Vol. 22, No. 6, pp. 493–520.
- Within the field of strategic management, there is a broad literature on the resource-based view. While there was already previous research on the resource-based view of the firm, most notably in 1984 with the article by B. Wernerfelt 'A resource-based view of the firm', *Strategic Management Journal*, 1984, Vol. 5, No. 2, pp. 171–180, this approach became popular in the mainstream management literature through the work of C.K. Prahalad and G. Hamel, 'The core competence of the corporation', *Harvard Business Review*, 1990, May–June, pp. 79–91 and G. Stalk, P. Evans and L. Shulman 'Competing on capabilities', *Harvard Business Review*, 1992, March–April, pp. 57–69. M. Peteraf provides a more recent academic perspective on the resource-based view in 'The cornerstones of competitive advantage: a resource-based view', *Strategic Management Journal*, 1993, Vol. 14, No. 3, pp. 179–191.
- In the article 'Towards a dynamic theory of strategy', *Strategic Management Journal*, 1995, Vol. 12, No. 8, pp. 102–105, M. Porter attempts to reconcile the market-based and the resource-based views of strategy.
- J. Rayport and J. Sviokla present the concept of the virtual value chain in 'Exploiting the virtual value chain', *Harvard Business Review*, 1995, November–December, pp. 75–85.

USEFUL WEBLINKS

- www.easyjet.com
- www.fedex.com
- www.porsche.com
- www.walmart.com

NOTES AND REFERENCES

1 Students in MBA or other programmes, and who have taken introductory courses in micro-economics, are already familiar with the concepts of value creation and value capturing. Yet they might find it of interest to look at these concepts in the specific context of e-business and electronic commerce.

2 C. Haney, 'Motorola's Iridium network set for decommissioning', *InfoWorld*, 2000, Vol. 22, No. 37.

3 There are numerous approaches available to estimate consumer benefit. They include (1) the reservation price method, (2) the attribute-rating method, (3) hedonic pricing and (4) conjoint analysis. For a more detailed discussion of these approaches, refer to D. Besanko, D. Dranove, M. Shanley and S. Schaefer, *Economics of Strategy*, John Wiley, 2003, pp. 416–419.

4 See also P. Kotler, *Marketing Management*, Prentice Hall, 2002, pp. 60–61.

5 For a detailed discussion of threshold features and success, see G. Johnson and K. Scholes, *Exploring Corporate Strategy*, Prentice Hall, 2002, pp. 149–156.

6 For an extensive discussion of the value chain concept, see M. Porter, *Competitive Advantage*, Free Press, 1998, pp. 33–61. A detailed discussion of the impact of IT on the value can be found in M. Porter and V. Millar, 'How information gives you competitive advantage', *Harvard Business Review*, 1985, July–August, pp.149–160.

7 Michael Dell describes the PC manufacturer's approach to supply-chain management in an interview with J. Magretta: 'The power of virtual integration: an interview with Dell Computer's Michael Dell', *Harvard Business Review*, 1998, March–April, pp. 72–84.

8 R. Waters, 'Dell aims to stretch its way of business', *Financial Times*, 13 November 2003, p. 8.

9 For a detailed discussion of customer relationship management in e-business, see D. Chaffey, *e-Business and E-Commerce Management*, Prentice Hall, 2002, pp. 330–370.

10 M. Porter, 'Towards a dynamic theory of strategy', *Strategic Management Journal*, 1991, Vol. 12, pp. 102–105.

11 For different types of strategic fit among activities, see M. Porter, 'What is strategy', *Harvard Business Review*, 1996, November–December, pp. 70–73.

12 Ibid.

13 See www.easyjet.com

14 J. Rayport and J. Sviokla developed this concept in 'Exploiting the virtual value chain', *Harvard Business Review*, 1995, November–December, pp. 75–85.

15 See C.K. Prahalad and G. Hamel, 'The core competence of the corporation', *Harvard Business Review*, 1990, May–June, pp. 79–91, and G. Stalk, P. Evans and L. Shulman 'Competing on capabilities', *Harvard Business Review*, 1992, March–April, pp. 57–69.

16 For this discussion, see also M. Porter, 'Towards a dynamic theory of strategy', *Strategic Management Journal*, 1991, Vol. 12, No. 8, pp. 102–105.

CHAPTER 6

Strategy options for value creation in market spaces

Chapter at a glance

Related case studies

Case Study		*Primary focus of the case study*
6	**Amazon *vs.* BOL**	Competitive advantage through opening up new market spaces
8	**Tesco**	Competitive advantage through differentiation
9	**ChateauOnline**	Competitive advantage through differentiation
12	**Nordea**	Competitive advantage through differentiation
17	**DoubleClick**	Competitive advantage through opening up new market spaces
25	**Online file-sharing**	Competitive advantage through opening up new market spaces

Learning outcomes

After completing the chapter you should be able to:

- Explain the generic approaches to strategy formulation.
- Understand the meanings of 'stuck in the middle' and 'outpacing'.
- Explain how firms can open up new market spaces and thereby create completely new types of value.

INTRODUCTION

When formulating a strategy, managers can choose between two basic options. First, they can aim to outperform competitors, either by having lower costs or by offering a superior product or service. Second, they can aim completely to redefine competition by changing the 'rules of the game', e.g. by opening up new market spaces and creating completely new types of value.

6.1 Exploring generic strategies in existing market spaces

The formulation of generic strategies is related closely to the creation of value. Porter proposes a generic strategy selection framework that builds on the type of value a firm creates (the 'what') and on the broadness of its target market (the 'where').[1] If a firm can create value primarily by achieving a low-cost structure, then it will most likely pursue a strategy of cost leadership within its industry. If, on the other hand, it can offer comparatively higher benefit than the competition to its customers, then it will aim for a differentiated strategy.

On the market side, the firm can either pursue a broad target where all customers are addressed, or focus on a certain segment within a market as part of a focused strategy. In both the broad and the narrow target, the choice is between cost leadership and differentiation. The two dimensions (i.e. *competitive advantage* and *broadness of target market*) open up the generic strategy option matrix, as shown in Exhibit 6.1. Since Section 4.2 discussed in great detail the issue of market targeting, we will focus here on the competitive advantage dimension of strategy development.

Exhibit 6.1 **The generic strategy options matrix outlines the four main approaches to strategy**

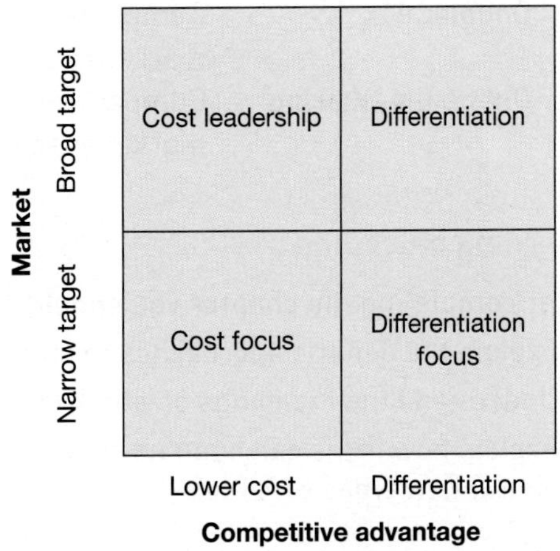

Source: Adapted from M. Porter, *Competitive Advantage*, Free Press, 1998, p. 39.

6.1.1 Achieving competitive advantage

Cost leadership

A firm that wants to attain a cost-leadership position in its industry needs to strive to fulfil the following two requirements:

- *Lowest cost position.* A firm that aims for a cost-leadership position has to be able to produce its product or service at substantially lower costs than its competitors. Lower costs enable the firm to earn profits even in an intensely competitive environment.
- *Benefit proximity.* Having the lowest costs, however, is not sufficient. In addition, a firm also needs to achieve benefit proximity relative to its competitors. This means that it must provide its customers with benefit levels that are still acceptable. If it is unable to do so, then it will eventually have to offer even lower prices, which reduces or eliminates the benefits gained through the low-cost position. For instance, through its unique direct sales model, Dell has established itself as a clear cost leader in the PC industry while, at the same time, achieving high levels of consumer benefit.

Several levers (including *scale effects*, *factor costs* and *learning effects*) help a firm to achieve a cost leadership position:

- *Scale effects* can reduce the individual unit costs of a product by spreading out fixed costs (i.e. the costs that do not depend directly on the number of products sold) over a large number of products (for a more detailed discussion of these issues, see Chapter 7 on the horizontal boundaries of a firm). For example, Amazon.com has made substantial investments in warehouses to organize the shipment of books and other products. As sales volumes increase, the warehousing costs that are incurred on each book continue to decline, which in turn provides Amazon.com with a significant competitive advantage. Other companies have had more difficulties realizing their cost-leadership strategy through scale effects. Webvan also wanted to attain cost leadership in its industry and decided to invest hundreds of millions of dollars to set up vast warehouses and logistics systems for its grocery deliveries. The company's managers made these investments assuming that they would be able to generate substantial scale economies. As it turned out, however, the number of customers remained much too small to justify the high investment, which eventually led to the bankruptcy of this Internet start-up (see the FT article 'Webvan's billion-dollar mistake', p. 24.)
- *Factor costs* represent a crucial cost driver, especially for retailing companies that act as intermediaries. The ability to bargain down input prices, for instance, through bulk purchasing can be an effective lever for lowering costs. Both low factor costs and scale effects are most likely to be realized through high volumes. Thus, a large market share in comparison to that of competitors is generally a prerequisite for being a low-cost provider. The goal of the online marketplace Covisint, for instance, is to pool the purchasing power of several car makers, thereby reducing factor costs.
- *Learning effects* can lower costs as a firm improves its efficiency over time, thereby reducing slack and wasteful activities.

Differentiation

Strategic position via a differentiation advantage can be achieved by providing comparatively more consumer benefit than competitors. The main questions that firms that strive for a differentiated positioning need to ask are: 'What creates consumer benefit?', 'What is unique?' and 'What cannot be imitated?' There are tangible sources for differentiation such as product quality, service quality and speed of delivery, and intangible sources, such as brand and reputation.

Similar to the cost-leadership approach, firms seeking a differentiated positioning need to ensure cost proximity to other competitors to guarantee superior value creation. This means that the cost disadvantage has to be small enough so the differentiation advantage can override it. It is not uncommon that firms overlook the need for cost proximity when they focus solely on providing the highest quality product in the market. Motorola's development of the Iridium phone is a prime example of a differentiation approach that did not pay close enough attention to costs.

6.1.2 Getting stuck in the middle

Porter argues that in order to have a unique and defendable competitive position, it is advisable to seek out one of the above two strategies.[2] The underlying assumption is that powerful strategies require trade-offs: high levels of quality usually entail high costs, while a cost-leadership strategy usually impairs the ability to provide above-average levels of consumer benefit. As a result, firms that try to be both a quality and a cost leader at the same time tend to end up getting 'stuck in the middle', a position that is characterized as neither low-cost nor differentiated.

Nonetheless, observers of Internet ventures have pointed out that there are firms, such as Amazon.com (see Strategy in Action 6.1) and eBay, that are outperforming competitors along both the price and the quality dimensions. They thereby effectively resolved the trade-off dilemma between quality and costs – an ability that is also called *outpacing*. From a theoretical perspective, the following factors can actually undermine this trade-off: (1) *the development of new technologies,* (2) *wastefulness* and (3) *economies of scale and learning effects.*

- *The development of new technologies*, as is the case with the Internet, offers innovative firms the opportunity, at least initially, to make large leaps on both the cost and the differentiation dimensions. Consider again the example of Amazon.com. Compared with other online book retailers, and also with most bricks-and-mortar book stores, it offers the most differentiated product and service, yet at the same time prices are highly competitive. This is possible because Amazon.com has been continuously improving its technology to lower costs.

  For instance, from 1999 to 2003, Amazon.com increased the volume-handling capacity of its warehouses threefold, which has helped to reduce warehouse operations cost from 20% of revenues in 1999 to 10% in 2003.[3] While this approach is possible as long as the technology is still evolving (and serious competition has not emerged yet), one may at least question its sustainability once the Internet and its associated back-end logistics become common-place.

  If Internet ventures can persistently have lower costs or offer higher value than their bricks-and-mortar competitors, then there will be two possible scenarios.

First, if both types of businesses (i.e. the online and offline business) continue to co-exist and serve different markets, then competition will take place between online Internet ventures. Second, if Internet-based firms (such as Amazon.com and eBay) turn out to be a substitute for bricks-and-mortar firms, then the latter will increasingly be driven out of business and the competition will start out all over again among Internet players. Either way, competition, and with it, the need to have a clear strategic positioning, is likely to increase.[4] Other more mature industries, where new technology developments are of only secondary importance, indicate that it then becomes necessary to seek a more precise positioning.

- *Many firms and industries are wasteful in their activities*, which makes it possible simultaneously to optimize quality while also reducing costs. When companies are highly inefficient they can make great strides without having to face the trade-off between quality and costs. Yet, at this point, we are also dealing not really with strategic decisions but with issues of operational effectiveness. During the Internet boom years, many start-up companies, such as the online fashion retailer Boo.com, were spending lavishly on marketing, parties and travelling (see the FT article 'Burning money at Boo', p. 21). Cutting costs in such situations is easy since there are no real trade-offs to be made.
- *Scale economies and learning effects* might allow a firm to generate significant cost advantages while still pursuing a differentiated strategy. They enable a firm to achieve both low costs (through scale effects) and a superior product offering.

In spite of the above factors, the trade-off between differentiation and cost is an important issue to consider in strategy formulation, because, more often than not, a firm cannot be excellent at everything it does.

STRATEGY IN ACTION 6.1

Amazon.com CEO Jeff Bezo's letter to shareholders

To our shareholders:

In many ways, Amazon.com is not a normal store. We have a deep selection that is unconstrained by shelf space. We turn our inventory over 19 times in a year. We personalize the store for each and every customer. We trade real estate for technology (which gets cheaper and more capable every year). We display customer reviews critical of our products. You can make a purchase with a few seconds and one click. We put used products next to the new ones so you can choose. We share our prime real estate – our product detail pages – with third parties, and, if they can offer better value, we let them.

One of our most exciting peculiarities is poorly understood. People see that we're determined to offer both world-leading customer experience *and* the lowest possible prices, but to some this dual goal seems paradoxical, if not downright quixotic. Traditional stores face a time-tested trade-off between offering high-touch customer experience on the one hand and the lowest prices on the other. How can Amazon.com be trying to do both?

The answer is that we transform much of customer experience – such as unmatched selection, extensive product information, personalized recommendation, and other new software features –

into largely a fixed expense. With customer experience costs largely fixed (more like a publishing model than a retailing model), our costs as a percentage of sales can shrink rapidly as we grow our business. Moreover, customer costs that remain variable – such as the variable portion of fulfillment costs – improve in our model as we reduce defects. Eliminating defects improves costs and leads to better customer experience.

We believe our ability to lower prices and simultaneously drive customer experience is a big deal, and this past year offers evidence that the strategy is working.

- First, we do continue to drive customer experience. The holiday season this year is one example. While delivering a record number of units to customers, we also delivered our best-ever experience. Cycle time, the amount of time taken by our fulfillment centers to process an order, improved by 17% compared with last year. And our most sensitive measure of customer satisfaction, contacts per order, saw a 13% improvement.

  Inside existing product categories, we've worked hard to increase selection. Electronics selection is up over 40% in the US alone over the prior year, and we now offer ten times the selection of a typical big box electronics store. Even in US books, where we've been working for eight years, we increased selection by 15%, mostly in hard-to-find and out-of-print titles. And, of course, we've added new categories. Our Apparel and Accessories store has more than 500 top clothing brands, and in its first 60 days, customers bought 153 000 shirts, 106 000 pairs of pants, and 31 000 pairs of underwear.

  In this year's American Customer Satisfaction Index, the most authoritative study of customer satisfaction, Amazon.com scored an 88, the highest score ever recorded – not just online, not just in retailing – but the highest score ever recorded in any service industry. In ACSI's words:

  > Amazon.com continues to show remarkably high levels of customer satisfaction. With a score of 88, (up 5%), it is generating satisfaction at a level unheard of in the service industry ... Can customer satisfaction for Amazon climb more? The latest ACSI data suggest that it is indeed possible. Both service and the value proposition offered by Amazon have increased at a steep rate.

- Second, while focusing on customer experience, we've also been lowering price substantially. We've been doing so broadly across product categories, from books to electronics, and we've eliminated shipping fees with our 365-day-per-year Free Super Saver Shipping on orders over $25. We've been taking similar actions in every country in which we do business.

  Our pricing objective is not to discount a small number of products for a limited period of time, but to offer low prices every day and apply them broadly across our entire product range ... To be sure, you may find reason to shop in the physical world – for instance, if you need something immediately – but, if you do so, you'll be paying a premium. If you want to save money and time, you'll do better shopping at Amazon.com.

- Third, our determination to deliver low price and customer experience is generating financial results. Net sales this year increased 26% to a record $3.9 billion, and unit sales grew even faster by 34%. Free cash – our most important financial measure – reached $135 million, a $305 million improvement over the prior year.

In short, what's good for our customers is good for our shareholders.

Jeff Bezos
Founder and Chief Executive Officer
Amazon.com, Inc.

Source: Excerpts taken from Amazon.com Annual Report 2002.

6.2 Opening up new market spaces

The generic strategy framework focuses on the traditional form of competition, which assumes a clearly defined set of competitors within an industry. The key performance measure is relative performance vis-à-vis competitors. As a result of this competitor-focused competition, improvements tend to be incremental through an increase of benefits or a decrease of costs. An alternative way to approach strategy development is to move beyond the sole industry focus and look for new market spaces across different industries.[5] Doing so allows a firm, at least temporarily, to break out of the cycle of ever-increasing competition within an industry, either by redefining the industry competition or by creating a new industry. The goal of this approach is drastically to increase consumer benefit while at the same time reducing price.

The concept of the value curve depicted in Exhibit 6.2 is used to illustrate how to redefine competition along different dimensions of benefit. In the book-retailing example, these dimensions include price, convenience, selection range, speed and face-to-face interaction. Obviously, on these dimensions, traditional and online bookstores offer varying levels of benefit. This is shown in Exhibit 6.2 where, on the vertical axis, a value of one refers to the highest level of benefit and a value of zero refers to the lowest level of benefit.

Exhibit 6.2 **The value curve provides insights into new market spaces**

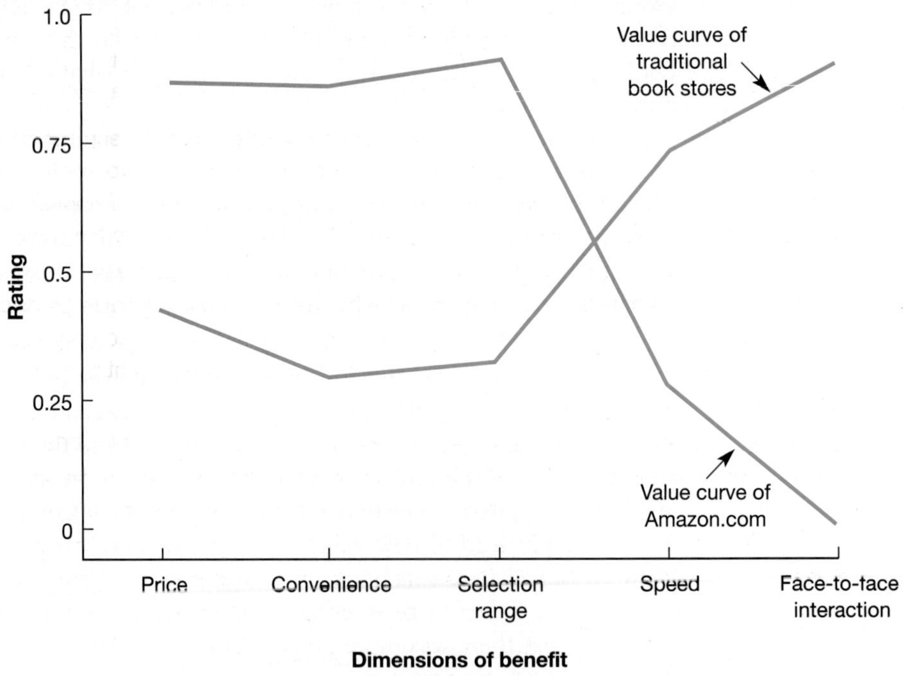

Source: Adapted with permission of *Harvard Business Review* [Exhibit 99105]. From 'Creating new market space' by C. Kim and R. Mauborgne, Jan.–Feb. 1999. Copyright © 1999 by the Harvard Business School Publishing Corporation, all rights reserved.

6.2.1 Looking outside one's own box

How can this type of revolutionary value creation be attained? A firm needs to analyze the way it wants to create value by 'looking outside the box', i.e. outside the standard business practices of its own industry. Doing so can lead to the discovery of uncovered market spaces between separate industries.[6] This can be done in different ways:

- *Looking across substitute industries.* The main question that needs to be asked here is how customers make trade-offs between different products (or services) that serve as substitutes. The goal is to determine why customers choose one product and not the other, and what criteria they use in making their decision. In the traditional business world, the most severe competition does not necessarily come from within the industry. Customers make trade-offs, for example, between using cash or a credit card, travelling by car or train, and using a pen or word-processing software. In the online world, customers make trade-offs between shopping online or going to the store, and between banking online or going to the bank branch. When Nordea Bank considered this trade-off, it found out that customers who go to the branch value the ease of use of over-the-counter banking. Thus, Nordea set out to develop a highly user-friendly online interface to offer the ease of use of a branch office with the benefits (and the lower costs) of an online channel.
- *Looking across strategic groups.* A strategic group consists of firms that produce the same type of products, for instance cars, for a certain customer segment. Firms usually compare themselves with competitors positioned in the same strategic group as themselves. Doing so usually does not lead to radically new insights since firms in the same strategic group tend to be similar in their product offerings. Looking across strategic groups means looking at what companies do that produce the same basic product for different customer segments, thereby finding out potential new ways of creating value. In car manufacturing, for instance, Mercedes, after analyzing lower-ranked strategic groups, developed the Smart car, which is offered at prices that compete with low-cost cars while still containing the Mercedes technology inside. Similarly, car manufacturers from lower-ranked strategic groups, such as Toyota, developed cars that possess many features of higher-ranked competitors while still maintaining a low price position.
- *Looking across chains of buyers.* The underlying logic of this perspective is that the person in charge of purchasing is not necessarily the one using the purchased product or service. For instance, the purchasing agent and the corporate user usually have different definitions of value. While price and the purchasing procedure are important for the procurement agent, users focus on ease of use. If a firm has previously considered only one of the two groups, taking on the other group's perspective might lead to new value creation. For example, the 12Snap case study featured in Part 4 of this book illustrates how the firm moved up the chain of buyers. While it first targeted end consumers with its online auctioning platform, it realized that there was more potential for value creation with corporate buyers of wireless marketing services.
- *Looking across complementary products and services.* Most products and services are not used in isolation, but instead need others to complement them. Computers,

for instance, require software in order to operate. Amazon.com recognized the power of complementary products when it launched its personalized book-recommendation service, which suggests customers a list of books that might be of interest to them based on their previous purchases. Nordea Bank wants to push the concept of offering complementary services even further through the use of a triggered database, which works as follows. When there is a change in a customer account – for instance, a large incoming money transfer, a change of address or a change in marital status – a trigger in the database is set off and informs the bank about this change, which then raises a number of questions regarding complementary products: what does this change mean for the customer in terms of financing, long-term payments, insurance and e-services? (See also the FT article 'Dell's move from PCs into complementary products'.)

FT

Dell's move from PCs into complementary products

If things go according to plan, Michael Dell could eventually become the Henry Ford of the information age. For a maker of desktop personal computers who founded his company, famously, in a University of Texas dormitory 20 years ago, this may sound unlikely. But the ambitions of Dell Inc are boundless – and thanks to a simple business idea that has proved highly adaptable, and a fearsome relentlessness, things at Dell have a way of going according to plan. Consumer electronics are about to provide what could well be the biggest test of the Dell way of doing business. Until now, the company has sold mainly to corporate customers: only a fifth of its sales in the US are to consumers, and much less than that elsewhere.

Yet executives at the Texas headquarters are now busy laying plans to take on some of the giants of the consumer electronics world. According to Kevin Rollins, the president and chief operating officer who has had much to do with its remorseless rise, there is no reason why Dell should not aim for 30–40 per cent of the global market for all the products it makes. Applied to the $800bn (£480bn) computing and consumer electronics markets that Dell now targets, that suggests it believes it could one day easily exceed the $160bn sales of General Motors. Mr Rollins says this is not a specific target that has been 'written down and pinned to the wall', but he does not shrink from the ambition.

Dell's simple but effective idea has been to sell standardised electronic products direct to customers, usually over the internet. That removes most of the research and development that is normally required, while also cutting out retailers and other middlemen.

Armed with the information it gets from taking orders directly from customers, Dell has gained two other powerful advantages. One is the ability to build products to match orders as they come in, slashing its inventory costs. The second is a highly efficient marketing machine that can adapt its message based on real-time results as orders arrive.

With its lower costs, Dell sets out to undermine profits in the markets it enters and destroy the margins that sustain its more entrenched competitors.

'Our goal is to shrink the profit pool and take the biggest slice,' says Mr Rollins. Consumer electronics companies, often with gross profit margins of more than 30 per cent, make an obvious target for this ruthless approach. 'Our gross margins are in the 18–19 per cent range: we don't need 40 per cent,' he says. A former ▶

partner from Bain, the Dell president applies the cool analytics and familiar jargon of the strategy consultant to this relentless expansion: search out the markets with the biggest 'profit pools' to be plundered; pick ones with close 'adjacencies' to those Dell already serves to reduce the risk of wandering into unknown territory; and apply its 'core competences' to conquering new ground.

As a textbook case of applying a proven and repeatable formula, Dell takes some beating. It used the formula to move from selling PCs to businesses to selling them to consumers. Next it followed its business customers into servers, then into storage hardware. Now it wants to follow consumers into other areas of electronics as well. It has started with products closely linked to the PC, such as MP3 digital music players and 17-inch flat-panel television sets that resemble computer monitors. According to Dell's rivals, success in the PC business in the US has disguised the fact that the company has found it harder to break into other products and new geographic regions. 'Dell's success is backward-looking,' claims Jeff Clarke, head of global operations at Hewlett-Packard.

According to Steve Milunovich, technology strategist at Merrill Lynch, not all markets are as susceptible to all aspects of the Dell approach as the PC business. Yet he adds that the company has shown great discipline in attacking only those areas where its strengths still give it a clear economic and operational advantage. Even most of the company's competitors concede that the shift in consumer electronics from analogue to digital technology plays to Dell's strengths. It is already the biggest purchaser of liquid crystal display screens and computer hard-drives, for instance, putting it in a strong position as these components come to play a bigger role in television sets and other household items. 'When you combine monitors and LCD televisions, we will blow away the consumer electronics guys,' says Mike George, chief marketing officer.

More importantly, Dell also benefits from the standardization that brings down the cost of components and removes the advantage once enjoyed by companies that invest in their own technology. As more of a product's functions come to reside in standardized components such as microprocessors and hard drives, the differentiation that comes from making new versions declines. The contrast with others is stark. Sony chief Nobuyuki Idei, for instance, told the FT two weeks ago that the Japanese company was putting a growing emphasis on proprietary components to differentiate its products. In the past four years, 70 per cent of Sony's investment has been in silicon chips.

While the digitization of consumer electronics may have played to Dell's core strengths, though, there are at least three things about the market that are likely to test its business model.

One is the fact that it will rely, at least for now, on manufacturing by other companies, reducing its ability to drive down costs. Also, the consumer electronics business is based on common products that are not configured individually for different customers: according to Mr Clarke, that removes one main advantages of Dell's build-to-order model, the ability to customize products for each buyer. Using outside manufacturers is also likely to mean the company 'will not be able to operate on inventory that is as thin as it is in PCs,' says Charlie Kim, a consultant at Bain. Company executives suggest that once manufacturing volumes reach a high enough level, Dell is likely to start production itself. Also, while the cost advantages may be less in 'back-end' activities such as production and sourcing, the real opportunity for Dell in consumer electronics lies in the 'front-end' marketing and sales area, says Mr Milunovich. 'There's a big chunk of money to be taken out of distribution,' he says.

Whether Dell can take advantage of this opportunity with its direct sales system will be the second big challenge. Retail stores suit consumer products best because they bring an instant mass market and let users test the look and feel of products, says Mr Clarke. That is particularly important for products such as television sets, which buyers want to see, or handheld devices, which they want to pick up, say rivals. Dell executives retort that similar

doubts were once expressed about its efforts to sell PCs online, and that its early sales of personal digital assistants suggest that consumers familiar with the quality and style of the company's PCs are willing to buy other items online too.

The third test will be whether the Dell brand and marketing approach can be adapted to suit the new market. High name-recognition helps, but will get Dell only part of the way. 'Everyone knows who Dell is – but it's still a PC-focused brand,' says Mr Kim at Bain. For a company that still relies heavily on selling to corporate customers, this will pose a big challenge. 'We're very humbled by the fact that there are virtually no other companies that are both consumer and enterprise brands,' says Mr George. He adds, though, that the basic attributes of the Dell brand – with its connotations of a certain level of value, quality and service – should extend across both types of market.

Overcoming obstacles such as these will stretch the Dell model in ways that it has never been stretched before. '[In the past] they've been able to push new products through their system without having to change it much,' says Mr Kim. 'Now, they're going to have to adapt.' Henry Ford, famous for designing the first system capable of mass-producing a standardised product, would have approved of what Dell has already done to the PC business. To do the same in the consumer electronics world, though, it will have to prove that it can constantly retune its business model without losing the power that has set it apart.

Talk to senior Dell executives and before long the phrase crops up: 'maniacal focus'. A ferocious attention to detail, applied to a tried and tested business model, accounts for the company's continuing edge, despite efforts by rivals to copy its methods. 'We don't let the paint dry on any process,' says Ray Archer, formerly a rear-admiral responsible for logistics in the US Navy and now in charge of Dell's supply chain. That is evident at the company's Texas assembly plant, where up to 25,000 machines are produced each day - more than double the plant's capacity when it was opened three years ago. Dell executives say they see no end to the continual adjustments that can be made, to speed the company's processes and bring down costs. Dell's way of doing business is no secret but the years of maniacal focus on fine-tuning the system make it difficult for others to catch up, says Mr Rollins. 'Why doesn't Kmart do what Wal-Mart does? It's built up over many years; it's in our DNA.'

Source: R. Waters, 'Dell aims to stretch its way of business', *Financial Times*, 13 November 2003.

- *Looking across functional or emotional appeal to buyers.* Products or services often focus either on functional or tangible characteristics (such as durability and breadth of choice) or on their emotional appeal, which is captured by the strength of the brand. Looking across boundaries by, for instance, turning functional products into emotionally appealing products can lead to a vast increment in the perceived consumer benefit. Take the example of the coffee house Starbucks, which has turned a functional mass product (i.e. coffee) into an emotional experience for its customers, thus being able to charge a premium price for it.
- *Looking across time.* By assessing early on the impact of future changes in the macro- or competitive environment, a firm can adapt its value-creation strategies based on the expected changes. For instance, Nordea realized in the 1980s the importance of electronic channels and swiftly introduced e-banking services. This helped Nordea to create substantial cost savings while at the same time significantly increasing customer benefit.
- *Looking across unrelated industries.* It is also possible to venture out and look across completely different industries to see how value is created there (see Section 2.3).

This is one of the messages that the case studies in this book convey. Looking across different industries requires creative leaps on your side, but it has the potential to create surprising insights. An insurance salesperson might ask, for instance, what lessons to take away from Ducati's exclusive Internet sales of new motorcycles directly to customers, and to what extent the learning can be adapted to the insurance business.

6.2.2 Pinpointing possibilities for new value creation

After looking across the above dimensions, different questions arise in the four areas listed below. Answering them opens up the opportunity for new-value creation potential.[7]

- *Eliminate.* Does what we do really create consumer benefit? If not, which components or features of our product or service should we eliminate? Even if a company has made a proper assessment of these issues at some point in time, then it should raise these questions again since buyers' preferences are dynamic by nature.
- *Reduce.* Where can we reduce our range of offerings? What costs us a lot of money but does not create benefit?
- *Raise.* Where should we raise the standard of products or services? Where can we increase benefit by expanding our existing offering?
- *Create.* What can we do that has not been done so far?

Tapping into hitherto uncovered market spaces provides firms with the opportunity not only to capture large parts of the market by taking away market share from competitors but also to expand the overall market size. Amazon.com, for example, did not just take buyers away from traditional bricks-and-mortar book stores. It also turned people who previously had not purchased many books into avid buyers through the depth of its offerings and the value-adding services such as the book reviews and personalized recommendations.

However, the move into new market spaces is not a one-time affair, since superior profit will last only as long as competitors do not move into this newly discovered market space. Just as it is with generic strategies, competitors will try to catch up if they believe that the new model promises attractive returns, thereby eroding profitability. The sustainability depends again on the uniqueness of the positioning and on how difficult it is to imitate this positioning.

SUMMARY

- This chapter focused on value creation in e-business. First, it reviewed generic strategy options for doing so. These options revolved primarily around cost leadership and differentiation strategies.

- Second, the chapter discussed the concept of being stuck in the middle, which refers to companies that focus on neither a cost leadership nor a differentiation strategy. They face the risk of not possessing any competitive advantage vis-à-vis more specialized rivals. However, there are also factors that can allow a firm to outpace its rivals by offering both lower costs and differentiation. These include the development of new technologies, wastefulness of companies, scale economies and learning effects.
- Finally, the chapter analyzed how firms can break away from traditional forms of competition and redefine their value proposition by opening up new market spaces. This can be done by looking across substitutes, strategic groups, chains of buyers, complementary products and services, functional and emotional appeal to buyers, time and unrelated industries.

REVIEW QUESTIONS

1 What generic strategies can a company use to create value for its customers?

2 What do 'benefit proximity' and 'lowest cost position' refer to?

3 What levers can a company use in e-business to create a cost or a differentiation advantage?

4 Why do companies end up being 'stuck in the middle'?

5 What are the factors that allow a company to pursue an outpacing strategy?

6 How can a company look for new market spaces outside its own industry?

DISCUSSION QUESTIONS

1 Illustrate each quadrant of the generic strategy options matrix through an e-business example.

2 Explain how the Internet can help a company to achieve a competitive advantage in the market place through (1) cost leadership and (2) differentiation. Illustrate each case through an actual example, other than those mentioned in this chapter.

3 Analyze how the Internet can help companies not to get 'stuck in the middle'. Refer to the Amazon.com letter to shareholders to explain your reasoning.

4 Discuss how an Internet venture can outperform its competitors along both the price and the quality dimensions. Provide some examples to support your arguments.

RECOMMENDED KEY READING

- M. Porter's book *Competitive Strategy*, Free Press, 1998, provides detailed accounts of different generic strategy types.
- B. Henderson emphasizes the importance of differentiation as a key element in strategy formulation when he compares strategy to biological evolution in 'The origins of strategy', *Harvard Business Review*, 1989, November–December, pp. 139–143.
- For an extensive discussion of market segmentation, see P. Kotler, *Marketing Management*, Prentice Hall, 2002, pp. 279–306.
- C. Kim and R. Mauborgne developed the concept of creating new market spaces by looking outside one's own industry in 'Creating new market space', *Harvard Business Review*, 1999, January-February, pp. 83–93. See also 'Value innovation – the strategic logic of high growth', *Harvard Business Review*, 1997, January–February, pp. 103–112.

USEFUL WEBLINKS

- www.dell.com
- www.smart.com
- www.starbucks.com
- www.toyota.com

NOTES AND REFERENCES

1 M. Porter, *Competitive Strategy*, Free Press, 1998, pp. 34–46.
2 Ibid, pp. 41–44.
3 F. Vogelstein, 'Mighty Amazon', *Fortune*, 26 May 2003, pp. 64–66.
4 For a discussion of the economic fundamentals, see S. Liebowitz, *Rethinking the Network Economy*, Amacom, 2002, pp. 115–117.
5 See C. Kim and R. Mauborgne, 'Creating new market space', *Harvard Business Review*, 1999, January–February, pp. 83–93, and also G. Johnson and K. Scholes, *Exploring Corporate Strategy*, Prentice Hall, 2002, pp. 132–133.
6 See C. Kim and R. Mauborgne, 'Creating new market space', *Harvard Business Review*, 1999, January–February, pp. 83–93.
7 A detailed discussion of this approach to value creation can be found in W. C. Kim and R. Mauborgne, 'Value innovation: the strategic logic of high growth', *Harvard Business Review*, 1997, January–February, pp. 103–112, and 'Creating new market space', *Harvard Business Review*, 1999, January–February, pp. 83–93.

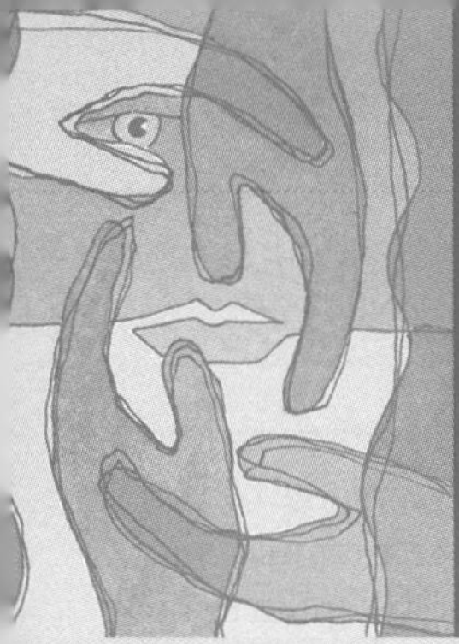

CHAPTER 7

Impact of the Internet on the horizontal boundaries of a firm

Chapter at a glance

7.1 Concepts of economies of scale and scope
- 7.1.1 Economies of scale
- 7.1.2 Economies of scope

7.2 Timing of market entry
- 7.2.1 Early-mover advantages
- 7.2.2 Early-mover disadvantages

Related case studies

Case Study	*Primary focus of the case study*
4 **Euro-Arab Management School**	Economies of scale
6 **Amazon *vs.* Bol**	Economies of scale and scope
8 **Tesco**	Economies of scale
1 **Minitel**	Early-mover advantage
5 **Alcampo *vs.* Peapod**	Early-mover disadvantage
26 **12Snap**	Early-mover disadvantage
22, 23, 24, **eBay**	Early-mover advantage

Learning outcomes

After completing this chapter you should be able to:

- Explain the concepts of economies of scale and scope.
- Understand the importance of the above concepts in the context of e-business.
- Recognize the advantages and disadvantages of being an early mover in e-business.
- Determine how Internet ventures can benefit from setting up virtual online communities.

INTRODUCTION

When looking at different industries, you will find that the average size of a firm varies drastically from industry to industry. At one end of the spectrum, a few very large companies dominate large parts of their industries. This is the case, for example, in computer chip production and car manufacturing. At the other end of the spectrum, hundreds of small product/service providers compete for customers. This is the case, for example, in the consulting and fashion industries, which are highly fragmented.

To a great extent, the two drivers that determine industry size are *economies of scale* and *scope*. Scale measures the quantity of goods sold, while scope measures the variety of products sold. There are two strategic questions that need to be addressed in the context of this chapter:

- How big should our firm be?
  - What size (scale) do we need to have to be able to operate profitably?
  - How much product variety (scope) should we offer?
- How quickly should we try to grow?
  - What are the crucial early-mover advantages in our industry?
  - What are the crucial early-mover disadvantages in our industry?

The next sections address the above two questions and their respective sub-questions. First, a close analysis of economies of scale and scope is offered. Then, the different types of early-mover advantages (and disadvantages) that a firm can exploit (or should avoid) are discussed.

7.1 Concepts of economies of scale and scope

7.1.1 Economies of scale

The basic concept of economies of scale is that as a firm increases its product output, it decreases its unit production cost.[1] Why is that so? In general, any production process consists of *fixed costs*, which do not change as output increases, and *variable costs*, which go up with an increase in output. Examples of fixed costs are software development, warehouses and machinery, while examples of variable costs are raw materials and postage for a package.

High economies of scale usually exist in production processes that have high fixed costs and low variable costs. As the cumulative production quantity increases, fixed costs are spread out over a larger number of products, thereby reducing the unit production costs (see Exhibit 7.1). Once existing production costs reach their constraints, fixed costs increase again as new facilities are required. Variable costs, on the other hand, increase proportionally with output. For instance, as a mail-order company handles more packages, postage costs increase proportionally.

Exhibit 7.1 Economies of scale lead to a decrease in per-unit costs as output increases, whereas diseconomies of scale lead to an increase in per-unit costs

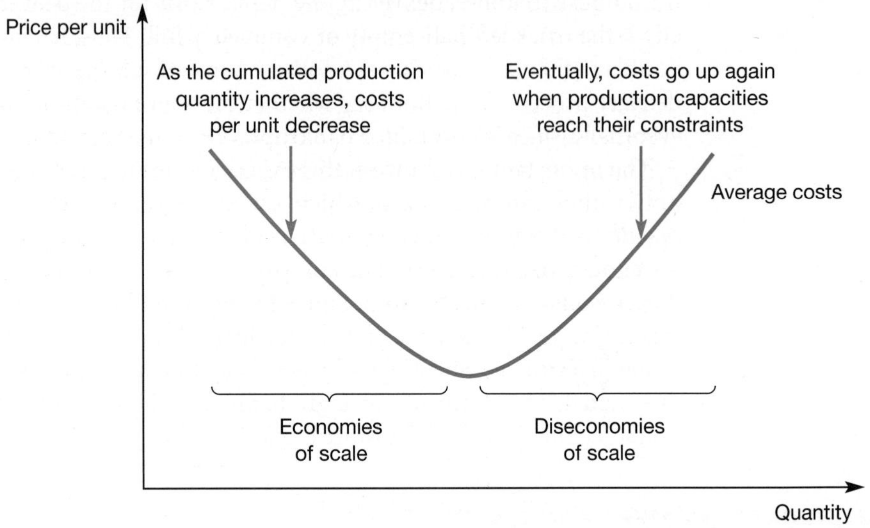

Due to extensive scale effects and efficient IT processes, WalMart in the USA can sell its products at massive discounts in comparison with competitors such as Ahold, Safeway and Kroger. For example, it sells Colgate toothpaste at 63% of rivals' prices, Tropicana orange juice at 58% and Kellogg's corn flakes at 56%.[2]

The expectation of high economies of scale was an important reason why Internet ventures were so popular with business managers and entrepreneurs and highly valued in the stock market. In the traditional book retailing and banking industries, for example, whenever a company wants to expand its offerings to new customer groups, it has to build new branches or sales outlets. Such physical infrastructure requires high capital investments, while providing only limited potential for scale economies.

Amazon.com and Advance Bank thought that they would be able to limit their investment to IT infrastructure, website management and call centres, and then scale up these facilities depending on customer demand. By doing so, they would not need to make any substantial additional investments, while still being able to provide a highly customized service (see also e-Business Concept 7.1).

The evolution of Internet-based grocery retailing and the different approaches taken by Webvan and Tesco.com illustrate further the concept of economies of scale. The strategy of Webvan relied heavily on the realization of economies of scale. It set up throughout the USA centralized and highly automated warehouses at a unit cost of $30 million. These were essentially fixed costs, since they were incurred independent of utilization. The expectation was that variable costs for each shipment would be very low, since the picking and packaging processes were highly automated, thereby reducing the need for expensive labour.

The business rationale was that Webvan would be able to position itself as a low-cost leader while still being able to deliver high levels of consumer benefit through the automated delivery process. It was thought that as customer numbers increased,

the warehouses would operate at capacity, which in turn would create substantial economies of scale. The latter were also crucial for the grocery-delivery process, whereby delivery trucks were filled at the centralized warehouse and then driven from house to house, delivering the items. Costs for the delivery varied only marginally if the truck left half-empty or completely full. Thus, having enough customers to be able to fill up the truck was another source of substantial economies of scale in the delivery process. We cannot say whether the above reasoning would have worked out eventually, since Webvan filed bankruptcy only one year after going public.

The important insight from this experience is that economies of scale are valuable only if they can be realized, which usually requires a large throughput. Tesco.com reached a different conclusion after analyzing the economies of scale potential of warehouse-based delivery. The company decided, contrary to the common wisdom, that it would be sensible to organize the order fulfilment and delivery process out of existing stores. By doing so, it was possible substantially to reduce the need for additional investment, which would have created high fixed costs. Furthermore, through this model, Tesco.com was able gradually to scale up its operations by adding additional regions on a store-by-store basis.

E-BUSINESS CONCEPT 7.1

Blowing up the trade-off between richness and reach

The trade-off between *richness* and *reach* focuses on the constraints that companies traditionally face when interacting with existing or prospective customers.[3] In this context, 'reach' refers to the number of people exchanging information. 'Richness' is defined by the following three dimensions:

- **Bandwidth**: this dimension refers to the amount of information that can be moved from sender to receiver in a given time. e-Mail requires only narrow bandwidth, while music and video require broad bandwidth. On a different level, face-to-face interaction provides a broad bandwidth. This offers an information exchange that goes beyond the content level by also including facial expressions, gestures and tone of voice. The telephone, on the other hand, is much more limited in its bandwidth since it cuts out the visual aspects of interaction. e-Mail is even more limited since it also excludes the voice component of the interaction.
- **Customization**: this dimension refers to the ability to address the needs and preferences of individual customers. For instance, a bank employee at a branch office can provide a much higher degree of customized service than a mass-mail advertisement.
- **Interactivity**: this dimension refers to the possibility of having bi-directional communication. Traditional one-way TV broadcasting has a very low level of interactivity. The Internet on the other hand is very interactive, since it allows for an almost instantaneous bi-directional exchange of information (see Exhibit 7.2).

Let us now turn to the historic trade-off between richness and reach. Traditionally, the communication of rich information required proximity to customers and also channels suited for transmitting such information. For instance, rich information exchange takes place in a bank's branch office, where customers talk in person to the bank agent.

Exhibit 7.2 The Internet can dissolve the trade-off between richness and reach

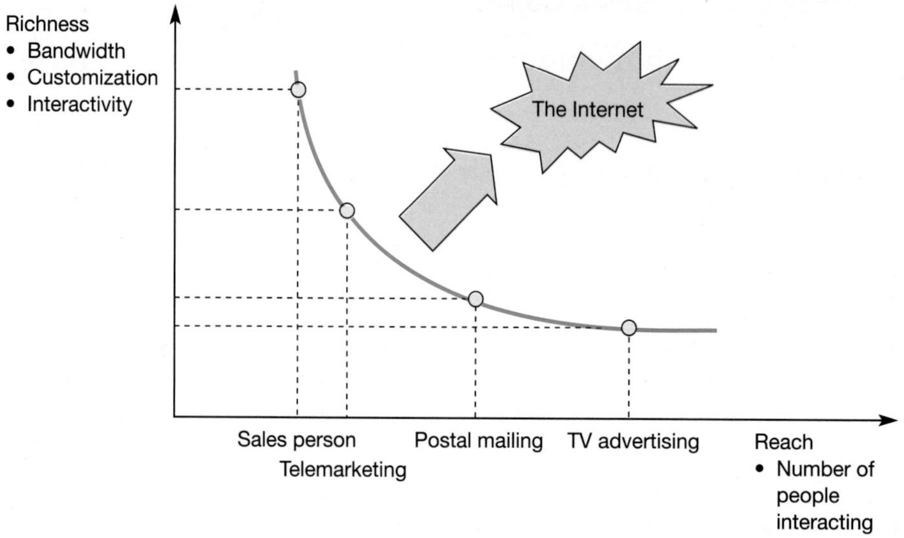

Source: Adapted with permission of Harvard Business School Press. From *Blown to Bits* by P. Evans and T. Wurster, Boston, MA, 1999, p. 24.

However, reaching a large number of customers used to come at the expense of richness, which was due to the limited bandwidth of most mass-media devices. This resulted in little customization and a lack of interactivity, as is the case, for example, with a TV advertisement. To achieve reach and richness at the same time used to require substantial investments in physical infrastructure and sales force. In other words, scale economies were very limited when a firm wanted to expand its customer base – i.e. expand reach – while still maintaining high levels of richness. Proof of this is the extensive branch network of universal banks through which banks can reach a large number of customers while serving each of them individually. As numbers of customers go up, so do the costs.

The main argument of the richness and reach framework is that two main drivers have blown up this trade-off between richness and reach. These drivers are: (1) *the increase in connectivity* made possible by the Internet and (2) *the development of common standards* such as the IP/TCP, HTML and XML. Connectivity and open standards have allowed firms to reach out to a larger number of customers, while at the same time ensuring a high degree of richness.

Does this concept stand up to reality? In many cases it does. A global auction place such as eBay would not have been possible in the pre-Internet days. Then, people could sell their used lawn-mowers and stamp collections at a local garage sale. There, they had very high levels of richness, where buyers could actually touch and try out the product; yet reach was very limited since, typically, it did not extend beyond the immediate neighbourhood. eBay has created a much more liquid market by connecting buyers and sellers across cities and countries, enabling them to share rich information about products as well as the reputation of buyers and sellers. Similarly, the Zshops at Amazon.com, where customers and other booksellers can sell their used books, also provide high levels of reach and richness. For setting up these business models, traditional assets such as a large sales force or an extensive branch network, which allowed for richness in the traditional bricks-and-mortar world, would have been more of a liability than an asset.

CRITICAL PERSPECTIVE 7.1

The limitations to blowing up the trade-off between richness and reach

Due to several reasons, the blow-up of the trade-off between richness and reach has not happened to the expected extent. On the bandwidth dimension, the Internet cannot replicate the richness of face-to-face contacts, which can only be achieved in the physical world. Nordea's branch network has by no means become obsolete. While the bank has rationalized its network, it still intensely uses the remaining branches to sell complex financial products that require a high level of trust.

Furthermore, the face-to-face interactions in a physical branch are also important for convincing more traditionally minded customers to start using the online banking service. For companies that do not operate physical branches, it is far more difficult to acquire customers, since they do not have a strong brand name or customer awareness, the building of which requires substantial investments and marketing efforts.

Even if direct personal interactions are not needed, physical branches can still be useful from a marketing viewpoint to help instil trust in customers who are inherently sceptical of pure online ventures. The latter do not offer a place for customers to turn to when problems arise.

Finally, expanding reach also poses the danger of undermining the strategic fit of a company's activities (see also Section 5.2.2). Thus, as a company expands its reach by adding new customers, it needs to ensure that by doing so it does not compromise its core activities.

7.1.2 Economies of scope

The logic behind economies of scope is similar to that of economies of scale. While economies of scale can be realized by increasing the production of one product type, economies of scope result from expanding the variety of products sold using the same R&D, production and delivery assets.

The main goal here remains the same: it is to spread fixed costs over a wider basis by adding new products or services to the existing offering. Economies of scope can be achieved by extending into different markets and sectors of an industry. Amazon.com, for instance, is trying to achieve economies of scope through the introduction of additional categories of goods on its website, thereby potentially increasing its share of the wallet of any given customer. Although it started out with just books, Amazon.com has since added new product categories, such as CDs, videos, electronics and clothes, using the same technology platform and delivery infrastructure.

So, economies of scale and scope should be considered within the context of a specific strategy and not pursued just for the sake of lowering costs. What always needs to be kept in mind is the type of value proposition that a company offers to customers. Adding scale by reaching out to new customer groups, or adding scope by offering new products, might help to reduce the cost position of a firm. In addition to costs, however, it is also important to consider the revenues that can be generated

after expanding into different customer segments or adding new product categories. Advance Bank, for instance, expanded its scale by moving into more price-sensitive customer groups, thereby threatening its overall value proposition. Thus, it is crucial to keep in mind that expanding economies of scope might compromise a firm's positioning and implicit trade-offs.

7.2 Timing of market entry

Early or first-mover advantages were a major driver for the Internet boom during the late 1990s. No potential entrepreneur or investor wanted to miss out on the profit potential that was promised to early movers. Thus, they all rushed into setting up or financing Internet start-ups, accepting large initial losses but expecting high return over time due to first-mover advantages.

Undoubtedly for some Internet start-ups, such as eBay, Yahoo and Amazon.com, early-mover advantages helped to pave the way for a dominant market position. In most cases, however, companies that started out early during the Internet boom have either gone out of business or were acquired by other firms that embraced the Internet much later.

Before moving into a more detailed discussion of early-mover advantages, we want to emphasize that a major difference between the Amazon.com-like ventures and the bankrupt Internet companies is that Amazon.com was not only early but also best in class. Since its launch in Seattle, USA, in 1995, Amazon.com has strived continuously to improve customer experience while simultaneously increasing operational efficiency, thereby reducing costs. In other industries, early movers were unable to compete with late entrants and eventually went out of business.

Similarly, Yahoo.com, eBay and other successful Internet start-ups managed to get the timing right and also deliver superior value on a continuous basis. Thus, while early-mover advantages are important, it is equally important that a firm maintains its quality or cost lead over competitors to keep its dominating position.[4]

In the following sections, we first analyze the different types of early-mover advantages and discuss how they impact Internet-based industries. Early-mover advantages can result from (1) *learning effects*, (2) *brand and reputation*, (3) *switching costs* and (4) *network effects*. We then analyze early-mover disadvantages, which are (1) *market uncertainty*, (2) *technological uncertainty* and (3) *free-rider effects*.[5]

7.2.1 Early-mover advantages

Learning effects

The idea of learning effects is that as output increases, a firm gains experience.[6] This allows it to conduct its business more efficiently, thereby reducing costs and increasing quality. When Amazon.com entered the German online book market in 1998, it was able to capitalize on its three years of experience in the USA where it had learned how to do online and offline marketing, make its website user-friendly and streamline its logistics and delivery processes.

Germany's Bertelsmann Online (BOL), on the other hand, entered the online book retailing business later and still had to go through the learning process, while Amazon.com kept improving at the same time. Ultimately, BOL was never able to provide a shopping experience that could compete with Amazon.com's, a shortcoming that contributed to the Bertelsmann Group's eventual decision to abandon BOL.

Brand and reputation

Companies that come to market first with a new product or way of conducting business impress consumers quite strongly, thus gaining reputation and brand awareness. Furthermore, media coverage creates free and strong publicity, which can enhance the brand and reputation. The business press is always interested in new business developments, successful or not, and covers them extensively. When Amazon.com went public in the middle of the 1990s, major business newspapers and journals wrote about it, thereby creating free and credible publicity. For instance, in 1996, *The Wall Street Journal* published a front-cover story on Amazon.com; on the following day, book sales on the company's website doubled.[7] Other early movers such as Yahoo.com and eBay have received similar levels of media coverage.

Being an early entrant in a market can also help to build up a strong reputation with customers, provided that the company can meet customer expectations during the first few contacts. This may seem obvious, but many Internet start-ups were unable to do so due to their badly designed websites and the lack of timely and reliable product delivery. More successful Internet start-ups such as Amazon.com managed early on to provide customers with a superior shopping experience. Customers who had a good experience with one provider are unlikely to switch to another. Therefore, any new competitor must provide a higher value than that offered by the early entrant in order to offset the uncertainty of being new and to induce the customer to switch over.

However, an established brand and reputation are no guarantee for a lasting success. The case of the search engine Google is an excellent example of how a newcomer managed to overcome the brand recognition and reputation of older and more established rivals such as Overture and AltaVista. Google was able to do so because it offered radically higher user benefits through higher speed and better search accuracy than all other companies. Without doing any serious advertising, Google quickly became the preferred search engine for millions of Internet users. (For more details, see the Google case study, p. 420.) In fact, Google has been so powerful that critics have launched a website (www.google-watch.org) to scrutinize the intrusive search techniques that Google uses.

Switching costs

Switching costs, also called self-compatibility costs, result from moving from one product to another. Even if a new product is superior to the one you already possess, you might still decide to keep the old product because of switching costs, which, in effect, create a weak form of lock-in. The expectation that switching costs on the Internet would be high was one of the main drivers behind the race for 'eyeballs' and 'clicks', whose levels determined the stock market valuation of many companies

(more traditional metrics such as price/earnings ratios were not considered to be suitable for Internet start-ups).

The common belief was that once customers got used to the set-up of a website, and once they had provided their customer information, they would not want to switch any more because of switching costs. This belief turned out to be fatal for many companies that spent heavily on marketing and customer acquisition only to find out that their customers were happily switching to other websites when a competitor offered better value.

Four sources of switching costs can be identified: (1) *switching costs from relearning*, (2) *switching costs because of customized offerings*, (3) *switching costs because of incompatible complementary products*, (4) *switching costs resulting from customer incentive programmes*. These are now defined:

- *Switching costs from relearning* are a result of having to get used to a new product. Users of software programs who switch from one provider to another often stick with the old product for as long as they can to avoid relearning costs. Consider the cases of Brun Passot and CitiusNet featured in Part 4 of this book. These companies had developed proprietary B2B software platforms to interact with their corporate customers. Once the customers got used to this software and had trained their personnel to use it, switching to a competitor would have entailed considerable relearning.

  Similarly, Internet users get used to the functionalities of a specific website and might not want to switch to another website. The more website-specific the knowledge is, the less likely it is that a person will switch to another website. In other cases, such as with search engines where the usage is easy and intuitive, switching costs are minimal. This was another reason that helped Google to become, within a matter of months, the most popular search engine. (At the same time, this lack of lock-in is also the greatest danger that Google faces today as competitors, such as Microsoft, start investing heavily into search-engine development.) As the Internet continues to mature and users become more accustomed to using it, relearning-induced switching costs are likely to decrease.
- *Switching costs because of customized offerings* result from a firm's ability to adapt a website to the specific needs and preferences of individual customers. For instance, as customers make purchases and search for books, Amazon.com learns about their preferences and is then able to make customized recommendations based on previous purchase patterns. If customers want to switch to a competitor, they first need to 'teach' their system through a number of purchases before the latter can provide them with the same level of customized offerings.
- *Switching costs because of incompatible complementary products* result from the inability to use the new product in combination with old products. An illustrative example of this was the introduction of the CD player, which rendered the existing vinyl record collection of music lovers worthless if they decided to switch to the new technology. Similar situations exist today as consumers are contemplating switching from the traditional video tape to the DVD or upgrading their PC, which might lead to incompatibilities with other hardware and software components.
- *Switching costs resulting from customer incentive programmes* occur when firms offer customers benefits in return for their loyalty. A prominent example here is

the frequent flyer bonus programmes offered by airlines, where passengers earn free upgrades or free tickets after having flown a certain number of miles with the specific airline. In the online world, ChateauOnline, for instance, awards frequent shoppers with webmiles to increase their loyalty.

For consumers, it is sensible to consider overall costs, including switching costs, when deliberating a new purchase. With hindsight, it is surprising that switching costs received so much attention during the Internet boom years, since the above mentioned types of switching had been around before. Therefore, there was really no need to gain market share as rapidly as possible and to invest heavily into new technology. History has shown that in most cases, if a new entrant offers a substantially better product, then it will most likely drive the weaker product out of the market, even if there are substantial switching costs.[8]

Network effects

Network effects are present when a product becomes more useful to consumers in proportion to the number of people using it.[9] There are two types of network effects: *direct* and *indirect*.

- *Direct network effects*. The strength of these effects depends directly on the number of users of a given device or technology that exhibits a network effect. An example of a product with strong direct network effects is the telephone. While a single telephone by itself is essentially worthless, it becomes very valuable when large parts of the population own a telephone and can use it to communicate with each other. Similarly, the Internet increases in value for the individual user as the number of users increases. Bob Metcalf found that the value of a network increases proportionally to the square of the number of people using it. Thus, if you double the number of participants in a given network, the value for each individual participant doubles, which leads to a fourfold increase in the overall value of the network.[10]
- *Indirect network effects*. Similar effects also apply with products that require complementary goods, such as video recorders and video games. Their value increases as the size of the installed user base increases, because more companies offer complementary products such as video tapes and games cartridges.

Whether a firm can benefit from network effects depends largely on the nature of the network. If network effects exist in a publicly owned platform that is open to all firms, then network effects benefit the whole community but do not accrue special benefits to any individual party. The telephone and the Internet, for instance, are open networks where the benefits of network effects accrue largely to customers. If, on the other hand, network benefits are specific to a particular website or community, then the operator of this site can reap benefits from these network effects (for a discussion of virtual online communities and network effects, see e-Business Concept 7.2).

In electronic commerce, a vivid example of network effects is eBay. On a stand-alone basis, this online auction platform is not very valuable at all; its value comes from the millions of users who post products for sale and search for products to buy. This results in a highly liquid market, where it is easy to match sellers and buyers.

Furthermore, the strength of the network effects is increased through the information that is posted about sellers and buyers, who both get rated by their peers on criteria such as timeliness of delivery, payment and quality of the products sold. eBay users who have received strong peer ratings are likely to continue using eBay because of their reputation, which makes it easier for them to sell items. eBay, as the operator of the community, can capture parts of the value, e.g. through fees for posting products.

Through its book reviews, Amazon.com has also created network effects. As more customers use its website and post their comments about books and other products, Amazon.com becomes more valuable to other customers, who can now retrieve information from many different reviewers about any given book. Other companies, such as ciao.com, have turned customer reviews into a complete business model, where they create a website that consists primarily of consumer ratings of different kinds of product.

In all of the above-mentioned examples, the value of the services offered by a firm increases with the larger number of users involved. Online file-sharing service providers such as Kazaa and Gnutella show similar network effects. The value of their service also depends largely on the number of users who are signed up and willing to allow other users to download music files from their computers.

From the individual customer perspective, switching from a network that is built around a large installed user base is sensible only if everybody else switches as well. It is possible, at least in theory, that a company with strong network effects can induce customers to stay in spite of the advent of new competitors with superior products. Users decide not to switch because they do not want to lose the compatibility with other users. If all users could agree to switch to the new product, however, then they would be better off to do so as well.

The logic of the Internet boom years was that if companies wanted to generate strong network effects, then they needed quickly to generate large market share, even if the costs for doing so were high. Part of this thinking was also that quality in comparison with competitors was not of central importance, because it was assumed that barriers to entry would increase as a result of network effects, making it difficult for newcomers to veer away customers. However, network effects, when they existed, often did not turn out to be strong enough to keep customers at one website. In fact, there are only very few instances, such as online auctioning, where network effects are sufficiently strong to have a substantial impact on user value.

Additionally, even if network effects are strong, this does not necessarily mean that consumers will not switch to a new, superior product. When choosing between an existing and a new product, customers do not look only at the existing situation; they also anticipate its future evolution – otherwise, CD players, for example, because of their need for CDs, would never have become popular. Thus, as has always been the case, in order to succeed new entrants need to demonstrate the superiority of their product and to give the impression among the general public that their product presents the most attractive features for the future.

E-BUSINESS CONCEPT 7.2

Virtual online communities and network effects

The concept of the *virtual online community* stems from the idea of moving a community from the physical marketplace to the digital market space in order to create network effects among participants.[11] To illustrate what a virtual online community is and what it looks like, we need to determine what purposes a community serves in the real world. Communities aggregate groups of people who have some kind of common interest (e.g. sports, cars, diseases, etc.). Communities in the physical world can be organized into clubs or teams, or they can be a loosely connected group of people. The common thread is, however, that people are drawn to communities because the latter provide an engaging environment in which one can connect with others and interact on specific interests.

The four essential purposes of communities are: (1) **communication**, (2) **information**, (3) **entertainment** and (4) **transaction.** The Internet can fulfil some, albeit not all, of these purposes as well as or even better than communities in the physical world. Building on these different purposes, it is possible to distinguish the following community types that focus on individual purposes:

- **Communities of interest and relationship** focus mainly on communication between users and sharing information. Users interact regularly on many different topics about their personal lives. Tesco.com, for instance, is partners with iVillage (www.ivillage.co.uk), the online community for women, which offers discussion forums on topics such as pregnancy, baby care, parenting, diet, fitness and relationships. (For more details, see the Tesco.com case study, p. 298).
- **Communities of fantasy** focus mainly on providing entertainment. In these communities, users, who in most cases are not aware of each other's identity, relate in a purely fictional setting while playing multiuser, Internet-based video games.
- **Electronic communities of transaction** are not communities in the traditional social sense; instead, they are focused primarily on selling and buying. eBay is the premier example of a transaction-centred community. Nordea's Solo marketplace, which brings together merchants from different fields, also has its main focus on transactions.

Virtual online communities have been trying to incorporate as much as possible from the above-listed community types into their own community, primarily to create a strong bond of loyalty between the community and its members. The underlying hope is that customers who see many of their needs met in a specific virtual online community are likely to build a high level of loyalty and to keep visiting this community over and over again.

The value of online communities depends primarily on the number of users visiting the website. Therefore, network effects are of utmost importance in the context of online communities. A firm that enters the market early can achieve a competitive advantage, since it has a head-start in building a critical mass of community members. These members provide the following benefits:

- **User-generated content**. By posting through the website classified ads and opinions on bulletin boards, community members can create a significant amount of user-generated content. The book reviews that customers write at Amazon.com provide additional information for other customers searching for books. Furthermore, the possibility of evaluating the quality of reviews by others further increases the value of user-generated content.

- **Data-mining.** Analyzing user activities provides insights about community members' needs, which in turn helps to refine offerings accordingly. eBay is constantly scanning the events and activities in its virtual communities, and adapts offerings and services accordingly.
- **Commercial content.** The larger the membership base of a community, the more attractive it becomes for advertisers as well as for product and service providers. The latter can place advertisements and hypertext links on the web page and offer discounted prices to community members.

The above features make a given community even more attractive for prospective members, who, upon joining in, add to this cycle of self-reinforcement (see Exhibit 7.3).

As always, creating value for customers is just one side of the equation. In addition, it is also essential to find ways to capture part of that value by charging customers (or other parties) for benefiting from online communities. Revenues in virtual communities are typically generated from the following sources:

- **Advertising** was the most popular source of revenues during the Internet boom days, since many firms were willing to invest heavily in online advertising. Many of these firms received vast amounts of capital from venture capitalists or through their initial public offerings (IPOs). Since their main aspiration was growth, they spent a large part of their budget on marketing and online advertising. Furthermore, although the effectiveness of Internet-based advertising had not been studied closely, its popularity, especially among online communities, was due to the inflated estimates of its impact. However, when the stock market collapsed and more detailed research showed that online advertising did not live up to its promise, the importance of advertising as a source of revenue declined significantly in comparison with other sources.

Exhibit 7.3 Virtual communities generate self-reinforcing effects once a critical mass of members is achieved

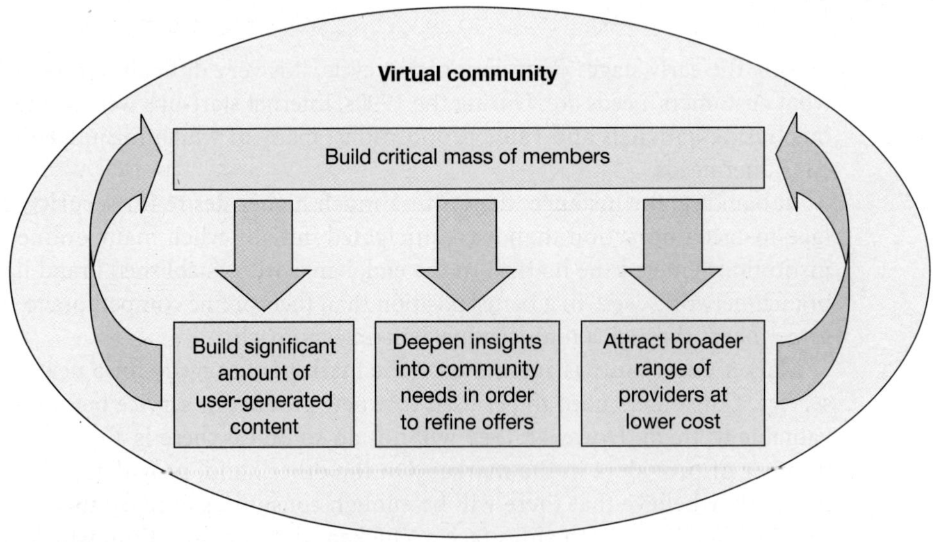

- **Usage fees** are charged for the actual time that a user spends in an online community. Many Internet service providers, such as AOL and Terra Lycos (see the case studies in this book), collect revenues from usage fees. However, the drawback of this approach is that it sometimes makes community members limit their usage as much as possible in order to reduce costs. This, in turn, also reduces the potential for other revenues coming from transaction or content fees.
- **Subscription** *fees* entail a flat monthly charge for the usage of an online community and have recently become more common. They are easy to collect, since they are based on a monthly charge and do not limit the time a user wants to spend in the community.
- **Content** *fees* are charged for the downloading of individual items such as a newspaper or magazine article or a song. In the early years of the Internet, content fees were difficult to charge because online payment systems were not developed enough to make payments for low-priced items (such as a newspaper article) economically viable. With the advent of online micro-payment systems (such as paybox.net, described in the case study, p. 570), charging content fees has become increasingly common.
- **Transactions** are at the core of communities that focus on the buying and selling of goods. The eBay community model, for instance, relies primarily on charging sellers a transaction fee for each transaction made. In the Solo marketplace, Nordea uses a combination of subscription fees and transaction fees for companies that sell through its marketplace.

7.2.2 Early-mover disadvantages

Firms entering the market early with a new technology do not necessarily achieve a competitive advantage over their rivals.[12] In fact, there are a number of reasons why a late entrant might actually accrue some benefits. These reasons are (1) *market uncertainty*, (2) *technological uncertainty* and (3) *free-rider effects.*

Market uncertainty

During the early stages of an innovation cycle, it is very difficult to establish clearly what customers' needs are. During the 1990s, Internet start-ups were trying out various business models and value propositions, many of which misjudged the actual consumer needs.

In banking, for instance, there was a much higher desire for security, trust and face-to-face interaction than was anticipated initially when many online financial institutions entered the market. In the end, banks with established brand names and branch networks were in a better position than their online competitors to fulfil customer needs through a multichannel banking approach.

Market uncertainty is aggravated if the market is not ready for a new product or service. Consumers need to get used to a new product or service before it becomes valuable to them. However, they will not do so unless there is already a sufficient number of providers in the market. On the other hand, providers will not invest unless they believe that there will be enough consumers to make their investment worthwhile. Thus, both sides face a 'chicken-and-egg' situation, which results in uncertainty regarding future developments.

Technological uncertainty

Betting on wrong technologies can be as problematic as overestimating market demand. In mobile electronic commerce, for instance, early adopters of the wireless application protocol (WAP) found that this highly praised technology did not deliver on its promises to create superior customer value. Instead, it proved to be very cumbersome to use, with a complicated 35-step procedure to configure a mobile phone for WAP access, long connection time (over 60 seconds) and the tiny screen space of a handset. As a result, market pick-up was much lower than expected.

When 12Snap launched its mobile auctioning service, the company did not know whether mobile technology with the small screens and clumsy keypads would be suitable for this type of business. As it turned out, it was not, and 12Snap had to overhaul its strategy completely by moving into a different business in order to survive.

Third-generation (3G) mobile phones are now facing the same type of uncertainty. European telecommunication firms bid billions of euros for the acquisition of 3G licences to be able to enter the market early. Yet it is still uncertain whether the investment in this specific technology will pay off.

Free-rider effects

Learning effects can constitute a first-mover advantage. However, if they cannot be kept proprietary, then competitors will benefit from them without having to make the same mistakes as the first-mover(s). In general, developing a market as a first mover is more expensive than just imitating it.

Many traditional bricks-and-mortar retailers who were initially hesitant to enter the online business and then embraced the Internet profited greatly from the failed experiences of the early movers. They leveraged their well-known brand and installed customer bases to overtake quickly their pure online competitors. Thus, for example, WalMart in the USA has become one of the largest Internet retailers by leveraging its strong brand name and synergies with its store network.

SUMMARY

- This chapter dealt with the impact of the Internet on the horizontal boundaries of a firm. It first analyzed the concepts of economies of scale and scope, where scale refers to the quantity of goods sold and scope measures the variety of goods sold.
- The chapter then analyzed the trade-off that companies traditionally needed to make between richness and reach, and how the Internet helps to dissolve this trade-off. Reach refers to the number of people exchanging information, while richness is defined by bandwidth, customization and interactivity.
- Next, the chapter discussed timing issues for market entry in e-business. More specifically, it analyzed the different types of early-mover advantages and disadvantages that an Internet venture can exploit (or should avoid). Early-mover

advantages include (1) learning effects, (2) brand and reputation, (3) switching costs and (4) network effects. Early-mover disadvantages include (1) market uncertainty, (2) technological uncertainty and (3) free-rider effects.

- Finally, the chapter discussed the rise of virtual online communities and their individual purposes (e.g. interest and relationship, fantasy and transactions). It also highlighted the self-reinforcing effects in virtual communities.

REVIEW QUESTIONS

1. Define the concepts of economies of scale and scope.
2. Why do companies need to make a trade-off between richness and reach? How can the Internet help dissolve this trade-off?
3. Outline the timing issues for market entry in e-business.
4. What are the advantages and disadvantages that early movers in e-business should exploit or avoid?
5. Define the concept of virtual online communities and their individual purposes. Explain the self-reinforcing network effects in virtual communities.

DISCUSSION QUESTIONS

1. Demonstrate through an actual example, other than those provided in this chapter, how the Internet has helped companies to achieve economies of scale and scope.
2. Illustrate each type of early-mover advantage through an e-business example. Discuss how an e-business venture can exploit early-mover advantage and whether they are sustainable over time.
3. Provide an e-business example for each type of early-mover disadvantage. Explain how an Internet venture can avoid these disadvantages.
4. Illustrate through an actual example each type of virtual community. Within the context of each example, discuss the extent of the self-reinforcing network effects.
5. Critically assess how the Internet helps companies to dissolve the trade-off between richness and reach. Defend your arguments through actual examples.

RECOMMENDED KEY READING

- For a discussion of economies of scale and scope, see D. Besanko, D. Dranove, M. Shanley and S. Schaefer, *Economics of Strategy*, John Wiley, 2003, pp. 72–95.
- A good discussion and critique of the effect of switching costs and network effects in e-business companies can be found in S. Liebowitz, *Re-thinking the Network Economy*, Amacom, 2002, pp. 13–48. C. Shapiro and H. Varian look at the same issues in *Information Rules*, Harvard Business School Press, 1999, pp. 83–226.
- S. Rangan and R. Adner discuss early-mover advantages in the context of electronic commerce, 'Profits and the Internet: seven misconceptions', *Sloan Management Review*, 2001, Summer, pp. 44–46.
- P. Evans and T. Wurster developed the concept of the trade-off between richness and reach in *Blown to Bits*, Harvard Business School Press, 1999, pp. 23–38.

USEFUL WEBLINKS

- www.aol.com
- www.ciao.com
- www.google-watch.org
- www.ivillage.co.uk
- www.tesco.com
- www.walmart.com
- www.yahoo.com

NOTES AND REFERENCES

1 A detailed discussion of the concepts of economies of scale and scope is contained in D. Besanko, D. Dranove, M. Shanley and S. Schaefer, *Economics of Strategy*, John Wiley, 2003, pp. 72–95.

2 'Make it cheaper, and cheaper', *The Economist*, 13 December 2003, pp. 6–7.

3 P. Evans and T. Wurster developed the richness and reach concept in their book *Blown to Bits*, Harvard Business School Press, 1999, pp. 23–38.

4 S. Rangan and R. Adner discuss the pitfalls of early-mover advantages in the Internet world in the article 'Profits and the Internet: seven misconceptions', *Sloan Management Review*, 2001, Summer, pp. 44–46.

5 For different types of early mover advantages, see D. Besanko, D. Dranove, M. Shanley and S. Schaefer, *Economics of Strategy*, John Wiley, 2003, pp. 438–446. W. Boulding and M. Christen point out that there are also important early-mover disadvantages in 'First-mover disadvantage', *Harvard Business Review*, 2001, October, pp. 20–21.

6 The importance of learning and experience first received attention through the development of the experience curve: B. Henderson, 'The experience curve reviewed', in C. Stern and G. Stalk (eds.), *Perspectives on Strategy*, John Wiley, 1998, pp. 12–15.

7 J. Cassidy discusses the story of Amazon in *Dot.con*, Perennial, 2003, pp. 135–150.

8 S. Liebowitz refutes the frequently cited QWERTY keyboard and VHS/Betamax examples in *Re-thinking the Network Economy*, Amacom, 2002, pp. 47–48.

9 A good discussion and critique of the impact of network effects on e-commerce companies can be found in S. Liebowitz, *Re-thinking the Network Economy*, Amacom, 2002, pp. 13–48. S. Rangan and R. Adner also discuss network effects in e-commerce in 'Profits and the Internet: seven misconceptions', *Sloan Management Review*, 2001, Summer, pp. 44–46.

10 George Gilder coined the term 'Metcalf's Law' in 1993. The article can be found at www.discovery.org

11 For a condensed discussion of the concept of virtual communities, see J. Hagel and A. Armstrong, 'The real value of on-line communities', *Harvard Business Review*, 1996, May–June, pp. 134–141. The same authors also wrote a more extensive book on the topic, *Net Gain*, Harvard Business School Press, 1997.

12 For a detailed discussion of first-mover disadvantages, see M. Liebermann and D. B. Montgomery, 'First-mover (dis-)advantages', *Strategic Management Journal*, 1998, Vol. 19, No. 12, pp. 47–49.

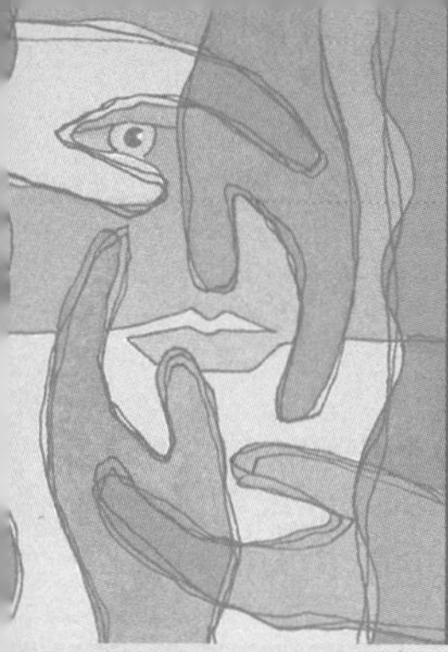

CHAPTER 8

Impact of the Internet on the vertical boundaries of a firm

Chapter at a glance

Related case studies

	Case Study	*Primary focus of the case study*
4	**Euro-Arab Management School**	'Make-or-buy' decisions in e-learning
6	**Amazon *vs.* BOL**	'Make-or-buy' decisions in retailing
10	**Advance Bank**	'Make-or-buy' decisions in financial services
14	**Ducati *vs.* Harley**	'Make-or-buy' decisions in manufacturing

Learning outcomes

After completing this chapter you should be able to:

- Describe the spectrum of 'make-or-buy' options.
- Identify the main reasons that favour 'make' decisions.
- Identify the main reasons that favour 'buy' decisions.
- Describe the concept of value-chain deconstruction and the role of the Internet within this concept.
- Understand the concept of unbundling the corporation.

INTRODUCTION

While horizontal boundaries determine the size of a firm, a firm's vertical boundaries focus on the degree of integration of individual activities in a firm's value chain. The main question is: 'Which activities within the value chain should a firm perform by itself and which ones should it outsource to external providers?'

Consider the merger of AOL and Time Warner in 2000. The two firms merged because they wanted to create an integrated value chain in the media industry that spanned from content production to content delivery. Substantial synergies were expected from this merger. As it turned out, these synergies proved difficult to realize and many critics argue that it would have been better to keep the two firms separate.

From a more historic perspective, let us consider the evolution of the PC industry. In 1985, IBM, which then dominated this industry, conducted all the activities of the value chain, from the development of micro-processors, to marketing, sales and distribution. As a result of open standards and the increased use of mass production, this integrated value chain became more fragmented over time. Today, as shown in Exhibit 8.1, companies focus on (and dominate) individual parts of the PC industry value chain.

The above-mentioned examples illustrate how companies can choose from a variety of options available to them for making a product or service. They can decide to perform some activities internally ('make') or 'purchase' them on the open market ('buy'). The different options that a companies can choose from are as follows:

- *Market transactions* entail the purchase from an external provider on an individual one-by-one contractual basis.
- *Long-term contracts* entail the purchase from an external provider on a contractual basis, spanning over an extended period of time.
- *Alliances* entail the close co-operation of two separate firms that join up in the production of a certain product or service.
- *Parent/subsidiary constellations* entail the set-up of a distinct firm that operates separately from, yet under the auspices of, the parent company.
- *Internal production* entails a process that is managed completely internally, without any outsourcing to external providers.

At one end of the spectrum, firms that rely heavily on input from external providers include car manufacturers, such as DaimlerChrysler and BMW, and sports-goods manufacturers, such as Nike and Adidas. Another example is Dell, which concentrates on tightly integrating different suppliers to deliver the components for the PCs that it assembles and sells. At the other end of the spectrum, highly integrated firms, such as Procter & Gamble and Nestlé, perform most functions internally, ranging from R&D and production to marketing and distribution.

Many e-business analysts have argued that the increased use of the Internet makes it more attractive to rely more heavily on external providers and perform fewer activities internally. In order to assess this claim, we need to analyze the different factors that favour 'make' and 'buy' decisions and determine how the Internet affects them.

Exhibit 8.1 During the 1990s, the PC industry became increasingly fragmented

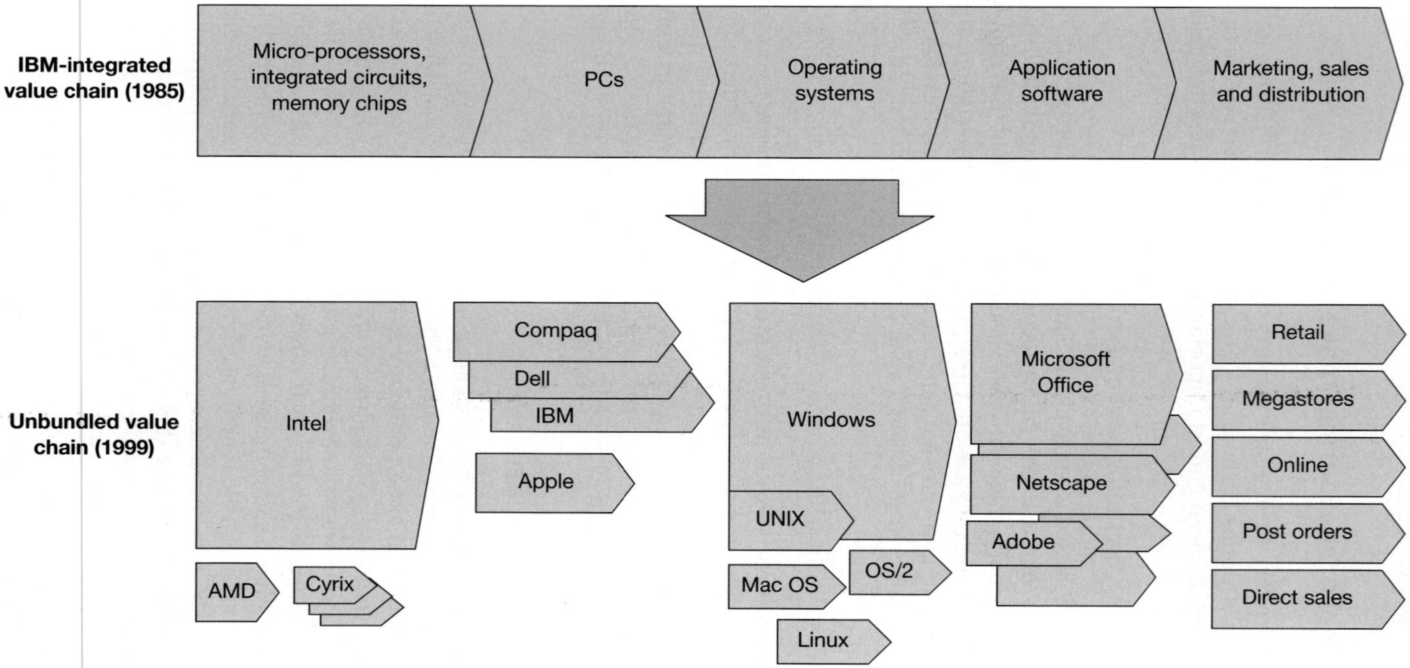

Source: Adapted from D. Heuskel, *Wettbewerb jenseits von Industriegrenzen*, Campus, 1999, p. 53.

8.1 Reasons determining 'make-or-buy' decisions in e-business

8.1.1 Reasons favouring 'make' decisions

There are three main reasons that favour performing activities in house (i.e. the 'make' option). These are (1) *a strong linkage between activities*, (2) *confidentiality of information* and, most importantly, (3) *high transaction costs.*

Strong linkage between activities

We discussed extensively in Section 5.2.2 the importance of linkage between activities. When it is crucial for a company to integrate tightly different activities of its value chain, these activities should be performed internally if that is the only way to realize the integration. Creating close links throughout the value chain can help a firm either to provide superior customer benefit through reinforcement of activities or to lower costs through an optimization of efforts.

Confidentiality of information

Confidentiality of information is another reason that can lead a firm to perform activities internally. The sharing with external providers of critical information about R&D processes, customer information and production methods may undermine the firm's competitive advantage. Microsoft, for instance, refuses to provide other software-developing firms with the source code for its software because it fears that doing so would eventually result in a leak in the public domain.

High transaction costs

Most important, however, are usually the costs relating to the actual transaction process, also called transaction costs.[1] These consist of costs that a firm incurs when it relies on the market to make a product or provision of a service. Transaction costs appear because buyers and sellers usually have diverging interests, which make them act opportunistically. The seller wants to maximize profits by charging as high a price as possible, while the buyer wants to keep costs down by paying as little as possible. To avoid *opportunistic behaviour*, a company needs to invest time and effort to search for an appropriate business partner, negotiate conditions, and monitor and enforce the contract.

Which factors determine whether a firm acts opportunistically, and how does the Internet influence these factors? We will now look at two main factors that drive opportunistic action and, therefore, strongly influence transaction costs: these are *asset specificity* and *information asymmetry.*

- *Asset specificity* refers to the investments that need to be made in order to set up a transaction between two or more parties. Before the advent of the Internet, companies that wanted to engage in electronic transactions with one another had to invest in proprietary electronic data interchange (EDI) systems, which were costly

to install and could generally be used with only a very limited number of partners. Once such a system was in place, the parties were locked into the agreement because of the high investment and the limited choice of partners.

Imagine the case of the tyre manufacturer Tire Inc., which sources rubber from the rubber producer Rubber Corp. In order to optimize the production flow, Tire Inc. has agreed to install an EDI system that connects it to the IT system of Rubber Corp. The two companies draw up a contract and delivery takes place as planned. Subsequently, Rubber Corp. informs Tire Inc. that it needs to raise prices by 20%, knowing that Tire Inc. needs to keep the business relationship going to recover the investment in the EDI system. Tire Inc. might decide to accept the raise, or to take Rubber Corp. to court, or to terminate the relationship altogether. In any case, there will be substantial costs involved for Tire Inc. Knowing what might await it next time, Tire Inc. decides to produce the rubber internally, thereby avoiding the transaction costs.

Now, let us think about what this scenario might look like today. Through the Internet, Tire Inc. would connect to the system of Rubber Corp., thereby substantially reducing the costs for specific IT investments. Rubber Corp. at the same time would not be inclined to try to raise prices because it knows that Tire Inc. could easily switch suppliers. Therefore, transaction costs are now much lower due to lower asset specificity, which makes it more likely that Tire Inc. outsources activities to external providers.

- The second important factor that influences transaction costs is the degree of *information asymmetry* between the involved parties. Often, a buyer lacks vital information about a seller because it does not know the track record of the seller, and vice versa. If a buyer can hide past cases of fraud, then it is much more inclined to act opportunistically in the future and to try to commit fraud again.

  This type of information asymmetry is also easier to remedy through the Internet. Through virtual communities, such as those at eBay, buyers can rate the quality of sellers, and sellers can rate the reliability of buyers. This has a twofold effect. First, any buyer who is considering a purchase can base its decision on the track record of the seller. If a seller has hundreds of positive ratings, then it is very likely that it will also fulfil its promises during the next transaction. Second, as the number of positive ratings increases, sellers are more likely to maintain their high standards in order to protect their reputation. Thus, a self-reinforcing virtuous cycle is set in motion through the rating system, which deters opportunistic behaviour, thereby also reducing transaction costs.

Because of the lower asset-specific investment and the improved information, it is sensible to assume that the Internet reduces transaction costs. This should, in turn, make it more attractive to outsource parts of the value chain to external providers.

8.1.2 Reasons favouring 'buy' decisions

Today, many companies rely heavily on sourcing parts and services from external suppliers. There are four main reasons for doing so: (1) *high economies of scale*, (2) *high capital requirements*, (3) *specialized know-how* and (4) *higher efficiency of the open markets*.

High economies of scale

A firm that produces only for its own use usually requires a much smaller quantity than a supplier that produces for many different firms. Therefore, the external supplier has the possibility to reap much larger economies of scale than the individual firm that decides to make the part by itself. Dell, for instance, could decide to build its own factories for producing the micro-chips that it uses in the PCs it sells. However, the investment required for doing so internally is too large, relative to the expected output, and would make every chip produced prohibitively expensive. Therefore, Dell sources the chips from specialized manufacturers, such as Intel and AMD, which also supply many other computer manufacturers with chips. In fact, Dell has chosen this approach with almost all its inputs. Since it is a large customer for most of its suppliers, it is in a position to capture large parts of the economies of scale in the form of low prices.

High capital requirements

If the production of a specific part requires a major upfront investment, such as the construction of a specialized plant, then it may be sensible to find an external supplier who already has the required facilities in place. Doing so might be more expensive on a per-unit basis, yet it reduces the overall risk. Webvan, for instance, might have fared better if it had relied more on external suppliers when it set up its online grocery business. Instead, Webvan organized by itself all parts of the value chain and invested heavily in a custom-built IT platform, highly automated warehouses and a large fleet of delivery trucks, only to find out that the business model did not work the way it was anticipated. The expensive IT platform, the warehouses and the trucks were later sold during the bankruptcy proceedings for a fraction of their original prices.

Specialized know-how

Specialization effects are likely to be related to economies of scale. A firm that produces large quantities of goods also tends to build up over time substantial know-how regarding R&D processes and production methods. This specialized know-how should then lead to lower-cost production and higher quality standards, or both. Consider Amazon.com's delivery system. The company owns large warehouses to organize the logistics of incoming and outgoing shipments. Yet, for the actual shipment process, Amazon.com relies on specialized logistics firms, such as UPS, DHL and Federal Express, which possess strong experience in logistics and delivery and have optimized their processes over time.

Higher efficiency of the open markets

Finally, external suppliers are often more efficient because they are facing permanent competitive pressure from other companies within their specific industry. If performed internally, the production of a sub-product or the provision of a service can become highly inefficient over time because of a lack of control, thereby causing unnecessary costs. External firms producing that same product, on the other hand,

do not enjoy the same type of 'protection' and are therefore forced constantly to maintain high levels of efficiency, thus keeping down costs.

8.2 Value-chain deconstruction through the Internet

The concept of *deconstruction* builds on the foundations of transaction cost theory.[2] The fundamental idea of this concept is that traditionally integrated value chains within industries get unbundled and are reconfigured as a result of two main developments. These are (1) the separation of the *economics of things (physical goods)* and the *economics of information (digital goods)* and (2) the *blow-up of the trade-off between richness and reach.* (The limitations of the concept of deconstruction are discussed in Critical Perspective 8.1.)

Let us take a closer look at the first point. How do the economics of things and information differ? When physical goods, such as a chair or a table, are sold, ownership is transferred from the seller to the buyer. Informational goods, on the other hand, can be used many times, with low (if any) incremental costs. Take a newspaper article that is published online. It does not impact costs much if it is read by 10 or 10 000 people. Furthermore, physical goods are location-dependent. They cannot be moved easily, and they often take up substantial space. Information, on the other hand, can be sent across the globe quickly and requires only disk storage space on a computer server.

In the past, the two different types of economics were combined within a unified business model, which led to compromises. Consider the example of a used-car dealership. What are the reasons for customers coming to used-car dealerships? They want to find out about different choices, go for a test drive, get an attractive financing scheme, and receive a warranty and maintenance services.

In order to provide the customer with as much information as possible about products, it makes sense to put many cars on display, so that customers can easily compare between different models and make a more informed purchasing decision. On the other hand, since the information about cars is held in the physical car, maximizing the number of cars in the showroom conflicts with the desire to keep down costs by limiting showroom space and inventory. A further compromise is that, for sales purposes, it is sensible to build large car dealerships in central locations to maximize the number of cars on display. For servicing purposes, however, it would be much better to have small repair shops located near the car owners' homes.

The Internet auction eBay has effectively deconstructed the used-car business, thus becoming the largest used-car dealership in the USA. Like a traditional car dealer, eBay tries to offer as wide as possible a choice of cars, but unlike physical dealers it is not constrained by physical space on a car lot. eBay acts as an integrated market maker for sellers, thereby offering unsurpassed choice. Through the deconstruction and reconfiguration of the value chain with external partners, eBay can offer higher benefits to consumers at reduced costs.

How does it work? Sellers wanting to sell their car on eBay face the problem of not being able to convince potential customers of the quality of their car. To remedy this,

eBay works in partnership with the certified vehicle inspection chain PepBoys, which inspects the car, for which the seller can download a coupon from the eBay website and then post this information on the eBay site. The information about the state of the car is even better than in the traditional marketplace, where the buyer, who normally does not know much about cars, has to inspect the car themselves. eBay has also partnerships with financing companies and with neutral third-party payment operators, who, to prevent fraud, act as a proxy and send the payment from buyer to seller.

Overall, this deconstruction leads to a development called *de-averaging of competitive advantage.* Here, a firm picks out individual parts of the value chain and decides to compete on only one dimension through larger scale, higher degrees of specialization, or other factors that contribute to competitive advantage, while outsourcing other activities to external providers.

CRITICAL PERSPECTIVE 8.1

The limitations of deconstruction and unbundling

How should we evaluate the applicability of the 'unbundling' concept? Its proposition is similar to that outlined in the concept of deconstruction.[3] Both state that different parts of the value chain, here called businesses, should be reconfigured so that the trade-offs and compromises inherent in integrated firms can be resolved. The examples of eBay and Dell, where deconstruction has worked out very well, thereby rewarding the two companies with high profitability, need to be contrasted with other companies engaged in e-business where this type of deconstruction has been more limited. There are different reasons why deconstruction might not be appropriate for a firm:[4]

- **Lack of linkage between externally and internally performed activities**. Amazon.com, for instance, initially set out with a highly deconstructed business model in which the focus rested on the front end of interacting with the customer. Back-end warehousing and logistics were to be left to external suppliers. However, integrating the front end with external logistics providers turned out to be more cumbersome than anticipated, and thus it became impossible to deliver the promised customer benefit in terms of speed of shipment, quality and reliability. Amazon.com therefore decided to reintegrate parts of the value chain by setting up a proprietary warehousing system.
- **Increased convergence and ease of imitation**. When key steps of the value chain that previously constituted substantial sources for competitive advantage are outsourced to external providers, this creates the risk that competitors turn to the same vendor, thereby making purchased inputs more homogeneous. Doing so decreases possibilities for differentiation and increases price competition. Furthermore, it also lowers barriers to entry because new entrants only need to assemble purchased inputs rather than build their own capabilities.

8.3 Unbundling the corporation through the Internet

The concept of 'unbundling the corporation' is very similar to the deconstruction approach.[5] It also argues that companies need to rethink the traditional organization and unbundle their core businesses (or core activities) as a result of falling transaction costs made possible by the Internet. (The limitations of this concept are discussed in Critical Perspective 8.1.)

The 'unbundling' concept recognizes that a corporation consists of the following three core businesses (see Exhibit 8.2):

- *Customer relationship management*, which focuses on the interfaces between the firm and its customers: these interfaces include activities such as marketing, sales and service. Their common goal is to attract and retain customers. For example, the branchless Advance Bank focused on the customer-relationship-management business while outsourcing its product innovation to external financial providers and minimizing its infrastructure requirements through its direct banking approach.
- *Product innovation*, which focuses on R&D but also includes activities further down the value chain such as market research to find out about consumers' preferences: the globally operating firm IDEO, which designs products and services for large corporate customers, is a prominent example of a company focusing primarily on the product innovation business.

Exhibit 8.2 The traditional corporation can be unbundled into three distinct businesses

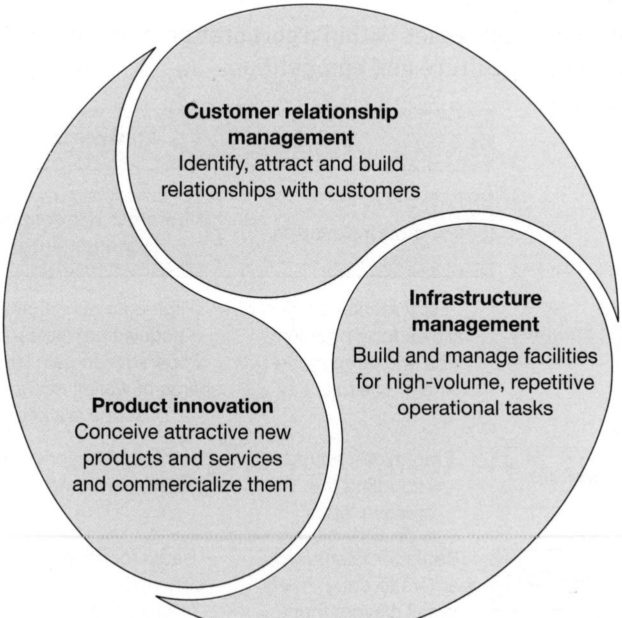

Source: Adapted with permission of *Harvard Business Review* [Exhibit 99205]. From 'Unbundling the Corporation' by J. Hagel and M. Singer, Mar.–Apr. 1999. Copyright © 1999 by the Harvard Business School Publishing Corporation, all rights reserved.

- *Infrastructure management*, which focuses on logistics and support functions: this business includes the building and management of physical facilities, such as plants, retail outlets and truck fleets, for high-volume production and transportation processes. Through its extensive physical retail network, Tesco.com is very strongly involved in managing the infrastructure business.

The reason why the different businesses conflict with one another is that they have differing economic, cultural and competitive imperatives (see Exhibit 8.3):

- *Economics.* In product innovation, speed, which allows a firm to introduce new products sooner than the competition, is the most valued asset. However, in the customer relationship and infrastructure management business, what matters most are, respectively, economies of scope (getting a large share of the consumer wallet) and economies of scale.
- *Culture.* Product innovation focuses on creative employees who are responsible for developing new ideas. This is mirrored in flexible pay schemes and work schedules that are designed to make employees content. The customer-relationship business, on the other hand, focuses on the external customers, while the focus of the infrastructure business is on costs. To operate large-scale operations efficiently, it is necessary to create a culture of standardization, predictability and efficiency.
- *Competition.* For a successful product innovation, it is essential to gain access to skilful and talented employees. Developing innovations often does not require large start-up costs, as is illustrated by the founders of some of the e-commerce success stories (e.g. Amazon.com, eBay, Yahoo!). Therefore, in product innovation, there are usually many small players, of which few will succeed. In both of the other businesses, however, competition tends to be driven by economies of scope and/or scale, which leads to a consolidation where a few big players dominate the competition.

Exhibit 8.3 Different businesses within a corporation have different imperatives regarding economics, culture and competition

		Businesses		
		Product innovation	**Customer relationship management**	**Infrastructure management**
Imperatives	**Economics**	Early market entry allows for a premium price and large market share; speed is key	High cost of customer acquisition makes it imperative to gain large shares of wallet; economies of scope are key	High fixed costs make large volumes essential to achieving low unit costs; economies of scale are key
	Culture	Employee-centred; coddling the creative 'stars'	Highly service-oriented; 'customer comes first'	Cost-focused; stress on standardization, predictability, efficiency
	Competition	Battle for talent; low barriers to entry; many small players thrive	Battle for scope; rapid consolidation; a few big players dominate	Battle for scale; rapid consolidation; a few big players dominate

Source: Adapted with permission of *Harvard Business Review* [Exhibit 99205]. From 'Unbundling the Corporation' by J. Hagel and M. Singer, Mar.–Apr. 1999.

The problem for integrated firms is the difficulty of optimizing simultaneously scope, speed and scale; therefore, firms need to make trade-offs. For instance, in order to maximize scope, a retailer should provide a vast variety of products, possibly also from external stores.

This is what Amazon.com has been doing with its Zshop system, which allows other used-book retailers to sell their products through the Amazon.com website. Doing so makes the site more attractive for customers because they find not only the new Amazon.com offerings but also used books, which are generally cheaper. From a scope perspective, this makes a lot of sense. However, if doing so leads to fewer orders originating from Amazon.com, then this would then result in a lower utilization of physical infrastructure, such as warehouses, thereby compromising the company's economies of scale.

SUMMARY

- This chapter dealt with the impact of the Internet on the vertical boundaries of a firm. It first analyzed the degree of integration of individual activities of the value chain. More specifically, it discussed which activities a firm should perform ('make') by itself and which activities it should source ('buy') from external providers:
  - Reasons that favour 'make' decisions in e-business include strong linkage between activities, confidentiality of information and high transaction costs.
  - Reasons that favour 'buy' decisions include high economies of scale, high capital requirements, specialized know-how and higher efficiency of the open markets.
- The chapter then discussed value-chain deconstruction through the Internet. This deconstruction results from the separation of the economics of physical goods and that of digital goods, and from dissolving the traditional trade-off between richness and reach.
- Next, the chapter analyzed the unbundling of the traditional organization as a result of falling transaction costs made possible by the Internet. The unbundling concept distinguishes three core businesses in a corporation: (1) product innovation, (2) infrastructure management and (3) customer relationship management. These three businesses have different imperatives regarding economics, culture and competition.

REVIEW QUESTIONS

1. Describe the different organizational options along the make-or-buy spectrum.
2. In general, which factors determine whether a firm should make or buy a product or a service?
3. Why should a company consider deconstructing its value chain through the Internet?
4. Outline the concept of unbundling the corporation, and explain its underlying rationale.

DISCUSSION QUESTIONS

1. Illustrate through different examples how the Internet enables companies to integrate activities across their value chain.
2. Provide examples of Internet ventures that favour (or have favoured) either 'make' or 'buy' decisions.
3. Explain how a company deconstructs its value chain through the Internet, illustrating your answers through an actual example.
4. Provide two examples from two different industries (one about physical products and one about digital goods) that demonstrate the concept of unbundling the corporation.
5. Critically assess the deconstruction and unbundling concepts, and show their limitations using e-business examples.

RECOMMENDED KEY READING

- R. Coase wrote the first influential article on transaction cost theory in 'The nature of the firm', *Economica*, 1937, 4, pp. 386–405. O. E. Williamson provided an additional foundational perspective on this topic in *Markets and Hierarchies: Analysis and Antitrust Implications*, Free Press, 1975.
- P. Evans and T. Wurster developed the concept of deconstructing the value chain in *Blown to Bits*, Harvard Business School Press, 1999. For a condensed version of this concept, see, by the same authors, 'Strategy and the new economics of information', *Harvard Business Review*, 1997, September–October, pp. 71–81.
- J. Hagel and M. Singer wrote the article 'Unbundling the corporation', *Harvard Business Review*, 1999, March–April, pp. 133–141.
- M. Porter criticizes the deconstruction and unbundling concepts in 'Strategy and the Internet', *Harvard Business Review*, 2001, March, pp. 72–74.

USEFUL WEBLINKS

- www.amd.com
- www.ideo.com
- www.intel.com

NOTES AND REFERENCES

1 Transaction costs are an important concept to explain firm structures. For a detailed discussion of the impact of the Internet on transaction costs, see A. Afuah, 'Redefining firm boundaries in the face of the Internet: are firms really shrinking?', *Academy of Management Review*, 2003, Vol. 28, No. 1, pp. 34–53.

2 For more detailed discussions of the concept of deconstruction, see P. Evans and T. Wurster, *Blown to Bits*, Harvard Business School Press, 1999, pp. 39–67, and D. Heuskel, *Wettbewerb jenseits von Industriegrenzen*, Campus, 1999, pp. 57–72.

3 J. Rayport and J. Sviokla developed a similar concept to the two concepts mentioned here. It proposes an unbundling along the dimensions of content, context and infrastructure. Since the findings are essentially the same as in the deconstruction and unbundling concepts, we do not elaborate further on this concept. However, for a detailed discussion of this concept, see J. Rayport and J. Sviokla, 'Managing in the market space', *Harvard Business Review*, 1995, November–December, pp. 141–150.

4 M. Porter, 'Strategy and the Internet', *Harvard Business Review*, 2001, March, pp. 72–74.

5 For a detailed discussion of this concept see J. Hagel and M. Singer 'Unbundling the Corporation', *Harvard Business Review*, 1999, March–April, pp. 133–141.

CHAPTER 9

Internal organization of a firm's e-business activities

Chapter at a glance

9.1 Choosing options for online interactions with customers

9.1.1 Information activities

9.1.2 Communication activities

9.1.3 Transaction activities

9.1.4 Distribution activities

9.2 Choosing online/offline distribution channels

9.3 Choosing the organizational structure for e-business activities

9.3.1 Separate e-business organization

9.3.2 Integrated e-business organization

Related case studies

Case study		*Primary focus of the case study*
8	Tesco	Online/offline channel management in grocery retailing
12	Nordea	Online/offline channel management in financial services
13	Ducati	Online/offline channel management in manufacturing
5	Alcampo *vs.* Peapod	Organizational structure: integrated operations *vs.* partnership
6	Amazon *vs.* BOL	Organizational structure: integrated operations *vs.* spin-off
14	Ducati *vs.* Harley	Organizational structure: integrated operations *vs.* spin-off
21	Covisint	Organizational structure: case of strategic alliance

Learning outcomes

After completing this chapter you should be able to:

- Understand the four virtual spaces of the ICDT (information, communication, distribution and transaction) model.
- Recognize the sources of online/offline channel conflicts and possible ways to resolve such conflicts.
- Understand the different options of organizing e-business activities.
- Assess the benefits and drawbacks of different organizational set-ups for e-business activities.

INTRODUCTION

This chapter focuses on the decisions a firm has to make regarding the internal organization of its e-business activities. It addresses the following questions:

- What kind of online interactions and capabilities should we offer to our customers?
- What activities should we perform online and offline, and how can we resolve possible channel conflicts?
- What organizational set-up should we have for our e-business activities?

9.1 Choosing options for online interactions with customers

As companies have developed their e-business activities, they have started to offer increasingly elaborate e-business capabilities. The ICDT (information, communication, distribution and transaction) model describes the main features that a firm can offer to its customers.[1] Essentially, there are four options, which are depicted in Exhibit 9.1.

Exhibit 9.1 **The ICDT model describes the four main usage dimensions of the Internet in the virtual market space**

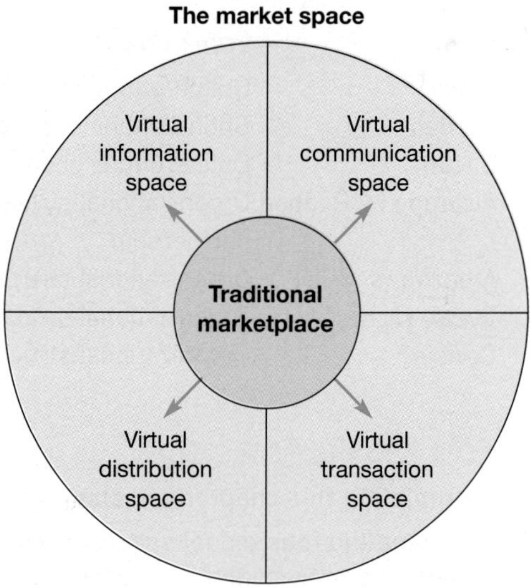

Source: Adapted from A. Angehrn, 'Designing mature internet strategies: the ICDT model', *European Management Journal*, 1997, Vol. 21, No. 1, pp. 38–47.

9.1.1 Information activities

Information activities include advertising and posting information on the company website. This includes company, products and services-related information. When the commercial use of the Internet became widely spread in the mid-1990s, companies first designed their web presence to provide customers with information about their products and services. At that point, the Internet was not yet tightly integrated with other marketing channels or enterprise resource planning (ERP) systems.

Since then, information provision has changed drastically. Today, many companies closely link their Internet advertising with other channels, as illustrated in the12Snap case study featured in Part 4 of this book. Furthermore, information provided over the Internet is not of a static nature any more. Instead, online catalogues are linked closely to warehousing and production planning systems, enabling customers to find out instantaneously when their order will be fulfilled and delivered.

As the Internet becomes increasingly common as an information medium, companies need to avoid information overload and be careful not to offend Internet users with unsolicited spam mail. The FT article 'When customer information turns into "spam"' illustrates the problems associated with spam mail and outlines possible solutions.

FT

When customer information turns into 'spam'

At a recent conference, a panel of chief technology officers was asked what they would do about spam. Brian Keating, chief technology officer of Safeway, replied: 'We sell it for £1.19 a tin.' Other CTOs would love to have such a convenient answer to the problem. Spam clogs up corporate networks, slowing down legitimate traffic and forcing businesses to deploy anti-spam software or let their users waste hours deleting the messages. Spam cost European companies €2.5bn ($3bn) in lost productivity last year, by some estimates. It is not just businesses that hate spam: individuals also have to wade through e-mail inboxes filled with junk and worry about their children being bombarded with unsavoury messages from pornographers.

For these reasons, the European Union decided to take action, bringing out a set of regulations on privacy in electronic communications that come into force on December 11. These impose restrictions on what businesses may and may not do in sending e-mails and mobile phone text messages to their customers, as well as covering communications by phone and fax.

At the core of the new regulations is the difference between opt-in and opt-out marketing. The latter has been the norm up to now: consumers have had the chance to opt out of marketing if they find it intrusive, for instance by asking to be taken off e-mail lists or by registering with the Telephone Preference Service, a form of 'do not call' list for telephone marketers. Under the new rules, opt-in will become the standard. Under this system, marketing messages can legally be sent only to consumers who have given their prior consent to marketing in some form. 'These regulations provide much stronger protection for people's privacy,' says Elizabeth Dunn, compliance manager at the office of the Information Commissioner.

So will it stop spam? No. The supporters and detractors of the new legislation are united on ▶

one point: they do not believe it will have much effect on the overall volume of spam that users receive, because most spam comes from areas outside the EU, such as the US and Asia, and the amount coming from these sources looks likely to grow. 'We all have to be honest about this: technological measures will stop spam more than regulations,' admits Ms Dunn.

Why regulate, then? Because it will stop some spam within the EU, establish a principle of privacy protection, set standards for reputable companies and assure consumers that their privacy is a concern for lawmakers.

The minimal impact this legislation is likely to have on spam has enraged critics. They believe that the inconvenience and expense of obtaining consent from the recipients of marketing represent an obstacle to business, while doing little to improve the lot of consumers.

John Higgins, chief executive of Intellect, the body that represents British electronics companies, argues: 'This legislation is not much use to anyone. To the good guys [who are considerate in their marketing], this adds an extra burden. The bad guys will just ignore it as always, and most are outside Europe. And consumers will not see their junk e-mails disappear.' He believes businesses will face additional and unnecessary costs in ensuring compliance with the new rules.

The Confederation of British Industry takes a softer line. Though it supported an opt-out, rather than an opt-in, regime as more conducive to support a fledgling e-commerce industry, the CBI now plans to focus on minimizing the cost and disruption to businesses, and monitoring the implementation of the directive in other EU member states. But reputable marketers have nothing to fear from the legislation, according to supporters, such as the Direct Marketing Association. Justin Anderson, chief executive of marketing agency Frontwire and a board member of the DMA, says: 'This provides a framework for legitimate marketing. The [e-mail and SMS] channels should not be used for general prospecting but if a user has given their consent, it can be effective.'

However, there remains room for confusion in the interpretation of the legislation as drafted, argues Andrew Sparrow, partner at Lecote Solicitors. For instance, the question of what constitutes informed consent is unclear. Do individuals have explicitly to request marketing materials? No, says the Information Commissioner. Customers can be assumed to have opted into receipt of such materials if they have established a relationship with the marketer. However, companies will be forbidden from contacting customers by e-mail or SMS in order to obtain their permission to send marketing messages, leaving them to find other means to make contact.

There is an exception to the requirement to obtain consent, the so-called 'soft opt-in'. To take advantage of this exception, marketers must satisfy three conditions. They must have obtained the person's contact details in the course of a sale or negotiations for a sale; they must be marketing similar products and services to those involved in the sale; and they must have offered the recipient the opportunity to opt out of further marketing when they obtained the contact details, and continue to provide an opportunity to opt out in every subsequent communication.

If customers have given their consent, marketers are still constrained to market to them only goods and services similar to those to which the consent applied. This could lead to uncertainty, particularly for companies selling a range of goods, such as supermarkets. 'It's the stuff of litigation,' says Mr Sparrow.

Organizations will also be restricted in sharing their customer information. For instance, could a company share its database with a sister company that has the same owner but a different brand? 'In my view, this would not be allowed,' says Paula Barrett, partner at Eversheds, the law firm. In the case of business-to-business marketing, companies may act more freely. Prior consent will not be necessary and the onus remains on the recipient to opt out. When sending out marketing communications to employees at other businesses who are identified by name,

companies must be sure to provide a clearly identifiable source for the communication, and an opportunity to opt out from further communications of the same sort. Yet businesses sending out messages to workers who are not identified by name do not have to allow them to opt out. 'There is nothing in the law to stop you continuing [in these circumstances] even if someone tells you to stop,' says Ms Dunn.

The new legislation also deals with 'cookies', which are pieces of software that websites can deposit with those who visit them, attaching to their web browsers usually without the user's knowledge. These programs enable the websites to track the user's movements, for instance from one website to another. Under the new rules, users must be given clear and comprehensive information about the use of cookies on any site, and the right to reject them unless they can be deemed necessary. The new legislation was drawn up with the pace of technological development in mind, and attempts to be technologically neutral. Mr Sparrow concludes: 'It's notoriously difficult to legislate in this area, because the technology changes so quickly. The law can't keep up.'

Meanwhile, users will have to find other ways to deal with the kind of spam that does not come in a tin. After December 11, UK companies operating within the European Union will face fines if they send electronic marketing messages (either e-mails or SMS messages by mobile phones) to individual consumers without prior consent. Companies using e-mail or SMS to market to other businesses do not need their consent but must provide an opt-out mechanism and must cease to market to named individuals within companies if requested to stop. 'Informed prior consent' may include a person ticking a box, for instance on a website, that explicitly requests marketing materials, and someone requesting a brochure, or buying goods and services from a company. When marketing to consumers, companies can use e-mail or SMS to market only goods or services similar to those in which the consumer expressed an interest.

Companies will not be allowed to share their lists of customers with a third party. But the UK's Information Commissioner has decided that lists of consumer contacts compiled before December 11 may continue to be used for electronic marketing, provided the marketing company offers the consumer an opt-out. This would cover lists of e-mail contacts that have been bought from list sellers or other third parties. Companies can go on using these lists indefinitely. The legislation also covers automatic machines that phone people with marketing messages, and unsolicited faxes used for marketing, and for the first time allows businesses to opt out of receiving such faxes by registering with the Fax Preference Service. While the new legislation is intended to reduce spam mail, it is expected to have little effect. This is because most spam originates outside the EU, most of it from unscrupulous companies with little regard for their reputation.

Source: F. Harvey, 'E-marketing in a straitjacket', www.FT.com 1 December 2003.

9.1.2 Communication activities

Communication activities include a two-way communication between a company and its online visitors and customers. This can take place via Internet applications such as e-mail and real-time chat. In order to make communication more personal, the online fashion retailer Landsend.com has included a Land's End live icon on its website. By clicking on it, customers can request to be called by a Land's End employee or to enter an online chat to ask questions and obtain specific product information.

In addition to facilitating communication between businesses and their customers, the Internet also facilitates communication between customers who are members of a

virtual online community. For some firms, such as eBay and Kazaa, the communication that takes place among customers and peers is much more important than the communication between the company and its customers.

9.1.3 Transaction activities

Transaction activities include the acceptance through the Internet of online orders (i.e. commercial transactions) and electronic payments (i.e. financial transactions). At the outset of the commercial usage of the Internet, there were two main drawbacks associated with online transactions.

First, most Internet users, who were afraid of fraud, considered making e-payments as too dangerous, which held back the evolution of e-commerce. However, as payment mechanisms mature and trusted e-payment companies evolve – consider, for instance, the case of Nordea – online transaction activities are becoming more and more common-place.

Second, since payments were limited to credit- or debit-card transactions, the offering of low-priced products or services (such as newspaper articles) was not economically feasible, since transaction costs would have been prohibitively high. The development of micro-payment services, such as the electronic purse in Portugal (featured in the case studies section of this book), address this shortcoming.

9.1.4 Distribution activities

Distribution activities include the online delivery of digital goods, such as software, videos, films, music and e-books, by letting customers download the purchased product(s). The main bottleneck that has limited online distribution so far is the limited bandwidth of online connections. As broadband access becomes more common-place, even in households, online distribution will be used increasingly with products and services that can be digitized.

First, the online distribution of music, games or even movies will become the norm over time, eventually replacing physical distribution through CDs and DVDs. Online file-sharing such as Kazaa has already provided a first glimpse of this revolution in distribution (see the case study in Part 4 of this book). Second, service providers from different realms, such as consulting and education, will use the Internet increasingly to deliver lectures, presentations and services to their customers and students.

9.2 Choosing online/offline distribution channels

Manufacturers and retailers that have, in the past, sold their products through physical outlets using sales forces fear that moving into the online sales channel will cannibalize their offline sales.[2] Their argument is that the new online channel is not creating a new market or extra sales but merely siphoning off existing sales.

To understand whether manufacturers should fear distribution channel conflicts, they need to analyze how new online channels affect their offline channels, and whether the various channels actually serve the same customer segments. For instance, companies may believe mistakenly that different channels are competing with one another when in fact they are benefiting from each other's actions. They may also believe that the loss of sales is ascribed to a new channel when, in reality, it results from the intrusion of a new competitor.

The channel conflict matrix (see Exhibit 9.2) analyzes how traditional bricks-and-mortar retailers should react towards possible conflicts between their offline and online channels. There are two main dimensions that determine how to deal with possible channel conflict: (1) the prospect of destructive conflict between different channels and (2) the importance of the existing channel that is threatened by the new online channel.

The resulting matrix provides insights into how to deal with possible channel conflicts. The four quadrants of the matrix are now described:

- *Quadrant 1.* If the prospect of destructive conflict between channels is high and the importance of the threatened channel is also high, then it is sensible to address the problem and find ways to reconcile the two channels. For instance, when Nordea bank started its online banking operations, it was positioned clearly in Quadrant 1. Branch-based banking was threatened severely by the rise of the online channel, yet it was of great importance to the overall functioning of the

Exhibit 9.2 **The channel conflict matrix analyzes how different types of channel conflicts should be resolved**

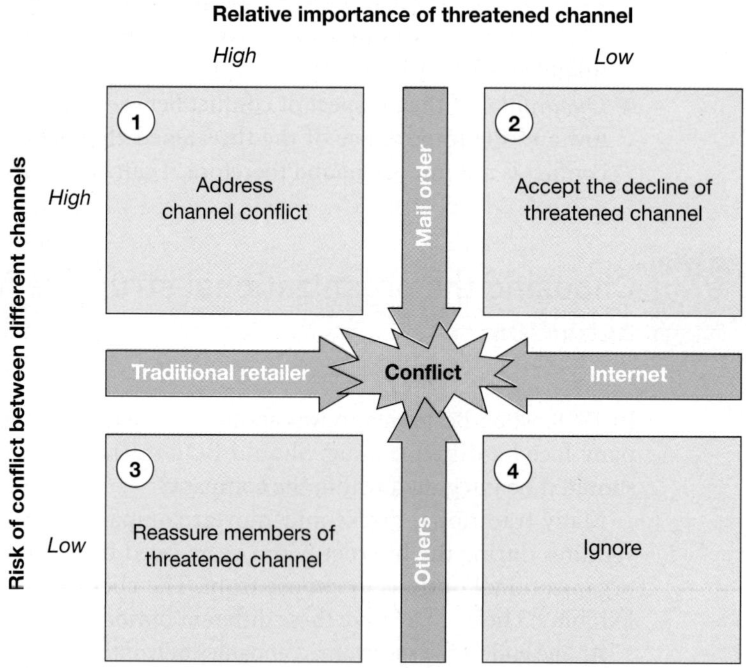

Source: Adapted from C. Bucklin, P. Thomas-Graham and E. Webster, 'Channel conflict: when is it dangerous?', *McKinsey Quarterly*, 1997, No. 3, pp. 36–43.

bank. Contrary to many other banks, Nordea decided to integrate fully its online banking within its physical banking operations, thereby eliminating possible competition between the two channels. In fact, branch employees were enticed to move branch customers over to the Internet. Ultimately, the ability to leverage the branches to move customers to the Internet, thereby eliminating the need for expensive marketing campaigns, was one of the main reasons why Nordea managed to acquire a dominant position in the online banking world.

- *Quadrant 2.* If the prospect of destructive conflict between channels is high and the importance of the threatened channel is low, then it is usually sensible simply to allow the threatened channel to decline.
- *Quadrant 3.* If the prospect of destructive conflict is low but the importance of the threatened channel is high, then the latter's employees need to be reassured that they will not be affected. This is the case, for instance, with Tesco's bricks-and-mortar retail store network. In spite of the drastic increase of online sales through the Tesco.com channel, retail stores continue to play a significant role. Thus, it is important to let employees know that the new channel does not present a threat to them. Similarly, when Ducati started selling motorcycles exclusively through the Internet, it was necessary to comfort the dealership network and reassure them of their continuing importance. To back up this claim, customers who ordered through the Internet had to identify the closest Ducati dealer to their address. The dealer was then informed and could either accept or reject processing the order. In case of acceptance, the dealer would receive a 10% commission of the total price, which was less than the average commission received on a normal Ducati motorcycle sale. However, with online sales, dealers had no inventory risk and no advertising or marketing costs. The goal of Ducati's online sales was not to cannibalize sales made through the offline channel but instead to expand into hitherto untapped market segments.[3]
- *Quadrant 4.* If the prospect of conflict between the online and off-line channels is low and the importance of the threatened channel is also low, then the channel conflict is not important and therefore, it can be ignored.

9.3 Choosing the organizational structure for e-business activities

In 1998, when Bertelsmann was about to launch its online bookstore BOL, the company faced a difficult issue. Should BOL operate as an independent business, or should it be integrated within the company?

Many traditional bricks-and-mortar companies that launched their e-business ventures during the Internet boom years faced the above question. They had several organizational options to choose from. The clicks-and-mortar spectrum shown in Exhibit 9.3 helps to analyze these different options.[4]

At one end of the spectrum, companies fully integrate their e-business activities within the firm. At the other end, the e-business operation is completely separated from the company and spun off. Both approaches have distinct advantages and disadvantages.

Exhibit 9.3 The clicks-and-mortar spectrum spans from integration to separation of a company's e-business activities

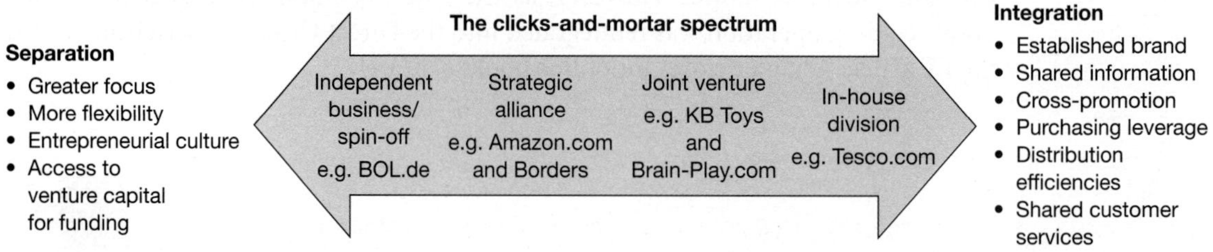

Source: Adapted with permission of *Harvard Business Review* [Exhibit ROO 313]. From 'Get the Right Mix of Bricks and Clicks' by R. Gulati and J. Garino, May–June 2000. Copyright © 2000 by the Harvard Business School Publishing Corporation, all rights reserved.

9.3.1 Separate e-business organization

Let us first consider separating the e-business activities from the parent company, an option that was particularly popular during the Internet boom years. Bertelsmann, for instance, decided to launch BOL as a separate business to enter the online market for book retailing. In the banking industry, Vereinsbank, which founded Advance Bank, set up a completely separate venture to enter the direct banking market in Germany. At the time, many other bricks-and-mortar companies chose this separation approach of their online activities because they believed that it gave them the following advantages:[5]

- *Greater focus.* Due to the fast-moving business environment and the increasing Internet-based competition, companies wanted to set up entities that focused solely on e-business activities and did not have to take into consideration the overall strategy of the firm.
- *More flexibility and faster decisions.* A separate e-business organization also allowed for a more flexible and faster decision-making process.
- *Entrepreneurial culture.* Established management approaches and business procedures were considered to be inadequate for the Internet world, where 'everything' had been turned upside down. To accommodate for this change, e-business ventures were often staffed with young individuals, having an entrepreneurial drive, strong IT know-how and analytical capabilities (yet often little knowledge of the industry).
- *Access to venture capital.* The soaring stock markets of the late 1990s was another reason for separating a dot.com business from its parent company. The outrageously high valuations of companies were focused primarily on pure dot.com businesses without any physical bricks-and-mortar structures to hold them back or dilute their business strategy.

With the burst of the Internet bubble in March 2000, many companies that had spun off their e-business activities could not exploit the synergies between their online and offline channels and operations and, therefore, were not able to pursue a clicks-and-mortar strategy. After wasting large sums of money on doomed dot.com businesses, shareholders wanted to see fewer fast decisions and more profitable and sustainable strategies.

As a result of the above developments, many of the companies that initially spun off their e-business operations have reintegrated them into the parent company. A

prime example for this development is the case of the Internet bookseller BOL, which started out as a completely separate business with its own management structure and business model. However, as the Internet boom subsided, the online book-retailing operation was reintegrated into the Direct Group of Bertelsmann (see the FT article 'Chapter closes for online books venture').

FT

Chapter closes for online books venture

The sound of dotcoms hitting the rocks across Europe has become so familiar since Boo.com started the trend last year that most problems now barely cause a tremor.

But Tuesday's decision by Bertelsmann to roll BOL, its books and CDs e-tailer, into its more mature book clubs is still significant. It signals the end of the home-grown challenge to Amazon.com's European dominance.

Heidi Fitzpatrick, an analyst at Lehman Brothers, says: 'It is another indication that the economics of pan-European e-tailing are just not there.'

Bertelsmann set up BOL as a stand-alone business in 1999 with the hope of spinning it off as a separate public company.

Despite being the second largest pan-European online bookstore – with 16 countries giving it the biggest geographical footprint – BOL has found it hard to achieve widespread brand recognition and has failed to catch up with Amazon's head start.

Tuesday's move illustrates that Bertelsmann believes it has to take advantage of all the available synergies such as sharing purchasing, warehousing and marketing costs with its book clubs.

Klaus Eierhoff, head of Bertelsmann Direct Group, said on Tuesday: 'By merging BOL with the book clubs we will have a combined entity that will generate a significant profit by 2003.' The international book clubs were set to become profitable next year by themselves and BOL was expected to break even in 2004.

Mr Eierhoff told Financial Times Deutschland that his company was talking to its US partners about folding Barnesandnoble.com, the US online bookseller, into its book clubs.

Talks are continuing over the future of BOL's French, Spanish and Japanese operations. The German, UK, Dutch, Italian, Swedish and Finnish branches will be merged with local book clubs while branches in Denmark and Norway will be closed.

Source: T. Barker, and B. Benoit, 'Amazon sees off Bertelsmann', www.FT.com, 16 May 2001.

9.3.2 Integrated e-business organization

Some companies chose right away to integrate tightly their e-business activities with their bricks-and-mortar operations. Office Depot seamlessly integrated its website with the physical retailing network. Thus, it was able to leverage its existing infrastructure with a call centre and a vast fleet of delivery trucks. Similarly, when deliberating whether to fulfil using its existing store network or warehouses, Tesco.com opted for the integrated in-store-based fulfilment approach.

Today, it seems that in most cases the benefits of an organizational structure that combines online and offline channels outweigh those of a separated organization. These benefits include:[6]

- *Established and trusted brand.* Companies moving from the physical world into the online world can leverage the brand they have established with their customers. Trust is a critical issue in e-business, and it increases when customers can resort to face-to-face interaction in case of problems.
- *Shared information.* Information about customers can be shared across different channels. For instance, Tesco.com uses purchasing information from its online channel to adapt offerings in the physical grocery outlets.
- *Cross-promotion.* Online and offline channels can benefit from one another through cross-promotion. Nordea uses its bank branches to convince clients to use the online channel. At the clothing company Gap, signs throughout physical stores point to the online presence of Gap.com.
- *Purchasing leverage.* Purchasing can be pooled for offline and online channels. This increases a company's bargaining power vis-à-vis its suppliers, thereby reducing purchasing costs.
- *Distribution efficiencies.* Different channels within a company can use the same infrastructure facilities, thereby increasing utilization and scale effects. Consider Tesco and its store-based picking approach. There, most of the picking is done during off-peak hours, when there are fewer customers in the store. At barnesandnoble.com, customers can browse and order their books online and pick them up at the physical store.
- *Shared customer service.* The offline channel is very useful for providing customer services for the online channel. It is much easier for customers to return defective or unwanted purchases to a physical store than to repackage them and return them by postal mail or courier service. Similarly, employees at physical stores can also help by providing maintenance and inspection work.

There are also some hybrid options spanning the two extreme choices of full separation and full integration. These include setting up joint ventures and strategic partnerships. These approaches seek to combine the technological know-how, nimbleness and entrepreneurial culture of an online company with the strong brand name and existing customer base of a bricks-and-mortar company.

Consider, for instance, the partnership between the Borders Group, one of the largest US book retailers, and Amazon.com. As part of this agreement, Amazon.com provides the Borders Group with an e-business solution containing technology services, site content, product selection and customer service for the co-branded 'Borders teamed with Amazon.com' site. Amazon.com records all orders that take place through the site and passes on a fixed sales percentage to the Borders Group. Through this agreement, the two companies leverage Amazon.com's strong technological know-how and the Borders group's extensive physical store presence. Depending on availability, customers who order through the website have the possibility to pick up their purchase on the same day at the nearest Borders store. Customers then receive an e-mail confirmation from Borders, informing them that the purchased item has been picked and reserved under their name for express in-store pick-up.[7]

SUMMARY

- First, the chapter presented the ICDT model and illustrated its four virtual spaces through some specific examples. These four spaces are (1) the virtual information space, (2) the virtual communication space, (3) the virtual distribution space and (4) the virtual transaction space.
- Second, the chapter discussed how a company can choose between online and offline channels to conduct its activities. It also offered a framework to assess the impact of possible channel conflicts and ways to resolve them.
- Third, the chapter analyzed how to choose an organizational structure for e-business activities. The following four options were discussed: (1) in-house integration, (2) joint venture, (3) strategic partnership and (4) independent business/spin-off. It also discussed the benefits and drawbacks of these different organizational options.

REVIEW QUESTIONS

1. Outline the ICDT model and describe how a firm can use it when deciding on its e-business activities.
2. Explain the online/offline channel conflict matrix and illustrate it through specific examples.
3. What are the different options that a company has when choosing the organizational structure for its e-business activities?
4. What criteria should a company use when deciding on whether to integrate its e-business activities in-house or whether to spin them off?

DISCUSSION QUESTIONS

1. Illustrate the ICDT model through the example of an Internet venture that you are familiar with.
2. Critically assess the ICDT model and pinpoint its shortcomings.
3. Consider the examples of Tesco.com and Ducati. Explain for each case the extent of the online/offline channel conflict.
4. Should a company refrain from launching an Internet venture if it judges the prospect of a destructive conflict with the offline channel to be high? Defend your argument.
5. Consider the examples of BOL.de and Nordea. Compare the integration/separation decisions that were made in each case, and explain their rationale.

RECOMMENDED KEY READING

- A. Angehrn describes the ICDT model in detail in 'Designing mature internet strategies: the ICDT model', *European Management Journal*, 1997, Vol. 21, No. 1, pp. 38–47.
- R. Gulati and J. Garino present the clicks-and-mortar spectrum in 'Get the right mix of bricks and clicks', *Harvard Business Review*, 2000, May–June, pp. 107–114.
- For a discussion of the channel conflict matrix, see C. Bucklin, P. Thomas-Graham and E. Webster, 'Channel conflict: when is it dangerous?', *McKinsey Quarterly*, 1977, No. 3, pp. 36–43.

USEFUL WEBLINKS

- www.barnesandnoble.com
- www.borders.com
- www.landsend.com
- www.officedepot.com

NOTES AND REFERENCES

1 The ICDT model is described in A. Angehrn, 'Designing mature internet strategies: the ICDT model', *European Management Journal*, 1997, Vol. 21, No. 1, pp. 38–47.
2 For a more extensive discussion of channel conflicts see C. Bucklin, P. Thomas-Graham and E. Webster, 'Channel conflict: when is it dangerous?', *McKinsey Quarterly*, 1997, No. 3, pp. 36–43.
3 T. Jelassi and S. Leenen, 'An e-commerce sales model for manufacturing companies: a conceptual framework and a European example', *European Management Journal*, 2003, Vol. 21, No. 1, pp. 45–46.
4 R. Gulati and J. Garino, 'Get the right mix of bricks and clicks', *Harvard Business Review*, 2000, May–June, pp. 107–114
5 Ibid.
6 Ibid.
7 'Borders and Amazon.com announce in-store pick up', www.writenews.com/2002/042602_borders_amazon.htm

Part 3

LESSONS LEARNED

PART OVERVIEW

This part suggests a roadmap for e-business strategy formulation, which consists of the following six steps:

- Formulating a vision
- Defining quantifiable business objectives
- Determining the desired customer value
- Deciding on the target market segment(s)
- Determining the organizational set-up for e-business
- Formulating the business model for the e-business venture.

Drawing on the strategic concepts and frameworks as well as on the insights gained from the case studies covered later in the book, this part aims at providing students and managers with a roadmap for e-business strategy development.

CHAPTER 10

A roadmap for e-business strategy formulation

Chapter at a glance

Learning outcomes

After completing this chapter you should be able to:

- Explain the six steps of the e-business strategy formulation roadmap.
- Link the individual steps of the roadmap to the different parts of the e-business strategy framework.
- Understand the main business and management issues involved in each stage of the e-business strategy formulation roadmap.

INTRODUCTION

To help you, as an executive, manager or manager-to-be, develop an e-business strategy for your company, this chapter proposes a roadmap consisting of the following six steps: (1) vision formulation, (2) business objectives definition, (3) customer-value creation, (4) market segmentation and targeting, (5) organizational set-up and (6) e-business model formulation (see Exhibit 10.1).

After having presented in Part 2 of the book an e-business strategy framework, what is the purpose of this roadmap? While the e-business strategy framework outlines from a structural perspective the key elements of strategy formulation, the goal of this roadmap is to propose from a process-oriented perspective the different steps involved in setting up an e-business strategy.[1]

In spite of their different perspectives, the roadmap and the strategy framework are closely interrelated. On the one hand, this roadmap aims at providing you with a practical way to develop an e-business strategy. On the other hand, the cross-references to the more extensive e-business strategy framework allow you to conduct more detailed analysis depending on your previous knowledge and the specific organizational situation at hand. As discussed in Section 2.4, the depth of the analysis depends on the issue at hand. If you do not choose carefully where to drill deep and where to stay at the surface, you increase the risk of over-analyzing issues with relatively low importance while overlooking other issues of critical importance.

You may also wonder why we chose to present the roadmap in Exhibit 10.1 using the same design as on the cover of this book. By doing so, we want to emphasize two important qualities of effective strategy formulation. Just as the four hands are

Exhibit 10.1 **The development of an e-business strategy addresses six interrelated issues**

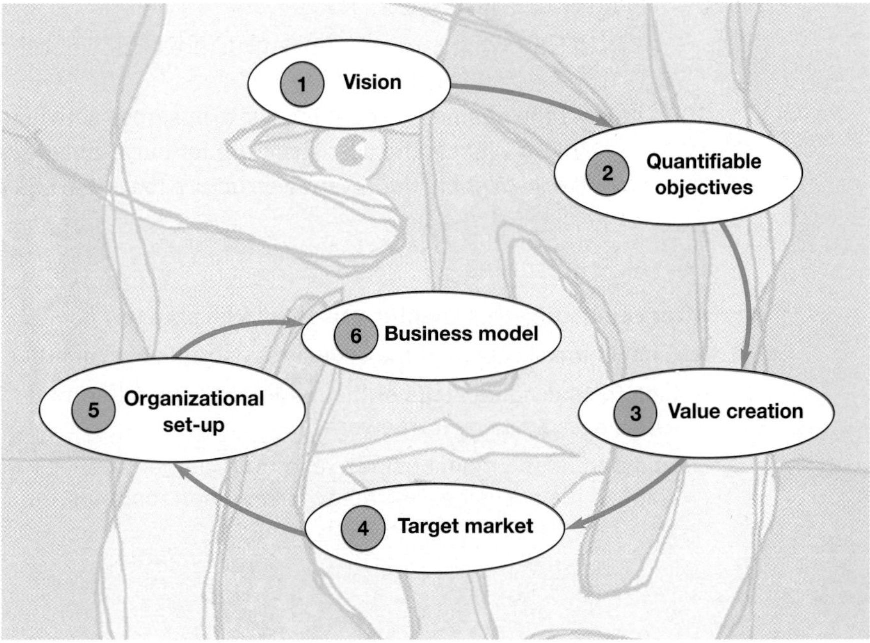

crossing one another on the picture, also all steps of the strategy formulation roadmap are closely inter linked. While the relative importance of each step will differ depending on the situation at hand, none of the six steps can or should be taken in isolation. The roadmap itself is represented in the exhibit as a flowing process. Yet, in reality, you should think of it as a web in which each dimension of the strategy connects to all the other ones. Undoubtedly, it is one of the key challenges for any manager involved in strategy formulation to delve deeply into each individual issue, while at the same time keeping in mind the inter-dependencies with the other issues. The goal of the roadmap and the e-business strategy framework is to make it easier for you to bridge this tension between breadth of analysis on the one hand and the depth of analysis on the other hand.

The second important relationship in the picture is that between the eye and the hands. Here, the eye symbolizes the vision and the creative dimension of strategy formulation. It stands for the act of looking outside one's own restricted perspective, and opening up new possibilities for value creation. The hands symbolize the more applied (or hands-on) dimension of strategy formulation. This includes particularly the analytical work that is required to determine the feasibility of creative ideas. As we discussed in Chapter 2, in order to develop effective strategies the catalyst for change needs to be able to switch back and forth between creative thinking and sound analysis.

10.1 What is the vision for our company?

As mentioned above, the vision presents the starting point of strategy formulation. It reflects the strategic intent of the firm and points to its desired future state.[2] As an example, consider the following vision statements made by some of the companies featured in the case studies section of the book.

The vision statement at Nordea Bank, for instance, explicitly mentions the importance of Internet-based financial services and solutions as part of the desired future state for the bank.

> We will be valued as the leading financial services group in the Nordic and Baltic financial market with a substantial growth potential. We will be in the top of the league or show superior profitable growth in every market and product area in which we choose to compete. We will have the leading multi-channel distribution with a top world ranking in e-based financial services and solutions.[3]

The 2002 Amazon.com Annual Report states that providing superior customer orientation and broad product selection are of fundamental importance to the future development of the company.

> We seek to offer the Earth's biggest selection and be Earth's most customer-centric company, where customers can find and discover anything they might want to buy online.[4]

The goals of formulating a company's vision are twofold:

- *To establish a direction*, thereby focusing the attention and effort of top management and employees around a common and shared task. It is crucial that top management is involved in the vision formulation and supports it, otherwise the vision is unlikely to be implemented.
- *To encourage creativity and innovation.* To formulate a vision, you need to expand your thinking beyond the existing boundaries of the firm and the current status quo. A vision states the direction to take and the aim to strive for, and yet it does not prescribe how you should go about achieving it.

However, developing a powerful vision that will be supported by all members of an organization over many years presents a challenging task. On the one hand, it needs to consider the specific characteristics of the company and its employees. On the other hand, it also needs to incorporate the broader context within which the company operates. Doing so can include asking questions such as: 'What are the major recent technological developments that we can leverage in the future?' and 'How are demographics changing in our society and what does this mean for our company in the long term?' For a structured approach to formulating these types of questions, it is helpful to analyze the different dimensions of the macro-environment, which are outlined in Chapter 3.

10.2 What are the quantifiable objectives for our e-business activities?

While a vision is important to establish the direction of your company, it is equally important that you select parameters to measure the success of your efforts towards achieving the vision. These parameters are the quantifiable objectives, which can include measures such as profits, sale, revenues and customer satisfaction levels.

Depending on the type of vision, the objectives will differ. Yet all of them should have in common the fact that they can be measured and quantified. Only then can they provide goals for the employees to strive for, and only then is it possible to track progress and make adjustments along the way in order to achieve the objectives.

Consider the example of the vertical e-marketplace Covisint, which is featured in Part 4. The founding car makers, General Motors, Ford and DaimlerChrysler, stated their objective to achieve $6 billion of savings per year through online collaboration, e-procurement and e-supply chain management.

10.3 What type of customer value do we want to create through e-business?

When answering this question, you need to determine why customers would want to buy your products or services. They could do so because of low prices or high quality, or both.

If your company decides to compete primarily on price, you need to strive to become a cost leader within your industry. The low-cost airline easyJet (see Strategy in Action 5.1, p. 109) is a prime example of a low-cost leader. The Internet is an integrated part of the company's strategy since it allows easyJet to cut out expensive ticketing offices and sales agents.

The other option is to strive for a differentiation advantage vis-à-vis rivals (see Sections 5.1.1 and 6.1.1). You can achieve this, for instance, by offering high levels of convenience, broad product selection, high service quality, or a superior brand name. Additionally, you can leverage information that is already available in your organization to create benefits for your customers (see Section 5.2.3 on the concept of the virtual value chain). FedEx has pioneered this service differentiation approach by allowing its customers to track and trace through the Internet the physical movement of their parcels until they reach their final destination (see Strategy in Action 5.2, p. 113).

Regardless of which of the two options you choose, it is important to create a strong fit between different activities by (1) aiming for consistency among them, (2) ensuring reinforcement between activities to increase customer benefits, and (3) optimizing overall efforts as to reduce costs (see Section 5.2).

Finally, you can also aim at achieving both cost leadership and differentiation advantages at the same time, similar to what Amazon.com, Tesco.com and eBay have achieved in their respective markets. However, doing so entails the risk of getting 'stuck in the middle', where you possess neither a cost nor a differentiation advantage vis-à-vis rivals (see Section 6.1.2).

The likelihood of outpacing your competitors along both the price and differentiation dimensions improves if you find ways to open up new and attractive market spaces (see Section 6.2). For instance, you can break out of traditional ways of conducting business by looking across substitute industries, strategic groups, complementary products or unrelated industries.

10.4 What market and customer segments are we targeting through e-business?

Closely linked to value creation is the decision about who your customers should be. Deciding on a target market entails two steps. First, you need to select criteria for dividing your potential market into segments. The chosen criteria will have a significant impact on the segmentation outcome (see Section 4.1.1). For instance, you can segment markets according to customer types (i.e. consumer, corporate and governmental/public-sector customers), or according to age or income.

Based on the market segmentation, you need to decide which segments to target (see Section 4.2) with what products and services that are tailored specifically to a segment's needs. Consider how some of the companies featured in Part 4 of this book have chosen target segments. Tesco.com, for example, focused initially on targeting upper-class shoppers with its online grocery service. Subsequently, it expanded into mass-market segments. Covisint targets exclusively corporate users at participating car manufacturers and suppliers. eBay, on the other hand, from the outset targeted the mass market with its consumer-to-consumer online auction platform.

10.5 What organizational set-up should we have for our e-business activities?

10.5.1 What scale should our e-business activities have?

The first important question to address in the context of the organizational set-up for the e-business activities deals with how large your company needs to be (see Chapter 7).

To determine the required scale, you need to analyze the (expected) cost structure of your e-business activities. This entails an analysis of each activity of the value chain and its underlying cost drivers. If costs are primarily fixed, as is the case with warehouses or website development, it is likely that they display high economies of scale. This, in turn, requires that your operations need to be sufficiently large in order to benefit from the cost reduction brought about by scale effects.

Beware, however, that scale effects are achieved only if your company is also able to generate the required sales volume. As the example of Webvan shows (see the FT article: 'Webvan's billion dollar mistake', p. 24), many companies during the e-business boom ramped up operations very quickly in order to achieve economies of scale. However, they did so without first having understood the underlying economics and customer demand. After having developed expensive proprietary technology platforms and putting into place vast physical warehouse infrastructure, it became impossible for Webvan to adapt the chosen strategy to meet the different market conditions.

The second main question in this context concerns how quickly you should enter the market and how fast you want to grow (see Section 7.2). Early market entry and fast growth can open up possibilities for achieving first-mover advantages such as strong learning and network effects. However, doing so requires substantial investments for aggressive marketing, while taking the risk of betting on the wrong markets or unproven technologies. As a late mover, on the other hand, you may benefit from the early movers' experiences and, thereby, avoid making their mistakes.

10.5.2 What scope should our e-business activities cover?

In addition to the size of the company, you also need to determine the breadth of products and services you want to offer. This breadth depends to a large degree on the target market segments that you want to serve (see Section 4.2). If your company wants to achieve broad coverage, you will, in all likelihood, need to offer a broad variety of products to meet the needs of different customer segments. This is the case, for instance, with the car manufacturer Volkswagen, which offers different models covering all target segments. If, on the other hand, your target segment is very narrow with well-defined preferences, as is the case with, for example, Ducati, then it is advisable also to limit the number of products offered. When thinking about an extension of scope, you need to consider the trade-offs involved. The opportunities are increased market reach and sales, while the risks include a possible loss of internal focus and a dilution of the brand name from a customer perspective.

In addition to a company extending product scope by itself, it can also leverage the Internet to establish partnerships with complementors (see Critical Perspective 3.1,

p. 70). Here, the critical question is: what else would your customers want to buy in addition to the products and services, which are currently offered? The online travel agency ebookers.com, for instance, has links on its website that point to weather reports, currency exchange information, car rental services and travel insurance. Amazon.com went even beyond the Amazon.com vision statement mentioned above. It invited all types of retailers to sell on its online platform their products (including new and used books), which might be in direct competition with Amazon.com's own product offerings.

10.5.3 How integrated should our e-business activities be?

When deciding on the degree of integration of the e-business activities, you need to analyze the value chain again and decide which e-business activities to perform in-house and which ones to outsource to external providers (see Chapter 8). The main reasons that favour 'make' decisions are strong linkages between individual activities and high transaction costs. Reasons that favour 'buy' decisions include high economies of scale, high capital requirements, specialized know-how and higher efficiency of the open market.

As the Dell example illustrates, making the right 'make-or-buy' decisions can present a major source of competitive advantage. Dell's success results greatly from its ability to find the right balance between activities that are sourced from external providers, thereby reducing costs, and those that the company performs in-house. Internal activities ensure differentiation from other competitors.[5] So far, the latter have been unable to imitate the unique Dell approach of manufacturing, selling and servicing computers.

10.5.4 How should we align our physical-world strategy with our e-strategy?

This step is applicable to bricks-and-mortar companies that are embarking on e-business activities and is, therefore, not applicable to pure Internet players. The alignment of a company's physical-world strategy and its e-strategy requires strategic decisions to be made on issues such as branding, pricing, IT and channel conflict. The guiding question here is as follows: for each one of these issues, what should we do regarding our physical operations and our Internet operations? For example, regarding branding, should we name our Internet activity after our physical world brand (e.g. Ducati.com at Ducati, Tesco.com at Tesco), or should we use an anonymous brand (e.g. oohop.fr at Carrefour or reflect.com at Procter and Gamble)?

Regarding the channel issue, when adding the electronic channel, you need to determine how to align it with the existing physical channel (see Section 9.2). This includes two main issues: dealing with potential channel conflict and setting prices for different channels.

Regarding the first issue, if the old and the new channels compete for the same group of customers, then this is likely to result in a conflict because of cannibalization effects. If the old channel is expected to remain important and the likelihood of

a channel conflict is high, then it is essential to address this conflict early on and to find ways to reconcile the interests of the two channels. This can be achieved, for instance, by creating one unified profit centre or, as in the case of Ducati, by providing dealers with added financial incentives if they support the online sales channel.

Regarding the second issue, what should be the pricing strategy for products and services across channels? For example, for Internet-based grocery retailing, should we:

- Apply the *same product prices* as in stores (the way Tesco.com does it in the UK) to convey the message that the value is elsewhere than in price savings?
- Charge *lower prices* (as Alcampo.es did in Spain) to attract, through this financial incentive, a large number of online shoppers and quickly build a critical mass of customers?
- Charge *higher prices* (the way Ahold does it) to reflect the extra costs involved in order fulfilment, packing and delivery?

In financial services, Nordea has used a differentiated pricing strategy. Customers pay a significantly lower fee for a given banking transaction if it is carried out online rather than in a physical branch office of the bank. This approach has helped Nordea attract customers to its Internet-based banking services.

10.5.5 What organizational structure should our e-business activities have?

As part of the internal set-up of your company, you need to choose the appropriate organizational structure for the e-business activities. At one end of the spectrum, this would mean completely integrating the e-business activities into your existing organization. At the other end of the spectrum, it would mean setting them up as a separate entity or a spin-off (see Section 9.3).

The benefits of setting up a spin-off include factors such as greater focus, a faster decision-making process and a higher degree of entrepreneurial culture. As valuations of online companies are soaring again (see the FT article 'eBay leads online revival as net hits the refresh button', p. 28) and IPO activities are picking up, access to venture capital might also become once more a relevant reason for spinning off online operations.

However, overall the favour has been tilted towards integrating e-business activities into the existing operations of the firm. By doing so, companies can leverage their established brands to attract customers to the online channel. Additionally, it becomes possible to provide multi-channel offerings, where customers can choose between online and offline interaction, depending on their individual preferences and needs. This opens up the opportunity for cross-promotions, shared information systems and integrated customer services, where customers can, for instance, return products purchased through the Internet to a physical store.

10.6 What is the business model for our e-business activities?

The final and most critical issue to address is with regards to the financials involved in the e-business activity. To find this out, you need to analyze the business model of your firm in terms of both the cost structure and the revenue structure.[6]

10.6.1 What is the cost structure for our e-business activities?

To determine the cost structure, you need to consider the individual parts of the value chain – such as production, IT, marketing, sales and after-sales service – and analyze their underlying cost drivers (see Section 5.2). This entails asking questions such as 'How will costs evolve as the scale of operations increases?' (see Section 7.1), and 'How can we use the Internet to lower costs across the value chain?'

As the focus of investors has shifted towards the profitability of e-business ventures, it has become much more important to control costs. Ultimately, the cost structure of your e-business venture determines the gross profit margins that your company must earn in order to cover overhead costs and generate profits. However, if from the beginning you start out with high costs due to, for example, high fixed costs or marketing expenses, then this limits your spectrum of business opportunities. Obviously, your cost structure dictates the types of revenue you need to generate in order to achieve the desired profitability. For instance, with cost-intensive infrastructure in place, you will generally find it difficult to justify targeting small markets (although these may be very promising), since they are unlikely to generate enough revenues to cover costs. In addition, you will also find it more difficult to adjust your venture's strategy if market realities do not meet your expectations.[7]

10.6.2 What is the revenue structure for our e-business activities?

In order to determine the revenue structure of your e-business activities, you need to analyze the different options for generating revenues. The latter depend on the type of business you are operating and can include the following sources (see e-Business Concept 4.1: 'The e-business market segmentation matrix', p. 79):

- *Advertising revenues* and *usage fees*, as is the case in P2P e-commerce.
- *Transaction fees* and *information postage fees*, as is the case in C2C e-commerce.
- *Transaction fees, hosting service fees, membership fees* and (monthly) *subscription fees*, as is the case in B2B e-commerce.
- *Transaction fees, advertising revenues* and *subscription fees*, as is the case in B2C e-commerce.

In addition to analyzing revenue sources, you also need to assess the sustainability of your business model, which depends to a large degree on the customer's ability to bargain down prices, intensity of competition, substitutes and barriers to entry (see Section 3.2).

In order to sustain revenues, you should consider the following two options, which are not mutually exclusive. The first option is constantly to 'reinvent' your e-business activities to stay abreast of changes and avoid being pushed out of the market. As the Internet matures, it becomes less likely that fundamental changes will throw over established business models (see Section 1.2.4). Nowadays, the rise of Internet-based start-up companies, such as Amazon.com and eBay, which revolutionized ways of doing business by using the Internet, is still possible; yet they become more unlikely as the technology matures and e-business applications have become established.

The second option is to aim at creating customer lock-in (see Section 7.2), which you can achieve through the following means.

- By setting up *customizable websites* (see e-Business Concept 4.2: 'Segments of one and mass customization in the Internet world', p. 83), where customers can adapt the company's website to their own needs. For instance, at Advance Bank customers can keep records of previous money transfers. At Tesco.com, online shoppers can store their shopping list for future purchases.
- By leveraging *data-mining techniques* to analyze customer information (age, gender, income, etc.), click-stream patterns, past purchases and comparisons with other like-minded customers. The information gathered by means of data-mining can then be used to make specific targeted service and product offerings based on individual preferences. Numerous companies, including Nordea, Amazon.com, Advance Bank, Peapod.com and eBay, all of which are featured in Part 4 of this book, have used data-mining extensively to build up loyalty among their customers.
- By leveraging *network effects*. To do this, you need to find ways in which your product or service becomes more valuable for customers as the overall number of customers increases (see Section 7.2 on network effects). The most popular way of achieving this is to set up virtual communities in which online users have the opportunity to interact with one another on topics that are of special interest to them (see Business Concept 7.2, p. 146).

SUMMARY

- First, the chapter suggested in broad terms a roadmap for e-business strategy formulation.
- It then described in detail each of the six steps involved in this roadmap and illustrated them through some examples and some of the cases contained in this book. These steps consist of

  (1) defining a vision,

  (2) setting up quantifiable objectives,

  (3) deciding on a specific type of customer value,

  (4) selecting target markets,

(5) deciding on the organizational structure for the e-business venture (including scale, scope, integration, alignment and organizational structure)

(6) establishing a business model that outlines the expected cost and revenue structure for the e-business venture.

REVIEW QUESTIONS

1 What are the six steps involved in the e-business strategy formulation roadmap?

2 What strategic issues does a company need to address when adding clicks to bricks?

3 What possible decisions can a company make regarding branding and goods' pricing across channels?

4 What options does a company have for solving the online/offline channel conflict?

5 What possible revenue streams can a company consider for its Internet activities?

DISCUSSION QUESTIONS

1 Illustrate the six steps of the e-business strategy formulation roadmap through a real-world example that you are familiar with.

2 What challenges do traditional companies face when moving from bricks to clicks?

3 Critically assess the three broad pricing strategies for goods sold online, which are outlined in Section 10.5.4.

4 Choose an e-business activity of your own and formulate it through the six steps of the e-business strategy roadmap.

RECOMMENDED KEY READING

- N. Venkatraman suggests a five-step approach for developing e-business strategies: 'Five steps to a dot-com strategy: how to find your footing on the Web', *Sloan Management Review*, Spring 2000, pp. 15–28.
- D. Chaffey presents different types of e-business strategy processes in *e-Business and e-Commerce Management*, FT Prentice Hall, 2002, pp. 164–169.
- C. Christensen and M. Raynor provide a detailed account of how to choose different strategy development processes depending on the type of innovation at hand: *The Innovator's Solution*, Harvard Business School Press, 2003, pp. 214–231.

NOTES AND REFERENCES

1 For an excellent discussion of different forms of strategy formulation processes, see C. Christensen and M. Raynor, *The Innovator's Solution*, Harvard Business School Press, 2003, pp. 217–234.

2 See also R. Grant, *Contemporary Strategy Analysis*, Blackwell Publishing, 2003, pp. 29–30, and G. Johnson and K. Scholes, *Exploring Corporate Strategy*, Prentice Hall, 2002, pp. 12–13.

3 Taken from Nordea company website.

4 Amazon.com, Annual Report 2002, Part I, p. 1.

5 C. Christensen and M. Raynor, *The Innovator's Solution*, Harvard Business School Press, 2003, pp. 170–171.

6 The term 'business model' has been used widely during the e-commerce boom, entailing many different elements. To keep it as simple as possible, we decided to include only costs and revenues in it. For a more expansive definition of the business model concept, see D. Straub, *Foundations of Net-Enhanced Organizations*, John Wiley, 2004, pp. 237–239.

7 For an insightful discussion of how companies should manage their cost structures during different stages of growing a new business, see C. Christensen and M. Raynor, *The Innovator's Solution*, Harvard Business School Press, 2003, pp. 216–231.

Part 4

CASE STUDIES

A guide to the main focus of cases

	Case name			Chapter 3		Chapter 4			Chapter 5		Chapter 6	Chapter 7		Chapter 8	Chapter 9	
				Macro-environment	Industry structure	B2C market segmentation	B2B market segmentation	Mass customization	Value creation	e-CRM/virtual value chain	Competitive advantage	Economies of scale and scope	Early-mover (dis-) advantages	'Make-or-buy' decisions	online/offline channel management	e-Business organizational structure
IT infrastructure and services	1	Minitel	209	●●					●		●		●●			
	2	CompuNet	224	●				●●	●●	●	●					
e-Government and e-education	3	e-Government	237	●●					●							
	4	Euro-Arab Management School	247									●●		●●		
B2C in retailing	5	Alcampo *vs.* Peapod	253						●				●●		●	●●
	6	Amazon *vs.* BOL	269		●●			●●	●●		●●	●●		●●	●	●●
	7	Nettimarket	288			●●										
	8	Tesco	298						●		●●	●●			●●	
	9	ChateauOnline	310			●●			●		●●					
B2C in financial services	10	Advance Bank	325					●●		●●				●●	●	
	11	Electronic purse	341	●●					●							
	12	Nordea	355	●					●	●●	●●				●●	
B2C in manufacturing	13	Ducati	371						●●						●●	
	14	Ducati *vs.* Harley	386					●●	●					●●		●●
B2C in media	15	Terra Lycos	400		●●					●●						
	16	Google	420		●				●●				●			
	17	DoubleClick	433						●		●●		●			
B2B e-commerce and B2B e-marketplaces	18	Brun Passot	449		●		●●				●					
	19	CitiusNet	462				●●		●	●						
	20	mondus	480				●●									
	21	Covisint	499				●●		●			●				●●
C2C e-commerce	22, 23, 24	eBay (A, B, international)	514–538						●●				●●			
P2P e-commerce	25	Online file-sharing	539		●●				●		●●				●	
Mobile e-commerce	26	12Snap	554			●●			●	●			●●			
	27	paybox	570	●					●		●		●			
	28	NTT DoCoMo	584	●●					●				●			

●● Primary focus of the case study ● Secondary focus of the case study

IT infrastructure and services

1 Establishing a national IT infrastructure: the case of the French videotext system Minitel

The case argues that establishing an advanced IT infrastructure can provide a competitive advantage not only for the country that develops it but also for the companies that use it creatively. It describes the development in France of the Minitel system, the world's most successful national videotext system, and highlights why it was successful while other systems in other countries have been commercial failures. It also stresses the strategic business impact of Minitel.

The case aims to explain the major decisions – political and technical – that led to the success of Minitel, understand the factors that influenced the management and implementation of large information technology, and illustrate how to leverage a national IT infrastructure to offer electronic commerce and eventually impact the way business is conducted and corporate competitiveness.

2 Business process redesign at CompuNet: standardizing top-quality service through IT

The case focuses on the turnaround at CompuNet from being traditionally an IT products reseller to corporate customers in Germany to becoming an IT services provider and an IT outsourcer. Key to this successful business transformation are the vision and entrepreneurial leadership at CompuNet. The case discusses the new value proposition that the company offers by bundling products and services to differentiate itself in the marketplace. It also analyzes how the company leveraged IT capabilities (namely, groupware applications, enterprise resource planning systems and computer–telephony integration) in implementing its new vision and redesigning key business processes in order to offer top-quality service and a lifetime guarantee for its IT products.

The new e-business platform allows all employees not only to share information (about competitors, customers and products) but also to exchange ideas and augment each other's knowledge and expertise. The case demonstrates the strong linkage at CompuNet between business strategy and IT, which enabled the company to implement a new service strategy and gain a competitive advantage in the marketplace.

e-Government

3 e-Government: the role of information and communication technologies in the modernization of government

The move to modernize government through the role of the Internet illustrates some important learning points in the general discussion of the strategic development of e-business. As governments across the globe explore ways to optimize the Internet as a complement to rather than a replacement of traditional services, they have created innovative ways to integrate e-functions with existing bricks-and-mortar activities. This has meant seeking new ways to turn data into accessible and meaningful information and to transform the relationship with citizens from passive to interactive. Far-reaching reforms to improve the quality of service delivery have led governments to address changes in organization, culture, leadership and management. These changes provide interesting examples of how the public sector is adopting the new model of the 'open-book organization' and creating a platform and common framework for inter-organizational structures and citizen-centric services.

e-Education

Teaching note available

4 The Euro-Arab Management School

The Euro-Arab Management School (EAMS) is an academic institution established in 1995 by the European Union and the League of Arab States in the city of Granada, Spain. The school is a virtual organization intended to offer educational programmes and services in the member states of its founding bodies. EAMS does not operate through traditional bricks-and-mortar facilities but instead offers programmes in an innovative manner that combines web-based learning with local tutoring. The case focuses on the management of a virtual organization and addresses issues of the future of education in the age of the Internet.

B2C in retailing

Teaching note available

5 To be or not to be on the shelf: grocery retailing through the Internet – Alcampo (Spain) *vs.* Peapod (USA)

The case discusses the business strategy of two Internet-based grocery retailers: Alcampo in Spain, which is a traditional, bricks-and-mortar supermarket chain, and Peapod in the USA, which is an Internet-only grocery retailer. The case describes the Alcampo move into Internet commerce and the way the company has developed and operates its online grocery shopping system. It highlights the challenges that this Alcampo move presents for reconciling both the physical and the virtual modes of

operation. The case contrasts the business model of Alcampo in Spain with that of Peapod in the USA and pinpoints the strengths, weaknesses and future potential that each approach presents. It also raises the cultural and technological factors underlying the two business approaches. The case concludes with issues related to the increasing competition in Internet-based retailing and the business opportunities offered in Internet-based grocery retailing.

The teaching objectives include: (1) to contrast the business strategies of a traditional, bricks-and-mortar supermarket chain and an Internet-based grocery retailer; (2) to assess the development and operation of an Internet-based grocery shopping system in Spain and the challenges of operating through both physical and virtual channels; (3) to stress the importance of relationship management in computer-mediated commercial transactions; (4) to determine ways of improving the business model and service quality of Alcampo's and Peapod's Internet-based businesses; and (5) to analyze the strengths and weaknesses of Internet-based grocery retailers and their future outlook.

Teaching note available

6 Fighting over the Internet: the virtual battle between Amazon.com (USA) and BOL.de (Germany)

The case contrasts the business strategies of two Internet booksellers: Amazon.com, a young Internet start-up, and Bertelsmann Online (BOL), a subsidiary of a traditional mass-media firm. It presents the global marketing approach taken by each firm, with a particular emphasis on their operations in Germany, highlighting the strengths and weaknesses of their respective competitive strategies. It also discusses the critical success factors in launching an Internet-based book store and sustaining its market growth and financial profitability.

The teaching objectives include: (1) to contrast two business strategies competing via the Internet in a global electronic market; (2) to discuss the building of customer relationships and loyalty in electronic commerce; (3) to suggest ways to sustain the market growth and financial profitability of an Internet-based venture; (4) to determine the facilitators and barriers for launching an Internet-based venture by a large traditional company, such as Bertelsmann, and a small Internet start-up firm, such as Amazon.com; and (5) to discuss the cross-cultural management issues that need to be addressed when adopting know-how between Germany and the USA and across countries in general.

7 Cyber-entrepreneurship: the Nettimarket.com venture in Finland

Despite much initial hype on the subject, only a fraction of the revenues from food and beverage sales is generated online in Finland, with the situation being similar in other countries as well. The main reason for customers' reluctance to shop online lies in the fact that initial web services have offered little added value for customers in comparison with traditional, bricks-and-mortar shopping.

The case suggests that there are four different ways in which customer value can be created in Internet-based grocery retailing, but that the chosen business model will set limits to whether – and to what extent – the online retailer will be able to offer each of the suggested customer benefits. The case describes how a couple of entrepreneurs

launched an Internet-based grocery retailing business in the city of Turku, Finland. It discusses the business strategy and business model behind this venture, and the marketing, operational and technical challenges that Nettimarket.com faces. The case also questions the long-term financial viability of this cyber-venture, especially in light of the increasing competition coming from the big players of the industry.

Teaching note available

8 The Tesco.com experience: is success at hand?

The case focuses on opportunities and challenges for a traditional, bricks-and-mortar retailer to use the Internet as an added channel. A major implementation issue, which raised a heated debate among retailers, concerns Tesco.com's order-fulfilment approach, based on in-store picking, rather than dedicated warehouses. It also shows how can one make Internet retailing a profit-making story.

The case objectives include: (1) to understand better how to optimize the mix of bricks and clicks in a retailing strategy; (2) to be able to address Internet-based retailing as a business rather than a technological issue; (3) to recognize the critical importance of operations and logistics in e-retailing; and (4) to realize that in e-retailing, profit-making results from a well co-ordinated, multifunctional implementation

Teaching note available

9 ChateauOnline

ChateauOnline looks at the situation of an e-tailer in 2001. The firm has done well and is a European leader. However, it faces the twin challenges of creating the online market for wine purchasing and the threat of entry by major players. The case explores the following themes: (1) value added: to understand how an online model can fit into established patterns of consumer behaviour; (2) the browser interface: to understand the role of the customer interface; (3) sustainable advantage: to understand the nature of on-line advantage; and (4) economic potential: to understand the potential of B2C retailers.

B2C in financial services

Teaching note available

10 Banking on the Internet: the Advance Bank in Germany

The case discusses the launch of Advance Bank, the branchless bank in Germany, which offers a full range of banking services and investment advice. A unique feature of Advance Bank is that it was built from scratch without relying on the products and banking infrastructure of its parent company, a branch-based bank. The bank's concept is that of a virtual company that sources its services and products from different financial providers spread out all over Germany and integrates them through a seamless interface with the customer. The case also discusses how a bank combines the offering of its services through a variety of distribution channels (telephone, PC and Internet). Customers can perform online standardized banking operations. For highly personalized and complex products, financial advice is offered by integrating telephone and Internet capabilities, thus allowing simultaneous voice and data

communication with the customer. The case concludes by highlighting the future challenges facing the Advance Bank.

The teaching objectives include: (1) to contrast the business models of a traditional, bricks-and-mortar bank and a virtual, branchless bank; (2) to assess the design and launch of the Advance Bank and to determine ways of improving its operations in Germany; (3) to analyze the roles of IT and the Internet in offering a highly customized banking service; and (4) to discuss possible strategies for the Advance Bank to fend off the increasing competition in branchless banking and to reach its break-even goal for 2001.

Teaching note available

11 The electronic purse in Portugal: a mere payment system or a socioeconomic revolution?

Typically, small-amount financial transactions cannot be paid through electronic means. In Portugal, in order to alleviate this problem, the inter-bank payments operator (known as SIBS[1]) launched in 1995 the PMB (Porta Moedas Multibanco) electronic purse. This project consisted of using chip-card technology to create a new payment system that makes daily coin operations more effective and puts a lot of 'pocket money' in bank accounts. This case investigates the technological, business and societal dimensions of the PMB electronic purse. It also analyzes the forces that motivated this innovation, the winners and losers, and the critical success factors of the project.

Teaching note available

12 From e-banking to e-business at Nordea (Scandinavia): the world's biggest clicks-and-mortar bank

This case focuses on the Scandinavian Nordea Bank's move from e-banking to e-business. It starts out by presenting Nordea's vision for e-banking and shows how the e-habit and e-trust among the Finnish population have contributed to fulfilling this vision.

The case continues by examining the main e-business services that Nordea currently offers to its private and corporate customers. These include e-identification, e-signature, e-billing, e-salary and e-payment. The case also discusses how Nordea integrates and manages the different banking channels to serve customers. These channels include (1) ATMs and pay terminals, (2) m-banking, (3) PC banking, (4) TV banking and (5) branch-based banking. As part of the channel management, Nordea also uses pricing schemes to entice customers to move online. On the technological side, the case discusses Nordea's authentication system, which is based on a one-time code (OTC). The case also considers the competitive threats from other physical banks and Internet pure players.

The case concludes by outlining future growth opportunities in existing markets and through new services. The latter include the usage of triggered data-mining techniques to improve customer service and the offering of risk-management services for e-businesses.

1 SIBS stands for Sociedade InterBancária de Serviços. It is a joint venture of 31 credit institutions established in Portugal.

B2C in manufacturing

Teaching note available

13 Ducati motorcycles (Italy): riding traditional business channels or racing through the Internet

This case discusses the e-business strategy of Ducati, an Italian manufacturer of high-performance motorcycles. It describes how, on 1 January 2000, Ducati sold exclusively through the Internet its new MH900e motorcycle at €15 000 per unit. It was the first motorcycle ever sold through the Internet, and the first-year production of the MH900e was sold out after just 31 minutes. The case also presents the way the company created the physical and the virtual 'World of Ducati'. The case objectives include: (1) to assess the business opportunities and risks that the Internet creates for a manufacturer; (2) to analyze how a manufacturer can exploit the Internet along four dimensions: context, content, commerce and virtual communities; and (3) to illustrate how a manufacturer can resolve the online/offline channel conflict and reconcile its e-commerce strategy with the business functions traditionally performed by its dealer network

14 Ducati (Italy) *vs.* Harley-Davidson (USA): innovating business processes and managing value networks

The case compares the e-business/e-commerce strategy of two leading motorcycle manufacturers and demonstrates how Ducati, unlike Harley-Davidson, has made the Internet today an inherent part of its corporate strategy, thus constituting a major change of direction for the firm. More specifically, the case describes how Ducati has successfully repositioned itself and adopted a new focus on R&D, marketing and sales, moving away from its initial manufacturing strength. It also analyzes how Ducati has fundamentally changed its business model, from traditionally operating through a narrow value chain to setting up a value network that has integrated online and offline processes and business partners. The case contrasts this approach with that of Harley-Davidson, which uses the Internet mainly as a communication channel with its dealers and customers, including the creation of a virtual online community. It also highlights the way each company manages its business processes and the roles that IT and the Internet play in R&D and design, purchasing, manufacturing and assembly, logistics, marketing and sales, and after-sales service.

B2C in media

Teaching note available

15 Terra Lycos: creating a global and profitable integrated media company

The case recounts the strategy of Terra Lycos, an integrated global media company formed by the October 2000 merger of Spain's Terra Networks and USA-based Lycos,

to achieve profitability and a leading market position. At the time the case was written (November 2001), Terra Lycos trailed its three heavy-weight contenders, AOL-Time Warner, Yahoo! and Microsoft/MSN. Teaching objectives are to discuss online media and the strategy of a major industry player in uncertain and negative market conditions. The case traces Terra Lycos's creation and its strategy to become an international player during the new economy slow-down through diversifying revenue streams and integrating online and offline media

16 Google.com: the world's number-one Internet search engine

The case examines the reasons for the success of Google.com, the California-based company Google Inc.'s Internet search engine. Google became the market leader leaving behind competitors like Netscape and AltaVista. The case explains the contribution of Google's technological innovations and focus on user-friendliness to its popularity. Google's unique business model, which made it one of the rare dot.coms to earn profits, is explained in detail. The case also provides details on various services and tools offered by Google to its corporate clients as well as Internet surfers. Finally, the case throws light on the problems faced by Google in 2003 and discusses their impact on its future prospects.

The case is designed to enable students to: (1) understand the concept of Internet search engines, the dynamics of the search engine market, and the circumstances that led to the development of the Google search engine; (2) understand the importance of technological superiority and customer-friendliness in the success of a dot.com venture; (3) understand the importance of an innovative and carefully planned business for successfully managing and running a dot.com company; and (4) understand the importance of constant innovation in the services offered to users to gain a competitive edge.

17 DoubleClick Inc.: a strategic transformation

DoubleClick was one of the companies present from almost the beginning of the commercial Internet. The growth of this infomediary acts as a primer for understanding the development of online advertising and marketing, while also tracing the company's subsequent move to become a technology provider. This case recounts the company's first breakthrough with its product DART and the DoubleClick Advertising Network, its subsequent delve into ASPs, and its acquisition of the offline infomediary Abacus.

The case seeks to show the strategies that DoubleClick has used in its development and growth as an infomediary, why and how DoubleClick shifted from being a pure media player to becoming a technology company, and where it should look for new growth opportunities. Finally, it debates the question of whether DoubleClick should aim to become the Bloomberg terminal of online advertising.

B2B e-commerce and B2B e-marketplaces

18 Competing through EDI at Papeteries Brun Passot: making paper passé

The case illustrates how Brun Passot, a small French company specializing in the distribution of office supplies, developed a set of tele-purchasing applications to differentiate customer service, shorten lead time and reduce management costs. It discusses the adoption and diffusion of electronic data interchange (EDI) and the company plan to leverage this technology in the evolving single European market.

The case objectives include: (1) to illustrate how IT influences business strategy formulation; (2) to demonstrate how EDI capabilities help a small company to change the competitive balance within an industry; and (3) to discuss IT potential as a competitive weapon in the evolving single European market.

19 CitiusNet: the emergence of a global electronic market

The case focuses on the emergence of electronic commerce and its business and organizational impact on trading partners. It presents CitiusNet, the first European B2B electronic platform offering multisectorial, online access to products and services. The case describes the technological components and functional capabilities of CitiusNet, emphasizing how the platform supports both the commercial aspects and the financial flows of a business transaction. The competitive dimension of this new locus of value creation is also highlighted.

The teaching objectives are: (1) to demonstrate how to leverage IT to successfully launch a new venture and compete in the emerging market space (as opposed to the marketplace); (2) to illustrate how companies can use IT to re-engineer business processes and relationships, and transform their business scope/business network, transcending traditional organizational and industry boundaries; and(3) to discuss the global opportunities of electronic commerce and the business implications of this new locus of value creation.

Teaching note available

20 B2B electronic commerce: mondus.com – an e-marketplace for small and medium-sized enterprises

This case describes the development and use of a neutral B2B marketplace (mondus.com) set up for small and medium-sized enterprises. It analyzes how mondus matches buyers and sellers through the request-for-proposals model. The case also describes the international expansion of mondus and the entrepreneurial leadership of its founders, and highlights the benefits and drawbacks for the e-marketplace players.

The case objectives include: (1) to demonstrate how the Internet helps streamline the purchasing process and creates value for all parties involved; (2) to analyze the information flows between the buyer, seller and e-marketplace operator during an online purchasing transaction; and (3) to discuss the business opportunities and risks that an e-marketplace operator faces.

21 B2B e-marketplace in the automotive industry: Covisint – a co-opetition gamble?

The case discusses the business drivers underlying the creation of Covisint, an Internet-based exchange platform set up in 2000 by General Motors, Ford and DaimlerChrysler. This global portal connects the car makers and their suppliers and supports online collaboration, e-procurement and supply chain management. The case analyzes the business strategy and business model of Covisint as well as the organizational and technological issues involved in developing and operating the platform. It also discusses Covisint's usage and the benefits it is expected to achieve thanks to its tremendous economies of scale. It also raises the difficulties for the 'Big Three' car manufacturers in developing this mega-exchange and in co-operating through this online venture while still competing in the marketplace. The case also highlights anti-trust concerns of whether Covisint, through the combined purchasing power of its participating car makers, could be anti-competitive for suppliers.

C2C e-commerce

22, 23, 24 eBay strategy A, B and international

eBay is, by most measures, one of the most successful pure-play Internet companies. It has been very successful in creating the world's largest person-to-person trading network. Its future growth is being driven by entry into foreign markets (in Europe and Asia) and evolutions in its business models, such as fixed pricing. This raises several interesting managerial issues for eBay, which are captured in the case studies. The eBay strategy (A and B) cases allow for a dicussion of the following aspects:

- Consideration of additional business models such as corporate stores, fixed prices etc.
- Consequences of the above on strategic postion, customer segment focus and dilution of core business model.
- Management decision-making under uncertainity.

The eBay international case study allows for a discussion of the following aspects:

- eBay's international expansion strategy, including choice of markets and mode of entry.
- Role of eBay's aquisitions, in particular of iBazaar in France.
- Exploration of 'global-local' issues in product and services offers.

P2P e-commerce

25 Online file-sharing: the music industry's paradigm shift

Ever since they succeeded in closing down the original Napster in 1999, the major music companies have struggled to deal with its successors, the peer-to-peer (P2P)

networks. Yet, is this really the paradigm shift that many claim it to be? Is P2P directly responsible for the tumbling sales of music between 1999 and 2003? Putting together the emotional response that many people have for music with the hard-nosed world of business is always likely to be a balancing act. This case study helps us to look at how established industries respond to threats and to consider the complexity of the value chain between the original producer of a product (the writer or performer) and the end user (the consumer who buys the CDs and merchandise).

Mobile e-commerce

Teaching note available

26 12Snap (Germany, UK, Italy): from B2C mobile retailing to B2B mobile marketing

The case analyzes the first years of operation of 12Snap, a German start-up launched in 1999 and today considered the largest mobile marketing channel in Europe. It focuses on the changing market positioning and business model of the company, which evolved from B2C mobile retailing to B2B mobile marketing. The objectives for this case are: (1) to understand how mobile marketing campaigns can be conducted and the underlying technologies that enable them; (2) to gain insights on a more aggregate level into how mobile applications can change marketing and advertising methods; and (3) to understand the entrepreneurial evolution (in terms of business strategy and business model) of a mobile marketing service provider.

Teaching note available

27 Paybox.net (Germany): a mobile payment service

Paybox.net, founded in 1999, is a front-runner in providing mobile payment services in Germany and other European countries. The case discusses the development and roll-out of the m-payment services, the business model and marketing approach used, the technological and organizational challenges that the company faced, and the sustainability of the paybox competitive position. The case objectives are: (1) to analyze the disruptive innovation dimension of mobile payment services compared with existing online and offline payment modes; (2) to demonstrate how an entrepreneurial firm adapts to a competitive business environment with a slow market uptake, risk-averse investors and a fast-changing technology; and (3) to understand the development, marketing and pricing of mobile payment services as an example of digital, network-based goods.

Teaching note available

28 NTT DoCoMo i-mode: value innovation at DoCoMo

As of November 2001, NTT DoCoMo was the only company that had been able to make money out of the mobile Internet. This case describes how, in a very competitive industry engaged in a technology race and strong price erosion, NTT DoCoMo has been able to achieve superior performance since it launched, in February 1999, its novel i-mode services. This was an immediate and explosive success. DoCoMo

now exceeds its parent company in terms of market capitalization as well as potential for profitable growth as we enter the age of mobile Internet. This case offers a value innovation perspective to analyze the success of i-mode with a particular emphasis on the business model used to exploit the i-mode innovation of DoCoMo. The case is designed to serve a variety of purposes in the 'value innovation and winning business ideas' teaching module of an MBA strategy course or executive education programme. It can also be used in an IT course in a module focusing on mobile Internet. Equally, the case can be used individually as a stand-alone module on value innovation or as part of a sequence of three to four sessions. In the first instance, the instructor can use it to cover the following topics: (1) the value innovation logic, (2) the value curve and six paths analysis, (3) the buyer utility map and (4) the price corridor of the mass and the business model guide. Alternatively, the instructor can use it to cover specifically the latter three topics.

Teaching note available

Case study teaching notes are available at **www.booksites.net/jelassi** where indicated.

CASE STUDY 1

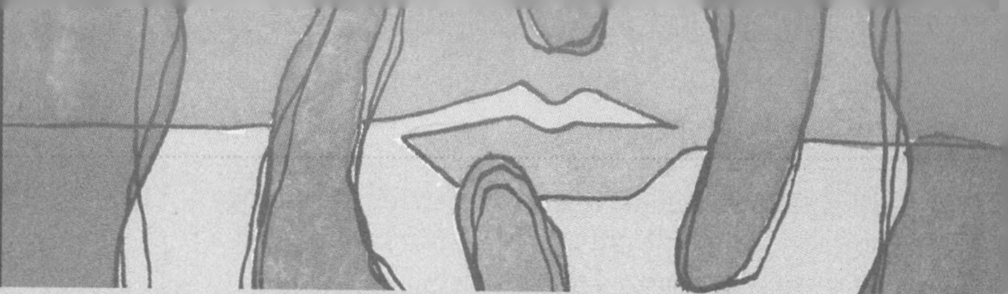

Establishing a national IT infrastructure

The case of the French videotex system Minitel

In the late 1970s, videotex[1] was an important fixture of the telecommunications landscape of most industrialized countries. Many national post, telephone and telegraph (PTT) companies and commercial ventures started pilot videotex projects. Some social commentators and researchers began discussing videotex as one of the driving forces in the movement towards an information society.

A decade later, most of the enthusiasm has evaporated. France's famous Télétel[2] (over six million subscribers and 17 000 services, as of December 1991) is the only commercially viable national videotex system so far. The limited success of videotex ventures is surprising, since there were at least 50 videotex projects in 16 countries of Western Europe, Japan and North America in 1982.

Indeed, Britain's Prestel (150 000 subscribers and 1 300 services) and Germany's Bildschirmtext (250 000 subscribers and 3 500 services), which rank second and third in the world, are considered commercial failures, and their prospects for growth are not very good.

What made Télétel such a success?

Information technology and French industrial policy

In the mid-1960s, particularly after the American Congress had denied a permit to export a large IBM mainframe computer to the French government, French political commentators started to voice concerns that France was falling behind the USA in information technology and that it would soon be in an intolerable situation of technological and cultural dependence. For example, President Valéry Giscard d'Estaing, in gathering support for moving France into the information age, stated: 'For France, the American domination of telecommunications and computers is a threat to its independence in the crucially significant if not overriding area of technology and in the field of culture, where the American presence, through television and satellite, becomes an omnipresence.' This line of thought continued to be voiced during the 1970s and became a central piece of the industrial policy of the country.[3]

1 Videotex is a generic term for an easy-to-use, computer-based, interactive system to access and selectively view text and graphics on a terminal screen. The content is usually organized into tree structures of pages that are selected from a series of hierarchical menus. Videotex systems typically offer a wide range of information-retrieval interactive and transactional services, such as directory and reservations systems, financial reports, home banking and shopping. Videotex was developed in Europe in the mid-1970s for consumer applications. Because of its consumer origins, videotex excels at delivering information to untrained and casual users. The user may use a dedicated videotex terminal or other access deliveries (e.g. PC). The primary objective of commercial videotex systems is the efficient delivery of value-added information and services to a maximum number of users profitably for both the system operator and the service provider.

2 The system is popularly known as Minitel. In strict terms, however, Minitel refers only to the dedicated terminal itself. Throughout this case, we use Télétel when we refer to the whole system and Minitel when we allude to the device.

3 Although the 'enemy' has changed and the main villain is now Japan, the policy is still very much in place today, as illustrated by the French government's decision in 1991 to save the consumer electronics companies Bull and Thomson from insolvency.

This case was written by William Cats-Baril, Visiting Professor at INSEAD; Tawfik Jelassi, Associate Professor at INSEAD; and James Téboul, Affiliate Professor at INSEAD. It is intended to be used as a basis for class discussion rather than to illustrate either effective or ineffective handling of an administrative situation.

In 1975, President Giscard d'Estaing asked two researchers, Simon Nora and Alain Minc, to suggest a strategy to computerize French society. The Nora–Minc report delivered in 1978 and published in 1979 went on to be a best-seller (a first for this type of report). Nora and Minc coined a new word, 'Télématique' (from telecommunication and informatique), and proposed it as the cornerstone of that strategy. Télématique was the merger of computers and communication technologies to create information-processing applications with broad societal impact.

Indeed, Nora and Minc predicted that eventually Télématique would affect all aspects of society – education, business, media, leisure and routine day-to-day activities. The way they saw it, Télématique would, by increasing access to information, lead to decentralization of government and business decision-making and therefore to an increase in national productivity and competitiveness and an improvement in the ability to respond to an increasingly fast-changing environment (Nora and Minc 1979). Nora and Minc's view, however, implied that a new national communication infrastructure was necessary for France to remain among the leading countries of the industrialized world. Their report also underlined that such a transformation would require a long-term strategy and co-operation between the government and business sectors.

One of the recommendations of the report was for the Direction Générale des Télécommunications (DGT), as France Télécom was then named, to encourage co-operation between computer services companies and hardware manufacturers to produce the technical components of the required infrastructure. Another recommendation was for the DGT to implement a research programme to develop applications that would leverage and take advantage of that infrastructure (Nora and Minc 1979).

These recommendations are typical of French industrial policy. The strategy of having the government orchestrate and subsidize large technological projects by creating alliances among companies and 'rationalizing' an industrial sector by encouraging mergers – the computer and electronics sector being a prime example – had been used before (e.g. Ariane, Airbus, Concorde, TGV). As a senior official of the French government put it, 'This type of large industrial project, or, as we [the French] call them, "les grandes aventures", has always captured the imagination of French politicians'.

The French telephone system in the 1970s

In 1974, when Giscard d'Estaing became President of France, the French telecommunication system was very weak. There were fewer than seven million telephone lines for a population of 47 million (one of the lowest penetration rates in the industrialized world, equivalent to that of Czechoslovakia), a four-year wait to get a new line, and manual switches still in use in most rural areas in the country (Chamoux 1990; Mayer 1988).

President Giscard d'Estaing decided to make the reform of the telecommunication infrastructure a top priority. In April 1975, the Conseil des Ministres (a cabinet-level meeting of the secretaries of all agencies) approved the President's programme under the banner 'Le téléphone pour tous' (a telephone for everyone).

Also in 1974, Gérard Théry took over as Director of the DGT. At that time, the strategic direction of telecommunication technology was set by the Centre National d'Etudes des Télécommunications (CNET). The CNET was, and continues to be, the research and development arm of the DGT. The CNET was dominated by engineers whose responsibility and vocation was the design of new products. They focused on technical prowess and innovation.

Once the design of a product was complete, the CNET negotiated the development and commercialization of the product directly with the telecommunication industry. Housel (1990) notes that because the CNET engineers were constantly trying new technologies without a clear technological migration plan, manufacturers were forced into short production runs, making manufacturing economies of scale impossible, driving up prices, and making network compatibility difficult to achieve.

Théry changed the orientation of the CNET. From an attitude of technological change for the sake of technological change, the CNET moved to a more pragmatic and commercial stance. The change in culture was difficult at first: most of the engineers went on a long and bitter strike. Eventually, Théry's vision prevailed. Not only did the internal focus of the CNET change, but a new relationship between the DGT and French telecommunication manufacturers was established (Housel 1990; Marchand 1987a, 1987b).

Théry's strategy to establish a more commercial orientation at the CNET was implemented by creating the Direction des Affaires Industrielles et Internationales

(DAII) and bringing in an outsider – Jean-Pierre Souviron – as its director. One of the principal functions of the DAII was to ensure standardization of equipment. The DAII invited bids not only from the traditional suppliers of the DGT (e.g. CIT-Alcatel, Thomson) but from others as well (e.g. Matra and Philips). In order to drive down equipment prices, the DAII announced that from then on an important criterion in choosing suppliers would be their ability to export and thus acquire larger markets.

The government push towards standardization and export was partially responsible for lowering subscription charges and more than doubling the number of telephone lines between 1974 and 1979. By the late 1980s, the penetration rate was at 95%, one of the highest telephone-penetration rates among the industrialized nations (Chamoux 1990; Housel 1990).

The transformation of the French telephone network from the 'joke of Europe' to Europe's most modern ('from the ugly toad to the handsome prince', in the words of a government official) took some ten years and very substantial resources. Indeed, from 1976 to 1980, the DGT was the largest investor in France, averaging around 4% of the total national investment in the country (Hutin 1981). The cost of the transformation has been estimated at around FF120 billion. The magnitude of the investment raised questions as to how to maintain expansion of the telephone network and how to leverage the modernization costs. In early 1978, with the telephone-penetration rate growing very quickly, Théry realized that telephone traffic alone would not be enough to leverage the telephone network and the public packet-switched network (Transpac).

Théry asked the CNET to generate ideas for new services and established a list of requirements that they would be required to fulfil. The services would have to: (1) provide greater access to government and commercial information for all citizens; (2) benefit as many elements of society as possible; (3) demonstrate the value of merging computing and telecommunications; (4) be flexible enough to avoid quick technological obsolescence; and (5) be profitable (Housel 1990).

In November 1978, Théry prepared a report for the Conseil des Ministres detailing six projects: the electronic telephone directory, the videotex, the videophone, the wide distribution of telefax machines, the launching of a satellite for data transmission, and the voice-activated telephone. The background for his presentation was the Nora and Minc report and the need to counter the threat of IBM capturing critical strategic markets if left unchallenged, as perceived by Théry. 'Let us be the Japanese of Europe' was his battle cry (Marchand 1987a). The Conseil des Ministres gave a green light only to the electronic telephone directory and the videotex. Three years after the successful launch of the 'Le téléphone pour tous' campaign, 'la grande aventure du Télétel' was about to begin.

Télétel: A brief history

Work on Télétel began in the mid-1970s. The first Télétel prototype was shown at the 1977 Berlin Trade Fair. At that show, the British demonstrated a very impressive operational system (CEEFAX, the precursor of Prestel). Théry realized he had to move fast. He persuaded the government to allow the DGT to pursue the videotex project (during the interministerial meeting of November 1978). It was agreed to test Télétel in 1979. Initially, there were plans for two applications: the development of an electronic telephone directory (ETD) and classified ads.

With the installation of seven million telephone lines from 1974 to 1979, the French telephone directory was obsolete as soon as it was printed (even printed twice a year). Also, the cost of printing the directory had gone up so rapidly that in 1979 the paper telephone directory lost FF120 million. Between 1979 and 1984, seven million additional lines were to be installed. The cost of printing the directory alone was expected to double in the next five years and the quantity of paper needed to quintuple from 20 000 tons in 1979 to a projected 100 000 tons by 1985. Directory assistance was hopelessly overloaded. It required 4500 operators to provide a barely acceptable level of service. The number of operators needed in 1985 was forecasted to be 9000 (Dondoux 1978; Marchand 1987a, 1987b).

Directory automation was proposed both to address the directory assistance problem, which was becoming a serious public relations issue, and to bring about savings by avoiding the costs of printing telephone directories. The success of the electronic telephone directory assumed that a great majority of the subscribers would be able to use it. This notion in turn implied that subscribers would need to have access to an easy-to-use, inexpensive terminal.

Exhibit 1 Rate of Minitel distribution

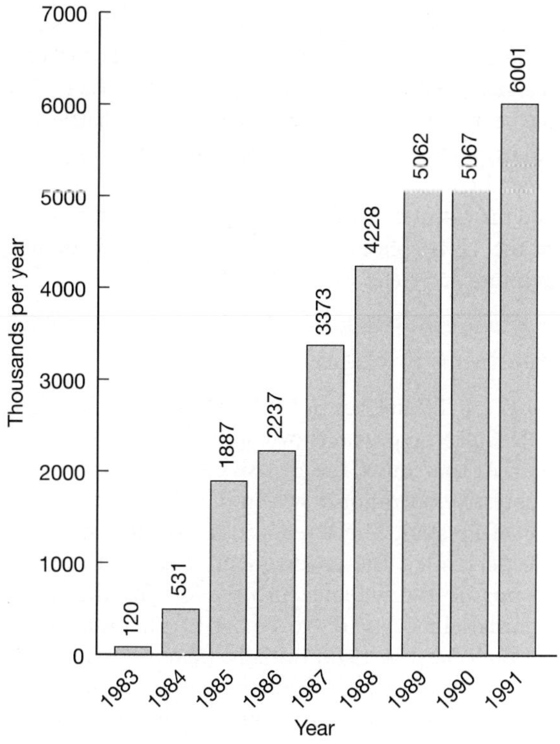

Source: France Télécom.

Exhibit 2 Growth of Télétel services

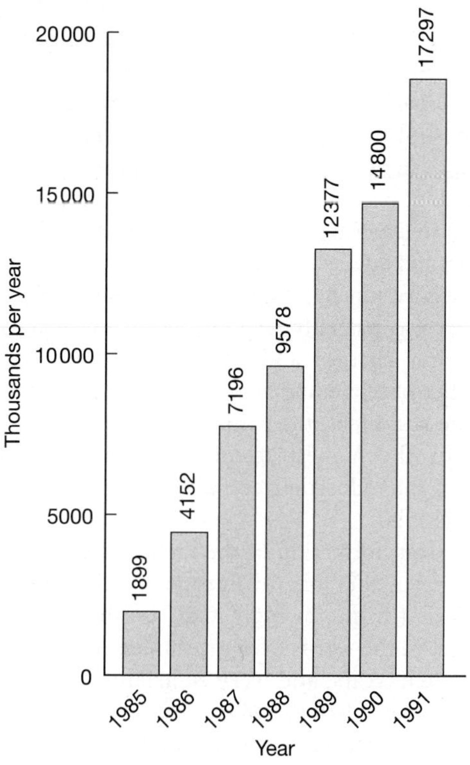

Source: France Télécom.

At the DAII, planners developed the scenario of distributing terminals free of charge to subscribers. They reasoned that as long as a dedicated terminal could be produced for FF500, then the cost of the terminal could be recovered in less than five years (the cost of each paper telephone book was FF100, and it was increasing). The government agreed to try out the electronic telephone directory concept during the Conseil des Ministres of November 1978. The first test was carried out in Saint-Malo, Brittany, in July 1980.

Another application that was discussed in order to help launch Télétel was offering classified ads. But after a vicious attack from the press and its powerful lobby, which saw their main source of income threatened, the DGT capitulated. On 12 December 1980, Pierre Ribes, Secretary of the PTT, stated unequivocally that there would be no classified ads offered through Télétel in the videotex experiment to be started in Vélizy, a suburb of Paris, in June 1981. The press has consequently dropped its resistance to the Télétel project (Marchand 1987a, 1987b).

The initial testing of the electronic directory began on 15 July 1980 in Saint-Malo.[4] The actual videotex experiment started in Vélizy (under the name Télétel 3V) in June 1981 with a sample of 2500 homes and 100 different services. After two years, the Vélizy test showed that 25% of the users were responsible for 60% of all traffic, one-third of the sample never used the device (this proportion of non-users has remained constant throughout the dissemination of minitels), and, overall, households had had a positive experience with Télétel. The experiment was considered a success in both technical and sociological terms (Chamoux 1990; Marchand 1987a, 1987b).

4 By comparison, the British television-based system Prestel had a field trial with 1400 participants in 1978 and started commercial service in the autumn of 1979. Full nationwide operation was established in March 1980. At the end of 1981, Prestel had only one-tenth of the users predicted for that time (Thomas and Miles 1989). This failure has been attributed to the late delivery and high prices of television monitors (Prestel needed a connection between the telephone and the television set), uncoordinated marketing and bad quality of the databases (Schneider *et al.* 1990).

Exhibit 3 **Total Télétel usage (including ETD)**

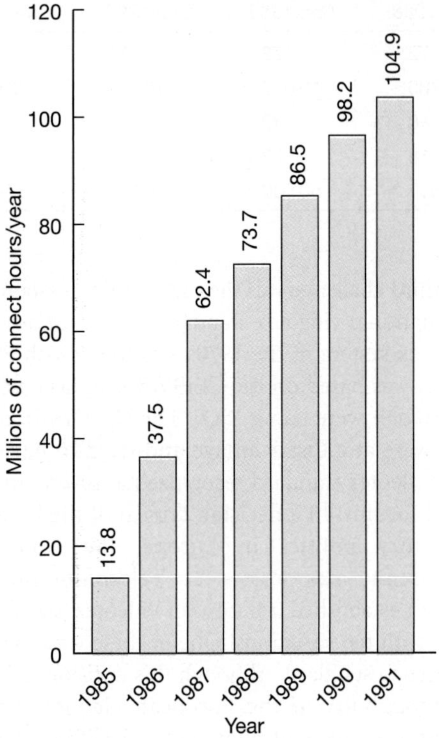

Source: France Télécom.

Exhibit 4 **Usage of the electronic telephone directory**

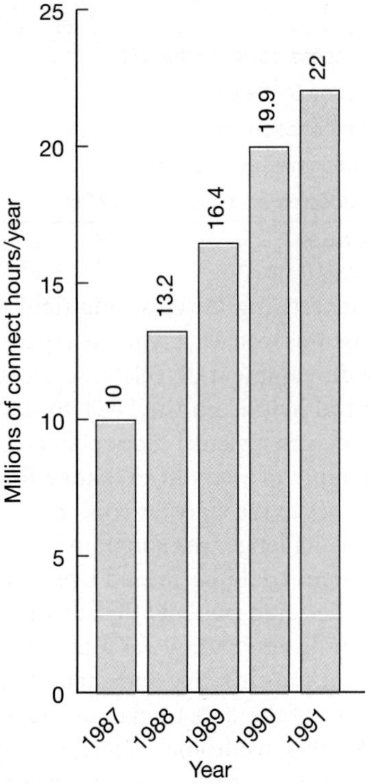

Source: France Télécom.

On 4 February 1983, a full-scale implementation of the electronic directory was started in the area of Ille-et-Vilaine. In the opening ceremony, Louis Mexandeau, the new Secretary of the PTT, exulted: 'We are here today to celebrate the beginning of a "grande aventure", an experience which will mark our future.' François Mitterrand had replaced Valéry Giscard d'Estaing as President of France, the 'left' was now in power, but the rhetoric on the importance of Télématique to the future of the country and the underlying industrial policy remained the same.

Soon after the successes of Vélizy and Ille-et-Vilaine, the free, public distribution of Minitel terminals was implemented: there were 120 000 Minitels in France by the end of 1983, over three million by December 1987, and more than six million by December 1991 (see Exhibit 1). Videotex services went from 145 in January of 1984 to 7000 at the end of 1987 to more than 17 000 by December 1991 (see Exhibit 2). Traffic on the Télétel system and on the electronic telephone directory has increased steadily over the past several years (see Exhibits 3 and 4). Moreover, these two systems have been continuously expanded and improved (see Table 1). In 1989, France Télécom created new organizational entities (e.g. Intelmatique) to export Télétel and the accompanying know-how.

Télétel had to overcome four serious challenges in the early years. First, there were vicious attacks by the newspaper owners, in particular François-Régis Hutin, owner of *Ouest-France*, who found among many philosophical reasons to stop videotex one very pragmatic one (Hutin 1981).[5] Videotex was a serious threat to the newspaper's main source of

5 Typical of the attacks is the call to arms by the political commentator George Suffert. He argued, in an article titled 'The fight of the century: Teletex versus paper', that it was dangerous to let the DGT have a monopoly on the videotex system. He wrote: 'He who owns the wire is powerful. He who owns the wire and the screen is very powerful. He who owns the wire, the screen, and the computer has the power of God.'

Table 1 Evolution of the electronic telephone directory (ETD) and videotex networks

	Dec 1987	*Dec 1988*	*Dec 1989*	*Dec 1990*	*Dec 1991*
Number of access points to the ETD	58	72	78	82	86
Number of ports to the ETD	14220	17280	19020	19020	20640
Number of information centres	31	40	42	44	47
Number of documentation centres	15	18	22	23	25
Number of videotex access points (VAPs)	43160	49611	50500	53000	57000

Source: France Télécom.

revenue: advertising. After a long fight, a political compromise was reached, giving newspaper owners a say in the development of Télétel services, subsidies and technical help from the DGT to develop their own services, and a virtual monopoly on services for the first couple of years in exchange for dropping their resistance to the videotex concept.

A second challenge was some politicians' feeling that the system could be abused by the state. These politicians declared publicly that this new mode of information dissemination was a potential threat to the liberty of the citizenry and that Télétel was the latest attempt of the state to manipulate information ('the Big Brother syndrome'). Later, the rapid proliferation of 'chat' services (*messageries*), some of which were considered pornographic (*messageries roses*), brought criticism from both government and private groups who were concerned that the state was billing and indirectly subsidizing immorality.

A third challenge was the early battle to establish an international videotex standard. The most advanced videotex system in the 1970s was the British Prestel. Prestel was based on the CEEFAX standard, whereas the French were using XXX. The DGT realized that they were at a disadvantage and tried to have their own videotex standard recognized at several international forums. In a decision typical of the byzantine regulatory politics in Europe, the Conférence Européenne des Postes et Télécommunications (CEPT) established a European videotex 'standard' in 1980, with ten variations! One of these variations was the French standard. Although this decision led to the incompatibility of the European videotex systems during the 1980s, it allowed the DGT to continue developing Télétel as planned.

The fourth challenge that Télétel had to meet was the negative publicity that surrounded the 'crash of 85', the only system failure since its inception. The

Exhibit 5 Minitel usage

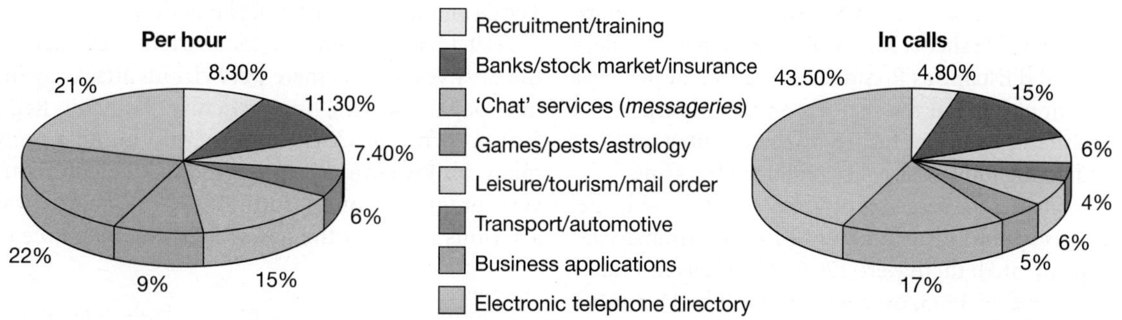

Table 2 **Demographic statistics of Minitel users**

	Minitel users population (%)	*French population (%)*
Sex		
Male	50.5	47.2
Female	49.5	52.7
Age (years)		
15–24	17.6	19.3
25–34	28.2	20.6
35–49	31.9	22.4
50–64	16.9	20.6
64 years	5.5	17.1
Job category		
Agriculture	4.6	6.0
Small business, handicraft, trade	12.1	7.7
Professions, executives	19.1	8.6
Office and skilled workers	36.2	24.7
Non-skilled workers	17.8	26.1
Non-working	9.8	26.8

Source: Adapted from 'La Lettre de Télétel', France Télécom, June 1992.

crash was the result of very heavy traffic of the *messageries* services. This heavy traffic caused an overload of the Transpac switching system, and the network went down. The technical problem was easy to solve: the switching system was changed to handle higher volumes, and there has not been another crash since. The perception that Télétel was mostly about sex lingered much longer, slowed down Télétel's development, and, paradoxically, increased its international visibility.

Overcoming these public controversies made Télétel stronger in the long run. Indeed, the political fury that Télétel generated in 1978–80 and later in 1985 led to a full and rich discussion on the issues of privacy rights, authority of the telecommunication agency, regulation of computer services, and the need to prevent the creation of a second class of citizens shut out of the information age. This discussion involved the President of France and the most notable political commentators and intellectuals in the country, and eventually created a broad national consensus on the use and limitations of the technology.

Today, Télétel is an integral part of the French society lifestyle. A survey conducted by France Télécom in October 1989 indicated that some 40% of the population had access to Minitels at home or at work. Another survey, conducted in 1991, showed that the system was used regularly by a broad cross-section of the population in a variety of ways (see Exhibit 5, and Tables 2 and 3).

The success of Télétel as a sociological development and its positive impact on the technological literacy of the population are unquestionable. The primary concern about Télétel now is whether it is a profitable operation. But before exploring this issue, let us describe some of the technical choices and characteristics that have made Télétel the only successful commercial videotex system in the world so far.

General characteristics of Télétel

A comparison of the technical characteristics and policies that were used in implementing Télétel with those of the other commercial videotex systems (e.g. American, British, German) explains to a certain degree the great success of Télétel and the rather tepid development of the others. The comparison of videotex systems can be made on the basis of four characteristics: (1) terminal design and strategy of terminal distribution; (2) system architecture and other

Table 3 **Minitel traffic statistics**

Télétel Traffic (including electronic telephone directory (ETD))	*1986*	*1987*	*1988*	*1989*	*1990*	*1991*
Total number of calls (millions)	466	807	1010	1242	1482	1656
Number of connect hours (millions)	37.5	62.4	73.7	86.5	98.2	104.9
Average usage per Minitel per month (minutes)	105.9	111.3	97.0	93.2	92.4	90.16
Average number of calls per Minitel per month	21.9	24.0	22.2	22.3	23.2	23.77
Average length of call to Télétel (including ETD) (minutes)	4.8	4.6	4.4	4.2	4.0	3.79
Average length of call to Télétel (excluding ETD) minutes)	6.3	6.1	5.8	6.5	5.5	5.3

Source: Adapted from 'La Lettre de Télétel', France Télécom, April 1992.

aspects of service provision; (3) billing system; and (4) regulatory environment (see Schneider *et al.* 1990).

Given the British experience, where the high price of the TV-based videotex set-up chosen became a barrier to implementation, and the DGT argument that the Télétel investment would be paid back through increased telephone traffic and savings in the production of the telephone directory, it was clear that Télétel's success was critically dependent on the development of an easy-to-use, dedicated and inexpensive terminal for mass distribution. The Vélizy experience also established the need for a user-friendly terminal with an easy-to-use interface. The motto for Télétel became 'make it simple' – simple to manufacture, simple to install, simple to use.

In an approach typical of French industrial policy, the government (rather than the consumer electronics industry) decided on the specifications of the videotex terminals. The DAII opened the procurement of terminals to multiple vendors and the promise of a production run of some 20 million terminals encouraged low bids. The total cost of the original basic Minitel terminal to the DGT was approximately FF1000.

The key decision on whether to distribute Minitel terminals free of charge generated intense controversy within the DGT. On the one hand, distributing Minitels on a free and voluntary basis gave the system an aura of democracy: those who wished to have a Minitel would not be impeded by cost. This also made it easier for the mass public to try out the device and the services it offered.

On the other hand, some senior officers at the DGT thought that a nominal fee on a per-month basis not only was sound policy from a financial point of view, but would also send an appropriate message to the users to counteract the 'if-it's-free-it-can't-be-very-good' syndrome. They reasoned that once the system was distributed for free, it would be practically impossible to charge for it later on without generating intense public resistance. In what turned out to be a critical decision for the success of Télétel, it was decided that Minitel terminals would be distributed free of charge.

Another critical success factor of Minitel was the decision to implement the Télétel concept by interfacing the public switched telephone network with the Transpac packet-switching data network. The subscriber was linked to the electronic directory or any other database via their telephone through a gateway – called a videotex access point (VAP) – giving access to the Transpac network to which the servers and host computers were to be connected.

This design approach had three basic advantages. First, Transpac charges are based on traffic (i.e. minutes of connect time) and not on distance, which means that any provider, independent of its geographical location, has equal access and equal costs in gaining a national audience. Second, it established a common standard protocol (i.e. the CCITT X.29), making connections to the system straightforward and relatively cheap (FF100 000), a crucial point in attracting service providers. Third, the networks were already in place, included the latest technology, and could support a rapid expansion in the number of subscribers and providers.

More importantly, the decision to use the Transpac network kept the DGT from becoming an information provider. With the exception of the electronic directory, the DGT acted as a common carrier and was responsible only for the transmission of information and administration of the network.[6] This is in contrast to the centralized solution offered by the British and German systems, where British Telecom and the BundesPost provided the design and storage of the databases. In Télétel, the storage and manipulation of information were left to the information providers.

The decision to build Télétel on a decentralized network and with an open architecture went a long way to (1) alleviating the 'Big Brother' concerns of the press and politicians and (2) encouraging innovation in information services, since clear telecommunications standards were used and the entry barrier to the information provider market was very low.

Another critical element in the success of Télétel is the billing system introduced by France Télécom in March 1984 and named the 'kiosk'. The billing is done by France Télécom, not by the service providers. The system was named after the newsstands where a variety of publications can be bought without leaving a record of what was bought or who bought it. The Télétel charges appear on the regular

6 That has now changed. France Télécom decided in 1990 to enter the information-provision business by offering what are called added-value services. Most of these services are offered through joint ventures with privately owned companies.

telephone bill as 'Minitel use', with no reference whatsoever as to what specific service was used.

The kiosk works as follows: when the connection to the desired service has been set up through the VAP, the VAP sends charging pulses to the subscriber's meter at a faster-than-usual rate to cover the cost of using the Transpac network and the cost of the service. The Transpac network keeps track of the connection time and pays each provider as a function of that time. The kiosk is a very clever idea because it protects the anonymity of the users (important on both financial and philosophical levels), because it does not require passwords or payments in advance, because service providers do not have to worry about billing and its associated administrative costs, and because it allows differently priced services to be offered easily through a series of different numbers.

France Télécom's monopoly position in basic telecommunication services and the fact that it did not have the return-on-investment pressures of a commercial firm provided Télétel with the necessary time to mature.[7] Infrastructure-based services like Télétel require a longer time horizon to assess and determine profitability. There is no doubt that the regulatory umbrella shielding Télétel in the early years is one of the critical factors in its success.

Another aspect of the French regulatory environment important to the development of Télétel was the ability of France Télécom to subsidize ventures out of its subscribers' revenue. Such subsidies are forbidden by American and British regulations. The subsidies allowed France Télécom to take a long and patient view on Télétel and helped amortize the free distribution of Minitel terminals, which amounted to a cost of FF6 billion over ten years.

Yet another specific benefit of this protective regulatory environment is described by Housel (1990). He notes that the ability to implement changes of tariffs quickly without going through a lengthy political process to justify them allowed France Télécom to respond quickly to changing market conditions. For example, there were many services that Télétel users could access and use without staying connected for very long. The user paid no fee because the tariff allowed free access. Because of the revenue-sharing arrangements with the service providers, however, France Télécom had to pay for each connection. France Télécom asked the regulatory bodies to charge subscribers a small access fee for every connection regardless of its duration. The request was barely scrutinized and the charge was approved without debate.

The regulatory environment in France also enabled France Télécom to run the kiosk billing system. The arrangement has come under fire on two fronts. First, the fact that the billing system results in the state (in the form of France Télécom) collecting fees for the distribution of services that may be deemed pornographic has been argued to be against the law. Second, it has been suggested that, even if it is not illegal, billing, which could be a very profitable stand-alone operation, should be a service offered by a third party and not by France Télécom. These criticisms have not stopped France Télécom from performing the billing.

The regulatory environment in Europe, with its myriad of standards and protocols, was also beneficial for Télétel initially because it served to protect the fledgling service from being battered by competition from abroad. However, that same environment has now become a barrier to Télétel's penetration of other European markets. Finally, one must note that it is to France Télécom's credit that in such a heavily regulated environment it pursued an open network architecture and stayed out of the information services business, with the exception of the electronic telephone directory.[8]

This policy of decentralization and liberalization of services, contrary to the centralization policies in Britain and Germany, led to an explosion of services. Indeed, while in France the number of providers has grown steadily and the number of services today surpasses 17 000, in Britain the number has stagnated at 1300 or so, and in Germany the number has not only stagnated but actually declined to around less than 3000 (Schneider *et al.* 1990). A comparison of the videotex systems in France, the UK and West Germany is shown in Exhibit 6 and Table 4.

7 France Télécom is directly accountable to the French government for all its ventures and is required to justify its fee structures. More than other state agencies, France Télécom is asked to demonstrate the viability of its investments and therefore is under some profitability pressures, mild as they may be.

8 Whether France Télécom would have taken such an enlightened position without the ferocious criticism of the press lobbies and consumer watchdog groups is debatable. Still, when it comes to Télétel, the executives of the DGT and France Télécom have consistently exhibited excellent judgement.

Exhibit 6 **Technical configuration of videotex systems in the UK, France and Germany**

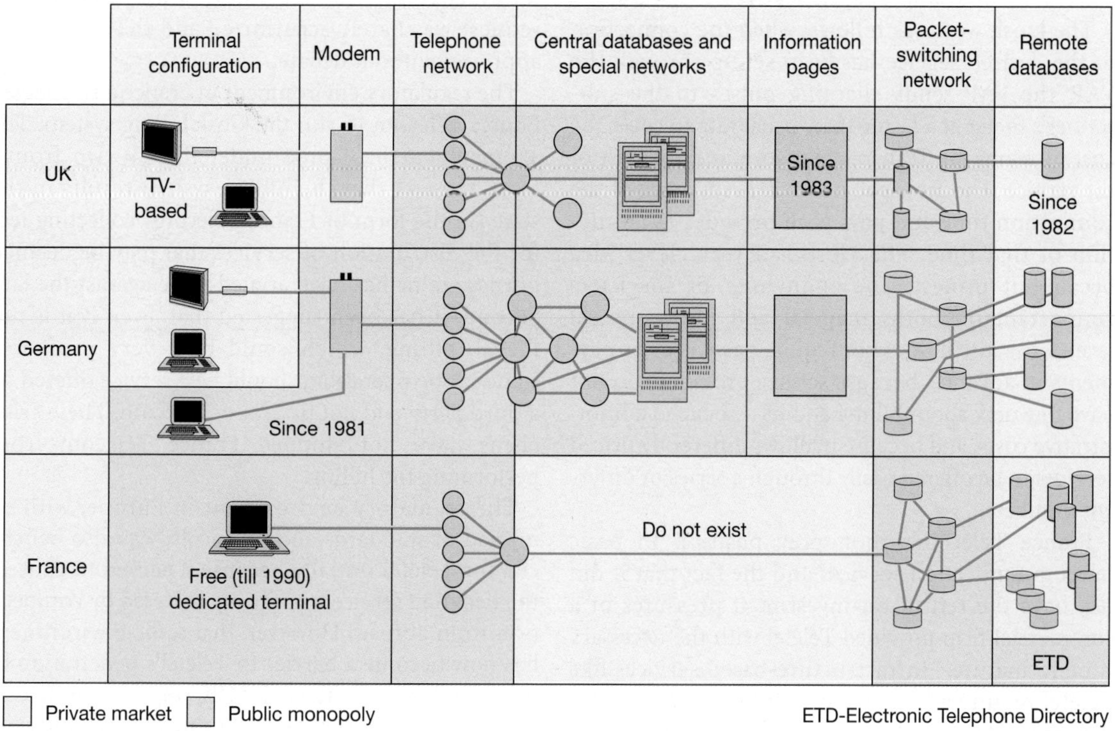

Source: Schneider *et al*. (1990).

Table 4 **Implementation strategies and structures of the videotex systems in the UK, France and Germany**

	UK	*France*	*Germany*
Terminal configuration	Adapted TV set provided by TV industry and to be bought by subscriber	Simple dedicated compact terminal (Minitel), free distribution (until 1990)	Adapted TV set provided by TV industry and to be bought by subscriber (change in 1986: multitels)
Network architecture	Several central databases, one update centre, closed system	Primarily privately owned databases, service computers connected to Transpac	Hierarchical network: one central datbase with regional sub-bases; interconnection to private computers
Information provision	Only by private IP (common carrier) (change in 1983: BT becomes IP)	Trigger service 'electronic phone book' by PTT; other services by private IPs	Only by private IP (common carrier)
Billing system	Subscription fees, page-based charges, phone-call charges	No subscription fees, time-based charges	Subscription fees, page-based charges, phone-call charges
Regulation political control	No specific regulations, less politicized	Specific regulations, liberal regime politicized, promoted by industrial policy	Specific regulations, very restrictive regime politicized

Source: Schneider *et al*. (1990).

Télétel: a sociological success

It would be a mistake to analyze Télétel exclusively on return on investment without taking into consideration its sociological impact. Although measuring the non-financial benefits (i.e. social, educational and political) brought by Télétel is difficult, the increase in technological awareness and literacy of society has to be factored in any cost–benefit analysis of the system.

Through its 17 000 services the Télétel system offers information about entertainment events, train schedules, television and radio programmes, jobs and classified ads, interactive games, banking services, grocery and home shopping, home banking, comparative pricing, and many other consumer services (Housel 1990; Marchand 1987a; Mayer, 1988; Sentilhes *et al.* 1989). Most services follow the same rules and command structures, and the same multicriteria search process (e.g. a subscriber deciding on whether to go to the movies can search for what films are showing in a given area, on a given topic, or starring a particular actor or actress), making it very easy for users to move from one application to another.

It is hard to assess the impact of Télétel on business, since this impact varies by company size and industry sector. France Télécom estimated in 1990 that the overall penetration of the business sector is at least 30% and growing and that the penetration for large companies (more than 500 employees) is 95%. Indeed, some industries have been profoundly affected by Télétel applications. For example, transportation companies using the Telerouting system have minimized the number of empty return trips for their trucks and moving vans by posting the schedules of return trips on Minitel and matching them to requests from customers (Marchand 1987a; Sentilhes *et al.* 1989).

Almost every French bank has developed its own Minitel-based home-banking system, allowing customers to check the status of their accounts, order cheques, pay utility bills and trade stocks.[9] Most retailers have also developed an electronic catalogue business and, although volumes are moderate at present, they are expected to explode as soon as payment can be done directly with the Minitel terminal.[10] Television stations run Minitel-based surveys every night. Travel agencies, insurance companies and consumer products companies have developed Télétel services.

Exhibit 7 Professional traffic as a percentage of all Télétel traffic

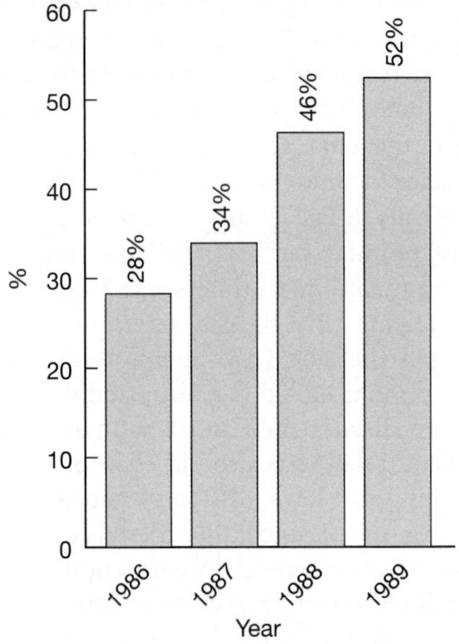

Source: France Télécom.

Whether the aim is to be in greater touch with the client, to increase efficiency in distribution, to gain market share, or to develop videotex products and services, Minitel has become an important component of the business strategy of companies operating in France. Exhibit 7 shows the increase in business-related volume over the years, and Table 5 shows the main applications for business users in 1991.

Table 5 Minitel main applications for business users

Electronic telephone directory	43%
Banking services, financial information, stock market	19%
Tourism/transport/hotels (timetables, reservations)	18%
Company-specific applications (including e-mail)	16%
Professional data banks	14%
General information (general databanks, newspapers, weather forecast)	32%

Source: Adapted from 'La Lettre de Télétel', France Télécom, June 1992.

9 For more information, see the case study by Tawfik Jelassi, 'Home banking: an IT-based business philosophy or a complementary distribution channel – CORTAL versus Crédit Commercial de France', INSEAD, 1992.

10 For more information, see the case study by Tawfik Jelassi, 'Minitel: a home retailing application,' INSEAD, 1992.

From a social point of view, Télétel has had an impact in a wide variety of ways. For example, the success stories of the various Télétel chat services (*messageries*) range from relatives separated by World War II finding each other to faster matching of organ donors and people in need of a transplant. Although the chat services have been in steady decline since the mid-1980s and represented only 6% of all the calls to Télétel in 1989, they are still one of the most popular services available (representing 15% of the total connect time; see Exhibit 5).[11]

The anonymity that the chat services provides have encouraged the sick (e.g. people with cancer or AIDS) and the troubled (e.g. drug addicts, divorced, abused) to discuss their more intimate problems with others. Télétel has also played a role in helping individuals who have difficulty getting out and around (e.g. the disabled, the elderly) to shop, bank and make reservations. Universities now use Télétel to co-ordinate student registration, course schedules and examination results. Other services give students access to help from teachers at all times.

Télétel services have been used in the political arena in innovative ways. During the last presidential election, a service allowed Minitel users to exchange letters with the candidates. Any voter accessing the service could view the open letters and the politicians' replies. Another example is the service sponsored by the newspaper *Libération*, which in December 1986 broadcast information on students' arrests as well as specific messages sent by the organizers of this unrest. These examples illustrate how broadly Télétel has been used as a decentralized, grass-roots vehicle for the discussion of a variety of societal issues. This utilization is very much in keeping with the original vision of Télématique proposed by Nora and Minc back in 1978.

Télétel: is it a financial success?

With a project of the magnitude of Télétel, it is very difficult to generate precise estimates of costs and revenues. There is a public perception, based in part on the free distribution of Minitel terminals, that Télétel is another Concorde: a high-technology, money-losing proposition. A recent report from the State Auditor General has stated that Télétel revenues have not covered its operating, depreciation and capital costs. The Secretary of the PTT, Mr Quilès, disagrees with that assessment.

On the one hand, the total investment in Télétel consists of the cost of the Minitel terminals plus the cost of the gateways to the Transpac network (VAPs) plus the cost of ports to the electronic directory network. The Minitel terminals cost approximately FF1000 per terminal, including R&D. The typical VAP has costs of around FF5 million. On the electronic directory network, one port costs approximately FF50 000. The following are approximate figures describing the investment of France Télécom in Télétel:

Minitel terminals	FF5.4 bn
Electronic directory	FF1.0 bn
R&D directory	FF0.2 bn
VAPs	FF0.6 bn
R&D (Télétel)	FF0.3 bn
Transpac	FF0.3 bn
Total	*FF7.8 bn*

On the other hand, the sources of revenues from Télétel include: (1) fees from revenue-sharing with information providers (France Télécom takes an average of 30% of the revenue generated by information providers); (2) advertising (of the Minitel offerings of some service providers); (3) electronic directory usage above and beyond the free allocation; and (4) rental of Minitels (Housel 1990).[12] Gross revenues from Télétel were approximately FF2 billion in 1989. Payments made by France Télécom to service providers for their share of Télétel revenues increased from FF278 million in 1985 to FF1.3 billion in 1987 and FF1.8 billion in 1989. By December 1991, they had reached over FF2.2 billion.

For purposes of cost-effectiveness analyses, however, the savings from printing fewer telephone books and having fewer directory assistance operators must be taken into consideration. Also, the additional revenues based on value-added tax from products, services and increased employment spawned by Télétel should be included but are difficult to calculate. Finally, the Transpac revenue generated by Télétel, almost 50% of all Transpac revenue (close to FF1 billion), needs to be considered. Quilès estimated that the total value-added of Télétel amounted to approximately FF6 billion in 1988.

11 The chat services are very lucrative, since both individuals 'talking' pay for the 'conversation', unlike a telephone conversation, where only one party gets charged for it.

12 Second- and third-generation Minitel terminals are not distributed; as of 1990, they must be paid for or leased.

France Télécom's official version is that Télétel revenues and expenses were in balance at the end of 1989 and the system is expected to start showing a significant return on investment in 1992. Unofficial estimates give a return on investment for Télétel during the 1980–90 period of between 8 and 12% (Housel 1990). Moreover, in 1991 France Télécom started to charge a monthly fee for the new Minitel terminals.

The view of senior officials of France Télécom is that this type of accounting may be a bit premature and potentially misleading, since Télétel is a major infrastructure project for which profitability needs to be measured on a long-term basis. Nevertheless, officials have been on record all along saying that the break-even point for Télétel would be ten years. Given France Télécom's numbers, those predictions seem to be right on target.

Exhibit 8 Growth of Télétel international usage via MinitelNet

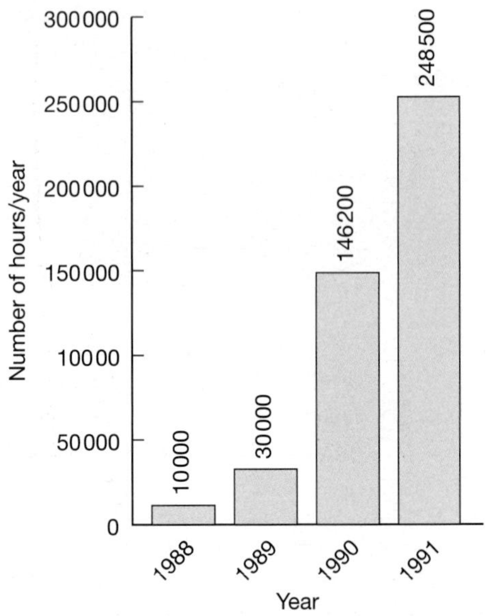

Source: Intelmatique.

Recent developments

From a hardware point of view, the line of Minitel terminals has been expanded to include eight models with varying levels of intelligence and functionality (e.g. colour screens, extended keyboards, compatibility with ASCII standards, service number memory). More than 600 000 terminals offering these capabilities had been installed as of 1990.

The new generation of Minitel terminals allows the user to prepare a message before placing a call, to monitor call set-up and to switch between voice and text transmission during a call. They also serve as automatic answering devices with protected access, and a portable Minitel that can be used over the cellular telephone network is available. Integrated services digital network (ISDN)[13] terminals have already been tested for the Télétel system.

From a software point of view, the kiosk now allows eight levels of pricing. A new routing capability allows information providers to use several host computers under a single Minitel access code. This new routing capability also allows the caller to access another service within Télétel without making a new phone call.

France Télécom is also experimenting with natural language interfaces for Télétel services. The Minitel Service Guide came online in 1989, with an interface that allows users to access the guide to Minitel services using French and without the need for special commands or the correct spelling.

With the internal market becoming progressively saturated and growth slowing down, France Télécom has made the international market a high priority. France Télécom has created Intelmatique – a division to sell videotex infrastructure and know-how. Recent clients include the Italian and Irish telephone companies.

Intelmatique markets the MinitelNet service, which provides foreign users with access to the Télétel network. The new service utilizes a multi-tariff billing scheme corresponding to the same tariffs on Télétel and greets foreign users with a personalized welcome in their native language. The service generated over 248 000 hours of traffic in 1991, an increase of almost 200% over 1990 (see Exhibit 8). Italy (52% of the traffic) and Belgium (15% of the traffic) were the two major markets (see Exhibit 9).

Major efforts are currently being made to export Minitel services to the US market. A number of companies (e.g. US West) have established gateways with the Minitel system. The Minitel Service Company, another entity of Intelmatique, was set up for the sole purpose of selling videotex know-how in the USA.

13 ISDN is capable of handling simultaneously data, voice, text and image transmission over a digital network.

Exhibit 9 MinitelNet: (a) markets and (b) usage

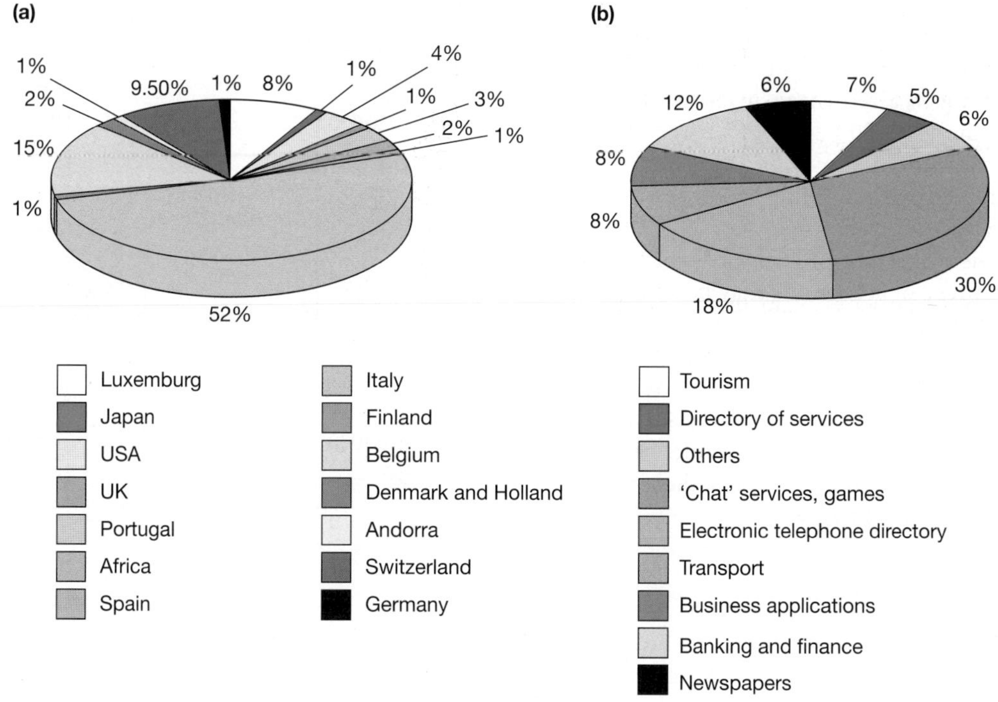

Source: Intelmatique.

Télétel is an example of a product spawned by government industrial policy. The Télétel story is about a successful government-directed technological push sustained by political will and technical vision. However, it is also a story about how, even within an enlightened industrial policy framework, good people are needed to make quick decisions to adapt to changing social, political and technological environments.

Although Télétel is a stereotypical case of the French industrial policy of 'les grandes aventures' and can be understood only by analyzing the industrial policy and political environment of France, there are some lessons from the Télétel experience that can be generalized to other products, services and contexts. The following questions serve as a guide in studying/reflecting on those lessons.

References

Chamoux, J. P., 'The French Télématique experience'. Paper presented at the Conference on IT/Telecommunications, Budapest, Hungary, 5–6 November 1990.

Dondoux, J., 'Problèmes Posés par la Présentation de l'Annuaire Téléphonique', Inspection Générale des PTT, Paris, 1978.

France Télécom, Annual reports and special documents on Minitel, 1985–92.

Housel, T. J., 'Videotex in France', manuscript, 1990.

Hutin, F. R., 'Télématique et Démocratie', *Etudes*, 1981, February, pp. 179–190.

Marchand, M., *La Grande Aventure du Minitel*, Paris, Larousse, 1987a.

Marchand, M., *Les Paradis Informationnels*, Paris, Masson, 1987b.

Mayer, R. N., 'The growth of the French videotex system and its implications for consumers', *Journal of Consumer Policy*, 1988, Vol. 2, pp. 55–83.

Nora, S. and A. Minc, *L'Informatisation de la Société*, Paris, Documentation Française, 1979.

Prévot, H., 'Report on the future of the PTT', September, 1989.

Schneider, V. *et al.*, 'The dynamics of videotex development in Britain, France and Germany'. Paper presented at the 8th Conference of the International Telecommunication Society, Venice, Italy, 18–21 March 1990.

Sentilhes, G. *et al.*, *La Minitel Stratégie*, Paris, Businessman/First, 1989.

Thomas, G. and I. Miles, *Telematics in Transition*, London, Longman, 1989.

DISCUSSION QUESTIONS

1. What are the critical success factors in the introduction and development of Télétel?
2. What types of services/applications benefit the most from Télétel?
3. Who should use Télétel rather than e-mail or electronic data interchange (EDI) solutions, and why?
4. What other telecommunication products could be introduced by France Télécom to exploit the Télétel experience?
5. What are some of the future directions for the development of Télétel?

CASE STUDY 2

Business process redesign at CompuNet

Standardizing top-quality service through IT

The goal of our business process redesign effort is to provide top-quality service in system support as a standardized, industrialized product.

Jost Stollmann, Chief Executive Officer, CompuNet AG

Company overview

CompuNet, founded in 1984 by Jost Stollmann, is regarded as the leader in reselling, networking, maintaining and supporting PCs in Germany. In addition to selling computer hardware and software, CompuNet offers a full spectrum of services developed around 'the networked PC'. The company became a multi-vendor systems integrator in 1990 when it extended its original line of IBM products to include such brands as Compaq, Hewlett Packard, Toshiba and Siemens Nixdorf. In October 1993, CompuNet acquired 75% of the loss-making Electronic 2000 Distribution Corporation (Vertriebs AG), whose product focus, and in particular the SUN and DEC workstations, was considered to be a strategic complement to the group's existing range of products and services.

CompuNet consists of 19 companies at 18 German locations, operating under the roof of a holding company, the CompuNet Computer AG. About 75% of CompuNet's 1256 employees work in service-related positions, including the technical customer service division where staff numbers are rising sharply to meet the strong increase in customer demand. (Table 1 lists CompuNet's services).

Table 1 CompuNet services

Consulting
Consulting for strategic IT planning, design and implementation of customized corporate IT architectures (client/server, Lotus Notes).

System engineering
Concepts and architecture for local networks, support in connecting and networking mainframes.

Project management
Nationwide project management providing large co-operations with products and services supporting complex networks – from purchasing and configuration to delivery and warranty.

Software support
User support, standard software training, hotline support.

Customer service
System configuration, system implementation, installation, repair and recycling of hardware, replacement of parts and repair service, life cycle warranty.

UNIX/computer centre integration
System engineering and support in heterogeneous networks, system integration of UNIX workstations and UNIX servers, integration of UNIX platforms into the computer centre.

European-wide service
Co-ordination and handling of European-wide projects through CompuNet's joint-venture partner International Computer Group BV.

Shift in business strategy

Originally, CompuNet's business strategy consisted of a focus on IBM products enhanced by peripheral

This case was developed by Claudia Loebbecke, University of Cologne, and Tawfik Jelassi, Professor of Information Systems at Theseus Institute and INSEAD. It is intended to be used as a basis for class discussion rather than to illustrate either effective or ineffective handling of an administrative situation.

The contribution to this case provided by CompuNet AG, in particular by Mr Patrick Bischoff and Dr Bernd Wirsing, is greatly appreciated.

products from other suppliers. The aim was to provide quality hardware and services and to ensure compatibility with systems already in place. At that time, services in general were offered mainly by the suppliers or by third-party service maintenance companies. Since 1990, CompuNet has changed its competitive position in two respects: first, CompuNet has moved away from its narrow focus on IBM products and turned itself into a multivendor systems integrator (see Table 2); second, the company has increasingly shifted its business focus towards value-added services, as an essential complement to its reselling business. Andreas Münchow, Aachener und Münchener Informatik-Service AG, points out:

> The particular value which CompuNet has, as a multivendor service provider, is that its staff is familiar with all systems platforms. It is not easy to find consultants among CompuNet's competitors who can demonstrate a depth of knowledge covering the broad range of PCs, UNIX systems and large mainframes, who understand their clients' needs, and who can implement forward-looking solutions to those needs.

Table 2 **Evolution of CompuNet's PC distribution (in units)**

	1990–91	*1991–92*	*1992–93*	*1993–94*
IBM	34 959	36 278	43 666	49 667
Compaq	4 988	8 665	16 071	29 432
Toshiba	856	1 222	1 285	2 374
Others (HP, SNI)	0	0	0	2 215
Total	40 803	46 165	61 022	83 688

Financial data

For the financial year ending June 1994, CompuNet's turnover amounted to DM924.6 million, up from DM684 million in the previous year. The company attributes these impressive results partly to the resurgence of demand in the market for brand-name vendors such as Compaq and IBM, both of which are now key CompuNet suppliers. CompuNet shipped 83 688 units, which represents an increase of 37% over the 61 022 units shipped in the previous year. Trading revenue increased by almost 32% to DM766.8 million in 1994, up from DM582.6 million in 1993. Concurrently, service revenues increased by 55% from DM101.5 million in 1993 to DM157.8 million in 1994. Billings for services represented 17% of CompuNet's total group revenue in 1994, compared with 14.8% in 1993 and 10.8% in 1992 (see Table 3).

Table 3 **Evolution of CompuNet's revenue mix (DM millions)**

	1989–90	*1990–91*	*1991–92*	*1992–93*	*1993–94*
Total revenue	340.4	625.7	678.3	684.1	924.6
Distribution	326.9	568.6	604.4	582.6	766.8
Service	13.5	57.1	73.9	101.5	157.8
% service	4.0	9.1	10.9	14.8	17.1

The balance-sheet sum increased by 5.8% from DM329.7 million to DM349.2 million. Between 1993 and 1994, current assets increased by approximately 2% to DM299.7 million. In 1994, inventories were reduced to DM101 million from DM126 million in 1993. To account for slow-moving items and depreciation, provisions of 5% against the value of inventories, and of 2% against spare parts, are made every 30 days. (Table 4 provides an overview of CompuNet's financial data.)

CompuNet in Europe

To leverage its experience in the European market, in 1989, in co-operation with Computacenter (UK) and Random (France), CompuNet founded the International Computer Group (ICG) BV. Headquartered in Paris, France, ICG consists today of 25 companies with 350 locations and roughly 10 000 people covering all of Western Europe, the Americas and Asia/Pacific Rim. ICG members are typically the leading providers of high-value-added systems integration and the related services in their markets. The group's Paris headquarters is staffed by multilingual specialists who provide project management, sales co-ordination, support marketing and information services. In 1993, ICG's turnover increased by 25% to US$4 billion from US$3.2 billion in 1992. Major customers of ICG include such companies as Kimberly Clark, Bang & Olufson, Coca-Cola, General Electric and Honeywell.

CompuNet's IT infrastructure

CompuNet's IT investment traditionally has been high, averaging about 2% of total turnover. In 1993–94, it

Table 4 **CompuNet's financial data** (all amounts in DM million)

		Consolidation and internal-growth		*Acquisition*	*Expansion*	
	1993–94	*1992–93*	*1991–92*	*1990–91*	*1989–90*	*1988–89*
Sales	924.6	684.1	678.3	625.7	340.4	175.9
Income from normal operating activities in (% of sales)	41.7	22.8	21.6	2.3	11.3	2.8
	4.5%	3.3%	3.2%	0.4%	3.3%	1.6%
Income before taxes[a] (% of sales)	41.7	22.8	21.6	2.3	11.6	2.8
	4.5%	3.3%	3.2%	0.8%	3.4%	1.6%
Consolidated earnings (loss) (% of sales)	32.5	14.0	13.7	(11.7)[b]	3.0	0.6
	3.5%	2.0%	2.0%	(1.9%)	0.9%	0.3%
Employees	1256	1097	1195	1128	489	307
Personal expense	116.4	99.9	100.2	86.5	37.5	19.1
Shareholders's equity	79.1	52.3	48.0	60.3	10.0	5.2
Internal financing[c]	110.9%	86.5%	95.6%	106.4%	44.2%	17.9%
Internal financing (%of total liabilities)	31.8%	26.2%	37.4%	36.9%	31.4%	17.7%
Dividend per share (DM)[d]	90.77	62.67	66.39	25.50	35.60	9.80

a Before profit transfers to silent partners.
b Not comparable with 1991–92 since losses could not be offset against profits.
c Including equity, silent partnership investment, and subordinated shareholder loans.
d Not including corporation tax refund.

Source: CompuNet's annual report 1993–94.

amounted to approximately DM15 million for the entire group. (See Table 5 for detailed IT costs.) The company employs 31 people in its central IT department: nine are assigned to mainframe management, 18 to SAP, and four to Lotus Notes. An additional one to two people are, among other tasks, responsible for the IT structure in each individual office.

SAP

In 1988, CompuNet first installed SAP,[1] soon after, the application package was turned into a company-wide IT platform for all business processes (accounting, inventory control, invoicing, purchasing, etc.). The system's ability to provide real-time information about all relevant business activities tremendously enhanced the transparency of corporate transactions. In 1994, SAP R/2 system supported in excess of 500 permanent CompuNet users with standardized business applications. Another 300 users have access to the system on a non-permanent basis.

SAP: R/2 *vs.* R/3

During 1995, the central warehouse administration system will be transferred to the new SAP R/3 system. For Jost Stollmann, 'R/3, running on a client–server architecture, will certainly be the IT backbone of the future'. The decision to switch to R/3 was not only motivated by the desire to build up expertise with the new system, but also was affected by the major cost differences involved. The choice was between an investment of DM2.58 million for R/2 and the necessary mainframe environment[2] or an investment of DM560 000 in SAP R/3 and its client–server environment.[3]

Leveraging the SAP experience

Control system

CompuNet managers are convinced that their five-year experience with SAP R/2 has provided the company with a competitive advantage regarding sophisticated business applications. For example, SAP has been used to establish an internal control system for business units and products. This system permits a comparative performance benchmarking of all operating units. Each kind of service (e.g. hardware sales,

1 SAP stands for systems, application and products in data processing.
2 DM2.5 million for CPU extension, DM20 000 for consulting and DM60 000 internal labour costs.
3 DM 270 000 for hardware and software, DM50 000 for consulting, and DM240 000 for internal labour costs.

Table 5 **IT costs (DM thousands)**

	1992–93	1993–94
Computer Center hardware cost	1596	2455
Computer Center operating system		
MVS	773	603
Tools	86	72
Carrier/network costs	646	651
SAP		3450
Lotus Notes Investment Cost (1992–94)		
Lotus Notes (switching cost from IBM PROFS to Lotus Notes, hardware, consulting, etc.)	2500	2500
Personnel (number of people, cost)		
Computer Center	14 (including network)	9
	918	834
Network administration		4
		335
SAP		18
		1900
Central spare parts sourcing/procurement system (1993)		
Development cost for central sourcing of repair materials		67
CN-KISS (customer information system)		
Customer information system cost in 1993–94		291
CallAS		
Since April 1994: 230 per month		550 (fixed)
External software development cost		
Applications design for SAP		278

technical support, systems consulting, software consulting) is separately monitored and measured against special performance indicators. Such a control system allows review of CompuNet's entire value chain. The availability of a transparent picture about company operations allows for more focused and effective concentration on core business activities such as purchasing, installing and maintaining PC networks. Plans have been made to extend the use of this concept and tool to monitoring customers.

Total quality management

Over the past two years, CompuNet has invested approximately DM1 million into a 'total quality management' (TQM) project, with the goal of building an efficient quality management system. In 1992, as a first step, CompuNet standardized all major business processes on a 'best practice' basis. During 1993, all employees (including all partners) were trained in TQM practices and concepts. By 1994, a broad set of TQM projects, ranging from simple tasks to re-engineering entire business processes, was in operation.

By using standard measurements that are common to everyone in CompuNet, the quality of individual departments can be measured continuously, and proposals leading to an ongoing improvement in quality can be implemented by the employees involved. Among other things, the 20 group-wide quality-measurement issues include the number and value of returned units and the percentage of customer complaints, as well as the availability and response time of the SAP system. The key to the success of the TQM effort is the broad, grass-roots involvement of all employees. (Table 6 lists CompuNet's quality statements.)

Lotus Notes

Lotus Notes is a technology platform that supports a process called 'workflow computing'. It offers basic applications such as e-mail and database capabilities,

Table 6 **CompuNet's quality statements**

Top quality within all our business processes is our prime objective
It is our prime objective to prioritize the quality of our processes to ensure continuous customer satisfaction.

The expectations and demands of our customers are at the centre of our work
Our doing is to ensure the competitive advantage of our customers. Therefore our performance must be better than that of our competitors. All our work has to at least fulfil if not exceed customer expectations.

The continuous striving for business improvement is the key issue for our corporate success.
We have to be outstanding in everything we do. This goes for our business performance, our relationships with the customers and, among ourselves, our social behaviour, our competitive style as well as our profitability.

The customer and the supplier are our partners
CompuNet ensures a mutually beneficial relationship with suppliers and buyers.

CompuNet's integrity does not allow for compromises
Our behaviour must be shaped by our honesty, fairness and social responsibility. Our company has to be respected for its integrity as well as its contributions to society. Nobody is to be discriminated against on the grounds of their race, nationality, religion, gender or views.

Source: CompuNet.

as well as advanced business modelling and simultaneous operations processing. Furthermore, Notes offers various sophisticated tools and an integrated macro language, which allow for the further development and customization of applications.

As a result of CompuNet's extensive use of Lotus Notes, it has become something of a pioneer in this technology in Germany. All employees use the package as the basis for their inter-office communication (data transfer volume: 12–14 gigabytes per month in 1993–94). Lotus Notes has replaced the previously used Office Vision, which was mainframe-based, thus avoiding the cost of an additional mainframe installation to assist the existing ES 9000/9121 computer.

However, Franz T. Mueller, Head of the CompuNet Computer Distribution GmbH in Kerpen, admits: 'Implementing Lotus Notes only for office communication would not make sense unless the company intends to use it to develop other applications.'

Crucial for CompuNet's decision to implement Lotus Notes was its ability to support integrated work processes. Says Ludwig Schlösser, Head of CompuNet Consult:

> We develop complex IT projects for our customers. Often, several of our [CompuNet] companies are involved in one project, and the expertise of the whole group is required. Lotus Notes seems to be the best product to support such projects with a state-of-the-art workflow based project management.

Lotus Notes helps a company to focus more on groups and processes than on individuals and functions. It supports document management and process monitoring, for example by enforcing 'workgroup computing', which reduces the importance of geographical distance. The issue is no longer where a task is carried out, or in which location the information is held, since departments are turned into logical units. Every employee can access all relevant facts through common Notes-based forums and databases, information can be read, and documents can be attached and then passed on to other employees.[4] Lotus Notes is also used for exchanging up-to-date data such as price lists or product information with CompuNet's external partners. Contrary to Office Vision, Lotus Notes supports a client/server distributed, decentralized data environment that fits well with CompuNet's corporate structure. Moreover, Lotus' implementation was facilitated by the company's extensive IT infrastructure. Each employee is equipped with a PC[5] that is part of a local area network (LAN) within each location as well as part of a corporate-wide area network (WAN). Thus, every employee can communicate with anyone within the organization at any time.

Compunet's business environment: the IT market

Overview

The IT industry is in the midst of a structural change. Manufacturers of mainframes and medium-sized computers are under pressure from worldwide overcapacity, while makers of PCs and workstations suffer from rapid technological changes and drastic price reductions. In 1992, the total turnover of the PC business declined by approximately 13%. While the producers of clones significantly increased their profits, brand-name manufacturers (including IBM and Compaq) lost market share due to their high prices and long delivery. In 1993, however, these manufacturers recovered lost market shares through rigorous pricing policies. Whereas the total PC market shrank by 4%, IBM and Compaq increased their PC sales by 25%. (See Table 7 and Exhibit 1 for an overview of recent developments in the German PC hardware market).

The German market for software and services in 1993 rose to US$13.27 billion, thus expanding by 11% from 1992. Desktop services are expected to

Table 7 **German PC revenue** (DM millions)

	1992	*1991*
Vobis	1096	793
IBM	910	1297
Escom	625	349
Compaq	585	606
SNI	456	517
Apple	445	426
Commodore	438	735
All manufacturers	8360	9619

Source: Info Corp Europe.

4 While previously the corporate IT department controlled the Office Vision communication tool, each business unit is now in charge of its Lotus Notes applications.

5 OS/2.11 and MS-Dos/Windows.

Exhibit 1 German professional PC market

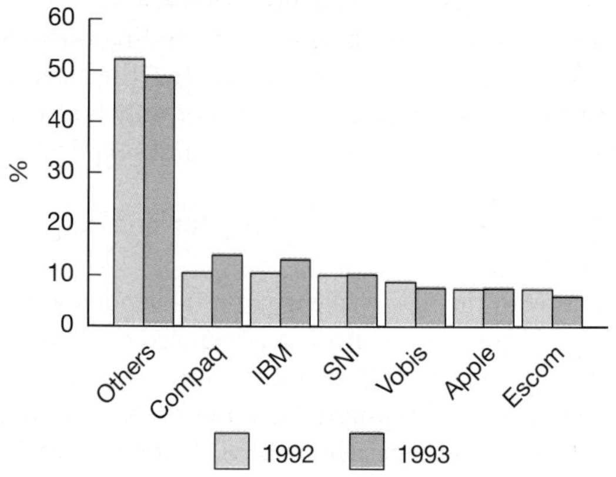

Source: IDC.

grow by 10% per annum until 1997, which would make Germany by far the largest software and services market in Europe. (See Tables 8 and 9 for developments in the German service market and Table 10 for the US market of LAN system integration services.)

Table 8 German market for IT

	1992		1997	
	Billion DM	*%*	*Billion DM*	*%*
Multi-user systems	9.4	18	9.9	14
Support services	6.8	13	7.8	11
Professional services	16.6	32	24.9	35
Packaged software	8.3	16	14.9	21
Data communications	1.0	2	1.4	2
Single user systems	9.9	19	12.1	17
Total	52.0	100	71.0	100

Source: IDC.

For large resellers like CompuNet, the industry trends are favourable. The US industry analyst Dillon Read has identified five positive trends:

- growing demand out of recession;
- trend to big-brand manufacturers;
- market-share gain by large resellers;
- more stable pricing environment;
- favourable terms and conditions for large resellers.

Although it is difficult to predict the end of the structural changes presently affecting the IT sector, the responsibility for corporate PC/workstation infrastructures is being increasingly transferred to external consultants (e.g. as CompuNet, M & S, ADA, debis Systemhaus, EDS, IBM, SNI, DEC, HP).

Customers' increasing interest in external service providers

In difficult economic times, companies often turn back their focus to their core competence. This change is accompanied by a detailed review of the IT value chain within the company, with the aim of reducing or eliminating the burden of some support activities, such as purchasing, installing, maintaining

Table 9 Estimated market growth services/networking per year (1993–97)

Segment	*Growth rate (%)*	*Source*
PC hardware sales	10.0	IDC
Traditional maintenance	3.0	Input
Network services		
LAN installation	18.5	Frost & Sullivan
LAN maintenance	30.0	Frost & Sullivan
Desktop services	30.0	Input

Table 10 US market for LAN systems integration services

Year	*Externally maintained LANs*	*Chargeable hours*	*Duration of maintenance (days)*	*Revenue per LAN (US$)*	*Sum (US$ millions)*
1990	3300	100	2.0	1600	5.3
1991	8500	110	2.7	2376	20.2
1992	15900	118	3.1	2926	46.5
1993	32500	127	3.6	3658	118.9
1994	46600	136	3.9	4243	197.7
1995	68400	140	4.5	5040	344.8
1996	95500	144	4.7	5414	517.1
1997	122600	148	5.0	5920	725.8

Source: Frost & Sullivan.

and upgrading PC networks, as well as providing the necessary software infrastructure. With the growing complexity of software applications and the ever-increasing professional use of PCs, the effective management of a company's IT infrastructure has become prohibitively expensive.[6]

According to the Gartner Group, the actual purchase value of PC hardware and software has been reduced to approximately 15% of the total PC life-cycle costs (approximately US$40 000 per PC). Another 15% covers technical support (e.g. help desks, application consulting, maintenance), while 14% is related to administrative tasks (e.g. purchasing, inventory management, audit). However, 56% of the PC life-cycle costs are devoted to end-user activities (including the operation, back-up, training and application development) and hence constitute the largest part of a company's IT cost. Due to the currently turbulent business environment, companies are seeking external assistance to manage their IT infrastructure and increasingly are opting for outsourcing solutions.

Business process re-engineering (BPR) 1: towards lean 'guarantee management'

The guarantee dilemma of a multivendor service provider

In an era of falling hardware prices, guarantee conditions have emerged as a competitive weapon for manufacturers struggling to retain market share. They are being used by these manufacturers as a differentiating factor in their market positioning.

From a customer's perspective, the wide variety of guarantee conditions has made the management of a large PC infrastructure much more complex, and therefore much more expensive. More specifically, since most companies have a heterogeneous PC platform, they have to deal with different guarantee conditions, depending on the product type and purchase date. In case of hardware failure, extensive checks are necessary in order to determine the corresponding manufacturer, the contact person, and the extent of the guarantee.[7]

For CompuNet, developing into a multivendor company while focusing more on services has led to a dramatic increase in the volume and complexity of company operations. CompuNet had to pass to its customers the different guarantee conditions and prices imposed on it by its various suppliers. As a result of this situation, each customer had numerous valid guarantee claims towards CompuNet. CompuNet ended up managing 65 000 hardware guarantee calls per year.

In order to compete in this demanding business environment, CompuNet recognized the need to streamline its business processes not only internally but also in relation to its customers and suppliers.

SAP as an enabling technology for business process re-engineering

Faced with the new challenge of multivendor service logistics, Jost Stollmann was convinced that further exploitation of SAP could create a competitive advantage for CompuNet. He thought that the company's five-year experience with SAP and the existing set of SAP applications could be leveraged for the handling of products and spare parts. The approach consisted of redesigning business processes so as to follow standardized SAP procedures for all business transactions. For Stollman, the PC serial number should be used to identify each customer's setting and relationships with CompuNet, thereby triggering all the necessary courses of action.

Re-engineering guarantee procedures leads to a new product

In late 1991, Rainer Borchardt recognized the difficulties resulting from CompuNet's increased focus on services. He analyzed the company's business processes aiming at optimizing the complex guarantee situation and benefiting from the new market demands. In January 1992, Borchardt and one of his colleagues took the initiative further: they completely redesigned CompuNet's value chain, mainly through simplifications of the core service activities.

The first principle underlying this redesign effort was to buy all products without any guarantee rights at accordingly lower prices. This would remove CompuNet's obligation to process individual reimbursements of guarantee claims with the manufacturer. However, the guarantee chaos from the customer perspective, and the resulting administrative difficulties at CompuNet, had yet to be solved. The concept of 'guarantee bundling' was then introduced,

6 PCs in this case study refer to personal computers and workstations.

7 Until recently, the standard guarantee offered in Germany was 12 months for defective parts. Travel to and from the customer site, as well as time spent, was usually invoiced. Such conditions changed with the PC market's price war.

and the PC Life Cycle Guarantee emerged as the solution to adopt.

The CompuNet Life Cycle Guarantee for new IT equipment runs for 48 months, which corresponds to the expected life cycle of the hardware. It covers repair, travel expenses for technicians, spare parts and all other costs related to equipment damages. CompuNet puts a special four-year-guarantee sticker on all hardware products that it delivers. These products have their own casing, electric cabling and serial numbers.

When CompuNet's service centre agent keys a given PC serial number into SAP, information about the corresponding product and customer is extracted and displayed automatically. Hence, the PC serial number has become the customer's 'entry ticket' to the service centre. This new SAP-based procedure has automated all guarantee-related transactions and, therefore, has eliminated all the paperwork and documents normally associated with guarantees.

Benefits of CompuNet's business process re-engineering

Since October 1992, all CompuNet products have been delivered with the new Life Cycle Guarantee, and every customer has only one contact person within CompuNet. Time-consuming searches for delivery notes and invoices have been eliminated, and customers now benefit from a state-of-the-art spare-parts delivery system and a real-time guarantee application within contracted time windows. These offerings simplify the guarantee procedures of large customers and therefore reduce their overall IT management costs.

For CompuNet, its BPR effort, resulting in the Life Cycle Guarantee product, has simplified its core activities significantly. Various guarantee-related transactions within the company, as well as with suppliers and customers, were eliminated, thereby reducing CompuNet's maintenance costs by 66–75%. Moreover, the time required to process guarantee cases has decreased sharply.

Pushing lean guarantee management further

To leverage the Life Cycle Guarantee concept further, CompuNet introduced two types of customer guarantees for existing PC installations that are either old or supplied by a third party: the so-called Refresh Guarantee and the Life Cycle Guarantee for Used PCs. For CompuNet, both guarantee types do not require management efforts beyond those associated with the Life Cycle Guarantee; they present, however, a promising business opportunity.

Both guarantee types for already installed PCs offer customers the same benefits as those of the new equipment guarantee (i.e. covering repair, travel and spare part costs related to PC damages) but have a different starting date for the guarantee. While the Life Cycle Guarantee for Used PCs begins on the installation date of the equipment, the four-year Refresh Guarantee starts once the hardware is checked and updated by CompuNet. These new guarantee types have been increasingly attracting customers who prefer to have total guarantee agreements with CompuNet for their existing hardware installations.

Business process re-engineering 2: towards customer-oriented support management

The core business activities of many companies increasingly depend on the availability and reliability of their IT infrastructure. Therefore, reducing the frequency as well as the duration of their system breakdown is of critical importance for them.

Call administration system (CallAS): the triggering idea

Since the introduction of the Life Cycle Guarantee and the resulting process simplifications, CompuNet's service business has increased dramatically. Hardware call volume per shipped PC has doubled every year and has led to diverse service requirements. For Walter K. Nagel, the partner responsible for the service business in the Cologne office:

> When it comes to defining their service requirements, customers' creativity has no limit. As a result of that, almost every contract has to be engineered to the exact specification that matches the corporate customer's requirements.

Making the PC service a standard product is difficult, but offering such a product in an effective and cost-efficient way is almost impossible. Since the variety of customer requests cannot be represented in SAP, delays for developing new software applications amount to approximately five years. In CompuNet's profit-centre-oriented structure, each company is responsible for increasing its own service business. In this context, the difficulties in managing the new service concept and the inappropriateness of

the SAP platform to support various service processes led to a new system development effort in the CompuNet Berlin office. There, in 1992, Andreas Thimm, a service manager, deviated from the official IT strategy for standardized products by developing a Lotus Notes application to manage his local service business better. While his personal initiative helped him to do his daily work, the resulting application did not meet the corporate IT standards. When asked to stop his initiative, he argued that the Lotus Notes application was his 'private effort', developed during his free time. Moreover, not only has Thimm continued his user-oriented 'spaghetti code' attempts to build CallAS, but he has also convinced his colleagues in other CompuNet branches of the advantages of Lotus Notes. Over time, an increasing number of companies within CompuNet adopted CallAS and adjusted it to their business needs and software-development concepts. Therefore, the CallAS adoption has led to the use within the company of different versions of the Lotus Notes application for service management. CallAS's 'guerilla approach' (as Jost Stollmann calls it) and the various 'spaghetti code' versions were incompatible with CompuNet's IT policy of providing company-wide applications and pursuing an open information policy that allows everyone to access the company databases. Furthermore, information security could hardly be controlled, and maintenance and support costs for the 15 different CallAS versions increased beyond a reasonable limit.

CallAS's official start

With the simplification of internal business processes and the success of the Life Cycle Guarantee, CompuNet's main challenge was to maintain a customer-oriented approach to service management, while remaining cost-efficient. Due to recent technological breakthroughs in information and telecommunication technology, it became possible to envision a service management system that would encompass physically dispersed support personnel. Therefore, Jost Stollmann decided to start, under his own leadership, an 'official' project to re-engineer CompuNet's customer service offerings completely, using IT and telecommunications support. His strategy was to merge the process-oriented Notes front-end tool and the central SAP back-end application into a comprehensive, distributed service-management infrastructure.

The concept was first formalized in May 1993 by Rainer Borchardt. Then an extensive specification chart was developed by a team that represented the different concerned parties. In October 1993, this chart of CallAS redesign and its integration into the SAP backbone was contracted to the internal consulting company, CompuNet Computer Consult (Cologne), for a fixed price of DM550 000. (Table 11 provides CompuNet Consult's five-year results.)

Table 11 **CompuNet Consult's financial results (in DM; figures in parentheses are losses)**

1 January–30 June 1989	(122 000)
1989–90	(871 000)
1990–91	82 000
1991–92	(51 000)
1992–93	101 000

Source: CompuNet.

Integrating SAP and Lotus Notes for a better CallAS

First steps

Beyond the use of Lotus Notes' capabilities, CompuNet Consult recognized the need to exploit the SAP backbone further. While SAP had been used only to support central business processes, Lotus Notes had served as a communication tool for the CompuNet Group since 1993. Due to the different hardware platforms that each of them requires (respectively, a mainframe computer and a client–server architecture), the SAP and Lotus Notes applications had been separated from each other.

However, in order to further simplify its service procedure, CompuNet developed a new service-management concept that integrates SAP and Lotus Notes. When a customer calls CompuNet's decentralized service department to report a PC problem, they need only to provide the serial number of the broken machine. This data item allows CompuNet's service staff to access immediately, through SAP and Lotus Notes, the product history and guarantee status, and to take the necessary service action(s).

Problems encountered

Early in 1994, a modified Lotus Notes version for sales support was installed, allowing the distribution

of maintenance and service-level contract data throughout Germany. A pre-release of CallAS was also installed to forward service calls between branches. However, the new networked version created total chaos. The CallAS application broke down at least six times a day, response times were unacceptable, and data and entire calls got lost. Recovering lost data was a source of frustration for everybody and, since problems were no longer fixed locally, all complaints were directed to CompuNet Consult. Service quality deteriorated dramatically, and customer complaints even led to the loss of some business relationships.

When reviewing the situation, CompuNet Consult identified the main reasons for the problem: (1) the branches had heterogeneous PC and LAN infrastructures and used different patch levels; (2) there was no real support structure for CallAS and Lotus Notes; and (3) the CallAS and Lotus Notes applications had some faulty features.

As CompuNet Consult was trying to turn its business into a profitable operation, its human resources were completely overwhelmed with work. Fixing CallAS, while at the same time working on external customer projects, led to drastic service problems. In the midst of this stressful and chaotic situation, it was decided to change the fixed-price contract relationship with CompuNet Consult. Instead, the CompuNet Group hired 13 of the best specialists of CompuNet Consult to be dedicated exclusively to the development of the IT support for CompuNet's service management. This brought focus and stability back into the operations and, in the subsequent months, the so-called 'Dream Team' made major progress.

Achieved goals

Initially, all incoming customer calls were represented in Lotus Notes and were also entered into SAP. The current version of CompuNet's SAP–Lotus Notes integration enables automatic communication between both software products through mouse-clicks. When using Lotus Notes, SAP information and dialogues can be accessed without leaving Lotus Notes. SAP data (such as customer number, order number and PC serial number) are integrated online into Lotus Notes documents, thereby allowing them to be processed further through Lotus Notes' graphical interface. Thus, different work procedures are 'melted' into one business process. This SAP–Lotus Notes integration is at the core of the advanced company-wide CallAS version and helps to improve further CompuNet's management of incoming customer calls and the resulting hotline activities.

With the new application, the contact person knows in subseconds what kind of product is damaged, whether it was damaged before, whether the spare parts needed for a potential repair are in stock, if and when a CompuNet engineer was at the customer's site before, and whether the service was handled remotely. Lotus Notes also makes it possible to find out immediately when an engineer with the necessary know-how will be available. The customer can then be informed about the date and time of the repair.

Furthermore, the schedule of support staff is managed and the necessary spare parts allocated. Technically speaking, customer calls are received in the PC-based Lotus Notes environment where online SAP data (such as customer address, contact person and PC-related information) are integrated. The calls are then processed as support orders for the different CompuNet offices.

Another crucial aspect of shortening the reaction time to a customer problem is the quick availability of information about technical staff engagements. CompuNet has developed a telephone-based central automated operator system (AOS) to complement CallAS functionalities. Technicians call the AOS before and after their customer visits, and all relevant data (e.g. reference number, date and time, status) are automatically processed and stored within the call documents of the Lotus Notes database. Moreover, in order to remind the technicians' supervisors of urgent actions, a built-in escalation mechanism automatically sends them an e-mail (Autopost) shortly before support deadlines. Upon request, several warning levels (e.g. different timeframes before the deadline) are accessible online to control continuously the processing of customer calls.

Achieved benefits

CallAS allows CompuNet to monitor predetermined service levels and to allocate its technical field personnel accordingly. The automation of most steps in the support value chain reduces order-processing time and provides continuous online information and control of any service activity, be it for in-house purposes or for CompuNet's customers. Thus, the second BPR project laid the ground for better service

management, including hotline and help-desk processes, and enabled CompuNet to offer unique customer service options in Germany. Ludwig Schlösser, partner responsible for the CompuNet Consult business, explains:

> For CompuNet, CallAS is the IT backbone to keep our service promises to our customers. Due to the fast processing of calls, we can guarantee our customers that they will regain the full functionalities of their PCs and networks nationwide within the contracted up-times of typically four to 24 hours.

Since CallAS had become the basis for fast, cost-efficient and high-quality PC support and maintenance, Jost Stollmann decided to leverage these new capabilities further and package them in an attractive way for his customers. This led CompuNet to add, in April 1994, another offer to its service product range: the Support Guarantee. This guarantee aims at eliminating all administrative processes from support management. It reduces support efforts at CompuNet and at the customer site to 'one bill, one site, and one phone number'. Comparable to the Life Cycle Guarantee concept, CompuNet ensures reducing system down-times – depending on the contract type – to one day, eight hours, or four hours. Paying an all-inclusive guarantee premium, the customer can call the same CompuNet phone number whenever and wherever a PC problem occurs.

Moreover, CompuNet has started to leverage its expertise further by offering the SAP–Lotus Notes integration to its customers. Andreas Thimm says:

> Altogether, the SAP–Lotus Notes integration has allowed for major synergies at CompuNet. Having put two already implemented application packages together, it is clear that the total is more than the sum of the parts.

Future use of CompuNet's SAP–Lotus Notes integration

Further development plans

For the near future, CompuNet's goal is to develop a concept whereby a customer can reach their contact person at a distributed maintenance and support department. This decentralized structure would not need to be grouped geographically but could be based on logical organizational units. Implementation-wise, an advanced telecommunications system will be used to transfer the caller's number, which will then automatically trigger a database search. As the incoming call reaches the service agent, historical data about the calling customer are displayed, providing the agent with information about the client, their IT infrastructure under CompuNet's guarantee, and past maintenance cases (what they were, when they took place, who handled them, etc.). Once the customer call is qualified, it will be routed within subseconds to the next appropriate, geographically independent service person who could offer some remote support. An even more advanced version of the system could be based on automatic voice recognition, at least with regard to the serial number of the broken PC.

While this project requires the co-operation of a telephone company, a specialist in automatic call distribution (ACD), and a network provider, the integration of all application modules (which include a case-based knowledge system) will be completed by CompuNet. Hence, a new integrated product for service support will be developed and marketed.

Expected benefits

To leverage the new service-management application (currently under development), CompuNet aims at increasing the percentage of remote services from today's level of 50% to 80–90%, a figure that is already common in the USA. Jost Stollmann expects that 'in the medium run, the only service requests requiring field service will be material fatigue and hardware upgrading'.

Customers' experience with Compunet's new services

Thyssen Handelsunion AG

Thyssen Handelsunion AG (THU) is one of Europe's leading trade companies, with sales of DM16 billion and 29 000 employees. It currently uses 800 PCs in its corporate headquarters in Düsseldorf, Germany. In order to manage its PC infrastructure cost-effectively, THU decided to outsource PC tasks such as purchasing, installation, software support and maintenance, and it chose CompuNet as its external service provider.

Mr Weide, project manager at THU, says:

> CompuNet was already known to us as a partner of many years standing. We believed that CompuNet was best able to meet our requirements due to its size, experience and knowledge of hardware, software and logistics. THU and CompuNet staff already work together as a team. This form of co-operation enables us to slim many processes quite extensively, and to eliminate duplication, both in-house and for our partners. Today, we can supply better service to our users at lower cost.

BEB Erdgas und Erdöl GmbH

BEB is a major supplier of gas in Germany (it provides approximately 20% of the country's gas requirements) and is also involved in the domestic oil extraction business. It has 2000 employees and its activities are spread over the entire country. Approximately 600 PCs are installed in the company headquarters in Hannover, and an additional 250 PCs are used at other locations connected to the headquarters via a WAN. After analyzing its IT expenses over the entire PC life cycle, BEB wanted to improve its service quality while at the same time reducing PC costs and making them transparent. Explains a BEB IT manager:

> We realized the need to tackle the substantial costs of IT service and support. CompuNet's offer to supply all required services for a flat fee meets this need. We now have a firm basis for our IT costs.

Aachener und Münchener Informatik Service AG (AM)

Together with Aachener und Münchener Informatik-Service AG, SWT Software-Technologie und Systemberatung GmbH and CompuNet developed a UNIX-based SAP R/3 application as the basis for an integrated insurance model built by KPMG, SAT and SWT (an AM subsidiary). The project team identified a way of connecting, via the existing SNA network, the individual PCs to the UNIX system. The problem was that the PCs could only be connected via the protocol TC/IP; however, the latter was not supported by SNA.

Regarding his joint work with CompuNet, Andreas Münchow, project manager at AM, said:

> CompuNet's value is the familiarity of its staff with all systems platforms. It is not easy to find consultants at CompuNet's competitors who can demonstrate a depth of knowledge covering the broad range of PCs, UNIX systems and large mainframes, who understand their clients' needs and who can implement forward-looking solutions to those needs.

General Electric (GE)

GE in Europe has 45 000 employees at 160 locations. Its major businesses include capital, plastics, medical appliances, power control and aircraft engines. GE annually purchases through corporate resellers approximately US$10 million of hardware, peripherals and services, and has an installed base in Europe of over 10 000 central processing units.

In order to reduce the total cost of procurement and support of PC hardware and software, GE decided to streamline and standardize its IT infrastructure. After choosing IBM and Zenith to provide the hardware, and Microsoft Office as a basic interface, GE looked for a reseller able to fulfil its requirements across all European countries with standard Europe-wide prices. Because of ICG's comprehensive European coverage and international account-management capabilities, GE chose ICG over EDS, ECS and KNP BT to be its pan-European supplier. ICG now provides delivery, installation and customization of hardware, peripherals and software add-ons, and on-site technical support for all GE locations across Europe, while CompuNet is responsible for the German operations of GE.

Outlook

For Jost Stollmann, the merger of IT and telecommunications technologies offers an opportunity for new service offerings and a more efficient in-house handling of service-related business processes. He says:

> Having heavily invested in IT since the very first years of CompuNet's existence, it will always be necessary to check where and to what degree our IT experience and infrastructure can be leveraged as additional competence across diverse business processes. The efficient use of IT has become a particular challenge in the context of our shift from a reseller to a service provider. It still remains a continuous effort to adapt our IT infrastructure, originally targeted towards reselling, to the needs of the service sector. It's not only the economics that are different between the reselling and the service business.

For Stollman, CompuNet's future developments should be in two directions: (1) the appropriateness of the company's IT policy and its business impact; and (2) CompuNet's competitive position. Regarding the first direction, he asked his assistant Patrick Bischoff to think about the following questions:

- Is an investment of DM230 000 per month for the 'Dream Team' appropriate to further develop CallAS?
- Is it justifiable to invest so much time and money into the service side of the business if services account for only 17% of total revenues?
- Is it a future-oriented choice or a strategic mistake to design Lotus Notes applications based on a telecommunication infrastructure that is not yet available in Germany?

- Do CompuNet's management concepts need to be adjusted once the business process redesign projects are completed? How?

Concerning CompuNet's competitiveness, Stollman wondered:

- How will the competitive environment of multivendor service providers change over time? Who are currently the main competitors in this business, and who will they be in the near future?
- To what degree does (or will) the complexity of multivendor service management require strategic partnerships? For what activities should CompuNet consider such a partnership, and who could its partner(s) be?

DISCUSSION QUESTIONS

1 Is it justifiable for a company such as CompuNet to invest a lot of money and effort into the service side of its business when service accounts for only 17% of its total revenues?

2 Is it advantageous or, rather, adventurous for CompuNet to design advanced IT applications that require an ISDN-based telecommunications infrastructure not yet available throughout Federal Germany?

3 How will the competitive environment change over time, considering CompuNet's shift towards a multivendor service provider? More specifically, who are currently the main competitors and who are they likely to be in the near future?

4 To what degree does/will the management complexity of a multivendor service provider require strategic partnerships? For what specific activities should CompuNet consider such partnerships, and who should it consider as potential partners?

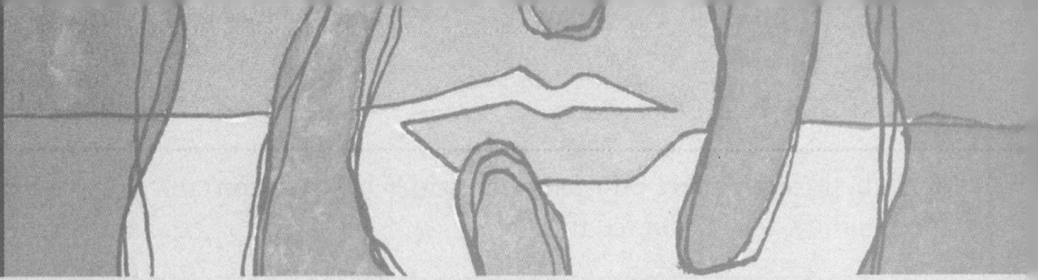

CASE STUDY 3

e-Government

The role of information and communication technologies in the modernization of government

e-Government is a key instrument for modernization and reform as governments face the continuing pressures of increasing their performance and adapting to the pressures of the new information society. As an example of the future, the Singapore government has created a new personalized system called My.eCitizen. Rather than searching through hundreds of services, individuals, based on their preferences and choices, receive a personalized system of alerts, messages and information from a wide range of government departments. This is an action to move the citizen from the fringes to the heart of government.

As Norris (2000) explains, cyber-optimists envision the Internet as a way to revive flagging civic energies. On the other hand, cyber-pessimists suggest that the use of the web will reinforce, but not radically transform, existing patterns of political communications and democratic participation, and even lead to a further widening between the engaged and the politically apathetic. In the same vein, Tolbert *et al.* (2002) suggest that the Internet may be a double-edged sword, with both the potential of online politics to expand civic partition to those previously disengaged in politics and the potential to widen existing disparities in participation, based on income and education.

Whether one considers oneself as an optimist or pessimist, there is persuasive evidence that the movement towards cyber-government is firmly established. First, it was estimated by the United Nations (UN) in 2002 that there were over 50 000 official government websites worldwide compared with just 50 in 1996 (Ronaghan, 2002). Second, in the new e-era, citizens have become increasingly accustomed to e-activities extending across society through business, cultural and recreational activities. It is no wonder that they are receptive to governments being able to offer a similar quality of service. Third, e-government initiatives contribute to the common policy objective of reducing government spending by promoting a greater efficiency in administration. e-Administration helps to eliminate time spent on repetitive, mass-processing tasks, and thereby speeds up general administration operations. This, therefore, generates savings on data collection, transmission and the constant doubling-up of information that is rife between departments, which allows for resources to be employed on higher-priority activities. Finally, new generations are increasingly computer-literate and are used to the e-lifestyle, if not already adapting to the m-(mobile) lifestyle.

Better government

Governments have the ability to be role models to both business and community by representing an example of best practice and demonstrating how to seize the opportunities presented by the information economy. A significant part of this is to promote the vision that e-functions are a complement to existing systems and, thereby, need to be aligned and integrated into the organization's overarching strategy. As an example, the Australian government sees its e-government activities to have had 'a significant demonstrator and

This case was written by Morven McLean, MBA participant (2003), and Tawfik Jelassi, Professor of e-Business and Information Technology, both at the School of International Management, Ecole Nationale des Ponts et Chaussées, Paris, France. It is intended to be used as the basis for class discussion rather than to illustrate either effective or ineffective handling of an e-government situation. Case released in 2004.

pull-through effect on Australia's wider information economy'. It has achieved this by:

- emphasizing governance and stakeholder partnerships;
- developing and co-ordinating its responses to strategic issues affecting the information economy;
- facilitating research and innovation that maximize the opportunities and benefits for government departments and agencies to put information and communication technologies to effective use;
- being involved in exemplar projects;
- providing information and advice as well as capturing and sharing learning.

In the UN study, there are a number of correlating economic factors that impact on a country's ability to implement an e-government strategy successfully (Ronaghan 2002). These factors include the state of a country's telecommunications, the diffusion of human technical skills, political will, scale of access to computers and political stability. As a result, there is a direct connection between a country's economic, social and democratic levels of development and its level of e-government implementation.

The UN benchmarking process assessed information and statistics concerning a country's official online presence, evaluation of its telecommunications infrastructure, and assessment of its human development capacity and created five stages of e-government readiness. These are as follows:

- *Emerging*: describes when a country has a formal but limited web presence that provides users with static organizational or political information. Sites may include contact information (e.g. telephone numbers and addresses of public officials) or, in rare cases, special features such as frequently asked questions (FAQs). This presently accounts for 16.8% of UN states.
- *Enhanced*: describes when a country has an online presence expanded to include a number of official websites. Content can consist of more frequently updated and specialized information, and sites link to other official pages. Government publications, legislation and newsletters are available, along with search features and e-mail addresses. This presently accounts for 34.2% of UN states.
- *Interaction*: describes when a country has a dramatically expanded presence on the Internet, with access to a wide range of government institutions and services, including a more sophisticated level of formal interactions between citizens and service providers, such as e-mail and post comments area. The capacity to search specialized databases and download forms and applications, or to submit them, is also available. Content is managed critically, and information is well balanced and frequently updated. This presently accounts for 30% of UN states.
- *Transaction*: describes when a country has complete and secure transactions, such as obtaining visas, passports, birth and death records, licences, ability to pay online for automobile registration fees, utility bills and taxes, and submitting bids for procurement contracts. Digital signatures may be recognized in an effort to facilitate procurement and doing business with the government. Secure sites and user passwords are also present. This presently accounts for 9% of UN states.
- *Transformation*: describes a state when a country has removed the demarcation between ministerial, departmental and agency borders, and services are clustered together along common needs and removed to cyberspace. None of the countries surveyed has reached this capacity.

Bonham *et al.* (2001) describe government-to-government (G2G) activities as the backbone of government. This involves sharing data and conducting exchanges between local, national and international government players. e-Solutions enable departments to streamline operations and trim costs, reinforcing the hopes of policy modernizers to restructure and reform government in a manner worthy of the new information age. The Internet is also fostering a new multifunctional information infrastructure that can enable the movement towards greater integration across both intra-government and inter-government activity. An example of this is demonstrated in the USA, where the US G2G site facilitates inter-governmental collaboration and interoperability between state, federal and tribal/native American governments. This is achieved by highlighting exemplary practices and innovations across governments, plus publishing web standards and protocols.

Governments also need to focus closely on their back-office capacity to deal with the unleashing and empowering of the citizen-engagement process. They

should offer such empowerment only if they have already addressed the necessary changes to structure, organization, resource allocation and available skills. The UN reports that creating sufficient back-office capabilities is the major concern of public-sector professionals (Ronaghan, 2002). This is particularly true in developing countries, which suffer from a chronic lack of resources and where the vision of providing a one-stop shop of government services is severely restricted.

The challenge for governments is to manage equally the front and back-office demand in order to provide public administrators with the necessary resources to cope with the demands of cyber-government where the traditional, 'physical' transaction and interaction space is replaced by a 'virtual' space. In e-commerce, Sviokla and Rayport (1994) describe this as the market-space model – a virtual realm where products and services exist as digital information and can be delivered through information-based channels. Similar dynamics apply in the public sector. If an organization can successfully transform its traditional organizational structure and embrace e-capability, then the digital market space can represent a great opportunity for increasing value to citizens. The Web represents a single platform for the entire value chain, and it will strengthen, completely restructure and even force some elements to become obsolete.

Visibility through the Web can increase trust between governments and citizens by enabling a more transparent and 'open-book' organization. Experience to date in the private sector highlights the importance of providing a bridge between the physical world of the bricks-and-mortar organization and the virtual world of the Internet. Known as a clicks-and-bricks strategy, there are a number of benefits that an integrated strategy and model like this can bring to an organization. Gulati and Garino (2000) point out a number of strategic consequences of converging the physical and virtual worlds. These are:

- Integration strategy gives greater *credibility* to an organization's website by leveraging the existing corporate reputation. An organization can also drive its current consumers and thereby provide immediate traffic, plus capitalize on the fact that new consumers will know the site is legitimate, reducing fears of fraud or security.
- Integration strategy for *management* provides an organization with a better alignment of strategic objectives, the chance to identify and exploit possible synergies, and leverage mutually beneficial knowledge.
- Integration strategy for *operations* should be based on the strength of a company's existing delivery and information systems and the feasibility of their transferability to the Internet. It can provide significant cost savings depending on consumers' uptake.

Governments, particularly in Europe and North and South America, have embraced the new cultural dynamics, and made moves towards developing an 'open-book' organization. However, such a new culture is unlikely to be embraced by states that operate restrictive regimes, as transparent and accessible government processes are a threat to their political systems. For example, several countries in Asia, the Caribbean and sub-Saharan Africa use the Internet for very singular and self-promoting purposes. As a counter example, in 1998, the South Korean government launched OPEN (Online Procedures Enhancement or Civil Applications) to allow citizens to track online the progress of their applications or services in a battle against corruption and, in particular, to expose bureaucrats who in the past demanded bribes to expedite applications.

Better information

Solid commitment to e-government implies that a country's leadership recognizes the fact that information has become a social and economic asset. The Organization for Economic Co-operation and Development (OECD) (2003a) explains that governments effectively engage citizens through the Web when they recognize that access to information is a basic pre-condition, that consultation should be central to policy-making, and that public participation is a relationship of partnership. However 'open-book' organization does not necessarily mean that everything is summarily dumped on the website. Unfortunately, there is still a profundity of information on government sites that is extremely citizen-unfriendly. Wanting to provide as much information as possible is encouraging; however, quantity, if it is not accompanied by quality, adds little value to enterprising e-government initiatives. Therefore, a clear distinction between access and accessibility must be reinforced.

Making information more accessible can be achieved by providing search engines, software for style-checking, multilingual translations of official documents, and online glossaries, and improving the intelligibility of government texts (OECD 2003a). Additionally, governments with increased demand and burdened with the pressure of information-transmission overload would do well to seek the assistance of infomediaries (either internal or external agencies), which can facilitate the translation, aggregation and presentation of government information to citizens. It is essential that governments make considered and strategically sound decisions concerning information management, because gathering, assimilating and storing information is costly.

Currently, governments hold data recording the many facets of our lives, including health, education, social welfare and security, and tax and revenue. Presently, the majority of countries store these data in different departments and agencies. However, the governments that have managed to amalgamate all this information have developed a new capacity to interact individually with citizens, thereby radically enhancing the ability to target and customize services to meet differing individual needs. With the information gathered and assimilated, governments can also offer citizens a 'one-stop shop' of information and services. An example of developing a one-stop shop solution for citizens is illustrated in Table 1.

As we can see from the tremendous range of activities listed in Table 1, the Internet can allow governments to manage information in a radically new way. Also, as citizens receive higher-quality and more focused online services, governments of course hope that this will increase confidence and allegiance in citizens towards the political process. One of the outlets for engagement is to use the Internet to enable citizens to contribute to specific policy outcomes as information is more easily disseminated through a common platform for discussion and feedback.

It is fair to conclude that concerning policy-making, citizens are most generally engaged during the agenda-setting stage of the policy cycle, with information being disseminated for online surveys and opinion polls, discussion forums, bulletin boards, e-petitions and e-referenda. However, there is no reason why online activities cannot be extended across all stages of policy making (OECD 2003b). For example, policy analysis could include electronic citizen juries, and policy formulation could be extended to include e-referenda amending legislation.

In addition, policy implementation could involve e-mail distribution lists for target groups, while policy monitoring could be aided by online surveys and opinion polls. Another example of citizen involvement across the spectrum is provided in the Civic Engagement exercise of the Department of Environmental Affairs and Tourism in South Africa. The National State of the Environment Report was launched on the Internet in October 1999 as a tool for individuals, communities, organizations and governments to implement effective environmental management. The government wanted, on a national level, to identify a common set of core environmental indicators with the assistance of all relevant stakeholders. The result was that the various participating groups contributed to defining the environmental agenda, formulating the key priorities, and monitoring the development of government activities.

Better services

Just as through e-commerce B2C transactions are faster and more convenient, so government-to-citizen services can also improve through the use of e-government. Across local, national, inter-governmental and international levels, different governmental agencies are able to supply a more specific range of services to different groups within the community – whether defined geographically, by interest, or by the specific demographic group they represent. An interesting example of a wide range of e-services being targeted to a specific demographic group is an initiative by the UK government aimed at encouraging older citizens to use the Internet. This initiative counters the idea that many older people do not see the Internet as relevant to their lives and therefore prefer traditional channels of contact. National Audit Office (NAO 2003) research has demonstrated that many older people could benefit from increased access to e-services for the following reasons:

- Older people are generally less mobile e.g. due to illness or disability, and therefore are accustomed to using call centres or remote interactive services to handle their affairs without having to travel.
- Internet portals and electronic kiosks could enable older people to gain information on health, consumer rights and benefits from a single source, saving them time and inconvenience.

Table 1 **A one-stop-shop solution for citizens: alphabetical listing of projects and activities**

A

Accessibility for people with disabilities
ADSL
Advancing with e-business
Agency online action plans
Assisting suppliers
Ausinfo guidelines for Commonwealth information published in electronic formats
Australian Government domain administration
Australian Government Gazettes
Australia's strategic framework
Authentication points of contact

B

Backing Australia's Ability (ICT Centre of Excellence)
Benefits of e-business
Better business
Better information
Better practice
Better practice in online service delivery
Bilateral activities
Bookshops
Broadband
Business environment for the information economy

C

Checklist, Commonwealth Agency website and Internet system security
Chemicals Gazette
Collaborative e-business/ITOL programme
Commonwealth electronic tendering system
Commonwealth government directory
Commonwealth government entry point
Communicating the government's e-procurement strategy

D

Digital authentication
Digital divide
Digital signature
Digital signature certificate
Disability issues and standards for accessing government web and online content

E

e-Business case studies
e-Business for small businesses
e-Business strategy
e-Business – where to start?
e-Commerce across Australia
e-Commerce: beyond 2000
Economic transformation through IT
e-Education
e-Government Benefits Study
e-Government events
e-Government strategies and implementation
e-Health
Electronic publishing and record keeping
e-Procurement demonstration implementations
E-Procurement update

F

FedInfo
FedLink
Foresight
Free trade agreements

G

Gatekeeper Type 3 Certificate – broad specification
Government agency website and Internet system security checklist
Government authentication
Government electronic satellite trial
Government e-procurement
Government information access network
Government online survey
Government public key authority
Government software agreements
govonline list-server – information and sign–up
Guidance for agencies – e-procurement
Guidance on departmental and ministerial websites
Guide to minimum website standards

H

Health

I

ICT skills
Image gallery
Improving confidence and trust
Integrated services
Interactive gambling
International dimensions
Internet Advocates Pilot Program
Internet Corporation for Assigned Names and Numbers
Interoperability for e-business

J

Job vacancies

K

Knowledge management

L

Library deposits

M

Media releases
Minimum website standards
Ministerial Council for the Information Economy

N

National co-ordination
National ICT Australia (NICTA)
National Registration Authority Gazette
National Tender Discoverability Project
NetSpots

O

Online Australia
Online banking
Online content regulation
Online council
Online gambling
Online information access network

P

People with disabilities
PO03 – concept of operations
Portals
Portfolio budget statement
Practice, communities of privacy
Privacy recommendations
Publications
Publications register
Publication services directory
Public key infrastructure (PKI) privacy guidelines

R

Regional Australia projects
Regional summits across Australia
Remittance advice
Resource centre

S

Save@Home
Security checklist, Commonwealth Agency website and Internet systems
Securing e-commerce/ e-business/e-government
Service providers signed to head agreements
Shaping global rules and standards
Shopping online
Solutions exchange
Solutions map
Spam

T

Tariff Concessions Gazette
Tax reform
Telecommunications
The information economy
TIGERS programme
Transport sector workshop report

W

WTO
Web and online content accessibility guidelines for Commonwealth agencies
What is e-business?
Who is doing what to get people online (survey)?
Whole of government telecommunications

Source: Australian Government National Office of Information Economy.

- Often, older people live alone or are far from relatives; e-mail would facilitate contact with friends and family.
- Many older people wish to maintain their independence; technology would allow them to consult doctors and monitor their health using telephone and video links, thereby avoiding the need to move into a nursing home.

Another example of how communities can be targeted, this time by geography and industry, is Bhoomi, an e-governance project of the Indian government that has succeeded in computerizing 20 million village land records of 6.7 million farmers. This system provides local farmers with the necessary data to buy and sell land, a process that was previously done manually and prone to endless errors. Additionally, the Bhoomi software enables policy-makers to generate various reports based on type of soil, land-holding size, type of crops grown, etc.

These examples illustrate that cultural, social and constitutional divides are being erased while the provision of more person-centred services emerges. Government-to-citizen functions were traditionally characterized by paper-laden government procedures. As governments create a more citizen-centric approach, they are exemplifying the concept of 'relationship' or 'one-to-one' marketing. This is defined by Peppers *et al.* (1999) as a move from mass standardization towards mass customization, and, most significantly, establishing a learning relationship with each customer. From a services point of view, this means building the capacity to identify, track and interact with individual citizens and reconfigure products and services to meet their specific needs.

Developing tri-sector partnerships and alliances can additionally multiply access points. Governments in partnership with private- and third-sector/voluntary organizations can promote Internet access through access points at work or other public spaces, such as recreation outlets, cultural spaces, libraries, transportation hubs, health centres, leisure facilities, community centres and schools. This promotes the concept that interaction with government can be 'out-of-the-box', and that engagement can happen across many focal points of our daily life. In order for the Singapore government to achieve its goal to 'delight customers and connect citizens by having an e-lifestyle prevalent in Singapore by 2006', it understands that convenient access must be provided to anyone who wants to transact online with the Singapore government. It encourages everyone without access to a computer to go to public libraries, supermarkets and community centres to get online. To provide this extended access, it has collaborated with grass-roots organizations and private companies to facilitate access to government e-services bundled with their normal services. For example, the Singapore Immigration and Checkpoints Authority has joined forces with a group of photo-developing outlets to help customers with their passport applications and renewals, with the incentive that the online registration fee for a passport is lower than for applications made over the counter.

Although online services will, on the one hand, increase the pool of potential users of government services, on the other hand it may create a greater divide between those that have and those that do not have Internet access – the so called 'digital divide'. The latter describes access differences related to income, education, age, family type, health and capabilities. Most often, this term describes the situation in developing countries, where factors impeding an enabling e-government environment include: institutional weakness, leading to inadequately designed systems and cost overruns, shortage of qualified personnel, creating insufficient technical support; erratic funding arrangements, leading to unfinished projects and high maintenance costs; and inconsistent technology and information changes, resulting in system incompatibility.

However, access issues are not exclusive to developing countries, as governments across the European Union (EU) have had to implement an array of initiatives targeting different segments of the population. Examples of these initiatives include training for adults through lifelong learning projects, providing public kiosks, promoting e-accessibility for people with special needs, and ensuring availability of e-learning platforms for teachers, pupils and parents. However, the OECD (2003b) report, 'The e-government imperative' insists that online services cannot be seen to diminish choice and that a principle of 'no wrong door' should be adopted. This means that everything that is offered online is also offered offline. This is to ensure that citizens continue to have the choice to interact 'physically' or 'virtually'. As an indicator of citizen usage, when con-

sidering the USA (one of the highest-ranked e-government nations), Marchionini et al. (2003) report that 68 million Americans (24% of the population) have used government agency websites, either in tandem with or instead of traditional means.

Better business

The government-to-business (G2B) sector is supportive of e-government developments from both sides. Much of the business community already utilizes e-activities across its operations, with B2B transactions conducted on the Internet accounting for up to 80% of all transactions carried out in e-commerce. Therefore, businesses would like to extend the cost savings and capability of their e-business platforms to also include government transactions and contracts. Second, policy-makers are driving cost-cutting initiatives and efficiency-increasing projects across government departments, particularly with regard to the potential to reduce procurement costs and increase competition. Procurement methods will be affected primarily through the introduction of 'reverse auctions', whereby companies will be able to bid openly against each other in real time to win a government contract. The purpose of reverse auctions is to drive down prices to market levels.

Better organization

It is a daunting task for governments to embrace the e-era; however, they can address the changes to their organizational structure and culture in an incremental and gradual process. For Hagel and Seely-Brown (2001), there are several starting points for an organization looking to provide its services and products online through a web-based services architecture. The first step begins by renting certain functionalities from an outside service provider and then carefully staging investments so as to purchase incrementally the technology that is needed. This allows an organization gradually to build up the architecture as an adjunct to its existing systems. Additionally, starting at the fringes of the organization and gradually working inwards allows for new systems to be tested first in less critical areas. Finally, a gradual process allows an organization to establish a common technical language with potential partners.

Embracing e-government means embracing a new organizational culture. Transforming a government into e-readiness is an intense and challenging process and is most likely to have an impact when it is delivered across agencies, whereby different departments are joined together vertically and department or agency managers work towards a high level of inter-operability through a common framework. New e-administration systems are likely to decrease hierarchical structures and increase vertical and cross-functioning systems; in this structure, managers will need to work together, sharing resources and even budgets. The OECD (2003b) recommends that governments will need to promote co-operative funding mechanisms, such as co-ordinated bids for new funds, and prioritize innovative, long-term investment. Therefore, projects need to have some certainty of future or repeat funding in order to encourage projects that are sustainable and that develop cost-effective solutions.

The resulting organizational structure and culture require appropriate leadership or, more precisely, managers that can provide their staff with sufficient encouragement, facilitate the necessary level of organizational change, and fit technology into the larger strategic vision. If the e-vision is to have any impact, then initiatives need to be supported publicly and endorsed by political leaders. This will be particularly effective in the early stages, when reforms are wide-sweeping and employees are reticent about the change and disruption that they fear information and communication technologies ICT will bring. This is especially true where the benefits from ICT may take a long time to emerge fully. From the onset, leaders should communicate clearly the process of change, expected outcomes and benefits.

The UN reports on an instructive experience in Estonia where, in 1997, President Lennert Meri launched 'Tiger Leap', an ambitious new programme to upgrade the nation's school system (Ronaghan, 2002). A key feature of Tiger Leap was a commitment to connect every school in Estonia to the Internet, a goal that has now been achieved. The programme is run by the Ministry of Education and used a combination of government and private-sector investment to create a new foundation that would match local government investments in computer equipment for schools. In addition to helping to fund computer purchases, Tiger Leap trains school teachers in computer skills and has sponsored the design of special educational software

packages, especially in the sciences. The President's direct promotion of this e-government initiative provided Estonia with strong e-vision and leadership.

Leaders needs managers with the training and skills to be responsive both to the traditional demands of government practice while, at the same time, challenging the status quo and finding innovative solutions to propel through modernization and reform. As the OECD report (2003b) describes it: 'they should be able to facilitate change through ICT rather than attempt to restructure public administration around current technology'. However, below-market salaries and the inability to offer private-sector-like benefits can frustrate government efforts to attract and retain skilled workers, thereby forcing it either to outsource certain projects or to delay implementation (Bonham, *et al.* 2001). On the positive side, over 100 countries have now appointed chief information officers, some with far-reaching access and some with seats within the cabinet. These posts are designed to co-ordinate initiatives and normally have a team or department working with them.

As an example, in the UK the Office of the e-Envoy was set up as a part of the Prime Minister's Delivery and Reform team based in the Cabinet Office. The primary focus of the e-Envoy team is to 'improve the delivery of public services and achieve long-term cost savings by joining-up online government services around the needs of customers and ensure that all government services are available electronically by 2005 with key services achieving high levels of use'. A specialized team can co-ordinate efforts towards addressing connectivity across departments plus education and training of government agency staff in an effort to increase the level of capacity, co-ordination and citizen focus, thereby making e-government operationally dynamic. The central element of consideration for an organization embracing the 'virtual' is that it still needs to represent itself as a single entity to consumers. So, even when competencies and service delivery have numerous providers, they need to be packaged in a user-friendly manner 'behind the stage'.

e-Government initiatives can be risky and expensive and require change and flexibility. Commonly cited problems include ineffective project management, technology failures, discontinued funding, unrealistic political demands, cost overruns, highly visible service-delivery failures, heightened privacy concerns, inability to keep up with technological evolution, and heightened fears of private–public relationships blurring boundaries (OECD 2003b). Regarding computer security and privacy, agencies must protect critical operations and assets from computer-based attacks (Bonham, *et al.* 2001). Areas of weakness commonly include security program management, access controls, software development and change controls, segregation of duties, operating systems controls and service continuity.

The risk of fraud and misuse of sensitive data can undermine trust considerably. Additionally, concerns about the use of 'cookies', sharing information between agencies, and the disclosure or mishandling of private information are frequent subjects of debate. Therefore, addressing the issue of privacy requires both a technical and a policy response. The Canadian government in Ontario has responded to this issue by developing the Privacy Impact Assessment (PIA) guidelines. These outline a process that helps to determine whether new technologies, information systems and proposed programmes or policies meet basic privacy requirements. They measure both technical compliance with privacy legislation, such as the Freedom of Information and Protection of Privacy Act, and the broader privacy implications of any given proposal.

Inter-organizational architecture will become a feature of the future and this should be of great interest to governments. For Dobbs (1998), through integrated value chains, multiple enterprises within a shared market channel could collaboratively plan, implement and manage, both electronically and physically, the flow of information, goods and services. In a manner that increases customer-perceived value, this new inter-organizational structure optimizes the efficiency of the whole value chain. For example, when the government of Hong Kong decided to launch its Electronic Service Delivery Scheme – 'EDS for an easy life' – it was faced with connecting together 20 agencies to deliver 70 services across leisure, marriage, household, health, personal growth, travel, business and citizenship via a single website. The InfoDev and Center of Democracy and Technology (2002) report recorded that when creating this infrastructure, policy-makers were aware of the multiple coding standards for Chinese characters and therefore they adopted ISO 10646 as their common Chinese language interface for message

exchange between the front-end ESD system and the back-end systems.

In reaction to the impending changes to its organizational structure, governments would be wise to consider a plan to: focus on core competencies and discard or outsource other functions; transform information from being a by-product into a source of customer value; seek closer integration with other service providers; and develop community-building initiatives. e-Communities (Armstrong and Hagel 1996) have the potential to facilitate virtual connections and communication between like-minded citizens. These activities are of particular value for individuals who feel their voice has greater impact on the political process when joined together with others who are like-minded. Additionally, virtual communities can provide a centre for citizen-to-citizen relations. 'e-Pals' is an interesting initiative by the City Marketing Division of the Seoul Metropolitan Government in South Korea, where individuals or groups can post contact points to meet friends or learn English and Korean.

Conclusion

By adopting ICT technology, governments are changing the shape of public administration and creating a more citizen-friendly interface. Additionally, Lanvin (2003) points out that governments are, at the same time, users of ICT and influencers on the development of the wider ICT environment. Traditionally, and still the situation in some countries, the ICT infrastructure was owned and managed entirely by the government, which wielded enormous influence on the entire market. Now, after mass privatization of the ICT sector, it is in the private sector where the most innovative activities emerge. With this in mind, Lanvin (2003) encourages governments to see their role not just as the rule producers (e.g. setting up legal and regulatory frameworks) but also as leaders and facilitators (e.g. taking ICT-related education initiatives and formulating policies to support market efficiency and transparency). No matter which nuances of this role governments play, they are major stakeholders in the development of the ICT industry – just as ICT will play a significant role in their modernization.

References

Armstrong, A. and Hagel, J., 'The real value of on-line communities', *Harvard Business Review*, 1996, May–June, pp. 134–141

Bonham, M., Seifert, J. and Thorson, S., 'The transformational potential of e-government: the role of political leadership', Panel 9–1, 4th Pan European International Relations Conference, European Consortium for Political Research, University of Kent, Canterbury 9 September 2001.

Dobbs, J., *Competition's New Battleground: The integrated value chain*, Cambridge Technology Partners, 1998.

Gulati, R. and Garino, J., 'Get the right mix of bricks and Clicks', *Harvard Business Review*, 2000, May–June, pp. 107–114.

Hagel, J. and Seely-Brown, J., 'Your next IT strategy', *Harvard Business Review*, 2001, October, pp. 105–113

InfoDev and Center of Democracy and Technology, *The e-Government Handbook for Developing Countries*, InfoDev and Center of Democracy and Technology, 2002.

Lanvin, B., *Leaders and Facilitators: The New Roles of Governments in Digital Economies. Global Information Technology Report 2002–2003*, Oxford University Press, 2003.

Marchionini, G., Samet, H. and Brandt, L., 'Digital government', *Communications of the ACM*, 2003, Vol. 46, No. 1, pp. 25–27.

NAO, 'Progress in making e-services accessible to all – encouraging use by older people'. Report by the Comptroller and Auditor General, HC 428 Session, 2002–2003: 20 February 2003.

Norris, P., 'Democratic divide? The impact of the Internet on Parliaments worldwide'. Paper presented at the Annual General Meeting. Political Communications Panel 38: 10 'Media virtue and disdain', American Political Science Association, Washington DC 2000.

OECD, 'Engaging citizens online for better policy-making', March 2003a.

OECD, 'The e-government imperative: main findings'. March 2003b.

Peppers, D., Rodgers, M. and Dorf, B., 'Is your company ready for one2one marketing?', *Harvard Business Review*, 1999, January–February, pp. 151–160.

Ronaghan, S., *Benchmarking E-government: A Global Perspective ... Assessing the member states*, United Nations Division for Public Economics and Public Administration and American Society for Public Administration, 2002.

Sviokla, J. and Rayport, J., 'Managing in the market space', *Harvard Business Review*, 72(6) 1994, November–December, pp. 141–151.

Tolbert, C., Mc Neal, R. and Mossberger, K., 'The democratic divide: exploring citizen attitudes about the Internet and political participation', presented at the Annual General Meeting, American Political Science Association, Boston, March 2002.

Useful weblinks

A – Z Index of US Government Departments and Agencies, US Government, www.firstgov.gov/Agencies/Federal/All_Agencies/index.shtml'.

Bhoomi Computerisation of Land Records, State Government of Kharnataka, www.revdept-01.kar.nic.in/

e-Accessibility: Design for All, European Commission, http://europa.eu.int/information_society/topics/citizens/accessibility/dfa/index_en.htm

e-Europe (2005) Action Plan, http://europa.eu.int/information_society/eeurope/2005/all_about/action_plan/index_en.htm

e-Government Action Plan II (2003–2006), Singapore Government, www.egov.gov.sg/egovt_action_planii.htm

e-Pals, Seoul Metropolitan Government, http://english.metro.seoul.kr/logic/bbs/user.cfm?snum=7001

ESDlife, Electronic Service Delivery Scheme, Hong Kong Government, www.esd.gov.hk/home/eng/default.asp

Government-to-Government, US Government, www.firstgov.gov/Government/Government_Gateway.shtml

My.eCitizen, Singapore Government, www.egov.gov.sg/delighted_customers_experience.htm

National Office for the Information Economy, Australian Government, www.noie.gov.au

National State of the Environment Report, Department of the Environment, Government of South Africa, www.ngo.grida.no/soesa/nsoer/project/index.htm

Office of the e-Envoy, Delivery and Reform Team, Cabinet Office, UK Government, www.e-envoy.gov.uk/Home/Homepage/fs/en

Privacy Impact Assessment (PIA) Guidelines, Access and Privacy Office, Government of Ontario, www.gov.on.ca:80/mbs/english/fip/pia/pia1.html#part1

Tiger Leap Foundation, www.tiigrihype.ee/eng/ index.php

Tiger Leap, Choices Magazine, United Nations Development Programme, www.undp.org/dpa/choices/2000/june/ p10-12.htm

DISCUSSION QUESTIONS

1 Considering the point of view of the cyber-optimists and the cyber-pessimists, which view do you think is most persuasive, and why?

2 What do you consider to be the main issues affecting government-to-government (G2G) activity, and how would you suggest strengthening a future G2G strategy?

3 How do you consider e-government adds or decreases 'value' to existing citizen and government relations?

4 What do you consider to be the key organizational and cultural changes affecting governments adopting a new e-administration?

5 Regarding the future, how can the private and public sectors work together to improve both e-business and e-government performance?

CASE STUDY 4

The Euro-Arab Management School

Tawfik Jelassi, Dean of Academic Affairs of the Euro-Arab Management School (EAMS), stared past the Alhambra Palace towards the distant snow-capped Sierra Nevada mountains on Spain's southern coast. The town of Granada, where he was located, was rich in cultural and political history. For centuries it had been regarded as a crucial bridge between the Arab and European worlds. Indeed, this was one of the main reasons why the European Union (EU), along with the League of Arab States and the Spanish government, had decided to locate the joint management school in this Andalusian centre.

It was January 1999, and Jelassi pondered the year ahead. Even though EAMS had been operating for over three years, this would be the first year that the school would take in students for its bicultural blend of management education. He felt that the school was ready for this step, although some lingering doubts did remain. Could a business school that counted only 14 full-time staff members on its payroll, from the janitor to the director, really compete with established academic institutions? Could a truly 'virtual' multinational organization be managed effectively? Had management education really come to the point where students would accept the learning model proposed by EAMS?

The Euro-Arab Management School

EAMS was formed in 1995 by the EU in the Barcelona Declaration as part of its contribution to the development of human resources, especially in the fields of professional training and education technologies. The venture was funded 100% by the EU, but it had the full support of the Arab League and the Spanish government. The EAMS mission was to prepare, through different educational, training and research activities, competent managers from the Arab world and Europe.

EAMS was owned by the Euro-Arab Foundation, a trust consisting of representatives from the EU Commission, the European Parliament, the Arab League and the Spanish government. The owners of the trust appointed a Board of Trustees to oversee the EAMS governance structure. The board appointed a Governing Council consisting of representatives of the EU Commission and the Spanish government Ministry of Education and Ministry of Foreign Affairs. This body, in turn, appointed the Executive Committee of the school, the group that managed the school on a day-to-day basis. The Executive Committee consisted of the director and the dean of academic affairs. The committee shared much of the managerial responsibility for the school with two other bodies, the Council of Partner Institutions, which approved the delivery of EAMS programmes in partner institutions, and the Academic Council, which granted the diplomas and degrees, set the admission and assessment policies, and controlled the quality of the content and its delivery. For a schematic representation of EAMS's governing structure, see Exhibit 1.

The school's mission statement stated that the goal of the EAMS was to 'deliver managers/entrepreneurs capable of working within the Euro-Arab marketplace, equipped with the skills to function in a rapidly changing business environment' and to 'extend the understanding of managerial, economic and social issues that confront Arab and European managers in dealing with each other'. The school would offer a one-year management diploma, a two-year MBA programme and various executive education seminars and customized programmes to

This case study was written by Sid L. Huff, Professor and Michael Wade, doctoral student, both at the Ivey School of Business Administration, University of Western Ontario, Canada. Case released in 1999.

Exhibit 1 The Euro-Arab Management School's governance structure

students and executives in the 15 countries of the EU and the 22 countries of the Arab League.

It was determined that even though the management school would be located in Spain, educational programmes would be offered throughout Europe and the Arab world. There was considerable debate early on as to the most efficient method of accomplishing this. It was considered impractical to establish a physical infrastructure in multiple locations. The cost of building and staffing multiple campuses was prohibitive. Other models were considered, including various self-directed learning options such as web-based education, correspondence courses and the like. However, it was felt that priority should be placed on some form of interaction between students and EAMS tutors and professors. After much consideration, a model was adopted that combined self-directed learning with local tutorship by EAMS trained and certified trainers.

The Master in Management Development Programme

The Governing Council of EAMS decided to work in collaboration with academic institutions throughout Europe and the Arab world to oversee the local delivery of EAMS programmes. EAMS would train tutors from these partner institutions at its Granada facility. The tutors, who were typically junior business professors or business PhD students, would meet for five modules, each lasting three weeks, during the one-year programme. The tutors would learn skills in bicultural (Euro-Arab) management and be exposed to the EAMS pedagogical structure and course content. Between sessions in Granada, the tutors would have to complete various pedagogical projects and assignments. Upon passing the course, tutors would be awarded a Master in Management Development Programme (MMDP) diploma. They would then return to their institutions to act as tutors to students taking EAMS courses locally in their native countries.

The role of the tutor was different from that of a teacher. Tutors did not teach EAMS programmes directly but acted as 'facilitators' or 'helpers' to students. Students received the course material either by mail or through the World Wide Web. Students would work independently on the course material and meet with the tutor, usually once per week for three hours or for a whole day every two weeks. The tutor would answer questions about the course material and provide advice on particular approaches or directions for projects and assignments. The tutors would also lead students in case analysis. Case-based learning was prioritized in the EAMS system.

The EAMS Academic Council had decided to follow a 'business-process' approach to learning, in contrast to the 'functional-area' approach adopted by most business schools. The functional area approach, which is characterized by learning from distinct perspectives such as marketing, finance, information systems, organizational behaviour and so on, was considered unrepresentative of actual business practices. The business-process approach analyzed a process, such as a new product launch or an expansion option, from a variety of perspectives. The consequences of business decisions on all functional areas were to be studied concurrently. Case-based learning lent itself particularly well to this style of learning. Another key function of the tutors was to help students to appreciate the cultural dimensions of the course material. An essential part of the programme was to provide students with an appreciation of the similarities and differences between European and Arab cultures. Part of the tutor's responsibility was to facilitate this type of learning.

Table 1 EAMS partner institutions

Algeria	Institute Supérieur de Gestion, Algiers Institute Supérieur de Gestion d'Annaba (ISGA), Annaba
Egypt	TEAM International, Cairo
Finland	Åbo Akademi University, Turku
France	Ecole Supérieure de Commerce (ESC), Toulouse
Italy	Scuola di Amministrazione Aziendale (SAA), Turin
Jordan	Applied Science University, Amman Institute of Public Administration, Amman Jerash University, Amman
Lebanon	TEAM International, Beirut
Morocco	Ecole Nationale de Commerce et de Gestion (ENCG), Settat Groupe Ecole Supérieure d'Informatique et de Gestion (ESIG), Casablanca Groupe des Hautes Estudes Commerciales et Informatiques (HECI), Casablanca Institut des Hautes Etudes de Management (HEM), Casablanca
Palestinian National Authority	Al-Azhar University of Gaza, Gaza Hebron University, Hebron Islamic University of Gaza, Gaza
Saudi Arabia	Arab Development Institute (ADI), Al-Khobar
Spain	Escuela de Administratión de las Empresas (ESADE), Barcelona
Sweden	Uppsala University, Uppsala
Tunisia	Ecole Supérieure de Commerce (ESC), Tunis Institut des hautes Etudes Commerciales (IHEC), Carthage Institut Supérieur de Gestion (ISG), Tunis
UK	School of Business, University of Bradford, Bradford

EAMS began taking in students for its MMDP (train-the-trainers programme) in October 1995. Students came to Granada for five three-week modules throughout the ten months of the academic year. Each module was organized around a particular theme, such as 'bicultural learning' or 'project management'. EAMS paid all the expenses of the admitted MMDP participants. This included tuition fees, travel between Granada and their home institutions (typically five round-trip air tickets), accommodation and a small weekly per diem rate while studying in Granada.

Most of the faculty would also travel to Granada to conduct the sessions, often for a week or a few days at a time. This was necessary, since EAMS staff was kept to a minimum (EAMS had 14 employees in December 1998). Instructors came from all over the world, although most worked for European academic institutions. The future tutors would typically receive instruction from 15–20 instructors during the year-long MMDP. All courses were conducted in English.

Two batches of tutors had graduated by the end of 1998. These two groups represented 30 tutors from 11 institutions in ten countries throughout Europe and the Arab world. A third group was set to graduate in early 1999. This group represented 18 future tutors representing an additional seven institutions and three countries. A fourth MMDP was set to begin in February 1999. By February 1999, EAMS would have graduated 48 tutors from 18 institutions in 13 countries, seven of which were Arab and six of which were European. By the end of 1998, EAMS had 24 partner institutions in 14 countries. See Table 1 for a list of these institutions and countries.

Student programmes

Once the tutors were in place throughout Europe and the Arab world, student courses could begin. The first course for students, the Euro-Arab Management Diploma (EAMD), was scheduled to be launched in October 1999. The EAMD was a ten-month management training course, which included, among others, modules on communications skills, managing people, conflict management, human resource management, planning techniques, organizational design, change

management, operations, marketing, information systems, data analysis, accounting and budgeting. Special emphasis was placed on bicultural contextual learning. In addition to regular course work, students would complete various projects and case analyses. Students would meet often with tutors in their native countries during the programme. The EAMD was estimated to require 450 hours of self-study time and 110 hours of study time with a tutor (three hours a week for nine months). In addition to course work, there was a major project component, which was estimated to add an additional 250 hours to the time required to complete the course, making a total of 810 hours to receive a EAMD.

In order to complete the EAMD, students must attend at least 90% of classroom sessions with the tutor. Assessment of the student would be made by the tutor monthly on a five-point scale (strong pass, pass, bare pass, bare fail, fail). The tutor also assessed project work. An EAMS-designed final examination would be administered by the tutor at the end of the course. Students must pass this examination in order to pass the course. Students who passed the final examination and completed their projects with a passing grade, and regularly attended tutor sessions, would be referred to the Academic Council, which made the final decision on whether to award the EAMD to the student.

To be admitted into the EAMD programme, candidates must hold an undergraduate university degree, have two years of work experience, be proficient in English, and pass the EAMD admission test. Candidates who fail to fulfil any of these requirements may still be admitted in exceptional circumstances, with special permission from the EAMS Executive Committee and the Academic Council. The EAMD targeted managers and entrepreneurs working or intending to work in an Euro-Arab context. Students who successfully completed the EAMD, and managers with substantial and related work experience, could apply to the Euro-Arab Masters in Business Administration (EAMBA) programme. The EAMBA was a ten-month course designed around the business-process model described earlier. It would be taught partly in Granada and partly in the student's native country, utilizing the same methodology as the EAMD programme, namely tutor-facilitated self-study. The first EAMBA programme was scheduled to be launched in October 2000.

Exhibit 2 The Euro-Arab Management School education delivery process

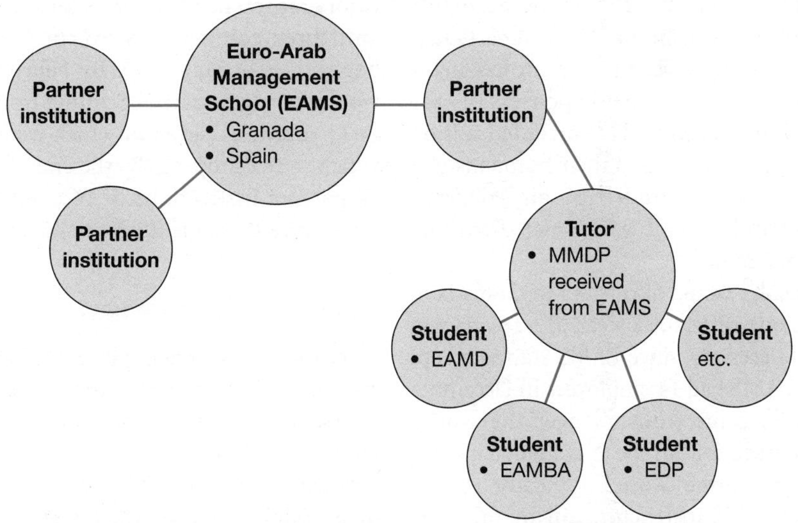

EAMBA, Euro-Arab MBA; EAMB, Euro-Arab Management Diploma; EDP, Executive Development Programme; MMDP, Master of Management Development Programme.

Tuition fees for students taking the EAMD programme would be collected by partner institutions. For example, students taking an EAMS course in Sweden would pay tuition fees to the EAMS partner institution in that country. That institution, in turn, would transfer a franchising fee back to EAMS, typically 20% of the gross tuition amount. EAMS recommended tuition fees for the EAMD programme to be between €3000 and €4000 (about US$3500–4600), although a certain amount of variability in this rate was expected to reflect local market conditions. While rates for the EAMBA programme had yet to be finalized, the tuition structure was expected to resemble that of the EAMD.

In addition to the flagship EAMD and EAMBA programmes, the EAMS offered public as well as company-specific executive education seminars that focused on bicultural management (Euro-Arab). EAMS also conducted research activities, primarily from its Granada headquarters. Research in 1998 focused on two areas – banking and finance and information technology and telecommunications. See Exhibit 2 for a schematic diagram of the EAMS learning model.

Academic quality

A concern with any virtual learning model is to ensure consistent quality of education. In an attempt to ensure the quality of its programmes, EAMS entered into a contract with the European Foundation for Management Development (EFMD), which had recently launched the European Quality Initiative (EQUAL). The EQUAL was designed to ensure a consistent quality of management education across Europe, in part by providing accreditation to qualifying members. The accreditation process involved a detailed audit of each institution's programmes and procedures. These included an audit of admission policies, pedagogical standards, assessment guidelines and so on. In addition to the standards imposed by EQUAL, EAMS decided that it would individually audit partner institutions and tutors on an ongoing basis.

Competition

EAMS was not the only institution offering accredited business education programmes on a 'virtual' basis. A number of universities had begun to offer various forms of distance learning options for students who wished to study remotely. The most established option offered by many institutions was distance learning through correspondence courses. These programmes typically followed a self-learning model, whereby students would receive learning material and assignments from an institution, often by mail, which they would complete and send back to the institution for marking. Correspondence courses usually involved minimal direct contact between students and faculty. Time periods for completion of these courses were often flexible.

The USA-based research organization, the Gartner Group, estimated that demand for online training would increase 10% per year between 1998 and 2000, to $12 billion. Another research organization, Quality Dynamics, also based in the USA, predicted that half of all corporate training would be delivered via technology by 2000.

Recently, many institutions had modified the traditional correspondence course learning model to take advantage of the speed, interactivity and ubiquity of the Web. Learning material was being posted on websites rather than being mailed, and students were given the option of returning assignments by e-mail and even corresponding with faculty through interactive means such as 'chat' programmes or video-conferencing. Other institutions had begun to offer full video-conferencing MBA programmes, whereby students would gather in small groups in remote locations and conduct classes with students from other remote locations and faculties, through the use of cameras, microphones and TV monitors.

The trend toward the 'virtual MBA' was being led by business schools in North America; yet by the end of 1998, some European universities had also begun to offer distance learning options. A number of schools in the UK, such as the Open University, Brunel University, Henley Management College, the University of Warwick and Leicester University, had established accredited MBA programmes that were administered remotely, mostly using some form of web-based learning. Some continental schools were also offering MBA programmes on a 'virtual' basis. This list included the Virtual University of Hagen in Germany and the Open University of the Netherlands. In addition to schools offering accredited programmes, there were many academic and

quasi-academic institutions that offered MBA programmes and other management degrees and diplomas over the web.

Jelassi was comforted by the fact that the mix of self-directed distance education and tutor-based learning, as adopted by EAMS, was unique in Europe. Also, EAMS was the only business school tailored to an Euro-Arab audience. Clearly, there were many students, both of Arab and European decent, who were interested in a bicultural (Euro-Arab) management education. Now that tutors were in place throughout Europe and the Arab world, these students would be able to study in their native countries through the EAMS systems. But how would they adapt to the EAMS distance learning model? And how would EAMS adapt to the inevitable changes and developments that would occur as new courses and new students entered the system?

DISCUSSION QUESTIONS

1 What do you think of the EAMS learning system? Does it seem to make sense to you? What are the strengths and weaknesses of the system?

2 How successful do you feel the EAMS will be in attracting students? From European countries? From Arab countries?

3 Who are the EAMS's competitors?

4 How should the EAMS market itself? To whom? Where?

5 More generally, what are some of the challenges of running a virtual organization? What can be gained or lost?

6 How do you seee the future of (management/higher) education? Do you think that in the future we will be taking most classes remotely? What technologies would be needed to make a virtual education experience as beneficial as a traditional one?

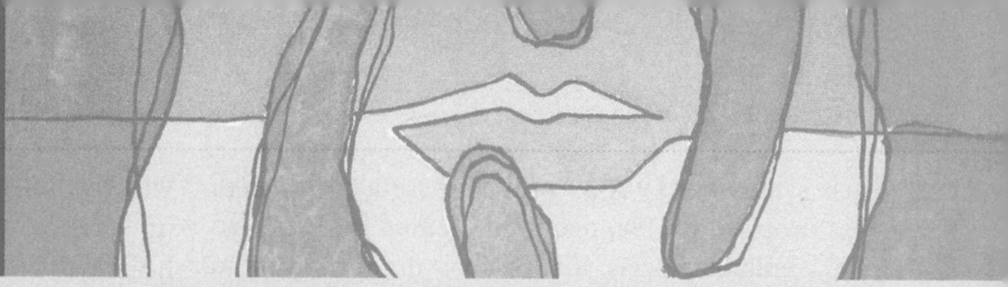

CASE STUDY 5

To be or not to be on the shelf

Grocery retailing through the Internet: Alcampo (Spain) *vs.* Peapod (USA)

It was a sunny spring morning in Madrid when Alberto Soriano, Director of New Sales Technologies at Alcampo, was recalling the trip he took to the USA in 1995 to find out about new developments in electronic commerce. He still remembers how his meetings at an online retailer and his visits to high schools and even private households made him aware of the advent of a new era: that of the networked corporation and the information society. Now, three years after that visit, he is pondering the best way to evolve in this new business area. The cautious words of Javier Liberal, a journalist for *Aral* retailing magazine, are still roaring in his ears:

> In Spain, leisure has a different meaning and shopping is an innate part of the Spanish way of life. Service quality, brand-name, and store ambience will determine whether traditional retail establishments will lose or gain customers after the advent of electronic commerce.

The *hipermercado* industry in Spain

Industry background

The following features characterize the *hipermercado* (large-scale supermarket, or 'hypermarket') industry in Spain:

- a store with a selling surface greater than 2500 square metres;
- self-service for customers;
- high-volume-consumption products, with an emphasis on grocery goods;
- extended and uninterrupted opening hours;
- large, free parking lots.

Spain has a ratio of five hypermarkets to one million inhabitants, compared with 16 to one in France, 13 to one in Germany, and ten to one in Belgium. However, in some other European countries (e.g. Portugal, Italy, Greece), this ratio is less than two hypermarkets to every one million people.

During the early 1990s, growth in the industry was strong in Spain, with over 20 new openings per year (with a peak in 1993, when 24 new stores were opened). Since then, this number has decreased to 19 openings in 1995 and only 15 in 1996. Furthermore, the overall turnover levelled off in 1996, due primarily to the stagnation of private consumption. Sales growth in the industry was a mere 3%.

The competitive environment

Today, five supermarket chains dominate the hypermarket industry in Spain and operate nationwide. In addition to Alcampo (which will be described later), the other supermarket chains are Pryca, Continente, Grupo Eroski and Hipercor. Pryca, which belongs to the French group Carrefour, is the industry leader in Spain, with a network of 54 hypermarkets (including four new openings in 1996). Investment for new construction in 1996 amounted to 30 143 million pesetas,[1] down 7% from the previous year, while

1 In April 1998, the average exchange rate of the Spanish peseta was as follows: €1 = 168 pesetas, US$1 = 153 pesetas.

This case was developed by Professor Tawfik Jelassi, Dean of Academic Affairs at the Euro-Arab Management School, Granada, Spain, and Albrecht Enders, Research Assistant from the Leipzig Graduate School of Management, Germany; the latter spent a research term at the Euro-Arab Management School. The case is intended to be used as a basis for class discussion rather than to illustrate either effective or ineffective handling of an administrative situation.

gross sales were 594 525 million pesetas. Although sales dropped by 1%, profits increased by 10.2% to 23 951 million pesetas; this profit is due primarily to the reduction of supply costs from 449 692 million pesetas in 1995 to 437 915 million pesetas in 1996.

Continente, a subsidiary of the French group Promodès, operates 48 hypermarkets nationwide (45 owned stores, three franchised stores), of which three were opened in 1996. Furthermore, in order to sustain its growth, Continente acquired a 34% share of the Andalusian group Luis Piña, which included the franchising rights to operate the three existing Luis Piña group hypermarkets as well as their future outlets. This agreement is the first of its kind in Spain that has granted the franchising rights to a competitor in the same industry. Continente's gross sales increased by 8% to 484 954 million pesetas due, according to company sources, to 'the intensification of price aggressiveness and the passing-on of the improved purchasing conditions to the clients'.[2]

The Eroski group operated 41 hypermarkets in 1996, achieving a sales turnover of 334 845 million pesetas. Eroski also owns 222 supermarkets (called Consum) and 36 self-service stores (called Charter), thus establishing the group as the leader in the Spanish food-distribution market. Constan Dacosta, President of the Eroski group, believes that due to increasing competition, alliances with other national or even international distributors will be central to Eroski's future business strategy.

Hipercor, a subsidiary of the El Corte Inglés Group (which also includes El Corte Inglés, Viajes El Corte Inglés, Informatica El Corte Inglés) achieved a consolidated sales volume of 1 093 251 million pesetas in 1996. Hipercor contributed 223 541 million pesetas, hence increasing sales by 11.5% compared with their 1995 figure. Hipercor invested 32 086 million pesetas in 1996, including 25 343 million pesetas used for acquiring real estate and machinery and for covering construction costs.

Regulatory developments and the 'ley de comercio'

In April 1985, the Decreto Boyer (named after the Spanish minister, Miguel Boyer), fully deregulated the opening hours in the Spanish retailing industry, which allowed retailers freely to determine their opening hours and even to open on Sundays and holidays. This deregulation allowed new retail formats, such as the hypermarket, to gain increasing market share at the expense of small merchants.

In December 1993, in response to protest by small retailers fearing for their existence, the Spanish government passed a national law that re-regulated retailers' opening hours. This new law limits the cumulative number of opening hours to 72 per week and allows retailers to open on only eight holidays (including Sundays) per year.

The *ley de comercio* (a state law to regulate commercial activities in Spain), passed in January 1996 after two years of intense parliamentary debates, furthermore limits the number of discounted sales to two per year and prohibits the underpricing of promotional items below ordering costs. To control the latter, hypermarkets are now required to present their product-purchasing orders and, in the case of proven underpricing, are charged with a fine ranging from half a million to 2 million pesetas.

In addition to regulating business practices, the *ley de comercio* also influenced the construction of new hypermarkets, for which two authorizations are now required: one from the municipality of the planned hypermarket site and one from the government of the concerned community. The granting (or not) of the second authorization is based on the potential impact of the planned hypermarket on the retail environment in the concerned area.

In 1996, in an attempt to protect small merchants, municipalities throughout Spain started to deny granting licences for building new supermarkets. Catalonia has led the way by imposing a temporary freeze (in 70% of the Catalonian community) on the expansion of stores with a surface area greater than 2500 square metres. (Building licences for projects for new Alcampo and Continente hypermarkets in this community have not yet been obtained.) Hipercor almost cancelled a project planned in Cornella, Catalonia. However, the new law does not affect stores with a surface area smaller than 2500 square metres. This has allowed hard-discount stores from Germany and France (which offer a reduced range of grocery products – between 600 and 700 items) to expand rapidly throughout Spain.

2 *Aral*, 1997, no. 1340, p. 32.

The Alcampo supermarket chain

> Our maxim at Alcampo is to sell more and more quality products at a better price than the competition to an increasing number of customers.
>
> Alcampo advertisement

Company background

Alcampo is the Spanish subsidiary of Auchan, a major supermarket chain in France. Auchan was founded in 1961 by Gérard Mulliez, who, by opening his first store in the northern region of France, implemented what was then a revolutionary new sales concept: for the first time, self-service and discount pricing were offered under one roof. The company is privately owned, with 85% of the shares held by the Mulliez family and the remainder held by the employees. In 1997, Auchan operated 199 hypermarkets, 471 supermarkets and 591 convenience stores in ten countries (France, Spain, Italy, Luxembourg, Portugal, Poland, the USA, Argentina, Mexico and Thailand).[3] It employed 107 000 employees worldwide and had in 1997 a turnover of US$25 billion.

In Spain, Alcampo opened its first store in 1981 in Utebo-Zaragoza; today, it operates 28 hypermarkets located throughout the country. The Alcampo presence in the Madrid area is especially strong, with nine hypermarkets (i.e. almost one-third of its total outlets). In 1997, the company plans to open three new hypermarkets in Marbella, Barcelona and Zaragoza.

In 1996, Alcampo's turnover reached 257 800 million pesetas, a decrease of 2.1% compared with 1995. For the parent company Auchan, the 'adaptation of the accounting structures to the *ley de comercio* and the stagnation of consumption in 1996'[4] were the main reasons for this turnover decline. However, profits increased by 6.6% to 4900 million pesetas, up from 4600 million pesetas in 1995.

As part of its expansion strategy, Alcampo acquired Pan de Azúcar in 1996. Through this acquisition, Alcampo added five Pan de Azúcar hypermarkets (called Jumbos) to its existing network. The hypermarkets reopened under the Alcampo banner and were adjusted to the Alcampo quality requirements. Consolidated turnover, including these five new stores, exceeded 300 000 million pesetas. Ten months after the acquisition, Alcampo stated that the integration had been 'extremely satisfactory for both parties, showing resounding approval by the customers who have showed their acceptance through a notable increase of sales in each [Jumbo] store'.[5]

The traditional Alcampo store

Alcampo's product range of over 60 000 items includes a mix of food products (60%) and a wide variety of non-food items (e.g. clothes, electronics, compact discs, furniture).[6] The average Alcampo hypermarket has a surface area ranging between 6000 and 14 000 square metres. Depending on the store's size, 400–800 employees serve between 5000 and 25 000 customers a day. The shopping system is based on a self-service system that offers customers 2000–4000 large-volume shopping carts and wide shopping aisles. Alcampo employees provide assistance and information in various departments, such as photography, electronics and groceries. A store has up to 70 checkout counters, with only one payment to be made for all merchandise. The Alcampo hypermarkets are usually part of large shopping malls, many of them managed by Alcampo itself (through its Immochan subsidiary). These malls consist of an Alcampo hypermarket and a variety of specialized stores (e.g. furniture, toys, electronics), restaurants and cinemas. To facilitate access to its hypermarkets, Alcampo provides free parking outside each store, with up to 5000 parking spaces. Each store is open Monday to Saturday, from 9.00 a.m. to 10.00 p.m.

Other Alcampo services

In addition to its supermarket chain, Alcampo also has a travel agency, Club de Viaje, and an insurance company, Línea de Seguros Alcampo. An independent travel agency, Viajes Ibermar, operates the Club de Viaje branches and offers pleasure and business

---

3 It operates under the names of Auchan, Atac and Mammouth in France; Alcampo and Sabeco in Spain; Jumbo, Pan de Açucar and Mini Preco in Portugal; and Auchan in the other countries where it is present.

4 *Aral*, 1997, no. 1340, p. 36

5 *Aral*,1997, no. 1340, p. 36

6 Food products include mass-consumer goods (grocery, liquids, cleaning products, toiletries) and fresh products (fruit and vegetables, meat, fish, frozen food, dairy products, delicatessen and bakery products). Non-food products consist of clothes (for men, women, children and babies), shoes, household goods (home furnishings, electrical gods, furniture, lighting, hi-fi and photographic equipment) and general products (car/DIY products, housework items, garden products, sport, toys, leather goods, drugstore items).

travel arrangements. Likewise, the Spanish bank Caja de Madrid has been operating an insurance agency since it signed an agreement with Alcampo, granting it the right to sell its insurance product line (life, car, retirement and home insurance) within the Alcampo hypermarket premises. Additional services offered by Alcampo include a shopping card, a home-delivery service and petrol stations on the Alcampo premises.

The 'Alcampo way of life'

According to the company, the 'Alcampo way of life' means the following:

- *Discount.* Alcampo's main vocation is to offer quality products at the lowest possible price.
- *Choice.* Alcampo offers a variety of choices within product lines and selects for each product group items from national and regional brand-names as well as Alcampo's own products.
- *Service and reception.* Alcampo hypermarkets are organized in such a way as to make shopping practical and to ensure the best reception and service.

The 'Alcampo Project'

In 1990, almost all Alcampo employees participated in a major project intended to define the Alcampo culture. The final document, called 'Proyecto de empresa Alcampo' (or 'Project of the Alcampo Enterprise') established the corporate foundation that has since then inspired all Alcampo actions. The company culture rests on the following three pillars:

- *Social.* Achieve customer satisfaction and continuously improve service quality.
- *Economic.* Generate profitability so as to allow the company to grow and innovate.
- *Human resources.* Foster the personal and professional development of all women and men working at Alcampo by (1) sharing information and knowledge and (2) encouraging initiatives and delegating responsibility, as well as allowing employees to own stock in the company.

Alcampo's virtual supermarket

> Our virtual supermarket is an innovation in Spain and is unique within the Auchan group world-wide.
>
> **Alberto Soriano, Director of New Sales Technologies Alcampo**

Project background

Alcampo's virtual supermarket is the first of its kind in Spain, and even in continental Europe. Before launching the project, Alberto Soriano, Director of New Sales Technologies at Alcampo, toured the USA and met with executives of Internet-based supermarkets (such as Peapod and Super Express) as well as some consumers in the San Francisco area in order to get acquainted with their experience with virtual shopping. Back in Spain, with new insights into electronic commerce, he outlined the following goals for the Alcampo Internet-based supermarket:

- To respond to the need for differentiated service and higher-quality interaction with customers.
- To meet customer desire for shopping through an Internet-based supermarket, hence increasing their leisure time (for some information on Internet users in Spain, see Table 1).
- To become the market leader in the online distribution channel.
- To acquire relevant know-how for online retailing and thus prepare Alcampo for the emerging information society.

The Internet-based supermarket project of Alcampo started in December 1996, and the system became operational on 28 May 1997 in the Madrid metropolitan area. Initially, Alcampo planned to roll out its Internet-based service nationwide by December 1997 and to the Canary Islands by the end of 1998. However, due to technical difficulties (which will be discussed below), the Madrid metropolitan area is still the only place where Alcampo's online shopping is offered.

Telefónica: Alcampo's electronic commerce service provider

> Since 1995, Telefónica has joined forces with leading players in different business segments to raise corporate awareness that future business will be conducted without the physical presence of buyers and sellers. Because of the current evolution rate, we are sure that it is going to be too late if you just wait for the new business to come; you rather have to create it [if you want] to be a major player in tomorrow's competitive environment.
>
> **Agustin Nuñez Castain, Director of Electronic Commerce, Telefónica Sistemas**

Alcampo and Telefónica (the Spanish telecommunications group) have jointly developed the Internet-based supermarket service. Telefónica not only

Table 1 Internet usage statistics in Spain

(a) Usage by region

	Population (thousands)	*People with Internet access (thousands)*	*Users in April 1997 (thousands)*
Andalucía	5966	160	109
Aragón	1060	47	31
Asturias	955	38	29
Baleares	651	43	27
Cantabria	458	10	10
Castilla y León	2186	43	19
Castilla-La Mancha	1384	47	21
Catalonia	5373	326	236
Extremadura	875	22	17
Galicia	2349	42	30
Madrid	4466	282	225
Murcia	899	9	9
Navarra	459	23	11
Com. Valenciana	3428	136	73
País Vasco	1833	69	43
La Rioja	234	6	6
Canarias	1410	38	21
Total (14 years +)	33986	1341	917

(b) Age and sex distribution among Internet users

Age group (years)	*Population (%)*	*With Internet access (%)*	*Users in April 1997 (%)*
14–19	10.5	10.7	10.6
20–24	9.9	21.4	19.5
25–34	19.1	35.2	37.8
35–44	16.3	22.1	24.5
45–54	13.9	7.8	6.5
55–64	12.0	1.7	1.0
65	18.4	1.1	0.1
Male	48.7	60.5	66.9
Female	51.3	39.5	33.1

(c) Access place

	Access places in April 1997 (thousands)
Home	425
Work	568
University	325
Other	110

(d) Services used

	Users in April 1997 (thousands)
World Wide Web	720
E-mail	623
File transfer	328
Other usage	292

Source: Asociación para la Investigación de los Medios de comunicación.

provides carrier services (for voice, data, etc.), but it is also a major player in the new electronic commerce business. Through its participation in the Alcampo Internet-based supermarket project, Telefónica aims to generate more traffic on its telephone network. Its subsidiary, Telefónica Sistemas, was in charge of developing the new system, the cost of which amounted to 100 million pesetas. The service centre of another subsidiary, Telefónica Servicios Avanzados de Información (TSAI), was responsible for the system operation and maintenance. For Agustin Nuñez Castain:

> The partnership with Alcampo will form a winning team if each party concentrates on its core business: marketing, selling and distribution for Alcampo, and technology platforms and electronic commerce for Telefónica. What a team like that could achieve is orders of magnitude better and faster than those who try to do everything inside the same company, particularly if it [the team] has the best-in-class know-how in both business and technology.

Prior to its agreement with Telefónica, Alcampo had negotiated a possible joint venture with financial institutions with electronic commerce expertise but thought that the terms and conditions these institutions offered were too expensive.

Besides its co-operation with Alcampo, Telefónica launched another online service called Intertiendas ('virtual shopping mall'), through which small and medium-sized enterprises can offer their products without incurring the typical large investments required in software and computer/telecommunications systems.

Implementation of the virtual supermarket

In order to implement the virtual supermarket project, a multifunctional team of 20 managers representing different Alcampo departments (including marketing, accounting, finance, logistics and legal services) was set up. The team had to address the following key issues related to various functions of the Internet-based supermarket:

Advertisement and promotion

> At Alcampo, you can also shop on holiday and we even deliver the goods to your doorstep!
>
> **Advertisement for Alcampo's Internet-based supermarket**

When choosing the coverage area for the launch of the Internet-based supermarket, the Alcampo project

team decided to start with the Madrid metropolitan area. However, advertising was limited because the system had not yet proven itself, and some initial problems were expected to occur. Instead of using large-scale TV promotion spots, the advertisement campaign was restricted to leaflets, newspaper ads, billboards, radio announcements and the main Internet search engines (such as Yahoo!).

Product catalogue and marketing

The product catalogue of the Internet-based supermarket contains the 10 000 most frequently purchased articles from five product categories (groceries, household articles, textiles, house appliances, beauty products). This selection is based on the findings of a study on customer purchasing at Alcampo hypermarkets. Although the listed groceries include perishable goods such as refrigerated and frozen products, items that need to be weighed individually (e.g. non-packed meat and fish, fresh vegetables and fruit in bulk) are excluded.

Since the price of an article varies from store to store, article pricing was a difficult issue. In order to avoid customer confusion and complaints, the project team decided that articles offered through the Internet-based supermarket should have the best price, i.e. the lowest price available for the offered products at any Alcampo store in the Madrid metropolitan area.

The product catalogue of the Internet-based supermarket went online in May 1997. Since then, it has been maintained by a workstation at the Alcampo hypermarket in Torrejon (a suburb of Madrid). This workstation can directly access the Alcampo website to change instantly the product selection or to adjust prices. Furthermore, the Torrejon site informs other hypermarkets about product selections in the catalogue, promotions and special sales, thus enabling them to adjust stocks accordingly.

Sales and shopping procedure

Compared with traditional stores, a major advantage of the Internet-based supermarket is the possibility for customers to shop 24 hours a day, seven days a week. Alcampo offers its service using Netscape's CommerceNet technology, which was initially designed to support small-quantity transactions rather than large volumes of commercial activities. Therefore, the system has a severe technical limitation in that it can process up to only 50 different articles per purchase order. Customers wishing to order more goods would need to place two or more separate purchase orders. To overcome this shortcoming, Alcampo plans to develop its own online shopping system without the use of commercially available standardized software packages.

Currently, the shopping process through Alcampo's Internet-based supermarket consists of the following steps (see Exhibit 1):

1. Upon accessing the Alcampo website (www.Alcampo.es), the customer is first required to key in the zip code of their residential area; this information is used later to assign a fulfilment centre for goods delivery.
2. The customer then chooses the items they want to buy and places them, through mouse-clicks, into their virtual shopping cart.
3. The customer may save selected items in a habitual shopping list, a feature intended to facilitate future purchases.
4. When shopping again at a later time, the customer needs only to access their habitual shopping list (which is retrieved automatically from the server)[7] and adjust it to their needs.

Alcampo's Internet-based supermarket does not require a minimum or a maximum purchase quantity. Furthermore, it allows customers to search for certain products or brand names as well as to shop through different 'department aisles' (e.g. groceries, household articles, textiles, house appliances, beauty products). Also, a complete section of the virtual supermarket is dedicated to special promotions and discounted sales for which items are listed under various departments (e.g. groceries, household articles, etc.).

Before sending the purchase order, the customer must key in their name and credit-card information. Presently, payment is possible through only a few credit cards: Alcampo, 4B and Visa.

Security of the system

> Payment and security are cultural problems. Financial institutions and merchants have propagated the unsafe

7 The server recognizes the physical location of the used PC and matches it with the corresponding habitual shopping list. However, it is possible to store only one habitual shopping list per PC.

Exhibit 1 **Alcampo's habitual shopping list**

> feeling of Internet transactions in order to discourage their current customers from going to global competitors.
>
> **Augustin Nuñez Castain**

The alleged lack of security is one of the major drawbacks of Internet commerce today. Many customers fear that hackers will be able to intercept non-encrypted credit card and consumer information, and this has restricted the growth of sales.

The security system of the Alcampo Internet-based supermarket currently uses Netscape's technology known as SSL (Secure Socket Layer). When a customer connects through the Internet to the virtual supermarket, all their personal information is encrypted before it gets transmitted over the Internet. The current SSL technology makes credit card payments over the Internet more secure for customers than giving credit card information over the telephone or in shops. According to Augustin Nuñez Castain:

> The risk of making a physical copy of a customer's credit card or giving credit card information through a MOTO [mail order, telephone order] is higher than breaking even the simplest 40-bit SSL browser. But in the end, it's the customer's education and culture that prevail.

In the near future, Alcampo plans to switch from SSL to the more advanced technology known as SET (secure electronic transaction). For Augustin Nuñez Castain, 'using SET [technology] is like putting a security guard in front of the supermarket gate and asking every customer to show his/her identification card to get in'.

Packing, shipment and delivery

> The project became publicly operational only six months after its launch, with 10 000 products in its [electronic] catalogue. Logistics of the delivery were the bottleneck [of the project], not the technological aspects.
>
> **Augustin Nuñez Castain**

Exhibit 2 **Flow of information and physical goods between Alcampo, Telefónica and final customers**

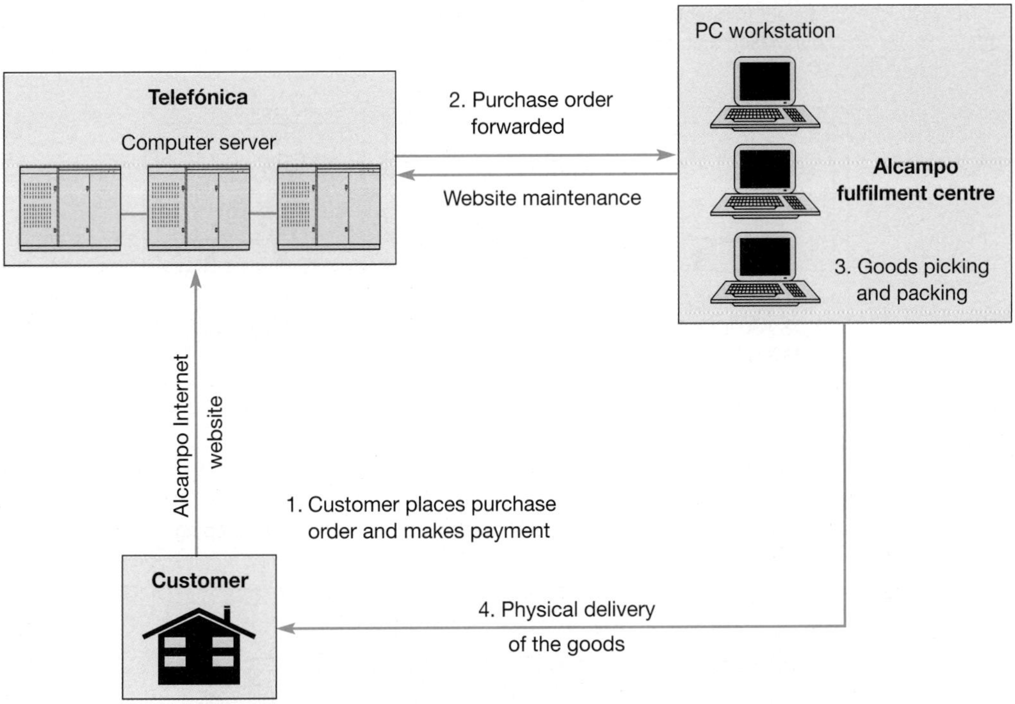

Purchase orders placed through the Internet-based supermarket are first received by Telefónica and then rerouted to the Alcampo stores (which act as fulfilment centres) according to the customer's zip code (see Exhibit 2). At night and during non-peak hours, Alcampo employees walk through the store aisles and put together the order; then they check it for completeness and pack it up.[8] Reusable, insulated boxes are used for frozen and refrigerated products, while all other items are packed in paper bags. Alcampo delivery personnel as well as external delivery companies transport the prepared orders using small vans and private cars. All delivery employees wear the Alcampo uniform.

Alcampo estimates the total handling cost for an average purchase order to be rather high, yet charges its customers a flat fee of only 950 pesetas for each goods delivery, regardless of the purchasing volume or distance travelled. In the future, Alcampo intends to adjust the delivery fee based on the physical distance between the fulfilment centre and the customer household.

Delivery takes places Monday to Friday, within 48 hours[9] of receipt of the customer's purchase order. However, when sending their orders, customers can specify a time window (within one week) for the delivery of the goods, to ensure that someone is at home when the order arrives.

> I think that Alcampo can improve on its customer service along two dimensions: the technological capabilities of the [Internet-based shopping] system and the quality of the goods delivery service.
>
> **Alberto Soriano**

Client service

Three Alcampo employees working at the Torrejon Alcampo hypermarket (the location where the product catalogue is maintained) operate the Client Service Department on weekdays from 8.00 a.m. to 10.00 p.m. They answer customer calls and respond to e-mail requests for information about Alcampo's Internet-based supermarket.

8 Fulfilment centres are required to have a large safety stock of all catalogue items so as to avoid running short of stock.

9 When designing its Internet-based supermarket, Alcampo planned on delivering the goods within 24 hours after receipt of the purchase order.

The Client Service Department is also in charge of calling customers when a purchased item is unavailable and offering a substitute product of equal or higher value. If the customer does not accept the offer, the Client Service Department cancels the charge made to that customer and issues a new adjusted charge. Customers can return items within seven days of their purchase. However, they first need to contact the Client Service Department, which then reroutes the request to the Alcampo hypermarket concerned.

Results to date of the virtual supermarket

> I think that the Alcampo experience is the first step but it has a long way to go. The key issue is: in what direction does the Alcampo [Internet-based supermarket] system have to evolve?
>
> **Joost van Nispen, Executive Board member, Spanish Electronic Commerce Association**

Telefónica believes that the massive traffic generated in Alcampo's Internet-based supermarket is much greater than the actual number of business transactions made through the system. But, says Agustin Nuñez Castain:

> We are sure that people who have accessed the system so far only to search for products and prices are coming back later to shop because the prices in the Internet store are cheaper than at any one of Alcampo's physical supermarkets.

Between July and October 1997, Alcampo's Internet-based supermarket generated a modest cumulative sales turnover. In October 1997 alone, the Internet-generated sales turnover represented 0.01% of the total sales turnover of all its supermarkets in Spain. For Agustin Nuñez Castain:

> Today the system has a mass of 200 regular customers who buy every 15 days. This figure is small but actually not bad if you consider that there was no proper TV campaign, nor a radio or press-based marketing, and also that the system is only open to the Madrid community. So in the next phase, this figure could be easily multiplied by a hundred. What is more important [to notice] is that customer satisfaction was proven since recurrent shopping means that those customers who come back are receiving the expected level of service.

Peapod in the USA

> Smart shopping for busy people.
>
> **Advertisement for Peapod's Internet shopping**

Company background

> We are encouraged by our [1997] third quarter results, particularly our growth in revenues and our ability to begin leveraging our centralized operations. We are continuing to pursue aggressive growth in membership, orders and geographic coverage. As membership and usage increase, we look forward to providing interactive research, promotion and advertising of increasing value to consumer package goods companies and to offering additional services to our members.
>
> **Andrew B. Parkinson, Chair and Chief Executive Officer, Peapod**

Peapod, founded in 1989, is the leading online grocery shopping and delivery service in the USA, as well as a provider of targeted media and research services. It operates its 24-hours-a-day shopping and delivery service through partnerships with high-quality grocery store companies in eight US metropolitan areas (including Jewel Food Stores in Chicago, Safeway in San Francisco, Kroger in Columbus, Ohio and Stop-in-Shop in Boston). When determining new markets in which to expand, Peapod considers numerous factors, including population density, demographic composition, PC prevalence, market condition, and the availability of a major high-quality grocery retailer. Peapod currently intends to focus primarily on the top 40 metropolitan markets in the USA.

As of March 1997, Peapod employed 225 full-time and 1075 part-time staff members (called 'shoppers', who are in charge of delivery), substantially more than in December 1995, when it had 90 full-time and 450 part-time employees. The Peapod service allows individual and corporate customers to order (via modem-equipped PC, telephone, fax or the Internet) and have delivered any item from the above stores. To prepare and place the purchase order, customers can download the necessary software from the Peapod website or call a toll-free number to obtain a free Peapod software kit.

In 1996, Peapod's customer base increased by 166%, from 21 200 to 56 300 members. Orders during the third quarter of 1997 reached 93 700, up by 114% from the 43 700 orders processed during the

same period in 1996. Revenues for the first nine months in 1997 were $41.6 million, up by 111% from $19.7 million for the same period in 1996. Revenue growth for the third quarter of 1997 was strong across each of Peapod's businesses. Net groceries sold increased to $10.2 million from $4.8 million a year before. Revenues from the sale of online marketing services grew to $0.6 million from $0.3 million, and member and retail services revenues increased to $3.4 million from $1.8 million in the same period of 1996. In 1997, Peapod added 37 new fulfilment centres to its existing network, thus covering an additional 3.6 million households (making the total number of households covered 6.6 million).

In spite of the remarkable growth, Peapod has incurred losses since its inception in 1989. This is due mainly to the substantial development, marketing and other expenditures related to its expansion programme.

Peapod's virtual supermarket

Upon first use of the Peapod software, the customer is asked to fill out an optional questionnaire that enquires about their education, marital status, household size, annual income, age group and sex. The rewards for providing this information are special sales and promotional items. The Peapod product range contains all products that are offered by its grocery store partners, i.e. groceries (including perishable goods), health/beauty products, household items, magazines and newspapers, stamps and pet food. Furthermore, Peapod offers a pick-up and delivery service for camera films and pharmaceuticals.

Peapod software offers customers four shopping methods: 'shop by personal list' (similar to the traditional grocery list, with the list stored on the customer's PC for the frequently ordered items), 'shop by aisle' (using an icon representation of the various grocery departments), 'find item' (based on a keyword search for finding specific brands or categories for recipes, menu planning or coupons), and 'shop from last order' (see Exhibit 3). Depending on the season, a special holiday section lists all necessary items for special meals, such as Thanksgiving and Christmas dinners. In addition to product prices and specials, Peapod's software allows customers to view the US Food and Drug Administration (FDA)-approved nutritional label. Products can also be accessed according to a variety of criteria, including calories, cholesterol, fat, fibre, sodium, protein and unit price. Customers can provide personal shopping instructions on any individual item, such as fruit ripeness, provide substitution preferences for out-of-stock items, and send comments and questions to Peapod, the grocery retailer or a specific consumer goods company.

Order fulfilment and delivery

Peapod electronically transmits customer orders to the fulfilment centre closest to the specified delivery address. There, in order to streamline the picking process, orders are organized according to the layout of the centre. Then shopping specialists collect the ordered goods, including fresh products (selected by specially trained produce shoppers), meat, fish and delicatessen items (which are custom-selected by the retailer's own experts). Shopping specialists also check prices and discounts and review member instructions, including substitution preferences for out-of-stock items. Packers organize and store goods before delivery, and a driver delivers the goods and collects payment and paper coupons. Drivers use either their own vehicles or vans leased by Peapod.

Besides delivering the goods, Peapod has also developed additional service options to meet member needs. For example, in the Houston market, it offers a 'drive-through pick-up' option, which reduces the cost to members and creates additional scheduling flexibility by allowing them to pick up the goods of their purchasing order.

To increase the efficiency and the quality of packing and delivery, Peapod has developed some field-operating standards and procedures, including employee training programmes and incentive plans for superior performance. Peapod University is the training programme for all Peapod fulfilment personnel: shoppers, packers, drivers and managers. A separate programme is conducted for produce shoppers to provide expertise in ensuring produce quality and freshness.

Peapod offers commercial and residential delivery to its customers, with varying service costs, depending on the city. In Chicago, for example, costs for residential service are $4.95 (for membership fee, including unlimited online time for shopping and e-mail, software upgrades, access to technical support and member services), and a delivery fee of $4.95 + 5% of the total order amount. For the commercial service, there is no membership fee; however, delivery costs are $9.95 + 9% of the total order amount.

Exhibit 3 Shopping at Peapod

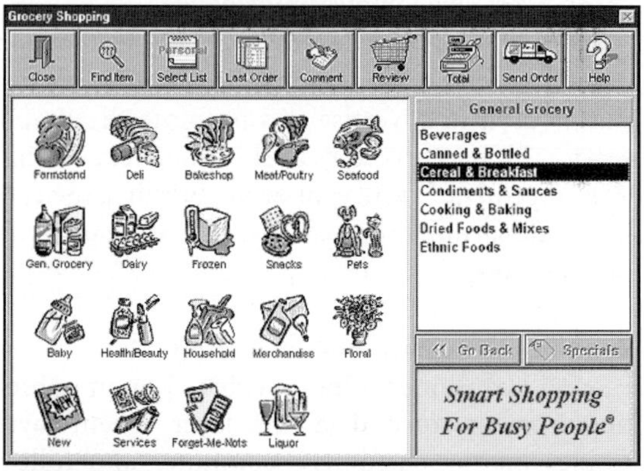

(a) **Selecting a shopping aisle**

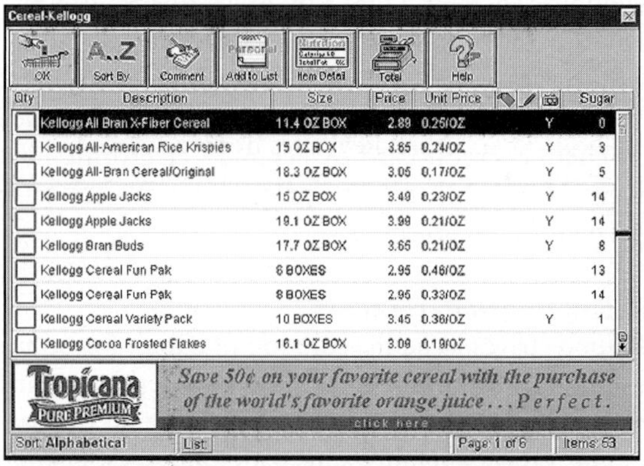

(b) **Product list sorted according to certain criteria**

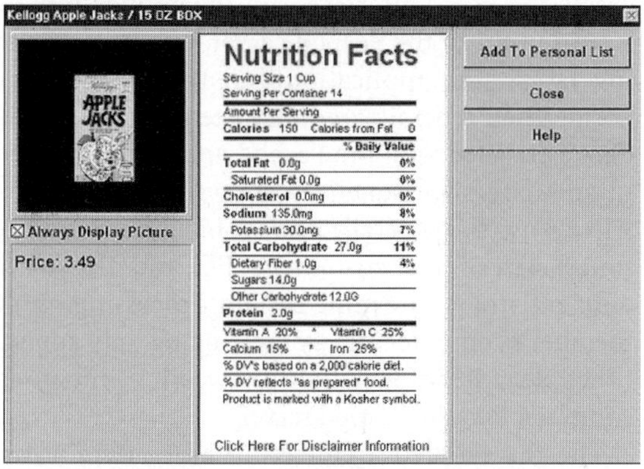

(c) **Detailed nutritional information available for each product**

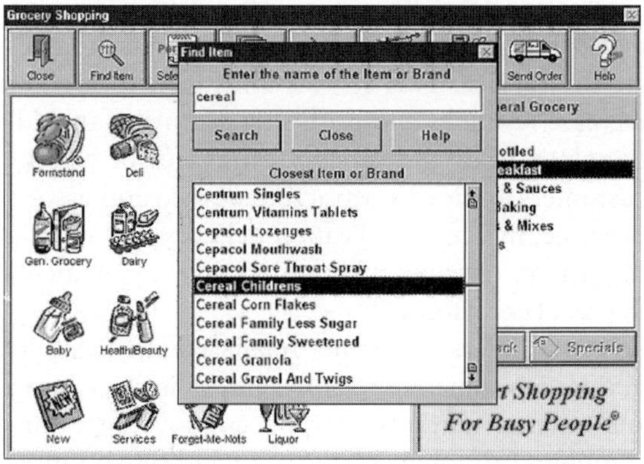

(d) **Search functions**

(e) **Personal shopping lists**

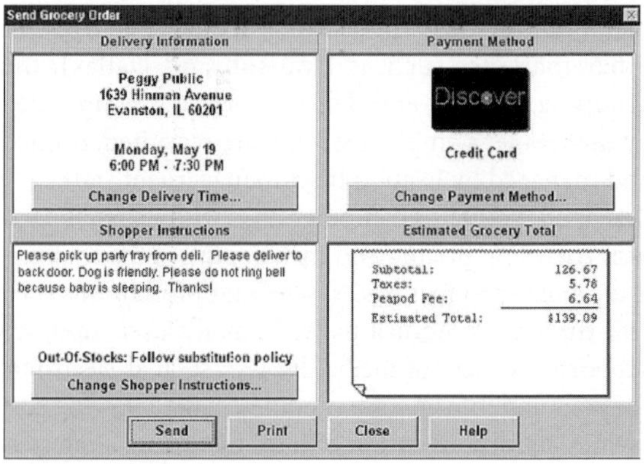

(f) **Ordering and paying**

For delivery, the customer can choose any day of the week (including weekends) and a 1.5-hour time window (e.g. 9.30–11.00 a.m. or 11.30 a.m.–1 p.m.). For an additional charge of $4.95, the delivery window can be reduced to 30 minutes. Payment occurs at the end of the delivery and must be made by cheque, credit card or Peapod's electronic payment (PEP). In order to protect the drivers, cash payment is not accepted.

Partnering with retailers

Peapod strives to be the solution of choice for online shopping and fulfilment services by offering varying levels of service and support, depending on the particular grocery retailer's needs. In all cases, Peapod provides its online shopping platform, including the application, the host computer system and the network-management capabilities necessary to operate the service. This service aims to help retailers increase revenues and profits by capturing an additional share of the grocery purchases of existing customers and/or by attracting new customers. For example, in Chicago, Peapod believes that most of the grocery revenues it has generated are incremental to Jewel Food Stores.[10]

Peapod offers its partner retailers some flexibility in their joint operation. For example, in the Chicago and Atlanta markets, Peapod employees perform complete fulfilment services, including shopping, packing and delivering groceries, while partners provide access to their retail stores within a particular metropolitan area for use as fulfilment centres. In other markets (such as Houston and Dallas), the shopping, packing and delivery services are provided by the retailer's employees, who are recruited, trained and managed by Peapod field-management staff.

Peapod maintains computer links with its retail partners regarding pricing and merchandise, thus enabling it to update product prices, sales and promotions on a real-time basis. Additionally, Peapod's user interface supports a variety of media displays, such as electronic coupons and information modules, hence allowing cost savings and the execution of local marketing strategies. Also, in order to reduce costs, enhance quality and increase volume scalability, Peapod is working closely with its retail partners to improve the order-fulfilment and product distribution model. For example, it is currently developing a hand-held scanning technology for the order-picking and packaging functions and is working with its retail partners to set up specialized distribution centres to lower distribution channel costs and improve profitability.

Retail partners pay Peapod fixed and transaction-based fees and provide annual marketing support that is used to advertise and promote the Peapod service. Either party may, at short notice, terminate this agreement before expiration, but in some cases the retail partner must pay Peapod a substantial termination fee.

Peapod's IT system and technology

Peapod's consumer software is based upon a three-tiered architecture. The first layer (client layer) resides on the customer's computer and follows instructions from the application server in order to create the user's interface, run the application and return input to the Peapod server. The two remaining layers, the application and the database, are maintained centrally and manage all the logic and data associated with the Peapod application, including members' personalized shopping lists. Peapod tries to use the generally narrow-bandwidth connection between the customer's PC and the server efficiently by performing certain processing on the member's computer and by exchanging only application-relevant information between a member's computer and the Peapod server.

The three-tiered architecture also offers a high degree of scalability, since the partitioning of the application and the databases enables Peapod to isolate and optimize the differing processing requirements of these layers. As the Peapod membership grows and the number of simultaneous users increases, Peapod can integrate additional application servers without impacting the rest of the application architecture. Through the 'thin-client' architecture, Peapod can also dynamically change much of the content and appearance of the consumer software without having to modify the client software on the member's computer. For example, in 1996 Peapod introduced Internet e-mail features to its members without any related modifications to the software residing on members' computers.

---

10 The average order size is five to six times the average in-store order size ($110). Although members may not, in the aggregate, be purchasing more consumer goods for their household, Peapod believes that they purchase from it household and other goods that they had previously purchased elsewhere.

For the latest version of the Peapod store (operational since early 1998), Peapod has licensed the use of the Internet Explorer 4.0 and ActiveX technology from the Microsoft Corporation. This version (5.0) will take advantage of the multimedia capabilities and standards of the World Wide Web (including graphics, animations, Hypertext Markup Language (HTML)[11] documents, video and audio) and of Peapod's WinSurfer, which provides high-performance application processing. Additionally, as new consumer technologies emerge and mature (such as Sun's Java programming language and inexpensive Internet appliances), Peapod can quickly adapt its consumer software to support those platforms.[12]

> The use of the Internet Explorer in our Version 5.0 further enhances our service by allowing us to offer customers a sophisticated multimedia web shopping experience, capable of easily integrating content from advertising and other parties. When combined with the performance features of Peapod's WinSurfer technology, we believe Version 5.0 represents the Internet's first shopping site to combine web multimedia capabilities with a powerful transaction processor.
>
> **Thomas Parkinson, Executive Vice President and Chief Technology Officer, Peapod**

Peapod's proprietary targeting engine enables the application system to target various forms of redeemable content, such as advertisements, electronic coupons, online surveys and product samples, to various Peapod members based on a range of criteria. The Peapod Universal Event Processor, a flexible, high-performance database application, manages the targeting and redemption of these events.

Peapod has also designed and integrated a business-support system that accompanies its shopping application in order to facilitate the administration of Peapod services. The Peapod fulfilment management applications, installed at the fulfilment centres, enable Peapod field-operation managers to access and print member orders according to store layout, manage delivery time availability and update the store-specific product offerings. The Peapod accounting systems provide for the billing, processing and collection functions associated with the transactions of the Peapod service. These include the electronic link of the processing of member credit-card payments and funds transfer. The member services and technical support systems provide Peapod's telephone representatives with real-time access to customer information, including order and online activity information, and this facilitates responsive service to the various member needs. The next fulfilment management application is being designed to incorporate hand-held scanning technology to enhance and streamline the order picking and packing functions as well as to integrate electronically the actual member order with the Peapod accounting system.

Peapod's discussion and information forums

> A market is a community and a community is a market. And if you're going to make a market in space, the first thing you have to do is to get users with common interests together. Then the transactions will follow.
>
> **Jeffrey Rayport, Professor, Harvard Business School**

Besides meeting shopping needs, Peapod's Internet supermarket (which includes a free e-mail account with unlimited use) also serves as a discussion and information forum for customers. Customers can, for example, submit their own recipes or search for recipes; Peapod chefs then test-cook the recipes and award shopping coupons to the authors of the best. Corporate sponsors such as Kraft can also post their recipes (which are updated according to the season, e.g. Thanksgiving or Christmas) and the needed (Kraft) ingredients can be ordered directly online by Peapod customers.

Other forums that have their direct links on the Peapod website include the American Heart Association (offering heart-healthy news, recipes and a virtual dietician), Working Mother (with tips for balancing working constraints and time with the children) and Your Kids (featuring articles about raising children). Furthermore, a pet-care section gives advice on how to clip dog toenails and how to remove fleas from dog fur.

In an additional section, members are encouraged to refer friends and family members to Peapod. For every new member acquired through a current member, the customer gets $20 worth of free groceries at Peapod and is entered into a lottery draw for a trip to Hawaii.

---

11 HTML is a way of presenting and transmitting data over the World Wide Web.

12 Version 5.0 is built with Peapod's scaleable remote framework (Surf), which allows programmers to create desktop applications (100% server-based) in the C++ programming language. Surf then uses Microsoft's ActiveX technology to present the application to the user via the Internet.

Leveraging core competencies: selling the IT system and know-how

Peapod believes that its IT systems, including the end-user interface and database applications, are the most advanced systems available for high-volume, online shopping transactions. Through its Split Pea Software division, Peapod now sells a non-exclusive licensing and system-management programme to select retailers. Under this programme, Peapod provides computer software, hosting and network management services, while the retailer manages, under a private label, the marketing, fulfilment, transaction-processing and customer-service components.

In September 1997, Peapod signed a letter of intent with Coles Myer Ltd, a leading Australian retailer and supermarket operator, to introduce its online grocery shopping system and delivery service in Australia. Peapod will provide the server-based shopping application, together with certain business systems such as the fulfilment management, product database administration, customer support and one-to-one content targeting engine. Furthermore, Peapod will provide Coles Myer with start-up training and advisory services related to the online grocery shopping system.

> We are excited to be partnering with Peapod. It [Peapod] has pioneered the online grocery shopping and delivery industry worldwide. Their technology and their know-how will be invaluable to Coles Myer as we introduce online grocery shopping, and potentially other online services, to consumers in Australia. We believe Australians will be attracted to the time savings and convenience of online grocery shopping and delivery.
>
> **Jon Wood, Managing Director of Direct Marketing, Cole Myer Ltd**

Peapod's diversification strategy

In September 1997, Peapod signed an agreement with the floral delivery service FTD Direct to launch an online flower shop in conjunction with Peapod's online grocery shopping and delivery service.

> We are thrilled about our new partnership with Peapod. Its aggressive marketing and business plans have impressed us, and are exactly what we look for when co-branding with other businesses. Peapod's customer base represents a very attractive sales channel for FTD, with characteristics that match those of typical Internet floral customers – those in need of convenient, time-saving shopping alternatives that make their lives easier.
>
> **Karl Immenhausen, Director of Floral Services, FTD**

The agreement between the two parties provides that Peapod will build an FTD-branded flower shop using the online shopping technology underlying its grocery service. This store will be launched during the first half of 1998 and will be available to Peapod members via the Internet. FTD responsibilities include the merchandising support and the fulfilment of floral orders through its international affiliate network.

> Peapod is very pleased to be partnering with FTD. The FTD floral shop is an important component to Peapod's strategy to selectively broaden its 'smart shopping for busy people' service beyond groceries. We believe that our members will find shopping for FTD floral products, particularly for gift purchases, to be very convenient via Peapod's online service.
>
> **John C. Walden, Executive Vice President, Peapod**

Peapod has also recently signed agreements to offer premium wines and greeting cards via its online services. Moreover, to expand further its online shopping service beyond its main grocery stores, Peapod is pursuing other retail relationships. In 1998, it plans to launch a gift service centre that will offer merchandise from numerous retailers who are likely to be attractive to Peapod members. The gift centre will utilize Peapod's extensive member data profiles in order to make targeted gift suggestions.

Peapod's interactive marketing services

Peapod started offering interactive marketing services in late 1995 and currently has agreements with several consumer goods and service companies, including Anheuser-Busch, Frito-Lay, Kellogg Company, Kraft Foods and Nestlé. To date, all interactive marketing sales have been made through sponsorship agreements, under which Peapod provides a variety of bundled interactive marketing products and services.

> As the leader in the in-store marketing industry, we are always looking to find innovative ways to better target consumers. By partnering with Peapod, we can now provide consumer packaged good manufacturers using our in-store marketing products and services with another unique way to reach customers at the point-of-purchase – which in this case will be the consumer's home.
>
> **Wayne W. LoCurto, President and Chief Executive Officer, Actmedia**

In September 1996, Peapod and Actmedia, the world's largest third-party provider of in-store marketing products and services, reached an agreement to provide consumer product companies with interactive, online

promotional opportunities via Peapod's online grocery shopping service.

> Peapod is pleased to have finalized a partnership with Actmedia. We believe Actmedia's leadership in store-based promotional service will enable Peapod to quickly broaden the awareness of its unique services among consumer product companies. Our companies are very complementary with respect to the interactive grocery shopping channel, and as the channel grows, we can offer increasing value to the manufacturer.
>
> **Andrew B. Parkinson, Chair and Chief Executive Officer, Peapod**

Actmedia markets Peapod's promotional, advertising and database-driven research services, which are designed specifically to be of value to Actmedia's customer base of consumer product manufacturers. Both companies envision their relationship to expand with the growth of online grocery shopping and delivery.

Peapod's software is designed to accommodate a variety of media and promotional events and is supported by a database containing extensive information about the shopping behaviour and preferences of its members. This information is not readily available from other sources. The interactive marketing system captures exposures, mouse-clicks, coupon redemption and sales and can report these data to consumer goods companies to inform them about the impact of the marketing programme. Peapod's database and membership profile, in conjunction with its proprietary targeting engine, enable it to deliver highly targeted, one-to-one advertising and promotions (such as electronic coupons) as well as to conduct cost-effective, high-quality marketing research. This accurate and comprehensive feedback is a valuable tool for consumer goods companies for pretesting and refining marketing programmes for execution in more traditional media.

The following are examples of interactive marketing services provided by Peapod:

- *Banner advertising.* A banner or a half-banner advertisement (including a direct link to a brand's online shelf location) that runs in the product 'home' screen and other high-traffic areas.
- *Enhanced content advertising.* Additional information module to explain the uses of an advertiser's product in detail, using an interactive format.
- *Electronic coupons.* Highly targeted, one-to-one promotion programmes (e.g. electronic coupons) using Peapod's database and membership profile. These programmes can be offered to all users or targeted to specific members, such as consumers of competing products.
- *Stimulus response testing.* Posting of online stimuli and incentives for customers with subsequent tracking of purchase behaviour among test and control households to calculate a return on investment.

Future outlook

In California, at the weekly meeting of the Peapod Management Committee, Andrew B. Parkinson was assessing proposals aimed at further differentiating the company from the increasing competition in the Internet-based supermarket business. Although he would approve the development of some multimedia applications that include, for example, different kinds of background music in the virtual supermarket sections (e.g. French music in the French wine department, Flamenco music in the Spanish ham section, etc.), he was struggling with some other, less obvious proposals. Should Peapod broaden its business scope by also offering its customers complementary products, such as online insurance and travel services? Would it be feasible and advisable for Peapod to introduce major technological innovations such as a new VRML-based[13] shopping system that would allow customers, through its three-dimensional store format, to walk down a virtual shopping aisle? Andrew B. Parkinson was also wondering about which ideas, other than those contained in the proposals, might be more useful at this stage for Peapod to make a financial turnaround.

In Madrid, as he looked through his office window at the hundreds of shoppers strolling through the aisles of the Alcampo supermarket facing the Madrid-based corporate headquarters, Alberto Soriano was pondering about the future of the Internet-based grocery shopping system, now operational for almost a year. How could the system sustain its growth in the future in spite of its technical limitations and logistical drawbacks? How could it strengthen customer relationship and loyalty? Furthermore, with the modest start of the project, what would be the best approach for a national roll-out of the system? How could the current 'chicken-and-egg' problem be solved?[14]

13 VRML stands for Virtual Reality Modelling Language.

14 That is, the problem of needing a large customer base in order to justify a national roll-out of the system, and the necessity of a national roll-out for generating a larger customer base.

DISCUSSION QUESTIONS

1 What should Alcampo's e-commerce 'pushers' (i.e. Alberto Soriano and his team) do in order to sustain the growth of the Internet-based grocery retailing system?

2 What business strategy should Alcampo's top management have for the Internet-based grocery retailing system and, more generally, for e-commerce?

3 Based on the case data, what specific actions would you recommend to Peapod in order to improve its financial performance and, hopefully, become profitable?

4 If you were an industry analyst, who do you think will, in the long run, dominate the Internet-based grocery retailing business? Will it be:

- The large, exclusively bricks-and-mortar, retail chains?
- Retail chains that offer customers a choice between shopping in stores or through the Internet?
- Online intermediaries with sophisticated IT platforms and partnerships with traditional retailers?
- New start-up companies?
- Players from other industries?

Defend your arguments.

CASE STUDY 6

Fighting over the Internet

The virtual battle between Amazon.com (USA) and BOL.de (Germany)

Businesses can do things on the Web that simply cannot be done any other way. We are changing the way people buy books and music ... Amazon.com provides a whole new level of convenience and customer service for book buyers. These are [virtual] stores that are open around the clock, even on Christmas Eve, where people can find the specific books, music CDs, videos, computer games, etc. they want and discover others they may also like to buy. It combines the power of the Internet with a very personalized experience.

Jeff Bezos, President and Chief Executive Officer, Amazon.com

On the afternoon of 29 April 1999, as Jeff Bezos was contemplating the new business strategy Amazon.com needed to fend off increasing competition in the Internet book sales in general and Germany's Bertelsmann Online (BOL) in particular, an urgent message from Wall Street blinked on his computer screen. It read: 'While Amazon.com, the most stellar of all electronic commerce stocks, started the week at $210 per share, it went down by today's close to $168.' This information made Jeff Bezos realize that his company's stock had not followed the positive trend of the technology companies in a month that was one of the best in the history of the US stock market. In light of the recent news, he began to ponder whether Amazon.com could continue to revolutionize retailing and to set a benchmark for electronic commerce while repeatedly incurring heavy losses. He was wondering whether, in spite of its disappointing financial results at home, the company should continue with its geographical expansion and the increase in product and service offerings.

The book industry in Germany

Industry overview

In 1998, the book industry in Germany had sales of DM11.2 billion.[1] Around 5500 book stores operated in the highly fragmented German market. The 80 largest book stores (as measured by sales) had only a 30% share of the whole market. Hugendubel leads this group, with sales of DM299 million, followed by Karstadt/Hertie (DM262 million) and Phönix/ Montanus (DM221 million).[2] Hugendubel operates 20 branches throughout Germany with a total selling surface of 24 000 square metres[3] and 740 employees (see Table 1). Industry-wide, annual sales per employee averaged DM288 500 and annual sales per square metre of selling surface were DM9120. In Germany, 3200 publishing houses published 78 000 new publications in 1997. One local bookstore serves about 17 000 customers and the average purchase is around DM27.[4]

Price fixing in the German book industry

A unique feature of the German book-retailing industry is the way in which book prices are fixed, requiring book retailers to sell their books at predetermined prices set by publishers. The book price

1 On 12 June 1999, the exchange rate between the Deutsch mark and the US dollar was: US$1 = DM1.864.
2 Buchreport 15, 1999.
3 One square metre = 10.76 square feet.
4 In the USA 270 000 customers are served on average by one book store.

This case was developed by Albrecht Enders, PhD student at the Leipzig Graduate School of Management, Germany, and Professor Tawfik Jelassi, Dean of Academic Affairs at the Euro-Arab Management School, Granada, Spain; the former author spent a research term at the Euro-Arab Management School. The case is intended to be used as a basis for class discussion rather than to illustrate either effective or ineffective handling of an administrative situation. Case released in 1999.

Table 1 The ten Largest physical bookstores in Germany

	Sales in 1998 (DM Million)	Number of outlets	Total selling surface (m²)	Number of employees
1 Hugendubel	299	20	24 000	740
2 Karstadt/Hertie	262	230	21 000	Not available
3 Phönix-Montanus	222	54	23 450	685
4 Kaufhof/Horten	174	122	22 000	Not available
5 Librodisk	169	240	23 000	430
6 Weltbild plus	125	118	18 900	410
7 Thalia	117	17	14 300	350
8 Mayersche	115	14	20 200	300
9 Bouvier	108	9	7966	290
10 Weiland	80	15	9270	286
71 Boulevard (Bertelsmann)	15	14	5535	Not available

Source: Buchreport 15, 1999

fixing is a voluntary agreement between all publishers, wholesalers and book retailers in Germany; it is meant to protect the German book-publishing industry and the small book stores. The supporters of book price fixing argue that the fixing is necessary for a variety of reasons. First, it protects smaller book stores (of which there are many in Germany) that cannot generate the same economies of scale as the large book-store chains, such as Hugendubel or Phönix do. If the book price fixing were to be abandoned, they argue, it would be impossible for the small book stores to compete against the discounts of large chains, which would have a stronger bargaining position vis-à-vis wholesalers and publishers. Second, it allows publishers to cross-subsidize the publication of seldomly bought books with the large profit margins from best-sellers. The publishers argue that they would not be able to provide such a wide variety of different books if they could not cross-subsidize, which is possible only as a result of the high prices that they can charge for their best-selling books. In 1984, the German parliament decided to maintain the system of fixing book prices arguing that 'without protection through fixing book prices, the German book publishing and retailing industry would not be able to fend off the multitude of dangers that threaten the "reading culture" in Germany'. Currently, the economics in the book-retailing industry in Germany are as follows: if the consumer pays DM100 for a book at the retailer, then this retailer paid around DM60–75 to the wholesaler, who paid about DM50 to the publisher. Critics of the price fixing argue that the book price fixing undermines competition, which ultimately hurts the customers, who pay more than necessary for their books. It is expected that price fixing will eventually be abandoned as the European Union (EU) continues to loosen up regulations within member states.

Response of traditional book retailers to the Internet

Traditional book retailers have shown mixed reactions to the increasing importance of online book retailing. As of today, of the 5500 book retailers in Germany, 1200 are present on the Internet.[5] A variety of Internet-based book retailing exists in Germany. In addition to Amazon.de, Bertelsmann Online (BOL.de) and other virtual book stores that ship their books through the postal service, there are other online book stores that rely on traditional retail outlets for distribution. For instance, customers choose their books from a selection of 800 000 titles displayed on Buchhandel.de's website and are then directed to a physical book store nearby, where they can pick up their purchase. Oliver Waffender, Manager of Electronic Publishing at Buchhandel.de, comments: 'We provide a high-performance Internet platform through which small and medium-sized book stores can connect.'

Other book stores are more sceptical about the possibilities of the Internet. Torsten Brunn, Director

5 Gesellschaft für Konsum und Absatzforschung (GFK), a marketing research company.

of Purchasing at Hugendubel (a company that does not yet have a website), comments:

> We have been following the developments in the online business for a few years now. As long as the online book market still remains a market for insiders, it doesn't make much sense for a mass provider like Hugendubel to enter the online book market. Only very few customers ask for a Hugendubel homepage. As long as we cannot fulfil the [online] expectations that are placed on us as a market leader, we will not go online. This [the preparation for offering online services] will probably take us until the end of 1999.

At present, 42% of all German households own a PC; 22% of all German citizens who are above the age of 14 use the Internet; and in the second half of 1998 2.4 million Germans shopped through the Internet.[6] Approximately 400 000 German Internet users purchased books online in 1998. The average purchasing amount for Internet book buying is approximately DM60–70.[7]

The media company Bertelsmann AG

> We have a broad range of media products in all fields. By the turn of the millennium, approximately half of our turnover will be in the print media industry, and the other half will be in the electronic media industry.[8]
>
> **Thomas Middelhoff, Chief Executive Officer, Bertelsmann AG[9]**

Company overview

Bertelsmann was set up over 160 years ago as a family-operated medium-sized publishing house. Today, Bertelsmann is a worldwide media group that operates in all areas of mass media. It is structured along five product lines, including book/magazine and newspaper publishing, as well as music, radio, television, movies and multimedia. Each business line is managed as a separate company, with its own board of directors. Bertelsmann's corporate headquarters, located in Gütersloh (a town of 50 000 inhabitants near Hannover), are responsible mainly for the company's financing and investment decisions as well as organizational development and group management. As a result of the decentralized organization, every company within the Bertelsmann group enjoys strong autonomy (in terms of its products and services, human resources, operating targets, etc.) and is responsible for its own business results. Mark Wössner, former Chairperson and Chief Executive Officer (CEO) of Bertelsmann AG, explains: 'We want the CEOs of the various Bertelsmann companies to feel and act like entrepreneurs. Our management structure is set up to put the "employee entrepreneur" in as analogous a situation to the "owner entrepreneur" as possible.'

Due to its decentralized organizational structure, one of Bertelsmann's challenges is to link effectively the different divisions of the company. Thomas Middelhoff points: that

> If we don't work together, we can't achieve any synergies. If Whitney Houston [a pop singer who is under contract with BMG[10]] wants to write a book, it should be self-evident that this book will be published by Random House.[11] [Similarly] members of Bertelsmann book clubs pay a special rate when signing on to AOL.[12]

With more than 600 individual companies, the Bertelsmann group employed in 1998 a total of 57 807 people in 53 countries (including 23 817 in Germany). Thomas Middelhoff (who is 46 years old), replaced Mark Wössner in the autumn of 1998. Before that, he had been a member of Bertelsmann's executive board in charge of co-ordinating the group's multimedia activities since 1994.

Compared with the previous year, the total sales in 1998 rose by 2.4% to DM23 billion, with Germany accounting for 30.5%, other European countries for 30.4%, and the USA for 30.5%. The remaining turnover was generated in other countries. After tax, income for the year increased by 9.8% to DM1.122 billion.

In order to achieve its business goals, Bertelsmann's guiding principles (as stated in company documents) are as follows:

- *Responsibility to society:*
  - Our publishing work serves mankind's communication needs. It imparts knowledge and education and promotes the free development of opinions within society.
  - We are a media enterprise with a pluralistic structure. The individual publishing houses and firms publish and circulate varied opinions and in each case develop their profiles. Freedom of publication and variety are ensured by decentralization and delegation of responsibility for programmes.

6 Buchreport 15, 1999.
7 *Die Zeit*, 2 February 1999.
8 Excerpt from 'A media company's strategies for the next millennium', keynote speech given at the 7th German Multimedia Congress, Stuttgart, 26 April 1999.
9 AG stands for 'Aktiengesellschaft', meaning corporation.
10 Bertelsmann Music Group.
11 Random House is Bertelsmann's USA-based publishing house.
12 America Online.

  - Given the international nature of our work, we intend to respect and promote national characteristics and cultural traditions.
- *Entrepreneurial leadership and organization:*
  - Entrepreneurial initiative through business-related decentralization.
  - Consistent delegation of tasks, authority and responsibility in accordance with individual operational business units and central staff and services.
- *Partnership in the company:*
  - Creation of areas of freedom for the individual so that they can fulfil the assigned task, and inclusion of the employees in the entrepreneurial decision-making process on a departmental and corporate level.
  - Implementation of a just compensation through wages appropriate to market conditions, compensation of executives in accordance with their success, and sharing by all employees in the profits and capital of the company.

These guidelines represent the framework within which each individual subsidiary creates its own identity.

The majority of the capital shares of Bertelsmann AG are held by the non-profit Bertelsmann Foundation. In September 1993, Reinhard Mohn, member of the founding family of Bertelsmann, transferred 68.8% of the capital shares of Bertelsmann AG to the Bertelsmann Foundation, the Mohn family kept 20.5% of the shares and the ZEIT Foundation kept the remaining 10.7%. For Reinhard Mohn, the reason for the renunciation of a large part of the family's property was to secure the continuity of the media company irrespective of family interests.

Bertelsmann's Buch AG

In the 1997–98 business year (ending 30 June 1998), Bertelsmann's book-publishing division (called Buch AG) had revenues of US$7.3 billion ($5.1 billion of which came from outside Germany), as compared with DM7.1 billion for the previous year. Sales revenues breakdown was 34% in German-speaking countries, 28% in the USA, and 36% in other European countries. During the same time period, the number of employees at Buch AG rose from 17 800 to 18 400.

Recent acquisitions by Buch AG include Random House (purchased at a price of $1.4 billion), which is where all the USA-based book publishing activities are integrated. The newly formed Random House Inc. group consists of autonomous publishing divisions of Bantam,[13] Doubleday, Dell and Random House with its 27 publishing companies. Random House now operates publishing houses in the USA, Canada, the UK, Australia and South Africa. It currently offers some 25 000 titles in hardback and paperback editions. Best-selling authors such as John Grisham, Danielle Steel and Michael Crichton (who have each sold more than a million copies of their books) are published by Random House. The acquisition of Random House made Bertelsmann the largest consumer book publisher in the English-speaking countries.

The main revenue driver of Buch AG is the book-club business, which accounts for 60% of the company revenues. Other revenues are generated from publishing (23%), professional information (10%) and direct marketing (7%). These clubs operate in Germany, Austria, France, Italy, Portugal, Poland, Spain, the Netherlands and China,[14] with a total of 26 million members. Through its book clubs and magazines, as well as AOL and CompuServe,[15] Bertelsmann has direct contact with more than 44 million consumers.

Bertelsmann's multimedia division

> We have a core competence in the generation of media content, whether for books, magazines, newspapers, television, the radio or the Internet.
>
> **Thomas Middelhoff**

The Bertelsmann multimedia division had consolidated sales of DM313 million in the 1997–98 business year and employed 930 people. The multimedia division is involved in the creation of content as well as services. It includes the subdivisions of new media, media systems and electronic commerce.

The new media division

The new-media division currently includes the following multimedia offerings that target the end customer (i.e. the consumer):

- *AOL.* With 15 million subscribers around the globe, AOL is the world's largest Internet service. AOL Europe operates as a 50/50 joint venture between

13 In 1997, Bantam Books had 32 best-sellers in the *New York Times*'s books rating.

14 The China Book Club, *Shanghai Culture Company*, has a membership of more than 600 000 subscribers.

15 Bertelsmann owns a 50% stake in both AOL and CompuServe.

AOL Inc. and Bertelsmann. It has more than 2.5 million subscribers, including 800 000 members in Germany and 450 000 members in the UK.

- *CompuServe.* CompuServe Europe is a joint venture between Bertelsmann and AOL. It provides online users with PC-relevant offerings and business solutions. It has 850 000 subscribers in more than 30 countries, including the UK, Austria, Switzerland, Germany, France and the Netherlands.
- *Game Channel.* The Game Channel is an Internet channel that offers multi-layer games (i.e. games that are played with several hundred participants over the Internet). It also offers news, chats, and an 'e-shop' from which hardware and software can be ordered.
- *Lycos.* Lycos is an Internet navigation system that is operated in Europe as a joint venture between Lycos Inc., Bertelsmann AG and Christoph Mohn. In addition to advanced search operations, Lycos offers current information such as daily share prices, news, sports, weather services, personal web guides and city information. Lycos is represented in the UK, Germany, France, Italy, the Netherlands and Sweden with services in their respective languages.
- *Sport 1.* Sport 1 is an Internet news channel that provides the latest sports information on soccer, Formula 1 motor racing and other sports. The offer includes videos with edited highlights of the latest Bundesliga events,[16] chat rooms, interactive games, and information from over 10 000 Bundesliga games.

Thomas Middelhoff states Bertelsmann's strategy for AOL, CompuServe and Lycos:

> We will continue to develop AOL, CompuServe and Lycos as Internet portals.[17] The number of AOL members in Germany has doubled within one year, from 400 000 to 800 000. We are striving to double this number again in the coming year. Together with CompuServe, we have about one million members. Throughout Europe, 2.5 million customers are with AOL and CompuServe; we project this [number] will grow to ten million within the next three years.

Media systems division

Bertelsmann's media systems division operates all computer centres and network infrastructures that operate within the Bertelsmann group and also offers services to external customers. It is comprised of the following subdivisions:

- *mediaWays.* mediaWays operates one of the largest TCP/IP[18] networks in Europe and provides network solutions ranging from intranets to IT systems management. The company is a joint venture between Bertelsmann and Debis Systemhaus (an IT services subsidiary of the DaimlerChrysler corporation).
- *Pixelpark.* Pixelpark is a multimedia agency that offers digital services for corporate as well as brand communications in the fields of electronic commerce, electronic finance and electronic marketing.
- *Telemedia.* Telemedia designs and implements Internet and intranet solutions in Germany, including regional online services and turn-key solutions for electronic commerce.
- *C@llas.* C@llas offers telecommunication services that integrate the multimedia assets of the Internet. Private and business customers can use C@llas for their telephone, fax, answering machine and e-mail services
- *NuvoMedia.* In June 1998, Bertelsmann made a significant investment in the California-based high-tech company NuvoMedia. The company core business focuses on the development and marketing of a portable 'electronic book' (called the Rocket Book), which allows users to load books from the World Wide Web via a network of online booksellers. The small appliance is the size of a pocket book, weighs about 600 g and can hold in its built-in memory at least 4000 pages of text (or the equivalent of ten novels). In Germany, the distribution of the electronic book, which will cost the customer around DM900 to purchase, will take place through the Bertelsmann Book Club. Its contents can be deleted at any time and replaced with new reading material. Henric Buettner, managing partner of Bertelsmann Ventures, explains:

> This complementary book distribution channel offers great opportunities. For the user it means good value and simple access to all published products. For the publishers the Rocket Book represents the latest move

16 The Bundesliga is the premier German soccer league.

17 Internet portals act as gateways to other sites. They vary from industry, product or consumer interest. They do not contain information at the site.

18 Transfer Code Protocol/Internet Protocol.

> in the rapidly growing online book business. It offers reliable and easy access to new readers who don't traditionally purchase in bookstores but are digitally open-minded.

Bertelsmann online venture

> Bertelsmann Online [BOL] will be the first truly international media retailing service, offering a comprehensive selection of titles in a variety of languages, supported by locally implemented customer marketing and fulfilment services.
>
> **Heinz Wermelinger, President and Chief Executive Officer, Bertelsmann Online**

Company history

On 25 February 1998, Bertelsmann announced that it had launched a project to develop an online bookstore in 1999. Klaus Eierhoff, member of the Board of Bertelsmann AG, explained: 'In just a few years time, the Internet will be a central distribution channel. Therefore, this is exactly the right time to launch BOL.'

By entering the online book market, Bertelsmann hopes to leverage the assets of its global network, including:

- a large database with more than 35 million active books and music club members in North America and Europe;
- access to a global inventory of available titles published in a wide range of languages;
- a well-established editorial and operational infrastructure in key countries around the world through the existing Bertelsmann direct marketing clubs;
- a close relationship with AOL through its equity stake in the parent company, which provides domestic Internet access service.

Markus Wilhelm, President and CEO of the US publishing house Doubleday Direct, further explains the rationale for launching BOL:

> Digital retailing is both a natural progression for our ever-growing international database marketing operations, as well as a potential to be a very attractive business in its own right. With the surging popularity of the Internet and online book buying becoming more prevalent, our expertise in how to reach the general-interest as well as niche consumer book market segments makes Bertelsmann Online an appropriate and exciting fit with our long-term growth strategy and our assets.

BOL was launched on 4 February 1999, simultaneously in Germany (through www.BOL.de) and France (through www.BOL.fr). Thomas Middelhoff elaborates on Bertelsmann's electronic commerce strategy:

> Now BOL is also operating in England and the Netherlands, with considerable start-up success there as well. This year, Spain and Switzerland will follow. It is our goal to become the number one in Europe. In the medium term we are planning the start of BOL in Italy and in Asia. We know today that books make up a quarter of all goods and services purchased on the Internet – and we recognize the tremendous potential that exists here.

BOL has entered new markets mainly through joint ventures such as the one it has with Havas in France, with Planeta in Spain and with Mondadori in Italy. Furthermore, it is currently looking for partners in Japan and Asia.

The IT system of BOL

Bertelsmann formed a partnership with Oracle, the database provider, to develop and implement the technology platform needed for the online bookstore. The platform was built in just nine months, a record time to market in the industry. Its open and modular features offer the scalability and flexibility needed not only to integrate software components from other providers but also to expand over time. All BOL stores use the same technology platform; the latter can be adapted easily to new market needs, new products, new currencies and new languages. Heinz Wermelinger explains: 'Our e-commerce platform is international. The individual stores, however, are adapted to the needs of the specific countries in which we operate.' The high quality of this technology platform enables BOL to set up a new store within six to eight weeks.

The BOL.de website

In Germany, BOL currently offers through its virtual store a selection of 500 000 book titles. Its website (www.BOL.de) provides customers with information about best-selling books as well as abstracts, contents, reviews and editorial recommendations about all listed books (see Exhibit 1). Customers are thus better informed before making their purchasing decision. Christoph Pech, a young manager at a large consumer goods company in Cologne, elaborates:

> It is fairly easy to find a specific book through the BOL website. The [site's dialogue] menu has a clear

Exhibit 1 BOL.de website

> structure, and the organization of the home page is very customer-oriented. With the links to the international activities of BOL, you can even find books in languages other than German. In a physical book store here, you normally have to wait for several weeks before receiving a book in French or English.

The BOL website also allows customers to create their personal profile ('My BOL'), which includes literary preferences,[19] payment mode and delivery address. To sign on to the personal profile, customers need to enter their e-mail address and a previously specified password. Once this information is given, they are informed on a regular basis about publications in their preferred literary areas/subjects or by their favourite authors when they access the BOL website. Dr Christof Ehrhart, Vice President for Corporate Communications at BOL, explains:

> Using your [i.e. the customer] profile in terms of preferred authors, topics, content, etc., 'My BOL' builds a store that is uniquely yours. This is a different level of personalization than sending out an individual e-mail as some competitors do. Furthermore, through our 'Mini-site' concept, we don't just show a book as a hypertext link that you click on, but we show a small-frame environment which contains additional content such as information about the author, reviews about the book, editorial recommendations, etc.

BOL gives customers the opportunity to submit book reviews, which are posted on the BOL website. Customers can also subscribe to a BOL newsletter, which provides customized news about preferred book types and authors. Furthermore, the purchasing process becomes easier, since all the necessary information about payment[20] and delivery mode does not need to be entered each time a book is purchased. It is also possible to track the progress of orders from the time they are placed to the moment of delivery. Jörn Dopfer, a theology student at the University of Leipzig, Germany, explains:

> I really like the layout of the BOL website. Although I don't know much about the Internet and technology in general, it's very easy for me to find my way around on the BOL website. I also like the incredible selection of books they have. I am very interested in theology literature, and I can find very specific books on the subject. But at the same time I feel bad for the small book stores which have to face this new competition, and I still try to go there. But they [the traditional book stores] just cannot offer this kind of selection, nor the search and browsing capabilities that BOL and Amazon.com offer.

Once a customer has selected a book, they can place it into their personal shopping basket by clicking on the mouse button. At the checkout, the customer is asked for their name, address and credit-card details (unless they have set up a personal profile that already contains all these data). If preferred, it is also possible to give the credit-card number to a BOL representative over the phone or send a bank cheque. Jörn Dopfer prefers the mode of payment at BOL to that at Amazon.com; he said:

> When I bought books at Amazon.com, I didn't like the fact that I had to pay by credit card. I really don't want to pass on credit-card information through the Internet. Who knows what might happen to it? At BOL, I can ask them to send me the bill and pay later. I have two weeks to pay. If I get the wrong book, I can send it back before paying.

At BOL, orders, personal information (name, address) and credit-card information are encrypted by means of Secure Socket Layers (SSL), a security standard that is supported by Internet browsers.[21]

In the future, BOL plans to build through its website a virtual community of book readers in order to facilitate communications among its customers through, for example, chat rooms. It also plans to expand its product range by including music CDs

19 The selection of preferences includes, among others, fiction, travel, education, business, computers and Internet.

20 BOL offers its customers three options: billing, payment by direct debit, and payment by credit card. While the first two options are most favoured by German and Swiss customers, British clients prefer to pay by credit card.

21 In case of misuse of credit-card information, BOL covers a deductible of up to DM100, provided that the error was not committed by the customer.

and videos. Furthermore, when it becomes technologically feasible, BOL intends to offer customers the possibility of downloading digitized content (book, music and film) through the Internet directly from the BOL website to the customer computer.

Order fulfilment and delivery

Order fulfilment is done in Germany through Bertelsmann's distribution company. In France, it is performed by France Loisirs, a 50%–50% joint venture between Havas and Bertelsmann. In the UK, it is managed by BCA, the Bertelsmann's book club there; and in the Netherlands, it is done through a public distributor owned by book publishers.

Delivery within Germany is free of charge,[22] and the average shipping time is two to three business days. In Germany, both Amazon.de and BOL deliver their books through the postal service. Upon receipt of the book package, the customer needs to sign a delivery form. If the customer is not at home when the delivery takes place, the postman leaves the package at the nearest post office, from where the customer can pick it up at a later time.

Strategic alliances

On 7 October 1998, Bertelsmann signed an agreement with Barnes & Noble, the largest physical book retailer in the USA, to establish a joint venture with its Internet subsidiary barnesandnoble.com. Bertelsmann paid US$200 million for a 50% stake in the joint venture. Bertelsmann and Barnes & Noble also each contributed $100 million to the capital of the joint venture. The arrangement between the two companies is that barnesandnoble.com focuses on the USA and Canada while BOL focuses on the rest of the world. Thomas Middelhoff explains the rationale for this strategic alliance:

> Barnes & Noble has one of the most recognized and trusted names in book retailing and we share great hopes for the potential of this new medium. Books have always been our core business, and we believe our e-commerce initiatives will benefit consumers, publishers and the entire book industry ... Through our e-commerce initiatives, Bertelsmann will continue to adhere to our principles of decentralized operations, which we have consistently followed throughout our history. Neither our English-language book publishers nor our consumers' direct marketing book clubs will be involved in the management or operations of barnesandnoble.com.

Launched in May 1997, barnesandnoble.com has become one of the 25 fastest growing websites and has over 700 000 customers. It offers a selection of 650 000 in-stock titles through the Barnes & Noble distribution centre and provides access to over 2.5 million titles from over 27 000 publishers. In the first six months of 1998, barnesandnoble.com generated sales of $22 million.[23] It is the exclusive bookseller to AOL's 13 million subscribers and has strategic partnerships with the top 20 websites, including CNN and Lycos.

Leonard Riggio, President and Chief Executive Officer of Barnes & Noble Inc., elaborates further:

> We are delighted to enter this exciting new phase of our e-commerce expansion with a partner of Bertelsmann's status. Their extensive expertise in direct marketing and their prominent position as a media company will strengthen our capital structure, enhance the quality of our offer, and most profoundly, provide barnesandnoble.com with immediate access to global markets.

In Germany, BOL signed an agreement with *Focus*, the German weekly news magazine, through which readers of the online version of *Focus* are connected directly with the BOL website. Heinz Wermelinger explains: 'The co-operation with *Focus* helps us to achieve a strong presence in the Internet right from the start. With its wide selection of books and the easy usage, BOL will be very attractive for *Focus* Online readers.' Jörg Buerosse, editor-in-chief of *Focus* Online, states his rationale for the decision: 'With BOL we have found the ideal partner to expand the services for our readers even further.' *Focus* had been offering its online service for four years; with 12 million hits a month, it is one of the most successful German websites.

Regarding BOL future plans, Christof Ehrhart said:

> For the short term, we'll add music products to our book selection. By the coming Christmas season, we'll have 500 000 music titles on sale through the Internet in Germany, France, the Netherlands and the UK. For the long term, we want to become a full-fledged online media store that offers any media product online, be it a book, a newspaper, a magazine, a music CD, or a video, and not only Bertelsmann products. Also, we want in the future not only to offer the opportunity to order online, but also to distribute online through the 'Rocket Book' technology [i.e. the portable electronic book].

---

22 In countries such as the UK where book prices are not fixed, BOL offers discounts of up to 40% of the book price but charges for the delivery.

23 barnesandnoble.com launched an initial public offering on 25 May 1999.

Amazon.com: the US Internet bookseller and music store

> I buy my books at Amazon.com because I am busy, and it's convenient. They have a big selection and they have been reliable.
>
> **Bill Gates, President and Chief Executive Officer, Microsoft**

Company history

In 1994, Jeff Bezos, a computer science and electrical engineering graduate from Princeton University, was the youngest senior vice-president in the history of D.E. Shaw, a Wall Street-based investment bank. During the summer of that year, an Internet statistic caught Jeff Bezos's attention: Internet usage was growing at 2300% a year! His reaction was that anything that is growing that quickly is going to be ubiquitous very soon. 'It was my wake-up call', recalls Bezos.

Jeff Bezos left his job and drew up a list of 20 possible products that could be sold on the Internet and quickly narrowed the prospects to books and music. Both had a potential advantage for online sales: there are far too many titles for any single store to stock. To start his venture, Bezos moved to Seattle, rented a house in a suburb, and started working out of his garage. He explains his rationale for having chosen Seattle as the company's headquarters:

> It sounds counter-intuitive but physical location is very important for the success of a virtual business. We could have started Amazon.com anywhere. We chose Seattle because it met a rigorous set of criteria. It had to be a place with lots of technical talent. It had to be near a place with a large numbers of book publishers. It had to be a nice place to live in – great people won't work in places they don't want to live in ... Obviously, Seattle has a great programming culture. And it's close to Roseburg, Oregon, which has one of the biggest book warehouses [operated by the book publisher Ingram] in the world.

Initially, Bezos chose the name 'Cadabra' for his new store, but he later dropped this because too many people mistook it for 'Cadaver'! He then selected the name of the river that carries more water than any other river in the world: Amazon. The new online store was incorporated in July 1994 in the state of Washington, and its website was launched in July 1995.

Currently, Amazon.com offers 2.5 million book titles, including most of the 1.5 million English-language books in print. Its virtual music store has 125 000 music titles, more than ten times the number of an average music store. The virtual video store offers more than 60 000 theatrical and general-interest videos and more than 2000 digital video disks (DVDs). Altogether, the Amazon.com store offers more than 4.7 million books, music CDs, videos, DVDs, computer games and other products.

As of 31 December 1998, Amazon.com had served 6.2 million customer accounts, up from 1.5 million accounts a year earlier. In the fourth quarter of 1998 alone, Amazon.com added 1.7 million new customer accounts. Repeat customer orders represented over 64% of orders placed on Amazon.com during the fourth quarter of 1998.

During the Christmas shopping season (from 17 November to 31 December 1998), Amazon.com achieved the following sales figures:

- More than one million new customers shopped for the first time with Amazon.com.
- Over 7.5 million items were shipped, more than the total company shipments during the entire year of 1997.
- During peak times, more than $6 million worth of parcels were shipped in a single day.

In addition to the corporate headquarters located in Seattle, Amazon.com has subsidiaries in Germany (Amazon.de) and the UK (Amazon.co.uk). In March 1999, Amazon.com signed an agreement with Samsung, the South Korean electronics manufacturer, to sell books in South Korea. This agreement allows Amazon.com to sell books through the Internet shopping website of Samsung. It also allows it to have large quantities of books in South Korea in order to reduce shipping time and costs. International sales, including export sales from the USA, represented approximately 20% in 1998, compared with 25% in 1997 and 33% in 1996.

Amazon.com website

The Amazon.com website (see Exhibit 2) offers the following features:

- *Browsing.* The website offers visitors a variety of subject areas and special features arranged in a simple and easy-to-use manner intended to facilitate book search, selection and discovery. It also presents a variety of products and information of topical interest or related to current events. To enhance the shopping experience and increase

Exhibit 2 Amazon.com website

sales, Amazon features throughout the virtual store a variety of books on a rotating basis.

- *Searching.* A primary feature of the Amazon website is its interactive electronic catalogue. Search capabilities for finding books and other products are based on the title, subject, author, keyword, publication date or ISBN.[24]
- *Reviews and content.* There are several forms of content to entertain and engage readers and to encourage purchases. These include cover content, synopses, annotations, interviews of authors and reviews by other readers, *The New York Times*, the *Atlantic Monthly* and Amazon's staff. Customers are encouraged to write and post their own reviews, and authors are invited to 'self-administer' interviews by answering predefined questions.
- *One-click ordering.* Customers can store their addresses and payment preferences with Amazon.com. During subsequent orders, this information can be accessed through one click of the mouse, thus shortening the ordering process.
- *Recommendations and personalization.* This includes greeting customers by name and providing them with instant and customized recommendations. Through the so-called 'eye service', customers are notified by e-mail about new publications that might interest them.
- *Gift-recommendation centre.* This feature, also called Gift Matcher, suggests gifts based on customer's interest. Amazon.com also offers paper and electronic gift certificates so that recipients can make their own gift selection. Instant e-mail gift certificates, sent within an hour, can solve the problem of last-minute shopping.
- *Virtual community.* The establishment of an online community is intended to invite customers to interact with each other. It also aims at encouraging them to visit Amazon's website frequently, hence promoting customer loyalty and repeat purchases.
- *Electronic auction.* This allows customers and small merchants to post and buy goods in 800 categories, including antique scientific instruments, animation art, Star Wars trading cards and digital cameras. Amazon.com charges users a fee for posting items and takes a small commission on each sales transaction. Amazon.com's auction guarantee covers purchases of up to $250 in the event that the buyer does not receive what the seller promised. Jeff Bezos comments on the auction site that was launched in March 1999:

> Our community of shoppers is the largest one online worldwide. Now for the first time, anyone can introduce products to that community. Whether you are a professional retailer or an individual with one item to sell, there's no other way to reach eight million pre-registered online buyers.

Sellers have their auctions automatically cross-merchandized across Amazon.com's book, music CD and video product pages. For example, a chair from Rick's Café in the movie *Casablanca* was auctioned at Amazon.com. This chair will be displayed simultaneously on the website pages where the *Casablanca* soundtrack, books, DVDs and videos are sold.

Marketing and sales

> Word of mouth remains the most powerful acquisition tool we have, and we are grateful for the trust our customers have placed in us.
>
> **Jeff Bezos**

Amazon.com offers discounted prices resulting in relatively low gross product margins. It offers discounts of 20%–40% on more than 400 000 books, including 40% on selected feature books, 30% on hardbacks and 20% on paperbacks. Prices are discounted for up to 40% on music CDs, including 30% off Amazon.com's 100 best-selling CDs. Amazon.com also invests heavily in marketing in order to strengthen its brand name, increase visits to its website and build customer loyalty.

24 International Standard Book Number.

Marketing and sales costs mainly include advertising, promotion and public relations, as well as payroll and related expenditures of staff engaged in marketing, sales and fulfilment activities. These expenditures, which rose from $40 486 million in 1997 to $133 023 million in 1998, were due mainly to increases in advertising and promotional expenditures,[25] higher payroll and greater credit-card fees resulting from stronger sales. The increase in 1998 was also due to Amazon.com's entry into the music and video online sales and the launch of the new venture in Germany and the UK.

For advertising, Amazon.com uses both paper-based outlets as well as the Web. Print advertisements appear in large circulation newspapers, such as *The Wall Street Journal* and *The New York Times* in the USA, and magazines, such as *Der Spiegel* and *Focus* in Germany (see Exhibit 3). Web advertising is made through Internet search engines such as Excite and Yahoo! as well as the websites of Amazon.com's online partners (see p. 282). It provides the company with information to assess the success of an advertisement based on the number of visits to Amazon.com's website and the number of visitors who actually made a purchase.

Customer service

Amazon.com seeks to achieve frequent communication with, and feedback from, its customers to continually improve its virtual store and online services. It offers a number of e-mail addresses to enable customers to request information (e.g. information on the status of their book shipment and information for investors) and to encourage feedback and suggestions.

The books return policy of Amazon.com is quite unique in the industry. It allows customers to return any book they purchased through its website, even after it has been read. Jeff Bezos explains: 'It doesn't matter how dog-eared or worn it [the book] is. Even if you ripped out the pages because you thought the book was so bad, you can still return the pieces to us for a full refund.'

Amazon.com clearly marks on its website which feature placements on its site are paid for and which are not. The company stresses that recommendations are not and have never been for sale to anyone. Only books selected by Amazon.com qualify for publisher-supported placement. Bezos explains:

> We have the largest staff of book editors online or offline, and for a book that does not meet our standards, there is no amount of money that would cause us to feature it. As a web-based store with a real community of book lovers, we're being held to a much higher standard than physical stores. And you know what? That's the way it should be.

Warehousing and order fulfilment

Many titles are available for shipment within 24 hours; others are available within 48–72 hours, and the remaining in-print titles within four to six weeks. Out-of-print titles are generally shipped within one to three months. Customers can choose from a variety of delivery possibilities, including overnight and various international shipping options, as well as a gift-wrapping service. Amazon.com uses e-mail to notify customers of order status under various conditions.

Total delivery time depends on the availability of the item that is ordered and the shipping option that is selected. For domestic delivery within the USA, customers can choose from the following shipping services:

- *Standard shipping service*, with three to seven days shipping time and a charge of $3 per shipment plus $0.95 per item.
- *Second-day air service*, with two business days shipping time (no weekend delivery) and a charge

Exhibit 3 **Amazon.de magazine advertisement**

25 Advertising expenditures alone increased from $21 million in 1997 to $60 million in 1998.

of $6 per shipment plus $1.95 per book/video ($0.95 per CD).

- *Next-day air service*, with one business day shipping time (no weekend delivery) and a charge of $8 per shipment plus $2.95 per book/video ($1.95 per CD).

For international delivery, Amazon.com offers three shipping services:

- *Standard shipping service*, with 2–12 weeks of shipping time and a charge of $4 per shipment plus $1.95 per item.
- *World mail service*, with 7–21 business days shipping time and a charge of $7 per shipment plus $5.95 per book/video ($0.95 per CD).
- *International priority*, with one to four business days shipping time and a charge of $30 per shipment plus $5.95 per book/video ($2.25 per CD).

Shipping time varies widely, depending on the destination. For example, standard shipments take about two to three weeks to Canada, six weeks to the UK, six to eight weeks to Japan and Australia, and 10–12 weeks to Brazil. For orders that contain multiple items with different availability dates, customers can choose to receive readily available products first and wait for later shipments or, in order to save shipping fees, to receive only one shipment once the complete order is ready.

Customs forms for all international packages list the value of an order's contents by product type. Orders containing books, music CDs and video titles will be listed, for instance, as follows:

Book value: $29.55
CD value: $ 9.95
Video value: $39.95

If the order is a gift, then the package is marked 'Gift'; however, the items' costs are still stated on the customs form. Any customs or import duties are levied once the package reaches its destination country. Additional charges for customs clearance have to be covered by the recipient of the package.

Amazon.com uses IT systems to process and ship customer orders. Through its proprietary software, it selects the orders that can be filled via electronic interfaces with suppliers, and forwards the remaining orders to its special orders group. Suppliers often ship the electronically ordered books to Amazon.com's warehouse within hours of receipt of the order. Bezos elaborates further: 'In 1999, we intend to build a significant distribution infrastructure. We must ensure that we can support all the sales that customers demand, with speedy access to inventory.'

Until recently, all shipping was done through the company's Seattle distribution centre (which has 93 000 square feet of space). In January 1999, Amazon.com set up a mechanized distribution facility in Fernley, Nevada, thus reducing the shipping time to key markets in the western US region by one day. The new 322 560-square-foot facility will also allow Amazon.com to increase significantly the number of books, music CDs and videos kept on hand for immediate delivery to customers. By the end of 1999, the Fernley centre was expected to employ more than 300 people. Amazon.com also has a 202 000-square-foot centre in New Castle, Delaware (near Philadelphia), which has been operational since November 1997.

Continuing its expansion, Amazon.com leased a distribution facility in Coffeyville, Kansas, which will enable faster delivery to Amazon.com customers across the mid-west and south-eastern USA. Plans for the existing 460 000-square-foot facility include expansion to over 750 000 square feet and the addition of automation, allowing the company to increase significantly the number of products kept on hand for immediate shipment to customers. The result is that customers in places such as Chicago, St Louis, Dallas and Minneapolis will receive their orders much more quickly, thanks to deeper inventory, faster processing and shorter delivery times. The Coffeyville facility was expected to begin operations during the second half of 1999.

Regarding the 1999 expansion plans of Amazon.com, Bezos said:

> We have begun and will continue to build out a significant distribution infrastructure. This will give customers greater availability, faster shipping times, and even better service. We will also continue to invest in systems, people, and product expansion, each of which helps us better serve customers. For the rest of 1999, we expect to invest more heavily than we have in the past. Our goal remains to build the world's most customer-centric company.

Amazon.com's IT systems and technology

Amazon.com developed not only its website but also its IT applications for order processing, invoicing,

payment, shipment, inventory management and procurement in-house. Its current strategy is to focus its IT development effort on creating and enhancing the specialized, proprietary software that is unique to its business, and to license commercially available technology, if judged appropriate, for other applications.

The company uses three Internet service providers (UUNet Technologies, InterNAP Network Services and Interconnected Associates) to connect to the Internet over multiple dedicated lines. All of Amazon.com's computer and communication hardware is located at a single facility in Seattle.

In the past, the company has experienced some system interruptions. For example, on 1 October, 1998, its Internet bookstore was shut down for ten hours for, according to company officials, 'maintenance work on the IT system'. Customers, who wanted to visit the website, and possibly make purchases, were greeted on the opening page with the following message: 'We are sorry. Our store is currently closed. If you leave us your e-mail address, we will notify you when we are open again.'

Employees

During 1998, the number of employees working at Amazon.com increased from 614 to 2100. In addition to its own staff, Amazon.com also employed independent contractors and other temporary employees in its editorial, fulfilment and finance departments. None of the employees is represented by a labour union. Part of the employee's salary consists of stock options on Amazon.com's shares.

Amazon.com's executives include eight people with an average age of only 37 years (their ages range from 33 to 46 years). Amazon.com does not have long-term employment agreements with any of its key personnel and maintains no 'key person' life insurance policies.

Jeff Bezos explains what he expects from Amazon.com employees:

> It's not easy to work here. When I interview people I tell them: 'You can work long, hard or smart, but at Amazon.com you can't choose two out of three.' But we are working to build something important, something that matters to our customers, and that we can tell our grandchildren about. Such things aren't meant to be easy. We are incredibly fortunate to have this group of dedicated employees whose sacrifices and passion build Amazon.com.

However, competition for qualified personnel is intense, particularly for software development and other IT skills.

Relations with suppliers

Large publishers

Amazon.com purchases the majority of its products from two major vendors: Ingram and Baker&Taylor. In 1996 and 1997, Ingram accounted for, respectively, 58% and 59% of the inventory purchases. However, after Barnes & Noble announced in November 1998 its acquisition of Ingram, Amazon.com decided to diversify its supplier base and to increase its direct purchasing from publishers. In 1998, Ingram remained the largest supplier of Amazon.com but accounted for only 40% of purchases.

Small publishers

> In order to match the power of Amazon.com's global distribution, independent artists, bands and labels would have to get their [music] CDs into an estimated 100 000 [physical] retail stores worldwide.
>
> **Mary Morouse, Vice-President of Merchandising, Amazon.com**

The Amazon.com Advantage Program allows small publishers to appear more often and more prominently throughout the Amazon.com catalogue. In the publishing industry, a book must reach a certain critical mass before it makes it into existing wholesale channels. Amazon.com has thus redefined what critical mass means. The programme allows small publishers to place a limited quantity of books in Amazon.com's distribution centres for immediate availability to customers. Those titles will then be upgraded in the Amazon.com website to 'usually shipped within 24 hours', instead of the usual four- to six-week delivery promise for special-order titles. Participating titles are assigned subject classifications to help surface the book through Amazon.com's browsing features. The book cover is also scanned at no cost to the publisher. Jeff Bezos explains:

> With more than 2.5 million titles in our catalogue from more than 50 000 publishers, Amazon.com has always provided an opportunity for small publishers to succeed. Now through Amazon.com-Advantage, a title from an independent publisher can have the same prominence, immediate availability and level of exposure as a title from a larger publisher who typically has more resources at their disposal.

The Advantage Program also includes music. It offers independent artists, bands and labels a solution to the problem of widespread distribution of CDs. Traditionally, such artists have difficulty getting their CDs into stores and selling their music. Through the Advantage Program, they can place a limited quantity of CDs in Amazon.com's distribution centres for immediate sales and delivery. Robert Haber, President of *CMJ*,[26] elaborates further:

> We are delighted to learn of Amazon.com's strategy for assisting these new artists in getting their music exposed to a potential audience in the millions. This is just the kind of program that makes the new medium of the Internet so exciting.

It is now easier for independent artists and bands to sell their CDs to customers worldwide through Amazon.com. On the website, they benefit from the same level of exposure as CDs from major artists and labels. Dara Quinn, member of the rock music band Rockin' Teenage Combo, explains:

> No matter how slamming your band is, it is really hard to get distribution without being signed to a major label. Even if we could get our CDs stocked in stores in every city we play in when we're on tour, who has the time and money to print and distribute all those CDs? Now, whenever anyone hears the buzz about our music, they'll be able to buy our CD at Amazon.com. What could be easier than that?

Acquisitions and online partnerships

Drugstore.com

In February 1999, Amazon.com acquired a 46% stake in the online drugstore Drugstore.com. This virtual store, based in Redmond, Washington, offers more than 15 000 brand-name personal healthcare products, extensive healthcare information, and a licensed pharmacy. Through this acquisition, Amazon.com aims to introduce customers to the new shopping experience at Drugstore.com. Peter Neubert, President and Chief Executive Officer of Drugstore.com, believes: 'People who like Amazon.com will like shopping at Drugstore.com. Amazon.com sets the standard for quality and excellent service and we at Drugstore.com are committed to matching that excellent service.'

Pets.com

In March 1999, Amazon.com agreed to obtain an ownership of approximately 50% in Pets.com, an Internet-based company that specializes in popular and rare pet accessories, and products and food for all types of animals. Jeff Bezos comments: 'Pets.com has a leading market position and its proven management team is dedicated to a great customer experience, whether it's making a product like a ferret hammock easy to find, or help in locating a pet-friendly hotel.' The financing will be used to fund Pets.com's further growth, develop the Pets.com brand, and build distribution through partnerships and alliances. Julie Wainwright, CEO of Pets.com explains: 'This is marriage made in heaven and clearly positions us as the online category leader.'

Bibliofind.com and MusicFile.com

In April 1999, Amazon.com acquired Exchange.com, the premier online marketplace for hard-to-find, antiquarian and used books at www.bibliofind.com and hard-to-find recordings and music memorabilia at www.musicfile.com. The acquisition aims to enlarge and enrich Amazon.com's core book and music offerings. It also provides thousands of independent dealers and retailers with the opportunity to sell and auction their hard-to-find books, recordings and memorabilia to Amazon.com's growing customer base.

LiveBid.com

In April 1999, Amazon.com decided to purchase LiveBid.com, a provider of live-event auctions on the Internet. LiveBid.com is a Seattle-based company that pioneered live-event-based auctions on the Internet, allowing auction houses to broadcast their auctions over the Internet. Online bidders can participate in the live auctions in real time, competing directly with bidders physically present at the auction site. Jeff Bezos comments: 'The big winners here are the world's traditional auction houses. Appraisal and authentication are important, and no one can do it better than established and expert auctioneers.'

Amazon.com online partnerships

Through Amazon.com's Associates Program, operators of other websites can create links to the Amazon.com homepage, through which customers are directed to the Amazon.com bookstore. The

26 *College Music Journal.*

website operators that participate in this programme, receive referral fees of 8% of the book value for sales generated by their sites. By the end of 1998, there were 200000 website operators participating in Amazon.com's Associates Program; this figure had increased to more than 260000 by 31 March 1999.

For industry analysts:

> Amazon.com knows that it will probably never be the very best site for rock climbing information or quantum physics discussions, but that the sites specializing in such subjects could be great places to sell books. A link to Amazon.com is an easy, and potentially lucrative, way for such a specialist to do that at one remove; a click on the link takes a viewer to the Amazon.com relevant page.[27]

In March 1999, Amazon.com and Dell, the PC manufacturer, agreed to offer linked websites and provide customized contents for Amazon.com and Dell customers. Both companies provide links to each other's websites from the checkout section of their respective sites. Michael Dell, Chair and CEO of Dell Computer Corporation, elaborates:

> Dell and Amazon.com have a shared vision of the future of online shopping. That vision is to deepen direct relationships with customers and deliver unique value and unparalleled service. Dell and Amazon.com will each offer our mutual customers customized services, competitive prices and easy navigation.

Dell currently sells more than $14 million in PC products over the Internet each day, which accounts for 25% of its business. Its website has over 25 million visits per quarter.

In addition, Amazon.com is present on several high-traffic websites, through marketing arrangements with Dell Computer Corporation, Microsoft and CBS SportsLine. Amazon.com is CBS SportsLine's online retail partner for books, videos and music in a co-branded store on the CBS SportsLine site. Through an agreement with Microsoft, Amazon.com functions as music merchant on Microsoft's MSN Shopping Channel, the MSN.com website, and other selected properties in the MSN network of sites.

Financial results

> It's all about the long term. We believe that a fundamental measure of our success will be the shareholder value we create over the long term. This value will be a direct result of our ability to extend and to solidify our current market leadership position. The stronger our market leadership, the more powerful our economic model.
>
> **Jeff Bezos**

Net sales of Amazon.com for the 1998 fiscal year were $610 million, which constitutes a 313% increase over net sales of $147.8 million for the 1997 fiscal year. In the fourth quarter of 1998, sales reached $252.9 million, which constitutes an increase of 283% over the net sales figure of $66 million for the fourth quarter of 1997. The net loss in 1998 amounted to $124.4 million, which included $50.2 million of merger- and acquisition-related costs. The net loss for the fourth quarter of 1998 was $46.4 million (see Tables 2 and 3). When asked about the continuing losses of Amazon.com, Jeff Bezos replied: 'We are going through a critical stage right now. We want to extend our offer on a global scale and we want to invest even more in customer service; that's all very expensive. This would be a miserable moment to make profits.'

According to industry analysts:

> Amazon's shares grew 966% in value in 1998. Between the beginning of December 1998 and early January 1999, its share price climbed a further 150% and the company's market value surged past $30 billion, overtaking Texaco, an oil company. Even now, Amazon is worth more than all America's bookstores, including Barnes & Noble and Borders Group Inc., put together.[28]

The following statements characterize the investment philosophy at Amazon.com:[29]

- We will continue to focus relentlessly on our customers.
- We will continue to make investment decisions in light of long-term market leadership considerations rather than short-term profitability considerations or short-term Wall Street reactions.
- We will continue to measure our programs and the effectiveness of our investments analytically, to discard those that do not provide acceptable returns, and to step up our investments in those that work best. We will continue to learn both from our successes and failures.
- We will make bold rather than timid investment decisions where we see a sufficient probability of gaining market leadership advantages. Some of these investments will pay off, others will not, and we will have learned another valuable lesson in either case.

27 *The Economist*, 10 May 1997.
28 *The Economist*, 30 January 1999.
29 As stated in the 1997 Annual Report of Amazon.com.

Table 2 **Amazon.com balance sheet**

	31 December		
	1998 ($1000s)	*1997 ($1000s)*	*1996 ($1000s)*
Assets			
Current assets			
Cash (and cash equivalents)	25 561	1 876	6248
Marketable securities	347 884	123 499	(included above)
Inventories	29 501	8 971	571
Prepaid expenses and other:	21 308	3 363	321
Total current assets	**424 254**	**137 709**	**7 140**
Fixed assets (net)	29 791	9 726	985
Deposits	626	169	146
Goodwill and other purchased intangibles	186 377		
Deferred charges	7 412	2 240	
Total assets	**648 460**	**149 844**	**8 271**
Liabilities and stockholders' equity			
Current liabilities			
Accounts payable	113 273	33 027	2852
Accrued advertising	13 071	3 454	598
Accrued product development			500
Other liabilities and accrued expenses	34 547	6 570	920
Current portion of long-term debt	$684	1 500	
Total current liabilities	**161 575**	**44 551**	**4870**
Long-term portion of debt	348 077	76 521	
Long-term portion of capital lease obligation	63	181	
Stockholders' equity			
Preferred stock			6
Common stock	1 593	1 449	159
Additional paid-in capital	300 130	66 586	9873
Note receivable from officer for common stock	–1 099		
Deferred compensation	–1 625	–1930	-612
Accumulated other comprehensive income	1 806		
Accumulated deficit	–162 060	–37 514	-6025
Total stockholders' equity	**138 745**	**28 591**	**3 401**
Total liabilities and stockholders' equity	**648 460**	**149 844**	**8 271**

Source: Amazon.com Annual Report.

Table 3 **Amazon.com statement of operations**

	31 December			
	1998 ($1000s)	*1997 ($1000s)*	*1996 ($1000s)*	*1995 ($1000s)*
Net sales	609 996	147 787	15 746	511
Cost of sales	476 155	118 969	12 287	409
Gross profit	**133 841**	**28 818**	**3 459**	**102**
Operating expenses				
Marketing and sales	133 023	40 486	6 090	200
Product development	46 807	13 916	2 401	171
General and administrative	15 799	7011	1 411	35
Merger and acquisition related expenses	50 172	(includes 42.6 million in goodwill amortization)		
Total operating expenses	**245 801**	**61 413**	**9 902**	**406**
Loss from operations	–111 960	–32 595	–6 443	–304
Interest income	14 053	1 901	202	1
Interest expense	–26 639	–326	–5	
Net loss	**–124 546**	**–31 020**	**–6 246**	**–303**

Source: Amazon.com Annual Report.

- We will balance our focus on growth with emphasis on long-term profitability and capital management. At this stage, we choose to prioritize growth because we believe that scale is central to achieving the potential of our business model.

Jeff Bezos elaborates further on his company's growth:

> When Barnes & Noble went online, most people thought we [Amazon.com] were going to get burned, and they called us 'Amazon.toast'. But it turned out differently. Then we had sales of $60 million a year. Today [in January 1999] we are up to more than $600 million. We are 12 times bigger than our closest competitor.

On 28 April 1999, Amazon.com announced its financial results for the first quarter of 1999. Net sales for the first quarter were $293.6 million, an increase of 236% over net sales of $87.4 million for the first quarter of 1998. Amazon.com reported a first-quarter pro forma operating loss of $30.6 million, or 10% of net sales, compared with an operating loss of $10 million, or 11% of net sales, in the first quarter of 1998, and a first-quarter pro forma net loss of $36.4 million, or $0.23 per share, compared with a net loss of $10.4 million, or $0.07 per share, in the first quarter of 1998. On a GAAP basis,[30] reported first-quarter net loss was $61.7 million, or $0.39 per share, and included $25.3 million of merger and acquisition-related costs.

Amazon.com announced that cumulative customer accounts increased by more than 2.2 million during the first quarter to more than 8.4 million on 31 March 1999, an increase of more than 250% from the 2.3 million customer accounts on 31 March 1998. Repeat customer orders represented more than 66% of orders during the quarter ending 31 March 1999.

Amazon in Germany: Amazon.de

> Our goal is to move quickly to solidify and extend our current position while we begin to pursue the online commerce opportunities in other areas. We see substantial opportunity in the large markets we are targeting. This strategy is not without risk. It requires serious investment and crisp execution against established franchise leaders.
>
> **Jeff Bezos**

In April 1998, Amazon.com prepared its international expansion through the acquisition of the German online bookseller ABC Bücherservices/Telebuch (which had, at the time, 96 000 customers). In that period, Amazon.com also acquired the UK-based Bookpages Ltd, also an online book store. Both Amazon.de and Amazon.co.uk opened their virtual stores on 15 October 1998.

Before launching Amazon.de in Germany, Amazon.com was also considering the possibility of entering a joint venture with Bertelsman. Jeff Bezos explains:

> Thomas Middelhoff and I met four times to talk about a joint venture [of Amazon.com and Bertelsmann] in Europe. Mr Middelhoff is a very smart and aggressive businessman, who I respect very much. But he wanted to have control over the business in Europe, and we wanted that as well. I believe that we know much more [than Bertelsmann] about electronic commerce, about the necessary customer service and the software.

Amazon.de is headquartered in Regensburg, near Munich, where it also has its distribution centre; the editorial and marketing offices are located in Munich. It offers 335 000 titles from German publishers and provides fast and easy access to 374 000 US titles. The store in England carries 1.2 million UK titles as well as fast and easy access to 200 000 US titles. Most popular US titles are ready for immediate shipment from the UK and from Germany, thus significantly reducing shipping time and cost. In March 1999, Amazon.de leased a new distribution centre in Bad Hersfeld, Germany; the facility was expected to begin operations during the second half of 1999.

The delivery of books within Germany is free. No additional taxes, customs or delivery fees apply (e.g. for books that are shipped from the USA). The average delivery time for most German and English books is two to three days; customers have a 30-day money-back guarantee. Like BOL.de, Amazon.de also delivers its books through the German postal service, which means that books that cannot be delivered because the recipient is not at home need to be picked up at the nearest post office.

Amazon.de is the exclusive book store of German and US titles on the search engines of Yahoo.de and Excite.de. Its website provides similar service features as the Amazon.com website. These include the following:

- *Search function*: allows searching the database of 900 000 titles in the Amazon.de online catalogue.
- *Browsing*: supports customers in their search for book titles in eight categories and 116 sub-categories.

---

30 GAAP refers to the US generally accepted accounting principles.

- *Bestseller-list*: lists the best-selling hardback and paperback titles from the Amazon.de site.
- *e-Mail service*: includes personalized book recommendations, articles, interviews and information on new book releases.
- *Reviews by experts and customers*: Munich-based staff of expert German editors develops reviews and recommendations of German-title books. Six editors review books and provide recommendations to customers.
- *Gift service*: picks out a book and selects the wrapping paper; gift certificates that the recipient can redeem at Amazon.de can also be ordered.

Customers who buy books from Amazon.de can return them within 30 days of the purchase date without having to explain the reasons for the book's return. They will not be charged any shipping costs, as long as the book is still in a very good condition.

For Michael Ulbricht, an MBA student, the service features offered by Amazon.de have been very beneficial. He says:

> I am currently working on my MBA thesis. Amazon has helped me immensely with my literature search because it provides recommendations based upon what other people have read. There is no other place on the Internet where I can find this kind of information and analysis.

During the fourth quarter of 1998, combined sales on the European Amazon sites in Germany and the UK increased significantly over the third quarter of the same year.[31] They established Amazon.com as the number-one online bookseller in these markets.

Future outlook

Generally, what will the future of electronic commerce look like? Will a large customer base embrace the Internet for commercial transactions (see Exhibits 4 and 5), or will traditional sales channels still dominate the business environment? Will the market confirm forecasts such as that of Dr Uwe Kamenz, Professor of Marketing at the University of Applied Sciences in Dortmund, Germany? He said: 'the potential market for mail-order purchases in Germany is only a mere 5%. With the Internet this might increase to 10%, which would present a huge increase. But this also means that 90% of all purchases will take place in traditional retail stores.'

Exhibit 4 e-Commerce sales forecast for Europe

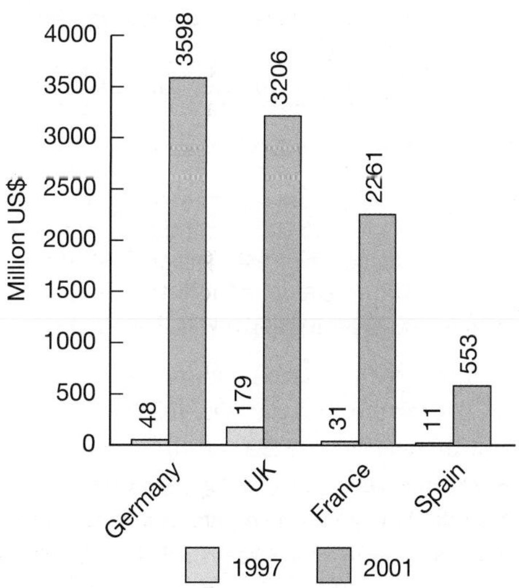

Source: EITO 1997, Roland Berger, Bertelsmann.

Exhibit 5 e-Commerce forecasts according to product categories

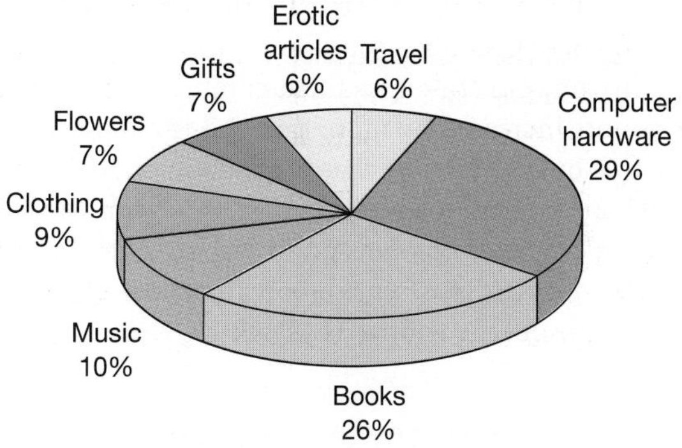

Total volume in Europe (2001): US$15.4 billion

Source: EITO 1997, Roland Berger, Bertelsmann.

Will follower companies such as BOL be able to steal customers from first movers like Amazon.de? Will they be able to attract clients such as Carsten Schmitz, for whom:

> There is no need to change since the service [of Amazon.de and Bol.de] is similar and the prices are

31 Separate financial data for Amazon.de and Amazon.co.uk are not made available through Amazon.com.

identical [due to price fixing in Germany]. I don't feel like learning how to use a new website and acquainting myself with a new content layout. I have been using Amazon.de since last year and don't plan to shift to BOL.

Will time prove that Jeff Bezos' business model is the right one? 'Ultimately, we [Amazon.com] are an information broker,' says Bezos. 'On the left side we have lots of products, on the right side we have lots of customers. We are in the middle making the connections. The consequence is that we have two sets of customers: consumers looking for products and [product] providers looking for consumers.' His objective, as stated in the 1998 Annual Report of the company, is to become the best place to buy, find and discover any product or service available online. He says:

> Amazon.com will continue to enhance and broaden its brand, customer base and electronic commerce expertise with the goal of creating customers' preferred online shopping destination, in the United States and around the world.

For Thomas Middelhoff:

> With over 300 profit centres in more than 50 countries, we [Bertelsmann] are the most international of media groups. We have the greatest treasure in the media world – over 44 million customers worldwide. And we do our best every day in the profit centres to satisfy these customers and to acquire new customers ... As of today [26 April 1999], we already hold second place, worldwide, in electronic commerce of media products with barnesandnoble.com, BOL and getmusic.com. Of all media enterprises, we are the most advanced on the Internet.

Clearly, for both chief executive officers, the sky is the limit. The global battle over virtual book sales and, more generally, Internet-based retailing is all but intensifying between Amazon.com and Bertelsmann Online. Both sides know that the business implications at stake are vital for their company's future. And this just makes the fighting today fiercer than ever before.

DISCUSSION QUESTIONS

1. Is it justifiable for a company like Amazon.com to continue investing so much money and effort in a business operation that not only has never made a profit, but is incurring heavier losses?
2. Will Bertelsmann benefit (or be hindered) by its physical organizational structure and management processes in its attempt to strengthen its position as an electronic commerce product/service provider? Defend your arguments.
3. In your opinion, what industries/companies would constitute a threat to Amazon.com and/or Bertelsmann's BOL over the next three to five years? Explain.
4. What success factors do you think are critical for online books (and mass-media) sales and, more generally, for launching an electronic commerce business?

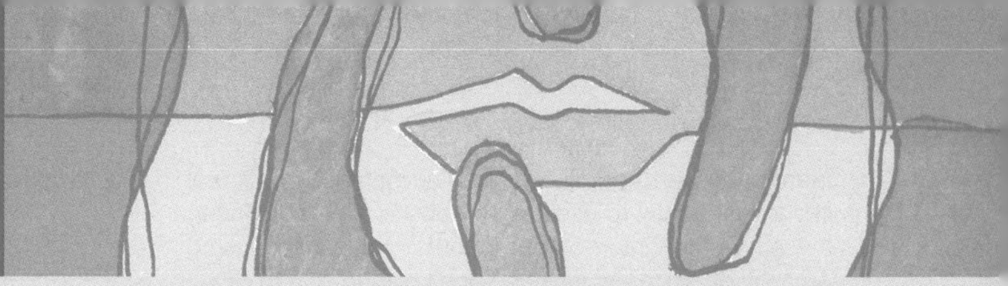

CASE STUDY 7

Cyber-entrepreneurship: the Nettimarket.com vcnturc in Finland

On a typical snowy day in early January 1998, as he was driving towards Helsinki, Aki Teranto spotted a poster on the motorway for Internet grocery shopping. The slogan read: 'Don't stand in line any more, just go online!' He thought: if it is possible to sell groceries online in Helsinki, why would it not be possible to do so in Turku?[1] A few months later, with the help of two partners and his wife Eija, Aki launched Nettimarket.com, the first Internet grocery shop in the Turku area. Today, the business is still in its infancy, but the signs of growth are already visible.

Company background

Aki had hardly any experience in the food or retailing business. He had been a truck driver for ten years, transporting food products for Veljekset U. Saari, one of the largest transportation companies in the Turku area. His job often took him to Sweden, and, in 1995, on one of his trips, he came across a type of flooring material, typically used to surface concrete floors, which he thought would have good market potential in Finland. He then decided to leave his job as a truck driver and, with a partner, founded his first company in May 1996. The flooring material company has been doing well: 'We make our living out of it', says Aki.

After reading the poster on that winter day, Aki pondered the idea of launching an Internet grocery store in Turku. Since there was, at that time, no competition there, he thought he might potentially gain a first-mover advantage. He had made up his mind before arriving home, upon which he informed his wife of his project. He did not carry out any analyses or benchmarking. He felt that he had a great idea and he was set to implement it. Nettimarket.com was founded in January 1998 with an initial capital of FIM25 000[2] and with two employees: Aki as the managing director and his wife Eija as the logistics manager.

Neither Aki nor Eija had any knowledge of information technology (IT). They both had a high-school-level education and were totally computer-illiterate. Aki learned about computers through self-study. 'Some of my visitors think that I am a computer wizard', says Aki. 'Actually, I never took a single course on the subject, but I spent all my weekends studying computer programming. My wife encouraged me, although she doesn't share my passion for computers!'

Aki and his wife wanted a name for the company that reflects the nature of its business, so they selected Nettimarket (i.e. 'the net market'). After the decision was taken to go into virtual business, Aki founded the company together with a partner, Jarkko. Aki's share is 60% of the company while Jarkko's share is 40%. Jarkko has a similar background to Aki's; although at first he did not play an active role in the in the company's operations, he

1 Turku is the fourth largest city in Finland and has approximately 180 000 inhabitants (including in the suburbs). Helsinki, the capital, has a population of one million, including in the nearby cities of Espoo and Vantaa (see Exhibit 1).

2 On 22 May 2000, the exchange rate of the Finnish Markka was as follows: US$1 = FIM6.5775.

This case study was written by Tawfik Jelassi, Dean of Academic Affairs, Euro-Arab Management School, Granada, Spain, and Pirkko Walden and Bill Anckar, both from the Institute for Advanced Management Systems Research at Åbo Akademi University, Turku, Finland. It is intended to be used as the basis for class discussion rather than to illustrate either effective or ineffective handling of a business situation. Case released in 2001.

Exhibit 1 **Map of Finland**

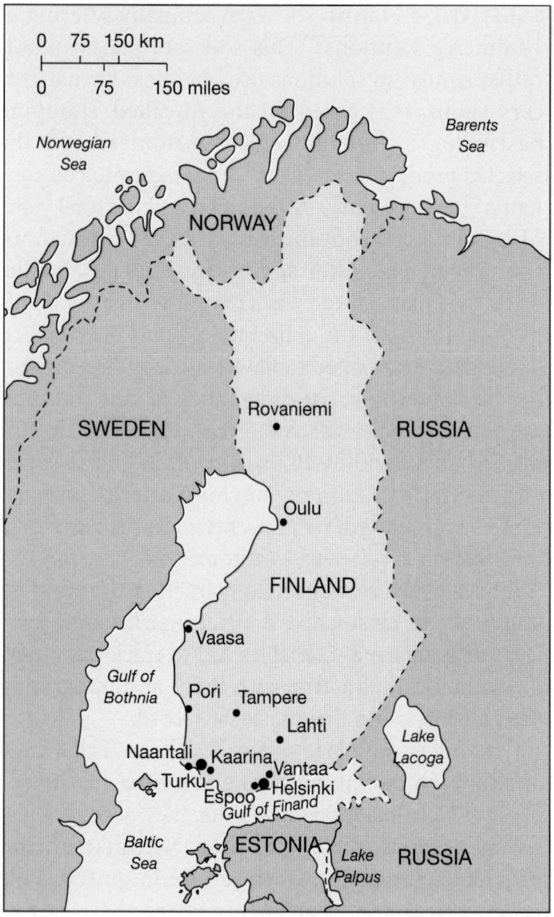

joined the team just before Christmas 1999 and now works at Nettimarket.com during the evenings and at weekends. Jarkko's wife Paivi has also joined the business and assists Eija in her duties.

Aki's and Jarkko's personal contributions were the share capital, which was assessed at FIM25 000 (approximately US$4100). The next step was to apply for a loan of FIM200000 and, three months later, for another loan of FIM200000. So far, total investments amount to FIM425000, which can be broken down as follows:

- Software: FIM110 000.
- Three PCs: approximately FIM50 000.
- Two printers.
- Phone installations.
- Server costs: FIM1500 per month.
- Leased van for goods delivery.
- Rented office space (100 square metres): FIM3000 per month.

The business model

Aki was convinced that, for reasons of convenience, customers prefer the 'one-stop shopping' concept, especially when shopping for groceries. However, an electronic market that allows customers to shop directly from producers is not conceivable in the grocery business, hence ensuring a strong role for wholesalers, distributors and retailers. Aki thought that most Internet grocery stores operate mainly as extensions of an existing physical retail business, aiming at attracting new customers and/or serving existing ones better. In Finland, these stores include www.eurospar.fi, Mestarin Herkku and s-kanava.net. This 'extended retailer' business model seems to be a logical solution in the early stages of electronic commerce, as online sales are still very limited and warehousing costs constitute a financial risk for start-up e-tailers. In fact, it is hard to imagine today a Finnish grocery business that operates only through the Web and generates enough revenues to justify maintaining its warehouse.

If customers are to give up traditional purchasing methods, then they must be offered certain value-added features in the virtual market space that are not attainable or available in the physical marketplace. A commonly stated consumer benefit of electronic commerce is the possibility for price reductions. These may take place as a result of: (1) increased competition as more suppliers are able to compete in an electronically open marketplace; (2) reduced selling prices due to a reduction in transaction costs; and (3) manufacturers internalizing activities traditionally performed by intermediaries. However, to date, virtual grocery stores do not generally offer prices lower than those of physical stores. The 'extended retailer' business model does not allow for price reductions in electronic markets, since in the traditional retail grocery stores customers play an important role in the distribution chain as they collect the goods and carry them home themselves. In Internet grocery shopping, the pick-up and distribution of goods become the responsibility of the seller and result in additional overhead costs. As the

extended retailer still has to pay for the cost of running a bricks-and-mortar business (i.e. physical infrastructure overheads and personnel costs), web-based grocery shopping is likely to remain unprofitable at least in the short run. Furthermore, it is likely to remain highly local due to the transportation costs of grocery goods.

In Aki's mind the 'extension' strategy is not a good one, since it would not make sense for the grocer to undertake services (such as goods pick-up, checkout, delivery, etc.) that customers have been carrying out themselves. Aki's strategy is therefore quite different; it is based on a partnership with a wholesaler since this solution eliminates warehousing costs (and risks), high physical infrastructure overheads, and checkout staff payroll. Aki negotiated with a wholesaler and even managed to rent the required office space within the wholesaler premises. For the wholesaler, Nettimarket.com is yet another customer, although it has a special relationship with it. As long as the wholesaler does not consider Aki as a competitor (a situation that may well change in the future), the two parties can co-exist and enjoy a mutually beneficial relationship. Aki does not believe that the role of grocery wholesalers will disappear in the future with the widespread availability of virtual grocery stores.

Theoretically, Aki's business model enables Nettimarket.com to compete on price. However, this is not yet the case, as the limited sales have forced Aki to charge an 18–20% margin, hence selling most items at a higher price than found in physical grocery stores. With smaller margins, Nettimarket.com cannot survive. Nettimarket.com's strategy is to operate as a truly virtual shop, offering customers the best products, a large selection of goods, premium customer service, just-in-time delivery and even ecological benefits (reducing traffic). The basic idea that underlies Nettimarket.com is similar to that of Amazon.com: instead of people going to look for books, make the books come to them.

The operational system

In order to build his Internet grocery shop, Aki looked for good software solutions. However, he found the offers that most consulting firms were making very expensive: his budget could not afford the several hundreds of thousands FIM price tag. He eventually bought a software solution developed by SuperWeb, a Finnish software company offering e-commerce solutions.[3] This software platform was rather similar to solutions used by most virtual grocery shops. It is based on the so-called 'shopping basket logic', through which customers add the selected products to a virtual shopping cart. The content of the basket may be modified and the total value of its content is conveniently displayed throughout the system. The order administration contains the order 'life span' all the way from ordering the goods to the printing of the collection list and the dispatch document. Aki wanted to have real-time data on visitors to the website, the orders they placed and their current status, as well as the sales turnover. He also needed the capability to print the bills and receipts, and to track customers' buying patterns. As customers register with Nettimarket.com, their personal information is stored in a customer database used by Aki to establish a one-to-one marketing relationship, and hence to personalize the Nettimarket.com service. The database also enables Aki to track customers individually, interacting with them and integrating their feedback into their database record.

Customers can place orders by phone, fax, e-mail and through the Internet.[4] The first time a customer uses the Nettimarket.com website, they need to register in order to place an order. Nettimarket.com provides a round-the-clock service in quite a wide geographical area that encompasses the cities of Turku, Kaarina, Naantali and Raisio. This space is divided into service areas according to postal codes.

In order to purchase products online, shoppers navigate through the hierarchical Nettimarket.com web pages (see Exhibits 2 and 3). The lowest-level menu allows the shopper to initiate the commercial transaction by selecting the goods to order, specifying their quantity and placing them in the virtual shopping cart. Furthermore, a search engine assists the shopper in finding the products of their choice (see Exhibit 2, lower left-hand corner). The search is

3 Although one of the software offers made to Aki was a solution used by a competitor, it did not meet the quality requirements of Nettimarket.com. Furthermore, this solution was almost ten times more expensive than the one that Aki finally acquired.

4 To place orders through the Internet, customers need to use a Pentium-based PC, an Internet (preferably with ISDN) connection of 33.6 Kbps, and Internet Explorer version 4.0 or Netscape version 4.0 or a later version.

Exhibit 2 **Searching for items at Nettimarket.com**

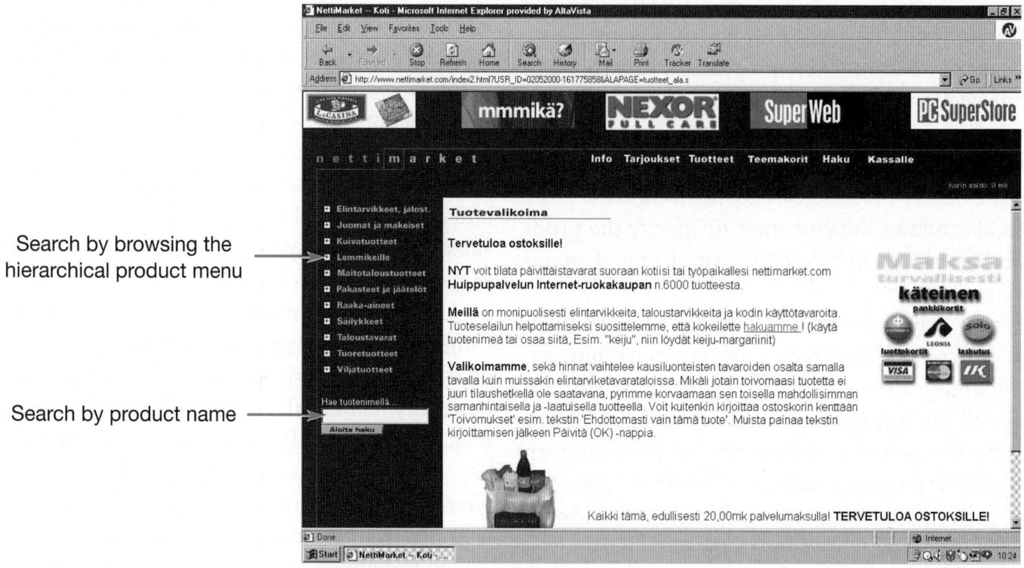

based on criteria including the generic name of a product (e.g. olive oil), its price range (e.g. less than FIM30) and its weight (e.g. 500 ml). In case a specific product is out of stock, the system suggests to the customer possible substitute products. In order to initiate the processing of the transaction, the customer must confirm their order and specify the mode of payment from the following options: ATM card, credit card (Visa, MasterCard, EuroCard), Solo system (Merita Bank) or cash (on delivery of the goods). Corporate customers may also choose to be invoiced. Upon receipt of the customer order confirmation, Nettimarket.com sends an e-mail message acknowledging receipt of the purchase order.

Exhibit 3 **Selecting goods at Nettimarket.com**

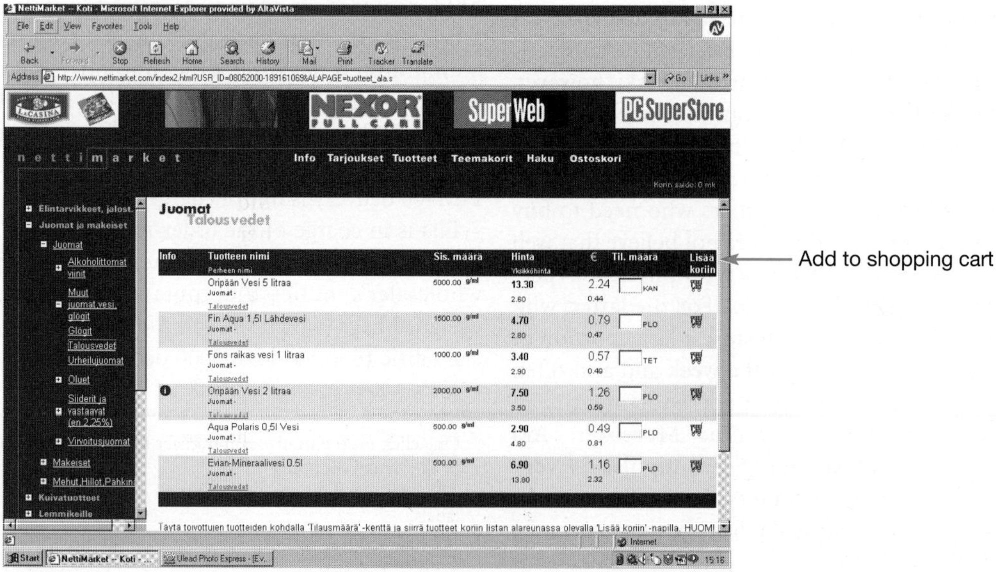

In order to simplify the buying process for customers, the system keeps a record of previous purchases. If the customer wants to buy the same goods as they did on their previous 'visit', through just one click their entire product list is moved to the virtual shopping cart. Moreover, the customer can put together several 'product baskets' in advance and move the basket into the cart by just one click.[5] The system also allows the customer to specify the product characteristics in free text format (e.g. 'I prefer my bananas green').

Aki is the only person in the company who maintains the website and updates product and customer information, discount lists and order processing. He also updates all the informational content of the website, including the e-mail messages sent to the customer. Through these messages, customers (who have agreed to receive such information) are informed every Monday about the special weekly offers on the Nettimarket.com website. Furthermore, the (SuperWeb) system provides Eija with a list of products ordered, specifying their respective quantity (or weight), which she uses to collect the goods from the wholesaler's outlet.

Product portfolio

Nettimarket.com's online catalogue contains approximately 6000 products, a product portfolio that is typically less than that offered in a physical supermarket store.[6] This product portfolio size, which is limited to that of Nettimarket.com's wholesaler (Wihuri Oy[7]), puts Aki at a disadvantage vis-à-vis physical retailers and also potential online competitors with a larger product assortment. Aki, however, feels that neither his Internet business nor other virtual grocery stores should be compared to physical supermarkets. For him, virtual grocery stores aim primarily at attracting customers who need to buy their everyday groceries; he does not believe that web stores will be able to compete with physical hypermarkets for weekend shoppers. For the latter, who typically buy from a physical store a large portion of the groceries needed during the week and also often look for gourmet items, product assortment is an important shopping criterion. Moreover, Aki acknowledges that shopping by impulse is very important for some customers, especially at weekends and during holidays – a feature that cannot be fulfilled by virtual stores.

Order fulfilment and delivery

Nettimarket.com suffers from a significant drawback: its online product catalogue is not linked to the wholesaler's warehousing system. This situation led to not being able to inform customers upon ordering whether their order can be delivered in full or whether some of the items are out of stock. In the latter case, and if already specified by the customer, a substitute product gets delivered provided it is in the same price range as the initially ordered product.

Nettimarket.com delivers the goods to the customer household typically within a couple of hours of receipt of the order, sometimes within a day. The company uses different handling and packaging means for the goods, depending on whether they are dry, refrigerated or frozen goods. In all cases, Nettimarket.com tries to ensure short delivery times from its premises to customers' households.

Goods deliveries take place between 10.00 a.m. and 9.00 p.m. on working days and between 9.00 a.m. and 3.00 p.m. on Saturdays. No deliveries take place on Sundays or holidays. Nettimarket.com requires that an order be placed at least half an hour before the required delivery time, which typically ranges from one to four hours. Since the volume of deliveries is not very high (on average, 40 delivery tours per week), Aki has not yet felt the need to use a computerized routing optimization system.

The order-fulfilment process, from receipt of the order to delivery of the goods to the customer household, requires on average 45 minutes of 'personal service'. At the beginning, Nettimarket.com required a minimum order of FIM100, but today there is no such minimum; however, orders of less than FIM100 are charged an extra fee of FIM7. There is a delivery charge of FIM20 per order, but for orders exceeding FIM400 delivery is free of charge.

Eija is in charge of the order-fulfilment and delivery process. She collects the goods from the wholesaler's outlet and puts them in specially designed bags (which she and Aki made out of a special fabric to last at least 5000 deliveries). These bags

5 One click on the mouse will transfer the entire list of products to the virtual shopping cart.

6 The online catalogue also contains 1000 product photos or labels.

7 Oy stands for '*osakeyhtiö*'; it means joint stock (or limited) company.

were tailor-made, taking into account the space available in the delivery van and the most frequently bought goods. For transporting ice-cream and other frozen food products, insulated bags with refrigerants are used.

Customer perspective

Since the start of Nettimarket.com, Päivi Hennula has been one of Aki's regular customers. Living outside Turku, Pävi has been buying from Nettimarket.com almost all the grocery needs of her household of four (including her husband and their two young children) since December 1998. 'It was quite a struggle at the beginning, but I did not give up,' she said. 'It was difficult to find products and it took a lot of time to order goods. Also, the shopping list disappeared during the process and the system did not work the way it was supposed to. I was seriously wondering whether it would ever work. Being an IT professional, I was well aware of all the system problems that could happen. I was really delighted when it finally worked. For me, buying groceries through the Net makes my life a lot easier.'

Päivi 'visits' Nettimarket.com once a week. For her, virtual shopping saves her a lot of time compared with going to a physical store, as she used to do. 'By shopping at Nettimarket.com, I save more time than I could have imagined. I spend all this extra time with my children. We now do a lot more enjoyable things than going to a store.'

Päivi's buying behaviour has also changed drastically. In the past, she never enjoyed shopping for groceries and her decisions were made on the spot in the store. She used to buy a lot more groceries than she actually needed, but she does not do that any more and spends less money on groceries:

> For example, I used to buy a lot of doughnuts and other bakery products. But today, I order the ingredients through Nettimarket.com and I do the baking together with my children. It gives us all a lot of pleasure. Honestly, before [having the possibility to order through the Net], I simply did not have time for baking doughnuts or bread. As I now bake my own bread and plan more carefully my weekly shopping list, my grocery bill has decreased by more than 30% per month, which really was an unexpected bonus.
>
> Some people think that it is important to choose your own vegetables and fruits. I do not share this view. In the store, I hate standing in line waiting for my turn to get fresh produce weighed or to pay for my groceries. Now I only go to the store to buy some gourmet items, which are not yet available through Nettimarket.com. I really enjoy it because I go there only when I want to, not feeling obliged to do so as was the case with groceries.

Initial difficulties

In the summer of 1999, although it was growing Nettimarket.com faced considerable financial problems. With 500 registered customers and only 200 regular online shoppers, the customer base was too small to sustain the business. Furthermore, the number of customers was growing very slowly, with on average just three new shoppers per month. Although the number of daily visits to the Nettimarket.com website ranged from 40 to 200, only one to five orders were placed every day. This situation resulted in daily gross sales of FIM1000–2000. In spite of these difficulties, which could have been seen as sufficient reasons for closing down the business, Aki still believed in eventually making Nettimarket.com a success.

Serving elderly people and disabled people: business expansion through a municipal decision

In Finland, recent increases in social expenditure have led to keeping elderly people and disabled people at home or with their families as long as it is more cost-effective to do so. For the same economic reasons, patients are also released from hospitals and returned to their homes earlier than before.

Elderly and/or disabled people who depend on home-helpers' assistance constitute an important customer segment for online grocery stores such as Nettimarket.com. Aki was thus pleased to know that the Turku social welfare office decided to outsource the shopping tasks initially performed by the home-helpers employed by City Hall. This decision was motivated by the increased demand for home-helpers. The latter typically visit their customers a couple of times per week to perform tasks ranging from taking care of the physical and mental health of elderly people to housekeeping and grocery shopping. Such shopping takes on average 45 minutes.

In order to make the home-helpers' work more effective at the 4000 households involved, the city of Turku decided to try, over a 15-month period, Internet-based shopping.[8] The social welfare office, which operates in the four Turku areas (north, south, east, west), decided to run the e-shopping trial only in the north and west areas. Of the nine Internet retailers (including Nettimarket.com) who participated in the bidding organized by the city of Turku, only three had some experience in online shopping. The goods delivery fees that these retailers offered ranged from FIM20 to FIM42.70; the Nettimarket.com fee was FIM27, with a guaranteed 30-minute delivery.

Nettimarket.com competitors in the bidding were Halinet Oy from Helsinki and Ruokamarkkinat Oy. 'I got the idea for my business when I was working at the social welfare office of the city of Lohja', said Harri Vilkko, Managing Director of Halinet Oy, a logistics service provider. 'Home-helpers can make better use of their time [with their clients] than waiting for their turn in a grocery store.' Halinet, which works with Ruokanet (an online grocery shop), is in charge of delivering the goods to the elderly and/or disabled people, educating the home-helpers and providing the city with the required IT equipment. Ruokamarkkinat Oy, which has been operating through the Internet since March 1998, is a subsidiary of Wihuri Oy, the wholesaler of Nettimarket.com.

Regarding financial transactions, the city of Turku did not specify the mode of payment but the customer has several options (as mentioned earlier). Purchasing orders are made mainly through the Nokia 9110 Communicator, which is a mobile phone with a large back-lit screen also enabling fax, e-mail and Internet communications. To use the Communicator, customers choose the Internet provider and the website application they are interested in and fill in the subscriber information. They can then surf the Internet at any time and almost from anywhere.

To run the e-shopping experiment, City Hall needed a budget of FIM77,000 to acquire 16 Communicators (of which Nettimarket.com bought two),[9] and FIM2.4 million to pay for the goods delivery to customers' households during the trial period. Some of the elderly people will contribute FIM10 per delivery, resulting in a net cost for the social welfare department of approximately FIM1.5 million.

In October 1999, the city of Turku selected Nettimarket.com for its Internet grocery shopping service for elderly and disabled people during the trial period from October 1999 to the end of December 2000. This has marked a surge in Nettimarket.com business, with approximately 1300 new customers in just two months (October and November 1999). The fees from goods delivery alone generated FIM1.3 million; with a conservative average order of FIM100 per customer per week, sales for 2000 were expected to reach FIM5 million. For Aki, City Hall's decision was a stroke of luck since before this he did not expect his business to break even before 2002. Furthermore, he would have had to rely on his floor-building company to support his family and to keep Nettimarket.com running.

Currently, Nettimarket.com employs 11 people. Four staff members (including Paivi, Jarkko's wife) take care of picking up the goods from the warehouse according to the orders; two of them work on the morning shift and two work on the evening shift. Besides Aki and Jarkko (the latter working only in the evenings and at weekends), there are two additional staff members who process the orders arriving through e-mail messages. Three drivers, using two leased vans, are in charge of the goods delivery. Currently, there are 75 delivery 'tours' per week; this number is expected to reach 120 in the near future. To cope with this drastic sales increase, Nettimarket.com needs to use a computerized routing optimization system. In addition to determining the routes, the system could also facilitate setting up the delivery timetable, a task that is becoming more complex, especially due to the fact that, in most cases, the home-helpers have to be present when the goods are delivered.

Witness accounts of City Hall's e-shopping experiment

The view of the home-helper services manager

Tuija Hassinen-Laine, the home-helper services manager of the city of Turku, is well aware of the difficulties in introducing an innovative service and the challenge of managing the subsequent resistance. She promoted the Internet shopping idea and tried to

8 A similar test was carried out by the cities of Helsinki and Espoo.

9 The unit price of the Communicator device is FIM5500.

have all the home-helper districts embrace it. Her supporting argument was that as the proportion of elderly and disabled people steadily increases, there is a need to use efficient platforms and tools enabling the provision of a better service.

At first, the home-helpers were very anxious about placing orders online. Numerous mistakes were made, either by the home-helpers or by Nettimarket.com. For example, some of the orders that were placed by the home-helpers never reached Nettimarket.com or were processed inaccurately. However, once the home-helpers got used to the online purchasing procedure, they started to appreciate the new service. It made their job physically less demanding and the home-helpers now have more time to take care of the health and housekeeping needs of their clients.

However, some customers, especially those living near a shopping mall, are not enthusiastic about the online ordering system. In spite of the home-helpers' efforts to explain the new e-shopping policy, several customers have difficulty understanding it. Furthermore, since they are used to buying special or brand-name products that are not available at Nettimarket.com, some customers demand that the home-helpers be allowed to buy these products in nearby shops as they used to do previously. They also want to be allowed, when taking a walk with their home-helpers, to visit a shop and purchase some goods.

For Tuija, careful planning is essential when buying online and everybody involved in e-shopping should learn how to plan. For example, customers should write their shopping list in advance so that the home-helpers can send the list online to Nettimarket.com. If a customer forgets to order a specific item that is urgently needed, then they can decide whether the home-helper should go to the traditional store to buy it.

Most of the orders are made through the Nokia Communicator device. For the home-helpers, this purchasing channel is much easier and more convenient than connecting to the Nettimarket.com website. On average, each home-helper orders goods from Nettimarket.com twice a week and typically services six customers daily. The online shopping system has led to providing a better grocery service as well as having more elderly and disabled people benefit from the home-helper services. Although the advantages of the new system clearly outrank its possible drawbacks, the Turku City Hall will make a formal assessment of the system at the end of the trial period.

The view of the customer

Although Anna-Lydia Candolin, one of the elderly people participating in the trial period, placed weekly online orders over a two-month period, several shortcomings in the new e-shopping procedure led her to withdraw from the City Hall's experiment. First, none of the shopping baskets that were delivered to her between October and November 1999 included all the goods that she ordered; certain items were always missing. Second, little information was shared with the elderly people before the experiment; for example, customers did not know how much to pay for the goods delivery, to whom and when. Third, prices were higher than those offered in most physical retail stores. Lastly, most of the invoices did not match the groceries delivered.

Regarding the first problem, customers were asked in advance whether they would accept substitute products. Since Anna-Lydia did not place the orders herself (she gave her home-helper a written shopping list), she was not even aware of this option and did not know whether she was signed up for this service. Since there was no alternative available to her to regularly get the groceries she needed, she reluctantly rejoined the experiment after a few weeks. However, before doing so, she shared her complaints with Aki, who acknowledged the problems and sent her a complete list of Nettimarket.com's assortment so as to facilitate her ordering process.

According to Anna-Lydia, by early 2000 she started receiving correct deliveries and the Nettimarket.com customer service improved. The delivered products have always been of good quality, and staff members have been kind and willing to help. However, she hopes that the prices will go down as the number of customers increase, and that Nettimarket.com will offer elderly people a special service, for example by placing the frozen and refrigerated items in the freezer/refrigerator upon delivery. With the current system, the home-helper needs to be present on delivery to unpack the purchased goods.

Competition

To date, Nettimarket.com has only one competitor operating in the Turku area – Ruokavarasto

(www.ruokavarasto.fi), which is part of Ruokamarkkinat Oy, the biggest private grocery retail chain in Finland, established in 1970. In 1988, it became a subsidiary of Wihuri Oy, the wholesaler of Nettimarket.com. Ruokamarkkinat Oy operates in the southern part of Finland and, in 1998, had a total sales turnover of FIM1300 million. Currently, Ruokamarkkinat Oy operates more than 130 physical retail stores under the brand name Ruokavarasto. Its Internet grocery operation is considered to be an extension of its business model, since the core of its activities still consists of traditional (physical) retailing. The product range offered by Ruokavarasto.fi is identical to the assortment available in the physical Ruokavarasto stores and all the goods are sold at the same price as in the physical outlets. Ruokavarasto.fi has rapidly expanded its geographical scale and now delivers groceries to eight cities in the southern part of Finland.

In the area of Turku, several supermarkets currently compete mainly on prices. They were able to drive out numerous small grocery stores that relied on service to build their customer base. For Nettimarket.com, providing customers with a unique, value-added service is its main competitive positioning.

Currently, there are only a few online grocery stores operating in Finland. For example Ruoka.net, which is based in Helsinki (approximately 160 km east of Turku), planned to broaden by December 2000 the geographical scope of its business so as to also cover the Turku area. According to its CEO, Timo Surma-Aho, 'technically everything is ready for this expansion. The only thing remaining is to "plug-in". Operating a virtual store over a large geographical area is difficult, especially managing the logistics associated with it. But now is the right time for us to expand the business.'

All large retailers and wholesalers in Finland also announced their intentions to do business over the Internet. For example, the S-ryhma group has six online grocery stores that have, so far, been serving only local markets. Another player, TOK-yhtyma, was about to launch its online store but the project got postponed.

For Osmo Laine, President of the Finnish Grocery Retailers Association (Paivittaistavarakauppa ry), since consumers are generally not interested in embracing the grocery e-shopping service, the Internet does not play an important role in the grocery business. Some data suggest that many customers have registered for the service but never placed a purchasing order online. Furthermore, during the trial period, several customers dropped out without any obvious reasons, such as quality or service-related problems.

Marketing activities

Nettimarket.com received a lot of coverage in the local press. Being the first truly virtual grocery store in the region has created genuine media interest, even before City Hall's decision to have the home-helpers shop online for elderly and disabled people.

At Nettimarket.com, every Monday Aki sends an e-mail message to his customers informing them about the special offers of the week. The content of this message is the same for all customers; no one-to-one marketing has been carried out so far, although technically Nettimarket.com could do so. Aki relies on online advertising on his own website; no banners are placed on other Internet sites. To ensure maximum visibility for the company, some ads placed in a local newspaper and the Nettimarket.com website address are displayed on the delivery vans as well as on the plastic bags in which the groceries are delivered. On the Nettimarket.com site, a frequently asked questions (FAQ) section is now available, but there are only a few posted questions, which might suggest that the system is rather easy to use.

Looking ahead

Most Nettimarket.com customers are middle-aged/career families or young (often single) people. They value quality of life and can be divided into two groups: those who spend (most of) the day at home with their children, and those who are hardly at home during the day. Several online retailers in Finland consider families with small children as their primary customer target. This customer base has been expanding very slowly, with the exception of the elderly and disabled people who are part of City Hall's e-shopping experiment. For Aki, the single most significant barrier to e-shopping is consumers' reluctance to change their attitudes; this constitutes a major challenge for Internet retailers.

Although Aki welcomes all individual customers, he believes that they will not provide a sufficient

customer base for Nettimarket's future. For him, corporate clients, such as companies and day nurseries, are important customer segments that he needs to tap into. However, Nettimarket's current priority is to make the service provided to elderly and disabled people a great success. The delivery schedules and the routing have to be optimized, and the add-on services as well as the business cost-effectiveness need to be enhanced. As of March 2000, no deliveries took place on Saturdays, and orders had to be placed at least two hours before the desired delivery time. Nettimarket.com's recent business expansion can no longer accommodate the 30-minute delivery time that was offered initially when the company made only a few deliveries per day.

Following the trial period, if City Hall's assessment of the e-shopping experiment is positive, then Nettimarket.com will also start serving the southern and eastern regions of Turku. Business-wise, this geographical expansion will allow the company to at least double its sales turnover. For Aki, it would mean that he could finally start paying himself a decent salary.

Further improvements

In any start-up business, there are always lessons to be drawn during the initial operational phase. For Nettimarket.com, certain problems need to be solved. First, since the orders placed by the home-helpers through e-mail use a free-text format, Aki must key them into the online grocery shopping system so as to be able to generate the goods pickings lists, invoices and delivery notices. This data-capture phase is time-consuming, error-prone and expensive and must be redesigned. Furthermore, Aki is also aware that the current shopping procedure relies heavily on the home-helper for (1) picking up the hand-written shopping list from the elderly, (2) placing the order over the Internet, and (3) being present at the goods delivery stage.[10]

While contemplating whether he will be able to improve the business significantly, Aki wondered whether the Turku City Hall would embrace e-shopping beyond the trial period. Does Nettimarket.com really stand a chance of surviving the emerging competition? Should he seek partners to further enhance and expand company operations? To what extent could he adopt (or adapt) the way American Internet retailers (such as Amazon.com) operate their cyber-stores? For Aki, one thing is sure: he has embarked on a long journey and the voyage of discovery has just begun.

10 Since Nettimarket.com does not offer the service of unpacking the groceries (something Aki should consider doing in the future).

DISCUSSION QUESTIONS

1 What suggestions would you make to Nettimarket to further enhance its value proposition?

2 Should Nettimarket broaden its current customer segment? How about expanding its business scope and geographical scale?

3 Does Nettimarket stand a chance of surviving the emerging competition?

4 Should Aki seek strategic partners to strengthen his business? If so, what type of partners should he consider and why?

CASE STUDY 8

The Tesco.com experience: is success at hand?

When dot-coms of any type in the UK ask me whom they should watch, I tell them they should be worried if Tesco decides to move into their space.[1]

Nick Jones, Analyst, Jupiter Communications

In spite of Tesco's apparently successful Internet-based grocery retailing business, there is still some internal debate within the company about its fulfilment ('in-store picking') approach and its possible limitations.

Company history

In 1924, Sir Jack Cohen founded the Tesco supermarket chain. Cohen invested his ex-serviceman's gratuity of £30 in a grocery stall, thus inaugurating the first store. The Tesco name was first used in 1929 for a shop in Edgware, London. The acronym presented the initials of the company's tea supplier – T. E. Stockwell – and Cohen's own name. Following the Great Depression, in 1932 Tesco was formally established as a private limited company. During the 1930s Tesco added more than 100 stores, mainly in London. After his visit to the USA to study the self-service supermarkets, Cohen developed Tesco's 'pile-it-high-and-sell-it-cheap' format, which was to become a central part of Tesco's retailing strategy in the years to come.

In 1956 the first Tesco self-service supermarket was opened in a converted cinema. During the 1950s and 1960s Tesco grew primarily through acquisitions. These included 70 Williamson's stores in 1957, 200 Harrow stores in 1959, 212 Irwin's outlets in 1960, and 97 Charles Phillips stores in 1964. By the 1960s Tesco had become a chain of 600 stores. The Tesco that opened in Leicester in 1961 had 16 500 square feet of selling space and entered the *Guinness Book of Records* as the largest store in Europe.

As customers began looking for quality and choice in the 1970s and 1980s, Tesco started to have severe problems and the company results slipped dramatically, so that in the 1980s few people thought that Tesco could survive. The primary reason for the dismal performance was that customers had a negative image of the company. Due to the sole focus on low prices, customers were faced with poorly maintained stores and a selection of items that was perceived as inadequate and of mediocre quality.

Tesco tried to respond to these developments by improving product quality and profitability. In 1977, it had already introduced private-label brands to strive for higher quality. In addition, 500 unprofitable stores were closed while simultaneously large-surface superstores were opened. Nevertheless, the situation did not improve significantly.

Lord MacLaurin, who had joined Tesco in 1959, led the company's turnaround. Upon becoming chair in 1985, he set about turning Tesco inside out. When he retired in early 1997, Tesco had become the largest, most profitable supermarket chain in the UK. His first move was to pour large amounts of money into the

1 Quoted in 'A British e-grocer takes on Amazon', *Fortune*, 12 June 2000.

This case study was written by Albrecht Enders, Research Associate at INSEAD, under the supervision of Tawfik Jelassi, Affiliate Professor of Technology Management at INSEAD, and Charles Waldman, Senior Affiliate Professor of Marketing at INSEAD. It is intended to be used as the basis for class discussion rather than to illustrate effective or ineffective handling of a management situation.

construction of new superstores in order to attract upper market segments. Simultaneously, new systems and technology were introduced in sales and distribution, which would enable Tesco to be positioned across a range of store formats and market segments.

The oldest and most established Tesco superstores offer customers a wide range of goods, a pleasant shopping environment and free car parking. These superstores have a minimum selling surface of 26 500 square feet and display 25 000–30 000 SKUs.[2] In the 1990s Tesco started to develop new store concepts such as Tesco Metro, a city-centre store meeting the needs of high-street shoppers and the local community. In addition, so-called compact stores (which are smaller than the superstores and have an average selling area of less than 26 500 square feet) were opened primarily on edge-of-town sites. This was followed by the launch of Tesco Express, which combines a petrol filling station with a local convenience store (Tesco is also Britain's largest independent petrol retailer). The latest store format is Tesco Extra, a hypermarket offering a wide selection of non-food items as a complement to, rather than at the expense of, the food assortment. The first Tesco Extra, which opened in 1996 in Pitsea, Essex, had a sales area of 102 000 square feet and displayed a total of 45 000 SKUs.

In 1995, Tesco introduced the first customer loyalty card, which offered benefits to regular shoppers while at the same time helping Tesco to analyze its customers' needs. Today, Tesco has ten million Clubcard member households.

Tesco's current CEO is Terry Leahy, who has worked for the company for 21 years. Much of Tesco's recent success is credited to his leadership ability. One of his former colleagues made the following comment:

> Anybody today who doubts that the current success isn't down to a mixture of both [Leahy and MacLaurin] – and more recently down to Terry Leahy – really doesn't know how retail businesses work.

When asked about Leahy's leadership style, another colleague said:

> When he [Leahy] took over as Chief Executive there were people in Tesco who missed the dash and the style of MacLaurin. But most of those people have now become fiercely loyal to Terry because he has a plan, he communicates it well and he is single-minded in going for it.

To respond to increased competition and declining prices in the food segment, Tesco has significantly expanded its range of products. The superstores now devote 40–50% of their shelf space to non-grocery items such as clothes and products for the home. In 2000, Tesco opened up a new front in retailing of consumer electronics, selling televisions, DVD players and mobile phones, which generated sales of £45 million.

For the year 2000, Tesco reported the following financial data. Overall group profit before tax increased by 12% to £1070 million. UK sales grew by 8.5% to £19.9 billion, of which 4.8% came from existing stores and 3.7% from new stores. International sales grew by 43% to £2.9 billion and contributed £74 million to profits, which presented a 48% increase over the previous year. Tesco's market share has grown steadily since the early 1990s and is currently about one-fifth of the UK market. Tesco employs 240 000 people worldwide.

Following an aggressive expansion strategy, today Tesco operates over 900 stores in the UK, Ireland, Hungary, Poland, the Czech Republic, Slovakia, Thailand, South Korea and Taiwan.

Tesco's strategy has four key elements, as stated in the Tesco 2000 Annual Report:

- *Strong core business in the UK*: We have continued to outperform the industry by offering value and innovation for customers against a background of difficult trading conditions. This business will continue to grow and compete effectively.
- *Non-food*: We are progressing with our aim to be as strong in non-food as we are in food. We are on track to secure a 6% share of the UK market. Non-food sales will grow faster than food as new space comes on-stream and as we extend global sourcing and global non-food capabilities. By 2002 we expect group non-food sales to be £5 billion.
- *Retailing services*: We follow the customer into new areas of expenditure as shopping habits change. We have the largest Internet grocery business in the world, we have doubled our mobile phone business in the past year and we are vigorously growing our financial services business.
- *International growth*: The pace of our international business is accelerating and experience is growing as we move through the development phase into profits and returns. By the year's end this business will be four times larger than it was four years ago and our lead countries, Hungary and Thailand, will be in profit. Overall, we are on track to 45% space overseas by 2002 and looking to expand into other countries in the longer term.

---

2 SKU stands for 'stock-keeping unit' and is a product reference number for inventory management purposes.

Tesco.com

> After spending around £40 million on getting its store-picking system right, Tesco has built up a profitable online food business with turnover of £300 million a year, making it the biggest Internet grocer [world wide].[3]

Tesco's online delivery service was initially launched in 1996–97. In so doing, Tesco became the first retailer in the UK to start this type of service, allowing customers to place orders by telephone, fax and via the Internet.

As of summer 2001, Tesco accounted for more than 50% of all online grocery sales in the UK and had expanded its Internet-based offerings into Ireland. Today, it has 750 000 registered customers and processes 70 000 orders a week. John Browett, formerly with the Boston Consulting Group and now Chief Executive Officer of Tesco.com, gives an overview of the financial developments at Tesco.com:

> We did £237 million in the year ended February 2001, and now we're at an annualized rate of more than £300 million. We lost a total of £9.5 million last year, due to the cost of rolling out [virtual] stores and starting five different non-food businesses – electronics, baby and toddler, fashion, entertainment and wine deals. But the grocery business is already profitable. Over the long run, there's no reason it can't be as profitable as retail stores, which now have an operating margin of 5.7%. We're not there yet.[4]

Although Tesco.com is one of the most frequently visited retailing websites in the UK (see Table 1), most of Tesco.com's registered shoppers are not yet regular users. The company is aiming to double the sales figures within three years and to build the business to 240 000 orders per week with £2 billion of turnover. Online shoppers tend to spend more than their brick-and-mortar counterparts. While the average store basket is about £25, the average Internet-based order is £90.

Tesco.com has a number of different online offerings, which include:

- *Groceries*: including fresh fruits and vegetables, fresh bakery, prepacked fresh meat and fish, chilled food, frozen food, store-cupboard items, beer, wine, spirits and pet care.
- *Books*: more than 1.2 million titles, ranging from fiction to children's stories to reference books.
- *Entertainment*: over 160 000 CDs, in addition to a wide range of videos and DVDs.
- *Electricals*: more than 1000 electrical products, from washing machines, refrigerators, kitchen appliances to hair dryers, TVs, stereos and game consoles.
- *You and your child*: brings together content, community and commerce by building on the community experience of iVillage (see below) and

3 *The Economist*, 30 June 2001.
4 'Online extra: Q&A with Tesco.com's John Browett', *Business Week Online*, 1 October 2001.

Table 1 **Most popular retailing websites in the UK**

	January 2001			*June 2001*	
	Visitors (1000s)	*Reach (%)*		*Visitors (1000s)*	*Reach (%)*
Amazon.co.uk	1509	11.7	X10.com	1581	10.4
Amazon.com	864	6.7	Amazon.co.uk	1496	9.8
Tesco.com	727	5.6	Amazon.com	1171	7.7
Argos.co.uk	537	4.2	Tesco.com	731	4.8
Jungle.com	432	3.4	WHSmith.co.uk	359	2.4
Shopsmart.com	430	3.3	Argos.co.uk	353	2.3
PCWorld.com	344	2.7	Jungle.com	327	2.1
Marksandspencer.com	312	2.4	Shopsmart.com	313	2.1
Etoys.co.uk	285	2.2	Streetsonline.co.uk	276	1.8
BOL.com	284	2.2	Beeb.com	272	1.8
Total retailing	6553	50.9	Total retailing	7772	50.9

Source: Webwatch, 2001.

the e-commerce knowledge gained from grocery home shopping and the baby and toddler catalogue business. With over 400 pages of content, subject areas range from feeding and health to clothing and advice for dads.

- *Home*: includes items such as cocktail shakers, dining-room furniture and computer tables.
- *Clothing*.
- *Personal finance*: the Internet activity also enables Tesco to build up its online banking service, Tesco Personal Finance. There exists a strong link between the food and financial activities: 70% of the clients who visit the Tesco Finance site also visit Tesco.com. Tesco Personal Finance has 15 products and services, two million customers, 400 000 savings accounts and 900 000 credit cards. John Gardiner, Tesco Chairperson, explains: 'Our superior economics allow us to be both profitable and fast-growing. Tesco Finance is one of the fastest growing retail banks in the country.' In addition to Visa card, Tesco Finance also offers savings accounts, Clubcard Plus, loans, pensions, credit cards, mortgages, savings products and insurance policies (for travel, pets, etc.).
- *Tesco.net*: Internet service provider with unlimited access to the Internet offered free of charge (excluding the cost of local calls).

Shopping at Tesco.com

Tesco.com customers have a number of different options to access Tesco's online services. As of July 2001, shoppers at Tesco.com can buy their groceries through mobile commerce applications. Through a partnership with Microsoft, Tesco.com launched Tesco Access, which allows users of hand-held computers and WAP-based wireless phones[5] to shop online. John Browett explains: 'Since the launch of Tesco Access, our customers can shop any time, any place, on any device, whether through the Internet, digital TV or pocket PCs.'[6]

In addition, beginning in June 2000, Internet cafés were opened up in stores across the country, including in some economic regeneration areas. One main goal is to bring customers online who are currently without computer skills. Tesco is also looking for ways in which customers can be given training in order to improve their understanding of computers and the Internet. Browett says:

> The big thing for us is educating the customer base. It is a bit like when self-service supermarkets were introduced, and people used to hand back their baskets and refused to do it. We have now passed the awareness stage and we have got to make this a habit.[7]

Terry Leahy explains the rationale behind all of these activities:

> We have spent nearly £55 million putting computers in virtually every classroom – many in less well off areas. And we're now rolling out our Internet cafés in our stores to provide access for our customers.[8]

Once customers have connected to the Tesco.com website, they register by providing delivery directions and choosing a username and a password. The website offers several types of functionality to facilitate the online shopping process. They include:

- *Shopping ideas*: help to buy relevant items for a special event such as Christmas, a barbecue or a party. Customers choose a specific list and then tick the lines of products that they want to add to their shopping basket.
- *My favourites*: includes a list of all the items that a customer has purchased recently. Customers then only need to click on any items that they want to buy again.
- *Online recipe book*: contains a large number of recipes. Customers can browse the ingredients and methods and see all the products needed for that recipe. Products are split into two groups: those that the customer probably has at home and those that are special to a particular recipe.

If customers have a preference regarding a product (e.g. they like their bananas yellow), they can mention this to their shopper using a special note facility that appears on the website next to each product (see Exhibit 1). If the ordered product is out of stock, Tesco.com offers either to choose a suitable substitute or skip that item, depending on the customer's choice. If Tesco chooses a substitute that the customer does not like, the customer can return it to the

5 WAP stands for Wireless Access Protocol.
6 'Online shopping: Tesco.com opens for WAP/PC orders', *Financial Times*, 21 July 2001.
7 'White van man trains sights on US: interview with John Browett, Chief Executive, Tesco.com', *Financial Times*, 14 July 2001.
8 Quoted in Tesco press release, June 2000.

Exhibit 1 Ordering yellow bananas at Tesco.com

Personal preferences

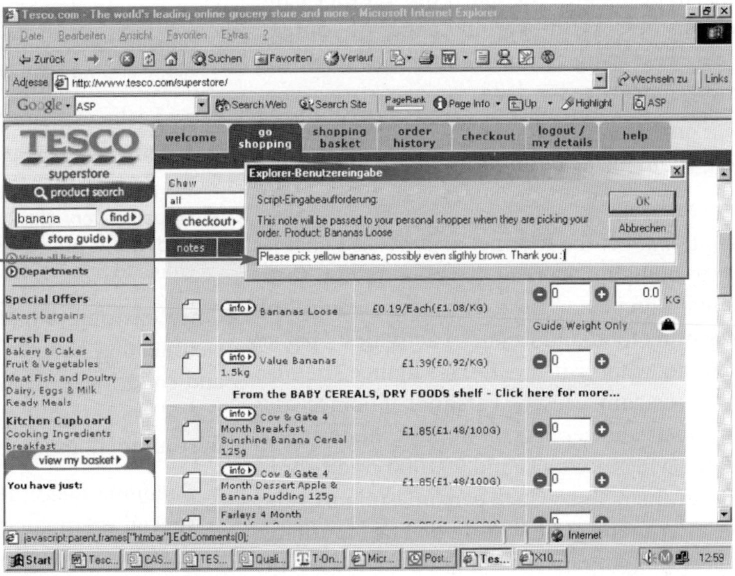

driver upon delivery and the amount is re-credited. After completing the online shopping, the customer can choose a delivery slot within a time window of one hour (see Exhibit 2).

The website stores the virtual shopping cart each time the customer leaves the virtual store, thereby making it easy for multiple family members to contribute to the shopping trip. Tesco is also trying to integrate the online and offline shopping experience. For instance, Tesco card members can enter their card numbers through the website and view recent purchases from offline stores.

Tesco.com's prices are the same as in the stores. In addition, discounts, promotions and special offers

Exhibit 2 Choosing a delivery slot at Tesco.com

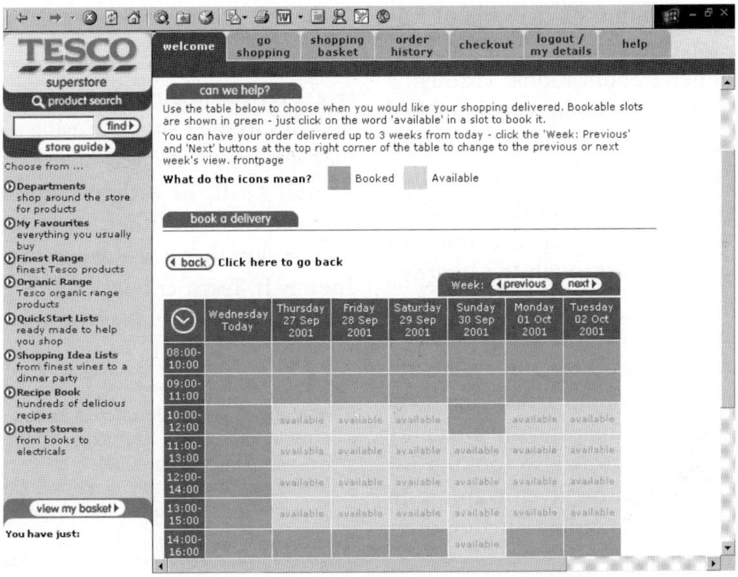

are made available to online customers. Service charge for delivery is £5, regardless of order size. Payment is made by credit card or debit card such as Visa, Mastercard, Switch, American Express and the Tesco Clubcard Plus. The account is debited when the packing is completed.

Improving the customer's online shopping experience is an ongoing effort at Tesco.com. In order to attract shoppers who have little or no Internet experience, Tesco relies on help and advice from external sources. For instance, Lynne Pullam, an Internet consultant for Tesco, determines what appears on the Tesco.com website. She explains: 'To me, a megabyte is a very large mouthful of food, and a hard drive is any journey on the M25 at rush hour, although I'm told that some people also use these terms to describe computers.'[9] She got the job after writing to Tesco about how the website could be improved. Now she is consulted on new features and every time the site is updated. For her services she is paid an hourly rate. Pullam explains her expertise: 'I may not be technically minded, but with almost 30 years of experience buying food for a hungry family, I can certainly tell Tesco whether shopping on the Internet is easy or not.' John Browett explains why Pullam was hired:

> Her experience as a busy mother of three is as valuable to us as an Oxbridge degree in computer science. If Lynne says 'No' Tesco won't go. She represents the voice of our customers, so if Lynne doesn't like the feature on our site, then we won't do it. The majority of customers using our online shopping know little about computer technology. For them, it's just a different, more convenient way of doing the shopping. A lot of these customers will be housewives and older people who have not experienced the Internet. If their first experience is too difficult, it could put them off for life.[10]

While growing its online business, Tesco is meanwhile benefiting from the Tesco Clubcard, which, with around 13 million registered consumers, represents an extraordinary database. For Karen Marshall, a spokesperson for Tesco, the card not only enhances customer satisfaction but also provides a valuable source of customer data for marketing efforts.

Shoppers' names and addresses and the category of products purchased are recorded and used for direct-mail campaigns and other promotions. For instance, when Tesco launched its pet insurance product, it was able to pitch to customers who had recently bought dog food and cat litter at its online store.

Clubcard evenings – complimentary in-store gatherings for certain Clubcard holders – are organized to promote products. Shoppers who have visited the wine or cheese departments at Tesco might be invited to a wine-tasting evening; those who purchased shampoo or cosmetics might be invited to a hair-care evening. 'It's a small "thank-you" to customers for shopping with us', claims Ms Marshall. 'The main idea is to help serve our customers better.' The popular evenings also provide an opportunity for personal contact with shoppers – something difficult to achieve in the mass-marketing age.

Tesco also sends Clubcard members a monthly magazine with recipe ideas, details of new product launches and other information tailored to particular demographic groups. Each separate edition of the magazine reflects the interests and lifestyle of a target market group such as young families, students or senior citizens.

It is impossible to register at Tesco.com without a Tesco Clubcard number. If a first-time online shopper already has one, the system will recognize that. In this way, Tesco is able to track how many online shoppers are its own customers and how many it is drawing from other chains. Tesco uses the extensive data it gathers on its customers' shopping habits to customize products and services – not, Browett insists, on a micro one-to-one level but on a broad demographic scale.

Tesco's fulfilment approach

> Think of the store as a warehouse. It is close to where people live, it is simple to pick from because the layout is designed for customers to navigate, infrastructure is there and it is already part of a supply chain.
>
> **Andrew Higginson, Finance Director, Tesco[11]**

When Tesco first started its delivery service, it was possible for customers to place orders through multiple devices: by telephone, fax and also via the Internet. However, the ordering system turned out to be too slow and inaccurate, as each order was captured manually. This led to frequent errors, which created frustration for customers. Delivery costs were also high, since the picking system was manual and

9 'What's a hard drive?', *The Mirror*, 27 July 2001.
10 'What's a hard drive?', *The Mirror*, 27 July 2001.
11 *The Economist*, 30 June 2001.

paper-based – pickers would walk around the store with their order lists and take the requested items off the shelves.

To overcome these initial difficulties, Tesco decided to automate its delivery service to a large degree and use the Internet as the sole ordering channel in order to streamline and improve order processing. When contemplating the delivery format for its online shopping, Tesco had to decide between two different approaches: either to pursue the warehouse model or to use its British stores as distribution centres. Both strategies had risks. Building huge warehouses would have cost millions of pounds, which Tesco was hesitant to spend on an unproven service. However, packing and picking groceries from stores might clog the aisles, thereby frustrating customers. So Tesco ran a series of calculations to identify the best delivery approach.

To get enough volume to justify the cost of building warehouses, Tesco determined that it would have to serve a large number of people from one location. In London, for instance, a single warehouse would have had to deliver to an area stretching from the northwest to the centre of town, a distance that would have taken hours to cover, as John Browett noted: 'The vans would have left on Friday and not returned until Saturday.'[12]

Browett explained the reasons for choosing store-based picking:

> We have done the maths. At current order volumes, you can't make warehouses work, because wherever you situate them, they are too far to reach your customers. What you may gain in [handling] efficiencies, you lose on delivery.

When asked about the scalability of the in-store picking approach, Browett said:

> There is no reason why we can't pick from the stores at night or continuously. You would have to pay staff more but in terms of efficiency it might be worth it. We are up to 600 orders a week in our largest store but you don't have to do very much to get that to 2000. In a typical superstore, we get 40 000 customers a week, so another 2000 is neither here nor there, particularly as Internet sales do not have to be scanned via the checkout where the most congestion is.[13]

In order to make a warehouse work, Tesco calculated that 10 000 orders a week were needed. Tesco.com picks around 70 000 orders a week from 300 British stores and could increase this number to 1000 orders for each store before needing to build warehouses. By delivering from local stores, no route takes longer than 25 minutes, since 94% of the population in England lives within a 25-minute radius of a Tesco store. The Boston Consulting Group assumes that the warehouse approach might make sense for the USA, with its wide catchment areas of stores, yet in Europe, where the density of supermarkets is much higher, the out-of-store approach seems to be a better option.

The out-of-store approach also greatly facilitated the roll-out of the online service. While other competitors had to invest a lot of time and money in the construction of extensive warehouse operations, Tesco gained an important first-mover advantage by using stores as warehouses. Tesco.com thus took an early lead in Britain, rolling out services in 100 of its 639 stores on a nationwide scale in 1999, thus attracting 250 000 customers.

The actual fulfilment process at Tesco.com works as follows. Customer orders go to an office in Dundee, Scotland, where they are grouped and sent to stores on the morning of the chosen delivery day. Each store's own computer system then sends the orders to shopping carts, equipped with mini-computers that give pickers a route through the shop for the orders in order to maximize efficiency. Each supermarket is divided into six zones – groceries, produce, bakery, chilled foods, frozen foods and 'secure' products such as liquor and cigarettes. Each picker covers only one zone, retrieving products for six customers at a time. Through the use of the route-planning computer and the division of the store into zones, pickers average 30 seconds of picking time per item, so that a typical order of 64 items can be fulfilled in 32 minutes. Pickers work during normal store trading hours but tend to go around stores when they are quietest: between 6.00 a.m. and 10.00 a.m. and between 11.00 a.m. and 3.00 p.m.

The pickers use carts that take six trays and can therefore pick for up to six customers at any one time. The trays are designed to slide in and out of the cart and are identified by stickers with the order

---

12 'Early winner in online food', *The New York Times*, 20 July 2001.

13 'Management of online retailing', *Financial Times*, 13 September 2000.

number. Gary Sargeant, head of Tesco Direct,[14] explains the reasons for the intensive use of technology:

> Everyone knows that £5 charged per order will not cover the true distribution costs, so we have to develop a high-tech solution to bring the handling costs down.[15]

The cost of picking for one order is around \$8.50, including labour and depreciation, with an average order size of \$123.[16] Tesco.com recovers its picking costs in a number of different ways. First, it saves about 3% of the order value by not using checkout staff. Second, online orders tend to have higher gross margins – more than 30% compared with Tesco's typical 25%, as has been shown by a Schroder Salomon Smith Barney analysis.[17] The reason for this is that online shoppers are more affluent and buy more profitable products, such as organic vegetables, quality meats, and private-label packaged goods. Tim Mason, Tesco's Marketing Director and chair of the dot.com business, admits: 'Our success is dependent on the fact that Tesco.com's margins tend to be higher.'[18]

In addition to cutting costs, Tesco also aims to minimize picking errors. Pickers scan the items they select and the system compares bar-code details with the item ordered on the customer's shopping list, sounding an alert if the wrong item is selected. With every item, the pickers inspect the sell-by date and check for damage. When asked about how she selects the products, Ms Sparks, a Tesco picker, said: 'Basically, it's common sense. You don't give a customer something you wouldn't buy yourself.'

In the storage area behind each store, different parts of each customer's order are grouped together. Orders are then loaded into vans, which are also designed to allow the trays to slot straight in. Tim Mason explains:

> Since its introduction, the system has had at least six big overhauls and countless minor ones. And still compared with what could be achieved, it is pretty rudimentary.[19]

Up to 15 orders can go into each van, depending on their size, and each vehicle has a separate area for frozen food. The 600 delivery vans make two daily runs. When dropping off the order, the van drivers also interact with the customers, who frequently make requests for additional services (see Table 2).

By charging customers for delivery, Tesco.com takes about \$27 million per year in fees, which is close to the estimated \$34 million cost of making the deliveries, according to Timothy Laseter, analyst at Booz, Allen & Hamilton, a consultancy.[20] Charging a delivery fee also increases the likelihood that customers are actually at home during the delivery time window, since they have to pay again for redelivery. In addition, imposing a fee has contributed to an increase in order size because customers want to get their money's worth. In comparison with the average

Table 2 Customer requests to Tesco delivery drivers

Most popular requests
Can I borrow your van to help me move?
Can you give me a lift?
I need some help to change a tyre.
Could you hold this ladder?
Does my bum look big in this?
Can you answer the phone and tell whoever it is that I am out?
Could you unblock my sink?
Unusual requests
Would you feed my pets while I am on holiday?
Do you want to join me for a candlelight dinner (after customer was stood up on Valentine's day)?
I need some marital advice.
Could you take a family photo?
I need someone to babysit.
Could you give us a lift to the wedding (after the car failed to turn up)?
Could you phone my office and tell them I am sick?
Would you drop the kids off at school?

Source: Tesco company documents.

14 Tesco Direct is a home-shopping catalogue service. The same products are available online, but for customers who do not have Internet access Tesco still provides a catalogue and a telephone ordering system. The catalogues available are 'Home and Living', 'You and Your Child', 'Gift' and 'Baby and Toddler'.

15 'Online grocery retailing', *Financial Times*, 6 September 2000.

16 'Tesco bets small – and wins big', *Business Week Online*, 1 October 2001.

17 'Tesco bets small – and wins big', *Business Week Online*, 1 October 2001.

18 'Tesco Bets Small – and wins big', *Business Week Online*, 1 October 2001.

19 'Online, in store, in profit and now in the US', *Financial Times*, 30 June 2001.

20 'Tesco bets small – and wins big', *Business Week Online*, 1 October 2001.

in-store transaction, online purchases are more than three times bigger.

As Tesco.com continues to expand its operations, a number of obstacles need to be overcome. Like many other online retailers, Tesco has run into trouble with orders for out-of-stock items. When the system was launched initially, customers were not informed as to whether products chosen were available. To remedy this problem, the web infrastructure was integrated with the inventory system, so that customers seeking items that were out of stock were informed immediately, not after they had placed their orders.

Optimizing delivery times presents a further hurdle. Customers typically prefer evening and weekend slots, which would mean an increase in the size of van fleets to cope with peak demand or risk losing shoppers to rival services. However, the labour and capital costs of running fleets during these times are considerable.

The quality of the products they receive is another main concern many customers express. Elizabeth Wolf, one of Tesco.com's customers, says:

> I am interested in it [online grocery shopping] because I work at a multimedia company and I'm quite familiar with the Web. But I'm very concerned with fresh food, and I've heard that the food being chosen and being delivered is, shall we say, not the best.[21]

In order to reduce the risk, many customers who are concerned with the quality of fresh products, choose to purchase only large and bulky items through the Internet. Heather Smith, a young mother of two who lives in West London, elaborates:

> I use Tesco.com mainly for items that I can't carry home with me. Since I am usually pushing a baby carriage, my carrying capacity is limited. In addition, I have been quite disappointed with the quality of fresh items delivered by Tesco.com. Therefore, I only buy bulk items and some packaged lettuce and tomatoes through the Tesco.com website.[22]

Other customers are more satisfied with Tesco's online service. Mike Smith reports on his first shopping experience:

> I registered on Tuesday evening and ordered the following to be delivered by Thursday morning at 11.00 a.m: ten free range eggs, one porter cake, a pint of milk, ice cream, a tin of fruit cocktail and a jar of coffee. I would have chosen more – I tried adding meat, a fresh cream sponge and some custard slices – but the site bizarrely decided that I had enough and wouldn't allow me to add any more items. The whole thing, including a delivery charge of £5, cost £15.59. I registered, entered credit card details and waited. The message the next day said the delivery would arrive between 11.00 a.m. and 1.00 p.m. on Thursday. At 10.45 a.m. everything arrived. The eggs weren't broken, the ice cream was frozen and things were generally OK. Maybe next time ... I'll order more.[23]

Other customers are also concerned about the environmental issues caused by the Tesco delivery trucks driving through town. However, Browett rejects this claim:

> This is environmentally friendly. We do 12 deliveries per run on one loop, instead of every shopper going back and forth. I think this is actually saving the planet.[24]

Finally, some customers, especially in the up-market community, dislike having Tesco white delivery vans in their driveways. In order to appease this segment, Tesco.com has bought a small fleet of green Range Rovers to deliver to their doors.

Alliances and acquisitions

Technology partnership with Interwoven

When launching its online store, Tesco's challenge was to create and edit the web files needed to keep abreast of inventory. Several web-design agencies were initially employed to develop the HTML[25] and ASP[26] files needed to illustrate Tesco's products and to contribute to Tesco.com's look and feel. While these agencies showed much creativity, Tesco found it difficult to incorporate new content into the existing website.

Leon Stoner, Tesco's webmaster, notes:

> There was no way for the agencies to test the ASP and HTML files before they went live. They'd develop a whole pile of pages for our review, then they'd send them to us via FTP[27] or e-mail in a zip file. Then, we'd

21 'British grocer Tesco tries to succeed where others have failed', *Hoover's Online*, 3 August 2001.

22 'British grocer Tesco tries to succeed where others have failed', *Hoover's Online*, 3 August 2001.

23 'Technology online grocer fails to deliver,' *Hoover's Online*, 24 July 2001.

24 'White van man trains sights on US: Interview John Browett, chief executive, Tesco.com', *Financial Times*, 14 July, 2001.

25 Hypertext Markup Language.

26 ASP, which stands for Active Server Pages, is an open Web application platform that combines server scripting with custom server components to create browser-independent web solutions and publish legacy databases to the Web.

27 File Transport Protocol.

> have to manually put them on a makeshift server, and give them a quick once-over ... then manually copy them from that test server to eight or more production servers. It was obviously quite time consuming, and a bit of a headache.[28]

The need for efficient management of its web assets became more pressing as the online operations continued to expand. Thus, Interwoven's TeamSite was selected to provide the required technology support. Two consultants from Interwoven worked with Tesco in London to customize the TeamSite technology to meet Tesco's needs. TeamSite manages content provided by about 15 web designers and authors. Tesco maintains 20 production web servers. When asked about the possibility of future expansion of the system, Stoner replied:

> We've been trying to arrange it so there is a generic implementation. We've designed the workflows and scripting behind the scenes so they're easy to maintain and manipulate. So when we decide to take the non-food sites through TeamSite, we can just take the existing scripts, tweak them a little bit, and then we'll just kind of roll the other sites over every four to six weeks. Eventually, we'll have the TeamSite running the national store.[29]

There are three important features that TeamSite provides for Tesco:

- *Templating*: the comprehensive templating framework allows Tesco's business managers to manage the timing and look and feel of online campaigns.
- *Smart context editing*: TeamSite offers a means for Tesco's external web design agencies to develop and check the quality of their work before submitting it to the online grocers.
- *Flexible workflow*: TeamSite allows line-of-business managers to assign work, control approval, and manage distribution to their offline and online customer channels.

For Stoner, using TeamSite has made a significant difference:

> TeamSite has allowed our agencies to test their work before they send it to us. This has been great because it cuts out a lot of our day-to-day maintenance role. Now we can develop new things, rather than just being reactive to the need for change on the current site. We have more time on our hands ... so we can take on more work.

Paul Arnold, a senior business consultant at Tesco, elaborates:

> TeamSite has enabled us to scale up quickly. Tesco Direct has gone from being a test site for a few stores to being the biggest online grocery site in the UK. The fact that we can create and merge store-specific content for all our retail locations has greatly improved our customer relationships. Plus, we can respond quickly to changes in pricing, inventories, and the like, which helps us operate much more efficiently. Best of all, our website can be easily managed by an internal team of only 12 people – we don't need a load of extra resources to keep things running smoothly, which definitely improves our bottom line.[30]

Partnership with iVillage UK

In July 2000, Tesco and iVillage Inc. agreed to create an international joint venture called iVillage UK to serve the women's online market in the UK and Ireland. The purpose of iVillage UK is to provide women with a community and various interactive online services such as content channels, planners, quizzes, message boards, chats and newsletters. John Browett comments on this alliance:

> There is great synergy between our two companies and category-leading brands, making this joint venture an ideal investment and strategic initiative for Tesco.com. iVillage UK will be using iVillage.com's clear advantage as the best site for women online and Tesco's rich knowledge of UK customers.

As part of the deal, Tesco.com receives a central positioning on the homepage of iVillage.co.uk and Tesco's products and services are contextually integrated throughout the iVillage network. Tesco.com also has central positions in a number of vertical content areas: Tesco Direct functions as the exclusive grocery partner of the iVillage's Food Channel. Tesco's Baby & Toddler Store is promoted throughout the Pregnancy & Baby Channel at iVillage. iVillage, on the other hand, receives marketing and promotional support from Tesco to drive traffic on to the iVillage website. These consist of in-store promotions, Tesco mailings, and positioning on Tesco's Internet service provider.

Acquisition of GroceryWorks

Deutsche Bank Research indicated in 2000 that it expected Tesco to roll out its online format into other markets:

28 Quoted in Interwoven company material.
29 Quoted in Interwoven company material.
30 Quoted in Interwoven company material.

> Tesco is likely to seek regional alliances via Tesco.com in Europe and some North American states. We strongly believe that this strategy is a good one, because consolidation in Europe is currently hampered by the excessively high cost of physical assets. Internet is a good means for Tesco to make regional alliances by bringing its technological and marketing expertise to local groups with strong renown in their area and access to food manufacturing groups. Involving a fairly limited capital commitment, this strategy enables Tesco to win market share in new segments without having to build stores.[31]

On 25 June 2001, Tesco did, indeed, announce a deal with Safeway, California's biggest food retailer. As part of this deal, Tesco is providing its technology and $22 million into GroceryWorks, a loss-making online retailer that is majority-owned by Safeway. GroceryWorks, which operated previously with warehouse-based distribution systems, plans to close these facilities and replace them with Tesco's store-picking system. In return, Tesco received a 35% stake in GroceryWorks. The deal attracted a lot of attention because a system developed in the UK for £40 million is to become the backbone for online shopping in the state that led the dot.com revolution.

> If Tesco can teach its new partner these skills and tricks, its 35% stake in GroceryWorks could turn out to be a goldmine, given America's avid Internet usage and Safeway's 1,700-strong network of stores, more than twice as big as its [Tesco's] own.[32]

In December 1999, GroceryWorks began delivering from warehouses. Two months later, its executives realized that their business model had severe flaws. Jeffrey Cushman, Chief Financial Officer of GroceryWorks, explained: 'We knew right away that we had to get the product costs down.' But without the buying power of a larger grocery chain, it could not get a competitive deal from suppliers. Furthermore, GroceryWorks also faced problems with its warehouse system. Cushman continued: 'A fulfillment center is so big that you never get the density until you run out of money.'[33] When asked about co-operating with Tesco, a Safeway spokesperson Debra Lamgert replied: 'We liked Tesco's track record. They understand how to combine technology with bricks and mortar.'[34]

GroceryWorks is closing its three distribution centres (built at a cost of approximately $7 million each) and is temporarily ceasing operations. When it reopens, it will operate under the Safeway name, using the Tesco model of store picking and packing. Tesco is expecting overall operating costs to be lower in the USA, since traffic congestion is less severe and fuel taxes are far lower.

Following the signing of the agreement, Terry Leahy commented on the deal:

> Retailing services are a key part of the Tesco strategy for growth. We have developed the best online grocery home shopping system in the world which we know can be of use to other retailers. Last year we outlined our desire to take Tesco.com into different markets, including the US. We admire Safeway Inc. greatly. They represent the best of US retail. With Tesco's know-how and the Safeway Inc. brand we have the perfect combination to bring [online] grocery shopping to the world's largest market.[35]

Future outlook: which recipe will taste best?

> Picking in-store is fine if there is low demand, but it is not good when the service ramps up – it disrupts the customers. When demand gets higher, then picking centers are the only route to market. We believe that a flexible model with a combination of stores and picking centers will deliver the best return.
>
> **Angela Megson, e-Commerce Director, Sainsbury Supermarkets**[36]

Thinking aloud about the capacity restrictions, Browett points out:

> We think we can go as high as £2–3 billion in sales using store-based picking and packing. And that's assuming no new stores and no significant productivity improvement, both of which are likely and would raise the number. Maybe someday we'll have a hybrid model with warehouses for dense areas like London, but the traffic just kills you. Plus, where would we put them? In any case, smaller places like Inverness, Plymouth, or Peterborough could never be served from warehouses.[37]

Marc van Gelder, Chief Executive Officer of Peapod.com (a USA-based Internet grocery retailer,

---

31 Deutsche Bank Research Report, 2000.
32 *The Economist*, 30 June 2001.
33 'Early winner in online food', *New York Times*, 20 July 2001.
34 'Tesco bets small – and wins big', *Business Week Online*, 1 October 2001.
35 Quoted in Tesco press release, 25 June 2001.
36 'Online grocery retailing', *Financial Times*, 6 September 2000.
37 'Online extra: Q&A with Tesco.com's John Browett', *Business Week Online*, 1 October 2001.

now part of Ahold, a Dutch retail chain) is not convinced by Tesco's business model. He said:

> We find Tesco's pure in-store model complicated from a quality perspective. Tesco has lower start-up costs but over time they have to naturally evolve to warehouses if they want efficiency.[38]

Like its dot.com rivals, Tesco has to offset direct expenses, such as vans and pickers, against its online revenues. In contrast to pure players, which also have to consider the running costs and depreciation charges of their warehouses, Tesco books these costs against its offline sales. This practice led some analysts and investors to question whether Tesco's online operation would be profitable if it were evaluated as a separate business unit. Jeff Matthews from Ram Partners, a hedge fund in Greenwich, Connecticut, says: 'Profits can be calculated in many different ways.'[39]

Tesco continues to build on its strong UK base through a concerted move into non-food markets and major store openings in Central Europe and Asia, in addition to its partnership in the USA with Safeway. In November 2001, Tesco expanded its online operations into South Korea, which has one of the highest penetrations of broadband Internet access. Currently, Tesco has seven bricks-and-mortar stores in South Korea and plans to open another 11 in the future. This international expansion may prove to be another opportunity for Tesco to roll out its successful Internet-based grocery retailing. It seems that for this new, scalable online business, the sky is the limit.

38 'e-Business: British grocer Tesco thrives filling web orders from its stores' aisles', *Wall Street Journal*, 16 October 2000.

39 'Supply chain management: shop or warehouse', *Financial Times*, 20 June 2001.

DISCUSSION QUESTIONS

1 What are the main opportunities and challenges in online grocery retailing?

2 In what ways does Tesco.com expect to benefit from its online initiative?

3 What role do logistics play in online grocery retailing in general?

4 What are the advantages and disadvantages of the different order fulfillment approaches (i.e. in-store *vs*. warehouse-based)?

5 What recommendations would you make to Tesco.com in order to consolidate its 'emerging' success?

6 What lessons would you draw from the Tesco.com case and other Internet-based grocery experiences you may be aware of, and what messages would you have for e-retailers in general?

CASE STUDY 9

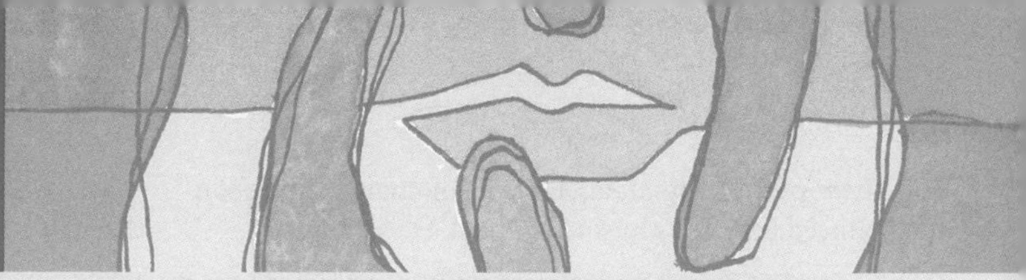

ChateauOnline

ChateauOnline, a three-year-old French wine e-tailer founded by a group of entrepreneurial MBAs and wine lovers, has pulled itself through the rise and fall of the B2C Internet boom. By early 2001 – with a staff of 80, a presence in seven countries, and sales of well over FF40 million in 2000 – ChateauOnline was one of Europe's leading online wine merchants. Yet the race was far from over. Hundreds of vineyards, warehouses, importers and start-ups were striving to capture a piece of the online pie. Global retailers like Carrefour were entering the online arena with all their muscle. Moreover, despite the obvious benefits offered by online shopping, consumer demand for Internet purchasing was not picking up as expected, and industry forecasters were revising their estimates sharply downward.[1] Worst of all, investors were losing patience and ChateauOnline was seeing many of its competitors abandon their expansion plans or verging on bankruptcy. The business proposition of online wine sales still seemed compelling and there was a great opportunity to gain market leadership that could later be expanded to other product categories, but ChateauOnline itself was struggling with financing, low conversion rates, and the ramping up of operations. How could it turn its wine e-tailing model into a viable, sustainable and profitable business – now?

ChateauOnline: vision and strategy

A passion for wine

The vision of the ChateauOnline founders was to promote and share their passion for wine with all wine lovers. Gregory Salinger, a Harvard graduate with banking, media and telecom/Internet experience, and Alexandre Basdereff, an ESSEC graduate with website-building and direct marketing experience, wanted to create a pan-European new-generation company – specifically, an Internet wine specialist that would bring 'e-quality' of life to everyone, not just an elite of connoisseurs. (For company history and values, see Exhibits 1 and 2.) ChateauOnline's information, discussion and service platform helps visitors to choose wines and enriches the wine lover's tasting experience with new, little-known quality wines; the site includes access to knowledge and advice from an independent professional sommelier at no cost. It covers *grands crus* and expensive specialities (e.g. a 1676 port priced at over FF150 000) as well as everyday table wines for just FF25. Wines are selected exclusively from a pool of over 12 000 wines and tasted by a panel of eight nationally acclaimed sommeliers led by ChateauOnline's 'cyber-sommelier' Jean Michel Deluc, former head sommelier of the Ritz Paris.

Guaranteed quality, and more

ChateauOnline's customers are a cross-section of typical Internet users and wealthier wine-consuming adults: 35- to 55-year-old, well-educated, urban males with higher-than-average incomes. They are mostly

1 Due to changed conditions and a range of e-commerce obstacles especially manifest in Europe, Gartner revised its prediction of global e-commerce reaching $7.3 trillion by 2004, downwards by $1.3 trillion, or 18%. 'Revised forecasts show how assumptions can crumble', *The New York Times*, 27 March 2001.

Mitti Snall, MBA, wrote this case under the supervision of Professor David Midgley, INSEAD, and Professor Timothy Devinney, Australian Graduate School of Management. It is intended to be used as a basis for class discussion rather than to illustrate either effective or ineffective handling of an administrative situation.

Exhibit 1 History and milestones of ChateauOnline

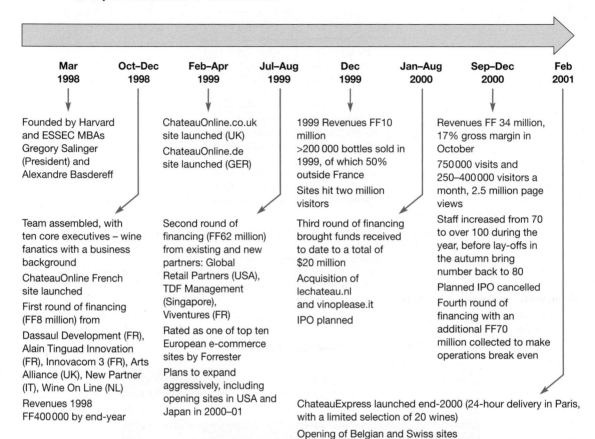

Mar 1998
Founded by Harvard and ESSEC MBAs Gregory Salinger (President) and Alexandre Basdereff

Oct–Dec 1998
Team assembled, with ten core executives – wine fanatics with a business background
ChateauOnline French site launched
First round of financing (FF8 million) from
Dassaul Development (FR), Alain Tinguad Innovation (FR), Innovacom 3 (FR), Arts Alliance (UK), New Partner (IT), Wine On Line (NL)
Revenues 1998 FF400 000 by end-year

Feb–Apr 1999
ChateauOnline.co.uk site launched (UK)
ChateauOnline.de site launched (GER)

Jul–Aug 1999
Second round of financing (FF62 million) from existing and new partners: Global Retail Partners (USA), TDF Management (Singapore), Viventures (FR)
Rated as one of top ten European e-commerce sites by Forrester
Plans to expand aggressively, including opening sites in USA and Japan in 2000–01

Dec 1999
1999 Revenues FF10 million
>200 000 bottles sold in 1999, of which 50% outside France
Sites hit two million visitors

Jan–Aug 2000
Third round of financing brought funds received to date to a total of \$20 million
Acquisition of lechateau.nl and vinoplease.it
IPO planned

Sep–Dec 2000
Revenues FF 34 million, 17% gross margin in October
750 000 visits and 250–400 000 visitors a month, 2.5 million page views
Staff increased from 70 to over 100 during the year, before lay-offs in the autumn bring number back to 80
Planned IPO cancelled
Fourth round of financing with an additional FF70 million collected to make operations break even

Feb 2001
ChateauExpress launched end-2000 (24-hour delivery in Paris, with a limited selection of 20 wines)
Opening of Belgian and Swiss sites

Source: ChateauOnline.

regular 'wine lovers' – as ChateauOnline calls them – although a few are true connoisseurs and some are less sophisticated mass consumers that purchase an odd bottle or mixed tasting case out of curiosity. As with wine purchases from a traditional retail outlet, some online purchasing depends less on particular customer characteristics and more on the usage, be it for a dinner, weekend lunch, gift or Christmas party.

One aspect of the value proposition offered by the company is the *bon vivant* lifestyle: 'ChateauOnline is not having the "chateau in Bordeaux" but "la vie de Chateau" – it is an overall quality of life, pleasure, having a high-rating life .... Right from the very beginning we invested in having a high quality selection, high quality brand.' Another aspect of its proposition revolves around communicating this quality to the customer in terms of guarantees and professionalism – having an independent wine selection evaluated by sommeliers, rather than promoting a certain vineyard's or retailer's products, as well as providing the tasting notes and professional advice. ChateauOnline's independent advice – together with secure payment systems, timely delivery and a money-back guarantee of satisfaction – all helps boost the customer's confidence in 'not having to be ashamed of the wine, knowing that it will be good'.

Wide offering, usage and recognition

By early 2001, ChateauOnline's site was attracting some 750 000 visits, including 250 000–400 000 visitors per month in France, and had a core customer base of 110 000 Wine Club newsletter subscribers Europe-wide. The site offered 1400–1700 wines from over 25 countries, all with online tasting notes and

Exhibit 2 Values and guarantees of ChateauOnline

Passion To promote and share the passion of the world's wine growers	**Curiosity** To discover the world through its vineyards
Intimacy To offer service to everyone in their homes, around the clock	**Honesty** To guarantee an unbiased choice of best wines, with transparent purchase policy

Guarantees to customers:

- *Quality and selection* – all wines tasted, full money-back guarantee if customer not satisfied.
- *Price* – competitive and transparent.
- *Personal advice* – individual response to questions within 48 hours.
- *Security* – payments protected by an internationally recognized protocol (Cybermut of Credit Mutuel).
- *Privacy* – all personal information treated with confidentiality.
- *Delivery* – rapid and safe delivery at minimum cost.

Source: ChateauOnline.

Exhibit 3 ChateauOnline UK website, April 2001

photos, and it had been recommended in the goodwebguide.co.uk. ChateauOnline offered webmiles for frequent users and had a broad affiliation programme feeding in traffic from other websites. The site also featured a gift shop, wine accessories, wedding and party services with recommended wines to go with the menu, venue and chosen budget, and advice on creating and managing one's own wine cellar. Corporate services included over 30 different gift baskets (with a catalogue of mail-order cards) and a range of vouchers and employee schemes. Some of the national sites featured small special sections for auctions and classifieds. (See Exhibit 3 for a view of the ChateauOnline UK homepage.)

The site had been mentioned in the press as an industry leader offering a good selection and competent advice. Public recognition had come from IBM, which had chosen the site for its year 2000 e-business advertising campaign, Forrester Research had ranked it among the top ten e-commerce sites in Europe in 1999 and, in 2000, and ChateauOnline held the e-commerce Grand Trophée for the best French site.

Exhibit 4 **Wine-consumption patterns in Europe**

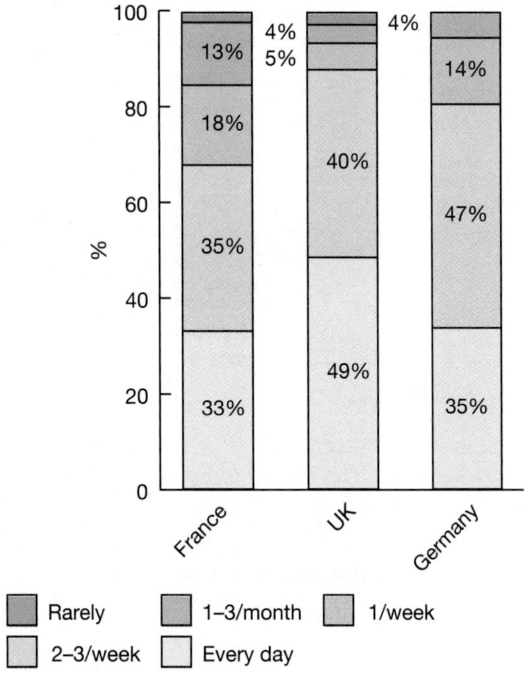

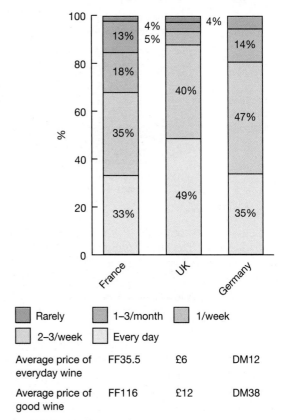

Average price of everyday wine	FF35.5	£6	DM12
Average price of good wine	FF116	£12	DM38

Source: ChateauOnline.

Wine retailing offline and online

The art of wine making starts in the vineyard, where producers carefully judge the grape varieties and growing conditions, plant and cull the vines, and selectively pick the ripe grapes to produce quality inputs. The grapes are crushed and the juice fermented, after which the 'raw wine' is generally matured in a variety of wooden and steel barrels for several months or years to add flavour and character. After sampling and evaluation, the wine may be blended, and the resulting product is bottled and sold. Typically, it continues to mature in the bottle until opened by the consumer – possibly dozens of years after production.

The European wine industry from winery to consumer

Today the European wine market is larger than the book or music industries, with an estimated $60 billion in sales representing some 60% of worldwide consumption. Between 70% and 90% of French, German and British adults drink wine several times a week. In 1999 wine consumption per person was 19 litres in the UK and 58 litres in France. Although the volume of individual consumption had been decreasing for some time (it has declined by 40% in France over the past 20 years), the quality of consumption was increasing steadily, and this was reflected in the higher average price paid. (See Exhibit 4 for European purchasing patterns.)

The wine industry in Europe is fragmented, with small wineries selling their products direct to the consumer as well as through a network of generalist and specialist wholesalers, exporters and retailers. There are up to 45 000 wine producers in France alone, producing well over 100 000 wines distributed through thousands of distributor and retail outlets, including small mom-and-pop shops, clubs and mail order (see Exhibit 5).[2] However, retail concentration is low, with the leading wine retailer in France holding only 1.5%

2 In the USA there are only 2100 wineries, of which just 49 produce 90% of wine and wholesaling has also consolidated. 'Those Musty Wine Laws', *The Wall Street Journal*, 1 June 2000.

Exhibit 5 Wine sales channels for home usage in France

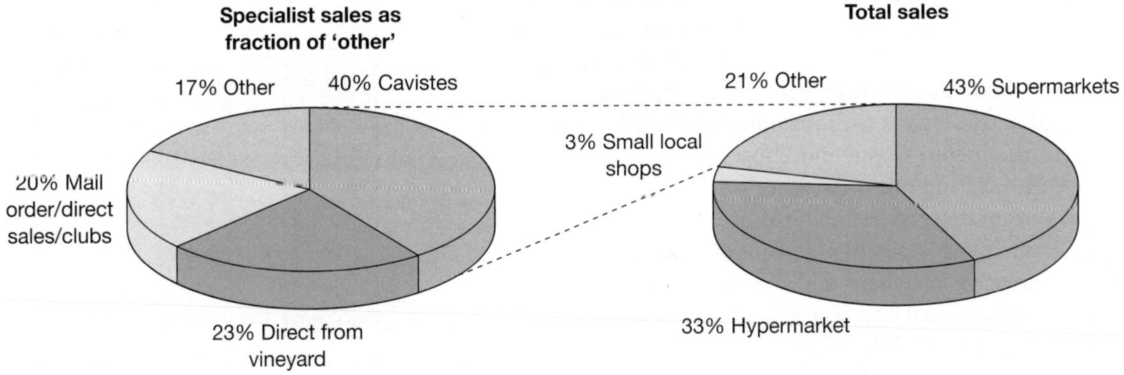

Source: Carrefour/verywine.

of market share. The biggest offline retailers in France are Carrefour, Leclerc and Nicolas. Due to the highly fragmented nature of the market, there is plenty of scope for entry and exit and thus opportunities to consolidate or streamline the market.

Wine online

Wine is a specialist product, distinguished by the grape variety, region and even place of growth, weather conditions in a given year, production methods and recipes, storage, image and taste. Despite efforts to discover what makes the difference between a good wine and a bad one, the art of wine making has only recently yielded to analysis.[3] Given that thousands of different wines of varying vintages are available, making a choice between even a small selection may prove difficult for the inexperienced consumer without assistance. These features make wine ideal for online sales, where large selections of wines can be systematically labelled, ranked, compared and sought, quickly and with little effort.[4] ChateauOnline's selection is already three times as wide as the normal supermarket selection of 400–800 wines and there are plans to expand it to 2000–5000 wines. Furthermore, it delivers across the European Union (EU) and Switzerland.

Adding to the suitability of wine as an online product is the fact that providing informational material such as wine descriptions and storing and serving instructions can create significant value. For aficionados, content and community features can be utilized to encourage online discussion. A wine bottle does not need to be touched before purchasing, it endures a slow delivery process as it is not perishable, and it does not lose value when stored. Consumption is often not immediate but planned in advance for an occasion, even if the choice between different wines is based originally on an impression or impulse. Wine is a popular gift, and wrapping and sending can be facilitated through the Internet. In addition, it provides the possibility of offering lower prices to the consumer while maintaining profitability by removing unnecessary wholesalers and importers from the traditional value chain (disintermediation). Conversely, as many wine consumers are relatively insensitive to price, there is also room for price premiums.

Some drawbacks of online sales remain, however. Wine bottles are heavy, breakable and require special delivery at high cost. Someone has to be at home to receive the delivery of what is an expensive and easy-to-steal item. Also, judging the value of the wine delivered and returning defective bottles would seem troublesome, as the criteria for a wine being spoiled or bad is ambiguous – wine online is not 'what-you-see-is-what-you-get', so you need either to know or to trust the product. To mitigate this,

3 'Can math predict wine? An economist takes a swipe at some noses', *International Herald Tribune,* 5 March 1990. V. Ginsburgh, M. Monzak and A. Monzak, 'Red wines of Medoc: what is wine tasting worth?', discussion paper, Catholic University of Louvain, April 1992.

4 In fact, making searching more convenient reduces price sensitivity for online wine purchasing. J. Lynch and D. Ariely, 'Wine online: search costs affect competition on price, quality, and distribution', *Marketing Science*, January 2000.

most online retailers give particular recommendations on the nature of wines and allow product returns without question.

Consumer reluctance

European markets seem particularly suited to online sales, as wine is already selling better than other consumer products via mail order.[5] However, France and many small nations are behind the UK and Germany in Internet adoption, and the French are also less inclined to online shopping (11% *v.* 26% in the UK and 22% in Germany), especially for groceries.[6] Historically, true wine lovers in Europe prefer to purchase from traditional sources and direct from a familiar winery. Older consumers may have difficulty with Internet usage, while younger potential purchasers may be too inexperienced to buy anything more than homepage special offers or ready-mixed trial cases. This leaves few obvious customer groups for a serious wine site, or at least increases the need for advertising and word-of mouth referrals. Further complexity is added by the cultural, linguistic, technological, transactional and regulatory heterogeneity between the European nations – indeed, some thought that Europe would not be at all easy to conquer 'virtually' with the exception of the highly wired and technologically inclined Scandinavian countries such as Finland and Denmark.

Even in the most Internet-enabled market of the USA, less than 0.9% of wine sales had migrated online by 1998, but an aggressive 5–10% were expected to shift to online providers by 2005.[7] In Europe, Internet sales had expanded more slowly, with an estimated lag of 1.5–2 years relative to growth in the USA.[8] In 2000 just 0.15% of the wine market was online; this was estimated to grow to a conservative 0.35% by the end of 2001, to 1.0% in 2002 and to 1.5% in 2003. Based on these estimates, total European online wine sales in 2000 should reach $90–110 million, with this figure doubling during 2001.[9]

The reasons for the slow uptake of wine sales on the Internet are simple. Rather than security concerns or lack of seeing and touching the bottle before purchase (barriers commonly cited), over a third of wine lovers surveyed had never thought of purchasing online because it was so easy to pick up a bottle while shopping for groceries. Almost a fifth thought their consumption too small to bother – for them the supermarket was fine and the cost of going online might be higher. Two-tenths each wished to maintain the spontaneity of offline purchasing, or disliked or felt uncomfortable with e-commerce (see Table 1).

Table 1 Reasons for not purchasing wine online

%	*Reason (multiple responses allowed)*
35	Don't know, or never thought that wine could be bought online
7	Find no need (e.g. own consumption so small)
17	Think local shop is just fine, or easier to use
17	Think the price or transaction costs are too high to justify online purchasing
13	Wish to buy wine at impulse, get it when in need
13	Dislike or are not used to online shopping
9	Don't know enough to buy wine online
4	Lack the time
4	Prefer to see the bottle before purchasing
4	Have security concerns that prevent purchasing

Source: Survey of 27 participants of four different wine-tasting classes in spring 2001 (wine-loving MBA students and their spouses).

The key purchase factors are the breadth of selection and the ease and convenience of finding and purchasing the right wine. Delivery and price were somewhat important, while accessing specialist products unavailable in normal shops was less so. Wine-related content was generally rejected as a reason to shop online.

Professional purchasers value roughly the same criteria but highlight the importance of the selection and the fact that a specified bottle is not out of stock when one tries to shop for it. Another key asset is the ability to purchase a variety of specialist wines in small quantities without the hassle of dealing with or visiting vineyards. Vineyards normally sell their own

5 4% of wine sales are by mail order compared with 2.8% of total consumer retail (ChateauOnline data).

6 'French increase inventories of groceries offered on Internet, but who's buying?', *The Wall Street Journal*, 25 September 2000.

7 Case estimates based on the Wine Institute statement and Salomon Smith Barney study in K. Steinriede, 'Online wine takes root', *Beverage Industry*, January 2000 and J. Spence, 'Online wine e-tailers are ripe for growth', *InfoWorld*, 21 August 2000.

8 Boston Consulting Group, 'The race for online riches: e-retailing in Europe', 2000.

9 Case estimates supported by Forrester data from ChateauOnline.

product by the case (minimum six bottles of the same wine), with a minimum order of 30–36 bottles. The direct purchase is generally confirmed by mail, paid for by cheque upon delivery, and takes up to three weeks to receive. This is in stark contrast to the convenience of purchasing online, especially if one knows what one is looking for. Given the flat delivery fee ranging from FF39 to FF59 and the 'reasonable' or discounted e-tailer price vis-à-vis the high street, ordering large quantities can be economical or at least can offset the delivery fees of online shopping. Here, again, content plays no role in purchasing, although an occasional article or fact is nice to have, if only for browsing.

Competition all around

Due to the relatively good fit of online sales, wine e-tailing attracted entrants into the business all around the world. After the pure-play era, the existing clicks-and-mortar wine merchants entered, followed by mail-order specialists, supermarkets, auctioneers and brokers. The last wave includes new models such as exchanges (e.g. Uvine, worldwineXchange). The fragmentation of the industry is illustrated and further amplified online, where players of all levels – from wineries to wholesalers to restaurants to clubs – push their homepages directly to the consumer. For example, in 2001 anyone searching via Altavista and Yahoo in the USA, the UK or France would obtain hundreds of hits. Some specialize in one region, chateau or consumer style and offer little more than an e-mail link or fax number for ordering; others employ sophisticated search tools and offer quality content to attract consumers. To quote one customer: 'Even doing a search does not help – you get too many names and don't know who they are.'

Despite the huge number of sellers, less than 20% of even the prime European Internet-using and wine-loving clientele surveyed had ever visited a wine site and just 7% had purchased wine online, none from ChateauOnline. However, 40% of online buyers surveyed had heard of ChateauOnline and 20% had even visited its site (see Exhibit 6). Why, then, had they not bought anything? As the example proves, customers are hard to come by and mainstream conversion rates remain low for everyone, at best at 1–2%.[10] Thus, ChateauOnline does not regard competition but sluggish demand as its primary threat:

Exhibit 6 **Funnel of purchasing wine online**

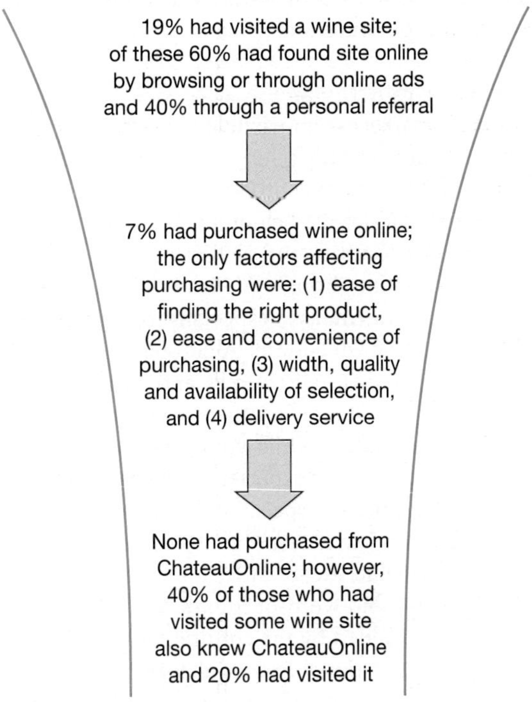

19% had visited a wine site; of these 60% had found site online by browsing or through online ads and 40% through a personal referral
7% had purchased wine online; the only factors affecting purchasing were: (1) ease of finding the right product, (2) ease and convenience of purchasing, (3) width, quality and availability of selection, and (4) delivery service
None had purchased from ChateauOnline; however, 40% of those who had visited some wine site also knew ChateauOnline and 20% had visited it

Source: Survey of 27 participants of four different wine tasting classes in Spring 2001 (wine-loving MBA students and their spouses).

> Is competition our problem? No, I don't think so. The big challenge is to *create a market*. We must create the market first.
>
> **Christophe Poupinel, Marketing Director, ChateauOnline**

ChateauOnline's capabilities

ChateauOnline considers a key strength to be its core team of young, experienced, international managers with graduate degrees and wide backgrounds in business development, marketing and wine or gastronomy. Having an innovative vision, the early establishment of the site and business platform and a subsequent brisk scale-up assured ChateauOnline of a strong position in the fledgling European online wine sales market.

10 Case estimates and hearsay of competitors' conversion rates. However, Amazon.com boasts conversion rates of 5–10%.

First-mover advantage and learning by doing

As theories about first-mover advantage and time-based competition point out, gaining hands-on experience in a new market ahead of others is a source of further competence, whose value can be judged only by the future decisions and additional degrees of freedom that the company has earned in the process. ChateauOnline has been through four tough rounds of funding, learned how not to get strangled by overpriced annual advertising contracts, and dealt with overstaffing and light-handed investments – all by trial and error. Fortunately, these mistakes were made at a time when the price of learning was not bankruptcy – which may well be a real risk in today's harsher economic climate.

Today, ChateauOnline is more seasoned and may even benefit from the forced focus caused by constrained financing. It has several months' (if not a whole year's) lead in being operational in multiple European markets, and it possesses skills that cannot be learned in a compressed timeframe, even if the competition invested more people and money in developing them. Also, as the European online market is more fragmented than that in the USA – the top ten online retailers in Europe account for only 26% of the market, whereas in the USA the top ten already held 43% in 1999 – ChateauOnline stands a good chance of participating in the upcoming consolidation game. Even though competition is fierce, the current fight is to build the market – consolidation has barely begun.

A centralized and integrated business model

ChateauOnline's operates an integrated, centralized Paris-based business system that allows for co-ordination and efficiency throughout the different steps of the value chain, even when handling multiple country markets (see Exhibit 7). It believes that this system allows it to maintain lean operations, uphold consistent standards and quality, and leverage the same skills, capabilities and concepts across Europe.

To ensure quality and acceptance of the wines sold, ChateauOnline has independent professional purchasers who source directly from abroad or domestic vineyards. Bypassing several layers of middlemen such as bottlers, wholesalers and importers, and cutting out their margins, allows ChateauOnline to act as an aggregator, squeezing out surplus from the value chain. As sales volumes are still small and the discounts received cannot be compared to those enjoyed by the large retailers, this streamlining creates room for end-customer discounts – something consumers have come to expect from Internet companies.

However, while the more strategic, customer-facing functions of purchasing, marketing, sales, customer service and the overarching IT platform have been kept under tight control, ChateauOnline has outsourced key parts of its value chain to logistics specialists, thus gaining speed and economies of scale. Danzas, Hays and UPS handle logistics to and from the company's warehouse in Paris. ChateauOnline owns many of the wines it lists but sells some under consignment for producers – some of which are stored at wineries, from where they are shipped directly. Centralization and low inventories enable easy, low-cost inventory management, crucial for a business with thousands of SKUs (stock-keeping units). (In contrast, Wine and Co. spread its warehouses across different countries and has recently withdrawn from some of its unprofitable foreign operations.[11]) ChateauOnline claims also to have benefited from having one central shipping location in France, because changing taxation and international regulation initially created arbitrage opportunities over domestic shipping in each target market. Competition has kept delivery costs low and, unlike some e-tailers, ChateauOnline has not attempted to make delivery a profit centre – perhaps wisely, as perceived high shipping costs are a key reason for abandoning Internet shopping carts.[12]

Marketing is the largest cost item for an e-tailer. Given tightening budgets, ChateauOnline (among others) has cut its mass-media advertising on TV and billboards and focuses on using public relations (PR) and variable cost marketing. An external PR agency has been hired to attract favourable free publicity. ChateauOnline also makes an active effort to partner with or place reciprocal long-term access buttons to suitable high-traffic online news sites, such as FT.com, Libération, Les Echos, Decanter and the main ISPs' homepages. Although banner ads are still used in seasonal campaigns, e.g. at Christmas, and ChateauOnline references itself regularly on European search engines and portal or directory sites, fixed sponsoring deals with large portals are passé.

---

11 'Interview with ChateauOnline' *Decanter*, February 2000.

12 McKinsey Internet Research, 'The race to scale', *McKinsey Quarterly*, April 2000.

Exhibit 7 **ChateauOnline's business system and value chain**

IT platform

Sourcing (suppliers)	Warehousing and logistics	Marketing and content	Sales and payment	Deliver and procurement	Customer service	After-sales (repeat)
• Professional purchasers who buy abroad and directly from vineyards; no wholesalers or importers involved	• Danzas inbound shipping • Hays inventory and service platform; all in Paris	• Little site customization except from central team • 1–3 people localize sites for content, pricing, site texts and product range • Local PR partnering and alliance management • Outsourced PR banner campaigns • Referencing • Buttons on partner sites • Webmiles • e-Newsletter • Deutsche BA frequent flyer club	• Effective purchasing but with complex add-ons (vouchers, promotional codes, etc.) • SuperMut security from Credit Mutuel	• Outsourced to UPS across EU and Switzerland • Break-even service where small orders subsidize large ones and cities subsidize remote delivery (fixed fee by region; different fees across area, e.g. within UK £5.99 and UK–EU £10.90) • 95% of deliveries are on time	• Multilingual call centre based in Paris • Usually e-mail but will call on critical occasion to rearrange shipping (e.g. Christmas wines)	• e-Newsletter (reminders)

Source: ChateauOnline interview.

Customer service is also centralized in Paris, where ChateauOnline employs multilingual agents to answer phone calls and e-mails. Although seemingly 'old-fashioned', the firm believes that sometimes calling the customer back may be a quicker way to find a replacement in case of a stock-out and has the added benefit of building brand and customer loyalty. Most customer response is handled via e-mail, however, and according to Helen Makin, Customer Service Manager, ChateauOnline customers find that the transaction, payment, order-processing and confirmation systems work well.

ChateauOnline's IT was initially designed as a state-of-the-art platform when cash was less scarce: 'It is sunk cost … now we have a fantastic infrastructure!' The centralized multilingual database is highly scalable and manageable. The localized site versions pick up different wine selections, also customized by price and tasting notes, to guarantee maximum competitiveness in the given environment. Although the maintenance burden increases as wine types, prices and regulatory issues, etc. need to be adapted for different locales, the database sub-categories can be managed centrally and all the IT-enabled operations remain more flexible, yet controlled, and cheaper than if the sites were separate.

Local and differentiated *vs.* global and controlled

ChateauOnline has the widest reach in Europe compared with its immediate competitors. The company derives over 50% of its sales outside its home market,

Exhibit 8 Cost breakdown of a bottle of wine (variable costs only)

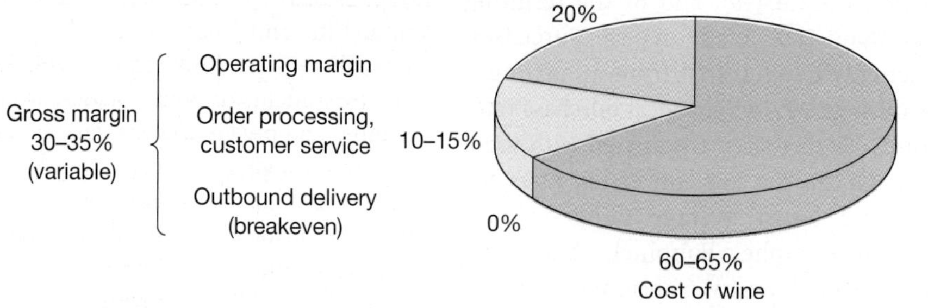

Source: ChateauOnline.

whereas the typical European retailer focuses solely on its domestic market.[13] Currently ChateauOnline has seven national sites but delivers throughout the EU and Switzerland. Five were developed as greenfield sites: France, UK, Germany, Switzerland and Belgium. The Dutch and Italian sites (www.lechateau.nl and www.vinoplease.it) were acquired. The Italian site, for example, stands out from the centralization policy in having its own warehouse from where a local selection is shipped. This has made integration more difficult. However, the rapid expansion of sites in local languages has allowed ChateauOnline to gain access to a larger potential consumer base than its competitors. It has also optimized its efforts by leveraging existing assets where cultural and language barriers can be overcome. For example, the Belgian site is modelled on the French and Dutch sites, the Irish site on the UK site, and the Swiss site on a combination of the French, German and Italian sites.

Furthermore, ChateauOnline has avoided attacking hopelessly small or difficult markets, such as the heavily regulated, sparsely populated and predominantly beer- and spirit-drinking Nordic countries, and Spain, where consumption is tilted towards restaurants and cafés rather than the home, and where the preferred domestic wines would have had to be double-shipped to Paris and back.

ChateuOnline's challenges

ChateauOnline's current and future challenges are related to the very viability of its business model: will European customers buy sufficient amounts of wine online? Will revenues be sufficient to generate profits? And, in the near term, will investors trust ChateauOnline's business judgement and finance its expansion and operations until profitability is reached?

Struggling to attract and retain customers

Examined qualitatively, ChateauOnline's position looks good. Nevertheless, when it comes to hard numbers, even with 4.5 million visits and 89–97% customer satisfaction, ChateauOnline produced revenues of just FF34 million in 2000 (up 2.9 times from 1999). Average order size was FF1200, with 35% repeat visitors purchasing on average 3.2 times a year. Voucher sales comprised 20% of the total. The problem is not variable costs, which are small enough to 'make money on all the orders' (see Exhibit 8). Such large purchases (with 15–25% operating margins) should be sufficient in the long term if combined with effective logistics, inventory and product-return management.[14] Rather, given that 80% of infrastructure cost is sunk and fixed costs are low, the greatest single expense facing ChateauOnline is marketing. Despite its best efforts at publicity, the implied conversion rate of only 0.1–0.7% of site visitors is simply not enough to support the business. Significant increases in volume are needed in the near future to cover marketing expenses and to keep the business going.

Purchase frequency and customer retention are the key drivers of e-tailer profitability – a 10% increase in conversion rate and repeat purchases has a direct impact of 10% improvement in the net present value of the e-tailer's cash flow. Also, the number of visitors and the revenues they generate drive capitalization in the stock market. In 1999, the e-tailers in McKinsey's

13 Total exports beyond national borders accounted for only 7% of European online retailers' revenue; exports out of Europe accounted for just 2%. Boston Consulting Group, 'The race for online riches: e-retailing in Europe', 2000.

14 J. Barsh, B. Crawford and C. Grosso, 'How e-tailing can rise from the ashes', *McKinsey Quarterly*, March 2000.

e-performance study had conversion rates of less than 4.5% (the lowest only 0.4%), and of the resulting shoppers less than 18% made repeat purchases. Conversion actually deteriorated from a maximum 4.5% to 2.5% during 1999, while repeat purchase rates improved from 10% to 18%.[15] Compared with these figures, ChateauOnline has low conversion rates but better loyalty and larger average purchase size. According to Christophe Poupinel, Marketing Director: 'We have good loyalty. Consumption in our target group is increasing. We can make them buy better quality and more products. We will have a larger share of their total purchasing.'

Competitive convergence

Not only is ChateauOnline hard-pressed to attract regular consumers, but it also faces competition from a handful of very similar start-ups: Wine and Co, 1855, Rouge et Blanc, MadAboutWine and, to a lesser extent, VinSurVins and ChateauNet. All its main pure-play competitors were founded between 1997 and 1999, often by students or wine fanatics, around whose personalities and preferences the business evolves. All offer a selection ranging from a few hundred to 4000 wines; MadAboutWine also features beer and spirits. Although the look and feel of the sites differ, their general features and value proposition are largely the same. (Table 2 and Exhibit 9 provide a snapshot of the main pure-play competitors.)

15 V. Agrawal, L. Arjana and R. Lemmens, 'e-Performance: the path to rational exuberance', *McKinsey Quarterly*, January 2001. J. D. Calkins, M. J. Farello, and C. Shi Smith, 'From retailing to e-tailing', *McKinsey Quarterly*, January 2000.

Table 2 **Comparison of competing sites** (usage features)

	ChateauOnline	Wine and Co	1855	Rouge et Blanc	MadAboutWine
Founded	1998	1999	1999 (end)	1997	1995/1999
Headquarters	France (UK)	France	France	France	UK
Management team	ESSEC, HBS students		HEC students France		Personalized around founders
Main offering	Wines (10 000 tasted, 1400 selection) Mixed cases Fine-wine cellar	Wines Mixed cases Fine wines	Wines (15 000) Fine wines	Wines (a few hundred) Mixed cases Fine wines Organic	Wines (4000) Mixed cases Fine wines Beers and spirits
Related products and services	Corporate gifts and baskets Corporate vouchers Gift shop Wine accessories Wedding services	Trade with corporations	Wine cellar Gifts under construction	Gifts Gift vouchers Wedding services (with planner)	Corporate accounts Gift shop
Presence	UK, Germany, France, Belgium, Switzerland, Netherlands, Italy (partners); Ireland advertised as upcoming	UK, Germany, France, Italy (Belguim, Singapore, Hong Kong, Japan, Netherlands upcoming)	France	France, UK, Germany	Japan, USA, UK, EU
Homepage	Special offers, ads Colourful, messy	Specials Empty, text-based Simple	Comprehensive, expert, small font, few pictures Structured	Flashy, messy Lots of text, huge pictures Difficult navigation	Easy to navigate, wealth of content, drawings

Table 2 continued

	ChateauOnline	Wine and Co	1855	Rouge et Blanc	MadAboutWine
Content	Sommelier's recommendations Nice, short news Feature articles Tip of the week Food-and-wine matching Links Prizes	Extensive tasting notes My Cellar Texts on wine, from basics to special Encyclopaedia Magazine FAQ	Descriptions of wines, with stars, temperature, age Usage statistics References to Hachette, etc. Food-and-wine matching under construction	Just wine descriptions	Not so detailed Lots of articles Expert advice on e-mail Recipes, food-and-wine matching Virtual wine-tasting class Party and cellar planning
Community	Food & Wine Champagne General, with fewer than six entries per month Expert's advice		Personalized account	Personalized account	Personalized account
Search	Inconsistent In addition to basic price, type, name, etc. also by region	Not functioning Also by grape, not region More countries	Excellent search, also by adjective (in addition to what all others offer)	Limited search	Good search
Browse	OK, size of category varies a lot	Through search	Great catalogue Step-wise, clear	Lists only	Through search, rather by category than catalogue
Commerce	Good, albeit a bit complex (vouchers, codes)	Simple, quick	Visa, MC, Amex	Complex, lots of codes and pages	Freight calculator
Payment	Visa, MC, EC Phone, fax, cheque	Visa, MC, Amex	SSL, Payline, Experian	Visa, MC, Amex	VISA, MC, others
Security	Credit Mutuel's Supermut security	SSL	49FF 10 days	SSL	SSL
Delivery	£5.99 in UK Throughout EU 7 days	£5 in UK, France, Italy, Germany 7 days	Press releases	£3.99/39FF (free) Across EU 3 days	£4.99 (Calculated) Worldwide 5–10 days
Promotional	Dossiers on regions Newsletter	Press section Newsletter and specials		Mailing list Wine Club	Mailing list
Club	Wine Club, not exclusive	Club Wine and Co			Wine Club

Table 2 **continued**

	ChateauOnline	Wine and Co	1855	Rouge et Blanc	MadAboutWine
Affiliation programme	Webmiles	Lots of deals, e.g. with Reuters, Yahoo!, Virgin Net Recommends, Freeserve, EMAP Online, X-Stream	Affiliate programme (aufemin, AOL.fr, Spray, La Tribune, Mageos, Caramail, MSN) Miles	Loyalty points	
Conclusion	Most commercial and communal, with widest reach, features and 'corners', but difficult to use	Simple, good learning tool for basics; more content on the art of wine making	Excellent advice and functionality; most technically advanced, with widest selection	'Plain vanilla', informal and hands-on; cheap and competes openly on price	Nicest and most entertaining to use, with lots of journalistic content; easy to enter and shop

Source: Case listing of features and analysis of sites, 18 February 2001, from the point of view of a new customer entering.

Exhibit 9 **Comparison of competing sites** (transaction sales revenues)

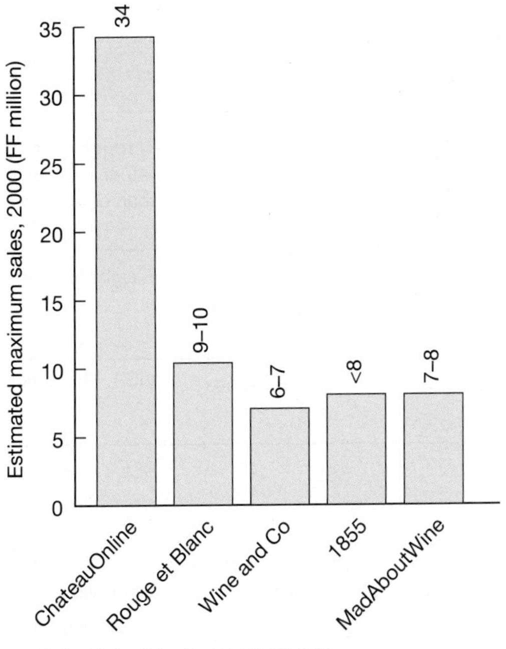

Source: ChateauOnline (interviews and public data).

Enter a powerful bricks-and-mortar incumbent

As the market gets crowded, some players will inevitably be marginalized and fail:

> It is a simple case of economics. Customer acquisition rates are way too high while too many companies are selling too little wine to too few people. There will be casualties ... Pure play is not sustainable at the moment.[16]

A big cause of casualties among start-ups is indeed the entry of traditional retailers. Bricks-and-mortar retailers already claim over two-thirds of European online retail and are expected to grab nearly 90% of it by 2005.[17] In France, Carrefour has launched its own site, verywine.com. As a dominant player on the supermarket and hypermarket scene, it has decided to gain a foothold in the specialist arena. Verywine features a complementary selection of specialist wines carefully avoiding overlap, price competition and thus cannibalization of Carrefour's in-store selection. The selection of 800 wines is expected to increase rapidly towards a target of 1200. Instead of sourcing from vineyards, Verywine relies on the Carrefour-owned bottler, the second largest in France, for preselection. The value proposition is to offer the same level of quality, advice and convenience as the

16 J. Stimpfig, 'Delivering net profit', *Decanter*, February 2001.

17 A. Leland, The cost of cross-border retail', *Forrester Research*, November 2000.

other sites – including two sommeliers – but to pair it up with Carrefour's familiar image and price discounts.

The imminent incumbent advantages that Verywine can count on are an established infrastructure, preferential supplier relations and pricing contracts and deep pockets to finance the venture. Likewise, it plans to leverage Carrefour's customer and credit-card databases and access to in-shop advertising, whereby it could reach well over 30% of all French households on a regular basis. Forty-three per cent of online shoppers prefer to buy from a site that has a physical store nearby,[18] a fact not lost on the Verywine managers. Other @Carrefour ventures, especially their successful U Shop concept, drive traffic. For example, when the @Carrefour sidebar was introduced, traffic to Verywine tripled. @Carrefour is building a newer, state-of-the-art IT platform for all its e-ventures and managing integrated customer accounts online. Verywine is patenting new revolutionary and customer-friendly features to be added to release 2.0, launched in summer 2001. Indeed, based on such factors, experts estimate the break-even point of a multichannel retailer is typically half that of its pure-play counterparts.[19]

Carrefour is not the only incumbent entering the online wine business. In the UK, the leading supermarket chain Tesco launched an 'e-grocer' business, including a 'wine warehouse' in 2000. By early 2001 this was seeing strong growth and receiving favourable press. Richard Branson's Virgin Group also created a wine e-tailer in 2000 (www.virginwines.com) and is looking to make acquisitions. Many specialist bricks-and-mortar wine retailers are also adding websites to their operations (e.g. www.oddbins.co.uk).

Show us the money

Until early 2000 the online wine industry was receiving more than enough venture capital funding[20] to cover the cost of expansion and operational losses. However, since then, euphoria and hype have been replaced by a cold dose of reality and an economic downturn. In the USA, the two leaders, Wine.com and WineShopper, merged and shed employees and soon after ran into near-bankruptcy with further lay-offs and a major restructuring. In Europe, WineShop folded and Wine and Co pulled out of its overseas ventures. The problems in the industry were exacerbated further by the cyclical nature of online sales,[21] making start-ups even more vulnerable to volatility in demand.

ChateauOnline may also be running out of time. Its aggressive expansion by acquisition is a thing of the past, its planned IPO in 2000 and ambitious overseas openings scheduled for 2001–02 were cancelled, personnel have been laid off, the launch of the second release of their website was delayed, and the company is struggling to convince its investors to finance the profitability gap. Notwithstanding, as ChateauOnline executives reviewed plans for the second quarter of 2001, there was room for considerable optimism. First-time sales continued to grow strongly, the website continued to receive plaudits, and more and more producers want to sell their wines through ChateauOnline. In comparison with many in this new industry, ChateauOnline was performing well.

Still, to prove to investors that its business model is viable and that the future is worth further investment, ChateauOnline needs to make a quantum leap, first in addressing the problems of conversion rates and margins, and second in demonstrating a definitive leadership position in the European market. If this could be done, then ChateauOnline would be very well placed to expand along with the growing European B2C market.

---

18 'Lessons from the online war for customers', *Harvard Management Update*, December 2000.

19 J. Barsh, B. Crawford and C. Grosso, 'How e-tailing can rise from the ashes', *McKinsey Quarterly*, March 2000

20 In spring 2000, six US online wine retailers received over US$200 million in pre-IPO funding rounds. 'The online wine players', *Upside*, April 2000; at the same time, LVMH invested FF100 million in Wine and Co in Europe.

21 30% of online retail in Europe takes place in the Christmas holidays. A. Leland 'Europe's retailers ring in the holiday season', *Forrester Research*, November 2000.

DISCUSSION QUESTIONS

1. What is the consumer decision process for buying wine and how well does the online model fit with this process? Which do you think are the segments with most potential for ChateauOnline? What value proposition does ChateauOnline provide to your target segment/s?
2. How well does the ChateauOnline website deliver this value proposition? How well does the site suit 'wine lovers'? How does it compare with that of other start-ups such as MadAboutWine (www.madaboutwine.com), Rouge et Blanc (www.rouge-blanc.com), or Wine and Co (www.wineandco.com)? Examining actual sites will give you a better sense for structure and interactivity than the case exhibits. How should we compare sites? Overall, how well would you rate ChateauOnline?
3. Does ChateauOnline have sustainable advantages, and from which capabilities of the firm do these derive? Where has ChateauOnline done well in developing its capabilities and where has it not?
4. Is there a viable market position for ChateauOnline to occupy longer-term – one that can provide an economically adequate return on the capital invested? What are the economies for ChateauOnline's partners?

Banking on the Internet

The Advance Bank in Germany

Walking through the bank's call centre in Munich on 28 March 1998, the two-year anniversary day of the bank, Volker Visser was wondering what suggestions he could make to the other members of the executive board of Advance Bank at their next business-strategy meeting. As he observed some agents answering customer calls, he wondered how to manage customer relationships better and whether new technological capabilities could be used effectively to create value in an electronic world. He knew that with the intensifying competition in the branch-less banking sector, his direct bank needed to customize further the financial advice it offered, especially if it wanted to achieve its goal of 250 000 customers by the year 2001. While recognizing the tasks that lay ahead in order to achieve that goal, he thought that the uniqueness of the Advance Bank concept would still be a strong competitive weapon in the marketplace:

> Marketing and winning over customers who fit our target profile is our key challenge. We are not afraid of current competitors or new entrants because we believe [that] we have a niche and a differentiated quality service ... Brick-and-mortar branches don't have a future. Why should the customer keep paying for their fancy branches in prime locations and for their large staff payroll, while dealing with restricted opening hours and lousy service quality?

The banking industry in Germany

The banking industry in Germany is dominated by large universal banks that offer comprehensive banking services to both private and corporate customers. Unlike in other financial systems, such as in the USA, German universal banks are allowed to offer both commercial and investment banking services. In order to exploit economies of scale and synergies, and to build global scale, many German banks have merged with one another. The largest bank merger in Germany took place in 1997, when the two Bavarian banks Vereinsbank and Bayerische Hypotheken und Wechselbank (Hypo-Bank) decided to join forces and create a single bank. Today, there are four major universal banks operating in Germany: Deutsche Bank, Vereinsbank/Hypo-Bank, Dresdner Bank and Commerzbank.

A central feature of the German banking industry is the strong link between banks and companies from other industries. For example, Deutsche Bank owns over 20% of Daimler Benz (valued at DM15 billion) and 10% of the insurance company Allianz (valued at DM10 billion). Allianz, on the other hand, owns 22% of Dresdner Bank.

Two important events have marked recent developments in the German banking industry. The first event, which took place on 1 July 1990, was the federal monetary union that integrated the states of the former German Democratic Republic into the West German monetary system. The inclusion of the five new *Bundeslaender* (states) opened up new market opportunities and motivated almost all banks to

---

This case was written by Professor Tawfik Jelassi, Dean of Academic Affairs, Euro-Arab Management School, Granada, and Albrecht Enders, Research Assistant from the Leipzig Graduate School of Management, Germany. The latter spent a research term at the Euro-Arab Management School. It is intended to be used as the basis for class discussion rather than to illustrate either effective or ineffective handling of a management situation.

The case was made possible by the co-operation of Advance Bank, Germany.

open branches in these states. The second important event was the launch of the European Monetary Union (EMU), which established, on 1 January 1999, the Euro as the single currency within the 11 European Union (EU) member states that had so far been admitted in the EMU.[1]

A second major trend in the banking industry in Germany is the rationalization of bank branches and the staff reduction that often results from it. Deutsche Bank, for instance, intended to cut the number of employees by 4100 by the year 2001 and to close 200–300 of its current 1600 branches. The German Employees Union foresees that overall staff reductions might amount to a loss between 100 000 and 140 000 positions during the coming years. To a large extent, this trend results from an increasing use of technology in banking, which is illustrated by the widespread use of automatic teller machines (ATMs), money-transfer terminals and direct banking institutions.

The competitive environment in direct banking

In 1996, the direct banking market in Germany was divided into two categories. First, traditional banks offered telephone banking delivery channels, built as extensions to their branch network, which provided increased availability for the customer beyond traditional business hours. In 1989, Citibank had launched a telephone banking service, and other banks (such as Postbank and Vereinsbank) had followed with a similar service. In 1994, the Direkt Anlage Bank started a discount brokerage, offering cheap transactions with only limited advice to the knowledgeable investor. The discount brokerage service was also appealing to other banks with a branch network, since the risk of cannibalization was considered to be low, thus allowing the branch network to co-exist with the new direct banking channel. Therefore, many traditional German retail banks, such as Commerzbank (with Comdirect), Berliner Bank (with Bank Girotel) and Deutsche Bank (with Bank24), started a direct banking service limited to discount brokerage services. In order to get a full range of banking services, customers still had to go to a traditional branch-based bank.

The strategic intent of Vereinsbank's new direct bank (called Advance Bank) was to go beyond the above-mentioned categories. It aimed instead at offering a full range of banking services and extensive investment advice through the telephone and later through the Internet.

In early 1998, direct banks in Germany had, cumulatively, 1.8 million customers. Market studies suggested that of the current 63 million customers of German banks, ten million were interested in direct banking; however, only three million customers intended to switch to direct banking in the near future. Commenting on this competitive environment, Hans Jürgen Raab, Member of the Executive Board at Advance Bank, said:

> The direct banking market is growing quickly, but not as fast as there are new competitors entering the market. In the spring of 1996, there were eight direct banks; today [in January 1998] there are already 39. About one third of them won't survive.

Vereinsbank's direct banking strategy

Vereinsbank is a large, regional bank in Germany with 22 000 employees and 770 branches nationwide. The branches are located mainly in Bavaria (the southern part of the country) and in the Hamburg area (in the northern part), with a few scattered branches in the rest of the country (see Exhibit 1). In 1993, the Vereinsbank board decided that in order to stay competitive and attract a larger customer base, it was necessary to expand the scope of the bank's operations to other parts of Germany. One possible option to achieve this goal was physically to expand the branch network to the central part of Germany; however, this option was discarded because of the high costs associated with it (a single branch would have cost DM1–3 million annually). The additional branch network of 100–200 branches needed to reach enough customers would have been too expensive. A second problem that needed to be addressed was the 'over-age' customer base of Vereinsbank, with a disproportionately large number of customers aged 50 years and above (see Exhibit 2).

In order to address these issues, Vereinsbank decided to launch a direct (branch-less) bank to offer ubiquitous access throughout Germany (via the telephone, letter, fax, PC and Internet) and to attract a younger customer

1 These member states are Austria, Belgium, Finland, France, Germany, Ireland, Italy, Luxembourg, the Netherlands, Portugal and Spain.

Exhibit 1 Vereinsbank's branch network in Germany

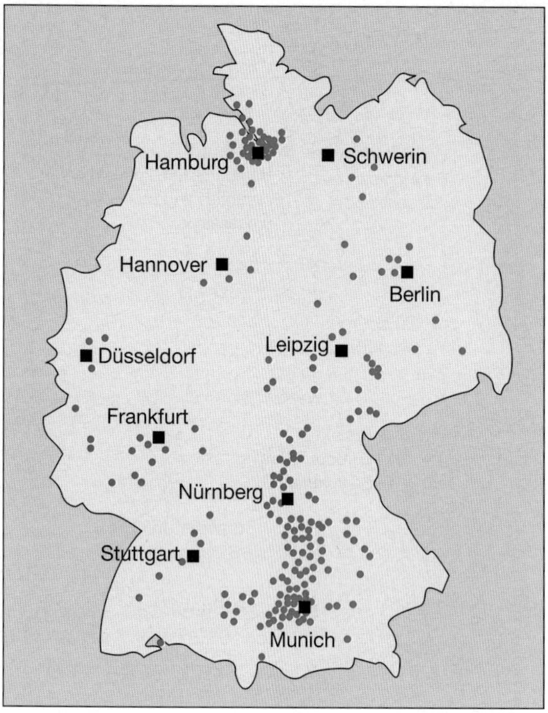

Source: Advance Bank.

base. In 1994, a feasibility study for the direct bank project was conducted, and it was agreed that the design and implementation of the new bank should be completed in just two years. Andersen Consulting was then selected to provide the required know-how and personnel. The three main challenges were: (1) to build from scratch a completely new banking system; (2) to align this system with the newly defined business processes; and (3) to implement this system within a completely new organization. Tasks allocated to Andersen Consulting included conducting a pre-study, designing the system, acting as general contractor for the system implementation, and training the personnel. Because of the new banking concept, Andersen consultants had to design by themselves large parts of the required software and hardware. During peak periods in the development process, over 100 Andersen consultants worked on the direct bank project at a total cost of over DM50 million.

In December 1996, the new direct bank employed 269 people,[2] 40% of whom had an academic degree and 55% a banking or business educational

2 This number includes part-time workers.

Exhibit 2 Vereinsbank's customer base

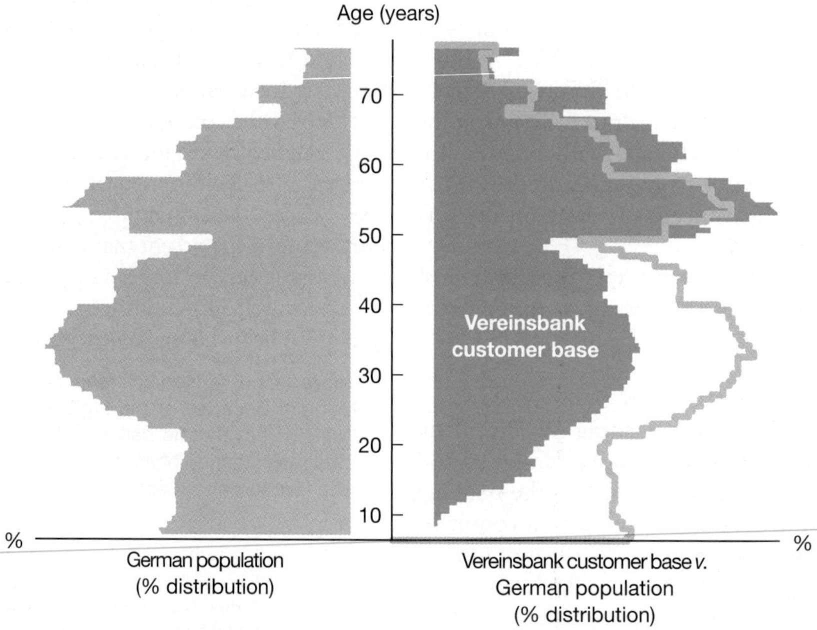

Source: Adapted from Advance Bank material.

background. In 1997, after the merger of the parent company Vereinsbank and Hypobank, Advance Bank was sold to Dresdner Bank, which is now the sole owner of Advance Bank.

The advent of a virtual bank

> We wanted to be the first direct bank in Germany that offers value-added service in terms of price-performance, [customer advice] objectivity, and convenience.
>
> **Frank Spreier, Manager, Organization and IT, Advance Bank**

Choosing a name for the virtual bank

When looking for a name for the new bank, many possibilities were considered, including 'First Choice' and 'Bank High 3'. However, they had to be discarded later because the name was either already patented or not accepted outside Germany, or there were some laws against using a particular name. Eventually, the bank's marketing group was left with only two choices: 'Quantum' and 'Advance Bank'. Volker Visser commented:

> During the first two years of the project, we thought it would be easy to find the right name for the bank, so we didn't think too much about it. That was a mistake.

Finally, the name selected was 'Advance Bank' because the word 'advance' (which was an artificially created word since it is missing the 'd' at the end) was thought to convey best the new bank's philosophy of being future-oriented and forward-looking. Another important advantage was that the first two letters of the name (i.e. 'a' followed by 'd') put the name at the beginning of almost any alphabetically ordered list. This characteristic will become more important as the Internet expands, since browsers typically sort their hits alphabetically.

The name for the new bank was then protected worldwide to keep open the possibility for an eventual international expansion of the business.

Key features of Advance Bank

An important feature distinguishing Advance Bank from other direct banks is that it was designed and built from scratch without relying on the banking infrastructure and products of the parent company. This independence, combined with advanced information technology, enabled Advance Bank to create a virtual bank that could source its services and products from different financial services providers spread out all over Germany (see Exhibit 3). When choosing a partner, Advance Bank looks throughout Germany for the best provider of a given financial service or product. Applying this best-of-breed strategy has resulted in having the individual parts of Advance Bank service assembled by different companies spread out all over the country. The bank's headquarters and main call centre are located in Munich; another call centre is in Wilhelmshaven (in northern Germany), an area where the unemployment rate is at 16%.[3] Furthermore, the accent that is spoken in that area of Germany is easy to understand, which facilitates the search for well-suited call agents. Regarding the selection of Wilhelmshaven, Volker Visser said:

> There is no reason to have all the call centres in Munich. Because of the high unemployment rate in Wilhelmshaven, the call agent salary is on average 29% lower than in Munich. This makes a big difference when we talk about costs.

Exhibit 3 Advance Bank: a virtual organization

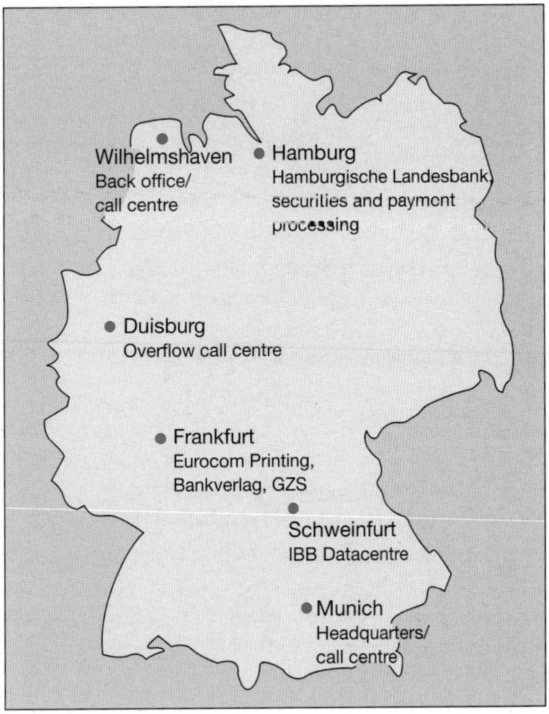

Source: Advance Bank.

3 Before choosing Wilhelmshaven, Advance Bank considered for its second call centre 29 possible locations, which were assessed based on 220 quantitative and qualitative criteria including availability of qualified personnel, wages, government subsidies, and real-estate prices.

IBB, a subsidiary of IBM, in Schweinfurt maintains the mainframe computer data.[4] Eurocom Printing in Frankfurt prints all letters and statements and distributes them together with brochures and leaflets. GZS, also located in Frankfurt, processes all incoming Euro-card statements, while the Hamburgische Landesbank (HaLaBa) in Hamburg processes securities and payments.

In order to integrate all of the above services provided by the different companies, a custom-designed front end of Advance Bank was necessary. A highly integrated, seamless interface with the customer has therefore been created, which gives the customer the impression of dealing with just one institution.

Security system

In order to ensure that customer information is kept confidential and secure at all times, Advance Bank relies on a complex security system. Upon opening an account with the bank, the customer receives a personal identification number (PIN) and a computer- generated six-digit secret code. Every time the customer accesses their account by telephone or Internet, they are first requested to provide their PIN; then, the bank's computer system asks randomly for three numbers from the customer's secret six-digit code (e.g. the first, the fourth and the fifth digits). Marc Hemmerling, an Advance Bank customer, explained:

> I am more concerned about security when I leave my credit-card number with the waiter in a restaurant or with the cashier at the gas station. I believe that the Advance Bank security system is reasonably safe.

This security system is used for two reasons. First, to ensure that even if someone were to intercept the customer message to the bank, then they would not have all the required information allowing them to access the account. Second, this system ensures also that even the call-centre agent handling the customer's call cannot know the customer's complete authorization code. An illustrative phone conversation between a call-center agent and a customer, with the relevant identification procedure, is shown below:

Claudia (Advance Bank agent): Advance Bank. Good evening. How may I help you?

Hr Schmitt (customer): Hello. This is Herr Schmitt. I would like to make a transaction.

Claudia: Would you please tell me your personal number, Herr Schmitt?

Hr Schmitt: My [personal] number is 92466503.

Claudia: Thank you. Then I also need the first, second and fourth digits of your authorization code.

Hr Schmitt: 9, 4 and 2.

Claudia: Thank you. Your account information is now being loaded into my PC, this will take a second. How much money would you like to transfer?

Hr. Schmitt: 2000 marks.

Claudia: 2000 marks. Which account do you want to transfer this money to?

Hr Schmitt: Account number: 1800 252191.

Claudia: And the number of the corresponding bank?

Hr Schmitt: 860 555 92.

Claudia: Who is the recipient?

Hr Schmitt: Thomas Schmitz.

Claudia: Thank you. 2000 marks will be credited to account number 1800 252191 at the Stadt und Kreissparkasse Leipzig. The recipient is Thomas Schmitz.

Hr Schmitt: Excellent. Thank you very much.

Claudia: Is this all you need?

Hr Schmitt: Actually, I also need 1000 US dollars in traveller checques.

Claudia: No problem. Shall I send the [traveller] cheques to your home address?

Hr Schmitt: Yes, provided that I get them before my trip to New York, which will be at the end of next week.

Claudia: You should receive them in three to four days. Do you need anything else, Herr Schmitt?

Hr Schmitt: No, thank you.

Claudia: You're welcome. Goodbye!

A few weeks later, Herr Schmitt called back Advance Bank. After being greeted by the call-centre agent and being authenticated through the identification procedure (explained above), the following dialogue took place:

Peter (Advance Bank agent): I hope that your visit to the US went well, Herr Schmitt. I heard that there was a major snow storm on the east coast [of the USA].

4 Initially, Advance Bank considered using the data centre of its parent company Vereinsbank. However, since this centre could not provide the required 24-hour accessibility, Advance Bank looked for another provider.

Hr Schmitt: Yes, indeed. However, I was quite lucky, since I left New York before the start of that storm.

Peter: I am glad you did! How can I help you this morning?

Within the bank, there are also various security systems to ensure that only authorized personnel can obtain and manipulate customer data. Depending on their user class, every call-centre agent works at a desktop with access to specific software applications. Every time they want to use one of these applications, they have to enter their user ID number and their personal password. When a call-centre agent wants to contact a customer, they must first provide a word code (already specified by the customer) to prove their identity to the customer.[5]

The above-mentioned security system seems to work well, since two years after its launch Advance Bank has had no security-related incident in carrying out its operations. However, in case a customer authorization code falls into the wrong hands, Advance Bank is liable for 100% of all damages, provided the customer informs the bank about it as soon as it has happened. If the customer does not find out about the misuse or does not notify the bank on time, then their maximum liability is only 10% of the caused damage; thus, personal risk is minimized.

Advance Bank's marketing strategy

Market positioning

We need to differentiate our bank from our competitors. Eventually, we will only be able to capture our target customer group if we can establish a well-known brand with a differentiated appearance and a clear profile.

Hans Jürgen Raab

An important marketing issue was to define the customer group that Advance Bank should target. The options were to offer either products that do not require financial advice (such as discount brokerage) or those that necessitate the bank's expertise. A marketing study showed that only 500 000 potential customers would be able to do their personal banking without any advice. Furthermore, the discount brokerage market was already crowded with players such as Bank24 and Comdirect bank. Advance Bank has thus carved a niche for itself by offering investment advice, hence targeting customers who are interested in joining a direct bank and who want to receive personalized advice.

Advance Bank targets the so-called 'individual customer' (IK) who typically earns more than DM5000 per month, owns or rents a house, lives in an urban area, enjoys sports and culture, and is self-employed, a freelancer or an executive (see Exhibit 4). Although this group represents only 17% of the potential customer population, it generates for the bank an average annual profit of DM2400 per customer. The other two groups consist of 'universal customers' (UK), who represent 80% of potential customers but generate an average profit of DM650 annually, and 'private investors' (PI), who generate an annual average profit of only DM5000 but who represent a mere 2% of the potential customer population. Additional information on the profiles of Advance Bank customers is provided in Exhibit 5.

5 Upon dialling the customer's telephone number, the call-centre agent can access on their PC that customer's password if, and only if, the customer picks up the phone. The call agent then asks whether they have the customer themselves on the phone; only then does the agent identify themselves as an Advance Bank employee and give the customer the word code.

Exhibit 4 Profile of the typical Advance Bank customer

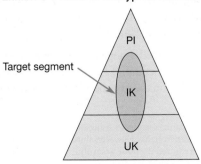

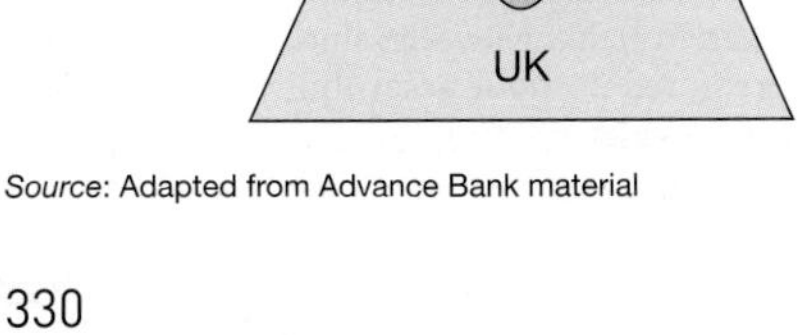

Age: 25–49 years
Education: high-school graduate and higher qualifications
Profession: self-employed, freelancer, executive
Income: >DM5000 net/month
Resident: urban areas (>200 000 population)
Housing conditions: tenant/owner of house
Hobbies: sports, culture
Other characteristics: high mobility (frequent traveller, etc.)

Source: Adapted from Advance Bank material

Exhibit 5 Adance Bank customer profiles (January 1997)

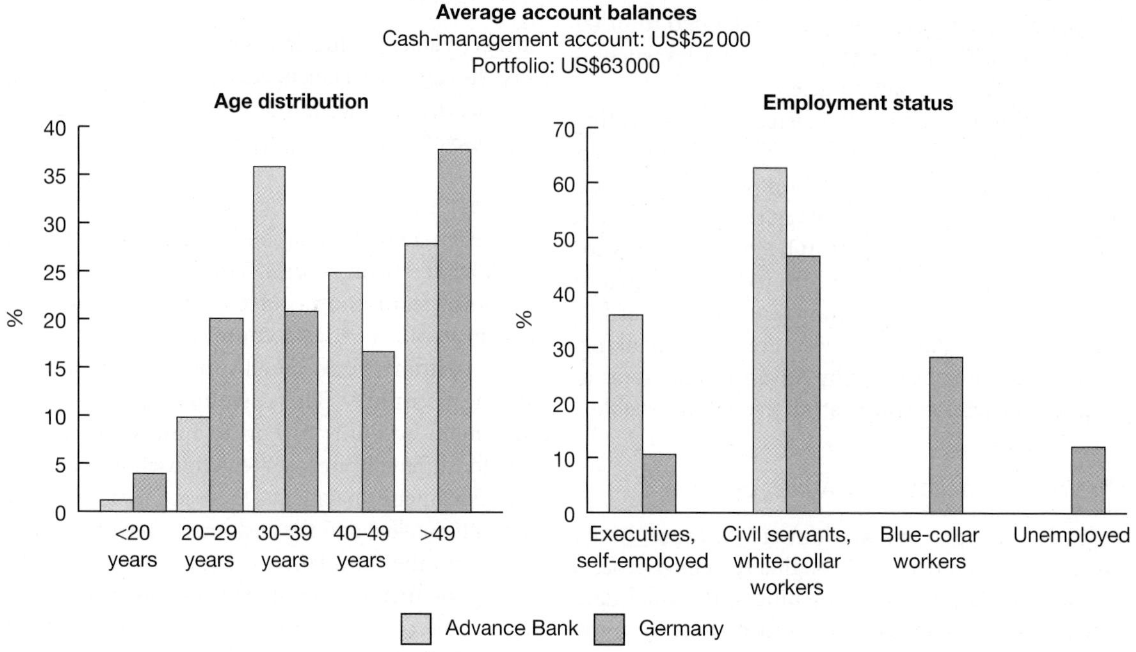

Source: Advance Bank.

Promotion and advertisement campaigns

In order to attract its target customer group, Advance Bank first started a direct mailing campaign to potential customers informing them in detail about the bank's product line. Besides being very expensive (due to the printed material and postage), these campaigns did not achieve much impact, since the 'Advance Bank' brand name was not yet known to the public. In the autumn of 1996, the bank had to stop all advertisement campaigns due to budget constraints. This action did not help to strengthen the brand name, especially at a time when the public had just started to take notice of the bank. In total, DM44 million was spent on marketing in 1996, of which DM22 million went into traditional advertising.

Having learned from the above mistakes, Advance Bank devised a new marketing strategy along two dimensions. First, a brand-image campaign was launched to make the name more known to the public. Part of this campaign was based on the sponsoring of the weather forecast during the nightly news programme 'Heute' on ZDF,[6] one of the most popular news broadcasts in Germany. The advertisement consisted of a short cartoon focusing only on the Advance Bank brand name; including more information would have been too expensive for the bank. Similar advertisements also appeared in other programmes (such as N-TV), which are popular among the above-mentioned target group. Second, a content advertisement campaign was launched through several high-quality German newspapers and news magazines aiming at conveying the benefits that customers can accrue through Advance Bank.

Acquiring new customers at Advance Bank

As of May 1998, Advance Bank had a customer base of 79 000 people. This relatively small number of customers resulted partly from the difficulty of pitching promotion campaigns at the desired target group and the high advertising costs involved.[7] To overcome these problems, Advance Bank has considered new ways of reaching potential customers, such as offering special rates to companies whose employees match the profile of the Advance Bank target customer. Companies that were first considered

6 ZDF is one of the two public television networks in Germany.
7 Each newly acquired customer costs on average DM600.

included those that were already co-operating with Advance Bank, such as Andersen Consulting and CompuNet.[8] This offer was later extended to other companies with similar employee profiles, such as McKinsey, Microsoft and Oracle.

Another approach has consisted of co-operating with other non-bank companies that offer products complementary to Advance Bank's financial products; this included the technology retailer TELIS and the Internet service provider AOL.[9] Through this co-operation, customers are offered a low-priced package solution (containing an ISDN[10] card, a modem and the Internet service) for online banking. This package is subsidized by Advance Bank so as to make online banking more attractive and accessible.

Opening an account at Advance Bank

In order to open an account at Advance Bank, prospective customers go through a screening process that assesses their credit-worthiness. Personal data (such as the income tax form, information from the SCHUFA,[11] marital status and employment) are used to rate them. This rating is necessary to reduce the loan default risk of new customers who, upon joining the bank, instantly receive a credit line of DM30 000.[12] Ninety-four per cent of all applicants pass the screening process; of the remaining 6%, half of them typically choose to make the required time deposit of DM30 000 and become customers of the bank.

Upon requesting the application material (through the Internet, phone, fax or mail), prospective clients receive a package including information about Advance Bank's products and services as well as the application form. Walter Klein, a new customer at Advance Bank, commented:

> Before choosing my direct bank, I requested information packages from both Advance Bank and Bank24. In the end, I found the Advance Bank offer more convincing.

The prospective client fills out the application form, attaches the income tax file as proof of income, puts these documents into a blue envelope (included in the package) and seals it. This envelope is then given to the post office, where the prospective customer presents their passport to a clerk as proof of identity. The post office forwards this envelope to Advance Bank.[13] Upon passing this screening, the customer receives from Advance Bank a confirmation letter containing the six-digit secret code mentioned earlier.

Advance Bank product portfolio and price/performance

Advance Bank's product line consists of two main products: the cash management account and the investment fund service. In addition to these products, Advance Bank also offers insurance and retirement funds.

The cash management account

The cash management account is the central piece of the Advance Bank service. This account offers the combined features of a current (chequing) account and those of a savings account; i.e. the availability of the customer funds at all times and an interest-bearing account.[14] The customer can sub-divide their main account into up to nine sub-accounts used for different purposes (e.g. household, car, rent, etc.). For interest payments, these accounts are automatically totalled and the customer receives (or pays) interest on the cumulative balance of both accounts. During the first quarter of 1998, the interest that the bank applied was 3.3% on deposits and 8.75% on loans. Philip Torsten, who has been a customer at Advance Bank since its creation, explained:

> Advance Bank charges more but also offers more service than other direct banks. I don't want to be checking the balance of my current account every two weeks to make sure that I don't have money sitting idle there that should better be put into an interest-bearing account. At the same time, I don't lose any interest whatsoever, and I don't end up paying interest for overdrawing one of my sub-accounts. This [service] is very important for me.

Customers can choose between the standard cash management account (which allows up to 50 free transactions per quarter) and the cash management account plus (which allows up to 150 free transactions

8 CompuNet delivers computer hardware equipment to Advance Bank.
9 AOL stands for America On Line.
10 ISDN (integrated services digital network) is capable of handling data, voice, text and image transmission over the same communication line.
11 SCHUFA, (Schutzgemeinschaft für allgemeines Kreditwesen) records the credit history of bank customers and provides this information to banks when customers want to open up a new account.
12 DM10 000 for each account, the Visa card and the Euro-Cheque card.
13 The German law requires every bank to confirm the customer's identity before opening an account.
14 In January 1997, the average account balance was the equivalent of US$52 000.

per quarter). A Eurocard Gold or a Visa Gold credit card (offering withdrawals of up to DM6000 per week) and a Euro-Cheque card (with withdrawals of up to DM5000 per week) are given free of charge once the account is opened.

Following an agreement with a group of German private banks (including Deutsche Bank and Commerzbank), Advance Bank allows its customers to use all the ATMs (which total 6000 in Germany) of these banks free of charge. In addition, Advance Bank customers have free access to all the ATMs of Vereinsbank, Hypo-Bank and Dresdner Bank. Furthermore, customers can also withdraw cash at any ATM in Germany (38 000 ATMs in total), and Advance Bank will reimburse each customer up to DM30 of ATM fees per quarter.

At the end of each month, each Advance Bank customer receives by postal mail a financial report (in an A4 format) containing detailed information on all transactions as well as changes in their main account and sub-accounts. Additionally, the customer is immediately informed when an incoming transfer that exceeds DM20 000 or an outgoing transfer of more than DM10 000 is made.

Every month, Advance Bank charges its customers a flat fee of DM16 if they hold a cash management account and DM28 if they have a cash management plus account. However, if a customer has a cumulative annual charge to their credit card of over DM8000, then the monthly fee is reduced to, respectively, DM13.50 or DM25. If this cumulative annual charge exceeds DM25 000, then the fee is waived for the cash management account holder, while it is lowered to DM12 for the cash management plus account holder.

Investment fund service

Through its investment fund selection service, Advance Bank offers 'objective' advice for selecting investment funds. In contrast with most other banks, which primarily sell their own funds to their customers, Advance Bank uses the expertise and experience of the Feri Trust investment specialists. Based on the information they receive, Advance Bank's financial consultants select the 50 best-performing funds out of a group of 2700 and recommend to the customer an individual portfolio strategy that takes into account personal investment goals, return and risk preferences, and the customer's tax situation, so as to maximize after-tax returns. Customers can choose from five different strategies:

- DM conservative;
- Germany conservative;
- international growth;
- international chance;
- European growth.

In addition to sending its customers a monthly market assessment and a personalized analysis of their portfolio, Advance Bank also sends up-to-date buying and selling recommendations. The fee the bank charges for managing the customer's asset portfolio is DM79 per year, regardless of the portfolio size. In January 1997, the average balance of a customer portfolio was the equivalent of US$63 000. Volker Visser commented on the average balances of the portfolio and of the cash management account:

> When you look at these average balances, you see that we are doing fine quality-wise. But we are not doing so well quantity-wise, and we need to increase the number of [Advance Bank] customers.

Advance Bank price/performance

To compensate for the fees it charges, which are higher than those of other direct banks, Advance Bank aims at offering a uniquely differentiated value through its all-inclusive banking services as well as its high customer service satisfaction. For example, before a trip abroad, a customer may deposit at the bank copies of important personal documents such as their passport; if one of these documents is lost or stolen, then Advance Bank would fax the customer a copy of it and also provide money within 24 hours. If a customer gets ill while abroad, they can contact the Bank's medical consultation service, where multilingual doctors are on call around the clock to give advice over the phone and, if necessary, to arrange for transportation back to Germany. Furthermore, to cover emergencies while abroad, customers receive up to 62 days of free insurance coverage, which fully covers treatment and medication costs and allows the customer to consult the doctor of their choice. All of the above-listed services are free for customers with a cash management account at the Advance Bank.

Advance Bank also decided to give the same benefits, including a free Euro-Cheque card, to heterosexual and homosexual couples when they open a

joint current account.[15] The bank's service quality is monitored constantly, and each customer complaint is answered within 24 hours. If the latter is not met, then the bank sends the customer a compensation gift (e.g. a jazz CD). In order to enhance service quality, complaints are tracked for each customer and aggregated under six categories: service, bank's appearance, competence, reliability, customer treatment and product range. These complaint records are also analyzed when designing new applications and processes or training call-centre agents.

Volker Visser elaborated on the price/performance issue at Advance Bank:

> We offer quality to our customers. We have to pay for quality and our customers are willing to pay us for this quality because in the end they profit from it. Our customers are not so much interested in low fees. They want the best information they can get to help them make money [by] investing into the funds we recommend to them. They don't care about the extra three marks that we charge for our services. If they did, they would do discount brokerage with another [direct] bank.

The call centre: the heart of Advance Bank

Since the call-centre agent is the only Advance Bank employee who has direct contact with the customer, special attention was given to the set-up of the call centre during the bank's design and implementation stages. The goal was to reach a high level of service quality by combining well-trained call-centre agents and sophisticated information technology to make the customer's banking experience as convenient, pleasant and efficient as possible.[16] This was done in order to remedy problems of traditional bricks-and-mortar branches such as these described below by Susanne Meier, another Advance Bank customer:

> When I was still a customer of a bricks-and-mortar bank, I had to deal with lots of incompetent people, who weren't able to help me out. In order to get hold of competent bank agents, I was often sent from one branch to the next before I got the service I wanted. Restricted opening hours also really got to me, especially during weekends when I would have had the time to sit down and do my banking. Now, every time I call up Advance Bank I receive good and qualified service quickly.

Key features of the call-centre architecture include:

- *Availability.* IT supports operations 24 hours a day, seven days a week (actual availability is at 99.91% of the time).
- *High service level.* 85% of all calls are answered within 15 seconds.
- *Personalized service.* Human contact is offered at all times.
- *Assured security.* All customer calls are recorded, and there is a secure customer verification.
- *Open architecture.* Standard hardware and software components are used.
- *Scalability.* The system can support up to 250 000 customers and beyond.
- *Interconnected call centres.* Incoming calls are routed automatically to available call-centre agents, independent of their geographical location.
- *Adequate technical support.* On-site service is offered within four hours for critical components.
- *Outbound dialling.*
- *Management reports.*

IT support for the call-centre

> We spend about 20–30% of the bank's budget on IT. This may sound exaggerated but it is not.
>
> **Frank Spreier**

Advance Bank call centres, located in Munich and Wilhelmshaven (with a staff of, respectively, 100 and 150 call agents), receive all incoming calls from current and prospective customers from 7.00 a.m. to 10.00 p.m., seven days a week.[17] Depending on availability, the automatic call distributor (ACD) routes the incoming call to the least occupied call centre. In order to optimize the call centres' utilization while reducing the wait time for incoming calls, Advance Bank designed a support system for the call centres that provides information on typical call frequencies (e.g. the breakdown of calls per day, week or month). The system also forecasts changes in call frequencies caused by special promotions, TV advertisements, mailings and newspaper/magazine articles, thus allowing the human resources manager efficiently to schedule personnel and to foresee possible bottlenecks.

15 The bank does not require homosexual couples to provide proof of their relationship.

16 Advance Bank was awarded the Grand Prix Customer Service Award for being the best call centre in Germany in 1997.

17 Calls coming in during night hours are rerouted to an overflow call centre located in Duisburg.

Exhibit 6 User interface of the integrated computer–telephony application

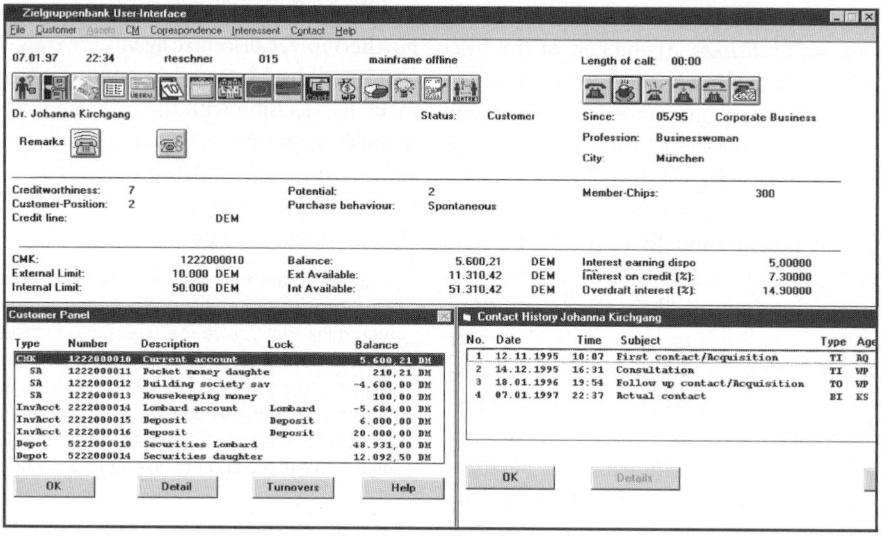

Call-centre agents work in teams of five to six members, with each agent using a multi-task workstation (with a large display screen) to access all relevant data while talking to the customer. The workstation integrates the functions of a PC and those of a telephone through a UNIX-based CTI[18] platform. It allows the call-centre agent to receive calls without having to pick up the receiver and simultaneously to transfer calls and call-related information to other agents in the call centre. Furthermore, the agent can place calls without having to dial, but simply by clicking on the customer's name on the screen. The agent can then talk to the customer through a headphone speaker set, which is connected to the computer workstation.[19]

Customer information

Upon receiving a call, the call-centre agent first enters the customer's personal identification number and the three digits provided by the customer from their security code. A pop-up menu is then displayed on the screen, which allows the agent to access and, if need be, modify the customer's personal account information (see Exhibit 6). The information includes:

- *Customer contact information*, such as home/office e-mail addresses and phone and fax numbers, as well as preferred contact times.
- *Customer credit rating*, which Advance Bank assigns to each customer in order to determine their credit line and the interest rate at which they can borrow money. This rating is first given to the customer when they open an account; it is then updated monthly based on the customer's transactions and other account activities.
- *Record of previous contacts*. When talking to the customer, the call agent can also view a detailed list of the past contacts the customer has had with the bank. This list shows the time and date of each contact, the name of the call-centre agent who handled the call, the issue discussed, and any other relevant comments that the agent deemed important to record.
- *Customer lifestyle*. The call-centre agent may also record customer lifestyle information. For instance, if a customer tells the agent that they need to withdraw $1000 in traveller cheques for a vacation in the USA, then the call-centre agent notes in the lifestyle information column that this customer likes travelling. Similarly, there are columns for musical taste, other cultural preferences, etc. Another column informs the call agent about individual customer characteristics, e.g. a hearing problem, so that each agent can take these

18 Through CTI (computer–telephony integration), databases are linked to the incoming call, allowing the call-centre agent quickly to access the file of the customer at hand.

19 For security reasons, all customer calls are recorded automatically.

characteristics into account when dealing with that customer the next time.

- *Customer likes and dislikes.* At the end of the first three months with the bank, every new customer receives the 'honeymoon' questionnaire, asking them to rate their satisfaction with the bank, its call-centre agents, the account-opening procedure and the intelligibility of the information material sent to them. Another survey is sent annually to the bank's customers, aiming at tracking their satisfaction level and finding new ways to improve the service quality and offerings. All surveys are scanned into the customer database and thus added to the already recorded customer information. When next talking to a customer, the call-centre agent can, from their workstation, instantly access this scanned information. Furthermore, to avoid annoying a given customer by repeatedly offering them a certain product or service, the call-centre agent has the option to block certain capabilities. For instance, if the agent finds out from a phone conversation that a given customer would rather not receive direct mailings from Advance Bank, then they can block this permanently by crossing out this function in the customer database record. Likewise, if a customer turns down a call agent's offer over the phone to open a cash management account, then the agent makes a note of this refusal in the corresponding database record.

Maintaining the human touch

> We can also talk about non-banking matters during our conversation with the customer. In fact, we are even encouraged to ask one question aside from banking to make things more human. By doing so, I create a positive atmosphere, where the customer gets the feeling that I am there to help him make a decision and not to push him over. Once I establish this atmosphere, the customer usually opens up and tells me more personal information, which then makes it easier to suggest the right product to him.
>
> **Klaus Eutin, call-centre agent, Advance Bank**

Making the customer feel comfortable and at ease while banking over the phone is one of the crucial challenges faced by a direct bank. Advance Bank tries to meet this challenge by authorizing its call-centre agents also to talk to customers about topics that are not banking-related. Klaus Eutin elaborated further on this matter:

> Some customers also ask personal questions, about your age, for example, or your hobbies. There are some call agents here in the office who met their future spouses while working.

Furthermore, call-centre agents are trained to keep the customer's best interests in mind. They are advised to make the decision with the customer instead of trying to 'push them over' and make the sale at any cost. The guiding principle of Advance Bank is to pull the customer and not to push them to buy a product. Marc Hemmerling elaborated on this point:

> It is important to build up a personal relationship with a call [centre] agent; this can only happen over time. When you think that you've really received excellent service and advice from a call agent, you'd like to come back to him and build on this good initial understanding. It's very much a psychological thing. I want an excellent product, but I also need to have the trust that the call agent is not trying to sell me something [that] I don't need.

The call-centre agent

> Initially, we thought that we needed to hire [for the bank's call centre] tele-marketeers and give them banking training. That turned out to be a mistake. Now we hire first-rate bankers and we give them a tele-marketing training.
>
> **Volker Visser**

Since call-centre agents are the crucial interface between customers and a direct bank, Advance Bank carefully selects, trains and motivates its call agents. Before getting invited to an assessment centre, applicants for call agent positions are first interviewed over the phone. During this interview, the recruiter has the opportunity to test the applicant's telephone 'appearance', which is the call agent's most important qualification. Besides having a warm and welcoming voice, a call agent must be able to communicate clearly and intelligibly over the telephone. Regional dialects are irrelevant, as long as the call agent can make themselves well-understood to the customer. Although call agents have varying educational backgrounds, they must have a service mentality when joining Advance Bank. Many of them have completed a banking apprenticeship, but there are also university students, former restaurant employees and housewives. After passing the telephone interview, applicants are invited to an assessment centre, where they have to demonstrate over two days that they are stress-resistant and also somewhat persistent, especially with regard to sales conversations.

Before starting their work, new call-centre agents undergo a six- to seven-week, full-time training

programme, during which they first get to know Advance Bank's philosophy, computer system and product portfolio. Call agents are then trained as to how to handle a phone conversation with a customer and how to talk to them. For example, instead of saying 'No problem', which might suggest to the customer that they are a problem, call agents are trained to say 'I will gladly do so' or similar non-judgemental sentences. During the final part of the initial training, which focuses on sales, call agents learn how to sell the bank's products to the customers using the following steps. First, the agent needs to establish a personal contact with the customer and create a rapport of trust. Second, the call agent needs to enquire about the customer's needs and then make the appropriate offer. The final step is closing the deal.

In order to improve the training quality, experienced call agents model the 'optimal call process' with its most frequently recurring parts, such as needs analysis, necessary explanations and possible customer objections. They then develop a script for the new call agents, to which they can refer. After the call agent starts their work, a team trainer provides coaching on the job, listens to customer conversations and gives instant feedback afterwards.

What next?

Internet-based banking

> I switched to Advance Bank because I want to be able to do my banking any time and anywhere, as long as there is a phone or an Internet connection available.
>
> **Rudolf Pfitzer, Advance Bank customer**

From the start, Advance Bank recognized the importance of the Internet as an additional information, communication, marketing and sales channel, as well as customers' willingness to use it to perform financial operations (see survey results in Table 1). The bank strategy stipulated the use of this technology-driven media to offer banking services. A website was set up to inform prospective customers about the bank's products and services (see Exhibit 7). Since summer 1997, customers have been able to access their main and sub-accounts through Advance Bank's Internet website without having to purchase any additional banking software and to perform all banking operations online (e.g. transactions, standing orders and funds management) from any computer with Internet access. As of April 1998, 42% of all money transfers

Exhibit 7 **Advance Bank's website**

Source: Advance Bank.

Table 1 Survey of Internet users (percentages)

				Age (years)					*Employment status*				
	Total	*Women*	*Men*	*<19*	*20–29*	*30–39*	*40–49*	*>50*	*Civil servant*	*Self-employed*	*Other*	*High school student/ apprentice*	*University student*
What kind of financial information would you like to access through the Internet? (Based on 8435 responses from Internet users)													
Information about stocks and investment opportunities	52.1	41.3	53.4	46.7	53.7	52.9	48.6	52.7	44.9	55.4	52.9	46.5	53.9
Information about insurance (prices, premiums, services)	36.1	33.7	36.5	16.7	36.5	39.9	36.7	34.0	38.4	38.8	40.7	18.5	30.1
Information about mortgages and real-estate financing	19.6	17.6	19.8	9.7	18.2	23.8	21.3	14.5	20.5	22.3	22.9	11.9	14.2
Databases with general financial information	38.1	32.7	38.8	22.2	37.9	41.2	38.4	38.0	30.5	44.0	40.5	25.1	34.5
Articles about general financial topics	32.0	27.4	32.6	25.9	32.5	33.9	30.2	29.6	30.2	35.0	32.3	26.8	32.8
Statistical tables and graphical displays	332.2	22.0	34.6	32.5	35.6	33.0	29.7	30.1	26.7	36.7	32.1	32.7	37.5
Stock quotations	48.1	38.1	49.3	48.6	51.1	47.8	44.4	42.6	37.0	49.5	47.9	47.3	52.1
Would you perform the following financial tasks through the Internet? (Based on 6292 responses from Internet users)													
Online banking (account management)	95.4	93.2	95.6	96.5	95.8	94.8	95.7	95.8	96.5	95.1	95.7	95.7	95.1
Purchasing shares	56.1	39.3	57.7	50.7	58.4	55.6	53.0	56.1	50.2	59.5	56.0	50.7	58.1
Purchasing real-estate mortgage	14.9	13.0	15.0	10.0	13.7	16.6	23.8	13.5	17.1	15.3	16.8	9.4	10.4
Purchasing car insurance	39.8	29.5	40.9	16.1	35.3	44.9	41.2	43.9	42.0	46.2	44.2	17.1	29.0
Purchasing liability insurance	34.6	28.8	35.3	12.0	29.9	40.0	33.9	36.1	38.1	39.7	39.2	12.8	23.2
Purchasing home insurance	33.3	29.5	33.7	11.1	28.3	38.7	33.0	37.1	35.8	37.3	38.2	11.1	21.7
Purchasing accident insurance	28.4	23.2	28.9	10.9	24.5	32.8	47.8	30.4	29.2	32.5	32.0	12.0	18.8
Purchasing life insurance	20.2	17.0	20.5	10.0	17.3	22.9	47.8	19.8	23.3	23.3	22.0	9.4	13.2

Source: Fittkau & Maass, 1997.

were conducted through Advance Bank's website. Susanne Meier added:

> With many other Internet banks, you need to install specialized software packages on your PC to access your banking account online. This limits the usage [of Internet-banking] to your home PC. With Advance Bank, I have universal access to my account as long as I can get a hold of a PC with Internet access. I could conceivably check my account in the US during vacation and make a transaction in case I have forgotten to pay my rent, for example.

However, for security reasons, the bank put a DM10 000 ceiling on transactions and transfers done through the Internet. Volker Visser explained:

> Our Internet transactions are very secure. For each transaction, we provide the customer with a transaction authentication number and a confirmation receipt.

However, if something goes wrong, for example a customer transfer does not reach its destination, we bear the cost and pay for it.

Towards a two-channel distribution system: integrating telephone and Internet banking

Banking through the Internet, without any human interaction, works well for selling standardized or simple financial products. However, for highly customized or complex products, such as a mortgage or a life insurance policy, the provision of customer advice is highly desirable, if not even required, by the client. For the latter case and in order to meet customer demands and expectations, Advance Bank intends to integrate the telephone into its Internet banking service to offer simultaneous voice and data communication between its call-centre agents and its customers (see Exhibit 8).

For example, when choosing a real-estate mortgage, the customer first provides through the Advance Bank Internet website some personal data (e.g. duration, amount, rate, etc.). These data are then used to produce instantaneously some 'what-if' analyses and scenarios. If the customer wishes to receive some personal advice, they then click on a specific icon on the screen. Subsequently, an Advance Bank call agent calls up that customer and discusses the matter with them; both parties have the possibility to look at the same document while talking and, if need be, to modify the mortgage data that the customer has entered on the Advance Bank Internet website. The resulting communication is very similar to the traditional form of communication at a bank branch; for instance, the call agent can suggest changing parts of the mortgage (e.g. the duration or the deposit) to obtain a better offer. Simultaneously, the agent can show on the web document what impact the change will have on the mortgage. Compared with traditional phone conversations, such an integrated telephone–Internet sales channel allows a reduction of call time, since the customer now enters the request parameters themselves, hence also reducing the number of possible entry errors.

In order to enhance its customer relationship further, Advance Bank plans to install video cameras on top of the call agents' workstations, thus allowing the customer to see the call agent on their PC screen while talking to them. In order to provide these complex services, the transmission speed of the Internet will have to increase greatly. Already customers are complaining about slow Internet connections to the Advance Bank website, as illustrated by Marc Hemmerling's comment below:

The main problem of Internet banking is that it takes too long to download the website. The initialization process [i.e. the online identification of the customer] also takes too long. When I think about the online fees, it is almost cheaper to do my banking over the phone or even to fill out a form and send it in by mail.

Exhibit 8 **Integrated Internet and telephone banking**

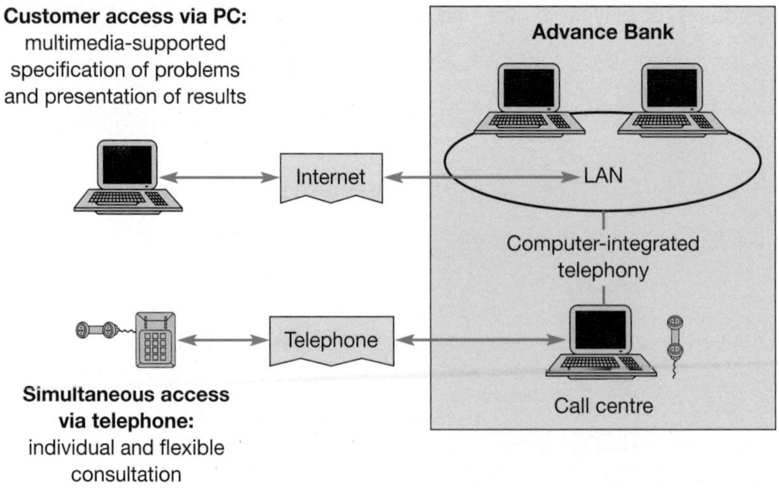

Source: Adapted from Buhl and Will, 'Finanzdienstleistungen auf Netzmärkten – Wandel der Märkte und Virtualisierung der Geshäftätigkeit' *Bank-Archiv*, 47, 6, p.430

Internationalization

Having gained good experience and expertise in offering direct banking services through its business operations in Germany, Advance Bank plans to expand its geographical presence by penetrating other European countries. This ambition to go international is not new at the bank, as stated by Volker Visser:

> Advance Bank is not a German bank. If we had wanted to be a German bank, we wouldn't have called ourselves 'Advance Bank' because Advance is not a German word. We would have called ourselves Hermann or Schmidt Bank. We chose an English name because we expect to expand throughout Europe.

Challenges ahead

Preparing for his next board meeting, Volker Visser was pondering the evolution of direct banking in Germany and in Europe, and the future of Advance Bank in the increasingly global and competitive business environment. What should Advance Bank do next in order to further attract new customers and build loyalty among existing ones? Should the bank broaden its business scope and extend its product portfolio? Should it go ahead at this stage with its plans to enlarge the geographical scale of its operations by launching its direct banking concept in other European countries?

Volker Visser was well aware that embarking on such ambitious projects is, at the same time, an opportunity and a threat for the survival and growth of Advance Bank. However, since the bank needed to achieve its goal of 250 000 customers by 2001 in order to break even, could it afford not to pick up the opportunity and take the risk that comes with it?

DISCUSSION QUESTIONS

1 Is the innovative use of IT one of Advance Bank's core competencies? Explain.

2 What should Advance Bank do next in order to further attract new customers and build loyalty among existing ones?

3 In your opinion, who will dominate the direct banking business in the long run? Will it be:

- the large, branch-based banks;
- the relatively new direct banks which operate only in a branch-less way;
- other financial service providers such as insurance firms and credit-card processing companies;
- new entrants from outside the financial services industry such as large retail chains and software houses, or players in other industries?

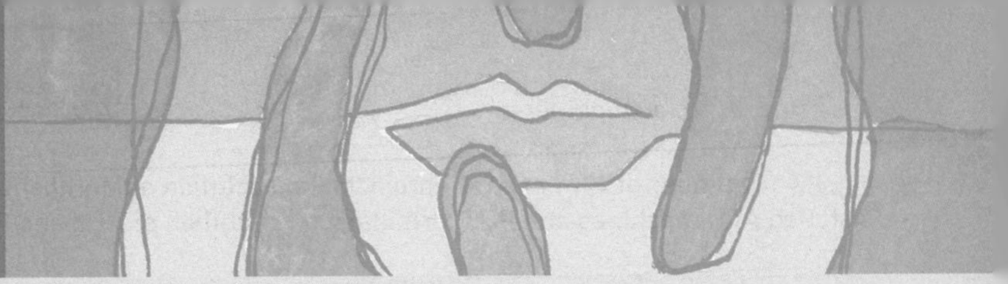

CASE STUDY 11

The electronic purse in Portugal

A mere payment system or a socioeconomic revolution?

The emergent chip-card technology that we are using in the electronic purse in Portugal will soon replace all the credit and debit card transactions worldwide. The main reason [for such a change] is security. The number of frauds in this segment is increasing so much that it will be cost-effective for all [credit and debit] card-processing companies to use this [new] technology.

Avelino Ribeiro, Project Manager, SIBS

Background

In October 1983, SIBS (Sociedade InterBancária de Serviços) was created as a joint venture of 31 credit institutions established in Portugal. At that time, banks were concerned by the increasingly large volume of paper-based transactions, the processing of which was very costly and time-consuming. The decision of 12 founder banks was therefore to initiate an ambitious IT project for automating routine operations. Since such a project needed to be co-ordinated at inter-bank level, SIBS was established. This joint undertaking allowed a major reduction of the financial investment that would have otherwise been required had the development of individual IT systems been the retained solution.

The long-term commitment to the project by the participating banks helped establish in Portugal a single inter-bank technical structure for electronic payments and clearance, representing more than 98% of the retail banking activity. Among the top five banks in Portugal in 1995, four participated in the project; these were Caixa General de Depósitos, Banco Espírito Santo, Banco Totta e Açores and Banco Português do Atlântico. The remaining one (Banco Comercial Português[1]) joined the group in 1987. By 1996, only five foreign or small banks had not joined SIBS.

Changes in banking introduced by SIBS

Several projects implemented by SIBS had a major impact on the banking sector in Portugal. This impact consisted of the creation of a network shared by all of the 1983 financial shareholders in the PMB project. This network enabled the creation of the Multibanco debit card, distributed since 1985 by all banks and acceptable at more than 4000 automated teller machines (ATMs). Through this card, customers could withdraw cash, consult the latest debit/credit transactions to their account, pay utilities and insurance bills, etc. The growth of the Multibanco card has been quite remarkable, since more than six million cards were issued by December 1996. The number of installed ATM machines and processed transactions also increased significantly (see Exhibit 1). Other projects developed by SIBS included the electronic funds at point of sale (EFTPOS or POS), the Interbank ATM/POS clearing service and the electronic purse PMB (Porta Moedas Multibanco) (see Table 1 for the impact of these projects on the Portuguese banking environment).

1 This bank was founded in 1986 and acquired Banco Português do Atlântico in June 1995.

This case was written by Tawfik Jelassi and Manuel João Pereira, who is from the Universidade Católica Poruguesa, Lisbon, Portugal. It is intended to be used as the basis for class discussion rather than to illustrate either effective or ineffective handling of a business situation. Case released in 1997.

The authors would like to thank Rui Santos and Avelino Ribeiro from SIBS for their co-operation in carrying out this field research.

Exhibit 1 **Number of ATM and POS projects: (a) evolution of Multibanco debit cards issued; (b) evolution of installed ATM machines and POS terminals; (c) evolution of ATM and POS transactions**

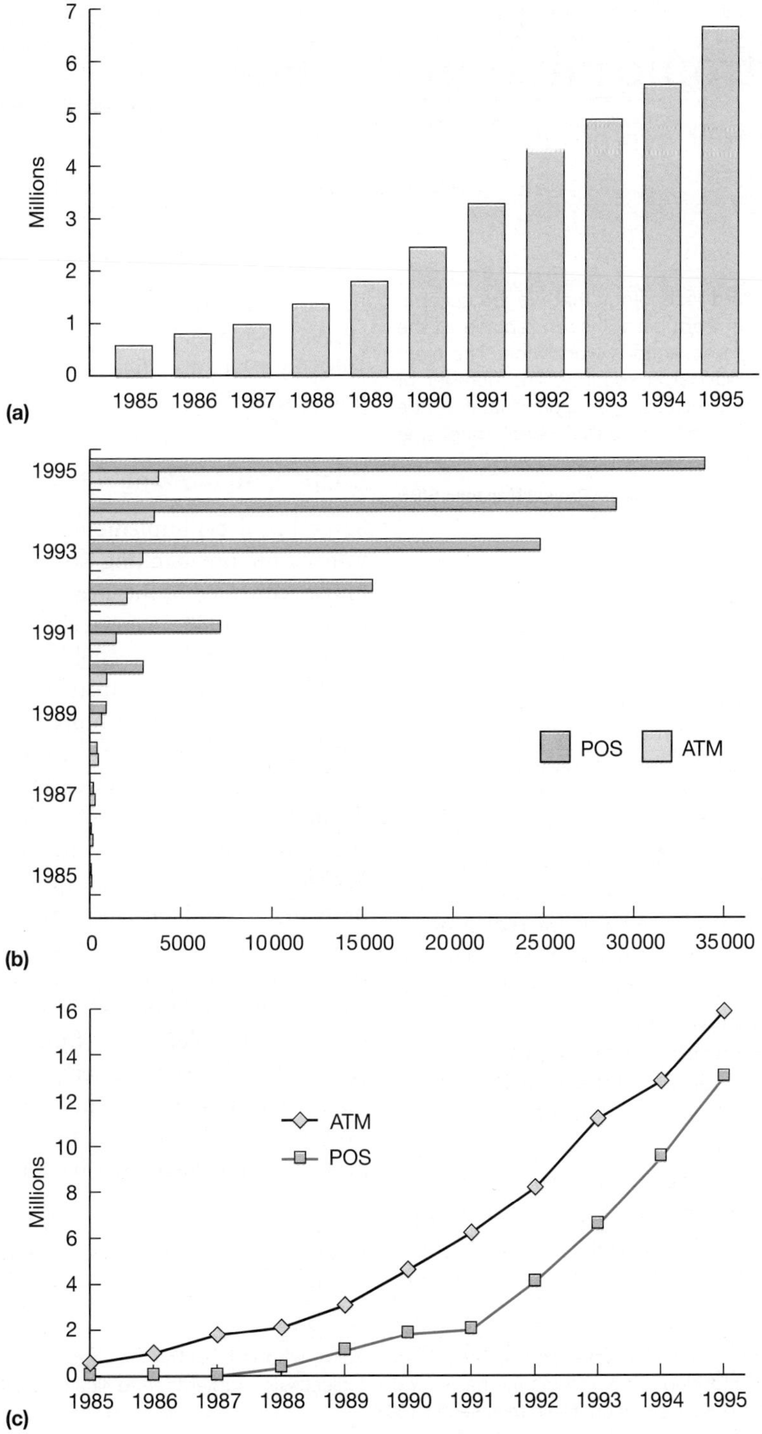

Table 1 Changes in the banking sector induced by SIBS projects

Date	*Project*	*Description*	*Changes in the banking enviroment*
November 1983	Start of the shared ATM network	Online mode of operation linking the SIBS central computer with each bank's computer Each ATM acts upon responses to its enquiries made to the central bank Effective control and monitoring of the network assuring a high security level	Clients of one bank can use ATM machines installed in other banks' branches Easier addition of new services to the network
September 1985	Caixa Automática Multibanco (ATMs)	Creation of the Multibanco debit card, which can be used in any ATM, and its distribution by banks. Accepts all the main international credit/debit cards, e.g. American Express, Visa, Mastercard, Eurocard, 4B, Edc/Maestro Main functions are: – money withdrawal from ATM machines (maximum $40 000 per day) – listing of last five credit/debit operations – money deposit – payment of services (e.g. telephone, electricity, water, gas) – purchase of tickets (e.g. for concerts) – payment of highway tolls (*via verde*) – offering of personalized bank products (e.g. stock market and investment funds)	Shorter queuing time to withdraw money, list past operations, or execute other banking operations Clients do not need to go to utility companies to pay their bills Improved service quality offered by banks Universal use: a bank client can use any ATM machine of the network 24 hours a day, seven days a week
February 1987	Pagamento Automáticon (EFTPOS or POS)	Providing shareholder banks with EFTPOS Electronic payments at POS using a terminal and the Multibanco card When a transaction is performed, updating both client and merchant bank accounts Accepting the same cards used in ATM machines	Extension of the shared network concept to suit the needs of the retail market Clients can pay their bills in convenient places, such as petrol stations, supermarkets and department stores Part of the ATM use to withdraw money is switched to the point of sale Reduction of clerical work for cheque processing
January 1991	Inter-bank ATM/POS clearing	Computing the balance of each credit organization participating in the Multibanco network Informing the Portuguese Central Bank (Banco de Portugal) to update its accounts Generating for each bank a detailed file of clients who used the network; accounts reconciliation across bank branches	Reduction of service costs and clerical work for all financial shareholders
March 1995	PMB – Porta Moedas Multibanco (electronic purse)	Inclusion of low-amount transactions (executed with coins) in the Multibanco network Allowing business transactions in 'non-online' environments to be executed through the Multibanco network	Clients do not need to carry a lot of coins to perform small-amount transactions Banks can include in their accounts a lot of money that clients used to keep in the form of coins

The PMB electronic purse

> One of our [customer] targets are the teenagers. We expect one day that the weekly money that they receive from their parents can be charged to their PMB card. The ice-creams, train/bus or metro tickets, fast food lunches, CDs and magazines are clearly transactions that can be paid for through this card.
>
> **Rui Franco, PMB Marketing Manager, SIBS**

The PMB concept

The PMB electronic purse, a chip-based card, was created as a substitute for coins. Each PMB card had a unique identification number and the image of the bank that issued it. Money amounts (ranging from 1000$00 to 40 000$00[2]) could be transferred on to the PMB card from any ATM machine, provided that its holder has a Multibanco account. The electronic purse could also be used to pay any small-value transactions. Since the PMB had no password check, if it was lost, anybody could use the card (just like someone finding money). However, to alleviate this risk, a customer could write (in a designated area of the PMB) their name and telephone number, so as to be contacted if they lost the card. Table 2 lists the operations allowed by the PMB card.

The PMB technology

Based on 'smart-card' (or chip-card) technology, a major advantage of the PMB is security, since all data are encrypted. Data are updated using an algorithm on the card, and the password (known only to the card holder) must match that stored in the memory of the card.

This chip-card technology is based on the EMV international standard and could be accepted at different terminal types. According to Rui Franco, PMB Marketing Manager:

> Three types of terminals were created for the chip-card technology: the PMB-94 portable terminal for market segments that can't be physically linked online with SIBS. This terminal is similar to a calculator and easy to operate; taxi drivers, small/fast-food restaurant managers, and 'kiosks'[3] can use it. There are also two other terminal types: the MS-94, which is basically a modified version of the POS and which also accepts credit/debit cards (including the Multibanco card), and the OEM-01 hardware card, which is used in coin-based vending machines (which typically sell tobacco, soft drinks, snacks, and parking/metro or bus tickets).

A PMB card was sold at 670$00, which is higher than the 50$00 unit price of a Multibanco debit card. This price could be seen as a barrier to the wide diffusion

2 The $ sign here refers to Portuguese escudos (US$1 = 155$00 escudos).

3 'Kiosks' are small outlets where you can buy magazines and convenience products.

Table 2 **Procedure to use the PMB electronic purse**

PMB clients/users	*Merchants with 'non-online' portable terminals*	*Banks*
Use ATM machines to load the PMB card with 1000$00–40 000$00 using only the Multibanco account	In the morning, open one set of transactions for the PMB portable terminal	During the day, process the loading of the PMB card and money transfer(s) from a client's Multibanco account to a special 'float account'
Use the PMB card to pay typical coins transactions, checking the available money on the PMB card and the amount to be paid	Execute transactions with the PMB card, allowing clients to see the amount of money they have on the PMB card and the transaction amount they need to pay	Use the money in the 'float account' in a similar way to the money in current accounts, and lend it subject to some restrictions
Through an ATM machine, may check the last 30 payments made with the PMB card	By day-end, close the set of transactions	By day-end, process merchants' PMB deposits. Transfer the total deposited amount from the 'float account' to the merchant's account. Determine the amount that the merchant needs to receive from each of the other banks
Use an ATM machine to load money on to the PMB card using the Multibanco account or any bank account	Using the PMB portable terminal, load the 'coins of the day' on a special chip-card called Merchant Deposit Card, which is different from the PMB card	By day-end, pay merchants using the 'float account' amounts paid by clients with accounts in other banks
PMB card is valid for a three-year period	Go to an ATM machine and use the Merchant Deposit Card to transfer money to the Multibanco account	

of the PMB, especially compared with the initial pricing strategy of the Multibanco card. A portable terminal for the chip-card technology cost approximately 30 000$00; however, SIBS also offered merchants a lease option of 1250$00 per month.

Factors behind the launch of the PMB project

Several forces motivated the launch of the PMB project:

- Financial transactions of less than 2000$00 were not covered by POS payment systems and ATM machines but could be accepted by the Multibanco network.
- The chip-card technology (which became available in the early 1990s) could be a substitute or complementary product to existing magnetic cards.
- Due to their 'non-online' nature, some businesses (such as taxis, mobile delis, etc.) did not have a telephone line and therefore could not be connected to a POS system. However, they asked SIBS for a convenient means that would allow them to accept electronic payments.
- The strong expertise and experience that SIBS had in developing network-based applications.

The aim of the PMB project was to use the chip-card technology to cover small-amount financial transactions (lower than 2000$00) mainly in a 'non-online' environment. The PMB payment system had to be secure and convenient (for both customers and merchants) and profitable for SIBS shareholders (i.e. the banks). The project was implemented using the existing SIBS network (shown in Exhibit 2).

Exhibit 2 **The Multibanco network, including ATM, POS and PMB terminals**

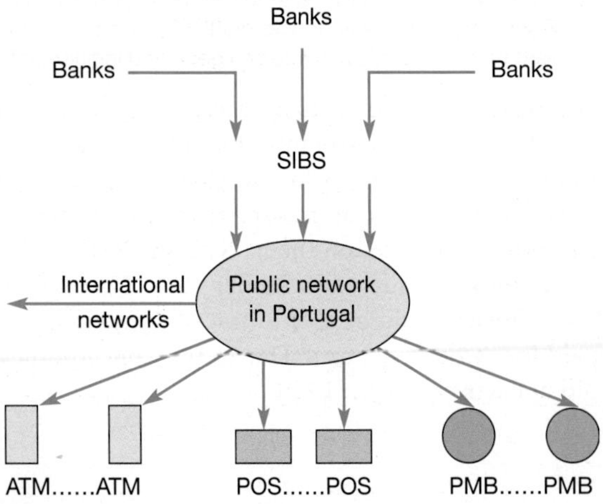

Potential winners with the PMB

The main PMB stakeholders were merchants, clients and banks.

Merchants

The main commercial segments that the PMB targeted were taxi drivers, small/fast-food restaurants, newspapers/magazines stores, parking/bus/train tickets vendors, and owners of stamp/tobacco/ice-cream/snack and soft-drink machines. In addition to improving their store image by adopting the PMB, merchants were interested in using this electronic purse as a mode of payment for three reasons:

- Since the PMB covers micro-transactions, accepting it might lead to achieving some sales increase – as did credit and debit cards, which also represent electronic money.
- Safety was another advantage, since storing cash on the electronic purse reduced the risk of robbery.
- The costs of controlling, transporting and depositing money stored on the PMB card were lower than their equivalent costs associated with traditional cash payments.

Clients

PMB clients were mainly people attracted by the novelty factor of the electronic purse and already having the Multibanco debit card.[4] Client segments included young individuals and teenagers who perceived the PMB card more as a high-tech status symbol than as an easy and convenient mode of payment. From a client perspective, the main objective was to be able to use the PMB card without facing any technical or physical problem. However, as Ana Rosa Coelho, a PMB user from Banco Espírito Santo, put it:

> Right now, even if we have the PMB card, we'll probably still have to use coins. Actually, only three out of ten 'coins operations' can be executed using the PMB. This is not motivating for users because they still need to search for places where the PMB card is accepted.

4 Since the PMB loading procedure was linked to the Multibanco card, it was easier to attract customers who already had this card.

If the PMB card could cover typical coins operations, then clients would use it widely instead of carrying coins or looking for change to pay for some small-amount transactions. Moreover, they could easily control their daily expenditures and enjoy the convenience of an electronic purse accepted by all Portuguese banks.

Banks

The substitution of coins with a nationwide electronic payment system helped banks to reduce clerical work (related to the handling of coins), lower the processing costs of small-amount cheques, build a banking relationship with teenagers who did not have bank accounts, and broaden the coverage scope for electronic payments in 'non-online' retail contexts. The national roll-out and use of the PMB card also represented a new source of revenues for banks. Although the system usage was free during the first year for merchants, thereafter banks charged a commission per transaction (this commission was lower than the 0.5–2% band used in POS transactions). Another major advantage for banks was the ability to introduce in bank accounts a large amount of money to finance some banking activities at a low cost. Since there was no interest paid on these accounts, they represented a good source of funding for banks. A SIBS analysis had actually predicted that 10% of total coins payments could be carried out by the PMB after ten years of the card launch, resulting in a significant funding benefit for banks.

SIBS

SIBS was also a winner in the PMB project. First, the volume of transactions in the network was expected to increase drastically since a large number of transactions under 2000$00 would be covered, thus generating extra revenues for SIBS. Second, the money involved in these transactions remained inside the bank electronic system (since first the customer loaded money on to their PMB card and then the merchant unloaded the money using the PMB terminal). SIBS charged both transactions while keeping the money inside bank accounts at all times.[5] (Exhibit 3 shows the information received by PMB card holders when loading money on to the PMB.)

City halls

City halls and government agencies were also important stakeholders in the PMB project. City halls were instrumental in the wide PMB adoption since most parking machines were technically ready to accept the card. The cost issue (who was going to pay what?) was an important one, but the agreement between the involved parties was beneficial to all Portuguese citizens.

Government

The government was an indirect winner of the PMB project, since the control of trade in Portugal would become electronic and tax payments were expected to increase.

Potential loses with the PMB

There were some negative perceptions regarding the PMB card and its capabilities; they came from merchants, clients as well as banks.

Merchants

Due to their social, cultural or educational backgrounds, some merchants preferred not to use 'high-tech' solutions such as the PMB. This was also the case for merchants operating in 'non-online' environments, such as taxi drivers and restaurant staff. As expressed by Miguel Correia, a taxi driver in Lisbon:

> The PMB accepts tips and it is quite easy to key them in. At the end of the day, when I do the balance with my boss, I receive the amount of tips according to the PMB listing. The problem is that my boss now knows exactly how much I make in tips and that's not good for me. This is why some taxi drivers make it difficult for customers who want to pay with the PMB. They would say: 'Sorry, the terminal is in the back of the car; do you want to wait five minutes so I can get it and initialize it?'

Some merchants who actually accepted the PMB did not like the extra control introduced by the card. For them, cash transactions for which no invoices were issued allowed them to not report related revenues and not to pay taxes on them. With the PMB, however, they wondered whether the Portuguese government would be able to trace the transactions paid for through the card. Due to this concern, they did not actively use the PMB.

5 This is different from a typical ATM withdrawal, in which cash is taken from the bank system.

Clients

Clients' negative perceptions of the PMB card were due to two factors: (1) many 'coin operations' could not yet be executed through the PMB, hence not meeting customers' expectations; (2) clients felt the need to carry a second card, a problem that could be overcome with the creation of one card integrating both the Multibanco debit card and the PMB.

Banks

Banks had some negative perceptions regarding the PMB. First, their sales force favoured other financial products that offered them better commission. Second, the PMB growth was slower than that of the Multibanco card,[6] but the investment required to diffuse it widely was higher. This was due to the fact that banks needed to cover a large number of 'coin operations' in so many places as to motivate customers to adopt the PMB card. Third, production costs represented another important stumbling block for the wide diffusion of the PMB, since the price of a chip card (670$00 as of June 1996) was 11 times higher than that of a magnetic card. Although the chip-card cost was expected to drop, the investment needed to produce millions of cards for the retail market was still very high, and return on that investment was foreseen for only the medium- to long-term.

PMB: From pilot tests to national diffusion

Launching the PMB card went through the following three phases: the technical pilot phase, the customer adoption test phase and the wide dissemination phase.

Technical pilot phase

The first phase of pilot tests was started in September 1994 and aimed at testing the technical features of the PMB card. This phase took place in closed, 'real-world' settings that included the Alvalade 'Cartier' in Lisbon, where the SIBS building was located. A PMB card was distributed to each one of the 220 SIBS employees, and PMB terminals were installed in 20 stores in Alvalade. The new building of Caixa General de Depósitos (the biggest Portuguese bank) was also a technical test site, and 2000 employees working there received the PMB card. PMB terminals were also installed there and, in some cases, only the PMB card was accepted (e.g. to pay for purchases from snack-food or soft-drink machines). These pilot tests helped the PMB project team to resolve some technical problems that were not detected in laboratory settings.

6 Supermarkets and hypermarkets had a major impact on the growth of the Multibanco card and its associated transactions volume.

Exhibit 3 Information received by PMB clients at ATM machines

* * * **Multibanco** * * *

ATM NUMBER: 035/0584/2 TRANSACTION NUMBER: 0115
DEBIT CARD NUMBER: 59032013595801 DATE: 25/07/96
ACCOUNT NUMBER: 0002012110011379 TIME: 01:30

LOADING OF ELECTRONIC PURSE PMB CARD
NUMBER OF MOVEMENT OF DEBIT CARD: 95
AMOUNT: *5.000$00

PMB CARD: 032 00001670 EXPIRES: 98/09
ISSUER BANK PORTUGAL
REFERENCE: 00001
PREVIOUS BALANCE: 320$00
CREDIT: 5.000$00
AVAILABLE BALANCE: 5.320$00

PMB – IT HAS CHANGE FOR EVERYTHING
ISSUER BANK PORTUGAL
ISSUERS BANK CARDS, ALL THE WORLD IN YOUR POCKET

* * * **THANK YOU** * * *

Customer adoption test phase

The second phase of pilot tests aimed at assessing customers' reactions to the PMB card. It took place in April 1995 in the city of Cascais, located approximately 30 km from Lisbon, the choice of which was motivated by the following factors:

- Cascais had the highest percentage in Portugal of people using the Multibanco card and was also expected to achieve a high usage rate of the PMB card.
- The ability to create in Cascais a closed environment allowing users to pay for their transactions without resorting to the use of coins.
- The proximity of Cascais to Lisbon meant that any technical problems could be handled and solved quickly, using the PMB technical development centre located in Lisbon.

SIBS asked its financial stockholders to launch a strong commercial campaign in Cascais with their main merchants (by offering them free PMB terminals) and with clients (by giving them free PMB cards). To do this, SIBS provided banks with 2000 terminals and 20000 PMB cards. In spite of this major commercial campaign, a negative perception of the PMB was created among both merchants and clients. It was due to the absence of nationwide coverage of the PMB terminals, the lack of training for branch managers throughout the country, and the long wait time that merchants had to go through after reporting a PMB terminal problem. Moreover, some banks did not seem to have a clear understanding of where co-operation ended and where competition started in dealing with matters related to the PMB joint venture.

Several lessons were learned from the Cascais pilot phase:

- The control of the PMB cards distribution in a co-operative development environment was an important success factor. Specific issues to address in the next PMB test phase included the need to have a quick after-sales service and an online help desk, and to train bank-branch employees.
- The necessity of having a good PMB distribution strategy: for example, in a first stage, offering PMB terminals to 'non-online' environments in cities where people actually performed a high volume of 'non-online' transactions. Then, in a second stage, rolling out the PMB terminals in the other cities.
- The need to motivate branch employees. This could be achieved by creating 'target objectives' (in terms of volume of transactions for PMB cards and terminals) and linking each employee's PMB performance with their work appraisal. Moreover, a national award (e.g. 'PMB manager of the year') could be set up to further motivate PMB employees.
- The perception that the PMB 'pull' and usage would be slower than that of the Multibanco card and POS terminals, although the potential volume of PMB payments per person was higher than that of Multibanco. POS had proven to be an effective payment system for hypermarkets and supermarkets (with an installation base of 60–100 POS per store), generating 80% of total POS transactions. However, since the PMB was a retail one-to-one product, its wide diffusion required contacting each merchant and client. Moreover, partnerships with professional associations (such as taxis or restaurant associations) were needed to foster the PMB diffusion.

Dissemination phase

The nationwide dissemination phase was launched in January 1996 and aimed at increasing the installed base of PMB cards and portable terminals among both customers and merchants. SIBS asked its member banks to offer merchants, over six months, free PMB portable terminals.[7] Afterwards, a 30 000$00 fee was to be charged. SIBS also requested offering free services during the first year of operation, after which charging a smaller commission than that applied to magnetic cards (which ranged between 0.5% and 2%).

This marketing strategy was successful, since at the end of the six-month period SIBS received more than 50 000 requests for the PMB portable terminals (see Exhibit 4), while it had initially expected to get only 15 000 requests. Although the number of requests was quite high (50 800 in June 1996), the number of terminals linked to SIBS was lower (31 470 in June 1996). Although the number of

7 During this period, SIBS covered the terminals' acquisition and installation costs.

Exhibit 4 PMB statistics: (a) evolution of the PMB in 1995; (b) evolution of the cumulative DMB money amounts in 1995; (c) evolution of the average PMB amounts in 1995; (d) PMB portable terminals: 'stand-alone' *vs.* 'linked' in 1996

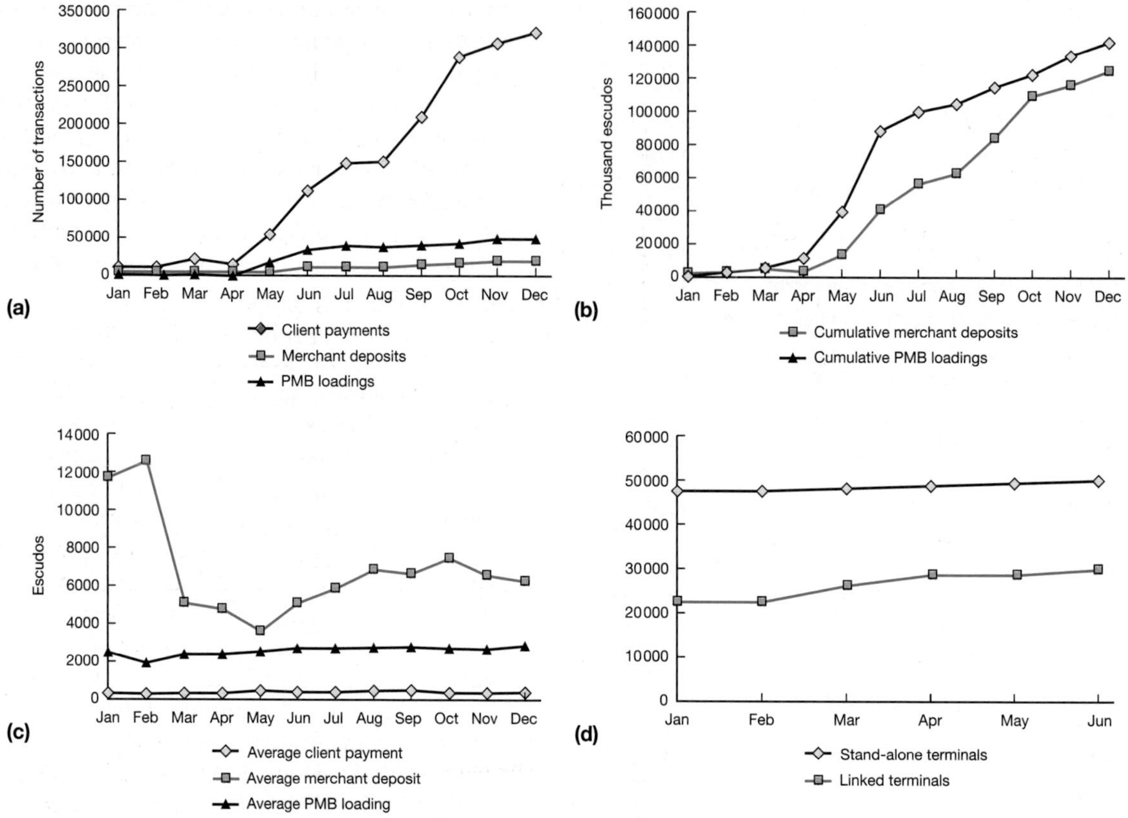

Source: SIBS.

stand-alone terminals had dropped from 54% in January 1996 to 38% in June 1996, there were still 19 330 PMB terminals not linked to the SIBS network. This was due mainly to a lack of merchants' training on how to process PMB payments and to the psychological effect of users accepting a 'free goodie'. SIBS aimed at decreasing the number of 'non-linked' PMB terminals to 15% by the end of 1996.

Emergent issues

Commercial segments that were especially interested in the PMB technology are listed in Table 3. It is interesting to notice that 66% of the demand came from 11 segments, while the other 140 segments represented the remaining 34%. The most important segments for the PMB were cafés, bars and soft-drinks/cookies shops (12.6%), followed by snack/fast-food and self-service outlets (11.8%). Retailing was the segment where the PMB was adopted quickly, in particular in the drinks and food business. The remaining 140 segments were expected to adopt the PMB terminal nationwide.

By January 1996, SIBS delivered 46 881 PMB portable terminals. Table 4 shows their geographic distribution per district and indicates that 53.2% of the terminals were in the three districts (Lisbon, Porto, Setúbal) with the highest population densities in Portugal. This situation is not expected to change over the next few years, since PMB usage is correlated with educated users having an active lifestyle and living in densely populated areas. The density factor means that more inhabitants live in a given geographical area, hence leading to a larger number of micro-transactions to be performed and therefore to a higher probability of adopting the PMB as an electronic payment system.

Table 3 Distribution of PMB portable terminals per segment (January 1996)

Economic activity code	*Commercial segment*	*Volume*	*%*
62011	Supermarkets and hypermarkets	2140	4.6
62014	General retail	2505	5.5
62022	Pharmacies	1178	2.5
62031	Textile, garment and fashion retailing	3118	6.7
62071	Petrol stations	1027	2.2
62093	Books and magazine stores	1842	3.9
62099	Other non-specific retail	4640	9.9
63110	Snack-bars, fast-foods, self-service	5522	11.8
63120	Cafés, bars, cookies/ soft-drinks shops	5886	12.6
71131	Taxis and rental cars	1792	3.8
93100	Education services	1195	2.5
	Other 140 segments	15 946	34.0
Total		*46 881*	*100.0*

Source: SIBS.

Table 4 Distribution of PMB portable terminals per district (January 1996)

Geographical district	*Volume*	*%*
Lisbon	14 433	30.8
Porto	7 018	15.0
Setúbal	3 444	7.4
Braga	3 068	6.5
Faro	2 812	6.0
Santarém	2 589	5.5
Aveiro	2 056	4.4
Leiria	1 875	4.0
Coimbra	1 659	3.5
Viseu	966	2.1
Viana do Castelo	914	1.9
Évora	883	1.9
Vila Real	791	1.7
Castelo Branco	782	1.7
Portalegre	685	1.5
Guarda	545	1.2
Bragança	520	1.1
Beja	534	1.1
Other	1 307	2.7
Total	*46 881*	*100.0*

Source: SIBS.

SIBS marketing campaign was customer-focused. It produced one million PMB cards (which represents one-tenth of the Portuguese population) and all its member banks initially gave these cards free of charge to their customers. Then banks started selling the PMB card, and prices varied from one bank to another. In June 1996, only 23% of all distributed cards were activated and used. In April 1996, following the second pilot phase, SIBS launched a national marketing campaign using a variety of mass-media outlets (TV, radio, newspapers, poster-based advertisement) to convey to citizens the benefits brought by the PMB card.

Table 5 shows the evolution of PMB usage in 1995. PMB distribution increased by 35% over a six-month period, illustrating the growth phase that the card is still in. The average payment per user was approximately 386$00 (U$2.44), confirming the micro-transactions usage of the card. The average amount of monthly payments and deposits was U$1181, similar to the average amount of monthly money loadings on to the card. It is worth noticing the impact of integrating the PMB card in the Multibanco network, namely how PMB accounted for only 0.2% of the overall network transactions and dealt with a small amount of transactions among SIBS main products. However, there was already a monthly sum of U$1333 in bank accounts that stayed inside the system and replaced coins. Moreover, it should be noted that the PMB as a product still has market growth potential and could attract a larger share of money transactions in the Multibanco network.

PMB *vs.* Mondex

Several national or global electronic purse projects were launched or have been already implemented all around the world (see Table 6). A wide-scale project among these is the Mondex electronic purse initiative developed by National Westminster (NatWest) Bank and Midland Bank of the UK. Like the PMB, Mondex is a computer-chip-based card used for small transactions that do not need to be authorized by the user's bank. The card can be used as a cash replacement to transfer value from one individual to another, and for high-street purchases. By autumn 1996, 17 banks from around the world subscribed for shares in a new private company being set up to

Table 5 Evolution of PMB services (first semester, 1996; figures on Escudos)

	January 1996	*February 1996*	*March 1996*	*April 1996*	*May 1996*	*June 1996*
Number of cards	168 010	182 733	198 170	207 676	217 387	227 359
Loadings						
Number	60 698	61 100	70 581	58 544	65 459	55 510
Amount (thousand escudos)	172 903	175 404	199 298	171 003	193 052	174 611
Average per user (escudos)	2850	287	282	292	295	315
Payments						
Number	411 087	468 243	569 677	491 632	553 845	431 230
Amount (thousand escudos)	156 186	169 559	200 983	177 579	195 736	166 565
Average per user (escudos)	380	362	353	361	353	386
Deposits						
Number	27 057	31 491	40 074	39 125	42 651	38 409
Amount (thousand escudos)	156 186	169 559	200 983	177 579	195 736	166 565
Average per user (escudos)	5 770	538	502	454	459	434

Source: SIBS.

Table 6 Electronic purse schemes using smart-card technology

Country	*Scheme Operator/Name*	*Sector*	*Status*
Belgium	Banksys/Proton	Banking	Trials started in December 1994
Czechoslovakia	Easy Card	Retailing	Roll-out underway in 100 stores
Denmark	Danmont	Multisectorial	Rolled out nationally
Finland	Avant	Central bank	Rolled out nationally
France	La Poste	PTT	Trial planned
Germany	GZS	Banking	Specification agreed
Netherlands	Primeur Card	Banking/retailing	Pilot under way
Portugal	SIBS/PMB	Banking	Rolled out nationally
Spain	SEMP	Banking	Trial under way
Switzerland	SWISS PTT/Postcard	PTT	Planning roll-out
UK	Mondex UK	Banking	Trial started in Swindon in July 1995
International	Visa/Mastercard/Europay	International	Agreeing specification/trials in 1996

Source: Ramanuuj *et al*., 1995.

incorporate the assets of Mondex.[8] Hence, Mondex aspires to become a worldwide payment brand with a worldwide ownership, superseding the traditional magnetic cards (such as American Express, Visa and Mastercard) as a key payment system in the emerging electronic commerce environment.[9]

The first pilot of Mondex began in July 1995 in Swindon, England, a city located 100 km from London and having an adult population of 190 000. In July 1996, 10 000 clients and 700 retailers were involved in this pilot. Later, another pilot was started in San Francisco, where over 500 employees of Wells Fargo were able to spend Mondex value at 22

8 The 17 banks (from Australia, Canada, Hong Kong, New Zealand, the UK and the USA) have already signed up for franchise rights to exploit Mondex in their respective geographical markets and own shares in Mondex International. NatWest receives a fixed sum of £6.5 million to pay back for the Mondex R&D costs and will receive deferred payments based on the future successes of the product globally.

9 For a discussion of electronic commerce and electronic markets, see, for example, Kalakota and Whinston (1997).

merchant sites, including drugstores, coffee shops, book stores and restaurants. In late 1996, three other pilot launches were established. The first pilot was conducted by Canadian Imperial Bank of Commerce (CIBC) and Royal Bank of Canada (RBC) in Guelph, Ontario, Canada, a community with 100 000 people situated 90 km from Toronto. The second pilot was conducted in Hong Kong by Hong Kong Bank; the third took place on the university campus of Exeter, in the south-west of England, and was conducted by the NatWest Group.

Description of the Mondex electronic purse

Mondex can be used to pay in shops, car parks, laundrettes and vending machines. The Mondex card was designed to replicate the anonymity and transferability of cash around the world as an alternative to coins, which can be used for everyday shopping as well as for electronic commerce. Unlike traditional credit and debit cards (which require clearance at payment organizations), Mondex is accepted immediately. A major difference between Mondex and the PMB electronic purse is the money-transfer procedure and its traceability: while all Mondex clients can transfer electronic cash among themselves without any bank control or traceability of the transaction, PMB-based money transfers are processed and stored centrally, hence making them traceable.

The loading procedure of the Mondex card allows banks to transfer electronic cash to and from customers via ATM machines and Mondex phones. Mondex phones can take the form of public or domestic phones and have a special drive where the Mondex card can be inserted. Using these phones, clients call the bank's account manager to request loading the card with the desired amount of money (be it national or foreign currencies). They can also use two Mondex telephones to make person-to-person money transfer.

Using the 'money transfer between cards without bank intervention' concept, Mondex created the Mondex wallet. This wallet allows clients to know the exact amount of electronic cash they have on their Mondex card and to make money transfers between two Mondex cards. As stated in July 1996 by David Hunt, President and CEO at AT&T Universal Card Services:

> Mondex offers customers an innovative array of services that can be packaged to meet their individual needs. Its ability to be used online, on the phone and at shopping malls makes it the most useful and exciting electronic payment system in the world.

Comparative strengths of the PMB electronic purse

Compared with Mondex, the PMB electronic purse has the following strengths:

- On a national level, the PMB card is based on a country-wide co-operative network shared by almost all Portuguese banks, hence allowing clients to execute PMB loading operations in any ATM machine.
- From a standards perspective, PMB cards follow standards used by Visa/Mastercard/Europay, which are different from those used by Mondex. Therefore, PMB cards cannot be used in Mondex terminals, and vice versa. The issue of standards is very important for retailers, since they do not want to have different terminals to be able to accept different payment cards. Visa/Mastercard/Europay still dominate the global commerce standards around the world, but it may be only a matter of time before they are superseded by other competitors. The later the global response of Visa/Mastercard/Europay to electronic purse cards, the bigger the market share of the Mondex global electronic purse business. On the other hand, as Catherine Adams, Mondex manager at the Royal Bank of Canada put it:

> Most terminal manufacturers can design products which will accept all cards, whatever the standard. We already saw in May 1996 inter-operable terminals made by manufacturers like Verifone and Dassault-AT. They proved their capability of accepting cards from Mondex and other payment schemes.

Mondex anticipates that terminal manufacturers will soon solve this problem. If Mondex has on a global scale the first-mover advantage (by having the highest number of installed terminals), then retailers may be faced with the inconvenience of having in their stores two or more terminals operating under different standards. Visa/Mastercard and Europay today hold the upper hand with the volume of their client base; however, a technological change from magnetic cards to chip-based cards will probably be followed by all clients. Many shareholders in Mondex

International are also conducting trials of alternative electronic purses. The actual impact of standards on the success of the PMB and Mondex cards remains to be seen.

- While one million PMB cards have already been distributed in Portugal (a country with a population of only ten million citizens), Mondex is still in a formative stage of maturity in bringing the electronic purse to the market. While some assessment can be made of the PMB socioeconomic impact, Mondex has yet to determine the type and extent of its effect on businesses and individuals.
- A nationwide dissemination strategy of an electronic purse is less risky than a worldwide one. Unlike the PMB card, Mondex will face the challenge of managing cultural differences across countries.

Critical success factors of the PMB

From the above analysis of the PMB electronic purse project, the following factors were critical for the successful development, implementation and national roll-out of the PMB in Portugal:

- *Ability to solve the PMB 'chicken-and-egg' problem.* The project success stems from a good geographical distribution of the PMB portable terminals. On the one hand, the wider the PMB coverage of traditional coins payments is, the stronger users' demand for the PMB will be. On the other hand, the larger the PMB client base is, the easier it is to broaden the PMB geographical scale and business scope.[10]
- *Reliability and security of the PMB electronic purse.* SIBS must ensure that if a PMB card with some money on it gets damaged, then the money is not lost and can be loaded on to another PMB card.
- *Creating a wide awareness of the PMB product.* Due to its novelty and high-tech factors, the PMB card can be adopted quickly and easily by social segments such as teenagers and youngsters. These target segments helped spread the word about the PMB and its advantages. Moreover, youngsters generally have the ability to persuade their parents to adopt the PMB card.
- *Sound software and technical choices.* The PMB software quality has minimized technical problems while enabling a quick execution, even during peak hours (through the use of more than one PMB portable terminal for each snack-bar or fast-food restaurant). From a security viewpoint, an interesting issue is whether it is wise to maintain the electronic purse without a password on it. On the one hand, a no-password card allows a faster execution speed and makes the PMB payment procedure similar to that used with traditional coins payments. On the other hand, it does not alleviate the security fear of some clients regarding the PMB use, and the PMB may be bypassed by new electronic purses that actually use passwords.
- *Managing the change process induced by the PMB.* This factor is critical for the cultural acceptance of the PMB electronic purse; it was achieved through specific actions that minimize the resistance of users (merchants, clients, city halls, banks).
- *Attractive cost/benefit ratio for both clients and merchants.* The price of the PMB card, its security risk, the fear of losing money and the lack of total market coverage represent costs that users have to incur and to trade-off with the benefits brought by the PMB.
- *Providing after-sales support to merchants.*
- *Keeping up-to-date with technological advances and international trends in the electronic purse market.* The chip-card market is changing rapidly, and new hardware and software offer more value-adding capabilities. It is therefore important for SIBS to leverage new technological advances and take into account the business evolution of other electronic purse companies, so as to enable the future integration of the PMB with global networks.

10 The 'chicken-and-egg' problem discussed above is a classical dilemma faced when introducing new technological innovations on a large scale. It was documented, for example, in the case of Minitel, the national videotext system in France (Cats-Baril and Jelassi 1994; Jelassi and Rapaport 1994).

References

Cats-Baril, W. and T. Jelassi, 'Establishing a national IT infrastructure: The case of the French videotex system', *MIS Quarterly* 1994, 18, 1–20.

Jelassi, T. and I. Rapaport, 'The technology of the Minitel system', in T. Jelassi, *Competing through Information Technology: Strategy and Implementation*, London, Prentice Hall, 1994, 216–243.

Kalakota, R. and A.B. Whinston, *Electronic Commerce: A Manager's Guide*, Reading, MA, Addison Wesley, 1997.

Ramanuuj, B., Penelope, O. and P. Richard, *The Case for Smart Cards*, 2nd edn, Hertfordshire, IBC Publishing 1995.

Turban, E.R., McLean and J.C. Wetherbe, *Information Technology for Management Improving Quality and Productivity*, New York, John Wiley, 1996.

Further reading

Pereira, M. J. and R. Magalhães, 'Key issues in the financial sector in Portugal: view of the managers', *Proceedings of the 4th European Conference of Information Systems*, Lisbon, 1996, 917–930.

Pommes, C., C. Taubman, Y. Doz and M. Hortwich, 'Banco Comercial Português', Fontainebleau, France, INSEAD, 1994.

SIBS, 'Evolution of the PMB service: 1995 and 1st semester 1996', Lisbon, SIBS, 1996.

SIBS, 'Statistics of Multibanco network – 1995 and 1st semester 1996', Lisbon, SIBS, 1996.

SIBS, 'MS-94 EFTPOS-Pinpad: user's and technical guide', Lisbon, SIBS, 1995.

SIBS, 'OEM-01 EFTPOS-payment module: user's and technical Guide', Lisbon, SIBS, 1995.

SIBS, 'PMB-94 Electronic purse-Eftpos portable terminal: user's and technical guide', Lisbon, SIBS, 1995.

SIBS, 'TA-94 and TP 94: user's and technical guide', Lisbon, SIBS, 1995.

SIBS, 'PMB electronic purse: a new Multibanco service', Lisbon, SIBS, 1995.

SIBS, 'PMB electronic purse: the role of the banks', Lisbon, SIBS, 1995.

SIBS, 'POS: guide of the service to banking agencies', Lisbon, SIBS, 1994.

SIBS, 'SIBS, the Portuguese inter-banking operator', Lisbon, SIBS, 1994.

Turban, E., E.R. McLean and J.C. Wetherbe. *Information Technology for Management: Improving Quality and Productivity*, New York, John Wiley, 1996.

DISCUSSION QUESTIONS

1. Should SIBS create a sales force to foster a wider diffusion of the PMB? Defend your argument.
2. How will customers react to this new electronic payment system that puts an end to physical money they can feel and touch?
3. How will digi-cash change consumer spending behaviour? Will the future of the electronic purse depend on the availability of an anonymous and untraceable mode of payment?
4. How will standards influence the world-wide diffusion of the electronic purse?
5. To what extent will the transfer of the electronic purse know-how be affected by cultural differences among societies?

From e-banking to e-business at Nordea (Scandinavia)

The world's biggest clicks-and-mortar bank

Nordea company background

> Our philosophy is both high tech and high touch, not either or.
>
> **Bo Harald, Head of Electronic Banking, Nordea**[1]

Customers entering Nordea's main branch in Helsinki at lunchtime on a busy weekday encounter something very different from what is typically seen at banks in other capital cities. Those long lines in front of the counter, so common at its competitors, have disappeared – even during peak hours.

During the past two decades, Bo Harald, Nordea's Head of Electronic Banking, has steadily and patiently moved the bank into the electronic age. As *Business Week* pointed out: 'Forget flash, fanfare and giant ambitions. This small Scandinavian outfit [Nordea] has quietly built the world's most successful Internet bank.'[2] Now that e-banking has become a reality at Nordea, the next big challenge for Harald is to move the bank into e-business:

> We are moving from e-banking to e-business. We are not moving into market places as such. What we are doing is taking our e-banking services and bringing them to the e-business value chain. We are an enabler for e-business.[3]

Company history

Nordea Bank is the product of several mergers between banks from four Scandinavian countries. Domestic mergers in Finland accelerated after a sustained economic crisis in the early 1990s caused by the collapse of the Soviet Union and the downturn of the global economy. The crisis strained Finland's timber-based economy and forced banks to cut costs.

The mergers took place over several years (see Exhibit 1). In 1997, the Swedish Nordbanken and the Finnish Merita merged to form MeritaNordbanken. In 1999, the Danish Unidanmark acquired TRYG and, later, Vesta. In 2000, Unidanmark and MeritaNordbanken merged to form Nordic Baltic Holding, which became Nordea after merging in 2000 with the Norwegian Christiana Bank Og Kreditkasse.

On completion of the merger process at the end of 2002, the market capitalization of Nordea reached €12.6 billion, making it the fifth largest company in the Nordic region and the fifteenth largest bank in Europe. Today, it is the largest financial group in the Nordic region with approximately €262 billion in total assets. Its market share in the Nordic banking markets ranges from 40% in Finland, 25% in Denmark, 20% in Sweden, to 15% in Norway. In the life insurance market, Nordea has a market share of 35% in Finland, 10% in Denmark, 9% in Norway and 6% in Sweden.

1 Nordea company presentation at Caisse d'Epargne Group, 13 June 2003.
2 'The dynamo of e-Banking', Business Week online, 16 April 2001.
3 Unless stated otherwise, quotations from Bo Harald were gathered during company interviews made in Helsinki in September 2003.

This case study was written by Albrecht Enders, Research Fellow at INSEAD (Fontainebleau), under the supervision of Tawfik Jelassi, Affiliate Professor of Technology Management at INSEAD, and Charles Waldman, Senior Affiliate Professor of Marketing at INSEAD. It is intended to be used as the basis for class discussion rather than to illustrate effective or ineffective handling of a management situation.

This case study was made possible by the co-operation of Bo Harald, Head of Electronic Banking at Nordea.

Exhibit 1 **The creation process of Nordea through mergers of Scandinavian banks**

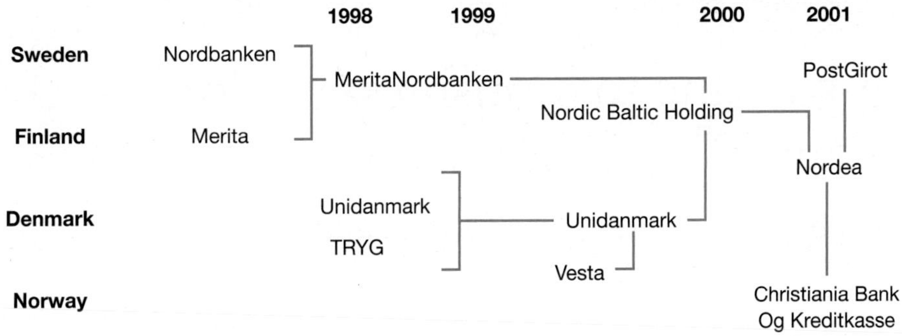

Source: Nordea Bank.

Retail banking represents the most important business area, constituting 74% of Nordea's income in 2002. Corporate and institutional banking accounted for 19%, asset management for 4%, investment banking for 2%, and group treasury for 1%.

At the end of 2002, Nordea had 10.6 million private customers, which the bank considers to be its main asset. Some 45% of the total population in the Nordic countries has either a main or secondary account with Nordea. At least 3.2 million customers are active e-banking customers (see Exhibit 2). In addition to its retail business, the bank also serves 950000 corporate customers. Nordea employs 35000 people and has 1260 branches throughout the Nordic and Baltic region (see Exhibit 3).

Exhibit 2 **Evolution of Nordea customers and e-banking**

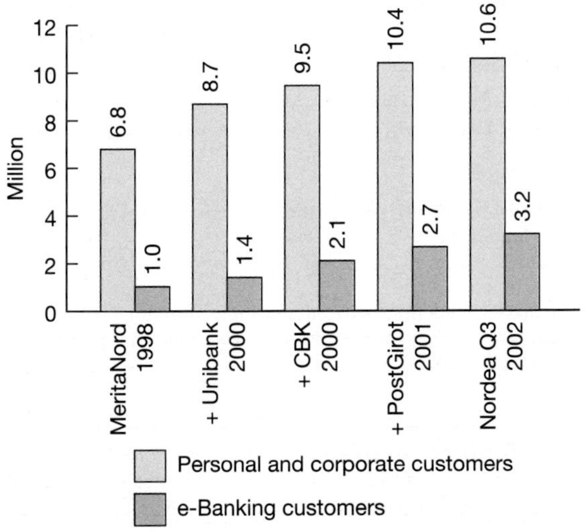

Source: Nordea Bank.

To outline the bank's purpose and goals, Nordea has formulated the 'Nordic Idea' and the 'Nordea Vision'. Its Nordic Idea states that:

- We share and exchange Nordic ideas.
- We are Nordic in operations while personal and local in delivering services. We think Nordic and act locally.
- Our market is of a size that makes it worthwhile to develop joint concepts, products and services.[4]

Nordea's vision for the future is built upon three main pillars:

- We will be valued as the leading financial services group in the Nordic and Baltic financial market with a substantial growth potential.
- We will be at the top of the league or show superior profitable growth in every market and product area in which we choose to compete.
- We will have the leading multi-channel distribution with a top world ranking in e-based financial services and solutions.[5]

Nordea's approach to e-banking

Bo Harald has been the main architect of Nordea's approach to e-banking. He joined the Union Bank of Finland in 1975 after studying law and economics, and opened the bank's first foreign office in

4 Taken from Nordea company website.
5 Taken from Nordea company website.

Exhibit 3 Nordea's European Branch Network

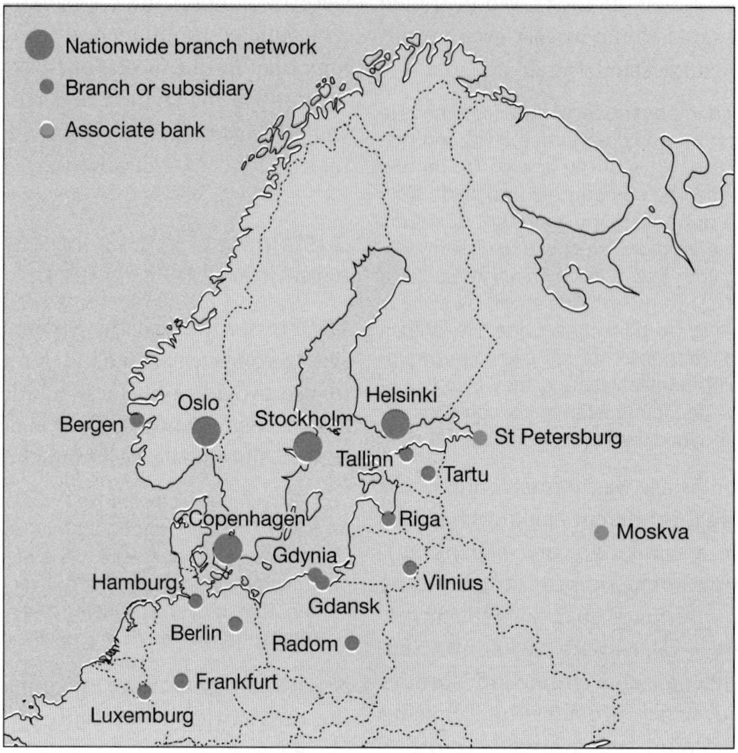

Source: Nordea Bank.

Luxemburg in 1977 and in Asia in 1980. His job assignments pushed him to use computers to carry out banking transactions:

> While away from home, I started using the computer to authorize payments. The beginning of PC banking in 1984 was a blessing for me. It became so much easier to do things from a distance.[6]

Union Bank introduced electronic payment systems and started to phase out cheques in 1982.

> I think the secret of our success was to start early. We started back in 1982 with telephone voice commands. By 1984, we added PC banking with a dial-up modem. It was like black and white compared to the color Internet, but it was a start and it gave us the experience.[7]

Starting out early also helped to keep costs down. Harald says:

> e-Banking is not expensive if you start early and you build it up gradually ... However, it can be very expensive if you wake up in the middle when things are already happening, because then you need to ask expensive consultants for advice and you end up buying all the expensive bells and whistles to outshine your competitors.

With the advent of the Internet, Bo Harald became Head of Internet Services at Merita Bank with the explicit mission to put as much business as possible on the Web in order to reduce costs and free up branch employees to focus on selling complex, higher-margin financial products.

Nordea's e-banking strategy evolved through different stages. The first was the creation of an 'e-habit' among its customers. To achieve this it was crucial to involve the 35000 branch staff who enjoyed the trust of customers and were in frequent face-to-face contact with them. In addition, the bank strived to keep e-banking simple to understand and use in order to

6 'Online extra: Q & A with Nordea's Bo Harald', Business Week online, 16 April 2001.

7 'Online extra: Q & A with Nordea's Bo Harald', Business Week online, 16 April 2001.

create a higher level of customer satisfaction. The underlying principle was that the bank's website should be designed in a way that would be easy even for 65-year-old customers to understand. Harald explains:

> I met the CEO of an important corporate customer. He had said before that he would never use a PC and that he would never retire. Now, at the age of 78, he had decided to retire. Then he came to me and said: 'Now that I am retired, I don't have my secretary doing my banking transactions anymore, so I have to do it myself. And I started using your Solo service [the Nordea online banking system] and it works extremely well.' Now he is really fond of our basic e-banking service. He is even talking about it to the people of his own age group. They tested it [Solo] themselves, and they also like it. That's how it works: first, our customers become believers [in e-banking] and then they become preachers.

The goal of the second stage was to interconnect customers by integrating the different banking channels: e-banking, mobile e-banking (or m-banking), branch-based banking, contact centre and providing different types of e-services such as e-payment, e-billing, e-signature, e-ID, e-salary and e-invoicing. All the Internet services are concentrated in Nordea's Internet bank, 'Solo', which provides the following banking services: account management, transfers between own accounts, domestic and foreign invoice payments, equity (domestic and foreign), mutual funds and bond investments, electronically signed credit facilities, as well as life and general insurance.

The goal of the third stage is to personalize further the e-banking services and customize offerings by tapping into the value of data-mines. But for Bo Harald, when developing new products and services at Nordea: 'We avoid asking customers directly. We would rather use our colleagues and their experience in the branches.'[8]

Getting top-management support for e-banking has not always been easy, Harald acknowledges:

> Either you have a CEO who supports e-banking right from the beginning and has the staying power to see it through, or he lets you take care of it yourself. I can't say that our CEOs early on were particularly excited about it. If you have someone on a high enough level who pushes e-business, then the CEO does not have to do it. Actually, I am a little bit afraid if CEOs become too obsessed with something. They have such a big voice that it might be overdoing it. It must be planted somewhere in the bank, and I have been lucky to have that role at Nordea. I would love to have had more support in the past, though. We would have taken off much earlier!

While Nordea and other Scandinavian banks were developing their e-banking know-how, their e-customers simultaneously built up other assets important for the success of e-banking. These included 'e-trust' (in the security and reliability of electronic banking channels) and 'e-habit' (the routine use of the Internet for bank transactions).

Sustaining Nordea's Internet lead: from e-banking to e-business

The e-trust and e-habit have prompted Nordea to leverage the competencies built up for its e-banking services to also provide e-business solutions. In fact, Harald believes that e-banking alone is no longer a way for a bank to differentiate itself from its competitors:

> e-Banking services are kind of passé. Every bank offers them. The really important thing is launching e-banking services for e-business. It's a huge market! Banks are getting their acts together but very slowly. So I am worried that banks are losing their opportunity to earn substantial income from e-business.

Nordea started to move into e-business by leveraging the capabilities it had built up for e-banking. Bo Harald explains:

> The underlying principle is that we try to reuse technologies that we already have. For instance, we have file transfers for accounts, so why not have file transfer for bills as well?

The main e-business services that Nordea currently offers to its private and corporate customers include e-idenfication, e-signature, e-billing, e-salary and e-payment.

e-Identification

Through Nordea's e-identification services, Nordea customers can identify themselves on the websites of other participating companies and governmental agencies. For the latter, the Finnish Ministry of Finance has officially stated that if customers need reliable identification, they can and should use the bank's identification standards. For example, consider the case of citizens who want to access the state pension system to find out the balance of their pension in order to decide how much to save for retirement.

---

8 'Learn from the largest Internet bank of the world', accessed at www.tietoenator.lv

Initially, they access the state pension system's website with links to all major banks in Finland that provide e-identification services. They then choose their bank, access the respective website and identify themselves with their one-time password. Upon registering there, they can switch to other services, including the state pension service, while staying within the identified area. 'This state pension site is accessed 2000 times a day', says Bo Harald.

> Our e-identification service is so convincing that the Finnish post office has stopped its own identification service. They use banks because it's very expensive to have a reliable identification service only for the post office. Why should they do it themselves?

e-Signature

The e-signature service came about 'by accident'. When Bo Harald told executives from Sonera, the largest telecom operator in Finland, that customers could get a loan online, they said: 'Look, if you can sign up for loans through your system, you should also be able to sign a phone subscription contract.' Within a few weeks, Nordea reached an agreement with Sonera to send all interested customers an online phone contract through a link to Nordea's Solo Internet bank website where they could identify themselves and then sign the contract. This system was later extended to other businesses that wanted to provide e-signatures for their contracts.

e-Billing

Through Nordea's e-billing services, companies can send their invoices electronically to the bank, which then forwards them to their customers who have e-banking agreements, while those customers without e-banking accounts automatically receive a printed invoice via the mail (see Exhibit 4). Customers who get their invoice through their e-bank connection are asked: 'Do you want to pay this bill?'; they approve the payment with a mouse-click and the bill is paid. This service was first used in 1998 by Finland's main telephone companies to send invoices to customers via Internet. Bo Harald comments:

> In Europe, there is a cost of $50 billion every year for paper invoices. Who pays for that? In the end, it is always the customer. We can eliminate that when we go to electronic invoicing. In Sweden, we are sending out invoice files to a Nordea switch, which are then distributed to private and large corporate customers [e.g. a telecom company that sends invoices to its customers].

Exhibit 4 **Nordea switchboard for invoice processing**

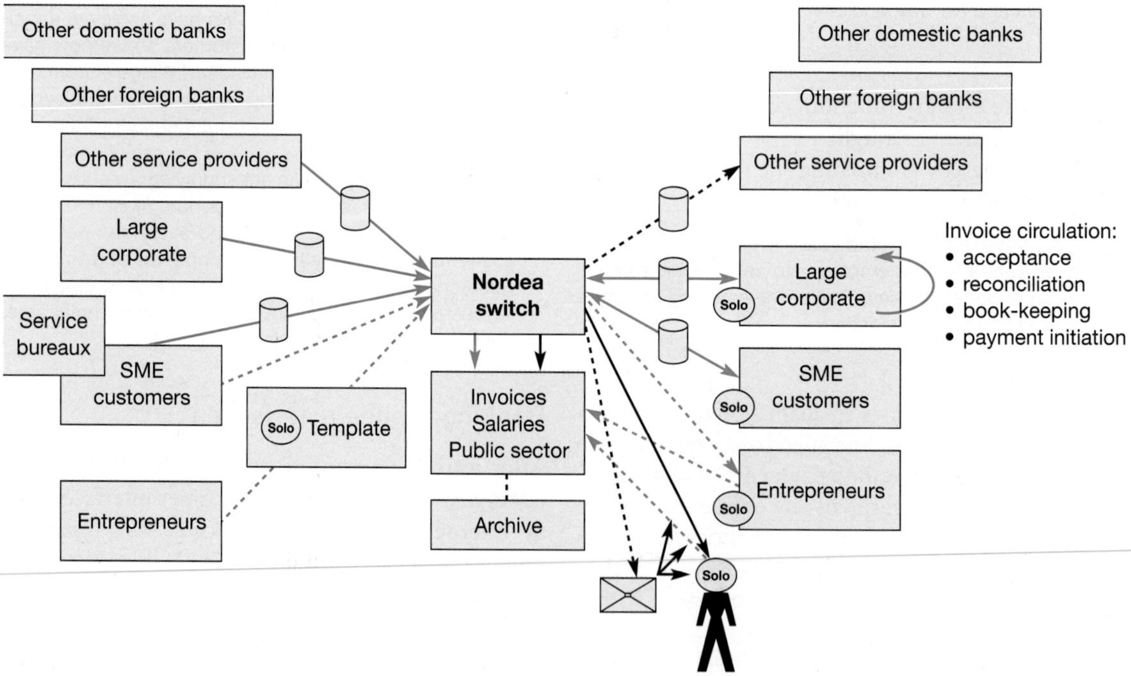

Source: Nordea Bank.

Exhibit 5 Evolution of banking devices at Nordea

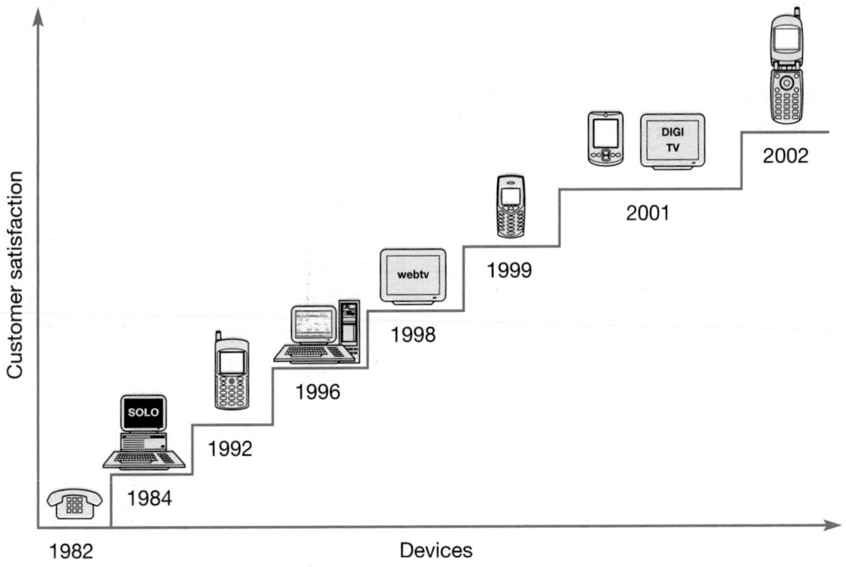

Source: Nordea Bank.

In the future, you will see it with other banks as well. What's fantastic about this is that if you are an entrepreneur you can pay your bills online and you can also send out your invoices easily and quickly. The party that is sending the bills doesn't have to worry. Isn't that the obvious way? We are already sending these bills to other banks in Finland, Sweden, soon to other banks in Denmark and Norway, and later to the rest of Europe.

e-Salary

Through the e-salary function, companies can send income statements straight to the e-bank of their employees, thereby eliminating the need for printed salary statements sent via mail.

If you have enough staff, say 10000 employees, it makes sense for the employer to send out e-salaries instead of paper salaries. That's where getting to a critical size really starts to matter.

e-Payment

The e-payment function is an adaptation of the invoicing function, which online merchants on the Solo platform can use for settling payments. It allows customers to go to the website of any online store in the Solo marketplace, place an order and click on a link to Nordea's e-payment system where they request an electronic invoice. After approving the payment with a mouse click, the amount is instantly transferred to the seller's account. This method has a twofold benefit: the merchant does not need to send out paper invoices or to worry whether the buyer pays. To ensure that there is no fraud on the merchant's side, Nordea conducts a reliability check on all 2000 merchants who sell goods in the Solo e-marketplace. Says Bo Harald:

For corporate customers, the value of the Solo e-marketplace grows exponentially with the increase in the number of retail customers ... We have achieved a critical mass among our retail customers so we now have people who want to buy all kinds of things – from CDs and stereo systems to kitchen appliances and bicycles. That's what we need for the e-marketplace. As part of this move into e-business, we see the evolution of value chains in which the banks are supplying essential parts. In the future, this is the most important reason for going into e-banking because each and every company and governmental agency is increasingly moving to digital value chains and the bank has a big role to play there for customer identification, direct payment in real time, invoicing, e-salary, e-pension and e-signature.

Banking channels at Nordea

After introducing online banking in 1984, Nordea continued to introduce new customer interfaces such as Internet banking, TV banking, WAP-enabled[9] mobile phones and digital TV (see Exhibit 5).

9 Wap stands for Wireless Application Protocol, a secure specification that allows users to access information instantly via handheld wireless devices

According to Bo Harald:

> When adding channels, a bank's main goal should be to add value ... But it is also crucial that all channels and services have the same look and feel so as to offer customers a consistent user experience. The key is to have one core to our electronic bank and then to keep adding doors to it.

Kaisa Juhanni, a Nordea customer from Finland, considers Nordea's reliable multi-channel services to be a major asset of the bank:

> I like the quick and instant access without having to queue up at a branch. I also like the flexibility of being able to do my banking any time and any place, be it from home, the office or through the mobile phone. The Solo system is also very reliable. The system has probably been down just once during the past six and a half years. Finally, Nordea has also a very large installed base of users in Finland which allows me to transfer money to them without any delays.

ATMs and pay terminals

Automatic teller machines (ATMs) and pay terminals still play an important role in cash withdrawal and other transactions. However, as card payments and Internet transactions become more important, the role of ATMs and cash in general becomes less relevant (see Table 1). Bo Harald explains:

> In our Danish organization, we have the highest number of card payments per capita in the world; the second highest is our Finnish organization. Actually, Finland has the lowest amount of cash in relation to GNP [gross national product]. As a result, ATMs have become less important. Earlier this year, we saw a fantastic development in Finland, which we consider as a laboratory. Compared to 2002, cash withdrawals have gone down by 15–16% in our branches and 8% from our ATMs. That's excellent because ATMs are very expensive: you have to keep the money there, you need to protect them and sometimes they are destroyed. Cash is actually the most expensive way to pay for things. Transactions at pay terminals are also quickly decreasing. We have started to charge people for using these terminals, so this year they should go down quite drastically. Just like ATMs, pay terminals are also unprofitable. Actually, I don't want to see them at all five years from now. People shouldn't be paying their bills in the street; they should do it at home. Why should people use cash at all? It's unhygienic, it's unsafe to carry around and there is a high risk of counterfeit money. It's irrational!

Table 1 Household transactions in Finland

	Transactions (millions)				*% change*
	1999	*2000*	*2001*	*2002*	*1999–2002*
Manual transactions	184.9	163.9	141.0	125.3	−32.2
Pay terminals	35.5	35.6	34.3	31.7	−10.7
Card payments	234.3	263.1	306.9	363.0	+54.9
Cash-withdrawal ATMs	197.9	202.5	207.2	204.4	+3.3
Direct debit	69	75.3	78.5	81.5	+18.1
Solo payments	32.7	58.2	78.2	97.6	+198.5
Total	754.3	798.6	846.1	903.5	+20

Source: Nordea Bank.

m-Banking

Nordea's wireless service started out with WAP phones in 1999. Through WAP-enabled phones, Nordea customers can track their account and credit card transactions, transfer funds between accounts, pay bills both domestically and abroad, trade equities and read customer mail. The WAP service extends to the mobile phone Nordea's Internet services originally available through Solo. In 2000, Nordea introduced stock trading and bank transfers via cell phone and also made it possible for customers to purchase movie tickets which are debited directly from their Nordea account. Adapting Internet services to the WAP cost Nordea less than €500,000; it mainly required adding a server for wireless services. However, Harald sees a lot of potential for wireless banking:

> I firmly believe that, with Nokia, Finland will continue to play a leading role world-wide in mobile phone technology. I was recently on a train from Arlanda airport [in Stockholm] and I saw a group of teenagers all using their mobile phones. These are our future customers.[10]

In January 2002, Nordea expanded its wireless services by providing a more elaborate m-payment version for Finnish customers who have GPRS[11] handsets and are connected with Telia's, Sonera's or Radiolinja's wireless communication networks. This service was made possible via a joint launch with Nokia of a dual-SIM[12]

10 'Online Extra: Q & A with Nordea's Bo Harald', Business Week online, 16 April 2001.

11 General Packet Radio Service (GPRS) is a technology used to send and receive data via packet delivery over a wireless network allowing the user to stay connected to the Internet.

12 A subscriber identity module (SIM) is the smart card inside a mobile phone that identifies the user account to the network, handles authentication and provides data storage for user data such as phone numbers and network information. It may contain applications that run on the phone.

handset for mobile transactions. The phone has two separate slots: one for the operator's SIM card, the other for the m-payment card issued by Nordea, which is based on wireless identification module (WIM).[13] Harald believes that customers should be free to choose the supplier of their banking services:

> You don't buy groceries from a furniture store, so why should you buy your banking services from the mobile operator? Plus, it's really not a big deal nowadays to make a handset with two chips.[14]

PC banking

> Wells Fargo, Citibank and Bank of America have, similarly, as many customers as our Internet Bank 'Solo'. But with 124 million payments over the Internet in 2002, no other bank can keep up [with us]! This number might be about twice as large as those of the previously mentioned banks combined.
>
> **Bo Harald[15]**

Online banking at Nordea started as early as the mid-1980s when Nordea allowed its customers to start doing transactions from computers at their workplace. Harald explains:

> In the mid-1980s, people didn't have computers at home, and if they did, they didn't have modems. So we asked our large corporate customers: 'Can't you allow your employees to log on to their banking account through the workplace computer? That will save you a lot of time and money because people won't have to go to the branch any more.' Ever since, workplace access has been a very important pillar for our e-banking.

e-Banking and bricks-and-mortar banking have never been in competition at Nordea. Rather, they are considered to be complementary, as Harald emphasizes:

> One of the main reasons for our success is the fact that we made e-banking already part of our branch business in 1982. We never considered it to be a competitor. e-Banking is not a separate profit center. That is important in order to quickly achieve a crucial size. Without the support of the branch employees, one is not able to reach that goal.[16]

However, direct online consultation from bank employees either in a branch or a call centre is kept to an absolute minimum:

> Nordea decided consciously to offer no consultation on the Internet and very little on the phone. You must keep your offer simple to succeed in Internet business and to gain the necessary confidence and trust of your customers. That's difficult but necessary, and if your offer is simple, you don't need to provide expensive instructions over the Internet. For complex [financial] products, customers go to the branch anyway. However, the shift of transactions to electronic channels frees up resources for improved service levels in the branch.[17]

Table 2 Evolution of online usage at Nordea

	Jan-July 00	*Jan-July 01*	*Jan-July 02*	*Jan-July 03*
Log-ons				
Denmark	6 091 418	8 924 759	11 721 765	14 659 759
Finland	17 495 518	20 582 125	24 671 753	28 199 328
Norway	1 595 000	3 562 704	4 528 822	6 118 581
Sweden	4 640 100	11 562 033	16 738 683	22 863 322
Nordea	29 822 036	44 631 621	57 661 023	71 840 090
Online payments				
Denmark	2 773 192	5 186 359	7 220 065	8 781 289
Finland	20 774 000	26 293 637	30 712 994	35 626 067
Norway	2 150 000	4 121 013	5 236 914	6 641 027
Sweden	6 660 147	18 845 501	25 202 502	31 401 953
Nordea	32 357 339	54 446 510	68 372 475	82 450 336

Source: Nordea Bank.

Tuukka Seppa, a Nordea customer from Finland, is fond of Nordea's banking services:

> What I really like is the simplicity of the authentication process and the website itself. It is also very helpful that it offers immediate transactions between two Nordea accounts.

Today, all Internet banking activities at Nordea take place through Solo, the company's online banking service, which has become increasingly popular (see Table 2). This is demonstrated by the following statistics (figures correspond to the highest month of usage):

- *Student loans*: 84% of all student loans are completely paperless. Students apply online by providing information about their financial status and the loan is approved within one hour through a computerized scoring system. Once approved, students sign by keying in their customer number once more and a one-time password.[18]

---

13 WIM allows users to identify themselves with digital signatures to confirm their banking transactions.

14 'Two slots are better than one', Silicon.com, 23 May 2002.

15 'Learn from the largest Internet bank of the world', accessed at www.tietoenator.lv

16 'Learn from the largest Internet bank of the world', accessed at www.tietoenator.lv

17 'Learn from the largest Internet bank of the world', accessed at www.tietoenator.lv

18 For more information on the one-time password, refer to the authentication section below.

- *Equity orders*: 80% of all equity orders are made through Solo.
- *Mutual funds*: 65% of all mutual funds are managed by Solo.
- *Foreign payments*: 59% of all private and small business foreign payments take place via Solo. Customers key the account number of the recipient into their computer (or mobile phone) and the money is received as fast as international transfers travel – within Nordea one day at most. Fees are €15 in a branch and €7 for online payments.
- *Currency deposits*: 30% of all currency deposits take place through Solo.
- *Foreign exchange*: 35% of all foreign exchange transactions occur with Solo.
- *Car finance*: 25% of all car financing takes place through Solo.
- *Home mortgages*: 24% of home mortgages come in through the Internet.

Bo Harald summarizes Nordea's challenge for 2005: 'All the numbers mentioned should be up to 80% or 90%. That's the challenge in our bank.'[19]

TV banking

TV-based banking was launched in 1996 through the use of a set-top box that connected to normal household TVs. Through this box, Nordea customers could log on to the Nordea banking system and carry out basic banking transactions. The underlying idea was that those people who disliked computers would use the TV to write e-mails and to check their account balance. However, as it turned out, TV banking has not so far fulfilled the high expectations associated with it. Says Bo Harald:

> Clearly, every family has a TV in their house, so in principle it should work well ... but we believe that people just do not want to check e-mails or do their banking in front of the whole family. Those are rather private things and that's why the TV in the living room is not well suited. That's the reason why we haven't invested more in this channel. We only offer basic services for e-payments. With the continuing convergence of the TV and the PC this might change, though.

Branch-based banking

The role of branch offices at Nordea has changed in recent decades. While in the past bank clerks spent most of their time keying in transactions manually, this has drastically decreased (see Table 1). For 2003, Bo Harald expect a further reduction of 20 million manual transactions:

> If every transaction takes one minute, what can you do with this time once customers start banking online? It frees up the branch staff to give customers advice. We use our branches primarily for establishing personal relationships with our customers, which is important when making a big decision (such as purchasing insurance or a pension scheme) that requires personal trust. In a sense, banking is local but it doesn't always require an expensive branch. Sometimes an office is enough. You don't have to offer transfers there but you will never be able to replace either the personal sales nor the fostering of personal relationships. To achieve this it is absolutely paramount not to create separate profit centres for Internet and branch banking because the two have to feed each other. There mustn't be competition but co-operation between the two channels. Combining and leveraging high-tech and high-touch is the key to success.

Nonetheless, the number of Nordea branches in Finland decreased significantly during the last decade – down from 1300 in 1991 to 400 in 2000. The number of employees shrunk to less than half during the same period, falling from 22 000 to 10 600 (see Exhibit 6). Getting strong and influential labour unions to agree to such staff reductions has not always been an easy task. Bo Harald recalls:

> We had to speak to the unions in great length and we had to hand out very generous packages since no employee was actually fired ... But we also tried to show that Solo [the Nordea Internet bank] had led to a great increase in customer satisfaction and that this would make Nordea a more competitive and stable institution in the future. We also showed the [labour] unions that Finland is absolutely world-class when it comes to Internet banking and that it was necessary to make changes in our organizational structure in order to maintain this lead. Finally, we pointed out that it was problematic to have people do this type of manual, repetitive, low-paid work and that it would be much more valuable if we educated these people to do a more creative and interesting job.

Today, Nordea operates 1 288 branch offices throughout the Nordic region and employs 34 600 people (full-time equivalents). In addition to the Finnish branches, there are 267 branches with 8500 employees in Sweden, 151 branches with 4400 employees in Norway and 348 branch offices with 9400 employees

19 'Learn from the largest Internet bank of the world', accessed at www.tietoenator.lv

Exhibit 6 **Evolution of Nordea's staff and branches in Finland**

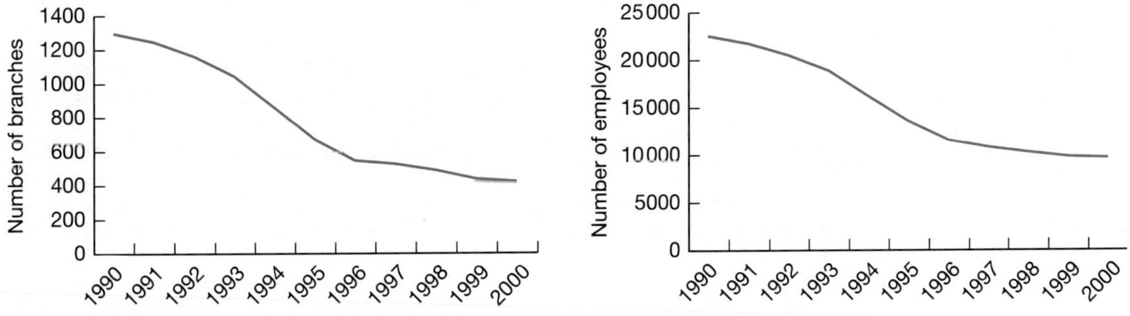

Source: Nordea Bank.

in Denmark. Says Bo Harald:

> We have been cutting branches for a long time, partly thanks to mergers and now thanks to the Internet ... Finland used to be over-branched, but now it is almost under-branched. The future is to change the way branches work: we are now opening teller-less branches in places such as shopping centers. The idea is to use the branch to sell and provide services, not to make transactions. The branch staff should add value for customers. They shouldn't do routine, uninspiring work.[20]

Marketing

Due to its early start in e-banking, Nordea has spent little on marketing its Internet initiatives in comparison with other online banks. From 1996 to 2001, Nordea spent about €18 million to market its Finnish Internet initiatives. This money was not directed primarily towards attracting new customers but instead towards getting the nine million branch customers to move to the Internet.

Because of its large size, Nordea takes a mass-market approach to its banking activities. Bo Harald explains:

> If you are as big a bank as we are, you can't afford not to target all customers ... There is also a misconception that there is a clear distinction between profitable and unprofitable customers. Of course, there are customers who come to the branch every day. They are unprofitable, but there is no way to get rid of them, so you might as well not even try. Another typical feature of less profitable customers is that they are young. However, soon enough they'll need a mortgage and a retirement plan. If you look at the older segments, you don't find that many unprofitable customers. Thus, when you want to talk about profitability, you really need to take a dynamic view of customers.

In its marketing activities, Nordea differentiates between two types of customer:

- *Internet believers.* These customers have been online for years and have the know-how and trust to navigate the Internet, to shop online and to do their banking online. To them e-banking is a normal day-to-day activity; something that is not worth talking about with their friends. From a marketing perspective, these customers are therefore considered to be 'infertile'.
- *Non-believers.* These customers are just starting to surf the Internet. They require substantial convincing to build enough trust and know-how to start doing e-banking. Friendly branch employees are best suited for removing that insecurity. Once they are online, however, these customers are amazed and proud of their accomplishments and want to pass the news on to their friends. After turning them into believers they take the next step and become preachers – a viral marketing effect where customers acquire more customers, as Harald emphasizes: 'When you get a critical mass of customers, they are the best sales force for you.'

At Nordea, the importance of a branch cannot be under-estimated when it comes to turning non-believers into believers. Says Harald:

> Just imagine an enthusiastic clerk serving a client, who says, 'Hey, why don't you also do e-banking? Everyone else does it' and then convincingly seals the deal ... The value of the branch network is absolutely fantastic. That's why you need to get employees to like it. Otherwise they won't move business into the online channel.

20 'Online extra: Q & A with Nordea's Bo Harald', Business Week online, 16 April, 2001.

In spite of having achieved a high penetration rate throughout Scandinavia, Harald still sees significant potential for the bank's e-banking services, especially among senior citizens:

> Even if you are the largest e-bank in the world, of course you still have a lot to do in the 60-year-old-plus sector. We feel a social responsibility to organize evenings – especially in the countryside – where senior citizens learn how to use the Internet. For those people, we organize senior citizens' clubs. We just had one in the east of Finland that was originally set up for 100 people. In the end, 1500 people wanted to participate. When someone in that age group finds out that they can send an e-mail to their children or their grandchildren, that's a big deal. The sooner they come on board, the better it is. And then they can take part in online communities and discussion forums. Finland is a country of associations; there is an association for everything, even for Siamese cats. Whatever it is they like, they can find it on the Internet. And they need e-payment, e-invoicing and e-identification. All those services are required to manage your Siamese cat association! Then, those senior citizens will get so much more out of their lives, because there is such a huge window that opens up into the world – a new dimension. And e-banking is just one part of it.

While targeting senior citizens with its e-banking, marketing these services to the younger, Internet-savvy generation is not at the top of Nordea's agenda. Bo Harald says:

> I wouldn't spend any money on marketing to people younger than 30; there is no need for that ... You can start with e-banking when you are 15; to get the message through to these people, you let them know what's possible. That's worthwhile putting some marketing money into. But from 18 to 30 or 40, there is not much you need to do. Instead, I would put all my money into the 60 years and above group.

Pricing

> e-Banking is not free because every transaction has a cost. Customers who use it should pay for it, not those who don't. If a bank comes out and says that their e-banking services are for free, they are lying. It is only a question of who pays.
>
> **Bo Harald**

Nordea's rates for retail customers contain fixed and variable elements. The monthly fee for basic services, regardless of usage, is €2 per month. Access to the credit card balance costs an additional 40 cents, and mobile WAP services an additional 30 cents; these charges are now being removed. Customers who want to do equity trading pay from €4 per month for a basic version and up to €20 for the most advanced version. Nordea's competitors tend to be cheaper. E*Trade, for instance, charges a fee of €10 per trade, a quarter of Nordea's price. However, Nordea's fees seem still to be reasonable, as Magnus Grann, a 40-year-old software engineer, points out: 'Nordea's fees just aren't high enough to make a difference.'[21]

But other customers struggle with the pricing of Nordea. Tuukka Seppa, a Nordea customer from Finland, points out:

> Nordea is definitely not cheap and charges some fees for every additional service. For instance, I really don't like it that there are additional monthly payments for accessing my investments.[22]

Tomas Bauer, a Nordea customer from Sweden, goes even further:

> I think Nordea's pricing practices are a little dubious. I actually feel that they tricked me into opening a savings account when they offered me an interest rate slightly above market level. After one year they dropped the rate to almost 1% below the comparable market level.[23]

On average, for its online services, Nordea generates revenues of slightly more than €2 per customer, which amounts to €7 million per month. These revenues cover all costs for the online banking channel and also generate a profit (which is not disclosed).

Corporate customers pay from €20 to €5000 depending on the level of service. To be a member of the e-marketplace, merchants pay a €200 connection charge up front and a monthly fee of €20. For each transaction, an additional fee of 35 cents is levied. In contrast to credit cards, the transaction fee does not depend on the volume of the purchase. This is due to the fact that with credit cards, the bank has to finance the period – up to 30 days – between when the merchant gets the money and when the customer pays the bill. Since the Solo direct payment is similar to a debit card, there is no time gap to be refinanced. Merchants benefit because they no longer have to send out invoices by mail. In addition, while previously they had to wait to be paid, they now receive payment in real-time before even shipping the goods, thereby eliminating their credit risk.

---

21 'The dynamo of e-Banking', Business Week online, 16 April 2001.

22 Personal interview, 5 October 2003.

23 Personal interview, 5 October 2003.

> We pay attention to the profitability of our e-banking operations. Our basic principle when introducing new applications is that we don't give added value for free. Our customers pay a monthly fee for Internet banking. If further services are taken up such as brokerage, credit card reporting or WAP, then it costs more. Customers accept it if they benefit from it, for example, if a transfer becomes more favorable and simpler. The added value which is created here cannot be free. Many companies have just started to understand it.[24]

The pricing of banking services is also used as an effective tool for steering customer business into certain channels. Bo Harald shares his personal experience:

> In 1983, we introduced a charge of 10 cents for all cheque forms, which were very popular at that time and my wife was very good at writing these cheques. But once this fee was introduced, she didn't write out one single cheque any more. In fact, chequebooks just disappeared because it wasn't worth even 10 cents to the people. Instead, they started to pay with a debit card and afterwards they used the debit card at payment terminals to pay bills. Those same people later on started using computers at their workplace to do the transactions. ... In the US, people write somewhere around 50 billion cheques a year. That amount of paper is transported by airmail to the banks and back. It costs somewhere around $75 billion a year to pay for these transactions and, on top of that, it's an environmental problem. It takes a lot of time and costs a lot of money. If you don't put an upfront price tag on costs, you still have to pay for them and you don't direct the activities of your customers. Showing the customer what it really costs allows the customer to make rational choices because they are paying for these costs.

Nordea has implemented similar pricing structures between branches and Internet banking to entice customers to move online. For instance, a foreign currency wire costs $7 online but $14 in a branch. Bill payment is free online, whereas it costs $3.50 per bill in a branch.

Customer authentication

Nordea's customer authentication procedure has been in place since the early 1980s. For all contact with the bank, whether via the Internet, mobile phone or call centre, customers use one identification number: the one-time code (OTC). These OTCs, which are printed on a card, are comparable to the transaction number which customers use for transfers. To access their bank account through any one of the above-mentioned electronic channels, customers need to have the OTC handy. Bo Harald considers the Nordea authentication approach to be superior to most others:

> To connect to Nordea, customers need to have their code, which is given after opening an account with us. The latter can be done only if the customer shows up in person at the bank branch and presents an ID document. Other banks, especially Internet banks, are not so rigorous. There, all you need to do is send in a phone bill where you can see the customer's address. That's easy to forge and then you can get into the money laundering business quickly.

He points out additional advantages of the OTC:

> With the one-time-password and the identification number they [the customers] get access to a safe e-business marketplace, which they can visit from everywhere and on which they can do much more than traditional banking transactions. For example, they can sign contracts with their energy and telecom suppliers, buy credit on-line, or assign attorneys. Plus, they don't need any pedantic installations of card readers or programs. At the moment, we have a very interesting situation since the Ministry of Finance recommends that for future transactions in the public sector which require an electronic identification this should be done through e-banking platforms. Again, that's trust, which upholds our services. 'You want to know something concerning your pension? Please click here.' We – and the other banks in Finland – offer the use of OTC to everyone who has to offer identification and signature possibilities. Millions of customers already have this code, and for them it's an additional service if they can interact with other companies or governmental agencies.[25]

However, the OTC is not popular with everyone. Kaisa Juhanni, a Nordea customer from Finland, points out: 'What I really dislike about the Nordea online banking is that you always need to carry the pass-code list with you in order to access the service.'

For the future, Nordea plans to develop a public-key infrastructure (PKI)[26] that would allow

---

24 'Learn from the largest Internet bank of the world', accessed at www.tietoenator.lv.

25 'Learn from the largest Internet bank of the world', accessed at www.tietoenator.lv.

26 Public key infrastructure is an electronic framework for trusted security. Participants in a PKI each obtain a digital certificate from a trusted certificate authority (CA), which then authenticates their identity when initiating a secure transaction. Individual transactions are encrypted by each participant using their own pair of electronic keys, one of which they keep for their own private use, while the other – the 'public key' – is made available to other participants. PKI has been widely adopted as the basis for secure Internet and web services transactions.

Exhibit 7 **Change of business structure to support the integration of IT and processes**

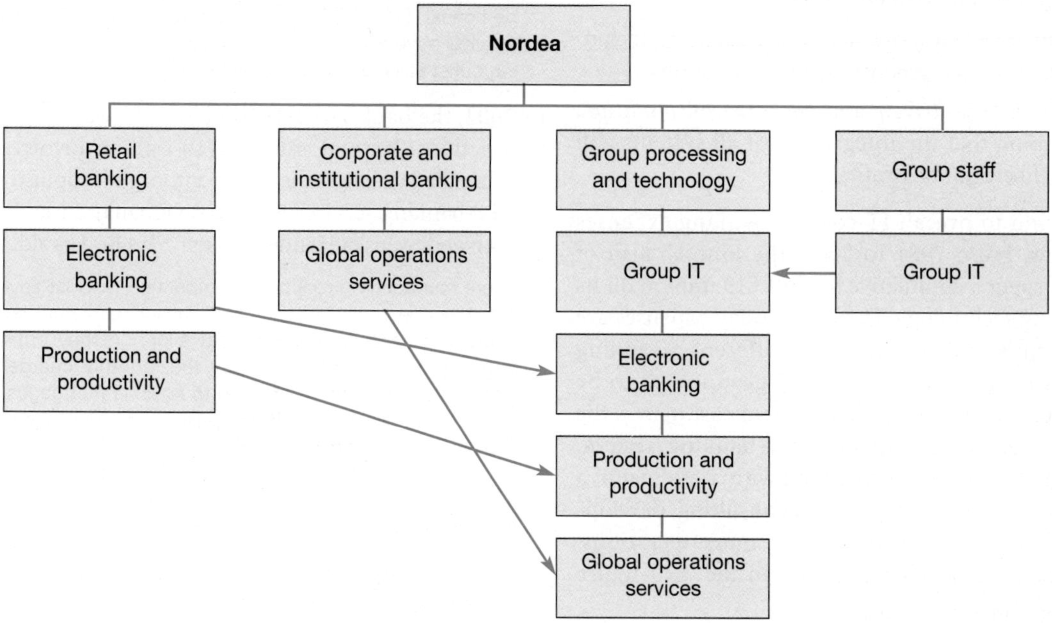

Source: Nordea Bank.

customers to log on to PCs or mobile phones using smart-cards equipped with chips.

Technology

The evolution of the technological platform at Nordea – the backbone of all its e-banking operations – has been strongly influenced by the original individual banks which all had different technology platforms. For instance, the Finnish Merita bank had an e-banking infrastructure that allowed customers to log on to their system with just a browser and a simple password system. At the Swedish Nordbanken, on the other hand, customers needed to install special software and get a smart-card reader before going online.

After the completion of the merger, Nordea was faced with a very complex IT infrastructure which included the following:

- *Production*: four main production centres with multiple platforms.
- *Applications*: roughly 9000 applications.
- *Networks*: four different branch networks.

Since then, Nordea has undergone efforts to integrate the various IT systems and organizational structure to streamline its activities. For example, real-time processing systems, which have been in place since 1985, needed to be aligned. On the organizational side, the changes are reflected in the increased importance of the group processing and technology unit (see Exhibit 7). The electronic banking and production and productivity units were moved over from retail banking. The corporate and institutional banking unit handed over the global operations services while group staff handed over the group IT. Several reasons led to this concentration of technology functions in one unit, including focusing on integration and cost efficiency, releasing time for business areas to focus on customers and capitalizing on change management.

Today, IT costs correspond to 20% of total expenses, averaging around €200 million per quarter. These costs are almost evenly divided between development costs (47%) and production costs (53%). Nordea has formulated a philosophy to drive its IT operations, which includes the following elements:

- *A comprehensive governance and control structure* on IT development and IT production.
- *Business-driven development*, i.e. business decides the 'what', IT decides the 'how'.

- *Strict prioritization of development* to support integration and cost efficiency.
- *Gradual creation of common Nordic platforms*, including consolidated production and applications.
- *Business-case-driven approach to consolidation*, assuming that the integration of all systems will most likely not be profitable.

In relation to overall IT costs, e-banking expenses were low. From 1981 to 2000, the Finnish arm of Nordea spent a cumulative total of €19 million on its e-banking technology. However, today expenses are significantly higher because 17 different e-banking systems throughout the Nordea group need to be maintained and improved. The main cost item is the development of an integrated e-banking system, which Nordea is jointly pursuing with TietoEnator, a Finnish company specializing in consulting, developing and hosting its customers' business operations. The annual e-banking costs are in the 'two-figure millions' range.

In the late 1990s, at the peak of the dot.com years, Nordea considered selling its technology systems to other banks in Europe. Bo Harald explains:

> In the end we didn't do it because all banks are very different and it would cost a lot of effort to make them work. Banking is a complicated business and if you really want to have the best return on equity, you should have high-touch and high-tech. We ended up making money but it wasn't enough to justify the effort of selling our technology. Instead, we decided to focus all of our energy on our customers.

Competition

Even though Nordea has achieved a dominant role in the Nordic region, a number of Swedish and Finnish banks compete head-on with Nordea – also with regards to e-banking services. Swedbank, for instance, which had 1.3 million online banking customers in 2002, is planning to allow its m-banking customers to view their mobile phone account statements, update their subscription contracts and access itemized calls.

Okobank in Finland has 720000 retail customers on the Internet. Matti Korkeela, Executive Vice-President at OKO, believes in the quality of the bank's e-offerings:

> We have estimated that active users of the system make up approximately 80% of our Internet-banking clients. I believe this figure is higher than that of our competitors. With OKO Bank, Internet banking per customer is more intensive than with most other banks. To be honest, I do not believe in pure Internet banking. We at OKO have a multi-service concept, where the banking outlet still plays an important role.[27]

In 2002, the bank saw a 48% increase in web-based transactions. In total, 40% of 110 million invoices were handled online. Other competitors with sophisticated e-banking services include Rabobank, Enskilda Banken and Svenska Handelsbanken. Says Bo Harald:

> There has been no real price competition ... Cost savings have been passed on in two ways. First, if you pay your bill in a branch today, you pay a lot of money, but if you pay it online you only pay the monthly charge. Second, competition has moved to housing mortgages. All the cost savings have been pushed into mortgages with margins down from 1.6% to 0.8%. Most banks have done the same thing and have passed on the cost savings, so it's always the customer who, in the end, wins the most.

At Nordea, pure online banks are not viewed as a major threat:

> We haven't lost a significant amount of business to pure e-players ... They may be cheaper than us but an e-bank has no personal selling capabilities, no customer base, and it costs them a fortune to acquire customers. I am convinced people value the safety of branches and a trusted relationship. Our vision is to be high-tech and high-touch. That will make us invulnerable to cyber-attacks. I believe traditional banks will play a central place in the e-economy. They have trust. They have established brands. Today, nobody would try to set up an Amazon.com-type bank any more. It's just too expensive and it doesn't work in our business.[28]

Customers who have been clients of Nordea for a long time are a major asset for the bank. Tuukka Seppa said:

> Initially, I was a customer of Kansallis-Osake-Pankki (KOP), which became Merita in 1976. For personal purposes, I started using the Solo online service in 1995. Through it I pay all my bills, review my account transactions as well as my credit card charges. I also use it to authenticate access to my electronic mailbox which is hosted by the Finnish Post.[29]

Where will new competition for Nordea come from? Will it be from software houses, large international

---

27 'The massive e-habit as a natural resource', Nordicum.com, No. 1, 2003.
28 'Online extra: Q & A with Nordea's Bo Harald', Business Week online, 16 April 2001.
29 Personal interview, 5 October 2003.

banks (such as Citibank or Deutsche Bank) or others? Bo Harald replies:

> These companies don't have the local branch structure and they don't have our cost-income ratios ... Telecom operators that have very broad access to their mobile phone customers might enter the competition.

However, contrary to popular belief, he does not believe that customer retention has gone down as a result of e-banking:

> The idea that the next bank is only one click away is absolutely not true. To become a customer, you need to go to the bank and open up an account. When you are used to one system, you don't want to change.

Growth opportunities

In its domestic markets, where Nordea operates its branch network, there is limited opportunity for growth. Bo Harald explains:

> We can't grow very much in Finland. In Sweden, we are the second biggest bank. In Denmark and Norway, we are still too small in private and corporate banking, which leaves plenty of room for growth. In neighbouring markets such as Estonia, we are already the third largest bank with substantial growth potential. In Poland, we bought four banks, which we now need to consolidate before we can start thinking about further growth.

Moving into other European markets as a pure e-bank without a branch network is not a real option for Nordea:

> As a pure play, you might be able to attract the tech-savvy people who are constantly checking interest rates. Those guys easily sign up for anything new but this market segment is very small. Our experience has been that if you don't have a strong brand name and a solid branch structure that allows you to get in personal contact with your customers, you will have problems addressing the mass market. I mean, if we went to southern France and said, 'Hi, we are Nordea. Come and do your banking with us on our great website!' – what would people say? That's why we have never tried to penetrate foreign markets where we don't have a physical branch network.

In addition to expanding geographically, another main growth area for Nordea is expanding its service range:

> Even in our Finnish market, we can expand quite a lot by offering new services that we didn't have before. If you look at these services, you can only offer some of them over the Internet, but not at a branch. For instance, customers won't come to the branch to check the balance on their credit card but would like to do it through their mobile phone.

For Nordea, there are two promising future e-business opportunities. First, to develop further customer relationship management, the bank is turning towards triggered data mining, which works as follows: when there is a change in a customer account – for instance, a large incoming money transfer, change of address or marital status – a trigger in the database is set off and informs the bank of the change, which then raises a number of questions: what does it mean for financing, for long-term payments, for insurance and e-services? Based on the answers to these questions, Nordea plans to make an offer either via mail or face-to-face in a branch. While Bo Harald sees substantial value in this approach, he wants to go a step further:

> Triggered data mining is not enough because it looks into the past. Instead, we should ask the customer directly: What are you going to be doing next? What's your next life event, as we call it? For instance, the most important thing that can happen to a man in Finland is the purchase of a new car. We want to invite the customer to tell us about it and then ask ourselves: What can we do? What can the private sector do? What can the public sector do? Well, he'll have to look for a car. Our Solo partners can send him car offers. He'll have to buy the car and sign a contract – this can be done through e-signature. He'll have to pay for the car – this opens up the opportunity for financing arrangements. He'll have to have his car inspected – again an opportunity for one of our partners on the Solo marketplace ... Of course, when we think about these services, a major concern is always the issue of data privacy, to which we are very sensitive. Nordea never shares any information with anyone outside the bank. Customers voluntarily decide to share information with, say, the car seller. During the initial stage it's even possible to have a protected identity which is unknown to the merchant.

The second major opportunity is risk management services for e-businesses:

> In the electronic world, business partners do not know each other well. At the same time, market volatility is very high, which has led to numerous big crashes. Therefore you shouldn't trust anybody. To accommodate this you can either use direct payment [e-payment as explained above] or get credit ratings. Today, most companies have a lot of people working in risk management. They pay tens of millions for credit information and insurance in order to reduce credit loss. In general this works well but it raises the question: How much should you pay? If you could use the bank's knowledge and its ready-made credit information and integrate it into the billing process, you could save a lot of money. That's what we plan to make available in the future. Every company in the world has a bank and usually the

bank has made a credit evaluation of that company and established a credit line. These banks have the most in-depth information and therefore it's probably the best credit evaluation anybody can get. If all banks made these evaluations available electronically by issuing trade-related bank guarantees on the Internet, companies could save a lot of money. It would be a lubricant on the e-business machinery. This is a very obvious idea but sometimes the things that are so simple and self-evident don't take off. That's the way the world works – never quite perfectly.

Future outlook

In spite of its successful e-banking and e-business initiatives, Nordea's stock performance has been below average in the last few years, falling 28% in 2002. This was due, in part, to a drop in the bank's total income which fell by 4% while expenses increased by 2%. However, Harald believes that another important factor is that investors do not value e-banking activities appropriately at the moment:

> Those who know e-banking know that we are the number one in the world. During the dot.com bubble we had investment bankers and analysts here every single day – I could've spent all my time just talking to them! They told me: 'You shouldn't really be classified as a bank, you should be an IT company and have a valuation that is ten times higher than your current valuation.' Actually, our valuation went up quite a bit. But now, how many analysts come to see us? What I am complaining about are the analysts. Now that the real thing is happening, why are they not interested in it? They were only interested in sensation. The underlying problem is that people tend to overestimate new technology in the short run but underestimate its influence in the long term.

Regarding the future, he sees the importance of e-banking and e-business in a broader perspective:

> Getting people accustomed to e-banking is really a social task to make Europe more competitive. We can't afford not to do it. e-Banking services can be used to make people more productive to compete with the US and the Far East. Due to our high costs and our powerful [labour] unions, we can't afford not to increase productivity. To achieve this, the all-important thing is the national resource of e-habit that we have been building up [over the years]. That's the key to the future. Nonetheless, you can't plan or foresee the future, you can only create it – and that's exactly what we want to do at Nordea.[30]

30 'Learn from the largest Internet bank of the world', accessed at www.tietoenator.lv.

DISCUSSION QUESTIONS

1 Analyze the current competitive environment of Nordea (you may want to use the five-forces industry model of Porter (see Exhibit 3.1 p. 65) or any other framework that you deem fit for your analysis).

2 What are Nordea's core competences? How unique and sustainable are they?

3 How does Nordea use its virtual value chain to leverage its customer information? What value can it create for its customers?

4 What should Nordea do next in order to maintain its world-wide lead in e-banking and e-business?

5 To what extent can the Nordea approach be applied to other industries where the online and offline channel conflict is paramount? Explain.

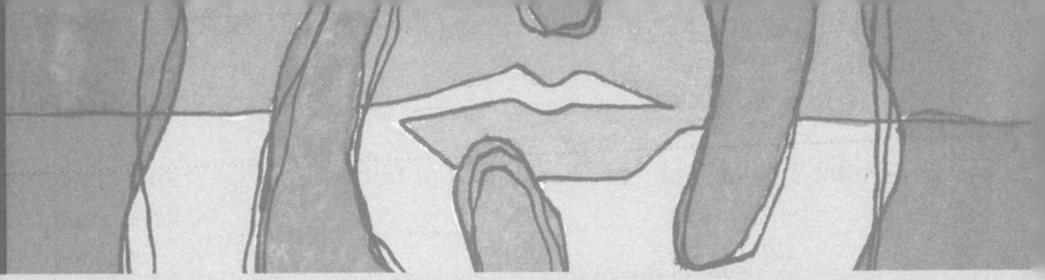

CASE STUDY 13

Ducati motorcycles (Italy)

Riding traditional business channels or racing through the Internet

We believe that, thanks to the wild success of the MH900e, the first [motor]bike ever to be launched and sold over the Internet, the Internet will become a strategic tool in the future growth of the Ducati businesses.[1]

Federico Minoli, Chair and Chief Executive Officer, Ducati Motor SpA[2]

The MH900e is a high-performance, hand-built motorcycle that was produced as a limited edition. It was sold at a unit price of €15 000[3] exclusively through the Internet starting on 1 January 2000 at 00.01 a.m. GMT.[4] The first year's production was sold out in just 31 minutes, before production had even started. With its online sales of the MH900e motorcycle, Ducati became one of Italy's largest e-tailers.

Ducati: company overview

The Ducati brothers founded their company in 1926, with headquarters and production facilities located in Bologna, Italy. Ducati is a leading premium price manufacturer of high performance motorcycles. Since the 1950s, Ducati motorcycles have dominated the World Superbike Championship. As a result, over the years racing has inspired the company's four model lines: Superbike, Super Sport, Sport Naked (also called Monster) and Sport Touring.

The company competes in the sport sub-segment of the road market segment with engine capacities of over 500 cc.[5] Ducati categorizes the motorcycle market into four segments: the motor-scooter market, the off-road market, the road market with engine capacities of less than 500 cc, and the road market with engine capacities of over 500 cc. The road-market segment with engine capacities of over 500 cc includes four sub-segments: sport, touring, dual and cruiser. Motorcycles in the sport sub-segment are built for, or inspired by, racing. Those in the touring and dual sub-segments are designed for comfortable, long-distance travel and for both on-road and off-road riding. The cruiser sub-segment comprises heavy motorcycles with classic American design.

The four Ducati models differ in design, technical features and target customers. The most popular model line is the Monster (52.1% of revenues in 1999), followed by the Superbike (25.2%), the Super Sport (14.3%) and the Sport Touring (8.4%). The flagship product, Superbike, has gained much ground over the past three years.

Besides motorcycles, Ducati sells parts, accessories and apparel in 40 countries worldwide, with a focus on Western Europe and North America. In 1999, these regions accounted for 85% of overall sales, with the remaining 15% generated in Asia and Australia.

Ducati has a global distribution network. In Belgium, Italy and Sweden, it sells motorcycles and

1 Ducati press release, 6 March 2000, Bologna, Italy.
2 SpA. (Società per Azioni) is a joint stock company.
3 On 31 December 1999, €1 = US$1.0041.
4 GMT stands for Greenwich Mean Time.
5 cc stands for cubic centimetre, a measurement for the motor cylinder capacity.

This case study was written by Stefanie Leenen, participant in the Master programme of the Leipzig Graduate School of Management, Germany, and Tawfik Jelassi, Affiliate Professor of Technology Management at INSEAD, Fontainebleau. It is intended to be used as the basis for class discussion rather than to illustrate an effective or ineffective handling of a management situation.

The case was made possible by the co-operation of Ducati Motor SpA (Italy).

Exhibit 1 Geographical distribution of Ducati 1999 revenues

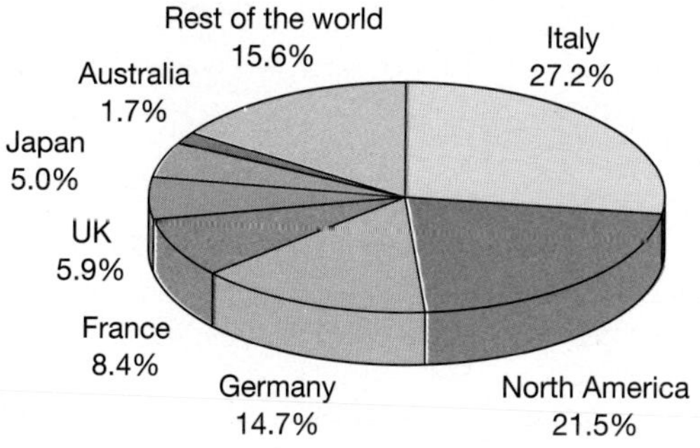

related products to its retail dealers directly out of Bologna. In other key markets (including Germany, France, Japan and the USA), wholly owned subsidiaries are responsible for Ducati's wholesale distribution. Ducati enhanced its control over key markets (see Exhibit 1) by increasing the number of subsidiaries, replacing underperforming distributors and appointing new distributors to enter new markets (such as Bahrain, Chile, Malta and Thailand).

In Italy, Ducati started restructuring its dealer network by turning dealer outlets into special Ducati retail outlets (called Ducati stores and Ducati corners). In the remaining countries, independent distributors function as intermediaries between Ducati Motor and retail dealers. In all markets (except Belgium, Italy and Sweden), dealers purchase Ducati products from subsidiaries or distributors and sell them to the final Ducati customer.

In 1983, Ducati became part of the Caviga group, an Italian manufacturing conglomerate. In September 1996, following a liquidity crisis at Caviga, Ducati Motor Holding (DMH) was created. Through a series of transactions, the USA-based Texas Pacific Group (TPG) and Deutsche Morgan Grenfell Capital Italy (DMGCI)[6] acquired 51% of DMH. In July 1998, the

6 DMGCI is the Italian subsidiary of Deutsche Bank's asset-management and private banking arm.

Table 1 Financial data, product mix and registration data of Ducati (L millions)

Twelves months ending 31 December	*1997*	*1998*	*1999*
Motorcycles	347.2	401.8	491.9
Spares parts, accessories, apparel	15.5	52.1	71.8
Miscellaneous	16.3	11.2	6.6
Total net revenues	379.0	465.1	570.3
Cost of goods sold	(234.6)	(287.4)	(341.8)
Gross profit	144.5	177.7	228.4
Gross profit (% of net sales)	38	38	40
Other operating revenues	1.0	2.3	3.4
Operating income (loss)	32.4	41.4	51.1
Net profit (loss)	5.2	(2.4)	17.3
EBITDA	65.1	79.1	98.3
EBITDA margin (%)	17	17	17
Net debt	284.5	290.4	217.5
Total shareholders' equity	142.6	139.0	253.8
Net debt/total net capitalization (%)	66	67	46
Twelve months ending 31 December	*1998*	*1999*	*Change over previous year (%)*
Total motorcycle units shipped (per model line)	28 011	33 124	+18
Sports Segment (Superbike and Super Sport)	13 368	13 461	+1
Monster	11 994	16 770	+40
Sport Touring	2 649	2 893	+9
Total motorcycle units registered (per region)	27 304	32 135	+18
North America	3 739	4 805	+29
Europe	20 019	23 302	+16
Japan	1 383	1 418	+3
Rest of the world	2 163	2 610	+21

remaining 49% of Caviga shares were purchased by TPG, which still owns 33% of Ducati Motor. All other shares are traded over the New York Stock Exchange and Borsa Italiana SpA, the Italian stock exchange. Following the transfer of Ducati ownership in 1996, a turnaround programme was initiated, aiming at increasing production and net sales. Ducati paid outstanding obligations to suppliers, increased its working capital to raise production levels, installed a new management team, and hired 250 professionals worldwide. The company rebuilt its sales, marketing and public relations departments, revamped its corporate image and is streamlining its assembly process and introducing new models.

As of December 1999, Ducati's revenues totalled L570 billion,[7] an increase of 22.6% over the previous year (see Table 1). In the same period, registered motorcycles, a key measure of retail sales, increased by 17.7% to 32 135 units. The net profit was L17.3 billion[8] compared with a loss of L2.4 billion in 1998[9] and a net profit of L5.2 billion in 1997.

Ducati competes mainly with four Japanese manufacturers (Honda, Suzuki, Yamaha, Kawasaki), two European manufacturers (BMW, Triumph) and, to some extent, with the USA-based Harley-Davidson's Buell Division. The Japanese manufacturers are generalists competing in all segments, from scooters to large-capacity motorcycles, while BMW and Triumph only manufacture motorcycles for various sub-segments in the large-capacity road market. Harley Davidson focuses on a niche market, the cruiser segment, although it also offers Sport Naked motorcycles. Within its specific business segment, Ducati's market share increased in 1999 to reach 6% of the Western European market. Japanese competitors have a greater market share worldwide, with Honda accounting for 26%, Suzuki for 23%, Yamaha for 17% and Kawasaki for 17%. Harley Davidson, BMW and Triumph have market shares of 5%, 4% and 2%, respectively. Ducati estimates reaching a market share of 17% in Italy, 6% in the UK, 4% in North America, 3% in France and Germany, and 2% in Japan.

Ducati's business strategy

> In this era of laziness, instant gratification and armchair comfort, the motorcycle is the real, physical anti-Internet experience.
>
> **Cristiano Silei, General Manager of Ducati.com**

Since the 1996 acquisition of the company by TPG and DMGCI, Ducati has been trying to increase its sales and profitability. In order to attain this goal, it broadened its product portfolio, restructured and strengthened its distribution network, focused on developing the Ducati brand and tried to raise production efficiency. 'We are not trying to do things that we can't do', explained David Gross, Director of Strategic Planning at Ducati. 'Our competence is making and selling motorcycles. We build relationships with other people who are attracted by the excitement of our product and will help us to broaden the World of Ducati.'[10]

Ducati motorcycle features (such as its design, the valve control and the L-twin engine with its special sound) constitute the basis of a distinguished product that attracts customers and builds loyalty. Besides introducing new models, Ducati continuously upgrades its existing motorcycles through design and technical innovations. In this way, the company aims at satisfying customer demands and strengthening its brand name.

The company's short-term aim is to increase the number of registered Ducati motorcycles worldwide by an average annual growth of 15%. To achieve this goal, Ducati decided to broaden the boundaries of its market niche by leveraging its brand name. 'That's where our strength is', explained Christopher Spira, Head of Investor Relations at Ducati. 'We have a global brand behind us.' Ducati motorcycles are positioned in the niche 'Function/Performance' (see Exhibit 2), emphasizing strong functionality and high performance. However, Ducati wants to expand its niche boundaries towards the quadrant 'Comfort/Lifestyle' and also wants to introduce new motorcycle-related products, such as motorcycle accessories and apparel, while remaining faithful to its niche.

---

7 On 31 December 1999, 1000 Italian lire (L) = €0.5165; L1000 = US$0.5186.

8 Financial reporting at Ducati is in accordance with both US GAAP (generally accepted accounting principles) and Italian GAAP.

9 The 1998 loss was due to non-recurring operating expenses of L16.9 billion, caused by the write-off of debt issuance costs and cash settled for warrant rights to credit institutions that arranged prior financing. Ducati had no similar non-recurring expenses in 1997.

10 The 'World of Ducati' is described below.

Exhibit 2 **Expansion of Ducati's niche boundaries**

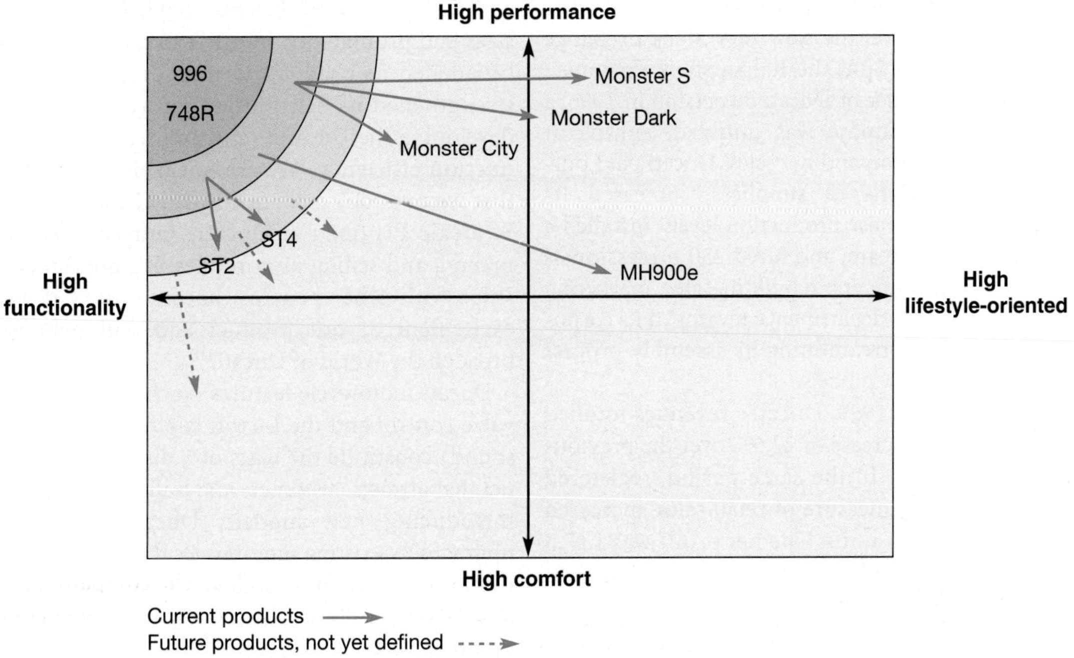

The 996 and 748R are models from the Superbike line; ST2 and ST4 are Sport Touring models and the Monster Dark, Monster City and Monster S are models from the Monster line. The Sport Touring (launched in 1997) as well as from the Monster (lanuched in 1993) models and the MH900e were launched in order to meet particular market needs and expand the niche boundaries. This expansion is illustrated by the concentric circles and the direction of the future product arrows. The number of future products and their features still have to be defined.

Source: Adapted from Ducati document, March 2000.

In November 1999, Ducati increased its stake in Gio.Ca.Moto, an Italian technical accessory company, from 50% to 99.9%. 'This represents a strategic step in our development of the World of Ducati', explained Federico Minoli. Accessories are marketed under the Ducati Performance brand name and are used to personalize the Ducati motorcycle to customer needs. Through co-operation with Dainese, a leading Italian manufacturer of technical riding gear, Ducati sells its products under the Ducati–Dainese brand name. In 1999, sales of motorcycle-related products amounted to 4.2% of total revenues, while motorcycle sales accounted for 86.3% (spare parts accounted for 8.3% and other miscellaneous items accounted for the remaining 1.2%).

The company's short-term goal is to increase motorcycle-related sales to 10% of revenues. Furthermore, Ducati selectively licenses the Ducati brand and plans to forge additional strategic alliances with companies that add value to the Ducati image and do not ask for any financial exchange.

For Ducati, distribution is a strategic pillar in its drive towards increased market share and higher profitability. In 1997, the company restructured its distribution system with the goal of maximizing retail sales and getting closer to the customer. Motorcycles, spare parts, accessories and apparel are sold worldwide via 800 independent privately owned dealers. The reduction of dealer outlets was one part of the turnaround programme that was started in Italy. Between 1996 and April 2000, the number of Ducati dealers was reduced from 165 to 61. The most important selection criteria for dealer outlets were geographical location, relationship with the dealer, sales turnover and Ducati's relative importance compared with other brands sold by a dealer.

Dealers received style guides and graphic packages to convert their outlet into a Ducati store. Such conversion requires not only offering sufficient space in order to display the Ducati products, but also having adequate workshop facilities and qualified staff. 'The

main prerequisite for opening a [Ducati] store is passion for this distinguished brand', stated Carlo Simognini, Director of Sales and Marketing at Ducati. 'This is the only reliable basis on which to build true commercial success.'[11]

Ducati stores are exclusive Ducati outlets, selling motorcycles, spare parts, accessories and apparel. They offer a customized retail environment as well as an increased level of service and technical support. In the medium term, Ducati expects to set up about 200 Ducati stores worldwide. Today's 40 independent Ducati stores outsell the ordinary dealer outlets by significant margins.

Ducati corners are a compromise between the exclusive Ducati store and the ordinary dealer outlet. If the market is not big enough to justify setting up an exclusive Ducati store, then a Ducati corner can be set up in a large dealer outlet offering a number of brands. David Gross explained:

> You walk in a store [and] you see motorcycles of all different brands everywhere, but in one corner you see this whole kind of Ducati experience. You have the walls, the panels, the colours, the design [and] the purity of the lines.

With the growing number of Ducati stores and Ducati corners, Ducati aims at further developing the Ducati lifestyle image. Furthermore, the company introduced a Ducati store on its Internet website. Besides using the traditional dealer-based sales channel, Ducati started selling over the Internet with the introduction of the MH900e model.

Ducati increased its production efficiency by rationalizing the manufacturing process and reducing complexity. The number of motorbikes made per production employee increased from 78 units in 1998 to 83 units in 1999. EBITDA[12] also increased in 1999 by 24.3% to L98.3 billion, which is 17.2% of total revenues, one of the highest EBITDA margins in the industry.

The 'physical' World of Ducati

> Ducati is more than just a motorbike. It's the ultimate expression of performance motorcycling.
>
> **Massimo Bordi, General Manager of Ducati**

To strengthen its brand image, Ducati created the 'World of Ducati' containing motorcycles and motorcycle-related products and services (see Exhibit 3). The core products, consisting of motorcycles, accessories and apparel, are complemented by six categories: racing, advertising, the Ducati Desmo Owners Club (DOC), events, the Ducati Museum and the Ducati University.[13] Each category contains several sub-categories; for instance racing includes sponsorship, a hospitality unit, the racing school,[14] Desmobid,[15] racing apparel, technical support and sales. The single categories are interconnected and are part of other categories (e.g. racing is a category in its own right as well as being part of advertising). Thus, the World of Ducati aims at strengthening Ducati's core products and image and thereby increasing Ducati sales and profitability.

Motorcycles and complementary products

> Once you want a Ducati ... you won't buy anything else.
>
> **Ignacio Romero Morell, Ducati dealer in Granada, Spain**

All Ducati motorcycles are produced in Borgo Panigale, just outside Bologna. The company started several production initiatives aimed at reducing production costs and improving the underlying process. In January 1999, Ducati introduced a production software that monitors the information flows from receipt of the customer order to the delivery of the motorcycle. Through customized material requirement planning (MRP) capabilities, the system automatically generates production schedules based on sales forecasts, optimizes warehouse volume levels, generates orders for purchasing materials and manages flows of materials for production.

Another Ducati production initiative is the implementation of the 'platform' approach, through which suppliers become responsible for delivering the key motorcycle components and managing their own sub-component providers. This reduces the number of suppliers, increases the volume of components provided by each supplier and thereby strengthens Ducati's bargaining power. Since several motorcycle models share common components, Ducati is able to maintain efficiency even at relatively low volumes.

11 Information found at www.microsoft.com/industry/km/business/casestudies/ducati-ms.stm. Page now removed.

12 EBITDA stands for earnings before interest, taxes, depreciation and amortisation.

13 Ducati managers and technicians give lectures worlwide at universities and polytechnics on Ducati and its products.

14 The racing school teaches motorcycling at all levels.

15 Desmobid is a Ducati memorabilia auction on the Ducati website.

Exhibit 3 The World of Ducati

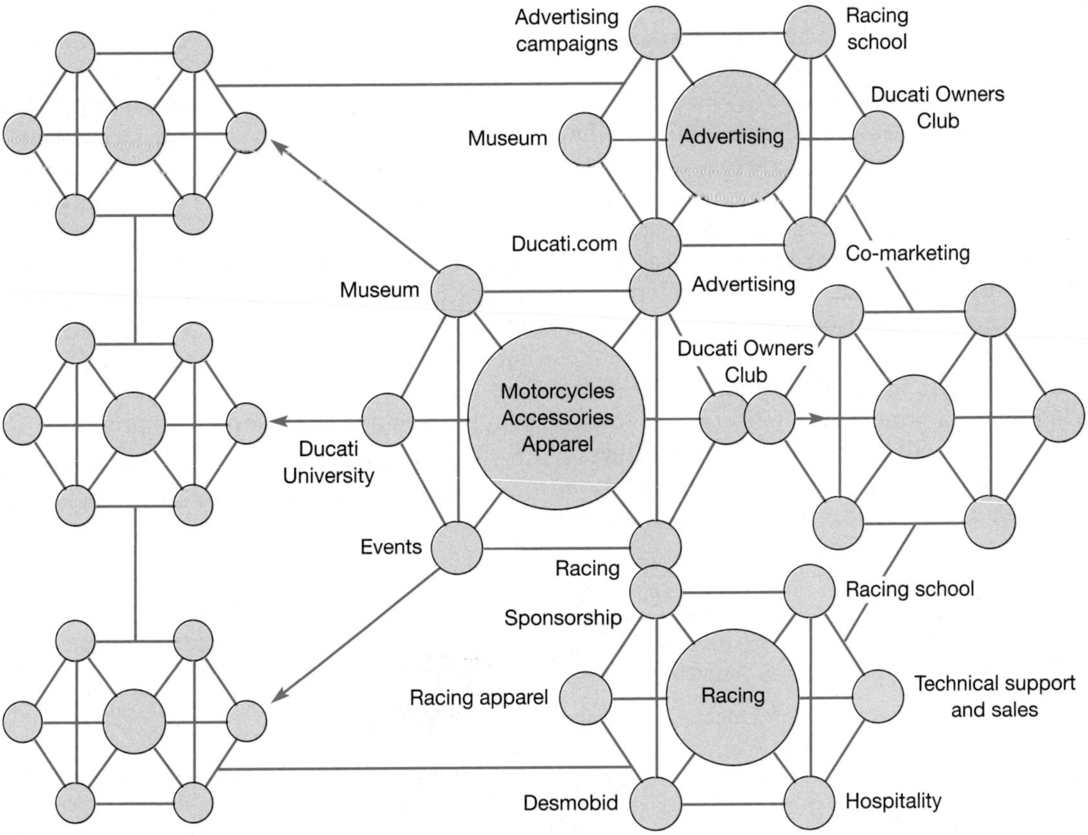

Source: Adapted from Ducati document, March 2000.

'We outsource 85% of our production cost', said Christopher Spira:

> Our factory could be anywhere. We are an assembly plant, an R&D centre and a design centre. We also have a large commercial area and a PR operation. We have outsourced all of our logistics.

Having outsourced the production of most of its components, Ducati essentially focuses on designing and assembling engines and motorcycles, and testing their quality. As a result, the fixed cost structure is relatively low. Direct and indirect labour costs amount to 15% of total costs incurred. Due to production initiatives, the daily rate of Ducati motorcycle production increased from 25 in September 1996 to more than 200 in May 2000. 'This achievement is not a final goal, but an incentive to improve and satisfy the requests of our Ducati enthusiasts', commented Massimo Bordi.[16] In order to reduce the number of key motorcycle components, Ducati tries to co-develop new components with its key suppliers. Currently, 59 platform projects are planned that will optimize production and involve outsourcing non-strategic activities.

In 1999, sales of spare parts accounted for 8.2% with total sales, compared to 8.3% in 1998, and are among the highest-margin products sold by the company. The spare-parts catalogue and order processing are managed electronically. By December 1999, over 93% of all spare-part orders were fulfilled in Europe within 48 hours of receipt, and within 72 hours in the rest of the world. Logistics are outsourced to Saima Avandero, an Italian logistics company located just north of Bologna, which is responsible for the physical movement of the spare parts, their storage and the automation of the Ducati spare-parts warehouse.

16 Ducati press release, 17 May 2000, Bologna, Italy.

In order to personalize Ducati motorcycles, Gio.Ca.Moto designs and distributes performance and custom-made accessories, such as specialized exhaust systems, fenders, fairings and custom-painted fuel tanks. These accessories and apparels have high margins. 'Our customers resemble fans rather than mere buyers', said Carlo Simognini.[17] Since 1998, Ducati Gear has been providing Ducatisti[18] with technical riding gear. Leather racing suits, jackets, gloves, boots and helmets are developed and produced in co-operation with Dainese. Ducati T-shirts, caps and memorabilia are also commercialized.

'One way of guaranteeing maximum exposure without having to dedicate large funds to advertising is by doing promotional marketing and forging strategic alliances', commented Christopher Spira. In 1999, Ducati signed a partnership with Infostrada SpA, an Italian telecommunication company that became the title sponsor of the Ducati World Superbike Championship team and provided technical support in establishing Ducati's communications network. Ducati also established co-operation agreements with other companies, such as Mattel, Maisto, Majorette and Virgin Entertainment.

In the future, Ducati intends to focus its activities on the motorcycle-related business, enriching the World of Ducati with the licensing of motorcycle model replicas, toys, video games and 'online' racing, allowing fans to compete 'virtually' with each other through the Internet. Products not related to the racetrack (such as boxer shorts, perfumes, etc.) will not be licensed by Ducati. Such activities aim at increasing Ducati brand awareness among the general public and also creating additional revenue streams.

Racing

> Ducati has won eight of the last ten World Superbike Championship titles and more individual victories than the competition put together.[19]

Racing helps Ducati to enhance the company image and to increase the demand for its products. The components of the World of Racing are sponsorship, hospitality, the racing school, the online auction Desmobid, technical support, sales and racing apparel.

Ducati signed a major multi-year renewable sponsorship contract with Infostrada and a multi-year sponsorship and supply agreement with Royal Dutch Shell. Shell will be the official and exclusive lubricant supplier not only for the racing team but also for Ducati's motorcycle production. A hospitality unit at the racetrack was created, and the racing school offers riding courses.

In October 1998, Ducati created a subsidiary, Ducati Corse, involved exclusively in racing activities. Besides its track-winning objective, Ducati Corse aims at leveraging Ducati's technological racing expertise into commercially oriented applications. It supports the Ducati team as well as other racing teams with technical knowledge, racing apparel, specialized motorcycles and engines. In 1999, costs amounted to L20 billion, compared with L17.5 billion in 1998. Revenues from sales and sponsorship increased from L6.5 billion in 1998 to L13.4 billion in 1999, covering 67% of racing costs in 1999, up from 37% in 1998. Through the racing success of Ducati motorcycles, Ducati has enjoyed high visibility in the media and demonstrated the high-performance characteristics of its motorcycles.

Advertising

> We find that we are lucky enough not to have to pay for any advertising [apart from ads in the motorcycle press]. Indeed, it is part of our strategy not to pay for advertising. We build alliances with famous international brands that help us at our events and activities, and we do the same for them.
>
> **David Gross**

In order to establish Ducati as a global brand, a universal, homogeneous marketing strategy was introduced after the 1996 acquisition of the company. A new corporate identity was created by standardizing the corporate logo and lettering as well as the promotional and marketing material.

In order to reinforce the brand, Ducati advertises only in the sector press. The first global advertising campaign, called Ducati/People, featured company employees. This campaign attempted to communicate authenticity, simplicity, consistency and the uniqueness of the Ducati brand. Instead of the colourful images typically used for advertising in the motorcycle industry, Ducati tried to demonstrate the nature of the brand as well as the design and style of its motorcycles.

17 Information found at www.microsoft.com/industry/km/business/casestudies/ducati-ms.stm. Page now removed.

18 Ducatisti are Ducati employees and Ducati fans owning Ducati motorcycles.

19 Ducati press release, 31 January 2000, Bologna, Italy.

Given Ducati's racing performance, the motorcycle press often writes articles on Ducati. Furthermore, the non-sector press (such as *The New York Times*, *The Wall Street Journal*, the *Financial Times*, CNN and Bloomberg) have published articles on Ducati. The brand enjoys a 'pull' effect, demonstrated by the attraction of Hollywood celebrities, Formula One racers, music stars and Ducati enthusiasts. Ducati motorcycles are shown in special museum exhibitions such as 'The Art of the Motorcycle' at the Guggenheim Museum in New York. Ducati also frequently lends bikes for photograph sessions in fashion, style and design magazines.

Ducati also fosters its advertising through the Ducati website (www.ducati.com), which is available in Italian and English. Its traffic is increasing, and in March 2000 it received on average more than 150 000 hits a day. About 17 000 fans subscribe to the racing site in order to receive timely press releases and racing results. The Ducati Owners Club site had 20 000 users after just three months of operating.

Co-marketing is carried out with other major international brands. In 1999, Sotheby's, an international auction house, had Ducati's MH900e on the cover page of the 'Motorcycles and Bicycles' auction. A whole section of the auction was dedicated to Ducati, offering racing and antique parts. DKNY, an American fashion company, provides on-the-track apparel for the Ducati racing teams and sells a limited collection of such apparel. Harrods of London exhibited Ducati motorcycles in its showcases during the 1998 Christmas season, offering them for sale. Ducati motorcycles have featured in several films and British television series (*Fled, Armageddon, The Professional*). 'We build strategic alliances with brands that add value to our brand without [requiring] any financial exchange', explained David Gross. 'We [Ducati] exchange promotion, public relations and marketing initiatives [with these partners].'

Over 400 Ducati clubs exist worldwide, linking up the Ducatisti. The company sponsors some of the club activities, such as the World Ducati Weekend, which was held in 2000 at the Misano racetrack in June. People were able to race, and visit the Ducati factory and the museum in Bologna.

The Ducati Museum is part of the Bologna headquarters and features the 'history of the men and machines that have raised the pulse rate of enthusiasts everywhere'.[20] The exhibition starts with the Cucciolo (i.e. 'Puppy'), which was constructed in 1946 and was no more than a 48-cc, four-stroke engine bolted to a bicycle frame, and continues with a display of the whole Ducati motorcycle dynasty.

By the 1950s, Ducati had built the Marianna, which won several races during that decade. The engineer, Fabio Taglioni, who constructed this motorcycle was also the designer of the Ducati special valve-control system 'Desmodromic'. Ducati also created the Ducati Desmo Owners Club, with its DesmoCard, as well as the DesmoNet, Ducati's extranet connecting dealers with each other and with the factory.

The Ducati Desmo Owners Club (DOC)

> DOC was a dream; now it's a reality. We want to build it up together with all our Ducatisti friends to make it the main point of reference for fans of the Desmodromic [motor]bike.
>
> **Federico Minoli[21]**

In 1999, the DOC was set up in the physical as well as in the virtual online world. Ducati Motor founded the club with the aim of interlinking members and their interests: their enthusiasm for riding Ducati motorcycles and opportunities for entertainment under the Ducati trademark. The Club is a nonprofit organization; any Ducatisti can join it by filling in an application form.

Joining DOC allows members to make new friends, participate in club events and benefit from exclusive services. Since January 1999, the DesmoCard, which is free of charge, has been giving new Ducati owners special discounts on Ducati merchandise, Superbike Championship tickets and hotel rates worldwide. Furthermore, members-only sections offering DOC activities are provided by Ducati stores and the DOC's website (www.ducatidoc.org). At present, the club operates only in Italy, and the main DOC event offered is the World Ducati Weekend. Ducati recognizes that DOC features need to be more specific as well as developed and implemented in other markets.

The 'virtual' World of Ducati

> We want to put a virtual layer on the real World of Ducati.
>
> **Cristiano Silei**

20 Ducati SportTouring brochure, 1999.
21 www.ducatidoc.com

The goal is to build the World of Ducati online and to reinforce the Ducati brand. Ducati plans to enhance the existing homepage, which currently delivers mainly content, and create 'Ducati.com tomorrow'. In the near future, the site is expected to offer electronic commerce capabilities, host virtual communities,[22] and provide motorcycle-related content, entertainment and financial services. Furthermore, the site will offer the opportunity to set up a personal homepage and to bet on motorcycle races.

Although the average Ducatisto/a is relatively young (27–30 years old),[23] Ducatisti use the Internet in a limited way. 'I am not the typical Ducatisti, as I own two Ducatis that are more than 40 years old', explains Federico Hansberg, an Italian Ducatisto. 'If I need information [on Ducati and its products], I would access the Ducati website, although I wouldn't purchase any spare parts or any other product through the Internet.'

Ducati.com today

Today, Ducati.com serves as an umbrella for several other Ducati sites, such as ducatidoc.com, memorabilia.ducati.com, ducaticorse.com and ducatistore.com (see Exhibit 4). It focuses on the content of the Ducati products, services and news. Ducatisti can apply online for membership to the DOC, customers can find addresses for technical services, and individuals searching for a job at Ducati can send their CVs online. Ducati fans can also communicate with the company and send suggestions regarding the company's website and products through the website.

Ducati.com today focuses neither on the virtual community nor on commerce. Online sales are limited to the sale of the MH900e and to the online auction site (memorabilia.ducati.com). Other products, services and context features are not yet available online.

Exhibit 4 Structure of the current Ducati website

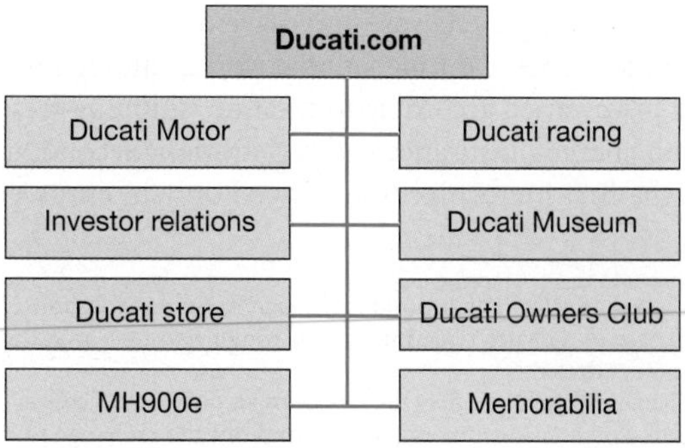

Source: Ducati document, March 2000

Content

Ducati.com today contains information on the company, its motorcycles, accessories, apparel, spare parts, stores and dealers, races and the museum. Each of its four motorcycle model lines and the MH900e are presented visually along with their technical data, new features and the service provided by Ducati. The virtual Ducati store supplies information on the nearest physical Ducati store and the complete range of motorcycles, clothing and accessories for customizing a Ducati motorcycle. It encourages clients to call or visit their local dealer and provides information on how to become a Ducati dealer. The visitor can also access information on the Ducati brand, current events and the latest news (e.g. the inauguration of a new Ducati store, new products, etc.). Ducati racing provides racing-related content but does not yet broadcast races over the Web.

In case a customer requires further information on Ducati products, services, prices and dealers, e-mail addresses and telephone numbers are provided, but there is no 24-hour hotline service yet. Customers can use the online dealer search to find an authorized Ducati dealer located close to their home.

The website also offers information on the company's history and the latest news as well as having an investor relations section. Investors or visitors to the web page can look up press releases and subscribe to its mailing lists. They can find financial data on Ducati and its stock performance, which are updated every 20 minutes. Although the website delivers much content, it lacks help functions such as a search function or a site map.

Commerce

Ducati.com today offers only limited electronic commerce capabilities. In the B2C e-commerce category, the website supported the online sale of the MH900e and the launch of the Desmobid, but not

22 Virtual communities are groups of people with common interests and needs who come together online. They form a critical mass of purchasing power and exchange information on issues such as product price and quality.

23 Ducati customer survey, November 1999.

that of other motorcycles, accessories and apparel. B2B e-commerce initiatives only account for the Ducati DesmoNet. The site still does not offer any C2C e-commerce service.

Business-to-consumer: the unexpected success of the MH900e

> Although I haven't visited the Ducati website, I would buy a [motor] bike or certain specific accessories over the Internet. But I would need to see the product first.
>
> **Vicente Juan Perez, Spanish Ducati customer**

In 1998, Ducati presented its MH900e[24] prototype at the Intermot motorcycle show in Munich. MH are the initials of Mike Hailwood, who rode Ducatis and dominated the Grand Prix from 1958 until 1967. As a homage to him, capturing the emotion of the historic motorcycles of the era, Pierre Terblanche, Director of Ducati Design, took the initiative and built his 'dream bike'.

Since the MH900e press reviews were very positive and people the world over were requesting the product from Ducati, the company inserted a questionnaire on its website for two weeks to find out whether fans would actually buy the handcrafted MH900e. Three hundred Ducatisti responded positively. 'The press was so enthusiastic that Federico Minoli and Massimo Bordi decided to go into production', recalled David Gross. 'The market wanted it.' Federico Minoli decided to produce a limited edition of 2000 MH900e units and to sell it online starting on 1 January 2000 at 00.01 a.m. (see Exhibit 5). It was the first motorbike ever to be sold exclusively over the Internet, although it was to be delivered through the dealer network.

When ordering an MH900e, customers had to identify their nearest dealer and give their credit-card details. Upon checking the availability of funds, the order was transmitted to the selected Ducati dealer, who could either accept or reject processing it.[25] If the dealer agreed to process the order, then the customer's credit card was charged 10% of the MH900e price (i.e. €1500). A confirmation reference number was assigned and the client was added to the official MH900e owner registry. Afterwards, the Ducati dealer sent the customer the purchase agreement and informed them of the delivery status and the final price. Customers could track their motorcycle order status through the MH900e owner registry, which is available online.

If the customer cancelled their purchase order within five days of its placement, they got the 10% deposit back. Past this deadline, no refund would be made. The remaining €13 500 was to be paid upon delivery. The company planned to deliver the first ten motorcycles as a special event during the World Ducati Weekend in June 2000. Normal delivery through dealers started in the summer of 2000.

Since several MH900e features were not yet defined, the production costs and the final dealer commission were not fixed, although the dealer's commission would be less than the average one received on a normal Ducati. Approximately 1% of all dealers to whom MH900e orders were forwarded rejected them, although all the dealer has to do as a final check is to set the mirrors, deal with the registration documentation and hand over the keys to the owner. 'I think it's fair to say that the dealers' effort is minimal', explained Cristiano Silei. 'For them [the dealers], it's a no-brainer. They receive a margin, but they have no inventory risk, no advertising cost [and] no marketing cost. We take care of all that at [Ducati] headquarters through our PR effort.'

The pricing policy was innovative: first, the retail price was the same throughout the world, although the final price varied according to taxation, shipping fees, set-up charges, insurance and registration. Second, it was the first motorbike to be priced only in euros.[26]

Exhibit 5 The MH900e on the Ducati.com website

24 'e' stands for the Italian world *evoluzione*, meaning evolution.

25 In case of a dealer rejection, the customer had to search for another dealer.

26 The Ducati website offers the service of an online euro conversion. Potential customers can thus find out the exchange rate of the euro for their currency.

Although the suggested retail price was €15 000, Ducatisti who did not order over the Internet had to pay a higher price. 'We ordered the MH[900e] on 4 January [2000] to sell it at our outlet', explains Pablo April, employee at the Ducati dealer outlet in Granada. 'We suppose [that] the MH900e, which is only sold through the Internet, will be a collector's motorcycle. Therefore, we hope to find a Ducatisti who likes it and to whom we can resell it at a far higher price.'

Besides the few dealers who ordered the MH900e, most purchases were made by individuals from 20 different countries, including New Zealand, Singapore, Portugal, the USA, Turkey, Spain and Sweden. Of the customers, 30% were from Europe, 30% were from the USA and 39% were from Japan. According to Ducati officials, the surprisingly high percentage of Japanese orders suggests that the Japanese do more Internet commerce than other nationalities and that they are keen on collecting technical and designer products.

By selling the MH900e through the Internet, Ducati was aiming not at taking away business from the dealers, but rather at attracting new customers and helping bring more business to the dealers. 'I don't see any competition coming from the Internet', says Ignacio Romero Morell. 'If I think of my customers, they are not Internet users. I assume people want to see the motorcycle and touch it.'

Although the MH900e production did not start before June 2000 (at a daily rate of five to six units), the first year's production was sold out within 31 minutes[27] of the year 2000. A catalogue was developed to customize the MH900e. Customers are passionate about Ducati, and they put their trust in the brand to the extent that they are willing to leave a deposit of €1500.

Business-to-consumer: the online memorabilia auction

The memorabilia auction website, Desmobid, gives fans all over the world the opportunity to acquire Ducati motorcycle parts that have been used and signed by a racing champion and to make a virtual visit of the Ducati racing box. The idea originated from enthusiasts coming to the Ducati box after a race and asking if they could have a valve, a piston or a fairing that had been damaged during the race.

In order to bid, Ducatisti must first register, which is free of charge. This gives them a password and an identification number. The memorabilia merchandise is divided into two categories: SBK Bikes Memorabilia, used at the World Superbike Championships, and Museo Ducati Memorabilia, which contains collectors' items. Two Ducatisti, nicknamed Mira and More-desmo, accessed the online auction rooms and became the winning bidders for an official Ducati Corse racing-team shirt. Mira paid US$240 while More-desmo paid US$235.

Business-to-business: the Ducati DesmoNet

In order to better control customer order management, facilitate information exchange between sales outlets and headquarters, and offer an improved customer service, Ducati has introduced an extranet service called DesmoNet. This links Ducati stores with one another and with Ducati's headquarters. DesmoNet was introduced in Italy at every Ducati store and set up during the year 2000 in other European countries (including France, Spain and the UK), starting with subsidiaries and distributors. The staff at Ducati dealer outlets, many of them in their late 50s and not accustomed to working with computers, often refused to use DesmoNet, although training was given. Since Ducati headquarters can monitor the use of DesmoNet by users, feedback is given if usage is too low. When running out of a certain item, it is possible to check whether a nearby dealer has it in stock, in which case the part can be transferred quickly.

The DesmoNet provides headquarters with real-time information, which serves as a basis for generating sales reports, optimizing stock, developing new services and distributing marketing questionnaires to the dealers to 'feel the pulse' of the market. Customers can use the DesmoCard to receive information from any dealer regarding their motorbike (including repairs made), as all information is stored on a computer system.

Virtual community

The Ducati virtual community is still in its early stages. The initiatives taken by Ducati.com today is limited to the Ducati Owners Club and the online auction Desmobid. DOC's website (ducatidoc.com) links Ducati headquarters with Ducati clubs and

27 The remaining units of the limited edition produced in 2001 were sold out in the following weeks.

individual Ducatisti. At present, the website contains an introduction to DOC, information on their affiliates, rides and tours, the latest news and DOC events. It also contains an online application form and associated articles. There is no section dedicated exclusively to members. In the 'Rides & Tours' section, Ducatisti can describe their travel experiences, report on their routes and areas of interest, and post photos of their trips. A special Ducati team manages the DOC's website, plans visits to the Ducati factory and museum, and helps organize DOC events and activities.

Ducati.com tomorrow

> Thanks to the passionate support of Ducatisti the world over, the Ducati brand has consolidated its position as the best in the world of sports motorcycling. We see our investment in Ducati.com as the next step in the development of the global Ducati performance lifestyle.
>
> **Federico Minoli[28]**

28 Ducati press release, 6 March 2000, Bologna, Italy.

Exhibit 6 **Structure of the future Ducati website**

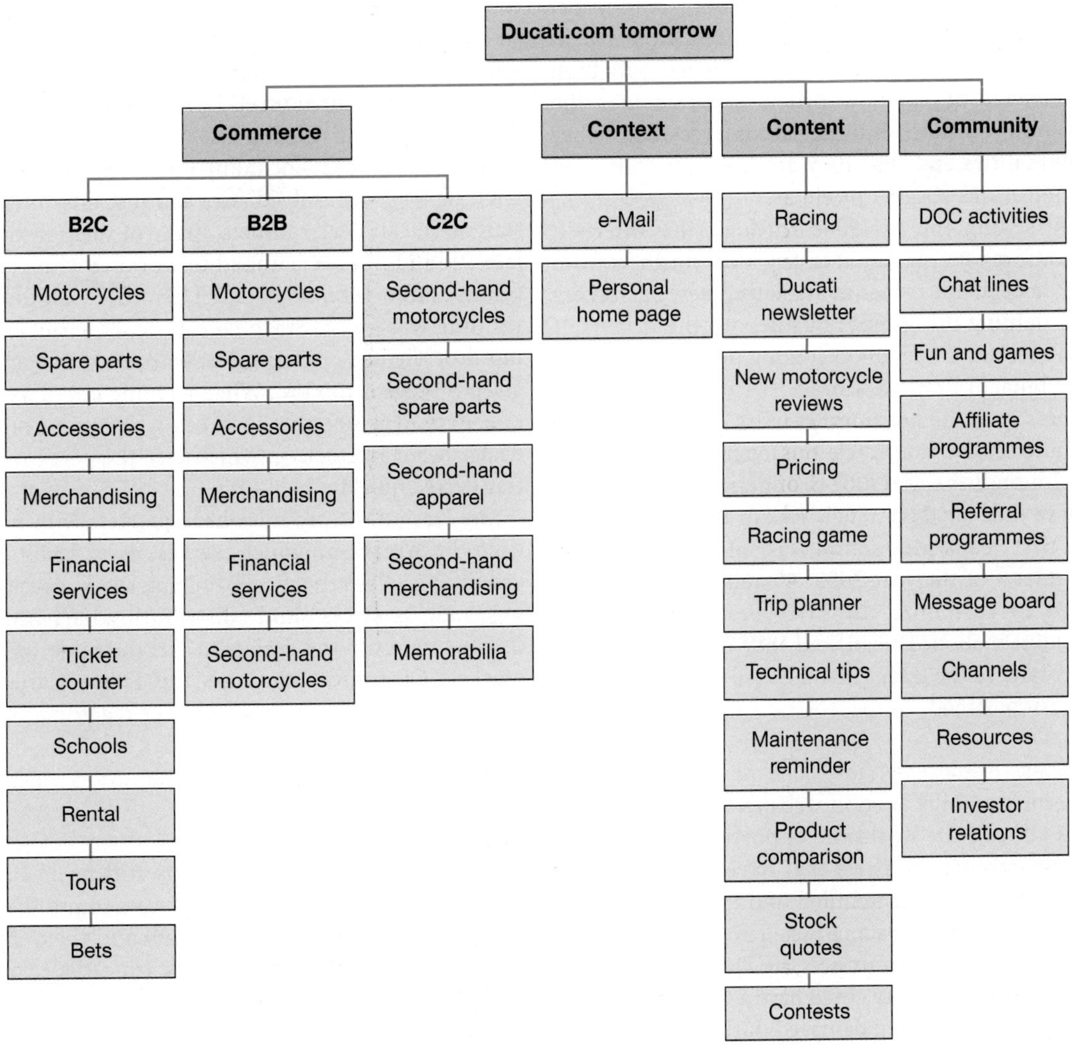

Source: Adapted from Ducati document, March 2000.

Ducati.com tomorrow aims at becoming a vertical Internet portal[29] dedicated to the Ducati lifestyle and the world of motor racing. It is the first initiative of its kind in the motorcycle world and will be based on the four 'Cs', i.e. content, commerce, community and context (see Exhibit 6). The functions of the current website will be enhanced and new functions, such as C2C activities, will be added. The launch of Ducati.com tomorrow has not yet been fixed.

Ducati tries to move fast. A new division, based in Bologna, was set up as a separate unit from Ducati Motor SpA dedicated to building Ducati.com tomorrow. The new venture plans to hire 15 e-commerce and Internet professionals during the start-up phase, in addition to its current staff of 15 employees.

Content

The future website is intended to build on the content delivered by Ducati.com today and to broaden its information scope. There are plans to expand the existing content with motorcycle reviews, pricing, racing games, trip planners, technical tips, a maintenance reminder, a Ducati newsletter, competitions and product comparisons.

Commerce

Ducati intends to enhance the different categories of its e-commerce applications (i.e. B2B, B2C and C2C). An important feature of B2B will be the trading of second-hand motorcycle parts. Cookies[30] will be used to analyze the behaviour of site visitors and derive knowledge about Ducati's markets and products. However, the integration of the e-commerce applications within the legal systems and databases constitutes an important challenge for Ducati.

Business-to-consumer

> We will use the Internet to reach out to customers [whom] we wouldn't have been able to access otherwise.
>
> **Cristiano Silei**

Ducati's e-commerce strategy is to use the Internet to promote and sell only limited editions of its motorcycles rather than all of its product lines. Furthermore, Ducati aims at selling services, accessories, apparel and spare parts through the Internet. Products sold online will be different from those offered at dealer outlets, in order to avoid competition. For Ducati, expensive items such as leather suits are difficult to sell through the Internet. However, they will be displayed online in order to refer customers to their local dealer outlet, where they can try them on and buy them. Thus, the website complements the existing dealer network while providing convenience to potential customers. 'It [our Internet strategy] keeps dealers very much in the loop', commented Cristiano Silei. 'It brings new clients to them and makes the dealers feel that they are very much part of all these business initiatives.'

The range of online financial services that Ducati provides to customers will include insurance and product financing. The company sees itself at an early Internet stage where several strategic decisions still need to be made. Motorcycle fans will have the opportunity to use the online ticket counter for buying tickets and betting on races. They will also be able to book tours and courses at the Ducati racing school as well as rent bikes over the Internet.

Business-to-business

B2B e-commerce will be done through DesmoNet. Eventually, purchasing will be electronic. B2B will have similar functions to those available through B2C, including the sales of motorcycles, spare parts, accessories and merchandising. It is expected to increase product availability. Financial services in the form of investment aids will be offered to the retail system. Furthermore, second-hand motorcycles will also be sold through the Internet.

Consumer-to-consumer

Ducati's C2C e-commerce will consist of selling memorabilia and trading second-hand items such as used motorcycles, spare parts, apparel and merchandising. Through its C2C offering, Ducati aims at strengthening its community of Ducati users and fans.

Virtual community

Through the Ducati.com virtual community, Ducati hopes to develop the company brand and attract new customers. Ducati.com will offer chat lines to its

---

29 A vertical Internet portal (vortal) specializes in a particular industry or product category. It offers the web browser personalized information and advice as well as access to a community with common interests.

30 A cookie is an item of information that is retrieved by a web browser and that remembers specific information about a unique visitor, such as location of the last visit, time spent or user preferences.

motorcycle fans, a message board, fun and games, information for investor relations, special DOC activities, and affiliate and referral programmes. Furthermore, club members can access the Ducati virtual community through the dealer channel and DOC organizers and are provided with resources in terms of dealer staff and Ducati products.

Context

Ducati.com tomorrow will offer Ducati customers and non-customers the option of setting up their own websites. In addition to having a personalized homepage, they will be able to have their own mailing system. Ducati encourages Ducati fans who set up their own homepage to collaborate with the company. Ducati can offer them access to the company logo (with the correct dimensions and colour) and customers can provide other fans with information, e.g. about their Ducati experiences.

Outlook

> We hope to imbue the new Ducati.com business with all the passion we have demonstrated during the last three years.
>
> **Federico Minoli**[31]

The Internet penetration rate in Italy is one of the lowest in Western Europe. As of June 1999, only 9% of the 57 million population used the Internet.[32] This may constitute a stumbling block for Ducati's Internet strategy and drive towards offering additional online applications. In spite of this, Ducati plans to continue investing in its new online venture. However, special features still need to be defined. For example, should Ducati control chat-line information exchanges between members of the DOC virtual community? Should it intervene if deemed necessary? Should the launch of Ducati.com tomorrow be a gradual process, or would a 'big bang' be preferable? Can Ducati find enough skilled employees to build up the vertical Internet portal? Will Ducati turn Ducati.com tomorrow into reality, or will it always remain a dream for tomorrow?

The World of Ducati has to move faster and expand, in both the physical and the virtual dimensions, as competition in terms of vertical Internet motorcycle portals has already started. Motoride.com, launched in 2000, claims to be the first portal in the two-wheel industry. The website, which was featured in major newspapers and magazines, is the result of a new venture co-ordinated by the Boston Consulting Group (BCG), Piaggio (the European leader in the motorcycle scooter industry and manufacturer of Vespa) and Deutsche Morgan Grenfell (the Piaggio majority shareholder). Motorride.com planned to offer a fully operational portal by December 2000.

While Ducati continues to consolidate its brand, selling an image and associated lifestyle, the company tries to expand the boundaries of the World of Ducati by offering motorcycle-related products, e.g. accessories and apparel. This product portfolio expansion can be done through strategic alliances and partnerships. However, Ducati will continue to focus on its core products: high-quality and high-performance motorcycles.

In order to increase sales revenues and profitability, Ducati intends to expand into new markets and further rationalize its distribution network. It aims at reducing the number of ordinary dealer outlets and replacing them with Ducati stores and Ducati corners. Ducati-owned subsidiaries are increasingly taking control of the distribution network.

Obviously, the above company initiatives raise several key issues. In order to broaden the product portfolio, should Ducati also offer accessories and apparels that are not related directly to motorcycles? What will the dealers' reaction be to Ducati's restructuring of its distribution network? Will Internet-based sales of limited edition motorcycles cannibalize dealer sales of other model lines? Will Ducati be selling accessories, apparel and all its motorcycle models over the Internet in the near future? Indeed, should it actually do this? Will the online electronic sales channel be a major threat to the dealers' *raison d'être*, despite the fact that Ducati's Internet sales were not expected to exceed 3% of total revenues in 2000? Or will the Internet prove to be a valuable source of information for customers and increase dealer sales?

Clearly, many business issues need to be addressed and strategic choices made. Ducati has just embarked on a voyage of discovery and its e-business journey promises to be a challenging but potentially rewarding one.

---

31 Ducati press release, 6 March 2000, Bologna, Italy.

32 *CIA World Factbook*, July 1999; InternetNews, June 1999.

DISCUSSION QUESTIONS

1 Do you think that Ducati's decision to sell exclusively through the Internet its MH900e motorcycle model was a risky decision or a safe bet? Explain.

2 Since Italy is the main market for Ducati and the Internet penetration there is one of the lowest in Western Europe, is it advantageous or adventurous for Ducati to focus its business strategy on electronic commerce? Defend your arguments.

3 Following the successful online sale of the MH900e model, what do you recommend to Ducati's top management to do next? In particular, do you think they should sell other products through the Internet? If so, how soon should they do it and what specific products should they offer?

4 'Success in the new economy will go to those who can execute clicks-and-mortar strategies that bridge the physical and virtual worlds.'

Discuss the above statement and provide your views as to how companies can get the right mix of bricks and clicks in order to win the distribution channel war. You may consider one or more industries as a business context for your answer.

Ducati (Italy) *vs.* Harley-Davidson (USA)

Innovating business processes and managing value networks

In 2001, as Ducati celebrated its 75th anniversary, some executives wondered whether the recent corporate restructuring had repositioned the company successfully. As part of this, the Italian motorcycle manufacturer had adopted a new focus on R&D, marketing and sales, moving away from its initial manufacturing strength. In addition, the company had embraced the Internet, deciding in January 2000 to sell its new motorcycle, apparel and accessories exclusively online. Though this had been a risky decision, it had been tremendously successful. Federico Minoli, President and CEO of Ducati.com, and Chair of the Board of Ducati Motor Holding, announced with pleasure that:

> Since 1 January 2000, we have sold over 2500 motorbikes online with the help and involvement of our official dealer network, proving the validity of our Internet strategy. With this success, we further confirm the value of our brand and our product.

Ducati: company overview

Ducati Motor Holding SpA[1] (DMH) was a manufacturer of expensive high-performance motorcycles. Since 1926, the medium-sized company, based in Bologna, Italy, has been developing and producing racing-inspired motorcycles, winning the World Superbike Championship uninterruptedly for decades. In 1996, Ducati's parent company Caviga faced a major financial crisis which led to the sale of a 51% stake in DMH to the USA-based Texas Pacific Group (TPG) and Deutsche Morgan Grenfell Capital (Italy). A new management team initiated a turnaround programme aiming at increased production efficiency, net sales and profit. 'Since 1996, we were really working against a backdrop that wasn't so far removed from bankruptcy', said Carlo di Biagio, Chief Executive Officer of DMH. 'Now our situation is different. Sooner or later, we think investors will see that.'

By 2001, the company had restructured its value chain activities, outsourcing 90% of its production and, in order to decrease costs, introducing a platform strategy that provided a common technical base for Ducati motorcycles. All models subsequently shared a fundamental engine configuration (L-shaped twin-cylinder engine), tubular trestle frame and many generic or commoditized parts. In addition, all models (excluding the ST2) used one of only two types of engines: two-valve – or four-valve – making assembly easier and manufacturing less costly. Furthermore, DMH restructured its distribution network by reducing the number of its dealer outlets and replacing multibrand dealers with Ducati-designed stores. Thus, after the restructuring, DMH consisted essentially of an R&D and design centre, an assembly unit and a marketing and sales department. Support and logistics were also outsourced.

One of Ducati's key strengths is its brand name and product innovation capability. The company has successfully revamped its existing product line and

1 SpA (Società per Azioni) is a joint stock company.

This case was written by Stefanie Leenen, doctoral student at the University of St Gallen, Switzerland, and Tawfik Jelassi, Affiliate Professor of Technology Management at INSEAD, Fontainebleau. It is intended to be used as the basis for class discussion rather than to illustrate effective or ineffective handling of an administrative situation.

The case was made possible by the co-operation of Ducati Motor SpA (Italy).

introduced several new motorcycle models, accessories and apparel. The new products were sold either through the traditional dealer network or exclusively over the Internet.

Ducati's e-commerce activities were first launched on 1 January 2000, when a new, limited-edition MH900e motorcycle, priced at €15 000 was sold exclusively over the Internet. The entire first year's production of the MH900e was sold out in just 31 minutes, despite the fact that production was not scheduled to start before June 2000. Industry-wide, it was the first event of its kind. 'Produce what is already sold' thus became a new motto for Ducati, and it subsequently set up an independent online entity, called Ducati.com on 6 March 2000.

In countries where Ducati took control of its distribution network, the company experienced a significant rise in motorcycle registrations, a key measure of retail sales. In 2001, Ducati announced the fifth consecutive year of record profits, amounting to €10.5 million (see Table 1). For the same period, the company sold 38 969 motorcycles, with revenues of €407.8 million and EBITDA[2] up by 10% to €66.1 million, i.e. 16.9% of revenues. In 2001, Ducati had a 6.4% share of the Western European market.

On 2 April 2001, DMH joined the STAR[3] segment of the Mercato Telematico Azionario of Borsa Italia SpA, a new high-standard stock segment.[4] Ducati was among the first 20 Italian companies to qualify for the STAR segment. Thereby, the company tried to obtain greater visibility in the financial markets and to enhance shareholder value through increased liquidity.

Table 1 **Ducati financial data** (million euros)

	1999	*2000*	*2001*
Total revenues (motorcycles, accessories, apparel, spare parts, etc.)	294.5	379.5	407.8
Accessories and apparel	37.1	55.9	61.4
Gross profit	118.0	150.6	166.5
Registration (units)	32 135	38 130	38 969
EBITDA	50.8	60.0	66.1
Depreciation and amortization	(24.3)	(29.6)	(34.6)
Financing expense	(14.3)	(19.4)	(12.1)
Non-recurring items	4.5	6.7	(28)
Income tax and minority interest	(7.8)	(7.2)	(8.9)
Net profit	8.9	10.5	10.5
Net debt	112.3	97.4	112.9
Total shareholders' equity	131.1	143.1	154.6
Total net capitalization	243.4	240.5	267.5
Net debt/total net capitalization (%)	46.1	40.5	42
Net debt/EBITDA	2.2×	1.6×	1.7×

Source: Adapted from Ducati documents, July 2001 and January 2002.

Harley-Davidson: company overview

Another major motorcycle manufacturer was the USA-based Harley-Davidson, which was in the market niche of cruisers and touring motorcycles (see Exhibit 1). Like Ducati, Harley-Davidson offered motorcycles, spare parts, accessories, apparel and general merchandise. Harley-Davidson Inc. was active in two business segments: motorcycles and related products with Harley-Davidson Motor Company and Buell Motorcycle Company,[5] and financial services with the Harley-Davidson Financial Services (HDFS). The latter provided wholesale and retail financing and insurance programmes to Harley-Davidson/Buell dealers and customers, including credit, insurance and production options, the Harley-Davidson Extended Service Plan[6] and the Harley-Davidson Visa card.

In June 1981, 13 Harley-Davidson senior executives bought Harley-Davidson Motor Company from its former parent company AMF, through a leveraged buy-out. At the time, the company suffered from a reputation for poor quality and low reliability, and it lacked innovative product design and development. A turnaround programme was begun, comprising of a 40% reduction of the overall workforce, a 9% wage-cut, and the introduction of new products. Over 20 years later, as it celebrated its 100th anniversary, Harley-Davidson was one of the most successful motorcycle manufacturers in the world, enjoying strong brand recognition and an innovative design

2 EBITDA stands for earnings before interest, taxes, depreciation and amortization.

3 STAR stands for Segmento Titoli con Alti Requisiti. This means a stock segment with high requirements.

4 The Mercato Telematico Azionario of Borsa Italia SpA is a screen-based stock exchange dedicated to small and medium-sized capitalization companies in Italy that operate successfully in traditional sectors of the economy and satisfy a series of requirements in terms of transparency, liquidity and corporate governance.

5 Buell Motorcycle Company produces sport motorcycles in addition to motorcycle parts, accessories and apparel.

6 The Harley-Davidson Extended Service Plan covers motorcycle repairs.

Exhibit 1 Expanding the niche boundaries of Ducati motorcycles: the move from performance, functional motorcycles to comfort and lifestyle-orientated motorcycles

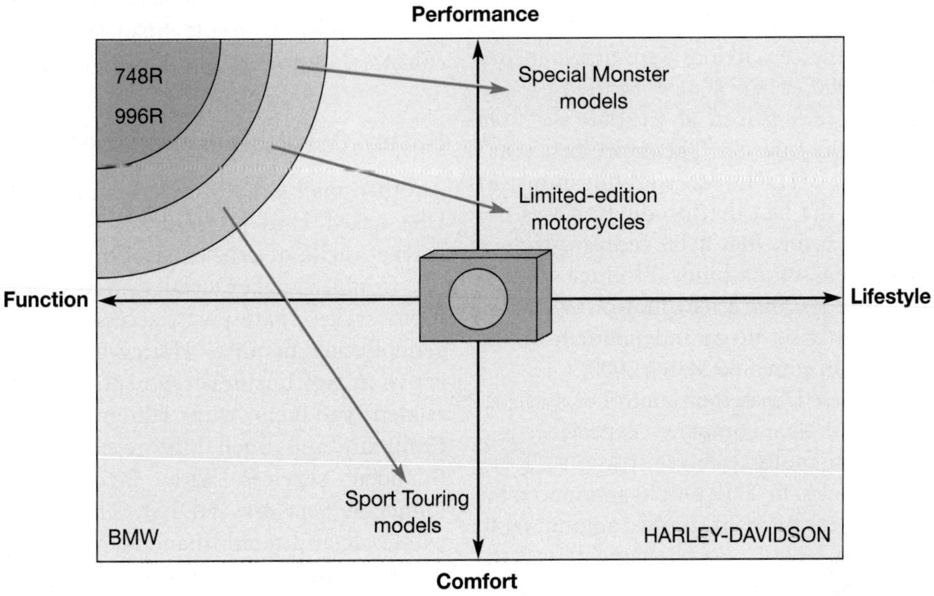

Source: Adapted from Ducati document, September 2001.

Table 2 Harley-Davidson financial data (US$ million)

	1999	*2000*	*2001*
Total revenues (motorcycles, accessories, apparel, spare parts, etc.)	2453	2906	3363
Costs of goods sold	1617	1915	2183
Gross profit	836	991	1180
Financial services income	133	140	181
Financial services interest and operating expense	105	103	120
Operating income from financial services	28	37	61
Net income	267	348	438
	2000	*2001*	*Change (%)*
Revenues			
Total motorcycles (Harley-Davidson and Buell)	2304	2692	16.8
Motorcycles parts and accessories	448	507	13.3
General merchandise	151	164	8.3
Other	2.6	0.2	(92)
Registration (units)	204 500	234 461	14.6
Harley-Davidson motorcycles	10 189	9925	(2.6)

Source: Harley-Davidson Annual Report, 2001.

and development capability. In 2001, Harley-Davidson was elected Company of the Year by *Forbes Magazine*, and was described as one of the 'most admired companies' in the USA.

In 2001, Harley-Davidson announced record revenues and net earnings for the 16th consecutive year. The company's revenues were US$3.4 billion, an increase of 15.7% over the previous year (see Table 2). Revenues of the Harley-Davidson motorcycle division increased by 17.1% to US$2.6 billion. Net earnings of the company grew by 25.9% to US$438 million. Harley-Davidson Financial Services' net earnings amounted to US$61 million, i.e. 14% of the company's total.

For its third quarter 2002, Harley-Davidson announced record revenue and earnings, with revenues of US$1.14 billion, an increase of 31.8% over the third quarter of 2001. 'As we began our year-long 100th anniversary celebration, we achieved our biggest quarter ever, setting new records in revenue and earnings', said Jeffrey L. Bleustein, Chair and Chief Executive Officer of Harley-Davidson Inc. 'The commemorative products for our 100th anniversary celebration were a major driver for our exceptional

third quarter performance and are a great springboard for growing demand for the future.'[7]

Ducati's business strategy

> Despite the challenging business environment in 2002, we are continuing to invest in innovative products and brand-building activities to lay the ground for strong and sustained future growth.
>
> **Carlo di Biagio**

Since the 1996 company turnaround, Ducati aimed at the following objectives: improving production efficiency, developing high-margin motorcycle-related businesses, leveraging the Ducati brand, pushing the boundaries of the Ducati products' niche, reinforcing the company's core niche position, improving the distribution network, and developing Internet and e-commerce activities.

Although Ducati was continuously learning and enhancing its products and processes, the company believed that it had attained its goals. To improve production efficiency, the company introduced several projects, including the Ducati Improvement Process (DIP). Sales of high-margin, motorcycle-related products such as spare parts, accessories and apparel increased by 9.8% from €55.9 million in 2000 to €61.4 million in 2001. The company also leveraged its brand through the sales of apparel and accessories. Ducati expanded its niche boundaries of high-performance, functional motorcycles with the Sport Touring models, special Monster models, and limited-edition motorcycles such as the S4 Fogarty (see Exhibit 1). At the same time, it reinforced its core niche position, for example with the sale of the top-of-the-line motorcycle model 996R, and by focusing on its core competencies.

By February 2002, the company had 92 Ducati stores worldwide. These retail outlets were designed to help the company gain more control over its distribution network, develop closer contact with its customers, increase profit margins and reduce lead times. Ducati had also been selling limited-edition motorcycles, accessories, apparel and memorabilia exclusively over the Internet. Some of the products sold online, particularly motorcycles, were delivered to customers through the dealer network. Products sold online were normally not available at the dealer outlets. The dot.com line offered restyled, classic motorcycles, and collector's items. The latter included limited-edition new motorcycles not yet launched at dealers and limited editions of enhanced or redesigned current motorcycle models. With its online sales, Ducati tried to strengthen rather than undermine dealers through increased sales volume and increased cross-selling opportunities.

After announcing the successful online sale of the MH900e motorcycle, the biggest Internet-based sale ever made in Italy, DMH's share price on the Milan Stock Exchange increased by an impressive 11.7%. 'It was at the time when the Internet bubble was at its peak', reflected Christopher Spira, Head of Investor Relations at DMH. The Internet since became an inherent part of DMH's corporate strategy. By 2001, the company was trying to integrate the separate Ducati.com operation into the real 'World of Ducati'. Hence, through trial and error, the company was fine-tuning its e-strategy and trying to adapt quickly to the changing business environment.

Ducati's business model had fundamentally changed from operating through a narrow value chain to setting up a value network, which integrated online and offline processes and business partners (see Exhibit 2). The value network included customers, suppliers, dealer outlets, marketing partners and sponsors. Through its network marketing partners and sponsors, Ducati tried to expose and leverage its brand.

As a result, Ducati had closer contact online and offline with its customers and a better understanding of their needs. 'The Internet changes your relationship with customers', commented Federico Minoli. 'Your customers become your marketing department. They tell you what kind of bike they want.' Indeed, the company considered customers a valuable source of information and took into account their preferences and views when making strategic decisions. For instance, Ducati conducted a major online survey asking Ducatisti[8] whether the company should participate in the World Grand Prix Championship. The 4500 positive responses reassured Ducati executives in their decision to participate in this major event.

The role of suppliers also became more important as Ducati outsourced most of the manufacturing of

---

7 www.harley-davidson/investor relations/pressrelease, 15 October 2002.

8 Ducatisti are Ducati employees and Ducati fans owning Ducati motorcycles.

Exhibit 2 The Ducati value network: Ducati in-house, networked and outsourced activities

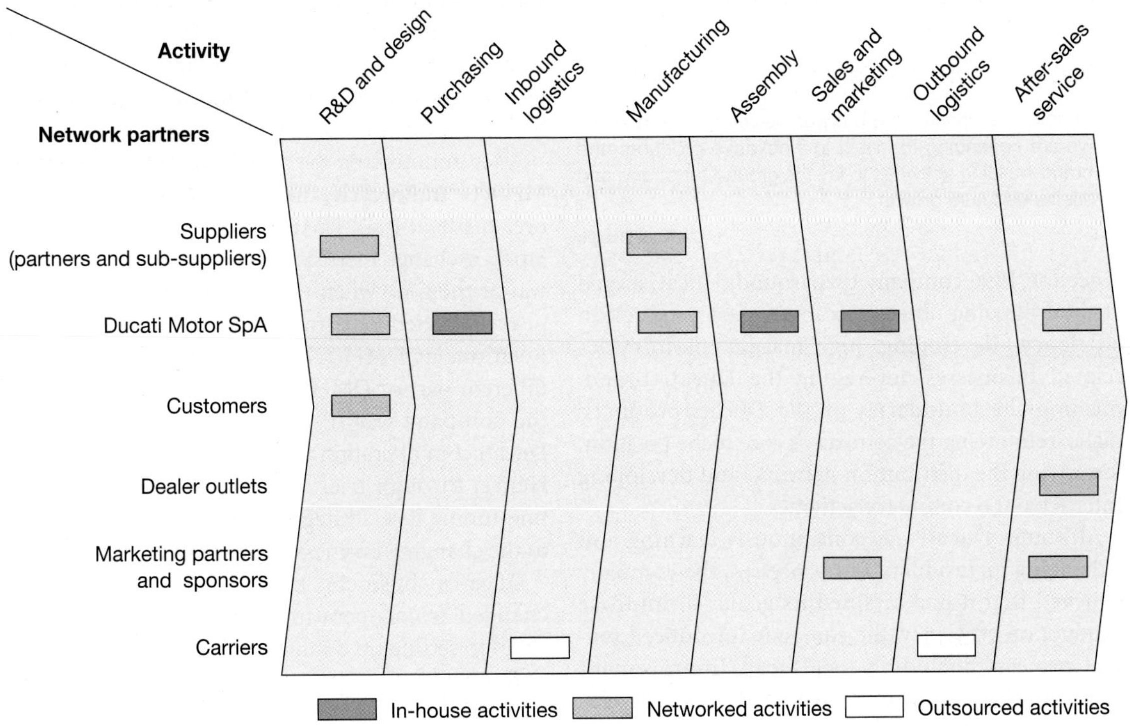

Source: Based on infomation provided by Ducati.

parts and components. At Ducati, the decision to outsource or keep in-house a certain activity was based on a two-by-two matrix (see Exhibit 3). If the

Exhibit 3 The insourcing/outsourcing decision matrix

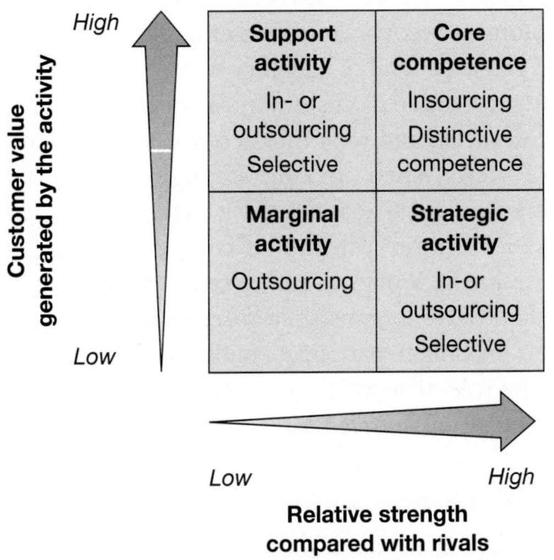

Source: Adapted from Ducati document, September 2001.

customer value generated by a given activity was low and Ducati's relative strength compared with rivals was also low, then the activity was marginal and should thus be outsourced. If the value of both criteria was high, then the activity was considered a core competence of the firm and kept in-house. If the value of one criterion was high and the value of the other one was low, then the decision to insource or outsource was made selectively.

Ducati's relationship with suppliers tended towards a long-term partnership, which involved suppliers in several activities of the value chain: R&D, design, manufacturing and assembly. To improve efficiency, Ducati was intending to establish electronic linkages with its suppliers through electronic data interchange (EDI).

With its distribution network, Ducati strengthened its ties both on- and offline. First, technical training and support were intensified. Second, through the virtual Ducati store, traffic was generated to the Ducati dealer. Third, Ducati stores became virtually integrated through B2B software called Softway,

which provided an electronic catalogue of spare parts and took orders and tracked processing electronically.

The value network also included marketing partners and sponsors such as Virgin Entertainment, Mattel and Maisto. Offline, Ducati partnered on the racetrack with companies such as Royal Dutch Shell, signing sponsorship and supply agreements with them. Online, Ducati.com had multiple partners such as the Italian telecommunication company Infostrada, which was a principle sponsor of the Ducati World Superbike Championship, and supported Ducati technically in establishing its communications network. Ducati.com offered dynamic partnership opportunities to drive traffic to partners' websites, enhance partners' brand exposure, and/or provide content to a wider audience.

As the value network partners were increasingly integrated into Ducati's single value-creating activities, communication became more important. Reflecting on the past actions of Ducati and the possibilities provided by the Internet, Carlo di Biagio said: 'We should have communicated more, better and earlier ... Once you create an Internet-based relationship with your network partners, you cannot abandon them.' As a result, DMH subsequently provided its customers with weekly news on the latest production of the motorcycle M4 Fogarty.

Harley-Davidson's business strategy

> It is one thing for people to buy your products. It's another for them to tattoo your name on their bodies.
>
> **Harley-Davidson Inc.**[9]

Part of Harley-Davidson's success lay in its ability to understand its products and the marketplace. Executives knew what the brand stood for and how to appeal to its customers' 'heart, soul and mind'.[10] The company also aimed at having a smooth relationship with its dealers. One initiative of Harley-Davidson's turnaround programme was to focus on its core customer base, expanding it to include CEOs, lawyers and doctors. By 2002, about 70% of the customers of the William Bartels Californian dealership were 'rubs' (rich urban bikers). Another project was the Harley Owners Group (HOG), founded in 1983 and aimed at helping Harley-Davidson dealers attract and retain customers. In 2001, there were more than 660 000 HOG members in over 115 different countries.

Despite the business climate, Harley-Davidson announced it was raising its 2002 motorcycle production to 263 000 units, up by 12% from the 234 500 in 2001. For 2003, the target was set at 289 000 units, another 10% increase over 2002. Celebrating its 100th anniversary in 2003, the company declared that its aim was to 'sustain growth...the next 100 years'.[11] More specifically, Harley-Davidson attempted to increase demand for its products and enhance its production with the goal of growing earnings faster than revenues. The company stated that its success drivers were its strong brand recognition, exciting products and services, mutually beneficial relationships with suppliers, and experienced management team supported by an empowered workforce. With its extensive 100th anniversary celebrations, the company sought to increase its brand exposure, celebrate with family and friends, and reach out to new customers. Several events were planned, variously entitled the 'Open Road Tour', the 'Ride Home', the 'Celebration' and the 'Party'.

Although Harley-Davidson recruited 500 additional workers to increase its production capacity in 2002, it still could not meet demand. In fact, the company preferred not to do so. Some dealers even charged 20% premiums over the manufacturer's suggested retail price (MSRP) or forced customers to wait up to 18 months for products. Impatient customers often refused to wait, resulting in the fall of Harley-Davidson's US market share from 48% in 1997 to 44% in 2001. 'Harley's true earnings and cash flow generating power are held back by production', said Joe Yurman of Bear Stearns, a US investment banking, securities and brokerage firm.[12]

In 2002, Harley-Davidson had more than 1300 dealer outlets in 48 countries. Furthermore, satellite stores located in shopping malls and other high-traffic locations were convenient for customers in search of gear

9 Harley-Davidson sponsors an annual rally in which the tattoo contest is a keenly anticipated event. G. Hamel, *Leading the Revolution: How to Thrive in Turbulent Times by Making Innovation a Way of Life*, Plume, 2002, p. 84.

10 'Marketing: the five best companies', www.forbes.com/2002/08/01/0801marketers.html

11 www.harley-davidson.com/investor relation/resources/events and presentations

12 http://www.forbes.com/best/2001/0910/008.html, 10 September 2001.

and collectables. Motorcycle sales rose by 19% during the first nine months in 2002. 'This, together with better than expected accessories and motor clothes sales in a difficult economy, gives us confidence in the robust demand for our products', said Bleustein.

Innovating the physical and virtual value networks

> I am like a priest for Ducati and my religion is innovation. We are pushing innovation in a broad sense. This means that we innovate our products, processes and organization, and also the way we do business through our online community.
>
> **Carlo di Biagio**

> Our [Harley-Davidson's] success didn't happen overnight. It was built on a foundation laid by generations – past and present. And it will continue to grow well into the future.
>
> **Harley-Davidson Inc., Annual Report, 2001**

R&D and design

Before the reorganization, it typically took seven years to develop a new motorcycle prototype at Ducati. R&D and design involved a long sequence of activities, with just a single activity carried out at any one time and requiring the involvement of not only the R&D and design departments but also manufacturing, external designers and suppliers. Christopher Spira explained how the process had changed:

> With this linear procedure, each time one unit of the company did a little bit they passed on the hot potato to another unit. Today, we have cross-functional experts, including those concerned with the end of the project, such as [the] marketing [department]. They work together right from the beginning, all the way through the end of the [new product development] process.

This new product development process at Ducati used a network-based design approach, enabling the company to reduce the time to develop a motorcycle prototype from seven years to four years. Starting with the R&D and design phase, several processes were carried out simultaneously, with all relevant internal and external departments and groups participating in a given process. These typically included R&D, design, manufacturing, quality control, sales and marketing as well as suppliers and sub-suppliers.

In 2000, Ducati invested almost €13 million, or 3.4% of total sales, in R&D and design activities. This sum represented an increase of 32% over the previous year. Over 150 people were dedicated to R&D and design, including 38 engineers. 'We also have a section on our website to integrate our customers in our R&D work', said Christopher Spira. The engineers used the latest CAD[13] and CNC[14] technology to design for assembly. 'We can use the parts developed for racing for our model line', commented Christopher Spira. 'Over a period of two to three years, all the innovations trickle through the model line.' R&D and design innovations were first introduced in racing and later used in the model lines, starting with the top-of-the-line models and subsequently integrated into less prestigious models.

Purchasing

Ducati

Back in 1996, the relationship between Ducati and its suppliers was tense. Suppliers were sending components in an unreliable and inconsistent manner, and Ducati's payments were often overdue. Thus, the company needed to win back supplier trust. It began by drastically overhauling its purchasing strategy: by 2002, 90% of part and component production was outsourced to suppliers and sub-suppliers, with all components delivered directly to Ducati. A hierarchical structure of four different layers of components and suppliers was developed to replace the formerly flat system. Sub-suppliers supplied to other sub-suppliers, or to Ducati partners, or directly to Ducati (see Exhibit 4); in recognition of the importance of their role, the company has developed a long-term partnership with sub-suppliers. In order to reduce costs, Ducati requested a constant supply of quality goods and services through an optimized process. Since 1998, the company has reduced the number of its suppliers by 26% to 175, while increasing purchasing costs by 59% to €196 million and increasing motorcycle production by 43% to 40016 units.

Several criteria were used to select suppliers. First, goods and services had to be priced competitively and combined with best-practice quality. Second, the company's philosophy and values had to be shared. These requirements enabled Ducati to have consistent and reliable supply, trust in its employees, and

---

13 CAD stands for computer-aided design.

14 CNC stands for computer–numerical control.

Exhibit 4 Ducati's supply management model

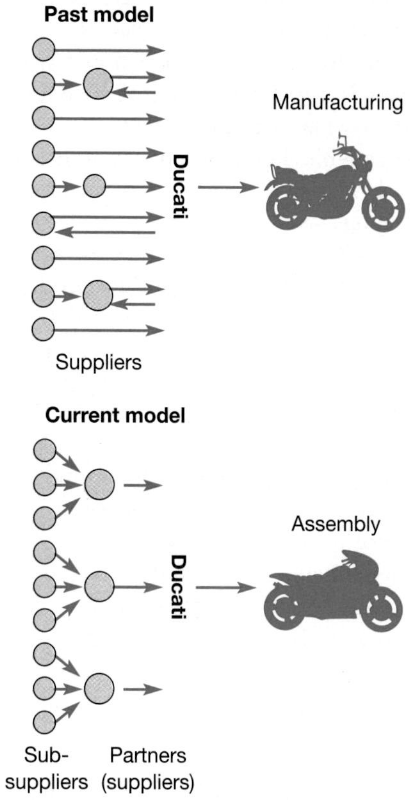

Source: Adapted from Ducati documents, September 2001.

solid financing and business continuity. Third, the supplier had to be large enough to benefit from economies of scale and to be able to invest in R&D, production technology and IT infrastructure. Fourth, the supplier had to constantly improve its processes and efficiency. Lastly, the supplier had to be able to implement innovative, personalized solutions and to react flexibly on demand as well as to deliver quickly and reduce lead time.

Several projects were under way to improve Ducati's supply network. The Ducati Evolution and Supply Management Optimization project (DESMO) examined the flow of material and information from sub-suppliers to supply partners, and from them to Ducati's production and assembly department, including outbound and inbound logistics. The objectives were to: (1) standardize the communication strategy with all companies; (2) reduce expenditure through cost analysis; and (3) enhance product and service quality.

Ducati's B2B e-commerce activities were still limited. As most of its systems were custom-designed rather than generic goods, the company was not keen on using electronic marketplaces. However, Ducati planned to launch its own e-marketplace for non-essential standard products. Other parts, including spark plugs, chains, tyres and lamps, could be purchased by joining Motoclusters, an online procurement system for the motorcycle industry set up by Giuseppe Narducci, Ducati's former Head of Purchasing.

More important to the company was its EDI connection to its major suppliers. A pilot web-based EDI project was carried out with five suppliers, aimed at electronically integrating them over the medium term with the Ducati IT system.

Harley-Davidson

At Harley-Davidson, purchases were already conducted online through traditional or Internet-based EDI. All Harley-Davidson suppliers were expected to become EDI trading partners. EDI was an effective, cost-saving way to transact business and minimize paper.

In 1996, Harley-Davidson redesigned its supply chain process. Given that over half of Harley-Davidson's products were made up of parts from outside suppliers, worth US$1 billion per annum, efficiently managing the supply chain was critical to Harley-Davidson's production and financial improvement. The company reduced the number of its suppliers by 80% from 4000 to 800. Product development time decreased by 30%, as did defective parts, from an average of 10 000 to 48 parts per million for over 75% of its suppliers. This resulted in a high reduction of waste and assembly-line down-time. Harley-Davidson's operating margins increased as a result of this redesign, going from 15% in 1997 to 18.4% in 2002.

In 2002, Harley-Davidson's online platform was still being rolled out. Even in its early phase, it offered secure access to the company's six-month billing history and to its 52-week demand forecast for parts from each of Harley-Davidson's five US plants. Suppliers could also access detailed information on purchase-order terms and conditions, e-commerce information, packing and shipping requirements, quality-assurance standards and Harley-Davidson news.

Manufacturing and assembly

> The historical achievement [of producing more than 200 motorcycles a day] is not a final goal, but an incentive to improve and satisfy the requests of our Ducati enthusiasts.
>
> **Massimo Bordi**

Part of Ducati's turnaround programme was to introduce lean production and assembly in order to improve its key production indicators. These aimed at: (1) enhancing motorcycle quality by reducing the number of defects; (2) decreasing costs by developing serial production; and (3) improving delivery service by trimming down the faulty parts at the assembly line. The company used a number of tools, such as the Kaizen[15]/Ducati Improvement Process (DIP), the zero-defects concept, the one-piece-flow principle and the total productive maintenance approach to ensure production reliability and reduce machine down-time.

Besides its radical process innovations, Ducati also carried out incremental improvements. While radical innovations required long and costly planning and implementation processes, the Ducati Improvement Process (DIP), introduced in 1999, aimed at continuously improving the company's processes using a step-wise, bottom-up approach, as opposed to a top-down approach. To optimize the internal production procedure and synchronize processes with suppliers, DIP was carried out at three levels (see Exhibit 5): on the shop floor (operative orientation), within the company's functions (tactical orientation), and company-wide (strategic orientation).

Exhibit 5 Ducati Improvement Process (DIP): development of the DIP project

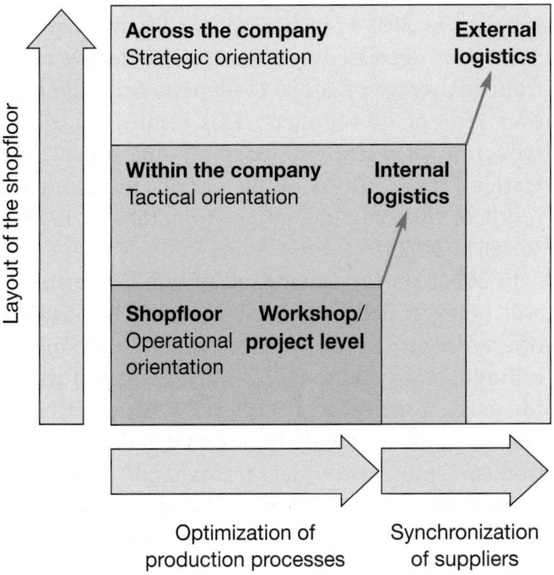

Source: Adapted from Ducati documents, September 2001.

DIP activities in manufacturing aimed at achieving a 98% availability of parts and reducing wait periods and change-over time. For assembly, the company tried to eliminate buffers, reduce the assembly stock and assembly time, and introduce production standards. Through DIP activities, the production process was redesigned to reduce operator ways (km/day) by 20%, material ways (minutes) by 34%, lead times by 50%, the default pieces by 21% and the workforce by 16% (see Exhibit 6).

To reduce stock, investment, lead time and requisite space, Ducati applied synchronized production and one-piece-flow. Hence, a maximum number of parts and components were manufactured simultaneously both in-house and by suppliers to be made ready for assembly. Since the production process redesign, daily motorcycle production increased from 25 units in 1996 to 225 in 2001, although staff numbers remained constant at 980.

In June 2002, Ducati introduced its 999 Testastretta motorcycle model. Since the previous 998 Testastretta model, the company had streamlined its assembly and decreased the component parts by 30%. Clean, renewable energy sources such as bio-gas, photovoltaic, wind, solar and biomass of agricultural and forestry derivation were all used in production.

By 2002, the dealer network provided Ducati with the company motorcycle sales forecasts, which formed the basis for production. While it typically took the company 37 days to manufacture and assemble one motorcycle, with an optimized process this would require just two days. Once produced, the motorcycle was stocked at DMH and shipped to the dealer outlet, which it typically reached four months after the order was placed. Carlo di Biagio explained the cyclical constraints on production:

> Most consumers buy their [motor]bike between March and June. The season is very short. I think it's less probable that one day we'll build to order. I know that there's a lot of pressure [from the market] in this direction. There are several constraints to deliver on order,

15 The Japanese word 'Kai' means 'change', 'zen' means 'better'.

Exhibit 6 **Impact of introducing Kaizen and one-piece flow on Ducati's efficiency: the case of the Alberi Motors workshop**

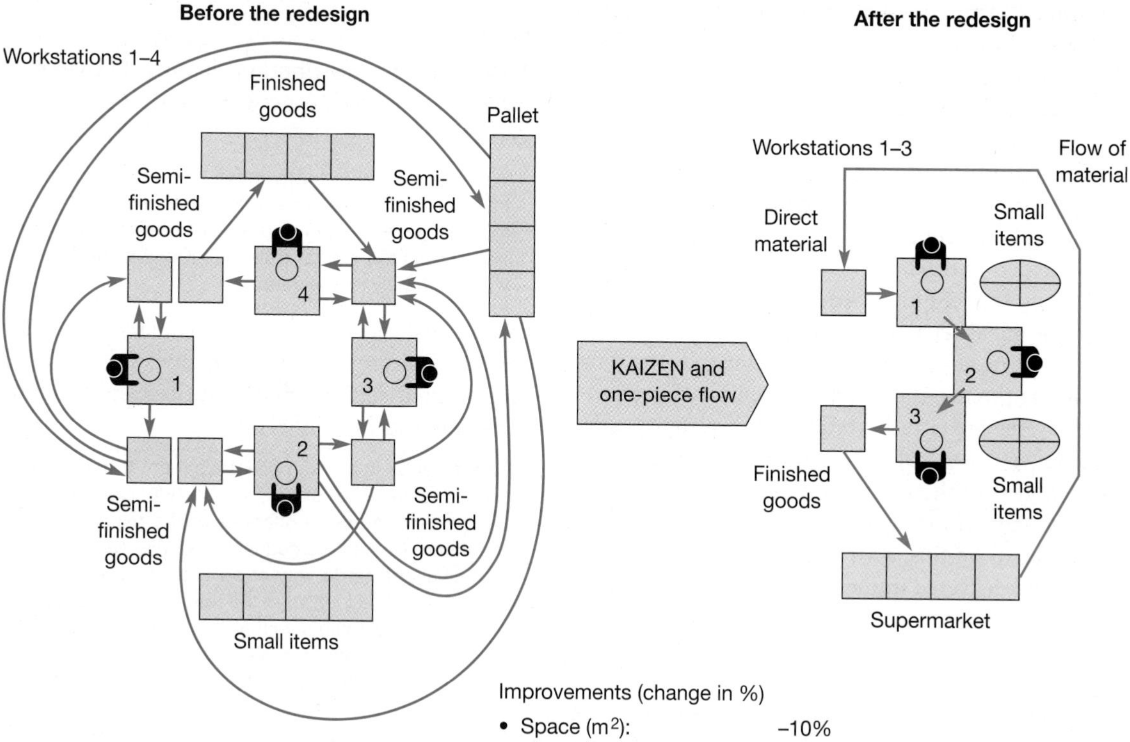

Improvements (change in %)

- Space (m^2): –10%
- Lead time (days): –50%
- Quality (default pieces): –21%
- Operator ways (km/day): –20%
- Material ways (minutes): –34%
- Production time: –27%
- Operators needed: –16%
- Operator training +100%

Source: Adapted from Ducati documents, July 2001.

including the quantity of supplies. If the customer now orders in March, we end up delivering in June and that is too late in the season.

Logistics

With its turnaround programme, Ducati tried to redesign its logistics process to align it with business strategy. As inbound and outbound logistics were considered non-core activities, they were outsourced to a specialized firm. Ducati still carried out its in-house logistics, which supplied the production line with parts and components, although the warehousing of spare parts and finished goods was outsourced. Giovanni Giorgini, Director of Manufacturing elaborated:

> Ducati sells 80% less in December compared to March. A service company managing stocks employs people throughout the year. It can easily even out seasonal ups and downs. But we can't change a shopfloor worker in March to [become] a warehouse operator in December.

In 2000, as part of the Ducati Improvement Process, the company launched several projects to optimize logistics. They included the reduction of expenditure and material flow within the factory as well as improving delivery punctuality. These projects were prioritized based on their duration and cost-saving potential, and were to be implemented throughout the end of 2004. The company first sought to improve its internal flow of material. For example, while in the past incoming parts remained in stock for four days before being assembled, they would henceforth be used the same day. Second, a logistics

control procedure was introduced. Third, the transportation of incoming material by carriers was optimized. The punctuality of part and component delivery, for example, increased from 75% to 97%. Furthermore, inbound quality-control functions were transferred to suppliers.

Ducati tried to pass on the just-in-time (JIT) delivery process not only to its suppliers but also to its sub-suppliers. The underlying premise of JIT is that supply functions provide what is needed, when it is needed and where it is needed. The aim is to reduce or even eliminate lead time, down time, space used, as well as repairs and faults.

Furthermore, the company changed its parts supply at the production and assembly line from a push system to a pull system. This system, called Kanban, consisted of having boxes containing parts located next to the production line. Once a box was empty, shop-floor workers filled out a purchase order. Based on this, a kit was prepared in the warehouse and delivered immediately to the assembly line (see Exhibit 6).

Marketing and sales

While Ducati's target customer was an athletic male with a median age of less than 30 years, Harley-Davidson's customer median age was 45 years (see Table 3). In 2001, the average household income of Ducati customers was below that of Harley-Davidson customers (which was US$78 300). Customers of both companies are brand-loyal: repeat purchasers at Harley-Davidson represented 41% of sales, while at Ducati they were 65%. Also, there were more female riders at Harley-Davidson (9% of total customers) than at Ducati (5%).

Table 3 Demographic profile of Harley-Davidson customers

	1997	*1998*	*1999*	*2000*	*2001*
Gender					
Male (%)	93	93	91	91	91
Female (%)	7	7	9	9	9
Median age (years)	44.6	44.4	44.6	45.6	45.6
Median income per household (US$1000s)	74.1	73.6	73.8	77.7	78.3

Harley-Davidson purchasers, 2001:
41% had owned a Harley-Davidson motorcycle previously;
31% had come from competitive motorcycles;
28% were new to motorcycling or had not owned a motorcycle for at least five years.

Source: 'Demographics' on Harley-Davidson Investor Relation website.

Ducati

Ducati used two distribution channels to market its products: the dealer network and the Internet. Feederico Minoli stated:

> We have the proof that we can sell products over the Internet that are expensive and complicated. And the Internet gave us the opportunity to better understand and assess the market potential of countries [in which] we were hardly represented.

Since its first successful sale on 1 January 2000 of the MH900e motorcycle, the company sold two additional limited-edition motorcycles exclusively online. Christopher Spira pointed out:

> The MH900e is a pure collector's item. It has an emotional value. The price [of €15 000 per unit] was extremely aggressive because of the experiment and the nature of the [Internet] initiative. We were offering a sort of avant-garde way of purchasing a very special item. We had no idea what the reaction was going to be and wanted to make sure that the price wouldn't be the hindrance. Actually, the MH900e online sale was not very profitable, the main return being in terms of marketing and brand building. We could have probably sold the MH900e for more, but that's one of the issues you can never really answer.

Ducati's second exclusive online sale took place on 12 September 2000, with the new, limited-edition 996R motorcycle, which went for a unit price of €26 000. The entire annual production (350 units) was sold out in just a day. A year later, on 21 June 2001, the third online sale met with almost as much success. Within three days, the annual production (380 units) of the limited-edition S4 Fogarty, priced at €18 000, was sold out. 'With the Fogarty S4, we were taking the Monster S4 [model] as a base, adding a few more performance parts, giving it a special sort of colour scheme and promoting it', said Christopher Spira. Apart from the S4 Fogarty, all other motorcycles of the 2001 model year were sold through the Ducati dealer network.

For every motorcycle sold offline, the dealer receives a 12–15% commission. However, for every motorcycle sold online that the dealer delivers to the customer, the dealer gets 5–10% commission. Carlo di Biagio commented on this mix:

> The dealers agree that we have to use the Internet to reach out to the Ducatisti. It's right for special-edition

> [motor]bikes to sell them through the Internet. I firmly believe that for normal bikes, the normal distribution channel [i.e., the dealer network] adds more value because in the end you need the dirty hands of a mechanic to prepare the bike for a customer.

In September 2002, Ducati announced the online sale of a bicycle developed in co-operation with Bianchi, the 125-year-old Italian manufacturer of high-performance racing bicycles. The limited-edition series included 200 units, which were made to measure for each customer, priced at €5500 each, and sold exclusively on the Ducati.com website from 5 November to 5 December 2002.

Harley-Davidson

Harley-Davidson had a key strength in marketing and selling its products by emotionally involving its customers. Some of the appeal that a motorcycle could exert on customers was explained by one HOG member, Walter Durandetto:

> If you come along riding a Harley, people seem to notice you more. It isn't the fastest motorcycle but sounds the best. It's still a myth, a legend. Everybody I grew up with wanted to have one. Now, I have two of them and many of my friends have one. We take trips together. It's more than a bike. It's the people, the camaraderie.

In 2001, the company's motorcycles revenues reached US$2.6 billion, accounting for over 78% of total sales (see Table 2). Parts and accessories revenues also increased by 13% to over US$500 million, i.e. 15% of total sales. General merchandise grew by 8% to US$164 million, i.e. 5% of total sales. In 2001, the company had a market share of 44% in the USA and Canada, followed by Honda (21%). In Europe, Harley-Davidson had a 6.7% market share. Through its Custom Vehicles Operation (CVO), Harley-Davidson also sold limited-edition motorcycles.

Harley-Davidson Financial Services was the largest speciality motorcycle-insurance company, insuring 300 000 motorcycle owners worldwide. The company also had a motorcycle-leasing business operating in over 32 US states as well as in Canada, Costa Rica, France, Germany, New Zealand and the UK.

The Harley-Davidson website showed every motorcycle model, described its technical details and enabled the website visitor to compare various Harley-Davidson motorcycles. It offered financing and insurance options and emphasized the emotional content of Harley-Davidson products. It also illustrated the 'Harley lifestyle' with facts and figures from engine history to motorcycle rider tips. HOG members received a 15% discount when signing up for motorcycle rallies on the Harley-Davidson website. Furthermore, Harley-Davidson used the Internet to communicate with its dealers about technical tips, service bulletins and sales information. Dealers could also place orders, pass on warranties, and receive information on a motorcycle's service history.

In October 2002, Harley-Davidson increased the convenience of browsing the 4500 accessories catalogued on its consumer website, Harley-Davidson.com. The accessories section of the site was organized by model and year, so that users could view a catalogue of accessories designed for every Harley-Davidson model dating from 1984. 'Customers can view a complete selection online, from year-round riding gear and accessories to limited-edition 100th anniversary merchandise', said Jeanne Winiarski, e-Commerce Operations Manager at Harley-Davidson Motor Company. For example, a customer could enter the name of a specific vehicle, year and model and subsequently access a catalogue of accessories designed for that model, such as trousers, boots, gloves, eyewear, etc.

For Harley-Davidson customers, the online catalogue was the source of the most current information on new and updated accessories. While purchasing accessories online became possible in 2001, the company was still keen to send customers into its dealerships, stating on its website:

> For Harley-Davidson stuff, go to a Harley-Davidson dealer. Besides, it might do you some good to get away from your computer and see the real world, maybe even do a little shopping.[16]

Alternatively, customers could combine both, selecting limited-edition products online and adding them to a 'wish list' that could either be printed or e-mailed to the Harley-Davidson dealer. Riding gear, accessories and collectables could also be purchased online from the convenience of the home or office.

After-sales service

Ducati pursued its strategy of getting closer to end customers online through Ducati.com and offline though its dealer outlets. The company's high-

16 www.harley-davidson.com

margin after-sales sector yielded a higher percentage of total sales every year. In 2001, Ducati's online and offline sales of spare parts, accessories and apparel amounted to €62 million, i.e. 15% of total revenues, compared with 14.7% of revenues in 2000 and 12.6% in 1999. In some geographical areas, Ducati provided technical assistance through 'flying doctors', based on customer needs and location.

At its dealer outlets, Ducati had a 93% availability level for its spare parts. This was made possible by the platform strategy. Dealers could order parts using Softway, the online catalogue listing over 15 000 items. Outlets were connected electronically, and each dealer could place orders and track them online. Partnerships with carrier service companies such as DHL and SAIMA meant that products could be available at any dealer outlet worldwide within 24–48 hours.

Through Ducati.com, the company leveraged the Internet to raise levels of customer service and to develop an online community of Ducati aficionados. To increase traffic on its website, content posted on the website was constantly enriched. For example, in 2001, in co-operation with the Italian motorcycle magazine *Motociclissmo*, Ducati tried to strengthen its community through a series of five two-day courses aimed at teaching women the basics of motorcycle riding. The registration fee for this course was €100, which covered riding lessons, accommodation and meals. After the announcement was made in the magazine, 600 women applied for the 150 available slots.

Harley-Davidson's approach to creating an online community differed slightly. It opted against a chat room for HOGs, deciding that it did not fit with the company image. The company's website stated: 'Chat rooms are for people who drive cars. We prefer to chat in the middle of a national park with a few thousand of our friends.'

Future outlook

Ducati

> Ducati's priority for the future is clear. We will stay focused on building our brand around the globe, revamping operations in the US, and above all, innovating our products to drive our growth.
>
> **Carlo di Biagio**

Since the 1996 launch of its turnaround programme, Ducati has successfully set up a value-added network with its suppliers, customers and sponsors. Through this value network, the company aims at improving efficiency while enhancing product and service quality.

For Ducati, its 'new' core competencies were R&D and design as well as assembly, marketing and sales. Its online activities enabled it to strengthen its relationship with customers, dealers and suppliers. However, in spite of its incremental improvements through DIP, Ducati still suffered from an uneven quality of supply, out-of-stock problems and the need for bigger stocks. To alleviate these problems, Ducati planned to replace its unstable production planning system. Would this help the company to schedule production better according to the variations in seasonal demand? Could Ducati quickly implement its multiple projects with its partners? Was the decision to outsource the manufacturing process, which used to be Ducati's core activity, a wise one? How would employees perceive the changes in Ducati's corporate culture and processes? Would the human dimension in managing the new business processes become a stumbling block towards Ducati's future success? Could the company fully exploit B2B e-commerce opportunities, or would this remain a longer-term goal? Christopher Spira commented:

> We would certainly like to reach a stage where customers give us an order over the Internet telling us what they would like us to have in their motorcycle. We are not there yet, and it is probably a long way from here to achieve that.

When – if ever – would Ducati be able to use a mass-customization business model?

Harley-Davidson

At Harley-Davidson, would the company succeed in its ambitions of sustaining growth for the next 100 years? Would it retain its leadership in motorcycle branding? Would it be able to effectively manage its human resources, specifically since Rich Teerlink, Harley-Davidson's former CEO and current board member, said:

> We still have people who just want to bring their bodies, and not their whole selves, mind included, to work.[17]

17 *Harvard Business Review*, 2000, July–August, p. 52.

DISCUSSION QUESTIONS

1 How would you compare the e-business/e-commerce strategy of Ducati and of Harley-Davidson? How would you explain the wide gap between these strategies among two leading, global motorcycle manufacturers?

2 What are the advantages and drawbacks for Ducati through outsourcing particular activities in its value chain?

3 Do you think that Ducati's decision to diversify its products with the exclusive online sale of a limited edition of motorcycles could be the starting point of a new strategy?

4 More generally, what future actions would you recommend to Ducati management in order to sustain their lead in e-business and e-commerce? Be as specific as possible.

5 What lessons would you take away from the Ducati *vs.* Harley-Davidson case study? How unique are these lessons compared to other case studies on e-business and e-commerce?

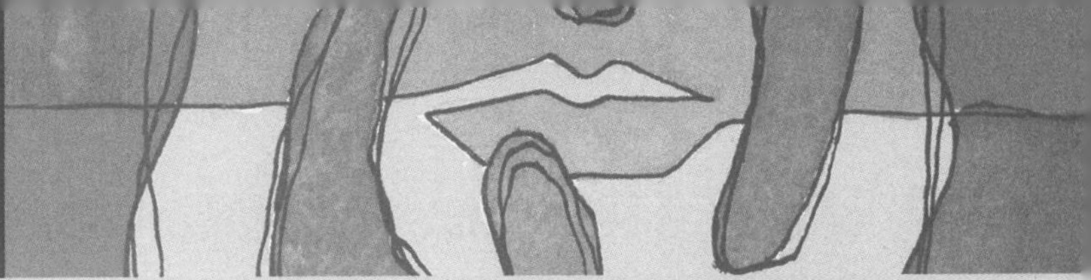

CASE STUDY 15

Terra Lycos

Creating a global and profitable integrated media company

Market leadership is a challenge within our reach, but requires us to achieve several objectives: consolidating our product offerings to make our portals the most comprehensive and compelling on the World Wide Web, taking advantage of our extraordinary cash position to grow profits and extend our website network, and finally offering small and medium-sized businesses effective e-commerce solutions. Terra Lycos must make full use of our advantage in the convergence of media, communications and interactive content, thanks to strategic alliances with Telefónica, our majority stockholder, and Bertelsmann.

Joaquim Agut, Executive Chair, Terra Lycos

The bright mid-September morning had not started well for Rafael Bonnelly, Terra Lycos's Vice-President of Content Management. He had just found out that FIFA,[1] the governing body of the soccer World Cup, had given the nod to Yahoo! to design and manage the official 2002 World Cup website. In knocking them out of the competition, FIFA had overlooked two of Terra Lycos's greatest strengths: the company's product diversity and its global reach, especially in Latin and South American markets, where football – or soccer – was more a religion than a sport. Disappointedly, he eased back in his chair and surveyed the colourful website print-outs plastering the walls. They represented another strategy to be deployed – one that would hopefully boost Terra Lycos to profitability and a top-tier position. A battle might have been lost, but the war was still on.

This case recounts the efforts of Terra Lycos, an integrated global media company formed by the October 2000 merger of Spain's Terra Networks and USA-based Lycos, to achieve profitability and a leading market position (Appendix 1). At the time this case was written (November 2001), Terra Lycos trailed its three heavy-weight contenders, AOL–Time Warner, Microsoft/MSN and Yahoo! (Appendix 2).

In the highly competitive and rapidly changing portal environment, contenders found themselves facing a clearly Darwinian challenge – adapt or risk extinction. By reviewing the evolution of the portal environment with its successes (AOL and Yahoo!) and failures (Snap.com and Excite@Home), what lessons could Terra Lycos extrapolate in developing its strategic focus? Was the market large enough to allow Terra Lycos a leadership position? What kinds of revenue streams should it explore to achieve positive earnings as quickly as possible? How should the organization change in order to support Terra Lycos's drive to profitability and market leadership? And finally, how great a role would issues such as management, branding and international market reach play in the drive to achieve a positive bottom line?

The wake-up call

It was the Big Bang of the Internet industry: the announcement on 10 January 2000 by America Online Inc. (AOL) that it was merging with Time Warner Inc. to create a multi-brand, media and communications behemoth. The new company would

1 Federation Intérnationale de Football Association.

This case was written by Patricia Reese, Research Associate, under the supervision of Soumitra Dutta, The Roland Berger Chaired Professor of e-Business and Information Technology, and Theodoros Evgeniou, Assistant Professor of Information Systems, all at INSEAD. It is intended to be used as a basis for class discussion rather than to illustrate either effective or ineffective handling of an administrative situation.

have more than \$30 billion in combined revenues, with diverse online and offline brands such as AOL, Time, CNN, Warner Brothers, Netscape and Looney Tunes.

While growth by acquisition was not new in the Internet world, the sheer size and breadth of the AOL Time Warner deal threatened to reshape completely the Internet portal landscape in one masterstroke. What would such a deal mean for independent companies like Yahoo! and Lycos?

Post AOL–Time Warner merger musings

In the purple and yellow Yahoo! boardroom, Chief Yahoo, Jerry Yang, CEO Timothy Koogle and President David Mallet debated this question.

> After four hours, a pot of Koogle's bitter coffee, and umpteen squiggles on the white board, the trio reached consensus: they would not follow AOL's lead. All of Yahoo's chips would remain on the Net.[2]

Lycos's response would eventually be its October 2000 merger with Terra Networks of Spain. In fact, Lycos was ahead of its time. At least a year before the AOL–Time Warner merger, Lycos had already attempted to walk to the altar with USA Networks, but Lycos's shareholders had balked and the deal was cancelled.

While some analysts had reacted positively to the USA–Lycos deal, others felt that the call-off was just another opportunity for Lycos to merge with the likes of Time Warner, Microsoft, NBC and News Corporation – all considered possible suitors at the time. Others thought that money-making Lycos should continue to forge ahead on its own: 'Lycos goes back to being Lycos, which is one of the best-run, most aggressive players in the Internet space', recounted one analyst.[3]

Creating Terra Lycos

Yet it was clear that the AOL–Time Warner merger put pressure on smaller, second-tier web portals like Lycos to merge or risk sinking even further. A mere month after the merger, representatives of Terra Networks approached Lycos's CEO Bob Davis about joining the two companies.

The first meeting in February 2000 between Davis and representatives of Terra Networks did not go well. Davis recalled slamming the door after only 15 minutes when he realized that Terra was interested in buying out Lycos, not in establishing a joint venture as he had been led to believe.[4] Yet Terra persisted, eventually getting Bertelsmann Chair and CEO Thomas Middelhoff, a friend of Davis, to bring him back to the table. Terra also brought in some very big guns – its Spanish telecommunications parent, Telefónica, which had net profits of €2.5 million and billed more than €28 billion in 2000.

By 16 May 2000, the parties had hammered out a \$12.5 billion stock deal, which closed on 27 October 2000 at \$6.5 billion due to their sagging stock prices. Telefónica promised a rights offering that would give the new company €2.2 billion in operating capital – some of the deepest pockets around for an Internet company – and gave Terra a 49% stake in a new wireless joint venture called Terra Mobile, together with Telefónica Móviles, the mobile subsidiary of Telefónica. Bertelsmann, which owned 18.4% of Lycos Europe,[5] agreed to a five-year \$1 billion deal to make out cheques for advertising and services to Terra Lycos. The German media company also gave Terra Lycos exclusive access to its content, including BMG artists such as pop star Christina Aguilera and Random House authors Louis L'Amour and Danielle Steel.

The deal was seen as being positive, as it combined Terra's obvious strength in Latin American markets, the deep pockets of Telefónica, and access to one of the world's largest wireless networks, with Lycos's brand name, online properties, strong US presence and a positive bottom line (see Appendix 2 and Exhibit 1). Touting itself as the newest global media company in the world, Terra Lycos could boast of operations in 37 countries in 19 languages. It controlled 120 websites, reaching 94 million unique users, who racked up 400 million page views per day. The total number of subscribers jumped from one million to just under seven million. Terra Lycos was now ready to take on the market leaders. 'It makes it

---

2 Ben Elgin, Linda Himelstein, Ronald Grover and Heather Green, 'Inside Yahoo!', *Business Week*, 21 May 2001.

3 Jim Hu, Sandeep Junnarkar and Tim Clark, 'Going solo may not work for Lycos', CNET News.com, 12 May 1999. Quote from Paul Noglows, an equity analyst at Hambrecht & Quist.

4 Robert Davis, *Speed is Life: Street Smart Lessons from the Front Lines of Business*, New York, Doubleday, 2001.

5 Eric Bovim, 'Lycos Europe open to Terra or Bertelsmann takeover', Reuters, 22 May 2001. Bertelsmann and Lycos co-founded Lycos Europe in 1997. Terra Lycos has a 29.6% stake in Lycos Europe, and Christoph Mohn, CEO of Lycos Europe and the son of Bertelsmann Foundation Chair, holds 11%.

Exhibit 1 **Terra Lycos group chart**

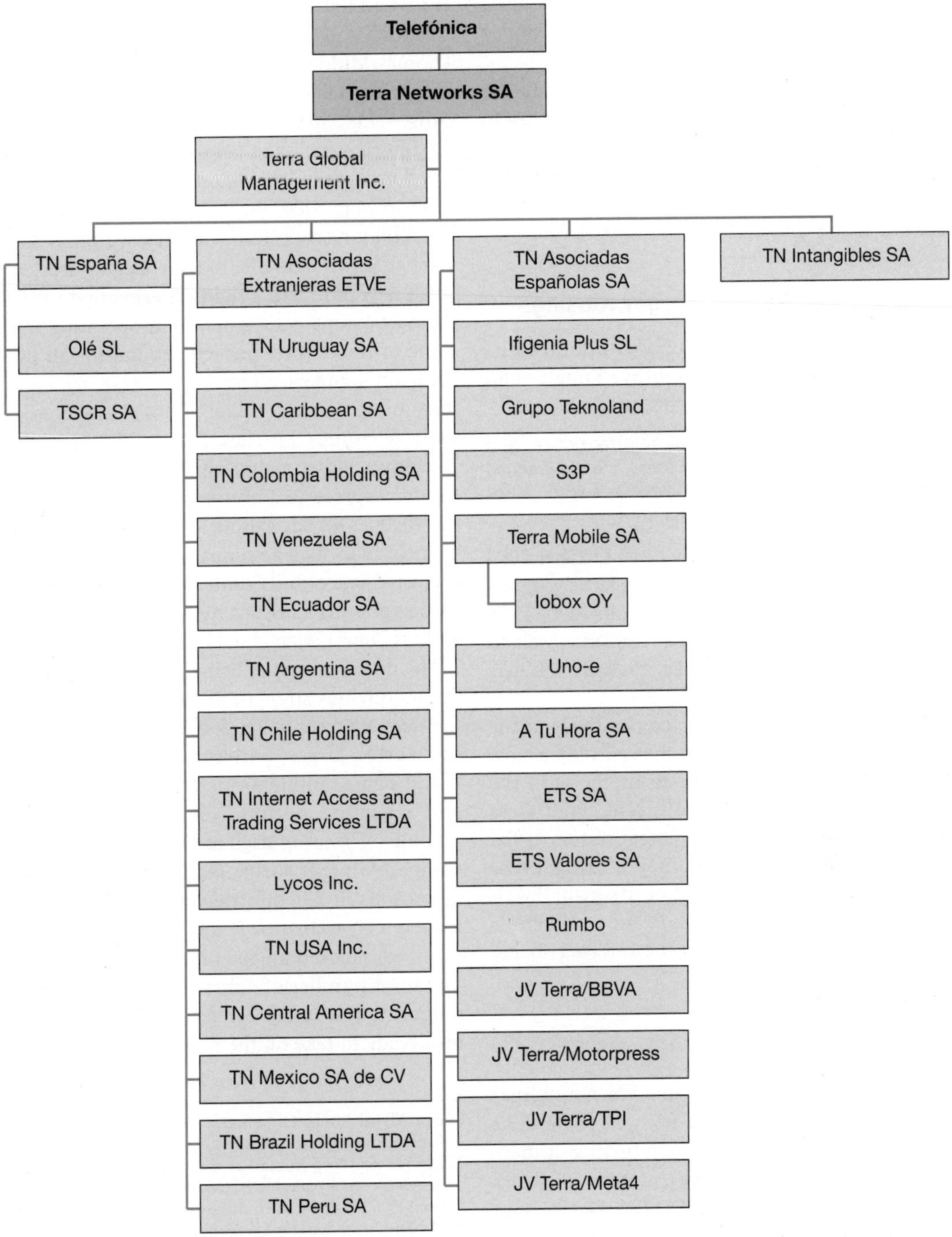

Source: Terra Lycos, internal company presentation, August 2001, p. 12.

a real equal of the Yahoos of the world and a great near-equal for AOL', noted one shareholder.[6]

Seeing red? Combining US and Spanish management

Only two months after the merger was announced, and before it was even complete, the company faced its first major test. Since Lycos was the first American portal to be bought out by a non-US company, analysts were paying particular attention to the melding of American and Spanish management and corporate cultures.[7] Although Lycos had joint ventures in Europe and Asia, it was an American company run by Davis from its Waltham, Massachusetts, headquarters. Terra's hold on the Hispanic market extended to the USA, but it was a Spanish company, headquartered in Barcelona, with marching orders given by Juan Villalonga, then Chair and CEO of Telefónica and Chair of Terra Networks.

Initially, Davis and Villalonga had agreed that Davis would run the new company. However, Villalonga was ousted from both Telefónica and Terra in July 2000 and replaced by Joaquim Agut, a former General Electric (GE) executive. From the start, Agut made it clear he would be the boss: 'I am the executive chairman of the company. The only one. Basta!'[8] In Spain, the Executive Chair's post is much like that of a CEO.

On 1 February 2001, four months after the merger was completed, Davis declared he was stepping down as CEO and would become the non-executive Vice-Chair of the company.

A high-level shake-up followed, rattling investor confidence and causing the stock price to slump. The key players were quickly replaced, however, and Agut subsequently worked hard to get the company back on track.

Reworking Terra Lycos's business model: looking for new revenue streams

Agut's first priority was to push the company into the black. While the year 2000 was a spectacular one for Terra Lycos, with an 87% increase in revenues and 336% more subscribers,[9] the tech bubble continued to deflate. Advertising revenues sunk and the newly combined company's share price kept heading south, dropping from a high of $27.12 to a low of $4.50 between October 2000 and 2001. In June 2001, the *Financial Times* named Terra Lycos the second worst performer of 2000, with a negative shareholder return of minus 87%.[10]

The company needed to introduce and exploit new online and offline revenue streams as quickly as possible, but which ones? Bonnelly believed Terra Lycos's best hope to be in reaching that sweet spot, or intersection, between customer relationship management (CRM), business and brand objectives. 'If we are able to execute on these three, then we stand a chance of breaking into the majors', he stated.[11] Concretely, how could Terra Lycos translate this three-pronged strategy into bottom-line results?

CRM objectives: Six Sigma and putting the customer first

In making the customer number one, Agut's blue-chip background proved extremely useful. One of his first acts to get the company on track was to introduce Terra Lycos managers to 'old-economy' standardized tools and measures to contain costs and increase revenues. The most far-reaching of these is Six Sigma, a 'highly disciplined process' embedded in the culture of his former employer, GE:

> The central idea behind Six Sigma is that if you can measure how many 'defects' you have in a process, you can systematically figure out how to eliminate them and get as close to 'zero defects' as possible.[12]

The process places the customer at the heart of its analysis 'to satisfy customer needs profitably'[13] (see Appendix 3). This customer focus is expected to allow the company to create specific offers for targeted

6 'Lycos, Terra complete merger', *Bloomberg News*, 27 October 2000. Quote from Brian Grove, a principal at Vaughan Nelson Scarborough & McCullough.

7 Mary Hillebrand, 'Terra Lycos deal faces rocky road', *E-Commerce Times*, 18 May 2000.

8 Richard Waters and Leslie Crawford, 'Spanish win Internet bust-up', *Financial Times*, 2 February 2000, p. 28.

9 Terra Lycos Annual Report 2000, p. 9.

10 Martin Dickson, 'European Performance League 5: lack of strategic focus among the also-rans: poor performers', *Financial Times*, 29 June 2001, p. 5.

11 Rafael Bonnelly, classroom presentation, INSEAD, Fontainebleau, France, 29 May 2001.

12 www.ge.com/sixsigma/makingcustomers.html, 16 October 2001.

13 Terra Lycos, presentation, 'DFSS (Design for Six Sigma) for e-Business,' September 2001, p.3.

consumer groups, such as the Spanish MTV site for teens, interactive games like Banja (http://banja.terra.es) for teens and males aged 18–35, personal finance offers for adults, and so on. It also explains why the company recently spearheaded a comprehensive CRM effort across all of its business lines and geographic units, which it labelled 'Project Transform'.

The CRM–Six Sigma effort also has clear bottom-line implications. Applying Six Sigma to its e-business has helped Terra Lycos to identify the gaps in its income and processes and produce targets to revise them. Six Sigma is present in all of its business units and across all of its functions. It touches on projects from achieving profitability to new product launches and the selection of software vendors. This attention to process-related development differs vastly from the frenzied, undisciplined growth-at-all-costs approach that many start-ups and established companies seemed to adopt at the height of the dot.com craze. Cost-reduction targets have now been fixed; 'it's unthinkable to miss them', noted one company executive. Before the 11 September terrorist attacks in the USA, the company predicted that it would break even in the second quarter of 2002, but it later pushed the deadline to the end of 2002.

Business objectives

Global reach and revenues

When Terra joined up with Lycos to create the world's first global new media company, Lycos added its properties in the USA, Asia and Europe to Terra's properties in 17 Latin American countries. There was no region, apart from Antarctica, that the two did not have a leading market share in. This was an inherent advantage over its rivals but not necessarily a key driver of current profits.

In studying the origins of the company's business, the vast majority of profits come from the USA, 56% in all.[14] While Internet growth rates for Asia and Latin America can be spectacular – for example, Goldman Sachs foresees the number of Internet users rising in Latin America from 20 million in 2001 to almost 75 million by 2005[15] – companies are being held back by financial volatility, low Internet penetration rates, intense competition, and higher telephone, tax and distribution rates.

Currently, Terra Lycos maintains leading positions in certain markets, especially the Latin American and Hispanic markets, European markets (through Lycos Europe) and individual markets such as Japan, Korea and Canada. This makes it the most widespread ISP/portal service geographically (42 countries), but the key top-tier players – AOL, Yahoo! and MSN – are moving quickly: AOL was present in 16 countries (it created AOL Latin America in 1999), MSN in 33 countries and Yahoo! in 24, as of July 2001.

Still, when looking where the next growth spurt will come from, many analysts point their fingers eastward. Asian markets have proved that they are quick on the uptake of new technologies, and per-capita incomes are increasing steadily. International Data Corporation estimates that there would be 240 million Internet users in Asia-Pacific, excluding Japan, by 2005.[16] In fact, some analysts are predicting that given technology adoption rates, the US market is close to saturation, with 63% of US households already online and the number of PCs bought dropping.[17] Terra Lycos is already looking to the east: Lycos Asia, a 50–50 joint venture with Singapore Telecommunications, was launched in December 1999, and MyRice.com, one of mainland China's top 20 websites, was bought in a deal estimated at $10–13 million in autumn 2000.

From ISP to integrated media channel

Terra Lycos's business strategy is currently focused on moving from a pure ISP player to an integrated media channel. When the economy slowed down, advertising – the major source of revenue for most portals – started to dry up. Given that the Terra Lycos current revenue mix is heavily advertising-dependent, to the tune of 75% with the other 25% coming from its ISP business, the company was hit hard by the downturn (see Appendix 4). It adjusted its revenue objectives downward for 2001 in May, from $900 million to between $625 million and $650 million, and moved back its earnings before interest, tax, depreciation and amortization (EBITDA) break-even point from the fourth quarter of 2001 to the second quarter of 2002.[18]

14 Rafael Bonnelly, interview, Madrid, Spain, 7 May 2001.
15 Goldman Sachs, 'Terra Lycos Equity Report', 10 July 2001, p. 25.
16 Goldman Sachs, 'Terra Lycos Equity Report', 10 July 2001, p. 25.
17 Julia Angwin, 'Has growth of the net flattened? Consumer adoption rate slows in replay of TV's history; bad news for online firms', *Asian Wall Street Journal*, 17 July 2001, p. 7.
18 Goldman Sachs, 'Terra Lycos Equity Report', 10 July 2001, p. 38.

Terra Lycos's management, like that of most other portals, needed to find new sources of revenue – and quickly. The April 2000 tech crash had shown that profits mattered. Although online advertising is expected to make an eventual come-back and surpass traditional advertising, diversification is the key to weathering such down-turns. The softness in the advertising market has made the company look to its user base as the best source of new revenues.

And therein lies the problem: how does one get customers to pay for a service that previously was free and still is – on your own or someone else's website? Terra Lycos, like other portals, is exploring the possibilities: upgrading content, broadband services, acquisitions and alliances, mobile portals, subscriptions, e-commerce and new product development, to name a few. Some of the possible revenue streams look promising, but it's like putting your chips on the table before the roulette wheel spins; each number looks good until the ball drops.

Is paid content king?

So far, very few sites – apart from sex sites – are actually charging for content. Of those non-sex sites that are doing so, very few seem to be pulling in a profit. The online version of *Consumer Reports* does,[19] but the wsj.com, Dow Jones' online version of *The Wall Street Journal*, with 600 000 subscribers paying $59 per year, still had not made money.[20] As Bonnelly remarked:

> We see our role as making your offline life easier. If we make it easier for you, then you are probably going to pay ... Content is what helped AOL become a huge corporation, out of reach in terms of its revenues. No other entity can generate those kinds of numbers – not even Yahoo! That is why we have to get the balance of user-generated and network-generated content right. It will allow us to compete with the likes of AOL and MSN.[21]

AOL's market dominance and continued ability to generate revenues in the face of flagging advertising has other portals looking to follow in its footsteps. AOL borrowed the subscription concept from cable companies that have succeeded in getting people to pay because their programming is considered 'premium' vis-à-vis the free channels and, thus, worth paying for. Noted Terry Semel, CEO of Yahoo!: 'There's lots of great programming on CBS and NBC for free ... Yet many people pay to watch *The Sopranos* [HBO's TV series on the mob].'[22]

Nonetheless, the difference between charging for a few extras and actual monthly billing (and revenues) is like the difference between using a computer that runs on a 386-MHz micro-processor and one running at 2 GHz. Others are already starting to follow AOL's lead: Yahoo! is introducing more paid services, and Terra Lycos is looking at a similar 'cable' strategy.

Making the link: OPB cable strategy

Terra Lycos has conceived an open, basic, premium (OBP) plan, a three-pronged strategy to upgrade its subscribers from free to paying services through the packaging of different service levels and products (Tables 1 and 2).

Instead of going for an all-or-nothing payment plan, Terra Lycos has created a model whereby it hopes to retain those subscribers who have zero tolerance for paying fees while at the same time encouraging others to upgrade to a better level of service and functionality. It is a low-risk strategy that minimizes the possibility of losing its subscribers or 'eyeballs' that advertisers pay for.[23] But even when Terra Lycos ends its free ISP service, as it did in Brazil in May 2001, or raises its access fees by 50% in Brazil and Mexico, it finds that it loses few of its subscribers.[24] It does, however, try to nudge consumers to upgrade to better services where the value of its customers is greater. Terra Lycos uses a content-analysis method, developed in collaboration with Jupiter Media Metrix (see Appendix 5), to evaluate the viability of its paid content and to help it determine and classify those content areas able to generate the most in revenues. Thus, the company can focus on categories, such as personal finance and publishing, where potential income is greatest. Thus, it has found that a typical Lycos user generates only 0.04¢ of income per month, whereas a Quote.com subscriber generates $58.

Enrique Pareja Rodríquez, Vice-President Access, commented that integrated and seamless access is

---

19 Timothy J. Mullaney, 'Sites worth paying for?' *Business Week*, 14 May 2001.

20 Stefanie Olsen, 'If you post it, will they pay?', CNET news.com, 29 March 2001.

21 Rafael Bonnelly, classroom presentation, INSEAD, Fontainebleau, France, 29 May 2001.

22 Brad Stone, 'Learning the ropes,' *Newsweek*, 30 July 2001, p. 31.

23 One of the ways in which websites charge for advertising is CPM, or cost per thousand. It reflects the number of times an ad is viewed.

24 Goldman Sachs, 'Terra Lycos Equity Report', 10 July 2001, pp. 3, 12, 33.

Table 1 **Competitive analysis of paid services**

	Lycos	*Yahoo*	*AOL*	*MSN*	*Terra*
Search					
Spidering	F	P	P	P	
Personal Publishing					
Web page building	F	P	P	P	
Web pages – extra disk	F	P	F		
Web pages – HTML tools	F	P	F		
e-Mail extra disk	F	P	F	F	F
Entertainment					
Video	F	F	F	F	
Online personals	P	F	F	P	F
Music downloads	P	F	F		
Online gaming	F	F	P	F	F
e-Books	P				
Business and finance					
Finance/quotes	P	P	P		
Small business services	F	P	P	P	F
Small business directory	F	P	F		F
Business cards	P	P	P		
P2P payment	F	P	P	P	
Bill payment	F	P	P	P	
Funds transfer	F	P	P	P	
Domain registration		P	P	P	F
Access and communication					
Mobile services	P				F
ISP			P	P	P
e-Commerce					
Auctions	P	P	P	P	P
Reserve auction	P				
Travel	P	P	P	P	P
Careers	P	P	P	P	F
Consumer reports		P			

F, free; P, paid.

Source: Adapted from Terra Lycos, internal documents, 2001.

what will help push business from one part of the company to another. 'The idea is to leverage the company's portal integrated access for TVs, PCs, PDAs or mobiles and permit customers to connect with all possible offerings – media, communications, services and applications', he emphasized.[25]

You've got a friend: partners and allies

Another priority revenue-generating area for Terra Lycos is establishing and deepening its relationships with partners (Table 3). It already has two crucial 'in-house' partners that will help it over the positive EBITDA hurdle through cross-selling and marketing: Telefónica and Bertelsmann. With Telefónica's 67 million wireless subscribers, Terra Lycos has a perfect opportunity to develop mobile services and portals for an almost captive audience. It owns 49% of the joint venture, Terra Mobile. The two have already started linking services such as Telefónica's yellow pages unit (TPI), which will market services to SMEs for Terra Lycos. In addition to its $1 billion advertising deal with Terra Lycos, Bertelsmann is also working with Terra Lycos to develop platforms to deliver music and books via the Internet. Bertelsmann and Terra Lycos both hold stakes in Lycos Europe.

Terra Lycos is also leveraging its global presence to form alliances with bricks-and-clicks. These exclusive deals can provide another sorely needed revenue boost or, at the least, allow the companies to barter goods and services. The company has signed deals with Unilever (manufacturer of Lipton tea, Dove soap, Magnum ice-cream), food giant Danone (Dannon in the USA) and IBM. Raúl de la Cruz Linacero, Vice-President of Sales, explained the deal with Unilever:

25 Enrique Pareja Rodríguez, interview, Madrid, Spain, 17 September 2001.

Table 2 **Packaging different service levels and products**

Open (free)	*Basic (paid)*	*Premium (paid)*	*Pay-per-view, pay-per-use*
Search	Free web hosting	Gaming and gambling	Real-time events
News and information	Personalization	Personal finance	Content on demand
Communication services	Youth communities	Travel services and information	e-Commerce
	Shopping	Streaming (music, video)	e-Learning
	Real estate		

Source: Terra Lycos, internal documents, September 2001.

Table 3 **Examples of Terra Lycos's alliances, partnerships and joint ventures (JVs)**

Company	*Description*	*Date*
Amadeus	Terra signed an agreement with Amadeus Global Travel Distribution (Air France, Lufthansa, Iberia) to create a JV to book and sell e-tickets. It created Rumbo, a 50-50 JV in March 2000 and went on to buy Travelone.com in the USA.	July 1999
BBVA	Already a strategic partner of Telefónica, Banco Bilbao Vizcaya Argentaria (BBVA) is one of Spain's largest banks. Terra Lycos has a 49% participation in BBVA's online interactive bank, Uno-e. Banco Uno-e had 80 000 clients in March 2001, a 54% increase over the previous quarter, and was managing €358 million, 128% more than 2000. In March 2000, Uno-e merged with Internet financial services provider First-E of the UK. Called UnoFirst Group, it is valued at $2.25 billion with Uno-e-Com holding 67.5% and the UK partner 32.5%.	Jan. 2000
Dannon	The two partners fashioned a marketing deal to have Terra Lycos's children's site, Lycos Zone, featured on some 200 million Danimals yogurt cups and bottles in the USA.	June 2001
IBM	Inked a two-year deal with IBM to buy technology and services for its IT infrastructure to reduce costs and increase network capacity. The IBM system will link together the company's systems, including web servers, CRM and enterprise resource planning (ERP). In return, IBM agreed to buy advertising on Terra Lycos's websites. Both companies will also explore opportunities for common marketing agreements and work on developing new technologies and applications. The deal is estimated to be worth $70–80 million.	July 2001
MTV	Terra Lycos signed an exclusive agreement to distribute MTV content through Latin American and Hispanic websites. The agreement also allows Terra to create co-branded sites with MTV. Ad space is usually sold out.	NA
Unilever	Established a partnership to showcase its products in its Hispanic markets through joint advertising, e-CRM strategies, data-bank management, targeted content production to women, and other e-commerce initiatives.	May 2001
Telepizza	A Tu Hora is a 50–50 JV that markets books, videos, CDs, prepaid phone cards and entertainment products, with distribution and delivery times from one to 24 hours.	April 2000
Telefónica	The parent company of Terra Lycos and its biggest stockholder at 36.27%, Telefónica created Terra Mobile during the merger. The wireless operator had three million registered users in March 2001. The two work together to develop mobile products such as information listings through TPI, the yellow pages unit of Telefónica, cross-marketing of products, etc.	July 2000

> Unilever knows everything there is to know about how its female customers aged 25-38 will behave in a shopping aisle, but they don't understand how these same customers react to the same products and promotions online.[26]

This integrated online marketing approach means that Terra Lycos is capable of offering more than just banners, he noted. Companies such as Unilever can use Terra Lycos portals to learn about specific online patterns and behaviours to refine their offerings and products.

Such an integrated approach to advertising seems to be a winning solution:

> As the summer of 2000 wore on, the biggest traditional advertisers began looking for online marketing ideas beyond Yahoo's banner ads, which elicited less and less interest from consumers – even as Yahoo's audience continued to grow. These corporations wanted ad campaigns integrating the Internet, TV, and radio. The soon-to-be-merged AOL Time Warner could offer that. Not Yahoo.[27]

And now, of course, Terra Lycos with its partners could offer the same.

Shopping around: vertical acquisitions and developing e-commerce capabilities

In terms of content development, the company is also buying stakes or launching new companies in areas where it does not necessarily have all of the required expertise but can add value in the form of its Internet expertise (Table 3). Such is the case with Uno-e, an online bank started by Banco Bilbao Vizcaya Argentaria (BBVA), one of Spain's leading banks, in which it owns a 49% stake. Uno-e served 80 000 clients in Latin America and Europe as of

26 Raúl de la Cruz Linacero, interview, Madrid, Spain, 17 September 2001.

27 Ben Elgin, Linda Himelstein, Ronald Grover and Heather Green, 'Inside Yahoo!', *Business Week*, 21 May 2001.

March 2001.[28] Other examples of its strategic partnerships and launches include its travel holdings: a 27.73% stake in the US booking site OneTravel.com and a 50–50 joint venture in the Latin American travel site Rumbo with Amadeus, the travel technology provider owned by Air France, Lufthansa and Iberia. Terra Lycos is also moving into B2B car sales with BBVA and B2E (business-to-employee) e-business centres with Emplaza, a joint venture with software company Meta 4, to fulfil administrative functions for small and medium-sized enterprises. Here, it is clear that Terra Lycos is interested not only in content but also in converting its users into online customers.

28 Terra Lycos, Annual Report 2000, p. 23.

Table 4 Examples of Terra Lycos products and offerings

Product/service	*Launch or acquisition*	*Description*
Angelfire.com*	August 1998	Web community
Banco Uno-e	January 2000	Online banking services in Europe and Latin America
Banja	December 1999	Online community interactive game for teens. Had 32 000 registered users in February 2001
Bumeran.com	December 2000	Latin American career site
CIERV	July 1999	Designs communications products (web pages, intranets, virtual communities)
Disney Blast	June 2000	Latin American children's site, featuring interactive games, songs and videos
Gamesville.com*	November 1999	Interactive gaming site
Lycos 411	April 2001	US service where operators provide mobile users with information and can send e-mails
Iberwap	January 2001	Mapping service
Ifegenia Plus	June 2000	Virtual education and cultural content portal
LYCOShop*	October 1999	Online shopping, e-commerce
Magazines (print)		*Punto net* (Chile), *Lycos Business Magazine* (Spain), etc.
Matchmaker.com*	June 2000	Personal classified ads
Myrice.com (Lycos Asia)	January 2001	Chinese portal, one of China's 20 most popular sites
OneTravel.com	November 2000	Number-four travel booking portal in US
Ordenamiento de Links Especializados (Olé)	April 1999	Internet search engine
Quote.com*	December 1999	Multimedia financial vortal. Also transmitted via iTV with jagfn.tv
Rumbo.com	March 2000	Online travel agency serving Spanish- and Portuguese-speaking markets
Raging Bull	January 2001	Financial services site
Sonique*	August 1999	MP.3 player
Terra Networks Intangibles	July 2000	Provider of Internet services
Tripod*	February 1997	Personal-page builder, web community
Virtual studios	NA	Offer complete audio and visual production. Transmit around 400 live events per day
Wired Digital (Hotbot, Webmonkey, Hotwired, Suck.com, WiredNews)*	July 1999	Comprises a search engine, developer's news, tech news, and commentary
Whowhere*	August 1998	Online directory

*Acquired through Lycos merger.

Before the merger, both Terra and Lycos were on the buying path, aggressively scooping up properties (Table 4). Terra acquired nine properties in a little over a year, and Lycos acquired seven, between January 1998 and August 2000. While Terra Lycos does have a healthy cash position of €2.2 billion, the buying spree has been calmed somewhat by an obsessive focus on its return to profitability.

Agut told shareholders that Terra was interested in vortals specializing in finance, travel, real estate and entertainment:

> I am only interested in acquiring an audience that I can turn into paying clients ... Vertical portals that add content or technology, or that sell services, are more important for me than page hits or viewing figures.[29]

For example, the company acquired Raging Bull for $10 million in January 2001 and Quote.com when it merged with Lycos. These two financial sites have boosted Terra Lycos's content in an area (personal finance) where user-generated income is high.

These vortals will help to differentiate and fill the gaps in Terra Lycos's content, making it more attractive to paying customers. And once the ad market picks up, Terra Lycos will have another advantage as the new trend is towards advertising on vortals and other niche websites. Forrester Research estimated that ad revenues for vortals should grow to 32% (up from 24%) by 2004, whereas for those portals not in the top three, ad revenues would fall to 3% of total Internet ad revenues.[30]

While Terra Lycos considers its launches and acquisitions as a driving growth factor that diversifies and strengthens its bottom line, there are inherent difficulties, such as switching acquired companies over to the same platforms and software, resolving branding issues, getting new employees from different countries to embrace a single company culture, and trying to create a coherent range of services, to name but a few. To illustrate this, recent acquisitions have meant that the company suddenly found itself juggling four different content-management systems. It acquired and started installing a global content management system in June 2001.

New media, not old: new technologies as revenue generators

Like other Internet companies, Terra Lycos closely follows new developments in technology and tries to match its offering to demand, while turning a profit. Areas such as broadband, m-commerce and interactive television, or iTV, are all being studied. Again, Terra Lycos's multimedia stockpile (through Admira, the media holding of Bertelsmann and Telefónica) gives it an advantage over most of its rivals. Some of the statistics look promising – like broadband, where revenues were estimated to increase to $60 million by 2005,[31] and the increase in wireless customers, up to 100 million for Telefónica alone by 2004 (from 67 million in 2001).

But dark clouds still hang over the new technology horizon. For example, the failure of the public to adopt Wireless Application Protocol (WAP) Internet-enabled mobiles looms large over mobile portals, putting the future of next-generation mobiles (3G) in doubt.[32] Unfortunately, the new technologies are sometimes more expensive and promise more than they can deliver, making consumers loath to adopt them and causing companies to backtrack on their development and rollout. Both Lycos and Yahoo! announced in May 2000 that they were stepping back from their broadband plans,[33] and cable ISP Excite@Home declared bankruptcy in September 2001.

Branding objectives

How do I brand thee? Let me count the ways

One of the company's first acts was to appoint a task force in September 2000 to consider the issue of branding. A strong brand allows portals to distinguish themselves from the competition, pull off successful brand extensions, and bring in revenues. Yahoo! is a clear example where branding has helped it to become not only one of the world's most recognized brands but also to maintain its leading market position.

In terms of branding, the news is good and bad for Terra Lycos. In bringing together the two companies,

29 Leslie Crawford and Richard Waters, 'Terra Lycos signals shift in US strategy', *Financial Times*, 7 June 2001, p. 31.

30 Charlene Li, *et al.*, 'The parting of the portal seas', *Forrester Report*, December 1999, p. 9.

31 Jean-Christophe Féraud, 'PC et TV profiteront ensemble de l'envol de haut débit', *Le Nouvel Hebdo*, 27 July–2 August 2001, p.17.

32 'Is there a future for WAP?', The Pfeiffer Report 2 October 2000, www.pfeifferreport.com/trends/ett_wap.html

33 Corey Grice and Jim Hu, 'Lycos, Yahoo step back from ambitious broadband plans', CNET news.com, 1 May 2000.

it wed the Lycos brand, well-known in the USA and European markets, with the Terra brand, strong in Latin American and Hispanic markets. Yet the branding strategies the two companies used before the merger differed greatly. One of the company's biggest challenges has been working out how to combine the two.

Before the merger, Lycos followed a multibranded 'network' approach, offering a variety of stand-alone brands. It bought diverse properties, leaving the new properties with their original names. Thus, Lycos increased its offering, while hoping to retain surfers within its network:

> The Lycos Network combines the best aspect of the network television model – its incredible reach – and the best aspects of the cable television model – its terrific audience segmentation – and puts those assets into the far more trackable, more accountable framework for the Web.[34]

But this approach never really seemed to work.

One analyst noted:

> Lycos was a victim of their own strategy because they never did figure out how to integrate all those properties they bought. Lycos ended up with seven or eight different brands, some of which were directly competitive with each other. They never presented a clear vision.[35]

While Lycos claimed that it had a 95% recognition rate among web surfers,[36] no one was really sure what the brand stood for: '[Lycos] doesn't mean anything to consumers, but it does mean something to advertisers. But it can't survive on one side of that equation. They must unify both sides of the equation,' said another analyst.[37] Another lamented that the Lycos brand 'certainly has not achieved as much of a brand appeal and unique sensibility as Yahoo! or America Online'.[38]

Terra, on the other hand, took an umbrella approach, rolling its multiple brands into the Terra fold. This is the strategy that Yahoo! used to build its brand into the most recognizable name on the Internet. Noted Tim Koogle, Chair and CEO of Yahoo! (January 1999 to April 2001):

> Some of our competitors, like Lycos, Infoseek, and Excite, built an array of fragmented brands, and they never reach critical mass. We built a big consumer base and then extended off of that. Comprehensiveness and integration of services under one consistent brand is hugely powerful, and it drives serendipitous consumption.[39]

Terra Lycos is slowly moving towards an overall brand strategy that it hopes will help to monetize its users. It wants to reduce the number of brands, currently 16, to around three, noted Pablo Aranguren, a brand manager.[40] He pointed out that a study found that most Tripod users were unaware that it was owned by Lycos, so having a multibrand network provides little value to the master brand. The same study also concluded that the Terra brand was almost unknown outside of Latin American markets, and the Lycos brand was clearly seen as a second-tier brand.

One of the biggest outcomes of the new branding strategy has been the company's decision to redesign the Lycos website: '60% of the Lycos home page was generating 10% of the traffic', Aranguren said. Code-named Project Genesis, the redesign was launched in October 2001 and gave Lycos more of a Terra look. The new design also promoted the company's open–basic–premium content strategy. Terra websites would also be redesigned in 2002, but the change would not be as radical.

Offline brand extensions

Terra Lycos is also looking at how to extend its brands in the offline world: 'Can we take these brands we have developed on the Internet and put them everywhere else?' Bonnelly asked. Why should the company limit itself only to those consumers who have Internet access?

Terra is looking to emulate experiences like Endemol's show *Big Brother*. This widely syndicated reality TV show has spun off merchandise, video, magazines, games, websites, wireless applications, and so on. In fact, Terra Lycos is now working on creating magazine, radio and television shows for its online personals service, Matchmaker.com.

Co-branding is another revenue-generating possibility. Bonnelly pointed out that by co-branding a

---

34 Lycos press release, 'Lycos acquires wired digital', 6 October 1998, www.lycos.com/press/wired.html

35 John Ince, 'Portals: who gets the bigger slice?', *Upside*, March 2001, pp. 166–174. Quote from Barry Parr of International Data Corporation.

36 Terra Lycos, Annual Report 2000, p. 13

37 Jim Hu, 'Is there room for sites other than AOL or Yahoo?', CNET news.com, 27 April 2000. Quote from Charlene Li of Forrester Research.

38 Whit Andrews, 'Commentary: what does Lycos offer Terra Networks?', Gartner Viewpoint, CNET news.com, 16 May 2000.

39 John Ince, 'Portals: who gets the bigger slice?', *Upside*, March 2001.

40 Pablo Aranguren, interview, Madrid, Spain, 17 September 2001.

website with Endemol's Argentinean version of *Big Brother*, Terra Lycos moved up from the number-six to the number-two spot in the country: 'The Internet is only one more distribution channel for brands, and it is the relationship of users with these brands that will create value', he said.[41]

The company also publishes print magazines such as *Punto Net* in Chile and *Lycos Business Magazine* in Spain. However, falling advertising revenues means magazines are folding or cutting back. In some new industry titles, such as *Wired* and *Fast Company*, advertising was down as much as 30% in 2001.[42] Other titles filed for bankruptcy, such as *The Industry Standard* in August 2001. Some conglomerates are selling their print publications: Vivendi Universal sold off its trade magazine division of approximately 50 titles to the private equity group Civen for €2 billion in July 2001. On the other hand, others are buying up publications: AOL–Time Warner bought British IPC Publishers (which publish *Marie Claire*) for $1.64 million in July 2001.

Conclusion: some progress but the road remains uncertain

In its move from pure play to a multi-integrated channel, Terra Lycos's central aim is breaking into the top tier of portals dominated by AOL–Time Warner, MSN and Yahoo!. In comparison to its rivals, the company feels closest in match to MSN, but it wants to add in the financial power of a captive subscriber base like AOL. MSN acts as a showcase for Microsoft products, develops proprietary technology such as its Instant Messenger and Explorer browser, and has big bucks to throw behind its marketing. Terra Lycos wants to do the same type of cross-marketing and selling on its sites, and it also has a large cash pile, thanks to Telefónica, to carry it through. AOL is envied for its subscriber base, which has captured 40% of the US market, worldwide brand recognition, ability to offer offline promotions and its enormous media resources, thanks to its acquisition of Time Warner. Like Yahoo!, which is expanding in the corporate marketplace through Yahoo! Corporate Portals (revenues of $60 million in 2000), Terra Lycos is also looking to new marketplaces such as B2B and B2E.

Off to a rough start initially, Terra Lycos has since tightened up the ship, bringing in former GE executive Joaquim Agut to guide the company through this crucial period. In adapting 'old-economy' tools to this 'new-economy' company, Agut pushed cost-cutting and revenue diversification to try to reach the 'can't-miss' goal of positive EBIDTA in 2002. Yet given that in the portal environment innovation is followed quickly by imitation, what kinds of revenue streams will prove most useful in helping Terra Lycos to distinguish itself from its competitors?

In terms of its profile, Terra Lycos is trying to reorganize itself around a new brand strategy, moving away from Lycos's network brand strategy and rolling its brands into one recognizable brand. But can the company pull all of these brands together into a coherent strategy that will help propel it to a dominant market position and bigger profits?

Although it holds a leading position in most of the fastest-growing markets in the world, the net revenues from such regions are paltry sums when compared with what a portal can ring up in the USA: should Terra continue to spread itself throughout the world while preparing for the next Internet gold rush in Latin America and Asia, or should it concentrate on expanding in the US market, where the profits are greatest for now?

Terra Lycos does see some bright spots on its horizon, but it is also facing some distinct challenges on the road to profitability and increased market share. Although the company has a strong cash position of €2.2 billion and the best geographic positioning, it still trails the Big Three – AOL–Time Warner, Microsoft/MSN and Yahoo! – in market reach, branding recognition and, most importantly, profits. In merging Terra Networks with Lycos Inc., it has become a serious contender for one of these top spots, but can Terra Lycos come up with a strategy that will help propel it into a top-three position?

---

41 Rafael Bonnelly, classroom presentation, INSEAD, Fontainebleau, France, 29 May 2001.

42 Michelle Kessler, 'Tech publications pull the plug', *USA Today*, 29 August 2001, p. 9A.

Appendix 1 Background information

Terra Lycos and partners

When Terra and Lycos joined forces in October 2000, they became a power to be reckoned with.

Terra started life in December 1998 as Telefónica Interactiva, a spin-off of Spanish-telecom giant Telefónica, and was rebaptized Terra Networks in November 1999. The company targeted the Spanish- and Portuguese-speaking markets with a combination of Internet access, content and services for consumers and small office/home office (SOHO) users. It grew quickly, snapping up nine companies in key Latin American and Hispanic markets (Spain, Argentina, Brazil, Mexico, Chile, Peru, Venezuela, Guatemala and the USA) by the end of March 2000, and established a leading position in these markets.

As employee number one at Lycos, Bob Davis built the company from the ground up. Lycos began as a search engine, with technology developed and licensed by Carnegie Mellon University. Lycos quickly started adding other features and sites, and soon the search engine had transformed itself into one of the USA's leading portals. The company also expanded aggressively in other parts of the world – usually as joint ventures – forming Lycos Europe in May 1997 (in 11 countries at the time of the merger) and Lycos Asia in December 1999 (in nine countries at the time of the merger). Lycos was also one of the few real success stories in the Internet world: at the end of June 2000, a few months before the merger, it reported a gain of $23 million.[43]

The deep pocket behind Terra Lycos, Telefónica,[44] was created in the early 1920s as Telefónica Nacional de España. It held the state telephone concession from 1924 to 1939 and was nationalized in 1945 by General Franco. With the EU's opening of telecom markets in 1998, the state monopoly was privatized in 1997. It revamped its corporate structure, cut 10 000 jobs, and changed its name from Telefónica Nacional de España to Telefónica SA.

Today, Telefónica is the leading telecommunications operator in the Spanish- and Portuguese-speaking world, operating in 48 countries on five continents. Its biggest markets are in Latin and South America. It is the number-one Spanish multinational by market capitalization,[45] and it is one of the largest private telecommunications companies in the world. At the end of March 2001, the company had 66.9 million managed customers for its fixed and mobile telephony lines and pay TV (71.3 million total customers).

Telefónica is organized along global business lines: fixed telephony, its Internet business (Terra Lycos), customer relationship management (CRM) business, directories and guides, audiovisual media content production and diffusion, mobiles, business data and services, B2B e-commerce development, and Emergia, the development of a submarine fibre-optic network linking the Pacific and the Atlantic.

Bertelsmann's history begins in 1835, when the printer Carl Bertelsmann founded a book-printing plant in Gütersloh, Germany.[46] The company has been family-managed ever since. A non-listed stock corporation, Bertelsmann AG's shareholders are the Bertelsmann Foundation, Groupe Bruxelles Lambert, the Mohn family and the ZEIT Foundation. In the mid-twentieth century, a fifth-generation family member, Reinhard Mohn, laid the foundations for Bertelsmann's evolution into a modern, international media company. From theology tracts to fiction, book clubs, magazines, records and then radio and television, the company's prestigious stable of brands includes Random House, BMG Music, RTL Television and Radio, UFA Sports, Springer Verlag, Barnes&Noble.com and CDNow. Since branching into Spain, its first international market in 1962, Bertelsmann has become one of the world's most international media companies, present in 60 countries. It posted $16.5 billion in revenues in 1999–2000.

---

43 Andy Robinson and Norm Alster, 'Terra Lycos: mano a mano with Yahoo?' *Business Week*, 8 January 2001, p. 54.

44 R. Hernández, J. A. Larraz and M. Menéndez, 'Terra networks SA', INSEAD MBA Industry and Competitive Analysis Paper, 20 April 2000; and corporate website, www.Telefónica.com

45 At the time this case was written (summer 2001).

46 www.bertelsmann.com.

Terra Lycos Timeline

June 1995	Lycos Inc. founded.
April 1996	Lycos raises $46 million with its IPO.
December 1998	Telefónica creates Telefónica Interactiva
	Internet. Becomes Terra Networks in September 1999.
November 1999	Telefónica Interactiva's IPO raises approximately €550 million. Approx-imately 15% of the company is floated in Spain and in the USA (Nasdaq).
May 2000	Spain's Terra Networks declares it will buy Lycos in an all-stock deal valued at $12.5 billion, or $97.55 a share. It is the first time a foreign company buys an American portal. The next day, shares of Lycos fall by $15.03, or more than 20%, to $57.59, after several financial analysts downgraded the stock.
July 2000	Terra and Telefonica Móviles establish Terra Mobile.
August 2000	Joaquim Agut replaces Juan Villalonga as Chair of Terra Networks.
October 2000	Terra Networks completes the $6.5-billion acquisition of Lycos (the lower price due to falling stock prices). Thanks to a rights offering by Telefónica, Terra Lycos possesses €2.2 billion in cash, more than Yahoo! and AOL.
1 November 2000	Terra Lycos's first day of trading on the Madrid Stock Exchange.
January 2001	Terra Lycos launches a Spanish and English wireless portal (wap.terra.com).
February 2001	CEO Robert Davis steps down, replaced by Chair Joaquim Agut. Other high-level departures follow. Stephen Killeen, former Chief Executive of Raging Bull, becomes President of US operations.
May 2001	Terra Lycos announces a 15% reduction in staff. It had 3300 employees in 42 countries at the end of March. Revenues for 2001 were projected at $624–650 million, down 31% from the previously announced $900 million. Positive EBITDA was pushed to second quarter 2002, six months later than expected.[47]

Appendix 2 Terra Lycos and the competition

In positioning itself as a 'global provider of integrated services', Terra Lycos is hoping to beat at least one of the three industry leaders, AOL–Time Warner, Microsoft/MSN and Yahoo!, for a place in the 'first tier' of web portals.

Terra Lycos has the most widespread audience geographically (42 countries, 19 languages) compared with AOL (16 countries, eight languages),[48] MSN (33 markets, 17 languages) and Yahoo! (24 countries, 12 languages). Figures are for July 2001.

Like AOL–Time Warner, Terra Lycos also has access to a trove of media resources through its partnership with Bertelsmann. However, while AOL–Time Warner is concentrating more on developing these resources (development of interactive media, attempt to buy AT&T Broadband, etc.), Terra Lycos is positioning itself as a services provider, hence its push into e-commerce (online shopping, car sales, etc.) and developing services (travel services, portals for SMEs, Internet banking, etc.). This is why Terra Lycos feels closer in spirit to MSN than to Yahoo! or AOL.

In terms of revenues, however, everyone wants what AOL has – its subscription base. A $1.95 hike in unlimited monthly access fees for 29 million AOL customers in May 2001 translated into $56.5 million of extra revenues.[49] Terra Lycos, like Yahoo!, is trying to wean itself off its overt dependence on advertising revenues.[50]

Where is there a place for Terra Lycos? It is clear that Terra Lycos does not, at least for the time being, pose much of a threat to MSN or AOL–Time Warner, which have the financial resources, product range and brand recognition necessary to retain and

47 After the terrorist attacks of 11 September 2001, it was revised to fourth quarter 2002.

48 'Worldwide AOL membership surpasses landmark 30 million milestone', *Business Wire*, 25 June 2001.

49 Jim Hu, 'AOL raises monthly rates 9%,' www.cnet.com, 22 May 2001.

50 In the first quarter of 2001, Yahoo cut its advertising revenue expectations by 42%, down to $180 million. B. Elgin, L. Himelstein, R. Grover and H. Green, 'Inside Yahoo!', *Business Week*, 21 May 2001.

increase their market positions.[51] Yahoo!, however, is another story. In a commentary crediting Steve Case with the foresight to use AOL's overly 'inflated currency' (stock price) to buy out Time Warner in 1999, it is predicted that at some point in the future, one company will be rubbing its hands, in looking back at its acquisition of Yahoo! for a 'song'.[52]

On top of competing with the big three on a worldwide basis, Terra Lycos must also contend with regional competitors. In Europe, that means rivals like Deutsche Telekom's T-Online and France Telecom's Wanadoo. In Asia, there are Chinadotcom and Goo (Japan), to name only a few. In its Latin American and Hispanic markets, Universo Online (UOL) and StarMedia represent two of Terra Lycos' biggest market-share headaches.

51 MSN launched a $50 million advertising blitz in May 2001 to steal AOL customers, and the two have waged battle over bids for AT&T's cable unit, online service fees and icon placements on desktops, among others.

52 John Ellis and Seth Godin, 'In my humble opinion', *Fast Company*, 2001, October, p. 82.

Lycos and Terra Networks, Terra Lycos[a]

($ millions)	*1998 (Lycos)*	*1999 (Lycos)*		*1998 (Terra)*	*1999 (Terra)*		*2000 (Terra Lycos)*
Revenues			Revenues			Revenues	
Advertising	41.8	93.4	Subscriptions	4375	6192	Media	431.4
e-Commerce, licensing, other	14.3	42.1	Advertising	554	1159	Access, services	139.7
			Corporate services/other	3812	5716		
Total	56.1	135.5	Total	8741	13 067	Total	571.1
Cost of revenues	12.5	28.7		NA	NA		229.6
Gross profit	43.5	106.8		NA	NA		341.5
Operating expenses (loss)	75	173.8		(10 252)	(28 737)		(664.3)
Sales and marketing	35	78.8					(398.4)
R&D	26.7[b]	26.3		NA	NA		(137.4)
General and administrative	5.6	16.3					(128.5)
Net income (loss)	(28.4)	(52)		(1511)	(15 670)		(566.3)

a All amounts in US GAAP, except for the 1998–99 figures for Terra (Spanish GAAP) and Terra Lycos's 2000 net loss.
b Reflects 'in process research and development' expense recorded in with company acquisitions.

Amounts might not total due to rounding.

Source: Lycos, Inc., 'SEC Form 10-K', 29 October 1999; Terra Networks, 1999 Annual Report, p. 111; Terra Lycos, '4Q 2001 Results', p. 8, www.terralycos.com/investor/pdf/4q€01all.pdf

Microsoft

($ million)	1998	1999	2000
Revenues			
Windows platforms	6236	8570	9265
Productivity applications and developer	7458	8636	10089
Consumer, other	1765	1854	2718
Reconciled amounts	(197)	687	884
Total	15262	19747	22956
Cost of revenues	2460	2814	3002
Gross profit	4490	7785	9421
Operating expenses (total)	8848	9819	12019
Sales and marketing	2828	3231	4141
R&D	2601	2970	3775
General and administrative	433	689	1009
Net income (loss)	4490	7783	9421

Amounts might not total due to rounding.

Source: Microsoft, 'SEC Form 10-K', 28 September 2000.

Yahoo!

($ million)	1998	1999	2000
Revenues			
Advertising	226.3	535.4	1004
Business services	18.8	56.4	106
Total	245.1	591.8	1110
Cost of revenues	52.2	102.6	158.4
Gross profit	192.9	489.1	951.7
Operating expenses (total)	207.6	440.6	653.9
Sales and marketing	125.0	223.9	419.7
Product development	34.1	72.3	117.2
General and administrative	24.6	42.4	74.5
Net income (loss)	(13.6)	47.8	70.7

Amounts might not total due to rounding.

Source: Yahoo! Inc., 'SEC Form 10-K', 16 March 2001.

Competitive benchmark September 2001

	Terra Lycos	AOL–Time Warner	Yahoo!	Microsoft/ MSN
Subscribers (million)	7.5	30	–	6.5
Unique visitors (million)	100	140	200	200
Reach (%)	30	45	66	66
Page views per month (billion)	20	28	30	NA
2000 revenues (millions)	€571.1	$7703	$1110	$22956

Source: Terra Lycos internal documents 2001; and information from previous tables.

AOL–Time Warner

($ millions)	1998 (AOL)	1999 (AOL)	2000 (AOL–Time Warner)
Revenues			
Subscriptions	2765	3873	4777
Advertising commerce	612	1240	2369
Content and other	496	610	557
Total	3874	5724	7703
Cost of revenues	(2538)	(3324)	(3874)
Gross profit	NA	NA	NA
Operating expenses			
Sales, general and administrative	1034	1390	1902
Acquired, in-process R&D	(80)	–	–
Amortization of good will	(49)	(68)	(100)
Merger and restructuring charges	(50)	(123)	(10)
Settlement charges	(18)	–	–
Net income (loss)	115	1027	1152

Amounts might not total due to rounding.

Sources: AOL-Time Warner, 'SEC Form 10-K,' 27 March 2001.

Top ten websites, June 2001

Rank		Unique visitors (1000s)	Digital media reach (%)
	All digital media	195172	100.0
1	Microsoft sites	125226	64.2
2	AOL–Time Warner Network	107891	55.3
3	Yahoo!	106072	54.3
4	**Lycos sites**	**37360**	**19.1**
5	Excite Network	36911	18.9
6	X10.COM	34896	17.9
7	About/Primedia	33407	17.1
8	**Terra Lycos**	**29967**	**15.4**
9	Infospace infrastructure servers	27470	14.1
10	eBay	26711	13.7

Source: Media Metrix, 'Global top 20 web and digital media properties (Argentina, Australia, Brazil, Canada, Denmark, France, Germany, Italy, Japan, Norway, Spain, Switzerland, United Kingdom and United States combined) June 2001 – at home'.

Top ten US websites, July 2001

Rank	Top web and digital media properties	Unique visitors (1000s)	Total usage minutes (millions)	Average minutes per month
	All digital media	94392	117111	1240.7
1	AOL Time Warner Network	77310	40580	524.9
2	Yahoo!	64388	8721	135.5
3	Microsoft Sites	63894	9604	150.3
4	X10.COM	39567	54	1.4
5	**Terra Lycos**	**37631**	**726**	**19.3**
6	Excite Network	28685	1082	37.7
7	About/Primedia	28496	486	17.1
8	Ebay	22129	2169	98.0
9	Vivendi-Universal Sites	21707	546	25.2
10	**Amazon**	**21576**	**346**	**16.0**

Source: Adapted from Media Metrix, 'US top 50 web and digital media properties unique visitors – at home and at work combined in the US measurement period July 2001'.

Appendix 3 Six Sigma

Developed by Motorola University, Six Sigma[53] is a highly disciplined, customer-oriented quality process designed to eliminate product and process defects, with the aim of getting as close to 'zero defects' as possible (3.4 defects per million opportunities for each product or service). Six Sigma is used by companies such as General Electric (GE), Motorola and Nokia. GE first began using Six Sigma in 1995, and it is estimated that the company saved more than $10 billion in the first five years it was implemented. GE proclaims: 'Six Sigma has changed the DNA of GE – it is now the way we work – in everything we do and in every product we design.'[54] The methodology was introduced into Terra Lycos as soon as Joachim Agut, a former GE executive, took the reins in August 2000.

The Six Sigma methodology merits its own dictionary. It has generated terms such as DFSS (Design for Six Sigma), DMADV (Define, Measure, Analyze, Design, Verify) for new product development, and DMAIC (Define, Measure, Analyze, Improve, Control) for improving an existing process or product. It is a 'full-company' experience, leaving no department or service untouched and requiring intensive employee and management interaction. It achieves this through the use of 'Black Belts' team leaders who work full-time on the project and 'own' the process. The methodology is flexible, and companies can adapt it to fit their particular industry and specifications. Results are linked directly to financial savings and/or consumer satisfaction.

Terra Lycos has adapted Six Sigma throughout the company. Examples of projects where it has been used include new e-business introduction, next-generation improvements on existing web services, B2C, B2B and B2E projects, and electronic networks.

The methodology starts with a DFSS, which defines the product or process, with an emphasis on collecting data from the customer's viewpoint. Once the data are analyzed, a 'business case' is written, in which defects are defined and improvements proposed. Then, the phase of quantitative data collection begins. Analysis of the data collected should reveal 'variances' or changes in process or business practices. Only then can the company begin working on the improvement of the process or product in question. When as many defects as possible have been

53 Sigma, the eighteenth letter of the Greek alphabet, is a statistical term measuring process performance.
54 www.ge.com/sixsigma

eliminated, quality-control measures are put in place to monitor the product or process improvements and to ensure continued savings.

For Terra Lycos, DFSS[55] means:

- identifying key customers by segments;
- conducting customer research and data collection;
- specifying CTQs[56] customer requirements;
- measuring current performance and competitors;
- prioritizing, analyzing and implementing new features.

Terra Lycos: DFSS model fo e-business

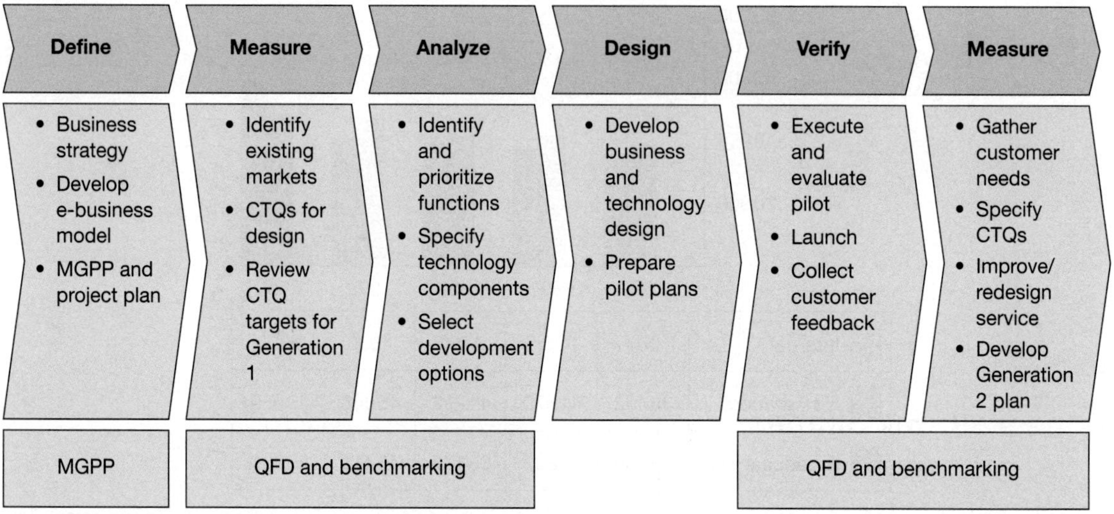

MGPP, multi-generational product plan: do as much right as possible for the first time (Generation 1), improve later, adding new features (Generation 2) and then add more features (Generation 3); QFD, quality function deployment: a document that converts the voice of the customer (VOC) into technical requirements. For more information on Six Sigma, consult www.isixsigma.com and www.ge.com/sixsigma

Source: Terra Lycos, internal company presentation, August 2001, p. 12.

Appendix 4 Advertising

Internet advertising has continued to increase since its inception, as has competition for ad dollars. In March 1999, 110 companies controlled 60% of all US minutes online. In March 2001, the 110 became 14, an 87% decrease, Jupiter Media Metrix reported.[57] Forrester Research estimated that the top three portals, AOL, Yahoo! and MSN/Microsoft, garner only 15% of Internet traffic but pocket 45% of Internet advertising dollars (and this should increase to 57% by 2004). Second-tier portals pull in only 5% of advertising receipts, and this was predicted to shrink to 1% by 2004.[58] In general, however, worldwide Internet advertising was expected to grow to $42 billion by 2005, making it comparable to what is currently spent on TV and newspaper advertising.[59]

55 Terra Lycos, internal presentation, 'DFSS design for Six Sigma for e-Business', September 2001, p. 8.

56 CTQ, or critical to quality, is a measurable customer-performance requirement key to the customer's perceived quality.

57 'Fewer companies dominating time spent online,' *News Bytes News Network*, 8 June 2001.

58 Charlene Li, *et al.*, 'The parting of the portal seas', *Forrester Report*, December, 1999 p. 7.

59 Jim Nail, *et al.*, 'Online advertising eclipsed', *Forrester Report*, January 2001, p. 14.

Terra Lycos culls around 75% of its revenues from advertisers, Yahoo! 90%. Yahoo! saw its market capitalization dive from a dizzying $110 million in January 2000 to $11 million by May 2000.[60] Terra Lycos was hit equally hard: its shares shrank by 10% the same day that Yahoo! announced its profit losses for the year. An analyst stated: 'Terra ... is the European company with the biggest exposure both to the US and to online advertising in general'.[61]

US advertising spending by media

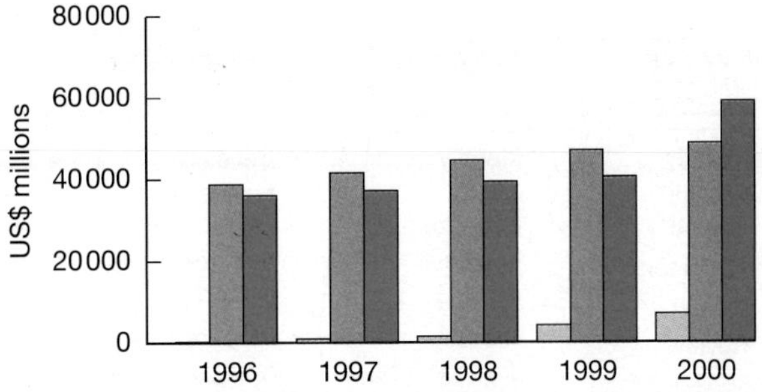

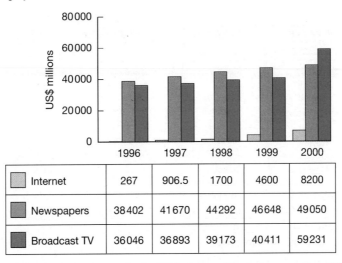

	1996	1997	1998	1999	2000
Internet	267	906.5	1700	4600	8200
Newspapers	38402	41670	44292	46648	49050
Broadcast TV	36046	36893	39173	40411	59231

Source: Adapted from the Television Bureau of Advertising (Universal McCann) 'Estimated annual US advertising expenditures 1995–1997 and 1998–1999' and the Internet Advertising Bureau (IAB)/PricewaterhouseCoopers ©2000.

Appendix 5 Paid content viability analysis

Terra Lycos uses the paid content viability analysis (developed in collaboration with Jupiter Media Metrix), a leader in the measurement and analysis of the Internet and new technologies on commerce and marketing. Instead of taking a stab in the dark as to what content should be developed, dropped or revamped, the company uses the index to gather and process quantitative data, allowing it to make strategic decisions on how to use the content. The index defines and measures three areas: content, market and financial attributes.

In *content attributes*, the index gauges the proposed content's enrichment value (the customers' perception of how the content will improve their lives), its quality, its exclusivity (whether similar online content exists and at what price) and its entertainment value. The index also takes account of the *market*, through the size of the potential audience and its discretionary budget, and *financials*, in discerning the costs for staff, marketing, technology, production, potential for cannibalization online and offline. The *net value* assesses the content's inherent qualities: whether it is searchable, its instantaneity, its special depth, its absences of geographic and temporal limits, and whether it facilitates interaction and a sense of community with authors or like-minded consumers.

The index yields a *total*, which then determines the prospects for the content:

10–20 = low near-term prospects.
20–30 = fair near-term prospects.
30–40 = good near-term prospects.
40–50 = very good near-term prospects.
50–60 = excellent near-term prospects.

60 Elgin, et al., 'Inside Yahoo!'

61 Paul Abrahams and Thorold Barker, 'Yahoo! slides amid staff and profit turmoil', *Financial Times*, 9 March 2001, p. 34.

Paid content viability analysis

	Content attributes				Net value	Market attributes		Financial attributes	
	Enrichment value	Content exclusivity	Content quality	Entertainment value		Audience discretionary budget	Potential market size	Synergistic potential	Financial feasability
Weighting	2	1.5	1	0.5	1–3	2	1	1	1
Score	a	b	c	d		e	f	g	h
Weight × score	2a	1.5b	1c	0.5d		2e	1f	1g	1h

2a+1.5b+1c+0.5d=A

2e+1f=B

1g+1h=C

A × **NV** + **B** + **C**

= **Total**

Source: Adapted from Terra Lycos, internal presentation, 'Paid Content Viability', © Jupiter Research 2000.

Once the content has been analyzed, Terra Lycos can integrate the content into its OBP (open, basic and premium) plan. Content with low promise will be integrated into the open or free plan, content with medium promise into the basic plan (flat-fee payment), and content with high promise into the premium plan (most profitable).

So, for example, in analyzing its personal publishing offering, Terra Lycos finds that it yields an overall potential total of 45.66, indicating that it has very good near-term prospects. However, the company's current offering reaches only 39.46, meaning that it still has the potential to increase the viability of its product and hence its value to a paying audience. The rating of 45.66 indicates that personal publishing is a high-end, lucrative product that should be included in Terra Lycos's premium plans.

DISCUSSION QUESTIONS

1. Which types of portal revenue streams could be considered 'traditional'? What other revenue streams could online portals exploit?
2. What new revenue streams could emerge from synergies with the offline world?
3. Discuss Terra Lycos's strategy for reaching its top dual objectives (positive revenues and becoming a first-tier online media player).
4. Should Terra Lycos pursue global expansion, given that the USA seems to be the most profitable market right now?
5. Discuss the competitive market conditions: will competition lead to convergence?
6. What are some possible scenarios for the future of online media players?

CASE STUDY 16

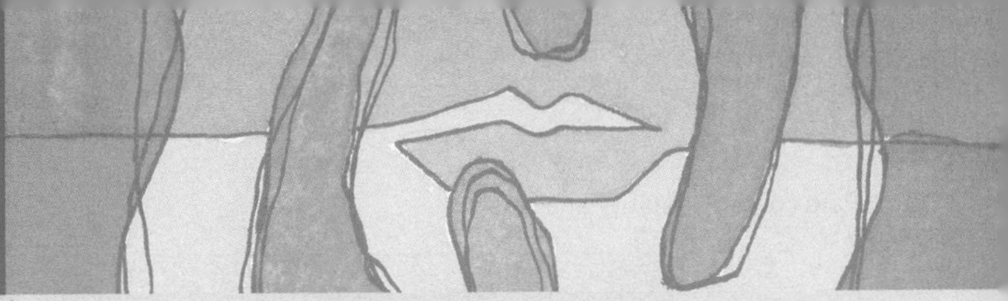

Google.com

The world's number-one Internet search engine

A profitable dot.com is a rare thing. For one founded only in late 1998, and – worse – a dot.com that includes advertising as one half of its business plan, Google's progress is a feat. But then it could be argued that Google has been flying in the face of conventional wisdom since its launch.

Neil McIntosh, 'Seeking search engine perfection', *The Guardian*, January 2002

Google had not had a single print or television advertisement so far and most people felt that when it was launched there was not a market for another search engine. But with all other search engines developing into portals, Google stuck to the basics and now it is better than every other search engine.

Matthew Ragas, consultant, 'The cult runs deep', *Economic Times*, March 2003

The most preferred seach engine

In early 2003, Google.com (Google), the California-based company Google Inc.'s search engine,[1] was named Best Search Engine by *Pandecta* magazine. Google also received the Outstanding Search Service award by *Search Engine Watch*.[2] The *Search Engine Watch* newsletter claimed that Google was the most heavily used search site by Internet browsers. These developments were not a major surprise for Google, which had received many such awards and recognitions since its inception in 1998 (see Table 1).

Google was preferred by millions of browsers over search engines such as AltaVista, Infoseek, Netscape and Lycos. Not only did Google rank much higher than other search engines in terms of efficiency and effectiveness, but it also scored over others in terms of layout due to its uncluttered look (see Table 2 for a comparison of popular search engines). Google searched more than three billion Web pages and processed more than 200 million search requests every day. The search engine could search for every possible file type on the World Wide Web, in 36 languages, and provided interface in 86 languages.

The fact that Google had become a household name (reportedly, even a generic term for search engines) without spending a penny on print/television advertisements or online banners was regarded as a commendable achievement. Its success was attributed largely to its constant focus on providing the best search services online, in terms of both speed and accuracy. Larry Page, CEO and co-founder of Google commented: 'It is through our maniac pursuit to offer only the best technology and search experience that Google has earned its reputation.'

Background note

The founders of Google, Larry Page and Sergey Brin, graduated in computer science from Stanford University in 1995. By January 1996, the duo began working on extending their summer project work on a search engine. They wanted to develop a technology

1 A search engine is an Internet-based utility that helps surfers search for specified keywords by displaying a list of documents (web pages) on the World Wide Web that contain those keywords. Different search engines use their own proprietary software to provide faster, more accurate and more meaningful search results to their users. Most popular search engines, such as Google and AltaVista, are free to use.

2 *Pandecta* is a monthly e-business magazine for Internet entrepreneurs. *Search Engine Watch* is a leading Internet technical guide for web developers and search engine users.

Table 1 Google: awards and recognition

Date	*Award*
December 1998	*PC Magazine*: Top 100 Websites: Search Engines
September 1999	*USA Today*: Hot Site *Shift Magazine*: 100 Best Websites *PC Magazine:* Top 100 Websites: Search Engines *POV Magazine*: Top 100 Websites *PC Magazine*: Technical Excellence Award for Web Applications
December 1999	*Time Magazine*: Top Ten Best Cybertech of 1999
January 2000	Wall Street Executive Library: Best of the Net About.com: Top Ten of 1999 Best of the Net *Smart Computing Magazine*: 50 Hot Technologies Yahoo Internet Life: Best Search Engine on the Internet
March 2000	*The Net*: Best Search Engine *Interactive Week*: 25 Unsung Heroes of the Net *San Francisco Chronicle*: Best of the Web 2000
April 2000	*PC Magazine*: Top 100 Websites: Search Engines
May 2000	Time Digital: Top 10 Sites *Upside Magazine*: Upside's Hot 100 Private Companies The Webby Awards: People's Voice Awards The Webby Awards: Best Technical Achievement
June 2000	*ID Magazine*: Silver Award, Interactive Media Design
July 2000	Yahoo Internet Life: 10 Internet Essentials
August 2000	*Internet World*: 25 Shapers of the Net *PC World Magazine*: Best of the Web 2000 CNET: Editor's Pick
September 2000	*Forbes*: Best of the Web *PC World*: Best Bet Search Engine Technologic Partners: Top 10 Investors Choice
October 2000	WIRED Readers Raves: Most Intelligent Agent
November 2000	*PC Magazine*: Editor's Choice and Best Internet Innovation
December 2000	Yahoo Internet Life: 100 Best Sites for 2001
January 2001	Search Engine Watch: Most Webmaster Friendly Search Engine and Outstanding Search Service
February 2001	Mobility Award 2001: Technical Achievement of the Year, Honourable Mention
March 2001	*PC Magazine*: Top 100 Websites Search and Reference *Pandecta*: Best All-round Search Site
May 2001	*Forbes*: Best of the Web The Net Awards 2001: Best Site and Best Search Engine Premi Cambrescat Internacional: Best Business Initiative on the Internet Basex Excellence Award: Knowledge Management The Industry Standard's Net 21: Monika Henzinger–The Sage of Search PC World's World Class Awards 2001: Best Search Engine
July 2001	2001 Webby Award: Best Practices
October 2001	Com! Online: German OnlineStar 2001 Award *PC Magazine*: Top 100 Websites
January 2002	Scripting News Awards for 2001: Best Weblog Utility/Distraction
February 2002	2001 Search Engine Watch Awards: Outstanding Search Service, Best Image Search Engine, Best Design, Most Webmaster Friendly Search Engine, Best Search Feature
April 2002	Russian Online Top: Best Foreign Website of the Year MIT Solan eBusiness Award: MIT Students Choice
June 2002	PC World's World Class Awards 2002: Internet Product of the Year and Best Search Engine 6th Annual Webby Awards: Best Practices, Best Practices – People's Voice, Technical Achievement – People's Voice
July 2002	12th Annual Software Development Jolt Awards: Product Excellence Award Enterprise Systems: Top 100 Power Picks.
August 2002	*Linux Journal* 2002 Editor's Choice Awards: Best Website
September 2002	IDGNow! Internet Awards: Best Search Engine *San Francisco Business Times* 2002 HotTech Awards: The Crowd Pleaser
November 2002	Premio www 2002: Best Search Engine, Econnet 100 2002
December 2002	Future UK Internet Awards 2002: Best Search Engine/Directory
January 2003	The Pandia Awards 2002: Best Search Site 2002 Search Engine Watch Awards: Outstanding Search Service 4th Annual Wired Rave Awards: Business People of the Year
February 2003	2003 ClickZ Marketing Excellence Awards: Best Paid Search Program *Pandecta Magazine* Awards: Best Search Engine BrandChannel: Brand of the Year

Source: www.google.com

Table 2 Comparison of various search engines

	Google	AltaVista	HotBot	Lycos	Overture	Yahoo!	Vivisimo
Truncation	No	Middle, end using *, up to 5 characters	Front, middle, end using *, but erratic	No	Automatic	Automatic or * for short words	Automatic
Case-sensitive	No	Only in phrase searches	Yes	No	Yes	No	No
Limits	Language, file format, date, occurrences, domains	Language, date	Date, language, media type, domains, page depth	Language	Domains	Directory sites, date	Domains
Sorting	Popularity, relevance, proximity	Relevance	Relevance	Relevance	Relevance, location, frequency, links, date	Run by Google, same sorting	Frequency, ranking used by search engine, group clustering
Translation	60 languages	6 languages	No	No	6 languages	No	No
Size (11 December 2001)	2 billion pages	550 million pages	500 million pages	625 million pages	500 million pages	1.7 million pages	Depends on other search engines
Type of engine	Search engine	Search engine	Search engine	Search engine	Search engine	Directory	Meta-search engine

Source: Adapted from www.ucalgary.ca/library/netsearch/compchart.html

that would retrieve a relevant set of data from a massive database of information. They named their search engine 'BackRub' because of its ability to identify and analyze 'back links' that pointed to a given website. Larry began creating a new kind of server[3] environment that used low-end personal computers (PCs) instead of big, costly machines. For this, they needed to buy several low-cost PCs. However, due to shortage of cash, they had to borrow PCs from the university.

By 1997, BackRub gained a lot of popularity due to its unique approach to solving search problems on the Internet. Throughout the first half of 1998, Larry and Sergey focused on perfecting their technology. To store huge amounts of data, they bought a terabyte of memory disks (one trillion bytes equal one terabyte) at bargain prices. Larry used his dormitory room as a data centre, while Sergey used his room to set up a business office. By now, they knew that their search technology was superior to any other technology available. They started looking actively for potential partners interested in licensing the same.

They contacted many people, including friends and family. One of the people whom they got in touch with was David Filo, the founder of Yahoo!, a leading portal.[4] Filo complimented them for the 'solid technology' they had built but did not enter into any agreements with them. Instead, he encouraged them to start their own company. The owners of many other portals also refused to invest in their technology. One such portal's CEO told them: 'As long as we are 80% as good as our competitors, that is good enough. Our users do not really care about search.'

During the late 1990s, the dot.com fever was at its peak in the USA, and almost everyone was opening a dot.com company. Though Larry and Sergey were not very keen on opening their own company, they decided to set one up, since they were unable to

3 Servers are computers or devices that manage the resources in a network. For instance, users on a file server can store files on the server, which is essentially a storage device dedicated to storing files. In a search engine, database servers are used to process database queries.

4 A portal is a website featuring commonly used services as a starting point and a common gateway to the Web (a web portal) or a niche topic (vertical portal/vortal). The services offered by most portals include a search engine, news, e-mail, stock quotes, chat, forums, maps, shopping and customization options. Large portals include many additional services.

attract any partners. However, they had first to clear off the debts they had accumulated to buy the memory disks and to move out of their dorm office. The duo put their PhD plans on hold and began looking for a prospective investor for their business.

Help came in the form of a faculty member who introduced them to Andy Bechtolsheim, one of the co-founders of Sun Microsystems. Andy saw their presentation and knew instantly that it had a lot of potential. As Andy was in a great hurry to attend a business meeting that day, he closed the deal by writing the duo a cheque for $100 000. However, the cheque was made out in the name of Google Inc.,[5] an entity that did not yet exist. Since Larry and Sergey could not deposit the cheque in their accounts, they decided to set up a corporation named Google Inc.

After collecting another $1 million from their families, friends and acquaintances, they opened their office on 7 September 1998. The office was located in the garage of a friend's house in Menlo Park, California. The name Google, although chosen by accident, indicated the company's mission to sort out and organize the immense data available on the Web. The website www.google.com became operational when Craig Silverstein joined the duo.

Google soon became popular among Internet browsers. Still in the beta stage (any software's trial-run phase), Google was answering 10 000 search queries every day. Its technology, which gave precise search results for queries, attracted the attention of the press, and articles on the website appeared in *USA Today* and *Le Monde* (leading US and French newspapers, respectively). By December 1998, Google was named by *PC Magazine* as one of the world's leading technology publications, and as one of the top 100 websites and search engines for that year.

Google shifted its office to University Avenue in Palo Alto in February 1999. The company increased its staff strength to eight and was by now answering 50 000 queries each day. Google's phenomenal growth within a short span of time attracted many corporate customers, and Red Hat[6] signed on as its first commercial customer. Google also secured a venture capital of $25 million from Sequoia Capital and Kleiner Perkins Caufield & Byers.[7]

Three new members, Mike Moritz (of Sequoia), John Doerr (of Kleiner Perkins) and Ram Shriram (CEO of Junglee), joined Google's board of directors in June 1999. Soon after, Omid Kordestani (of Netscape) and Urs Hölzle (of UC Santa Barbara) joined as the Vice-President of Business Development/Sales and Vice-President of Engineering, respectively. Google shifted its office to Mountain View, California, to accommodate the increasing number of employees. By mid-1999, Google was attracting a lot of attention from its clients, users and the press.

AOL/Netscape, a leading USA-based Internet services company, selected Google for providing its search service. Google helped AOL/Netscape to increase website traffic to over three million searches per day. In September 1999, Google was moved out of the beta stage and declared a fully fledged search engine. The reason behind the company's astounding growth was very simple – a focus on giving Internet browsers an easy, accurate, clutter-free and user-friendly search experience. All this was made possible by the founders' attention to technological excellence.

Google's technology: the success secret

From the very beginning, Larry and Sergey focused on building a search engine that would fetch precise search results. Larry said: 'We want to build a search engine that understands exactly what you mean and gives you back exactly what you want.' They wanted to overcome the limitations of the existing search engines, which used a group of large servers to perform search operations. The performance of such search engines slowed down during peak loads, which meant that the greater the number of queries, the higher the response time.[8]

5 The name Google was derived from the word 'googol', which denotes the number one followed by a hundred zeros. It was coined by Milton Sirotta, nephew of Edward Kasner, an American mathematician.

6 Red Hat is the world's largest and most recognized provider of open-source technology (Linux).

7 Sequoia and Kleiner Perkins are leading USA-based investor companies that have financed companies such as Cisco Systems, Apple Computer, Yahoo!, Linear Technology, Amazon.com, America Online, @Home, Excite, Healtheon, Intuit and Sportsline.

8 The IBM Directory of Computing describes response time as 'the elapsed time between the end of an enquiry or demand on a computer system and the beginning of a response'.

Larry and Sergey realized that they would have to develop a new kind of server set up to provide a fast and accurate search service. So, Google made use of large clusters (around 10 000) of Linux[9] PCs so that search queries could be answered quickly. The system consisted of three types of servers: a web server, an index server and a doc server. A typical query was answered in the following manner: Google sent the user query to a web server (which acted as a query processor), which in turn forwarded it to the index servers. The index servers searched for keywords and phrases that matched the search query. Thereafter, the doc server did the job of retrieving the actual documents that contained the search results. These results were then returned to the user (Exhibit 1 shows the lifecycle of a query).

This innovation helped Google to achieve greater scalability[10] at lower costs and faster response times, even during peak loads. At the front end, Google made use of a search technology that carried out a series of simultaneous calculations to process a query. This ensured that the entire search took only a fraction of a second to complete.

Google had a comprehensive database of web content running into over three billion web pages. In addition, Google stored a cached copy of every indexed web page so that users could access the web page even when the main server was down or the link was broken. Thus, Google accessed more information on the Internet and presented it in a more searchable format than any other search engine.

Google's database is composed of the following four categories of documents: indexed web documents (73.10% of total web-related data), un-indexed URLs[11] (25%), other types of files (1.75%) and indexed web pages/refreshed daily (15%) (see table 3).

Most search engines used the number of times a word appeared on a web page as the criteria for ranking a page. Therefore, a page in which a search word appeared ten times would be ranked higher than a page in which the same word appeared five times.

9 The Linux operating system was developed by Linus Torvalds at the University of Helsinki, Finland, to provide PC users with a free or very-low-cost operating system. Traditional systems like UNIX were very expensive. Linux is reputed for being a very efficient and fast operating system. Google's set-up was one of the biggest ever commercial Linux server clusters.

10 Scalability is defined as the ability of a computer (hardware or software application) to perform well even when it is changed in size or volume in order to meet a user's need.

11 URLs (Universal Resource Locators) refer to the addresses of resources and documents on the World Wide Web. Each file on a particular website thus would have a different, unique URL.

Exhibit 1 Lifecycle of a search query on Google

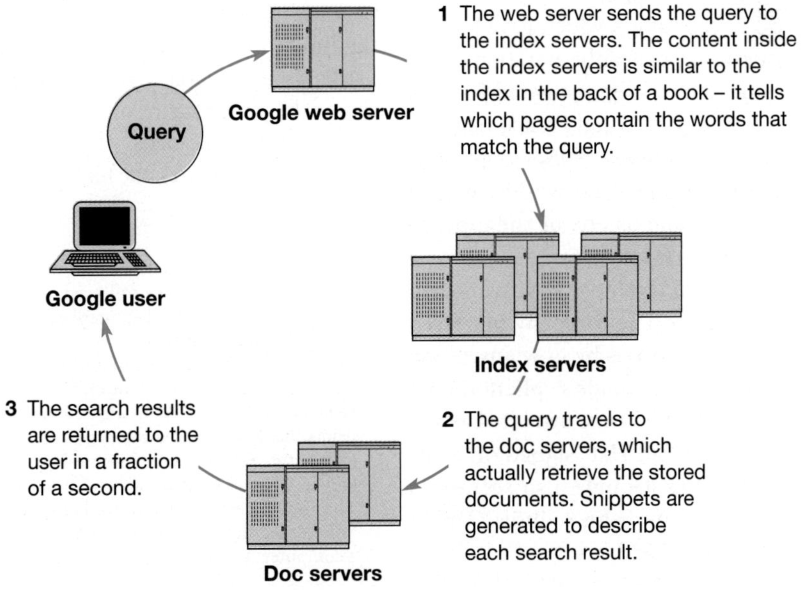
Google web server
1 The web server sends the query to the index servers. The content inside the index servers is similar to the index in the back of a book – it tells which pages contain the words that match the query.
Query
Google user
Index servers
3 The search results are returned to the user in a fraction of a second.
2 The query travels to the doc servers, which actually retrieve the stored documents. Snippets are generated to describe each search result.
Doc servers

Source: www.google.com

Table 3 The Google database

Indexed web documents	Simple Hypertext Markup Language (HTML) web pages that browsers come across
Unindexed URLs	Only the URLs are specified but the database does not contain any indexed copy of the page
Other types of files	Files other than HTML pages, such as Adobe Acrobat PDF Files, Microsoft Office documents (Word, Excel, PowerPoint), WordPerfect, Flash and others
Indexed web pages/ refreshed daily	The same as the indexed web pages but updated more frequently, such as news-based websites and pages

Source: www.topsitelistings.com

Thus, web-page editors could use a particular word many times to make their web pages appear higher up in searches, even if the contents of the web page were irrelevant.

To avoid this problem, Google used the PageRank technology to rank web pages. PageRank examined the entire link structure of the Web to determine which page should be ranked higher. This software did an objective measurement of the degree of importance of web pages by solving an equation of more than 500 million variables and two billion terms. For example, unlike other search engines, which counted direct links, Google interpreted a link from page A to page B as a vote from page A to page B. This way, it determined the importance of a page by the number of votes it received.

PageRank software also analyzed the quality of every page that cast a vote. That is, if a page that was already ranked 'important' voted for another page, then the linked page was considered to have greater value. Thus, 'important' pages received higher ranks and appeared at the top of search results. This way, Google's software made use of the 'collective intelligence' of the Web to assess the importance of a web page. Google's technology was fully automated and did not use human editors to judge a page's importance, thus avoiding manipulation of search results.

Apart from PageRank technology, Google also used Hypertext Matching Analysis to analyze the content of a Web page. Factors like font size and type, subdivisions of text and also the precise location of each word were taken into account. Google also analyzed the content of other web pages on the same site. This way, it ensured that the results were relevant to the user's query.

In September 1999, Google introduced a new feature, GoogleScout, on its website. This feature was introduced to make surfing and navigating the Web much easier and faster. A GoogleScout link was provided with every website result in the search results page. By clicking on the GoogleScout link, a user could get a list of additional site links related to the required search. This feature enabled Google to provide highly accurate information to the user and reduced the amount of time a user needed to spend on the Internet for searching.

Google's business model

Most search-engine companies spent a lot of money on marketing to build their brands. Google, however, focused solely on building a better search engine. Its superior search technology was the primary reason for its popularity among Internet surfers and corporate clients. Sergey said:

> We developed our approach to search technology to address the very real challenge of finding information on the Internet. Everything we do – from the development of our advanced technology to the design of our user interface – is focused on delivering the best search experience on the Web. We are delighted with the response we have received from Google users around the world who have enthusiastically embraced our approach to search.

Word-of-mouth recommendation became the main force driving traffic to the Google website. Within three years of its launch, the website was answering more than 200 million searches a day. With traffic increasing constantly, it became clear to Google that it could develop its business around two revenue streams, online advertising programmes and search services. Half of Google's revenues came from the two main search services it provided to its clients: Google WebSearch and Google SiteSearch.

Google search services

Launched in mid-1999, the WebSearch service enabled clients (destination sites and portals) to offer Google's search services to their members. The client could use the results page for selling its own advertisements on the Web. The WebSearch service provided many useful

features, such as cached links, directory definitions, file types, 'I'm feeling lucky' (a button that allows users to bypass all results and go to the first page that was returned for a query), and a spell-checker.

The Google SiteSearch service provided clients with a fully customizable search on the (client) company extranets and public websites. SiteSearch improved site navigation and usability and also increased site stickiness.[12] Visitors to a website using the SiteSearch service could easily locate a specific product or service and find company information. This not only enhanced customer communications but also reduced the number of customer service calls to the company. This in turn helped clients improve sales opportunities by providing product and service information quickly to the customer. Using SiteSearch thus increased the chances of customer loyalty for the (client) company and also reduced the need for customer support.

In 1999, many companies signed up as Google's clients. The list included Virgilio (an Italian portal), Virgin.net (Britain's leading online entertainment guide), *The Washington Post*, Cisco Systems, Sony, Procter & Gamble, MarthaStewart.com, Hungary Minds.com, eBoodle.com, Real Names Corporation, *The New York Times*, AskJeeves, AT&T, Bizrate, Dealtime and Earthlink. The year 1999 also brought with it a lot of awards for Google. Google was ranked first among 13 search and portal sites[13] in a survey conducted by NPD Online Research[14] for user satisfaction and loyalty. The company received the Technical Excellence Award for Innovation in Web Application Development by *PC Magazine*. A high point was the company's inclusion in *Time* magazine's Top Ten Best Cybertech list for 1999.

The list of clients signing up for Google's services kept increasing in 2000. Apple Computers, a popular computer manufacturer, signed up Google to create its company-specific search engine. Go2Net's Meta Crawler and Dogpile Metasearch (two of the Internet's popular meta-search services) also became Google's clients. In January 2000, Google offered the Free WebSearch service facility to its customers. This customizable service allowed small or entry-level websites to take advantage of Google's advanced search technologies free of cost. Within a month and a half, the company had registered 13 000 subscribers.

In February 2000, Google launched a new set of browser tools called the Google Browser Buttons. These add-ons could be downloaded for free from Google's website. The set included the Google Search button, the Google Scout button and the Google.com button. The Google Search button helped users to search the Web simply by highlighting a word or phrase on a web page. Clicking on a Google Scout button helped users to get web pages similar to the current page. Clicking on the Google.com button took users to Google's homepage.

In April 2000, Google announced a host of search services that were fully automated and customizable (at low cost): Silver WebSearch, Gold WebSearch and the Silver/Gold WebSearch (see Appendix 1). In the same month, Google also brought out the industry's first comprehensive wireless search engine service. This facility enabled users of WAP (Wireless Application Protocol) mobile phones[15] and other Internet-enabled hand-held devices connected to a wireless modem to search the Web.

Google's advertisement programmes

Google earned half of its revenues from the advertising programmes it offered to its customers. The company did not permit advertisements on its website, but it allowed advertisements based on keyword targeting on its search results pages. Advertisements based on keyword targeting ensured that the ordinary run-of-site advertisements did not appear indiscriminately on every page. Google ensured that only those advertisements that were relevant to the search appeared on each search results page. Hence, not all search results pages carried advertisements.

Unlike most search engines, Google did not accept any pop-up advertisements or advertisements that used rich media, such as graphic images, flashing logos and animations. All Google advertisements were plain-text-based advertisements, and they were

12 The stickiness of a website refers to its ability to make visitors stay longer and/or return again and again.

13 Other companies included AltaVista, AOL, AskJeeves, Excite, Go Network, GoTo.com, HotBot, LookSmart, Lycos, Netscape, WebCrawler and Yahoo!.

14 The NPD group is an international marketing information company headquartered in Port Washington, New York. The company was the ninth largest market research firm in the USA, based on 1998 revenues.

15 WAP is a telecommunications protocol that allows users to access information through hand-held wireless devices such as mobile phones.

all clearly identified as 'Sponsored Links'. Thus, Google attracted better click-through rates[16] (two to three times higher than the industry standard) by keyword-targeted advertising than by flashing banner advertisements appearing randomly. Normally, a 2% click-through rate was considered good by advertisers. However, as users become familiar with banner advertisements, the click-through rate reduced to well below 1%. Thus, by making use of keyword-targeting-based advertising, Google could make many browsers get interested in the advertisements/sponsored links as well.

In early 2000, Google offered its clients an advertisement programme called Premium Sponsorships. Under this, the company offered clients an opportunity to reach a highly targeted audience with minimum effort. The advertiser/client provided Google with a set of keywords (as many keywords as required), which Google used to create a text-based advertisement. Each keyword was then matched to different creative executions. Advertisers could also purchase predetermined keywords or keyword phrases from Google, which were used by Google to match a user's query to a closely related advertisement.

These advertisements appeared as links on top of the search results page (see Exhibit 2). Once these advertisements were put in place, the company constantly monitored them to improve their performance (i.e. by selecting more appropriate keywords and rewriting the text of the advertisement). Google charged approximately $10 000 or more per quarter for the Premium Sponsorship advertisement programme.

Impressed by the efficiency of the services provided by Google, Yahoo! entered into a partnership with Google in June 2000. This added to Google's reputation of being a leading technology provider (by now, it was answering 18 million user queries every day). Google entered into partnership deals with companies from other countries as well, including leading portals in China and Japan–NetEase and NEC's BIGLOBE, respectively.

In mid-2000, Google brought out a cheaper alternative to Premium Sponsorship in the form of the AdWords programme. Under this programme, Google allowed customers to create their own advertisement

16 Click-through rate can be defined as the percentage of times viewers of a web page click on an advertisement causing a request for the advertiser's website to be opened to the viewer. For instance, if two of every 100 visitors to a web page clicked on an advertisement, then that advertisement would have a 2% click-through rate. Many advertisers rate the success of an advertisement on the basis of its click-through rate alone. However, some also take into account the actual viewing of the advertisement by the visitor.

Exhibit 2 Google's Premium Sponsorship programme

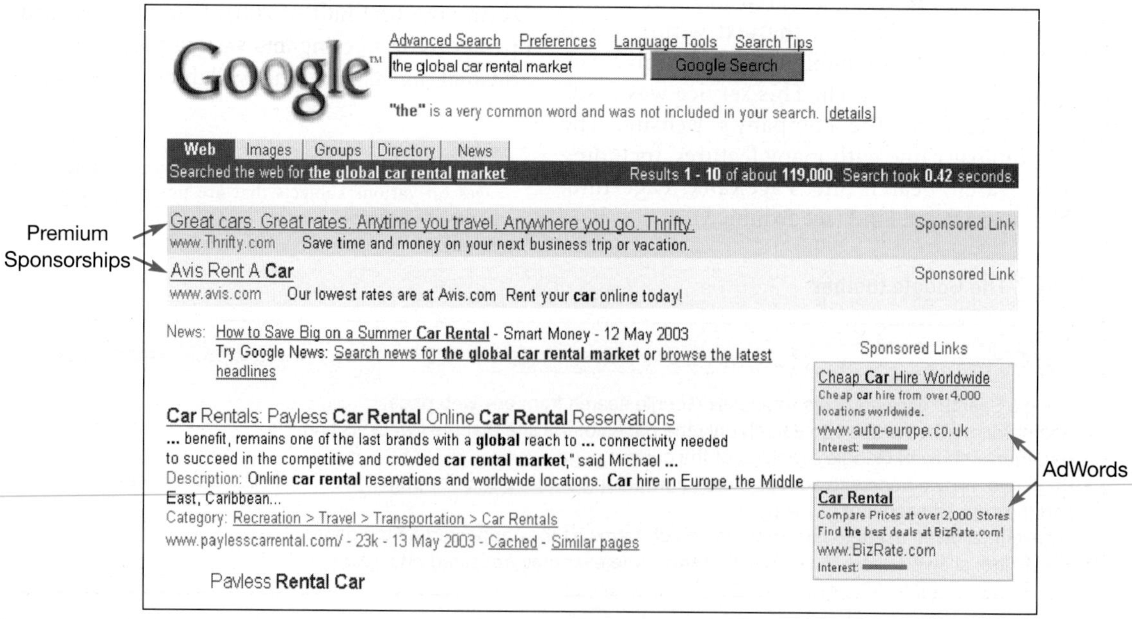

Source: www.google.com

text or purchase carefully selected keywords to target potential customers. The results for AdWords were highly targeted and advertisements appeared only if a user entered the same keywords or phrases that an advertiser had purchased. For example, if a user entered a query 'dental insurance' into the Google search box, then it would produce search results and text-based advertisements relating to the purchase of dental insurance online. The advertisements brought out under the AdWords programme appeared adjacent to the search results (see Exhibit 2).

Google makes searching easier

In mid-2000, Google took its first step in the direction of aggressive global expansion by announcing that its search engine would be available to users in ten languages other than English. Now, users could conduct searches in Swedish, Finnish, French, German, Portuguese, Dutch, Norwegian, Italian, Spanish and Danish. In September 2000, Google increased the number of foreign languages to 14, by adding Japanese, traditional and simplified Chinese, and Korean. The company also planned to support 15 more languages, including Hebrew, Greek and Russian by the end of 2000.

To make it easier to find information, Google launched the Google toolbar in December 2000. This innovative browser plug-in enabled a user not only to search from the Google search box but also to search by right-clicking on the text within a web page. A user could also highlight keywords in a web page and conduct a search. This service was made freely available on the company's website. The Google toolbar came with many features, including Google Search, Search Site, PageRank, Page Info, Highlight and Word Find (see Exhibit 3).

Google experienced significant business growth and expansion of services in 2000 and 2001. In January 2001, to build its credibility in the market, Google offered the Google SiteSearch service free of cost to universities and educational institutions worldwide. As a result, many educational institutions, including the University of Chicago, Duke University, Mills College, Rice University, Rochester Institute of Technology, Stanford University, and the Universities of California at Berkeley and Irvine signed up Google as their default search engine.

The company acquired Deja.com's Usenet Discussion[17] service in February 2001. Google integrated the vast information in the Usenet archives into a searchable format and made it available to web surfers under Google Groups.

In early 2001, Google won the Search Engine Watch awards in two categories of Outstanding Search Service and Most Webmaster Friendly Search Engine, leaving behind competitors such as AltaVista, AskJeeves, Fast, GoTo, iWon and Lycos. Commenting on the success of Google, Danny Sullivan, editor of Search Engine Watch, said:

> Google undoubtedly deserves to win as outstanding search service. I consistently receive positive feedback from my readers and members of the public who are impressed with the relevancy and accuracy of Google's results. There is no doubt that Google has raised the bar on the quality users should expect from a web search service.

During the first half of 2001, Google expanded its operations by entering into various partnership deals and making its services available to a worldwide

17 Usenet refers to a collection of user-submitted notes or messages on various subjects that are posted to servers on a worldwide network.

Exhibit 3 The Google toolbar

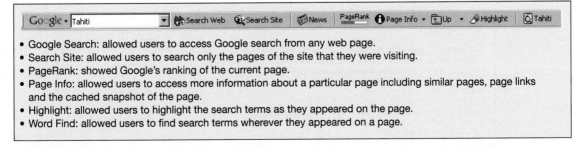

- Google Search: allowed users to access Google search from any web page.
- Search Site: allowed users to search only the pages of the site that they were visiting.
- PageRank: showed Google's ranking of the current page.
- Page Info: allowed users to access more information about a particular page including similar pages, page links and the cached snapshot of the page.
- Highlight: allowed users to highlight the search terms as they appeared on the page.
- Word Find: allowed users to find search terms wherever they appeared on a page.

Source: www.google.com

audience of mobile phone users. Its clients included users of i-mode mobile phones (Japan), users of wireless Internet in Asia, users of AT&T wireless (a leading IT services provider in the USA), Sprint PCS (USA-based global communications company) and Cingular (second largest wireless carrier in the USA). In July 2001, Google won the title Model of Overall Excellence and the Webby Award for Best Practices at the prestigious fifth Annual Webby Awards function held in San Francisco, USA.

In late 2001, the company acquired the technology assets of Outride Inc., a California-based developer of information retrieval technologies. Google also entered into a deal with Universo Online (UOL), Brazil and Latin America's leading portal, to provide Google search services for Latin America. In December 2001, Google launched the Google Zeitigeist, a real-time window that provided information about the top search queries on Google for 2001. Google also launched the Google Image Search and Google Catalog Search which enabled users to search for more than 250 million images on the Web and over 1100 mail-order catalogues that were previously available only in print. By the end of 2001, Google offered more than three billion searchable documents on the Internet.

Sufing into the future

Google's good fortunes continued in 2002. It was recognized as a Top Business Media Property by *BtoB*, America's leading marketing publication. Google's inclusion in the top ten rankings of the Media Power 50[18] made it the most preferred consumer brand online.

In February 2002, Google announced a major change of the AdWords programme. The company announced that it would start charging advertisers according to cost-per-click (CPC) rates. That is, advertisers would pay Google depending on the number of times their advertisements were clicked on. This way, advertisers could control their advertising costs. Google charged only $5 for activating a client's account (this could be done online within a few minutes). This programme was cost-effective for small as well as large businesses.

To increase the aesthetic appeal of the website, the Google homepage featured Dilbert, a highly popular cartoon creation by Scott Adams in May 2002. This move was in line with the company's corporate culture of changing its homepage logo frequently. The company had altered its logo time and again to commemorate holidays, events and even international celebrations, including the Burning Man festival, the Olympics, Bastille Day and Christmas.

In mid-2002, the company launched Google Labs to allow Google's in-house engineers to present their ideas to a larger audience. This way, web surfers could get acquainted with several work-in-progress projects at Google and provide feedback. Another service, Google News, was launched in September 2002. Offered as a free service, the Google news link provided access to more than 4500 leading news sources on the Internet. News content was updated automatically with the help of a computer program.

In December 2002, Google launched the Froogle search service, which provided access to information about products for sale on the Web. This service provided users with a searchable index of products online and a directory of products by category. It also allowed users to narrow searches by price range. Apart from the above services, Google also offered the Google Directory service, which made use of Open Directory Pages[19] to search information on the Web. The Google Directory contained more than 1.5 million URLs.

Another service, Google Preferences, helped users to customize their search preferences. Users could select the number of results per page, filter web content using SafeSearch filtering, select the language in which the search results were to be viewed, and request translation of web pages. Google also offered its users a free service called Buddy link to Google. Users had to incorporate in their website a small code that the company offered to get the Google search button on their (the user's) website. Other services offered included Google Web APIs (application programming interfaces), a service that could be

18 The Media Power 50 is compiled by a panel consisting of B2B editors and media buyers who select the most valued and effective B2B venues among many media outlets, including print, broadcast, online and outdoor media. Google was ranked first among others including *The Economist*, *The Wall Street Journal*, *Fortune*, CNET and CNN.

19 Open Directory Pages are a part of the Open Directory Project (ODP), which is a large database of web pages maintained by Netscape. A group of editors from around the world evaluate websites for inclusion in the directory. These web pages are arranged according to various categories and sub-categories.

used by software developers to incorporate Google's code in their applications, and Google Answers (a paid service), in which experienced researchers answered user queries.

Recognizing the value of the services provided by Google, the UK-based net ratings firm Nielsen, named Google the top website of the year 2002.[20] Reportedly, Google Inc. was one of the few dot.coms in the world that was posting profits. Though the company did not release financial information, according to a *BusinessWeek* article revenues for 2002 were in the range of \$50 million to \$100 million, with a profit margin of 30%.

Problems at the search engine giant

In spite of its growth, popularity and profitability, Google faced several problems in late 2002. As competition from other search engines intensified, some of Google's corporate clients and website users objected strongly to its policies. The first sign of trouble can be traced to changes in Google's relationship with its long-time partner Yahoo!.

In 2001, Yahoo! had signed a \$7.1-million contract with Google. Under the contract, Google agreed to provide Yahoo! with exclusive web search results. However, Yahoo! dropped the 'exclusive' part of the contract in October 2002, at the time of the deal's renewal. Yahoo! agreed to pay Google a fixed rate depending on the number of search queries served by the latter. This implied that Yahoo! could make use of other search services providers if it wanted to. In another announcement in December 2002, Yahoo! declared that it would buy the web-search business of specialized search engine service provider Inktomi. Analysts felt that this was a clear indication of Yahoo!'s gradual withdrawal from Google.

Sources at Yahoo! stated that Yahoo! had 'grown tired' of Google's popularity and was moving away from it.[21] Commenting on the situation, Jason Kellerman, CEO of LookSmart (search-technology company), said: 'The portals have started to get fed up. Over the last three years, Google has stolen 40% of the search market directly at the expense of AOL, MSN and Yahoo.'

Google also faced stiff competition from other search engines like Verity and Overture. Verity had grown to become a leader in the corporate search market, while Overture had strengthened its position in the paid search listings business. Overture had signed a series of contracts with various businesses, the most significant being contracts with CNN and CNN's various online properties. These developments were a cause for concern for Google, as it earned approximately one-third of its revenues in 2002 by being a third-party search results supplier.

However, Google remained confident of its position for a variety of reasons. Google had a strong tie-up with AOL and provided most of the portal's web-search capabilities. According to Nielsen NetRatings, a web traffic tracker, AOL and Google together got six times the search traffic of Yahoo! in late 2002. Also, Google had a strong user response from its clients, including AOL, Yahoo! and many media customers who used Google's services, most importantly its news sections, to draw visitors.

Analysts were, however, rather sceptical about optimistic projections regarding Google's future. Analyst Danny Sullivan of Search Engine Watch said:

> The bulk of Google's business these days is built around Google.com. If partners continue to grumble, the pendulum could swing – and Google may end up facing a mutiny and a world full of hostile competitors, each seeking a piece of the king of search.

Google faced another setback in February 2003 when Google Watch website[22] nominated it for the Privacy International's 2003 Big Brother Awards.[23] Google was accused of, among other things, recording all the personal information it could through its cookies,[24] retaining all data indefinitely, and not mentioning

---

20 As mentioned in a BBC news article dated 31 December 2002.

21 Yahoo! had played a vital role in Google's popularity. It encouraged Google to create its own search engine and became one of the first clients to license Google's search services for its portal. However, gradually Google began introducing other search services, such as news and shopping pages, which competed directly with Yahoo!'s services. In order to lessen its dependence on Google, Yahoo! bought Inktomi, a specialized search engine service provider, for \$279.5 million in March 2003.

22 Google Watch was formed by Daniel Brandt in mid-2002 and is backed by a non-profit organization named Public Information Research.

23 Privacy International's Big Brother Awards are given to those websites that are found guilty of privacy violations on the Internet.

24 Cookies are small text files placed on a computer's hard disk by a website through the web browser. They are used to store information that enables websites to identify users between visits.

why it needed such data. Google toolbar was also suspected of being spyware.[25]

However, Google did not make it to the final list because Privacy International did not find the company to be a major threat to Internet privacy. An analyst at Search Engine Watch commented:

> Nevertheless, the nomination has caused some to wonder about the privacy of their search requests at Google. In addition, some allegations made in the nomination have been transformed by others as proof of privacy violations, without being closely examined.

In spite of these unpleasant developments, Google continued to be popular among users. The receipt of a *Pandecta Magazine* award and the Business People of the Year award by *Wired Magazine* in early 2003 indicated that Google had strong growth prospects. Problems and threats notwithstanding, Google continued to be regarded the world over as the 'perfect search engine'.

In early 2003, analysts remarked that Google could even go public in the near future, like many other successful Silicon Valley ventures. Whether the company decided in favour of taking on the pressures of stock-market performance, analysts expected Google to continue innovating and developing breakthrough technologies. In line with these expectations, a Google source stated: 'Whatever is to come in the way of search technology, you can be assured that Google is working to make it faster, more accurate and even easier to use.'

Appendix Google WebSearch services[26]

- *Free WebSearch*: designed for personal homepages or low-traffic websites; provided free of charge.
- *Silver WebSearch*: designed for small or growing websites (more than one million queries per year). Google charged $599 as a monthly fee for providing additional customization, the ability to place ads in the search results pages, and monthly reports.
- *Gold WebSearch*: designed for big websites with heavy traffic (more than four million queries per year). Google charged $1999 as a monthly fee for this service.

Standard Google WebSearch features include:

- *Quick set-up*: Google's WebSearch could be set up within an hour.
- *Co-branding*: Google's logo featured on the customer's website and search results pages.
- *Customization*: search results retained the look and feel of the customer's site.
- *Service*: Google provided a user-friendly process that enabled clients to sign up and implement WebSearch services.
- *Additional features*: included with all WebSearch services are Google's specialized search and navigation features, such as Google Scout.
- *Preview customizations*: clients could view how Google search results complemented any website before registering for the service.
- *Ads in the results page*: customers could place their own advertisements in the search results page.
- *Enhanced customization*: further customization included support for navigation bars and menus, which ensured that Google's search results page had the look and feel of the customer's site.
- *Monthly reporting*: reports included the number of search queries performed per day.

25 Spyware refers to software that gets installed in a user's PC and sends information about the user, all without their knowledge. The information gathered is typically about the user's activities on the Internet and is transmitted to the makers of the spyware. This information is used for marketing purposes, either by the spyware developers themselves or by third parties who purchase the information.

26 www.google.com

DISCUSSION QUESTIONS

1 In what ways were the services offered by Google different from those offered by other search engines? Discuss with specific reference to technology, corporate client servicing and customer-friendliness.

2 Most dot.com companies relied heavily on online advertisements as the primary source of revenue, and many also spent a lot of money on advertising their brands. However, Google did not do so – and was still rated as the world's most preferred search engine. Critically discuss Google's business model in the light of the above. Was Google's decision not to use conventional advertising a wise one?

3 'Over the last three years, Google has stolen 40% of the search market directly at the expense of AOL, MSN and Yahoo!' Do you think Google's leadership position is going to become a threat to the company's future growth and survival? What measures should the company take in order to sustain its position as the leading Internet search services provider in the future?

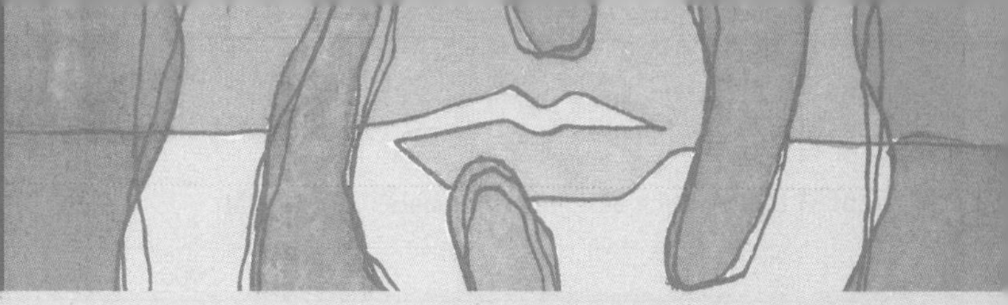

CASE STUDY 17

DoubleClick Inc.

A strategic transformation

Ideally, we would like to become the Bloomberg terminal for online marketers and advertisers.

Kevin Ryan, CEO, DoubleClick Inc.

It is a story that has become a mantra for DoubleClick's CEO, Kevin Ryan. Not only does it exemplify the success of his company, but it also illustrates the rise of the online advertising market:

> When Kevin O'Connor and I went out to raise money in 1996, we told venture capitalists: 'In 1995 the Internet advertising market generated $50 million in revenues. We think you should invest in our company because in the year 2001 it will be $3 billion.' Yet we were thrown out of so many offices ... The incredible thing is that if you could have looked into the future at that point, you would have seen that not only was the market going to surpass $3 billion and hit $5 billion, but there would be people [distressed by the dot.com bust and its adverse effect on online advertising] who are sitting around moaning, 'It's so terrible, it's really horrible. You must be so depressed ... It's really not working, is it?' People have such short-term memories; they can only think in comparison to last year.[1]

Exhibit 1 **Business breakdown**

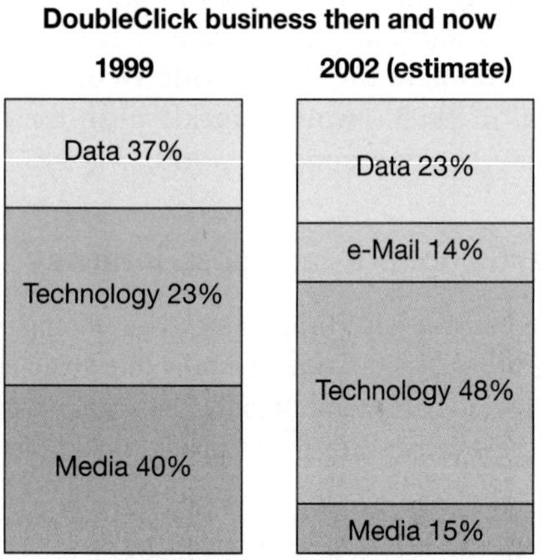

Source: DoubleClick corporate presentation 3Q02, p. 24.

As one of the companies present from almost the beginning of the commercial Internet, DoubleClick can legitimately stake a claim to being called one of the 'founding fathers' of Internet advertising. DoubleClick can also lay claim to the title of infomediary, a type of business that flourishes in the world of bytes and bandwidth.[2] (Appendix 1 and Table 1 provide selected statistics and financial data for DoubleClick.)

In outlining the rise and transformation of DoubleClick (see Exhibit 1 and Appendix 2), this

1 Kevin Ryan, interview, New York, 29 January 2002.

2 For the purposes of this case, we define an infomediary as a company using state-of-the-art technology to collect and/or manage aggregate information across a network of companies and/or websites. Such companies derive their revenues from the sale of their proprietary analysis of collected information.

This case was written by Patricia Reese, Research Associate, under the supervision of Soumitra Dutta, The Roland Berger Chaired Professor of e-Business and Information Technology, and Theodoros Evgeniou, Assistant Professor of Information Systems, all at INSEAD. It is intended to be used as a basis for class discussion rather than to illustrate either effective or ineffective handling of an administrative situation.

Table 1 **DoubleClick selected financials (US$ 1000s)**

	2001	*2000*	*1999*	*1998*	*1997*	*1996*
Revenue						
Technology	206999	203391	74695	24965	9823	1939
(external customers)	(195911)	(179543)	(66834)	(6008)	(673)	(NA)
Media	129336	253827	125499	74180	29924	6514
Data	81329	72355	65961	46979	30971	17532
Total revenue	417664	529573	266155	138724	67926	25985
Cost of revenue	177397	246570	107156	69191	29741	3780
Gross profit	228250	259041	151138	69533	38185	2734
Operating expenses						
Sales and marketing	182782	227229	103578	52525	24855	3079
General and administrative	65695	83227	35004	19424	11948	2145
Product development	53447	44789	28364	12194	5108	618
Total	511669	448158	209853	84503	42013	5842
Net income (loss)	(265828)	(155981)	(55821)	(18039)	(7741)	(3954)
Basic and diluted net loss per share	(2.02)	(1.29)	(0.51)	(0.21)	(0.16)	(0.07)

Source: DoubleClick 10K SEC filings 1998, 1999 and 2001; company information.

case recounts the company's first breakthrough with its product DART[3] and the DoubleClick Advertising Network, its subsequent delve into application service providers (ASPs), and its acquisition of the offline infomediary Abacus. The case seeks to generate discussion around the following questions: what strategies has DoubleClick used in its development and growth as an infomediary? Why and how did DoubleClick shift from being a pure media player to becoming a technology company? Where should it look for new growth opportunities?

DoubleClick: the beginning

DoubleClick was the brainchild of Kevin O'Connor and Dwight Merriman, respectively the company's current Chair and Chief Technology Officer. The two, convinced of the Internet's potential, spent six months in O'Connor's basement formulating as many as 100 ideas on how to capitalize on the Internet.

They came to the conclusion that advertising would be a crucial element to making money on the Internet. The Internet Advertising Network (IAN)[4] was born, powered by a cutting-edge ad-serving product, DART (Exhibit 2).

At the time IAN was conceived, very few websites were household names, much less making money, and the Internet was still the domain of 'tech heads'. But the web was on the cusp of mainstream acceptability: search engines like AltaVista were multiplying, the Netscape browser was on millions of desktops,[5] and a little web directory called David and Jerry's Guide to the World Wide Web' – rebaptized Yahoo! in 1995 – would quickly push the Internet into households around the world.

Advertising: pre- and post-Internet

Before Internet advertising came of age, companies that wanted to advertise would typically hire an ad agency to run their ad campaign. Broadly, the agency would produce the creatives[6] for the campaign, make suggestions

3 Dynamic Advertising Reporting and Targeting.

4 The company was renamed DoubleClick in 1996, following the merger of IAN with 'DoubleClick', the Internet sales group of ad agency Poppe Tyson (now Modem Media).

5 In the summer of 1995, Netscape's market share was estimated to be 80%. By 2002, it had fallen to less than 5%: www.hmetzger.de/netscape/netscape_history.html, 24 August 2002; and Matthew Broersma, 'Tech doesn't buoy Netscape browser', CNET News.com, 28 August 2002, http://news.com.com/2100-1023-955734.html, 3 September 2002.

6 An advertising term that describes the mock-ups or creative work produced by the ad agency. They enable the client to preview and select the advertising campaign.

Exhibit 2 How DART delivers online ads

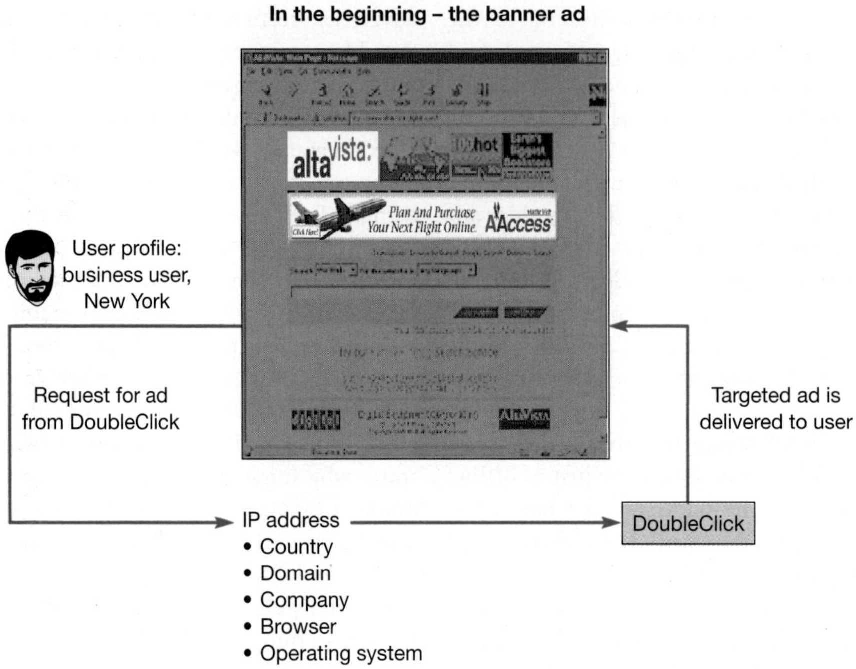

Source: DoubleClick corporate presentation 4Q01.

on what types of media to use (TV, radio, print, billboards, direct marketing, etc.), and where to buy (local markets, national, international). The client (advertiser) would preview and approve the campaign, and then the advertising agency would produce it.

Translating this process into dollars meant that an advertising campaign that cost $1 million in media buys could, for example, generate $200 000 in creative fees for the agencies. On top of that, the ad agency would charge a percentage of the media buy, traditionally around 10%, bringing the total cost for the advertiser to $1.3 million, of which the agency would receive $300 000. Internet advertising, however, threatened this cash cow, as Christopher Saridakis, Senior Vice-President for Global Sales and Client Services,[7] explained:

> You can get a lot for $1 million online. Creating that banner, music space or streaming media doesn't cost $200 000 ... In fact, you don't even need a story board any more. It's only going to take some programmers a day or two to put together a bunch of banners for $1000.[8]

More importantly, Internet advertising could offer more than just cost savings; it could also offer accountability. Before software like DoubleClick's DART, online advertising was a leap into the dark: advertisers had no way of knowing which advertisement was seen by whom, how often, and, most importantly, whether the viewers were even in their target audience. Advertisers would buy space on websites, drawing assumptions based on traffic, unique visitors, number of hits, etc. Then along came DART and its innovative use of cookies[9] to deliver audiences to advertisers. Before DART, banner ads were blind, put up and charged at will – exactly like offline advertising.

7 Saridakis was Senior Vice-President for Global Techsolutions at the time of his interview.

8 Christopher Saridakis, interview, 30 January 2002, New York.

9 DoubleClick's cookies are small amounts of data that are stored on a user's computer on a temporary or more permanent basis. DART generates a cookie unique to each IP address – and even to a particular campaign – that tracks the surfers in the DoubleClick Network of sites. When a surfer visits a site in the DoubleClick Network, the cookie is used to exchange information between the visitor and the DoubleClick server, including data on surfing habits, preferences and how often a particular ad has been viewed by this visitor across the network – all in about 15 milliseconds.

In using DART, online advertisers could pinpoint – with a precision greater than that of traditional media – which visitors to their sites or to the DoubleClick Network were viewing which ads and their responses to those ads. It was the online equivalent of what the Nielsen Ratings did for network television in the USA, starting in the 1950s.

Saridakis recalled advertisers rushed to adopt DART because it permitted them to manage their ads by audience segment, geographic distribution – practically just about anything an advertiser wanted. 'The better you could target, the more you could charge – classic supply and demand', he said. 'People knew that our technology was the only one that could do it.'[10]

For websites, DART meant that they could at last charge for their advertising inventory just as offline companies had done, by CPM or cost per thousand.[11] Even better, DoubleClick's technology would also eventually permit network members or technology customers to price ad space by the number of actions generated (cost per click, cost per lead, cost per sale and cost per download) rather than using the less precise cost-by-impression metric. Its unique technology, which could 'target an audience and deliver volume to advertisers', gave the DoubleClick Network a clear advantage over its competitors.[12] DART permitted network members – especially smaller websites that did not have the pull of a large website – and technology customers to move their unsold advertising inventory quickly.

For the ad agencies, on the other hand, DART was a rose with some substantial thorns. While the technology undoubtedly helped the agency to serve its online ads, it also placed a larger burden on the agencies' shoulders: DART can determine almost immediately whether a campaign is working because the results are measurable in real time. An online campaign can be changed in a matter of minutes if DART metrics show that the ad is missing its target audience. Is the bright orange background too powerful? Change it to a soothing blue. Think the message is too direct? Tone it down. Want to add in free shipping for orders over $75? Done. Compare that to a billboard, magazine ad or television spot, which are virtually unchangeable once they are running, and it becomes crystal clear what one of online advertising's biggest benefits for advertisers is. This advantage explains why many advertisers seem to love it. It also means ad agencies shoulder more responsibility for results when running online campaigns.

But even with these advantages, traditional blue-chip companies were – and some still are – sceptical about the effectiveness and impact of online advertising.[13] They were also appalled by the astronomical rates some sites were charging and needed little incentive to steer clear of the medium. Since the decline of Internet hype, though, traditional companies are appearing online, attracted by the large inventories and the subsequent rate drop (Exhibit 3).

The case of Doritos, a brand of tortilla chips owned by Frito-Lay (a division of PepsiCo), illustrates why some traditional advertisers are moving online. In January 2001, Doritos bought air time for one 30-second Super Bowl[14] television spot for around $70,000 per second. In 2002, the company completely pulled out of the Super Bowl, and tripled its online budget. Why? It realized that its target audience was 12–24-year-olds who preferred surfing online to watching the Super Bowl.

Not only was it not reaching them through the Super Bowl, noted Susan Sachatello, DoubleClick's Chief Marketing Officer, but with the cost of one 30-second Super Bowl spot running to $2.1 million, Doritos could spend the same amount and reach them all year long online. She continued:

> This has been a phenomenal move for the community because Frito-Lay will never sell a single Doritos chip online, but they have found that the brand impact and the ability to reach their consumer are much more effective online than off.[15]

---

10 Saridakis, interview.

11 CPM is a variable rate charged every time 1000 users view an ad. Rates in 2002 ran anywhere from a tenth of a penny to nearly $100. M comes from the Roman numeral for 1000.

12 Judith Messina, *Crain's New York Business*, 16 June 1997, 13, 24, p. 1. Quote from Mario Dell'Aera, a partner at KPMG Peat Marwick, DoubleClick's auditor at that time.

13 One of the reasons why DoubleClick has invested so heavily in research is to prove the effectiveness of online advertising and marketing to such sceptics.

14 The Super Bowl is the American football championship that takes place each year. It is one of the top-viewed US events, and subsequently commands some of US television's highest advertising rates.

15 Susan Sachatello, interview, 30 January 2002, New York.

Exhibit 3 Potential for growth of online advertising: ad budgets will follow consumers online

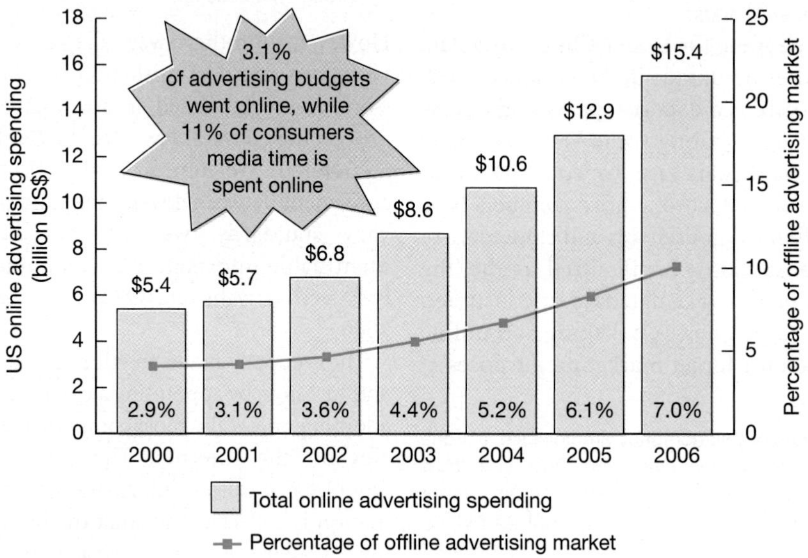

Source: DoubleClick corporate presentation 4Q01.

The network effect

A key reason for DoubleClick's quick success was its very early creation of an online network, which emulated an offline media network. It is the same principle behind US television networks, where a small hometown station is more interesting to bigger, national advertisers as an affiliate of one of the 'big three' US networks, for example, rather than as a stand-alone local station.[16]

Likewise, DoubleClick created its network to sell advertising via a collection of websites. As Kevin Ryan explained, many sites do not have the mass appeal of Yahoo! or AOL and are too small to pull in lucrative advertising contracts on their own. The DoubleClick Network offered to sell such ad inventory to an advertiser as part of a package of other websites. He pointed out that:

> The big media buyers are never going to talk to a small site, but as part of the DoubleClick Network, not only will the technology make a small site more valuable, but our dedicated online sales teams will sell the inventory on these sites. We take 40% of any revenues that we generate to cover our technology and sales costs, and give your site a cheque for the remaining 60%.[17]

The network effect compounded: by October 1998, two years after it was founded, the company represented 120 websites such as Travelocity, United Media, Edgar-Online, US News, AltaVista and Fast Company – from 35 in April 1996. Company revenues rose as well, shooting from $6.5 million in 1996 past $138 million in 1998. And this was only the beginning of the company's interest in networks, which could add to its core businesses and bottom line.

Riding the offline network: acquiring Abacus

Though DoubleClick had locked down the online advertising market with DART and the DoubleClick Network, the company had bigger ambitions: 'We want to be in anything that has to do with measurable media', Ryan said. 'We took a look at the area and asked, "What data out there are important in the long term? What about the direct marketers who are

16 ABC (American Broadcasting Co.), CBS (Columbia Broadcasting System), NBC (National Broadcasting Corp.).

17 Ryan, interview.

offline?"'[18] Such thinking ahead led them to their 1999 acquisition of the world's largest database of buyer transactions, Abacus.

Abacus is a gold mine for DoubleClick – or a data mine, to be exact – and unique in the business world. The Abacus Alliance is a data co-operative that collects and shares data among some 1800 catalogue companies and publishers (see Appendix 3). From the data that are shared, co-operative members have access to 90 million US households and close to three billion sales transactions. It bills itself as the 'the nation's largest proprietary database of consumer, retail, business-to-business, publishing and online transactions used for target marketing purposes'.[19] Exclaimed Ryan:

> The fundamentals of this company are colossal. It's one of the best businesses I've ever seen! Once you know what everyone has purchased, there's nothing more predictive. If I know that you have bought gardening supplies and have three kids, then obviously I should send you children's clothing and gardening-supply catalogues.[20]

Though the company posted $70 million in 2001 revenue with a 30% profit margin, it was not evident in the beginning that it would become so successful. After all, Abacus was asking its members to share their bread-and-butter customer lists with the other members of the co-operative. Ryan sympathized with their distress:

> It's extremely hard for them to do this because they're thinking, 'This is my customer list!' But we have 1800 companies that have given us their data because then Abacus allows its members to buy names from it at half of normal market rates. So why do it? If those names perform for me and they are cheap, then it's great business for them. They just have to give us their data. Plus, if everyone gives their data to Abacus, no one can challenge that business.[21]

Though information between direct competitors is not shared, Abacus can create models of those households actively buying via catalogues and turn up those households. For example, a children's clothing catalogue might ask for the addresses of households that have bought highchairs or playpens in the last six months.

The acquisition of Abacus presented a new opportunity for the online advertiser. Noted one journalist:

> Mr. O'Connor [then DoubleClick's CEO] realised that, by marrying the two, he could identify individual web users and not only track, but also predict their behaviour – making online advertising even more science than art. And he would have data that advertisers would pay through the nose for.[22]

However, soon there were allegations about privacy violations and data mishandling. The Federal Trade Commission launched an investigation, and privacy groups filed several lawsuits.[23] DoubleClick quickly responded. 'We commit [today], that until there is agreement between government and industry on privacy standards, we will not link personally identifiable information to anonymous user activity[24] across websites', O'Connor stated in March 2000.[25]

The company made an effort to reassure the public and investors by appointing a chief privacy officer, and adopting one of the most comprehensive privacy policies on the Internet. The policy explains how DoubleClick collects information, what kind of information is collected and what the information is used for.[26] Under the current privacy policy, surfers must 'opt-in' to have their personal information included in a DoubleClick database. The company also participates in the self-regulating Network Advertising Initiative, audited by PriceWaterhouseCoopers.

DART: selling the secret weapon

> It's a classic business school lesson: if you don't do it, someone else will. I'm not going to walk away from a great market.
>
> **Kevin Ryan**

Looking back at DART's stellar early success, it could be attributed to two key factors: first, the early adherence of website 'heavyweights' in DoubleClick's stable of network websites – such as AltaVista,

---

18 Ibid.
19 www.abacus-direct.com/, 29 July 2002.
20 Ryan, interview.
21 Ibid.
22 'The Internet's chastened child', *The Economist*, 11 November 2000, p. 80.
23 The FTC investigation was concluded in March 2002 without any charges being filed. All private lawsuits have also been either dismissed or settled.
24 The company can, however, merge the two as long as the users remain anonymous.
25 Kevin O'Connor, 'Statement from Kevin O'Connor, CEO of DoubleClick', company press release, 2 March 2000. www.doubleclick.com/us/corporate/presskit/pressreleases.asp?asp_object_1=&press%5frelease%5Fid=2395, 29 July 2002.
26 www.doubleclick.com/us/corporate/privacy/privacy/default.asp, 29 July 2002.

Netscape and Travelocity – created a snowball effect that attracted more and more websites to the network. At its peak in 2000, the network represented some 2000 websites. It was a classic case of network dynamics reinforced by a unique technology.

Second, for DoubleClick's media representatives, DART constituted a key competitive advantage. As Saridakis stated, DART was the only system that allowed advertisers to target eyeballs (surfers) using criteria such as frequency capping,[27] geographic location, domain names and even browser types. Handing over the technology to other aspiring network creators was viewed internally as a life-or-death matter. And this was exactly what would go on the table.

In 1996, the company was negotiating with the Wall Street Journal Online to bring it into its media network. While DoubleClick felt its arguments were solid – a tried-and-true online sales force, its network reach, and a brilliant technology – the WSJ was convinced that its media sales team had already longstanding relationships with advertisers, and it did not need to outsource its online ad sales. Its counteroffer: to buy DART, and only DART, as an ASP solution.

The WSJ proposition set off a volcanic in-house debate. The media sales team was passionately opposed to selling the technology. For them, selling DART technology to others was unthinkable. They argued that it would mean that DoubleClick would have to approach engineers and chief technology officers – clients substantially different from the creative and marketing directors that DoubleClick was used to seeing.

But the company realized that if it did not sell its ad-serving software, others might sell theirs. At that point, they had a lock on the market with 'a lot of guys in the middle', as Saridakis pointed out, but no one had a technology that could compete with DART in segmenting audiences and targeting information. Yet a patent dispute or competitor's technology development could change that. So DoubleClick seized the moment and began commercializing the system separately.

The financial arguments helped make the decision less painful: the margins on selling DART as an ASP solution were far higher than the return on media sales; furthermore, DoubleClick would not have to hand over 60% of what it charged to those websites it represented in its network. The green light was given in August 1996, and the WSJ Online became DoubleClick's first technology customer. DART for Publishers, or DFP, was born – and a new company vision with it.

A shifting model: from media to technology

By January 2002, the company had made a strategic shift from operating essentially as an online advertising sales network to becoming an online technology solutions company, centred around five product poles: Media, TechSolutions, Direct Marketing (Abacus), e-Mail Marketing and Research (Diameter) (see Exhibit 4 and Table 2).

In the beginning media sales were hot, parallelling a rise in online advertising. They initially accounted for 100% of the company's revenues. However, the first sale of its DART technology to the Wall Street Journal Online started moving DoubleClick in another direction that has exploded, accounting for 70% of the company's revenue in 2001.

The company has continued its industry dominance by spinning off successful product adaptations of DART, such as DART for Advertisers (DFA) and DART Enterprise. DoubleClick takes its cue for development from the market, as had happened with DFA. As Ryan noted:

> Advertisers and agencies were coming to us, saying, 'Look, here's our challenge: when we buy ads on the WSJ Online, we get a DART report. We love that but we advertise on 20 different sites, so it's a nightmare for us. I get this report, that report and that report.' Some reports are DoubleClick, some are not. The accounting methodology is different. It's the equivalent in financial terms of multiple stock reports for a portfolio. The boss asks, 'How did your portfolio do?' and you say, 'I don't know'.

Additionally, DART permitted online advertisers to streamline operational issues such as campaign management:

> An advertiser, Ford for example, says, 'This ad campaign is not working well and we want to change it. We're displaying the blue car; let's go with the red car instead.' What they had to do was call up and ask the ad agency to change the ad. With DFA, they can change the ads as much as they want – every day, every three days, every week.

27 Limiting the number of times an ad is viewed by a particular surfer.

Exhibit 4 DoubleClick's products and services

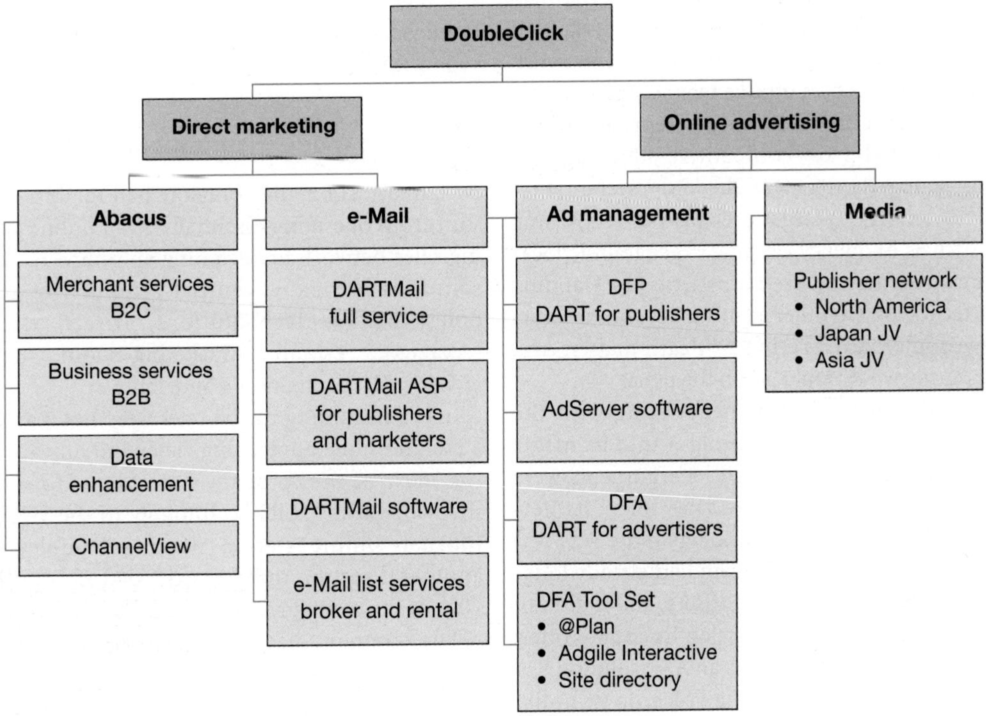

Source: DoubleClick corporate presentation 4Q01.

Table 2 DoubleClick's products and services

(a) Online advertising

Product	*Description*	*Statistics*	*Comments*
DART® for Advertisers (DFA)	A hosted web-based ad management and serving application that enables advertisers to target users for ad viewing. Also allows advertisers and their agencies to streamline the ad management process through analytical reporting and manage their online campaigns.	Served 682 billion ads in 2001. 400 clients in 2002. Used by all of the top 10 advertising agencies.	The product that launched DoubleClick. Uses cookies for geographic targeting and frequency capping (limits the number of times a person sees the same ad). Patented technology (September 1999).
DART® for Web Publishers (DFP)	A hosted web-based ad management and serving application geared to publishers, allowing them to traffic, target, serve and report on ad campaigns for their advertisers. Provides integrated ad delivery and inventory management. Offers an API (application programming interface) to integrate legacy systems.	817 clients in 2002.	Integrated rich media in 2001. Commercialized in January 1997.
DART® Enterprise	In-house licensed software that permits web publishers and merchants to target, serve and report ads online. Can also be used for other digital channels such as kiosks and iTV. Can be integrated with back-office systems.	407 customers in 2002.	Rebranded in March 2002. Formerly known as AdServer.

Table 2 **continued**

(a) Online advertising cont.

Product	*Description*	*Statistics*	*Comments*
Site Directory	A web-based searchable database for ad buyers. Contains media planning information (audience, advertising specs, etc.) for thousands of websites. Provides web publishers exposure to top media buyers and planners.	NA	The online 'yellow pages' for media buyers.
MediaVisor™	A web-based media planning tool designed to streamline the planning, buying and trafficking process for agencies and advertisers. Can be used with DART and Site Directory or integrated into in-house systems.	NA	Started development in February 2002.
mDART	Version of DART for wireless ad serving on mobile telephones.	NA	

(b) e-Mail marketing

Product	*Description*	*Statistics*	*Comments*
DARTmail® Service (self and full)	A web-based application and licensed software using DART allowing publishers and direct marketers to plan, execute and track their e-mail campaigns (self-service). A fully out-sourced, turnkey version also exists.	300 clients in 2002. Served 2 billion e-mails in first quarter 2002.	Incorporates January 2002 MessageMedia and April 2001 FloNetwork acquisitions.
UnityMail™	In-house licensed software for e-mail deployment and tracking.	NA	

(c) Marketing analytics

Product	*Description*	*Statistics*	*Comments*
ChannelView™	A web-based application that allows marketers to see the results of their direct mail campaigns across multiple order channels, including websites, catalogue call centres and retail stores.	NA	Introduced in January 2002.
SiteAdvance™	A hosted website software for online merchants. Allows online merchants to analyze the interactions between site traffic and transactions. Combines website metrics with multi-channel marketing data.	NA	

(d) Database marketing

Product	*Description*	*Statistics*	*Comments*
Abacus Alliance	Offers direct marketers transactional data, prospect lists, list optimization, advanced statistical modelling (housefile modelling) across different channels (direct mail, e-mail, Internet advertising) on information collected from members.	1800 members. 2.9 billion transactions. 90 million US households covered.	Bought Abacus in 1999 for $1.7 billion (founded in 1990). Bought remaining stake in Abacus Direct Europe in 2002.
B2B Alliance	Co-operative database focusing on directly marketed business-to-business products and services.	850 million business transactions. 250 participants.	

Table 2 continued

(e) Media

Product	Description	Statistics	Comments
DoubleClick Network	Allows advertisers access to a collection of branded sites. Uses DART and DARTmail. Promises to build brands and generate leads for direct marketers, publishers and advertisers. Operates Gravity Direct website, allowing surfers to opt in for direct marketing offers	Reached 53% of US users in December 2001 according to Jupiter Media Metrix.	Sold 85% of European business to AdLINK in January 2002. Sold US media business to rival L90 (now MaxWorldwide) in July 2002.
DoubleClick Sweepstakes	Provides tools for building and tracking customized online sweepstakes, rewarded registration form or rewarded survey in minutes.	NA	

Statistics for 2002, unless indicated otherwise.

The DART product line has also been successfully replicated and exported throughout the world, establishing an international standard that accounts for a large part of its success, with some 1600 clients currently using a DART product. In addition to its successful extension into new product areas, the company continues to dominate because it also upgrades and adds new features to its existing products, as with its latest release, DART 5. The company made the system more open, allowing client companies to integrate it into their billing systems.

The deflating Internet bubble accelerated DoubleClick's move away from media sales into technology. Falling advertising sales in 2001 forced the company to cut its staff by 25%, cutting the total headcount from 1929 to 1450. While the company took the critical decision to start selling its technology as an ASP solution, what will it do in light of the fact that the dot.com bust has also deflated revenues for DART, down 51% between August 2000 and 2001?[28] On the bright side, it seems that blue-chip advertisers are now getting more interested in web advertising. They accounted for 66% of DART's revenue between August 2000 and 2001.[29]

Yet despite such bright spots, the company has essentially divested itself of its media network. In January 2002, DoubleClick sold its European media sales network to Germany's AdLINK for €30.5 million, 36% equity and a 10-year deal with AdLINK to use DART technology. The company wants to continue working with media, but without the associated costs. 'We want to focus on our core competencies in technology and data', Saridakis said. 'If we look at the spin-off to AdLINK in Germany, it's rather seamless. They have always been a client of our technology – we just have a closer relationship with them.'[30]

On the heels of this sale, DoubleClick followed up by selling its US media operations to a struggling competitor L90 in July 2002 for $5 million in cash and 4.8 million shares. DoubleClick will hold a seat on the board – and get a share of profits – in the new company, MaxWorldwide.

Where to now?

> The question is: what are the next big areas we are going to go after?
>
> **Kevin Ryan**

For DoubleClick's CEO, growing the business means improving processes and developing products for markets in which DoubleClick either has a first-mover advantage or those sectors in which existing competitors (Table 3) have a year or less head start. It also means shedding core businesses, if deemed necessary.

Ryan calls these opportunities for growth 'open areas'. One such area is e-mail marketing. Though DoubleClick's activities in e-mail marketing are currently centred on e-mail targeting and delivery, future activities in this sector might lead to the eventual takeover of the entire process of data

28 *Information Week*, 20 August 2001.
29 Ibid.
30 Saridakis, interview.

Table 3 Examples of DoubleClick's competitors

DoubleClick business line or product	*Examples of competitors*
Advertising sales	Web publishers (AOL, Yahoo!, Terra Lycos, etc.) Other media (television, cable, radio, print) Ad agencies (Ogilvy & Mather, DDB Worldwide)
Networks	24/7 Media, Ad2One, CCI, Engage, L90, MSN Network
Ad serving	AdForce, Avenue A, Mediaplex, Real Media, Sabela Media (a unit of 24/7 Media), companies' internal tech departments
e-Mail marketing	Annuncio, Cheetah Mail, Digital Impact, Exactis (a unit of 24/7 Media), Kana, Lyris, MSN Advantage Marketing, Responsys, NetCreations, (list broker), YesMail (list broker)
Diameter (research)	Dynamic Logic, Ipsos-ASI Interactive, Jupiter Media Metrix, Millward Brown Interactive, Nielsen//NetRatings
Data aggregation	Acxiom, Dun & Bradstreet, Harte-Hanks, InfoUSA, TransUnion
Information, marketing research	Engage, iBehavior, Junkbusters, Prefer.com, Z-24 (a unit of Experian)
CRM products	E.piphany, Kana

Source: DoubleClick 10K SEC filings 2000–01, online research.

management in online marketing – hosting, merging and purging data for clients.

Offline, companies already outsource their data management to specialists such as Acxiom or Experian. But Ryan smells change in the air:

> The old thinking is 'Give these data to Acxiom because I don't want to handle them'. Now, we have a new generation of companies who are thinking differently and have different needs, and the old generation of data management companies is not ready to handle this.[31]

While DoubleClick's strategic success has been driven by leveraging available opportunities, the company is setting its sights and hopes on its technology, on providing the power and brawn that makes direct marketing work online – and eventually offline. It is continually adding the pieces one by one, improving its offering, and developing new features like Channelview for the catalogue industry or a service for interactive television.

If, however, a market turns unprofitable or detracts from its new core vision, DoubleClick does not hesitate to make difficult choices, including divesting itself of its original businesses. Recent actions seem to substantiate this hypothesis: the sales of its media network in Europe and the US, of its ad effectiveness business to Dynamic Logic, and of @plan, DoubleClick's data research division, to Nielsen//NetRatings.

It is a bumpy evolution towards new terrain. And when all is said and done, even Ryan admits that DoubleClick is hard to pin down in terms of its core businesses. One thing, though, seems clear in his mind:

> What we do does not exist anywhere else. For example, on Wall Street, billions of dollars are being spent, and technology is there tracking every second of it. There are no legacy systems, nothing written in Fortran.[32] It's all new because it's worth it to have. Similarly in the marketing industry, there are billions of dollars floating around. A major automobile company is going to spend $2 billion on marketing. Do they know exactly what worked and what didn't? No, they have a vague idea ... The question is: could that process be improved and can you reduce costs? Absolutely. The role of technology and data in marketing is becoming much more significant.[33]

If Wall Street is tracking every second of the billions of dollars spent, does the advertising industry need to do the same? What is DoubleClick's role in this? Should and could DoubleClick become the 'central' Bloomberg terminal for marketers? Or should it just provide the standard technology for others to handle this?

31 Ryan, interview.
32 Fortran (FORmula TRANslation) was the first widely used, algebra-based programming language, designed for mathematics, scientific and engineering applications.
33 Ryan, interview.

Appendix 1 Quick facts and statistics

- Global HQ: New York
  - Regional HQs: Europe – Dublin, Asia – Hong Kong
  - 26 offices in 12 countries
- Employed 1361 (532 in sales and marketing) in May 2002
- 20 data centres around the world
- Listed on NASDAQ (DCLK)
- Revenues: 2001 – $406 million; 2000 – $506 million; 1998 – $138.7 million
- Global customer base in July 2002:
  - Database marketing (Abacus) – 1800
  - Ad-serving clients (DART technology) –1624

DoubleClick statistics

	2002	2000	1998	1996
Ad-serving customers (DART, DFA, DFP)	1624	2023	570	35
Sites in network[a]	238	1658	340	NA
Ads served on DoubleClick Network via DART	730 billion[b]	621 billion	34 billion	10 million
e-Mails served per quarter	2 billion	90 million	0	0
Employees	1361	1929	482	13
Stock price				
High	$13.88[c]	$135.25	$77.13	IPO: $17.00
Low	$4.68[c]	$8.00	$13.50	PO: $34.44

a Sold to rival L90 (renamed MaxWorldwide) in July 2002.
b Projected.
c 52-week range on 18 July 2002.

Sources: Company statistics, 6 May 2002; DoubleClick 10K SEC filings 1998–2001; Interactive Advertising Bureau, www.iab.net; Network Wizards Internet Domain Survey, Internet Software Consortium www.kltprc.net/policynotes/gifs/fig_009_1.htm, 18 July 2002; online research.

Internet statistics

	2002	2000	1998	1996
Internet users	490 million	259 million	113 million	19 million
Internet hosts	160 million	72.4 million	36.7 million	16.7 million
Internet advertising revenues	$10.3 billion*	$8.2 billion	$1.92 billion	$267 million

* Projected

Sources: Company statistics, 6 May 2002; Interactive Advertising Bureau, www.iab.net; Network Wizards Internet Domain Survey, Internet Software Consortium www.kltprc.net/policynotes/gifs/fig_009_1.htm, 18 July 2002; online research.

Appendix 2 Timeline 1996–2002

The initial idea for DoubleClick sprung out of an eight-month-long basement brainstorming session in 1995 between Kevin O'Connor and Dwight Merriman. At the time, the two were working together at the Atlanta-based software company Attachmate.[34] Convinced of the Internet's potential, they began formulating ideas that would capitalize on it. One hundred ideas later, they deduced that online advertising would be key to the Internet's business model. Thus, the model for the DoubleClick Network was born, with DART as its backbone.

34 O'Connor was the company's Chief Technology Officer and Vice-President of Research, responsible for new markets. Merriman was the company's Research Engineer.

April 1995	Poppe Tyson (now Modem Media) forms an Internet sales group called DoubleClick.
August 1995	Kevin O'Connor and Dwight Merriman form the Internet Advertising Network (IAN).
January 1996	IAN and DoubleClick merge to form DoubleClick Inc.
March 1996	The DoubleClick Network launches to provide media buyers with branded sites, content and mass reach through one entry point.
September 1996	DART is offered as a service solution for the first time to web publishers outside the DoubleClick Network. DART for Publishers or DFP is born. The Wall Street Journal Online becomes the first client.
November 1996	Delivers first advertisement on AltaVista.
June 1997	Raises $40 million in venture capital.
August 1997	First international office opens: DoubleClick Japan.
January 1998	Organizes sales force to sell DART technology.
February 1998	IPO raises $62.5 million (offered 3.5 million shares of common stock at $17 per share).
July 1998	Launches DoubleClick Local (for regional and local advertisers).
October 1998	Launches DART for Advertisers (DFA), known at the time as Closed-Loop Marketing Solutions.
December 1998	Secondary offering nets $93.7 million (offered 2.5 million shares of common stock at $34.4375 per share).
July 1999	One billionth ad served.
October 1999	Completes its merger with NetGravity, a California-based industry leader of software for interactive online advertising and direct marketing. Completes its $1.7 billion merger with Colorado-based Abacus Direct, an information and research provider to the direct marketing industry.
November 1999	Moves to its new corporate headquarters in Manhattan.
December 1999	Completes acquisition of Colorado-based Opt-In Email.com, which provides e-mail marketing, publishing and list management. Announces its launch into e-mail marketing with DARTmail. Acquires the remaining 90% of DoubleClick Iberoamerica in a $2.5 million deal with Terra Networks.
January 2000	Lawsuit filed to prevent DoubleClick from collecting personal information on Internet users without their prior written consent. Several class-action lawsuits follow. DoubleClick takes a 30% equity stake in ValueClick Inc., an advertising network that utilizes a cost-per-click model, for $85 million in stock and cash. Completes a two-for-one stock split of common stock.
February 2000	The US Federal Trade Commission (FTC) launches an investigation into DoubleClick after the Electronic Privacy Information Center accuses it of planning to merge anonymous online data with Abacus's identifiable household data. Announces creation of chief privacy officer position.

May 2000	Acquired for $19.6 million New York-based Flashbase Inc., a creator of completely automated solutions for the design and management of online sweepstakes.
July 2000	Names Kevin Ryan as CEO. Kevin O'Connor to continue as Chair.
November 2000	Appoints Brian Rainey as President of Abacus. Hires Susan Sachatello as Chief Marketing Officer.
December 2000	Announces it will break even, beating expectations by $0.02 per share. Terminates merger agreement with e-mail marketer NetCreations, Inc. Receives break-up fee of $8.6 million.
January 2001	FTC closes its investigation into DoubleClick's data-handling practices. Finds no violation of the company's privacy policy.
February 2001	Finalizes acquisition of @plan for $104.3 million in cash and stocks.
March 2001	Serves one trillionth ad. Divides ad business into two networks – audience and brand. Announces 10% cut in workforce (200 jobs).
April 2001	Acquires B2C Toronto-based e-mail marketer FloNetwork Inc. for $52.7 million in cash and stocks. Launches Diameter.
May 2001	Acquires technology assets of Sabela Media from competitor 24/7 Media.
June 2001	Launches DART 5.
September 2001	Acquires media buying and planning technology from interactive media agency Adgile Interactive based in San Francisco.
October 2001	Purchases rival L90's ad-delivery technology.
December 2001	Sells off ad effectiveness research practice to Dynamic Logic, an online research firm, for a 10% equity stake. Promotes David Rosenblatt to President. Names Bruce Dalziel as Chief Financial Officer. Hires Mok Choe as Chief Information Officer.
January 2002	Announces a positive pro forma EPS of 0.01¢ per share. Reorganization of sales force by customer group: TechSolutions (publishers, marketers, agencies and direct marketers) and Media (brand advertisers and agencies). Completes $12.5 million all-stock acquisition of MessageMedia, a provider of permission-based e-mail marketing and messaging solutions. Sells its European media business to Germany's AdLINK Internet Media AG for €30.5 million and a 15% equity stake.
March 2002	Agrees to a settlement on privacy litigation. Under the two-year agreement, the company will give clear notice of its privacy policy and explanations of its services; ensure that users must opt-in to have personally identifiable information combined with anonymous online information; serve 300 million consumer privacy banner ads; carry out routine purging of collected online data; and limit the life of new ad-serving cookies to five years. infoUSA buys DoubleClick's e-mail list services division for an undisclosed sum, obtaining 40 million opt-in addresses, 28 million postal names and addresses and 45 branded lists.
May 2002	Nielsen//NetRatings and DoubleClick form a strategic data partnership. DoubleClick sells @plan research tools to Netratings for $18.5 million in cash and stocks. Pledges to integrate the tool into its DART and MediaVisor software.
June 2002	Buys remaining 50% stake in Abacus Direct Europe launched in 1998 (26 million households, 250 retail companies) from Claritas Europe, a Dutch data-research company, to expand in Europe. Claritas will continue to provide data products to Abacus's European operations for five years.
July 2002	Reports a net profit of $4.1 million or $0.03 per share. Sells US media operations to its Los Angeles-based competitor, L90, which renames itself MaxWorldwide, for $5 million and 4.8 million shares. Will get seats on the board of the company, plus $6 million if MaxWorldwide is profitable in the next three years.

Appendix 3 Abacus Direct

Started in 1990, Abacus was conceived of as a data alliance: companies that shared their data would receive prospective customer lists and data modelling in return. Initially, the company grew slowly because, as Kevin Ryan pointed out, companies were reluctant to share their 'bread-and-butter' customer lists with potential competitors. However, cataloguers quickly realized that the positives far outweighed the negatives, and business picked up steam. DoubleClick merged with Abacus Direct in 1999 in a $1.7 billion deal.

Today, the Colorado-based company has chugged ahead to become the US's 'largest proprietary database of consumer, retail, business-to-business, publishing and online transactions used for target marketing purposes.'[35] It contains almost three billion transactions from more than 90 million US households, including geographic, demographic, lifestyle and behavioural data. The company uses the sales data for consumer behaviour modelling and helps catalogue companies to analyze and maximize their own mailing lists.

It provides its members with the following products and services:

- *Channelview* is a web-based, multichannel analysis tool that allows direct marketers to follow a campaign across multiple channels such as websites, retail stores and catalogues.
- *Housefile modelling* rates customers' propensity to make repeat purchases, weeding out unresponsive consumers.
- *Optimization modelling* allows cataloguers to select customers most likely to make repeat purchases on a given list.
- *Prospect modelling* allows cataloguers to identify and add new customers to their lists.
- *Market research* provides information on customers, business, competitors and the marketplace.

Competitors include ACNielsen, to which DoubleClick sold its research tools in May 2002, Acxiom, Experian, Harte-Hankes and infoUSA, which bought DoubleClick's e-mail list services division in March 2002.

35 Company website: www.abacus-direct.com, 16 July 2002.

Superior data drives customer results

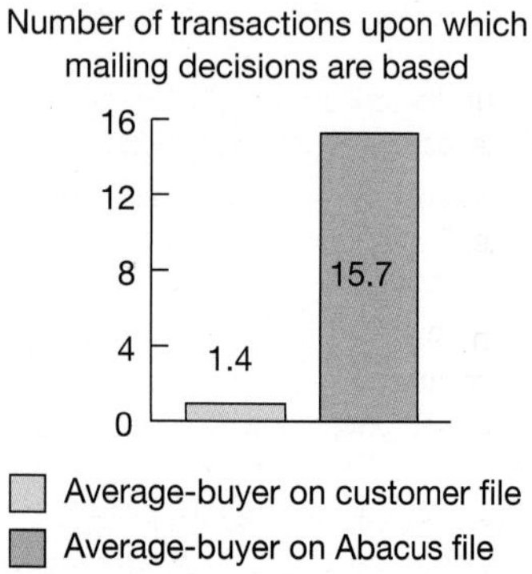

Typical merchant customer profile	Abacus customer profile
• Lives in an affluent postal code • First-time customer • Purchased $100 of apparel • Two weeks ago	• Lives in an affluent postal code • First-time customer • Purchased $100 of apparel • Two weeks ago
	• Purchased $1000 in apparel in past six months from catalogues, online and retail • Purchased £300 in gifts in past 12 months • Purchased $600 in home/garden • Purchased $250 in accessories • Opted in and clicked on e-mail offers • Female, household income = $75–100K

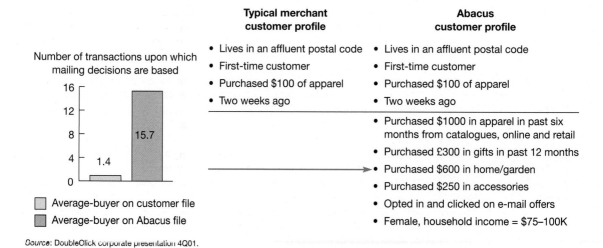

Source: DoubleClick corporate presentation 4Q01.

DISCUSSION QUESTIONS

1. Is DoubleClick a media network, a technology company, or neither? What really are its core competences?
2. Is DoubleClick the online version of the offline advertising agencies or something different? If the latter, what are the differences, and does Internet-based advertising compare with the traditional offline?
3. What is the role of the DoubleClick network? Was it instrumental for the growth of the company?
4. What was the idea behind the acquisition of Abacus? What is the key competitive advantage of Abacus?
5. Why did DoubleClick sell its technology? What is the breadth of data it has in the marketing tools arena?
6. Does DoubleClick really have to be either a technology or a media (network) company? Where would you suggest that DoubleClick go to now?

Competing through EDI at Papeteries Brun Passot

Making paper passé

We've tripled gross revenues in five years, while maintaining manpower at a constant level. The increased efficiency came primarily from implementation of EDI [electronic data interchange].

Jean-Philippe Passot, Deputy Managing Director, Brun Passot

Industry overview

The office supplies industry in France is highly fragmented; the principle players are the manufacturers, distributors and customers. Many highly specialized manufacturers are often dedicated to a single product line. The distributors, like Brun Passot, are of different sizes and degrees of specialization. The total number of distributors in France is about 5000. This figure sharply contrasts with the one in the UK where approximately 100 distributors share a slightly larger market.

Approximately 25% of the French office products suppliers market is held by the four main companies: Guilbert, Gaspard, Saci and Brun Passot. The remaining 75% of this FF11 billion[1] market is divided among small players. The annual growth rate of the market is 3–4%; it is constant and mainly driven by the high level of innovation and the number of new products.

The size of the office supplies market in the European Community is FF175 billion, with the two main players being Germany and the UK, who have a share of respectively FF35 billion and FF15 billion. Some large American and British firms are expected to approach the French market over the next few years. Their high volume and global operating capabilities are likely to have a severe effect on the French industry.

Company overview

Brun Passot is a French PME[2] founded in 1949 by André Passot as a family business located near Lyon. The 60-person company initially specialized exclusively in paper processing, a renowned business in the Rhone–Alpes region. In 1970, it started diversifying its activities into the distribution of office supplies and products related to computer and office equipment.

In 1992, Brun Passot employed 160 people including a salesforce of 22 persons. It had recently significantly enlarged its direct customer base to include major industrial and service organizations (e.g. Renault, Alcatel, Dassault, Péchiney, Crédit Lyonnais, Shell, Philips and DEC France) as well as several governmental agencies (such as Electricité de France, France Télécom, the French Armed Forces and the national railroad company SNCF). Through its network of 11 branches and one warehouse centre, Brun Passot offered 12 000 products to 6 000 customers at 15 000 delivery locations throughout France. From a mere FF15 million in 1970, the company's turnover reached FF254 million in 1991.

The growth of Brun Passot over the years, coupled with higher diversification and more products and partners (customers and wholesalers), has increased the business complexity for the company. In the early 1970s, its top management decided to use IT to help

1 US$1 = FF 5.85, as of 25 August 1993.
2 PME ('Petite et Moyenne Entreprises') refers to small and medium-sized enterprises.

This case was written by Tawfik Jelassi, Associate Professor at INSEAD. It is intended to be used as a basis for class discussion rather than to illustrate either effective or ineffective handling of an administrative situation.

Financial support from INSEAD Alumni Fund European Case Programme is gratefully acknowledged.

manage Brun Passot operations. In 1978, the first step consisted of networking the corporate headquarters with the central warehouse, providing a platform for developing real-time applications. Aware of the potential of this new IT platform and at the stimulus of several large customers, Brun Passot established an electronic link between their purchasing departments and Brun Passot's supply information system. Several routine tasks, including orders generation, inventory inquiries and statistics, could now be handled in a more efficient, less paper manner, resulting in a number of benefits for both parties.

Brun Passot's business strategy

According to a national study,[3] an employee of the service or manufacturing sector uses on average FF2200 of stationery (i.e. writing materials) per year; this figure excludes the purchase of paper, preprinted forms, and computer-related equipment. Purchasing this stationery requires, on average, 16 purchase orders, each containing 70 product lines. Brun Passot has estimated the costs for companies, to process these orders and manage the subsequent inventory, to range from 38 to 145% of the purchase value[4] (see Exhibit 1). As Jean-Philippe Passot said:

> Companies suffer from what I call 'the sugar syndrome'. On average they stock sufficient office supplies to cover four to ten months of consumption.

In 1980, Brun Passot sought to distinguish itself from the competition by offering a distinctive customer service based on the concept of 'just-in-time' purchasing (or telepurchasing). Because of telepurchasing's potential for reducing the costs of acquiring, storing and managing office products, the company saw it as a means to win the loyalty of existing customers. Other customers, it was hoped, could be stolen away from its rivals. Such benefits are especially important in the highly competitive office supplies market where profit margins are small (3–4%) and price sensitivity very high. Jean-Philippe Passot added:

> The impact of such a change in the relationship [with the customer] shifts the entire focus of classic commercial procedures, wherein the seller presses the buyer according to his own interests [in] selling a large volume of goods with a high profit margin.[5]

Exhibit 1 Costs of office supplies for customers (for a purchase of FF2200/office worker/year)

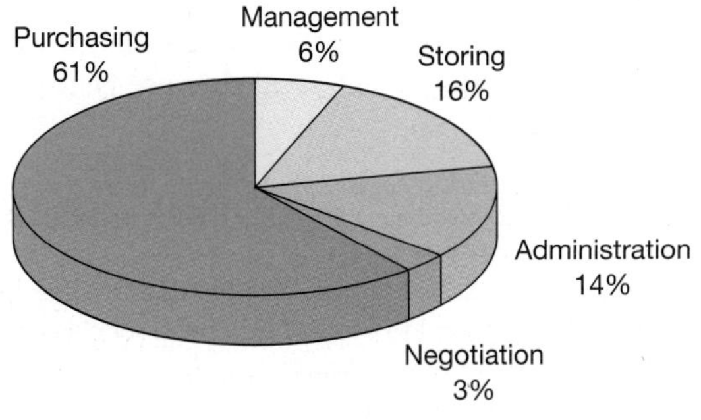

Source: Brun Passot.

Brun Passot's telepurchasing applications

In 1980, in order to implement telepurchasing, Brun Passot considered setting up IBM computer terminals at customer premises which would be connected to its supply information system through a specialized communication line. However, it quickly realized that only a few customers could afford the cost of such an electronic link. It then found in the emerging videotex platform, which became publicly available in France in 1982, an interesting vehicle for developing the telepurchasing service.

Three reasons led Brun Passot's management to adopt Minitel: first, France Télécom provided the terminal free of charge (this has changed since 1990); second, Minitel was widely used throughout France (there were 120 000 terminals distributed in 1983 and this number was expected to increase significantly in time);[6] and third, the Minitel terminal

3 A study made in France in 1989 by the Institut National des Statistiques et des Etudes Economiques (INSEE), Paris.

4 These figures are based on a representative sample of 80 customers with a total number of employees ranging from 300 to 5000.

5 'Telesupplies, the Brun Passot Bureautel System', *Minitel News*, No. 2, 1991.

6 That prediction was confirmed since the distribution of Minitel terminals increased to 531 000 in 1984, then to over two million in 1986, and approximately seven million in 1992. In addition to electronic telephone directory, Minitel terminals offer information services, professional databases, banking services, electronic mail, order processing, cash management, portfolio management and accounting. (For more information on the development and diffusion of Minitel, see: Cats-Baril, W. and Jelassi, T. 'The French videotex system Minitel: an example of a successful implementation of a national information technology infrastructure', INSEAD Working Paper Series, 1993. For examples of business applications of Minitel, see, in the INSEAD Case Study Series, Jelassi, T. and Loebbecke, C. 'Home banking: An IT-based business strategy or a complementary distribution channel – CORTAL versus Crédit Commercial de France', 1993; also Jelassi, T. and Murthy, G. 'Minitel, a home retailing application', 1993).

allowed for connection to a computer network. With the help of France Télécom, Brun Passot developed Bureautel in 1982, the first Minitel-based telepurchasing service offered in France. This non-EDI application is one of the three telepurchasing services that the company has developed, the other two being a basic EDI application (called SICLAD) and an advanced one.

Bureautel 2000

Bureautel 2000 was developed in one year by four members of Brun Passot's nine-person information technology grroup. In March 1983, its two application modules became available; they were aimed at two different user categories:

- One application module concerned supply, which allowed the sending of electronic orders in a validated and secure way (each customer has an identification number and a password).
- The other concerned managerial decision-making; it allowed routine inquiries of Brun Passot's inventory and provided reports on the status of purchases to date and cash flow.

An enhanced version of Bureautel, developed in 1989, allowed customers to follow up on their supplies. Based on the LECAM[7] technology, it gave users direct access to Brun Passot's order entry application. Brun Passot issued its own credit card that had a predefined maximum purchase limit per customer department for a certain time period. As orders were placed, the value of the items was subtracted from the department budget. Using reports provided by Bureautel, users/departments were able to trace their expenses. The benefits of the system included: (1) it substituted for a purchase order and hence reduced paper work; (2) users no longer needed to request management approval or go through a centralized purchasing department to order office supplies; and (3) careful monitoring of the use of their office supplies budget was ensured since they could not exceed it without getting their supervisor's approval. This card was not used for actual payment; instead orders resulted in the issuance of a regular invoice.

Customers with any computer equipment were attracted to Bureautel but others found it less appealing. Some large customers pushed Brun Passot into developing a PC-based telepurchasing service. As Olivier Figon, Head of the IT Department at Brun Passot, explained:

> Some of our customers refused [to use] Minitel and strongly preferred the PC. Not developing an application on the PC, which was becoming widely used in companies, would have resulted in one missing out on a whole market.

Initial EDI development

The first EDI application at Brun Passot was developed in-house in 1985 by a five-member team. The software, called SICLAD (Système Informatisé de Commande Locale pour Approvisionnement Décentralisé), was PC-based. As Olivier Figon said:

> The PC had several advantages over Minitel. It is cheaper for the customer since, with the PC, data input is free[8] while with Minitel he pays for the phone connection while keying-in the data [the purchase orders]. Moreover, Minitel has no memory storage capability; we can't save a file on it. The PC is also faster than Minitel, more user-friendly, and allows the use of colours and having a LAN [local area network] configuration.

The SICLAD software was offered free of charge to Brun Passot customers; it ran on Macintosh and IBM-compatible PC environments either in standalone or LAN configurations. The LAN version supported up to 32 customer PCs, with anyone permitted to access the external network. This provided centralized control over placing orders, while still giving customers the convenience of generating from multiple offices. Olivier Figon said:

> Apart from some bugs in the application programs which we fixed, the other technical problem that we faced was due to the type of network our customers had. Even those [networks] with the same type, such as Novell or Ethernet, didn't work from the start.

SICLAD allowed customers three ways to access the Brun Passot server by way of the customer's private automatic branch exchange[9] in three different ways: first, over the telephone network through the use of a

---

7 LECAM (Lecteur de Carte à Mémoire) is a device that can be attached to a Minitel terminal to read magnetic-stripe cards.

8 The customer can key in a file his/her purchase orders before getting connected to the data network to electronically transmit that file.

9 A private automatic branch exchange (PABX) provides for the transmission of calls to and from the public telephone network and allows internal dialling from station to station within the company's premises. It also allows Brun Passot to determine the telepurchasing application used for placing an order (i.e. Bureautel, SICLAD-EDI, or point-to-point EDI) and hence to measure the volume of transactions made over each medium.

Exhibit 2 **Access methods to Brun Passot's telepurchasing applications**

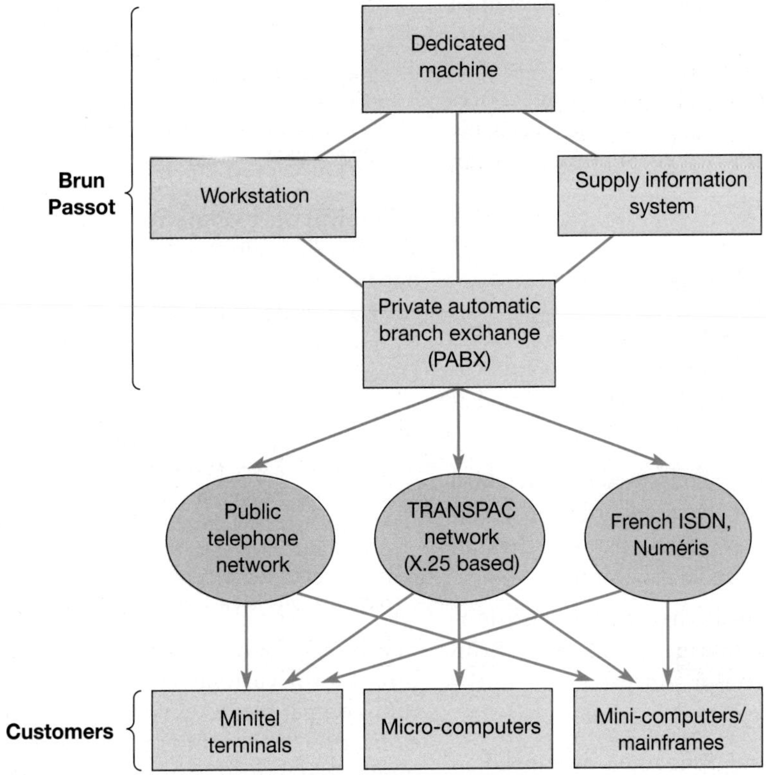

Source: Adapted from *Télécom Magazine*, No. 33, April 1990.

modem; second, over the TRANSPAC[10] network; and third, over the French ISDN[11] network Numéris (see Exhibit 2). The choice of the path depended mainly on the volume of transactions that a customer has with Brun Passot.

Customers could use SICLAD to send purchase orders electronically and receive receipt acknowledgements. Invoices and catalogues were not available over the network. Olivier Figon explained:

> Purchase orders and receipt acknowledgements are what I call peripheral documents. They don't directly impact the information system of the customer. This is not the case for products information and invoices, which are both central to the customer files, databases and accounting systems.

Three technical limitations restricted electronic distribution of the catalogue and invoices. First, the typical PC did not have sufficient memory space to store a huge volume of data.[12] Second, more sophisticated software would have been required. Third, incompatibility of data formats would have required customers to rekey invoice data. Olivier Figon added:

> To avoid entering the data in their [computer] systems, some of our customers asked us to develop a front-end interface between SICLAD and their internal IT applications. But we didn't want to get into this business. Plus, since each customer has a different IT system, how many interfaces would we have ended up developing?

An enhanced version of SICLAD, developed in 1989, used Numéris, the French ISDN service. It provided colour photos of each product using an image database. Customers accessed this database either by locally looking up the images of the 200 products[13] stored on the hard disk of their PC, or by remotely

10 TRANSPAC (Transmission par Pacquets) is based on the X.25 packet-switching standard.

11 ISDN (integrated services digital network) is capable of handling simultaneously data, voice, text and image transmission over a digital network.

12 Storing just the 12 000 products catalogue would have required a minimum of 10 megabytes.

13 This figure represents the average number of office supplies frequently purchased by large customers and which correspond to products of ongoing consumption. These products slightly differ by customer (by a factor of 10%).

getting connected to Brun Passot's workstation. In the latter case, the entire image database for 12 000 products was accessible.

In spite of the added functionality, ease-of-use and convenience that the various versions of SICLAD brought over Bureautel, some of Brun Passot's large customers still did not want to adopt it. Olivier Figon explained:

> Bureautel and SICLAD are [telepurchasing] services with a single supplier; they are proprietary systems of Brun Passot. What some of our large customers wanted are multi-supplier [telepurchasing] services. Their attitude represents an emerging trend in the market.

Advanced EDI development

SICLAD allowed customers to place purchase orders and receive the corresponding receipt

Exhibit 3 Information flows between Brun Passot and its business partners

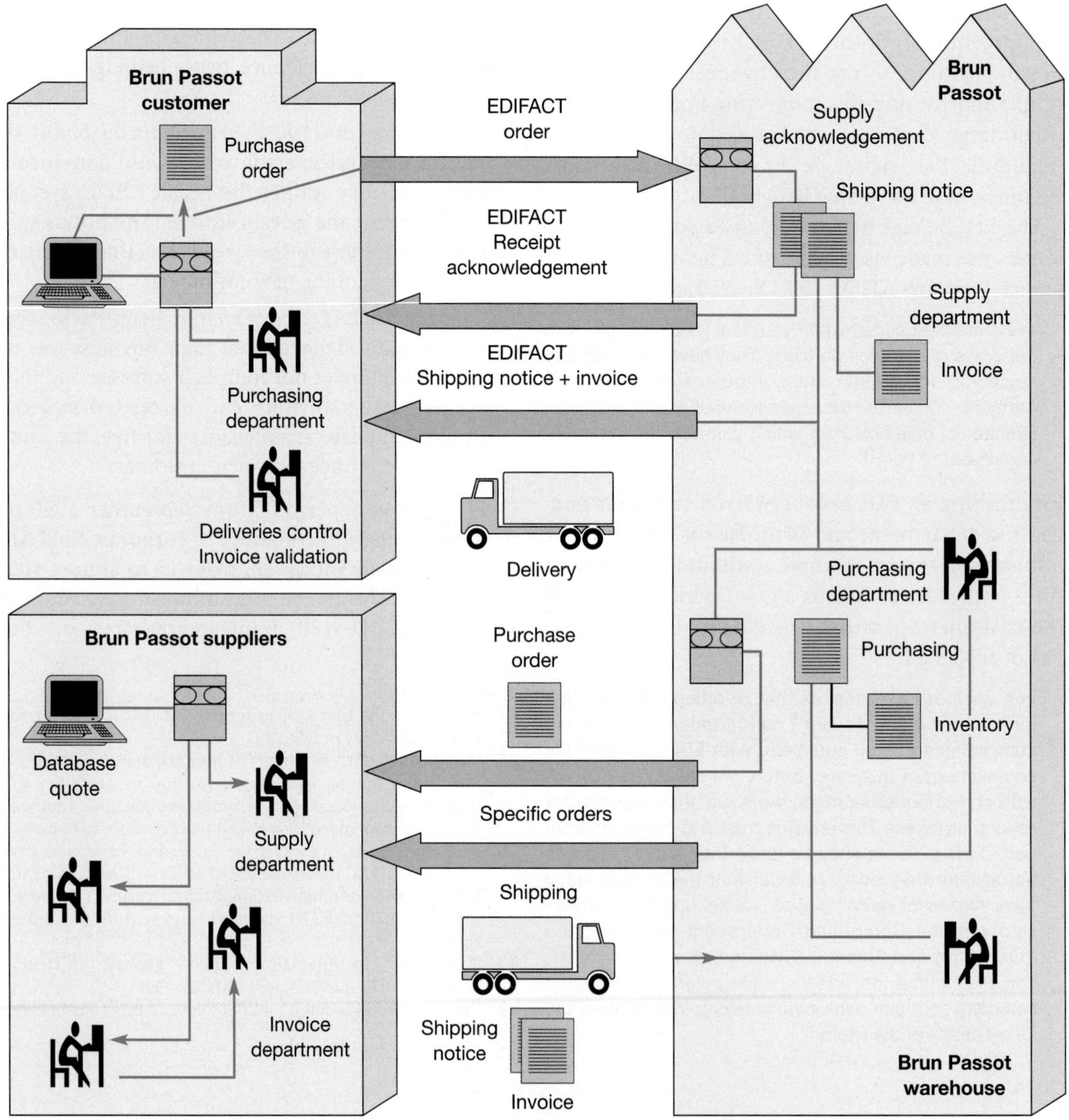

Source: Adapted from *Télécom Magazine*, No. 33, April 1990.

acknowledgements. In order to offer other capabilities, Brun Passot developed in late 1989 an advanced EDI application through which it also electronically sent product files, delivery status reports, purchase quotes, shipping notices, invoices as well as payments and related bank details (see Exhibit 3). However, a hard copy of each invoice was generated for archival purposes. According to Monique Coupaud, Manager of the EDI Project at Brun Passot: 'We still print our invoices on paper, because electronic invoices are not yet recognized by the [French] judicial system.'

In late 1989, the French subsidiary of Digital Equipment Corporation (DEC) was the first Brun Passot customer to use the advanced EDI application.[14] Shortly after this pioneering implementation, other large customers connected to the system, including Electricité de France, Elf Aquitaine, Péchiney, Matra and Spie Batignolles.

The EDI linkage between Brun Passot and its customers was made via a value-added network (VAN),[15] France Télécom's ATLAS 400. Olivier Figon said:

> VANs are best suited when you deal [electronically] with hundreds of business partners. They have good security since you don't 'enter' the computer systems of your partners. You leave messages for your customers in an [electronic] mail box from which you also retrieve messages sent to you.[16]

Establishing an EDI link between a customer purchasing department and Brun Passot's order entry information system requires commitment and trust from both sides as well as a good understanding of the customer operating procedures. Jean-Philippe Passot explained:

> In a business as banal as that of office supplies, you tend to get a lot of what I call flirtation between big companies and their suppliers. With EDI, you need the commitment of true love. Before we set up an EDI link with one of our customers, we study their logistics for as long as a year. This requires trust and openness from both parties. In the end, we know their supply patterns better than they do ... In order that the system really takes root in major companies, we set up a real partnership with the Computing Department as well as the Purchasing and Finance Divisions of our customers. This means that the system is integrated into the client company so it can evolve while taking into account the future needs of the users.[17]

Organizational/business changes induced by EDI at Brun Passot

Three actions by Brun Passot top management helped diffuse customers' adoption of the telepurchasing applications while building internal commitment. These actions, which also led to some organizational changes inside the company, were:

- *Creating in 1989 a new marketing unit* exclusively in charge of promoting the diffusion of SICLAD and in particular its Numéris version. This unit, which had three full-time members, had been participating in a variety of fairs and industry shows throughout France, hence helping the company salesforce.
- *Establishing in 1990 a new financial bonus* to reward each salesperson who would convince a customer to adopt the basic EDI system (SICLAD) or the advanced one. The bonus was paid in addition to the already existing financial reward for winning new customers.
- *Offering SICLAD free of charge*: Brun Passot top management believed that their business was to sell office supplies not computer software and that by giving the software and its related services (training, update, maintenance) for free, the company could attract some new customers.

Over a two-year period (from September 1990 to September 1992), the number of corporate SICLAD users drastically increased, from 15 to almost 100. Moreover, all the new large customers[18] have adopted either SICLAD (80 implementations) or the

14 It was also the first EDI experience of this nature for the French subsidiary of DEC.

15 VAN (value-added network) is a network that provides additional value to basic leased lines. It connects computers and provides new services such as electronic mail, facsimile transmission, and enhanced terminal-to-computer communications.

16 Exchanged messages between the sender and the receiver were on the EDIFACT format (EDIFACT – Electronic Data Interchange For Administration, Commerce and Transport – is an international EDI standard suggested by the United Nations).

17 'Electronic documentation offers greater efficiency', *International Herald Tribune*, 14 March, 1991.

18 Large customers account for about 90% of Brun Passot client base.

advanced EDI service (seven implementations). Olivier Figon said:

> The larger number of SICLAD implementations was due to any of three factors. First, those companies [who adopted SICLAD] didn't have the required computer equipment for the advanced EDI service. Second, they were in the process of restructuring their information systems and they didn't want to add a new major operation. Or, third, they found the investment [required for the advanced EDI service] too heavy.

The advanced EDI service had also affected the organizational relationship of Brun Passot with some of its customers, especially the large ones. Olivier Figon explained:

> We became in 1990 the single supplier of office products to DEC France. This evolution in the relationship with our large customers is quite typical. It also happened with Péchiney in Grenoble and Matra Espace in Toulouse.

However, the scale of this success was rather limited. Olivier Figon added:

> Some customers, who have been using SICLAD, thought they should not deal with only one supplier. I find this nonsense. There is nothing strategic in [products such as] pencils, erasers, paper, staples and pens.

Investment in telepurchasing and resulting benefits for Brun Passot

For Brun Passot, the initial investment made for Bureautel and SICLAD amounted to a total of FF250 000 (FF150 000 for acquiring additional hardware to the existing large computers[19] and FF100 000 for developing the software). Subsequent investment to purchase microcomputers as well as to use EDIFACT and Numéris amounted to FF300 000. Maintenance costs reach approximately FF100 000 per year, an expense covered by the FF280 monthly subscription fee to the system that only Bureautel users pay.

The return on this investment became visible rapidly. In 1984, Bureautel contributed 2% (or FF4.5 million) to total turnover with 18 000 electronic orders processed, a figure that reached 22% (or FF27 million) in 1988, corresponding to a volume of 180 000 electronic orders. In early 1991, the contribution of all three telepurchasing applications reached about 50% of total turnover[20] or a value of approximately FF120 million, with Bureautel contributing FF41 million, SICLAD FF28 million and the advanced EDI application FF44 million. Brun Passot's management thought that, although the contribution of Bureautel reached a ceiling, that of SICLAD and especially the advanced EDI application would continue to increase over the next several years.

Moreover, the introduction of the telepurchasing applications at Brun Passot simplified the supply procedure and the related administrative work. This freed up 25 people to do more sales and customer visits. Telepurchasing also enabled the company to predict more accurately customer needs and, consequently, to have a better idea of what goods to order from the wholesalers and when it should be done. This improvement led to faster stock rotations (from 9 times in 1977 to 11 times in 1983 to 16 times in 1989) and, therefore, to reduced inventory management costs by 7%.

Qualitative benefits were also achieved. The telepurchasing applications enabled Brun Passot to differentiate itself from the competition by first establishing Brun Passot as an innovative user of new technologies and then by sustaining this advantage over time through the continuous enhancement of these applications. Jean-Philippe Passot said:

> The development of our telepurchasing service has helped improve the image of our company. It has made for faithful clients, and at the same time, helped us improve our productivity.

Moreover, the videotex- and EDI-based offerings allowed Brun Passot not only to provide a quality service to its customers but also to view its relationship with them differently. Jean-Philippe Passot explained:

> The development of this type of service represents the archetype of a new relationship that a company can establish with its suppliers. The service aspect becomes the basic component of a partnership between the two parties, as much because of increased productivity as due to the methods and culture it introduces. In this way, the 'goods' are relegated to their proper position, [that of] a qualified, quantified, regulated and controlled flow of physical objects.

---

19 The telepurchasing applications run on a PRIME 6350 computer (with a processing power of 10 MIPS), connected locally to a VAX 3400 (having 4.5 MIPS) and remotely to five other PRIME computers. There are 150 terminals, local and distant, connected to the network, as well as over 1000 videotex terminals.

20 The remaining contribution comes from sales made through the traditional modes (i.e. mail, telephone and fax).

Customers' use of telepurchasing and resulting benefits

Today, Brun Passot's telepurchasing applications are used by 1120 customers who connect to the system on average 400 times every day (approximately 10000 times each month) for a duration of about 7 minutes per connection. The applications are mainly used for placing orders (78% of the traffic), but also for generating control reports (8%), sending e-mail messages (8%) and getting cash flow statements (6%).

Brun Passot claims that, based on a survey of 50 of its customers,[21] its telepurchasing services can save companies 20 to 60% of their present office supplies budget.[22] Compared to the traditional paper-based procedure, these services decrease the lead time by two to four days and reduce the rate of errors (due to re-keying the information contained in the paper documents) by a factor of five.[23]

Exhibit 4 shows costs incurred by Brun Passot's customers through the four different ways of acquiring office supplies: Economat (which refers to the traditional paper-based method), Bureautel, SICLAD and the advanced EDI application. These costs are related to a purchase value of FF2200 and are given for each associated function, i.e. purchasing, storing, distribution and management accounting. The costs of the EDI acquisition method are only a small fraction of the corresponding Economat costs.

Exhibit 4 Costs of office supplies for customers based on four purchasing methods
(for a purchase value of FF2200)

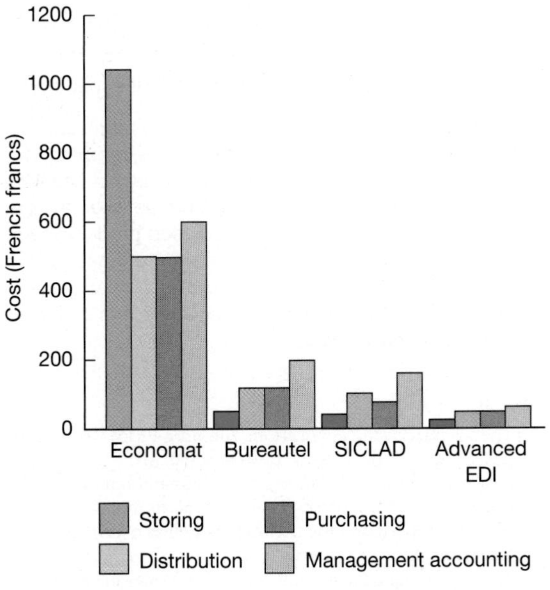

Source: Brun Passot.

Users' perspective on SICLAD

Customers are convinced of the benefits of adopting the telepurchasing applications. For example, COGEMA (Compagnie Générale des Matières Atomiques), which is located in Vélizy (outside Paris), has for the last two years been using the simplest version of SICLAD which operates on a stand-alone PC station. Mr Maslard, a manager in the Purchasing Department of COGEMA, said:

> My goal vis-à-vis my internal customers was to offer them a good, fast service by means of a simple procedure. I realized that I needed a PC-based system [for telepurchasing] and Brun Passot had the best one [available] on the market.

After an eight-month period, during which Mr Maslard discussed the telepurchasing idea with the company management, SICLAD was adopted and the system smoothly implemented. Today, his 700 internal 'customers', located at 72 delivery points, submit their orders of office supplies to him on a paper-based document. He then keys these orders in the PC and forwards them through SICLAD to Brun Passot. Mr Maslard said:

> The investment was very minimal: FF2500 to buy a modem for my PC and about FF240 per year to pay for telephone charges. But every year we save 30 to 40% of the cost of [our previous] manual procedure.

The savings are due to the reduction of inventory and the elimination of one staff position as well as mailing costs. Aware of the additional benefits to be gained from eliminating the paper-based documents filled by the internal users, COGEMA decided to implement the network version of SICLAD by late 1993. Mr Maslard explained:

> I can't do it before then. Connecting all users' PCs to my PC [which SICLAD runs on] requires using the internal phone exchange and installing a modem on each PC. This would be very costly. We preferred to wait till the internal PC network is implemented.

---

21 Brun Passot commissioned in 1989 a French business school, the Ecole Supérieure de Commerce de Lyon, to conduct this survey. The latter was based on a mail questionnaire which, in some cases, was followed up by telephone interviews.

22 '*Une Entreprise, Une Application Télétel*, France Télécom, February 1990, No. 19.

23 Ibid.

Matra Espace, an aeronautics company employing 2000 people and with headquarters in Toulouse, installed the network version of SICLAD. The company, which purchases office supplies worth FF2 million from Brun Passot annually, has been using SICLAD as part of its new purchasing procedure. Throughout the week, secretaries key in their office supplies orders on the company computer network. On Friday, the purchasing manager reviews these orders and then transmits approved orders to the Brun Passot server. The following Tuesday, Brun Passot delivers the ordered products to the company offices. According to Mr Boutty a purchasing manager at Matra Espace:

> The benefits have been tremendous. We have been saving FF700 000 to FF800 000 per year since we adopted SICLAD. It is due to the reduction of personnel [needed] to prepare the paper-based documents and to the elimination of xeroxing and mailing costs as well as following up, by phone or fax, on the orders we placed ... The statistics that we get from SICLAD have been very helpful. Before we were in the dark. We didn't know what had been expended. We couldn't know.

For Matra Espace, in order to set up SICLAD the only significant investment made was in management time to hold a series of meetings. Hardware was not an issue due to the highly computerized corporate environment. Although the conversion to SICLAD went smoothly and a training programme was given, a few secretaries (about two in ten) who were used to the old manual procedure had some difficulty in adjusting to the new computerized system. In the summer of 1993, the Toulouse division of Matra Espace started using the advanced EDI application of Brun Passot, now its single supplier of office products.

The successful experience of the Toulouse division of Matra Espace with Brun Passot has attracted other divisions of the company. Matra Vélizy has recently adopted SICLAD and other companies of the Matra Group are considering switching from their current supplier (who uses the traditional, paper-based approach) to Brun Passot.

Users' perspective on the advanced EDI application

The research centre of Péchiney, a major chemicals company, employs 400 people in its Grenoble offices. A pilot installation of Brun Passot's advanced EDI application was set up over a 18-month period; then the use of the system to the entire centre was generalized. Mr Bouchailler Head of the Purchasing Department, explained:

> Due to the nature of our work and the profile of our employees who are mainly engineers and technicians, we are big users of office products. A lot of work was needed to acquire and manage these low-priced products; we call it here the 80–20 rule. I suggested to the management that they adopt a system like Brun Passot's so we can make users responsible for their purchases.

Today, purchasing of office supplies is decentralized at Péchiney with each department managing its own budget. Once a week, each department secretary looks up the Brun Passot's catalogue on their computer screen, keys in the products to order, and transmits them via the EDI system to Brun Passot. The latter delivers the ordered products to each requesting department. Mr Bouchailler added:

> The required [EDI] investment was small, but we have significantly reduced our overall [office supplies] budget. There aren't any more misuses or abuses such as 'the start of schools' phenomenon. We have made significant time savings since everything is now done directly between Brun Passot and the final user without going through us [the Purchasing Department]. The system works well and our [internal] customers like it.

Péchiney stopped acquiring office products from the small suppliers it used to deal with and now does all its business with Brun Passot. However, the company does not think that the EDI system caused a 'lock-in' effect vis-à-vis Brun Passot. Mr Bouchailler said: 'We will keep using EDI but we are totally independent of any supplier. We can easily switch to other players in the market, to Guilbert or Gaspard if we want to.'

The issue of customer independence/lock-in has been central to the on-going debate at Brun Passot. Some managers prefer to 'push' SICLAD further because they think the proprietary nature of this software would lock-in customers. Other managers favour diffusing the advanced EDI application because of the additional capabilities and enhanced customer service it provides.

DEC France, another EDI user with Brun Passot, has an annual volume of 8000 orders, averaging a value of FF700 per order. These orders total about 60 000 item lines generated from over 1 000 internal departments within DEC France. In the past, four paper-based documents were generated per order:

the purchase order, the receipt acknowledgement, the shipping notice and the invoice. The associated procedure was error-prone (due to re-keying the data), costly and time consuming. Since October 1989, about 1 100 terminals located in 24 sites within DEC France have been connected through the company network to Brun Passot's server. Through these terminals, users place their office supplies orders in an autonomous yet controlled manner, without having to go through a centralized purchasing department.

According to a manager at DEC France headquarters in Evry, 'We have achieved a time saving of 8–12 days for processing an order. It corresponds to a gain of FF400 000 to FF700 000 per year.'

Since 1 January 1990, Brun Passot delivers office products to all the 24 sites of DEC France.

Brun Passot guarantees delivery of the ordered products to the customer premises within 48 hours of receipt of the electronic purchase order. This factor allowed Spie-Batignolles, a major construction company employing 3500 people, to go one step further than DEC France and the other customers. It decided to abolish its FF2 million stock of office supplies, which required ten full-time employees to manage. Since then, Brun Passot delivers three to four tons of products daily to Spie-Batignolles.

Facilitators and barriers to the use and diffusion of the EDI applications

Several facilitators and barriers helped/hindered the development, use and diffusion of Brun Passot's telepurchasing applications.

Facilitators

Some of the facilitators were due to a clear business strategy and sound management decisions; others were the result of good timing and luck. These were:

- *The perception of telepurchasing and EDI as the core of a business strategy* and not just an IT project. Jean-Philippe Passot said:

  > From a technological perspective, there is nothing exceptional about EDI. The real value that we add is our know-how and experience. We had to go through a 'cultural revolution' ourselves and to adjust our marketing approach [to the use of the technology].[24]

- *The long-term commitment and involvement of Brun Passot management*: Jean-Philippe Passot, the 39-year-old Deputy General Manager with a background in Law and Management, has been a fervent champion of the telepurchasing projects since he joined the company in 1980. For example, he was the key sponsor of these projects at Executive Committee meetings, defending them and winning approval for their development and funding.
- *The strong financial support of IT activities at Brun Passot*: the corporate IT budget over the years has been between 4% and 5% of total turnover, a figure that is double the average IT budget in the industry.
- *A 'motivated' organizational environment* for developing the EDI applications, due to the already available Bureautel service. Moreover, SICLAD helped launch the advanced EDI application. Olivier Figon said, 'SICLAD was an intermediate step. For us, it was a springboard to [reach out to] some of our large customers.'
- *The availablity of new technologies* (such as TRANSPAC, Numéris and ATLAS 400) developed by a public third-party (France Télécom). This factor has made the development of SICLAD and the advanced EDI application easy, fast and quite inexpensive.
- *The adoption by Brun Passot of an evolutionary approach* to allow for future enhancement and growth of its inter-organizational relationship.
- *A strong business pull* (as opposed to a technology push) at the very start and throughout the development of all the telepurchasing applications. This pull came mainly from some large customers who believed in the benefits of establishing an electronic link with Brun Passot.
- *The close interaction with customers* to define the 'what, where, when and how' of the product supply chain so that both customer and supplier can benefit from the added value; also *customers' reactions* to a promising tool that simplifies procedures and reduces time and cost.
- *Competitors' late development of telepurchasing*: the other major players in the French office supplies market already have their own Bureautel-like system but not yet an EDI-based service. Guilbert,

24 Translated from an interview to *Décision Micro*, No. 68, 27 January 1992.

the market leader, has just developed a SICLAD-like system with the help of a software company; however, it has not really attracted customers. Mr Maslard, from COGEMA, said, 'I looked at their system; it's very good. But I won't take it because Guilbert sells it for FF55 000; it runs only on a 486-PC and requires strong technical knowledge.'

Barriers

There were only a few barriers to the use and diffusion of Brun Passot's EDI applications. These were:

- *The rapid success of Bureautel* (i.e. its wide adoption by customers and its rapid contribution to Brun Passot's total turnover) constituted a barrier for the diffusion of SICLAD and the advanced EDI application.
- *The Brun Passot decision to keep offering the Bureautel service* after introducing both SICLAD and the advanced EDI application. The rationale for this decision was keeping customers, who had a small transactions volume and who were especially sensitive to costs, for whom Bureautel was best suited.
- *The relatively weak bargaining power of Brun Passot* vis-à-vis its customers due to the non-strategic nature of the products it markets.
- *The relatively heavy investment needed on the customer side* to use the advanced EDI application.

Going beyond the 'basic' use of EDI

Brun Passot has already started leveraging its EDI infrastructure through several on-going projects. As reflected in an internal document, the company intends to use EDI as the 'Trojan horse' for further growth.

> At Brun Passot, EDI spells the future. It is 'paper-less trading' relying on 'people-less administration' ... The beauty of these [EDI] applications is that they need not be confined to the procurement of office supplies, but can be developed to encompass all purchasing undertaken by the company.

Establishing EDI links with wholesalers

Brun Passot has started extending its information system backwards to the wholesalers in order to get access to a more diversified product offering (from the current 12 000 to 120 000 products). Both parties would benefit from this electronic linkage since Brun Passot could increase the products penetration rate with its customers. Moreover, a just-in-times (JIT) purchasing system can generate savings (due to reduced inventories) for both sides.

Operationally, the JIT purchasing system is used as follows. Due to its strong knowledge of the nature and quantity of products its customers order, Brun Passot needs to send, for replenishment purposes, electronic orders to its wholesalers only once a week. In some rare cases where a customer requests an exceptional quantity of products, Brun Passot places right away an urgent order with its wholesaler(s) without waiting for the regular weekend consolidation. Jean-Philippe Passot said:

> We aim, by the end of 1992, to do 80% of our transactions with wholesalers through EDI. We are considering setting up an electronic link with a supplier as an opportunity to assess its business performance in terms of logistics costs, quickness of delivery, and quality of service. In some cases, this assessment led us to stop doing business with some of our traditional suppliers.

Rerouting

For Brun Passot, rerouting is a natural extension to its present telepurchasing capabilities. The idea consists of setting up 'electronic bridges' using TRANSPAC or Minitel which would allow customers to access, through a single connection to the Brun Passot network, different servers related to a given market. For example, a user connected to one of Brun Passot telepurchasing applications and requesting some information on product lines (e.g. those of 3M France) that Brun Passot markets, gets automatically rerouted to the server of that company. Rerouting takes place while customers are still logged on to the Brun Passot system; once they have completed all enquiries about those product lines, they get disconnected from the host server and taken back to the original telepurchasing application.[25] This new capability alleviates Brun Passot from the task of having to include such data on its server.

Offering complementary products

Another planned enhancement consists of providing access to products marketed by other firms which are complementary rather than competitive with Brun

25 Rerouting can be thought of as a multi-windowing facility through which, for example, a software package gets called upon or executed from an already activated application.

Passot's. Examples of such products include office furniture and cleaning materials. This will allow Brun Passot to extend its telepurchasing applications into a broader electronic market place.

EDI expertise as a product

The availability in France of a large diversified telecommunications network[26] allows many companies to install or to enhance inter-company electronic communication through EDI. However, many suppliers are PMF that often lack the financial basis and the technical expertise necessary for implementing EDI systems. Having been a pioneer and an innovative user of telepurchasing over the last decade, Brun Passot has decided to leverage its expertise in this area through SATELITE, a new subsidiary set up to offer services in the development and implementation of EDI systems. Jean-Philippe Passot said, 'We have moved from the business of distributing office supplies to that of a service provider in this [industry] sector'.[27]

Diversifying EDI capabilities

Brun Passot also intends to diversify its EDI capabilities by offering 'financial EDI' applications. This automation would eliminate the costs of banking transactions for both customers and suppliers. Jean-Philippe Passot explained:

> It makes no sense to separate the commercial and physical exchange of documents from the financial payment. Once [business] partners communicate with each other using the same mode, e.g. EDIFACT, they can process all their transactions operations. A supply [of goods] is not completed unless [its related] accounts are updated. The administrative work of a transaction has its financial aspects as well.

Business plans for the evolving single European market

The advent of the single European market

The single European market, established by the 12 EC nations and born on 1 January 1993, consisted of 344 million consumers, which is 50% more than in the USA, and has the potential to grow even larger. Although the formation of this $4-trillion market seems inevitable and beneficial to the European economy, full implementation is being delayed because of many remaining fiscal (taxation policy), legal (antitrust law), monetary (single EC currency) and operational problems (e.g. passport controls). Nevertheless, the elimination of customs and all other barriers that prevent the free flow of goods and capital has already started and many companies have prepared themselves for increasing competition as new players (both European and non-European) enter or expand their operations in the EC market. Preparations made in anticipation of 1993 resulted in major investments in Europe and a wave of corporate restructuring and mergers within those industries most directly affected, such as banking, insurance, and airlines.

Restructuring of the office supplies market

In the office supplies market and in anticipation of the 1993 event, some American companies which had already established themselves in England (such as Basic Net) as well as some British and German firms (e.g. Spicers and Herlitz respectively) made plans to expand their operations in Europe. Due to the threat such a move represents to the market share of French companies and in order to create a barrier for foreign penetration, some alliances and acquisitions have already taken place. For example, Brun Passot merged with Saci, another distributor of office supplies with similar market share. The new larger group, called Groupe FIDUCIAL, aims at increasing profitability margins by benefiting from economies of scale, strengthening bargaining power vis-à-vis wholesalers and customers, as well as further leveraging Brun Passot telepurchasing applications.

Brun Passot plan for European expansion

Brun Passot has taken several steps towards expanding its geographical coverage to other European markets. First, it developed a multilingual (English and Spanish, in addition to French) version of its telepurchasing applications that uses the X.25 packet switched networks already available in several EC member states. This new application will help provide an integrated service to national as well as

---

26 Industry analysts consider the French telecommunications system better than that in other Western countries. This is due to the availability of a fully digitized telephone network as well as of a nationwide videotex, ISDN and packet-switched networks.

27 Translated from an interview to *L'Usine Nouvelle*, No. 2327-2328, 29 August 1991.

pan-European corporate customers. Jean-Philippe Passot said:

> Salespeople have some difficulty in selling in foreign markets due to linguistic and cultural differences. With our telepurchasing applications, we will be able to talk in a language that our international customers can understand, that of convenience, ease of use and savings.

Second, it approached some of its multinational customers who have expressed their interest in reducing the number of suppliers they are dealing with across Europe. Brun Passot plans to start its European operations with DEC, who had decided, by the end of 1993, to centralize on a single computer all the purchase requests generated at its different European subsidiaries. The information system residing on this computer would then select, based on the geographic location of the requesting party, the best suited supplier to provide the goods.

Brun Passot considers 'winning' the European subsidiaries of its present multinational customers as a good business opportunity for quick penetration of the single European market. Among management plans to implement the geographical coverage expansion are acquiring or joint venturing with some national companies as well as setting up some distribution centres near potential new European customers. The challenge for Brun Passot is to be able to move products around the continent as efficiently as it is done at present within the French borders and to offer bottom-line savings to the new European customers.

The different projects for leveraging its EDI infrastructure coupled with the future business trends mentioned above show the multi-faceted dimensions of Brun Passot's business strategy and market ambitions. In 1993 Jean-Philippe Passot said, 'By 1994, we want to achieve a turnover of FF800 million with 80% of our transactions electronically made and processed, and with only 15% of personnel increase ...'.

DISCUSSION QUESTIONS

1. What factors (business, managerial, technological) were critical for the successful development of the telepurchasing applications at Brun Passot?
2. If you were a Brun Passot manager, what would be your position with respect to the ongoing internal debate mentioned in the case (i.e. favouring 'pushing SICLAD' versus 'diffusing the advanced EDI application')?
3. Assess the success potential of Brun Passot's future projects for leveraging its EDI infrastructure, in particular the company's intent to broaden the business scope and geographical scale of its operations.

CASE STUDY 19

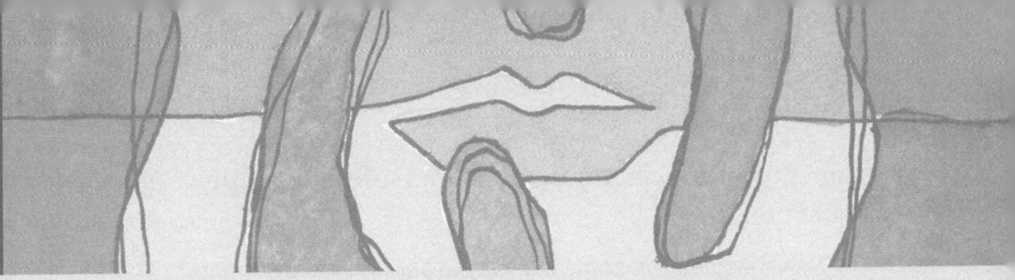

CitiusNet

The emergence of a global electronic market

Citius, Altius, Fortius[1]

Le Barron Pierre de Coubertin, founder of the modern Olympic Games in Athens in 1896

Looking out of his office window on the last Friday of summer 1992, Jean-Philippe Passot, Chief Executive Officer of Brun Passot, pondered the consequences of the critical decision he was about to make. Should he continue his successful office supplies distribution business or embark on a new venture to build a global electronic market place? As he watched the high-speed TGV trains enter the Lyon station, he debated whether the concept of business-to-business electronic commerce could attract corporate customers, or whether it was a risky technological adventure. Mr Passot felt that he was at a crossroads and he had to decide in what direction he wanted to go.

Background: the successful Brun Passot Inc.

Brun Passot, a 60-person strong family business, was founded in 1949 in Lyon, in the Rhône–Alps region of France. Initially the company specialized exclusively in the paper processing business. Then, in the 1970s, it diversified its activities into the distribution of office supplies and products related to computer and office equipment. As a law graduate, and after having gained some industry consulting experience, Jean-Philippe Passot joined his father at Brun Passot and, in 1980, became its Managing Director. By 1992, the company had several major customers such as Renault, Alcatel, Dassault, Péchiney, Crédit Lyonnais, Shell, Philips and Digital Equipment Corporation. In addition to industrial and service organizations, the customer list included several governmental agencies such as Electricité de France, France Télécom, the French Armed Forces and the national railroad company SNCF. With one central warehouse and 11 branches, Brun Passot offered 12 000 products to 6000 customers with a total of 15 000 delivery locations throughout France. The company's turnover in 1991 reached FF254 million[2] from a mere FF15 million in 1970.

In 1978, realizing the potential benefits of information technology (IT) to improve Brun Passot's business operations, top management decided to link electronically the corporate headquarters with the central warehouse. The real-time link between the company's sales offices and the central supply application, built on a network platform, significantly improved the order-to-delivery process. In 1983,

1 Meaning 'Faster, Higher, Stronger', the Latin motto of the 1992 Olympic Games that were held in Barcelona, Spain. The product names of CitiusNet Inc., a company created in October 1992, were inspired by this motto.

2 In January 1996, the average exchange rate between the French Franc and the US dollar was approximately \$1.00 = FF5.00.

This case was prepared by Han-Sheong Lai, Research Assistant, and Tawfik Jelassi, Professor of Information Systems. It is intended to be used a basis for class discussion rather than to illustrate either effective or ineffective handling of an administrative situation.

Financial support from the 1995 European Union–ASEAN Scholarship Programme and the British Council is gratefully acknowledged.

Brun Passot decided to differentiate its service from that of the competition by developing a telepurchasing application. The resulting system, Bureautel, became the first Minitel-based[3] telepurchasing service implemented in France. Quite revolutionary at that time, it allowed customers to connect to Brun Passot's computer system and enter their purchase orders electronically.

Despite the initial success of Bureautel and due to the growing business use of personal computers, some large customers pushed Brun Passot to develop a PC-based telepurchasing application. In 1985, a five-member team from Brun Passot developed SICLAD,[4] a PC-based EDI[5] software that featured data storage operations, a user-friendly interface (including colour display) and networking capability. Although superior to Bureautel, SICLAD had some shortcomings: it allowed customers to send electronic purchase orders and receive acknowledgment notices but not to receive product information or invoices electronically. In 1989, an advanced EDI application was developed; it allowed customers to access product files and get delivery status reports, purchase quotations, shipping notices as well as invoices. Moreover, it provided Brun Passot with the customer's payment-related details. The added functions have not only led several large companies (such as DEC France, Elf Aquitaine, Pechiney and Electricité de France) to adopt the new telepurchasing application, but they have made Brun Passot the exclusive provider of office supplies to some customers. The latter include the construction company, Spie-Batignolles, to which Brun Passot delivers four tons of office supplies daily.

Although the advanced EDI application met users' expectations, it still had a major drawback. Through it, customers were able to link up electronically with only a single supplier (i.e. Brun Passot). In fact, they needed a multi-supplier telepurchasing system that would allow them easily to place orders with different product/service providers.[6]

The birth of CitiusNet Inc.

> We want to develop an electronic market with multiple suppliers and purchasers in France, Europe and the world ... In 1995, our sales turnover was FF7.5 million. Our goal is to reach FF50 million by 1997.
>
> **Jean-Philippe Passot, Chief Executive Officer CitiusNet Inc.**

In October 1992, Jean-Philippe Passot created the new company, DDP & Associés,[7] with an initial capital of FF5.5 million and 15 employees. Most of the staff had an IT/telecommunications background; nine of them have been working in R&D and the rest were in charge of administration, marketing and sales. The underlying business objective of DDP was to extend the telepurchasing application developed at Brun Passot from a single supplier system to a multi-vendor electronic market. After a 12-month development period by a team of nine employees, DDP launched CITIUS as the first European platform for business-to-business electronic commerce. The new system aimed at positioning itself as a multi-supplier, multi-sectorial telepurchasing application. Recalling the origin of the business idea, Mr Passot said:

> The CITIUS concept was to set up a global, virtual market by electronically linking up different customers and suppliers through the same system. Depending on their business requirements, companies can interface with CITIUS even through their existing [internal] applications such as SAP.[8]

By late 1995, the company had expanded worldwide, with subsidiaries in the USA, Canada, Switzerland, Austria, the Netherlands, Belgium, Luxembourg,

---

3 Minitel is the national videotex platform which was developed by France Télécom and has been commercially available in France since 1982. For more information on Minitel, see the chapters 'Establishing a national IT infrastructure: the case of the French videotex system' and 'The technology of the Minitel system' in Tawfik Jelassi's book, *Competing through Information Technology: Strategy and Implementation*, London, Prentice Hall, 1994.

4 SICLAD stands for 'Système Informatisé de Commande Locale pour Approvisionnement Décentralisé'.

5 EDI stands for 'electronic data interchange' and refers to the direct exchange of data between computer applications (without human intervention in the process). With EDI, computer systems can exchange purchase orders, confirmation and other information, without the need for multiple input operations or correspondence via the post service.

6 For detailed background information on Brun Passot Inc., see the chapter on 'Competing through electronic data interchange at papeteries Brun Passot, or making paper passé' in Tawfik Jelassi's book, *Competing through Information Technology: Strategy and Implementation*, London, Prentice Hall, 1994.

7 In September 1995, the company changed its name from DDP & Associés to CitiusNet Inc. to reflect its main product name (CITIUS).

8 SAP stands for system application processing; it is also the name of the German company that markets it. It is a software product that supports company-wide business operations in an integrative way.

Exhibit 1 CitiusNet subsidiaries, January 1996

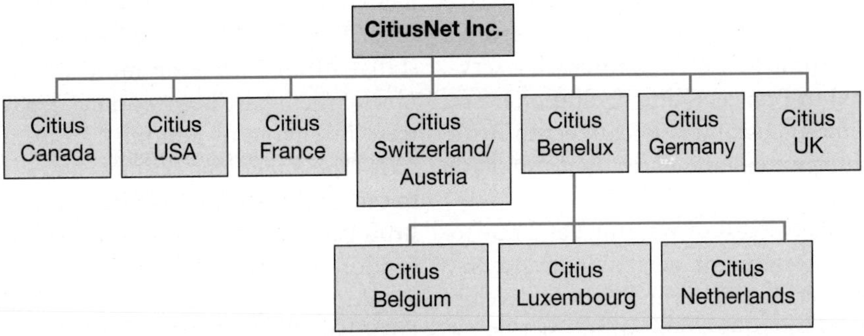

Germany and the UK (see Exhibit 1). CitiusNet in France is responsible for setting the overall business strategy, co-ordinating R&D activities world-wide and ensuring the inter-operability of the country-specific servers. CitiusNet international subsidiaries are in charge of the local marketing and sales as well as customer service activities.

CitiusNet's business applications

CitiusNet plays an electronic intermediation role between purchasers (corporate departments or end users within a company) and suppliers (such as manufacturers, wholesalers and distributors). It provides electronic access to a large number of products and services, and supports the different stages of a commercial transaction (from issuing a purchase order to settling the invoice). Typically, when a purchasing company joins CitiusNet, it brings with it its suppliers (or at least a subset of them) and the trading partners start doing business electronically. However, in some instances, CitiusNet plays the matchmaker between purchasers and suppliers.

Conceptually, the CitiusNet environment connects, through EDI, three main parties (see Exhibit 2): the purchaser, the CitiusNet server and the supplier. Purchasers place their orders through CitiusNet to the suppliers who then deliver the physical goods according to the specified time and destination. After receiving the invoice, the purchaser sends the payment electronically to the supplier through CitiusNet.[9] The CitiusNet platform consists of three components: CITIUS (the 'transaction processing' module), ALTIUS (the 'information provision' module) and FORTIUS (the 'financial settlement' module).

Exhibit 2 Purchaser/supplier relationship through CitiusNet

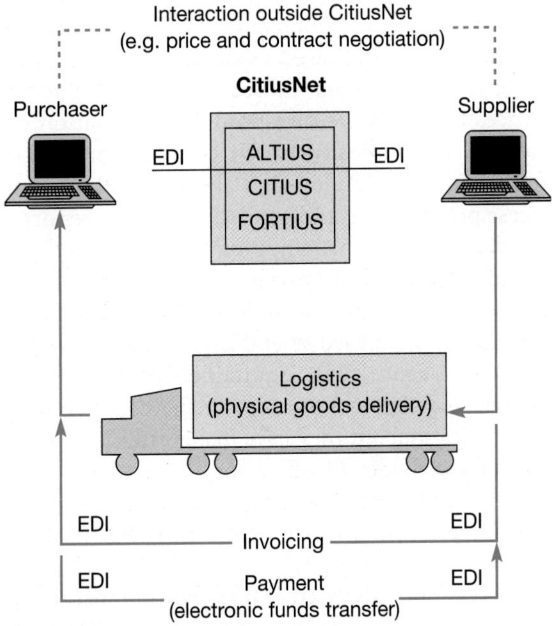

Source: Adapted from CitiusNet internal documents.

Functionally, the CitiusNet platform allows a supplier to become a purchaser and vice-versa, depending on the specific business situation. It supports different ways of channelling electronic purchase orders: end

9 This latter feature of electronic funds transfer was operational by mid-1996.

users (i.e. staff members) can send purchase orders directly to CITIUS, or, alternatively, first to their local (or corporate) purchasing department for consolidation and subsequent transmission to CITIUS (see Exhibit 3). Through ALTIUS, product catalogues can be structured in three different ways: public, sector-specific, or company-specific offerings. The public cluster allows any inter-company linkages, regardless of the business sector involved. The sector-specific cluster contains product information relevant to a particular business sector such as construction, health care or car manufacturing. The last cluster provides company-specific product information. The other module of CitiusNet, FORTIUS, facilitates the financial operations (such as invoice settlement) associated with commercial transactions.

Technically, CitiusNet provides a company with typical EDI functions such as the CITIUS purchasing application interface, the EDI message translation and the communications transfer (see Exhibit 4). The subsequent message transmission can take place through a telecommunications network or a value-added network (VAN). The format of commercial documents (such as purchase order, acknowledgment receipt, shipping notice and invoice) is standardized for both trading partners, thus preventing data inaccuracies and improving inter-company communications. Moreover, with the capability of converting the different EDI

Exhibit 3 Electronic linkages between CitiusNet and trading partners

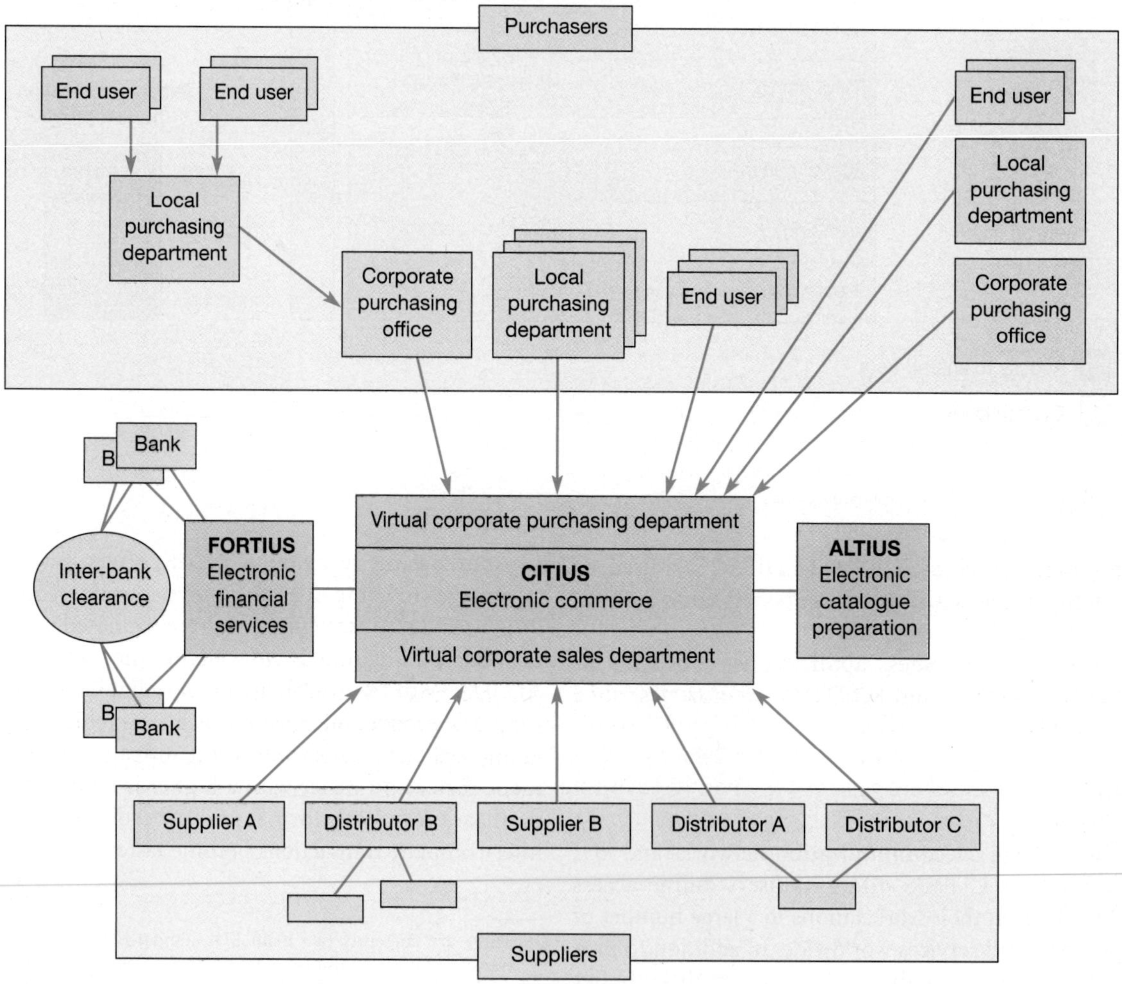

Source: Adapted from CitiusNet internal documents.

Exhibit 4 Functions of the CITIUS purchasing application

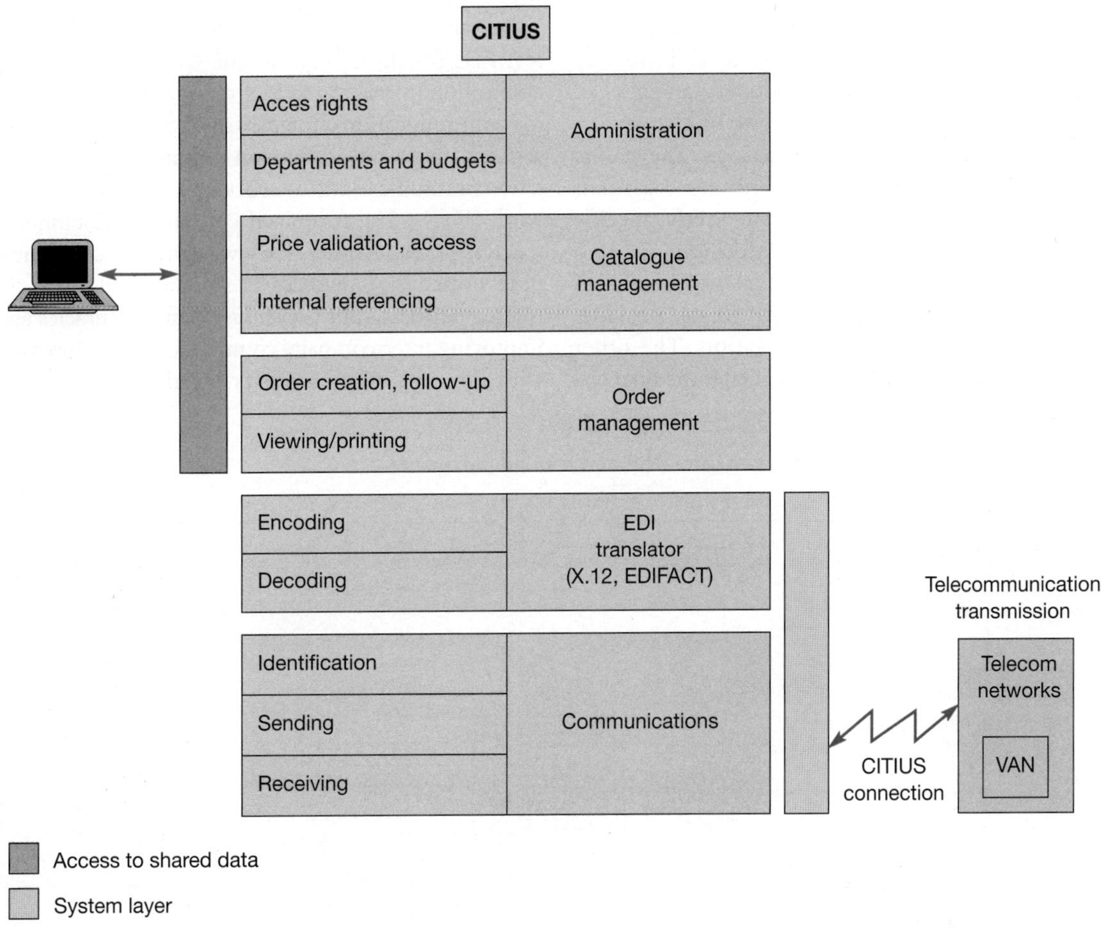

Source: Adapted from CitiusNet internal documents

standards (such as X.12 and EDIFACT)[10] used by trading partners, CitiusNet can be viewed as a multi-standard commercial platform.

CitiusNet's business applications, consisting of CITIUS, ALTIUS and FORTIUS, are now described in detail.

CITIUS

Using global telecommunication networks and EDI technology, CITIUS offers its users online access directly from their workstations to a large number of products and services worldwide. In addition to providing a new capability (i.e. the multi-supplier feature of CITIUS) and a more flexible approach to the purchasing function, CITIUS offers several advantages to companies. For purchasers, large and bulky product catalogues can be eliminated since product cataloguing is now maintained through ALTIUS. With the availability of an online display of suppliers' product information such as graphical diagrams and technical layouts, company purchases are made faster and easier with a higher level of standardization in both format and procedure. Hence inter-company transactions become faster and more

10 There are currently two main EDI standards used for the transfer of business information: ANSI X.12 (which is mainly used in North America) and EDIFACT (which is sponsored by the United Nations and used worldwide).

accurate. Product prices are automatically updated in the CITIUS network each time suppliers introduce price changes (due to, for example, price discounts).[11] As an electronic intermediator, CitiusNet converts EDI formats for each supplier and customer interface only once at the installation stage (all the necessary EDI formats and conversion capabilities are available in CITIUS).

The CITIUS interface module for purchasers, depicted in Exhibit 4, consists of the following components:

- *Administration*: management of users' access rights,[12] department/supplier links and approval rights, as well as setting budget limits (per department, user, purchase order or specific product).
- *Catalogue management*: browsing supplier catalogues, entering customer reference related to a supplier product, and validating article/price updates made by suppliers and transmitted through CITIUS.
- *Order management*: creating new purchase requests/orders and viewing historical purchase orders.
- *EDI translator*: encoding and decoding outgoing and incoming EDI messages respectively.
- *Communications*: identifying the document destination, dispatching purchase orders electronically to the CITIUS server, and receiving supplier-provided information (such as acknowledgment receipt of purchase orders, updated product prices, etc.).

ALTIUS

Upon joining CitiusNet, suppliers need to have their product catalogues converted (by ALTIUS) to an EDI format. The conversion task involves the creation of a supplier database and the corresponding electronic product catalogue, either from paper-based documents or from an existing electronic form. This conversion can be performed by importing product information either from a spreadsheet application or from the supplier's internal information system and, alternatively, by keying in product information to the ALTIUS application. The electronic product catalogue is customized for each purchaser based on the products they are interested in and the specific prices offered to them by the supplier.

In addition to creating product catalogues, ALTIUS manages supplier-provided updates such as adding new products, deleting obsolete ones and changing the value of some data items (e.g. product price). ALTIUS is also in charge of forwarding such data updates to purchasers and integrating them into their local database. Exhibit 5 shows a sample screen of suppliers' product categories made available to purchasers.

FORTIUS

FORTIUS handles the inter-organizational financial flows associated with the purchasing activity performed through CITIUS. The different steps involved in the commercial transaction (from ordering through payment) are shown in Exhibit 6. The sequence of these steps is as follows:

- The purchaser sends, through CITIUS, an electronic purchase order to the supplier.
- The supplier sends, via CITIUS, an acknowledgment receipt and subsequently a dispatch notice to the purchaser.
- The supplier delivers (physically) the ordered goods to the purchaser.
- The supplier transmits, via FORTIUS, the invoice to the purchaser.
- The purchaser sends, via CITIUS, a goods receipt notice to the supplier. (Note that this step could take place prior to invoicing.)
- The purchaser sends, via FORTIUS, a payment order to their bank (i.e. bank B) to pay the supplier a given amount on a specific date.
- Bank B sends, via FORTIUS, a remittance advice to the supplier notifying them of a forthcoming payment.
- Bank B makes the payment to the supplier's bank (i.e. bank A) through the inter-bank clearance network.
- Bank B sends, via FORTIUS, a debit advice to the purchaser.

11 Product catalogue information (with the exception of prices) is the same on the supplier, purchaser and CITIUS servers; any update is automatically replicated on all three sites.

12 The term 'user' is employed throughout the case in a generic sense to refer to an end-user, a manager, an administrator or a superviser. This sequencing reflects an increasing authority level within a purchasing company for approving purchase requests.

- Bank A sends, via FORTIUS, a credit advice to the supplier.

FORTIUS is quite a novel component of CitiusNet, offering features that are complementary to those of CITIUS. Jean-Philippe Passot said: 'An electronic market that doesn't handle the financial side of a commercial transaction cannot succeed in the future.'

Revenues and costs for trading partners

CitiusNet revenues are generated from the fees paid by the trading partners: a one-time entry fee, a monthly subscription fee and a transaction fee. The entry fee, which ranges from several hundred to a few thousand US dollars depends, for suppliers, on the size of the product catalogue and, for purchasers, on the number of workstations connected to CitiusNet.[13] This entry fee also covers the installation of the CitiusNet purchasing software (with a customized product catalogue) and training. The monthly subscription fee covers both maintenance of the server and management of the product catalogue. The transaction fee varies depending on the volume of commercial transactions conducted through CitiusNet.

As an example, a medium-sized purchasing company having 100 terminals connected to CitiusNet pays an entry fee of US$5000, a monthly fee of US$500 and a usage fee of US$1 per transaction.[14] Obviously, the above fees can be much higher for a

Exhibit 5 **Sample screen of product categories menu**

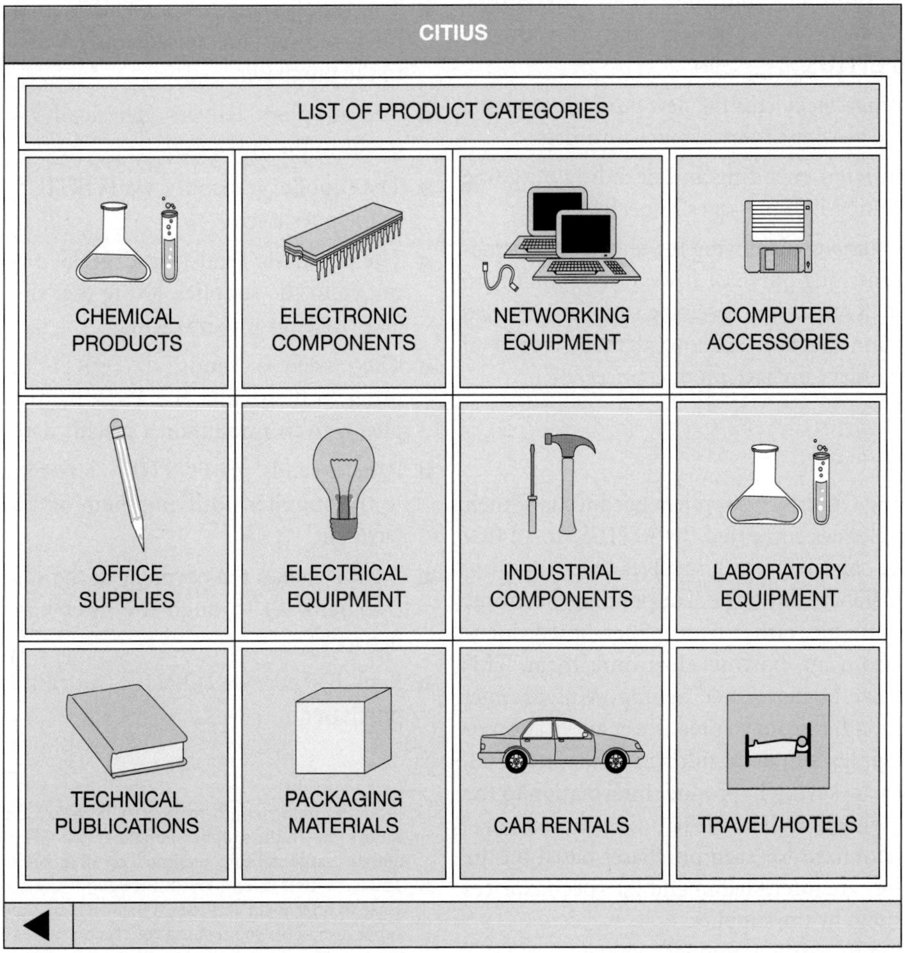

Source: Adapted from CitiusNet internal documents.

large purchasing company; for example, Rhône-Poulenc pays US$20 000 per month for its 10 000 terminals connected to CitiusNet.

For a small supplier, an entry fee of approximately US$1000 covers preparing the product catalogue in an EDI form and loading it on the CitiusNet server. A supplier also pays a monthly subscription fee ranging from US$100 to US$1000 and a $1 charge for every transaction conducted through CitiusNet.

Typical CitiusNet costs for a small-sized supplier and a medium-sized purchaser are shown in Table 1. The figures are based on the use of one PC for the supplier and a commercial volume of 100

Table 1 Typical CitiusNet costs

Cost element	*Purchaser ($)*	*Supplier ($)*
Entry fee (one-time fee)	5000	1000
Monthly subscription fee	500	400
Transaction fee	100	100
Total	*5600*	*1500*

13 The minimum technical requirement for a workstation to be connected to CitiusNet is a 486-chip PC with 4 megabytes of RAM (random access memory) and 5 megabytes of hard disk per 10 000 product items.

14 The transaction fee covers the whole procurement cycle from placing a purchase order to acknowledging payment.

Exhibit 6 CITIUS/FORTIUS: electronic commerce and financial intermediation

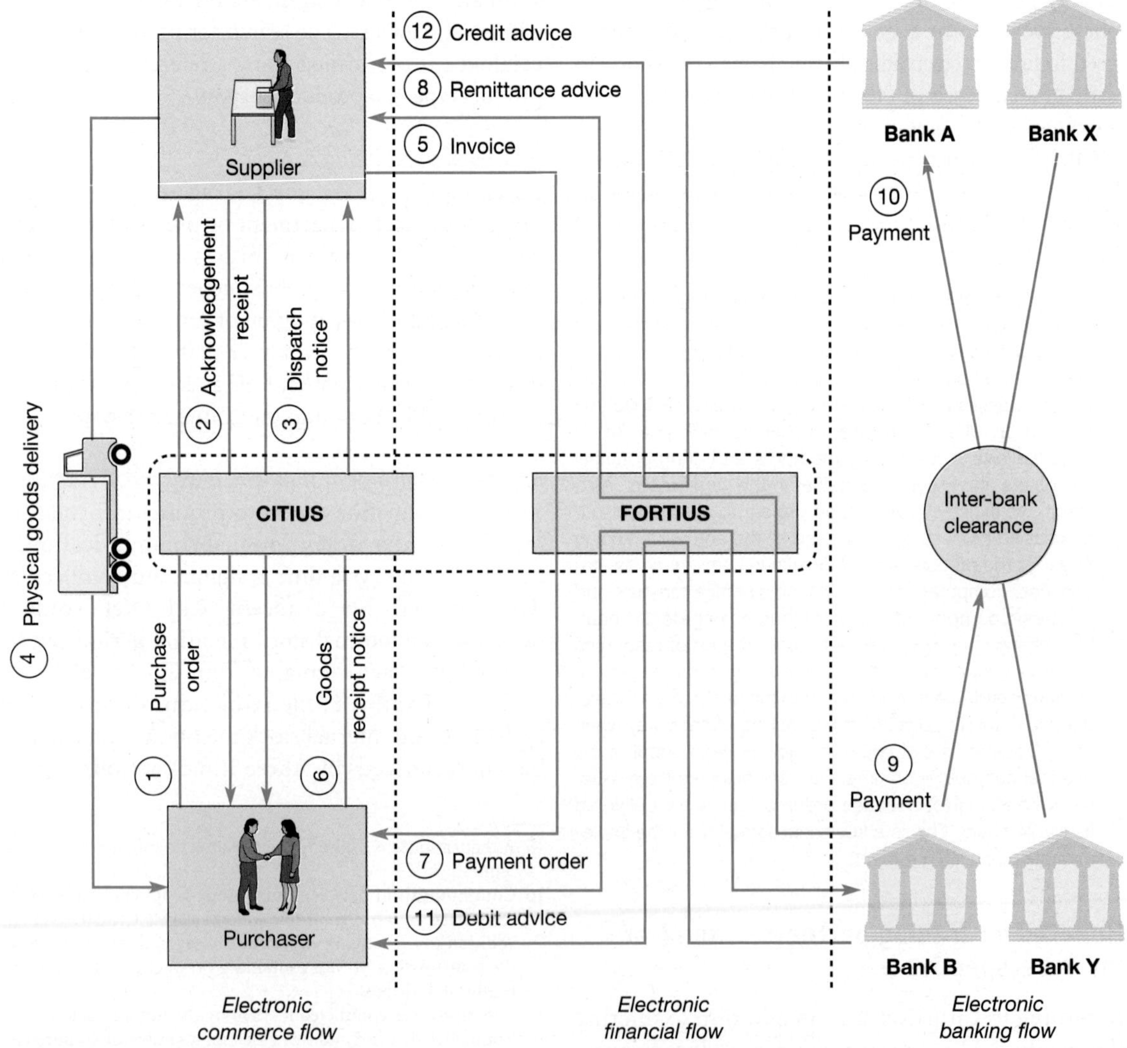

Source: Adapted from CitiusNet internal documents

transactions per month. For the purchaser, the figure assumes that 50 terminals are connected to CitiusNet and the commercial volume is also 100 transactions per month. It must be noted that the total costs shown in Table 1 represent only the charges incurred during the first month of CitiusNet usage, based on the aforementioned business assumptions.

Implementation issues

Implementation issues faced by CitiusNet include: (1) cultural differences in purchasing practices among customers; (2) the electronic conversion and maintenance of large product catalogues; and (3) the management of a variety of EDI standards already adopted by different trading partners. In some cases, the implementation phase proved to be even more challenging due to the need to link up electronically purchasers and suppliers with different levels of IT sophistication (i.e. 'high-tech', 'medium-tech' or 'low-tech').

Christian Kaermmerlen, Purchasing Director for Europe at Texas Instruments (a major user of CitiusNet), commented on the implementation of CitiusNet in France:

> We met Mr Passot in mid 1994 when he came to us with what he called a 'marvellous product'. My first reaction was: 'How many suppliers have you got [on the network]?' He said they had only two or three! When he visited suppliers, he was again asked: 'How many customers do you have on CITIUS?' The answer was almost the same. So we said: 'Let's take the bull by the horns and bring potential customers and suppliers together in the same room.' As a result, we initiated a very good project to re-engineer our purchasing process by eliminating all the non-value adding tasks for the procurement of low-value items (such as stationeries, computer accessories, small office furniture and electronic components). For the purchasing department, processing such procurement required a lot of resources and was costly and time-consuming. So the idea was to empower end-users by letting them place purchase orders, through CitiusNet, directly with suppliers. What is key when using CitiusNet is that you must pick the right supplier, the one that can deliver on time. Our requisitioners[15] are satisfied with CitiusNet because ordered goods are delivered within 24 hours. This is a key success factor for the implementation of such a system.

Benefits for trading partners: CitiusNet Inc.'s perspective

According to CitiusNet Inc., in addition to offering the traditional EDI benefits (such as reduced paperwork, faster processing, improved data accuracy and reduced inventory), the CitiusNet electronic commerce platform provides purchasers, suppliers and, potentially, banks the following benefits.

Benefits for purchasers

Access to multi-sectorial product databases

Purchasers can access multi-sectorial product databases (available in different languages) as opposed to mono-sectorial ones as is the case in traditional (point-to-point) EDI (see Exhibit 7). Purchasing costs can be reduced as a result of competitive bidding since product information from different suppliers is available through CitiusNet. Furthermore, corporate purchasing managers or local departments within a company can select suppliers for inclusion in their CitiusNet database. The search for products within a catalogue is performed using a reference number, a product type or a product category.

Improved purchasing control

Purchase orders are checked against pre-defined budgets for each department or user within a company. Moreover, purchase orders can be assigned a ceiling amount and a global budget can be set up for corporate purchases at different time periods (yearly, quarterly, monthly, weekly or daily). Jean-Philippe Passot said: 'Management feels at ease because all the controls can be built into the [CitiusNet] system.'

Shorter procurement time and lower stock retention

With faster on-line access to product information and better inter-organizational communication,[16] the purchasing cycle time is significantly reduced as demonstrated by a recent CitiusNet study.[17] Similarly, the internal stock retention period can be reduced by a factor ranging from three to eight. As shown in Exhibit 8, the reduction of purchasing cycle time and internal stock retention can generally be characterized by three time periods which

15 A requisitioner is typically the person who initiates a purchase request.

16 Communication between purchasers, suppliers and banks is supported by an e-mail-like system called CitiusDirect. In addition to exchanging electronic messages, this system allows the transmission of files containing product information and technical drawings.

17 This study was conducted in 1993 by the Ecole Supérieure de Commerce de Lyon and was based on a sample of 40 purchasing companies operating in France.

Exhibit 7 Traditional EDI and CitiusNet multi-sectorial platform

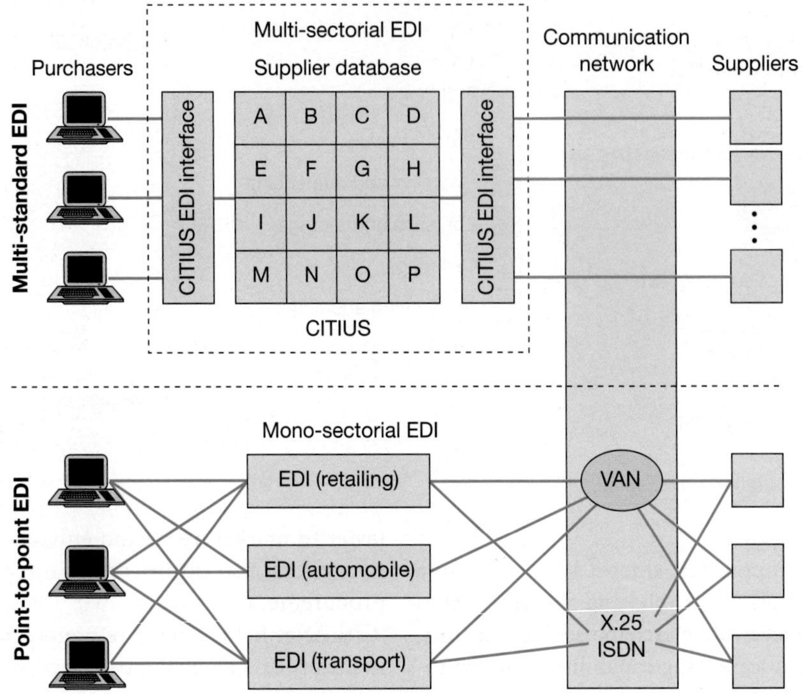

Source: Adapted from CitiusNet internal documents.

correspond to different levels of CitiusNet impact. These time periods are: (1) the first six months of CitiusNet introduction in a purchasing company, during which the impact is typically low to medium; (2) the second six-month period, during which a drastic reduction of cycle time and stock retention takes place and the impact of CitiusNet is very high; and (3) after one year of using CitiusNet within the company, when the impact of CitiusNet decreases and a plateau is reached.

Exhibit 8 Reduction in purchasing cycle time and stock retention time

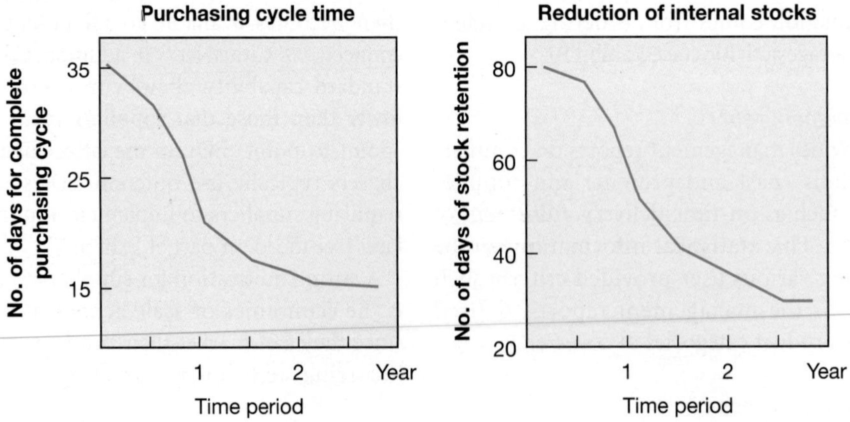

Source: Adapted from CitiusNet internal documents.

Exhibit 9 **Potential reduction of purchasing cycle costs with CitiusNet** (for a purchase order of US$1000)

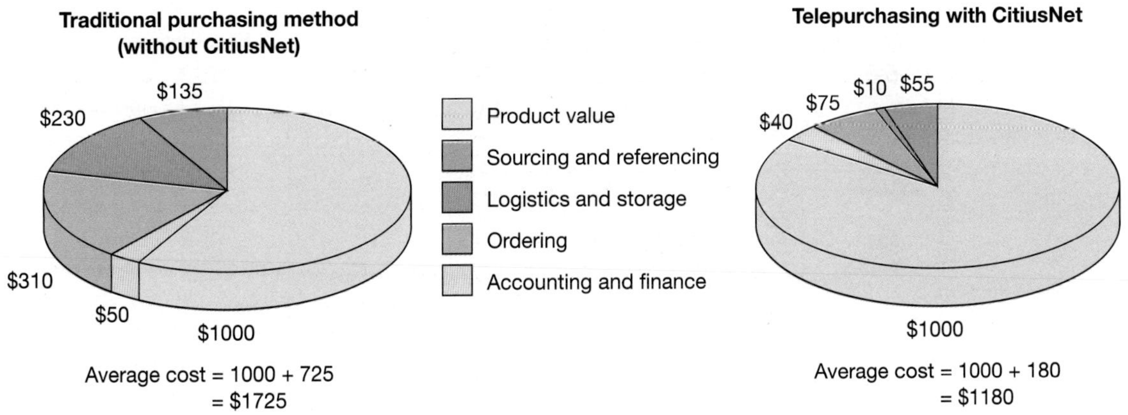

Source: Adapted from CitiusNet internal documents.

Empowered end-users

End-users feel empowered since CitiusNet allows them to perform all the purchasing functions from placing orders to receiving merchandise. Furthermore, a built-in budget monitoring capability allows management to control purchasing commitments (in amount terms), manage ceiling levels and consolidate summarized statistical information.

Reduced purchasing costs

The CitiusNet study mentioned above also revealed that administrative costs related to corporate purchasing can be reduced by 20% to 80%. For example, for a product worth US$1000, the total purchasing cost is reduced from US$725 when using the traditional (paper-based) purchasing method to US$180 with CitiusNet. The main cost reduction comes from ordering as well as logistics and storage activities (see Exhibit 9).

Timely management reports

CitiusNet provides management reports on commercial transactions (past and present) and supplier performance such as on-time delivery, fulfilment of the orders, etc. This statistical information can be produced using various user-provided criteria such as frequency of the management reports, desired level of detail, product categories to cover, etc.

Enhanced competitiveness

The electronic integration of buyers' and suppliers' value chains allows both trading partners to react faster to market needs and enhance their competitiveness. It also improves the inter-organizational procurement process. Mr Passot explained: 'CitiusNet helps clients re-engineer their procurement process by evaluating their business strategy and its supporting information systems.'

Benefits for suppliers

For suppliers, CitiusNet shortens the time-to-market and also provides access to new potential purchasers. Moreover, it handles the electronic interface and conversion between different application formats and EDI standards, a task which is often beyond the IT sophistication or financial means of small suppliers.

Furthermore, CitiusNet requires only a one-time EDI conversion of suppliers' product information which then becomes available to all potential purchasers connected to CitiusNet.[18] In addition, CitiusNet's multi-standard capability allows conversion costs that are lower than those that suppliers incur in traditional (point-to-point) EDI. In the latter environment, purchasers typically use different EDI standards, hence requiring suppliers to implement multiple EDI interfaces (see the lower part of Exhibit 7).

A strong motivation for suppliers to join CitiusNet is the economies of scale achieved by the network since they can market their products widely without incurring additional marketing investments. For

18 There is however an exception for the 'price' data item which is determined between the supplier and the individual purchaser.

example, in co-operation with the publishing company Hachette and the French Ministry of Industry, CitiusNet has developed CEDEVIN, which is a special online service for the pan-European wine market. Currently the number of vineyards that offer their products through CitiusNet is 14000, and is expected to reach 140000 vineyards across Europe. Mr Passot explained:

> As we establish more [CitiusNet] servers around the world, the business opportunities for suppliers are really becoming exponential. Just think how much leverage small enterprises, for example, could get from electronic commerce.

Potential benefit for banks

FORTIUS, as the financial intermediation component of CitiusNet, does not eliminate the traditional services that banks provide; on the contrary, it could offer them a new business opportunity. Once a purchaser instructs their bank to pay a given supplier on a specific date,[19] the bank could offer that supplier an earlier payment at a small interest. The risk involved for the bank is rather low since purchasers are typically large and reliable companies such as Texas Instruments, Rhône-Poulenc and GEC Alsthom. Hence, banks could become providers of electronic factoring services.

CitiusNet's growth through partnerships

Once the development of CITIUS was completed, CitiusNet Inc. started marketing its product in France and, through partnerships, abroad, with the aim of becoming a key player in the emerging market of electronic commerce. In May 1993, using commercially available telecommunications infrastructure, CITIUS was officially launched in France, hence becoming the first European inter-company platform for electronic commerce.

In December 1994, CitiusNet Inc. signed a contract with Bell Canada, a major Canadian telecommunications operator, allowing it to develop new CitiusNet servers in North America. Moreover, with the help of Bell Canada, the Federal Government of Canada and two provincial governments (Ontario and Quebec) selected CitiusNet as a platform for redesigning their purchasing process. The first applications included the procurement of spare car parts for the police department and of general purchases for 15 local prisons. In December 1995, through its partnership with the Canadian company Québécor Multimédia, Citius Canada extended its operations to the USA and Mexico.

At the end of 1994, CitiusNet Inc. was selected by the European Union as the telepurchasing platform to support its procurement function. In February 1995, CitiusNet Inc. was invited to make a presentation at the G7 Global Conference on the Information Highway which was held in Brussels (Belgium). In August 1995, CitiusNet Inc. formed a joint venture with France Telecom named CITIUS France with an initial capital of FF2.5 million[20] in which the French telecommunications company is responsible for marketing and sales. By late 1995, CitiusNet Inc. had signed similar contracts with companies in Switzerland, Austria, the Benelux countries (Belgium, Luxembourg and the Netherlands), as well as Italy and the UK.

In January 1996, CitiusNet customers in France included large organizations such as Rhône-Poulenc, GEC Alsthom, Texas Instruments France, Compagnie Bancaire and La Poste (the French postal authority). Moreover, 80% of French office supplies companies (mainly wholesalers and distributors) have joined CitiusNet. Jean-Philippe Passot commented:

> We had to prove ourselves in our home market to gain credibility abroad ... It's in a way like Dassault; if it can't sell its [military] jets to the French airforce, how can it hope to equip foreign armies?

Partners' and customers' perspectives

Until now, most of CitiusNet's customers and partners have been based in Europe. The latter are responsible for the marketing and sales of CitiusNet in their respective countries. Some of the most frequently cited benefits and drawbacks of CitiusNet are provided below.

Organizational impact

One of CitiusNet's business partners is Conexus Global Information (Germany) which is both a CitiusNet user and an R&D partner. It is currently developing technologies to connect CitiusNet to the

19 There is typically a credit period of two to three months for the purchaser to actually pay the supplier.

20 CITIUS France has an ownership structure of 72% for CitiusNet Inc. and 28% for France Télécom.

Internet and is also offering CitiusNet services in German-speaking countries such as Austria, Germany and Switzerland. Chief Executive Officer Hans U. Schmid said:

> CitiusNet's biggest benefit is its ability to extend the concept of lean production to organizational processes through the involvement of both suppliers and customers. That results in reduced costs, lower inventory and faster information exchange.

Advanced product features

For Mrs Van Rijbergen, who is from IN Connection and is a CitiusNet Partner in the Benelux countries, CitiusNet has overcome some major drawbacks of traditional EDI. First of all, the platform is flexible and supports multiple IT environments. For example, suppliers can easily accommodate, through CitiusNet, the various EDI standards used by their trading partners in different industries. This task can be complex and expensive with traditional EDI solutions. Secondly, CitiusNet has a strong product cataloguing capability to create and maintain catalogues at different geographical locations, a feature which is especially useful for multinational companies. Mrs Van Rijbergen said:

> Because of such advanced electronic commerce features, the response to CitiusNet in the Benelux has been very positive. In particular, chemicals companies, textile manufacturers and makers of electronic components are very interested in CitiusNet. Typically, users are mainly large multinationals which suffer from slow and expensive purchasing procedures. For them, CitiusNet provides a way to streamline the procurement process.

Budget control capability

CitiusNet allows different ways of enforcing management control over purchases. First, corporate purchasing departments can set an overall purchasing budget per product category for a given time period (yearly, quarterly, monthly, etc.). Second, management can allocate individual departments or users with a fixed budget for their purchases. Third, a ceiling on the total amount per purchase order can be defined. When pre-defined budget ceilings are reached, authorization is needed from higher management levels.

Reduced purchasing time

For Texas Instruments France, electronic catalogue solutions (such as CitiusNet) have significantly reduced the purchasing cycle time and improved the productivity level of non-strategic purchases. According to Mr Kaemmerlen, since the company no longer requires prior approval for purchasers of low-value items,[21] CitiusNet electronic catalogue and ordering capabilities have helped reduce the order processing time from an average of eight days with the traditional paper-based method to virtually zero (see Exhibits 10 and 11). Furthermore, a Texas Instruments study conducted in 1993 revealed that system costs for processing a line item internally within a purchase order decreased from US$15–20 to approximately US$1–2.[22] The total costs for a complete procurement cycle (from order request, approval, issuing of purchase order, receipt of goods to payment), including system costs, have dropped from $200 to $5.

Mr Kaemmerlen added:

> Now we have a cut-off time for sending electronic purchase orders [through CitiusNet] of 12.00 noon and physical goods delivery by our suppliers at 8.00 a.m. on the following day. So the cycle time is now even less than 24 hours! Prior to using CitiusNet, the traditional paper-based order-to-delivery time took approximately a week. That's a significant improvement ... From a purchaser's perspective, thanks to the multi-standard feature of CitiusNet, we only need one interface with the CITIUS server. Also the extensive product catalogue provides purchasers with much more choice for product sourcing. For suppliers, developing an electronic catalogue [with CitiusNet] is a one-time effort since it can be customized.[23] It is clear that the larger the number and geographical coverage of CitiusNet users [i.e. suppliers and purchasers] are, the higher the benefits of such a [electronic] commerce platform will be.

Texas Instruments France is currently considering the use of CitiusNet for strategic/higher-value items once FORTIUS becomes operational. At the same time, the company's worldwide headquarters are evaluating the adoption of CitiusNet as a global purchasing platform for non-strategic, low-value transactions.

Enhanced productivity

For José Drevon, corporate purchasing manager at LKR (a subsidiary of GEC Alsthom, with a turnover

21 This procedure was adopted by Texas Instruments France although CITIUS can support multiple levels of management approval.

22 System costs include computer processing, transmission, hardware and IT personnel costs.

23 The only data item in the catalogue that varies from one customer to another is the price column, which can only be accessed by the customer concerned.

Exhibit 10 Traditional procurement process

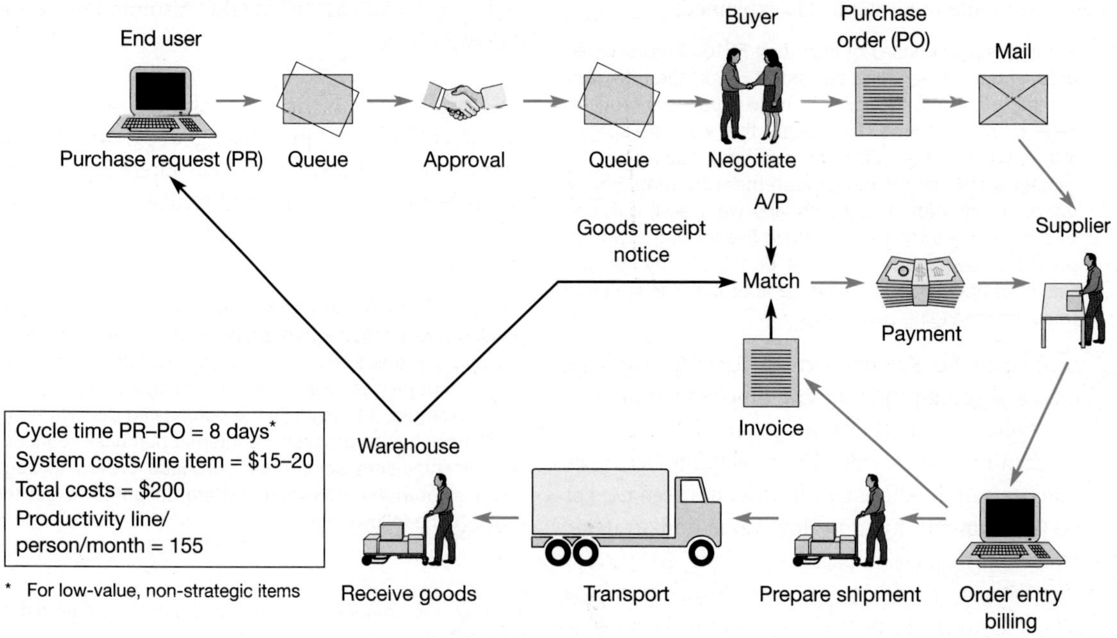

Source: Adapted from Texas Instruments (France) internal documents, January 1996.

Exhibit 11 Improvement achieved through electronic commerce at Texas Instruments, France

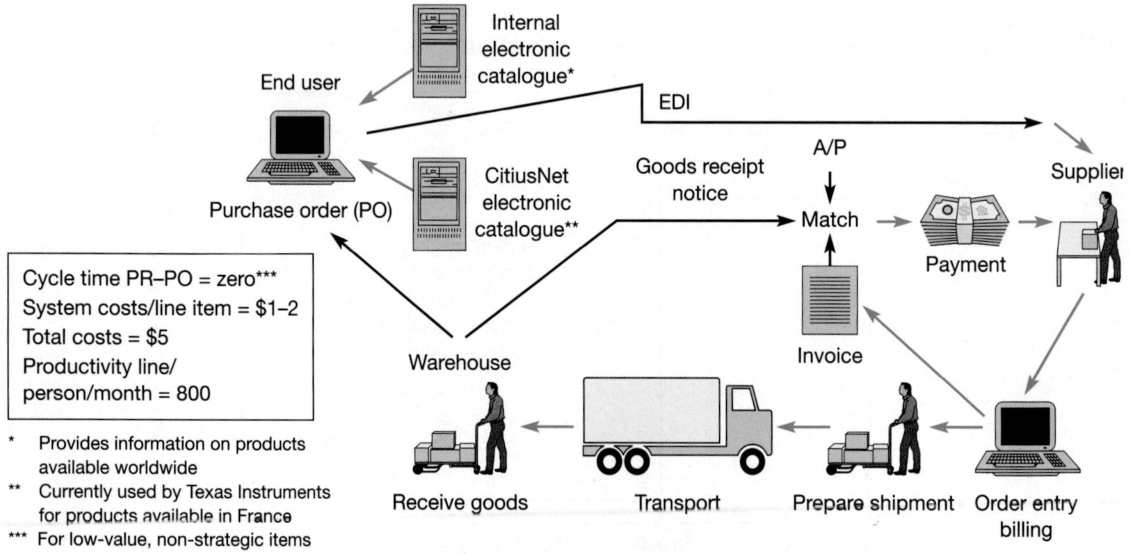

Source: Adapted from Texas Instruments (France) internal documents, January 1996.

of FF350 million and a staff of 600 people), the benefits that his company has achieved through CitiusNet have been quite remarkable. He explained:

> In the past, purchases of less than FF1500 represented 60% of our transactions but only 4.5% of the total procurement budget. Processing these purchases required 50% of my staff time. This meant that we were spending only the other 50% of our time managing the remaining 95.5% of the procurement budget! So we adopted CitiusNet in July 1994 and we used it with one of our suppliers.[24] Today we have five [of our] suppliers on the network and they will be 12 shortly. So far, CitiusNet has helped us save 22% of the time we used to spend managing purchases.

According to Mr Kaemmerlen at Texas Instruments France, as a result of purchasing time reduction, productivity has increased in some purchasing situations more than five times: from 155 to 800 line items per person per month. Although CitiusNet has been used at Texas Instruments for only low-value/non-strategic purchases, its financial impact is significant. As revealed by the internal study (mentioned above), purchase orders at Texas Instruments France that make up 80% of the purchasing transactions[25] are worth less than 5% of the annual cumulative value[26] of purchase orders (see Exhibit 12). As shown in a 1993 benchmarking study conducted by Texas Instruments France, the above phenomenon is common to other large purchasing companies like Texas Instruments USA, Europe and Asia (excluding Japan), as well as GEC Alsthom France and IBM Worldwide.

Job enrichment in the purchasing function

CitiusNet frees the purchasing department from keying in purchase requests, checking ceiling amounts and the pre-defined budget, and sending purchase orders to suppliers. LKR GEC Alsthom's José Drevon explained:

> Our staff is released from routine tasks which add no value to the procurement process. We feel better valued and our job is enriching ... Before CitiusNet, the procurement process was time-consuming and error-prone. For example, it took us [in the purchasing department] a full week just to process the internal purchase requests. Now end-users send their purchase orders through CitiusNet in the afternoon and are delighted to get the goods the following morning!

---

24 Today, the company has two workstations connected to CitiusNet.

25 A purchasing transaction refers here to the complete purchasing cycle that includes purchase requisition, goods delivery, invoicing and payment acknowledgement.

26 This cumulative value is of all line items for all purchase orders.

Exhibit 12 Procurement of non-strategic items at Texas Instruments, France

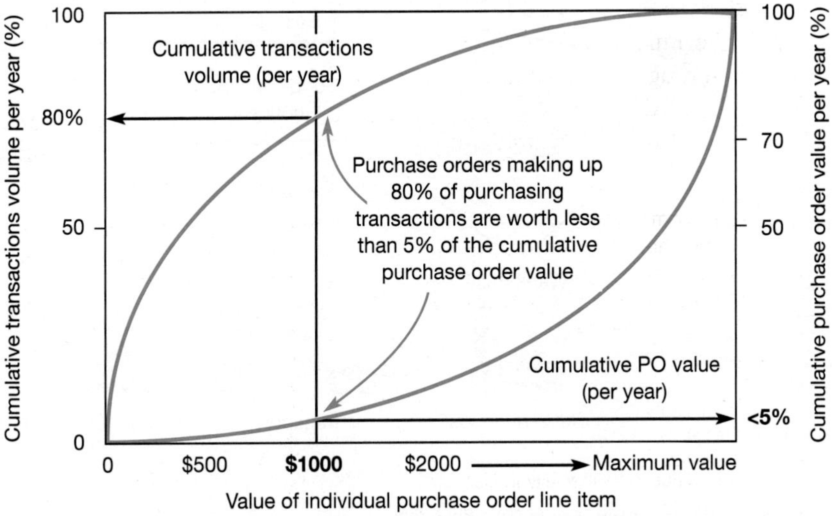

Source: Adapted from Texas Instruments (France) internal documents, January 1996.

Further improvement of CitiusNet

For José Drevon, product information provided through CitiusNet can be further enhanced. He said:

> Product descriptions, for example, should be improved. Currently, they are more suited for suppliers than for customers. Also the technical product information [on the server] should be more elaborate than what it is now. Suppliers should invest some time to change this.

Compagnie Bancaire, the French financial services group, is another CitiusNet customer. There, staff members send purchase orders through an internal computer system to the company's corporate purchasing department which, after consolidation, forwards the orders via CitiusNet to the suppliers. Abdallah Hitti, Corporate EDI Manager at Compagnie Bancaire, said: 'We think CitiusNet is a good [electronic commerce] solution. However, we want it to be more interactive, so we can put it on every [staff member's] desk.'

For Mr Schmid of Conexus, CitiusNet can be further improved. He said:

> Purchasers are attracted to CitiusNet because of the range of products and their associated information [such as general product information, price, and product pictures] that the system can offer to potential customers. However, the number of CitiusNet servers needs to be increased worldwide so as to support cross-border shopping on a wider scale.

Market growth for CitiusNet

From 1992 to 1995, the number of commercial transactions conducted through CitiusNet had been growing at a steady rate (see Exhibit 13).

Regarding CitiusNet's future, Mr Schmid commented:

> I would assume a 100% compound growth per year over the next three years. That's high but achievable when you look at the projects currently underway and in part sponsored by the G7 countries. I think it's possible. It's not a question of potential but rather a matter of keeping up with the development and having sufficient and qualified personnel.

For Mrs Rijbergen of IN Connection:

> There is a lot of interest in CitiusNet especially in Belgium where the European Union is using it. This has given CitiusNet a major boost in the Belgian market. Furthermore, the European Union's suppliers, which are mainly based in Belgium, will have to start using CitiusNet.

Exhibit 13 Number of commercial transactions conducted through CitiusNet

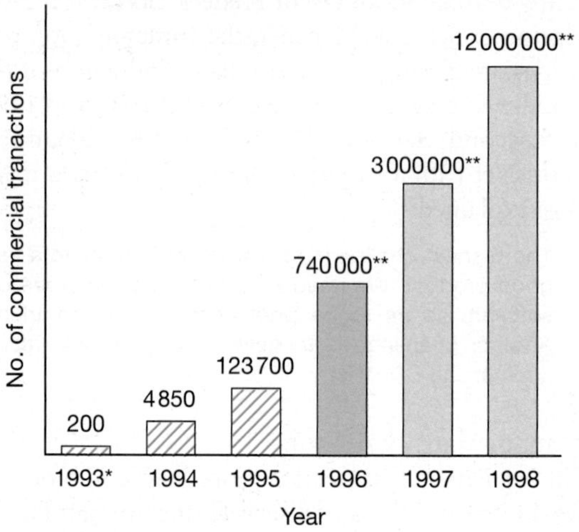

*1993 is considered an R&D year
**Forecast

Source: CitiusNet SA.

For Laurent Demilly of Gaspard, an office supplies distributor with 5000 products in its electronic catalogue, user-friendliness and response time are two key features of CitiusNet. According to Texas Instruments' Kaemmerlen, CitiusNet is the 'right' approach. He said: 'I feel that simplicity and user-friendliness are important.' He later added:

> We also look forward to using FORTIUS. And this is when we need to be more involved as there will be direct financial implications and even more so if we use CitiusNet for purchasing strategic items.

For José Drevon of LKR GEC Alsthom, it is obvious that FORTIUS will enhance the market interest in CitiusNet. He said:

> A financial [services] component, such as FORTIUS, is necessary in electronic commerce if we want to optimize the whole [order-to-pay] chain. However, it will require a 'cultural revolution', especially in our accounting department.

CitiusNet challenges

> Our challenge is to manage [CitiusNet's] business growth and the technical complexity associated with a global electronic market. It represents a new form of economy and CitiusNet is like a continuously changing 'puzzle' that involves different [business] players around the globe.

Jean-Philippe Passot

Technical challenges

Approximately 40% of CitiusNet's budget is currently devoted to R&D. For Frédéric Bost, CitiusNet's Customer Services Manager, the company's top priorities are: first, speeding up the introduction of the Windows version of CitiusNet expected by mid 1996, and second, developing new interfaces to connect CitiusNet with a variety of application software. Mr Bost explained:

> The biggest challenge for CitiusNet is to have a very good product. We need to continuously improve our software so as to be present in [various] markets. Another challenge is to develop ways of interfacing Internet and CitiusNet.

Management challenges

For Mr Passot, CitiusNet is more than a web of networks, workstations and servers; the 'human factor' is an important element for its diffusion. Although the hardware and software constitute the backbone of the system, the success of CitiusNet depends to a large extent on the company's ability to manage the different corporate cultures and business procedures of various trading partners in their respective countries.[27] Due to the difficulty in implementing successful applications of electronic market abroad, CitiusNet has adopted what Mr Passot calls a 'task-force'-based marketing approach whereby representatives from CitiusNet Inc. and its foreign partners work together on setting up a local server and on marketing CitiusNet. Mr Passot said:

> Like a 'small atom', a business task force works with CitiusNet to jointly open new markets in new regions. Its job is to market products and to find customers, suppliers and local partners. As an electronic commerce [service] provider, we don't want to favour one supplier over another; the customer will choose.

International challenges

Mr Passot added:

> We want to build an international company, neither European nor American but a worldwide enterprise that encompasses different cultures. Technically, this can be done by interconnecting CitiusNet servers [around the world] so that each one of them can access databases from other servers. It is also important that we can exchange ideas with our international partners in each market that we develop. From December 1995, in addition to the server in France, we have set up servers in Canada (one in Montréal and one in Toronto), in Denver, in Barcelona, in Zurich and in Brussels. By the end of 1996, CitiusNet will cover most of Western Europe and parts of Central and Eastern Europe. In the longer term, we plan to set up servers in other parts of the world; for example, in the Asia Pacific region.

The international expansion approach of CitiusNet is based on equity partnerships with local companies. In addition to setting up local servers, partners are responsible for marketing CitiusNet and developing the pricing policy for their respective regions. For CitiusNet, this expansion approach is more appropriate than setting up a few large central servers to cover operations worldwide.

Marketing challenges

According to Jean-Philippe Passot, today electronic market services are mainly offered by software companies capable of developing state-of-the-art computer interfaces between different IT systems. He said:

> These companies, however, lack substantial experience in commerce. The strength of CitiusNet as a vendor is precisely its strong knowledge of the market, products, suppliers and customers' purchasing behaviour. It is also our ability to manage the product database and its related information, a key success factor in electronic commerce.

For CitiusNet Inc., continuous financial investment in both technical personnel and product development is needed to leverage new technologies and cope with changing business environments. Moreover, the profit margin from selling electronic commerce packages will shrink over time, as is the case for most software products. The challenge is therefore to develop a pricing policy with entry, subscription and transaction fees that are high enough to ensure profits but low enough to attract new customers. Such a policy is a critical element of the company's marketing strategy to win new markets, especially abroad. Mr Passot added:

> To enter the UK market, we had to first customize the [CitiusNet] product to the American market because it's easier to transit through the US to get to the UK than to try to sell a French product to the British! In a similar way, it was easier to sell CitiusNet in the US as an American product rather than as a European one.

---

27 The issues of corporate cultures and business procedures, among others, have been discussed at recent meetings of the Citius Users' Club which was created in January 1995. Members of this club include purchasers, suppliers, business partners and CitiusNet Inc. management.

Looking ahead

As he looked at the lit towers of La Défense[28] from the window of the Citius France office, Mr Passot wondered whether his technology-based business adventure could lead quickly to success. For him, it was clear that the further diffusion of CitiusNet would rely heavily on an effective marketing strategy. He said:

> The [CitiusNet] product must be well-known and for this we have to make more effort in promoting it. We also need to further enhance its capabilities. The next two years are going to be critical for us. Our aim is to make CitiusNet a standard of electronic markets. The challenge is that we only have a short time window to achieve this goal.

28 La Défense is a Manhattan-like area located just outside Paris in which the corporate headquarters of numerous companies are located.

DISCUSSION QUESTIONS

1. Assess the business model of CitiusNet. What improvements would you make in order to generate more revenues?
2. More broadly, what recommendations would you make to the management of CitiusNet in order to enhance the value-added of its e-marketplace?
3. How would you compare CitiusNet with electronic data interchange (EDI)-based e-procurement solutions and also with internet-based e-marketplaces? What advantages and drawbacks does it have for its users?
4. With the increasing use of the Internet in the late 1990s, what opportunities and threats (from a business and technological perspectives) does CitiusNet face? Explain.
5. How sustainable is CitiusNet as a global e-marketplace? What exit strategies would you consider? Defend your arguments.

CASE STUDY 20

Business-to-business electronic commerce

Mondus.com – an e-marketplace for small and medium-sized enterprises

Back from London, after having presented his business plan at the Catapult Competition,[1] Alexander Straub, a 26-year-old German, was wondering whether he had been able to convince the competition's expert panel of his e-marketplace business idea. When the telephone rang, the last thing he was expecting was to be told that he had just won the 1999 competition:

> From that day on, my student life changed tremendously. It was no longer a question of being a doctoral student at Oxford University, sitting in the hall with only dreams, but suddenly with US$1.7 million in my pocket ...
>
> **Alexander Straub, co-founder and Vice-Chair, mondus.com ltd**

Background: e-commerce

e-Commerce emerged in the 1980s with the use of electronic data exchange (EDI) in the retail and automotive industries. At that time, only 1% of companies used EDI for the business-to-business (B2B) exchange of electronic documents.[2] Today, widespread growth of the Internet has opened up numerous business opportunities and new sources of revenues. While in 1998, worldwide B2B revenues amounted to US$43 billion, they were expected to reach US$1.3 trillion by 2003. This figure will represent approximately 90% of the dollar value of e-commerce and 4% of the world economy, a percentage that will reach 30% by 2010.[3] Also the way of doing business will change. Today, 87% of all deals are settled directly between companies; it was expected that by 2004 most transactions (53%) would be done through electronic marketplaces.[4]

The emergence of mondus

> In my student time, I was faced with the basics of the net economy.

When Alexander Straub started studying mechanical engineering at the University of Darmstadt, Germany, in 1991, he acquired his first e-mail address. He witnessed the advent of browsers at Cornell University in 1994. When he later joined Stanford University, he accessed disk storage space allowing him to host a web page and heard about the new evolving businesses such as Netscape and Yahoo!. In 1996, he was awarded a Rhodes Scholarship[5] to study in the UK. He explained: 'I left for the sake of completing my Doctorate, but I was actually really ready to create my own company.' During the evenings, he and some

1 A competition jointly run by *The Sunday Times* and 3i, the UK venture capital firm, awarding a prize to the best Internet start-up.
2 Timmers, P. (1999), *Electronic Commerce: Strategies and Models for Business-to-Business Trading*, New York, John Wiley & Sons, p. 4.
3 Timmers, P. (1999), pp. xi and 4.
4 Forrester Research (2000), 'eMarketplaces boost B2B Trade', *Forrester Report*, February.
5 A prestigious scholarship granted to foreign students to study at Oxford University. Bill Clinton was also a Rhodes Scholar in 1968.

This case was written by Michael Müller, a participant in the Master programme of the Technical University of Aachen, Germany, and Tawfik Jelassi, Affiliate Professor of Technology Management at INSEAD. It is intended to be used as a basis for class discussion rather than to illustrate either effective or ineffective handling of an administrative situation.

The case was made possible by the co-operation of mondus.com.

friends would meet in the college halls and brainstorm over new business models and opportunities.

In 1998, as an intern in Goldman Sachs' private investment area, Alexander Straub attended discussions on Internet start-ups:

> At that time I thought there was something tremendous about the Internet ... It was no longer just a marketing tool, nor just about information, but it was also about transactions. It was especially interesting for transactions where you have highly fragmented markets and inefficiencies. It goes beyond what B2B software solutions in ERP[6] systems can provide.

When he heard about the Catapult Competition, he wrote a business plan on his Internet start-up idea and submitted it. In February 1999, six submissions out of 1600 were invited to make a presentation in London. 'For me it was the first time I had ever presented my business plan to venture capitalists', remembered Alexander Straub. 'I didn't expect it to go well. But they liked it very much and called me the next day.'

Rouzbeh Pirouz, the co-founder of mondus, was a Canadian of Iranian origin who studied international relations and politics at Stanford University and at the Kennedy School of Government in Boston. He was also a Rhodes scholar and had met Alexander Straub at a farewell party in New York before they left the US. They both had an entrepreneurial spirit and often discussed business ideas. He was in Iran conducting research on the Iranian democratic movement when Alexander informed him about the Catapult prize. Pirouz decided to return to Oxford and help his friend launch mondus.com ltd. The name mondus.com had already been registered in 1997, when it was created by a group of students that included Straub and Pirouz. It was derived from *mundus*, the Latin word for 'world', and was supposed to be easy to pronounce and without a meaning that could lead to bias.

After setting up an office, Straub and Pirouz invited some friends, companies and consultants to reflect on their business model. While the original focus was on virtual community, commerce and content, they quickly discovered that, for a viable start-up, it was important to concentrate on transactions. They asked businesses about their procurement problems, analyzed different product categories and looked at market potential as well as the Internet adoption rate. Pirouz explains:

> The opportunity for businesses to use the Internet as a tool for growth was the driving factor. The main reasons for this are cost, opportunity to compete against 'big players' and access to serious, reputable buyers and suppliers. All these factors were taken into consideration when developing mondus.[7]

On 1 April 1999, 3i transferred the Catapult prize of US$1.7 million to mondus.com. The company needed large premises to house the marketing and web design specialists who were hired, along with the database designer and the technical support team. The first website became operational in July 1999. At that time, customers were able only to register and to gain information about mondus.

By August 1999, mondus.com was valued at US$60 million, after Eden Capital, a venture capitalist firm, committed US$12 million for the company's expansion into the US and Germany. New offices were opened in New York and Hamburg. In September 1999, the UK website mondus.co.uk was officially launched. One month later, the US website mondus.com became operational and another venture capitalist, Zouk Ventures, invested US$3 million. Since the local telecommunication company could not set up the Internet connection any earlier, the German website mondus.de started in November 1999. Two months later, an office was opened in Paris and mondus' fourth national website, mondus.fr, became available just one year after the initial business plan had been submitted. The company's original name was mondus.com ltd. On 19 May 2000, it was changed to mondus ltd[8] (see Exhibit 1). Its headquarters were located in Oxford, England.

The business model

> We offer products and services in the horizontal categories. These are not goods in category A or category B, but category C. For example, not the tyres that are produced or the rubber that was used to produce the

6 Enterprise resource planning (ERP) systems are computer applications that allow companies to manage their business operations (e.g. finance, requirement planning, human resources and order fulfilment) using a single, integrated set of corporate data. ERP solutions are offered by software vendors such as SAP, Baan or PeopleSoft.

7 www.mondus.co.uk/mori/mori.cfm

8 Throughout the case, the term 'mondus' will be used to refer to mondus ltd.

Exhibit 1 Organizational structure of mondus.com ltd, 8 May 2000

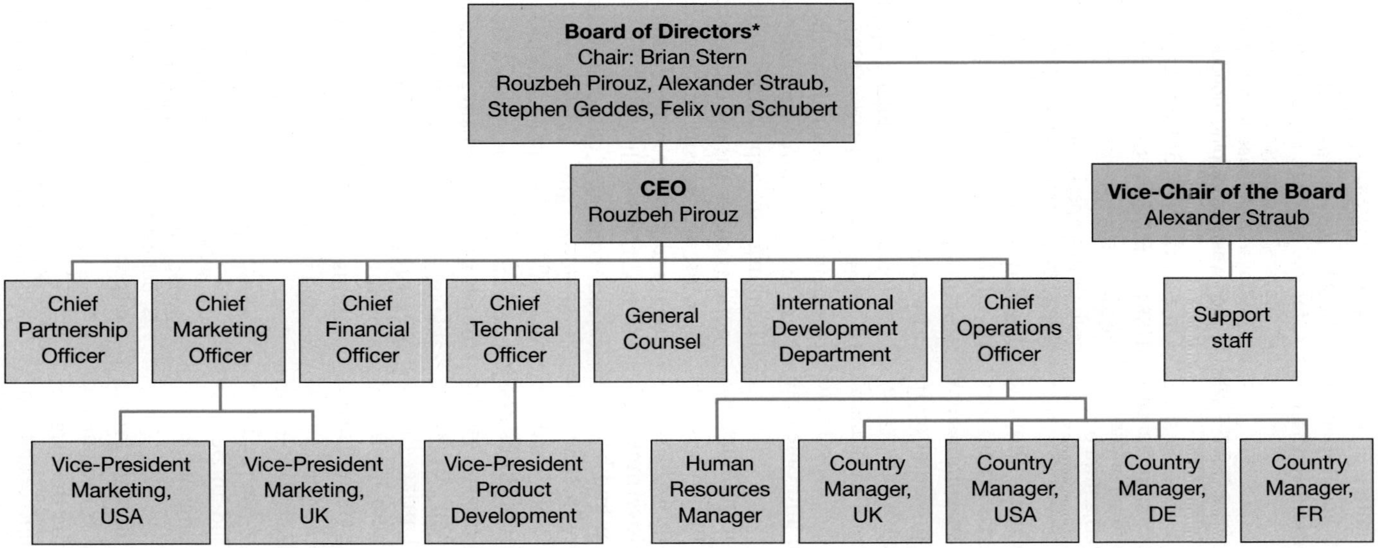

* Brian Stern was Senior Vice-President of Xerox Corporation and President of Xerox Technology Enterprises. He has served as Vice-President of Corporate Business Strategy, President of the company's Personal Documents Products Division and President of the company's Office Document Products Group. In these capacities, he oversaw the development and implementation of products for small businesses and home offices through retail distribution channels and the worldwide marketing of the industry's broadest line of office copiers. Stephen Geddes and Felix von Schubert are partners at Eden Capital and Zouk Ventures respectively.

Source: mondus.com ltd.

> tyres, but in fact what I would call business needs such as office supplies, office services, human resource services, or financial services.[9]
>
> **Marcus Gerhardt, Head of Communication and UK Country Manager, mondus**

Mondus was a horizontal web-based B2B marketplace.[10] It aimed at offering a one-stop procurement solution to small- and medium-sized enterprises (SMEs) by matching buyers and sellers through its website. The reason why mondus chose the horizontal approach (see Table 1) was because of branding. 'We spoke with a Goldman Sachs analyst back in the summer [1999]', explained Marcus Gerhardt:

> He indicated that a horizontal brand was far easier to establish and to create [than a vertical brand]. In fact it meant that you would have leverage over the vertical markets. We have seen this with a few Scandinavian players who had very strong and successful businesses.

9 Categories A, B and C are derived from the ABC analysis that attempts to classify procurement needs based on the ratio of value and volume. While there are only a few products in category A, of great importance to the company, C-type goods have a low value and account for most of the procurement needs. Category B goods are in between the two.

10 A horizontal marketplace refers to an application that is offered to a wide range of industries. In contrast, vertical markets only focus on a specific industry.

Table 1 Purchasing categories of mondus.com, 8 May 2000

Computer equipment	*Marketing services*
Desktop PCs	Direct marketing
Laptop PCs	Mailing lists
Apple systems	Public relations
Computer software	Telemarketing
Computer accessories	CD business cards
Monitors	Banner advertisements
Printers	*Office services and equipment*
Computer services	Fax machines
Software development	Copiers
Network services	Projectors
Corporate hospitality	Scanners
Catering	Printing refills
Event planning	*Printing and related services*
Couriers	Printing services
International couriers	Business cards
Messenger services	Business stationery
Nationwide couriers	*Professional services*
Human resource services	Translation services
Executive recruitment	*Promotional items and services*
Temporary staffing	Corporate apparel
Payroll services	Corporate gifts
Internet services	Promotional staffing and entertainment
Internet service providers	*Telecom and communications*
Website design	Paging
Website hosting	Video-conferencing
Server hosting/colocation	Telephones and accessories
Internet security	*Training services*
Transaction services	Business and sales training
Web traffic analysis	Computer training
Intellectual property services	Language training
Patents	Office support training
Trademarks	

Source: mondus.com ltd.

Exhibit 2 **Matching buyers and sellers through mondus.com**

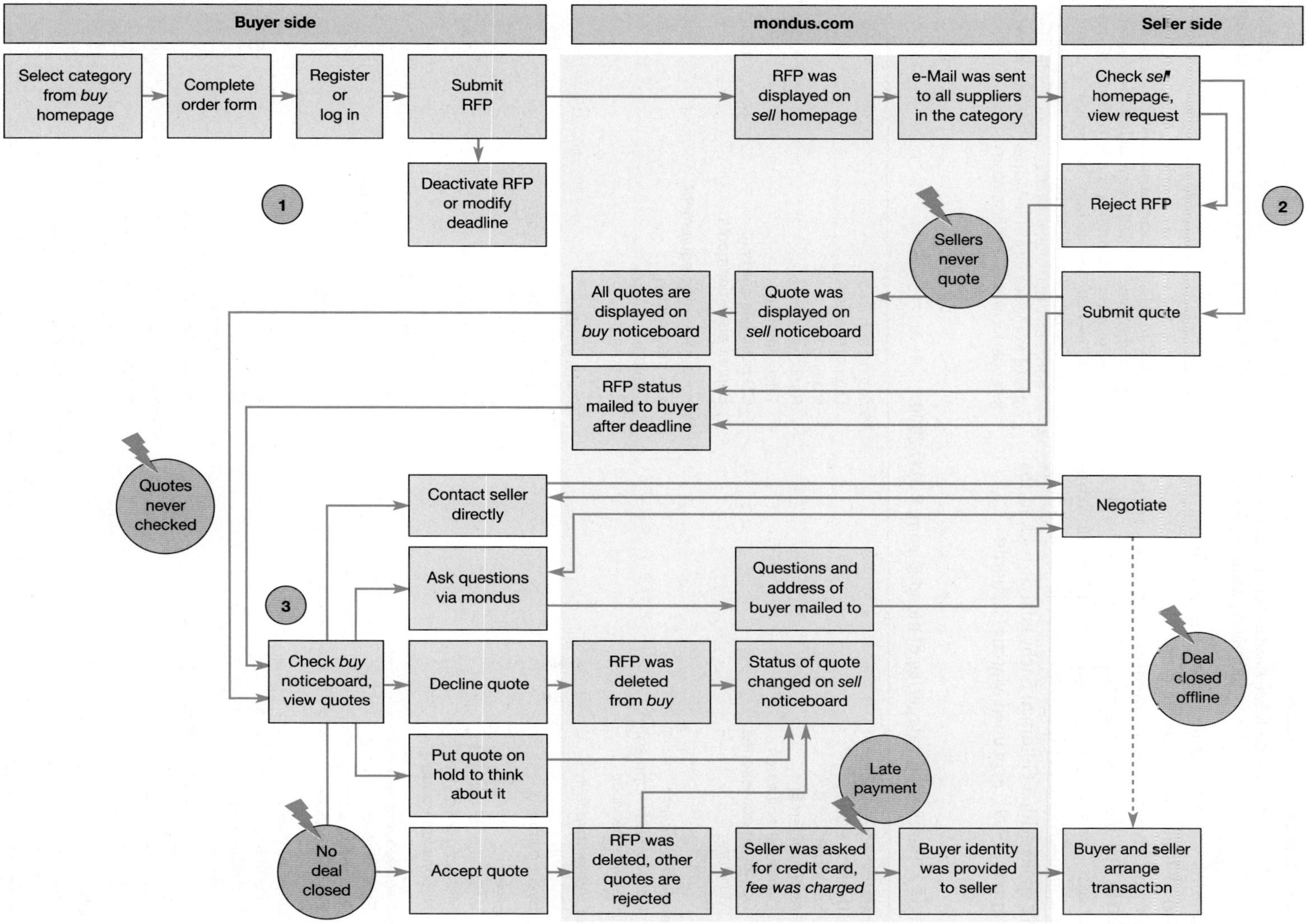

> They came up with a vertical [approach and] it was very difficult for them to sustain their brand in the horizontal space and actually go beyond Scandinavia or into other markets because nobody recognizes their brand. Mondus was different; it was taking the horizontal approach. We aim at becoming the one-stop solution for the procurement needs of SMEs.

Mondus' market model was based on the use of a request-for-proposal (RFP). The matching of buyers and suppliers was a three-step procedure. First, the buyer placed a request. Second, one or more suppliers replied to the request by submitting a quote. Third, the buyer viewed all the quotes, if necessary negotiated with the sellers, and accepted or rejected the received quotes (see Exhibit 2).

The above process was facilitated through the mondus homepage, which was divided into a buy section and a sell section (see Exhibit 3). In the buy homepage, buyers requested the product or service they needed. In the sell homepage, sellers could view the requests currently submitted and place quotes. All users of the system had a personal noticeboard (my mondus) that informed buyers through the buy noticeboard about the current status of their requests, and sellers through the sell noticeboard about their quotes. There was also a 'How to' section containing information on mondus.

Exhibit 3 Structure of the mondus.com homepage

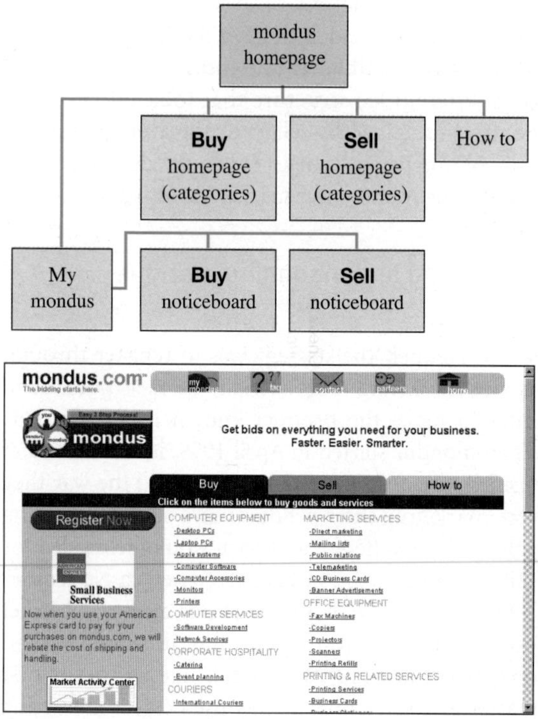

Placing a request for proposal

The buyer selected on the buy homepage the category of products or services they were looking for. A standardized order form popped up and the buyer was asked to specify their needs. Possible answers were provided for each question. It was also possible to use an open-format query or to attach a file with more detailed information. With every question made by the system, online help was provided (for example to explain what a hard disk is, how its size was defined and what size was necessary). Alternatively the buyer could look up the frequently asked questions (FAQs), call a toll-free number or send an e-mail to the helpdesk. Mondus set up call centres in the local markets and trained the centre agents to answer queries about any aspect of the site without having to redirect the caller. The aim was to answer all e-mail messages within an hour of their receipt, which, at the time this case was written, was true for 74% of all incoming calls. A global customer relation strategy tried to provide the same service everywhere.

After the buyer defined the service or product they needed, they were asked for the delivery date, the maximum number of quotes to be received and a deadline for the quotes. To submit the RFP they could either log on or register. When a new customer registered as a buyer, they were asked for their name and address, the name and size of their company, their position and a password; they were then assigned a username. After a request was submitted, it could be deactivated or its deadline extended.

Placing a quote

Once an RFP was submitted, it was posted on the sell homepage and an e-mail sent to all suppliers that had registered for that category. If a seller registered, they had to provide the same information as the buyer and the categories for which they could supply goods. They could decline to be notified daily about RFPs submitted in their categories. It was possible to specify the geographical area in which a seller could provide their products or services, a short description of their company (including its age) as well as the return of goods and guarantee policies.

The e-mail contained the identification number of the RFP. Sellers could go to the sell homepage, enter the RFP number and view the request. Alternatively they could check any category on the sell homepage and view all submitted quotes. The information shown to the seller did not contain the identity of the buyer nor any quotes made by other suppliers. Mondus believed that displaying competitors' prices might prevent vendors from making quotes, and that customers did not make their purchase decision based only on price but rather on the complete offer they received.

After a seller viewed an RFP, they could submit a quote or reject the request. When placing a quote the vendor had to specify the delivery date, the volume, the price and give a short description of the offer. Additionally they were asked whether their quote exactly met the buyer's request. In order to submit a quote, the seller had to log in or register. Quotes were binding and not retractable.

Selecting a quote

All quotes submitted were displayed on the buy noticeboard and could be viewed by the buyer. If the deadline expired, an e-mail was sent to the buyer to inform them of all the quotes. If no quotes were submitted, they were also notified and asked to call mondus for further help. In those cases, the customer service departments checked the requests and tried to call suppliers individually. In order to proceed, the buyer had to open the buy noticeboard. They could decline quotes, put them on hold or accept them. The buyer's choice was automatically displayed on the sell noticeboard to keep the vendor informed of the status of their quotes.

The buyer could also contact the vendor and ask them questions or negotiate with them. They could do this either directly, because each quote contained the seller's address, or via mondus. In the second case, the buyer entered the questions and their address into a query provided on the buy noticeboard. The information was then forwarded to the supplier who was asked to contact the buyer.

Once a buyer accepted a quote, all other quotes were automatically rejected. The selected vendor was asked for their credit card details and a fee was charged by mondus. The vendor then received the buyer's address and both arranged the details of the transaction. In the end, mondus asked the buyer for feedback on the seller's performance.

The revenue model

> In B2B [e-commerce] the buyer has the power and was the one that decides how things work. If, in bricks-and-mortar businesses, the buyer was sitting in his chair and the salesperson was trying to impress him, in an Internet-based solution this balance of power has to be reflected as well.
>
> **Dr Florian Heupel, Director of Business Development, mondus.de, Germany**

Mondus did not only want to consider buyer-centricity through its matching procedure (where sellers submitted binding quotes and buyers chose from these), but also through the revenue model set in place. Mondus only charged sellers a fee on successful transactions settled through mondus. All services provided to the buyer were free. Initially, sellers were also charged for submitting quotes, but mondus changed its policy to motivate vendors to quote and to increase the number of quotes submitted per RFP. Registration was free of charge for both sellers and buyers.

The transaction fee charged was 2% of the transaction volume. Though originally mondus planned to apply different percentages depending on the product category, it finally preferred to charge a flat fee. 'The RFP is a fairly new model and customers first have to get used to it', explained Christoph Pech, Manager of International Development at mondus. 'That's why we decided to keep the billing structure as simple as possible.' In the future, mondus could use a different fee structure that took into account the margins gained by sellers or the average transaction volume per category. Fees could also be used as a marketing tool to offer market incentives.

Developing and managing mondus

Marketing

For Dr Heupel, 'the strategy was to register through various marketing tools as many users as possible in order to make the product known to the market'. When mondus started in April 1999, it first looked at business-to-consumer (B2C) players and the way they were marketing their products and services. Having realized that a different approach would be needed for B2B e-commerce, mondus performed in November 1999, with the help of an advertising agency, a market test. Based on the test results, mondus launched an integrated marketing campaign in the UK in the first quarter of 2000, which mainly used direct marketing

Exhibit 4 **Information attached to the letter sent to potential sellers – part of the test campaign in the UK, November 1999**

techniques. Marcus Gerhardt explained: 'Envelopes or direct mail [were] sent out to buyers and suppliers followed by an e-mail and a telephone call and another e-mail and telephone call. At the same time [we did] some radio advertising to create market awareness.' Advertising in the printed press and on TV did not seem to be effective. The information sent to customers was different for potential buyers and sellers; it contained a letter and a small brochure (see Exhibits 4 and 5). Mondus obtained the customer information from telecommunication and computer providers. 'The point is not that we used lists of computer suppliers, but in fact databases that came from companies that are active in the computer area', explained Marcus Gerhardt.

> The reason is that you can assume that this kind of environment feeds into the early adopters. They will have companies [in their customer databases that] are well aware of computers and the Internet and are therefore happier than others about adopting that kind of trading platform.

The marketing campaign led to a significant increase in customer registration, though it did not have an impact until late February. In February 2000, 17 000 customers were registered worldwide; however, within one month this number had grown to 60 000. Also the number of RFPs increased twice within the same period of time (see Exhibit 6).

A marketing campaign was launched in Germany, its design based on experiences gained in

Exhibit 5 Letter sent to potential buyers – part of the UK marketing campaign, first quarter of 2000

www.mondus.co.uk

9999999 X 99999

Mr A Sample
Any Job
Any Company
1 Any Street
Any Town
Anyshire
XY1 1XY

The more quotes you get the better the price you'll find

Dear Mr Sample,

But getting quotes takes time. Time is money. And time and money are two things you don't want to waste.

Now you don't have to. Thanks to mondus.co.uk

mondus is a new on-line service that gives you access to a whole range of top quality suppliers - fast. Whatever you're looking for, from IT to printing, office equipment to human resources, you'll get a bigger selection of competitive quotes by visiting www.mondus.co.uk And because the service is completely free to buyers, all you'll need to invest is a few minutes to register.

The easy way to save time, money and hassle

You don't need to be an experienced internet user to benefit from mondus. Just click onto our website, register and fill out an order form. It really is as easy as that.

Then, we will forward your request to all our relevant suppliers. Every one of them who can meet your specification and deadline will send their quotes to us, and we'll e-mail them to you. You choose the best quote and the deal is done.

For help or advice you can always call our dedicated customer helpline on 0800 100 123. And if you register at our site before 31st March 2000, we'll enter you in our free prize draw to win a brand new Alfa Romeo 156. Quite a reward for next to no effort.

For more details read the enclosed leaflet or, better still, visit our website at **http://www.mondus.co.uk** and find out how you can save time, money and hassle.

Yours sincerely

Audrey Roser
Customer Care Manager

Oxford Centre for Innovation Mill Street Oxford OX2 0JX
VAT No. 715196318 Company Reg. 3466138

the UK. Online banners were displayed in different websites and in newsletters of other companies starting on 22 March 2000. A one-page advertisement was placed in the major business and non-business newspapers as well as in weekly journals. Additionally radio-based advertising took place in Frankfurt and Hamburg, and direct mailing in combination with telemarketing was used. The best results with respect to customer registration were gained through telemarketing. However, these customers had not placed many RFPs. While advertising in weekly magazines seemed a cost efficient method of increasing the number of RFPs, radio advertising had no significant effect (see Table 2). It could only be used to generate brand awareness and attract customers to the website in the long run.

Another way to attract customers was via the affiliate scheme. Mondus offered companies an

Exhibit 6 **Evolution of the number of customers and RFPs in Germany and worldwide**

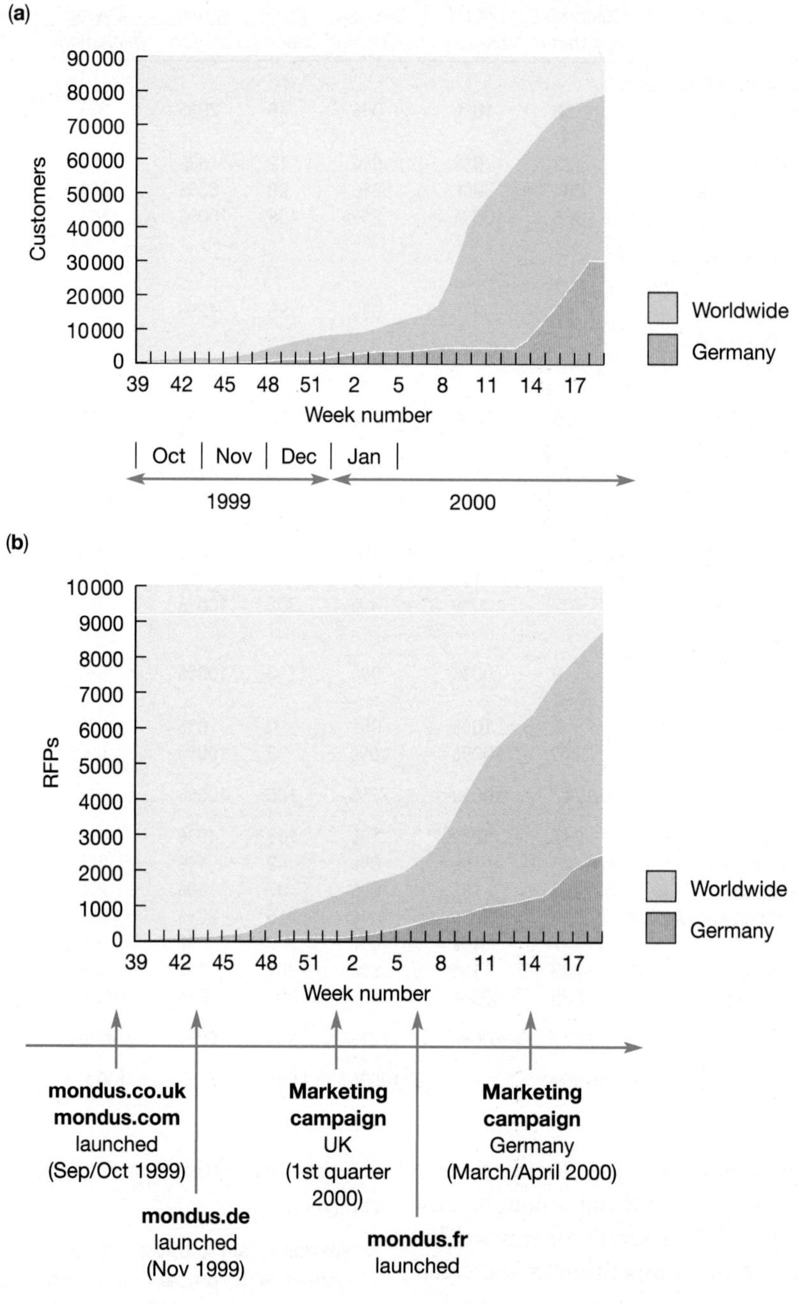

Source: mondus.com ltd.

exchange in links and logos. Affiliates displayed the mondus logo on their website and mondus placed the affiliate's logo in its so-called recourse library, a special section on the web page.

Partnerships

According to Marcus Gerhardt, there were three objectives in creating partnerships: 'To attract traffic to the mondus site, to complement our service, and

Table 2 Effects of the mondus.de marketing campaign in Germany, 5 May 2000

		Customers registered	*Within category*	*Overall percentage*	*RFQs placed*	*Within category*	*Overall percentage*	*Contacts (1000)*	*Total cost (1000 DM)*
Online (lbanner)	Web sites of IT related businesses	59	16%	0%	46	29%	3%		
	Other companies' newsletter	23	6%	0%	12	8%	1%		
	Other web sites	284	78%	2%	98	63%	5%		
	Total online	*366*	100%	*2%*	*156*	100%	*9%*		
Print	Daily newspapers *(FAZ, Süddeutsche Zeitung)*	65	9%	0%	35	12%	2%		
	Daily business newspapers *(German FT, Handelblatt)*	158	23%	1%	62	21%	3%	383	192
	Weekly magazine *(Focus)*	338	48%	2%	133	44%	7%	972	237
	Weekly business magazine *(Wirtschaftswoche)*	137	20%	1%	70	23%	4%	270	96
	Other journals	4	1%	0%	2	1%	0%		
	Total print	*702*	100%	*4%*	*302*	100%	*17%*		
Radio	Local radio station in Hamburg	9	90%	0%	3	100%	0%	750	65
	Local radio station in Frankfurt	1	10%	0%	0	0%	0%		
	Total radio	*10*	100%	*0%*	*3*	100%	*0%*		
Telemarketing		*12 747*	100%	*77%*	*106*	100%	*6%*	25	1 163
Others	Letters	247	50%	1%	108	49%	6%	100	182
	Press articles	75	1%	0%	42	1%	2%		
	Telephone	66	1%	0%	37	1%	2%		
	Promotion in exibitions	9	30%	0%	5	27%	0%		
	TV	7	1%	0%	5	1%	0%		
	Others	429	1%	3%	201	1%	11%		
	Total others	*833*	100%	*5%*	*398*	100%	*22%*		
No information		*1 911*	100%	*12%*	*859*	100%	*47%*		
Total		16 569		100%	1 824		100%		

to support it with technical services.' Partnerships in Internet business were 'crucially important, because you do not just open the market up for yourself, but you close it down to the competition as you create these partnerships'.

Accessing new customers

Mondus tried to co-operate with Internet companies that had strong brands in their markets. Partnerships signed by mondus included those with Internet.com,[11] SmartOnline.com,[12] Yahoo.co.uk, Compaq, British Telecom and vertical marketplaces. Marcus Gerhardt explained:

> We don't want to become a vertical market but we could partner with vertical players. For example, we have a partnership in the UK with doctors.net. We don't offer bandages or pharmaceutical equipment, but doctors also

11 Internet.com was a provider of real-time news for the Internet industry and experienced Internet users.

12 SmartOnline.com was an application service provider (ASP), offering productivity applications and information resources to SMEs.

> need desks, computers and telecommunications. So we provide the C category of goods to doctors. In Germany we just closed a deal with farmpartner.com, which was a very active vertical Internet site for the farmers.

There were also agreements signed with non-profit organizations, such as the German Federal Association for Procurement and Logistics (BME).[13] Through this agreement, mondus offered its marketplace to all BME members and supported the association through information campaigns on electronic markets.

Extending the business model along the value chain

In addition to setting up partnerships, mondus tried to extend its business model through co-operations. The service provided by mondus only extended to the point at which the deal was closed. A co-operative agreement set up with Dun & Bradstreet helped to check customers' credit ratings. Dun & Bradstreet provided a large database of information on companies, ranging from trading styles to financial statements. When a customer registered, whether as a seller or a buyer, their company was searched through the Dun & Bradstreet database. If found and the feedback was positive, a Dun & Bradstreet logo was displayed next to the customer's name on the sell or buy noticeboard.

For Alexander Straub:

> In the long run you must help the buyers along the whole value chain. The next step was payment and logistics. We are [also] looking into financing. Another area which will be a challenge to the marketplace in general is to get the ERP systems on both the buyer and seller side [integrated].

Banks and logistics companies could profit from partnerships with marketplaces such as mondus because new business opportunities could be created. Mondus aimed to extend its business into payment and logistics by the third quarter of 2000 and into financing by the end of the year 2000. Of special interest, mondus and a certain bank were developing a trust account to help increase the number of SMEs that trusted the mondus marketplace. Furthermore, mondus planned to offer integration into the ERP by summer 2000.

Market models

As stated above, a key assumption underlying mondus' business model was that B2B markets were mainly buyer-driven. However, in addition to the RFP, other buyer-centric models existed, which included multi-catalogues and reverse auctions. Multi-catalogue models worked like mail order companies. Different products were offered with fixed conditions to customers who could choose from a list. The selected goods were then shipped to the buyer. In reverse auctions, a buyer specified their need and sellers were asked to submit the lowest price. In some models, the buyer could also define the price and sellers could either accept or reject it. The RFP model was the most flexible solution since it allowed vendors to compete on price and any value-added feature. Dr Heupel said:

> The RFP was a fairly new model and we are now asking ourselves: Does this model work? ... From what we have seen so far, people are extremely interested in this model, which was more suitable for some categories than for others. For low volume transactions, it was probably not a good model. However, to find services, it seems to be an excellent model. In the future there will probably be more than one product offering in terms of what model you are using. We are currently extending into multi-catalogues and reverse auctions.

Multi-catalogues

Mondus believed that multi-catalogues were most suitable for urgent needs and small transaction volumes. Alexander Straub explained that a major problem for catalogue businesses was that customers could act as buyers only.

> It is very difficult for catalogue businesses to attract buyers and it is often not cost efficient. We haven't seen the same problem at mondus since, in our marketplace environment, the buyer can also act as a seller and the seller as a buyer. People basically foster themselves.

Mondus did not want to own the catalogues, but to leverage its customer base when using multi-catalogues on its website.

Reverse auctions

Reverse auctions were usually applied in high value purchases, for instance, of A and B category products. The process itself was quite complicated because vendors had to be qualified and goods thoroughly specified. Mondus believed that for high-volume orders (e.g. purchasing 1000 laptops), this model was

13 BME stands for Bundesverband Materialwirtschaft, Einkauf und Logistik e.V.

the best choice. When integrating reverse auctions into its website, mondus relied on standard auction engines that could be bought 'off the shelf'. The multi-catalogue and reverse auction models were to be operational by the third quarter of 2000.

Seller-centric models

For some product categories, seller-centric models could be more suitable, especially in categories with few suppliers, such as electricity, gas or telecommunications. To offer such a service, mondus intended to select some power-suppliers[14] and co-operate with them. Leveraging the purchase power of its customers, mondus hoped to gain better prices. Negotiations were under way with Royal Dutch Shell. British Petroleum had also contacted mondus.

In the long run, Alexander Straub believed that extending into consumer-to-consumer models would be possible. 'Some people have maybe used equipment that they now want to sell for half of the original price, or put into an auction.'

International activities

International expansion

From the very beginning mondus focused on its international expansion. Subsidiaries were soon to be launched in Canada and Scandinavia, with others to follow in Spain, Poland, Austria and South Korea. Also market entry studies were to be conducted for Italy and Ireland. Because of Switzerland's multinational character and small market size, a future website would only provide links to the German, French and Italian sites. Christoph Pech explained how the international organization would look:

> A local office will be set up in each of the countries and run as a subsidiary of mondus.com ltd. The IT back office for all European activities will be located in the UK. For North America it will be in the US. When expanding to Asia a local back office will probably also be needed there. While a team based in Oxford will develop categories that work equally all over the world, the local offices will only be in charge of products and services related to their specific region.

Mondus also tried to have partnerships with multinational companies that offered their services in any country where mondus was present.

International sales

Although most SMEs did not sell their products and services nor fulfil their procurement needs globally, mondus believed that this situation would soon change. Straub explained: 'What I think is most attractive for international categories is everything that has to do with intellectual property and which can be delivered in a digital format and shipped across borders.' For example, software and translation services could be the first global categories.

Competition

The e-commerce market targeting SMEs was underdeveloped and fragmented. Market entry barriers were minimal since new competitors could launch, at relatively low cost, websites offering services and products to SMEs. In the Canadian and US markets, there were then two competitors providing an RFP model to the same customer segment (BizBuyer.com and Onvia.com). While Bizbuyer.com's business model was equivalent to that of mondus, Onvia.com initially started with a multi-catalogue model designed for small-sized enterprises.[15] From November 1999, it also provided an RFP model for business-related services as well as content (e.g. news, notices and downloads such as business plan checklists). Onvia.com had its initial public offering (IPO) in March 2000. In Germany, it had just begun working in co-operation with Mercateo.de, which could be accessed at Onvia.de. Mercateo.de also offered a multi-catalogue system and an RFP for services. In addition it tried to establish so-called pool buying, through which, based on the number of buyers willing to buy a product, the price of the product varies. That year, Mercateo.de planned to expand its operations into different European countries. The main competitor in the UK was buy.co.uk, which tried to sell not only to private businesses, but also to public agencies.

Furthermore, other Internet sites offered multi-catalogue models to SMEs, including Digitalwork.com and Works.com. Some sites originally targeting the consumer market also sold to small-sized enterprises (e.g. Beyond.com, Buy.com and Onsale.com). Large Internet players like Yahoo!, America Online and Microsoft also offered B2B e-commerce services or planned to do so in the near future. In addition,

14 Power-suppliers refer to suppliers with which mondus built a special relationship.

15 The company was founded as MegaDepot in 1997; in May 1999 it changed its name to Onvia.com.

e-marketplaces set up by traditional multinational companies (such as the one in the automotive industry set up by General Motors, Ford and DaimlerChrysler, or the one in retailing owned by Sears, Roebuck and Carrefour) could attract SMEs due to lower prices resulting from their bargaining power. However, Dr Heupel believed that mondus had a first-mover advantage: 'It must be our strategy to have a pool of users set up very quickly, so that we don't have to get customers off other websites but that others have to get them off ours.'

Customer perspective

The number of worldwide customers had increased significantly since mondus launched its first website in October 1999. As of 8 May 2000, there were 86,892 customers registered worldwide, 76% of whom were buyers (see Table 3). The average number of orders per active buyer was 1.9 (this percentage should be taken qualitatively only since some sellers had also placed RFPs). Active sellers had placed, on average, 9.7 bids. The most popular categories for RFPs were desktop and laptop PCs, computer accessories, printing services and web design; these were also the top five categories for quotes. A third of all quotes were submitted for web design and 13% for desktop PCs.

The average volume of quotes was about US$3000 worldwide; however, there was much data variation from week to week (see Exhibit 7). This was largely due to the different transaction volumes in the various product and service categories (e.g. transaction volumes for web design were significantly higher than for printing refills).

Buyer benefits

SMEs' demand for category C goods varied and trading volumes were usually small. Unlike large companies, SMEs could not effectively leverage their liquidity and bargaining power to streamline the procurement process and cut costs.

Streamlining the procurement process

Through mondus, the procurement process could be simplified, thus resulting in time and cost savings. Instead of selecting and negotiating with customers individually, procurement needs could be specified only once and quotes would be automatically requested and forwarded to the buyer. The buyer could then compare the offers and choose the one that best suited their requirements. Through its database of suppliers and the variety of services and products offered, mondus aimed to provide a one-stop procurement solution and increasing market and price transparency.

Using mondus, I didn't have to call all my suppliers. The system will list the quotes in a way that makes it easy

Table 3 **Customer statistics per country for the period from the launch of the website until 8 May 2000**

	UK	*Germany*	*France*	*USA*	*Total*
Website fully operational since	*October 1999*	*November 1999*	*January 2000*	*October 1999*	
Customers	51660	19227	354	15651	86892
Buyers	46488	15755	107	4065	66415
Who have placed RFPs	2304	1235	33	174	4846
Sellers	5172	3472	247	11586	9013
Who have placed quotes	1432	738	32	1124	3326
Who have placed RFPs	642	409	28	393	1472
Total number of PRFs	4086	2464	76	2387	9013
Total number of quotes	17904	6334	61	8188	32487
Quotes rejected	4015	1113	13	915	4056
Quotes accepted	129	82	0	33	244
Mean value of accepted quotes	£826	DM1904	–	US$2468	

On 8 May 2000, the exchange rates were: £1=US$1.5279; 1 DM=US$0.4586.

Source: mondus.com ltd.

Exhibit 7 **Development of the average volume and the ratio of quotes per RFP in Germany (mondus.de)**

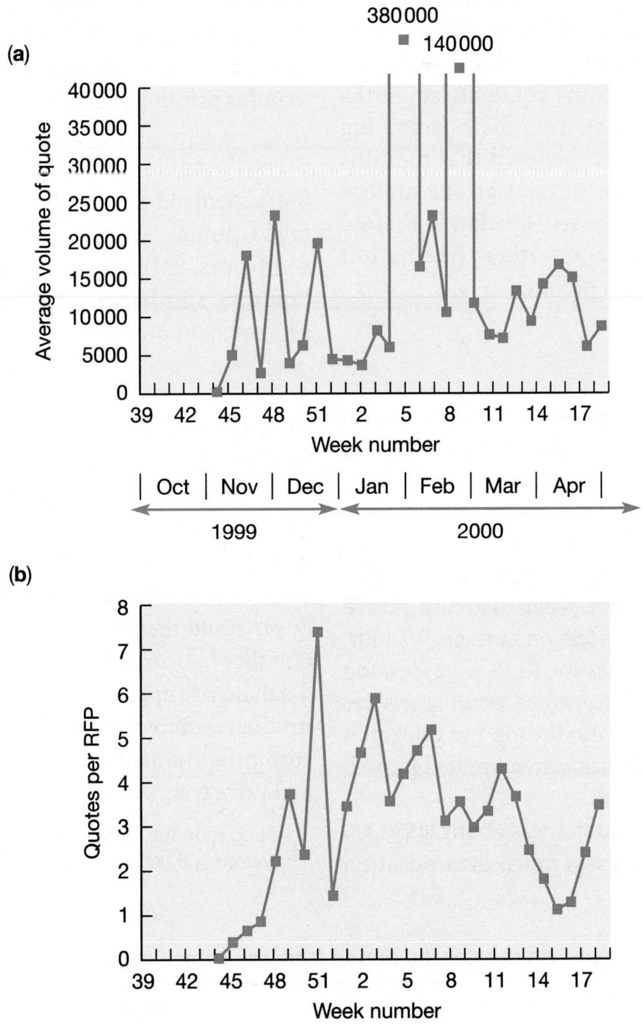

Source: mondus.com ltd.

for me to decide. It also helps me to get a better feeling for the market and possible prices.

Marco Keilholz, Managing Director, Office Forum, Germany

Convenient and easy procedure

Customers found the mondus homepage and the matching process well structured, and both on and offline help was provided. The implementation of standardized request forms offered a quick and easy specification of products and services. Through the buy noticeboard, the buyer was kept informed of the current status of their requests. They could also view previous RFPs and quotes. Furthermore the website was available 24 hours a day, seven days a week.

Low investment and cost

Requirements to run the electronic mondus marketplace were minimal. Only a PC with a standard web browser, an e-mail programme and access to the Internet were required.

Customization

Although most of the RFP process was standardized and automated, individual specifications could be added to the request form using the open-format

query or attached files. Quotes did not contain information only on the product and the price, but also on the guarantee and the goods' return policies. If needed, buyers could contact vendors and negotiate with them individually. It was also possible to extend deadlines and cancel an RFP at any time.

Confidentiality and safety

The buyer's identity was kept confidential until they accepted a quote or they contacted the seller. Through customer feedback, mondus was kept informed of supplier performance. Since mondus did not act as a seller itself, bias was avoided. For security reasons, encryption was used when credit card details were transmitted and customers were logged out automatically if they did not use the system for 20 minutes.

Seller benefits

Access to online trading and new market opportunities

As a study by MORI, a UK-based research institute, revealed: 'Most companies selling to SMEs see the Internet as a unique opportunity to gain and retain customers, with time and cost savings playing a major role in the drive to trade online.' However, for most SMEs trading online meant a massive commercial upheaval. They could lose online sales if they did not have the resources needed to launch professionally designed websites.[16] Mondus therefore proposed that, through its system, vendors could sell online without having to set up and maintain their own website as well as undertaking marketing activities. Access was provided to potential new customers with less lead-time and with reduced financial outlay. New distribution channels and sources of revenue could be created and possibilities for national and international expansion offered. According to Rouzbeh Pirouz:

> By trading through mondus, companies have the ability to exploit new markets without the expense of a bricks-and-mortar presence, or even a website. It presents the opportunity for small businesses to compete in new markets, against more established organizations.[17]

> Mondus offers a huge spectrum of potential customers to me. Through its system I can get in contact with potential buyers that I would never have reached otherwise. Using mondus for four weeks, 30% of my revenues were already generated through it.

Andreas Schacky, owner of Schacky's Computer Laden, Germany explained:

According to Marco Keilholz, his company had not yet generated substantial business through mondus, but he believed there was a huge potential. 'You don't have to access customers individually and ask for their needs. Instead, the buyer specifies the product or service needed himself. This allows a seller to make individual offers without any acquisition costs.' He added:

> From my perspective another benefit was that customers using mondus are generally open-minded about the Internet and new technologies. These are the customers that I'm interested in and that I like to do business with.

Using the mondus brand

It was often very difficult for SMEs to establish a brand. By aggregating the expertise of various suppliers, mondus eventually created a brand for specific services or products and drove customers to its website.

> My company offers training. But there was always a trade-off because you can't make acquisitions and give courses at the same time. Through mondus, I hope to leverage their brand and get customers even when I'm teaching.
>
> **Alex Reyss, owner, Step4word, Germany**

Gaining a competitive advantage

With SMEs gaining access to a larger market, they could leverage their smaller overheads against bigger competitors. Through customer-oriented offers, such as individual distribution arrangements or product-related services, SMEs could establish a niche in the market and possibly gain a competitive edge.

How customers used mondus

> People have been using the site for purposes other than for what we intended.
>
> **Audrey Roser, Global Head of Customer Relations, mondus**

Most buyers used the site to check prices, the number of quotes they could receive and the time it took. A survey revealed that 66% of all buyers just used mondus to see how it worked. Also a lot of suppliers used the website pretending that they were buyers to check the prices offered by their competitors.

16 'SMEs are flocking to buy and sell via the Internet', MORI, April 2000.
17 www.mondus.co.uk/mori/mori.cfm

Dropping out

Because of the revenue model adopted, it was important for mondus that customers followed through the process to the end and performed the transaction through mondus. Investigation showed customers dropping out of the process at different stages. First, not all vendors submitted quotes and RFPs could be left unanswered. In addition, most buyers did not get back to their buy noticeboard to check the quotes. Because buyers had the option to contact sellers, the parties could go offline and close the deal without notifying mondus. Audrey Roser explained: '[If customers] go offline we have no way to track that effectively.' In other cases, buyers could decide to stick by their traditional suppliers or never close the deal. Because most SMEs, at least in the UK, did not have credit cards, invoices had to be sent, resulting in delayed payment.

Customers' complaints

Buyers' complaints

According to Audrey Roser, there was a lot of interest in the mondus concept but some quotes were not price-competitive and sometimes customers did not get enough quotes. Some buyers complained that they got quotes that did not match their RFP and thus were not relevant. Furthermore, others were unwilling to accept quotes from companies they did not know. However, according to mondus' research, customers would overlook brand if prices were good enough. In addition, response time was an important issue for buyers.

Sellers' complaints

Most vendors complained that they never got feedback on their quotes. One reason was that the majority of buyers never viewed the quotes they got nor followed them up. Other suppliers stated that they did not have the time to go through all the RFPs and send quotes for each of them. Many vendors felt unable to compete because they thought other suppliers offered better prices. This situation improved slightly once mondus no longer displayed the lowest quote. Others were frustrated with the model because the buyer was kept anonymous until the end unless the buyer contacted the vendor directly. This prevented the seller from doing their sales job. Some vendors stated that they could not give a price without actually talking to the buyer. 'If you were a supplier of a website, there was no way that you can give a price for a website based on the answers to ten questions.' Other customers suggested that mondus should ask buyers to shortlist some suppliers, which could then contact the buyer directly. Mondus in this case might charge the vendor for the service. At first there were also many complaints regarding technical problems as well as incorrect registrations that either prevented suppliers from accessing the right information or resulted in the receipt of RFP numbers for goods they were not selling.

Challenges for mondus

As a one-year-old company, mondus faced several challenges. How could it increase the number of deals closed? Could mondus recruit sufficiently qualified people to implement its expansion strategy? How was it going effectively to manage all of its activities in so many countries?

Increasing the number of deals closed

It was important for mondus to ensure that sufficient quotes were submitted on RFPs. Audrey Roser explained: '[The idea] was to have a lot of power suppliers, which are suppliers that agree to quote on a competitive level and with which we develop relationships. Currently we have power suppliers only for some categories but not [in] all of them.' Dr Heupel believed that there would be more quotes as the number of sellers grew and customers used the system more frequently. 'At first, there was only one offer per request. The number of offers was growing at a higher rate than that of registered users and RFPs. On average today you receive four offers per bid.'

Mondus also called buyers to validate orders and to ask for details that could prevent sellers from quoting. Once quotes were submitted, the customer service department called the buyer four days before the offer deadline expired to motivate them to look at their quotes and decide. Mondus hoped that this would also help filter out customers that were just testing the system (in this case mondus rejected all quotes and gave sellers instant feedback). If buyers rejected quotes, the system asked them for feedback and offered different answers to choose from. By these means mondus hoped to get more information on customers' needs and decision criteria.

A major problem was that buyers and sellers only used mondus to get in contact with each other. Then

they went offline and never returned to the system. Alexander Straub explained: 'We open the system up to the end, so negotiations can happen. We believe that this was very important to get the value to our business, especially in highly complex service categories.' He argued that mondus could prevent customers from staying offline if it offered additional services such as logistics, financing and insurance. 'At that time we know the whole process and we know the whole volume and we know about the charges.' Dr Heupel was not very worried about the small number of deals currently closed through mondus: 'Getting into the arithmetic was very difficult since often people register, look at our system and become active users later on. Plus we are growing very rapidly. So on what do you base your percentage?'

Recruitment

For Marcus Gerhardt, recruitment was one of the critical management issues at mondus. 'We are growing at a rate where it is very difficult to find qualified and relevant people who fit into our organization and still bring along the experience.' At first, mondus recruits were former university friends. Straub explained: 'At that time we had no other choice. People [in Europe] didn't know much about stock options.' In particular, professionals from the technical side preferred fixed salaries rather than share options. For Marcus Gerhardt recruiting through networking also had the advantage that 'at least you know the spirit was going to be right and you foster a certain company culture'.

Since those networks were by their nature limited, mondus had to use other means. Headhunter agencies were employed to find executives such as chief financial officer, chief operations officer and country managers. In terms of finding directors and assistant managers, these agencies were 'not helpful since they really didn't understand our needs and couldn't meet them very well', remembered Gerhardt. Instead mondus found the Internet to be a useful tool.[18] 'Our Director for Marketing and our Director for Business Development have come to us through the Internet. They were early adopters of the Internet and brought along eight or ten years of experience in their field', he added.

Management challenges

Effectively managing all its activities was yet another major challenge for a rapidly growing company such as mondus. Dr Heupel noted:

> Focusing on the financial side to get enough money in, on the marketing side to get customers in, on the product development side in tailoring the product into a suitable form and balancing all these needs, that's a very difficult task.

The co-ordination of the four national markets and their office activities especially was a logistical challenge that needed a good communication structure in place.

Furthermore, the company was in a state of transition. While its vision was still founder-led, in terms of its processes mondus had already found its own way. Alexander Straub said: 'I have realized that very experienced managers with 10–15 years' work are much more effective than me because they know the processes.' In January 2000 Straub stepped down as the head of the US office and became Vice-Chairman of the Board of Directors. Whether Rouzbeh Pirouz stayed in the long-term as the CEO of mondus was still an open question.

Future outlook

Mondus was planning an initial public offering at the end of 2000. 'The timing of the IPO will depend primarily on whether it suits the company's development and on market conditions', explained Marcus Gerhardt.

> As for evaluation, it won't make any sense to engage now in any projections, especially in light of the current market volatility ... In the future, it will be important for mondus to consolidate the four markets [where we currently operate] without becoming an overburdened organization. The high level of productivity was our big plus over established players that have the SME relations that we are seeking, the money that we could never hope to get and the resources that we would never have.

Whether mondus could sustain its business model in the medium- to long-term was still an open question. According to AMR Research, 'bankruptcy, mergers, and acquisitions could swallow up as much as 90% of the current crop of online B2B marketplaces.'[19] George Reilly, Research Director at the GardnerGroup, shared this view: 'There will be a consolidation of [electronic] marketplaces. And the winners will be those that can execute transactions with value added.'[20]

18 Most people applied through Internet sites like hotjobs.com, topjobs.com or monster.co.uk.

19 Enos, L., 'Report: most online marketplaces will vanish', *e-Commerce Times*, 26 April 2000.

20 Dembeck, C., 'B2B ventures losing their allure', *e-Commerce Times*, 11 April 2000.

DISCUSSION QUESTIONS

1 What would you have done differently to mondus in designing, implementing and operating a B2B electronic marketplace?

2 If you were Rouzbeh Pirouz, the Chief Executive Officer of mondus.com, what strategic actions would you consider for the near- and medium-term to enhance further mondus' value-added and increase its market share? Defend your arguments.

3 Beyond the context of small- and medium-sized enterprises described in the case, what unique features (in terms of capabilities as well as potential advantages and drawbacks) can electronic marketplaces offer to large companies? You may answer this question in generic terms and/or in the context of one or more specific industries.

4 What criteria should a company use when choosing an electronic marketplace for its procurement activity?

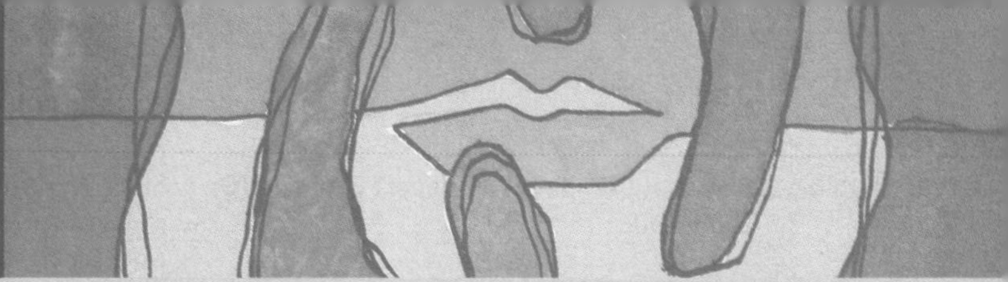

CASE STUDY 21

B2B e-marketplace in the automotive industry

Covisint: a co-opetition gamble?

On 25 February 2000, G. Richard Wagoner Jr, Jacques A. Nasser and Jürgen Schrempp, Chief Executive Officers of General Motors, Ford and DaimlerChrysler, respectively, announced in Detroit (Michigan) the joint creation of a businessto-business (B2B) integrated supplier exchange for the automotive industry. This new venture, in which the three car manufacturers would have an equity stake, would operate as a separate independent business, offering open participation to all companies in the automotive industry, i.e. automotive manufacturers and suppliers alike.

> As we continued to build our separate exchange sites, we quickly realized traditional, individual stand-alone models weren't the winning strategy for us, our industry, our suppliers and, ultimately, our customers. By joining together, we can further increase the pace of implementation, thereby accelerating the benefits to everyone involved. We are excited about the opportunity to build on what each of us started separately and creating the best trade exchange in the world.
>
> **G. Richard Wagoner Jr, President and Chief Operating Officer, General Motors Corporation[1]**

Industry overview

The automotive industry can be characterized by the following factors:[2]

- *Globalization of the industry*, driven by a search for economies of scale and market share and also by nationalistic investment strategies, has produced significant near-term overcapacity worldwide. This has led to unexpected side effects, such as downward pressures on real pricing, tighter margins, and significant mergers and acquisitions activity.
- *Excess capacity*[3] has grown from approximately 12 million units to 24 million in 1998, while utilization rate[4] has decreased from 80% to less than 70% over the same time period. This has led to several mergers and acquisitions in the industry, most notably the merger in 1999 of Daimler-Benz and Chrysler (see Exhibit 1). Through consolidation, it is expected that utilization rates will

Exhibit 1 Global excess capacity and utilization

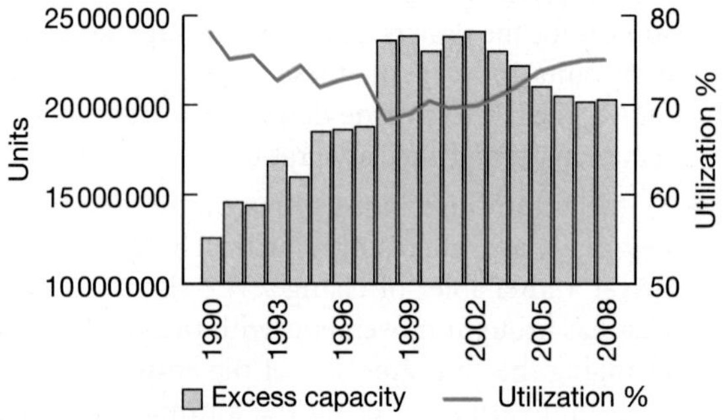

Source: The Global Automotive Outlook Summary, 2001, First Quarter, Autofacts, PricewaterhouseCoopers.

1 Detroit, 25 February 2000.
2 The Global Automotive Outlook Summary, 2001, First Quarter, Autofacts, PricewaterhouseCoopers.
3 Excess capacity = capacity – assembly (in millions of units).
4 Utilization rate = assembly/capacity.

This case was written by Tawfik Jelassi, Affiliate Professor of Technology Management at INSEAD, and Carlos Faria, MBA graduate of the Catholic University of Lisbon, Portugal. It is intended to be used as the basis for class discussion rather than to illustrate an effective or ineffective handling of a management situation.

Exhibit 2 Regional Combined Transport Group (CTG), 2000–2008

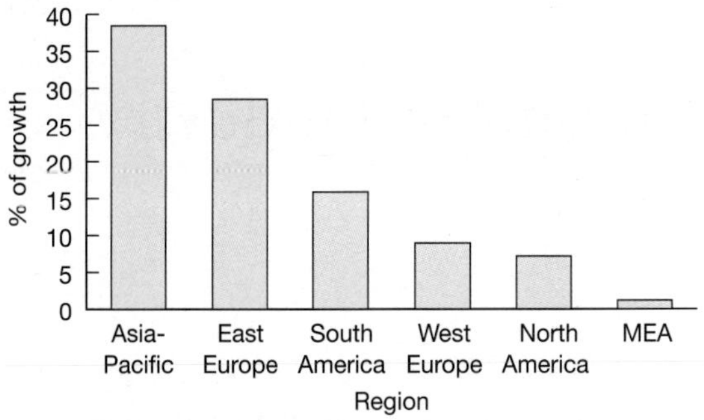

Source: The Global Automotive Outlook Summary, 2001, First Quarter, Autofacts, PricewaterhouseCoopers.

increase to approximately 76% by 2008 and excess capacity to 20 million units per year.

- Unlike mature markets, *emerging markets* (such as Asia-Pacific and Eastern Europe) represent the highest potential for future growth (see Exhibit 2).
- In order to meet their customers' needs, mergers and acquisitions at the original equipment manufacturers (OEM) caused a similar effect at the Tier One, Tier Two and Tier Three levels. On the *retail side and at the aftermarket level*, consolidation followed suit. Downstream activities are traditionally revenue sources for the dealers and the OEM suppliers. New e-entrants focused on these activities while the OEMs started to pursue downstream revenues in service, parts and ancillary products (see Exhibit 3).
- As the automotive industry restructures, *technology* plays an increasingly critical role, both as driver and enabler of change. The rise of e-business has brought movements with the potential of changing the configuration of the entire industry with innovations altering the automotive value chain. However, firms still need to find ways of organizing their activities and processes in order to derive the maximum benefit from e-business.

The emergence of Covisint

> Today's announcement is another example of how the Internet is transforming every piece of our company and our industry. It's exciting; it's dramatic, and it's only going to accelerate. We'll push this transformation even further to bring sustainable benefits to our customers, our suppliers and our dealers.
>
> **Jacques A. Nasser, President and Chief Executive Officer, Ford Motor Company**[5]

Since November 1999, GM and Ford have been working on their own Internet exchanges. Ford has formed its AutoXchange, General Motors (GM) its TradeXchange and DaimlerChrysler (DCX) its e-extended enterprise. Their plans, which were substantially different at the beginning of the exchange wars, were rapidly converging. TradeXchange initially focused on electronic purchasing. AutoXchange, on the other hand, focused on going beyond procurement towards supply chain management with broader initiatives such as advanced planning and scheduling, demand forecasting and design collaboration.

Soon after its first exchange announcement, GM changed its strategy to include a supply chain management tool similar to that of Ford. It quickly envisioned a web-enabled automotive production process, from ordering production materials to forecasting future demand to making cars to consumer specifications. Mark Duhaime, at that time Director of Ford's Program Management, explained this convergence: 'As we came out of the gate and ran for the last couple of months, you could see that our strategies were becoming more and more similar.'

While developing the exchanges, the 'Big Three' OEMs had difficulties in bringing their most important suppliers on board. Soon, the suppliers wondered how they would save any money by having to build three separate versions of the same commerce technology in order to do business with the 'Big Three' car manufacturers. Joining the different exchanges seemed to be the sensible action to take. According to Mark Duhaime: 'There has been a history of the suppliers dancing to the OEMs' tune. But we want to build true partnerships with our suppliers ... If we are telling the supply base that this is good for them, we can't give them a model that drives inefficiencies.'

In May 2000, the new exchange received the name of Covisint, which is intended to reflect the business drivers underlying its creation. The letters 'Co' refer to collaboration. 'Vis' represents the visibility that the Internet provides. The letters 'Int' refer to the integrated solutions the new venture will provide. Peter Weiss, former Co-CEO of Covisint,[6] explained:

> Connectivity and visibility are the promises of e-business. Connectivity is about connecting buyers and sellers into a single network. Visibility means real-time

5 Detroit, 25 February 2000.

6 Prior to the April 2001 appointment of Kevin English as CEO of Covisint.

Exhibit 3 Value chain activities in the automobile industry

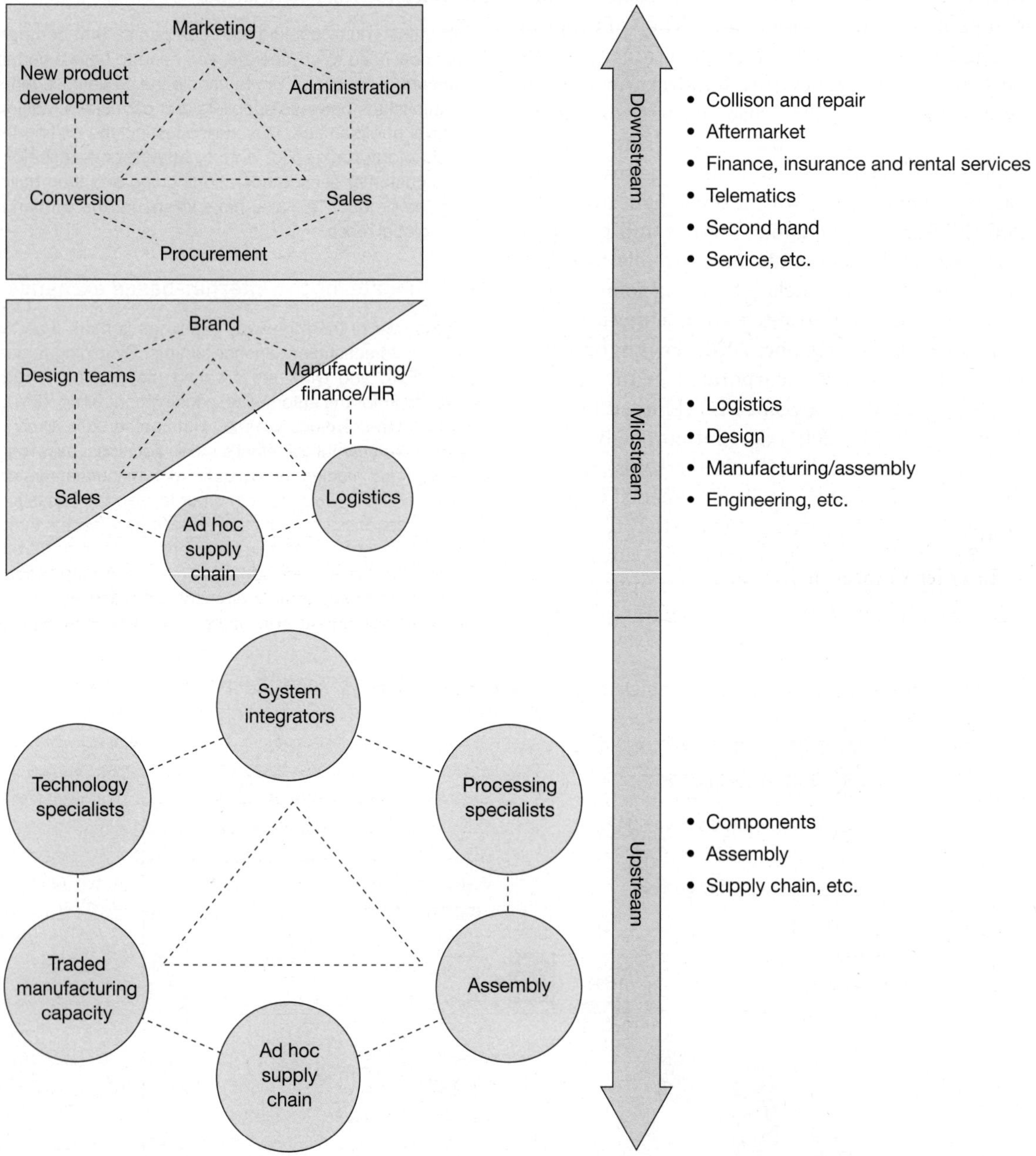

Source: The Global Automotive Outlook Summary, 2001, First Quarter, Autofacts, PricewaterhouseCoopers.

information presented in a way that speeds up decision making and enables communication through every level of a company's supply chain anywhere in the world.

On 14 April 2000, Renault and Nissan announced their decision to join the exchange. Three days later, Toyota Motor Corporation announced its intention to use the exchange, but without committing capital to the partnership.

In late March 2000, the Federal Trade Commission (FTC) decided to investigate the mega-exchange. Its

concern was to determine whether the combined purchasing power of the automakers could be anti-competitive for suppliers. The European Commission and the German government's anti-trust regulatory agency (the Bundeskartellamt, or BKA) followed suit. Silke Schau, in charge of marketing and communication at Covisint Europe, explained the delays caused by the anti-trust investigations. 'While waiting for the green light from FTC and the Bundeskartellamt, Covisint and the other (existing) exchanges could not formally have any communication. This delayed making some important decisions, and no integration activities could take place.' On 11 December 2000, Covisint became a legal entity and was incorporated in the state of Delaware (USA) as Covisint LLC (Limited Liability Company). In May 2001, Covisint Europe BV began operations in Amsterdam (the Netherlands), and one month later Covisint Asia-Pacific opened in Tokyo (Japan). At the same time, the European Commission gave its formal approval to Covisint.

In April 2001, Kevin English was appointed as CEO, who, prior to that, was in charge of Credit Suisse First Boston's e-commerce operations. He explained the challenges ahead:

> Any time you're dealing with companies that compete but now need to co-operate, you need to have a certain amount of finesse ... So, to handle the sometimes tense relationships between suppliers and carmakers requires a level of diplomacy. The challenges include getting the technology rock-solid, getting customer acquisitions and customer service operations going and then building the product. We also have to ensure the exchange has global reach.

The rationale for the Internet-based exchange

> The power of the three-way exchange is more than the sum of its constituent anchor tenants. By joining forces, GM, Ford and DMX are creating the dominant trade exchange for the automotive industry, controlling 46% of industry transactions volume, with another 20% likely to join in the near future. What's more, additional passenger vehicle and medium/heavy duty truck manufacturers are likely to join the exchange in order to reap the benefits of the tremendous economies of scale. In fact, such a three-way exchange could gain sufficient momentum that its scope broadens to include other manufacturing verticals including construction equipment, off-highway, marine, railroad equipment and others. DCX's involvement in

Exhibit 4 Percentage of global light vehicle supply chain transactions ($1300 billion)

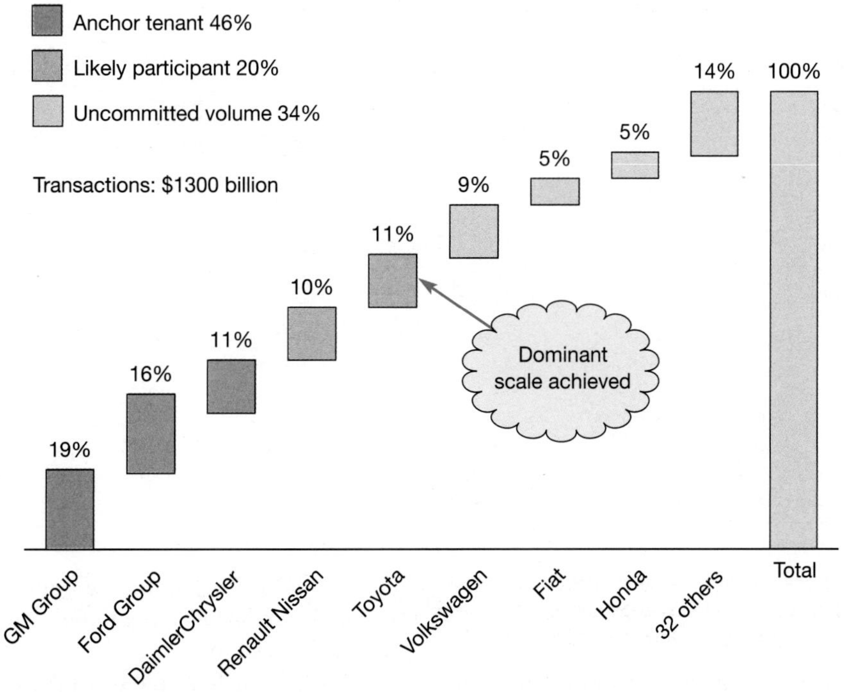

Does not include medium/heavy-duty transactions at DaimlerChrysler.
Source: GS Research estimates.

some of these areas, as well as its DASA aerospace unit, are not lost on the participants.

Gary Lapidus and Chris Laporte, Goldman Sachs Investment Research

The partners of the exchange have a joint world market share of 61%,[7] which could reach 72% if Toyota joins in with its 11% (see Exhibit 4). The world's total transaction volume is estimated at US$1300 billion.[8] The four companies' joint purchasing from their suppliers amounts to approximately US$300 billion.[9]

The exchange could bring a total supply chain cost reduction of US$1064 per vehicle, where the OEMs could save US$368 and the suppliers US$695.[10] For the suppliers, the cost savings would result from less scrap and rework (US$147), finding lower cost vendors (US$94), improved purchase processes (US$84), improved productivity (US$187), volume discounts (US$70), reduced inventory cost (US$67) and more detailed part specifications (US$46). For the OEMs, the cost savings would come from improved productivity (US$115), reduced scrap and rework (US$91), purchasing processes (US$76), fewer warranty repairs on cars (US$50) and reduced inventory cost (US$36) (see Exhibit 5).

The present value of Covisint could exceed US$40 billion.[11] In a potential initial public offering (IPO), besides the cost reductions and depending on the pricing and value strategies followed, the OEMs owning the exchange could increase their own indvidual share valuation in the stock market beyond what would be achievable individually.

The business strategy

Covisint aims at becoming the leading Internet-based B2B exchange platform in the automotive industry worldwide. It considers the worldwide reach of the Internet as crucial for the automotive industry in which both OEMs and Tier One companies are global

7 GM 19%, Fiat 5%, Ford 16%, DCX 11%, Renault-Nissan 10%; Lapidus, Garry and Laporte, Chris, 'e-Automotive', March 2000, Goldman Sachs Investment Research; Brewers, Janine, 'Mergers and acquisitions in the fast lane', *Corporate Finance*, April 2000.
8 Lapidus, Garry and Laporte, Chris, 'e-Automotive', March 2000, Goldman Sachs Investment Research.
9 Lauren Gibsons, Paul, *CIO Magazine*, 15 April 2000.
10 Lapidus, Garry and Laporte, Chris, 'e-Automotive', March 2000, Goldman Sachs Investment Research.
11 Ibid.

Exhibit 5 **Dollars per vehicle: global light vehicle supply chain transactions**

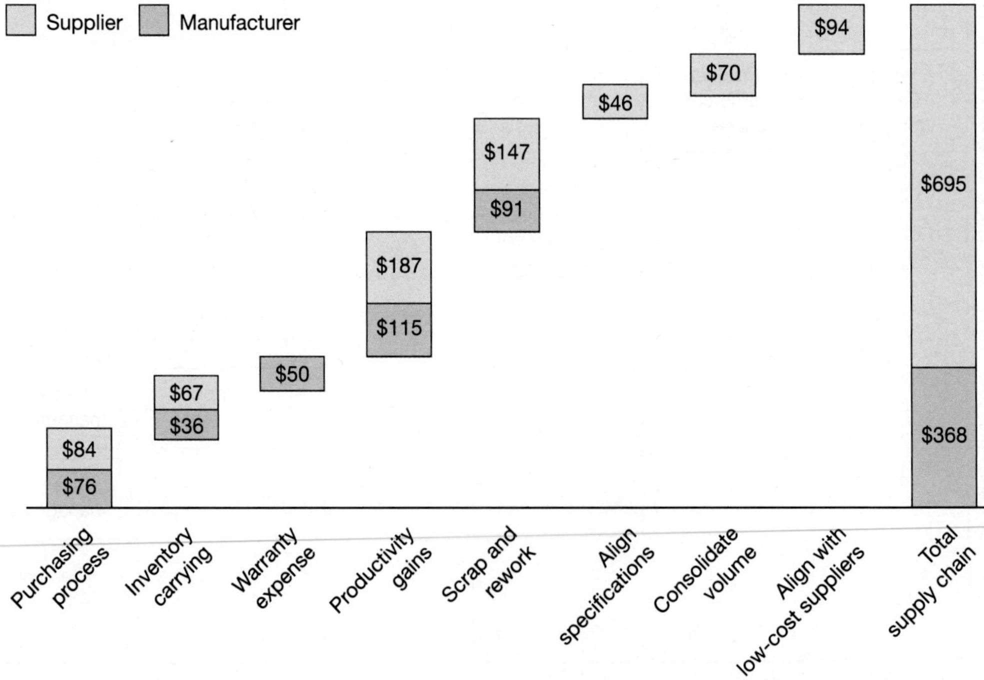

Source: GS Research estimates.

players. By linking the participants' supply chain and managing their inter-organizational information flows, Covisint expects to eliminate non-value-adding activities through the automation of some business processes. It also aims to contribute, through its tools, to meeting some of the major challenges the automotive industry faces: the reduction of the development cycle time of a vehicle, the compression of the order to delivery cycle, and the reduction of operating costs (including those of its suppliers).

Philipp Hartmann, Co-CEO of Covisint Europe,[12] explained:

> The vision is to become the leading exchange in the automotive industry. How far Covisint can go in the supply chain depends on the shareholders' value creation, keeping in mind that our target is to be a profitable organization. This drives the whole speed of how we work.

The business model

Covisint is a global Internet B2B exchange focused on the automotive industry, providing an open, standard-driven and secure platform to perform the key business processes of the industry. Its business model consists of linking OEMs and suppliers to reduce procurement costs, speed up information flows and enhance new product development. Covisint's capabilities include e-procurement, supply chain management and collaborative product development.

e-Procurement

Covisint supports purchasing processes and routine buying procedures, both for direct and indirect materials. The platform offers the following B2B purchasing models (see Exhibit 6):

- *Online catalogues* can be custom-made or community-based. Buyers and sellers authorize, through a mutual agreement, access to data held within Covisint. Custom-made catalogues comprise lists of approved products a buyer has with a supplier

12 Prior to the appointment of Kevin English as CEO.

Exhibit 6 **Covisint activities**

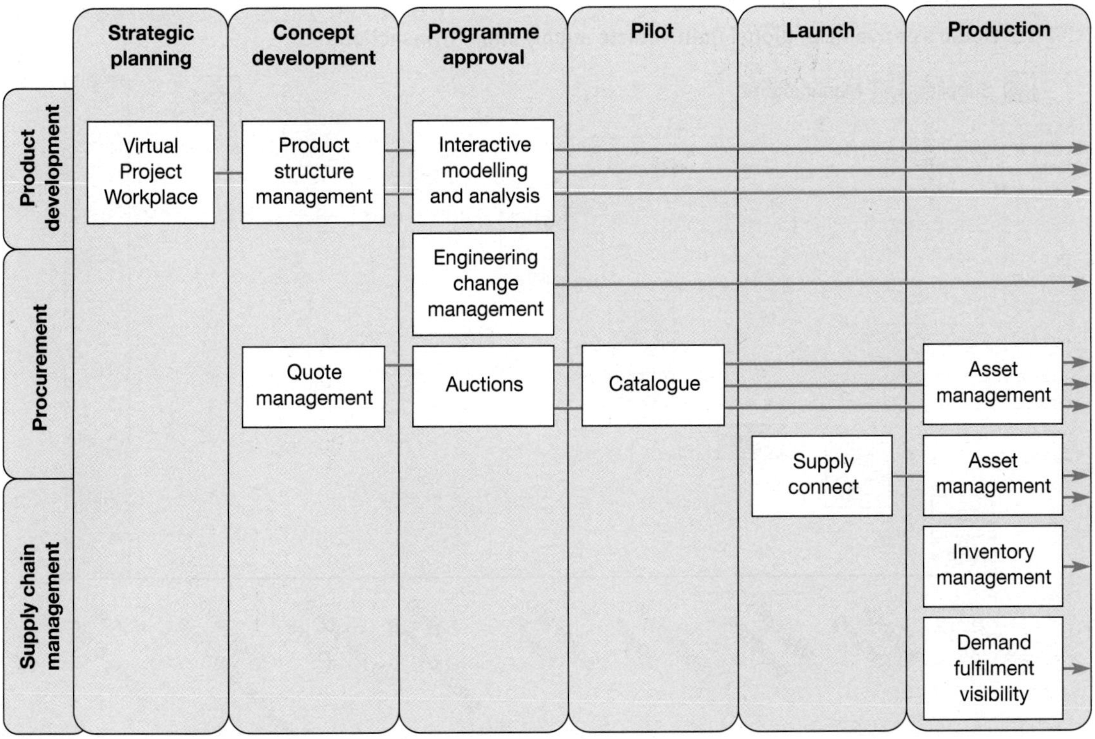

Source: Covisint.

with pre-negotiated prices. Community catalogues are multi-supplier-based and use market prices.

- *Online bidding events*: Buyers or sellers can organize online bidding events. Sellers' auctions are designed to launch an online bidding for excess or obsolete assets. The seller sets the timeframe and rules for the bidding process. Bidders submit their offers through a separate web-based user interface, while the seller monitors the event throughout. In buyers' auctions, bidders (sellers) submit price offers; they can submit multiple proposals or just a single bid. Through web-based tools, buyers review the incoming bids and select the winning bid, based on some criteria (such as price, quality, delivery terms, warranty, etc.). Actual contracts are still signed offline.
- *Quote management* consists of the electronic assembly, communication and response to sourcing requirements. It is the linking piece to online catalogues and auctions. It allows putting together complex bids, controlling document routing, managing workflows, approving electronic signatures, controlling user access from multiple organizations, posting and viewing documents in multiple formats, and sending e-mail notifications of document postings and revisions.
- *Asset management* enables tracking idle assets within a company for potential transfer, sale or scrap. It uses a database of valuation information that enables quick location of resources. Covisint offers the following three asset management services: idle asset database, asset valuation and fixed price listings.

Supply chain management

> GM says that when a customer orders a car with leather seats, the cow should wince. We want [to have] that type of communication from the dealer back through the chain, all the way down to the steel supplier that makes the steel bars that go into the forging that goes into the gear that goes into the power train.
>
> **Doug Grimm, Director of Global Strategic Sourcing, Dana Corporation (a Tier One supplier)**

Covisint's supply chain management (SCM) applications support the flow of online information between customers and suppliers. They enable participants to collaborate on production plans, based on capacity availability and constraints as well as inventory levels throughout the supply chain.

SCM key processes are the following:

- Planning and scheduling, which include forecast and capacity, metrics as well as messaging and alerts.
- Developing material releases, which involve engineering change notices, inventory visibility and pull system empowerment.
- Receipt of supplied items and parts, including transportation scheduling.
- Goods production.
- Packing and shipping, which include customs documentation, container management, network optimization, as well as freight payment and audit.

Covisint offers standard solutions (Supply Connect), allowing production controllers to manage communications, administration and reporting. Communications are managed through an individual mailbox, which can be organized by document type or trading partner. The mailbox includes the following folders: inbox, in process and sent. Files can be downloaded, and the information they contain (e.g. pictures, special instructions, etc.) used by the production controller.

The fulfilment service gives partners the possibility of quickly sharing critical information, such as inventory levels, usage history and patterns, forecast, in-transit inventories, receipts and other relevant information. The reporting feature offers a transactions log capability to review when a document was sent, received or acknowledged. It also provides a transaction summary to trace the routing history of a document.

Product development

Product development, also referred to as Virtual Project Workspace (VPW), is designed for multi-enterprise product development teams to manage information and communications. It also enables interaction, virtual meetings, product-specific data sharing and process automation. It aims at enhancing efficiency, while ensuring a high quality and low cost work process.

VPW applications support the management of data files, pictures (in 2D and 3D) and interactive multimedia files. They also support communications between teams within and across organizations and geographical locations. These communications include sharing information on work activities and

Exhibit 7 **Global organizational chart**

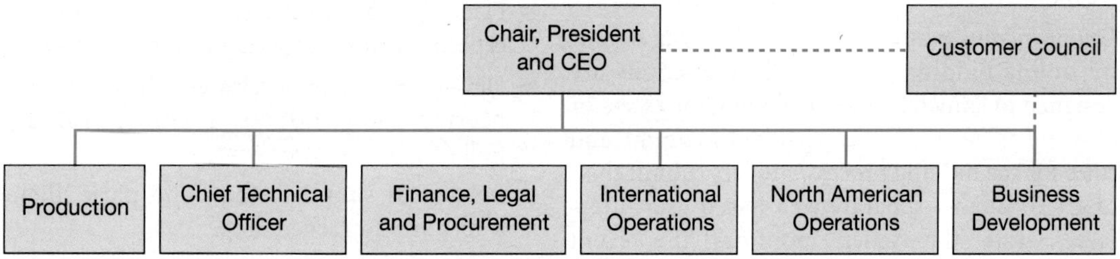

Source: Covisint.

schedule assignments as well as acknowledgement receipts. All data generated are then stored in databases and made available to authorized parties.

Covisint worldwide organization

> Covisint has gone from a vision to a planning organization to a company in less than 12 months. This unprecedented partnership is making history on many levels and Covisint is poised to assume a leading role in providing services to customers in the global automotive marketplace.
>
> **Dan Jankowski, spokesperson for Covisint**

Since its inception, and until April 2001, Covisint was managed by three Co-CEOs in the USA (Alice Miles from Ford, Peter Weiss from DCX and Rico Digirolamo from GM) and two Co-CEOs in Europe (Philipp Hartmann from DCX and Marc Siellet from Renault/Nissan). In April 2001, Kevin English was appointed CEO of Covisint (see Exhibit 7 for the organizational chart).

Covisint's worldwide headquarters are located near Detroit, Michigan (USA), where the main corporate functions are centralized. The Amsterdam-based European headquarters and the Tokyo-based Asian office of Covisint are in charge of sales and customer support activities for their regional markets. In addition, feedback is provided for future product and service offering developments.

Covisint Europe

Originally, the European operations of the exchange were located in Stuttgart, Germany. (See Exhibit 8 for the organizational chart of Covisint Europe.) In June 2001, it was moved to Amsterdam, which was selected

Exhibit 8 **Organizational chart of Covisint Europe**

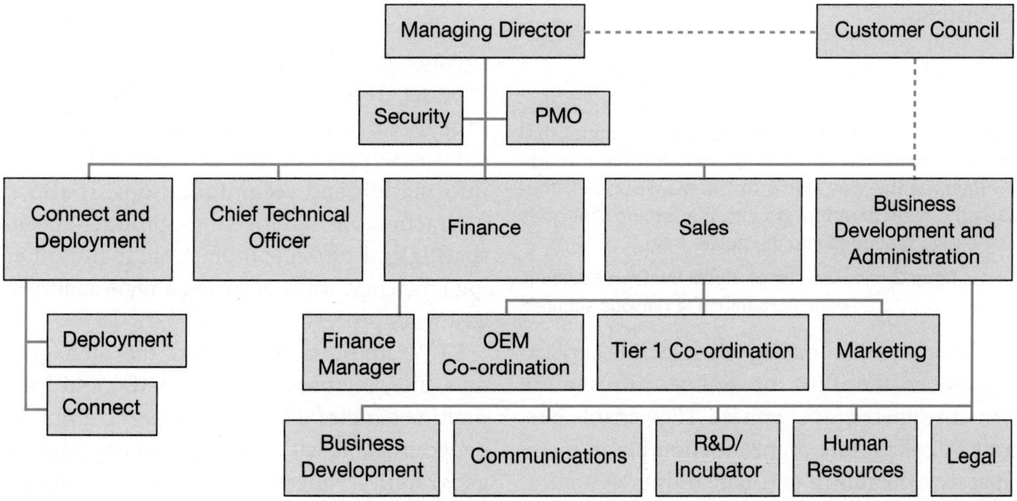

Source: Covisint.

for the international environment as well as the excellent infrastructure and facilities that it offered.

Major issues distinguishing Covisint Europe from the worldwide organization are the specificity of European customers, human resources, marketing and sales, and customer support. Philipp Hartmann commented:

> Do we want to serve our customers from our European office or do we want to tell them to use our servers in Chicago, which is technologically possible? All this depends on the strategy we want to have, the investment we want to make, and the attitude of our shareholders. Now, we have a data centre in Chicago, where the applications are run. A customer who logs on in Europe is actually working with the servers in Chicago. The question is whether to tell the engineers in Sindelfingen (Germany) that their new design data for the S-Class (Mercedes car) is lying somewhere in a data centre in Chicago. Does that work from a business point of view? Or do we think that it's better to tell him that there is a data centre in the Netherlands or in Germany?[13]

Human resources management

Since its inception, Covisint Europe has sought to recruit skilled people who are flexible and readily available to join the company. Henry Paccalin said:[14] 'When hiring middle managers, we look for mobility, international spirit, open-mindedness, people who are team players and fun to work with.' In September 2001, Covisint employed 170 people in the USA and 30 in Europe.

Before launching its recruitment process, Covisint defined its human resources and financial objectives, encompassing all the stages from establishing hiring needs to formulating work contracts. For every staff position to be filled, a job description was prepared, including the specifications of the skill set required. An appraisal system, called 'Performance Management Process', was also developed to serve as a basis for personnel evaluation.

Marketing

Covisint's founding car makers are promoting the exchange by using it to carry out their business activities. The OEMs are committed to Covisint, and conduct most of their transactions through it.

Covisint communication strategy focuses on three key issues:

- To clearly communicate to all players in the marketplace what Covisint is about.
- To keep all prospects and stakeholders informed about developments at Covisint.
- To keep all prospects actively engaged.

Covisint is promoted at industry events and conferences as well as through the Covisint portal and one-on-one marketing communications to key target groups. In October 2000, an advertising campaign was launched using major newspapers and aiming at creating brand awareness. Silke Schau explained: 'This does not bring any short-term advantages, but it creates awareness about our name.'

Product development

> In each of our product lines [procurement, supply chain management and product development], we have functionalities available that we enhance over time. In procurement we have auctions, catalogues and quote management. In the next release, we will introduce new functionalities. The biggest challenge is to meet customer needs.
>
> **Philip Hartmann, Co-CEO, Covisint Europe**

At Covisint, the product development process comprises the following stages:

- Build the business case. This stage includes evaluating the proposed project, establishing a value proposition, listing the expected benefits and analyzing the financial impact of the project.
- The business case is submitted to the product development team in the USA.

The product development team gathers from the USA, Europe and Asia all the information that is relevant to the proposed project. To decide whether to offer a given new product, Covisint addresses the following questions: What problems will the new product offering solve? Are these problems industry-wide or company-specific? Currently, Covisint proceeds with the development of a new product only if it can benefit the automotive industry as a whole and not just one company. Furthermore, it uses a 'best-of-breed' technology strategy while ensuring the integration of its solutions.

Information technology

Covisint IT strategy is based on the use of open standards to work with the ODETTE EDI[15] protocol for supply chain management. This allows Covisint to

13 Interview held in Stuttgart in February 2001.
14 Ibid.
15 ODETTE is the electronic data interchange (EDI) standard in the automotive industry.

Exhibit 9 **Structure of the Covisint IT platform**

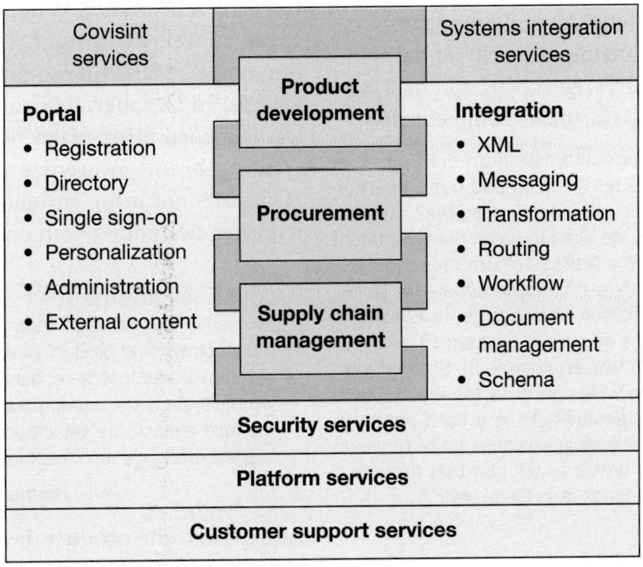

position itself between IT standards and the organizations working on business standards. Thus Covisint uses existing protocols that allow neutrality and enable customers to keep their legacy EDI systems or use XML.

Silke Schau said:

> Covisint should have an infrastructure as open as possible. Whatever systems customers have internally, Covisint should easily be adapted to them, so that the data transfer could be done easily and quickly. We want to avoid having customers handling or keying in data twice just because they use Covisint.[16]

Covisint technology consists of the following components arranged along a U-shape (see Exhibit 9):

- A front-end customer interface, which is browser-based.
- A back-end integration interface.
- XML-based message format.
- Communications handled by middleware, providing data integrity and delivery guarantee.
- Encryption based on SSL3 (Secure Socket Layer) or S/mime (asymmetric keys).

Access to the exchange is password-protected. It allows any member company to choose the partner(s) it wants to communicate with. It is only the member companies that can provide access to their partners.

Covisint set up internal procedures to enforce security, including the development of a corporate policy document on confidentiality issues and having internal staff look after physical security. More specifically, security is technically enforced at the following three levels:

- Physical security through the establishment of a secure data centre.
- Logical security through encryption, users' authentication, authorization and integrity.
- Organizational procedures such as subcontracts with hackers to test the platform.

Finance

> People are looking and saying where's the beef? [They say] prove to me that you can build a durable, profitable company and you'll get the valuation. I think the hype has been taken out of the equation – and thank goodness for that.
>
> **Kevin English, CEO, Covisint Worldwide**

In addition to its founding members (i.e. Ford, GM and DaimlerChrysler), Covisint's shareholders today include Renault/Nissan and PSA Peugeot Citroën and technology partners (from the beginning) Oracle and Commerce One. Bernard Jentner explained: 'We are in the start-up phase of a new business. We have to learn from experience and

16 Interview held in Stuttgart in February 2001.

adjust our business plan and revenue model accordingly.'[17]

The payback criteria that Covisint used are based more on market valuation than on the net present value (NPV). The exchange was aiming for an IPO in 2002 or 2003, soon after reaching its expected first profitable quarter, and planned to float its shares on the New York Stock Exchange. Bernard Jentner said:

> For an IPO, the market has to assess several quarters in order to produce its analysis [of the company]. It has to check the fundamentals underlying our industry, the validity of our concept, our ability to achieve profits and our growth potential. The IPO will probably take place in 2002 or 2003, depending on our ability to meet our ambitious business plan. We want to break even before going for an IPO. Of course, the sooner we can reach our break-even point, the better it will be.[18]

Robyn Meredith, an industry analyst, had a sceptical view of Covisint's achievements to date and of its future potential. She said:

> Fourteen months after the creation of Covisint, nothing has worked as smoothly, as quickly or as profitably as planned. The B2B exchange is floundering and has no hope of living up to its hype ... Covisint's owners have spent a combined US$170 million on their fat company, including US$50 million on a pack of consulting firms. The site now burns through US$12 million a month. The partners expect to spend up to US$350 million before Covisint breaks even, which they hope will be before the end of 2002. And for all that cash, Covisint last year handled less than 1% of the carmakers' purchases. This year, it aims for 30%, US$75 billion, a nearly impossible goal.[19]

The revenue model

> Covisint revenues will primarily come from subscription fees for various services, but also from transaction fees and set-up fees. We are competitively priced in the market ... Online exchanges like Covisint will move to a subscription fee model that bundles a variety of e-business tools.
>
> **Kevin Vasconi, Chief Technical Officer, Covisint USA**

The Covisint revenue model is based on transaction fees, subscription fees, service charges and hosting fees. The exchange provides consulting services to its customers to integrate their own IT systems into the Covisint platform. Charges for these services are made on an hourly fee basis.

For the e-procurement applications, the fees that are charged for using the online catalogue and auction tools depend on the transaction volume being handled. The seller pays a fee ranging from 1% to 4% of the value of the contract;[20] this fee varies according to the participant's size. For the supply chain management and the product development (VPW) applications, a subscription fee per user is used. This fee varies according to the specific package(s) used.

Covisint usage

From the beginning of operations until September 2001, Covisint had over 2600 companies registered for using the platform. By September 2001, online auctions were the most used tool, with over 1000 online bidding events organized and cumulative transactions totalling US$45 billion. More than 200 online catalogues were in use, offering 2.5 million individual items (or SKUs)[21] and resulting in 61 000 transactions. The supply chain management tools were used by 1500 companies and had 2300 seats sold. The Virtual Project Workspace (VPW) tool, which was aggregated, with the quote management tool, had more than 500 seats sold and in use (see Table 1).

Customers' perspective

> Participating in Covisint underscores our commitment to be an industry leader in OEM business-to-business initiatives. We believe Covisint will provide benefits to the entire automotive industry by promoting innovative product solutions, following common standards and creating an infrastructure that reduces system inefficiencies through improved communications between suppliers and customers. Given Collins & Aikman's unique position as both a key Tier One and major Tier Two supplier, participation in Covisint will not only enhance our own business opportunities, but will also provide benefits for our customers and suppliers worldwide.
>
> **Thomas E. Evans, Chair and CEO, Collins & Aikman**

In order to create momentum, it was important, from the beginning, for Covisint and for the OEMs to get from some of the most important Tier One suppliers support and commitment for the use of the exchange. Some suppliers actually wanted to be the first to do so to show to the OEMs their commitment. They also hoped to have a privileged business relationship with the OEMs.

---

17 Ibid.
18 Ibid.
19 'Harder than the hype', *Forbes Global*, 16 April 2001.
20 'Culture: fear of the unknown may be the worst', www.news.cnet.com
21 SKUs stands for strategic key units.

Table 1 **Covisint metrics**

	Accumulated			
	Until December 2000	*End of February 2001*	*End of June 2001*	*End of September 2001*
Auctions				
Events	100	325	420	>1000
Volume transactions ($ million)	350	1500	36 000	45 000
Companies involved	NA	800		
Catalogues				
No. of catalogues	NA	250	>200	>200
No. of stock keeping units	NA	NA	2 500 000	>2 500 000
No. of transactions	NA	NA	>20 000	61 000
SCM				
No. of seats sold	NA	NA	>1500	2300
VPW/quote management				
No. of seats sold	NA	200	>500	>500
No. of companies involved	NA	6	NA	NA
Registration				
No. of companies registered	NA	NA	>1000	>2600

For the OEM users of Covisint, the results they have achieved to date through the exchange have been satisfactory. However, they shared suppliers' fears regarding the conflict of interests in the margins shared between customers and suppliers.

Recently, Ford tried out a reverse auction for tyres, which are considered a true commodity by most carmakers. Brian Beursmeyer, the e-Business Strategic Planning Manager at Ford commented on this successful experiment:

> Five tire manufacturers went online early in the morning, starting with an initial bid set by Ford. Twelve hours later, they were still bidding, and the suppliers kept lowering the price. The market tension that this created was dramatically different from the traditional buying process. You're going to see a ripple effect through the whole supply chain as a result of this. Ford understands that achieving lower prices alone may not lead it to true supply chain nirvana. Squeezing people on price isn't that good if you can't make your suppliers more efficient.[22]

After the numerous mergers and acquisitions that have taken place over the past few years, some companies in the automotive industry are relying on Covisint to help them better integrate their information systems and business processes worldwide. This was the case, for example, for Lear Corp., one of the world's largest manufacturers of auto interiors, which joined Covisint in 2000. 'Many of our facilities around the world were acquired in the past four years, and their IT systems don't always communicate', said Jim Vandenberghe, Vice-Chair of Lear Corp. He continued:

> Using phone, fax, and mail to exchange data between supply chain tiers leads to errors and a slow response time. Covisint is a key part of our strategy to integrate our operations around the world. There's no way that we can get on our own the same kind of efficiency that an exchange like Covisint offers for our supply base.[23]

Industry analysts' perspective

Some industry analysts have been sceptical about the way Covisint was formed, its hybrid structure and exquisite format. The complexity of the project, the size of the exchange and its target impact in the medium- and long-term are additional sources for this scepticism.

Robyn Meredith commented:

> In some ways, it is remarkable that Covisint has survived this long. It was created for the wrong reason – as much to cash in on a dot-com stock sale as to overhaul parts buying. It was born to a dysfunctional family of three parents given to fierce infighting. Its technology comes from two companies with a poisonous rivalry,

22 www.forbes.com
23 www.cio.com

> Oracle and Commerce One. Auto suppliers, its would-be customers, view Covisint as a transparent attempt to divert their profits to carmakers, forcing it to resort to discounting and arm-twisting to bring them on board. Even Covisint's mission is split: it must be both a cooperative cost-cutting tool and, eventually, a profitable, stand-alone company.[24]

PricewaterhouseCoopers has advised its customers that are suppliers to the OEMs to join a public exchange and also to invest in their own e-systems.

Future challenges

> We want to be the dial-tone for the car industry. That's absolutely still the vision, but over time. I've never known a company that can be all things to all people on day one. This is all about flawless execution.
>
> **Kevin English**

Competitive environment

Covisint's main competitor is SupplyOn.com, another electronic marketplace founded by the OEMs. The recent recruitment of PSA Peugeot Citroën should boost the build up of Covisint operations in Europe, where the exchange has had a lower profile than in the USA. However, it still leaves Volkswagen and BMW, who have private exchanges, outside Covisint's reach, while in Asia, the main hold-outs are Toyota (who has a 'wait and see' attitude by not revealing to what extent it will use the exchange) and Honda.

In the upstream area, there are several exchanges (e.g. e-steel, which is co-operating with Covisint) that have specialized in different products that are also used by the automotive industry. FreeMarkets.com is another competitor that has specialized in online auctions and successfully generated significant business from some companies operating in the automotive industry (see Exhibit 10).

Coping with change

One of the challenges that Covisint faces is being able to cope with a changing business environment and continuous technology advances. Philip Hartmann explained:

> If you have a leading edge business, things change very quickly. Because while you think you are on the right track, suddenly you see that there are new influences, which you have never thought about before. Or you develop new ideas to go into the next business, for example to provide guidance and support to your customers.[25]

Philip Hartmann further elaborated:

> For Covisint to get fully established, it'll take a lot more than just pursuing a plan within a certain timeframe. It involves many complex issues, including people and change management ... We work hard every day on getting Covisint fully established. The difficulties and challenges are becoming clearer. Certain things are going very well and others aren't progressing as well as expected. It's not so much about the implementation of the exchange, but about its integration into customers' business processes. How would users accept it? How would they adapt their business procedures and IT infrastructure? If you use daily a business process and suddenly you have to change it to fit a new tool, some steps will fall out due to the increased efficiency.[26]

Extending Covisint to other industries

Covisint can be extended, in the medium- to long-term, to other industries. 'We are seeing if it makes sense, if our customers need that and if their response would be positive', said Philip Hartmann.

> For example, we have just linked Covisint to e-steel [the Internet exchange in the steel industry]. This would allow a buyer in the automotive industry to connect through Covisint and its different applications to e-steel and buy steel. We would extend the industry scope of Covisint only if there is a good fit and customers' demand for it.[27]

Covisint may be well positioned to establish standards in the automotive industry. However, whether it will be able to set standards in other industries (for example, by forging strategic alliances with other industry players) remains to be seen.

Enhancing the value proposition

> We're coming out with a new suite of next-generation [software] product that will let us 'plug and play' ... It will be a much easier and more cost-effective way into their legacy systems. So I think we're going to improve our value proposition over time.
>
> **Kevin English**

Time-to-market

In the time it has taken Covisint to get established, the OEM and some big suppliers have decided to

24 'Harder than the hype', Meredith, R. *Forbes Global*, Vol. 167, No. 9, 16 April 2001.
25 Interview held in Stuttgart in February 2001.
26 Ibid.
27 Ibid.

Exhibit 10 **Competitive environment**

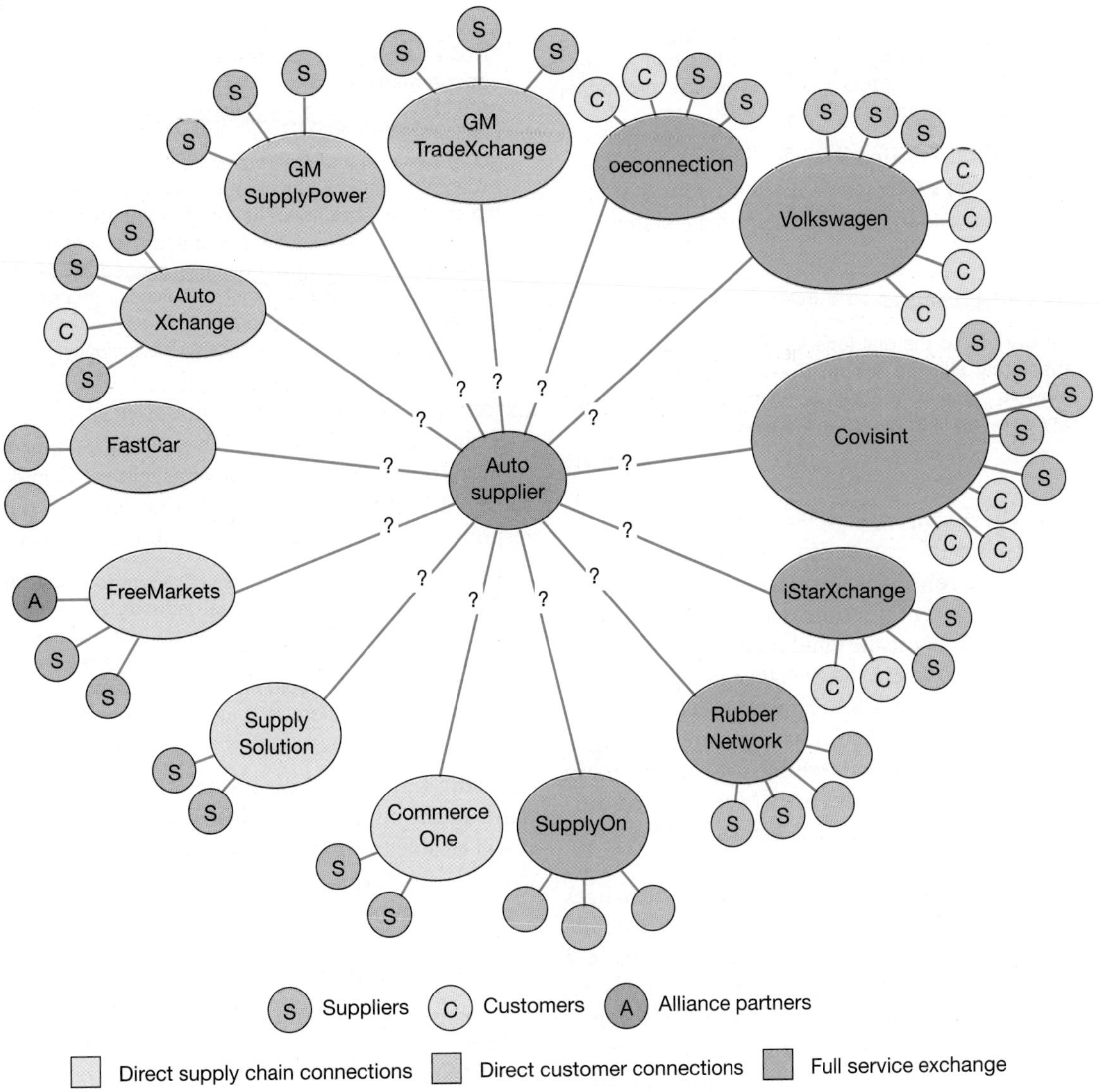

Source: PricewaterhouseCoopers.

construct their own e-business systems, aiming to use these to deal with their own supply base. Kevin English said:

> I'm not sure that some of the suppliers who have decided to do their own thing understand the hidden costs, the time it takes … The business-to-business exchanges that haven't worked have all lacked industry sponsorship. Covisint has huge industry sponsorship … It will just take some time to get this thing to the scale we want … The suppliers I have talked to are very interested, but we represent revolutionary rather than evolutionary change – and revolutionary change takes time.

As stated above, Covisint obviously faces several important challenges. However, it remains to be seen whether it can achieve its objectives and eventually become a B2B industry standard, or whether it proves to be a losing co-opetition gamble. Clearly, the jury is still out …

DISCUSSION QUESTIONS

1 What is, in your opinion, the unique selling proposition of Covisint? Can it lead to achieving a competitive advantage?

2 Assess the suitability of the revenue model used by Covisint (as described in the case). What changes would you make to this model?

3 If you were the CEO of Covisint, how would you address the challenges that the company faces today?

4 In some ways it is remarkable that Covisint has survived this long. It was created for the wrong reason – as much to cash in on a dot-com stock sale as to overhaul parts buying. It was born to a dysfunctional family of three parents given to fierce infighting. Its technology comes from two companies with a poisonous rivalry, Oracle and Commerce One. Auto suppliers, its would-be customers, view Covisint as a transparent attempt to divert their profits to carmakers, forcing it to resort to discounting and arm-twisting to bring them on board. Even Covisint's mission is split: it must be both a cooperative cost-cutting tool and, eventually, a profitable, stand-alone company.

From 'Harder than the hype', Robyn Meredith, *Forbes Global*, Vol. 167, No. 9, 16 April 2001.

Provide your own analysis of and position on the views expressed above. Defend your arguments.

CASE STUDY 22

eBay strategy (A)

> eBay is my life. It is my freedom!
>
> eBay gives me a fun way to bring a little cheer to people who really want to find something and I have it. I have met some wonderful people through my buys and sells.
>
> **Comments from members of the eBay community**[1]

Conceived in 1995 on 'a really good idea' from Pierre Omidyar, a 31-year-old software development engineer in California, eBay had grown beyond the wildest imaginations of its founder into one of the successes of the Internet revolution. 'While its peers burned their start-up cash, eBay became a phenomenon – a Silicon Valley company that has always made a profit and is the world's most successful Internet group.'[2] (Table 1 provides a summary of selected financial and operational data on eBay.)

From humble roots in enabling trade in candy dispensers, eBay has grown to become the world's largest online marketplace for the sale of goods and services by a diverse community of individuals and businesses. Between 1998 and 2002, the number of confirmed, registered eBay users grew from approximately 2 million to 62 million worldwide. In the fourth quarter of 2002, eBay boasted 195 million listings, and in that whole year had completed transactions totalling US$14.9 billion.[3] According to Media Metrix measures in September 2002, eBay was the fifth ranked Internet portal in terms of reach (28%) and fourth ranked in terms of minutes/user (111). For a firm that reported less than US$100 million in after-tax profits, eBay boasted a market capitalization of some US$21.2 bn.[4]

Was eBay just a very lucky firm that had caught the wave in time? Or was it doing something fundamentally different and insightful?

Company background

> eBay is a place where small people can be big.
>
> **Michael van Swaaij, VP Europe**

In company documents, eBay defined its mission as helping 'practically anyone trade practically anything on earth'. The eBay trading platform was an automated, topically arranged, easy-to-use, online service that was available on a 24-hours-a-day, seven-days-a-week basis and that enabled sellers to list items for sale and buyers to bid for and purchase items of interest.

eBay's big start was in tapping effectively into a segment of individuals that traded collectables – one-of-a-kind items that usually came with a story or some unusual feature. Michael van Swaaij explained:

> There were no efficient means of trading collectables. Collectors found it very difficult to get in touch with other collectors who may want to buy their collectables.

1 http://pages.ebay.com/community/aboutebay/community/profiles.html
2 Paul Abrahams and Thorold Barker, 'eBay, the flea market that spanned the globe', *Financial Times*, 11 January 2002.
3 eBay Company Update, February 2003.
4 Amazon's market capitalization on the same date (6 December 2002) was US$8.6 billion. Earlier, on 8 March 1999, eBay's market capitalization was US$21 billion, as compared to US$19 billion for Amazon.

This case was written by Soumitra Dutta, The Roland Berger Chaired Professor of Business and Technology, and Subramanian Rangan, Associate Professor of Strategy and Management, both at INSEAD, as a basis for class discussion rather than to illustrate either effective or ineffective handling of an administrative situation.

> The physical marketplace for trading collectables, prior to eBay, was very inefficient. eBay created an efficient marketplace for trading collectables and gave easy access to this marketplace to collectors. The marketplace was open. *Everyone* could go there. This was really important.

The principle of operating a non-exclusive marketplace was an anchor of eBay's strategy. One consequence was that eBay's item mix expanded rapidly from primarily collectables to include practical everyday items, such as household goods, computers, consumer electronics and other tradables (such as tickets to sporting events). Item proliferation and the patterns of interest they generated would guide the creation of new categories. The aim of introducing new categories was to keep search simple and ease of use high. Patterns of user interest also guided marketing (especially where to advertise to draw users to the eBay site).

Beyond the proliferation of categories, another consequence of the non-exclusive policy was reflected in the growing diversity of the user base. eBay's user base had grown from individual consumers to also include merchants, small to mid-sized businesses, and, eventually, global corporations, and even government agencies. Still, in 2002, 95% of the value of total transactions on eBay was generated by individuals and small businesses.

Between June 1999 and October 2002, the daily average number of bids at eBay had increased from 0.9 million to 5.25 million, and the daily average number of page views had increased from 54 million to 460 million. Furthermore, even while the number of registered users and transactions increased, gross merchandise sales (i.e. transaction value) per customer had remained relatively stable at around US$65. (Appendix 1 provides a summary of the trading experience on eBay, and Appendix 2 provides a brief description of the major services available on eBay.)

eBay's revenues came primarily from fees that users paid for listings and completed transactions. To list items for sale, sellers on the site paid a nominal listing fee. (Appendix 3 describes the fee structure of eBay.) By paying incremental placement fees, sellers could have items featured in various special ways. For example, a seller could highlight their item for sale by utilizing a bold font for the item heading, or opt for the Buy-It-Now feature, which enabled a seller to close an auction instantly, once a specified price was reached. eBay also collected (relatively small) fees when transactions were completed.

Also, through the acquisitions of Butterfields and Kruse, eBay had entered the 'offline' auction business. Butterfields, established in 1865, was the largest auction house headquartered on the west coast of the USA. It specialized in fine art, antiques, and collectables. Kruse, which operated in the state of Indiana, was established in 1971, and was one of the world's leading collector car auction companies.

Trading platform

The eBay trading platform was composed of a user interface and transaction processing system based on internally developed proprietary software. The eBay platform supported the complete sale process, including notifying users via e-mail when they initially registered for the service, placed a successful bid, were outbid, listed an item for sale, and when an auction ended. The platform also sent daily status updates to active sellers and bidders.

The platform regularly updated a text-based search engine with the titles and descriptions of new items, as well as pricing and bidding updates for active items. eBay's proprietary software also helped its product managers keep close tabs on the relative growth or decline of the sales of different items. These trends were used to decide when to split highly successful categories into sub-categories or to merge less successful categories.

The cost of eBay's internal development efforts totalled about US$25 million in 1999, US$56 million in 2000, and US$75 million in 2001. (See figures under 'Product development' in Table 1).

A business based on trust

To get people comfortable with the idea of trading online, eBay had created the Feedback Forum – a system of mutual user feedback. The system encouraged every user to provide comments and feedback on other eBay users with whom they interacted, and offered user profiles that included feedback ratings and incorporated user experiences. The Feedback Forum required feedback to be related to specific transactions. eBay prohibited

Table 1 eBay selected consolidated financial data

(a) Consolidated statement of income data

	Year ended 31 December				
	1997	1998	1999	2000	2001
	(in thousands, except per share data)				
Net revenues	$41 370	$86 129	$224 724	$431 424	$748 821
Cost of net revenues	8 404	16 094	57 588	95 453	134 816
Gross profit	32 966	70 035	167 136	335 971	614 005
Operating expenses					
Sales and marketing	15 618	35 976	96 239	166 767	253 474
Product development	831	4 640	24 847	55 863	75 288
General and administrative	6 534	15 849	43 919	73 027	105 784
Payroll expense on employee stock options	–	–	–	2 337	2 442
Amortization of acquired intangible assets	–	805	1 145	1 433	36 591
Merger related costs	–	–	4 359	1 550	–
Total operating expenses	22 983	57 270	170 509	300 977	473 579
Income (loss) from operations	9 983	12 765	(3 373)	34 994	140 426
Interest and other income (expense) net	(1 951)	(703)	21 412	46 025	46 276
Impairment of certain equity investments	–	–	–	–	(16 245)
Income before income taxes	8 032	12 062	18 039	81 019	170 457
Provision for income taxes	(971)	(4 789)	(8 472)	(32 725)	(80 009)
Net income	$7 061	$7 273	$9 567	$48 294	$90 448

Source: eBay Annual Report, 2001.

(b) Consolidated balance sheet data

	Year ended 31 December				
	1997	1998	1999	2000	2001
	(in thousands)				
Cash and cash equivalents	$12 109	$37 285	$221 801	$201 873	$523 969
Short-term investments	–	40 401	181 086	354 166	199 450
Long-term investments	–	–	373 988	218 197	286 998
Restricted cash and investments	–	–	–	126 390	129 614
Working capital	(1 881)	72 934	372 266	538 022	703 666
Total assets	62 350	149 536	969 825	1 182 403	1 678 529
Long-term debt	16 307	18 361	15 018	11 404	12 008
Total stockholders' equity	$9 722	$100 538	$854 129	$1 013 760	$1 429 138

Source: eBay Annual Report, 2001.

(c) Online, US and international net revenues

	1999	Per cent change	2000	Per cent change	2001
	(in thousands, except per cent changes)				
Online net revenues					
Transactions	$179 895	94%	$348 174	73%	$602 671
Third-party advertising	2 030	541%	13 022	544%	83 853
End-to-end services and promotions	608	4 959%	30 756	(9%)	27 881
Total online net revenues	182 533	115%	$391 952	82%	714 405
Butterfields	31 319	(6%)	29 405	(14%)	25 251
Kruse	10 872	(7%)	10 067	(9%)	9 165
Total offline net revenues	42 191	(6%)	39 472	(13%)	34 416
Total net revenues	$224 724	92%	$431 424	74%	$748 821

Table 1 continued

(c) Online, US and international net revenues cont.

	1999	Per cent change	2000	Per cent change	2001
		(in thousands, except per cent changes)			
US net revenues	$222 130	81%	$402 446	58%	$634 659
International net reveneus	2 594	1 017%	28 978	294%	114 162
Total net revenues	$224 724	92%	$431 424	74%	$748 821

Source: eBay Annual Report, 2001.

(d) Supplemental operating data

	1999	Per cent change	2000	Per cent change	2001
		(in millions, except per cents and per listing amounts)			
Confirmed registered users at end of year	10.0	125%	22.5	89%	42.4
Number of items listed	129.6	104%	264.7	60%	423.1
Gross merchandise sales	$2 805	93%	$5 422	72%	$9 319

Cost of net revenues for eBay's online business consists primarily of costs associated with customer support and site operations, such as employee compensation and facilities costs for customer support, site operations compensation and Internet connectivity charges. Cost of net revenues for eBay's offline business consists primarily of employee compensation for auction, appraisal and customer support personnel as well as direct auction costs, such as event site rental.

Product development expenses consist primarily of employee compensation, payments to outside contractors, depreciation on equipment and corporate overhead allocations.

eBay's third-party advertising revenue is derived principally from the sale of online banner and sponsorship advertisements for cash and through barter arrangements. The duration of the banner and sponsorship advertising contracts has ranged from one week to three years, but is generally one week to three months.

eBay's end-to-end services and promotions revenues are derived principally from contractual arrangements with third parties that provide transaction services to eBay users. The duration of these end-to-end services and promotions contracts have ranged from one to three years.

Source: eBay Annual Report, 2001.

actions that undermined the integrity of the Feedback Forum,[5] such as a person leaving positive feedback about themselves through multiple accounts or leaving multiple negative feedback for others through multiple accounts. Users that developed positive reputations had colour-coded star symbols displayed next to their user names to indicate the number of positive feedback ratings they had received. Before bidding on items listed for sale, eBay users were encouraged to review a seller's feedback profile to check their reputation within the eBay community. Users receiving a threshold rating of negative net feedback had their registrations suspended, and were not allowed to bid on or list items for sale.[6] Michael van Swaaij elaborated:

> On eBay, users can be anonymous.[7] Behind the user ID, no one need know whether there is an individual working from a bedroom or a large corporation. However, once you start trading, our feedback system gives you an individualized personality. It gives you a reputation within the marketplace that is critical for your trading success. Would you send money to a seller that you do not trust?

In addition to the Feedback Forum, eBay had created the SafeHarbor programme, which provided guidelines

5 The Feedback Forum had several automated features designed to detect and prevent some forms of abuse. For example, feedback posting from the same account, positive or negative, could not affect a user's net feedback rating (i.e. the number of positive postings less the number of negative postings) by more than one point, no matter how many comments an individual had made. Also, a user could only leave feedback on completed transactions.

6 Description from company documents, including the eBay 2001 Annual Report.

7 On eBay, users could also publicly disclose their identity and provide information about guarantees. For example, sellers could give their physical location and contact details and guarantee the quality of their merchandise.

for trading, information for resolving user disputes, and responded to reports of misuse of the eBay service.

Marketing

eBay employed a variety of methods to build brand awareness and interest, including trade shows, participation in certain events, public relations and word of mouth. To attract new users, eBay used online advertising in local areas in which eBay believed it could reach a target audience. Malte Feller of eBay Germany commented:

> We believe strongly in the value of local business development. We have more than 60 employees at eBay Germany devoted to local sales and marketing. Their function includes the identification of local opportunities for building and sustaining customer interest in eBay. For example, if we started a new category in antique cars, they would search out the associations, meetings and publications for people interested in selling and buying antique cars, and actively use those venues to promote eBay.

The aim in established markets such as the USA was to nurture the brand, acquire new users, and increase the activity of existing users. Accordingly, eBay focused on producing a consistent image through online, television, and print and radio advertising. Also, under the rubric of eBay University, representatives conducted free seminars in various local markets to help eBay members to buy and sell more effectively.

A sense of community

> eBay exists because of the strength and spirit of our community. At the very core of this online company is a community of people who have built it to become the largest Internet marketplace.
>
> **Meg Whitman, eBay CEO[8]**

Apparently, eBay members came together to do more than just buy or sell – they shopped around, got to know one another, had fun, and sometimes pitched in to help. Through the eBay public discussion and chat boards, members got to know one another and discussed topics of mutual interest. The community also helped ensure that all members followed the eBay guidelines. eBay encouraged open and honest communication throughout the community and the company. Frequently, members of the community organized grassroot movements to improve the environment in which they worked and shopped.

The sense of community was alive offline, too. Some eBay members had planned vacations together, chipped in and bought a special item for another member, and even spent vacation time doing home repairs for an eBay member in need. Michael van Swaaij gave an example of the camaraderie that existed between members of the eBay community:

> We once heard of a collector in Florida who picked up a shoebox of postcards from a garage sale. He knew from a previous trade an eBay member in France who collected postcards. He sent the entire box of postcards over from Florida to France with the note, 'Take what you like, pay me what you want and send the rest of the postcards back to me'. This is what makes eBay unique.

In the summer of 2002, eBay held an 'eBay Live' event in Anaheim, California. Its purpose was to bring together community members from across the world and expand their online relationships.

Industry and competition

The Internet had emerged as a global medium enabling millions of people worldwide to share information, communicate, and conduct electronic commerce transactions. According to Nua Internet Surveys,[9] as of February 2002, more than 544 million people worldwide had access to the Internet either from home or from work. In the USA, eBay users were fast becoming the largest users of the postal service. In other countries like Germany (the third largest e-commerce market in the world, after Japan) eBay accounted for a high proportion – nearly 40%, by some estimates – of total e-commerce traffic.

To be sure, eBay's position had been, and was still being, challenged and contested. eBay users could buy and sell similar items through a variety of competing channels, including online and offline retailers, catalogue and mail order companies. For instance, in December 2000, Amazon launched the Amazon Marketplace, a platform that integrated new and used merchandise. In October 2001, Yahoo! launched Yahoo!Warehouse, a channel for liquidating excess inventory. Although competition was expected to intensify in the future as current offline and new competitors launched online retail sites, eBay appeared to be forging further ahead. (Table 2 provides a brief summary of rivals vying for the space that eBay occupied.)

---

8 eBay press release, 13 March 2002.

9 www.nua.com

Successful strategy: accidental or engineered?

By 2002, the Internet hype had totally evaporated. The bubble around this new technology had collapsed within the short span of a year or two. Yet eBay stood tall; one of the few genuine success stories among the so-called 'pure play' Internet firms. Was there more than luck and first mover advantage to the firm's success? Had eBay deciphered an economic code embedded in the technology of the Internet?

Table 2 **eBay competitors by category**

Category	*Primary competitors*
Broad-based competitors	Wal-Mart, Kmart, Target, Sears, Macy's, JC Penney, Costco, Office Depot, Staples, OfficeMax, Sam's Club, Amazon.com, Buy.com, AOL.com, Yahoo! Shopping, MSN, QVC and Home Shopping Network/ HSN.com
Antiques	Christie's, eHammer, Sotheby's, Phillips (LVMH), antique dealers and sellers
Coins and stamps	Collectors Universe, Heritage, US Mint, Bowers and Morena
Collectables	Franklin Mint, Go Collect, Collectiblestoday.com, wizardworld.com, Russ Cochran Comic Art Auctions, All Star Auctions
Musical instruments	Guitar Center, Sam Ash, Mars Music, Gbase.com, Harmony-Central.com, musical instrument retailers
Sports memorabilia	Beckett's, Collectors Universe, Mastro, Leylands, ThePit.com
Premium collectables	Christie's, DuPont Registry, Greg Manning Auctions, iCollector, Lycos/ Skinner Auctions, Millionaire.com, Phillips (LVMH), Sotheby's, other premium collectables dealers and sellers
Automotive (used cars)	Autobytel.com, AutoVantage.com, AutoWeb.com, Barrett-Jackson, CarPoint, Cars.com, Collectorcartraderonline.com, eClassics.com, Edmunds, CarsDirect.com, Hemmings, imotors.com, vehix.com, newspaper classifieds, used car dealers
Books, movies, music	Amazon.com, Barnes & Noble, Barnesandnoble.com, Alibris.com, Blockbuster, BMG, Columbia House, Best Buy, CDNow, Express.com, Emusic.com, Tower Records/Tower Records.com
Clothing	Bluefly.com, Dockers.com, FashionMall.com, The Gap, J. Crew, LandsEnd.com, The Limited, Macy's, The Men's Wearhouse, Ross
Computers and consumer electronics	Best Buy, Buy.com, Circuit City, Compaq, CompUSA, Dell, Fry's Electronics, Gateway, The Good Guys, MicroWarehouse, Radio Shack, Shopping.com, 800.com, Computer Discount Warehouse, PC Connection, computer, consumer electronics and photography retailers
Home and garden	IKEA, Crate & Barrel, Home Depot, Pottery Barn, Ethan Allen, Frontgate, Burpee.com
Jewellery	Ashford.com, Mondera.com, Bluenile.com, Diamond.com, Macy's
Pottery and glass	Just Glass, Pottery Auction, Go Collect
Sporting goods/ equipment	dsports.com, FogDog.com, Footlocker, Gear.com, Global Sports, golfclubexchange, MVP.com, PlanetOutdoors.com, Play It Again Sports, REI, Sports Authority, Sportsline.com
Tickets	Ticketmaster, Tickets.com, ticket brokers 49
Tools/equipment/ hardware	Home Depot, HomeBase, Amazon.com, Ace Hardware, OSH
Business-to-business	Ariba, BidFreight.com, Bid4Assets, BizBuyer.com, bLiquid.com, Buyer Zone, CloseOutNow.com, Commerce One, Concur Technologies, DoveBid, FreeMarkets, Iron Planet, labx.com, Oracle, Overstock.com, PurchasePro.com, RicardoBiz.com, Sabre, SurplusBin.com, Ventro, VerticalNet, Amazon.com, Surplus Auction, uBid, Yahoo! Auctions

Source: eBay Annual Report, 2001.

Appendix 1 The eBay trading experience

Registration

To bid, list or purchase an item, buyers and sellers had first to register with eBay by completing a short online form and confirmation process.

Buying on eBay

Buyers typically entered eBay through its home page, which contained a listing of major product categories, featured items and theme-oriented promotions. Users searched for specific items by browsing through a list of items within a category or sub-category and then 'clicking through' to a detailed description of a particular item. Users could also search specific categories, interest pages or the entire database of listings, using keywords to describe their areas of interest. eBay's search engine generated lists of relevant items with links to detailed descriptions. Each item was assigned a unique identifier so that users could easily search for and track specific items. Users could also search for a particular bidder or seller by name to review their listings and feedback history and search for products by a specific region or other attributes. Once a user had found an item and registered with eBay, the user could enter a bid for the maximum amount they were willing to pay at that time, or, for listings that offered the Buy-It-Now feature, purchase the item by accepting the Buy-It-Now price established by the seller. In the event of competitive bids, the eBay service automatically increased bidding in increments based upon the current high bid, up to the bidder's maximum price.

Selling on eBay

Registered sellers could list a product for sale by completing a short online form or using 'Mister Lister, "Seller's Assistant"' or third-party tools that facilitated the listing of multiple items. The seller selected a minimum price for opening bids for the item and chose whether the sale would last three, five, seven or ten days. Additionally, a seller could select a reserve price for an item, which was the minimum price at which the seller was willing to sell the item, and was typically higher than the minimum price set for the opening bid. The reserve price was not disclosed to bidders. Sellers with appropriate feedback ratings could also choose to use the Buy-It-Now feature at the time of listing, which allowed sellers to name a price at which they would be willing to sell the item to any buyer. Listings that offered the Buy-It-Now feature were run in the normal auction-style format, but would also feature a Buy-It-Now icon and price. Until the first bid was placed, or in the case of a reserve auction, until the reserve price was met, buyers had the option to buy the item instantly at the specified price without waiting for the auction to end. When an auction ended, the eBay system validated whether a bid had exceeded the minimum price, and the reserve price if one had been set. If the auction was successful or if the buyer opted for the Buy-It-Now feature, eBay automatically notified the buyer and seller via e-mail, and the buyer and seller could then complete the transaction independently of eBay. At the time of the e-mail notification, eBay generally charged the seller a final value transaction fee. eBay did not take possession of the item being sold or the buyer's payment for the item. Rather, the buyer and seller had to arrange independently for the shipment of and payment for the item, with the buyer typically paying for shipping.

My eBay

eBay also offered My eBay, which permitted users to receive a report of their recent eBay activity, including bidding, selling, account balances, favourite categories and recent feedback.

Value-added services

eBay also provided a variety of 'pre-trade' and 'post-trade' services to enhance the user experience and make trading easier, safer and fun. 'Pre-trade' services simplified the listing process and included photo hosting, authentication and seller productivity software. 'Post-trade' services made transactions easier and more comfortable to complete, and included payment processing, insurance, vehicle inspections, escrow, shipping and postage.

Source: eBay Annual Report, 2001.

Appendix 2 Major services on eBay

Billpoint

At the time of writing, Billpoint was eBay's preferred online bill payment service that facilitated credit card payment between buyers and sellers. With Wells Fargo Bank, Billpoint offered expedient and secure completion of each transaction. By giving sellers the convenience of credit card acceptance, and providing buyers the ease to pay more quickly than writing a cheque or filling out a money order, Billpoint provided for a hassle-free and reliable online payment solution on eBay.

Half.com

The eBay community benefited from a marketplace combining traditional auction-style trading and Half.com's fixed-price trading. Half.com offered an organized online marketplace to buy and sell high quality, previously owned mass-market goods. Unlike auctions, where the selling price is based on bidding, the seller set a fixed price for items at Half.com at the time an item was listed.

eBay International

Users on eBay come from many countries. With eBay's vision and global business strategy, the company offered its service and brand abroad. For instance, eBay users in Korea have bought items from users in the US, or users in Australia have bought from others in France.

eBay Motors

At the time of writing, eBay Motors had become the Internet's largest auction-style marketplace for buying and selling all things automotive. At any given time, eBay Motors had a wide variety of vehicles listed for sale, from Acuras to Volvos, and all makes and models in between. The site also featured collector cars, motorcycles, as well as auto parts. eBay Motors provided end-to-end online services such as financing, inspections, escrow, auto insurance, vehicle shipping, title and registration, and a lemon (defective car) inspection.

eBay Stores

eBay Stores expanded the marketplace for sellers by allowing them to create customized shopping destinations to merchandise their items on eBay. For buyers, eBay Stores represented a convenient way to access sellers' goods and services. Buyers who shopped at eBay Stores could make immediate and multiple-item purchases for fixed-price and auction-style items.

Buy-It-Now

Buy-It-Now was an optional enhancement for item listings. It allowed buyers to buy an item at a specified price without having to wait for the end of an auction. It gave sellers an easy and convenient method of selling items fast at a specific price. Listings with Buy-It-Now also ran as an auction. However, once an auction bid was placed, the opportunity to 'buy it now' ended.

eBay Professional Services

Professional Services on eBay served a fast growing and fragmented small business marketplace by providing a destination on eBay to identify professionals and freelancers for various business needs such as web design, accounting, writing and technical support, among others.

eBay Local Trading

eBay had local sites in 60 markets in the US. These localized eBay sites allowed users easily to find items located near them and browse through items of local interest. eBay's local sites delivered a distinctive regional flavour, and gave users the convenience to shop for more difficult-to-ship items such as automobiles, furniture and electrical appliances.

eBay Premier

eBay Premier was a specialty site on eBay, which showcased fine art, antiques, fine wines and rare collectables from leading auction houses and dealers

from around the world. Through its 'Premier Guarantee' programme, all sellers on eBay Premier stood behind and guaranteed the authenticity of their items.

eBay Live Auctions

Live Auctions provided live, real-time online bidding on items being sold on the sales floor of the world's leading auction houses. A proprietary technology developed by eBay, Live Auctions empowered traditional auctioneers to extend their sales beyond the auction house floor and reach millions of potential buyers online. Buyers gained easy access to exclusive, high-end property with the convenience and comfort of bidding from their home or office.

Source: eBay Annual Report, 2001.

Appendix 3 eBay's fee structure

Invoices for listing, feature and final value fees are sent via e-mail to sellers on a regular (at least monthly) basis. eBay requires all new sellers to have a credit card account on file. Sellers who pay eBay by credit card are charged shortly after the invoice is sent. A summary of eBay's fee structure, as of 1 March 2002, is provided below.

Listing fees

Minimum bid, opening value or reserve price	*Listing fee*
$0.01–9.99	$0.30
$10.00–24.99	$0.55
$25.00–49.99	$1.10
$50.00–199.99	$2.20
$200.00 and up	$3.30

Special categories	*Listing fee*
Passenger vehicles or other vehicles	$40.00
Motorcycles	$25.00
Real estate	$50.00

Feature fees

Seller feature	*Description*	*Feature fee*
Home Page Featured	Item is listed in a special featured section and is also rotated on the eBay home page	$99.95
Featured Plus!	Item appears in the category's Featured Item section and in bidder's search results	$19.95
Highlight	Item listing is emphasized with a coloured band	$5.00
Bold	Item title is listed in bold	$2.00
Buy-It-Now	Allows the seller to close an auction instantly for a specified price	$0.05

Final value fees

Sale price	*Final value fee*
Up to $25	5.25% of sale price
$25.01–1000	Above plus 2.75% of amount over $25
Over $1000	Above plus 1.5% of the amount over $1000

Source: eBay Annual Report 2001.

DISCUSSION QUESTIONS

1. What were the effects of eBay's decision to be a non-exclusive marketplace? How does the company benefit? What are the drawbacks of this approach?
2. Explain the Feedback Forum system. To what extent does it help to lock-in customers (see also Section 7.2.1, p. 142 on switching costs)?
3. How do customers benefit from the online community at eBay? Does eBay also benefit? If so, explain why.
4. To your mind, what are the most serious competitive threats that might endanger the success of eBay? What are eBay's greatest assets that help the firm to sustain its lead over competitors (see also Section 7.2.1, p. 144 on network effects)?

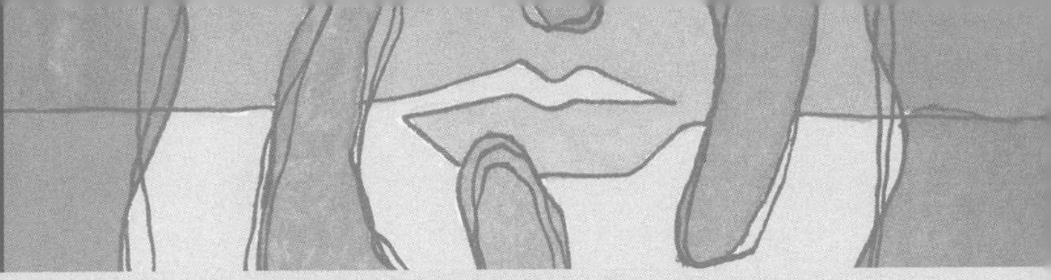

eBay strategy (B)

> Perhaps what sets our business model apart from practically all others is its ability to produce increasing returns on the income statement and generate tremendous amounts of cash. In our marketplace model, investments in growth flow directly through the income statement, leaving minimal amounts capitalized on the balance sheet to be amortized in future periods. The combination of our powerful business model and a strong, sustainable top-line outlook has made eBay one of the strongest young companies in recent history.
>
> **Pierre Omidyar, founder, and Meg Whitman, CEO, eBay Inc.**[1]

Founded in 1995, eBay has grown to be the world's largest online person-to-person marketplace for the sale of goods and services. In mid-2002 (after the Internet bubble had collapsed), the firm still boasted a market capitalization of US$14 billion.[2] Between 1998 and 2001, the number of confirmed registered eBay users had risen from approximately 2 million to 42 million. In 2001 eBay users listed more than 423 million items and completed transactions totalling US$9 billion. Although the USA remained eBay's biggest market, the firm operated in more than two dozen countries. (Table 1 presents selected financial and operational data on eBay.)

Now, Meg Whitman, CEO of eBay, was intending to take the firm to an entirely different level of performance – tripling the firm's revenues and gross merchandise sales by 2005 to US$3 billion and US$35 billion, respectively.[3] eBay's stock price-earnings ratio of 130 suggested that investors did not expect much less. The challenge, even though eBay had virtually no cost of goods, no inventories, and lean marketing, would be considerable. For one thing, growth in online transactions was slowing down. 'In the quarter to September [2001], US online transaction revenue grew by just 4%, quarter on quarter, and 54% on year, compared with 7% and 61% in the previous quarter.'[4] The tragic events of September 2001 in the USA and the ensuing global economic slowdown had not helped matters.

Macro-economic factors aside, the growth goals raised fundamental questions about the firm's business strategy going forward. In particular:

- To what extent should eBay expand aggressively beyond collectors, individuals and merchants, to cater to other customer segments such as corporations? Should standard and unused items (such as computers and cell phones) and high-ticket items (such as cars and real estate) be allowed to become an even larger percentage of items listed?
- Would it make sense to allow fixed-price formats to grow and possibly overshadow the classic auction format that eBay was founded on?
- Should eBay use its much valued 'virtual real estate' to seek advertising revenues (rather than

1 eBay Annual Report 2001.
2 As compared with Amazon's market capitalization of US$6 billion on the same date (9 May 2002). On 8 March 1999, eBay's market capitalization was US$21 billion as compared with US$19 billion for Amazon.
3 By comparison, American retailers J.C. Penny and Wal-Mart reported revenues of US$33 billion and US$217 billion, respectively, in 2001.
4 Paul Abrahams and Thorold Barker, 'eBay, the flea market that spanned the globe', *Financial Times*, 11 January 2002.

This case was written by Soumitra Dutta, The Roland Berger Chaired Professor of Business and Technology, and Subramanian Rangan, Associate Professor of Strategy and Management, both at INSEAD, as a basis for class discussion rather than to illustrate either effective or ineffective handling of an administrative situation.

Table 1 eBay selected consolidated financial data

(a) Consolidated statement of income data

	1997	1998	1999	2000	2001
	Year ended 31 December (in thousands, except per share data)				
Net revenues	$41 370	$86 129	$224 724	$431 424	$748 821
Cost of net revenues	8 404	16 094	57 588	95 453	134 816
Gross profit	32 966	70 035	167 136	335 971	614 005
Operating expenses					
Sales and marketing	15 618	35 976	96 239	166 767	253 474
Product development	831	4 640	24 847	55 863	75 288
General and administrative	6 534	15 849	43 919	73 027	105 784
Payroll expense on employee stock options	–	–	–	2 337	2 442
Amortization of acquired intangible assets	–	805	1 145	1 433	36 591
Merger related costs	–	–	4 359	1 550	–
Total operating expenses	22 983	57 270	170 509	300 977	473 579
Income (loss) from operations	9 983	12 765	(3 373)	34 994	140 426
Interest and other income (expense) net	(1 951)	(703)	21 412	46 025	46 276
Impairment of certain equity investments	–	–	–	–	(16 245)
Income before income taxes	8 032	12 062	18 039	81 019	170 457
Provision for income taxes	(971)	(4 789)	(8 472)	(32 725)	(80 009)
Net income	$7 061	$7 273	$9 567	$48 294	$90 448

Source: eBay Annual Report, 2001.

(b) Consolidated balance sheet data

	1997	1998	1999	2000	2001
	Year ended 31 December (in thousands)				
Cash and cash equivalents	$12 109	$37 285	$221 801	$201 873	$523 969
Short-term investments	–	40 401	181 086	354 166	199 450
Long-term investments	–	–	373 988	218 197	286 998
Restricted cash and investments	–	–	–	126 390	129 614
Working capital	(1 881)	72 934	372 266	538 022	703 666
Total assets	62 350	149 536	969 825	1 182 403	1 678 529
Long-term debt	16 307	18 361	15 018	11 404	12 008
Total stockholders' equity	$9 722	$100 538	$854 129	$1 013 760	$1 429 138

Source: eBay Annual Report, 2001.

(c) Online, US and international net revenues

	1999	Per cent change	2000	Per cent change	2001
	(in thousands, except per cent changes)				
Online net revenues					
Transactions	$179 895	94%	$348 174	73%	$602 671
Third-party advertising	2 030	541%	13 022	544%	83 853
End-to-end services and promotions	608	4 959%	30 756	(9%)	27 881
Total online net revenues	182 533	115%	$391 952	82%	714 405
Butterfields	31 319	(6%)	29 405	(14%)	25 251
Kruse	10 872	(7%)	10 067	(9%)	9 165
Total offline net revenues	42 191	(6%)	39 472	(13%)	34 416
Total net revenues	$224 724	92%	$431 424	74%	$748 821

Table 1 **continued**

(c) Online, US and international net revenues cont.

	1999	Per cent change	2000	Per cent change	2001
	(in thousands, except per cent changes)				
US net revenues	$222 130	81%	$402 446	58%	$634 659
International net reveneus	2 594	1 017%	28 978	294%	114 162
Total net revenues	$224 724	92%	$431 424	74%	$748 821

Source: eBay Annual Report, 2001.

(d) Supplemental operating data

	1999	Per cent change	2000	Per cent change	2001
	(in millions, except per cents and per listing amounts)				
Confirmed registered users at end of year	10.0	125%	22.5	89%	42.4
Number of items listed	129.6	104%	264.7	60%	423.1
Gross merchandise sales	$2 805	93%	$5 422	72%	$9 319

Cost of net revenues for eBay's online business consists primarily of costs associated with customer support and site operations, such as employee compensation and facilities costs for customer support, site operations compensation and Internet connectivity charges. Cost of net revenues for eBay's offline business consists primarily of employee compensation for auction, appraisal and customer support personnel as well as direct auction costs, such as event site rental.

Product development expenses consist primarily of employee compensation, payments to outside contractors, depreciation on equipment and corporate overhead allocations.

eBay's third-party advertising revenue is derived principally from the sale of online banner and sponsorship advertisements for cash and through barter arrangements. The duration of the banner and sponsorship advertising contracts has ranged from one week to three years, but is generally one week to three months.

eBay's end-to-end services and promotions revenues are derived principally from contractual arrangements with third parties that provide transaction services to eBay users. The duration of these end-to-end services and promotions contracts have ranged from one to three years.

Source: eBay Annual Report, 2001.

just listing and transaction fees)? To what extent ought the integration of value-added services be pursued as a source of revenue and profit growth? CEO, Meg Whitman, was quietly confident: 'We are a global trading platform. There are more opportunities than we can chase.'[5]

New customers and products

eBay defined its mission as helping 'practically anyone trade practically anything on Earth'. eBay's roots, however, lay in effectively tapping into a segment of individuals that traded collectables – one-of-a-kind items that usually came with a story or some unusual feature. The success of eBay among collectors was legendary.

> Stories abounded in the press of people who had closed their antique shops and stopped going to flea markets and trade shows because they found that they could make more money by selling exclusively through eBay. Whitman estimated that 20 to 25% of online users were sellers and, of those, approximately 25% made their full-time living selling on eBay.[6]

Now, eBay's user base had grown from individual consumers to include also merchants, small to mid-sized businesses, global corporations and even government agencies. Large corporates, still a small proportion of total trade value on eBay, promised to bring a larger range of merchandise to eBay, and were also capable of paying higher fees for exposure to eBay members and a variety of eBay value-adding services. Expanding the user base to include large sellers also

5 Paul Abrahams and Thorold Barker, 'eBay, the flea market that spanned the globe', *Financial Times*, 11 January 2002.
6 Kelly A. Porter and Stephen P. Bradley, eBay Inc., Harvard Business School Case No. 9-700-007, June 2001.

created some concerns for eBay. Michael van Swaaij, Managing Director eBay Europe, explained:

> Large buyers might squeeze out other sellers by virtue of their brand name and the number of items that they can list. Large sellers might influence how the eBay marketplace is run. This might threaten the non-discriminatory (i.e. non-exclusive) access that eBay provides all its members. If smaller sellers find that people are not buying their items any more, they might go away. It raises an important business dilemma: how do we balance the benefit of having millions of small sellers with that of having larger corporate sellers?

Further, as eBay evolved, its operations expanded to more categories of items, and to a broader and more global user base. In 2000, eBay launched eBay Motors in association with AutoTrader.com. This created the Internet's largest auction-style website for consumers and dealers to buy and sell used cars. eBay users had grown the breadth and depth of the marketplace, going from 8000 categories in the year 2000 to more than 18 000 categories in early 2002. In early 2002, three of eBay's top-level categories – autos, computers, and consumer electronics – were US$1 billion businesses, as measured by gross merchandise sales, and three more, collectables, books/movies/music, and sporting goods and memorabilia, were expected to reach the US$1 billion milestone by the end of 2002.

Beyond auctions

eBay had been launched on an auction format, and a variety of auction formats were now available (see Table 2). eBay charged fees for listing and closing auctions, as indicated in Appendix 1. The fee structure was designed to reduce incentive for members to take final transactions offline.

That history notwithstanding, eBay was introducing other formats, such as fixed price. Michael van Swaaij explained:

> Initially, auctions made sense as people were trading collectables, and it was hard to determine what the fair market value was. As the range of products expanded from collectables to practicals, other pricing models, such as fixed pricing, started becoming popular. New segments of users have developed over time. These users are regular consumers. They want to compare prices. They want the product quickly. They do not want to wait for seven days to buy a product.

Fixed price was available to eBay buyers in different variations. eBay sellers could opt to pay a minimal extra fee and choose to list a 'Buy-it-Now' price when they listed their items for traditional auction. For such items, buyers could opt to pay the 'Buy-it-Now' price and obtain the item without waiting for the

Table 2 **Auction formats available on eBay**

Auction format	*Description*
Reserve price auctions	Bidders know there is a reserve price, but they do not know what it is.
	In order to win the auction, a bidder must meet or exceed the reserve price and have the highest bid.
	If no bidders meet the reserve price, neither the seller nor the high bidder is under any further obligation.
Private auctions	Bidders' e-mail addresses will not show up on the item or bidding-history screens.
	When the auction is over, only the seller knows who bought the item.
Dutch auctions	Sellers start by listing a minimum price, or starting bid, and the number of items for sale.
	Bidders specify both a bid price and the quantity they want to buy.
	All winning bidders pay the same price – which is the lowest successful bid.
	If there are more buyers than items, the earliest successful bids get the goods.
	Higher bidders get the quantities they have asked for.
	Bidders can refuse partial quantities.
Restricted access auctions	To view and bid on Adult-Only items, buyers need to have a credit card on file with eBay.
	Sellers must also have credit card verification.
	Items listed in the Adult-Only category are not included in the New Items page or the Hot Items section, and are not available by any title search.

Source: eBay Inc.

auction to end. The attractiveness of the fixed price model appeared strong.

In addition to listing products in the eBay marketplace, sellers could list a broad range of products at fixed prices for lower fees within their own eBay stores. A low fixed insertion fee was charged for each listing, regardless of whether one or one hundred of the same item was listed. Three different monthly fee levels – US$9.95, US$49.95, US$499.95 – were set for eBay stores, depending upon the level of exposure offered to the store on eBay's site. In order to open an eBay store, sellers were required to have a certain minimum feedback rating (of at least 20) or become ID verified. User search on the general eBay marketplace did not include the eBay stores; buyers had to specifically enter eBay stores to buy products listed there.

To deepen its fixed-price offer, eBay acquired Half.com in July 2000.[7] Founded in July 1999, Half.com operated a fixed-price, online marketplace to buy and sell high quality, new, overstocked, remaindered and used products (such as books, CDs, movies, video games, computers and consumer electronics) at discounted prices. Unlike auctions, where the selling price was based on bidding, the seller set the price for items at Half.com at the time an item was listed. There were no fees to list items on Half.com, and sellers were charged a commission on each sale only after an item was sold. Appendix 2 provides details on Half.com's business model.

These new non-auction formats raised inevitable questions about whether eBay would eventually be competing with the likes of Amazon on the one hand and Wal-Mart on the other. Michael van Swaaij added:

> Auctions also provide a 'thrill-of-the-hunt' and encourage interactions between members of our community. Those aspects are likely diminish with the fixed price formats. One has to carefully judge the strategic impact of this change on our community.

Evolving the revenue model and the trading platform

Alone, and through a host of partnerships, eBay provided a variety of 'pre-trade' and 'post-trade' value-added services to enhance the user experience and make trading easier. 'Pre-trade' services made listing items for sale easier and included photo hosting, authentication and seller productivity software. 'Post-trade' services made transactions easier and more comfortable to consummate, such as payment facilitation, insurance, vehicle inspections, escrow, postage, and shipping. Specific value-added services on eBay included:

- Billpoint, which enabled person-to-person payment on the Internet;[8]
- eBay Picture Services, powered by iPIX, which provided eBay users with an easy-to-use, robust set of imaging services to aid selling;
- the addition of Saturn and its retailers to provide a nationwide automobile inspection service as part of eBay Motors.

There was debate however: should the firm own some of these value-added services (and take the associated revenues, costs, and profits) or should it provide them through strategic partnerships (as it currently did)? Van Swaaij elaborated:

> Many of the value-adding services have very interesting business models. We work with a single platform and the platform costs do not necessarily grow proportionately with the number of transactions. Thus, there is significant cost leverage. The question then arises: should we go for this leverage? And if the answer is yes, what kind of services should we integrate into our platform?

There was also the question of advertising revenues. eBay's trading platform obtained billions of page views every day and provided a valuable opportunity to raise revenues via online advertising (see Table 1). Advertising revenues could come from two sources: advertising for other online retail sites and advertising for services (such as payment and shipping) that helped members of the eBay community to conduct effective trades. The sheer size of the global eBay community raised the important question of whether the company should do more to exploit online advertising as a source of revenue growth. Van Swaaij put it this way:

> We can generate revenues off advertising. We have done so in the past and can possibly do a lot more of it in the future. The real question that we have to answer is: how does it add value to our members? Does it help us to grow our business for the future?

Beyond this, eBay was also focused on continually improving its trading platform. In 2000, eBay intro-

7 Half.com made national and international news when it launched its site in January 2000 by collaborating with Halfway, a small town in Oregon. The town had changed its name to Half.com and had become the first 'dot.com' city in the USA.

8 In February 2000, eBay announced a strategic relationship with Wells Fargo & Co., in which Wells Fargo purchased a 35% equity interest in Billpoint and entered into a long-term payment processing and customer care contract with Billpoint.

duced the API (application programming interface). The API allowed eBay to be fully integrated into independent sites across the Internet. A new site was able to use the eBay commerce engine to power its business, eliminating time and expense from the start-up process. Larger businesses could directly tap into the eBay trading platform from their own manufacturing, sales, and inventory systems. A second benefit was that API allowed eBay and its commercial partners more easily and rapidly to add eBay's services to new devices, such as wireless telephones and hand-held computers. For example, eBay launched eBay Anywhere, a comprehensive mobile strategy that aimed to make eBay accessible from any Internet-enabled mobile device.

The next five years

In 2002, eBay was, without doubt, one of the most successful firms in the online retail space. Equally clearly, it was on the move now. Yet, the challenge ahead of delivering significant profit growth promised to be daunting. Van Swaaij observed modestly: 'For much of the past five years, eBay's growth has happened almost naturally. We are now entering a phase in which we shall have to manage the future growth of the firm.' It was in this spirit that eBay was revisiting all three fundamentals of its business strategy: what, for whom, and how?

Appendix 1 eBay's fee structure

Invoices for listing, feature and final value fees are sent via e-mail to sellers on a regular (at least monthly) basis. eBay requires all new sellers to have a credit card account on file. Sellers who pay eBay by credit card are charged shortly after the invoice is sent. A summary of eBay's fee structure, as of 1 March 2002, is provided below.

Listing fees

Minimum bid, opening value or reserve price	*Listing fee*
$0.01–9.99	$0.30
$10.00–24.99	$0.55
$25.00–49.99	$1.10
$50.00–199.99	$2.20
$200.00 and up	$3.30

Special categories	*Listing fee*
Passenger vehicles or other vehicles	$40.00
Motorcycles	$25.00
Real estate	$50.00

Feature fees

Seller feature	*Description*	*Feature fee*
Home Page Featured	Item is listed in a special featured section and is also rotated on the eBay home page	$99.95
Featured Plus!	Item appears in the category's Featured Item section and in bidder's search results	$19.95
Highlight	Item listing is emphasized with a coloured band	$5.00
Bold	Item title is listed in bold	$2.00
Buy-It-Now	Allows the seller to close an auction instantly for a specified price	$0.05

Final value fees

Sale price	*Final value fee*
Up to $25	5.25% of sale price
$25.01–1000	Above plus 2.75% of amount over $25
Over $1000	Above plus 1.5% of the amount over $1000

Source: eBay Annual Report 2001.

Appendix 2 The Half.com fixed-price format

Half.com offered a fixed-price, online website to buy and sell high-quality, previously owned goods at discounted prices. Unlike auctions, where the selling price was based on bidding, the seller fixed the price for items at the time an item was listed.

Registration

While any visitor to Half.com could browse through the site and view the items listed for sale, in order to buy an item or to list an item for sale, buyers and sellers were required first to register with Half.com.

Buying on Half.com

Buying at Half.com was similar to the shopping experience at other leading online retailers. Shoppers could easily search for specific books, CDs, movies and video games or browse for items that were categorized and surrounded with product descriptions, reviews and artwork. Just like any online retail store, shoppers could fill their shopping cart and check out with a credit card. Customers could also see real-time price comparisons of new versions of the same item through an on-screen shopping agent that showed prices from other Internet retailers.

Selling on Half.com

Sellers wishing to sell items on the Half.com site simply typed in the ISBN or UPC bar code number, selected the item's condition, confirmed the sale price, and the item was immediately listed. Half.com automatically added descriptions and pictures to each listing, so sellers did not need to do it themselves. There were no fees to list items on Half.com. In an effort to help users price their products competitively, Half.com provided a suggested selling price. The suggested selling price for an item was calculated as a percentage of the best online retail price for a new copy of the item, depending on the quality of the item. The Half.com pricing recommendations as percentages of the best online retail price were as follows:

Condition	*Suggested percentage*
Like new	50%
Very good	45%
Good	40%
Acceptable	35%

How transactions were completed

When a buyer selected an item for purchase, sellers were sent an e-mail notifying them to ship the item. Once the seller confirmed that the item was being shipped, the buyer's credit card was charged. At least once a month, sellers were sent a cheque from Half.com for all items sold during the previous period, less Half.com's 15% commission. Sellers also received an allowance for shipping costs.

Buyer protection policy

Half.com reserved the right to suspend the membership of any buyer or seller that Half.com felt had attempted to commit fraud by misusing the Half.com Buyer Protection Policy for their own personal gain.

Source: eBay Inc.

DISCUSSION QUESTIONS

1 Why did eBay decide to expand its user base from individual consumers into merchants, small to mid-sized businesses and corporations? What dangers are associated with this expansion?

2 Using the concept of economies of scope (see also Section 7.1.2, p. 140), why do you think that eBay expanded into more categories of items such as cars?

3 Is it sensible for eBay to offer fixed-price sales on its auction place website? What are the benefits and drawbacks of doing so?

4 What other value-added services has eBay started to offer in addition to its auction place? If you were CEO of eBay, in which other direction would you expand eBay's business?

eBay international

> If eBay is to achieve its ambitious goal of US$3 billion revenues in 2005, it will have to replicate its US success around the world.
>
> **Thorold Barker, *Financial Times*, 11 January 2002**

At the busy intersection in Paris of Rue de Flandre and Rue de Stalingrad, traffic was noisy and people were bustling about. Upstairs, on the fifth floor of a nondescript building, where a firm called iBazar operated, Michael van Swaaij, an INSEAD MBA, and now VP of eBay Europe, was huddling with his boss, Matt Bannick. Should eBay acquire rival iBazar in France or should it grow organically, as it had done successfully in the UK?

Bannick, a Harvard MBA, and now head of eBay's international operations, had his own quandaries. Japan had shaped up as a giant market in person-to-person auctions, second only to the USA. Yet, Yahoo!, in a joint venture with Softbank of Japan, had made deep inroads into Japan, and was now seemingly undisplaceable there. Should eBay cut its losses and pull out of the Japanese market?

Van Swaaij was tantalized, not only by iBazar, but also by the possibility of cross-border person-to-person trade. eBay prided itself on 'making impossible commerce possible, and on making inefficient commerce efficient'. But commerce even on eBay was still largely national. In the future, would a French person trade rare wine with an Austrian, and would the latter sell their violin to a buyer in Italy? The possibilities were inherent in the many-to-many technology that was the Internet. Indeed, the British and the Americans were already showing the way by trading collectables and other items across the Atlantic. Van Swaaij wondered to what extent the idea of a marketplace formed by a community of buyers and sellers could span national borders. Could cross-border trade develop into a growth engine for eBay in Europe?

Bannick, too, wondered about these possibilities. He had just received reports from Australia. The news was positive, but, to do even better, Australia wanted a site more customized to its local needs. The significant (approximately half-million dollar) expense of doing this aside, Bannick wondered what, if anything, in a 'pure play' Internet business, was different in terms of global strategy. Ought eBay to become a 'brand global, act local' player? What implications would that have for global cross-border trade?

eBay background: 1995–2001

eBay was launched on Labor Day in 1995 in Campbell, California, by Pierre Omidyar, a software engineer. His (now) wife, Pam, a collector of candy dispensers, found it difficult to link up with others with a similar interest. Omidyar believed he could use the burgeoning technology of the Internet to create a marketplace for physical goods that would be as efficient as the stock exchanges were for trading stock. Thus, eBay (settled on as a domain name since Echo Bay, the name Omidyar had first requested, was taken) was born as an Internet-based community

This case was written by Soumitra Dutta, The Roland Berger Chaired Professor of Business and Technology, and Subramanian Rangan, Associate Professor of Strategy and Management, both at INSEAD, as a basis for class discussion rather than to illustrate either effective or ineffective handling of an administrative situation.

where members, primarily collectors, could list items for sale by auction, and interested others could make bids for those items. The auction closed when the seller was satisfied (on average, after one week), and the highest bidder won. eBay thus made it possible for thousands to indulge their hobbies and enjoy the thrill of the deal without leaving the comfort of their homes or offices.

The response was overwhelming. Within one year of starting, tens of thousands of individuals had posted their items for trade and had made purchases. The venture capital community spied an opportunity and eBay was transformed into a business venture. Incorporated in San Jose, California, in 1997, eBay spread nationally within the USA. Thanks to word of mouth and Internet marketing, listings from outside California had grown. The business's infrastructure (of servers and software) resided in California, but access was, of course, nationwide.

The model was simple and surprisingly successful. Unlike at other Internet firms, such as Amazon, at eBay customers performed most of the value added. They chose what to list and for how long, and they described and uploaded photos of the items. If a sale materialized, they packed, insured, and shipped items to the buyer. The buyer handled payment and verification. Importantly, customers monitored one another by rating their trading partners. The system policed itself. eBay neither took possession of the items, nor did it physically handle items, money, or documents. For these reasons, the model was truly 'scalable' (i.e. expandable without proportional increase in cost).

For its part, eBay oversaw and optimized the entire process and user experience. It made listing items and uploading photos relatively simple. It made search intuitive and accurate. eBay managers, who created category directories (under which featured items were listed) were tuned in to how people thought about and browsed for items. eBay also made auction bidding and notification interesting, yet efficient. It made feedback and rating simple, yet valuable. Also, working with 'complementor' firms, such as iPix, Lloyds and Billpoint, it facilitated photo-loading, insurance and payments. If there was a problem, eBay was willing to step in, investigate and sort out the matter. For this efficient, trust-efficient trade service, eBay charged a modest listing and transaction fee. (A car, for instance, could be sold on eBay for fees totalling around US$50.)

eBay goes international

By 1998, eBay was receiving hundreds of listings a day from Canadian residents. The major international markets, however, were turning out to be Germany and the UK. In both these markets, local imitators had emerged, and, indeed, eBay itself was witnessing bids and listings from the UK. The logic of critical mass appeared quite important. Because the probability of successful transactions was higher on a 'thick' rather than a 'thin' market, individuals would tend to tip to the more trafficked sites. eBay would have to get going in these international markets if it was not to be locked out.

Accordingly, in 1999, eBay ventured into the UK, Australia, and Germany. Through similar reasoning, in 2000, eBay launched sites in Japan, France and Canada.

iBazar in France

Shortly thereafter, eBay became the leading auction site in Canada. (It was estimated that eBay was 50 times as large as the next auction site in Canada.)[1] Success in the USA had certainly given the firm considerable publicity and credibility that had spilled over north of the border. More surprisingly, by the first quarter of 2000, eBay was pulling even in the UK with QXL (pronounced 'quick sell'), the first mover there in person-to-person (P2P) auction-based trading.

In France, the country of birth of eBay's founder, Pierre Omidyar, the story was different. France was an important market in Internet commerce. By 2005, e-commerce revenues there were projected to be the fourth highest in the world (see Exhibit 1). Alas, eBay had entered France in October 2000, well after an upstart local firm, iBazar, had adapted the eBay model and launched an Internet auction site there in 1998.

As iBazar built traffic, eBay France languished. The problem, eBay felt, was actually worse than it appeared. iBazar was founded and run by a couple of web entrepreneurs, Pierre-François Grimaldi and Marc Piquemal, but it was funded by a financial investor. At the time, building up traffic and registered users was considered critical. With the aim of maximizing this, iBazar offered free listings and charged

1 eBay Analyst Day presentation, 29 October 2001.

Exhibit 1 Projected e-commerce revenues in (US$ billion) top 20 countries 2005

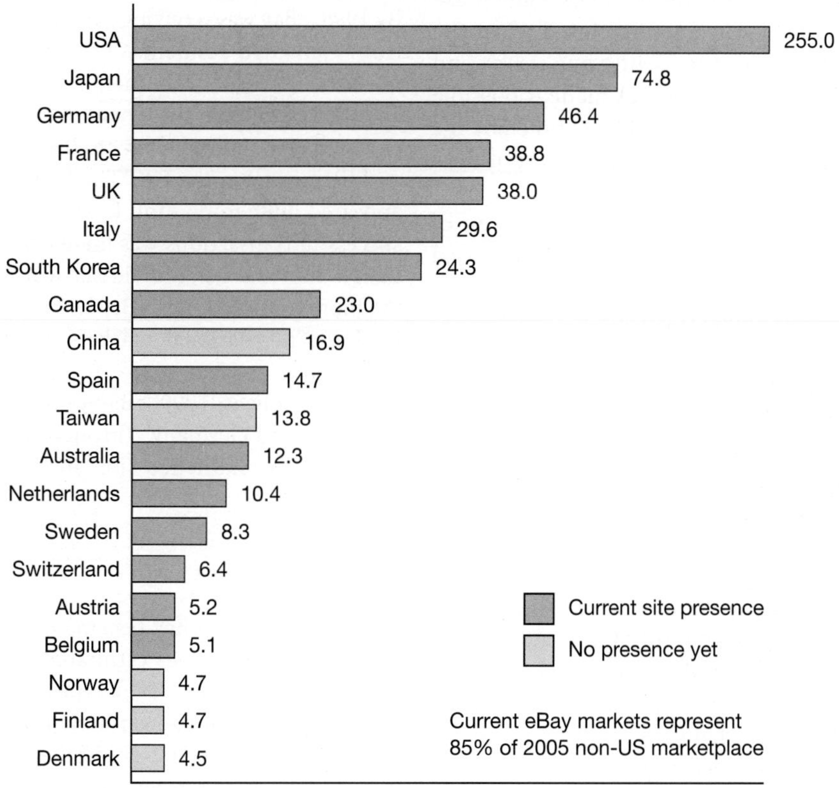

Source: IDC; eBay Analyst Day presentation, 29 October 2001.

relatively small fees for transactions, while promoting the site heavily through television advertising. Its revenues and profits were to come from advertising. Under this model, users flocked to the site and listed anything and everything. Critically, unlike eBay, iBazar focused on the trade of practicals. Collectors and hobbyists did not really warm to the site, and the users that came did not become repeat traders.

As listings and trades rose in France, van Swaaij at eBay Europe became increasingly apprehensive about the following. First, how could eBay build up listings on its own French site? Second, if iBazar attracted the good and the not so good (in terms of items listed), French users would have a poor experience, and the entire budding P2P market in France risked being compromised. Third, if users grew accustomed to listing without fees and to the 'classifieds' model of iBazar, this could be detrimental to future 'monetization' of traffic by eBay or, for that matter, others.

A Dutch national, van Swaaij had previously worked at AOL in London. In the fairly new world of e-business he was relatively experienced. He had dealt with international expansion, with competition, and had lived and studied in France. Flying to France from his office in Switzerland, van Swaaij kept hovering between two major options. The first was to stick it out and wait for iBazar to self-destruct. After all, if he was right about the potential pitfalls in iBazar's approach to the business, the firm would run out of cash. (iBazar had grown from two to a staff of 200; outside guesses put its 'burn rate' at well over US$1 million per month; and it was taking in only 20–30% of that figure in revenues.) The downside was that it was difficult to predict how long this would take, and whether iBazar would take the whole French market down with it. Not to mention, iBazar was also already exporting its 'weak model' into other southern European markets.

Table 1 **eBay selected financial data**

	Year ended 31 December			
	1997	1998	1999	2000
	(in thousands of US dollars)			
Net revenues	US$ 41 370	US$ 86 129	US$ 224 724	US$ 431 424
Cost of net revenues	8 404	16 094	57 588	95 453
Gross profit	32 966	70 035	167 136	335 971
Operating expenses				
Sales and marketing	15 618	35 976	96 239	166 767
Product development	831	4 640	24 847	55 863
General and administrative	6 534	15 849	43 919	73 027
Payroll expense on employee stock options	–	–	–	2 337
Amortization of acquired intangible assets	–	805	1 145	1 433
Merger related costs	–	–	4 359	1 550
Total operating expenses	22 983	57 270	170 509	300 977
Income (loss) from operations	9 983	12 765	(3 373)	34 994
Interest and other income (expense) net	(1 951)	(703)	21 412	46 025
Income before income taxes	8 032	12 062	18 039	81 019
Provision for income taxes	(971)	(4 789)	(8 472)	(32 725)
Net income	US$ 7 061	US$ 7 273	US$ 9 567	US$ 48 294
Supplemental operating data	(in millions)			
Number of registered users at end of period	0.3	2.2	10.0	22.5
Number of items listed	4.4	33.7	129.6	264.7
Gross merchandise sales	US$95	US$745	US$2 805	US$5 422

Source: eBay Annual Report, 2001, p. 18.

The second option was for eBay to acquire iBazar. Of course, in order to make this happen, van Swaaij would have to convince headquarters in San Jose, California, to fork out hard cash today to take out a bad player. (In 2000, before the Internet stock bubble collapsed, it was rumoured that iBazar considered itself to be valued at over a billion dollars.) Headquarters was bound to ask why eBay France was not delivering in the face of competition, when eBay in the UK was. Further, given iBazar's different approach (which focused on practicals as opposed to collectables), would the business evaporate once the television advertising stopped? Notwithstanding, the financial investor at iBazar was bound to put the squeeze on in terms of price. He was likely to perceive that eBay had more to gain than he had to lose. He could also be under the impression that iBazar, which, after all, had a couple of million registered users, would turn the corner any day and become a money-maker. Last but not least, Wanadoo, the leading Internet access provider in France (and a unit of France Télécom), was expressing interest in iBazar, as was Yahoo! Europe. Timing was vital; a smart acquirer would wait until the current owner was predisposed to selling, but would have to move before the others did.

It was for the purpose of discussing and deciding on this that van Swaaij had invited Bannick and eBay Chief Financial Officer, Rajiv Dutta, to Paris to a meeting with François Grimaldi and the financial investor in iBazar.

Japan calling

If France posed challenges for eBay, it was not the only foreign market to do so. Japan was, in some ways, an even more vexing case. Japan, the second largest economy in the world, was also the number-two market in P2P e-commerce. Japanese city-dwellers were considered 'tech savvy', and the younger population, in particular, was mobile phone and Internet friendly. By some estimates, P2P e-commerce in Japan was expected to reach US$75 billion by 2005.

The problem was that Yahoo!, the leading Internet portal firm, had also become aware of these trends and had entered not only the portal but also the auction business in Japan. Its joint venture with

Table 2 **eBay revenue breakdown**

	1999	*Per cent change*	*2000*
	(in thousands of US$, except percentage changes)		
Online net revenues			
Transactions	US$ 179 895	94 %	US$ 348 174
Third-party advertising	2 030	541 %	13 022
End-to-end services and promotions	608	4 959 %	30 756
Total online net revenues	182 533	115 %	US$ 391 952
Butterfields	31 319	(6%)	29 405
Kruse	10 872	(7%)	10 067
Total offline net revenues	42 191	(6%)	39 472
Total net revenues	US$ 224 724	92 %	US$ 431 424
US net revenues	US$ 222 130	81 %	US$ 402 446
International net revenues	2 594	1 017 %	28 978
Total net revenues	US$ 224 724	92 %	US$ 431 424

Source: eBay Annual Report, 2001, p.24.

Softbank, at the time the leading Japanese venture capital firm, gave it considerable resources in Japan. In auctions, Yahoo! had torn a page from the eBay book. In Japan, it meticulously channelled its portal traffic to its auction site and built a business model similar to that of eBay. By the time eBay launched its site in Japan in 2000, Yahoo! was well under way.

The challenge of working out what to do in Japan fell to Matt Bannick, the Head of eBay International. An American, and the youngest member of eBay's relatively young top management team, Bannick had worked in the US State Department and travelled the world. Now entrusted with leading eBay's international operations, Bannick had to deliver profitable growth. On the US stock market, the firm was trading at extraordinary premiums (more than a hundred times earnings), which, without doubt, were premised on expectations of growth (see Tables 1 and 2). International operations were expected to be a sure and significant contributor to this growth.

Unlike in France, in Japan, the option of acquiring the leader did not exist in any real sense. Yahoo! was already a giant in the USA and elsewhere (with a market capitalization that was sometimes as large as that of eBay, and often larger). Further, eBay did not see itself getting into the portal business. However, Yahoo! was attracted by the P2P e-commerce and auction business. It offered auctions in the USA as well, although there, until now, eBay had dwarfed it.

Unappetizing as it was, one option was to pull out of Japan. Japan, being a major but distinct market, necessitated a customized site and local presence. Competition, however, was bruising. Consequently, the burn rate there for eBay was relatively high. Cash flows were interconnected and the firm would have to consider carefully to what extent the drain in Japan would cause financial analysts to mark down eBay's stock. If the stock price dipped, a key currency for other acquisitions would fall. Besides, the value of employee stock options would take a hit as well. Clearly, continued bad results in Japan would be harmful to the firm.

The other option in Japan was to stay and fight. If eBay could trump Yahoo! in auctions in the USA and other parts of the world, it should be able to vanquish it in Japan as well. Besides, by pulling out of Japan now, would eBay be conceding that market permanently to Yahoo!? Would Yahoo! use free cash flows generated there to attack eBay in other Asian markets (such as China and Taiwan, two potentially important e-commerce markets that eBay had not yet entered)?

Bannick, who worked out of the same building and same second floor as CEO, Meg Whitman, was to meet with her and brief her on an optimal course of action. At Whitman's next conference with analysts, she was certain to be asked about eBay's strategy in Japan.

Cross-border trade and the 'glocal' model

Separately, in the background, there remained the question of cross-border person-to-person trade. The prospects for this were inherent in the Internet. It was clear that, at least in terms of the cost of the search for potential trading partners, the Internet shrank distance substantially. After all, local P2P markets (including garage sales, *vide greniers* and flea markets) were, to some extent, being displaced by the electronic marketplace that eBay had pioneered and was perfecting. This electronic market, however, was still largely regional and national. Bigger opportunities for 'arbitrage' lay in bridging greater distances and especially national borders.

The prospects of this cross-border P2P market intrigued van Swaaij. Europe, after all, was a continent of nations in the process of unifying further and further. How could he tap into this potential for cross-border trade? Already, certain categories, such as stamps, had shown promise in this area. Rough estimates indicated that cross-border transactions accounted for close to 10% of total activity at eBay. There was also the question of the magnitude of resources to be devoted to the project. One person was already dedicating half their time to keeping an eye on and fostering cross-border transactions. But a more fundamental question for van Swaaij was what could, and should, eBay do to actively promote global trade? Should eBay remain an 'enabler', allowing global traders to work out how and what to trade cross-border, or were there key barriers that eBay could help lower, but that individual traders were ill-equipped to tackle by themselves?

Of course, potential for cross-border trade would depend on the compatibility of the technological platform across various eBay markets. Bannick felt that it would be ideal if eBay looked like 'Intel to us, but Unilever to our customers'. That is, global on the inside but local on the outside. Indeed, in most international locations, eBay had a local site that listed items in the local currency and within local categories. In small, new markets (like Austria and New Zealand) eBay operated a 'slimmed down' version, whereby it hosted a local home page that drew from the US site. In these cases, items would not be listed in local currency or within local categories. As and when trade grew, eBay would invest in developing a 'full site' (as it had done in the UK and Germany). In all cases, however, the sites would be based and built on the same global platform.

Although this approach centralized and leveraged the costs of developing and upgrading the platform, while maintaining the potential for cross-border trade, it raised the issue of whether concept and platform development, driven primarily outside the US, would be in eBay's best long-term interest. How, for instance, to ensure that innovative concepts from markets outside the US, would eBay find sufficient and timely expression in the common platform? On what aspects, beyond currency and categories, would it make sense to encourage local adaptation? Lastly, since the 'glocal' approach was not very different from the centralized-but-adapted model that firms like McDonald's had used in their internationalization, the question arose as to what, if anything, was different about global strategy in a so-called 'pure play' Internet company.

Decision time

In 2001, over US$9 billion worth of transactions (gross merchandise sales) had been conducted on eBay. The firm reported revenues of US$750 million, and operating income and net profits of US$140 and US$90 million, respectively. eBay was the only Internet firm to be reporting steady and growing profits. The firm's market capitalization had hovered at between US$10 and US$20 billion. Outside the USA, eBay operated in some 20 countries. In 2001, international operations accounted for about 16% of eBay revenues. This proportion was expected to rise to one-third of the total by 2005. Although international listings generated lower revenues in terms of percentage of gross merchandise sales (5 to 6%, compared to more than 8% in the USA),[2] eBay reported that its operations in Canada, Germany and the UK had turned profitable.

Now, it fell to Bannick, van Swaaij, and the others on the international team to take eBay's non-US revenues from US$114 million in 2001 to the over US$800 million projected for 2005. If 2005 seemed some time away, the dilemmas in France, Japan, and Europe were at hand now. Competition at home and abroad was not going to go away. The decisions were likely to have important implications for eBay's future.

---

2 eBay Analyst Day presentation, 29 October 2001.

DISCUSSION QUESTIONS

1. Using the concept of economies of scale (see also Section 7.1.1, p. 136), explain how the business model from eBay differs from other online retailers such as ChateauOnline or Amazon.com.
2. Why did iBazar in France present a threat to eBay's aspirations in that market? What would you recommend to eBay?
3. How should eBay behave in the Japanese market? Would it be better to compete against Yahoo! or pull out of the Japanese market altogether? Defend your argument.
4. Referring to the eBay technology platform, how do you evaluate the concept of being 'global on the inside, local on the outside'? What are the specific benefits and drawbacks of using this approach?

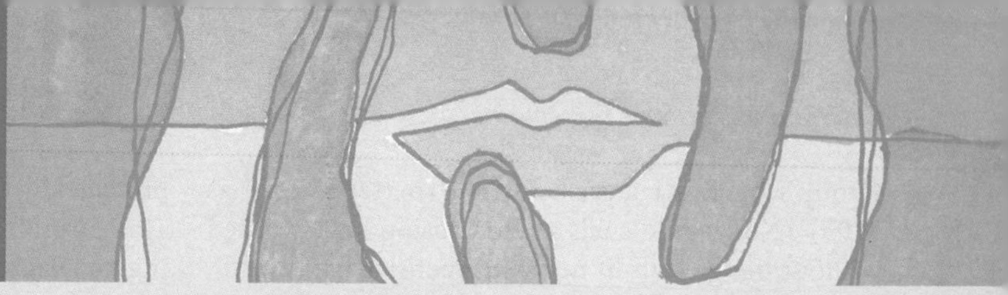

CASE STUDY 25

Online file-sharing

The music industry's paradigm shift

This will be decided not in the courts, but around American dinner tables.

Cary Sherman, President of the RIAA[1]

I am all for destroying their machines ... [damaging an accused pirate's machine] may be the only way you can teach someone about copyrights.

Orin Hatch, Chair of the US Senate Judiciary Committee

In the late 1990s the music industry experienced an unparallelled period of growth. The coming of age of the compact disc (CD), and the economic boom at the time, made music a worldwide boom industry. Unfortunately, the same technology boom that was driving consumer spending was also driving a new technology that would threaten, if some observers are to be believed, the very livelihood of the industry and the musicians and artists who provided the content that made the industry so successful.

Between May and November 2003 the RIAA issued over 911 subpoenas to Internet service providers demanding the names of clients who were still offering music on file-sharing networks. In June 2003 Jesse Jordan, a 19-year-old college student, was one of the first individuals to be hit with a lawsuit by the RIAA. Mr Jordan settled the suit by paying $12 000 to the RIAA. On 29 September 2003 Alan Davis was sentenced to six months in jail for criminal music copyright infringement, and on 2 October 2003 four individuals pleaded guilty to criminal copyright infringement charges.

Many people are passionate about music: the people who buy it, the people who write it, the people who perform it and usually the people who sell it. A considerable body of economic theory also shows that the usual relationship between price and utility changes significantly when consumers add such an emotion to their purchasing decision, and for decades this has driven almost continuously rising revenues and profits for the music industry.

In late 1998 everything changed. Shawn Fanning, a young computer whizz-kid, put the Internet, music lovers and traditional file-sharing together in an explosive cocktail that took on Fanning's hacker handle for its name: Napster. File-sharing, over Usenet, bulletin board systems, cassettes and eight-tracks, had been around for years, although the level of activity had never really posed a major threat to the record industry in its established markets.

Fanning's ignition of the taper was his decision to create a system that was 'presence aware' and that actively encouraged users to share their own material: any user logging on to Napster could now see what was being shared by all the active users (replacing the frustration of trying to download something that was on a computer that was not connected) and could painlessly share their own files without having to endure a complicated process to do so.

Napster would never have taken off without the creation of an acceptable compression algorithm to shrink music files from around 10Mb[2]/minute of music to 1Mb/minute – the Motion Picture Expert

1 RIAA, Recording Industry Association of America.

2 Mb, megabyte. One byte represents one character or piece of information; there are 1 048 576 bytes (1024 × 1024) in a megabyte.

This case was prepared by Timothy Lennon and Leslie Diamond, MBA participants (2003), and Tawfik Jelassi, Professor of e-Business and IT, all at the School of International Management at the Ecole Nationale des Ponts et Chaussées, Paris, France. Case released in 2004.

Group's MPEG-1 layer 3 format (better known as MP3)[3]. Nor would such an innovation have worked without the growth in mass, inexpensive bandwidth, or the fall in mass-storage prices. Nevertheless, the ability to share music on a scale not seen before sent shockwaves through the music industry. Early on, music CD sales began to decline as what the industry describes as the 'LP/CD upgrade cycle' – the music industry cash cow that has seen music buyers upgrade old collections from eight-track to LP,[4] to cassette, to CD – faltered.

In the best traditions of the music business and the people who work with it, the industry began to eat itself: Metallica sued Napster and immediately became the target for industry alumni and other bands, with some making recordings attacking Metallica and others joining the RIAA suits against Napster and the clones that soon began to spring up.

The sharing of music has been around since music itself, but its frequency has increased dramatically as new media have become available to the general public. The advent of the cassette, for example, led to a long and eventually unsuccessful record industry campaign with the tagline 'Stop home taping; it's killing music'. More recently, those who wanted to share their music moved to dialling directly into one another's computers using bulletin boards.

With widespread Internet availability, however, major changes began to take place. Initially, music aficionados would use File Transfer Protocol (FTP) servers and their own homepages and websites. For nearly three years after 1995, this was recorded as the most common method for sharing music.

In 1998, however, Shawn Fanning's Napster finally put together the components needed to make file-sharing a major force. Fanning was helped by a motley crew of dot.com wannabes, including his uncle, to turn Napster into a runaway success, with millions of worldwide users sharing huge numbers of songs.

Not surprisingly, it was not long before the lawyers were on the scene: the RIAA sued Napster for $100 000 for each song that was copied, on the basis of infringement of copyright. By early 2000, Napster had entered into a relationship with German media giant Bertelsmann. Hoping to provide a legitimate service to the millions of people who had downloaded the Napster client, they attempted to block sharing of hundreds of thousands of songs on a list provided by the RIAA. This failed and the RIAA sued again. Combined with other woes, such as the blocking of Napster traffic by some universities – the biggest source of such traffic – this proved to be the final straw: in late 2001, Napster had closed down.

In January 2002, Bertelsmann, which had invested US$85 million in the company, offered to buy the remains for $20 million. In-fighting followed, and the tattered remains of the business, including the brand name and rights thereto, were sold to Roxio.

The rise of peer-to-peer

The fall of Napster was not the end of the story for savvy Internet users who wanted to listen to music. While the RIAA was smothering Napster in legal judgements, America OnLine (AOL) was purchasing a small company called Nullsoft, one of whose projects was to become the Gnutella network. AOL quickly cancelled the project, but by then it was too late and the code and design were in the public domain.

Gnutella was the first of the peer-to-peer (P2P) networks. With no central server or presence that could be shut down by litigious copyright owners, it was a supposedly safe way to share one's files. All that was required was that someone wrote the client software, which would allow Internet users to connect to this network. This was accomplished quickly and, just as quickly, competitors began to spring up.

Most file-sharing applications allow the user to share files of all types as well as MP3s. They run on Windows, Macintosh, Linux, Sun and other computing platforms. The applications operate essentially along the same lines, whereby they offer:

- searching ability (by artist, genre, or other meta information);
- multi-tasking (it is possible to operate multiple searches and multiple downloads at the same time);
- integrated file libraries;
- browsing abilities (when someone else is online, it is possible to browse the contents of their shared folders);

3 MP3 is a compression algorithm that allows data to be compressed and expanded 'on the fly', given sufficient computing power. However, the algorithm is 'lossy' to provide better compression; it strips some of the data from the original source, thus making any MP3 file an imperfect copy of the original.

4 LP, long-play disc.

- interchangeable colour schemes ('skins');
- availability in different many different languages;
- speed of downloads (most sharing systems allow users to download a track from multiple locations and attempt to optimize use of bandwidth and download times).

These systems not only allow for sharing music but also encourage users to publish their original works and share these works with the general public. Because the systems allow multiple users to exchange the same information, the effect is that the information is more easily accessible and quicker to obtain.

The user downloads the desired program, be it Kazaa, Gnutella, Morpheus, Grokster, etc.; with that program, the user is allowed to search other users' hard drives that they have made available and that are running on the same program. For example, a user using Kazaa or the Kazaa Media Desktop (KMD), which is owned and operated by Sharman Industries, can search the shared files on the hard drive of someone else who is running KMD. For example, Dorothy and Albert, as well as a lot of other people, are running KMD. Dorothy searches for 'Where did our love go?' by the Supremes. Dorothy runs the search, the program finds the song on Albert's hard drive, and Dorothy downloads it to her computer. As sharing is the name of the game and the ability to swap content (music or other) is key, the program requires the user to set up a folder ('My shared folder') in which the user stores material that he or she wants to share. The file-sharing services urge users not to make their entire hard drive or 'My documents' folder available and to keep the folders from which they would like to share information separate and well marked to avoid unwanted infiltrators. (A report in 2002 found that most users had little idea as to precisely what they were sharing, evidence borne out by some of the users named by the RIAA's latest legal cases.[5])

The philosophy behind the file-sharing programs is to make available and share information. Users are encouraged to share responsibly at least as much information (content) as they download. Kazaa rewards those who actively participate in downloading as well as making content available by rating each user's participation level. The level of participation is then used when a user is searching for information. When a file is requested by another user and it has already been requested by someone else, the user with the highest participation level will be given priority. (This would matter, of course, only in terms of a highly desired file.)

To date, the most popular of these is the FastTrack network, which can be accessed using clients offered by Kazaa and Grokster. As of 26 May 2003, Kazaa had become the most downloaded piece of software ever on the Internet, with 203 million copies downloaded.

Since Gnutella and FastTrack, a number of alternative networks have emerged, all operating on a similar business model. On any given day, millions of people are typically active on these networks, as shown in Table 1 (numbers obtained 7 December 2003 at midday).

Table 1 Peer-to-peer networks and user numbers

Network	*Users*
FastTrack	3 941 240
eDonkey	1 598 842
iMesh	1 311 015
Overnet	688 128
MP2P	279 254
Gnutella	191 650
DirectConnect	189 899
Ares	57 446
Filetopia	4,284
Total	*8 261 758*

Source: www.slyck.com, 7 December 2003.

P2P revenue streams

Currently, the companies selling or offering clients to P2P networks have three revenue streams:

- Subscriptions from users who choose to purchase the clients.
- Advertising revenue from partners who advertise through the P2P clients (typically using a product like Cydoor or Gator[6]).
- Payments from Altnet for hosting specific files.

5 Brett Glass, 'Kazaa and others expose your secrets', www.extremetech.com

6 Both Cydoor and Gator are considered by hardcore users as 'spyware': they install small software clients, which watch a user's surfing behaviour in an attempt to target the user with more appropriate advertisements.

Subscriptions

The number of subscriptions purchased for P2P clients appears to be low, with as few as 1% of completed downloads resulting in a subscription. However, this still represents some 2.5 million subscriptions (based on a P2P community of roughly 250 million people),[7] based on typical subscription fees of $20–35. Given the reluctant attitude towards paying for services that is held by many Internet users, it is hard to see how subscriptions will provide meaningful revenue streams for the P2P companies. However, the issue of subscription was recently caught up in the RIAA subpoenas: one of the first people to be targeted was a 12-year-old New York girl, whose mother believed that since she had paid Kazaa a $29.95 subscription, her daughter was free to use the software (and the material downloaded using it) as she wished.

Advertising

Of the three revenue streams, the second seems to be the hands-down winner in terms of generated revenue. Figures are not directly available because online advertising rates fluctuate hugely and P2P companies are shy of releasing such figures; however, recent speculation suggested that a number of the key figures involved in the creation of various P2P networks have made handsome returns from their creations:

> Niklas Zennstron and Janus Friis [founders of Kazaa and FastTrack] ... may be sharing up to US$70m ... on an annual basis. ... Elan Oren formed iMesh in 1999 ... Slyck estimates that iMesh has earned the Israeli owner a cool US$100m.[8]

Anecdotal information – as well as any examination of the essential technology involved – suggests that a P2P network once set up can be extremely profitable. Providing a network has sufficient users to interest advertisers, then the incremental revenue from customers is almost entirely profit.

Altnet

Streamwaves, the first music service backed by major record companies, approached Kazaa to find a way in which file sharers would pay for downloaded music. Streamwaves' Altnet pays Kazaa for the right to place its clients' files on the top of search results. Those files are scrambled to deter piracy and in some cases require users to pay to play them. Under the deal, Kazaa users who search for many major-label artists will find a link to Streamwaves at the top of their search results. Clicking on that link will launch Streamwaves' software, providing samples of songs by the artist and related performers from an online jukebox. Streamwaves streams music to users rather than offering downloadable tracks. Altnet's files are protected by electronic locks (i.e. DRM,[9] see later) that control how files are opened and used. Altnet also offers to pay users to share files authorized for distribution. They are able to accumulate what are called 'peer points' which could amount (in theory) to $250 000 worth of prizes each month to those who transmit the most files to other Kazaa users. But the only files that earn points are Altnet files; the non-paid-for downloaded files from Kazaa cannot be used. Hence, Altnet is using honey to try and rid Kazaa of what the RIAA terms illegally downloaded files while the RIAA's vinegar seems to be antagonizing users.

Future revenue streams

Partly because of its close association with Kazaa and Sharman Networks, Altnet is not an option that is liked by most of the P2P industry, who set up their own lobbying group, P2PUnited, in mid-2003.

Other P2P companies are looking at similar revenue models that do not embrace such proprietary solutions. In a recent interview, Limewire's CEO Greg Bildson described his company's attempt. Called 'Magnetmix', it allows artists to cheaply publicize their content without the expense of hosting that content, and offers users a higher value-added experience beyond simply searching for a specific item and downloading it.

Because P2P networks essentially allow users to share data easily, and with a low cost to them, they are already making small inroads into areas such as online gaming, telephony solutions and software distribution. How the networks – the people who make the software – succeed in making money from such services remains to be seen; perhaps the type of data-sharing envisaged in these applications will become such a seamless, unseen part of users' operating systems that the software vendors will be swallowed up by operating system suppliers.

---

7 Over 500 million downloads have been made of P2P clients, but there is no agreed methodology for assessing the actual number of people on all the file-sharing networks.

8 Ciarán Tannam, 'P2P millionaires on the increase', www.slyck.com, November 2003.

9 DRM, digital rights management: software that controls how DRM-protected material can be used, by restricting copying, etc.

Music industry background

The music industry as we know it was started by Thomas Edison, whose invention of the first phonograph in 1877 paved the way for music to be reproduced in one's own home. From these early beginnings, records came into popular usage from the turn of the 20th century, and the industry experienced its first boom.

This continued until the 1920s, when radio became a mainstream medium. Fearing the loss of their livelihoods and their monopoly, the musicians' unions forbade their members from recording for radio or licensing their material to the nascent radio networks. This all changed when Louis Armstrong and a host of largely black, non-unionized musicians began to record for radio: their rapid rise to popularity convinced the unions and the recording companies that radio – far from threatening their livelihoods – was driving an overall growth in the market for music consumption.

Especially in the USA, industry growth continued with little interruption throughout the inter-war years and the Second World War. Throughout this period, the record was the sole mass medium for people to listen to their music on demand. In 1940 RCA Victor awarded Glenn Miller the first ever gold disc for selling one million units of 'Chattanooga Choo-Choo'.

The invention of the cassette in 1964 spelt the beginning of a long, slow decline in sales of records. Since their original design, with a mono soundtrack recorded at 78 rpm, and made from thick bakelite (an early type of plastic), records had moved on to stereo and quadrophonic recording (although the later was a commercial failure) and were now available as full LPs on 33 rpm.

Philips chose to license widely its cassette technology, driving rapid uptake and incurring the wrath of music industry executives, who treated the cassette as the second coming of radio, believing that it would drive piracy and shrink the overall music market. In fact, although piracy grew as a result of the introduction of this new technology, the overall music market grew sufficiently to far outweigh this loss of revenue. Furthermore, extensive independent research suggested that although cassettes allowed consumers to share music in a fashion that had not previously been possible, this sharing of music broadened general tastes in music consumption and led indirectly to an overall growth in per-capita consumption of music.

In 1978 Philips demonstrated the compact disc, sounding the beginning of a long but initially slow decline in cassette sales. Just as the cassette was eating away at vinyl sales, so would CDs eat into the market share of both vinyl and cassette. Surely enough, in 1988 CDs sold more units than vinyl, and by 2002 the IFPI[10] estimated that CDs provided 89% of global music industry revenue (see Table 2).

Table 2 **Global value of music industry sales by format**

Media	*Value share (%)*	
CD		89
Others		11
of which	Singles	40
	DVD video	27
	Cassette	24
	VHS video	6
	Vinyl	2
	Other audio	1

Source: IFPI Recording Industry World Sales Report, April 2002.

In 1991, Sony introduced the Mini-Disc (MD), hoping to replace the cassette with a medium that offered the flexibility of the cassette with the technology of the CD. Despite Sony's earlier success with the Walkman, which revolutionized the consumer electronics and music markets, the MD has been less of a trend-former, being rapidly overtaken by recordable CDs and MP3 players.

The music industry today

Throughout its history, the music industry has seen extensive mergers and acquisitions activity. From the humble beginnings at the turn of the twentieth century, the music industry is now a sprawling multi-billion euro monster. In 2002, the world music market was worth US$32.23 billion, with the USA the largest single market (see Tables 3 and 4).

Much of this activity is either controlled by, or at some point touches on the businesses of, five major players: Sony Music, Universal Music and Distribution, Bertelsmann Music Group (BMG), AOL Time Warner and EMI. Around one-quarter of the

10 International Federation of the Phonographic Industry.

Table 3 International music markets and sales breakdowns

Market	*% of world sales*
USA	39
Japan	16
UK	9
France	6
Germany	6
Canada	2
Italy	2
Spain	2
Australia	2
Mexico	1
Others	15

Source: IFPI Recording Industry World Sales Report, April 2002. NB Slight errors introduced due to rounding.

Table 4 Regional summary of market changes, 2001–02

	Unit change (%)	*Value change (%)*	*Value (US$ billions)*
World	−8.40	−7.20	32.2
North America	−10.10	−8.20	13.2
Europe	−4	−4.10	11.1
EU	−2.90	−3.90	10
Asia	−12.80	−10	6
Asia (excluding Japan)	−15.20	−13.40	1
Latin America	−5.40	−9.80	1
Australasia	−2.80	−5.40	0.6
Middle East	−20.50	−15.50	0.2
Africa	−3.10	1.40	0.1

Source: IFPI Recording Industry World Sales Report, April 2002.

Table 5 Worldwide market share ('Big Five' and independents), 2002

Company	*Worldwide market share (%)*
Universal	25.9
Sony	14.1
EMI	12
Warner	11.9
BMG	11.1
Independent labels	25

Source: Forbes Magazine, August 2003.

market is controlled by so-called 'indie' labels – labels independent of these groups (see Table 5).

Making music

The process of making and selling music seems, in many respects, very simple. However, a look at the industry's value chain[11] and a look at the cost breakdown of a typical CD (see Table 6) shows how many people can be involved in the production and sale of a single or LP: depending on the agreements signed by an artist and the other creative people and businesses who have an input into a recording, a contract can look more confusing than the King of Spain's early attempts to 'share' the wealth of the New World with those who had travelled there and enslaved the locals on his behalf.

The complexity and opacity of this system is perhaps one of the reasons that so many musicians are publicly disgruntled with the music business. Even before The Beatles formed Apple in the late 1960s, there had been high-profile defections from major record companies. However, this was only one high-profile example of a number of ways in which artists 'get back' at the industry majors:

- Mariah Carey signed a £70-milion deal with EMI's Virgin subsidiary in 2001. After the failure of the first album ('Glitter'), EMI paid Carey £19 million to extricate itself from the contract.
- Prince took to using a symbol for his name, then called himself 'the artist formerly known as Prince', then just 'Artist' in order to make his point to his then label Warner Bros. about the music he wished to pursue.[12]
- George Michael fell out publicly with Sony and ended up in court. After losing the case, Michael reached an agreement with Sony so that the latter could avoid expensive and embarrassing litigation: he moved to Virgin/Dreamworks and Sony received a lump sum payment.[13]
- Courtney Love famously took the industry to task in 'Courtney Love does the math[s]', published

11 R. Schulze, (1994) quoted in Shuman Ghosemajumder, *Advanced Peer-based Technology Models*, MIT Sloan, 2002, identified up to 15 different organizations that might seek a share or payment from an artist's work, from recording studios, managers, agents and distributors to sound engineers, retailers and marketers (obviously, some organizations might perform a number of these functions).

12 Ann Harrison, *Music: The Business*, Virgin Books, 2002.

13 Ibid.

online in *Salon* magazine. She wrote: 'Piracy is the act of stealing an artist's work without any intention of paying for it. I'm not talking about Napster-type software. I'm talking about major label recording contracts.'

- Robbie Williams signed a US$80-million deal with EMI in 2002, including the record company in his merchandising, concerts and other commercial activity.
- Janis Ian attacked the industry in May 2002 for its negative approach to file-sharing and the opportunities she said it offered (www.janisian.com).

In a 1999 report, one consultancy reported that any given album release in the USA had a 0.4% possibility of becoming a million-selling release, with a majority of the 30 000–40 000 albums released there each year losing money.[14] Courtney Love did her maths well from an artist's point of view, but she ignored the unpleasant reality that record companies simply do not know who will be a financial success and thus they need successful acts to subsidize less successful acts.

To the uninitiated, for example, a £250 000 advance is a lot of money. However, when one 'does the maths', the economics of the record industry start to become a little clearer. The record company is advancing £250 000 to a promising artist or band to get their first album. The band then needs to cover its living expenses for up to three years and to make some or all of the following payments: legal costs, accountancy costs, management fees, studio fees for album, tax, and cost of video production.

At this point, if the band fails to come up with material that the record company feels able to release, then the company is out of pocket by £250 000 in cash, plus whatever value it puts on management time and other resources it has devoted to helping the band members get their act together.

Assuming that the album is 'up to standard' – in any case, this is a highly subjective judgement – the record company now needs to commit time and money to the promotion and marketing of the album: another black hole into which limitless cash could be poured.

The music industry's response

Shutting down the file-sharing services

The RIAA joined forces with the film industry in 2001 by filing a copyright infringement suit against the larger P2P networks (including Morpheus and Grokster). Napster used a central server in order to co-ordinate and distribute the music and hence was held responsible for the infringement of the copyrights by the users of the service. File-sharing programs like Kazaa, Morpheus and Grokster use a decentralized network, where files are distributed from and by the user(s). Napster, being incorporated in the USA, was wholly vulnerable to legal action, whereas file-sharing services like Kazaa and iMesh are incorporated offshore and therefore inaccessible to US courts. Therefore, it is not as easy to file a law suit against the decentralized services as there is no one to sue. (Kazaa is based on software that was commissioned by two Scandinavian businessmen; the programmers are Estonian; and the right to license the program was acquired by an Australian-based company, Sharman Networks, which has no direct employees and is incorporated in Vanuatu, a tiny island in the South Pacific.)

Under the 1998 Digital Millennium Copyright Act, a federal judge in Washington, DC, was able to rule in January 2003 that Verizon Communications Inc., a provider of landline-based and wireless communications, was forced to identify an Internet subscriber accused of illegally making available 600 songs from well-known artists. Verizon subsequently appealed against this ruling and won, partly on the basis that an ISP is not responsible for data held on its client's computers.[15]

Suing the users

Realizing that it may be too difficult to prove that the music file-sharing programs were committing copyright infringement, the RIAA decided to file suits against individuals who use file-sharing software and has hence announced that it would begin preparing hundreds of lawsuits against individuals, demanding $150 000 per song downloaded.

In April 2003, the RIAA filed lawsuits against four students at three different American universities, accusing them of operating music file-sharing programs like Napster. The RIAA's aggressiveness is antagonizing not only university officials but one of their largest target

---

14 Ashish Singh, *Cutting Through the Digital Fog*, Bain & Co., 2003.

15 www.eff.org/cases/Riaa_v_verizon/opinion-20031219.pdf

audiences (students) as well. The President of Michigan Technological University, one of the universities cited in the suit, stated in a letter to the RIAA:

> Had you followed the previous methods established in notification of a violation [copyright infringement], we would have shut off the student and not allowed the problem to grow to the size and scope that it is today. I am very disappointed that the RIAA decided to take action in this manner.

Many file-sharing users tend to be students using high-speed campus computer networks, and many colleges believe that blocking P2P networks would be contradicting academic freedom. Record industry executives and online music companies are now working with colleges and universities to find ways in which to offer legitimate sources of free or deeply discounted music to students in order to stop the use of unauthorized file-sharing, although colleges and universities would then be obligated to block unauthorized downloads. Discussions are still in the early stages.

Other means

The record industry has also pursued less conventional ways to combat music file-sharing by harassing music file-sharing systems and users alike by posting corrupt or empty files. The industry has actually looked at legal ways to 'lock up' any computer that uses the file-sharing software. So far, the Big Five of the music industry have refused to partner with any of the file-sharing programs. Ever since 1999, Napster and its successors have made numerous attempts to reach some form of concord with the industry, including an ill-fated attempt by Napster to filter out illegal content and more recent efforts by Kazaa and Grokster to offer distribution deals to the industry.

Despite efforts thus far, the industry has behaved in what appears to be an extremely reticent manner, refusing to accept that file-sharing services have any form of future and refusing almost point-blank to deal with them.

The Big Five have asked major recording artists, such as Eminem, Madonna, Elton John and Luciano Pavarotti, to speak out against music file-sharing and to deliver personal messages in the media. Some high-powered musicians have even testified at US Federal and State Government hearings on illegal file-sharing. On the other hand, some artists, including Courtney Love, Joni Mitchell, Jimmy Buffet and Janis Ian, have been outspoken as to how the music industry has been taking advantage of artists all along and now the tide has turned. In 'Love's manifesto',[16] Courtney Love sets out explicitly how she believes the music industry has profited from artists and how the artists have not received their due.

The music executives who are recruiting these big stars to come out against file-sharing are also the same people who are desperately trying to work out how to turn this around so that they too may profit from the Internet distribution systems. Adding to the soup, some of the Big Five are also part of organizations that are selling computers with CD burners and other equipment for copying music (Sony is an excellent example of this).

Signing up universities

The rejuvenated Napster (now a division of Roxio) signed in December 2003 a deal with Pennsylvania State University, allowing the students access to the new Napster and most of its library, although the service makes heavy use of Windows-embedded DRM technology. Precisely what the cost is to Penn State, or what the contract between the university and Roxio contains, or even whether such a deal is for publicity purposes or is repeatable, are all still in debate.

Legal file-sharing services

The music industry has launched alternatives to the P2P networks, supporting legal online music services such as MusicNet, eMusic, Pressplay, Rhapsody, iTunes and Buymusic.com. MusicNet has been touted as the industry's best response to music file-sharing. For $9.95 a month, a user can download 100 songs streamed to them. Of course, these services are not as popular, not only because they are paying services but also because some of them offer monthly subscriptions rather than selling individual songs and albums. How is the music industry going to get the public to purchase something that they have been able to obtain for free?

Online retail

Through their control of most of the popular catalogues, the music majors are busy trying a number of different ways to sell to online users, as described

16 Courtney Love, 'Courtney Love does the math', 14 June 2000, *Salon.com magazine* (San Francisco and New York), http://dir.salon.com/tech/feature/2000/06/14/love/index.html

later. With a tiny number of exceptions, these follow their current model, using a third party to interact with music buyers.

DRM

A key element of a number of industry responses is the use of digital rights management (DRM) technology. A simple concept, good DRM is very difficult to get right, as Sony has found out with its ATRAC-3 system. Essentially, the technology allows the vendor of a piece of digital media to decide:

- how long the user can listen to the music for (e.g. one week);
- whether, and how many times, the track can be duplicated;
- what media the track may be duplicated to;
- whether the track can be translated into another format (e.g. from WMA to MP3).

At present, however, DRM systems are proving generally to be cumbersome and complicated. For example, if you download tracks from some music services, you are unable to install them on your MP3 player unless it is on a list of approved and tested equipment. Or perhaps you have two computers and wish to use the track on both: most DRM systems will not allow this, despite the fact that such use clearly falls within applicable copyright and reproduction laws in both the USA and Europe.[17]

Other revenue sources

Traditionally, record labels have largely only earned money from the sale of recorded music. EMI Group was the first of the Big Five to make an all-encompassing deal with Robbie Williams, the British pop star. EMI paid Robbie Williams around $80 million to become a full partner in all of Williams's earning: publishing, touring, merchandising and record sales.

In a presentation on 3 May 2003, EMI Executive Vice-President John Rose stated that EMI is actively looking for a strategy but it is still relying heavily on law enforcement rather than looking to partner with any of the file-sharing programs. Some of the strategies that he mentioned include the following:

- Tighter pre-release management.
- Keeping a tighter internal inventory so as to avoid leaks and letting songs and/or content reach the Internet too quickly.
- Becoming better informed about customers.
- Making it more difficult to rip and burn CDs by embedding the CDs with technology that limits the customer's ability to copy the music.

All of these ideas are well and good, but none of them is aggressive enough or will react fast enough to the changes occurring in the industry. Any technological encryption will probably be broken relatively quickly, which means spending more and more time and personnel to constantly re-invent ways in which to make CD copying more difficult.

The music industry realizes that it must change its business model. Besides Streamwaves' partnership with Kazaa, the music industry has been very reluctant to form any sort of partnership with the file-sharing companies. Mr Rose stated that it must now seek new revenue sources such as Internet and physical sales, DVD music videos, Internet radio, turning telephone ring tones into ring 'tunes', and digital downloads. EMI realizes that it must fully integrate digital distribution into its business model.

Response from other parties

The advent of file-sharing appears to be affecting the industry far more than earlier incarnations of music-sharing, such as cassettes and eight-track tapes. Who are the other parties who are involved here?

Artists

For some artists, the advent of the Internet has revitalized their careers and their finances. The most frequently quoted case is that of Janis Ian, who has famously published two articles providing what she describes as 'an alternative view'.[18]

The Internet has allowed artists to take more control, at lower expense, of their promotion and marketing, where they are allowed to do so by their contract, and for some this is a huge boon: they can gather more of the revenue from their products – whether this is a music download or a mail-order CD – than was possible previously. A look at the

17 The most famous attempt at DRM was the SDMI (Secure Digital Music Initiative). The creators (in 2001) offered a US$1-million prize to whoever could crack it: a group of Princeton researchers took 48 hours and were promptly sued into silence.

18 www.janisian.com

available analyses of CD costs shows that record companies, distributors and record shops, whether online or on the high street, take a large part of the actual consumer cost of a CD (see Tables 6 and 7).

Table 6 **Revenue shares from an £11.61 ($16.98) CD**

Company overhead, distribution, shipping	£2.29	19.72%
Pressing album, printing booklet	£0.51	4.39%
Retailer mark-up	£4.26	36.69%
Advertising, retail discounts	£0.58	5.00%
Artist royalties	£1.36	11.71%
Marketing	£1.47	12.66%
Signing and producing record	£0.74	6.37%
Label profit	£0.40	3.45%
Total	*£11.61*	*100%*

Source: Billboard, CNN.

Table 7 **Estimated revenue breakdown for a $0.99 music file download**

Telecoms company (bandwidth)	$0.02
Publishing	$0.08
Retailer margin (e.g. MSN)	$0.12
Service provider	$0.21
Artist royalties	$0.09
Marketing	$0.20
Overhead/A&R	$0.19
Corporate profit	$0.08
Total	*$0.99*

Source: Financial Times, 1 September 2003.

Importantly, artists from both ends are threatening the semi-hegemony enjoyed by the Big Five record companies. Where people like Janis Ian are taking their own responsibility for selling a broad catalogue to a comparatively small audience, groups such as Simply Red are also taking responsibility for their own products; for example, the release of Simply Red's latest album is being handled entirely 'in-house' by the group, thus depriving their former label of millions of euros in potential revenue.

Of course, for any artist, the greatest fear is that of anonymity, and the Internet does not necessarily offer a cure for this. Shuman Ghosemajumder found that many artists who had submitted work to MP3.com had received almost no sales as a result, or had sales that were derisory in terms of their effort and expense. He also pointed out that in 1993, 90% of UK artists generating income from copyright received less than £1000 for the year, with 31% receiving less than £25.

Although it is difficult to establish clearly how the Internet, along with the easy portability and downloading of music, is affecting some artists, it seems sure that the two sides who are using it successfully are either the most well-established, well-known groups, or the lesser-known but still long-established groups with a clear fan base.

Service companies

It is extremely difficult to get any figures relating to the amounts of money that the industry spends on efforts to eradicate the online sharing of music. Particularly in developed markets, where this is perceived as a problem, there are a number of businesses that appear to be making healthy profits from working with music companies to create 'spoof' recordings, to flood P2P networks, to target users on the networks, and of course to try to drag sharers to court.[19]

Consumer electronics companies

The uneasy relationship between the music industry and the companies who make the equipment on which people listen to their product is best epitomized by the marriage of Sony's music and consumer electronics divisions. Jealous of Apple's iPod, senior staff at Sony seem to have spent much of 2002 trying to work out how to keep their businesses ahead in both markets.[20] Sony's dilemma is encapsulated in devices like its USB-compatible MiniDisc: unlike many other devices designed to carry music around in a quickly erasable/rewriteable format, Sony's latest generation of MiniDisc players uses a copy-protection system that some may consider to be somewhat cumbersome or unfriendly.

Other companies, such as Philips, Apple, Samsung, Nokia and Creative, have been happy to create a bewildering array of players for MP3 tracks, allowing consumers, in some cases, to carry around more than 7000 songs (30 Gb or more of data) on a small player.

19 'Spoofs' are corrupted or unusable files that record companies pay intermediaries to host. The purpose is to render music downloading a less pleasant, more frustrating experience. The most famous was the 'release' of tracks from Madonna's new album in mid 2002; rather than the actual tracks, the MP3 contained an endlessly repeated clip of Madonna saying: 'What the **** are you doing?'

20 Frank Rose, 'The civil war inside Sony', *Wired*, February 2003.

Recent initiatives have supposedly brought together many of the key players, in an attempt to agree secure standards for such devices.[21] However, this activity has not stopped the design of more and more sophisticated and user-friendly MP3 players. In fact, as pointed out in Rose's article, the relative sizes of these two industries suggest that the leverage of music companies is limited: although they control the content creation, the availability of software to 'rip' anything produced by the industry secures consumer electronics companies from any accusation of open complicity in file-sharing. Ripping, in this context, means the duplication of a digital stream, and commonly refers to the uploading of a CD's contents to a hard drive, hence Apple's advertising campaign in late 2000 featuring the catchphrase 'Rip, Mix, Burn': tracks could be 'ripped' or copied, mixed (i.e. gathered in the order chosen by the user) and 'burnt' (transferred) to a new (blank) CD.

Online music retailers

The music industry has certainly not stood still in its response to people sharing music online. A number of efforts have been made to attract people to the purchase of music online, with varying degrees of success, and there have been a number of reviews of the different services. To make comparison easier, we examine some of the newer online businesses to look at the options being explored by the industry.

The iTunes music store

Launched in May 2003, the iTunes music store is a composite part of Apple's iTunes software. Available to all Macintosh users (less than 10% of the worldwide PC community), iTunes is a program for managing music and audio files on a Macintosh.

Apple has managed to get a number of major record companies on board, leading to a fairly broad content availability (of around 200 000 titles in July 2003). This content is easily accessed through a simple interface that is based heavily on the album-cover images (see Exhibit 1). To use the music store, one simply connects, clicks on the tracks one wishes to purchase, and either downloads them immediately (at 99 cents each) using a 1-Click[22] payment interface, or stores them in a 'basket' for group purchase later on.[23]

21 '17 leading companies form a working group to simplify sharing of digital content', Philips press release, June 2003.

22 An online payment interface that allows consumers to purchase items with a single click once they have set up their credentials on that website.

23 In November 2003, Steve Jobs, Apple's CEO, cast doubt on the economics of this price point, claiming that with over ten million downloads, Apple had failed to turn a profit on the service, with 'almost every cent going to the music companies'. Even so, Wal-Mart's offer of tracks at 88 cents each set a new base price in late December 2003.

Exhibit 1 The iTunes music store

Source: Download via www.apple.com/itunes, May 2003.

Music is downloaded as 128 Kbps AAC[24] format files and is almost infinitely transferable, whether to another computer or to an MP3 player or writeable CD. This was an issue with some respondents to CNet's review of the music store, which pointed out that for a track to be CD quality, it should be recorded at bit rates of at least 192 Kbps. The other main issue is, of course, the fact that the service is available only to Apple users. Nevertheless, in December 2003 Apple reported that 25 million tracks had been downloaded from the store since its inception.

BTOpenWorld's dotmusic on demand

dotmusic (www.dotmusic.com/ondemand) is a relatively new player built for the European market (iTunes is currently available only in the USA). It is wedded to Microsoft's WMA[25] music format. This goes to the extent of requiring users to have Windows, Internet Explorer and Windows Media Player all installed before they can use the service.

Users of the service have a number of options when joining, from paying for individual tracks (ranging from 99p to £1.49) to a full subscription (at £9.99 a month), which includes unlimited streams and unlimited downloads (see Exhibit 2). The dotmusic streaming service includes a number of radio stations (whose content is changed every fortnight)

Exhibit 2 **Dotmusic pricing options**

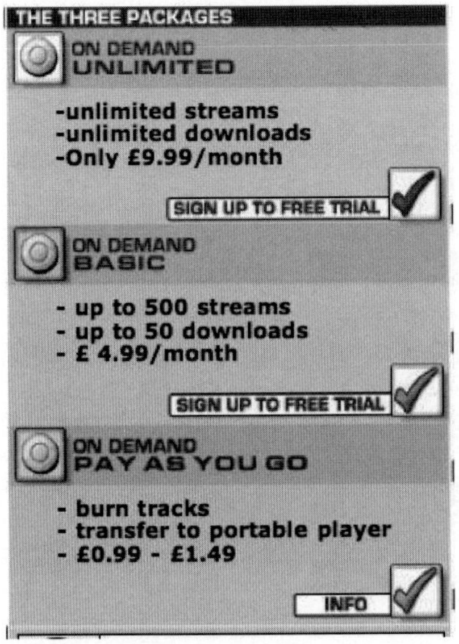

Source: www.dotmusic.com/ondemand, May 2003.

and also all of the music available on the website. (Since streams tend to be at much lower bit rates than downloads, they are good for previewing whole tracks or albums, or simply listening to something online. The quality is not usually acceptable, however, for a reusable format, i.e. burning on CD.)

The site claims to contain around 170 000 tracks (in May 2003) and is operated on behalf of British Telecom by OD2, which also operates Freeserve's[26] music service on many of the similar basics (WMA, similar track selection, subscription service, etc.).

eMusic

A subsidiary of Vivendi Universal (the parent company of Universal music) and founded in 1998, eMusic had 70 000 subscribes by December 2003. The eMusic service offers unlimited downloads for a monthly subscription, using 128-Kbps MP3 files as the standard music format. As the website says:

> Since it was founded in 1998, eMusic has been a pioneer in the digital distribution of music. In July of 1998, eMusic became the first commercial site to begin selling singles and albums in the popular MP3 format. In the Fall of 2000, eMusic became the first company to launch a downloadable music subscription service.[27]

The site had around 70 000 subscribers for its 250 000 songs in December 2003, but it did manage to generate some negative publicity in May of that year, when it advised some customers that downloading several thousand tracks over a single month was not considered to be 'fair use'.

For many commentators, eMusic's service is the future for a large part of the music industry, offering users effectively unlimited music for a constant revenue stream. Perhaps the poor support of the service by music companies demonstrates their fear that music consumers are moving further from their marketing reach and that consumers will become further accustomed to getting more music for the same outlay.

---

24 Kbps, kilobits per second: a measure reflecting the amount of sound data captured – the higher the figure, the greater the fidelity to the original recording. AAC, Advanced Audio Coding, or MPEG 2 layer 3.

25 WMA, Windows Media Audio, Microsoft's proprietary music compression format, which contains a number of DRM features.

26 www.freeserve.com/entertainment/music

27 www.emusic.com

Exhibit 3 CNet's 2002 comparison of online music purchasing services

	BurnItFirst	eMusic	FullAudio Music Now	Pressplay	Listen.com Rhapsody 1.5	RealOne MusicPass
Free trial	Yes, but 30-second previews only	Yes; 30 days, 50 downloads	Yes; 30 days, 100 downloads	Yes; 3 days, unlimited streams and downloads	Yes; 7 days	No; 14-day SuperPass trial includes video content but not music
Number and price of plans	One plan: $9.95/month	Two plans: $9.95 (12-month commitment) and $14.95 (3-month commitment)	Two plans: $7.49 and $14.99	Three plans; $9.95 or $17.95 per month, $180 per year	Four plans: $4.95 to $9.95	One plan: $9.95/month (plan with video content also available)
Number of songs streamed in each plan	No full streams, but unlimited number of 30-second streamed previews	No full streams, but unlimited number of 30-second streamed previews	No full streams, but unlimited number of 30-second streamed previews	Unlimited	Unlimited	100
Number of downloads in each plan	20	Unlimited	50/100	Unlimited (downloads that expire with membership); 0/10/120 (permanent downloads)	None	100
Downloaded songs accessible after membership	Yes	Yes	No	Yes, 10 per month with middle plan, 120 per year with highest plan	NA	No
Can burn songs to CD	Yes, three times each	Yes	No	Yes, permanent downloads only	No	No
Can transfer tunes to a portable player	Yes, some players	Yes	No	Yes, permanent downloads only	No	No
Songs are copyright-protected	Yes	No	Yes	Yes (the unlimited downloads expire)	NA	No
Quick whole-album downloads	Yes	Yes	No	Yes	NA	No
Approximate number of tracks in catalogue	2100	22000	50000	100000	135000	75000

Source: www.cnet.com, May 2003.

Other services

Exhibit 3 shows the results of a CNet review carried out in 2002, and compares some of the biggest services then available. As is clear from this exhibit and from the other services described above, there is a huge range of options in terms of the way that one can download and listen to music online.

Looking carefully at the different services available, it is clear that while the industry has learnt a lot from the operation of other online businesses, it is still seeking a model that customers 'like' – so far, downloadable music as a business has no Amazon.com trailblazing the way it deals with customers. Almost all of the services looked at are seeking a way to make customers more 'sticky', and many seem to be almost experimental, considering the different ways in which customers can interact. It was found that customers can get their music in a number of different ways:

- Streaming[28] audio, based on song or playlist selection.
- Streaming audio based on radio channels created by the services (e.g. MusicMatch MX).
- Downloadable tracks that are non-transferable and that expire with a period of time or with membership.
- Downloadable tracks that are transferable in specific fashions to specific devices.
- Downloadable tracks that have no DRM system and are infinitely transferable (i.e. to CD, MP3 player, etc.).

Other proposals

The music industry provides a heady combination of big business and high emotion: consumers respond to purchasing music in a different way to purchasing washing machines. Largely as a result, there is no shortage of advice available to the industry, ranging from Orin Hatch's quickly withdrawn proposal at the beginning of this case study to advocates of free goods supporting the complete destruction of the music business as we know it.

Some of the more (and less) possible suggestions being proposed, aside from those discussed above, include:

- Licensing P2P companies and paying the proceeds to artists.
- Requiring compulsory DRM installation on equipment.
- Banning P2P networks.

Next steps

With the two sides of the debate so polarized, a solution seems a long way away. Record companies seem loath to abandon what they see as decades of growth based on their existing distribution and business models, and the P2P companies – along with their users – are continuing to refuse to share the revenue with what they consider to be the overbearing and stifling Big Five.[29]

Certainly in the USA, it is clear that action in the courts will continue apace, and recently the IFPI announced that it was planning to begin similar actions in Europe. It is clear that such action has an effect – however temporary – on the downloading of music. However, the negative effect that this action is causing for the industry, as well as the prospect that P2P services will be around for the indefinite future (in 2001, Intel's Andy Grove described P2P as 'the future of computing'), call for a far more permanent and customer-friendly solution.

Consumers may have more and more leisure euros to spend, but the music's share of that cash has been falling. The two divergent but interconnected questions that observers worldwide are trying to decide are the following:

- How do you carry on giving consumers the music they want while paying the people who actually make it?
- Where do the P2P businesses go from here?

---

28 Streaming refers to a constant digital stream between the service provider and the customer, operating in a very similar fashion to a radio station. Sound quality tends to be lower, but streams are effectively available on demand.

29 One mailing list included the following anecdote: 'Wayne Rosso yelled to a room packed with people anxious to be involved in legitimate online music distribution at the iHollywood Conference – "I'm not going to pay you guys a damn thing!"' (referring to a conference held in December 2003).

DISCUSSION QUESTIONS

1. How could the music industry have responded differently to the rise of Napster?
2. What should peer-to-peer (P2P) networks do to grow their business?
3. Could the various protagonists have 'seen it coming'? Were there any warning signs that might have helped them to respond?
4. What is the music industry's biggest problem – is P2P a disease or a symptom?
5. What can other industries learn from the major music companies' response to online file-sharing?
6. What can we learn from the response of parties other than the music companies and the P2P file-sharing facilitators?

12Snap* (Germany, UK, Italy)

From B2C mobile retailing to B2B mobile marketing

Some of the mobile marketing campaigns are getting 20-30% response rates. That is outstanding compared to direct mail, where you get a 2% response rate if you are lucky. The mobile phone is intensely personal. It is yours, it is in your pocket and every message gets read. It is very powerful.

Andrew Hughes, Executive Secretary of the Wireless Marketing Association, UK[1]

12Snap: company background

The launch phase (September 1999–June 2000)

In the midst of the e-commerce boom in 1999, Michael Birkel, Andreas Müller, Cyriac Roeding, Alexander Brand and Bernd Mühlfriedel – all employed at consulting companies such as McKinsey and A.T. Kearney – were contemplating how to launch a 'new economy' venture. Andreas Müller was inspired by former high school friends who had founded Alando.de, an Internet-based auction platform, and sold it after only three months of operation to e-Bay.com for €30 million: 'Alando.de was the one new economy success in Germany. I felt that that we had to build something ourselves.'[2]

Through their different educational backgrounds and consulting work, the founders of 12Snap combined a broad range of experience in the fields of strategy, technology, marketing, finance and project management. While still working for the consulting companies, they came up with 80 business ideas for their new venture and considered three possible areas: wireless applications, business-to-business e-commerce, and broadband technology.[3] Michael Birkel, Chief Executive Officer of 12Snap, explains the rationale for choosing the wireless applications area: 'Rather than jumping on the internet bandwagon, we wanted to address the next wave'[4] (see Exhibit 1).

Andreas Müller, Chief Strategy Officer of 12Snap, adds:

> After deciding to focus on mobile technology, we asked ourselves: what can we do with a mobile phone? Eventually, we decided that we should do something that would be fun.[5]

Birkel and Müller decided to start with mobile auctions. With the help of a creativity agency, they chose '12Snap' as the company's name. Müller explains:

> Snap stands for impulsiveness. A '1' at the beginning is good as it puts us on top of all lists, even before A. '12Snap' represents the consumer process of a fun mobile auction.[6]

---

* Reads 'one-two-snap'.

1 'The novelty could quickly wear off', Financial Times.com, 17 July 2001.

2 Company interviews, which the authors conducted in November 2001.

3 Broadband is a transmission medium that can carry signals from multiple independent network carriers on a single coaxial or fibre optic cable, by establishing different bandwidth channels.

4 '12Snap gets crackle and pop', *European Venture Capital Journal*, 1 November 2000.

5 Company interviews, which the authors conducted in November 2001.

6 Ibid.

This case study was written by Albrecht Enders, Research Associate at INSEAD (Fontainebleau), under the supervision of Tawfik Jelassi, Affiliate Professor of Technology Management at INSEAD, and Charles Waldman, Senior Affiliate Professor of Marketing at INSEAD. It is intended to be used as the basis for class discussion rather than to illustrate effective or ineffective handling of a management situation.

Exhibit 1 Evolution of mobile phone users in Germany

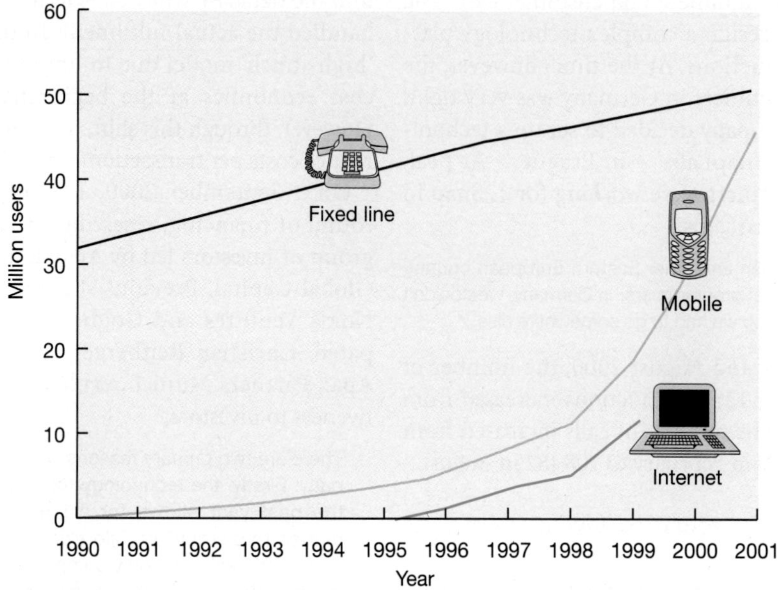

Source: International Data Corporation, Wirtschaftswoche

On 6 September 1999, in order to acquire venture capital, the 12Snap founding team presented its business plan to executives from Mannesmann, a German mobile telecommunications firm. The result of the meeting was a mutually exclusive co-operation agreement with D2 (now D2 Vodafone) and an appointment with an investment manager at Viventures, a venture capital fund based in Paris specializing in IT and media ventures. The fund, established by the Vivendi Group, is backed by companies including British Telecom, Mannesmann, Siemens, Nokia, Cisco and Omnitel. The next morning the team presented its business plan to Viventures, which agreed to fund a first round of financing with €2.55 million.

On 15 September 1999, the 12Snap's founding members simultaneously quit their jobs and started developing the technology for the auction platform, hiring staff and seeking co-operation agreements with product suppliers. On 14 December 1999, the company conducted its first online auction test among the 12Snap board members. The item auctioned was a chewed-off piece of dental gum: its final strike price was DM14387.[7] Cyriac Roeding, Head of Marketing at 12Snap, comments on this first experience: 'It was even more fun than we could ever have imagined.'[8]

On 20 December 1999, the team ran the first live auction for test customers in which 190 people participated. The item auctioned was a Sony PlayStation. After testing the system with 250 auctions, 12Snap went live on 21 January 2000. Michael Birkel commented:

> There comes the moment when you have to stop analyzing things. You just have to jump into the cold water and start the business. Speed is crucial. Growth gets crippled if it's not pushed with insane speed. Then pragmatism and improvisation have to prevail over perfection.[9]

Looking back at the initial experience, Müller comments:

> At the beginning, speed was everything. We built the technology platform in just three months and we were very proud of it. We even worked over Christmas. What I feel now is that had we moved slower, it might have been better. Until June 2000 we kept working with the same business model. Because we were all caught up in operations, we forgot about rethinking and reanalyzing things. We then substantially decreased the speed and this has helped us.[10]

12Snap's mobile auction business comprised the following steps: product selection and ordering from

7 €1 = DM1.95.
8 Quoted on 12Snap website.
9 Ibid.
10 Company interviews, which the authors conducted in November 2001.

suppliers, production of the auction, running the auction, payment, fulfilment and customer care. The company had to design a complex technology platform to run the auctions. At the time, however, the market for programmers in Germany was very tight. Eventually, the company decided to set up a technology lab – called 'SnapLabs' – in Prague.[11] At peak times, 45 programmers were working for 12Snap in Prague, as Müller explains:

> We could've chosen any other Eastern European country where you could get programmers. In Germany, we couldn't get programmers, so we had to go somewhere else.[12]

Between February and August 2000, the number of registered users for 12Snap's auctions increased from 9370 to 136854. The number of calls increased from roughly 20000 calls in February to 108482 in August.

The shift from 'high touch' to 'low touch' mobile commerce

After running the business for six months, 12Snap management realized that the internal handling of all the steps involved in an auction – from software development to operations – was very costly. At the same time, because of the focus on business-to-consumer (B2C) auctions, the model proved to be less scalable than, for instance, the consumer-to-consumer (C2C) auction model used by Internet companies such as eBay.

In the summer of 2000, 12Snap conducted an activity-based cost analysis to gather detailed information about the actual costs of running mobile auctions, which it would also need for the next round of financing from external investors. The analysis showed that the auctions created substantial costs in the internal operation areas. Alexander Müller, International Controlling Manager at 12Snap, comments:

> We took a snapshot of the financial situation of 12Snap at that time. We tried to actually analyze the data in terms of the underlying business models. We divided the figures into transaction-related and mobile marketing-related. When we had the actual results we were, in a way, surprised at how obvious it was for us.

With the existing business model, total costs were €26.7 per transaction. Further calculations showed that optimizing the existing model would reduce costs to €20.1 (see Exhibit 2).

In order to reduce costs, the company decided to shift from the 'high-touch' business model, where all operations were handled internally, to a 'low-touch' model in which 12Snap simply entered the products into the database while an external logistics provider handled the actual fulfilment. Initially, it chose the 'high-touch' model due to limited scale and fixed-cost economics at the beginning of operations. However, through this shift, the company was able to reduce costs per transaction to €14.6.

On 3 September 2000, 12Snap secured a third round of financing, receiving €37.2 million from a group of investors led by Apax Europe IV and Argo Global Capital. Previous shareholders Viventures, Nokia Ventures and Goldman Sachs also participated. Christian Reitberger, Assistant Director at Apax Partners Munich, explained 12Snap's attractiveness to investors:

> There are two primary reasons why we backed the company. Firstly, the technology that it has developed over the past year allows for a large number of access modes to execute mobile transactions. As far as we know, 12Snap is the only company with a working high-performance, high-throughput multi-model platform. Secondly, 12Snap has customers! With the launch of the mobile auction service it became the only company to have tested its platform under real-world conditions. While other companies will undoubtedly develop their own open-access platforms, 12Snap has experience and a huge first-mover advantage.[13]

The shift to the Media Model

During summer 2000, 12Snap realized that even the 'low-touch' model would not be profitable because of the limited scalability of shopping revenues due to the B2C focus. In addition, margins were extremely low because a bargain-buy mentality prevailed among users. At the same time, it was necessary to invest heavily and continuously in marketing activities in order to attract new customers. It also became obvious that it would not be possible to retain young customers simply by offering shopping.

To address the above challenge, 12Snap decided to scale down the shopping component by limiting the product choice and to add content instead: entertainment and mobile marketing activities. This new approach was referred to as the 'Media Model'. External benchmarks – such as the NTT DoCoMo's

---

11 Prague was chosen because it was the home city of the CTO's wife.

12 Company interviews, which the authors conducted in November 2001.

13 '12Snap gets crackle and pop', *European Venture Capital Journal*, 1 November 2000.

Exhibit 2 **Activity-based costing analysis at 12Snap, summer 2000** (in euros).

Results activity-based costing

Cost	Status quo	Optimized	Low touch	Low-low touch
Per transaction	7.1	2.7	2.7	1.3
Per shopping offer	16.7	14.8	14.8	1.8
Per new item (1st order)	122.9	67.4	67.4	0.0
Item registry & soundfile	88.8	44.1	44.1	0.0
Order cost per item	34.1	23.3	23.3	0.0
Supplier acquisition	916.7	916.7	916.7	916.7
Customer registry	3.0	2.9	2.9	2.9

#Transactions/day	150
#Auctions/day	50
Average # products/item order	20
# Times an average item is re-ordered	1.5

Status quo: initial business model

Status quo

Source	Cost	Per transaction	Per transaction/ cumulated (status quo)
IVR costs/transaction	4.9	4.9	12.0
Shopping offer	16.7	5.6	17.6
New item registry	88.8	1.8	19.4
Item order cost	34.1	1.7	21.1
Average shipping Cost of shipment (kamino)	5.6	TOTAL/ transaction	26.7

Optimized: business model after first optimization

Optimized

Source	Cost	Per transaction
IVR costs/transaction	4.9	4.9
Shopping offer	14.8	4.9
New item registry	44.1	0.9
Item order cost	23.3	1.2
Costs/shipment (kamino)	5.6	TOTAL/ transaction

Low touch

Source	Cost	Per transaction	Per transaction/ cumulated (status quo)
IVR costs/transaction	4.9	4.9	7.6
Shopping offer	14.8	4.9	12.6
New item registry	44.1	0.9	13.4
Item order cost	23.3	1.2	14.6
Cost of shipment charged by supplier	0.0	TOTAL/ transaction	14.6

Low-touch: business model after second optimization with outsourced logistics

Low-low touch

Source	Cost	Per transaction
IVR costs/transaction	4.9	4.9
Shopping offer	1.8	0.6
New item registry	0.0	0.0
Item order cost	0.0	0.0
		TOTAL/ transaction

Low-low-touch: calculation for further cost reduction (not implemented)

Source: 12Snap company calculations.

i-mode system in Japan – demonstrated the power of entertainment to attract and maintain active customers. In addition, the entertainment features that were built into the 12Snap service from the beginning had been instrumental in driving traffic to 12Snap. The goal of the new Media Model was to turn customers into 12Snap addicts, as Andreas Müller explains:

> People have a natural desire for entertainment. Therefore, we decided to focus on mobile entertainment services. The auction service was already a mélange between

> transaction and entertainment ... The main goal of providing entertainment is to attract customers and to make them happy. It's just like standard TV – you have to offer entertaining programmes that attract viewers but don't generate revenues. You make money by offering advertisement slots to marketers. In addition, we needed the shopping service to find out what our customers buy. Therefore, we needed to offer transactions.[14]

In October 2000, 12Snap's business shift towards the Media Model was accompanied by a corporate restructuring which involved laying off 20 employees from the purchasing, operations and marketing functions. Also, in order to increase 12Snap's attractiveness, an entertainment channel targeting different customer segments was established at the beginning of 2001. It was aimed at different target segments according to customer preferences.[15] It used both text messages (SMS) and mobile broadcasting technology and was divided into the following thematic zones:

- *'High-tech' passion zone* for customers with an interest in technology, hi-fi, games and computers, offering news, tips, test results and logos for downloading.
- *'Party' passion zone* offering movie and music packages and tickets, mobile games and the latest show-biz news.
- *'Style' passion zone* offering body and fashion advice, tips about restaurants, workout centres, etc.
- *'Love' passion zone* offering romance-related services such as dating and through SMS offering love horoscopes, psycho tests and 'products for two'.

The schedule of the channel was designed to correspond with users' behaviour: during the week the channel had special offers during lunch breaks (from midday to 2.00 p.m.), while on weekends the offers ran from midday to 10.00 p.m. All passion zones also offered mobile sweepstakes.

The shift to mobile marketing

The new 12Snap strategy launched in autumn 2000 still had a strong B2C focus and the company realized that it would be increasingly difficult to attract new customers without a major investment in marketing. Andreas Müller elaborates:

> To acquire customers as an online or a mobile shop, you have to spend a lot on advertising and marketing. That, for example, is what Amazon.com did. However, in the adverse venture capital conditions that we were facing at that time, this option was not viable anymore for us.[16]

In December 2000, 12Snap management realized that mobile shopping would not work under the financial and technological constraints they faced and decided to reposition the company once again. An analysis conducted in April 2001 showed that 90% of the margin came from mobile marketing (see Table 1), as Andreas Müller explains:

> We realized that we would never have deep enough pockets to make transactions work because of the market crash and the slower-than-expected development of mobile technology. We also realized that there wasn't enough money to continue content and entertainment. The solution that came to mind was that we needed to leverage the power of other players with deeper pockets such as big media and telecommunication companies. We decided to concentrate on mobile marketing.

Regarding the frequent strategy shifts at 12Snap, Müller says:

> The strategy of a start-up depends strongly on the situation of the financial market and other factors beyond a small company's control, such as overall development of industry technologies. With the bursting of the [new economy] bubble and the much-slower-than-expected progress in mobile technology development, we knew that we would never get enough money to sustain our business model until the market had developed. That's why we had to shift again. In addition, the strategy of a start-up is a learning process. We have to be extremely flexible as an organization and to adapt until we figure out the right business model that is profitable.[17]

12Snap's shift towards mobile marketing again led to staff lay-offs. Out of 53 employees in the technology field, only six remained to manage the internal knowledge base (see Table 2). The company also sold its 'SnapLabs' and decided that it would be more cost efficient to outsource technology development. Additionally, the 12Snap subsidiaries in the UK and Italy built up small local technology teams who worked directly with local salespeople.

---

14 Company interviews, which the authors conducted in November 2001.

15 Users provide detailed preferences when they sign up for the auctioning service.

16 Company interviews, which the authors conducted in November 2001.

17 Company interviews, which the authors conducted in November 2001.

Table 1 12Snap's profit and loss statement for the period January–April 2001 (in euros)

Description	*Total company*	*Total transactions + mobile marketing*	*Transactions*	*Mobile marketing*	*Overhead + other*
Income statement					
Revenues					
Sales transactions					
Sales total	29 234.83	29 234.83	29 234.83		
12Snap commission	−1 287.79	−1 287.79	−1 287.79		
Intercompany sales total	625.51	625.51	625.51		
Other revenues	2 956.66	2 956.66	2 956.66		
Sales transactions total	**31 529.21**	**31 529.21**	**31 529.21**		
Sales mobile marketing	**263 403.69**	**263 403.69**		**263 403.69**	
Sales telco revenue sharing	125.82				125.82
Revenues total	**295 058.72**	**294 932.90**	**31 529.21**	**263 403.69**	**125.82**
		100%	**11%**	**89%**	
Cost of goods sold (COGS)					
12Snap COGS					
12Snap COGS	−30 461.38	−30 461.38	−30 461.38		
Intercompany COGS total	−515.66	−515.66	−515.66		
12Snap other COGS	−1 416.80	−1 416.80	−1 416.80		
Cost of goods sold total	**−32 393.84**	**−32 393.84**	**−32 393.84**	**0.00**	**0.00**
		100%	**100%**	**0%**	
Gross margin 1	**262 664.88**	**262 539.06**	**−864.63**	**263 403.69**	**125.82**
		100%	**0%**	**100%**	
Operating expenses and income 1					
Operating expenses and income	−19 389.13	−19 389.14	−8 694.36	−10 694.78	
Store/sales (refers to storage costs for the auction business)	−729.08	−729.08	−729.08		
Fulfilment costs	−12 759.48	−12 759.48	−12 759.48		
Technology costs	−64 243.38	−64 243.38	−63 041.86	−1201.52	
Operating expenses and income 1	**−97 121.07**	**−97 121.08**	**−85 224.78**	**−11 896.30**	**0.00**
Gross margin 2	**165 543.81**	**165 417.98**	**−86 089.41**	**251 507.39**	**125.82**
		100%	**−52%**	**152%**	
Operating expenses and income 2					
Research & development total	−137 646.76	−137 646.76	−137 646.76		
Marketing & selling total	−1 163 082.72	−770 372.23	−451 399.65	−318 972.58	−392 710.49
General & administration total	−348 218.56	−30 236.41	−30 236.41		−317 982.15
Other operating expenses and income total	−7 145.12				−7 145.12
Operating expenses and income 2	**−1 656 093.16**	**−938 255.40**	**−619 282.82**	**−318 972.58**	**−717 837.76**
		100%	**66%**	**34%**	
Operational result	**−1 490 549.35**	**−722 827.42**	**−705 372.23**	**−67 465.19**	**−717 711.94**

Table 2 Evolution of the staff headcount at 12Snap

Function	*Q1/00*	*Q2/00*	*Q3/00*	*Q4/00*	*Q1/01*	*Q2/01*	*Q3/01*
Management	6	6	7	7	7	8	8
Business development	0	2	2	1	2	4	0
Operations	5	9	12	9	9	10	0
Purchasing	0	6	7	5	5	5	0
Marketing	1	3	4	2	2	1	0
Business intelligence	0	0	0	0	0	0	4
Sales	0	0	1	1	1	3	6
Technology	1	33	50	58	48	53	6
Finance	1	6	6	7	4	6	3
Administrative	2	7	7	5	4	3	3
Total	*16*	*72*	*96*	*95*	*82*	*93*	*30*

The new business shift led to a lower cash burn rate for the company and thus increased its corporate life expectancy. Bernd Muehlfriedel, 12Snap's Chief Financial Officer, adds:

> Ever since we placed the focus on mobile marketing as our sole business line, we have improved EBIT[18] by over 60%. This is true not only because of significantly lower operating costs, but also due to a strong increase in revenues. This distinguishes 12Snap from many other start-ups which often have been forced simply to scale down their cost base to become 'living deads' without a clear business strategy in mind. If the mobile marketing market continues to pick up, we are confident to achieve break-even in the first half of 2003. Given our current cash balance and the current as well as planned monthly EBIT, this still leaves us with some room if things turn out to be less favourable.[19]

12Snap today: a mobile marketing service provider

The value chain of mobile marketing consists of different activities. 12Snap covers the following:

- *Concept development.* This includes the development of mobile marketing concepts that can be integrated into the overall marketing concept of a company, e.g. combining TV spots with a mobile marketing campaign;
- *Application development.* This refers to the merging of technology and concept. Usually it entails the adaptation of existing applications (e.g. an SMS quiz) to the specific requirements of a given product or company. The combination of SMS, voice and sound allows for a wide array of campaign types.
- *Access and selection of the customer base.* There are two different ways to do this. First, by sending customers (who have given their permission) targeted SMS messages ('push' mode). The second is to use a different media type (such as TV or print) to find customers for a mobile marketing campaign, present a question and ask viewers to reply via SMS ('pull' mode).
- *Production and implementation.* This entails the provision of infrastructure such as SMS-gateways, connecting to mobile phone providers, application server and other infrastructure services. 12Snap also produces sound files for advertising messages.
- *Reporting and data mining.* This covers the reporting of response rates. Because all responses can be matched to a specific mobile phone, it is possible to gather very detailed information about users and their profiles, allowing a finer segmentation for future marketing campaigns. For instance, someone who participated in a campaign for the Sony PlayStation II might subsequently be interested in various PlayStation game releases.

12Snap's approach to mobile marketing

Marketing campaigns over mobile phones are very sensitive and companies who engage in this type of marketing need to be careful not to offend users. Will Harris, Global Marketing Director for Genie, British Telecom's mobile internet service, points out:

18 EBIT stands for earnings before interest and taxes.

19 Company interviews, which the authors conducted in November 2001.

'Sending unsolicited messages is tantamount to brand suicide. Our business is entirely dependent on the goodwill of our customers.'[20]

In Europe, the mobile advertising industry is striving to protect mobile phone users by establishing guidelines for responsible advertising. Two supervisory bodies – the Wireless Advertising Association (WAA), a US-oriented global body, and the Wireless Marketing Association (WMA), which operates in the UK, Germany and Italy – have been established to oversee the industry. The main principle of these guidelines is consent, i.e. consumers agree or opt-in to receive ads. In addition, they must be given a clear understanding of what their personal data are being used for and, if they wish, be able to remove themselves from advertisers' databases. Through its membership in the Mobile Data Association, the WMA and the WAA, 12Snap is actively involved in regulating the mobile advertising industry. Cyriac Roeding, who serves as the European Co-Chair of the WAA, explains the Association's goals:

> We are trying to regulate the market by defining rules and standards that all players in the field have to adhere to. The risk remains that there are irresponsible players out there who just send out messages, thereby destroying the market for all of us.

In its business practice, 12Snap adheres to strict standards to avoid offending mobile phone users and to ensure consistent quality of its campaigns, in which only those mobile phone users who give an explicit opt-in are included. This drastically reduces the number of participants, in contrast to including all users who do not explicitly opt-out. Referring to the spamming issue, Andreas Müller comments:

> First of all, all users that we approach have given us their permission. Secondly, they can turn off our channel whenever they feel like doing so – either via the mobile or through the internet. Interestingly, not a lot of users do so, which shows that they appreciate our service. And thirdly, since we target individual segments we don't approach all end users all the time. This obviously reduces the number of messages that each user gets.

Due to these strict standards, 12Snap must find ways to entice customers to opt into their mobile marketing campaigns. Cyriac Roeding explains why many companies have difficulties attracting mobile phone users:

> A lot of companies make the mistake of coming to this from a technological angle, rather than thinking about what the consumer wants. If advertising is entertaining, if it engages the emotions, it will be accepted.[21]

Ulrich Pietsch, senior manager at 12Snap, explains the company's approach:

> We don't consider ourselves to be just an advertisement broadcaster, but rather an entertainment channel. We develop campaigns for mobile marketing which are fun for the consumer and use them as interactive amplifiers of classical advertising formats.[22]

For 12Snap, the following factors are critical for developing successful mobile marketing campaigns:

- *Interactivity.* When contacting recipients, it is possible to receive immediate feedback. Since the mobile phone is usually always on, it offers an excellent opportunity for interaction.
- *Entertainment.* Interaction is only fun for users if they find the advertisement exciting. Therefore, mobile campaigns need to combine advertising and entertainment so that users are willing to give their time to an advertisement.
- *Emotion.* To attract users, advertising also needs to have an emotional component. Text, however, especially if shown on a small mobile phone screen, can hardly convey this emotional dimension. Emotion can be created through the combination of voice and sound. A music jingle, such as a short sequence of the sound track of the movie *Titanic*, can be used as the opening for a partner test or an activity aimed at single people.
- *Incentive.* To increase the willingness to participate in interactive mobile games, there is a need to offer incentives. This might include sweepstakes with product samples or prices. This only entails brand-affinity incentives such as free brand logos for the mobile phone, which are strongly appreciated by users.

The overall goal is to create a game, an image or a jingle so compelling that it is no longer seen as an ad and takes on a value of its own. 12Snap's experience has shown that the best response rates are achieved through a combination of games with multiple difficulty levels and small perks such as free logo downloads. Cyriac Roeding explains:

20 'The novelty could quickly wear off', Financial Times.com, 17 July 2001.

21 'The novelty could quickly wear off', Financial Times.com, 17 July 2001.

22 'Nestles Mobile Marketing Kampagne erfolgreich abgeschlossen', www.gsmbox.com, 26 June 2001.

> If I can weave myself into the life of the young target group in an entertaining way, then they like it and it works. If I do it in a simply annoying way, then it backfires. The difference between traditional marketing and mobile marketing is that I, as a user, can't escape because it [the SMS] will be in my inbox on my mobile phone. I have to delete it myself, while with a TV ad I can just walk away if I don't like it. Therefore, if we don't want to upset people, we need to be even more creative. Our approach is that it needs to be entertaining and doesn't even feel like advertising. This is very different from the approach taken by other mobile marketing firms. It is not 'Buy this' or 'Get the new two-litre Coke bottle now'. That's a nightmare!

As of autumn 2001, 12Snap had two revenue streams in its mobile marketing activities. A small amount is generated through kickbacks, i.e. revenue-sharing agreements with telecommunication providers. Andreas Müller explains:

> Kickbacks depend on the country where you are doing business. We don't have the power to change the rules of the market. In the UK, for instance, you get something for the call; in Germany, providers pay for the SMS. Usually, we get about 20% for SMS and about 25% for calls. However, we don't consider these kickbacks a strategic part of our business. In mobile marketing, our customer is the marketer, the one who spends the money, and the end user. It's not the mobile operator.

12Snap's main revenue generating business is the provision of mobile marketing services to corporate customers. Its clients include the following firms:

- *McDonald's.* As part of a joint marketing campaign started in January 2001, 12Snap launched a one-year mobile advertising campaign for McDonald's for a fee of DM1 million. The focus of the campaign was interactive mobile games and an evaluation of McDonald's products. The campaign targeted mobile phone users who have activated the 12Snap service. By activating the service, i.e. sending an opt-in SMS to McDonald's, participants receive automatic messages when music CDs or vouchers are raffled off.
- *Nestlé.* In March 2001, 12Snap launched a mobile marketing campaign for Nestlé's 'KitKatChunky' chocolate bar. The campaign ran from 28 March to 8 April 2001 to complement the overall marketing effort consisting of TV and radio spots and the website www.chunky.de. The campaign worked as follows: an SMS offered community members the opportunity to win a one-year supply of KitKatChunky if they called a specified number. Callers were shown via their phone screen the face of a taxi driver who appears in a KitKatChunky TV commercial and two other new characters presenting riddles. An automated voice then explained: 'Each of the three protagonists names a number which makes him shut up. Once you have discovered the number, push the appropriate button on your mobile, a 'KitKatChunky' is stuck in his mouth and you go on to the next round.' In the first round, 400 000 users were identified and received a kick-off SMS at the beginning of the campaign. In the following rounds, only those players who had actively opted-in in the first round received an SMS. In order to maximize the number of responses, 12Snap sent alert messages to members of its database the day before the ad's TV premiere and again 30 minutes before the show, when the questions were sent. In total, 12Snap sent 5 888 text messages, achieving a response rate of 7.8%.

  Frank Schübel, Marketing Executive for Nestlé Chocolate, commented on the success of the campaign: 'The response rate was higher than expected and we were able to increase awareness for our product in the desired target segment.'[23] This SMS campaign was also the first to invite entrants to answer questions on a TV ad. Dan Rosen, Mobile Marketing Director at 12Snap, points out the potential that cross-media marketing campaigns represents: 'It is not a question of mobile advertising versus other media. Mobile can be used to optimize other kinds of advertising.'[24]

  The final evaluation of the campaign took two different forms: first, direct participants were counted; second, a telephone survey was used to evaluate the media mix and the singular effect of the mobile campaign. 25% of the users found the mobile phone-based campaign 'funny', 10% of the respondents ranked the campaign positively 'entertaining', whereas only 3% did not consider the campaign to be 'valuable'.
- *Wella.* In August 2001, Wella, a manufacturer of hair products, developed with 12Snap a mobile marketing campaign featuring a 'mobile kiss'.

---

23 'Nestlés Mobile Marketing Kampagne erfolgreich abgeschlossen', www.gsmbox.com, 26 June 2001.

24 '12Snap launches TV ad tied to SMS campaign', New Media Age, 12 July 2001.

Exhibit 3 12Snap's mobile marketing campaign for Wella Design: Susan is addressed directly via SMS

Source: 12Snap.

Users can send a kiss message to their friends, who receive a voice file with a kiss sound (see Exhibit 3). This is followed by an SMS which tells the receiver who has sent the kiss and also provides the chance to send back a kiss. Other components of this mobile campaign include an SMS quiz and a free kissing-lips logo for the mobile phone. Stephan Maasen, e-Business Manager at Wella, comments: 'Through the mobile phone, we can address exactly the target group for the Wella-Design line – the 14–29-year-old people.' Ulrich Pietsch elaborates: 'The kiss campaign combines voice and sound elements which appeal to the user's emotion. Responding to the SMS only requires hitting one button.' The campaign led to an increase in awareness within the target group from 40% to 90%. Andreas Müller explains the reason for the success: 'This campaign is a great example of viral marketing. Because people sent the kiss to all their friends, we eventually had more people who we didn't know before participating in this kiss than people who we had contacted through our database!'

- *Vodafone and 20th Century Fox.* On 13 August 2001, Vodafone and 20th Century Fox chose 12Snap to launch a mobile marketing campaign in the UK. The campaign, aimed at two million 16–24-year-old Vodafone customers, functioned as publicity for the 20th Century Fox summer release of *Planet of the Apes* – a post apocalyptic movie where apes rule over humans who struggle to survive. The campaign started two weeks prior to the UK release of the movie. In keeping with the theme, Vodafone customers were invited, via text and voice on their phone, to survive a variety of challenging games based on the movie. 12Snap developed interactive voice response and text games named Ape s-cape, Ape@tak, and Ape IQ. Successful respondents who completed one of the games could win different *Planet of Apes* theme awards, such as a trip for two to the NASA space camp in the US.
- *YourMobile.* In September 2001, 12Snap started a partnership with YourMobile Networks, a mobile entertainment company that focuses on wireless multimedia content distribution to network operators, mobile device companies and media companies. The partnership provides 12Snap with access to YourMobile's database of over 2.2 million mobile numbers from which 12Snap creates opted-in databases in the UK. In return for access to the mobile numbers, 12Snap supports

YourMobile with a mobile marketing campaign to relaunch the YourMobile website, involving a text-based prize draw competition to win £100 000,[25] a Ferrari, or an all-expenses-paid shopping trip to New York City. Each recipient can choose to receive targeted messages and be involved in future mobile marketing promotions. Anne de Kerckhove, Managing Director of 12Snap UK, explains the benefits of this partnership: 'With such a massive, targeted database and with such willing recipients, we are an invaluable marketing tool for media channels across Europe. No other company can give such immediate access to so many people in any mobile marketing campaign in Europe.'[26]

Building the 12Snap brand

When 12Snap started its operations at the beginning of 2000, the main focus was still on business-to-consumer relationships. Therefore, it was necessary to build a strong and appealing brand name to bring customers into the 12Snap channel. By August 2000, 12Snap had become one of the most well known start-ups in Germany (see Exhibit 4). Cyriac Roeding says:

> By August 2000, we had achieved an aided awareness rate of 33% within the age group of 18–35-year-olds and 50.2% in the 15–20-year-old bracket ... That rate compares to 60% for H&M [a large fashion retailer]. So we were only 10–15% below H&M after eight months with a total spending of DM8 million. That was quite extraordinary. We also compared ourselves to other start-ups which were launched at the same time and their [awareness] rate was between 8 and 14%.[27]

Exhibit 4 12Snap's aided awareness development

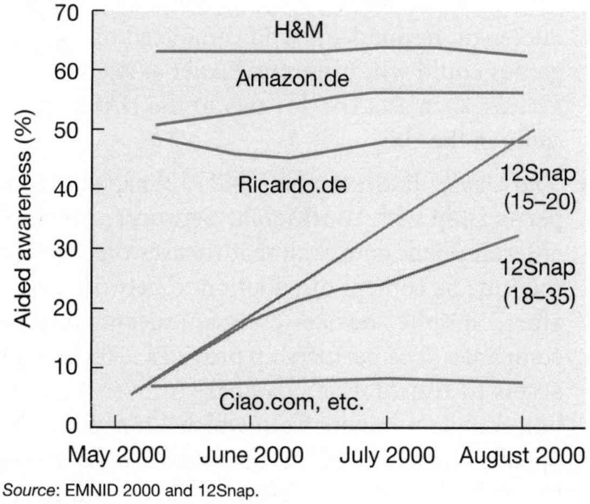

Source: EMNID 2000 and 12Snap.

Acknowledging this marketing success, the *Media Strategy* magazine awarded 12Snap third prize in a brand awareness contest it organized, behind Deutsche Post and Peugeot, which both spent between €30 and €50 million on their respective campaigns.

12Snap's use of non-traditional marketing approaches helped build the company's brand, as Cyriac Roeding comments:

> We didn't believe in using money to convince the target group; rather we create stories. We decided that, for us, marketing means telling stories that others – especially the press – want to talk or write about. That saves us a lot of money, plus it is much more credible than if we speak about ourselves. Our job was to set little impulses to get things moving, and then everything else followed almost automatically.[28]

12Snap started out with a number of 'guerrilla' marketing activities, jointly developed with BrainWash, a small creativity firm. During a Bundesliga[29] match between the Borussia Dortmund and the 1860-München teams, a parachute with a 12Snap logo dropped out of the sky on to the middle of the soccer field, thus interrupting the game for five minutes. Within six minutes of the landing, 12Snap was being talked about on national radio. Cyriac Roeding explains this 'accident':

> It wasn't our fault that the parachute landed in the stadium. We had permission for landing outside the stadium but the wind took the guy into the stadium. We were extremely sorry for what happened![30]

Even so, Cyriac Roeding and the whole management team, which happened to be watching the game in the stadium, were very pleased with the outcome of the campaign:

> We were immediately on the news. That's what we always wanted to achieve. We wanted people to laugh and have fun and we didn't want to disturb anyone. The whole stadium was laughing. The guy landed and the game had to be interrupted. The cameras were all on it, because the game was transmitted live. So it was quite cool!

25 £1 = €1.55.
26 12Snap press release, 20 September 2001.
27 Company interviews, which the authors conducted in November 2001.
28 Ibid.
29 The premier soccer championship league in Germany.
30 Company interviews, which the authors conducted in November 2001.

A second 'guerrilla' campaign featured the infamous German prince August von Hannover, known for his violent outbreaks against journalists. Alluding to the prince's personality trait, 12Snap ran an advertisement in the Cologne, Hamburg and Munich editions of *Bild*, the largest German tabloid, cities which happen to have the highest concentration of journalists in Germany. The advertisement, which bore the 12Snap logo, showed a picture of the prince with an ambiguous message: 'Hier kann jeder zuschlagen', which can either be taken to mean (1) 'Here everyone can get a bargain', but also (2) 'Here everyone can punch'. The unconventional advertisement drew widespread attention and, as a result, the following day *Bild* featured a story about it in the national edition. Cyriac Roeding comments on the success of the campaign:

> In fact, we used *Bild* as a launchpad for journalists to write about us because the first thing they do in the morning is to read *Bild*. The total campaign cost us €35 000. We ended up getting total coverage worth €600 000 because the national TV stations RTL and Sat 1 had reports on it during prime time.

Following the initial 'guerrilla' activities, 12Snap decided to target the mass market with a television commercial. In April 2000, the manager of Lothar Matthäus, a German soccer legend, called 12Snap to inquire about a possible co-operation as Matthäus was an avid mobile phone user. Cyric Roeding comments: 'Matthäus was exactly the right guy for us to move things forward.'

Each of his appearances in public received front-page coverage in *Bild*.

> I told his manager the conditions, which were much lower than he wanted. I only offered him a small cash amount and stock options. This was the first time that a star was paid in stock options. He thought it was interesting. On top of that, we said that we would do the spot only if Matthäus brought his girlfriend along. Our purpose was to have a story that others would write about. We knew that bringing his girlfriend in would create massive attention because she was much younger than him.

The spot was produced in days while it usually takes four months to produce a TV commercial. Two days before the shoot the team still didn't have permission to film in New York City where Matthäus was living at the time. Finally, the four video clips and radio spots were produced in six hours. The spot showed Matthäus and his girlfriend, Maren, coming back from a shopping trip in New York City. Suddenly his mobile phone rings and an SMS comes in. Maren asks, 'Did you get a message from Franz?'[31] and Lothar replies, 'No, but I 'snapped' an iron for you'.[32]

The spot went live on German TV a week later. Pilot Media, a media agency, had previously estimated that 8000 to 10 000 people would call after viewing the TV ad. In fact, 360 000 people called in and registered for the 12Snap service.

By spending DM2.5 million on the TV spot, 12Snap managed to get coverage worth more than DM5 million. This was possible because the TV station Premiere World, which covers mainly major sport events in Germany, had come along to tape the filming of the commercial. Cyriac Roeding explains:

> I sent it [the video clip] to all TV stations so they could show it because Lothar and Maren were together on TV for the first time. RTL showed it during their prime time news for free whereas one spot with RTL usually costs €40 000. In addition, we gained much more credibility because they showed the making of it [the spot]. The major German business newspapers, *Handelsblatt* and *Financial Times Deutschland*, also wrote stories on this TV commercial because it was the first time that a star was paid in stock options.

After shifting away from the end-consumer business to mobile marketing for corporate customers, 12Snap's marketing expenditures were drastically reduced. Alexander Müller explains:

> If you are in the consumer business you have to do the marketing. If you are in B2B, you don't because somebody else does the marketing for you. However, what becomes more important is being present in specialized trade fairs.

The biggest obstacle has been the reluctance of the industry to use mobile marketing. Alexander Müller says:

> A marketing agency manager once told me, that we'll only be able to convince companies when we show them the figures that mobile marketing actually works. That's also the reason why we can only run campaigns when we are convinced that they will be successful.

Cyriac Roeding elaborates on the process of acquiring corporate customers:

31 Franz Beckenbauer is another German soccer legend.
32 For 12Snap, 'to snap' means to win an auction.

> What we do now is relationship marketing. I don't see myself as a salesman but rather an architect of relationships. If I want to approach a big company like Nestlé, I can't just talk to a product manager. Even if he likes my proposal, he won't be able to sell it to his boss. So I need to talk to the top guy and getting there is my main job everyday. I need to find out who knows the top guy and how I can speak to him. Rather than making cold calls, I always use an indirect way and have someone else call the big guy for me.

Andreas Müller, who is also involved in the acquisition of advertising partners, adds:

> It is quite painful. We go out, give speeches and arrange meetings with people who have the right connections. The success rate is not high – 15–20% at most. So, every fifth time we present something, a deal comes out. That's the biggest barrier. For the most recent contracts, we leveraged our networks. For instance, our relationships that we still have from our time at McKinsey help us quite a bit. We need the networks because it [mobile marketing] is a new idea and marketing people are quite conservative. They don't want to take risks, so what we need are senior people from these companies who understand the potential business value of mobile marketing.

Financial situation

In 2000, 12Snap revenues consisted mainly of sales from auctions, which reached almost €600 000. Total revenues for that period were €651 000. The cost of selling goods was €684 664. Total losses for 2000 were approximately €16 million (see Table 3).

Following the addition of mobile marketing activities in 2001, the revenue structure shifted rapidly towards the new business (see Exhibit 5). During the first quarter of 2001, mobile marketing activities generated €263 403, representing 89% of total revenues of €295 058. At the same time, transaction revenues fell to €31 529. Overall losses were €1.5 million (see Table 1).

Bernd Muehlfriedel explains:

> When we saw the numbers, it looked very obvious. We still had a large cash position but it was also clear that, under current financial market conditions, we would have to use this money to get to break-even. In practical terms, this means we have to concentrate on the most promising business and become truly excellent in one area rather than just good in several areas. Only by doing so would we be able to significantly improve EBIT in a fairly short-term and thus preserve the financial stability of the company for the years to come.

Table 3 12Snap's profit and loss statement for the year 2000 (in euros)

Income	*Total*
Revenues	
Sales transactions	
Sales	
12Snap sales	
12Snap returns	
12Snap discounts	
Sales total	511 613
12Snap commission	28 674
Other revenues	59 424
Sales transactions total	599 711
Sales mobile marketing	51 129
Sales telco sharing	333
Sales betting	
Revenues total	**651 173**
12Snap COGS total	–675 909
12Snap other COGS	–8 755
Cost of goods sold total	**–684 664**
Gross margin 1	**–33 490**
Operating expenses and income	
Personnel costs total	–3 060 038
Amortization and depreciation total	–449 140
Communication total	–604 680
Travel/diverse expenses total	–902 536
Insurances total	–20 257
Infrastructure total	–968 811
Store total	–13 566
Fulfilment total	–30 162
Customer care total	–1 086 704
Total production	–31 618
Technology total	–1 455 438
Marketing total	–4 909 266
Company expenses total	–66 868
Legal fees total	–364 345
Business development total	–56 175
Recruitment training total	–458 165
Finance and accounting total	–414 186
Other operating expenses total	–974 422
Other operating income total	19 029
Operating expenses and	**–15 847 348**
operational	**–15 880 839**
Financial income and expenditure total	90 437
Earnings before taxes	**–15 790 402**

Source: 12snap.

Exhibit 5 **Evolution of 12Snap's revenues**

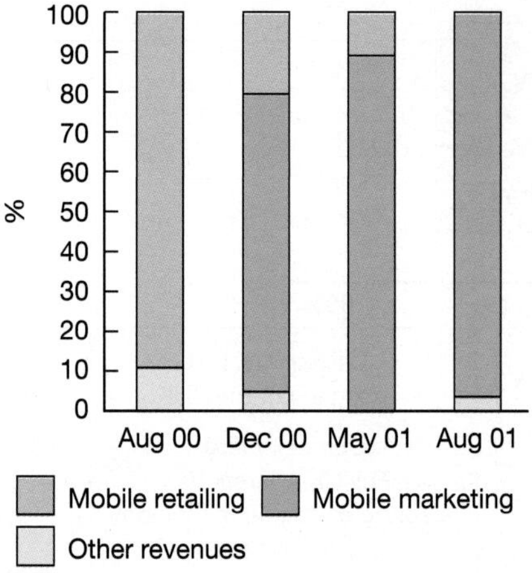

Source: 12Snap.

After the financial analysis, 12Snap management also reviewed mobile marketing industry trends and overall trends in the mobile telecom sector before recommending to its supervisory board to focus on mobile marketing. Bernd Mühlfriedel recalls:

> When the supervisory board approved our strategy shift, we knew that the most difficult was yet to come. We had learnt to analyze and draw logical conclusions based on external and internal analysis from our consultancy experience but we did not have the experience actually to turn around a company. The following months of preparing for the shift and then implementing it were the most strenuous and tough months in my professional life. Never before had I been under such stress, both time-wise and emotionally, but never before did I learn so much. What helped was the strong conviction that what we were doing was necessary to ensure long-term stability of the company.

Will 12Snap run into the financial difficulties that caused the failure of many 'new economy' start-ups? Says Alexander Müller:

> 12Snap is different from other companies in so far as it has had a very strong financial focus from day one ... In addition, we are very cautious when we make financial projections. When we look at the budget, we first take out all the revenues and ask ourselves 'How long are we going to survive?' We look at our cash burn rate as expenditure. Whatever revenue comes in, it is on top – at least for the time being.'[33]

An eventual IPO was on the founders' mind when 12Snap was launched in early 2000. However, the idea was shelved due to the business model shifts and the financial markets' downturn. Alexander Müller elaborates:

> It [the IPO] is still in the back of our minds. When we decide on accounting standards, for instance, that's something we think about. However, it's not crucial for us financially. Eventually, though, we might need additional capital to enter new markets and to acquire competitors.[34]

Regarding the future, Mark Grondin, Chief Technology Officer at 12Snap, admits:

> There isn't a lot of funding out there for another round or to go public, so we aren't going public now. In the next couple of quarters, there is no such a thing as a high growth, high-risk business model. It's our job to create money and a viable business, and that's the focus for now.[35]

International expansion

In October 2000, 12Snap launched a subsidiary in Italy and, two months later, entered the UK market (see Exhibit 6). Birkel explains the rationale for the latest expansion: 'Given the 83% increase in mobile subscribers in the UK in the past year, this is an ideal market for our pan-European expansion.'[36] Andreas Müller says:

> To recruit people for our European subsidiaries ... I used my network of contacts and sent out e-mail messages in London through the Boston Consulting Group and in Italy through McKinsey. The interesting thing was that everyone wanted to start a company at that time and become an entrepreneur. The people we talked to had already their own teams assembled. They loved our business approach because they have to build up everything themselves. All they got from us was the idea and the money.[37]

Regarding further international expansion, Andreas Müller says:

> We are thinking of expanding further, but not by investing a lot of money. Instead, we are looking for strong partners who can do the financial investments themselves. Right now, we are looking into possible

33 Company interviews, which the authors conducted in November 2001.
34 Company interviews, which the authors conducted in November 2001.
35 'It's as easy as 1, 2, Snap!', *Connectivity Today*, No. 1, 2001.
36 '12Snap enters UK market', *Revolution UK*, 7 December 2000.
37 Company interviews, which the authors conducted in November 2001.

Exhibit 6 **12Snap's group organization, 30 November 2001**

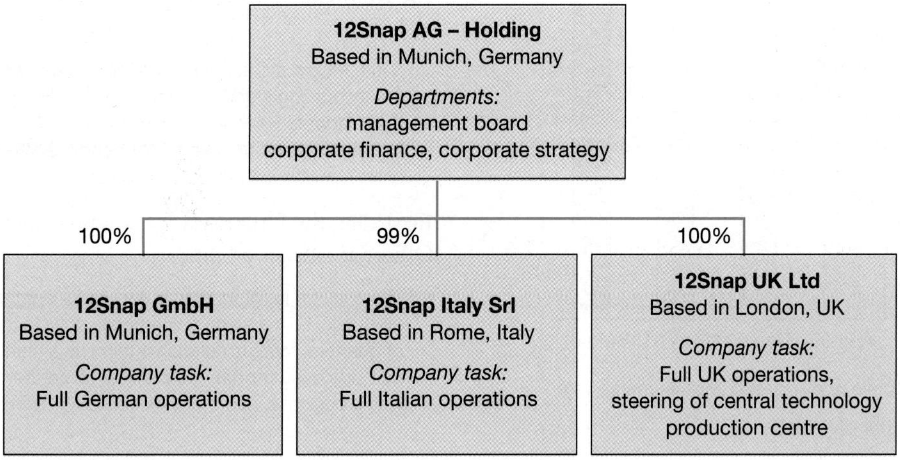

Source: 12Snap.

> agreements in Argentina and Portugal. The people there know that we are the experts in this arena. They contact us and say, 'We have the money, please help us set it [the business] up'. We want to give them initial consulting or give out licenses and then get a part of the equity in return, but we want to let them run the business in their country.

Competition in the mobile marketing industry

Because of the novelty of mobile marketing, there are not many companies in this market yet. Nevertheless, Andreas Müller expects the competition to pick up soon:

> It could come from telecommunication companies, though I don't see them there. It's more likely that standard marketing players, like creative agencies, will move into our market. Right now, it's still a new medium for them. Eventually though, they will learn about it, just like [they did] with the Internet. At the beginning there were specialized boutiques, then traditional agencies also figured out the new medium. So I see stronger competition from that side – but that's still sometime in the future, not today. Right now, we are competing in the German market with five start-up companies which are smaller than us.[38]

One of these competitors is Mindmatics, which is working with the mobile phone operator D1. It pays mobile users if they agree to receive a certain number of text-based advertisements. Andreas Müller comments:

> I am not convinced by this approach. They [Mindmatics] send text messages only, without any entertainment. What helps them is that they offer standardized campaigns which are smaller and also much easier to handle. But, I don't see how they can grow this business.[39]

Future outlook

> We are still fighting to get in the deals quickly enough. With some ideas we had, we were too early because the market wasn't there yet ... Mobile marketing might develop much later, which might force us to reduce the cash burn rate that we have even more, so that we can survive until the market takes off. We know that we are creating value, so the business idea is proven. The challenge is whether we can convince [corporate customers] quickly enough.

In spite of the above challenge, Andreas Müller is not eager to move back into the B2C or even the C2C business. He says:

> C2C is clearly the better business model because it's easily scalable. That's what allowed eBay to really take off. However, that type of business model isn't possible on mobile phones because C2C requires much more information than can be delivered over the mobile. If you want to buy a chair, you need to have a lot of information about it. What you can do over the mobile is to sell standardized products that everybody knows, like a Sony PlayStation, for example. That's why we probably won't go back into mobile retailing.

---

38 Company interviews, which the authors conducted in November 2001.

39 Ibid.

However, Andreas Müller does not rule out the possibility of expanding the target groups:

> Currently we are reluctant to run campaigns for older people. I have already rejected offers to target older people because the market isn't there yet, especially when it comes to SMS. I actually taught my father how to use SMS. He didn't know that he got an SMS once there is a message on his voice mail. He just asked: 'What's that little box there?'

Another expansion possibility could come from the business potential of some new IT capabilities. Says Andreas Müller:

> With the rise of location-based technologies ... the mobile phone might become interesting for wireless services that help people get from A to B. However, that's something the operators have already started doing because it's more technical and their engineers love it. But when it comes to youth entertainment, that's something they don't understand. Gaming communities might be an opportunity. Our 'Fishsnapper' [game] is a testing ground for those people who play with it. But then again, that is also only a pure entertainment application.

DISCUSSION QUESTIONS

1. Analyze the competitive business environment of 12Snap (you may want to use the five-force industry model of Porter (see Exhibit 3.1, p. 65) or any other framework that you deem fit for your analysis).
2. Based on your analysis above, what opportunities and threats are there for mobile marketing companies (such as 12Snap)?
3. How would you assess the current target user group and revenue model of 12Snap? What changes would you make to these dimensions in order to improve on them?
4. Do you think that the four factors for developing mobile marketing campaigns (as mentioned in the case on page 561) are critical for success, or are there others? Defend your arguments.
5. Would you recommend that 12Snap expands its business into other European countries? Defend your arguments.
6. Should 12Snap move back into the B2C business or consider launching a C2C business through mobile phones? More generally, what future actions would you recommend to the management of 12Snap?

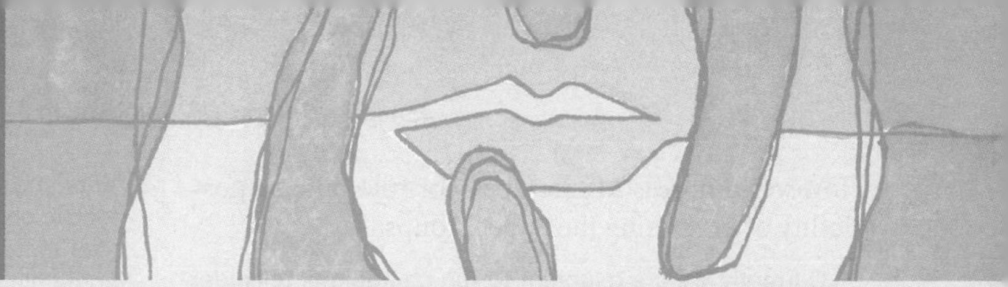

CASE STUDY 27

Paybox.net (Germany)

A mobile payment service

Our goal is to establish the international standard for paying via the mobile phone.

Mathias Entenmann, Chief Executive Officer, paybox.net AG

With these words, Mathias Entenmann addressed the journalists who had gathered in Hannover (Germany) for CeBIT 2001, which is the world's largest information technology trade fair. Prior to his address, Entenmann was awarded the CeBIT Innovation Prize for his payment solution, a prestigious industry award which, before paybox.net, went to other innovative companies such as Microsoft and Napster.

Six months later, the board of paybox.net met at the company headquarters near Frankfurt to decide whether to market paybox to business customers as a B2B2C (business to business to consumer) product called PIA (Paybox Intelligent Architecture). The PIA business model would be similar to that of credit cards: companies would license the paybox brand name and have their payment service operated by paybox employees and technology. Selling the PIA could, in the short run, mean improved revenues for the fledgling company, and, in the longer term, stimulate the European m-payment market, which has, so far, been slow to materialize. However, on the negative side, paybox would allow other companies to capitalize on its technological capabilities and surrender end customer relationships to their new partners.

Paybox.net: the initial idea

In July 1999, Mathias Entenmann left his management consultancy job to found paybox.net AG, with the help of a recent graduate and two university students. The company focused on developing a secure and convenient mobile payment service for online and offline transactions. Entenmann had the idea for such a service during a trip he made to Finland in 1998. He read about an experiment that took place there where one could buy a drink from a vending machine and pay for it with the mobile phone. The buyer would, on their mobile phone, dial a number printed on the vending machine for a particular drink, which would then dispense the beverage. The call charge for the dialled number would include the price of the drink.

Entenmann thought that the use of such a system could be expanded. 'That's great for a simple purchase of a beverage, but think of all the phone numbers you would need [to assign to the different books] for a moderately sized bookstore.' His paybox.net start-up would be built on this idea, but would be more versatile.

The system matches a special personal identification number (PIN) with the caller's mobile phone ID ('caller-ID'). To initiate a standard transaction, the payee dials the paybox.net transaction phone number and is identified via the caller-ID, which is automatically transmitted by the calling phone. The

---

This case study was written by Philipp Leutiger, MBA graduate of the Leipzig Graduate School of Business, Germany, and Tawfik Jelassi, Affiliate Professor of Technology Management at INSEAD. It is intended to be used as the basis for class discussion rather than to illustrate an effective or ineffective handling of a management situation.

The case was made possible by the co-operation of paybox.net (Germany).

payee then enters the phone number of the payer as well as the amount to be paid. An interactive voice response (IVR) then transmits this information to the paybox.net server, which immediately calls the designated payer. The latter is asked to confirm the payment via a four-digit PIN. The server then confirms the payment to the payee, thus completing the transaction. Afterwards, paybox.net initiates a money transfer from the payer's account to the payee's account. 'The beauty is', says Entenmann, 'that paybox works with any mobile phone network, any phone, and any bank account. Our focus is the market, not a specific technology.'

In May 2000, paybox.net released its mobile payment ('m-payment') service in Germany. It was a proactive move to seize the business opportunities that lay ahead. Indeed, according to a May 2001 Forrester poll, bricks-and-mortar companies, as well as online retailers, expected that, in three years' time, 10% of their transactions would be paid for via mobile phones.

By April 2002, paybox.net had 750 000 customers in Europe, and successfully launched its operations in Austria, Spain, Sweden and the UK. A total of 10 000 merchants accepted the payment service. Further international expansion was considered and planned.

Launching paybox.net

To implement his business plan, Mathias Entenmann persuaded four friends, some from his previous management consultancy, to join him. They took over the responsibilities for the product development, finance, marketing and operations activities of paybox.net. Entenmann also sought funding from some financial institutions and venture capitalists, but no deal was in sight. Nevertheless, he decided not to approach telecommunications operators so as to avoid becoming a proprietary m-payment system for a single network. He thought that such a dependency would limit the business potential of his m-payment solution.

Despite the lack of financial investors, Eckhard Ortwein, paybox.net's Chief Technology Officer, forged ahead and built a prototype of the system, with the help of two small software companies, financed by the personal funds of the paybox.net board members. The trial test ran on a Compaq desktop computer with the use of a computer telephony integration (CTI) card that received and placed the voice calls required. The system became operational in December 1999.

'It proved to be a breakthrough', recalls Entenmann. 'We could simply walk up to a potential investor and say, "just take this phone, Sir, and let's assume I want you to pay me some money". We'd punch in some numbers, and the person's phone would ring, prompting him for a PIN. People were quite amazed!'

A number of potential investors then became interested in paybox.net. After some consideration, the company decided to turn down the venture capitalists' offers and instead struck a deal with Deutsche Bank in February 2000. The bank paid for a 50% stake in the start-up, with the option to participate in any additional capital offering, so as to maintain its equity share. In addition, the bank agreed to handle the 'back office' billing and money transfer operations of paybox.net.

In March 2000, the funding enabled the company to move to larger offices in nearby Wiesbaden and to employ 25 people, in addition to involving several outside IT systems integrators. Product development began in earnest with the development team working hard to build a scalable and reliable payment solution. In April 2000, the first transactions using the new paybox.net system were made. At the same time, a marketing campaign was launched aiming at winning merchants and especially online retailers. Stefano Nepute, then Chief Marketing Officer of paybox.net, explains:

> The reason [for this focus] is quite simple: you would need thousands of bricks-and-mortar shops to gain a national coverage; yet you will only have a minimal selection of products. But on the Internet, merchants who sell the goods you want and who are willing to accept the paybox.net payment service are only a click away from you.

The initial reaction to the paybox.net product was positive, with the new payment service being presented in several national newscasts. In June 2000, *Business Week* named, in its international edition, Mathias Entenmann one of the '50 Stars of Europe'. Mathias Entenmann and Jochen Schwiersch, Chief Financial Officer of paybox.net, started building a network of alliances and partnerships, laying the groundwork for the internalization of the payment system. At the same time, paybox was restructured, with paybox.net becoming a holding organization and national paybox companies being founded for each

Exhibit 1 Paybox ownership structure

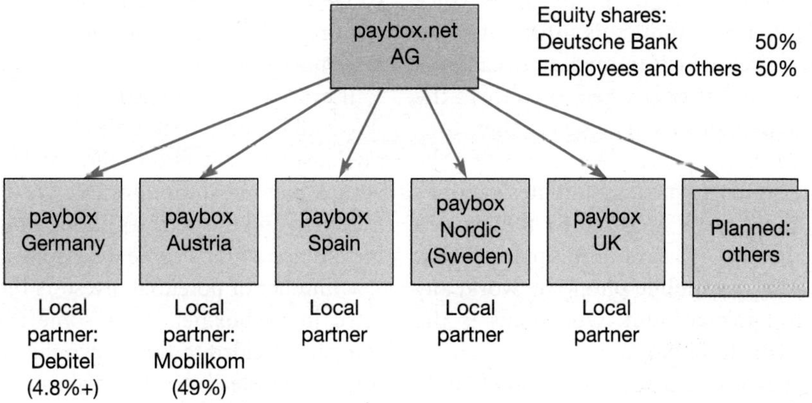

market. The company sought sales and infrastructure co-operation partners in every market, with mobile telecommunications network re-seller, Debitel, taking the lead as sales partner for paybox.de, the German subsidiary (see Exhibit 1 for the company structure).

However, the paybox team also suffered some setbacks. It was hard to convince major anchor clients to join the system. Many merchants required 'split billing' (for example, if a customer bought several books online but not all of these were delivered, only a partial sum would be billed). Also, some alliances to gain customers took longer to implement than initially thought, or were not as effective as expected. Furthermore, in December 2000, Stefano Nepute left the company.

Still, the service roll-out continued; it included mobile merchants like taxi drivers and pizza delivery personnel. By December 2000, paybox.net served 4300 merchants and 120000 customers. The company moved again to larger offices near Frankfurt and employed a total of 100 people, including those working in national offices.

Paybox.net service offering: a variety of online payment systems

The current paybox.net service is quite different from Entenmann's original idea. In March 2001, the company identified the following types of online payment transactions (see Exhibits 2–6)

Exhibit 2 Internet-to-paybox payment process

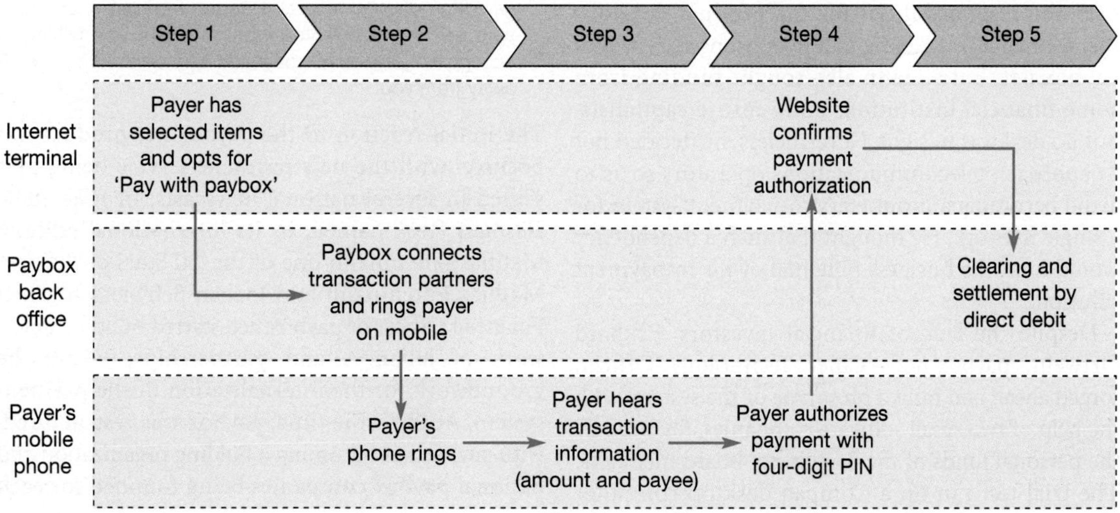

Exhibit 3 **Paybox-to-paybox payment process**

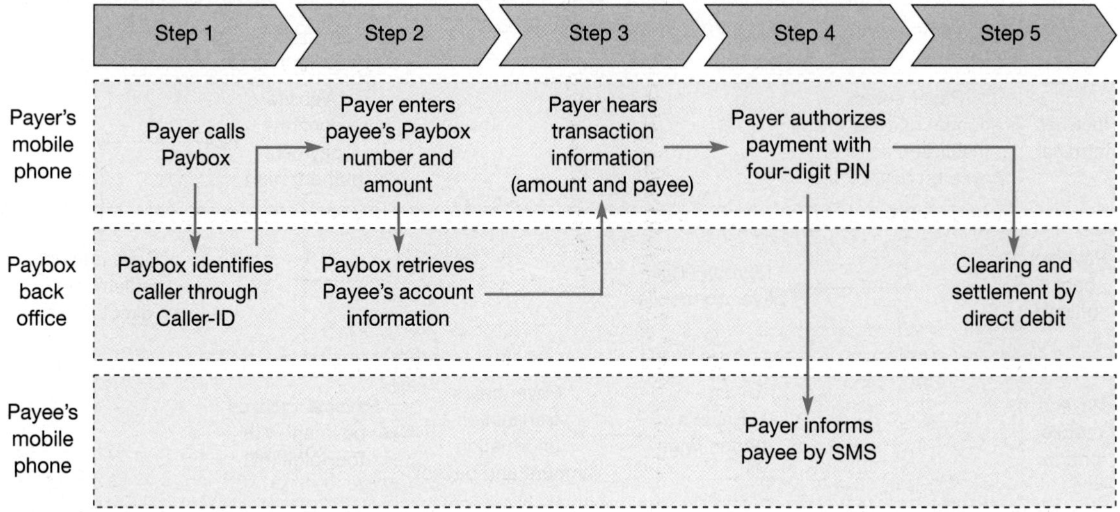

Exhibit 4 **Mobile-to-paybox payment process**

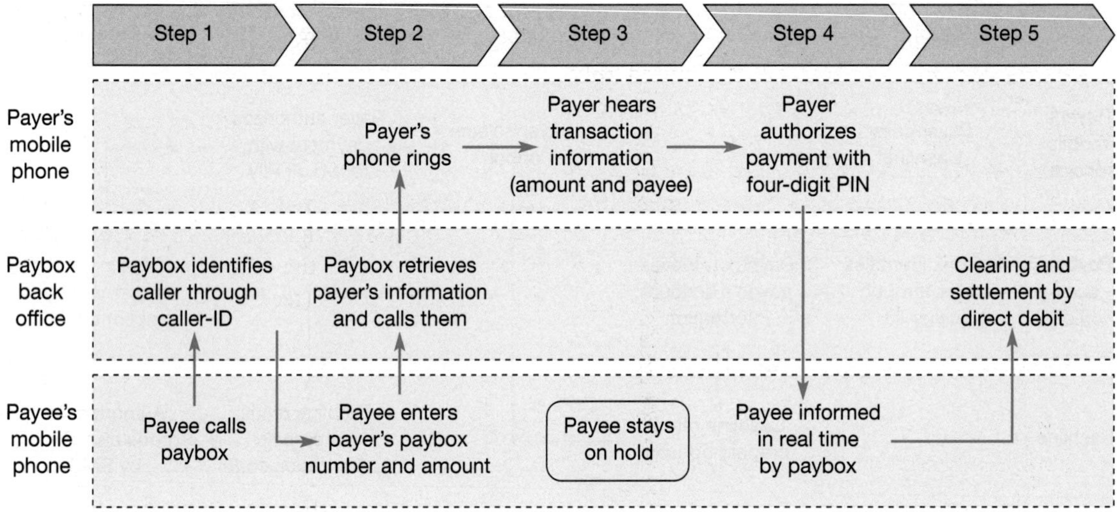

Internet-to-paybox (I2P)

This type of transaction is designed for all sorts of online purchases. A consumer first selects items at an online store in much the same way as with any other payment system. At checkout, however, they select 'pay with paybox' instead of any other regular payment method (such as a credit card). They are then asked to enter their mobile phone number, including the international access code. Within seconds, the customer receives an automated call on their mobile phone asking them to verify a transaction of the stated amount. To approve it, the customer enters their paybox PIN. The payment instruction is then stored and Deutsche Bank later completes it through direct debit. By March 2001, Internet-to-paybox already accounted for 10% of all purchases made at the German Internet bookstore buch.de.

The main advantage for the consumer is the increased security over regular credit card transactions. Instead of transmitting a credit card number, the only information sent over the Internet is the payer's mobile phone number. Fraud is only possible

Exhibit 5 **Money transfer with paybox**

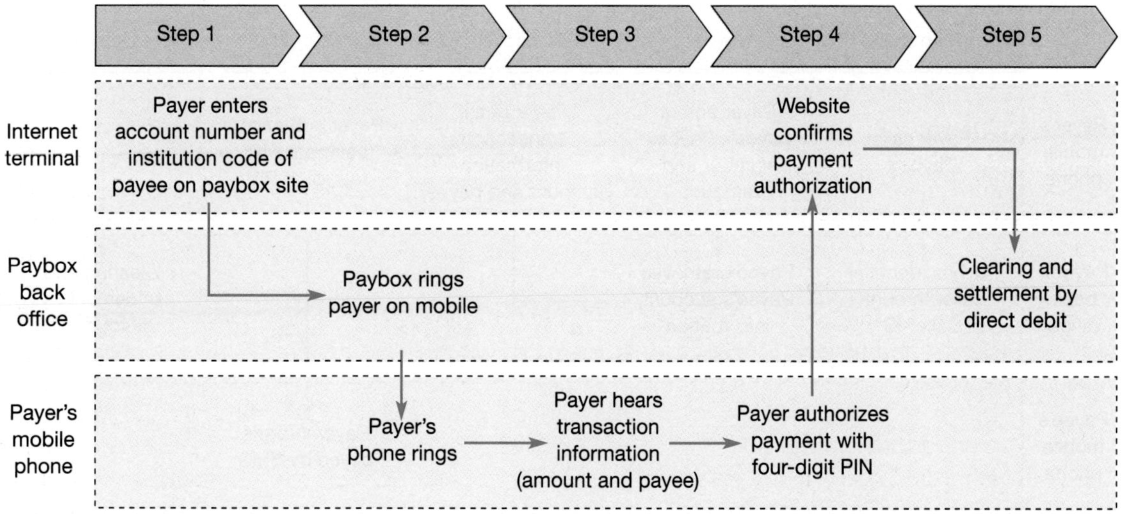

Exhibit 6 **Debitel Cashline**

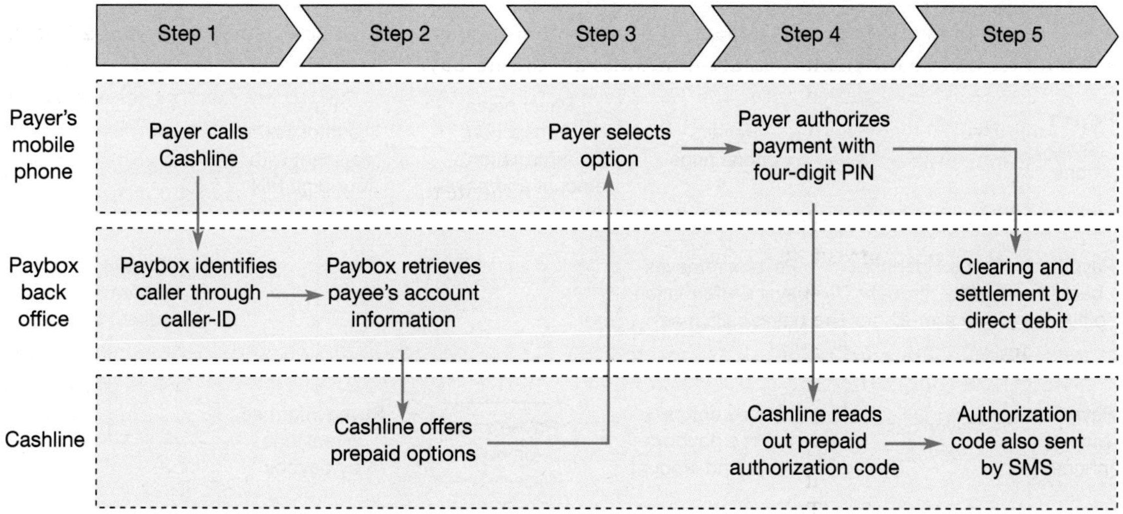

if the offender has access to the switched-on mobile phone (or knows the mobile's PIN) and also has knowledge of the paybox PIN. 'We believe this is even more secure than a bricks-and-mortar use of a credit card', says Peter Seipp, Chief Operating Officer of paybox.net. 'After all, most people use their credit card only once every couple of days, so stealing one could go unnoticed for a while. But everyone notices immediately when they lose their mobile phone, because it is viewed as a personal item.' According to online surveys in Germany, approximately 90% of the visits to Internet merchants, where shopping carts were filled, did not result in any sales, because of consumers' security concerns.

Paybox-to-paybox (P2P)

This service allows users to transfer money among themselves. The payer calls the paybox server through their mobile phone. The system automatically identifies them due to the caller-ID. The payer then enters the paybox number of the payee as well as the amount involved. Paybox asks for the PIN in

order to validate the transaction. Then, within seconds, the payee is informed about the transaction via SMS (short message system). 'Unlike any credit card, paybox-to-paybox is a peer-to-peer service', says Joerg Ziesche, responsible for consumer marketing at paybox.de. 'In addition, you can use it to transfer money to a mobile phone that is currently not paybox enabled. The owner of the phone can then leave his account information with us or sign up as a payboxer (i.e. a paybox customer) and have the money transferred to his account.' In October 2001, the paybox-to-paybox mode was already well established as the preferred payment method for many auctioneers at eBay.de.

Mobile-to-paybox (M2P)

This payment method closely resembles Entenmann's original concept, with the payee triggering the transaction by calling paybox.net and staying on the phone until the payer has completed the transaction. 'It was very difficult to explain this process to our customers', says Ziesche. 'It has remained our transaction method of choice for mobile merchants because it includes a guaranteed real-time confirmation for the payee. That's important in business transactions, where payer and payee don't usually know each other.'

Money transfers over the Web

Paybox.net users can also visit the company's website to make money transfers. In addition to their phone number, they key in either the payee's phone number or the standard bank information (account number and institution code). After entering the amount to be paid, the payer is called on their mobile phone to validate the transaction. Thus, money transfers can be made over the Internet without the complicated use of transaction numbers (TAN), the current standard for online banks.

Debitel Cashline

Debitel Cashline is a service with which Debitel prepaid phone customers can recharge their prepaid cards by using paybox, without having to go into a store. Users call the Cashline phone number, order an increase on their spending limit, and authorize a payment over this amount with their PIN. Then, the prepaid code is read out by the paybox call server and sent to the user via SMS. The user can then call the regular recharge hotline and enter the code the same way the code bought on a card would be entered. Since the complete transaction with the customer is done over the mobile phone, paybox markets this service as the first m-commerce solution.

Additional services

Paybox.net users who are concerned about their privacy can get a paybox alias on the website. This number can be entered for any paybox transaction instead of providing the user's cellular phone number. The paybox database matches the phone number and the alias. Also, paybox users have access to the 'myPaybox' personal site, which includes a history of transactions and the personal information of each customer. The site is not accessed through a password, as is common for other personalized pages. Instead, the user is authenticated over the mobile phone: they enter their phone number on the website and are immediately called by the paybox server. After entering their PIN on the phone, the personal page is displayed.

In the autumn of 2001, approximately half of the online payment transactions made at paybox.net were of the Internet-to-paybox type. However, the number of money transfers, a service introduced in March 2001, has been growing fast and is likely to dominate the other online payment offerings.

The market incumbent: credit card companies

The credit card industry was thought to be a duopoly between the two largest players, Visa and Mastercard. A firm like Visa is actually a co-operation between all card-issuing banks, called member banks. A typical transaction between a consumer and a merchant in Europe is depicted in Exhibit 7. The consumer would present their card upon purchase, with which the merchant would create a credit card receipt either with an online terminal, or, where no online connection is available, imprint a carbon copy of the card information using a special manual press. The payer would sign the receipt, thereby confirming the amount and validating the transaction. The merchant would hand the transaction information to its bank, which would identify the consumer's card-issuing bank and inform it about the payment. The card-issuing bank would collect all incoming receipts and send the consumer a monthly statement of their

Exhibit 7 **Regular credit card transaction**

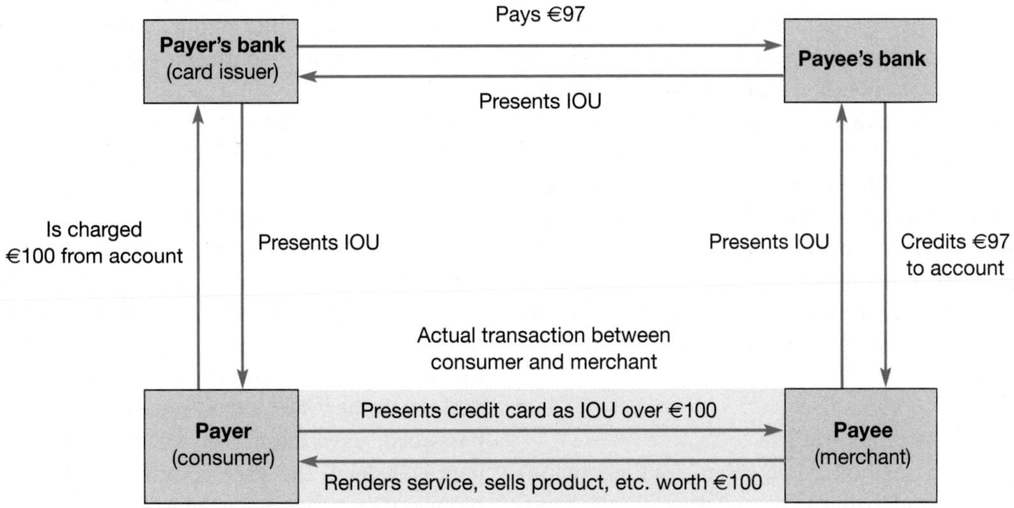

payments. It would then withdraw the required funds from the consumer's bank account. This money, less a commission (called *disagio*), which the card-issuing bank retains, would be transferred to the merchant's bank, which would credit the money to the merchant (minus a commission).

In addition, the card-issuing bank charges the consumer an annual card membership fee, while the merchant's bank charges the merchant a subscription fee as well as a service fee. In return, consumers benefit from the convenience offered and a later debit date. For the merchant, the card-issuing bank guarantees payment if the card was physically present at the time of purchase.

Although they are a considerable force in the market now, credit card companies had faced an uphill struggle over many years in the European markets. After their launch in the early 1970s, it took the credit card industry a full 22 years to attract 500000 customers in Germany.

The paybox.net business model

The paybox.net revenue model is similar to that of a credit card company, described above. Paybox charges consumers an annual fee of €5. Merchants usually pay a fee for the integration of the payment system (€500 to €2500 for Internet shops) and are charged a yearly fee. This fee is €100 for the basic transaction functionality, which requires manual payment requests from the merchant at the time it ships its goods. For premium service, which includes automated billing, the annual fee is €300. Moreover, for every transaction, the company charges merchants a *disagio* in the single digit percentage range. The minimum charge per transaction is €0.25, which enables the company to break even on a payment. Anchor merchants, as well as launch merchants, pay less. For paybox-to-paybox transactions, the company charges €0.25 for each €25 of transaction volume. The company competes with credit card companies on the payment guarantee dimension. As paybox does not have a banking licence, it is legally not allowed to promise guaranteed fulfilment. The contractual basis is that merchants 'can expect payment', coupled with the understanding of both paybox as well as the merchant that paybox would bear the burden of customer insolvency. Paybox payment days for merchants are every 14 days, which is slightly shorter than the monthly cycles of credit cards. For all transactions, paybox.net uses direct debits operated by Deutsche Bank.

Establishing a mobile payment solution

Five market segments for a mobile payment system can be identified. The first distinction is between micro-payments (amounts of €10 or less for parking tickets, bus fares, vending machines, or online content) and macro-payments (e.g. for books, petrol, groceries, etc.).

This classification is important because transaction costs are relative to the total cost of goods sold, and many payment methods used for macro-payments are too expensive or too time-consuming for smaller amounts. Micro-payments can be made either for mobile content (such as location-based services), online purchases (Internet content), or offline purchases (e.g. from vending machines). Since it is unlikely that mobile content applications will charge more than €10, the two possibilities for macro-payments include online purchases and offline purchases.

CEO Entenmann identifies the following six key factors for the success of an m-payment system:

- All user groups must have access to the payment method – using any phone, over any network. Systems using proprietary technical solutions in handsets will fail because of the required upgrade of all handsets. Systems focusing on the users of a single network operator will not attract merchants who would need four to six payment systems serving customers in Germany alone.
- The payment system must have universal applications for m-commerce products as well as online and offline stores. This increases the versatility of the system and thus the customer benefit derived from it.
- The payment system must be easy and convenient to use. The steps required to trigger a transaction (i.e. entering a PIN for authentification), should follow a procedure that consumers and merchants alike are familiar with.
- Security concerns of consumers and merchants have to be addressed.
- The transaction cost of the payment system must be priced attractively for the consumer.
- The system must be internationally accepted.

Interest in mobile payment is generally high, especially among merchants. They cite enhanced customer service, increased sales and reduced cash handling as the main advantages of m-payment. Internet merchants, in particular, are desperately searching for a payment method that could convince their customers of its security features. Many Internet merchants fear dependence on credit card transactions and would prefer an alternative, strong and efficient payment method. However, common fears concerning m-payment are high transaction costs due to the relatively high call charges of mobile phones.

Consumers, on the other hand, having already resisted other radically new payment methods, seem unlikely to join m-payment solutions in droves. The challenge is to dispel their worries over data privacy and security issues in order to attract customers beyond the initial early adopters.

Driving customers' adoption

> We have the coolest product. I've never met anyone who didn't get enthusiastic about it once I explained to him how paybox works. The problem is [that] I don't have the time to speak to everyone in person.
>
> **Mathias Entenmann**

Paybox.net has been focusing on online macro-payments, since its minimum charge of €0.25 is not suited for micro-payments. 'We provide the service for those who want to offer it, but it doesn't really make sense to promote it', says Ralph Westenburger, Head of Merchant Acquisition at paybox Germany. 'When you are selling a new ring tone for a cell phone for €1, you don't want to pay that much just to have the transaction confirmed.' Nonetheless, to achieve a critical mass of customers, paybox started several alliances, referral programmes and advertisements.

Partnership with Debitel

In September 2000, paybox forged its partnership with Debitel, a telecommunications network reseller. In exchange for an equity stake in paybox.net, Debitel markets paybox in its retail outlets in conjunction with mobile phone contracts. In addition, paybox and Debitel launched Cashline, which enables all prepaid customers to reload their accounts via paybox. The equity stake could be increased depending on the number of paybox customers acquired by Debitel. Mobilkom Austria, a major player in the Austrian mobile phone market, also bought a stake (49%) in paybox Austria. Paybox is actively searching for similar co-operation partners in its other national subsidiaries. The current ownership structure of paybox.net is depicted in Exhibit 1.

Co-branding and referrals

To gain consumers quickly, paybox co-branded its payment system with a number of alliance partners. For this, the paybox registration and payment

processes are integrated in the current offering of an online partner, or contracts and information brochures are made available at the partner's offline locations. Online partnerships include the German portal web.de, Ciao.com, as well as the mobile portal jamba!. Paybox was also advertised as a mobile wallet at AOL Germany, on eBay.de, and on the website of Deutsche Bank 24 (which is Deutsche Bank's retail arm). In the offline world, paybox alliances include the students' magazine *Unicum*, MTV and Debitel. Paybox usually pays its partners a customer acquisition fee per registered paybox consumer and co-brands the product. Eckhard Ortwein says:

> The success of the co-branding effort relies heavily on the integration efforts of both partners. Web.de, for example, was exemplary in incorporating paybox into their unique look and feel, and including our payment options on their website.

To instigate referral links on private websites and word-of-mouth between friends, paybox also paid consumers a €5 referral fee per signed up customer. Word-of-mouth referral was especially powerful when paybox-to-paybox enabled consumers to send money to any phone. 'Repay your debt to someone conveniently and earn €5 as soon as that person signs on, how good is that?' says Ziesche, a consumer marketing firm.

Another agreement was drawn up with Norisbank, whose bank account E@sy Mobile Giro now features Internet brokerage, home banking and a paybox registration. 'This was possible with Norisbank because they are one of the smaller retail banks, and are thus under higher competitive pressure in over-banked Germany', says Ortwein.

Merchant integration and reselling

Paybox.net set up several alliances aimed at getting merchants to accept its m-payment system. In partnerships with e-commerce platform providers and merchant associations, the company standardized its system integration process with that of the merchants.

This integration was especially successful with online stores. Paybox.net set up an alliance with Pago and launched its payment solution to Pago merchants in February 2000 (three months before the actual launch). Similar agreements were made with other online hosting providers, such as Brodos.de. Furthermore, a software cartridge was developed in co-operation with Intershop and other e-commerce software providers to allow the easy integration of the paybox system. 'A partnership that is really going well in this regard is the hosting provider 3C Systems', says Westenburger. 'Some hosting providers simply don't have a stable hosting environment. And things then do not run well. In general, the hosting providers are our main partners for rolling out the system. We would never have the resources by ourselves to integrate so many merchants.'

A similar partnership was implemented with taxi companies. However, the mobile-to-paybox solution proved to be a major stumbling block. 'We have showered those cab drivers with tapes [containing usage instructions] and stickers. Product awareness was certainly boosted; however, only one third of the taxi drivers offering paybox are fervent missionaries. The mobile-to-paybox solution still requires a lot of data entry from the taxi driver', says Westenburger. To improve this situation, the paybox team tried to integrate the payment system into information terminals already existing in taxis. However, as Ortwein puts it: 'There is room for improvement.'

Until a solution with a stronger value proposition for all involved can be implemented, paybox.net has scaled down the taxi driver acquisition effort and used the currently integrated taxis to raise awareness of its payment method. 'This is what we call the "lighthouse concept"', says Westenburger.

Innovation and image

Paybox is pursuing its drive to establish its brand with merchants and end users. The first aspect of this was innovative new product designs. At Munich's Systems in November 2000, CTO Ortwein unveiled a cigarette vending machine without a coin slot. Cigarettes could only be bought through the mobile phone. 'The system could potentially prevent teenagers from buying cigarettes, because paybox could check the age of the payer', says Ortwein. A new WAP-based 'push-paybox' was also unveiled at Munich's Systems, in co-operation with the mobile portal jamba!. The system was built to demonstrate micro-payments for mobile content. At CeBIT 2001, paybox presented two bricks-and-mortar cashier systems that were paybox enabled. 'In general, these are great products that create some buzz. But the tech industry is very short-lived. You need to follow up

immediately to gain the most of these inventions', is Westenburger's experience.

The second important factor that paybox emphasizes is its security image. Prior to the launch of its payment solution, paybox partnered with Experian, a real-time customer scoring system. The company was also proud of obtaining, in May 2000, the certification for its Trusted Shop money back guarantee.

Third, paybox highlights its growing acceptance network by presenting anchor clients such as eBay.de, Karstadt Reisebüro (a bricks-and-mortar travel agency) and Kinowelt (a movie-theatre chain). 'These opinion leaders are really central to any product establishment', comments Westenburger. 'Get one of the big names and they all come. However, negotiating a workable contract with these fellows takes time. In the beginning, large companies would turn you back and say: "come back when you have shown that it works." Well, they don't say that any longer.' A major coup in this regard was the Madonna Greeting Campaign launched in September 2000, when the online demo of the paybox system included a teaser of a Madonna song launched in Germany at that time. Ziesche remembers: 'That was when people out there realized: paybox is a company to reckon with.'

Advertisements and promotions

Paybox also started regular advertising campaigns. In June 2000, a TV campaign on MTV was launched, combined with a paybox–MTV lottery. Conventional print media advertisements followed, as well as a second campaign on national TV stations in April 2001. Promotional activity included a Loveparade lottery, where payboxers (paybox users) could win a ride on the paybox truck at the Berlin Loveparade 2000, as well as free business cards for paybox users at Web.de and flower vouchers at online flower service Valentins.de. 'In general, I find that European customers are a bit suspicious of cash offers, like our €5 referral fee. Our promotions with Valentins.de or Web.de better match their tastes', says Ortwein.

In addition, paybox has a number of continuous offers. For example, it dropped its €5 annual fee for the first year of membership and switched, in autumn 2000, all incoming phone calls to free call numbers. Soon afterwards, it dropped all transaction charges for consumers, making merchant fees the major revenue source. 'The *disagio* is our cash generator', says Jochen Schwiersch.

End users' perspective

For end users, the widespread availability of the paybox solution (across computer networks and phone systems), Deutsche Bank's backing and support of paybox, and the security system underlying the paybox offering are important features of the product. However, they think that the system also has some shortcomings:

- In the Internet-to-paybox payment mode, it is the merchant who decides when the charged amount should be withdrawn from the payer's account, while credit card companies typically execute the actual debit at a later date than the merchant does.
- Sometimes, the system cannot be used due to bad phone connections or low battery power of the mobile phone. Also, in some peak periods, the mobile telecommunications network is very congested and, therefore, the paybox system cannot be used. (One consumer reported that he could not pay a taxi driver one New Year's Eve due to the above problem.)
- Consumers argue that they would need to have two mobile phones if they wanted to enjoy the convenience they are used to from corporate and personal credit cards.
- The internationalization of Internet merchants has not progressed as much as online customers would have wished, especially since the latter shop at international sites such as Amazon.com or eBay.com.

Technology factors

The paybox payment infrastructure is presented in Exhibit 8. Paybox does everything to ensure safe and reliable transactions. The payment servers, which consist of several Hewlett Packard Unix machines, are hosted by Lufthansa Systems at their Frankfurt data centre, where many other data centres of banks are also managed. The IT department remains an integral part of the paybox.net parent company. Although marketing, sales and operations offices are also set up in the other European countries where paybox is to be launched, the complete technological backbone is developed, hosted and administrated in the company headquarters in Raunheim and the nearby data center. Calls are routed from the paybox call servers

Exhibit 8 **Regular paybox transaction**

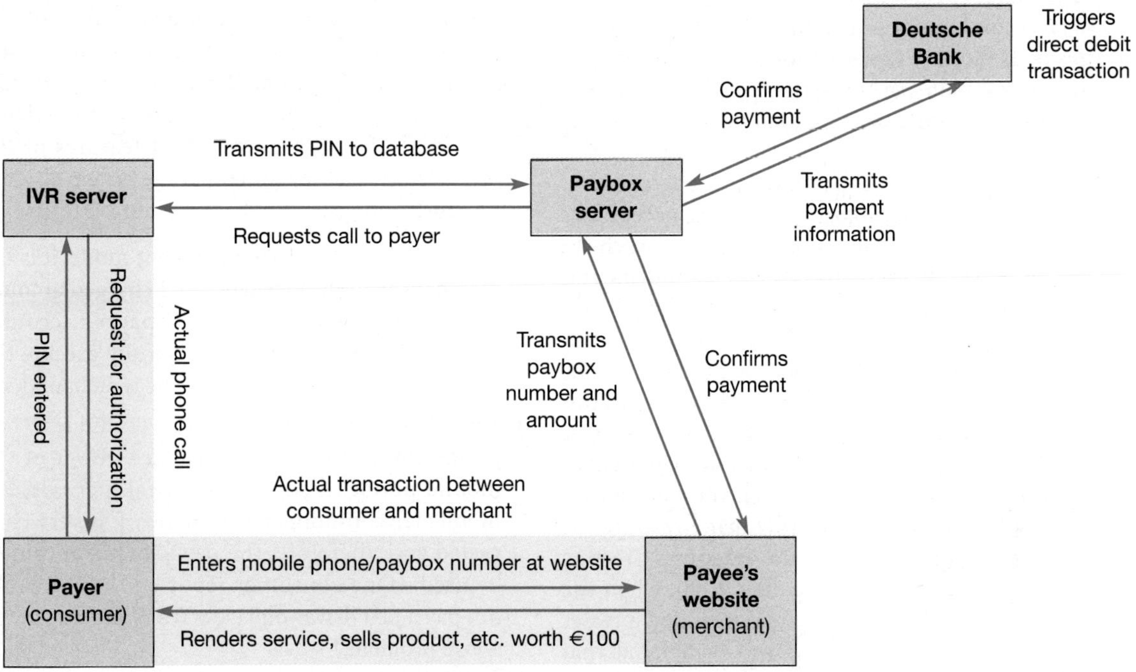

via voice-over IP to the respective countries where the transactions are actually made. The company is in close contact with its database vendor, Oracle, as well as the provider of the computer–telephone interface, Envox, that manages the voice calls.

Although over 99% of the transactions confirmed by paybox are processed by Deutsche Bank, around one in seven transactions fail to be confirmed in the first place because the connection to one of the transaction partners is lost during the transaction. Ortwein says: 'Of course, we don't know for sure whether someone just hung up or had a technical problem.' The reason for this is the technological set-up of the telephone network: it does not differentiate between lost connections and normally finished calls.

In addition, transaction times are fairly long. While the phone call to the payer (in Internet-to-paybox payment mode, for example) averages 25 seconds, calls by payees average 90 seconds. This is, of course, partly due to the fact that users are not yet very familiar with the system and require more time than necessary to enter the data correctly. The cost of these calls adds to the paybox cost per transaction, and makes it higher than that of a credit card processing company, if fraud is not taken into account.

Ortwein is unfazed by these apparent limitations:

> That may be the current state of affairs, but technology is advancing quickly. We will not stop at authentication over voice calls. With the always-on data functionality of mobile phones, which will be possible, starting with GRPS-networks, we will only need to send a short data packet. We will be faster, more convenient and cheaper than a credit card.

Competition

> We are no longer a regular start-up. We are a fledgling company on its way to becoming an international player. Exceptionally qualified and professional employees[1] are just as important for our success as the quality of our paybox products.
>
> **Mathias Entenmann**

During the launch preparations, paybox employees were debating the success in the US of PayPal, a payment system that enables peer-to-peer transactions using e-mail or personal digital assistants (PDA). PayPal is a free system that has financed itself since a couple of days after float, and from charging, like

1 By April 2002, paybox.net employed in its Raunheim headquarters 80 people, representing 25 nationalities.

paybox, a €5 referral fee. Two years after its launch, PayPal had 5 000 000 users, and became the number-one method of payment at eBay.com. Ortwein admits: 'So far, we haven't made a breakthrough similar to that of PayPal' (see Exhibit 9). 'However,' added Entenmann:

> PayPal's value proposition in the US is very different from whatever existed there before. People relied on postal mail to send cheques, with transaction times peaking at 14 days. PayPal was therefore launched to meet an urgent market need. Obviously, this situation in the US, where wireless transfers are also virtually unknown, doesn't compare with the one in Europe.

Paybox is not very worried by the possible entry in Europe of PayPal. 'PayPal, like most US products, is PC-centred', says Peter Seipp. 'European consumers are mobile phone-centred. Besides, PayPal's service in Europe would be far less convincing because the banking system here is only slightly less convenient than PayPal.'

Recently, numerous m-payment systems have been introduced in Germany. These include prepaid cards (such as PaySafeCard) and SMS-based solutions (like PayItMobile). Like paybox, these systems can operate over any mobile phone, any telecommunications network, and via any bank account. However, the PaySafeCard solution would require recharging the account as is already the case with prepaid phones. SMS-based systems are triggered via a website to send an SMS to the consumer's phone, which is then entered at the website by the consumer. These systems are cheaper to operate than paybox, but the SMS is not guaranteed to arrive within a specific time frame. Furthermore, unlike paybox, the use of SMS-based systems does not require a PIN; therefore, anyone with access to the phone could trigger the payment transaction.

More sophisticated ideas include storing credit card information on the cell phone's SIM[2] card. This solution, heralded by some credit card companies, is still in its testing phase. However, it is hampered by the cost of integrating the system into the telecommunications network and exchanging users' mobile phones and SIM cards.

In March 2001, Durlacher research categorized different international m-payment services along two dimensions: the strength of the payment service and the stage of development, implementation and acceptance (see Exhibit 10). Although PayPal scored higher in the second dimension, the report emphasized the strong market position of paybox.

In general, possible entrants include the major telecommunications operators, banks and credit card companies. However, nearly all of the rival systems are still in the test or launch phase. 'Large telecommunications companies have underestimated the complexity of the online payment process', says

2 SIM stands for subscriber's identification memory.

Exhibit 9 Paybox growth figures

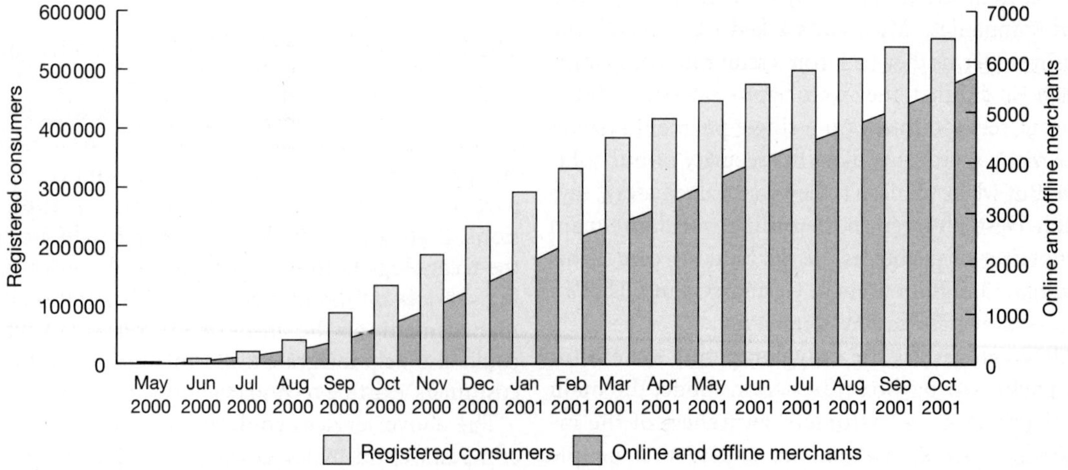

Exhibit 10 **Comparison of macro-payment solutions**

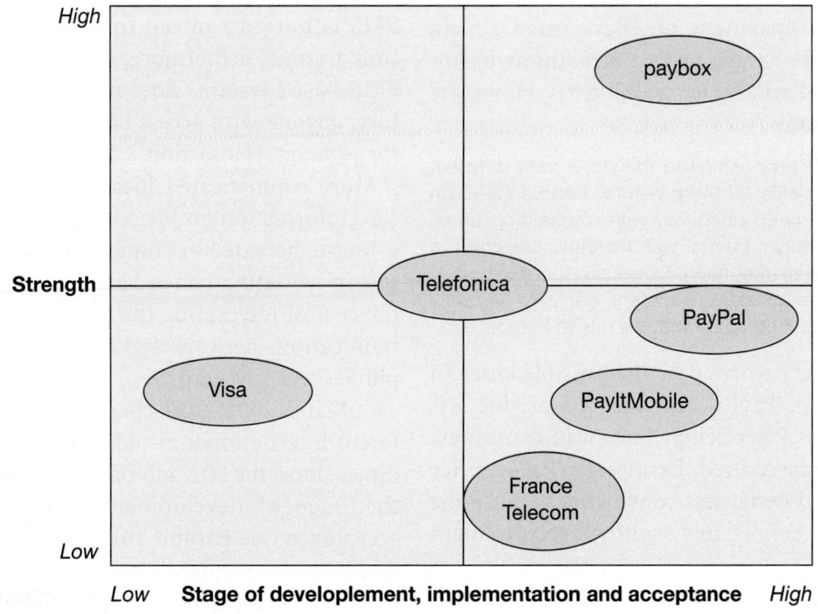

Source: UMTS Report, Durlacher Research, March 2000.

Entenmann. 'Credit card companies, instead of worrying about m-payments, have been busy trying to make their cards safer for the online world', states Ortwein. 'Banks have been content to fund small start-ups, like PayPal or paybox', adds Seipp.

With directly competing m-payment systems still to come, the real competitors may prove to be the entrenched market incumbents. In the Internet-to-paybox transaction mode, paybox is similar to credit card companies. 'Merchants asked us to match the [business] terms they had from credit card companies. When we did that, they were happy since they didn't want to rely too much on a single payment system; plus many merchants liked the security of our solution. But when we didn't, they just walked away', says Ralph Westenburger. In the offline world, the main competitor of paybox is the EC banking card. 'This card has 55 million users in Germany alone. That's a huge critical mass', says Westenburger.

Although cash is the only competing system for the paybox-to-paybox transaction mode, the main barrier to entry is customers' awareness of the m-payment system. 'We have to ensure that people think of paybox the next time they need to pay someone. The idea is just too new and will take some time to make its way through', says Eckhard Ortwein. 'Overall', explains Entenmann, 'I think that a bunch of dauntless [m-payment] competitors could help us spread the word and educate consumers. After all, competition is good for business!'

The PIA proposal

The Paybox Intelligent Architecture (or PIA) proposal is about creating these 'dauntless competitors', although they would also use the paybox technology platform. The architecture is planned to be a modular, global application infrastructure comprising all parts of the paybox service and its various applications. Paybox.net would wholly or partially license the technology to interested parties and sell consulting services on the implementation, operation and management of the m-payment service. Paybox could also help integrate its payment system into the customers' existing technology infrastructure.

The above services could interest banks, service companies and major corporations for which the

paybox system may complement their existing customer loyalty programmes. They could also appeal to telecommunications companies, especially to second- or third-generation mobile network operators. They could all leverage the PIA technology to create co-branded paybox products.

'With our existing base of 750000 consumers using the paybox solution every day, we have proved that our system works', says CTO Ortwein. 'Other companies have failed to create a mass-market system. With PIA, they can buy the most successful, off-the-shelf [m-payment] solution. So why wait?'

Paybox has invested heavily in its consumer business and intends to keep this operation:

> We have a strong customer base and are growing steadily. However, with the functionality to submit standard payment transfers, we have finally found a killer application; we have established backward compatibility ... In the last few months, we have driven growth by taking only small fees or no fees at all, especially where consumers are concerned. Our main challenge now is how to make money from the paybox-to-paybox transaction mode and from money transfers.

DISCUSSION QUESTIONS

1. Beyond the information given in the case, what are the advantages and disadvantages of paybox compared to other payment services?
2. What factors were critical for the success of paybox.net?
3. How would you assess the current revenue model of paybox.net (in terms of its strengths and weaknesses)? How would you improve on it?
4. If you were Mathias Entenmann, Chief Executive Officer of paybox.net AG, what would be your strategy regarding the following issues:
   - to increase the usage of the paybox service;
   - to implement or not to implement the Paybox Intelligent Architecture (PIA) proposal;
   - to foster the internationalization of the company?

CASE STUDY 28

NTT DoCoMo i-mode™

Value innovation at DoCoMo

Every ten years, Japanese companies come up with a new mobile device that shakes the world. Sony's Walkman was launched in 1979 and Nintendo launched Gameboy in 1989. And in 1999, we invented i-mode.[1]

Mari Matsunaga

Kouji Ohboshi is a worried man. It's early 1999, and NTT DoCoMo's Chair is anxiously waiting to hear how the press conference for i-mode – his company's new mobile Internet system – has fared. He has every reason to be nervous. Although DoCoMo is a leader in the Japanese mobile industry, the market is showing signs of saturation and Ohboshi has gambled a large stake of his company's future on the development of the new system. The report arrives and his worst fears are realized: the press conference was a debacle.

The launch of i-mode couldn't have gone worse. With only seven reporters attending, i-mode's extravagant debut had fallen on deaf ears. Those journalists present were among Japan's least charitable. With the Internet boom waning, reporters were more sceptical than ever. Mobile Internet services had failed elsewhere so why should they work in Japan? Why not wait, like everyone else, for the third-generation (3G) global wireless Internet protocol? Ohboshi knew that unfavourable or – worse – weak press coverage in Japan's trend-driven mobile phone market could spell disaster.

Had he made the wrong decision to shift the company's strategic focus? Were his sceptical colleagues at DoCoMo right? What Ohboshi didn't know at the time was that in the weeks to come, i-mode would become an explosive success. Like the Walkman and Gameboy that preceded it, i-mode was to be more than simply a commercial success – it became a phenomenon. What explains this amazing success in Japan? How did DoCoMo turn a highly competitive industry with declining growth potential into an attractive business opportunity?

NTT DoCoMo's troubled birth

NTT DoCoMo was formed in 1992 as part of a partial government break-up of the powerful Nippon Telephone and Telegraph (NTT) telecom monopoly. Formerly NTT's mobile phone unit, it was cast from the nest to take over wireless communications sales and operations as an independent enterprise. Kouji Ohboshi, an energetic 60-year-old, was the first CEO of a company whose name DoCoMo is both a play on the Japanese word for 'anywhere' and an abbreviation of '*Do Co*mmunications over the *Mo*bile network.'

From the start, Ohboshi realized that DoCoMo had a tough road ahead. The mobile phone market was overregulated, transmission quality was poor, subscription fees were costly and mobiles were heavy.[2]

1 Interview: Ms Mari Matsunaga, formerly Manager, Gateway Business Dept., NTT DoCoMo, 20 August 2001.
2 M. Matsunaga (2000), *i-mode jiken [i-mode: The Birth of i-mode]*, Kadokawa Shoten.

This is a modified version of the original case 'NTT DoCoMo i-mode™: creating a solution for the masses' (number 05/2002-5036) written by Yasushi Shiina, INSEAD MBA 2000. Jason Hunter prepared this freely adapted version, under the supervision of Professors W. Chan Kim, Renée Mauborgne and Ben M. Bensaou. It is intended to be used as a basis for class discussion rather than to illustrate either effective or ineffective handling of an administrative situation.

Table 1 Number of regular mobile phone/PHS subscribers in Japan (millions)

	March 90	March 91	March 92	March 93	March 94	March 95	March 96	March 97	March 98	January 99
Mobile phones	0.49	0.87	1.38	1.17	2.13	4.33	10.20	20.88	31.53	39.79
PHS	–	–	–	–	–	–	1.51	6.03	6.73	5.86
Total	0.49	0.87	1.38	1.71	2.13	4.33	11.71	26.91	38.25	45.64
Pagers	4.25	5.08	5.91	6.69	8.06	9.35	10.61	10.07	7.12	4.27
Fixed-line	–	54.48	56.21	57.60	58.78	59.88	61.04	61.46	60.38	NA
Population	123.61	–	–	–	–	125.57	125.59	125.87	126.22	126.45

Source: Ministry of Public Management, Home Affairs, Post and Telecommunications (MPHPT), Telecommunication Carriers Association (TCA), Statistics Bureau and Statistics Centre.

Moreover, there was a palpable sense that the market had reached a plateau (Table 1).[3] Japan's economic bubble had burst and businesses had cut back mobile phone purchases. To add insult to injury, tough new government rules forbade the fledgling DoCoMo to ask NTT for financial assistance. By the end of its first year DoCoMo was saddled with a '10 billion yen loss ... and bankruptcy was a serious threat'.[4]

Faced with a looming crisis, Ohboshi went for broke, setting out to expand the market by bringing cellular phones to the masses. And he did so with a vengeance. During the next two years, Ohboshi invested ¥50 billion – a large sum for a company making a loss – to bring DoCoMo's mobile network services to everyday users.[5] His first move was to improve DoCoMo's network. In 1993 the company launched its new revolutionary PDC (personal digital cellular) standard, bringing crystal-clear calls, fewer interruptions and less background noise. Moreover, PDC helped DoCoMo use its limited allocation of radio spectrum more efficiently. Within a few months DoCoMo's PDC standard was adopted

3 The first Japanese cellular phone service was launched in December 1979. It was a disaster. The high service fees made the telephones unaffordable to all but the wealthiest of businessmen (*salarimen*). After putting down ¥200 000 deposit and a ¥72 000 subscription fee, users would hand over another ¥26 000 in monthly fees and a call charge of ¥280 for every three minutes. Moreover, the service area was limited, the sound quality was inferior to pay phones, and you had to be physically fit: first-generation cellular phones weighed 3 kg and were carried over the shoulder. With the stimulation of government deregulation and subsequent technological innovations it took a full ten years before cell phones became increasingly attractive to mass consumers. Carriers and telecom equipment manufacturers worked closely to improve both the usability of the phones and the quality of transmission. Rightly, they believed that reducing the size of handsets and extending their battery life were crucial improvements. By the end of 1998, the weight and the battery life of a standard phone reached 68 g and 330 hours respectively (Table 2 and Exhibit 1).

4 Interview: Mr Kouji Ohboshi, Chair, NTT DoCoMo.

5 Ohboshi (2000), *DoCoMo kyuseicho no keiei, [DoCoMo: management of rapid growth]*, Diamond Sha.

Table 2 Development of regular mobile phones in Japan

Year	*Height (mm)*	*Width (mm)*	*Thickness (mm)*	*Weight (g)*	*Battery life (hours)*
1979	140	50	210	2400	NA
1985	190	55	220	3000	8
1987	120	42	180	900	6
1989	175	42	77	640	9
1991	140	47	26	220	13
1994	143	49	29	185	20
1995	140	42	26	155	150
1996	130	41	23	94	170
1997	127	40	18	79	220
1998	123	39	17	68	330

Source: NTT DoCoMo, Panasonic.

Exhibit 1 Mobile phone rates

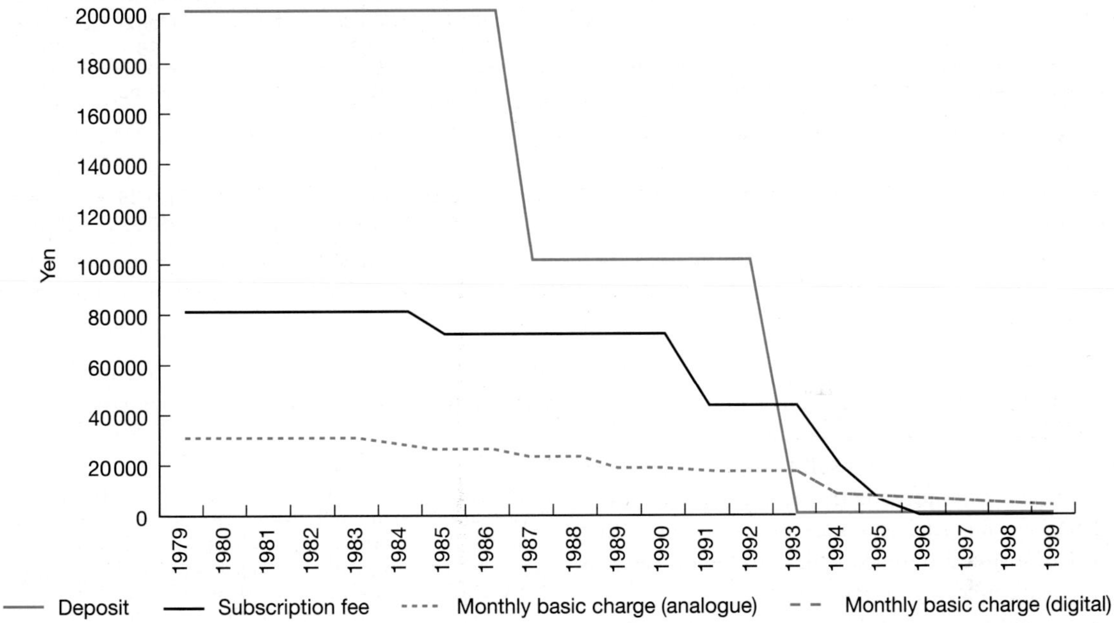

Table 3 Wireless telecommunication carriers in Japan, January 1999

	NTT DoCoMo	*DDI Cellular*	*IDO*	*J-Phone group*	*TuKa*
Year of founding	1979	1990	1988	1994	1994
Subscribers (million)	22.89	5.09	3.24	5.75	2.82
Market share (%)	57.53	12.79	8.14	14.41	7.08
System	PDC	TACS (analogue) PDC CdmaOne	NTT (analogue) TACS (analogue) PDC CdmaOne	PDC	PDC
Frequency	800 MHz	800 MHz	800 MHz	1.5 GHz	1.5 GHz
Operational region	Nationwide	Nationwide – excluding Kanto[a] and Tokai[a]	Kanto[a] Tokai[a]	Nationwide	Kanto[a] Kansai[a] Tokai[a]
PHS operations	NTT Personal	DDI Pocket	No	No	No
Major shareholders	NTT[b]	DDI[b] Kyocera[b]	Toyota Electric utility companies	Japan Telecom[b] Japan Railways[b] Vodafone Airtouch[b] British Telecom[b]	Nissan DDI[b] Hitachi[b] Motorola[b] Sony[b]

[a] Kanto: Tokyo area; Tokai: Nagoya area; Kansai: Osaka area.
[b] Fixed-line telecom carriers or telecom equipment suppliers.

Source: Company annual reports; Telecommunication Carriers Association (TCA); Goldman Sachs.

by competitor carriers across Japan. By December 1998, it would account for 98.7% of the Japanese market (Table 3).[6]

Next DoCoMo slashed prices. Its high deposit was abolished in October 1993 and subscription fees were cut in 1996. By March 1999 monthly basic charges had dropped 73%, the average charge for a three-minute call on DoCoMo falling 57.6% in the same period. Once again, the rest of the industry quickly followed suit by cutting fees (Exhibit 1). The lust for market share in the mid-1990s drove carriers to continue slashing prices to rock-bottom levels, even as monthly average revenue per user (ARPU) continued to sink (while monthly average minutes use remained relatively stable) (Table 4).

Table 4 Average monthly revenue and average monthly minute of use per user

	FY1995	*FY1996*	*FY1997*	*FY1998*
Average monthly revenue per user (Yen)	19720	15930	12570	10800
Average monthly minute use per user (minutes)	172	170	158	155
Churn rate	1.18%	1.20%	1.66%	1.97%

Source: NTT DoCoMo.

Ohboshi also attracted new customers by reducing the size of the phones. NTT had one of the largest R&D teams in the telecom industry and DoCoMo maintained close relationships with telecom equipment manufacturers.[7] Ohboshi leaned heavily on DoCoMo's engineers and its suppliers to reduce the size of phones and extend their battery life.

Although DoCoMo was feeling the effects of deregulation, it made the best of the gains offered by the new competitive environment. Within a year of Ohboshi's drastic measures, DoCoMo was still Japan's largest mobile telephone carrier, and its revenues and net income had soared.[8] By March 1999, DoCoMo's sales revenue ballooned to ¥3 118 billion with a net income of ¥205 billion, and market capitalization topping out at ¥11.2 trillion – about 60% of the size of its parent company, NTT (Table 5).

The wild, wireless East

NTT DoCoMo's emergence, together with deregulation, technological innovation, price reduction and the launch of new services, all contributed to the rapid expansion of the mobile phone market to mass users in Japan. In a ten-month period during 1998,

6 Tadashi Aoyagi (2000), *Daisansedai keitai business: nichibeiou no nerai [The third generation cellular phone business: aims of Japan, US and Europe]*, Ric Telecom.

7 DoCoMo inherited from NTT close relationships with four large Japanese suppliers (NEC, Fujitsu, Matsushita Communications Panasonic and Mitsubishi Electronics), who worked closely with NTT DoCoMo to break through technological barriers. This network soon became known as the 'DoCoMo Family', since its products were sold under the NTT DoCoMo brand, and the only way to identify the manufacturer of a cellular phone was to look at the first letter of the product number (e.g. 'N' for NEC). These relationships gave NTT DoCoMo considerable advantage, especially once its PDC standard was accepted as the only one in Japan.

8 It remained the nation's leading carrier; however, at times DoCoMo's market share dropped below 50% due to fierce competition.

Table 5 NTT DoCoMo's financial performance (million yen)

	March 95	*March 96*	*March 97*	*March 98*	*March 99*
Sales revenues	806982	1237176	1962850	2626120	3118398
Net income	16448	21379	28690	120628	204815
Operating margin	8.4%	9.9%	10.1%	15.7%	16.3%
Net income margin	2.0%	1.7%	1.5%	4.6%	6.6%
Market capitalization	NA	NA	NA	NA	11203920
Number of subscribers (thousands)	2206	4936	10960	17984	23897
Market share	50.9%	48.4%	52.5%	57.0%	57.5%

NTT DoCoMo listed its shares on the Tokyo Stock Exchange in October 1998.
The number of subscribers is for cellular phone services.
Source: NTT DoCoMo.

the market grew by an estimated eight million users, bringing the total number of subscribers to 39.8 million in January 1999 – fulfilling 87.2% of Japan's total wireless market (Table 1).[9]

Competition for market share in the late 1990s was cut-throat. Deregulation continued apace and by 1998 a flood of large foreign carriers and equipment manufacturers had entered the fast-growing market as the government lifted the last remaining limitations on foreign investment (Table 3).[10] Competition was equally fierce in the drive to offer new services. J-Phone shrewdly targeted younger users, launching the first SMS (short message service) and information services via the J-Sky web package. Using a similar approach, DoCoMo introduced the wildly successful 'Pocket Board,' a well-designed yet inexpensive mobile with e-mail and game functions.[11]

By January 1999, the wireless market in Japan had experienced seven years of rapid expansion (Table 1), with every third person owning a mobile phone. Although the size of the market was still small compared to that of fixed lines, its annual average growth rate of 68% was astounding compared to the anaemic growth (1.5%) of the fixed line market. Yet despite general optimism in the market, Ohboshi was once again getting nervous.

After victory, tighten your helmet strap

Ohboshi's marketing background had taught him that, 'fast growth means fast maturity, and faster speed for the market to move from maturity to saturation and then to decline'.[12] The market was once again moving to saturation both in the number of potential new users and in capacity, as available radio bandwidth increasingly limited market expansion.

It was time for action. To survive, Ohboshi believed that DoCoMo needed 'to create a new market, not by adapting to changes but by creating the changes through positively transforming their corporate strategy'.[13] Ohboshi told his employees that DoCoMo had to shift from simply increasing the size of the voice-based wireless market, to creating new value for customers. Shortly afterwards, in July 1996, the company formally announced its new strategic focus: 'from volume to value'.

Volume to value

At the heart of Ohboshi's 'volume to value' focus was non-voice-based wireless data transmission. With the explosion of Internet use during the late 1990s (Table 6), DoCoMo realized that the use of e-mail and the Web was quickly becoming a cornerstone of everyday life. From new market and social psychology research, Ohboshi was convinced that 'the daily needs and wants of the people in a mature society like Japan would shift from physical goods to communication, information, knowledge and entertainment'.[14]

Not only did the Internet offer new opportunities for filling customer demand, it also solved one of

9 The growth in subscribers was attributed to the increase in personal users. However, churn rates (subscriber termination rates) were also increasing, showing that customer loyalty was vulnerable in the new environment.

10 Airtouch acquired a 10–15% stake in the J-Phone Group of companies and offered its technical expertise; Motorola, a US electronic products manufacturer invested in the Tuka Group of companies.

11 For their part, DDI Cellular and IDO improved the quality of transmission substantially by adopting the US-based cdmaOne digital protocol. Although these services attracted new customers, these numbers were not significant enough to boost growth or change the structure of the market.

12 Ohboshi (2000).

13 Ibid.

14 Interview: Mr Kouji Ohboshi, Chair, NTT DoCoMo.

Table 6 **Internet users and the number of commercial (B2C) websites in Japan**

	December 96	*December 97*	*December 98*	*December 99*	*December 00*
Internet users (million)	NA	11.55	16.94	27.06	47.08
Penetration rate in Japan	3.3%	6.4%	11.0%	19.1%	34.0%
Penetration rate in the USA	NA	NA	32.4%	42.5%	58.9%
Commercial websites	2966	8245	13926	21634	NA
B2C e-commerce market (billion yen)	NA	NA	NA	336	770

Source: MPHPT, NUA, Nomura Research Institute, Accenture.

Table 7 Capital expenditure by carrier in Japan (billion yen)

	FY96	*FY97*	*FY98*
Fixed line NTT	1991.2	1886.9	1727.9
DDI	59.7	93.4	66.5
Japan Telecom	54.2	84.6	65.6
KDD	67.9	95.2	118.2
Fixed-line sub-total	*2173.0*	*2160.1*	*1978.2*
Mobile NTT DoCoMo	733.6	728.7	845.9
DDI Cellular	197.5 1	43.5	
IDO	119.5	15.4	137.6
J-Phone	181.7	182.7	166.1
Tu-Ka	84.1	57.6	42.8
DDI Pocket (PHS)	76.8	99.6	61.1
Mobile sub-total	*1393.2*	*1327.5*	*1253.5*
Total	**3566.1**	**3487.6**	**3231.7**

Financial year (FY) denotes the year from April to March of next year.
Source: Morgan Stanley Dean Witter (MSDW).

Ohboshi's greatest concerns: an increasingly congested radio spectrum. In contrast to traditional voice conversations that are sent via dedicated spectrum airwaves, Internet traffic is dispersed in small packets across the network to be reassembled at their destination (e.g. a user's telephone). If DoCoMo created an alternative mobile Internet network based on packet-switching technologies, it would completely circumvent the burdened voice network.

Within a year, DoCoMo was building one of Japan's first nationwide packet-switching networks.[15] The mobile computing team was strengthened and soon new products and services were introduced – albeit not very successfully – culminating in 1997 with the '¥10 e-mail service' (customers could send and receive 2 kilobytes of data for a mere ¥10).[16]

Although these early Internet initiatives were not big profit-makers for NTT DoCoMo, they created a new market by attracting customers who had never used cellular phones or e-mail before. As one of the team members involved in developing mobile computing services pointed out: 'Our intention was not to develop and introduce new products into the market, but to create and introduce new ways of using our traditional wireless services.'[17]

The new wireless world

In January 1997, Ohboshi asked Keiichi Enoki, a former electrical engineer and DoCoMo's new Director of Corporate Sales, to plan and launch a new mobile data communication service for the mass market embodying his 'volume to value' strategy.[18] He later reflected:

> About a year after we started launching new mobile data communication services, revenues from such new services increased to constitute 5–6% of our total revenues. With detailed marketing research and advice from external consultants, I felt a need to further boost these new services and asked Enoki, whom I trusted, to head a project specifically targeting the mass market. I assured him that he would have full discretion in choosing his staff and in using funds worth ¥5 billion, which is a lot of money.[19]

Enoki would have his work cut out for him. DoCoMo had a new strategic focus, but after two long years Ohboshi's team had yet to match vision with performance. Enoki had to create a winner. He was asked to develop a mobile phone service that would advance the Internet in the

15 This system would not only ease the use of congested radio spectrum capacity, but also serve as the basis for 3G services. Despite the optimistic market expectation and technological developments, the prospects for the 3G technologies were not necessarily bright. Although similar new data communication services attracted customers (e.g. WAP services in Europe), they had not proved to be adequate enough to boost the market, and it was feared that the same might be true of 3G cellular services. The introduction of new 3G technologies would also create huge additional costs for carriers, which had already incurred more than ¥1 trillion capital expenditure over the past few years (Table 7). Furthermore, competition would increase as other international carriers competed in a single global market.

16 In addition to these measures, Ohboshi and his successor Keiji Tachikawa, (then Vice-President), set up a small project team within the Corporate Strategy Planning Department, and very soon the first proposal for NTT DoCoMo's 'Vision 2010' was drafted. The year 2010 was deliberately chosen as 'it will be the time when wireless telecom technologies will make innovations from 3G to 4G and also the period of ten years is the longest possible for reasonable predictions to be made in a fast-changing environment.' Vision 2010 forecast huge opportunities for mobile telecom services in enriching personal lives and in supporting global corporate activities. In particular, it saw a greater role for mobile data services in fulfilling the needs of women, senior citizens and medical systems, important to a society characterized by a lower birth rate and an ageing population. In addition to these market projections, it also emphasized the need for DoCoMo to co-operate with other companies to expand the wireless telecom market, and summarized DoCoMo's operations towards the year 2010 in five key concepts or 'MAGIC' for short (Exhibit 2).

17 Interview: Mr Irukayama, Mobile Multimedia Business Department, NTT DoCoMo.

18 Ohboshi (2000).

19 Interview: Mr Kouji Ohboshi, Chair, NTT DoCoMo.

Exhibit 2 **NTT DoCoMo Vision 2010: 'MAGIC'**

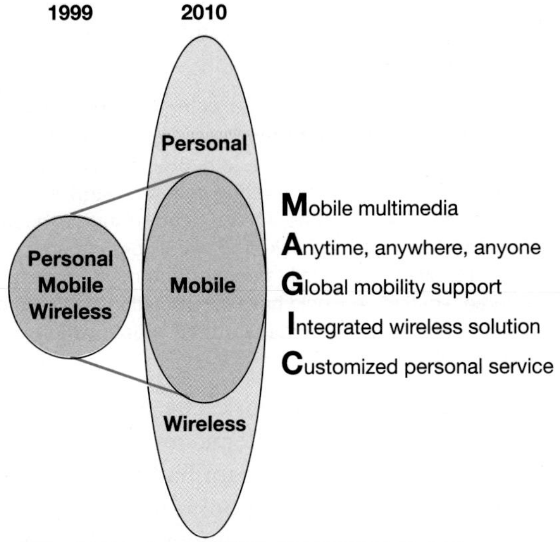

There are three words that characterize the business of DoCoMo – mobile, wireless and personal. Our aim is to make the most of the mobile communications market. DoCoMo's Vision 2010 is based on five key concepts that can be represented by MAGIC. However, MAGIC cannot be achieved by DoCoMo alone. We would like to create businesses and market opportunities through collaboration with other companies and organizations.

same way the Sony Walkman had advanced the stereo. But how?

'I got the first hints from my family', recalls Enoki:

> At that time, the pager was at the peak of its popularity. My daughter used the number pad as a form of data communication. My son could play a new computer game without reading the instructions. Their ability to adapt to new information technology and its ease of use convinced me that young people would accept a new data service that would give them the same kind of enjoyment.[20]

Now a believer, Enoki set out to tackle the new initiative by doing the unthinkable: recruiting new blood from the outside to lead the project. He first called Mari Matsunaga, a senior executive at Recruit Co., a job placement firm. Matsunaga was known for her marketing prowess and dramatic turnaround of Recruit's job placement magazine for women into one of Japan's hottest titles. She would head the content development team for DoCoMo's new service. Enoki then sought out a manager to devise a business model for the new mobile data communication service. He chose Takeshi Natsuno, a Wharton MBA and former head of Hypernet, one of Japan's first (and most hyped) web start-ups.[21]

Developing the electronic concierge service

Mastunaga set out to understand how the Internet works. What were the killer applications that provided web users with superior value? In studying the winners – such as AOL (America Online) – she found a positive correlation between the number of Internet users and the volume of content. As content increased, so did the number of users and vice versa.[22] Hence her conclusion: 'Content would have to be king on the new DoCoMo system'.

She also recognized that simply putting 'information' on the network would not differentiate the new service from the existing PC-based Internet, nor would it add value to users who were often lost in the sea of information on the Web. Matsunaga thus envisioned a service that would function like a 'hotel concierge', where users would be 'serviced' by content providers.

If DoCoMo could make it possible for users to access preselected websites on the screen of their handset, then they would capture Mastunaga's concept of an electronic concierge. The team set out to create such a user-friendly portal to serve both as an accreditation of quality for those preselected 'official' sites, as well as an easy way to navigate the whole wireless Web – similar to the service AOL provides its customers (Exhibit 3). Users could access other 'non-official' sites simply by typing in the URL address.

Meanwhile, Natsuno devised a business model for the new mobile data communication service based on what he saw as the 'Internet worldview' rather than the 'telecom worldview'.[23] The telecom worldview, according to Natsuno, is a zero-sum approach: carriers determine the standards and the services that can ride on their network, and are not interested in adapting to others' technology or in sharing profits with other

20 'A discussion with Keiichi Enoki, Senior Vice-President, General Manager of Gateway Business Department, Mobile Multimedia Division' in NTT DoCoMo Annual Report 2000.

21 By the time he joined DoCoMo, Natsuno had already left Hypernet before the free ISP fell from glory in a multi-billion yen crash in 1997.

22 Interview: Mr Kazuhiro Takagi, Director, Gateway Business Department, NTT DoCoMo.

23 Takeshi Natsuno (2000), *i-mode™ strategy*, Nikkei BP.

Exhibit 3 **Contents portfolio of the new service (i-mode)**

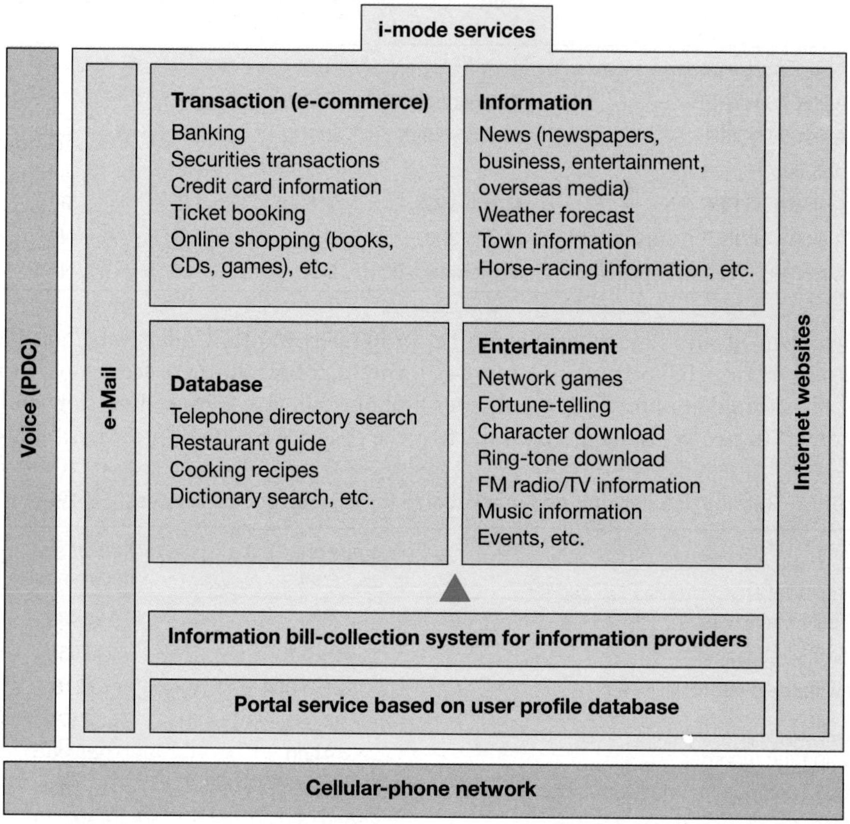

Source: NTT DoCoMo.

players in the value chain. Users must accept the infrastructure and services carriers offer them.

Conversely, the 'Internet worldview' is a positive-sum approach. As the Internet is an open network that can be accessed with various devices (e.g. computers, PDAs) whose specifications are not necessarily determined by either content providers or carriers – all parties are obliged to accept one another's technologies and services. In the Internet world, consumers choose the infrastructure they prefer. Specifications are thereby *de facto* standards determined not by their technological superiority but by the fact that they are so frequently used. In the Internet worldview, Natsuno believed, carriers have to work closely with other players, including information providers, to increase the number of users.

This 'win–win' relationship among players within the network became the foundation of Natsuno's business model. Accordingly, DoCoMo would not purchase content from providers or equipment from manufacturers but would rather accredit 'official' websites and mobile phones to be used with the new service. Interested partners would share both the risks and the rewards. Although this model restricted DoCoMo's role to simply that of a 'gateway' to the Internet, as the service attracted more users, the idea went, the network would attract more content. More content would beget more users; more users would beget more content, and so on,[24] thereby creating a virtuous circle where all parties benefit.

24 Similarly, content providers were inspired continuously to update their sites in order to keep their official status. And as content providers improved their websites, users were able to receive more 'useful' information from accessing the network, and thus all three players on the network benefited.

Table 8 **i-mode and regular handsets**

Phone	Date	Price (yen)	Weight (g)	Size (cm^3)	Battery life (hours)
Regular voice-based mobile phones					
Digital MOVA N207S HYPER	February 1999	32 700	96	85	300
Digital MOVA D206 HYPER	January 1998	30 100	93	99	320
i-mode mobile phones					
Digital MOVA N501i HYPER	March 1999	42 800	115	99	270
Digital MOVA N503i HYPER (i-application)	March 2001	Open	98	NA	460
Digital MOVA N501iS HYPER (i-application)	September 2001	Open	105	NA	450

Natsuno's 'win–win' business model would also be applied to the new service's billing system. A number of the 'official' sites would be subscription-only sites requiring customers to pay fees ranging from ¥100 to ¥300 per month. Under Natsuno's plan, DoCoMo would collect all these fees as part of its monthly phone bill, take a 9% commission, and then pass on the rest to the content providers. This service would

Table 9 **Retail price per unit and market size for various goods/services** (FY 1999)

Items	Average retail price (Yen)	Market size (thousands)
Weekly magazine	300	138 480
Monthly magazine	550–540	214 630
Newspapers (monthly)	3 925–4 384	72 218
TV set	97 130	434 171
Radio tape recorder	19 680	24 233
Mobile computer game (Gameboy)	8 900	23 970
Computer game software (Gameboy)	3 000–4 900	NA
Home PC	207 000–227 000	14 311
Telephone (fixed-line)	21 270	58 470
i-mode handset	35 900–42 800	–
Mobile phone (voice only)	28 200–42 800	–
PHS handset	16 700–30 100	–
Pager	6 300–13 900	3 766
TV licence fee (monthly)	1 345	–
Internet connection charge (monthly: fixed)	8 050	
	¥2.7 per minute	–
Telephone bill (fixed line: monthly)	8 198	
	¥10 per 3 minutes	–
Telephone bill (mobile: monthly)	9 270	
	¥45–120 per 3 minutes	–
Telephone bill (PHS: monthly)	5 550	
	¥30–130 per 3 minutes	–
Pager bill (monthly)	2,697	–

Telephone bills are estimated from average revenue per user or operating revenues.
Market size of TV, radio tape recorder and home PC are estimated from their penetration rates.
Market size of Gameboy is estimated from its outstanding units sold.
Source: MPHPT, NTT DoCoMo, NTT, TCA, Dentsu Institute for Human Studies.

Table 10 i-mode packet transmission charges

	Charge (¥)	
My menu	2–3	
Menu list	3–4	
Mobile banking (balance information)	20–21	
Mobile banking (funds transfer)	59–60	
News	17–18	
Airline seat availability	24–25	
Restaurant guide	37–38	
TOWNPAGE (NTT telephone directory)	35–36	
Share prices (searching by issue code)	26–27	
Image download (downloading one still image the size of the display)	7–8	
i-melody (downloading one three-chord melody approximately 15 seconds in length)	2–3	
i-anime (downloading one moving image the size of the display)	10–11	
i-mode mail transmission charges	*Sending (¥)*	*Receiving (¥)*
20 full-size characters	0.9	0.9
50 full-size characters	1.5	0.9
100 full-size characters	2.1	1.2
150 full-size characters	3.0	1.5
250 full-size characters	4.2	2.1

Source: NTT DoCoMo.

be attractive not only to content providers who could reduce their internal cost structure, but also to users who would appreciate not having to pay several separate bills. And by giving content providers a means to charge users, i-mode would ensure that there was plenty of high-quality content available.

Lastly, Natsuno recommended that the new service adopt existing widely-used technologies. For example, although there were better text languages such as WML (Wireless Markup Language), DoCoMo adopted c-HTML for its new service. With this compact version of HTML, the language widely used to create websites for the PC environment, content providers could quickly, easily and at low cost modify their PC-based websites into a new version to be displayed on the new DoCoMo service. New handsets were also developed that closely resembled existing cellular phones used exclusively for voice communication. Manufacturers were asked to reduce the size and weight of the new handsets while increasing screen size, data capacity and battery power.

The launch of i-mode

Almost a year had passed since Ohboshi had taken the decision to develop the new mobile data communication service, and pressure was mounting on him to perform. Although NTT DoCoMo had managed to maintain its position as the largest mobile telecom carrier in Japan, the cost of developing the new data service was taking its toll on Ohboshi's credibility and threatening the financial stability of the company. Colleagues peering in from outside Enoki's group were confounded by the project. 'Why were we wasting our time and resources on unproven Internet phones, instead of concentrating on the still growing, regular voice-based communication services?' they wondered. By late 1998, opposition to 'volume to value' was growing and Ohboshi was once again under fire.

Enoki and his team finally launched the new service as 'i-mode' on 22 February 1999 – the 'i' representing 'interactive', 'Internet' and the pronoun 'I'.[25] Looking at the phones, a user would notice little difference from the latest models, except for a slightly larger liquid crystal display and the central feature: the i-mode button (Table 8). This connected users to the Internet, where they could send and receive e-mail, access sport scores and weather, read the news, and download pages from the Web.

The new i-mode handsets were priced from ¥35 900 to ¥42 800, about 25% more than regular phones (see Table 9 for comparison with other goods/services). Users were charged ¥300 per month to access the i-mode network, and another ¥100 to ¥300 to access any of the subscription-only sites. Unlike regular mobile services, users were charged by the volume of data transmitted to their mobile phones rather than the length of time on the network. For instance, it would cost ¥0.3 per packet transmitted and ¥4.2 to send (¥2.1 to receive) an e-mail of up to 250 characters (Table 10).

Data transmission over mobile phones would become increasingly important for DoCoMo's bottom line: as revenue from voice calls continued to fall – from an average of $100/subscriber per month in 1997 to $65 in 2001 – data revenue amounting to an average of $17 per subscriber/month would increasingly fill the gap.[26]

25 Natsuno (2000).

26 'Peering around the corner', *The Economist*, 11 October 2001.

Exhibit 4 Number of i-mode-compatible sites

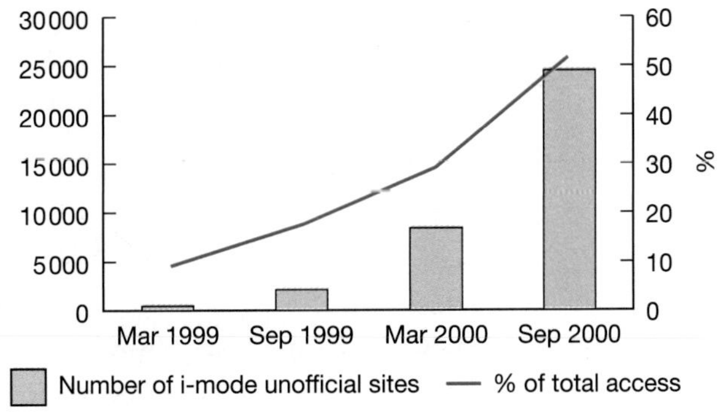

Number of sites in March 1999 is the number on 5 April 1999.

Source: Natsuno (2000), p.187.

Initially 67 content providers participated in the new service, with sites ranging from banking to Karaoke.[27] In the days that followed, dozens of 'unofficial' sites sprang up, even though they were excluded from DoCoMo's official portal. A venture company developed a search engine for unofficial sites just 11 days after the launch of the new service as their number reached 190 (twice as many as i-mode official sites) within two months (Exhibit 4).[28]

i-mode was aggressively promoted through DoCoMo's nationwide network of shops. A how-to book on i-mode was also published, followed by over 100 books and magazines within a year.[29] The number of subscribers exploded, reaching Natsuno's 'critical mass' of one million users by August 1999 (Exhibit 5).[30] By March 2001, i-mode subscribers reached 21.7 million (Exhibit 6), and revenues from packet transmission services increased from ¥295 million to ¥38.5 billion within a year after launch (Table 11).[31] i-mode also contributed to an increase in revenue from regular voice services, even as price competition drove down average monthly revenue per subscriber to ¥7 770 in March 2001.[32] In

27 'Mobile internet saizensen' ['Frontiers of mobile internet'] *Shukan Diamond*, 18 March 2000.
28 Natsuno (2000).
29 Ibid.
30 Ibid.
31 According to one senior official at NTT DoCoMo, 'i-mode surprisingly attracted not only young customers who were generally fond of new technologies, but also old customers who used it as a tool to communicate more often with their grandchildren'. In March 2001, 27% of the total i-mode users were above the age of 40, compared to 20.3% for PC-based Internet (Table 12).

Exhibit 5 i-mode monthly subscriber trend

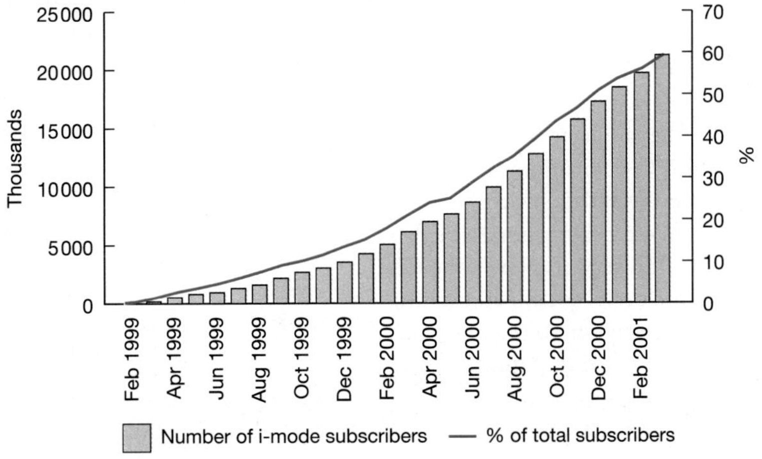

Source: NTT DoCoMo.

Exhibit 6 Number of subscribers for mobile data services on cellular phones

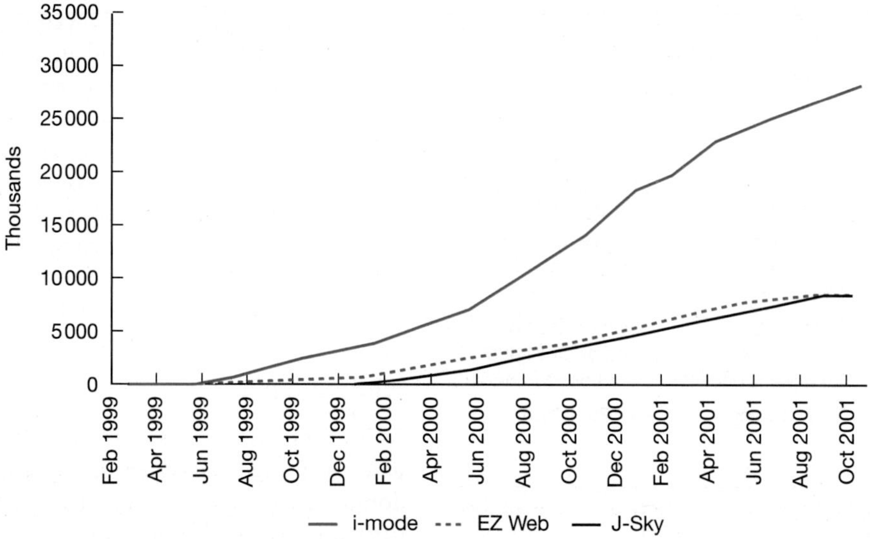

Source: TCA.

Table 11 NTT DoCoMo's financial performance since the launch of i-mode (million yen)

	March 99	*March 00*	*March 01*	*March 02E*
Sales revenues	3118398	3718694	4686004	5297000
Revenues from packet data communication	295	38500	NA	NA
Net income	204815	252140	365505	390000
Operating margin	16.3%	14.7%	16.6%	17.4%
Net income margin	6.6%	6.8%	7.8%	7.4%
Market capitalization	11203920	40314960	20977333	NA
Capital expenditures	845900	876058	1012795	1070000
R&D expenses	41100	89100	95400	NA
Average monthly churn rate	1.75%	1.61%	1.39%	1.32%
Average monthly revenue per user (ARPU: yen)	9270	8740	8650	8580
ARPU from cellular phone service (yen)	N/A	8620	7770	7160
ARPU from i-mode (yen)	N/A	120	880	1420
Average monthly minutes of use per subscriber	164	177	189	195
Number of subscribers (thousands)	23897	29356	36026	40300
Number of i-mode subscribers (thousands)	140	5603	21695	29800
Market share	57.5%	57.4%	59.1%	NA

Source: NTT DoCoMo.

addition, the important customer churn rate began to drop from 1.97 in FY1998 to 1.39 in FY2001, while DoCoMo's market share in the cellular market climbed to 59.1% in March 2001 (Tables 4 and 11).

32 This increase in revenue was due to the fact that 'subscribers were using i-mode and voice-based communication services together, as they made phone calls after they searched restaurants and hotels on i-mode'. ('Interview: Keiji Tachikawa' *Shukan Diamond*, 18 March 2000).

Table 12 Comparison between i-mode and the Internet

	i-mode	*Internet*
Sex of users (male:female)	57:43	58:42
Age of users (years)	Under 19: 7% 20–24: 24% 25–29: 20% 30–34: 12% 35–39: 8% Above 40: 27% Unknown: 2%	Under 19: 2.6% 20–29: 38.1% 30–39: 38.1% 40–49: 15.6% Above 50: 4.7% Unknown: 0.9%
Price	Monthly basic charge of ¥300 + ¥0.3 per 1 packet	Monthly basic charge of ¥1 480 + + ¥8 per 3 minutes
Number of users (March 2001)	21.70 million	17.25 million

Prices exclude monthly basic charges for cellular phone and fixed line telecom services. Price for the Internet is based on KDDI's IP service rates.

Number of users for the Internet is the number of contracts with Internet providers excluding mobile telecom carriers.

Source: MPT, NTT DoCoMo, KDDI.

Playing catch-up

Two months after i-mode's extraordinary launch, two competitors, DDI Cellular and IDO, announced their own mobile data communication services, called 'EZ Web' and 'EZ Access' respectively. Similar to i-mode, customers could subscribe to their services to access the Internet via their mobile phones.[33] However, with an eye towards future markets abroad, DDI and IDO asked their content providers to code their pages in HDML (Handheld Device Markup Language) used for the Wireless Access Protocol (WAP).[34]

Unsurprisingly, due to the costs and difficulties in transforming existing HTML-based Internet websites to EZ Web sites based on HDML, only a handful of content providers were willing to participate in the new service, driving DDI Cellular and IDO to purchase content until the number of subscribers was high enough for content providers to bear such costs voluntarily. In 2000, the two carriers merged to create (AU access to you). Although the number of DDI and IDO subscribers was much smaller than DoCoMo's i-mode subscribers, they still remained competitive with 6.7 million subscribers in 2001 (Exhibit 6).

DoCoMo's other main rival, J-Phone, responded to i-mode's success by concentrating on improving transmission quality and adding content to its existing service (J-Sky Web), and upgrading its J-Sky service so that users could send and receive large e-mail messages (3000 characters each) and view Internet content.[35] As with i-mode and EZ Web, all official J-Phone sites were accessible via the J-Phone portal and classified into nine categories.[36] By 2001, the new J-Sky service continued to attract many new – particularly adolescent – customers, totalling 6.2 million subscribers in March 2001 (Exhibit 6).

Without a net

As its competitors played catch-up, DoCoMo continued to power ahead in its quest for i-mode dominance in Japan. In March 1999, a month after the launch of i-mode, it formed a strategic alliance with Sun Microsystems. Through the partnership, Sun and DoCoMo developed i-appli, a new i-mode application platform that allowed users to run a

33 In addition to Internet access, the new EZ Web service offered subscribers e-mail services. They could now send e-mails of up to 250 characters and receive e-mails of up to 2000 characters on their cellular phones. Furthermore, DDI Cellular and IDO offered PIM (personal information management) services that were not offered by their competitors. By paying a ¥100 premium for address, schedule and task list functions, EZ Web subscribers were able to use their cellular phones more like PDAs (personal digital assistants). DDI Cellular and IDO initially offered these new EZ Web services by using circuit line switching technology that was also used for their voice-based telecom services. None of them had yet a packet-switching network. Thus, unlike i-mode, they charged EZ Web subscribers for the connecting time rather than for the volume of data transmitted to cellular phones (Table 13).

34 DDI and IDO also asked a number of their content providers to connect directly to DDI Cellular and IDO's EZ Web servers, in order to secure confidentiality and stable transmissions.

35 The amount of viewable content was also increased by allowing access not only to its own 'official sites', but also to HTML-based Internet sites and even to c-HTML-based i-mode sites by introducing MML (Mobile Markup Language) as the language for content. MML was another simplified version of HTML developed for simple mobile computing devices by J-Phone and Keio University in Tokyo. Although it was not accepted internationally like c-HTML or HDML, it was very similar to HTML and made it easy for content providers to adapt their existing Internet websites, or even their i-mode sites, into MML-based J-Sky websites.

36 In a strategy to attract younger customers, J-Phone's content focuses on entertainment. 'Keitai denwa, PHS kanzen test ['Cellular phones, PHS: perfect test',] *Nikkei Trendy*, September 2000.

Table 13 Mobile data communication services on mobile phones (September 2000)

	NTT DoCoMo	DDI Cellular (AU)	IDO (AU)	Tu-Ka	J-Phone
Service	i-mode	EZ Web	EZ Access	EZ Web	J-Sky
Functions	Internet access Internet mail transmission	Internet access Internet mail transmission PIM services	Internet access Internet mail transmission PIM services	Internet access Internet mail transmission PIM services	Internet access Internet mail transmission (J-Sky Walker)
Network platforms	PDC (800 MHz)	cdmaOne (800 MHz)	cdmaOne (800 MHz)	PDC (1.5 GHz)	PDC (1.5 GHz)
Communication method (speed)	Packet-switching technology (9600 bps)	Circuit-switching technology (14.4 Kbps) Packet-switching technology (14.4 Kbps)	Circuit-switching technology (14.4 Kbps) Packet-switching technology (14.4 Kbps)	Circuit-switching technology (9600 bps)	Circuit-switching technology (9600 bps)
Content	c-HTML	HDML (WAP-based)	HDML (WAP-based)	HDML (WAP-based)	MML
Content providers	Official: 1000 Unofficial: 24 032	Official: 368 Unofficial: 1 600	Official: 368 Unofficial: 1 600	Official: 368 Unofficial: 1 600	Official: 258 Unofficial: 2 700
e-Mail size	Send/receive: 250 full characters	Send: 250 full characters Receive: 2000 full characters	Send: 250 full characters Receive: 2000 full characters	Send: 250 full characters Receive: 2000 full characters	Send/receive: 3000 characters
Fee collection services	February 1999	March 2000	July 2000	June 2000	April 2000
Monthly basic charge (yen)	300	Standard: 300 Premium: 400	Standard: 200 Premium: 400	Standard: 200 Premium: 300	J-Sky Web: No charge J-Sky Walker: 250
Access fees	¥0.3 per 1 packet (= 128 bytes)	First 15 seconds free and ¥10 per 30 seconds thereafter Packet comm.: ¥0.27 per 1 packet (= 128 bytes)	¥10 per minute Packet comm.: ¥0.27 per 1 packet (= 128 bytes)	First minute ¥3 and ¥10 per minute thereafter	J-Sky Web: ¥2 per single request/reply J-Sky Walker: ¥8 per message transmission
Handset (nominal/real retail prices: yen)	NEC N502i (39 000/18 800) Mitsubishi D209i (34 600/16 800)	Panasonic C308P (44 300/1 800) Sony C305S (45 800/1 800)		Sharp J-SH03 (42 000/9 800) Toshiba J-T04 (42 000/7 800)	Panasonic TP01 (open/4 800) Toshiba TT02 (open/4 800)
Subscribers (% of market)	12.6 million (64.2%)	3.9 million (16.5%)		0.7 million (3.3%)	3.1 million (16.0%)
Service start	February 1999	April 1999		November 1999	December 1999

Source: NTT DoCoMo, KDDI, MSDW, CSFB, TCA, 'Nikkei Trendy'.

wider variety of programs, from video games to online financial services on their mobile phones.[37] A similar strategic partnership with Symbian, a UK-based wireless operating system company, led to the development of a new operating system adaptable to both PCs and mobile phones.

On the content side, in the two years after launching i-mode, DoCoMo struck a number of partnerships with new content providers, ranging from Japan Net Bank (the first Internet bank in Japan) and Playstation.com, to AOL and Walt Disney. Furthermore, i-mode pioneered so-called machine-to-machine or M2M communications that allow i-mode users to purchase soft drinks and other sundries from Japan's huge network of vending machines. A joint venture with Dentsu, the largest advertising agency in Japan, led to the introduction of advertisements on i-mode, thereby providing a new source of revenue and attracting new content providers to the network. Through these and other partnerships the i-mode network swelled to 42 720 sites (1 620 official and 41 100 unofficial) by March 2001.

Looking into the near future, DoCoMo had great hopes for entering the European and American markets and establishing i-mode as a global standard. In recent years, the Japanese mobile giant had been building its equity stakes in various foreign carriers (Tables 14 and 15), as well as applying for 3G licences in markets inside and outside Japan. In January 2001, while NTT DoCoMo was announcing plans to introduce i-mode in Europe[38] a number of crucial questions needed answers. Were i-mode and its success easily transferable outside Japan? Could DoCoMo make it work outside Japan and should it use the same strategy?

Despite i-mode's runaway success, DoCoMo faced a number of key domestic challenges. Its capital expenditures continued to soar as it built its new 3G services. Network congestion and interoperability

37 i-appli is based on Sun's popular, highly compatible Java programming language. Java allows application sharing across operating systems (e.g. between Microsoft Windows and Macintosh).

38 These initiatives are in partnership with KPN Mobile and Telecom Italia Mobile (TIM).

Table 14 NTT DoCoMo's major overseas operations since 1999

2 March 1999	Joint test of 3G mobile communications system with Telephone Organization of Thailand and NEC
17 March 1999	Establishment of local corporation in Brazil
30 September 1999	Establishment of US subsidiaries
8 October 1999	Establishment of Joint Initiative toward Mobile Multimedia (JIMM) with eight foreign carriers
2 December 1999	Capital investment in Hutchison Whampoa (Hong Kong)
27 January 2000	W-CDMA field trials in South Korea with SK Telecom
9 May 2000	Equity participation in KPN Mobile (the Netherlands)
27 June 2000	Establishment of representative office in Beijing, China
12 July 2000	Announcement of 3G mobile multimedia strategic co-operation with Hutchison Whampoa and KPN Mobile
2 August 2000	Launch of Japan-South Korea roaming service with SK Telecom
29 September 2000	Establishment of UK subsidiary and research lab in Germany
30 November 2000	Capital investment in KG Telecom (Taiwan)
30 November 2000	Capital investment in AT&T Wireless (USA)
7 December 2000	Establishment of advisory board in USA
18 January 2001	Announcement of pan-European mobile Internet alliance with KPN Mobile and TIM (Italy)
22 January 2001	Launch of international roaming service in Europe, Asia, Africa and Oceania
7 November 2001	Agreement with KPN Mobile to transfer and license technologies for i-mode-like services in Europe
18 February 2002	Agreement with E-Plus (Germany) to transfer and license technologies for i-mode-like services in Europe (service launched on 16 March 2002)
1 March 2002	Listing of stocks on London and New York Stock Exchanges

The dates shown above are the dates of press releases from NTT DoCoMo.

Source: NTT DoCoMo.

Table 15 Other major partnerships to promote mobile multimedia services

15 March 1999	Increased level of relationships, Symbian (UK)
16 March 1999	Technological partnership, Sun Microsystems (USA)
17 March 1999	Fusion of technologies, increased level of cooperation, Microsoft (USA)
14 June 2000	Increased level of relationships, 3Com (USA)
27 September 2000	Joint development of new Internet services, American Online (USA)

The dates shown above are the dates of press releases from NTT DoCoMo.

Source: NTT DoCoMo.

between newer mobiles and the i-mode system continued to plague the company. In March 2001, under intense political pressure, DoCoMo was forced to reduce interconnection fees to other mobile phone operators. And with Vodafone's acquisition of a controlling stake in J-Phone, DoCoMo's guaranteed preeminence in the Japanese market came under an increasingly dark cloud. How sustainable was NTT DoCoMo's advantage and what should its future moves be?

Keiji Tachikawa, Ohboshi's successor, believed that NTT DoCoMo's future was bright. In the three years since the launch of i-mode, DoCoMo had become the only company to make money out of the mobile Internet. Its net income continued to rise to an all-time high of ¥365.5 billion in March 2001, and its market capitalization far exceeded its parent company, NTT. In the autumn of 2001, DoCoMo launched FOMA ('freedom of multimedia access'), the world's first 3G mobile network capable of video-telephony and the use of data and voice services simultaneously) while other promised 3G initiatives around the world languished. As Tachikawa said, 'Anything mobile in society is a business opportunity for NTT DoCoMo'.[39] Maybe Mr Ohboshi can finally get a good night's sleep.

39 'Interview: Keiji Tachikawa' *Shukan Diamond*, 21 April 2001.

DISCUSSION QUESTIONS

1. How would you assess the attractiveness of the telecom industry in Japan at the time of the launch of i-mode services? What would you conclude from a five-forces industry analysis (see Exhibit 3.1, p. 65)?
2. How did NTT DoCoMo create distinctive value at low cost? How did DoCoMo combine the strengths of the mobile phone and the PC-Internet? How did the value curve of DoCoMo's i-mode differ from those of the mobile phone and the PC-Internet?
3. Where and how did i-mode create new buyer utilities? What is i-mode's business model?
4. How did NTT DoCoMo make profits out of its i-mode services?

APPENDIX

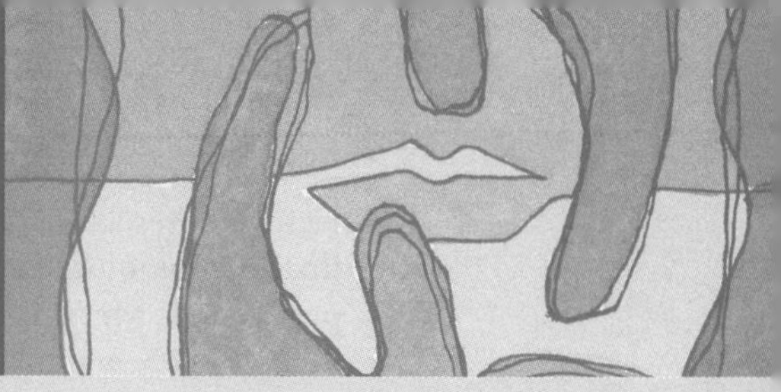

Technologies for electronic and mobile commerce

1 Introduction

Since this book offers a strategic business perspective on electronic and mobile commerce, this Appendix aims at providing readers with a basic understanding of the key technologies underlying the concepts and applications mentioned in the previous chapters. After a brief overview of the evolution of IT and its key milestones, a distinction will be made between wired and wireless technologies. Their definition, specific features and possible use will be presented, and illustrative examples and applications will be provided.

2 IT evolution overview

A key milestone in the evolution of IT is the beginning of the mainframe computer and the launch, in 1964, of the IBM System/360 product line. In 1969, the US Defense Advanced Research Projects Agency (DARPA) developed the Internet for exclusive military use. During the following years, other major IT advances took place; these included the development in 1970 of relational database management systems and of the compact disc technology, the launch in 1971 of Intel's first micro-processor, as well as the development in 1972 of the Ethernet by Xerox and of the UNIX/C programming language by Bell Labs. Between 1975 and 1981 several firms began to offer increasingly integrated personal computers (PCs). The year 1979 witnessed the first widely sold spreadsheet and 1984 the first liquid crystal display (LCD). In 1981 IBM entered the PC market and by 1983, held 42% market share. It set a quasi industry standard for PC hardware and enabled the development of two other standards: Intel's micro-processors and Microsoft's operating systems.

Between 1991 and 1995 the 'www' (World Wide Web) gained momentum through the development in 1991 of Enquire (a program that lined documents from various computers around the world), in 1993 of Mosaic (a program that allowed people to

This Appendix was prepared by Hans-Joachim Jost, MBA participant (2003), and Tawfik Jelassi, Professor of e-Business and IT, both at the School of International Management at the Ecole Nationale des Ponts et Chaussées, Paris.

view pictures as well as words), and in 1995 of the Netscape browser, enabling the first Internet business to evolve. In 1998 the price of one MIPS (million instructions per second, which is a measure for the computing power) was US$1, down from $120 in 1985. A similar development took place for the whole IT hardware industry, thus bringing computers to almost every household. Since then, IT has developed at an ever greater pace, culminating with the Internet hype of the late 1990s, the subsequent crash of the bubble in 2000, and the recent consolidation of the clicks and the bricks-and-mortar worlds.

2.1 The Internet, intranet and extranet

2.1.1 The Internet

Today, the Internet is a network of thousands of computer networks, connecting hundreds of millions of people, organizations, businesses and governments around the globe. A major reason for the rapid and global development of the Internet is the fact that it is a self-stabilizing network, and not just a set of connections. This means, thanks to flexible routing mechanisms, that the Internet works even when parts of it are broken down. Basically, the Internet uses a part of the public telecommunications network. This data interchange enables the development of many applications, with the most important being electronic mail or 'e-mail' (see 3.5.2 below). Yet recent technological developments also allow real-time voice and video transmission.

The most important part of the Internet is the World Wide Web (www), which connects web pages through hyper text links (see 3.2.2). When 'clicking' on such links, the web visitor is instantly transferred to the target site. Internet browsers (see 3.2.2) enable access to millions of available websites.

2.1.2 Intranet

An intranet is an Internet-based application, which is usually used to exchange data within an organization. It is sometimes referred to as B2E (business-to-employee) and represents a sort of 'private Internet'. An intranet basically consists of LANs (local area networks – see 3.4.2) and WANs (wide area networks – see 3.4.3) and possesses at least one gateway to the World Wide Web. To ensure privacy and security, an intranet generally makes use of a VPN (virtual private network – see 3.4.6) and is protected against the Internet by a firewall.

2.1.3 Extranet

An extranet is an Internet-based application, which is accessible to a closed external user group outside the firm, such as customers, suppliers and business partners. There is a need for privacy and security, usually beyond that available on an intranet. Extranets are widely used to do business, both in the field of B2B as well as B2C. Extranet applications may affect virtually all of a company's business functions, from R&D to logistics to sales. They include, for instance, joint R&D, training programmes, as well as shared access to manufacturing and warehouse facilities. In B2C,

extranets can group different companies' access to customers, e.g. in providing a shared online payment system.

2.2 Client-server and peer-to-peer models

2.2.1 Client-server

The term 'client-server' refers to two programs, of which the first (the client) sends a request to the second (the server – see also 3.2.7), which in turn processes the request and sends the result back to the client. This principle can be handled within a single computer, yet it is used to its full potential in networks and distributed systems (see also next section). Therefore, today's business applications are mostly written based on this model and the TCP/IP packaging protocol (see 3.2.5). Typically, multiple client programs share the services of a common server program. The latter is usually a 'daemon'; i.e. a program constantly checking whether there is a certain event (in this case, a client's request). To illustrate the client-server concept, consider that an Internet browser on a requesting computer can be referred to as a client, whereas the requested website comes from a (web-) server.

2.2.2 Peer-to-peer (P2P)

In addition to the client-server model, there are at least two other program relationships which should be mentioned. First, there is the 'master-slave' model, in which one program (the master) is in charge of all other programs. Second, there is the peer-to-peer (P2P) model, in which either one of the two programs can initiate a transaction. A well-known example of a network which evolved from a centralized server to a P2P network is Napster and its follower file-sharing platforms (e.g. Gnutella, Morpheus and Kazaa.com). The world-wide decentralized structure of Kazaa.com, for example, illustrates that there is no clear leading server or master, in spite of an exponentially increasing number of users. Currently, there is an increasing number of P2P based applications, and market research predicts that P2P infrastructures will increasingly replace client-server architectures.

3 e-Technology

3.1 Hardware

Hardware is the physical part of IT; however, nearly all hardware already includes some kind of software (for instance, a motherboard in a computer). From an IT management perspective, two important hardware issues are compatibility and scalability. The former refers to the possibility of having two pieces of hardware properly working with each other. The latter refers to the possibility and limitations of enlarging a (hardware) system. Most people assume that enlarging the capacity of one computer is simply putting a second one 'beside' the first. This can be less trivial than it may seem, especially for complex IT infrastructures which include a large number

of computers, databases, hubs, switches, routers, etc. Hence, it is crucial that managers have a mid- to long-term vision of the expected capabilities from an IT infrastructure and that they involve IT staff in these planning decisions to avoid compatibility and scalability limitations.

3.2 Software

3.2.1 Operating systems (OS)

An OS is the master software program which is automatically loaded when starting the computer (i.e. during the booting process). The OS controls the applications, i.e. the other programs running on the computer. In particular, it determines in which order applications should run. If the OS supports multi-tasking, then several programs can ran in parallel and the OS determines what share of the processing capacity of the CPU (central processing unit) of the computer each program gets. The OS manages the sharing of memory and handles inputs and outputs from the connected devices (such as scanners, printers and disk drivers). In turn, the applications use the OS to request specific services. Application Program Interfaces (API) enable two-way communications between programs. Users can also directly communicate with the OS (for more details on interfaces, see 3.2.6).

3.2.2 Browsers

A browser is a client program that provides access to all web content on the www. To 'browse' means basically 'to navigate through and read'. A browser works (mainly) on the HTTP (Hypertext Transfer Protocol). The visualization of a web page's content can differ slightly if different browsers are used. The first browser used was Mosaic; then in the mid-1990s Netscape became the first widely used browser before losing out to Microsoft's Internet Explorer. To be able to navigate the Web, a browser needs a 'target' and uses either an IP (Internet Protocol) address or a URL (Unified Resource Locator – see 3.2.4). Given the need for security and special effects of most web pages, today's browsers have built-in security functions and various plug-ins (e.g. for Java applications or Flash animations).

3.2.3 Free, open source and commercial software

As its name suggests, free software is programming capability that is offered free of charge. However, users may not be able to include it in their further application developments unless the free software is also free of copyright (which is, in practice, quite rare). A recent development in this area consists of programs that are basically free, although their programmers ask for donations.

Open source operating systems refer to a piece of software whose code is completely disclosed and can be further developed by anybody. The most widely known example of open source is the Linux operating system.

An alternative to the costs and restrictions of commercial software (such as Microsoft Windows) is a combination of free and/or open software. An example here

is the combination of Linux, the web server Apache, the script language PHP and the database system MySQL to implement dynamic, secure and performing website applications.

3.2.4 Uniform Resource Locator (URL)

A URL is a type of URI (Uniform Resource Identifier); it represents the address of a file or a program, which can be accessed with an Internet browser. A URL (for instance http://www.yourcompany.com/en/welcome.html) is composed of several address parts: the protocol (http), the domain name (yourcompany.com), the path within the domain (/en/welcome) and the programming language (html).

3.2.5 Internet programming languages and protocols

For the Internet, HTML (Hypertext Markup Language) is the most frequently used language to program static content for websites. Although it is quite simple and easy to use, it does not support the dynamic content that most websites require. To overcome this limitation, programmers use PHP (Personal Home Page Tool), ASP (Active Server Pages), JavaScript, Java, JSP (Java Server Pages) or CORBA (Common Object Request Broker Architecture). However, for security reasons, some of these dynamic programming tools (e.g. JavaScript) may not work when firewalls are activated.

XML (eXtensible Markup Language), in combination with a DTD (Document Type Definition), offers a sort of 'common grammar' to interchange data between companies, independent of their respective programs and systems.

Protocols serve as rules for transmitting files and content between two network nodes or addresses. The TCP/IP (Transmission Control Protocol/Internet Protocol) consists of two layers. The higher layer, TCP, takes care of the 'packaging'; i.e. slicing a message into pieces at the sender's side and reassembling them on the receiver's side. The lower layer, IP, manages the address part; i.e. enabling the sending and receiving of the sliced packages, which may be routed differently around the globe.

Other protocols are usually packaged with TCP/IP. The most common ones are HTTP (Hypertext Transfer Protocol) for downloading data and FTP (File Transfer Protocol) for uploading data from a client computer to a server. Security-related protocols and standards are HTTPS/SSL, TLS and SET. e-Mail is also included in the TCP/IP suite, notably SMTP (Simple Mail Transfer Protocol) to send messages, POP3 (Post Office Protocol) to receive messages, and PPTP (Point-to-Point Tunnelling Protocol) to build virtual private networks (see 3.4.6).

3.2.6 Interfaces

Interfaces refer to a physical (hardware) or a logical (software) arrangement which supports the attachment of a device. The latter can either be a user interface or a programming interface. A user interface simply allows the user to communicate and make use of a program; e.g. the Graphical User Interface (GUI). A common application of a user interface is the HBCI (Home Banking Computer Interface). Programming interfaces, on the other hand, provide communication (e.g. data,

functions and statements) between programs or programming languages. Examples of these interfaces include an Application Program Interface (API), a Common Gateway Interface (CGI), Structured Query Language (SQL), and Object-Oriented Database Management System (ODBMS).

3.2.7 Server types, platforms, architectures and infrastructures

A server is a software program that provides services to other programs (see client-server models in 2.2.1). The computer hardware on which a server program runs may also be referred to as Web-, Application-, Proxy-, FTP-, POP3-, SMTP-, Firewall-, DNS- (Domain Name Service), or DB (Data Base)-Server.

A platform is the basis upon which a given architecture is built. It is often determined by a certain type of system; e.g. a UNIX platform. More complex forms of architecture are then called infrastructure, which usually refers to a (sub-) network; e.g. a company's or a division's infrastructure.

3.3 e-Security

e-Security is a crucial factor for the success of e-business and e-commerce, especially in terms of privacy of content and electronic payment. Trusted communications on the Internet require the following four e-security pillars: confidentiality, authentication, integrity and non-repudiation. To achieve e-security, several concepts are used including digital signatures, cryptography, public and private keys, and e-security standards (such as SSL and SET).

3.3.1 Confidentiality

Confidentiality refers to the invisibility of a message to non-authorized parties. Besides physical access protection, the main measures to achieve confidentiality are encryption and digital signatures.

3.3.2 Authentication

Authentication is achieved when a sender can be correctly and uniquely linked to a message or request, i.e. when there is a proof that a person or an entity is, in fact, the party it declares to be. Commonly, this is done through the use of log-on passwords. Yet authentication requires previous identification to validate the password correctness, not the identity of the transmitter, hence the risk of revealed or stolen passwords. In practice, authentication is implemented using mainly PIN/TAN-based systems and digital signatures.

3.3.3 Integrity

Integrity is achieved when the content of a message (e.g. an e-mail message or payment data) is unchanged. It is implemented through the use of digital signatures or cryptographic hash sums, with the latter being able to reveal content changes caused by computer viruses.

3.3.4 Non-repudiation

A message is non-reputable if the signature can be attributed to the signer; i.e. when the sender of a document cannot claim not to have sent a message. Subsequently, non-repudiation has juridical implications. It is an important pre-condition for e-commerce (e.g. when buying and selling goods online or participating in e-auctions). Practical measures to achieve non-repudiation are encryption (with a trusted exchange of keys) and digital signatures.

3.3.5 Digital signature

Digital signatures and cryptography are two means that provide the e-security required for trusted online communication and e-commerce. They guarantee the identity of the sender and – with hash sums – the integrity of content, thus also providing non-repudiation. Digital signatures are easily transportable and hard to imitate.

Digital signatures are not digital certificates. A digital signature can be used with any kind of message, whether it is encrypted or not. The hash sum of a document is a mathematical summary which can be calculated with special software. The hash value and the signature are sent to the receiver through two separate transmissions. The verification can only be carried out with an identical key; i.e. the public key of the sender. The hash is usually time-stamped and thus different for every use. The encrypted hash becomes a digital signature. Obviously, the hash sum of the original document and the decrypted message must be identical.

3.3.6 Cryptography, private key and public key

There are differences which have to be understood in order to make a management decision regarding the weights of security level, complexity, feasibility, time and user-friendliness – and hence the what, when and how – of encryption. The two basic modes of encryption are symmetric and asymmetric encryption.

Symmetric encryption works with only one secret key, which serves on the one hand to encrypt the plain text at the sender's side (in order to create a cipher text to be sent, for example through the Internet) and on the other hand to decrypt the cipher text back into plain text at the receiver's side. The advantage of symmetric encryption is the relatively quick calculation for the conversion. The disadvantage is the problem of a trust worthy exchange of the secret key.

Asymmetric encryption makes use of two different keys from both parties. A private key is only possessed by the owner, whereas the public key can be used by third parties. Hence, the asymmetric encryption works by using one's private key in combination with the public key of the other party – on the sender's side as well as on the receiver's side. The major advantage of asymmetric encryption is that the private key is only known by the owner and there is no risk related to the exchange of a secret key. However, the major disadvantage is the time-consuming calculation of algorithms.

3.3.7 Key management, signature, certificate and PKI

A satisfactory management of security keys can be enforced by a 'trusted third party' or a 'web of trust'. The latter makes use of combined 'triangle relations': if, for example, party Y does not trust party X, but party Z trusts party X and party Y trusts party Z,

then party Y may well trust party X. With an increasing number of such parties, a web is built up. A well known 'web of trust' is the PGP (pretty good privacy), which can be set up between the employees of a company.

The 'trusted third party' model (which is similar to the 'web of trust') has gained increasing importance. In this case, a reputable third party (i.e. the trust centre) issues certificates to a large number of parties which do not trust each other (or which do not know each other). The trust centre (examples are Verisign and Identrus) makes keys and signatures available, thus setting up a public key infrastructure (PKI).

A trusted third-party issues digital signatures and digital certificates. The latter include, besides the digital signature, an identified user and a key, thus guaranteeing the authenticity of the signature. Furthermore, the digital certificate contains the digital signature of the certificate-issuing authority itself. To some extent, a digital certificate file can be regarded as a digital wallet or an online credit card, with the expiration date of the public key replacing the expiration date of a physical card. In practice, PKIs include the following components: security guideline, certificate instance, registration instance, index service for certificates and applications which can deal with PKIs. Parties involved in PKI include application developers, PKI hosting partners, smart-card producers and Internet service providers.

3.3.8 Smart-cards and biometrics

Smart-cards are plastic cards with a small chip on them. They are used in various ways and provide a higher level of security than password-based systems, although the level provided by PKI cannot be fully matched. Using smart-card-based log-in (via a computer) provides additional security because a potential abuser would have to get hold of the smart-card (device). A common application is Internet banking.

The use of biological data for IT security is referred to as biometrics; it currently provides the highest level of security. Such biological data can be obtained, for instance, from fingerprints and hand characteristics, the voice, the eye or from entire facial patterns. This sort of security system can only work if two conditions are fulfilled. First, there is a way to capture and convert the biological features into digital data. Second, this data is stored and available at the point of data comparison for authentication. An emerging standard, called BioAPI, supports the necessary interactions between different biometrics software systems.

Smart-cards and biometrics can be combined by putting biometric data on the chip-based cards. A user would then have a smart-card containing their biometric data, which can be matched at the point of authentication with the biometric data measured on the spot. However, a concern in using biometrics is data privacy. One way to alleviate this problem is to encrypt the data captured and then immediately delete the original data.

3.3.9 Secure Socket Layer (SSL) and Transport Layer Security (TLS)

SSL makes use of public and private key encryption systems, including a digital signature, and uses a program layer between the HTTP and the TCP (layer 5 of the OSI model). Although originally developed by Netscape, SSL became the de facto standard for secured data interchange on the Internet, built not only into the Netscape Navigator but also into Microsoft's Internet Explorer, other browsers, as well as most

web servers and client-server applications. The HTTPS protocol uses SSL as a sub-layer to the 'normal' HTTP in order to build up a secure channel for data transmission. Although SSL users understand TLS messages, the two technologies are not fully interoperable.

TLS consists of two layers. First, there is the TLS Record Protocol, providing connection security, usually with an encryption method. Second, there is the TLS Handshake Protocol, which allows authentication as well as negotiation of encryption. TLS has widely taken over the de facto standard role of SSL.

3.3.10 Secure electronic transaction (SET)

In comparison to SSL and TLS, SET is a specialized system for financial transactions. It not only makes use of Netscape's SSL, but also of Microsoft's STT (Secure Transaction Technology) and S-HTTP (Terisa System's Secure Hypertext Transfer Protocol). However, SET makes use of only some aspects of PKI. Usually, there are three major parties involved in a SET transaction: a buyer, a seller and a bank. A very practical example of how SET works is the following.[1]

Assume that a customer has an SET-enabled browser and that the transaction provider (e.g. a bank or a merchant) has an SET-enabled server:

- The customer opens a Mastercard or Visa bank account.
- The customer receives a digital certificate. This electronic file functions as a credit card for online purchases or other transactions and includes a public key with an expiration date.
- Third-party merchants also receive certificates from the bank. These certificates include the merchant's public key and the bank's public key.
- The customer places an order over a web page, by phone, or through other means.
- The customer's browser receives the merchant's certificate confirming that the merchant is valid.
- The browser sends the order information. This message is encrypted with the merchant's public key, the payment information that is encrypted with the bank's public key (which cannot be read by the merchant), and information that ensures the payment can only be used with this specific order.
- The merchant verifies the customer's authenticity by checking the digital signature on the customer's certificate. This may be done by referring the certificate to the bank or to a third-party verifier.
- The merchant sends the order message along to the bank. This includes the bank's public key, the customer's payment information (which the merchant cannot decode), and the merchant's certificate.
- The bank verifies the merchant's authenticity and the message. The bank uses the digital signature on the certificate with the message and verifies the payment part of the message.
- The bank digitally signs and sends authorization to the merchant, who can then fulfil the order.

---

1 www.whatis.com, 14 April 2003.

The major advantage of SET over existing security systems is the addition of digital certificates that associate the cardholder and merchant with their financial institutions and the respective SET payment brands.

3.3.11 Portable Document Format (PDF)

An indirect but practical aspect of e-security, in particular for data integrity, is the use of PDF files. In comparison to standard word-processed documents, PDF files cannot be changed. However, they offer a similar range of functionalities to that of other Microsoft Word documents; i.e. search functions or the possibility to copy text or graphs. PDF files have become widely used when exchanging documents such as contracts or bidding offers.

3.3.12 Protection

A company can protect its infrastructure with a range of software. This software includes firewalls (which are often installed on separate hardware), routers (hardware-based) and intrusion detection software. The latter not only supervises the system but can also provide active defence on (potential) attacks.

3.4 Networks

3.4.1 What is a network?

A network is made up of interconnected nodes. Networks are often clustered or grouped, have hierarchical structures and may interchange data. The basic configuration of node interconnectivity is referred to as topology; the most common ones are 'bus' and 'token ring' topologies. Networks can be classified by the data transmission technology (e.g. TCP/IP), by signal carriage (data or voice), by users (private or public), by spatial distance, or by other characteristics. The classification below is based on the spatial distance criterion.

3.4.2 Local area network (LAN)

LANs consist of a closed group of computers and associated devices which are usually related to central resources such as servers or databases. A LAN may include just a few associated users or it may involve all users of a large organization. In both cases, it covers a limited geographic ('local') area such as, for example, an office complex. The most widely installed LAN technology is Ethernet, which typically uses coaxial cable or special grades of twisted pair wires. A common Ethernet system is called 10BASE-T (providing data transmission speeds of up to 10 Mbps). Its devices are directly connected to the cable and compete for access using the Carrier Sense Multiple Access with Collision Detection (CSMA/CD) protocol.

3.4.3 Wide area network (WAN)

If a LAN is geographically wide, it is referred to as a WAN. WANs typically use the public telecommunication infrastructure. A common example of a WAN is when linking field workers and/or geographically dispersed corporate sites.

3.4.4 Metropolitan area network (MAN) and campus network

In terms of its geographical coverage, a MAN is an intermediate form of the two network types described above. The term MAN refers to the interconnecting of (through backbone lines) different networks within a city into a single larger network. An example of a MAN is a university's network (also referred to as a campus network).

3.4.5 Storage area network (SAN)

A SAN is typically part of an overall corporate network, serving a special purpose inside the firm. It is usually designed to inter-connect different data storage devices, offering users within the larger network high-speed access to data.

3.4.6 Virtual private network (VPN)

A VPN is a private data network that uses the public telecommunication infrastructure. Companies use a VPN, for instance, for extranets and wide-area intranets. A common example is field workers remotely connecting their portable computers (through public telephone lines) to their company's intranet. In order to save the high costs of private communication lines, companies also use a VPN to inter-link their different locations. Basically, a VPN is built up by connecting two or more computers and laying a secure 'tunnel' over this connection, thus resulting in a quasi-private (virtual) company network. The privacy is obtained by encrypting data before sending it off. The protocol used to transmit the data is the Point-to-Point Tunnelling Protocol (PPTP). At the other end of the tunnel, the data is decrypted. To make this transmission even more secure, the sender's and recipient's network addresses are also often encrypted. Usually companies integrate VPN software into their firewall servers.

The latest developments are multi-protocol-label-switching VPNs. Such MPLS-VPNs combine independently the advantages of common layer-2-based VPNs (bandwidth and run time guarantee) with additional IP address information.

3.5 Applications

3.5.1 e-Information

The display of information on a website is one of the most basic uses of e-technology. It can formally be separated into static and dynamic content display, with the latter being triggered either as push (company-wise) or pull (by the user). The electronic exchange of information between trading parties has been used for over two decades through electronic data interchange (EDI) technology, which is actually older than the commercial Internet. Depending on the nature of the data involved, EDI is increasingly being replaced by XML (see 3.2.5).

3.5.2 e-Mail

The exchange of electronic text messages was one of the first broadly spread uses of the Internet. Today e-mail is used more than ever before, thus representing a

significant share of Internet traffic. The advantages of e-mail over physical mail include speed of transmission, possibly multiple recipients of the same message, further processing, as well as indexing and archiving. Furthermore, attachments to an e-mail message could include any information type, from images to sound and video. Besides traditional messaging, there is instant messaging, which is the quasi real-time transmission (through Internet relay chat, or IRC) of messages between two or more parties connected to the Internet. The main drawbacks of e-mail are spamming, pri vate use at work and computer viruses.

3.5.3 e-Telephony, Voice Over Internet Protocol (VoIP) and computer-telephony integration (CTI)

e-telephony (or IP-telephony) is the use of the Internet to make voice calls and send faxes or video-sequences. From a business viewpoint, it can significantly cut costs, as these are reduced to local Internet access costs even if calls are made world-wide. Computer-based telephony uses standard components (usually Ethernet with an interface to the Web) and specialized software.

An e-telephony standard is Voice Over Internet Protocol (VoIP), which uses the Real-Time Protocol (RTP) to deliver sufficient quality; i.e. time-consistency. The latter is important as the voice data is cut into discrete (digital) packages which must arrive on time and be reassembled. Related to the above concept is computer-telephony integration (CTI), which manages telephone calls with computers. It is commonly used in call centres where calls can be routed to the 'right' agent, who then automatically receives the customer's data history on their computer screen.

3.5.4 e-Portals

An e-portal is a website that serves as a door to a wider range of other websites and services. Usually such websites are quick-loading and text-rich, and are often used as an anchor or 'boot' site (e.g. Yahoo!). Most portals offer a set of similar core features, such as the provision of short news articles, online weather, financial tickers on shares and currencies, an e-mail service, a chat forum, a search engine, a lifestyle section and some 'special offers'. It is also very common for e-portals to have large public sections and a premium area with a personal log-on. Most e-portals can be customized in terms of the overall content structure and also advertising.

3.5.5 e-Marketplaces

An e-marketplace is a virtual space where several (potential) buyers and sellers interact with each other online. It involves the following players to complete a transaction from the initial stage to the settlement: a host, an access provider, a content provider, a bank for clearing and settlement, and (horizontally or vertically-oriented) buyers and sellers.

3.5.6 e-Customer relationship management (e-CRM)

e-CRM aims to help a company manage the relationships with its customers in an organized manner. The use of IT-based CRM-tools enables a company not only to store customer data electronically and more systematically, but also to collect it and aggregate it meaningfully, and make it quickly available to all relevant people (including marketing and sales staff as well as call centre agents).

Although just seen initially as a means to make customer data processing more efficient and transparent – often only using a (CRM-) database – CRM has become a strategic enabler, which is at the heart of business models in various industries, for instance at Dell,[2] Amazon.com,[3] or Advance Bank.[4] At these companies, CRM plays a key role in implementing a mass-customization model based on treating each customer as a 'segment of one'.

Practically, there are proprietary as well as standard e-CRM products, often integrated into ERP systems (see 3.5.7) and/or combined with data-mining tools (see 3.5.9). Depending on the definition of 'customer', CRM is sometimes referred to with other labels such as SRM (supplier relationship management), which is frequently used in the logistics field.

The quality of the captured data is a pre-condition for successfully leveraging this data. Websites can be used as an important source for electronic data collection. Cookies – or whole cookie streams – are used to make up a 'picture' of a user. Basically, a cookie is information which a website (or server) places on the hard disk of the user's (or client's) computer in order to be able to access this information at a later date. This is necessary, as a server has no 'memory'; i.e. each HTTP request is identical from the server's point of view. The value added for the customer provided by cookies can range from faster websites over saved personal preferences to completely customized website layouts. Yet, as stated above, a company may also use the cookie data from its website users in order to fill up its e-CRM database and to leverage the resulting 'picture' of the customer.

For instance, if a customer of Amazon.fr browses or buys mainly IT books in English, Amazon.fr can adapt the personalized website for this customer by making appropriate offers on the welcome screen; for example regarding the most recently published IT books in English rather than offers on DVDs, games or French novels. The problem of most media, including the Internet, is that 'the' customer is often a – heterogeneous – group rather than one person. Usually, several people share a computer; e.g. a four-member family interested in classical music, video games, novels or comic DVDs. User-specific log-on might solve this problem, yet from a practical point of view this is not always applicable. This is where m-CRM comes to play an important role since wireless devices are much more personal than computers (see 4.2.2).

---

2 M. Porter and Rivkin, J. 'Matching Dell', *Harvard Business Review*, 1999.

3 See the case study 'Fighting over the Internet: the virtual battle between Amazon.com (USA) and BOL.de (Germany)' – in Part 4 of this book.

4 See the case study 'Banking on the Internet: the Advance Bank in Germany' in Part 4 of this book.

3.5.7 Enterprise resource planning (ERP)

ERP is an integration of several software applications, including (relational) databases. It can therefore be best described as a multi-module application or pre-integrated suit. Some of the basic ideas behind ERP are the better integration of organisation, communication and infrastructure and the reduction of costs for integration and ownership by not using various software companies' module applications. Classic ERP systems comprise modules for operations (e.g. purchasing, order tracking, inventory management and supplier management) and corporate services. A finance and human resource module is frequently offered as an add-on. Increasingly, ERP systems also offer pre-integrated CRM systems. The introduction of an ERP system has a significant impact not only on IT but usually also on the core business processes of a firm. Often, the introduction of ERP is in some way linked to a business process re-engineering. Due to their high costs, ERP systems have so far been largely a matter for bigger companies. However, ERP providers (including the open-source Linux) have been increasingly targeting small and medium-sized enterprises.

3.5.8 e-Supply chain management (e-SCM)

e-SCM aims at managing a company's flow of products and information to reduce inventory and delivery time, while ensuring a high level of availability. It impacts the whole supply chain, from sourcing (upstream) to in-house value creation, to distributors and buyers (downstream). However, the most significant information flow uses the opposite direction; i.e. from the point of sale back to the point of sourcing. State-of-the-art SCM solutions cross the traditional boundaries of the firm; i.e. information and product flow along the supply chain is integrated among different companies. Such integration provides a supplier, for example, with real-time information on stock and sales data of, say, a supermarket retail chain, thus enabling the supplier to make further deliveries without receiving an explicit order from the retail chain. ERP systems usually provide a foundation for building SCM solutions.

3.5.9 Data mining

Data mining goes beyond searching for particular data sets within a database. The objective of data mining is to reveal new and unknown patterns as well as correlations of data hidden in existing databases. This information is often of high value to a company, allowing it to predict outcomes or customer behaviour. Subsequently, this data allows the company pro actively to shape its products and markets rather than reactively respond to customer behaviour.

3.5.10 e-Content management system (e-CMS)

The purpose of a CMS is to manage a company's content on a website. A CMS allows employees, who are not familiar with any kind of programming, to publish and modify the website content. The company can provide a set of standard format templates for the authors to use, thus facilitating corporate design and corporate identity.

A CMS basically consists of two parts. The first is content management application (CMA), which facilitates the content treatment by the employee. The second is content delivery application (CDA), which provides the control and display of the data. Common CMSs also have integrated search functions. Even so, they provide an archive mechanism which tracks the history of content as well as information on who made which change of content at what point of time. This information is not only useful, but may for some businesses/countries be a legal requirement. Principally, a CMS can include documents, images, audio and videos. Obviously, each element adds some complexity, as does the CMS-based management of a website with various languages.

In combination with cookies and click-stream analysis, a CMS can be used to customize the content of the website for individuals and thus allow web-based one-to-one marketing.

3.5.11 Integrated services digital network (ISDN) and digital subscriber line (DSL)

ISDN is an Internet connection service that provides data transmission of up to 128 Kbps. Data transmission can be based on common copper phone lines or other media, as long as the user has an ISDN adapter instead of a modem. ISDN integrates analogue voice data and digital data within one network. It works with two types of channel, a B-channel which carries the data, and a D-channel, which carries the control and signalling information. The 128 Kbps are obtained through the use of two 64 Kbps B-channels in parallel.

Although ISDN offers higher speed than traditional analogue data transmission, DSL can further improve this speed, typically between 512 Kbps and 1024 Kbps (downstream), and theoretically even up to more than 6 Mbps. This enables the quasi real-time transmission of high-quality multimedia applications, e.g. video streams. xDSL refers to various forms of DSL; e.g. ADSL. A pre-condition for the use of DSL, however, is that the telephone line provider offers this service, necessitating a DSL service hub in relative proximity to the users. DSL offers, similar to ISDN, the transmission of analogue and digital signals, with the digital data part being permanently connected.

4 Wireless technology

Unlike e-technology, wireless technology is based on the use of mobile devices (such as cell phones, hand-held computers, and personal digital assistants) and wireless communication networks. Its main advantages lie in its ability to offer personalization and ubiquity. The former enables establishing a one-to-one relationship, while the latter is based on location sensitivity as well as temporal and geographical reach. Wireless technology therefore truly offers 'anytime' and 'anywhere' connectivity.

First, this section offers a comprehensive overage of m-technology, from both a hardware and software perspectives. It then provides illustrative examples of m-commerce and m-business applications.

4.1 m-Technology

4.1.1 Subscriber identity module (SIM)-cards

SIM-cards are a special kind of smart-card developed for mobile communication. They have an integrated micro-processor, enabling the processing and storage of data. With their input and output ports, as well as their compatibility with (embedded) Java, SIM-cards can be regarded as small computers. The main difference between SIM-cards and the bulk of smart-cards is that SIM-cards do not only carry data, but also the means to process this data.

Initially, SIM-cards were developed in conjunction with the GSM standard (see 4.1.3) and they served to store network information and access data. Due to improvements in SIM-cards' storage and processing capacity, further applications became possible. For example, SIM-cards serve today to authenticate a user (key and certificate storage), to encrypt data, to make international roaming possible and to customize services (e.g. storage of bookmarks and preferences).

4.1.2 Bandwidth and wireless networks

Bandwidth

Bandwidth refers to the data transmission rate, which is a measure for the speed of data flow (digital signals). Usually, the data transmission rate is measured in Kbps (kilobits per second) or in Mbps (megabits per second). Technically, bandwidth refers to analogue signals and the width of the frequency range of the electronic signals (between the lowest and the highest). It is determined by the number of cycle changes per second, usually measured in kHz (Kilohertz) or MHz (Megahertz). Today, bandwidth is a major bottleneck for the further development of m-business and m-commerce.

Wireless local area networks (WLAN)

Similar to the fixed-line LAN, explained in 3.4.2, a LAN may also work on a wireless basis. A WLAN must meet high-capacity, short-distance coverage, full connectivity and broadcast capabilities. The determining factors are therefore power, bandwidth and interconnectivity. The most widely spread standards are currently Bluetooth and WiFi, and, in the near future, probably UWB (see 4.1.3).

WLAN applications are not restricted to connections of fixed-line computers, mobile phones and handheld devices, but include all kinds of remotely controlled and wirelessly communicating devices. Examples of the latter include household devices as well as the recently developed robots of Honda ('ASIMO') and Sony ('SDRX4'), where all external communication of the robots takes place within WLANs.

Wireless wide area network (WWAN)

Beyond the reach of WLANs, wireless WANs (WWANs) represent the network for mobile communication, which is used, for example, by cell phones. Currently the WWAN's standard is in a transition from 2G (second generation) to 2.5G and 3G (UMTS). The latter offers a data transaction speed of up to 2 Mbps under stationary

conditions. Current WWANs make use of 2.4 and 5.7 GHz frequency ranges, with the 2.4 GHz usually being used by commercial applications and 5.7 GHz used by private and military applications. Within the next ten years, 4G technology is expected to be introduced, offering a maximum speed of 100 Mbps. It will operate on 'IPv6'; i.e. every WWAN node will have an IP address.

4.1.3 Network technologies

The major bottleneck in the development of the mobile internet has been the limited bandwidth and hence the long transmission time for rich applications and services. Starting from analogue transmission, the bandwidth could be increased step by step with the evolution of GSM, HSCSD, GPRS, EDGE and lately UMTS / 3G. Accordingly, applications and services have become richer, evolving from pure voice transmission to multimedia exchange.

Global System for Mobile Communication (GSM)

GSM is a digital circuit-switching system based on a time-division multiple access (TDMA) frame structure. It charges users on a 'pay-for-connection-time' basis. Data is compressed before it is transmitted as one of three separate data streams (with the remaining two containing user data). These data streams are transmitted in different time slots. GSM uses two frequencies for data transmission, 900 or 1800 MHz. Although it is hardly used in the USA where the standard is code division multiple access (CDMA), the GSM standard is very common in Europe and Asia. The number of users has led to a relatively broad range of applications, yet the limited data transfer rate of the 2G network (9.6 to 14.4 Kbps) has, until recently, prevented a real breakthrough. The fact that the GSM has hardly penetrated the US market made it difficult to use common GSM-based mobile devices there. The so-called tri-band cell phones overcome this standardization problem.

High-Speed Circuit-Switched Data (HSCSD)

HSCSD is not a different technology. It is based on GSM and uses four channels in parallel, thus achieving transmission rates of 38.4 to 57.6 Kbps. HSCSD is referred to as part of the 2.5G network. A major problem for applications is the relatively long set-up time of more than half a minute. Hence, HSCSD represents only an interim step between GSM and GPRS (see below), with the prevailing application being wireless e-mail access.

General Packet Radio Service (GPRS)

GPRS also works on the GSM network. However, compared to the GSM circuit-switching technology, GPRS supports IP to enable a data packet-based technology, making it a 'pay-for-data' system. This means that the connection is quasi always on and the user is only charged for the transmitted data packets. Therefore, GPRS does not require set-up time, nor middleware; two factors which so far have slowed down the speed of applications for wireless systems. GPRS provides data transmission rates of between 56 and 114 Kbps. In addition to the IP, GPRS also supports X.25, a common European packet-based protocol. Thus, GPRS is an important technological step towards full mobile Internet access.

Enhanced Data GSM Environment (EDGE)

EDGE enables data transfer rates of up to 384 Kbps (the average is below 200 Kbps). Technologically, it uses the existing time-division-based GSM standard by combining eight channels in parallel. EDGE is a broadband alternative for those European telecommunication operators that did not obtain a UMTS / 3G licence; it is considered to be at the upper limit of the so-called 2.5G network.

Universal Mobile Telephone System (UMTS)

Like GPRS, UMTS is based on the data-packet switching mode. The terms UMTS and 3G (third generation) are, in practice, often used interchangeably. UMTS is a global network standard, allowing the use of only one mobile device anywhere in the world. Physically, transmission is enabled through a combination of terrestrial and wireless and satellite systems. The bandwidth transmission rate ranges from 384 Kbps up to 2 Mbps, thus enabling more multimedia applications than ever before, including mobile video-conferencing or remote interactive mobile games. In the 3G field, Japan is currently the leading country, in terms of the number of 3G users (reach), richness (quantity of information) and range of applications and services offered. During the technological transition period, some mobile devices offer a multi-mode system that enables switching from a previous technology to UMTS.

Bluetooth, Wireless Fidelity (Wi-Fi) and Ultra-Wide-Band (UWB)

Bluetooth is a short-range wireless standard for the interconnection of various devices, such as computers, mobile phones and PDAs. The maximum range is about 10 metres. Connection requires a transceiver chip on each device, and transactions can be made either P2P or multi-point. The technology enables sending, receiving and replicating data and voice (via up to three parallel voice channels). A frequency of around 2.5 GHz (varying to some extent from country to country) enables data transmission at a speed of 1–2 Mbps (the latter is offered by the 2G network). Bluetooth is important when it comes to the convergence of e- and m-technology. From a security point of view, Bluetooth provides encryption and verification.

The high-frequency WLAN Wi-Fi offers a data transmission speed of more than 10 Mbps (even more than 50 Mbps for IEEE[5] 802.11a). Yet the trade-off is the required power supply. In contrast to Bluetooth, which is the low-power option, Wi-Fi cannot be used for battery-powered devices. It uses the Ethernet protocol and CSMA/CA (carrier sense multiple access with collision avoidance).

UWB offers the combined benefits of Bluetooth and Wi-Fi; i.e., it provides high data transmission speed at low power. UWB is a frequency-jumping technique, which can be applied to any base frequency. Within the next ten years, it is expected to provide a data transmission speed of up to 100 Mbps, thus providing a network technology for any multimedia application. Furthermore, given its frequency hops in the range of nano-seconds, UWB is more secure than other technologies.

4.1.4 Service technologies

In the subsequent sub-sections we want to assess the service technologies in a broader sense, i.e. the transport-bearing technologies for applications and services.

5 Institute of Electrical and Electronics Engineers.

Short Message Service (SMS), Enhanced Messaging Service (EMS) and Multimedia Message Service (MMS)

SMS allows the sending of P2P text messages as a push (similar to pagers). Messages usually contain up to 160 characters.[6] In order to avoid the problem of inconvenient typing (e.g. pressing the key '9' four times in order to print a 'z'), most handset producers have developed a built-in intelligent application which 'guesses' the words according to the sequence of pressed keys. In addition to mobile phones or handhelds, SMS can also be sent from websites with an SMS gateway. SMS only requires the GSM standard (but works on more advanced ones).

EMS is very similar to SMS, but allows richer services, e.g. formatted text in order to produce italics or bold letters.

MMS offers capabilities beyond those of SMS and EMS. It enables transmitting multimedia data like images, photos, video-clips or mobile video-conferencing.

Cell broadcast (CB)

The difference between CB and SMS is the number of connections set up in parallel. Whereas SMS is a pure P2P or one-to-one service, CB provides the possibility for one-to-many broadcasting, i.e. the mass-distribution of mobile messages. The most common example are messages sent by network operators to roaming users when crossing a border. CB is also important for various push-services and mobile marketing (for privacy reasons the message receiver has to subscribe explicitly to such services).

Unstructured Supplementary Service Data (USSD)

USSD is similar to SMS. However, unlike the offline-service SMS, USSD is an online service which only works as long as an opened session is not ended. This GSM-based technology is important with respect to applications that require real-time data interchange and confirmation, notably m-brokerage or m-payment (see 4.2.2). USSD is supported by SAT and WAP.

SIM Application Toolkit (SAT)

SAT provides a standardized execution environment for applications stored on the SIM-card. It also permits users to download and write on SIM-cards via SMS or cell broadcast. SAT uses asymmetric encryption – with the private key stored on the SIM-card – and is therefore very important for m-security (see 4.1.6). SAT allows the updating of existing mobile devices in order to make them usable for new applications, e.g. e-banking. Also, SAT permits writing and storing whole applications on the SIM-card (thus turning the mobile device into a fat client). Initially SAT was only seen as a short-term intermediate solution with various limitations, such as the problem of incompatibility with certain devices using proprietary software.

Wireless Application Protocol (WAP)

WAP works on top of standard data-link protocols such as GSM. WAP is an open standard which specifies communication protocols and which supports GPRS. Therefore, it opens, technologically, the way for mobile devices to use applications such as e-mail. Although WAP overcomes the problem of incompatibilities due to the proprietary solutions of various manufacturers, it is not without its drawbacks,

6 Or up to 224 when run in a 5-bit mode.

primarily concerning convenience, due mainly to limited screens (in size, resolution and colour) and data transmission rates.

Compact Hypertext Markup Language (c-HTML)

c-HTML is a smaller and compacter version of HTML. Applications based on c-HTML are faster than those based on the open WAP standard and offer direct access to HTML-programmed fixed line Internet sites. The c-HTML-based system widely used is currently NTT DoCoMo's i-mode (see the case study in Part 4 of this book), which holds a significant market share in Japan and is increasingly penetrating other markets, especially in Europe.

Mobile station application Execution Environment (MExE)

Like WAP, MExE is designed as a standard, working on networks from GSM to GPRS to UMTS. However, unlike WAP, MExE allows full application programming based on Java, requiring a JVM (Java Virtual Machine) to be stored on the mobile device. This enables users, for instance, to upload and download applications from and on to their mobile devices. Furthermore, MExE supports a wide range of person–machine interfaces, such as voice recognition. Through the storage of richer data and applications on the SIM-card, mobile devices become 'thick clients', requiring considerable storage capacity and significant processing resources, offered only by the latest mobile devices. A fundamental paradigm shift triggered by MExE is the need for comprehensive security solutions, similar to those on computers linked to the fixed line Internet, in order to prevent unauthorized remote data access.

4.1.5 Location technologies

Global Positioning System (GPS)

To make GPS work, there are 24 satellites in the orbit, roughly 17 km above the Earth. These GPS satellites are spaced in such a way that any point of the Earth's surface is covered by an 'umbrella' of four such satellites. The geographic position (longitude and latitude) can be determined by three of these satellites, and, with the help of the fourth, the altitude can also be obtained. Technically, it is possible to determine the exact position with an accuracy of just one metre, but for non-military applications this accuracy is 'diluted' to about 10 metres. By adding a set of measurements over time, GPS may not only determine the position, but also the direction and speed. Important commercial applications are the use of tracking systems within integrated supply chains, e.g. for parcel services. Also, car manufacturers have developed systems which create considerable value-added for car drivers (e.g. security issues) and manufacturers (e.g. after-sale data collection of user and product data). There is also a huge potential for mobile marketing, as the real-time location information enables the move from a broad customization to highly personalized one-to-one marketing.

Time of arrival (TOA), angle of arrival (AOA) and enhanced observed time difference (E-OTD)

TOA and AOA determine positioning based on triangulation, whereas E-OTD makes use of surrounding base stations. The latter calculates the position by evaluating the time differences of signals from the base stations to the mobile device. All three location technologies are currently lagging behind the development of GPS.

4.1.6 m-Security

Like e-security, m-security has four basic pillars: confidentiality, authentication, integrity and non-repudiation. Yet one must bear in mind that m-security comprises two different 'locations' of security: first, the security regarding the wireless network from a mobile device (e.g. a cell phone) to a gateway or network provider, and second, via the fixed-line Internet further to web-servers. GSM, for instance, refers only to the in-the-air security. Moreover, issues of digital signature, cryptography, private and public key certificates, as well as PKI, play a similar role for m-security as they do for e-security.

Smart-cards are of much more practical use for m-security than they are for e-security since in most cases they are already embedded in the device anyway. The SAT, which defines the communication interface between input/output devices like cell phones and the SIM-card, makes the GSM standard more secure by providing end-to-end security (through asymmetric encryption) instead of in-the-air-only security. TSL (and hence SSL) has its equivalent in WTLS (wireless transport layer security), which builds up a secure m-channel. SET, however, not yet has a comparable standard based on mobile technology.

In addition to the two 'locations' of security mentioned above, there is the nature of mobile communication which makes specific security protection necessary, particularly with possible unauthorized remote access on user data with technologies such as MExE. The latter turns the mobile device into a computer-like upload and download-enabled processing unit. A Wi-Fi WLAN for instance can be quite susceptible to unauthorized access. Mobile VPN (see 3.4.6) or WEP (Wired Equivalent Privacy) are therefore highly recommended when using WLAN within a corporation.

Despite all difficulties and particularities, m-security also offers business opportunities. Paybox.net, for instance, intended to replace credit card payments with a safer, m-technology based payment procedure.

4.1.7 Programming languages and protocols

This section does not intend to cover the vast range of programming languages, protocols and standards for wireless technology, although some have already been discussed in 4.1.4 on service technologies.

WML (Wireless Markup Language) is the equivalent to HTML. It is part of WAP and enables mobile devices to display the text content of Internet websites through wireless access. However, an important evolution is VoiceXML, which was initially mainly used to develop applications for the visually impaired but has now gained a broader interest with advances in wireless technology. VoiceXML serves the so-called 'acoustic web' in making XML structured data (see 3.2.5) not only available for the fixed line web, but also for wireless mobile devices, i.e. software developers may write audio applications with a standardized programming language. Practically, this means that text can be converted into audio language and, as such, it can be sent to a server or a mobile phone. Thus, VoiceXML enables the programming of dialogues between people and machines via menus and forms.

4.2 Devices and applications

4.2.1 Devices

Mobile phones are usually the first item thought of in the context of mobile technology devices. Their use has developed from pure voice transmission to text messages and ultimately, to multimedia transmission – including the capturing of digital photos. Computers are commonly associated with the fixed-line technology. However, wireless cards have turned them into a part of the mobile network.

Another group of devices are personal digital assistants (PDAs), characterized by their small size and integrated services such as phone book, time planner, notes manager and calculator. Recent PDA versions offer e-mail and Internet access as well as word processing and more sophisticated computation programs. Given the PDA's physical size limitation, there are several input possibilities, reaching from cell-phone-like keys to extensible computer-like keyboards, to handwriting recognition, and, to some extent, voice recognition.

Dual SIM adapters are a means to put two SIM-cards into one physical device. The cards are alternatively served by round robin; i.e. by switching the device (usually a cell phone) off and on again, the other card is activated.

4.2.2 Applications and services

Voice, text, pictures and movies

Basically, there are two different message types which offer various features. Voice, text, pictures and movies form the main underlying message types. The required network and service technologies have been discussed in the previous sections of this appendix. Similar to the message types, there are different application types, mainly comprising conversation, information, location, commercial transactions, payment, entertainment, advertising and marketing.

The combination of information and location offers a business opportunity which has so far only taken off on a broad basis in Japan, probably because in Europe and the USA the 'chicken-and-egg-problem' is prevalent; i.e. service providers require a broad existing customer base before offering a service and customers demand a large service offering before joining in. Technologically, the information provision (pushed or pulled) is triggered by the location service; i.e. customers can, for instance, ask for a list of restaurants within walking distance of where they are physically located at that moment. Obviously, this combination is closely linked to (location-based) advertising and commercial transactions. However, advertising and marketing can be independent of location sensitivity and based rather on the much higher personalization and temporal reach of mobile devices compared to that of fixed-line computers. An important limitation in this context is, however, data privacy.

The development of mobile entertainment is gaining more and more momentum. This boost is associated with improvements in bandwidth, colour, battery power, local memory and processing capacity, which are about to surpass a required minimum these days.

m-Shopping, m-payment, m-infomediaries

Due to the current limitations of wireless technology, such as the display size of the mobile device and the limited bandwidth, m-shopping cannot match the capabilities

offered by e-shopping. However, m-payment for physical shopping, whereby the customer pays for physical goods or services via the mobile device, is attracting more and more users (see the paybox.net case study in Part 4 of this book). Such payment systems are partly WLAN- and WWAN-based, and some of them use infra-red data transmission from the (chip of the) mobile device. However, no commonly accepted standard for m-payment has evolved so far. Yet there is a strong need for m-security and the use of passwords must be accompanied by a PKI infrastructure encryption. A particular m-payment which is worth mentioning here is the pre-paid (e- or m-) purse where money is stored on the mobile device and anonymously transferred at the point of sale. This system also offers the advantage of being faster and cheaper than other systems such as credit-card-based payments.

The mobile network seems to follow the development of the fixed-line Internet with respect to the opportunities offered for infomediaries. The latter build their entire business model on the provision of information as an intermediary stakeholder in the value chain between seller and buyer. The 12Snap case study (contained in Part 4 of this book) is an example of an m-infomediary which is focused on mobile marketing.

m-Banking and m-brokerage

m-Banking (push or pull information and transactions, such as remittances) as well as m-brokerage (trading of shares and the like) were probably the first mobile applications which gained relatively broad acceptance. As in the case of e-banking and e-brokerage, the main business drivers were (and still are) the high personal dimension in banking as well as the not so convenient opening hours of most bricks-and-mortar banks. In particular, with respect to m-brokerage, the time value of information can be crucial, as is m-security for m-banking and m-brokerage. Beyond these similarities to e-technology, it is obvious that the mobile technology offers on the one hand the advantage of real mobility and built-in smart-cards, but on the other hand the disadvantage of (still) very limited comfort regarding display, input and speed. A technological precondition for the development of m-banking was SAT, allowing the writing of data on to a mobile device. The online service USSD provides a technology that automatically ends a (not terminated) process once the session is interrupted (see 4.1.4).

Mobile customer relationship management (m-CRM)

Compared to e-CRM, m-CRM offers higher personalization, localization sensitivity as well as geographical and timely reach.

Since a cell phone is highly personalized (see 4.1.1 on SIM-cards), the data collected and presented through the mobile channel has a significantly higher quality and accuracy. The second major advantage of m-CRM is its location sensitivity (see 4.1.5 on GPS). Innumerable possible applications come to mind where m-CRM is therefore superior to any e-CRM solution. The third advantage is reach since, on the one hand, the number of mobile devices has already outnumbered the number of computers, and, on the other hand, a PC in the office (or at home) cannot be used once a person leaves work (or the home). However, a mobile device such as a cell phone is nearly always on and almost always at hand.

An example for an m-CRM application which leverages all three advantages is the following. Imagine the customer of a major department store (e.g. Galeries Lafayette)

walking along the Grands Boulevards in Paris. A sophisticated m-CRM solution would then detect that the customer (who had opted to receive SMS-based advertisements) is within 500 metres of the store and could, during the opening hours, send a SMS text message with a special offer – completely personalized, i.e. according to the time and the customer's location as well as their preferences derived from previous sales (e.g. 10% off for all ties if bought within the next two hours).

Another example is telematics applications in the automobile industry. Chips (like SIM-cards) built into cars do not only allow location-based services (such as navigation and road assistance), but, in the case of an accident, permit features such as automatic ambulance calls and transmission of the driver's key health data (e.g. blood group, allergies, etc.). Car producers may gain much better 'real' data via such m-CRM solutions than they did from conventional CRM.

Although m-CRM solutions have a strong potential, they also have some major limitations. These include data privacy (especially for applications with multimedia content), limited bandwidth and, therefore, limited information richness.

Automatic speech recognition (ASR) and text-to-speech (TTS)

With ASR, it is possible to use human speech entry instead of key-typed input for further digital processing. Frequent applications are in banking, intra-company systems and telephone distribution centres (e.g. to channel calls at insurance companies or hotlines). This makes it possible to reduce or eliminate low-value-added tasks like forwarding incoming calls to the appropriate staff member.

The more basic ASR technology-based systems allow the recognition of single-word entries such as numbers or yes/no entries. More advanced versions also make it possible to enter more complex inputs, such as, for instance, requests for driving directions. This complexity, in turn, offers far simpler input and output instructions. Given this complexity as well as the diversity of human speech, quality problems still exist in a number of current applications.

TTS is often used together with ASR to convert digital data into sound (e.g. as help instructions, query outputs and e-mails). This technology is crucial for applications targeting the visually impaired, but also for those applications making a visual reading difficult or undesired (e.g. in the case of navigation systems).

i-mode

i-mode is a service offered by NTT DoCoMo, initially in Japan and now in many other countries, especially in Europe. Therefore it could eventually become a de facto world wide standard. i-mode was the first wireless system to offer a web browsing service for mobile phones. Today, i-mode does not only handle the above-mentioned applications (e.g. m-banking, m-brokerage and m-shopping), but also wireless e-mail and Internet access, mobile video-conferencing and m-portal functionality.

The technological reason for the packet-based i-mode system to offer mobile services before other telecom operators could, is mainly based on the use of lean and simplified standard versions, from HTML (see c-HTML in 4.1.4) or WML (c-WML) to a compressed version of Java. i-mode does (so far) not support standard WAP and WML. (For greater details on this system, see the online file-sharing case study in Part 4 of this book.)

INDEX

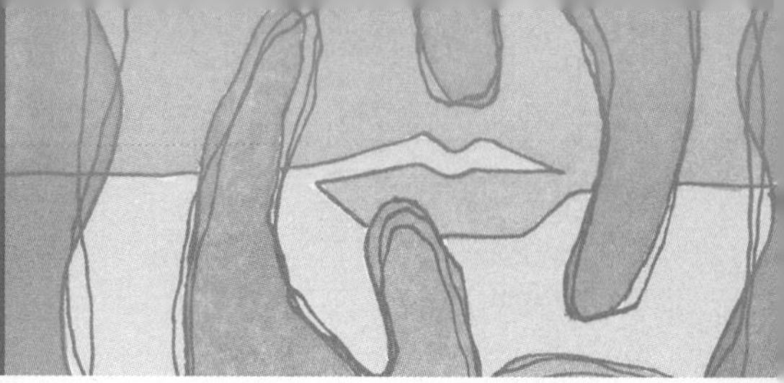